THE PAPERS OF

THOMAS JEFFERSON

BARBARA B. OBERG
GENERAL EDITOR

THE PAPERS OF
Thomas Jefferson

Volume 40
4 March to 10 July 1803

BARBARA B. OBERG, EDITOR

JAMES P. MCCLURE AND ELAINE WEBER PASCU,
SENIOR ASSOCIATE EDITORS

TOM DOWNEY AND MARTHA J. KING,
ASSOCIATE EDITORS

W. BLAND WHITLEY, ASSISTANT EDITOR

LINDA MONACO, EDITORIAL ASSISTANT

JOHN E. LITTLE, RESEARCH ASSOCIATE

PRINCETON AND OXFORD
PRINCETON UNIVERSITY PRESS
2013

Published by Princeton University Press, 41 William Street,
Princeton, New Jersey 08540
In The United Kingdom:
Princeton University Press, 6 Oxford Street,
Woodstock, Oxfordshire OX20 1TW

ISBN 978-0-691-16037-5

Library of Congress Number: 50-7486

This book has been composed in Monticello

Princeton University Press books are printed on
acid-free paper and meet the guidelines for permanence
and durability of the Committee on Production
Guidelines for Book Longevity of the
Council on Library Resources

Printed in the United States of America

DEDICATED TO THE MEMORY OF

ADOLPH S. OCHS

PUBLISHER OF THE NEW YORK TIMES

1896-1935

WHO BY THE EXAMPLE OF A RESPONSIBLE

PRESS ENLARGED AND FORTIFIED

THE JEFFERSONIAN CONCEPT

OF A FREE PRESS

SUPPORTERS

THIS EDITION was made possible by an initial grant of $200,000 from The New York Times Company to Princeton University. Contributions from many foundations and individuals have sustained the endeavor since then. Among these are the Ford Foundation, the Lyn and Norman Lear Foundation, the Lucius N. Littauer Foundation, the Charlotte Palmer Phillips Foundation, the L. J. Skaggs and Mary C. Skaggs Foundation, the John Ben Snow Memorial Trust, Time, Inc., Robert C. Baron, B. Batmanghelidj, David K. E. Bruce, and James Russell Wiggins. In recent years generous ongoing support has come from The New York Times Company Foundation, the Dyson Foundation, the National Trust for the Humanities, the Florence Gould Foundation, the "Cinco Hermanos Fund," the Andrew W. Mellon Foundation, the Pew Charitable Trusts, and the Packard Humanities Institute (through Founding Fathers Papers, Inc.). Benefactions from a greatly expanded roster of dedicated individuals have underwritten this volume and those still to come: Sara and James Adler, Helen and Peter Bing, Diane and John Cooke, Judy and Carl Ferenbach III, Mary-Love and William Harman, Frederick P. and Mary Buford Hitz, Governor Thomas H. Kean, Ruth and Sidney Lapidus, Lisa and Willem Mesdag, Tim and Lisa Robertson, Ann and Andrew C. Rose, Sara Lee and Axel Schupf, the Sulzberger family through the Hillandale Foundation, Richard W. Thaler, Tad and Sue Thompson, The Wendt Family Charitable Foundation, and Susan and John O. Wynne. For their vision and extraordinary efforts to provide for the future of this edition, we owe special thanks to John S. Dyson, Governor Kean, H. L. Lenfest and the Lenfest Foundation, Rebecca Rimel and the Pew Charitable Trusts, and Jack Rosenthal. In partnership with these individuals and foundations, the National Historical Publications and Records Commission and the National Endowment for the Humanities have been crucial to the editing and publication of *The Papers of Thomas Jefferson*. For their unprecedented generous support we are also indebted to the Princeton History Department and Christopher L. Eisgruber, president of the university.

FOREWORD

THE PERIOD covered by this volume reaches from the first day of Jefferson's third year as president, 4 March 1803, through 10 July. For all but three weeks of this time he was in the nation's capital. In the early spring and summer he and his cabinet had to navigate a complex diplomatic maze of relations with the Barbary States and the possibility that war might again break out between France and Great Britain. In preparation for the 8 April cabinet meeting, Jefferson received summaries of the voyages of the frigates *Constellation* and *Chesapeake*. Richard V. Morris's ineffectiveness as commander of the Mediterranean squadron was the first topic of discussion, and although there was as yet insufficient information for a plan of action, by 16 June the decision was made to recall him. As Jefferson told the secretary of the navy, nothing would be accomplished against Tripoli while the frigates in the Mediterranean were under Morris's command.

The cabinet also determined in April that "all possible procrastinations" should be used in dealing with France, but that discussions with Great Britain ought to move forward as well. Lafayette warned Jefferson that it would be dangerous for the United States to become entangled with the British, but Jefferson signaled in his private correspondence that Americans saw Great Britain as a "bulwark against the torrent" being unleashed by France and would consider a rapprochement with Britain if necessary. Using a pamphlet on agriculture as his excuse for writing, the president shared his reflections with Sir John Sinclair, a member of Parliament who had been instrumental in creating the British Board of Agriculture, and William Strickland, whom he had not written in several years. Jefferson left it up to them to communicate his opinions to their acquaintances in the British government and correct the misimpression that Americans were partial to France. The president also shared his views with David Erskine, the 11th Earl of Buchan. The renewal of war between the two powerful European nations would have significant consequences for the future of the United States, and "peace is our passion," Jefferson insisted.

Still alarmed by the closing of the right of deposit at New Orleans the preceding fall, the president confronted the potential consequences of the retrocession of Louisiana to France, which might stop American access to the Mississippi. But he resisted pressures to take New Orleans by force, urging patience and negotiation instead. In January 1803, he appointed James Monroe as special envoy to France, where he would participate with Robert Livingston in negotiations to purchase New Orleans and the Floridas. Monroe arrived in Paris on 12 April to confront a reality radically different from that which existed when he left the United States. While he was en route, Bonaparte instructed Barbé de Marbois to offer the United States all of Louisiana. By 30 April, the details of the agreement were set. For what in the end proved to be about 828,000 square miles of land, the United States would turn over $11,250,000 plus another $3,750,000 to pay off claims against France held by Americans. One of the American envoys' achievements was a plan, based on six-percent stock, that would spread the payment of the funds over several years. Jefferson was convinced that "by pursuing the ways of peace & reason," rather than going to war as many Federalists wanted, the United States had been rewarded with not just New Orleans but all of Louisiana. Livingston called the acquisition more important than the "purchase of Germany would be for france."

On 3 July, word of the stunning agreement reached Jefferson in Washington. The following day, the anniversary of the Declaration of Independence, the news appeared in the *National Intelligencer.* Several months earlier, Jefferson had begun to consider whether a constitutional amendment would be necessary, or at least "safer," for such a large expansion of the nation. Within days of receiving the dispatches from France, Jefferson's thoughts on an amendment to Article 4, Section 3, took on new urgency. He prepared a draft and showed it to members of the cabinet. The secretary of the Treasury, Albert Gallatin, thought that the powers Jefferson sought were already in the Constitution. Attorney General Levi Lincoln feared that having to wait for the passage of an amendment might bring down the whole project. All thought his draft went into too much detail. Jefferson, however, was seeking a mechanism by which most of the newly acquired territory could be reserved for Native Americans and therefore allow a consolidation of farming settlements east of the Mississippi. By late summer he would abandon his insistence on the necessity of a formal amendment.

Jefferson's concern with Louisiana did not end with its acquisition. In his inquisitive and studied way, he formulated a series of questions to help resolve the issue of how to bring into the United States a territory that had lived under a foreign political, legal, and economic system. His aim was to obtain the information and understanding that Congress would need in order to achieve a successful incorporation, he said. Albert Gallatin had also been at work on a list of queries, and after receiving his suggestions and meeting with him, Jefferson compiled the final list. The subjects included boundaries and the size of the population, whether the inhabitants could generally read and write, what language they spoke, whether they were litigious and their courts corrupt, and how the clergy was supported.

In January, Congress had given its approval and authorized funds for a westward exploratory expedition, to be led by Meriwether Lewis. During the spring and early summer, preparations moved forward for his journey. On 19 June, he invited William Clark to join him. By 8 July, he was at Harpers Ferry, Virginia, waiting for a second wagon to transport the supplies. He examined the articles that had been made for him there, "shot my guns," and reported that he would set out within the hour.

Just as Jefferson was involved in the enlargement of U.S. borders, he was also attentive to the design and construction of buildings in the nation's capital. He appointed Benjamin Henry Latrobe surveyor of the public buildings, requesting that he make a "flying trip" to Washington to urge the contractors to commence work right away. Latrobe submitted a lengthy report on the ground plan of the Capitol's new wing, a revision of the plan originally designed by William Thornton. He included a detailed account of the inconveniences of the construction that he had discovered. Concerned that a sufficient pace be maintained, Jefferson received almost weekly reports from John Lenthall, Latrobe's foreman, on the progress of the stone work on the south wing. The president also actively participated in the landscape design of the city, offering suggestions on the best placement of trees—oaks, elms, and Lombardy poplars—so as to provide a "shaded mall," or even, "at a future day," a canal. He received a proposal for the erection of a theater in Washington, to be built by private individuals on a public lot. Claiming that he lacked authority from Congress to donate public lands for purely private purposes, Jefferson denied the request, as he did a petition from directors of the Eastern Branch Bridge Company for a bridge, despite their argument that it would make travel and the transportation of goods across the Anacostia River more convenient.

Several years earlier, Jefferson had promised his friend Benjamin Rush that "one day or other" he would communicate his views on the Christian religion. In April 1803, Jefferson, having had time to reflect upon the subject, drew up an outline, or a "syllabus," comparing the merits of the doctrines of Jesus with those of other thinkers. He was opposed to the corruptions of Christianity, but not to the "general precepts of Jesus himself," Jefferson wrote. He dispatched the work to his two daughters, Rush, Joseph Priestley, Henry Dearborn, and Levi Lincoln, asking that his thoughts not be circulated. Such attention would expose him to the "malignant perversions of those who would misrepresent anything" he said.

Throughout his life, Jefferson claimed, he had "scrupulously refrained from" writing for newspapers. He apparently deviated from this practice and published three anonymous writings during the months of May and June. In May, he provided Samuel H. Smith with a brief analysis of Connecticut election returns, which appeared in the *National Intelligencer* as "Plain View of the Politics of Connecticut," to show that although the Republicans had lost seats in the state legislature, they had actually gained votes in the recent gubernatorial election. On 1 June he sent "Fair Play," an articulation of his policy on appointments and removals, to the Boston *Independent Chronicle*. Later that month in the Richmond *Examiner* as "Timoleon" he offered an impassioned defense against charges of financial impropriety some twenty years earlier. Two were political pieces relating to the Republican Party; the third a strong defense of his honesty.

In early May, having completed his second year as president, Jefferson prepared a chart listing and analyzing all of his personal expenditures from 4 March 1802 to 4 March 1803 (MB, 2:1098-9). From wines and provisions, to lands bought and buildings acquired, to the hire and maintenance of slaves, Jefferson captured most of his expenses, but some were only conjecture. The bulk of them he could cover from his annual salary of $25,000, tobacco, rents, and the sale of nails. According to his calculations, on 4 March 1803, he had in hand $293. The following month, as he informed his Georgetown banker, John Barnes, he took "an exact view" of his financial affairs and realized, once again, that he could not discharge his debts immediately. Ever optimistic, however, he was certain that he could soon begin to make regular payments to his many creditors, especially John Barnes and William Short, and continue them until the entire amount was discharged.

Public affairs were at the top of his mind during these months, and the election to Congress of his two sons-in-law, Thomas Mann Randolph and John Wayles Eppes, brought the public and the personal parts of his life together. His correspondence with his daughters was infrequent, but through letters to and from their husbands he kept up with the family and conveyed his concerns. He was pleased that his 18-month-old grandson, Francis Eppes, had recovered from the measles. He longed for a visit from both daughters but feared their health would deteriorate should they be in Washington during the unhealthy season. He also fretted that he would be too occupied with business for them to have a proper family visit.

ACKNOWLEDGMENTS

MANY individuals have given the Editors the benefit of their aid in the preparation of this volume, and we offer them our thanks. Those who helped us use manuscript collections, answered research queries, assisted with translations, or advised in other ways are William C. Jordan, Princeton University; Neil Ann Stuckey Levine for German translations; in the libraries at Princeton, Karin A. Trainer, University Librarian, and Elizabeth Z. Bennett, Colleen M. Burlingham, Stephen Ferguson, Daniel J. Linke, Deborah T. Paparone, AnnaLee Pauls, Ben Primer, and Don C. Skemer; Timothy Connelly of the NHPRC; James H. Hutson, Barbara Bair, Julie Miller, and the staff at the Manuscript Division of the Library of Congress, especially Frederick J. Augustyn, Jennifer Brathovde, Jeffrey Flannery, Joseph Jackson, Patrick Kerwin, Bruce Kirby, and Lewis Wyman; Peter Drummey, Elaine Grublin, and the library staff of the Massachusetts Historical Society, especially Nancy Heywood for providing digital scans; Robert C. Ritchie, Sara N. Ash Georgi, Juan Gomez, and Olga Tsapina at the Huntington Library; Anna Berkes, Lucia C. Stanton, Endrina Tay, and Gaye Wilson of the Thomas Jefferson Foundation at Monticello; Nicole Bouché, Regina Rush, and the staff of Special Collections at the University of Virginia Library; Beatriz Hardy and Susan A. Riggs, Swem Library, the College of William and Mary; the late Sara Bearss and Brent Tarter, Library of Virginia; Dennis Northcott and the staff of the Museum of Missouri History; Martin Levitt, Roy Goodman, Charles B. Greifenstein, and Earl E. Spamer of the American Philosophical Society; the staff of the New York Public Library; the Gilder Lehrman Institute of American History and Jean W. Ashton and Edward O'Reilly of the New-York Historical Society; Joy Holland of the Brooklyn Public Library; Charles M. Harris of the Papers of William Thornton, and our fellow editors at the Thomas Jefferson Retirement Series at Monticello, the Adams Papers at the Massachusetts Historical Society, the Papers of George Washington and the Papers of James Madison at the University of Virginia, the James Monroe Papers at the University of Mary Washington, and the Papers of Benjamin Franklin at Yale University. For assistance with illustrations we are indebted to Alfred L. Bush of Princeton, Bonnie Coles of the Library of Congress, and Anne Bouin and Alain Pougetoux of the Musée National des châteaux de Malmaison et Bois-Préau. Stephen Perkins, Helen Langone, and Jason Bush of dataformat.com provided essential technical support for us with the XML preparation of these volumes. We thank Alice Calaprice for careful reading and Jan Lilly for her unparalleled mastery of what a Jefferson volume must be. We appreciate especially the support and leadership of Peter J. Dougherty, Director of Princeton University Press. Others at the Press who never fail to give these volumes the benefit of their expertise are Adam Fortgang, Dimitri Karetnikov, Neil Litt, Elizabeth Litz, Linny Schenck, and Brigitta van Rheinberg.

For many volumes of *The Papers of Thomas Jefferson*, Robert W. Hartle skillfully and patiently assisted us with transcriptions and translations of French documents. We extend our deepest gratitude for his knowledge and dedication.

EDITORIAL METHOD AND APPARATUS

1. RENDERING THE TEXT

Julian P. Boyd eloquently set forth a comprehensive editorial policy in Volume 1 of *The Papers of Thomas Jefferson*. Adopting what he described as a "middle course" for rendering eighteenth-century handwritten materials into print, Boyd set the standards for modern historical editing. His successors, Charles T. Cullen and John Catanzariti, reaffirmed Boyd's high standards. At the same time, they made changes in textual policy and editorial apparatus as they deemed appropriate. For Boyd's policy and subsequent modifications to it, readers are encouraged to consult Vol. 1: xxix-xxxviii; Vol. 22: vii-xi; and Vol. 24: vii-viii.

The revised, more literal textual method, which appeared for the first time in Volume 30, adheres to the following guidelines: Abbreviations will be retained as written. Where the meaning is sufficiently unclear to require editorial intervention, the expansion will be given in the explanatory annotation. Capitalization will follow the usage of the writer. Because the line between uppercase and lowercase letters can be a very fine and fluctuating one, when it is impossible to make an absolute determination of the author's intention, we will adopt modern usage. Jefferson rarely began his sentences with an uppercase letter, and we conform to his usage. Punctuation will be retained as written and double marks of punctuation, such as a period followed by a dash, will be allowed to stand. Misspellings or so-called slips of the pen will be allowed to stand or will be recorded in a subjoined textual note.

English translations or translation summaries will be supplied for foreign-language documents. In some instances, when documents are lengthy and not especially pertinent to Jefferson's concerns or if our edition's typography cannot adequately represent the script of a language, we will provide only a summary in English. In most cases we will print in full the text in its original language and also provide a full English translation. If a contemporary translation that Jefferson made or would have used is extant, we may print it in lieu of a modern translation. Our own translations are designed to provide a basic readable English text for the modern user rather than to preserve all aspects of the original diction and language.

2. TEXTUAL DEVICES

The following devices are employed throughout the work to clarify the presentation of the text.

[. . .]	Text missing and not conjecturable.
[ ]	Number or part of a number missing or illegible.
[roman]	Conjectural reading for missing or illegible matter. A question mark follows when the reading is doubtful.
[*italic*]	Editorial comment inserted in the text.
<*italic*>	Matter deleted in the MS but restored in our text.

3. DESCRIPTIVE SYMBOLS

The following symbols are employed throughout the work to describe the various kinds of manuscript originals. When a series of versions is recorded, the first to be recorded is the version used for the printed text.

Dft	draft (usually a composition or rough draft; later drafts, when identifiable as such, are designated "2d Dft," &c.)
Dupl	duplicate
MS	manuscript (arbitrarily applied to most documents other than letters)
N	note, notes (memoranda, fragments, &c.)
PoC	polygraph copy
PrC	press copy
RC	recipient's copy
SC	stylograph copy
Tripl	triplicate

All manuscripts of the above types are assumed to be in the hand of the author of the document to which the descriptive symbol pertains. If not, that *fact is stated*. On the other hand, the following types of manuscripts are assumed *not* to be in the hand of the author, and exceptions will be noted:

FC	file copy (applied to all contemporary copies retained by the author or his agents)
Lb	letterbook (ordinarily used with FC and Tr to denote texts copied into bound volumes)
Tr	transcript (applied to all contemporary and later copies except file copies; period of transcription, unless clear by implication, will be given when known)

4. LOCATION SYMBOLS

The locations of documents printed in this edition from originals in private hands and from printed sources are recorded in self-explanatory form in the descriptive note following each document. The locations of documents printed from originals held by public and private institutions in the United States are recorded by means of the symbols used in the National Union Catalog in the Library of Congress; an explanation of how these symbols are formed is given in Vol. 1:xl. The symbols DLC and MHi by themselves stand for the collections of Jefferson Papers proper in these repositories; when texts are drawn from other collections held by these two institutions, the names of those collections will be added. Location symbols for documents held by institutions outside the United States are given in a subjoined list.

CSmH	The Huntington Library, San Marino, California
CU-BANC	University of California, Berkeley, Bancroft Library
CtY	Yale University, New Haven, Connecticut
DCU	Catholic University of America, Washington, D.C.
DLC	Library of Congress
DeGH	Hagley Museum, Greenville, Delaware
MH	Harvard University, Cambridge, Massachusetts
MHi	Massachusetts Historical Society, Boston
MWA	American Antiquarian Society, Worcester, Massachusetts
MdAA	Hall of Records Commission, Annapolis, Maryland
MdHi	Maryland Historical Society, Baltimore
MiU-C	University of Michigan, William L. Clements Library
MoHi	State Historical Society of Missouri, Columbia
MoSHi	Missouri History Museum, St. Louis
MsJS	Jackson State University, Mississippi
NBLiHi	Long Island Historical Society, Brooklyn
NBuHi	Buffalo & Erie County Historical Society, Buffalo, New York
NHi	New-York Historical Society, New York City
NN	New York Public Library
NNC	Columbia University, New York City
NNPM	Pierpont Morgan Library, New York City
NcD	Duke University, Durham, North Carolina
NjMoHP	Morristown National Historical Park, New Jersey
NjP	Princeton University

OClWHi	Western Reserve Historical Society, Cleveland, Ohio
PHC	Haverford College, Pennsylvania
PHi	Historical Society of Pennsylvania, Philadelphia
PPAmP	American Philosophical Society, Philadelphia
PWW	Washington and Jefferson College, Washington, Pennsylvania
PWacD	David Library of the American Revolution, Washington Crossing, Pennsylvania
ViU	University of Virginia, Charlottesville
ViW	College of William and Mary, Williamsburg, Virginia

5. *NATIONAL ARCHIVES DESIGNATIONS*

The National Archives, recognized by the location symbol DNA, with identifications of series (preceded by record group number) as follows:

RG 26	Records of the United States Coast Guard	
	MLR	Misc. Letters Received
RG 36	Records of the United States Custom Service	
	LR	Letters Received
RG 42	Records of the Office of Public Buildings and Public Parks of the National Capital	
	LRDLS	Letters Received and Drafts of Letters Sent
RG 45	Naval Records Collection of the Office of Naval Records and Library	
	LSO	Letters Sent to Officers
	LSP	Letters Sent to the President
	MLS	Misc. Letters Sent
RG 46	Records of the United States Senate	
	EPFR	Executive Proceedings, Foreign Relations
RG 59	General Records of the Department of State	
	CD	Consular Dispatches
	DD	Diplomatic Dispatches
	GPR	General Pardon Records
	LAR	Letters of Application and Recommendation
	MLR	Misc. Letters Received
	MPTPC	Misc. Permanent and Temporary Presidential Commissions

PTCC Permanent and Temporary Consular Commissions
RD Resignations and Declinations

RG 75 Records of the Bureau of Indian Affairs
LSIA Letters Sent by the Secretary of War Relating to Indian Affairs

RG 76 Records of Boundary and Claims Commissions and Arbitrations
MR Misc. Records

RG 107 Records of the Office of the Secretary of War
LRUS Letters Received by the Secretary of War, Unregistered Series
LSMA Letters Sent by the Secretary of War Relating to Military Affairs
LSP Letters Sent to the President
MLS Misc. Letters Sent
RLRMS Register of Letters Received, Main Series

RG 217 Records of the Accounting Officers of the Department of the Treasury
MTA Misc. Treasury Accounts

RG 233 Records of the United States House of Representatives

6. *OTHER SYMBOLS AND ABBREVIATIONS*

The following symbols and abbreviations are commonly employed in the annotation throughout the work.

Second Series The topical series to be published as part of this edition, comprising those materials which are best suited to a topical rather than a chronological arrangement (see Vol. 1: xv-xvi)

TJ Thomas Jefferson

TJ Editorial Files Photoduplicates and other editorial materials in the office of The Papers of Thomas Jefferson, Princeton University Library

TJ Papers Jefferson Papers (applied to a collection of manuscripts when the precise location of an undated, misdated, or otherwise problematic document must be furnished, and always preceded by the symbol for the institutional repository; thus "DLC: TJ Papers, 4:628-9" represents a document in the Library of Congress, Jefferson Papers, volume 4, pages 628 and 629. Citations to volumes and folio numbers of the Jefferson

Papers at the Library of Congress refer to the collection as it was arranged at the time the first microfilm edition was made in 1944-45. Access to the microfilm edition of the collection as it was rearranged under the Library's Presidential Papers Program is provided by the Index to the Thomas Jefferson Papers [Washington, D.C., 1976])

RG Record Group (used in designating the location of documents in the National Archives)

SJL Jefferson's "Summary Journal of Letters" written and received for the period 11 Nov. 1783 to 25 June 1826 (in DLC: TJ Papers). This register, kept in Jefferson's hand, has been checked against the TJ Editorial Files. It is to be assumed that all outgoing letters are recorded in SJL unless there is a note to the contrary. When the date of receipt of an incoming letter is recorded in SJL, it is incorporated in the notes. Information and discrepancies revealed in SJL but not found in the letter itself are also noted. Missing letters recorded in SJL are, where possible, accounted for in the notes to documents mentioning them or in related documents. A more detailed discussion of this register and its use in this edition appears in Vol. 6: vii-x

SJPL "Summary Journal of Public Letters," an incomplete list of letters and documents written by TJ from 16 Apr. 1784 to 31 Dec. 1793, with brief summaries, in an amanuensis's hand. This is supplemented by six pages in TJ's hand, compiled at a later date, listing private and confidential memorandums and notes as well as official reports and communications by and to him as Secretary of State, 11 Oct. 1789 to 31 Dec. 1793 (in DLC: TJ Papers, Epistolary Record, 514-59 and 209-11, respectively; see Vol. 22: ix-x). Since nearly all documents in the amanuensis's list are registered in SJL, while few in TJ's list are so recorded, it is to be assumed that all references to SJPL are to the list in TJ's hand unless there is a statement to the contrary

V Ecu

f Florin

£ Pound sterling or livre, depending upon context (in doubtful cases, a clarifying note will be given)

s Shilling or sou (also expressed as /)

d Penny or denier

₶ Livre Tournois

℘ Per (occasionally used for pro, pre)

7. SHORT TITLES

The following list includes short titles of works cited frequently in this edition. Since it is impossible to anticipate all the works to be cited in abbreviated form, the list is revised from volume to volume.

Ammon, *Monroe* Harry Ammon, *James Monroe: The Quest for National Identity*, New York, 1971

ANB John A. Garraty and Mark C. Carnes, eds., *American National Biography*, New York and Oxford, 1999, 24 vols.

Annals *Annals of the Congress of the United States: The Debates and Proceedings in the Congress of the United States...Compiled from Authentic Materials*, Washington, D.C., Gales & Seaton, 1834-56, 42 vols. All editions are undependable and pagination varies from one printing to another. The first two volumes of the set cited here have "Compiled...by Joseph Gales, Senior" on the title page and bear the caption "Gales & Seatons History" on verso and "of Debates in Congress" on recto pages. The remaining volumes bear the caption "History of Congress" on both recto and verso pages. Those using the first two volumes with the latter caption will need to employ the date of the debate or the indexes of debates and speakers.

APS American Philosophical Society

ASP *American State Papers: Documents, Legislative and Executive, of the Congress of the United States*, Washington, D.C., 1832-61, 38 vols.

Bear, *Family Letters* Edwin M. Betts and James A. Bear, Jr., eds., *Family Letters of Thomas Jefferson*, Columbia, Mo., 1966

Betts, *Farm Book* Edwin M. Betts, ed., *Thomas Jefferson's Farm Book*, Princeton, 1953

Betts, *Garden Book* Edwin M. Betts, ed., *Thomas Jefferson's Garden Book, 1766-1824*, Philadelphia, 1944

Biog. Dir. Cong. *Biographical Directory of the United States Congress, 1774-1989*, Washington, D.C., 1989

Biographie universelle *Biographie universelle, ancienne et moderne*, new ed., Paris, 1843-65, 45 vols.

Brigham, *American Newspapers* Clarence S. Brigham, *History and Bibliography of American Newspapers, 1690-1820*, Worcester, Mass., 1947, 2 vols.

Bryan, *National Capital* Wilhelmus B. Bryan, *A History of the National Capital from Its Foundation through the Period of the Adoption of the Organic Act*, New York, 1914-16, 2 vols.

Bush, *Life Portraits* Alfred L. Bush, *The Life Portraits of Thomas Jefferson*, rev. ed., Charlottesville, 1987

CVSP William P. Palmer and others, eds., *Calendar of Virginia State Papers... Preserved in the Capitol at Richmond*, Richmond, 1875-93, 11 vols.

DAB Allen Johnson and Dumas Malone, eds., *Dictionary of American Biography*, New York, 1928-36, 20 vols.

DHSC Maeva Marcus and others, eds., *The Documentary History of the Supreme Court of the United States, 1789-1800*, New York, 1985-2007, 8 vols.

Dictionnaire *Dictionnaire de biographie française*, Paris, 1933- , 19 vols.

DNB H. C. G. Matthew and Brian Harrison, eds., *Oxford Dictionary of National Biography, In Association with The British Academy, From the Earliest Times to the Year 2000,* Oxford, 2004, 60 vols.

DSB Charles C. Gillispie, ed., *Dictionary of Scientific Biography*, New York, 1970-80, 16 vols.

Dubin, *Congressional Elections* Michael J. Dubin, *United States Congressional Elections, 1788-1997: The Official Results of the Elections of the 1st through 105th Congresses*, Jefferson, N.C., 1998

DVB John T. Kneebone and others, eds., *Dictionary of Virginia Biography*, Richmond, 1998- , 3 vols.

EG Dickinson W. Adams and Ruth W. Lester, eds., *Jefferson's Extracts from the Gospels*, Princeton, 1983, *The Papers of Thomas Jefferson*, Second Series

Evans Charles Evans, Clifford K. Shipton, and Roger P. Bristol, comps., *American Bibliography: A Chronological Dictionary of All Books, Pamphlets and Periodical Publications Printed in the United States of America from...1639...to...1820*, Chicago and Worcester, Mass., 1903-59, 14 vols.

Ford Paul Leicester Ford, ed., *The Writings of Thomas Jefferson*, Letterpress Edition, New York, 1892-99, 10 vols.

Gallatin, *Papers* Carl E. Prince and Helene E. Fineman, eds., *The Papers of Albert Gallatin*, microfilm edition in 46 reels, Philadelphia, 1969, and Supplement, Barbara B. Oberg, ed., reels 47-51, Wilmington, Del., 1985

Garner, *Black's Law Dictionary* Bryan A. Garner, *Black's Law Dictionary*, 8th ed., St. Paul, Minn., 2004

Grainger, *Amiens Truce* John D. Grainger, *The Amiens Truce: Britain and Bonaparte, 1801-1803*, Rochester, N.Y., 2004

HAW Henry A. Washington, ed., *The Writings of Thomas Jefferson*, New York, 1853-54, 9 vols.

Heitman, *Dictionary* Francis B. Heitman, comp., *Historical Register and Dictionary of the United States Army*, Washington, D.C., 1903, 2 vols.

Heitman, *Register* Francis B. Heitman, *Historical Register of Officers of the Continental Army during the War of the Revolution, April, 1775, to December, 1793*, new ed., Washington, D.C., 1914

Higginbotham, *Pennsylvania Politics* Sanford W. Higginbotham, *The Keystone in the Democratic Arch: Pennsylvania Politics 1800-1816*, Harrisburg, 1952

Jackson, *Lewis and Clark* Donald Jackson, ed., *The Letters of the Lewis and Clark Expedition, with Related Documents, 1783-1854*, 2d ed., Urbana, Ill., 1978

JCC Worthington C. Ford and others, eds., *Journals of the Continental Congress, 1774-1789*, Washington, D.C., 1904-37, 34 vols.

Jefferson Correspondence, Bixby Worthington C. Ford, ed., *Thomas Jefferson Correspondence Printed from the Originals in the Collections of William K. Bixby*, Boston, 1916

JEP *Journal of the Executive Proceedings of the Senate of the United States...to the Termination of the Nineteenth Congress*, Washington, D.C., 1828, 3 vols.

JHR *Journal of the House of Representatives of the United States*, Washington, D.C., 1826, 9 vols.

JS *Journal of the Senate of the United States*, Washington, D.C., 1820-21, 5 vols.

King, *Life* Charles R. King, ed., *The Life and Correspondence of Rufus King: Comprising His Letters, Private and Official, His Public Documents and His Speeches*, New York, 1894-1900, 6 vols.

Kline, *Burr* Mary-Jo Kline, ed., *Political Correspondence and Public Papers of Aaron Burr*, Princeton, 1983, 2 vols.

L & B Andrew A. Lipscomb and Albert E. Bergh, eds., *The Writings of Thomas Jefferson*, Washington, D.C., 1903-04, 20 vols.

LCB Douglas L. Wilson, ed., *Jefferson's Literary Commonplace Book*, Princeton, 1989, *The Papers of Thomas Jefferson*, Second Series

Latrobe, *Correspondence* John C. Van Horne and Lee W. Formwalt, eds., *The Correspondence and Miscellaneous Papers of Benjamin Henry Latrobe*, New Haven, 1984-88, 3 vols.

Leonard, *General Assembly* Cynthia Miller Leonard, comp., *The General Assembly of Virginia, July 30, 1619-January 11, 1978: A Bicentennial Register of Members*, Richmond, 1978

List of Patents *A List of Patents granted by the United States from April 10, 1790, to December 31, 1836*, Washington, D.C., 1872

McLaughlin, *Jefferson and Monticello* Jack McLaughlin, *Jefferson and Monticello: The Biography of a Builder*, New York, 1988

Madison, *Papers* William T. Hutchinson, Robert A. Rutland, J. C. A. Stagg, and others, eds., *The Papers of James Madison*, Chicago and Charlottesville, 1962- , 35 vols.

Sec. of State Ser., 1986- , 9 vols.

Pres. Ser., 1984- , 7 vols.

Ret. Ser., 2009- , 2 vols.

Malone, *Jefferson* Dumas Malone, *Jefferson and His Time*, Boston, 1948-81, 6 vols.

Marshall, *Papers* Herbert A. Johnson, Charles T. Cullen, Charles F. Hobson, and others, eds., *The Papers of John Marshall*, Chapel Hill, 1974-2006, 12 vols.

Mattern and Shulman, *Dolley Madison* David B. Mattern and Holly C. Shulman, eds., *The Selected Letters of Dolley Payne Madison*, Charlottesville, 2003

MB James A. Bear, Jr., and Lucia C. Stanton, eds., *Jefferson's Memorandum Books: Accounts, with Legal Records and Miscellany, 1767-1826*, Princeton, 1997, *The Papers of Thomas Jefferson*, Second Series

Miller, *Alexandria Artisans* T. Michael Miller, comp., *Artisans and Merchants of Alexandria, Virginia, 1780-1820*, Bowie, Md., 1991-92, 2 vols.

Miller, *Treaties* Hunter Miller, ed., *Treaties and Other International Acts of the United States of America*, Washington, D.C., 1931-48, 8 vols.

Moulton, *Journals of the Lewis & Clark Expedition* Gary E. Moulton, ed., *Journals of the Lewis & Clark Expedition*, Lincoln, Neb., 1983-2001, 13 vols.

NDBW Dudley W. Knox, ed., *Naval Documents Related to the United States Wars with the Barbary Powers*, Washington, D.C., 1939-44, 6 vols. and *Register of Officer Personnel and Ships' Data, 1801-1807*, Washington, D.C., 1945

NDQW Dudley W. Knox, ed., *Naval Documents Related to the Quasi-War between the United States and France, Naval Operations*, Washington, D.C., 1935-38, 7 vols. (cited by years)

Nichols, *Architectural Drawings* Frederick Doveton Nichols, *Thomas Jefferson's Architectural Drawings, Compiled and with Commentary and a Check List*, Charlottesville, 1978

Notes, ed. Peden *Thomas Jefferson, Notes on the State of Virginia*, ed. William Peden, Chapel Hill, 1955

OED J. A. Simpson and E. S. C. Weiner, eds., *The Oxford English Dictionary*, Oxford, 1989, 20 vols.

Parry, *Consolidated Treaty Series* Clive Parry, ed., *The Consolidated Treaty Series*, Dobbs Ferry, N.Y., 1969-81, 231 vols.

Pasley, *Tyranny of Printers* Jeffrey L. Pasley, *"The Tyranny of Printers": Newspaper Politics in the Early American Republic*, Charlottesville, 2001

Peale, *Papers* Lillian B. Miller and others, eds., *The Selected Papers of Charles Willson Peale and His Family*, New Haven, 1983-2000, 5 vols. in 6

PMHB *Pennsylvania Magazine of History and Biography*, 1877-

Preston, *Catalogue* Daniel Preston, *A Comprehensive Catalogue of the Correspondence and Papers of James Monroe*, Westport, Conn., 2001, 2 vols.

PW Wilbur S. Howell, ed., *Jefferson's Parliamentary Writings*, Princeton, 1988, *The Papers of Thomas Jefferson*, Second Series

RCHS *Records of the Columbia Historical Society*, 1895-1989

RS J. Jefferson Looney and others, eds., *The Papers of Thomas Jefferson: Retirement Series*, Princeton, 2004- , 9 vols.

S.C. Biographical Directory, House of Representatives J. S. R. Faunt, Walter B. Edgar, N. Louise Bailey, and others, eds., *Biographical Directory of the South Carolina House of Representatives*, Columbia, S.C., 1974-92, 5 vols.

Seale, *The President's House* William Seale, *The President's House*, Washington, D.C., 1986, 2 vols.

Shaw-Shoemaker Ralph R. Shaw and Richard H. Shoemaker, comps., *American Bibliography: A Preliminary Checklist for 1801-1819*, New York, 1958-63, 22 vols.

Shepherd, *Statutes* Samuel Shepherd, ed., *The Statutes at Large of Virginia, from October Session 1792, to December Session 1806...*, Richmond, 1835-36, 3 vols.

Sowerby E. Millicent Sowerby, comp., *Catalogue of the Library of Thomas Jefferson*, Washington, D.C., 1952-59, 5 vols.

Stanton, *Free Some Day* Lucia Stanton, *Free Some Day: The African-American Families of Monticello*, Charlottesville, 2000

Stets, *Postmasters* Robert J. Stets, *Postmasters & Postoffices of the United States 1782-1811*, Lake Oswego, Ore., 1994

Sturtevant, *Handbook* William C. Sturtevant, gen. ed., *Handbook of North American Indians*, Washington, D.C., 1978- , 14 vols.

Syrett, *Hamilton* Harold C. Syrett and others, eds., *The Papers of Alexander Hamilton*, New York, 1961-87, 27 vols.

Terr. Papers Clarence E. Carter and John Porter Bloom, eds., *The Territorial Papers of the United States*, Washington, D.C., 1934-75, 28 vols.

TJR Thomas Jefferson Randolph, ed., *Memoir, Correspondence, and Miscellanies, from the Papers of Thomas Jefferson*, Charlottesville, 1829, 4 vols.

Tulard, *Dictionnaire Napoléon* Jean Tulard, *Dictionnaire Napoléon*, Paris, 1987

U.S. Statutes at Large Richard Peters, ed., *The Public Statutes at Large of the United States...1789 to March 3, 1845*, Boston, 1855-56, 8 vols.

VMHB *Virginia Magazine of History and Biography*, 1893-

Washington, *Papers* W. W. Abbot, Dorothy Twohig, Philander D. Chase, Theodore J. Crackel, Edward C. Lengel, and others, eds., *The Papers of George Washington*, Charlottesville, 1983- , 57 vols.

Confed. Ser., 1992-97, 6 vols.
Pres. Ser., 1987- , 16 vols.
Ret. Ser., 1998-99, 4 vols.
Rev. War Ser., 1985- , 21 vols.

Weber, *United States Diplomatic Codes* Ralph E. Weber, *United States Diplomatic Codes and Ciphers, 1775-1938*, Chicago, 1979

WMQ *William and Mary Quarterly*, 1892-

Woods, *Albemarle* Edgar Woods, *Albemarle County in Virginia*, Charlottesville, 1901

CONTENTS

1803

CONTENTS

CONTENTS

APPENDICES

ILLUSTRATIONS

Following page 320

PROPOSED DESIGNS FOR PENNSYLVANIA AVENUE

In March 1803, Thomas Munroe, the superintendent of the city of Washington; Nicholas King, the surveyor of the federal district; and William Thornton conferred about improvements to Pennsylvania Avenue. Afterward, Munroe sent President Jefferson a letter from King that included this set of diagrams made "for illustration, to the President." At the top, labeled "No. 1," is the profile of the street as it was at the time, with a crowned roadway of gravel in the center, a walkway for pedestrians along one side, and no landscaping. The other three cross sections show proposed designs for roadways, walks, and rows of trees. The number 3 plan, Munroe indicated, had originated with Jefferson. The outer flanks of the avenue were the same in the three proposals, including the rows of trees closest to the sides of the avenue. While they waited for the president's choice of design, King began to survey the lines for those outermost rows of trees and Munroe expected to begin acquiring young Lombardy poplars from Mount Vernon and Mason's Island at a cost of 12½ cents each. Jefferson responded from Monticello on 21 Mch. with a diagram of his own of a compromise design, which modified the second of King's diagrams to include fewer rows of trees (King to Munroe, 12 Mch., in DLC; Munroe to TJ, 14 Mch.; TJ to Munroe, 21 Mch.).

Courtesy of the Library of Congress.

ROBERT R. LIVINGSTON

John Vanderlyn painted this portrait of Livingston in Paris in 1804. During a previous residence in France from 1796 to 1801, Vanderlyn, a New Yorker, had developed his skills and become familiar with styles and techniques of French neoclassical painting. For that visit, Aaron Burr gave him financial assistance, encouragement, and letters of introduction that helped Vanderlyn form acquaintances with Fulwar Skipwith, Elbridge Gerry, and other influential Americans. He returned to Europe in 1803 at the age of 27 with recommendations to Livingston, who needed someone to collect replicas of paintings and statues for the new fine arts society and academy in New York presided over by his brother Edward. Vanderlyn also became friends with James and Elizabeth Monroe. Although he executed a number of portrait commissions in his career, he was more interested in painting historical and allegorical scenes and panoramas. He made this likeness of Livingston in hopes that it would stimulate the arts society to provide funds for travel to Italy, ostensibly to search for items for the study collection. In the painting, Livingston's hand rests on a paper headed "Plan for establishing an Academy of Fine Arts in New York." Nearby on his table is a letter addressed to him as the United States minister to France (Salvatore Mondello, "John Vanderlyn," ANB; Lillian B. Miller, "John Vanderlyn and the Business of Art," *New York History*, 32 [1951], 33-44; Vol. 39:363-4, 407).

In March 1803, before Vanderlyn left for France, Jefferson paid him $20 as subscription for two views of Niagara Falls drawn by the artist at Burr's urging. Vanderlyn had the Niagara pictures engraved in England. After Jefferson received his copies of the engravings in 1805, he displayed them in the dining room at Monticello. In a letter printed in this volume, Jefferson referred to Vanderlyn as "a first rate painter" (MB, 2:1093; Vol. 32:xxxvi-xxxvii; TJ to Joseph Sansom, 25 May 1803; Vanderlyn to TJ, [on or before 31 Dec. 1805]).

Vanderlyn's portrait of Livingston is in oil paints on canvas and measures 46¼ inches by 35¼ inches (New-York Historical Society accession number 1876.1).

Collection of the New-York Historical Society.

JAMES MONROE

This pastel portrait captures Monroe's appearance probably not long after his return to the United States following the Louisiana negotiations and his service as minister to Great Britain. The image has been attributed to Felix Sharples. Although Sharples's parents, James and Ellen, were prolific creators of portraits in pastels and members of the family often made copies of each other's creations, Felix was working in Virginia and could have made this portrait from life around the period 1807-1811. The picture is on paper and measures nine inches by seven inches (Doris Devine Fanelli and Karie Diethorn, *History of the Portrait Collection, Independence National Historical Park* [Philadelphia, 2001], 231; Lee A. Langston-Harrison, David Meschutt, and John N. Pearce, eds., *Images of a President: Portraits of James Monroe*, Fredericksburg, Va., 1992], 9; Vol. 29:xxxviii; Vol. 36:xlvii-xlviii).

Courtesy of Independence National Historical Park.

MAP BY NICHOLAS KING

As Meriwether Lewis prepared to lead an expedition across the continent, an initiative by Albert Gallatin to bring together geographical information about the region between the Mississippi River and the Pacific Coast resulted in this map drawn by Nicholas King. Gallatin informed the president on 14 Mch. that he had asked King "to project a blank map to extend from 88 to 126° West longitude from Greenwich & from 30° to 55° north latitude." Gallatin expected King to work out the metrics of the map's projection and draw the meridians of longitude (which in this projection converge toward the North Pole) and parallels of latitude. The secretary of the Treasury thought that he would then add the map's features himself. In the end, however, Gallatin left the meticulous cartographic work to King, who utilized the sources that Gallatin had identified.

King's map shows the continent from the Great Lakes region to the western sea. It illustrates the unevenness and imperfect nature of the available geographical knowledge. The map is richest in detail in the northern zone, portions of which had been described and charted by British overland and seaborne explorations. Knowledge of the region to the south was much thinner, and King left the bottom half of his map largely empty. He did not even show the southerly continuation of the Rocky Mountains, even though one of his sources, the 1802 map of North America by Aaron Arrowsmith, did so. King did attempt to show the upper reaches of three south-flowing rivers: the

Colorado on the west, the Rio Grande on the east, and, between them, the Gila—which he labeled the "Rio des los Apostolos."

With King and Gallatin, a third collaborator in the creation of this map was Lewis, who made a few additions and changes (Gary E. Moulton, ed., *Atlas of the Lewis & Clark Expedition* [Lincoln, Neb., 1983], 5).

Drawn in ink on two joined sheets of paper, King's map is 20 inches tall and 30⅓ inches wide. The vertical band running down the center of the map is the pasted seam of the sheets.

Courtesy of the Library of Congress.

UPPER MISSOURI RIVER

In instructions drafted during the spring of 1803, Jefferson directed Lewis to travel up the Missouri River until he could make a portage through the mountains from the headwaters of the Missouri to a river flowing to the Pacific (see Drafting Instructions for Meriwether Lewis, in this volume at 13 Apr.). The detail of King's map illustrated here shows a region of primary importance to the expedition, the upper branches of the Missouri. Here King followed, with some modifications, Arrowsmith's map, and like Arrowsmith he used dashed lines to indicate the lack of precise information about the courses of the rivers. King's speculative charting of the streams does contain inaccuracies, yet the major branches of the upper Missouri are recognizable. The stream to the north is the main branch of the upper Missouri. The long tributary below it, which joins the main river in the center right of this detail, must be the Yellowstone River. King, however, mistakenly attached it to the lower part of another river, the Little Missouri, which he labeled the "Lesser Missesouree." (Arrowsmith made a similar error, but he combined the Yellowstone and the Knife.)

For one section of the Missouri in this detail, King had accurate data—better than Arrowsmith's—and could use solid lines rather than dashes. This was the river's Great Bend, to the right of the junction of the two main branches. Mandan and other Native American villages along that part of the river were tied to British trading networks. The North West Company had charted the area, including coordinates of latitude and longitude, and Lewis gained access to that map, probably through the British chargé d'affaires. It was on that section of the Missouri River that Lewis, with William Clark and the Corps of Discovery, spent the winter of 1804-1805 before proceeding upriver.

Visible in the lower part of this detail is the word "Conjectural" that King spread across the middle of his map. Again using dashed lines, he also indicated a river that some people thought flowed westward from the central part of the continent toward the Pacific. In the lower right of this detail are the "Sources of the Rio Norte according to De Lisle." When Jefferson learned that Gallatin was relying on old maps, including one by Guillaume de L'Isle, to locate the origin of the Rio del Norte (the Rio Grande), he suggested the use of John Mitchell's 1755 map instead. King perhaps drew the river from L'Isle's map before Gallatin received that advice from the president, or perhaps King and Gallatin did not want to exclude the possibility that the headwaters of the Rio Grande were where L'Isle had put them. In the upper right of this detail are some of Lewis's changes in a different ink (Aaron Arrowsmith, "A Map Exhibiting all the New Discoveries in the Interior Parts of North America" [London, 1802]; Moulton, *Atlas*, 5, 16n; Gallatin to TJ, 14 Mch.; TJ to Gallatin, 20 Mch.).

THOMAS JEFFERSON

This likeness of Jefferson, drawn on paper in a black chalk with white chalk highlights, became a definitive image in France through the publication of a stipple engraving. That print, the mirror image of this original, was published in 1801 and put on display that year at the Salon, the prestigious annual art exhibition in Paris. This picture copies a popular engraving by Cornelius Tiebout that Mathew Carey published in Philadelphia at the time of Jefferson's inauguration. Tiebout's print was itself a reproduction of the oil portrait of Jefferson painted in 1800 by Rembrandt Peale. Continuing the progression of duplicates of Peale's work, the stipple engraving published in France became the source for other versions, including one that found its way onto British ceramics.

This drawing, the published copies of the stipple engraving, and another crayon drawing, very similar to this one but privately owned in the United States, are all signed "Bouch." The name presents a mystery, for biographical information about any artist of that name active at the time—even a first name or nationality—is lacking. The mystery is compounded by the fact that the full name of the engraver of the French print, who signed the engraving as Auguste Desnoyers, was Auguste Gaspard Louis Boucher Desnoyers. It has been suggested that Boucher Desnoyers the engraver was Bouch the artist. There appears to be no evidence, however, that Desnoyers used the name Bouch. Nor can Desnoyers be connected to a small portrait in pencil and watercolors of John Jervis, the Earl of St. Vincent, made in 1797 and now at the National Portrait Gallery in London, which is also signed Bouch. A portrait painter and drawing teacher named Bouché worked in Maryland in the 1790s, but no tie between him and the Bouch of the Jefferson and St. Vincent portraits is apparent.

In 1814, when Josephine, the former empress of France, died, this picture was part of the collection of art in the château at Malmaison. Josephine purchased the estate in 1799, and it was her residence after Napoleon divorced her in 1809. The couple used the house frequently while he was first consul. When the Bonapartes acquired this picture is not known. The first consul met Desnoyers, the engraver, on at least one occasion, and Bonaparte probably would have been aware of the stipple engraving of the Jefferson portrait from its exhibition at the Salon. It seems likely that this picture, as an engraving and perhaps as the original drawing, formed Bonaparte's mental image of Jefferson when, in the spring of 1802, the first consul was introduced to James Monroe and plied him with questions about the American president (see Robert R. Livingston's letter of 2 May in this volume). This, in effect, was the Jefferson to whom Bonaparte sold Louisiana.

Without its frame, the picture is 9⅞ inches high and 7⅞ inches wide. The artist dated it Year 9, which began in September 1800, but the fact that the picture copies Tiebout's print means that it was not created before late spring or summer 1801. In private hands from 1829 to 1958, the drawing is once again in the collections of the Musée National des Châteaux de Malmaison et

Bois-Préau, Rueil-Malmaison, France (Alain Pougetoux, *La Collection de peintures de l'impératrice Joséphine* [Paris, 2003], 181-2; Bush, *Life Portraits*, 40; Nicole Hubert and Alain Pougetoux, *Châteaux de Malmaison et de Bois-Préau, Musées napoléoniens de l'Ile d'Aix et de la Maison Bonaparte à Ajaccio: Catalogue sommaire illustré des paintures et dessins* [Paris, 1989], 70; J. C. F. Hoefer, *Nouvelle biographie générale depuis les temps les plus reculés jusqu'a nos jours*, 46 vols. [Paris, 1855-66], 13:866-9; *Dictionnaire*, 6:1216-17; Tulard, *Dictionnaire Napoléon*, 977-8, 1122-4, 1524-6; David Saywell and Jacob Simon, *Complete Illustrated Catalogue: National Portrait Gallery, London* [London, 2004], 545; Noble E. Cunningham, Jr., *Popular Images of the Presidency: From Washington to Lincoln* [Columbia, Mo., 1991], 25-7; George C. Groce and David H. Wallace, *The New-York Historical Society's Dictionary of Artists in America, 1564-1860* [New Haven, 1957], 67; Baltimore Museum of Art, *Two Hundred and Fifty Years of Painting in Maryland* [Baltimore, 1945], 31-2).

Courtesy of Réunion des Musées Nationaux / Art Resource, New York.

INVOICE FOR ENCYCLOPÉDIE MÉTHODIQUE

In February 1803, Jefferson wrote to the Parisian bookseller Charles Pougens about books to be acquired for the Library of Congress. He also included a request for something for his personal library: installments he had not yet acquired of the ambitious, serially published reference work known as the *Encyclopédie méthodique*, which was published in unbound segments called *livraisons* (see Vol. 39:458-62). In June, Pougens's assistants packed up a mixed shipment of books, some for Congress and some for the president, and prepared three lists. One list was of the books being shipped for Congress, another detailed books desired for Congress but not yet obtained, and the list illustrated here itemized the sections of the *Encylopédie* going to Jefferson. The invoice, made by a clerk in Pougens's shop, begins with parts of the third and fourth volumes on agriculture, includes sections of a variety of other volumes, and concludes with collections of illustrative plates (*planches*).

After Jefferson received the invoice in the latter part of September, he carefully reviewed it, making checkmarks and notations in pencil alongside the clerk's entries and more notes in ink in the margin and at the bottom of the page (see Pougens's letter of 9 June). A stamped circular seal of the Library of Congress appears in the upper right quadrant of the manuscript.

Courtesy of the Library of Congress.

U.S. CENT

In April 1803, Thomas T. Tucker, the treasurer of the United States, notified the secretary of the Treasury that according to a forgotten provision in a 1792 act of Congress, a ban on the use of copper coins except U.S. cents and half cents was three years overdue. The Mint had produced more than $100,000 in cents and half cents by 1803, double the amount needed to institute the prohibition. Informed of the situation by Albert Gallatin on 9 April, the president the next day authorized the "annunciation" of the rule. Observing, however, that Congress might not be committed to keeping the Mint in operation, Jefferson advised a delay in issuing the regulation to give legislators a chance to forestall it if they wanted. Tucker published the notice in mid-August.

Illustrated here is a copper cent struck in 1803. Introduced by Mint engraver Robert Scot on silver coins in 1795, this portrait of Liberty appeared on the cent beginning in 1796 and on the half cent beginning in 1800. It replaced a pattern that had also featured the head of a female Liberty, but the earlier image included a liberty cap on the end of a staff. Emblems from Roman times of the transition from bondage to freedom, the cap and staff became, in the 1770s, American symbols of resistance to British tyranny and subsequently found an important place in the iconography of the French Revolution. According to comments by a director of the Mint later in the 19th century, Scot engraved the new portrait of Liberty from a drawing by Gilbert Stuart. If so, direct evidence of Stuart's involvement is lacking. Along with dropping the motif of the liberty cap and staff, the new design changed another of Liberty's customary symbols: her loose, windblown hair. Stuart reputedly said that he made Liberty into a "steady matron." She would have now a proper coiffure, secured with a ribbon, in place of those earlier chaotic tresses.

Some numismatic historians speculate that Stuart's Liberty was Anne Willing Bingham, wife of Philadelphia capitalist William Bingham. Mrs. Bingham sat for a portrait by Stuart in the mid-1790s, and he had made studies of her face a decade earlier, for a group portrait of the Binghams with their daughters that he never completed. In 1796, the Binghams persuaded a reluctant George Washington to pose for the painting by Stuart that became known as the Lansdowne portrait. Nevertheless, Stuart's relations with the Binghams were generally frustrating for the artist. Anne Bingham died in 1801 at the age of 36. Scot, who became the engraver of the Mint in 1793, had designed Indian medals for the state of Virginia in 1780 and 1781, when Jefferson was governor of the commonwealth (Mort Reed, *Encyclopedia of U.S. Coins*, rev. ed. [Chicago, 1972], 25, 85, 90-1; Don Taxay, *The U.S. Mint and Coinage: An Illustrated History from 1776 to the Present* [New York, 1966; repr. 1983], 105-7, 112-13; James Ross Snowden, *A Description of the Medals of Washington; of National and Miscellaneous Medals; and of Other Objects of Interest in the Museum of the Mint* [Philadelphia, 1861], 177; Walter Breen, *Walter Breen's Complete Encyclopedia of U.S. and Colonial Coins* [New York, 1988], 165-8, 189-91, 337; Yvonne Korshak, "The Liberty Cap as a Revolutionary Symbol in America and France," *Smithsonian Studies in American Art*, 1 [1987], 52-69; Lawrence Park, *Gilbert Stuart: An Illustrated Descriptive List of his Works*, 4 vols. [New York, 1926], 1:153-6; 3:55-6; Allida Shuman McKinley, "Anne Willing Bingham," ANB; Robert C. Alberts, *The Golden Voyage: The Life and Times of William Bingham 1752-1804* [Boston, 1969], 149-50, 290-3; Vol. 4:xxxvii, 35-7, 106 [illus.]; Vol. 6:43; Vol. 27:192n).

The cent pictured here is $1\frac{1}{8}$ inches in diameter, much larger than a 21st-century penny. The half cent looked the same as the cent picture here, but the words on the reverse side are "half cent" and the denomination is "1/200." The half cent was $\frac{7}{8}$ inch in diameter (Reed, *Encyclopedia of U.S. Coins*, 85, 91).

Courtesy of the American Numismatic Society.

Volume 40

4 March to 10 July 1803

JEFFERSON CHRONOLOGY

1743 • 1826

1743	Born at Shadwell, 13 April (New Style).
1760	Entered the College of William and Mary.
1762	"quitted college."
1762-1767	Self-education and preparation for law.
1769-1774	Albemarle delegate to House of Burgesses.
1772	Married Martha Wayles Skelton, 1 Jan.
1775-1776	In Continental Congress.
1776	Drafted Declaration of Independence.
1776-1779	In Virginia House of Delegates.
1779	Submitted Bill for Establishing Religious Freedom.
1779-1781	Governor of Virginia.
1782	His wife died, 6 Sep.
1783-1784	In Continental Congress.
1784-1789	In France as Minister Plenipotentiary to negotiate commercial treaties and as Minister Plenipotentiary resident at Versailles.
1790-1793	Secretary of State of the United States.
1797-1801	Vice President of the United States.
1801-1809	President of the United States.
1814-1826	Established the University of Virginia.
1826	Died at Monticello, 4 July.

VOLUME 40

4 March to 10 July 1803

6 Mch.	Offers Benjamin H. Latrobe appointment as surveyor of public buildings in Washington.
7 Mch.	Leaves Washington for Monticello, arriving 11 Mch.
30 Mch.	Calculates tobacco crop for 1802 at Poplar Forest to be 45,139 pounds.
31 Mch.	Leaves Monticello for Washington, arriving 3 Apr.
8 Apr.	Cabinet unanimously agrees to "buy peace of Tripoli."
13 Apr.	Pledges to use "best endeavors" to remove discussion of Walker affair from newspapers.
23 Apr.	Sends Benjamin Rush his comparative view of the doctrines of Jesus.
2 May	Robert R. Livingston writes that New Orleans and Louisiana "are ours."
4 May	Estimates total personal expenditures from 4 Mch. 1802 to 4 Mch. 1803 at $27,720.92.
9 May	Denies pardon request of convicted slave trader Nathaniel Ingraham.
17 May	Right of deposit officially restored at New Orleans.
18 May	Great Britain declares war on France.
8 June	Orders sale of his slave Cary as punishment for an assault on Brown Colbert at the Monticello nailery.
19 June	Meriwether Lewis invites William Clark to join him on western expedition.
25 June	Response to accusations by Gabriel Jones appears in the *Richmond Examiner*.
4 July	*National Intelligencer* publishes news of the Louisiana Purchase.

THE PAPERS OF
THOMAS JEFFERSON

From Joseph Anderson

George Town 4th March 1803
Sir friday morning.

In my letter of yesterday, I express'd an intention of waiting on you this morning—but as you will probably be much engaged, and as I am very anxious to begin my Journey, after so long an absence from my family—I have concluded, to decline doing myself that honor—As it is of importance however to my concerns, to be inform'd, upon the Subject of my letter—I have to request the favour of an early answer; Cou'd I receive it in a week or two, after my arrival at home, which will probably be about the twentyeth of March—It wou'd very much accomodate me—As Some arrangements respecting my *future pursuits*, will depend upon your answer—please to direct—to Cheeks Cross Roads, Jefferson County.—If you Shou'd think proper to favor this application—I take leave to Observe, that I have express'd a wish, to be of that board of Commissioners, who are to set in the County of Adams—

With Sentements of the Most respectful Consideration—

Jos: Anderson

RC (DNA: RG 59, LAR); endorsed by TJ as received 4 Mch. and "to be Commr. Missipi" and so recorded in SJL.

In his letter of yesterday, Anderson requested a place as one of the commissioners to settle land claims in the Mississippi Territory. A statute approved by Congress on 3 Mch. for "regulating the grants of land, and providing for the disposal of the lands of the United States, south of the state of Tennessee" authorized the establishment of two land offices in the territory, one in Adams County and one in Washington County, to dispose of lands lying west and east of the Pearl River, respectively. In addition to a register of lands and a receiver of public money, each county was to have two commissioners, who, with the register, would decide cases of claims to land from British or Spanish grants or under the April 1802 agreement between the United States and Georgia (U.S. Statutes at Large, 2:229-35; Vol. 37:343-5; Matthew Clay to TJ, 28 Feb.).

To Joseph Anderson

DEAR SIR Washington Mar. 4. 1803.

I have this moment recieved your favor of this morning, but as I suppose from it that you were then on the point of departure, this can only follow you. the appointment which is the subject of it will not take place till autumn, and in the mean time we shall no doubt be recieving applications. you are sensible that it will be our duty to select from the whole number of candidates, & not knowing now who they will be, it is impossible now to say on whom the selection will fall. I thought it candid to say this much to you lest your arrangements might be affected by my silence. a multiplicity of business, visits of leave &c. obliges me to break off here with a tender of my friendly salutations & respect. TH: JEFFERSON

PrC (DLC); in ink at foot of text: "Joseph Anderson."

To Justus Erich Bollmann

SIR Washington Mar. 4. 1803.

Your favor of Feb. 28. is recieved, and if the box of the wine of the quality I selected, is not reserved for your own use, I shall certainly be very glad to recieve it, and I will ask the further favor of you to import for me a gross of bottles of the same quality: for I observe that it's price places it among those wines which are to be used pour faire bonne bouche, and not for ordinary consumption. is it designated by any particular name, or the particular place of it's growth known? I think it will be pleasing to you to know that Congress have given to the Marquis de la Fayette 11,500. acres of land, which may be located any where, and is probably now worth 4. or 5. times as many dollars. Accept assurances of my respect & consideration.

TH: JEFFERSON

PrC (DLC); at foot of text: "Doctr. J. Erich Bollman"; endorsed by TJ in ink on verso.

TJ never learned the PARTICULAR NAME or place of origin of the Hungarian wine he obtained from Bollmann, despite the latter's efforts. Because of commercial restrictions established under the Austrian empire and the relative passivity of Hungarian growers, wines from the region could be difficult to obtain (Zoltán Halász, *Hungarian Wine through the Ages* [Budapest, 1962], 164-9; Bollmann to TJ, 10 Oct. 1804).

In 1794, Bollmann had attempted to rescue the MARQUIS de Lafayette from a prison in Olmütz, an act that earned him some celebrity on both sides of the Atlantic, as well as a stint in the same prison (Paul S. Spalding, *Lafayette: Prisoner of State* [Columbia, S.C., 2010], 84-124; New York *Argus, or Greenleaf's New Daily Advertiser*, 11 Jan. 1796; Bollmann to TJ, 11 Dec. 1802).

From John Dawson

Dear Sir, George Town—March 4. 1803

I have reason to believe that you think favourably of Captain Barney—an intimate acquaintance with him convinces me that that impression is a just one, and that he is a man of merit.

he does believe that he was ill treated by the late Post master general, on account of his politicks, and that he has been neglected by the present—coud he be employ'd I am convinc'd that he woud do justice and credit to the public, and therefore I take the liberty of recommending him to you—he will explain his wishes!

With much respect Yr friend & Sevt J Dawson

RC (DNA: RG 59, LAR); endorsed by TJ as received 13 May and "Captain Barney for employment" and so recorded in SJL. Probably enclosed in John H. Barney to TJ, 13 May.

John H. barney, a stage line operator and former postmaster at Havre de Grace, Maryland, had written TJ requesting to succeed Joseph Habersham as postmaster general, but TJ appointed Gideon Granger to the post instead in November 1801 (Vol. 33:415, 429, 670, 677).

From Henry Dearborn

War Department
4th. March 1803.

Sir,

Walker K. Armistead, a Cadet in the Corps of Engineers, having on examination, received honorable testimonials of his progress in science and of requisite qualifications to sustain a Commission in the Army of the United States, I take the liberty of proposing to your consideration, the appointment of said Armistead, as a second Lieutenant in the Corps of Engineers.

With high consideraton &c.

FC (Lb in DNA: RG 107, LSP). Recorded in SJL as received from the War Department on 4 Mch. with notation "nomn Armistead."

The following day, 5 Mch., Dearborn wrote walker k. armistead to inform him that the president had approved his appointment. Armistead would go on to serve as chief engineer of the U.S. Army from 1818 to 1821 (DNA: RG 107, LSMA; Heitman, *Dictionary*, 1:169).

To Rolfe Eldridge

Dear Sir Washington Mar. 4. 1803.

On the reciept of your favor of Feb. 26. I had enquiry made at the clerk's office of the Supreme court, & recieved information that no such suit as that of Ld. Granville v. Davie or any others is on their docquet, nor any papers relating to it in their possession. Accept assurances of my esteem & best wishes. Th: Jefferson

PrC (DLC); at foot of text: "Mr. Eldridge"; endorsed by TJ in ink on verso.

your favor of feb. 26: that is, Eldridge's letter of 14 Feb., which TJ received on 26 Feb. Eldridge had requested information on a lawsuit that threatened land claimed in the Granville District of North Carolina by his wife and her sisters.

From James Jackson, Abraham Baldwin, and Peter Early

Sir, Washington, March 4h, 1803.

The Act disposing of the lands of the United States South of Tenessee, having required the appointment of two Commissioners, besides the land register for each of the districts, of Adams and Washington; and Georgia being as much interested in their duties, as any State—We take the liberty to state, that we hope it will be deemed proper to take one Commissioner of each board, from the Citizens of Georgia; and therefore recommend as proper Characters, William H Crawford, and James McNeil esquires, to fill those stations, and perhaps as much (if not better) acquainted with the state of lands there, as any others which could be selected.

We are Sir, with the highest respect, & consideration

Jas Jackson
Abr Baldwin
Peter Early

RC (DNA: RG 59, LAR); in Jackson's hand, also signed by Baldwin and Early; at foot of text: "The President of the United States"; endorsed by TJ as received 4 Mch. and so recorded in SJL with notation "Commrs. Missipi"; also endorsed by TJ: "Wm. H. Crawford H. Mc.Neal to be Missipi Commrs."

Peter Early (1773-1817) was born in Virginia, graduated from the College of New Jersey at Princeton, and studied law in Philadelphia before moving to Georgia in 1795. He was a member of the House of Representatives in the Seventh, Eighth, and Ninth Congresses, afterwards serving as a judge in Georgia, as governor, and in the state senate (dab).

act disposing of the lands: see Joseph Anderson to TJ, 4 Mch.

Jackson had enthusiastically endorsed William H. crawford in a letter to TJ in July 1801. TJ did not name Crawford or McNeil to be land commissioners in Mississippi Territory (Vol. 34:592-3; TJ to Madison, 12 July 1803).

To Thomas Newton

DEAR SIR Washington Mar. 4. 1803

Your favor of Feb. 16. is recieved, and according to the permission therein given me, I will ask that two pipes of Madeira of the Brazil best quality may be imported for me annually while here. the two lately sent me by mr Taylor were recieved yesterday. I set out in a day or two on a very short visit to Monticello. if you will be so good as to address the bill for the cyder to mr Barnes of this place he will remit it in my absence. the return of mr Newton your son, will of course give you the Congressional news. Accept my friendly salutations and assurances of constant esteem. TH: JEFFERSON

PrC (MHi); at foot of text: "Colo. Newton"; endorsed by TJ in ink on verso.

TWO LATELY SENT: James Taylor, Jr., to TJ, 19 Feb.

From Samuel A. Otis

SIR Washington March 4th 1803

In addition to the enclosed I can only repeat that tis my wish to continue Secretary of the Senate so long as that honble body, who yesterday gave me an additional & flattering mark of their approbation, shall permit my continuance

The Senate have uniformly allowed me, after arrangeing their business, to retire during vacation. In the present, it would be agreeable could I be permitted to exercise the office of a commissioner; which I shall however not presume to do, without your express permission. And in which, should you Sir be of opinion there is any incompatibility I shall cheerfully abide your decision.

Repeating my assurances of being very greatfully impressed by the mark of confidence[1] you have done me the honour to confer, & wishing you a pleasant summer & every felicity,

I have the honour to be With every sentiment of respect Your most obedient & humble Servt SAM: A. OTIS

RC (DLC); at foot of text: "The President of the U States"; endorsed by TJ as received 4 Mch. and so recorded in SJL. Enclosure not found, but perhaps it was the 3 Mch. resolution of the Senate postponing action on the Convention of 1802 with Spain; the Senate ordered Otis to lay the resolution before the president (JEP,

1:447-8; TJ to the Senate, 11 Jan. 1803, fourth letter).

THEIR APPROBATION: on 3 Mch., the last day of the session, the Senate voted 15 to 7 to postpone "the election of a Secretary, and the other officers of the Senate," thus continuing Otis in office (JS, 3:286-7).

For Otis's appointment as bankruptcy COMMISSIONER, see Memorandum on Appointments, 6 July 1802. TJ decided to appoint Edward Jones in place of Otis to fill up the slate of commissioners for Boston (Vol. 39: Appendix I).

[1]MS: "cofidence."

From Louis André Pichon

G. Town 4th. March.

Mr. Pichon with his respects incloses herewith the Passport which the President of the United States did him the honor to ask and returns The Passport of Mr Thornton which had been communicated as a model.

RC (DLC); endorsed by TJ as received 4 Mch. and "passport" and so recorded in SJL. Enclosures: (1) Safe conduct pass, 1 Mch., in French, signed by Pichon, asking civil officials, military and naval officers, and citizens of the French Republic to give protection and aid to Meriwether Lewis and his traveling party, who under the authority of the president of the United States are undertaking a journey of discovery to explore the Missouri River and the western parts of North America; the purpose of the expedition is scientific only, and the party is carrying no more goods than are needed to secure the good will of Indians along the route (Jackson, *Lewis and Clark*, 1:20). (2) Safe conduct pass, 28 Feb., by Edward Thornton as British chargé d'affaires, asking British superintendents of Indian affairs and British subjects engaged in trade with the Indians to allow Lewis's party to pass, to give them aid and protection, and to advance the objects of their mission; the document seen by Pichon was evidently dated 1 Mch. (same, 19-20, 23).

DID HIM THE HONOR TO ASK: in a dispatch to Talleyrand dated 4 Mch., Pichon reported that in a conversation at the President's House the previous day, TJ had used a copy of Aaron Arrowsmith's 1802 map of North America to show him Lewis's expected route of travel. For some time, Pichon indicated, the president had hoped that an exploration of the upper Missouri River and the country beyond it would locate the headwaters of the Columbia River. Pichon explained to Talleyrand that while the expedition was for the advancement of science, TJ had to justify his request to Congress for an appropriation on the grounds of promoting trade. When TJ asked him to furnish a passport for Lewis, Pichon inquired if Carlos Martínez de Irujo would be granting such a document on behalf of Spain. TJ replied that Irujo was obliged to do so (in recounting what TJ said, Pichon used the French verb *devoir*). Pichon anticipated that the safe-conduct document he provided might only be needed for the party's return journey, for TJ told him that the journeyers would have to find some ship on the Pacific Coast to give them passage back to the United States (Jackson, *Lewis and Clark*, 1:22-3; Vol. 32:69n).

TJ also spoke to Edward THORNTON about the prospective exploration, outlining the plan in terms very similiar to what he said to Pichon. The president, Thornton wrote to Lord Hawkesbury from Philadelphia on 9 Mch., had contemplated such an expedition "for some years past." He was eager to see it through, believed Thornton, as a means of "distinguishing his Presidency by a discovery, now the only one left to his enterprize." The transfer of Louisiana to French control had apparently "accelerated the determination of the President, as he thinks it certain that on their arrival they will instantly set on foot enterprizes of a similar nature" (Jackson, *Lewis and Clark*, 1:25-7).

To Edward Savage

SIR Washington Mar. 4. 1803.

Your favor of Feb. 7. is recieved. you mention having enclosed in it one of your proposals for publishing the print of the Declaration of Independence, but none came. I sent to the door keepers of Congress to know if they could inform me of the terms of subscription, but they could not. I shall be glad to become a subscriber, & will comply with the terms whenever made known to me. Accept my best wishes & respects.

TH: JEFFERSON

PrC (DLC); at foot of text: "Mr. Savage"; endorsed by TJ in ink on verso.

DOOR KEEPERS OF CONGRESS: Thomas Claxton for the House of Representatives and James Mathers for the Senate (*Biog. Dir. Cong.*).

TERMS OF SUBSCRIPTION: Savage's print of the "Signing of the Declaration of American Independence," sold for $7 by advance subscription, $8 by regular subscription, $10 for nonsubscribers, and $12 for proofs. According to an advertisement, the print would be available for delivery within 18 months (New York *Morning Chronicle*, 26 Feb. 1803; Vol. 1:lviii, 415 [illus.]).

From Robert Smith

SIR, [4 Mch. 1803]

The Enclosed is submitted to your Consideration—I will have some Conversation with you upon the Subject in the Course of a few days—

Your Humbl Ser

RT SMITH

RC (DLC); undated; endorsed by TJ as received from the Navy Department on 4 Mch. 1803 and so recorded in SJL with notation "Tingey"; also endorsed by TJ: "Tingey's applicn for advancd allowance." Enclosure: probably Thomas Tingey to Smith, 1 Mch. 1803 (not found, but see Enclosure No. 1 listed at Smith to TJ, 12 Mch. 1803).

From Robert Smith

Nav: Dep:

Sir! 4th. March 1803

I have the honor to enclose Eight blank Commissions, & Twelve Warrants—to which I request your signature.

The Commissions are wanted for the Lieutenants lately appointed—& the Warrants will, it is presumed, be wanted during your absence—for Midshipmen & other Warrant Officers.

I have the honor to be, with the greatest respect & esteem, Sir, yr mo ob Sr

Rt Smith

RC (DLC); in a clerk's hand, signed by Smith; at foot of text: "President U:States"; endorsed by TJ as received from the Navy Department on 4 Mch. and "commissions & warrants" and so recorded in SJL. FC (Lb in DNA: RG 45, LSP).

For the lieutenants lately appointed to the navy, see Smith to TJ, 28 Feb. and TJ to the Senate, 1 Mch.

To Hore Browse Trist

Dear Sir Washington Mar. 4. 1803.

Doctr. Carmichael, the Collector at Fort Adams, having absented himself from his post great part of a year, and never yet returned a single account, which calls for an immediate removal under a general rule, he is accordingly removed. this place is *at present* believed to be worth more than the Secretaryship of the territory, but from it's *singular* position must in a very short time become the best office in the gift of the US. it has the benefit too of being permanent, whereas that of the Secretary is probably very shortlived, as it will cease whenever the territory advances to another grade of government, which under it's late enlargement of boundary, & opening of a land office, will probably be almost immediately. it leaves a person too more at liberty as to the state of expences he may chuse to adopt. as it became absolutely necessary to decide between these two offices for you, without the opportunity of consulting you, we have undertaken to judge for you as we believe you would have done for yourself, had you been consulted.—Commission will accordingly be sent to you for the Collectorship of Fort Adams, and mr Cato West is appointed Secretary to the territory. there has been some thought of removing the residence of the Collector to Natchez, and appointing at Fort Adams a Surveyor only, but I do not know that it will be done. all the states on the Missisipi, the Tennissee, Ohio, & Wabash will be paying their tribute to this office, and doubling it at very short periods. Mr. Gilmer was here lately and informed me your family was well. Dr. Bache I believe has sailed from Philadelphia for New Orleans, leaving mrs Bache behind. our late elections shew a wonderful growth of republicanism. 14. states are with us. we believe N. Hampshire will chuse a republican Govr. (Langdon) this month, and that Connecticut & Massachusets will have republican legislatures in one year more. Accept assurances of my affectionate esteem & respect, and present my friendly salutations to Govr. Claiborne.

TH: JEFFERSON

PrC (DLC); at foot of text: "Mr. Trist"; endorsed by TJ in ink on verso.

For John F. CARMICHAEL, see Vol. 38:255n; Vol. 39: Appendix I.

TJ had earlier suggested that Trist consider the SECRETARYSHIP OF THE TERRITORY, with a salary of $750 (Vol. 36:389). JUDGE FOR YOU: on 28 Feb., Gallatin wrote TJ noting that the president had to decide whether Trist was best suited for the position of secretary or collector. Trist's COMMISSION as collector for the District of Mississippi, dated 7 Mch., was immediately transmitted to him. He also received a commission, dated 9 Mch., as inspector for the port at Fort Adams. Trist commenced his duties on 18 May (commissions in DNA: RG 36, New Orleans, LR; Gallatin, *Papers*, 8:735; Gallatin to TJ, 14 Mch.). For Trist's appointment, see also Vol. 39: Appendix I.

MR GILMER: probably Peachy R. Gilmer who married Trist's cousin, Mary House, in September 1803. He was the son of TJ's friend and physician, the late George Gilmer (Richard Beale Davis, *Francis Walker Gilmer: Life and Learning in Jefferson's Virginia* [Richmond, 1939], 364).

John LANGDON did not win the governorship of New Hampshire until 1805, after three unsuccessful tries (ANB).

From Augustus B. Woodward

Mar. 4. 1803.

The senate having struck out the provision I contemplated in my late observations to the president, prevents any further attention to that point at this time. It is an object, which, for reasons that are obvious, interests me much; and I will be happy in the presidents retaining a recollection of it. A. B. WOODWARD

RC (DNA: RG 59, LAR); addressed: "The president of the united states"; endorsed by TJ as received 4 Mch. and "his father Collectr. Washn." and so recorded in SJL.

PROVISION I CONTEMPLATED: the House, on 24 Feb., amended the bill on new collection districts adding Washington, D.C., to the proposed ports of entry and delivery. The title of the bill as passed by the House and sent to the Senate on 25 Feb. began, "An act to make Beaufort, the City of Washington, and Passamaquoddy, ports of entry and delivery." On 26 Feb., the Senate referred the bill to Robert Wright, Dwight Foster, and Stevens Thomson Mason. Wright reported the bill with amendments on 28 Feb. The next day the Senate adopted the amendments and on 2 Mch. passed the bill and sent it back to the House. The amended bill, agreed to by the House, did not include Washington as a new collection district (U.S. Statutes at Large, 2:228-9; JHR, 4:365, 366, 382, 384, 387; JS, 3:273, 274, 276, 280, 282). LATE OBSERVATIONS: Woodward evidently recommended John Woodward, his father, as collector at Washington (see TJ's endorsement above; Vol. 33:212n).

To Isaac Briggs

DEAR SIR Washington Mar. 5. 1803.

I have something to propose to you much to your advantage: but it is necessary I should see you; & as I leave this the day after tomorrow, I have only tomorrow for an interview. I send the bearer express, to see if you could come here tomorrow (Sunday) Accept my best wishes.

TH: JEFFERSON

PrC (DLC); at foot of text: "Mr. Isaac Briggs"; endorsed by TJ in ink on verso.

SOMETHING TO PROPOSE: TJ offered Briggs the position of surveyor of Mississippi Territory. According to the 3 Mch. act for disposition of lands south of Tennessee, the surveyor was to supervise the laying out of lands previously owned by Indian tribes into townships and half sections in a manner similar to that used to survey the Northwest Territory. The statute authorized a salary of $1,500 for the position (U.S. Statutes at Large, 2: 233-4; Gallatin to TJ, 21 Mch.; TJ to Wilson Cary Nicholas, 22 Apr.).

From William Hylton

SIR! Savana' la mar Jamaica 5 March 1803.

Sensible how much it is your Excellencies desire, as president of the United States of America, to maintain Harmony; and a reciprocity of Interests, between *Your* and the British Nation; upon a just Understanding—I do not hesitate, to take the liberty of communicating *directly* to your Excellency, an occurrence, which however trivial in *itself*, has produced a difficulty; which left unexplained—may interrupt it!

The valuable Ship Alknomac, trading to this place from New York, and owned by Louis Simond Esqr. of that City, had taken on board, *part* of Thirty hogsheads of *Molasses*, intended to be shipped by me on her—when Mr. James Brown the Collector at this port, forbid the master (Capt. John Gore) from proceeding; and threatened "to seize his Ship and her Cargo, of near four hundred punchions of Rum, unless the molasses was *immediately* Debarked"—alledging, "that it was *Syrup*—because, an advertisement in the newspaper, offering *molas-*

ses for Sale, by the name of '*Syrup*' to give it a currency, had lately appeared!"

I endeavoured to explain away the objection, by shewing—the Definition given, by every English author of the word, *Molasses*—was, *the* general Term for *an article* made, or produced, from the *Raw material*, without any *Lixivium* to Granulate it! and was *that*, which the Act of Parliament *enumerated* and permitted, to be shipped in American Bottoms—that *Syrup*, was *Sugar*, diluted and boiled up with *Water*!

Finding these expostulations *ineffectual* I caused the molasses to be relanded; and at the moment of the posts departure, hastily wrote a Letter to the Attorney General of this Island, of which the inclosed is a Copy.

Mr. Simonds intercourse with this Country is very extensive; and may be, if necessary, explained by himself.

Subjects or Citizens of either nation, may be greatly injured, if not Ruined; *by* the *Decoy* of a word, if uninformed Customhouse officers, *are* permitted to give their own pervert Construction to it; And I humbly submit this Information to your Excellency, how far you may see it, a *point*, for the Interests of both Nations, to have promptly explained.

As it may be important that no time should be lost—I have presumed, to transmit a Copy of this notification to his Excellency Rufus King Esqr. at the Court of London—for whatever may be the result of the Atty Genl. opinion—I do not conceive the most learned Legal Character, competent to define the *local* Term in question.

If in obeying *emotions*, from consideration for the general good, I have committed obtrusion, I trust your Excellency will do me the justice to impute it to the Zeal I have for the existing intercourse between the Countries.

With very high Respect, I have the Honor to be Your Excellency's Very Obedt. and most humble servant WM. HYLTON.

RC (DLC); at foot of text: "His Excellency Thomas Jefferson Esqr. President &c. &c. of The United States of America Washington"; endorsed by TJ as received [8 Apr.] and so recorded in SJL. Enclosure: Hylton to William Ross, "Savana la mar," 1 Mch. 1803, regarding refusal of customs officers to allow shipment of Hylton's molasses "or Syrup boiled from *bad* or *tainted* Canes"; he argues that the attorney general will find that "it is usual and customary with Planters, when there is a taint in the *Liquor*, to send it to the molasses Cistern" and that he determined to divert his cane because much of it had been damaged by drought; the customs officials will not clear the shipment until they receive Ross's opinion; Hylton trusts that the proper definition of molasses "will not be left to the construction of every busy or envious man who takes in his head, the *Invidious* part of *Informer* to the Custom house officers" (Tr in same).

To George Jefferson

Dear Sir Washington Mar. 5th. 1803

In my letter of Feb 28 I informed you I had drawn on you in favor of Craven Peyton for a thousand dollars payable the 10th. instant, and that that sum should be remitted you from hence on this day. accordingly I now inclose you 18. bills of 50. D cash, and one of 100. making the sum of 1000. D branch bank of this place.

About the beginning of October, I left a box of [. . .] at Monticello to be forwarded to my address here. I believe 3. other boxes, containing busts belonging to Dr. Thornton & addressed either to him or me, [were] joined with mine. they have never been heard of. I have had enquiry made at home, & the information [is] that they were forwarded to you by the boats. do you know any thing of them? be so good as to address the answer to me at Monticello where I shall be from the 11th. to the 28th. Accept assurances of my constant attachment. Th: Jefferson

PrC (MHi); faint and blurred; at foot of text: "Mr George Jefferson"; endorsed by TJ in ink on verso. Recorded in SJL with notation "1000. D." Enclosures not found, but see below.

On the previous day, John Barnes sent TJ an itemized list of the bank bills used in the transaction, and TJ recorded the payment to Gibson & Jefferson in his financial memoranda (MS in MHi, in Barnes's hand, endorsed by TJ on verso: "Jefferson & Gibson. bills sent them Mar. 5. 1803"; MB, 2:1093).

To Daniel Carroll Brent

Dear Sir Washington Mar. 6. 1803

Mr. Scott, writer of the inclosed, is engaged in the life of Genl. Washington. it is not in my power to answer the questions he asks relative to his family, and I suppose the family would not do it *for him*, because Marshal's is to be their favorite history. I have thought it possible that your knolege of the family, and your means of making the enquiries, would enable you to procure for me answers to be sent to mr Scott, for which I should be thankful.

Will you be so good as to inform me of the case of Pickering, writer of the inclosed letters, on my return? Accept assurances of my great esteem & respect. Th: Jefferson

PrC (DLC); at foot of text: "Daniel C. Brent esq."; endorsed by TJ in ink on verso. Enclosures: (1) Joseph T. Scott to TJ, 25 Feb. 1803, recorded in SJL as received from Philadelphia on 5 Mch. but not found (see TJ to Scott, 6 Mch.). (2) William Pickering to TJ, undated, recorded in SJL as received 24 Jan. 1803 and "jail. pardon" but not found. (3) Pickering to TJ, 6 Mch., recorded in SJL as received 5 Mch. and "jail" but not found.

CASE OF PICKERING: during its March 1802 term, the U.S. Circuit Court of the District of Columbia found William Pickering guilty of knowingly receiving stolen property and sentenced him to three stripes and a fine of $10. In a written statement dated 12 Apr. 1803, U.S. attorney John Thomson Mason declared that Pickering was undoubtedly guilty and that the only circumstance "calculated to excite compassion" in Pickering's favor was his recent marriage to "a young woman of very respectable deportment & connections." Mason added, however, that Pickering had already suffered a long imprisonment, "during which time he has been very much diseased" (MS in DNA: RG 59, GPR; notation by TJ at foot of text, dated 21 Apr. 1803: "A pardon to be issued. Th: Jefferson"). TJ pardoned Pickering of his corporal punishment, fine, and court costs on 22 Apr. (FC in Lb in same).

From Andrew Ellicott

Dear Sir   Lancaster March 6th. 1803.

Your agreeable favour of the 26th. Ult has been duly received, and the contents noted.—I shall be very happy to see Captn. Lewis, and will with pleasure give him all the information, and instruction, in my power.—The necessary apparatus for his intended, and very interesting expedition, you will find mentioned in the last paragraph of the 42d. page of my printed observations made in our southern country, a copy of which I left with you.—But exclusive of the watch, I would recommend one of Arnolds chronometers, (if it could be had,) for reasons which I will fully explain to Mr. Lewis.—

Mr. Lewis's first object must be, to acquire a facility, and dexterity, in making the observations; which can only be attained by practice; in this he shall have all the assistance I can give him with aid of my apparatus.—It is not to be expected that the calculations can be made till after his return, because the transportation of the books, and tables, necessary for that purpose, would be found inconvenient on such a journey.—The observations on which Arrowsmith has constructed his map of the northern part of this country, were all calculated in England.

The week before last I adapted a grid-iron pendulum to my regulator, it is the first ever made in this country, and was the work of six sundays, the duties of my office not allowing any other time:—the rods, and bob of this pendulum together, weigh 18 pounds.—

I had a midling good observation on the beginning of the eclipse of the sun on the evening of the 21st. of last month.

I am in hopes Mr. Madison forwarded my observations to the national institute by Mr. Munroe.—Those on the 4th. satellite of Jupiter, have been lately written for by both la Lande, and Delambre.

I have the honour to be with great respect and esteem your friend and hbl. Serv. ANDW. ELLICOTT.

RC (DLC); at foot of text: "Thomas Jefferson President U.S."; endorsed by TJ as received 18 Mch. and so recorded in SJL. PrC (DLC: Ellicott Papers).

FAVOUR OF THE 26TH: a letter from TJ to Ellicott of 26 Feb. is recorded in SJL but has not been found.

Astronomical observations that Ellicott made during the survey of the SOUTHERN boundary of the United States appeared in the *Transactions* of the American Philosophical Society in 1802 and as an appendix to his *Journal* of the survey published in 1803. With reference to a set of his lunar sightings on the Gulf Coast to calculate longitude, Ellicott made these recommendations about apparatus: "From this example it may be seen with what ease, both the latitudes, and longitudes of places may be determined on land for common geographical purposes with a good sextant, a well made watch with seconds, and the artificial horizon, the whole of which may be packed up in a box of 12 inches in length, 8 in width, and 4 in depth" (*The Journal of Andrew Ellicott, Late Commissioner on Behalf of the United States ... for Determining the Boundary between the United States and the Possessions of His Catholic Majesty in America* [Philadelphia, 1803], appendix, 42; APS, *Transactions*, 5 [1802], 202).

ARNOLDS CHRONOMETERS: for observations to find longitude, Ellicott recommended timepieces produced in England from John Arnold's design (Vol. 34:118, 119, 120n).

CALCULATIONS: Ellicott and Robert Patterson used a lunar distances method for finding longitude on land. They taught Meriwether Lewis how to measure the angular separation between the moon and the sun or another celestial body and to make multiple observations of the sun's altitude each day. They did not expect him, however, to make the laborious mathematical calculations that their technique required for the computation of longitude from the observational data. In his orders for the western expedition drafted in April, TJ instructed Lewis to make careful observations, record the results accurately, and bring the information back to the War Department, which would have the responsibility of finding "proper persons" to make the lengthy computations (Richard S. Preston, "The Accuracy of the Astronomical Observations of Lewis and Clark," APS, *Proceedings*, 144 [2000], 168-91; Patterson to TJ, 15 Mch.; Document IV of the group of documents on drafting instructions for Lewis, at 13 Apr.).

Ellicott shared his information about the timing of the 21 Feb. ECLIPSE OF THE SUN with his acquaintance José Joaquín Ferrer y Cafranga, who had observed the eclipse in Havana, Cuba. Ferrer used the two sets of figures to calculate the longitude of Ellicott's location in Lancaster, Pennsylvania (APS, *Transactions*, 6 [1809], 158-64; Vol. 36:485).

During the survey of the boundary with Spain, Ellicott collected data on the disappearance and reappearance of moons of JUPITER to determine longitude. A few of those observations were of the planet's fourth moon (APS, *Transactions*, 5 [1802], 188-9, 191).

To Benjamin H. Latrobe

SIR Washington Mar. 6. 1803.

Congress have appropriated a sum of money (50,000. D) to be applied to the public buildings under my direction. this falls of course under the immediate business of the Superintendant, mr Monroe, whose office is substituted for that of the board of Commissioners.

the former post of Surveyor of the public buildings, which mr Hoben held till the dissolution of the board at 1700. Doll. a year will be revived. if you chuse to accept of it, you will be appointed to it, and would be expected to come on by the 1st. of April. indeed if you could make a flying trip here to set contractors to work immediately in raising freestone, it would be extremely important, because it is now late to have to engage labourers, and the quantity of freestone which can be raised, delivered & cut, in the season is the only thing which will limit the extent of our operations this year. I set out tomorrow for Monticello & shall be absent 3. weeks, but I shall be glad to recieve there your answer to this. Accept my friendly salutations & respects.

TH: JEFFERSON

P.S. on the raising of the freestone be pleased to consult Colo. D. C. Brent, who can give you better information & advice on the subject than any other person whatever, having been much concerned in the business himself.

RC (MdHi); signature clipped; at foot of text: "H. B. Latrobe esq." PrC (DLC); includes signature. Enclosure: TJ's letter of the same day to Latrobe.

The recently passed act "concerning the City of Washington" did not specify a SURVEYOR OF THE PUBLIC BUILDINGS, but the legislation made all repairs and alterations of the buildings subject to the president's discretion (U.S. Statutes at Large, 2:235-6).

As he predicted, TJ left Washington the following day for MONTICELLO, where he stayed from 11 to 31 Mch. (MB, 2:1094, 1096).

To Benjamin H. Latrobe

DEAR SIR Washington Mar. 6. 1803.

The letter in which this is inclosed being a public one, and to be produced whenever necessary as a voucher, I have thought it would be useful to add a word in one of a private & friendly nature. from the sum of 50,000 D. we shall take between 5, & 10,000. for covering the North wing of the Capitol & the President's house. the residue of 40. to 45,000. D. will be employed in building the South wing as far as it will go. I think it will raise the external walls to the uppermost window-sills, being those of the entresols; and I have no doubt Congress at their next session will give another 50,000. D. which will compleat that wing inside & out in the year 1804. before that period the repairs of their frigates will become so threatening that I have no doubt they will come into the proposition of the dry dock to rescue themselves from heavier calls. I mention these things to shew you the probability of a pretty steady employment of a person of your character here, tho' the present job has the appearance of being for the present season only, say of 8. or 9. months; and that your being in possession of the post will put all other competitors out of the question. should you think proper to undertake it, if you come here on a flying trip as suggested in my other letter, you can advise with mr Monroe, who will set into motion whatever you may desire; and if you can be here finally the first week in April, you will then find me here, & every thing may be put under full sail for the season. Accept my best wishes & respects. TH: JEFFERSON

P.S. I think a great quantity of sheet iron will be wanting.

RC (MdHi). PrC (DLC); endorsed by TJ in ink on verso. Enclosed in TJ's letter of the same day to Latrobe.

Congressional negotiations over the funding of the public buildings were based upon an estimate of $40,000 for construction of the Capitol's south wing, but testimony characterizing the roofs of the NORTH WING and President's House as "so leaky as to threaten both edifices with ruin" encouraged the appropriation of an additonal $10,000. Having decided to reroof Monticello with SHEET IRON, TJ seems to have also urged its adoption for the public buildings (*Annals*, 12:608; Seale, *The President's House*, 1:115-7; Latrobe, *Correspondence*, 1:325; TJ to James Dinsmore, 3 Jan.).

To Joseph T. Scott

SIR Washington Mar. 6. 1803.

I recieved yesterday your favor of Feb. 25. it is not in my power to answer your queries relative to Genl. Washington's family: but I have put your letter into the hands of Colo. Danl. C. Brent, who will be able to give me the information either of his own knolege or from enquiry which he has good means of making, & shall be forwarded to you. Accept assurances of my esteem & respect.

TH: JEFFERSON

PrC (DLC); at foot of text: "Mr. Joseph Scott Philada"; endorsed by TJ in ink on verso.

Scott's FAVOR OF FEB. 25 was recorded in SJL as received 5 Mch. but has not been found. See also TJ to Daniel Carroll Brent, 6 Mch.

Scott's QUERIES concerned a projected biography of George Washington, which he had proposed publishing as early as December 1799. In seeking out subscribers, Scott claimed to have "obtained in the course of an extensive correspondence, with many gentlemen of talents and information, a large stock of original materials concerning the life of this illustrious Citizen" (*Aurora*, 28 Dec. 1799).

To William Thornton

Th:J. to Doctr. Thornton Sunday Mar 6. [1803]

Could you do me the favor to come a quarter or half an hour before the company, say at three a clock & bring with you the plans of the Capitol, on which & the avenue I wish to consult you?

RC (DLC: William Thornton Papers); partially dated; addressed: "Doctr. Thornton."

Although William Thornton's original PLANS OF THE CAPITOL had been modified, he continued to discuss the construction of the federal city and conversed with planners Nicholas King and Thomas Munroe about the landscaping and design along Pennsylvania AVENUE (Gordon S. Brown, *Incidental Architect: William Thornton and the Cultural Life of Early Washington, D.C., 1794-1828* [Athens, Ohio, 2009], 29; C. M. Harris, ed., *Papers of William Thornton: Volume One, 1781-1802* [Charlottesville, 1995], 1: 309-10, 313n; Vol. 26:517-18; Enclosure No. 1 listed at Thomas Munroe to TJ, 14 Mch.; TJ to Thomas Munroe, 21 Mch.).

From James Monroe

Dear Sir New York March 7. 1803.

I recd. yours of the 25. ulto. with one to Mr. de Cepede, this morning, when I also recd. my instructions from the department of State, with all the other documents connected with my mission to France & Spn. The ship, Richmond, of abt. 400. tons burden whose cabbin I have taken, cleared at the custom house on saturday, my baggage was put on board, in expectation of sailing yesterday as Mr. Madison informed me my instructions ought to arrive by 6 in the morning; but it being sunday, they were delayd till to day. We are now detained by a snow storm and contrary wind, but shall sail as soon as it clears up, & the wind shifts.

The resolutions of Mr. Ross prove that the federal party will stick at nothing to embarrass the admn., and recover its lost power. They nevertheless produce a great effect on the publick mind and I presume more especially in the western country. The unanimity in the publick councils respecting our right to the free navigation of the river, and its importance to every part of the U States, the dissatisfaction at the interference of Spn. which will not be appeased while the power of a similar one exists, was calculated to inspire the hope of a result which may put us at ease for ever on those points. If the negotiation secures all the objects sought, or a deposit with the sovereignty over it, the federalists will be overwhelmed completely: the union of the western with the Eastern people will be consolidated, republican principles confirm'd, and a fair prospect of permanent peace and happiness presented to our country. But if the negotiation compromises short of that, and leaves the managment of our great concerns in that river, wh. comprize every thing appertaining to the western parts of the U States, in the hands of a foreign power, may we not expect that the publick will be disappointed and disapprove of the result? So far as I can judge, I think much wod. be hasarded by any adjustment which did not put us in complete security for the future. It is doubtful whether an adjustment short of that wod. be approved in any part of the union; I am thoroughly persuaded it wod. not to the westward. If they were discontented, there wod. grow up an union of councils and measures between them and the Eastern people wh. might lead to other measures & be perverted to bad purposes. The Eastern towns, wh. govern the country wish war for the sake of privateering: the western wod. not dislike it especially if they were withheld from a just right, or the enjoyment of a priviledge necessary to their welfare, the pursuit of wh. by force wod. create a vast expenditure of money among them. Their confidence is now reposed in the admn. from the best of motives a knowledge that it is sincerely friendly to their interests: it is strengthened by a distrust of these new *friends.* but an inquietude has been created by the late event, an inquiry has taken place which has shewn that every part of the union especially the Eastern is deeply interested in opening the river; that the attempt to occlude it on a former occasion was a base perhaps a corrupt intrigue of a few; their hopes and expectations have been raised, and it is probable they expect from the mission by a peaceful course every thing wh. their enemies promised by war. The consequences of a disappointment are not easily calculated. If it restored the federal party to power and involved us in war, the result might be fatal. It therefore highly merits consideration whether we shod. not take that ground as the ultimatum in the negotiation[1] wh. must in every possible event preserve the confidence & affection of the western people. While we stand well with them we shall prosper. we shall be most apt to avoid war, taking ten years ensuing together; and if we are driven by necessity into it, it is much better that it be under the auspices of a republican than a monarchic admn. These ideas are expressed in haste for yr. consideration for I have not time to give them method or form. I shall most certainly labour to obtain the best terms possible, but it is for you to say, what are the least favorable we must accept. you will have time to weigh the subject & feel the publick pulse on it before any thing conclusive may be done. I hope the French govt. will have wisdom enough to see that we will never suffer France or any other power to tamper with our interior; if that is not the object there can be no reason for declining an accomodation to the whole of our demands.

I accepted my appointment with gratitude and enter on its duties with an ardent zeal to accomplish its objects. I derive much satisfaction from a knowledge that I am in the hands of those whose views are sound, are attachd to justice, and will view my conduct with candour and liberality. under these circumstances I embark with confidence & am fearless of the result as it respects myself personally. I shall take the liberty to write you occasionally and shall at all times be most happy to hear from you and receive your commands.

Your private objects were attended to as I came here. I have the book for Mr Volney & left the bottle of wine in a train to reach its destination. will you be so kind as to forward the enclosed to Mrs. Trist & Major Lewis. that to Major Randolph you will I hope be able to present, as it respects a private object in wh. I am interested. Our best regards to our friends in Albemarle. It was cause of much regret that we cod. not see them before our departure, but the cause you can explain. I am dear Sir very sincerely affecy.

yr. friend & servt. JAS. MONROE

8th eight oclock in the morning, the wind has shifted and we expect to be on board in an hour.

RC (DLC); endorsed by TJ as received 18 Mch. and so recorded in SJL. Enclosures not found.

WITH ONE TO MR. DE CEPEDE: TJ's letter to Monroe of 25 Feb. enclosed one to Lacépède of the 24th.

For Monroe's INSTRUCTIONS FROM THE DEPARTMENT OF STATE, see TJ to Robert R. Livingston, 3 Feb., and TJ to Madison, 22 Feb. The OTHER DOCUMENTS included commissions and letters of credence for Monroe to present to the French and (if necessary) the Spanish governments, printed above in this series at 12 Jan. and 11 Feb. Madison sent all the papers to Monroe on 2 Mch. (Madison, *Papers*, *Sec. of State Ser.*, 4:364-82).

The RICHMOND lay at anchor off Staten Island waiting for Monroe. The ship's destination was Hamburg, with a stop at Le Havre to allow him and his family to disembark. SATURDAY was 5 Mch. (same, 4:340; *New-York Gazette*, 4 Mch.; New York *Mercantile Advertiser*, 9 Mch.).

See TJ to Thomas McKean, 19 Feb., for James Ross's attempt to pass RESOLUTIONS in the Senate authorizing the use of force to guarantee a place of deposit for American goods on the lower Mississippi River.

ATTEMPT TO OCCLUDE IT ON A FORMER OCCASION: in 1786, John Jay, as secretary for foreign affairs, sought to accept a proposal from Spain that would close the Mississippi River trade to Americans for 25 to 30 years. In Congress, Rufus King was the plan's leading supporter and Monroe and Charles Pinckney headed the opposition to it (Ammon, *Monroe*, 54-8; Samuel Flagg Bemis, *Pinckney's Treaty: America's Advantage from Europe's Distress, 1783-1800* [New Haven, 1960], 84-102; Vol. 33:622, 623n).

TJ had arranged for Monroe to take VOLNEY the latest volume of *Transactions* of the American Philosophical Society (TJ to Nicolas Gouin Dufief, 4 Feb.; TJ to Volney, 6 Feb.; Dufief to TJ, 1 Mch.).

Monroe had asked James LEWIS of Albemarle County to watch over his affairs in Virginia (Madison, *Papers*, *Sec. of State Ser.*, 4:280, 348; 5:20-1).

WE EXPECT TO BE ON BOARD: Monroe's wife, Elizabeth Kortright Monroe, and their daughters, Eliza and Maria Hester, accompanied him to France (Ammon, *Monroe*, 207).

[1]Preceding six words interlined.

To Thomas Munroe

SIR Washington Mar. 7. 1803.

On further enquiry & consideration I find it will be better to employ what is called here *foundation stone,* rather than brick: consequently that little brick will be wanting. your advertisement therefore may be[1] that there will be wanting large quantities of freestone, foundation stone & lime, and some brick. be so good as to mention this to mr Latrobe should he come.

Accept my best wishes & respects. TH: JEFFERSON

PrC (DLC); endorsed by TJ in ink on verso.

Munroe's ADVERTISEMENT, dated 8 Mch., called for proposals to supply "large quantities" of freestone, foundation stone, lime, sand, "and some bricks" for public use in Washington, D.C. Proposals would be received until 4 Apr. (*National Intelligencer*, 9 Mch. 1803; *Washington Federalist*, 9 Mch. 1803).

[1]TJ here canceled "for."

From Robert Smith, with Jefferson's Note

SIR, Monday Morng. [i.e. 7 Mch. 1803]

I came over this morning to submit to you the propriety of procuring Carronades for the Small Vessels we are about building. All practical men prefer them to Cannon. But the Cost of them not being Comprehended in my Estimate they cannot be Obtained but under the appropriation in Brackenridge's Bill.—I wish to have your Opinion upon this Subject

Respectfully RT SMITH

[*Note by TJ*:]

I should approve of the caronnades; but I recollect nothing in mr Breckenridge's bill which could be applied to them. that related to militia & an armory on the western waters. TH:J

RC (DLC: TJ Papers, 110:18886); partially dated; endorsed by TJ as received from the Navy Department and "Caronnades for schooners" and so recorded in SJL; also endorsed by TJ as a letter of 7 Mch., but recorded in SJL as a letter of 6 Mch. received the 7th.

CARRONADES: "A short piece of ordnance, usually of large caliber, having a chamber for the powder like a mortar; chiefly used on shipboard" (OED).

For the act of Congress authorizing the navy to build or purchase four SMALL VESSELS of war, see Smith to TJ, 19 Jan. 1803. The navy acquired the brigs *Argus* and *Siren* and the schooners *Nautilus* and *Vixen* in 1803 under the terms of the act (NDBW, *Register*, 68, 75, 77-8, 80).

BRACKENRIDGE'S BILL: by an act of 3 Mch., Congress authorized the president to call up to 80,000 militia into service and to erect one or more arsenals "on the western waters," and appropriated $1,500,000 and $25,000, respectively, for these purposes. The act originated as a resolution offered by Senator John Breckinridge of Kentucky (TJ to Thomas McKean, 19 Feb. 1803).

From Baron von Geismar

a Hanau pres de francfort sur le Main
Ce 8 de Mars 1803.

MONSIEUR!

C'est dans le plus grand embarras, n'aiant recu sur quatre de mes lettres a Votre Excellence aucune reponse, que je m'adresse encore a Elle pour la prier de ne pas me refuser son Assistance et ses bons Conseilles—

C'est sur Sa lettre encourageante de l'anné 1798 que non seulement je me suis entierement reposé, m'aiant assuré que lorsqu'il serait tems Elle remettrait mes Affaires entre les mains d'un Avocat, mais j'ai encore acheté un quatrieme Billet: Et presentement j'apprens non seulement de Toute part, que Jacob Mark a fait une Banqueroute, mais aussi par une lettre de La main propre a une Actionaire des Mines de la Nouvelle York, Madame la Baronne d'Osterhausen a Cassel, dont je joins une Copie, qu'il a remis Les biens fonds entre les mains de la Justice. Voila ce qui me console encore en quelque maniere, tout persuade que cela ne peut pas etre a l'insue de Votre Excellence: et qu'Elle se sera souvenue a cette Occasion de l'interet d'un ancien Ami—Si meme aucune de mes lettres et de mes dupliques, que j'ai fait partir depuis 4 Ans par l'Angleterre et la hollande ne Lui fussent parcevues; je suis cependant assure Elle aurra pris des mesures en ma faveur, aiant eté parfaitement instruit de mon affaire par mes deux premieres, aux quelles Elle m'a honnoré de Ses reponses—J'ose donc la prier encore instament de me pretter Son Secours pour me tirer d'affaire: et c'est avec une pleine Confiance que je m'adresse a Elle, Ses Sentiments d'équite et de justice m'ettant connues d'ancienne date

Je suis avec la plus haute Consideration Monsieur de Votre Excellence Tres humble tres obeisant Serviteur DE GEISMAR

P:S:

A [Stauüard] Ce 8 d'Aout 1803

Aiant repris Service cela fait que j'ai aussi changé de demeure L'Electeur de Wurtemberg, m'aiant honoré de la place d'adjudant Genl: auprès de sa Personne et du Titre de Generale Major dans le pays, cela fait que je me suis etablis dans la Residence de l'Electeur, à [Stauüard] Si Votre Excellence m'honnore d'une reponse je La prie de me la faire parvenir seul par notre Envoie a Paris ou tout droit à [Stauüard]—Celle ci partira par Paris ou elle sera remise au Ministre des Etats d'Amerique par l'Envoie de Wurtemberg, Baron de Steuben. GESMAR.

EDITORS' TRANSLATION

Hanau near Frankfurt on Main
8 Mch. 1803

SIR,

Not having received replies to four of my letters to your Excellency, it is with the greatest distress that I address you again to beg you not to refuse your help and wise counsel.

Based on your encouraging letter of 1798, assuring me that when the time came you would entrust my affairs to a lawyer, I not only trusted you implicitly but also bought a fourth note. Now I hear everywhere not only that Jacob Mark has gone bankrupt but also, from a letter given to me by the Baronness of Osterhausen of Cassel, a stockholder in the New York mines, a copy of which I enclose, that he has handed over the business to the justice system. This consoles me in some way, since I am fully convinced that your Excellency must know about it and will, under the circumstances, remember the interests of an old friend. Even if you did not receive any of the letters and copies I sent you from England and Holland over four years, I am nevertheless assured that you will have taken measures in my favor, having been fully briefed on my case by the first two letters, to which you did me the honor of replying. I therefore dare implore you to lend your help to get me out of this difficulty. I address you with full confidence, long aware of your sentiments of fairness and justice.

With the highest regard, Sir, for Your Excellency, I am your very humble and obedient servant. DE GEISMAR

P.S.

[Stauüard] 8 Aug. 1803

Having taken on a new function, I have also changed domicile, since the elector of Württemberg has honored me with the position of adjutant general on his staff under the title of major general in the region. I have therefore settled in the elector's residence [Stauüard]. If Your Excellency should honor me with a reply, I ask you to send it through our envoy in Paris or directly to [Stauüard]. This letter will go through Paris where it will be entrusted to the minister of the American states by the Württemberg envoy, Baron von Steube. GEISMAR

RC (DLC); endorsed by TJ as a letter of 8 Mch. and 8 Aug. received 13 Nov. and so recorded in SJL. Enclosure not found.

AUCUNE REPONSE: Geismar had written his four most recent letters to TJ in August 1798, February 1799, February 1800, and June 1801. TJ had not responded since receiving the two latest of those letters, both of which came to him in October 1801. His last letter to Geismar, which is recorded in SJL but has not been found, was dated 8 May 1800. Much of the correspondence between them, which primarily concerned Geismar's investments in the New Jersey Copper Mine Association, is now missing (Vol. 30:317n; Vol. 31:378-81, 570n; Vol. 34:468-70).

LETTRE ENCOURAGEANTE: one letter from TJ to Geismar in 1798 is recorded in SJL, under 13 Feb., but it has not been found; see Vol. 30:316.

MES DEUX PREMIERES: probably a communication from Geismar of 15 Oct. 1796, to which TJ replied in his letter of 13 Feb. 1798, and another from the baron of 11 July 1798, which TJ received in January 1799 and reciprocated on 23 Feb. of that year (same, 317n).

L'ELECTEUR: by a treaty with France in May 1802, Friedrich II, the duke of Württemberg, agreed to yield up his possessions on the left bank of the Rhine. Then in a reorganization of German states arranged by France and Russia and announced in February 1803, Württemberg acquired the status of an electorate of the Holy Roman Empire, making Friedrich an imperial elector, and he received control over significantly more population and revenue than he had given up across the Rhine (Parry, *Consolidated Treaty Series*, 56:319-22; Peter H. Wilson, *German Armies: War and German Politics, 1648-1806* [London, 1998], 326-9; C. T. Atkinson, *A History of Germany: 1715-1815* [London, 1908], 462; Tulard, *Dictionnaire Napoléon*, 1754; Harold C. Deutsch, *The Genesis of Napoleonic Imperialism* [Cambridge, 1938], 56-8).

L'ENVOIE DE WURTEMBERG: Christoph Erdmann Freiherr von Steube zu Schnaditz was the minister plenipotentiary of Württemberg to the French Republic (Ulrich Fleischmann and Ineke Phaf, eds., *El Caribe y América Latina: The Caribbean and Latin America* [Frankfurt-on-Main, 1987], 65n).

From George Jefferson

DEAR SIR Richmond 8th. March 1803

I forwarded some days since the remainder of the nail rod, & the hoop-iron, received some time ago.

I likewise forwarded by C. Becks's boat 31 packages lately received from George Town & Alexandria, together with a Hhd of Molasses & the 3 Casks Cyder.

I could not conveniently get the Molasses caskd, and therefore sent it without, supposing Becks to be perfectly honest, and very careful.

I some time ago desired Mr. Higganbotham to direct some safe person to call for these things, but he repeated the request he had before made, that we would forward them by a Negro who goes in J. Rowes boat, and in which I am told he is concerned—he says Mr. Silby has engaged that all your things shall be retained for this boat—if so, you will be pleased to inform us.

The freight from George Town I did not pay, for a reason I have explained to Mr. Barnes. nothing else of yours has yet arrived.

I am Dr. Sir Your Very humble servt. GEO. JEFFERSON

RC (MHi); at foot of text: "Thos. Jefferson esqr."; endorsed by TJ as received 12 Mch. and so recorded in SJL.

For instructions related to the NAIL ROD, molasses, cider, and other items, see TJ to George Jefferson, 8 Feb. 1803.

From James Madison

DEAR SIR Washington Mar. 10. 1803

The answers from the Govr. & Intendant at N. Orleans to the Spanish Ministers letter were recd. by him yesterday. The Intendant himself states that he had taken his measures, merely on his own judgment, without orders from his Govt. and in opposition to the judgment of the Govr: but it appears that his determination had not been changed by the first interposition of Yrujo. As his second letter written after it was known that the Intendant had proceeded without orders, must have spoken with more energy, it is possible that it may have more effect. Considering however the case in all its aspects, I have thought it proper to call on Yrujo for the peremptory injunctions which he seemed willing to undertake, and am just sending him a note for that purpose, which is approved by my several colleagues. He says he will do every thing that depends on decision; and will even, in a private letter to the Govr. urge him, if the Intendant should be refractory, to ship him off to Spain, which is the Ultima ratio it seems of Spanish Governors agst. Intendants. The despatches of the Marquis will be forwarded under my cover to Claybourne, and will go by an Express who it is hoped will overtake the Mail now on the way.

It appears by a letter of Novr. 24 from Obrien, thro' Cathalan, that the Dey of Algiers refused the cash payment which had arrived, and insists on the Stores with much irritation at the offer substituted.[1] Will you be pleased to say to Mr. Smith whether he is to forward them as soon as possible, as seems now to be indispensable.

With respectful attachment I remain Yrs. JAMES MADISON

RC (DLC); at foot of text: "The President of the U.S."; endorsed by TJ as received from the State Department on 16 Mch. and so recorded in SJL with notations "N. Orleans. Algiers."

RECD. BY HIM YESTERDAY: Carlos Martínez de Irujo wrote to Madison on 10 Mch. concerning replies he had received to his letters to Manuel de Salcedo, the governor of Louisiana, and Juan Ventura Morales, the intendant at New Orleans. Irujo expressed confidence that Morales had acted on his own authority, without orders from Spain, when he closed the right of deposit at New Orleans and that Salcedo opposed the decision. In his NOTE in reply to Irujo, Madison observed that the season had come for American products to begin moving down the Mississippi River and urged "an instant resort, to such peremptory injunctions as may reclaim the Intendant from his error, and by giving to the violated treaty its due effect, rescue from immediate danger the confidence and good neighbourhood which it is the interest of both nations to maintain." Madison offered the services of the U.S. government in conveying dispatches from Irujo to Louisiana by land and urged that duplicates be sent by sea. Irujo wrote to Morales and Salcedo on the 11th to say that the right of deposit must either be restored at New Orleans or opened in another location to avoid a confrontation that could cost Spain both Louisiana and the Floridas (Madison, *Papers*, *Sec. of State Ser.*, 4:408-10; John Brown to TJ, 26 Nov. 1802; TJ to James Garrard, 18 Jan. 1803).

ULTIMA RATIO: that is, the last resort.

King Carlos of Spain had recently made Irujo a MARQUIS (Irujo to TJ, at 9 Jan.).

UNDER MY COVER TO CLAYBOURNE: on 11 Mch., the same day that Irujo signed his new dispatches to Morales and Salcedo, Madison forwarded the documents to William C. C. Claiborne in Mississippi Territory with a request that they be given "as quick a conveyance as possible" to New Orleans (Madison, *Papers*, *Sec. of State Ser.*, 4:413-14).

Stephen CATHALAN, Jr., in a letter to Madison of 10 Dec., passed along the news from Richard O'Brien that the DEY OF ALGIERS, Mustafa Baba, had refused to accept payment in lieu of stores (same, 4:186, 408n).

On 9 Mch., the State Department received from William E. Hulings a copy of an order dated 30 July 1802 from Miguel Cayetano Soler, the Spanish minister of the treasury, to Morales, informing him of the decision to cede Louisiana to France. The intendant was to be ready to transfer the province to whatever commissioners might be authorized to receive it for the Republic of France. Soler indicated that Salcedo would also receive notice of the intended transfer and of the crown's intention to find new postings elsewhere for soldiers in the colony who wished to remain in Spanish service. TJ later received a copy of the order from William Dunbar (Tr in DLC: TJ Papers, 132: 22836, in Spanish, enclosed in Dunbar to TJ, 21 Oct. 1803; Madison, *Papers*, *Sec. of State Ser.*, 4:190).

[1]MS: "subsituted."

From Edward Savage

SIR New York March 10—1803

your favour of the 4th. is Just Come to hand. the miscarriage of Several Papers appears very Extraordinary, I am very Shure of Enclosing to you a Discription of the mountain Ram, and one of my proposals for Publishing by Subscription a print Representing the Declaration of Independence.

I put up at the Same time a packet containing thirty Proposals and twenty three Recipts fill'd up and Signed, Except a Blank for the Subscribers Name, it was Directed to Mr Foster—which he Sayes he never Recd neither Could he find them in the office in Washington. I Beg'd of Mr Foster when he Receved them to give them to the Doorkeepers of Congress Supposing Some of the Gentlemen would be pleased to Encourage the work.

I now take the Liberty to Enclose to you Sir the Discription of the Mountain Ram and one of my Proposals, I am very sorry that you have had So much trouble in Consequence of not Receving the papers at first

I am Sir with Great Esteeme your very Humble Sevt.

EDWARD SAVAGE

Mr Foster as he pass'd throw this City inform'd me, that you had not Recd your Proposal,[1]

RC (DLC); at foot of text: "Thomas Jefferson President of the United States"; endorsed by TJ as received 18 Mch. and so recorded in SJL. Enclosures not found, but see below.

MISCARRIAGE OF SEVERAL PAPERS: see Savage to TJ of 7 Feb.

A description of the My-Attic or MOUNTAIN RAM, provided by Duncan McGillivray of Canada to Savage, first appeared in the New York *Daily Advertiser* on 4 Dec. 1802. It became the basis for Savage's drawings of the animal for his museum and for an "Account of the Wild North-American Sheep," which Samuel Latham Mitchill published in New York in 1803 in the sixth volume of his *Medical Repository*.

MR FOSTER: possibly one of the Federalist brothers, Dwight Foster of Massachusetts or Theodore Foster of Rhode Island, both of whom left their Senate seats at the beginning of March, and, like Savage, hailed from Worcester County, Massachusetts (*Biog. Dir. Cong.*).

[1] Postscript in left margin perpendicular to text.

From William Short

New York, 10 Mch. 1803. Replying to TJ's letter of 3 Mch., he asks that TJ bring the bundle of papers relating to Short's affairs when he returns from Monticello, as he would like to have access to the maps and mortgage papers for his property. With regard to TJ's offer to repay the money he owes Short in two years, Short states that he was "indifferent" to that subject before he left France, but now that he is in the United States he wants to get his affairs arranged in person. He has made out his account with TJ, which revealed a small error, and the sum owed by TJ as of 1 Jan. 1800 was about $11,700. John Barnes's accounts do not show that TJ paid any interest in the three years since then. Short will give the same attention to his own affairs now that he formerly gave to public matters. He wants his lands offered for sale by George Jefferson, noting that ten dollars is "equal or nearly" to his expected price, and Gabriel Lilly should now make only year-to-year leases on the property. He refers to his diplomatic service. He understands that Henry Skipwith accepts arbitration in the dispute between them about Short's finances. He will be traveling from Philadelphia next month and will not be stopping at Washington, but letters addressed to him in New York will always find him.

FC (DLC: Short Papers); 1 p.; entirely in Short's hand, consisting of an entry in his epistolary record. Recorded in SJL as received from New York on 21 Mch.

From Edward Tiffin

Chillicothe Ohio
Sir— March 10th. 1803

Yours of feby—has been duly received, in which you request with as little delay as possable to be furnished with a return of the Militia, and of the Arms and Accoutrements of this state, and of the several counties or other geographical divisions of it. believing as I do, that none but an armed nation can dispence with a standing Army and that standing Armys are dangerous to Liberty, I was well aware of the importance & necessity of vigorous exertions on the part of the state Governments to carry into effect the Militia system adopted by the National Legislature, agreably to the powers reserved to them by the Constitution of the United States. I therefore as soon as I came into office called upon the Adjutant General of the Militia for a return agreable to Law. his answer received yesterday, justified my apprehensions, that both the late Governor St Clair, and himself had intirely neglected to carry the Militia Law into effect. it is therefore out of my power at present to comply with your request. the Legislature of this State is now in Session, and the Militia Law which requires much revision is before them, but from the manner in which the appointment of Officers is directed to be made by the Constitution, it will require a considerable time before the Militia can be organized, and a knowledge of its strength and situation acquired—no exertions on my part shall be wanting to accomplish these objects, which when accomplished shall be immediately communicated to you.

pardon the liberty I have taken to inclose a copy of my communication to the General Assembly, and accept the assurances of my sincere wishes for your happiness and welfare Edward Tiffin

RC (PHi); at foot of text: "The President of [the United] States"; endorsed by TJ as received 6 Apr. and so recorded in SJL with notation "W"; also endorsed by TJ: "to be filed in the W.O." Enclosure: probably Tiffin's message to the Ohio Senate and House of Representatives, dated 5 Mch. but presented on 4 Mch., in which he congratulates the legislature on the addition of "another sovereign, free and independent State" to the Union and calls their attention to the important work before them; Tiffin points out the auspicious situation of the country and is confident that "prompt and efficacious measures" by the president and Congress will quickly settle the current "irregularities at New-Orleans" and restore commerce on the Mississippi River; as legislators work to "raise the superstructure" of their new government, Tiffin notes the state's solid fiscal condition and calls attention to a series of topics for consideration, including the election of federal representatives, devising a tax system, establishing a state judiciary, conducting a census, revising the militia laws, and reviewing all remaining territorial laws; Tiffin offers thanks "to that Being who has so highly favored us" and urges legislators to encourage and cultivate education, religion, economy in public expenditures, peace with the Indians, and "industry, frugality, temperance, and every moral virtue" (*Journal of the Senate of the State of Ohio: First Session of the Legislature, Held Under the Constitution of the State, A.D. 1803* [Chillicothe, Ohio, 1803], 11-16; *Journal of the House of Representatives of the State of Ohio: First Session of the Legislature, Held Under the Constitution of the State, A.D. 1803* [Chillicothe, Ohio, 1803], 9-14).

Born in England, Edward Tiffin (1766-1829) came to America in the 1780s and eventually settled in Virginia. A physician and Methodist lay minister, he emigrated to the Northwest Territory in 1798 with his brother-in-law, Thomas Worthington. Tiffin quickly became a popular and influential Republican leader and won a succession of prestigious offices, including speaker of the territorial assembly and president of the Ohio constitutional convention. In 1803, Tiffin was elected overwhelmingly the state's first governor, serving until 1807. During his tenure, he and the Ohio legislature earned TJ's praise for their actions in thwarting the Burr conspiracy, "which entitle them to a distinguished place in the affection of their sister states." Tiffin later served briefly in the U.S. Senate and subsequently received an appointment as commissioner of the General Land Office from President James Madison (ANB; TJ to the Senate and the House of Representatives, 22 Jan. 1807).

YOURS OF FEBY: Circular to the Governors of the States, 25 Feb. 1803.

APPOINTMENT OF OFFICERS: as specified by Article 5 of the Ohio constitution, the governor appointed the state adjutant general, while the legislature chose major generals and quartermasters general. Companies elected their own captains and subalterns, while majors, colonels, and brigadiers were chosen by the officers of their respective battalions, regiments, and brigades (*Constitution of the State of Ohio*, 2d ed. [Chillicothe, Ohio, 1803], 17-18).

From John Willard

SIR Middlebury Vermont 11th of March 1803

By a letter from Mr Israel Smith received on the 7th inst I understand that complaint has been made to the President of the United States by Amasa Paine & Cephas Smith that I had officiated in the office of Marshal without giving bond, as the Law requires—being unacquainted with the particulars it will at present be out of my power to reply to the charges exhibited against me, in the mean time I beg leave to explain a circumstance from which I think it probable they originated their suggestions. The term of my first appointment was limited to the rising of the next session of the senate—at the expiration of that term not having received my second commission I felt myself in an unpleasant situation & was undetermined how to act I took advice of the best informed law characters on the subject who were all unanimous in the opinion that I ought to proceed in the exercise of my official duty otherwise there would be an interregnum in the office which it is presumed was never contemplated by the law—under those circumstances I continued to officiate untill the reciept of my commission which was late in the summer (the precise time I do not recollect)[1] notwithstanding the letter of the Secretary of state in which it was inclosed bore date April 28th by whom the commission was detained it may be impossible to determin, the purpose for which it was detained will not be so difficult to understand & will serve as an other proof of the necessity of reform in the subordinate branches of the Postmaster department—it woud be unreasonable for me to expect to escape persecution when I consider that the most pure & exalted characters in the present administration are the broadest marks for slander—it will be needless for me to make any remarks on the characters of Paine & Smith the complainants I presume sir you are not unacquanted with the peculiar virulence with which they pursue every measure of the government—

Conscious of having at all times endeavored strictly to comply with the law in the exercise of my official duty I shall meet any inquery into my conduct with pleasure in the mean time while I continue to hold the office my prime object will be to make every mean in my power subservient to the public interest but when in the opinion of the executive that interest will be better promoted by another I shall suffer no private consideration to come in competition with the public good but will chearfully retire from office in full confidence that all the measures of the present executive originate from this purest design to promote the public happiness—

The benign influence of the measures pursued by the administration has a visible effect on the public mind the great mass of the people manifest a rapid increase of their confidence the time is fast approximating when the body of the freemen will be concerned how much their interest & happiness has been promoted by the change of men & measures.

Last week we made a second attempt to elect a representative to Congress in this district—from the return of votes we have already obtained I am convinced there will be no choice the republican ticket stands the highest has gained ground at the second trial & in all probability at the next will be successfull

I have the honor to be sir very respectfully your obedient Servant

John Willard

RC (DLC); at foot of text: "The President of the United States"; endorsed by TJ as received 5 Apr. and so recorded in SJL.

Born in East Guilford, Connecticut, the son of a shipmaster, John Willard (1759-1825) became a seaman during the Revolutionary War and was captured by the British. Upon his release he became quartermaster of a Connecticut regiment. After studying medicine with a local physician, he moved to Middlebury, Vermont, where he set up a medical practice and entered politics as an early and constant advocate of the Republican cause. On 4

Mch. 1801, he delivered an oration at Middlebury to celebrate TJ's inauguration. Shortly after taking office, TJ appointed him marshal for the district of Vermont in place of Jabez Fitch, who, according to the president, was guilty of "cruel conduct." Willard's appointment was also part of TJ's effort to bring Republicans into the court system dominated by Federalists. In 1809, Willard married 22-year-old Emma Hart, the principal of the female academy at Middlebury. She founded the Middlebury Female Seminary in their home in 1814, after Dr. Willard experienced financial reverses as a result of being a director of the Vermont State Bank. He served as physician and business manager for his wife's increasingly successful endeavors in female education, moving first from Middlebury to Waterford, New York, in 1819, and two years later to Troy, where the Troy Female Seminary received local financial assistance and opened in 1821 under Emma Willard's leadership (John Willard, *An Oration Delivered at Middlebury, in the State of Vermont, on the Fourth of March, One Thousand Eight Hundred and One* [Bennington, 1801]; Alma Lutz, *Emma Willard: Pioneer Educator of American Women* [Boston, 1964], 16-17, 20-1, 35, 38-40, 56; *Rutland Vermont Herald*, 15 Nov. 1809, 17 Nov. 1813; Windsor *Vermont Republican*, 11 Nov. 1811; Vol. 33: 111-12, 219, 668, 673, 674).

In a 13 Jan. 1803 letter to Senator Stephen R. Bradley, AMASA PAINE called for the removal of Willard, charging that he had "wholly omitted to give bonds, or qualify under his last appointment" for "four months after his first appointment expired, & that notwithstanding he continually executed the office, tho unauthorized." Paine recommended Reuben Atwater, Bradley's brother-in-law, in Willard's place (Dorr Bradley Carpenter, ed., *Stephen R. Bradley: Letters of a Revolutionary War Patriot and Vermont Senator* [Jefferson, N.C., 2009], 204). In December 1801, Elijah Paine, a Federalist, wrote TJ recommending Atwater in place of Willard. At the same time, Moses Robinson defended Willard's character, abilities, and conduct as marshal (Vol. 35:684-5; Vol. 36:100). SECOND COMMISSION: Willard was confirmed by the Senate with other interim appointments on 26 Jan. 1802, and that is the date the State Department issued his commission for a term of four years. Willard's commission was renewed in December 1805 and again in 1809. He was removed from office in January 1811 (commissions dated 26 Jan. 1802 and 17 Dec. 1805 in DNA: RG 59, MPTPC; JEP, 1:403, 405; 2:5, 130-1; Windsor *Vermont Republican*, 28 Jan. 1811; Vol. 36:334, 336n).

ELECT A REPRESENTATIVE TO CONGRESS: in Vermont the candidate had to receive a majority of the total votes cast by freemen at town meetings in the district to win the election. Middlebury was part of Vermont's northwestern district. In the first election on 11 Jan., Republican Udny Hay received 1,289 votes, the highest number in the district but not a majority. The two Federalist candidates with the most votes were Martin Chittenden and Amos Marsh, with 841 and 545, respectively. At the SECOND TRIAL on 1 Mch., Hay garnered 1,980 votes. The Federalists again split their vote, with 1,237 cast for Chittenden and 834 for Marsh. At the third election, held on 9 May, the Federalists united behind Chittenden, giving him the victory with 2,319 votes against Hay's 1,938 (*Middlebury Mercury*, 19 Jan., 30 Mch., 13 Apr., 18 June 1803; *Biog. Dir. Cong.*; Vol. 35: 575n; Vol. 36:575; Vol. 38:357n).

[1]MS: "recollet."

From Lewis Harvie

Dear Sir [before 12 Mch. 1803.]

I take the earliest opportunity of answering your favour of the 28th of February. The experience which my visit to Monticello gave me of the mingled benefit and pleasure resulting from a residence in your house induced me to offer my services as Secretary, when the wishes of the American people were gratified by your accession to the Presidential chair. Although my situation has been since somewhat changed, the same motives influence me now to accept with the liveliest satisfaction the offer you have politely made. Previous to the reception of your letter I proposed to remain some time in Georgetown, & prosecute the study of the Law under Mr Mason, as preparative to my establishment in Baltimore, which the extreme irksomeness of a residence in this Gomorra of Aristocracy caused me seriously to contemplate. But a conviction that in what ever place I may ultimately resolve to pursue my profession my prospect of success will be enlarged by the information which must be received from an intercourse so desireable, gives the unequivocal assent of my judgment to those feelings which warmly urge the acceptance of the situation proposed. The duties of the office, I trust will not be incompatible with my bestowing a portion of the day on other avocations,—as their intire occupation of my time would diminish the pleasure I should take in giving them a strict attention. As to other arrangements, I have only to observe that I did not originally propose to receive any salary; but my late visit to Washington induces me to believe that the funds I can conveniently command would be inadequate without its aid to defray the expences I should necessarily incur. I shall probably bring with me a servant; I hope no inconvenience will attend it. I shall be prepared to fill the post by the 1st of April; you have not mentioned where you will then be; I shall proceed to Washington unless I again hear from you. I cannot conclude without remarking that I consider this opportunity of forming my political opinions under the direction of one whose conduct is sanctioned by the approbation of every friend to his country as the happiest event of my life.

Accept my compliments Lewis Harvie

RC (DLC); undated; endorsed by TJ as received 12 Mch. and so recorded in SJL.

gomorra of aristocracy: that is, Richmond, where Harvie had been spending most of his time (Vol. 39:361-3, 409).

From Joseph Barbier

Digne, le 21. Ventose an 11.
de la République française,
Président, une & indivisible. [i.e. 12 Mch. 1803]

Le Citoyen Serraire habitant de Cette ville de Digne me charge de Vous prier de donner des Ordres pour qu'il soit pris des renseignemens Sur françois Serraire son fils qui a été emmené de Marseilles par le Capitaine de Navire *Michel* qui l'a conduit à Philadelphie il y a environ six ans; Depuis cette Epoque le Pere n'a aucune nouvelle de Son Enfant, il attend de votre Bienveillance que Vous voudrez Bien ordonner les mesures propres à Lui En procurer.

à mon Particulier Je vous Prie D'agréer mon homage Respectueux.

J'ai L'honneur de vous saluer avec Respect Barbier

EDITORS' TRANSLATION

Digne, 21 Ventose Year 11
of the one and indivisible
Mr. President, French Republic [i.e. 12 Mch. 1803]

Citizen Serraire, an inhabitant of this city of Digne, has charged me with asking you to obtain information about his son, François Serraire, who was taken from Marseilles to Philadelphia about six years ago by the ship captain Michel. Since then, the father has had no news of his child. He hopes that your kindness will prompt you to order an investigation leading to news.

In my own name, I beg you to accept my respectful homage, and have the honor of greeting you with respect. Barbier

RC (DNA: RG 59, MLR); English date supplied; on printed letterhead stationery of the *secrétaire général* of the *département* of Basses-Alpes, with emblems of the French Republic; dateline printed in part, with blanks filled by Barbier; at head of text: "au Président des Etats unis d'Amerique"; endorsed by TJ as received 19 Aug. and so recorded in SJL.

Joseph Barbier (b. 1769) became the secretary general of Basses-Alpes in 1800, when Bonaparte's government divided France into 90 regional departments. The chief officer of a *département* was the prefect, who answered directly to the central government. Each department also had a secretary general, who oversaw the bureaus that handled day-to-day civil administration in the department (Christiane Lamoussière and others, *Le Personnel de l'administration préfectorale, 1800-1880* [Paris, 1998], 79; Brian Chapman, *The Prefects and Provincial France* [London, 1955], 17-32).

A brief notice asking anyone with information about FRANÇOIS SERRAIRE to contact the State Department appeared in the *National Intelligencer* a week after TJ received Barbier's letter in August 1803. Newspapers throughout the United States reprinted the notice, which contained the facts related by Barbier to TJ (*National Intelligencer*, 26 Aug.; Philadelphia *Aurora*, 30 Aug.; New York *Evening Post*, 31 Aug.; Boston *New-England Palladium*, 6 Sep.; Hudson, N.Y., *Bee*, 6 Sep.; Charleston *City Gazette*, 8 Sep.).

From Robert R. Livingston

I. RECIPIENT'S COPY, 12 MCH. 1803

II. RECIPIENT'S COPY, 12 MCH. 1803

III. EXTRACT, [AFTER 18 MAY]

EDITORIAL NOTE

On 12 Mch., Robert R. Livingston began a letter to the president that reported on his activities in general terms, mentioning his efforts to influence Napoleon Bonaparte about Louisiana, his discussions with the Spanish ambassador concerning the Floridas, and French attitudes toward the United States and Great Britain. The next day, a Sunday, Livingston interrupted his writing to attend an afternoon reception at the Tuileries Palace. When he sat down again to resume the letter, a new topic appeared, one that dominated much of the correspondence written in Paris in the days following the gathering at the palace: at the reception, Bonaparte had startled everyone by publicly confronting Charles Whitworth, the British minister to France, about the souring relations between their two nations and the prospect of renewed war (Grainger, *Amiens Truce*, 174-5).

After recounting the incident, Livingston closed his draft by returning to subjects similar to those with which he had begun the epistle, including his desire to resign his position. With the help of an unidentified assistant, he prepared two fair copies to be dispatched to the United States (to guard against accidents in transit). Livingston underscored some passages in his draft that his helper put into code by writing above the line. The amanuensis then copied the letter for Livingston's signature, using code for the enciphered text (Document I below). Livingston himself made another clean copy of the letter, also incorporating the codes (Document II). He added a postscript to each copy.

Jefferson received both documents at about the same time. He endorsed both, but made only one entry in his epistolary record, where he recorded the receipt of a 12 Mch. letter from Livingston on 18 May. In his endorsement on Document I, his date of receipt is obscured. Jacob Wagner also endorsed that copy, docketing its receipt on 19 May. That notation probably refers to the day on which the State Department received the document from the president, who complied with a request by Livingston that he pass its contents along to the secretary of state. Jefferson also endorsed the other version of the letter (Document II), noting its date of receipt as 18 May.

The president decoded the encrypted passages of Document I, which in all likelihood means that it came to him first. Generally, as shown by his and the State Department's handling of Livingston's letter of 2 June in this volume, the first version of a dispatch to come to hand was decoded, and no effort was made to decipher duplicate versions that arrived later. Document II also has interlined decipherment, but in Madison's hand. Whether Madison decoded the passages himself or copied Jefferson's decipherment is not clear. (Jefferson decoded the message, as shown by spaces he left between parts of some words that were compounds made up of more than one code element.) If the president and the secretary of state both unraveled the coded text, perhaps they did so concurrently and without knowing that they were duplicating the effort of decipherment.

Although Livingston wrote "Copy" at the top of Document I, that version in his assistant's handwriting was not an exact duplicate of Document II. Livingston and his helper both used his draft to make their fair copies, but the clerk probably went first, and certainly followed the draft more faithfully. When his turn came, Livingston varied the wording and made some new changes to the draft (see notes to Document I). Documents I and II parallel each other, with some variation, for about the first third or so of the text—that is, the portion that Livingston composed before he went to the reception at the Tuileries on the 13th. Greater variation of wording, and also of detail, occurs in the middle of the letter where Livingston discussed the interplay between Bonaparte and Whitworth. The first consul's reference to "vengeance that would await the breach of a solem treaty" appears only in Document II. In Document I, but not II, Whitworth gets the last word in, with an appeal to peace. In Document I, Bonaparte avowed "I must either have Malta or war," but in the other version the remark is "if you do not evacuate Malta there will be war." In Document II, Livingston did not label every shift of dialogue between the first consul and the British minister; in Document I, the speakers are clearly identified.

Following the narrative of the affair at the palace, the two texts come back into closer alignment, although still with some variation. Only in Document II, for example, did Livingston relate a belief of "people about court" that the British would back down to avoid war. Whereas Document I, following the original wording of his draft, stated that "I Suffered so much on my outward passage," in Document II Livingston's family were the sufferers.

Livingston probably completed Document II sometime after 14 Mch., for in it he said that news of the incident at the palace went to Britain by express "that very night"—that is, the 13th—and to other European countries "in the course of the next day." Whitworth sent a full dispatch to Lord Hawkesbury on the 14th. As Livingston mentioned in both versions of his letter to Jefferson, he spoke with Whitworth at the reception, and the postscript to Document II indicates that they talked again sometime afterward. Whitworth was Livingston's key source of information, for, as Livingston confessed in Document I, a "difficulty of hearing" (in his draft he originally wrote "deafness") had prevented him from catching what was said in Whitworth's exchange with Bonaparte. Although he said nothing of that in Document II, his condition was evident at the function at the Tuileries. A Briton who was there with Whitworth recorded in his diary that the first consul spoke with the British minister, moved on to talk briefly with a few others, then "accosted the American Minister who being very deaf did not hear, and B— was too impatient to repeat." A British clergyman who was present remembered, almost half a century later, that after the first consul left the room, Whitworth "addressed the American Minister, who was very deaf, and repeated what had passed"—repeated, that is, a conversation that according to Whitworth had been "loud enough to be overheard by two hundred people who were present" (Oscar Browning, ed., *England and Napoleon in 1803: Being the Despatches of Lord Whitworth and Others* [London, 1887], 115-17; J. P. T. Bury and J. C. Barry, eds., *An Englishman in Paris: 1803. The Journal of*

Bertie Greatheed [London, 1953], 93; "Bonaparte and Lord Whitworth," *Notes and Queries*, 5 [1852], 313-14).

From Whitworth sometime after the incident at the Tuileries, Livingston learned that the most striking detail of his narrative, Bonaparte's stark ultimatum of "Malta or war," had not actually been uttered at the palace assembly. Rather, as Livingston noted in his postscripts to both versions of his letter to Jefferson, that declaration was from "a private conversation" (Documents I and II). Malta did come up in the exchange between Bonaparte and Whitworth at the reception, and Bonaparte predicted that a failure by Britain to comply with the terms of the Amiens treaty would result in a great storm or tempest. It was in a meeting with Talleyrand two days earlier, however, that Whitworth had learned of the first consul's resolution to consider a refusal by Britain to evacuate Malta as "a commencement of hostilities" (Browning, *England and Napoleon*, 112, 116; *Correspondance de Napoléon 1er: publiée par ordre de l'Empereur Napoléon III*, 32 vols. [Paris, 1858-70], 8:247, 250-1; Bury and Barry, eds., *Englishman in Paris*, 93-4; "Bonaparte and Lord Whitworth," 314; Grainger, *Amiens Truce*, 171-2).

Tension between the two nations had been mounting for several weeks. The British government objected to actions by the French in Italy, Switzerland, and Holland, suspected that a reoccupation of Egypt, with an intention of pushing on into India, was in the offing, and worried that a concentration of French troops and ships in northern France and Holland foretold an invasion of Ireland or Britain. For its part, the French government was alarmed by recent steps to augment British forces as well as by the halting of the withdrawal from Malta. According to the British clergyman's recollections years later, Bonaparte never raised his voice to Whitworth, who "smiled very courteously" at one point in the conversation, and the British diplomat even made a small joke about the confrontation after Bonaparte left the room. Whitworth, however, believed that the incident was a demonstration of the "violence" of Bonaparte's temper and reported to Hawkesbury that the first consul had appeared to be "under very considerable agitation." The British diarist noted that the French leader's "eyes roved about the room" as he confronted Whitworth, he shifted his weight "from leg to leg," and he "gave threatening shakes of his head." By more than one account, including official French versions of the affair sent to the nation's envoys in London and St. Petersburg, Bonaparte declared that in the eyes of both God and men—"aux yeux de Dieu et des hommes"—the responsibility for a breach of peace would fall on the British if they failed to meet their responsibilities under the treaty. French citizens could be killed but never intimidated, he asserted to Whitworth and all who overheard: "England will weep tears of blood if she goes to war," he reportedly said afterward. Talleyrand downplayed the incident, but the British government responded by strengthening the force of the Royal Navy in the English Channel and the North Sea ("Bonaparte and Lord Whitworth," 313-14; Browning, *England and Napoleon*, 116, 126-8; Bury and Barry, eds., *Englishman in Paris*, 94; *Correspondance de Napoléon*, 247, 251; Grainger, *Amiens Truce*, 154-77, 189).

A shortened version of Livingston's letter is in the records of the United States Senate, filed with a message from Jefferson of October 1803 but likely conveyed to the Senate at some other time (Document III). Evidently working in haste without time to make a clean copy, clerks used Document I to make that extract. They omitted Livingston's postscript but retained the underlining he had used to mark the sentence to which it pertained. As a result, in Document III Bonaparte appears not only to have delivered an ultimatum at the public gathering in front of the diplomatic corps and other guests, but to have given it a particularly menacing emphasis unintended by Livingston: "*I must either have Malta or War.*" Among the passages left out of the extract were Livingston's admission that he had not heard the exchanges between Whitworth and Bonaparte because of his hearing loss, and his wish to resign his position. The clerks also misread Livingston's assistant's handwriting and gave the date of the British crown's message to Parliament as the "1st" rather than the "8th" of March. The version of Livingston's letter received by the Senate became, however, for all its faults, an official account of Bonaparte's conduct at the Tuileries Palace on 13 Mch. It appeared in print in the *American State Papers* (ASP, *Foreign Relations*, 2:547; TJ to the Senate, 17 Oct. 1803).

I. Recipient's Copy

DEAR SIR Paris 12 March 1803

I have delayed replying to your friendly letter by Madame Brougniart in the hope of having something important to communicate, but in the mean time have been so full in my letter[1] to the Secretary of State that I have left myself little to say on the Subject of our publick affairs—I can only tell you generally that we have been gaining ground here for sometime past & some propositions I had an opportunity to make *to Joseph Bonaparte* to be submitted to the Consul's inspection, & which connected our objects will contain[2] *personal ones and couched in the stile which* I believed to be particularly pleasing here,[3] had a considerable effect in rendering *me personally acceptable* tho' after full deliberation, my propositions so far as they related to *personal advantages* were not agreed to, yet the matter & the manner left a favorable impression, & I meant to renew the subject upon the same ground, but as Mr Munroe's appointment will render every thing of this kind impossible it is necessary[4] to send you our correspondence as I had intended, & the rather as the whole was unsigned, & unofficial—my letter to the first Consul which you will find couched in pretty Strong terms, & such as are not usual here, & so far as it related to the claims repugnant to the Minister's sentiments has been[5] attended with happy effects as you will find by the answer transmitted herewith to the Secretary of State—I think it impossible after this for him to go back, & I have accordingly given information to the American creditors, of the state of their affairs that they may not be speculated upon—

With respect to a negotiation for Louisiana, I think nothing will be effected here. I have done every thing I can *thro' the Spanish Ambassador to obstruct the bargain for the Floridas & I have* great hope that it will not be soon concluded. *The Ambassador tells me that the Consul often complains to him* of the delay that business meets with *and while Spain keeps the Floridas Louisiana will be* considered here as an object of little moment as they are absolutely without ports in the Gulph & So far facilitate your negotiations with Genl. Bernadotte. I have given his character to Mr Madison *and I shall take care that he come to you inclined to do all* in his power to promote the connection of the two countries—I have had many interesting conversations with him, & have nothing to complain of. Remember however neither to wound his pride or that of his nation, both being extremely irritable—your message has been much admired here, tho' the printing it with a short commendation in the English paper of Paris (*the Argus*)[6] has, as he alledges, turned the Editor out of his office, & placed that paper in other hands. it is impossible that the abuse & ribaldry of the federals can have any effect against the facts it holds out, & I think I may insure you the voice[7] of every state in the Union on the next election, whether the Consul's Sentiments[8] with respect to you is changed I cannot say, it is however certain that nothing can be more polite[9] than the language he holds in the note I transmit to the secretary of State—I think it would have a good effect to let that note be *public* without being *published*.[10] The British grow every day more disagreeable here to (which their news papers as much as any other matter contributes) I wish ours were more prudent, it is natural that they should be more attentive to us, & I am satisfied that the flourishing state of our affairs, & the firm attitude we have lately taken has contributed to procure us respect. I have strongly inculcated here the important light in which the British view us, & the absolute nullity of any Colonies that France may establish in America if the United States Should throw their weight into the British scale—

Mr Madison has never told me whether he has received two little essays calculated the one to raise our importance in the view of this Government as a naval power, & the other to disgust them with Louisiana preparatory to our future negotiations, they were both read with considerable attention by the First Consul, having had them translated for that purpose—

I broke off this part of my letter to attend Madame Bonaparte's drawing room where a circumstance happened of sufficient importance to merit your attention—it is usual on these days for the Ministers, their Ladies & all strangers male or female that have been presented to attend, they commonly occupy two rooms in the Palace—After they have met, Madame Bonaparte enters, & soon after is followed by the Consul each attended by a Prefect of the Palace, they walk their rounds, & adress themselves to every Lady, after which the Consul mingles in the crowd of Gent, & commonly speaks to the Ministers, & some other persons of rank—After the first Consul had gone the circuit of one room, he turned to me & made some of the common enquiries usual on these occasions, & then bowed to the Gent that were near me & Spoke a few words to the Danish Minister, he then returned to me & entered into a further conversation; when he quitted me he passed most of the other Ministers merely with a bow, & went up to Lord Withworth, & after the first civilities said—I find Milord your nation want war again— L.W—no Sir we are very desirous of peace— 1st C. you have just finished a war of 15 years—Ld.W.—it is true Sir, & that war was 15 years too long.— Cl—but you want another war of 15 years— L.W.—Pardon me Sir, we are very desirous of peace— Cl—*I must either have Malta or war*[11]—L.W—I am not prepared Sir, to speak on that Subject, & I can only assure you, Citizen first Consul that we wish for peace[12]—the Prefect of the Palace then came up to the Consul, & informed him that there were Ladies in the next room, & asked him to go in, he made no reply, but bowing hastily to the Company retired immediately to his cabinet without entering the other room—Lord Withworth came up to me[13] & repeated the conversation as I now give you presuming from my distance & difficulty of hearing[14] that I had not heard it distinctly, tho' as I understood from what I could hear there was rather more acrimony on the part of the Consul[15] than what I have stated.—I asked Lord withworth whether there were any pending negotiation relative to Malta,—he told me that there were that the conduct of France having convinced them that they still had views upon Egypt, & the guaranties to which they were intitled with respect to Malta, not having been executed they thought that they could not surrender it with Safety—but what brought on the business to day was a message from the king of Great Britain to the Parliament on the 8th which has just been received here speaking with distrust of the armaments in the French Ports, & in fact preparing them for war, this you will have sooner by the way of England than this letter—it is then highly probable that a new rupture will take place, since it is hardly possible that the first Consul would commit himself so publickly unless his determination had been taken—I am fearful that this may again throw some impediment in the way of our claims which I believed in so prosperous a train, in other views it may serve us, & I shall give all my attention to avail myself of circumstances as they arise, in which I hope shortly to receive the assistance of Mr Munroe—in another view too, his coming will be extremely pleasing to me, since I trust he will be empowered to take my place which I shall find a pleasure in quiting to him—I had in no event determined to remain here longer than till next Spring, & shall be very happy if I can so far anticipate upon my first intention as to retire by the beginning of next September—I suffered[16] so much on my outward passage that I would not wish to make my voyage latter in the season—I am sick of Courts, & the round of ceremony that is now established here—besides that, the state of my finances will not justify the expences I incur—my expences within[17] the last year came within a triffle to 30000$ exclusive of plate which I do not rekon because I suppose I may part with it, without much loss—this with the relinquishment of my office worth 2800$ a year, makes it necessary to pay early attention to my domestic arrangements—all accounts agree that the expences of a family have at least doubled here since the Revolution—& as the three Consuls occasion three courts that of dress & time is also greatly encreased—I am yet at a loss to know whether Mr Munroe comes here first or goes first to Spain. Mr Madison's letter would lead me to conclude that I am to have the pleasure of seeing him here first whereas other accounts speak of his earliest mission as directed to Spain—he will have pretty strong prejudices, & some enmities to contend against here but his prudence & good sense will enable him I trust get the better of both—I must pray you Sir, to have the goodness to furnish Mr Madison with such an extract from this letter as ought to be upon[18] his file of correspondence with me, since the fear of loosing the opportunity & the necessity of the Greatest activity at this interesting moment will deprive me of the pleasure of writing farther to him by this conveyance.

I have just received your letter relative to the books, & called upon Mr Pougens with the catalogue, he had only two days before received Mr Duane's letter—I have left the Catalogue in his hands with direction to put the price to the books that I may compare them with the demands of other booksellers, & I will at the first moment of leisure endeavour to see your commission properly executed.[19]

I pray you to believe that I am Dear Sir—With the most respectful attachment Your most Obt hum: Servt. Robt R Livingston

So much of this conversation at the Thuilleries as is scored was said in a private conversation & not as I at first understood Lord Witworth upon that occasion

RC (DNA: RG 59, DD); in a clerk's hand, signed by Livingston; postscript in Livingston's hand; completed no earlier than 14 Mch. (see Editorial Note above); at head of text: "Copy"; written partly in code (see Vol. 36:208n and Weber, *United States Diplomatic Codes*, 467-77), and words in italics, except as noted below, are TJ's interlined decipherment of coded passages; endorsed by TJ, date of receipt obscured by tape; endorsed by Jacob Wagner as received by the State Department on 19 May. Dft (NHi: Robert R. Livingston Collection); codes interlined by clerk above passages underscored by Livingston; lacks postscript. Recorded in SJL as received 18 May.

The FRIENDLY LETTER carried by Louise d'Egremont Brongniart was TJ's to Livingston of 10 Oct. 1802 (Vol. 38: 476, 477n, 481).

Not until May 1803 did Livingston send Madison details of the PROPOSITIONS he made to Napoleon Bonaparte through the first consul's brother Joseph. If the Bonapartes gave themselves title to New Orleans and the Floridas, he suggested, they would be providing themselves with a future refuge away from Europe. The United States, he offered, would pay ten million livres for the right to administer the territory. Livingston also proposed a second option, in which the United States would acquire New Orleans, West Florida, and all of Louisiana north of the Arkansas River. France would retain lower Louisiana, and the two nations would share navigation of the Mississippi (Madison, *Papers*, *Sec. of State Ser.*, 4:592-3, 594-5n).

MY LETTER TO THE FIRST CONSUL: Livingston wrote to Bonaparte on 27 Feb. The first half of the long letter concerned financial claims against France by U.S. citizens. Without explaining a basis for the figure, Livingston indicated that the principal and interest for the claims totaled twenty million dollars. Implying that France was finding it difficult to pay claims under the Convention of 1800 and noting that the United States had paid its share of obligations required by that pact, he argued that by a "moderate" estimate France must pay twenty million dollars a year for supplies purchased in the United States for the colonies in the West Indies. He suggested an arrangement whereby France would pay American creditors in stock, and he noted that some transaction involving Louisiana, if it should put the United States in obligation to France for an amount greater than what France owed to American claimants, could help preserve the value of the stock. Livingston went on to ask for assurances about the right of deposit at New Orleans, boundaries, and navigation of the Mississippi River on the terms previously agreed to by the United States and Spain. He also asked for some guarantee of navigation of rivers emptying into the Gulf of Mexico. Arguing that New Orleans and Florida would always be a burden to France, he suggested that a cession of some of that territory to the United States would be beneficial and help to fund the purchase of supplies in the United States for France's island colonies. The ANSWER, dated 19 Ventôse (10 Mch.), was from Talleyrand on instructions from Bonaparte. The republic's finances were in excellent condition, declared the minister of foreign affairs, and France could meet all its responsibilities under the Convention of 1800. Surprised that claims by Americans could amount to twenty million dollars, Talleyrand asked for a full accounting of the particulars. Once that statement was in hand, he indicated, France would pay its debts. The first consul, Talleyrand wrote, wished that Livingston had not combined Louisiana and the claims issue in a single letter. Bonaparte, aware of the concerns in the United States about the acquisition of Louisiana by France, was sending a minister plenipotentiary to the U.S. to collect information and report on the situation. The first consul, Talleyrand wrote in conclusion, wished to communicate his high regard for the United States. Livingston sent a copy of his letter with a dispatch to Madison dated 3 Mch. and enclosed the reply in a dispatch of the 11th (ASP, *Foreign Relations*, 2:538-40, 545-6; Madison, *Papers*, *Sec. of State Ser.*, 4:385, 410-13).

Livingston believed that he could work through José Nicolás de Azara, the SPANISH AMBASSADOR in Paris, to prevent the cession of the Floridas to France (Vol. 38:383, 391, 584).

In December, Bonaparte had named Jean Baptiste BERNADOTTE to be minister to the United States. Livingston informed Madison in January that Bernadotte, who was Joseph Bonaparte's brother-in-law, "is a very respectable man & has the character of a decided Republican." On 11 Mch., Livingston wrote Madison that Bernadotte's "dispositions are as friendly as possible to our Government and Country, & his ideas relative to the importance of our connection and the little importance of Louisiana exactly such as I would wish." Bernadotte's departure was delayed, and he never took up the post in the United States (Madison, *Papers*, *Sec. of State Ser.*, 4:277, 279n, 411).

The ARGUS, an English-language newspaper controlled by the French government, first appeared in October 1802. France's relations with Great Britain, not the paper's handling of TJ's annual message, probably lay behind the replacement of Lewis Goldsmith as editor in February 1803. Goldsmith sent TJ two of his publications in 1801, when the journalist was living in London (DNB; Vol. 34:149).

NOTHING CAN BE MORE POLITE: in the conclusion of the reply to Livingston's letter to Bonaparte, Talleyrand noted the first consul's high regard and friendship for the United States and "son estime et sa considération personelle pour le Premier Magistrat qui la gouverne"—his esteem and personal regard for its chief magistrate (ASP, *Foreign Relations*, 2:546).

THROW THEIR WEIGHT INTO THE BRITISH SCALE: early in January, Charles Whitworth informed his government that he had heard from Livingston that acquisition of the Floridas by France "would have the immediate effect of uniting every individual in America, of every party," with Britain—"none more sincerely" than Livingston himself. If that happened and someone of Livingston's "known political bias" joined in the sentiment, Whitworth surmised, the British would then have "few enemies remaining" in the United States (Browning, *England and Napoleon*, 37; George Dangerfield, *Chancellor Robert R. Livingston of New York, 1746-1813* [New York, 1960], 345).

Livingston's ESSAYS were "Thoughts on the Relative Situation of France, Britain and America, as Commercial and Maritime Nations" and "Whether it will be advantageous to France to take possession of Louisiana." He had had the tract on Louisiana printed for distribution to Talleyrand, Joseph Bonaparte, and other influential individuals (same, 504n; Madison, *Papers*, *Sec. of State Ser.*, 3:468, 470; Vol. 38:584, 588n).

ATTENDED BY A PREFECT OF THE PALACE: four *préfets du palais* under the supervision of a governor of the palace oversaw affairs at the Tuileries (Thierry Lentz, *Le Grand Consulat, 1799-1804* [Paris, 1999], 337).

Christof Vilhelm Dreyer was the DANISH envoy extraordinary and minister plenipotentiary in Paris (*Almanach national de France, l'an dixième de la République françoise* [Paris, 1802], 131; Emil Marquard, *Danske Gesandter og Gesandtskabspersonale indtil 1914* [Copenhagen, 1952], 241).

MESSAGE FROM THE KING OF GREAT BRITAIN TO THE PARLIAMENT: a special royal message to the House of Commons on 8 Mch. called for increasing British naval forces by 10,000 men and readying the militia (Grainger, *Amiens Truce*, 169).

MR MADISON'S LETTER: Madison wrote on 18 Jan. to inform Livingston of Monroe's mission (Madison, *Papers*, *Sec. of State Ser.*, 4:259-61).

TJ wrote to Livingston on 20 Nov. RELATIVE TO THE BOOKS desired for the Library of Congress.

SO MUCH OF THIS CONVERSATION ... AS IS SCORED: that is, Bonaparte's declaration "I must either have Malta or war," which Livingston underlined in the text to key it to the postscript.

[1] Dft: "letters."

[2] The preceding two words are a misreading by the copyist and should be, according to the Dft and Document II, "with certain."

[3] Word lacking in Dft.

[4] Dft: "unecessary," and see Document II ("unnecessary").

[5] Here in Dft Livingston interlined "on this point"; see Document II.

[6] Words underlined, not coded, in MS.

[7] Thus in Dft also, but see Document II ("vote").

[8] Word interlined in Dft in place of "language."

[9] Word interlined in Dft in place of "flattering."

[10] Livingston's aide put "public" and "published" into code and TJ deciphered them, although according to Document II Livingston underlined the words in the Dft for emphasis rather than for coding.

[11] Sentence underlined, not coded, in MS (see Livingston's postscript). In Dft, Livingston first wrote "I must either have Malta or war" before altering the passage to read "you must either evacuate Malta or war"; see Document II.

[12] In Dft Livingston interlined the preceding statement by Whitworth in place of "I give you this conversation as lord Witworth repeated it to me in the drawing room immediately after the con."

[13] Dft: "as soon as the consul left the room Lord Witworth came up to me."

[14] Preceding three words interlined in Dft in place of "deafness."

[15] Here in Dft Livingston interlined "(who invoked the vengeance of heaven on those that violated the treaty)."

[16] In Dft Livingston canceled "I" and interlined "my family" in its place; see Document II.

[17] Dft: "my expenditures for."

[18] Word supplied by Editors from Dft.

[19] In Dft, Livingston inserted this paragraph in the margin.

II. Recipient's Copy

DEAR SIR — Paris 12th. March 1803

I have delayed answering your friendly letter by madame Brogniard in the hope of having some thing important to communicate but in the mean time have been so full in my letters to the secretary of State that I have left myself little to say on the subject of our publick affairs. I can only tell you generally that I have been gaining ground for some time past & some propositions I had an opportunity to make *to Joseph Bonaparte* to be submitted to the consuls inspection & which connected our objects with certain *personal ones and couched in the stile which I* believed to be particularly pleasing had a considerable effect in rendering *me personally acceptable* tho after full deliberation my propositions so far as they related to *personal advantages* were not agreed to, yet the matter & the manner left a favourable impression, & I meant to renue the subject upon the same ground, but as Mr. Monroes appointment will render every thing of this kind impossible, it is unnecessary to send you our correspondence, as I had intended & the rather as the whole was unsigned & unofficial—My letter to the first consul which you will find couched in pretty strong terms & such as are not usual here, & so far as it related to the claims repugnant to the ministers sentiments has however as to this point been attended with the most happy effect as you will find by his note in reply transmitted to the secretary of State. I think it impossible after this to go back, & I have accordingly given information to the american creditors of the state of their affairs to prevent their being speculated upon. with respect to Louisiana I fear nothing will be done here. I have laboured thro *the Spanish ambassador to obstruct the bargain for the Floridas & I have* great hope that it will not soon be concluded *the Ambassador tells me that the Consul often complains to him* of the delay that business meets with *and while Spain keeps the Floridas Louisiana will be* considered here as an object of little moment as they are absolutly without ports in the Gulph & so far facilitate your negotiations with general Bernadotte. I have given his character to Mr Madison *and I shall take care that he come to you inclined to do all*[1] in his power to promote the connection of the two countries, I have had many interesting conversations with him & have nothing to complain of, remember however neither to wound his pride or that of his nation both being extreamly irritable. Your message has been much admired here tho' the reprinting it with a short commendation in the english paper of paris (the argus) has as he alledges turned the editor out of his office & placed the paper in other hands. It is impossible that the abuse & ribaldry of the federalists can have any effect against the facts it holds out & I think I might assure you the vote of every state in the union on the next election. Whether the consuls sentiments with respect to you are changed I can not say, it is however certain that nothing can be more polite than the language he speaks in the note I transmited to the Secy of State, would it not be well that this should be *public*, without being *published*. The british grow every day more disagreeable here to which their news papers greatly contribute I wish ours were more prudent. it is therefore natural that they should be more attentive to us, & I am satisfied that the flourishing state of our affairs, & the firm attitude we have latly taken have contributed to procure us respect. I have strongly inculcated here the important light in which the british view us, & the absolute nullity of any establishments that france may form in america if we throw our weight in the british scale. Mr. Madison has never told me whether he has recd two little essays which I wrote with a view by the one to raise our importance in the view of france, as a naval power, & the other to disgust her with her projects in Louisiana preparatory to our future negotiations, both were read with considerable attention by the first Consul having had them translated for that purpose.

I broke off to attend madame Bonapartes drawing room where a circumstance took place of sufficient importance to merit your attention. It is usual on those occasions for the ministers their families & all strangers male & female that have been presented to attend they commonly occupy two rooms in the palace. After they have met Mme

Bonaparte enters & is soon after followed by the first Consul, who walks the round of the ladies, speaking to each of them after this the Consul mingles in the round of gent. speaks to the ministers & others that he knows. When the first Consul had gone the round of one room, he turned to me & made some of those common questions usual on such occasions. He then went up to the danish envoy who was near me, & after speaking a few words returned to me, when he quited me, he passed most of the other ministers with a bow & accosted Lord Witworth with some warmth, told him that there would probably be a storm, Lord Witworth hoped not—You have had already a 15 years war says he—true & sir, & it was 15 too much—but still you are eager for another—pardon me Sir we wish for peace—He then made some observations on the vengeance that would await the breach of a solem treaty, & concluded "*if you do not evacuate Malta there will be war.*" The prefect of the palace then came to him & informed him that there were ladies in the other room. He made no reply but turning of suddenly he retired to his cabinet. You may easily surmise the sensation that this excited. Two expresses were dispatched to England that very night, & I dare say to every court in Europe in the course of the next day. As soon as the consul left the room Lord Witworth repeated the conversation to me as I have given you as nearly as I can recollect. I asked him whether there were any pending negotiations relative to Malta—He told me that there were that the conduct of France having convinced them that they still had views upon Egypt & the guarantees to which they were intitled not having been given they conceived that they could not surrender it with safety. but what brought on the business today was a message from the King of Great Britain to the parliament of 8th., which had just been recd here speaking with distrust of the armaments in the french & Dutch ports, & preparing the nation for war, this you will have by the way of England before this reaches you. It is now highly probable that a rupture will take place since it is hardly possible that the first consul would have committed himself so far as he has done before all the ministers of Europe unless his determination had been taken. The people about court however think otherwise & believe (which I do not) that England will receed. I am fearful that this may throw fresh embarrassments in the way of our claims which I believed in so prosperous a train, in other views it may serve us, & I shall give all my attention to avail myself of circumstances as they arise, in which I hope shortly to recieve the assistance of Mr. Monroe. In another view too his coming will be extreamly pleasing to me, since I trust he will be empowered upon contingencies to take my place, which I shall find a pleasure in quiting to him. I had in no event determined to remain here longer than till the next spring, & shall be very happy if I can so far anticipate my first intentions as to retire by the beginning of September. My family suffered so much on my outward passage that I would not wish to make my voyage later in the season. I am sick of courts and the perpetual round of ceremony, besides that, the state of my finances will not justify the expences I incur—My expenditures for the last year (counting from my arrival at L'Orient) amounted to (within a triffle) of 30,000$—exclusive of plate which I do not count as it is convertible into money with little loss. This with the relinquishment of an office of 2800$ a year makes it necessary to turn my attention to my domestic arrangments, all accounts agree that the expences of a family here have doubled since the revolution, & as three consuls occasion three courts that must be sedulously attended, that of dress & time is also greatly increased. I am yet at a loss to know whether Mr. Monroe comes here or goes to Spain first. from Mr. Madisons letter I should conclude that he was coming here, yet reports from America say otherwise. He will have pretty strong prejudices to contend with, but his prudence & good sense will I trust get the better of them. I must pray you Sir to have the goodness to furnish the Secretary of State with such an extract from this letter as should be upon his files, since the fear of loosing the opportunity and the necessity of the greatest activity at this interesting moment will deprive me of the pleasure of writing to him further by this vessel. I have but just recd your letter relative to the books. I called upon Mr. Pugens with the catalogue. He had only two days before recd Mr. Duanes letter. I have left the catalogue in his hands with directions to annex the price at which he will furnish the books which when he returns it I will compare with the demands of other booksellers & will endeavour to see the commission properly executed.

I have the honor to be dear Sir with the Most respectful consideration Your most Obt hum: Servt Robt R Livingston

PS. upon repeating the conversation with Lord Witworth I find the words scored were not said at that time but in a private conversation with Lord Witworth & he blended them together in speaking of it to me

RC (DLC); completed no earlier than 14 Mch. (see Editorial Note above); at foot of text: "Thomas Jefferson Esqr. president of the United States"; written partly in same code as Document I; words in italics in the opening section of the letter are Madison's interlined decipherment of coded passages (see note 1 below); endorsed by TJ as received 18 May.

WORDS SCORED: the passage earlier in the letter beginning "*if you do not evacuate Malta.*"

[1] All preceding words in italics are Madison's decipherment of coded passages. In the remainder of the letter, words in italics were not in code, but underlined by Livingston.

III. Extract

DEAR SIR, Paris 12th. March 1803

I have delayed replying to your friendly letter by Madam Brougniart, in the hope of having something important to communicate; but, in the mean time, have been so full in my letter to the Secretary of State that I have left myself little to say on the subject of my public affairs. I can only tell you, generally, that we have been gaining ground here for some time past; and altho some propositions which I had an opportunity to make, to Joseph Bonaparte to be submitted to the Consuls inspection,[1] were not agreed to, yet the matter and the manner left a favorable impression, and I meant to renew the subject on the same ground.[2]

My letter to the First Consul, which you will find couched in pretty strong terms and such as are not usual here, and, so far as it related to the claims, repugnant to the Ministers sentiments, has been attended with happy effects; as you will find by the answer transmitted, herewith, to the Secretary of State. I think it impossible after this for him to go back; and I have accordingly given information to the American Creditors of the state of their affairs, that they may not be speculated upon.

With respect to a negotiation for Louisiana I think nothing will be effected here. I have done every thing I can, thro' the Spanish ambassador, to obstruct the bargain for the Floridas and I have great hope that it will not be soon concluded. The ambassador tells me that the Consul often complains to him of the delay that business meets with: and, while Spain keeps the Floridas, Louisiana will be considered here as an object of little moment as they are absolutely without ports in the Gulph, and so far facilitate your negotiations with Genl. Bernadotte.[3] I have had many interesting conversations with him, and have nothing to complain of. Remember, however, neither to wound his pride or that of his nation, both being extremely irritable.

Mr. Madison has never told me whether he has received two little essays calculated the one to raise our importance in the views of this Government as a Naval power; and the other to disgust them with Louisiana preparatory to our future negotiations. They were both read with considerable attention by the First Consul; having had them translated for that purpose.[4]

I here broke off this part of my letter to attend Madam Bonapartes drawing room, where a circumstance happened of sufficient importance to merit your attention. ++++++ After the first Consul had gone the circuit of one room, he turned to me and made some of the common inquiries usual on these occasions. He afterwards returned and entered into a further conversation. When he quitted me he passed most of the other Ministers, merely with a bow, went up to Lord Whitworth,[5] and after the first civilities said: "I find my lord your nation want war again." L.W. No Sir, we are very desirous of Peace. First Consul. "You have just finished a War of fifteen years."—L.W. "It is true, Sir, and that War was fifteen years too long." Consul. "But you want another War of fifteen years." L.W. "Pardon me, Sir, we are very desirous of Peace." Consul "*I must either have Malta or War*." L.W. "I am not prepared Sir, to speak on that subject; and I can only assure you Citizen first Consul that we wish for Peace." The Prefect of the Palace[6] then came up to the Consul, and informed him that there were ladies in the next room and asked him to go in. He made no reply; but, bowing hastily to the company, retired immediately to his Cabinet, without entering the other room. Lord Whitworth came up to me, and repeated the conversation as I now give you. I asked Lord Whitworth whether there were any pending Negotiations relative to Malta. He told me that there were: That the conduct of France having convinced them that they still had views upon Egypt, and the guaranties to which they were entitled with respect to Malta not having executed, they thought they could not surrender it with safety. But what brought on the business to day was a message from the King of Great Britain to the Parliament on the 1st, which has just been received here, speaking with distrust of the armaments in the French ports, and in fact preparing them for War. This you will have sooner by the way of England than this letter. It is, then, highly probable that a new rupture will take place; since it is hardly possible that the first Consul would commit himself so publickly, unless his determination had been taken. I am fearful that this may again throw some impediment in the way of our claims, which I believed in so prosperous a train. In other views it may serve us; and I shall give all my attention to avail myself of circumstances as they arise: in which I hope shortly to receive the assistance of Mr. Monroe.[7]

I must pray you, Sir, to furnish Mr Madison with such an Extract from this letter as ought to be on his file of Correspondence with me.

Since the fear of loosing the opportunity, and the necessity of the greater activity at this interesting moment, will deprive me of the pleasure of writing farther to him by this conveyance.

I am &c ROB. R. LIVINGSTON

Tr (DNA: RG 46, EPFR, 8th Cong., 1st sess.); in multiple clerks' hands with several emendations; at head of text "Extract" and "Robert R. Livingston, to the President of the US." Filed with TJ to the Senate, 17 Oct. 1803; printed in ASP, *Foreign Relations*, 2:547.

ON THE 1ST: this is a clerk's misreading of "8th"; see Documents I and II.

[1]The clerks here canceled "and which connected."

[2]The clerks here canceled a set of five "+" signs set off by dashes.

[3]The clerks here canceled "I have given his character to Mr. Madison; and I shall take care that he come to you inclined to do all in his power to promote the connection of the two countries."

[4]This paragraph is an insertion on a slip of paper pasted to the MS.

[5]Preceding nine words inserted in margin.

[6]MS: "Palance."

[7]The clerks here canceled "In another view, too, his coming will be extremely pleasing to me. Since."

Petition from the Mississippi Territory House of Representatives

The memorial and petition of the House of Representatives of the Missisippi Territory.

Respectfully Sheweth.

That a considerable portion of the Inhabitants of this Territory are situated upon lands of the greatest fertility, watered by navigable Rivers, which have no communication with the Bay of Mexico, but through the dominions of his Catholic Majesty. The principal of those settlements being within the Bay of Mobille upon the Tom begby, a fine navigable river, extending its branches so as nearly to interlock with the waters of the Tenessee, is so situated as to be cut off from all communication with the settlements adjacent to the Missisippi by a Wilderness of at least two hundred miles; hence it results that the Inhabitants of that and other settlements can receive no supplies of a variety of articles, which the wants of man have rendered indispensible to the comforts of life, but thro' the indulgence of the Spanish Government. This indulgence disiriable as it may be in the existing circumstances of those countries and which may be withdrawn at any moment, can only be obtained, accompanied with inconveniencies which tend greatly to retard the prosperity of those settlements. The Spanish Government possessing an arbitrary power will permit only such traders as they shall be pleased to licence, to visit our settlements and perhaps for this licence a tax must be paid. It is unnecessary to present before the enlightened mind of your Excellency, the serious evils which must attach themselves to the planting interest, thus cramped and embarrassed.

The ardor of the cultivator is repressed and the new Establishments must languish until a remedy shall be applied to the source of the Evil.

The Treaty of navigation & limits with Spain has not brought into view a number of Rivers, which tho' not equally extensive with the Missisippi, yet whose navigation is equally necessary to the prosperity of a large & fertile region of the United States.

Your memorialists duly impressed with an assurance of the parental care which your Excellency as head of the Empire, unceasingly extends to the most distant portions of its territory, more particularly to this the youngest and most defenceless of its Colonies, are fully persuaded, that it requires only to be made known that a grievance exists, to excite in your benevolent mind a desire to apply an immediate remedy.

Your Memorialists therefore pray that your Excellency will be pleased to adopt such measures as may procure for the Citizens of the United States the free navigation of all navigable Rivers and water courses falling into the bay of Mexico from the Territories of the United States, and passing thro' the dominions of his Catholic Majesty.

William Gordon Forman
Speaker of the House of Representatives

Attest.
Samuel Sidney Mahon Clk.
House of Representatives
March the 12th. AD 1803.

MS (ViW: Tucker-Coleman Collection); in a clerk's hand, signed by Forman and Mahon; dated by Mahon; at head of text: "To his Excellency Thomas Jefferson President of the United States"; endorsed by TJ as received 3 May and "memorial & petn" and so recorded in SJL. Enclosed in William C. C. Claiborne to Madison, 15 Mch., requesting that he lay it before the president (Madison, *Papers, Sec. of State Ser.*, 4:423).

A native of New Jersey and graduate of the College of New Jersey, William Gordon Forman (1770-1812) emigrated to the Mississippi Territory around 1800, where he undertook planting and became a leader of the territory's Federalist faction (Ruth L. Woodward and Wesley Frank Craven, *Princetonians, 1784-1790* [Princeton, N.J., 1991], 113-17). Samuel Sidney Mahon later moved to the Orleans Territory, where he became a legislator, militia officer, and county judge (*Louisiana History*, 22 [1981], 434-5).

A resolution passed by the Mississippi Territory House of Representatives on 12 Mch. requested that the governor transmit the above MEMORIAL AND PETITION to the State Department (MS in ViW: Tucker-Coleman Collection; in Mahon's hand and attested by him as clerk of the House; enclosed with the petition above).

TREATY OF NAVIGATION & LIMITS WITH SPAIN: that is, the Pinckney Treaty of 1795, Article 4 of which granted free navigation of the Mississippi River to citizens of the United States (Miller, *Treaties*, 2:321-2).

From Benjamin Rush

DEAR SIR, Philadelphia March 12th 1803

The Solicitude I felt upon the account of your health, excited by your letter of last summer, is in a great measure removed by the history you have given me of your disease in your favor of the 28th. of February. Chronic diseases even in persons in the decline of life, are far from being incurable, and I have great pleasure in assuring you that complaints of the bowels such as you have described yours to be, have very generally yeilded to medicine under my care, and that too in some instances in Old People.—The Remedies which appear to me proper in your case are

1 A Diet consisting chiefly of *solid* Aliment, taken at *short* intervals. The Stomach should never be full, nor empty. Like a School boy when idle, it does mischief to itself, or to parts connected with it. Fish, and every other Article of food that disagrees with your bowels should be avoided. The most inoffensive vegatable that you can take with animal food, is the potatoe. Biscuit, or toasted bread or boiled rice should be taken when convenient, with all your meals. Sherry wine, or madeira when pure and old, may be taken in moderation alone, or with water daily. Port wine may be taken occasionally, but it is too gouty for habitual Use.

2 The utmost care should be taken to promote a constant determination of the powers of the System, externally, and of the discharges, thro the skin which are natural to it. Perspiration is an excretion of the first necessity to health and life. The means of promoting and encreasing it in your case should be the warm Bath in cool weather, and the cold Bath in Summer. The best time of using them is about 12 or 1 oClock. The System bears them best at those hours. With the warm and cold Baths, flannel should be worn next to your Skin, and uncommon pains should be taken to keep your feet constantly *warm.* They are the avenues of half the paroxyisms of all chronic diseases when cold. It will be the more necessary to promote warmth & vigor in your feet, as the disease in your bowels is probably the effect of a feeble, misplaced Gout.

3 Gentle exercise should be used at those times when you feel *least* of your disease. When your bowels are much excited, rest should be

indulged. Riding on horseback should be preferred to walking or riding in a Carriage. Avoid exercise of every kind before breakfast, in damp weather, and after Sunset. Your custom I recollect formerly was to breakfast as soon as you left your bed. That custom is now more necessary than ever to your health. Carefully avoid fatigue of body & mind from all its causes. Late hours, and midnight studies & business should likewise be avoided. It will be unsafe for you to sit up later than 1 oClock.

4 To releive the Diarrhœa when troublesome, Laudanum should[1] be taken in small doses during the day, and in larger doses at bedtime so as to prevent your being obliged to rise in the night. I have seen the happiest effects from a Syrup prepared in the following manner. Take of the powder of Oak Galls six drachms & Cinnamon two drachms. Boil them in a pint of water to half a pint,—then strain them, and add to the liquor half a pint of Brandy, and as much loaf Sugar as will make them over a slow fire into a Syrup of which take a tablespoonful, or more three times a day.—Pepper mint tea may be taken occasionally with both the above remedies for paroxysms of your disease. In cases of severe pain, an injection composed of forty drops of Laudanum mixed with a tablespoonful of Starch and half a pint of water will give ease. The Laudanum when thus received into the System, seldom affects the stomach with sickness, or the head with pain afterwards.—

5 If the above Remedies do not releive you, Blisters should be applied occasionally, & alternately to your wrists and ankles. Such is the Sympathy between the skin & bowels, that the irritation of the Blisters on the Skin suspend all morbid action in the bowels. In the mean while astringent medicines act with double, or perhaps quadruple force upon them.

6 If the Blisters in addition to the other Remedies that have been mentioned do not cure you, recourse must be had to as much mercury, either used internally combined with opium, or externally in an Ointment, as will excite a gentle salivation. This remedy is a radical One. I have not often been obliged to resort to it in obstinate Diarrhœas,—but when I have, it has seldom failed of performing an effectual, and permanent cure.—

To encourage you to expect releif from your present disease, I could furnish you with many histories of the efficacy of *each* of the above Remedies. I shall mention the effects of but One of them. The Revd: Dr Ewing late Provost of our University was cured of a Diarrhœa of several years continuance in the 66th: year of his age by the Use of the Cold Bath.

I have been much struck in Observing how seldom a diarrhœa (where the stomach is unimpaired) shortens the duration of human life. The late Wm Smith of New York Afterwards chief Justice of Canada, was affected with it for fifteen years in the middle stage of his life, and General Gates (now between 70, & 80 years of age) was seldom free from it during our revolutionary War, and I beleive for some years afterwards.—

I beg you would continue to command my Advice in your case. All your communications upon it, shall be confined to myself.

I shall expect to see Mr Lewis in Philadelphia, and shall not fail of furnishing him with a number of questions, calculated to encrease our knowledge of Subjects connected with medicine.

The Venerable Dr Priestley is now, we fear upon his last visit to our city. His health & strength have declined sensibly within the two last years, but his Spirits are unimpaired, or rather improved, and his conversation is as instructive & delightful as ever. The Philosophical Society did homage to his genius, and character a few days ago by giving him a public dinner. The toasts will be published shortly. They were confined wholly to philosophical characters and Institutions.—

Have you seen Acerbi's travels into Sweden, Finland, and Lapland? They are more interesting than any work of that kind yet published, inasmuch as they embrace both science & literature. The author is an Italian, but he writes in an elegant English Stile.—

I return Latude with many thanks. It is I find an abridgement only of a large work in which is contained an account of a hospital of deranged people with whom he lived for some time after he left the Bastile.

I have only to add a single thought foreign to the Subjects of this letter, & that is, fatal as has been the issue of the Struggle for Republicanism in Europe, and precarious as the tenure may be by which we hold our excellent republican[2] form of government, I still continue in my abstracted situation, and private pursuits in life, to admire and prefer it to all Others, as most consistent with the rational nature, and the moral and religious obligations of man.

With the most cordial Wishes for your health and every blessing that can be connected with it in public and private life, I am Dear Sir your sincere old friend BENJN: RUSH

PS: I recollect you were in the practice formerly of washing your feet every morning in cold water in *cold weather.*[3] It is possible that practice so salutary in early and middle life, may not accord with your present age. The bowels sympathize with the feet above any other external part of the body, and suffer in a peculiar manner from the effects of Cold upon them. As warm and cold water produce the same Ultimate effects upon the feet;—suppose you substitute the former, to the latter hereafter in the Winter Months. The warm water acts as a direct stimulant while the cold water produces Action, and warmth indirectly only, After first inducing weakness and cold in the parts to which it is applied. The *action* and *warmth* are induced only by reaction, and when the energy of the feet is not sufficient for that purpose (as is sometime the case in the decline of life) the cold water may do harm. The whole System will often react against Cold, when a part of it, especially a part remote from the heart & brain will not.—Hence a general cold bath will sometimes be inoffensive, & even Useful, when a partial one will be hurtful.

Should you conclude to Use the Cold Bath in summer begin with water at 90°: or 85° and let its heat descend gradually to 55°: or 60°:

RC (MHi); Rush added the numbering of paragraphs as an afterthought, inserting the numerals in the indentations of the paragraphs; endorsed by TJ as received 25 Mch. and so recorded in SJL.

The letter in which TJ discussed a problem of HEALTH was not from the summer, but 20 Dec. 1801 (Vol. 36: 177-8).

VENERABLE DR PRIESTLEY: in a special meeting convened for the purpose on 28 Feb., the American PHILOSOPHICAL SOCIETY resolved to invite Joseph Priestley to dinner "from their high respect for his Philos: Labors & discoveries, & to enjoy the more particular pleasure of a Social meeting." Priestley attended a meeting of the society on 4 Mch. and accepted the invitation. The event took place at Francis's hotel the next day, Saturday the 5th. According to one report the toasts given on the occasion "were appropriate to the object in view, and appeared to have the good fortune of being unexceptionable. It was pleasing to see all distinctions of religious sects and political opinion buried in the pleasing sentiments of fraternal esteem" (minutes in PPAmP; Concord, N.H., *American Republican Gazette*, 28 Apr.).

ACERBI'S TRAVELS: the first publication of the *Travels through Sweden, Finland, and Lapland, to the North Cape, in the Years 1798 and 1799* of the Italian lawyer, diplomat, and scholar Giuseppe Acerbi was in English. The two-volume edition appeared in London in 1802 (Peter Hainsworth and David Robey, eds., *The Oxford Companion to Italian Literature* [Oxford, 2002], 5; Robert L. Kahn, "Seume's Reception in England and America," *Modern Language Review*, 52 [1957], 65n).

A year earlier Rush had asked to borrow the memoirs of Henri Masers de LATUDE. Authorities in prerevolutionary France had confined Latude in the Bastille for many years and in a HOSPITAL for the insane (L. H. Butterfield, ed., *Letters of Benjamin Rush*, 2 vols. [Princeton, 1951], 2:848n; Vol. 37:68, 69n, 86).

[1] Rush here canceled "may."

[2] Word interlined.

[3] Preceding three words interlined.

From Robert Smith

Sir, Washington Mar. 12. 1803

In consequence of the Conversation I had with you some days since respecting the Compensation to be allowed to Capt Tingey I have Offered to him the same pay & emoluments which he would have been entitled to receive, if he had remained a Captain of the Navy. This he does not consider sufficient. Herewith you will receive Copies of my Letter & his answer.

I find that in the hurry of your departure hence you had omitted mentioning to Mr Madison that the idea of sending the Gun Carriages to the Emperor of Morocco was relinquished and that money was to be substituted. I take the liberty of recalling this to your recollection, because there ought not to be any delay in forwarding the money.

As soon as I shall receive your instructions respecting the stipulated Articles for the Dey of Algiers they shall be forwarded with the utmost expedition.

It may be proper to remind you that the Shipping Articles of the Crews of the Vessels now in the Mediterranean expire at the several times stated as follow

Enterprise	Feb. 17. 1803
Constellation	March 14.
Chesapeak	April 27.
Adams	June 10.
N. York Jno. Adams	} Oct.

With great respect & Esteem I am Sir, Y H S. Rt Smith

RC (DLC); endorsed by TJ as received from the Navy Department on 18 Mch. and "Tingey. gun carriages. Algiers. Mediterrn. crews" and so recorded in SJL. Enclosures: (1) Smith to Thomas Tingey, dated Navy Department, 11 Mch., acknowledging Tingey's letter of 1 Mch. and informing him that the president has authorized Tingey to receive for his future services the pay and emoluments of a navy captain, $1,784 per annum (Tr in DLC). (2) Tingey to Smith, dated Washington, 12 Mch., stating that he is willing to continue as superintendent of the Washington Navy Yard, but that he would "betray my duty to my Family" if he accepted the amount tendered; Tingey again asks Smith to use his "good offices with the President" to augment the sum to $2,500 per annum, otherwise Tingey "shall reluctantly be necessitated to resign—in which case it will oblige me, by appointing a successor as speedily as can be effected" (same).

For the most recent discussion among TJ and his cabinet regarding the gift of gun carriages for Morocco, see Vol. 39:493, 494n.

From Benjamin H. Latrobe

Dear Sir, Philadelphia March 13th. 1803

I received your favor of the 6th with the most grateful sentiments. It did not reach me till the 11th. I cannot better express the sense I have of your kindness, than by setting off for Washington as soon as I can leave my business with convenience, & safety. This will be in 2 or 3 days at furthest. I have already made my principal arrangements.—The failure of my partners Messrs. Bollmann, has thrown the weight of our Iron concern upon my shoulders, & renders it impossible for me at this moment to say that I shall be able to accept of your generous offer.—But I will devote myself to the compleat organisation of the business of the Season with the same zeal and activity, as if I could go through with it: and as I shall have the honor to see you at Washington, I will give you my decission then. My sincere wish is to be employed near you, & under your direction.—In the mean time, I beg you to believe me with the truest respect

Yours faithfully B Henry Latrobe.

RC (DLC); endorsed by TJ as received 21 Mch. and so recorded in SJL.

Justus Erich and Lewis BOLLMANN were the principal investors in the rolling mill that Latrobe and Nicholas James Roosevelt had devised to draw extra power from the engines of Philadelphia's waterworks. After the failure of the brothers' merchandising business, they were forced to auction off their share of the mill (Fritz Redlich, "The Philadelphia Water Works in Relation to the Industrial Revolution in the United States," PMHB, 69 [1945], 243-56; *Poulson's American Daily Advertiser*, 10 Mch. and 16 May 1803; TJ to James Dinsmore, 3 Jan. 1803).

From Jacob Lewis

Sir New York March 13th. 1803

In July 1801—I was hon'd with the Consular appointment for the British Territories In the East Indies—as soon after as Convenience wou'd admit of, I visited the Court of St. James's for the purpose of obtaining my Exequator, this I did from an opinion which I had previously form'd; that without being Acknowledged by the General Government, I shou'd be subject to the Caprice of the Colonial one, & cou'd only remain In office by Courtesy—In this situation, I cou'd niether assert my Contry's rights, or claim redress for individuals wrongs—therefore, shou'd not be able to do my duty towards my Government, or afford satisfaction, to the subjects of it—In this opinion I am Confirm'd, by experience had in a simulur appointment;—through Mr. King our Minister resident at that Court—London[1]—I made my application; after three months delay, through him, I received an answer, which was In the Negative; I soon after return'd to this Country, with a hope, that some appointment Equally Important wou'd be given to me, In this Expectation I applied to the Secretary of State, who Inform'd me, that I shou'd have the first vacancy In the Consular department, & at the same time, proposed for my acceptance, several, which were then vacant, either[2] of which I did not think an object to a person who has a family, therefore, declin'd the offer; & prefer'd to remain longer In the Chapter of accidents—received Mr Madisons renew'd promise, & returned to this City,—Since a few days, I have heard that Gunboats are to be built on the waters of the Missisippi, being Tired of a State of Suspense, & feeling In every particular Equal to the importance attached to such a Command—I hazard to offer my services, and shall be highly gratified if the honor Is Confer'd upon me—as a Nautical man I am Known to Genl. Mason. the Post master General. Genl. Dearborne, & to the Secretary of State through Mr. Erving our Consul at London. Its my intention to sail for New Orleans immediately for the purpose of reconatring the river from Its Mouth to the Natchez—& shou'd the climate & Country be Equal to my Expectations shall remove myself there—

I have the honor to be with the highest Respt yr. very obet. Huml Servt.

J LEWIS

RC (PHi); at foot of text: "President of the United States"; endorsed by TJ as received 25 Mch. and "to command a gunboat" and so recorded in SJL with notation "N."

CONSULAR APPOINTMENT: Lewis's commission as consul at the port of Calcutta was dated 29 July 1801. He learned that his APPLICATION for an exequatur had been refused in March 1802 (Vol. 34:656-7).

For George W. Erving's recommendation of Lewis as a NAUTICAL MAN, see Vol. 38:664n. In a 5 Mch. letter (now missing), the secretary of state offered Lewis another position. Writing from New York on 13 Apr., Lewis acknowledged Madison's offer, noting "it wou'd have been very acceptable to me, if it had been made a few days sooner." Now, determined to SAIL FOR NEW ORLEANS, he was making arrangements to depart for "the waters of the Missisippi" later in the month. Lewis concluded: "if my servises can be made usefull in that Quarter, I shall feel happy & gratified to Continue to possess the Confidence of my Goverment" (RC in DLC: Madison Papers; Madison, *Papers, Sec. of State Ser.*, 4:516).

[1] Word interlined.

[2] Interlined in place of "all."

From Joseph Dougherty

Sir City of Washington Mar. 14th 1803

The family is all well and Lives tranquil Sir. Stable jacks master is now here from the Easternshore. He proposes. the following terms to sell his Servant he will furnish me with a copy of his Uncles will who is Dead About four years & four months. jack was borne a slave under him and at his Death was to serve this Wm. Legg his present Master twelve years. At the Expiration of which time he is to be free. By this infirmation he has Seven years & eight months to Serve for which time he asks 210 Dollars. that is 30 D per year, but Sir. he may be bot for 200 Dollars I could Sir. give him no Satisfactory Ansr. without your approbation

I Hope Sir. we to our great satisfaction we will heare that you had a safe journey and is well. I am Sir

your moste obedt. Servt. Jos. Dougherty

RC (MHi); endorsed by TJ as received 18 Mch. and so recorded in SJL.

John (jack) Shorter was a livery servant and hostler at the President's House from the fall of 1801 until the spring of 1809 (Lucia Stanton, " 'A Well-Ordered Household': Domestic Servants in Jefferson's White House," *White House History*, 17 [2006], 9, 11; RS, 1:60n).

William legg lived in Centreville in Queen Anne's County on Maryland's Eastern Shore (Easton, Md., *Republican Star*, 10 Apr. 1804, 17 Jan. 1809).

From Albert Gallatin

Dear Sir Washington 14th March 1803

You will receive herewith an official representation dated the 5th instt., submitting the propriety of removing the collectors of Brunswick Georgia, Plymouth Mass., & Fort Adams, Mississ.; The Commissions for their three successors Turner of Georgia, Henry Warren & Mr Trist have already been received from the Secretary of State & transmitted to them. I had understood that a commission of register for the land office at Natchez was also to be made out in the name of the other Turner of the Mississippi territory; but upon application to the departt. of State, it was found that his name had not been transmitted by you; and being myself ignorant of his christian name, it was necessarily delayed. The sooner you can transmit his name, the better it will be, as, independent of other reasons, I think it eligible that the news of his appointment should, together with that of Cato West, be received in the Territory as early as that of Mr Triest.

I have issued a Warrant for the 2,500 dollars appropriated for the extension of the external commerce of the United States in favor of T. Tucker as Treasurer of the Military department, which will, of course, place the whole sum subject to the drafts of Gen. Dearborn as Secy. of War; but it is necessary that I should have for that purpose your authorization: a form is herein enclosed. Capn. Lewis leaves this place to morrow morning. I have requested Mr King to project a blank map to extend from 88 to 126° West longitude from Greenwich & from 30° to 55° north latitude; which will give us the whole course of the Mississipi and the whole coast of the Pacific ocean within the same latitudes together with a sufficient space to the North to include all the head waters of the Port Nelson River. In this I intend to insert the course of the Mississipi as high up as the Ohio from Ellicot's, the coast of the Pacific from Cook & Vancouver, the north bend of the Missouri & such other of its waters as are there delineated from the three maps of Arrowsmith & from that of Mackenzie, and the Rio Norte and other parts of the Missoury from Danville & Delisle. The most difficult point to ascertain is the latitude of the sources of the Rio Norte; and it is important, in order to know whether there would be any danger in following a more southerly branch of the Missouri than that delineated in Mackenzie's & in the manuscript transcribed from Mr Thornton's map by Cap. Lewis. I mention this because you may perhaps have some book at Monticello, which might throw some light on that subject or at least on the latitude & longitude of Santa Fe.

I do not perceive that there will be any thing of importance to be done in this department till your return—

With respect & attachment Your obedt. Servt.

Albert Gallatin

RC (DLC); endorsed by TJ as received from the Treasury Department on 18 Mch. and "Thompson, Watson, Carmichael, Turner, map" and so recorded in SJL with notation "Capt. Lewis." Enclosures not found.

Joseph TURNER replaced Claud Thomson as collector at Brunswick, Georgia. For the search for Thomson's successor, see Vol. 38:241, 243n, 259, 446, 447n, 462, 464. For the appointment of HENRY WARREN in place of William Watson at Plymouth, see Warren's letter to TJ of 10 Nov. 1802. In his list of appointments, TJ interlined the entries for all three of the new collectors at 3 Mch. (see Vol. 39: Appendix I).

REGISTER FOR THE LAND OFFICE: Edward Turner, a lawyer, who had joined his brother Henry, a merchant at Natchez, in January 1802. He was recommended for the office by Thomas Marston Green and John Breckinridge. By September 1803, he had received his temporary commission and instructions from Gallatin, dated 27 July. Recently married to Cato West's daughter, Turner feared local Federalists and others would try to prevent his confirmation by the Senate (*Terr. Papers*, 5:264-71; Gallatin, *Papers*, 8:572-6; 47:889).

The Senate confirmed the appointment of CATO WEST as secretary of Mississippi Territory on 3 Mch., and the State Department issued his permanent commission on that date (commission in Lb in DNA: RG 59, MPTPC; Matthew Clay to TJ, 28 Feb.; TJ to the Senate, 1 Mch. 1803).

EXTERNAL COMMERCE: the term used to ensure confidentiality when Congress appropriated $2,500 for the expedition to explore beyond the Mississippi River (see note to TJ to the Senate and the House of Representatives, 18 Jan., first message, and TJ to James Monroe, 25 Feb. 1803).

The map that Nicholas KING prepared at Gallatin's request covered an area from Lake Michigan on the east to the Pacific Ocean on the west, and from the junction of the Ohio River with the Mississippi on the south to beyond Lake Winnipeg on the north. Alexander Mackenzie's recently published *Voyages from Montreal* indicated that rivers such as the Saskatchewan, feeding into Lake Winnipeg and the NELSON River, formed a route between the western mountains and Hudson Bay. Other sources of geographical information that Gallatin expected to use for the map included Andrew Ellicott's chart of the Mississippi River completed in 1801, the explorations of James Cook and George Vancouver along the Pacific Coast, and maps of North America by the British cartographer Aaron Arrowsmith. Older French maps, such as those by Jean d'Anville and Guillaume de L'Isle, placed the sources of the Rio Grande—the Rio del NORTE—in the northern Great Plains, which would put the course of that river to the west of some tributaries of the Missouri. If that proved to be true, the headwaters of those branches of the Missouri would not be near the sources of any rivers running to the Pacific. The map that King produced from the information collected by Gallatin, in a large area marked "Conjectural," does show the upper part of the Rio del Norte to the west of the lower branches of the Missouri. The map posits, however, a main branch of the Missouri that has its headwaters near the mountains and loops around the head of the Rio del Norte. One segment of that hypothetical course of the Missouri River appears in detail, marking locations where the Pawnee and Mandan Indians lived. That information came from a map copied by Meriwether Lewis, apparently from one in Edward THORNTON's possession. It charted a portion of the river with coordinates of latitude and longitude from data collected by the North West Company (Gary E. Moulton, ed., *Atlas of the Lewis & Clark Expedition* [Lincoln, Neb., 1983], 5, plate 2; John Logan Allen, *Passage through the Garden: Lewis and Clark and the Image of the American Northwest* [Urbana, Ill., 1975], 74-90; King's map of western North America, in Geography and Map Division, DLC; map of bend of the Missouri River in Lewis's hand, same; W. Kaye Lamb, ed., *The Journals and Letters of Sir Alexander Mackenzie* [Cambridge, 1970], 110-16; Vol. 35:423; Vol. 37:565-6n).

From Ephraim Kirby

SIR Litchfield March 14th. 1803

It has been mentioned to me, that expectations of the removal of the Surveyor at Saybrook in this State, from office, are generally entertained. Should such an event take place, permit me to name Mr. George Wolcott as a candidate for the appointment. He is a Gentleman of fair and unblemished moral character, whose integrity, amidst the conflicts of party, I believe, has never been questioned; and whose competency to the duties of the office cannot be doubted.

Mr. Wolcott is a man of business habits—During the severe period of political persecution in 1798 & 99 he was deprived of an office under the State Government, which afforded handsome emolument, for no other cause, than his political opinions. His rank in society is respectable—he has frequently, & recently been elected to a seat in the Legislature of Connecticut.

Since you have been so good as to permit me to address you with freedom on subjects of this nature, I make no apology for the present communication.

I am with great respect Sir Your Obedt. Servt

EPHM KIRBY

RC (DNA: RG 59, LAR); at foot of text: "The President of the U. States"; endorsed by TJ as received 4 Apr. and "Wolcott George to be Surveyor Saybrook" and so recorded in SJL.

SURVEYOR AT SAYBROOK: Richard Dickinson. DEPRIVED OF AN OFFICE: Wolcott lost his position as deputy sheriff of Hartford County (Hartford *American Mercury*, 22 Mch. 1804; Pierpont Edwards to TJ, 25 Feb. 1803).

Wolcott represented Windsor in Hartford County in the state LEGISLATURE (*Windham Herald*, 22 May 1800; Hartford *American Mercury*, 24 Sep. 1801). He was also recommended by Pierpont Edwards; see Edwards to TJ, 25 Feb.

From James Madison

DEAR SIR Washington. Mar. 14. 1803

You will find in the gazette of this morning the letter from d'Yrujo, which he wished to be printed, and which will I hope do good. Pichon has also written a strong letter to the Govr. of Louisiana, summoning him on his responsibility, to see that the cession of that province to France be not effected, nor the amicable relations of the Republic to the U. States, be endangered by a perseverance of the Intendant in his breach of the Treaty. Both these Ministers are deeply alarmed at the apparent tendency of things, and seem willing to risk themselves for the purpose of checking it.

I have just recd. & decyphered the inclosed letters from Mr. Livingston. In general they wear a better aspect than heretofore; but it is remarkable, unless some intermediate letter has not been recd. that nothing is said of the written assurance which was to be given on the return of the chief Consul, that the Spanish Treaty would be faithfully observed by France. It is still more remarkable that he should undertake to prescribe measures, without hinting even the reasons for them. The whole of his postscript of Decr. 23. is an enigma; suggesting a fear of some hazardous finesse or some unwarrantable project,[1] rather than a hope of successful negociation. What inconsistency also in waiting for safe opportunities, and at the same putting his letter which contains confidential things not even in Cypher, into the hands of a British Minister. Surely a letter in Cypher might as well be trusted to a French post office; and then he might write as frequently & fully as he pleased, thro' England, and with a much better chance of despatch, than by direct conveyances from Paris.

OBrien says that the Dey of Algiers threatens war if the Stores be not sent, and allows three months only for their arrival. He demands, over & above the stores, 1000 barrels of Gun powder. The answer to this request he says must be in a separate letter from the President. But the importance of the subject requires that you should see the letter, and I therefore inclose it.

With respectful attachment I remain Yours

James Madison

RC (DLC); at foot of text: "The President of the U. States"; endorsed by TJ as received from the State Department on 18 Mch. and "Livingston & Obrien's lres, Yrujo & Pichon" and so recorded in SJL with notation "N. Orleans." Enclosures: (1) Robert R. Livingston to Madison, 20 Dec. 1802, and perhaps letters from Livingston to Madison of 11 and 14 Nov.; Madison deciphered the coded passages in all three letters (Madison, *Papers, Sec. of State Ser.*, 4:115-16, 121, 203-5). (2) Richard O'Brien to Madison, 23 Nov. 1802, from Algiers, stating that on the previous day he informed the Algerian government of the arrival of $30,000 in the place of timber and stores for the annuity from the United States, but Mustafa Baba has refused to accept the cash payment; the dey insists that unless the U.S. wants war, he must receive the items required by the annuity arrangement, plus 1,000 barrels of gunpowder, within three months' time; O'Brien estimates that the gunpowder now demanded by the dey would cost $40,000 with freight and insurance if sent from the U.S.; he believes that the dey wants to use the timber and stores in the construction of a frigate; he also discusses debts owed by the U.S. to financial houses in Algiers that play a role in relations between the countries; the amounts owed include $6,500 to repay the ransoming from Tripoli of men from the brig *Franklin* (same, 135-7).

GAZETTE OF THIS MORNING: under the heading "OFFICIAL," the *National Intelligencer* printed Carlos Martínez de Irujo's letter to Madison of the 10th. According to editorial comments in the newspaper, the Spanish minister's letter made clear that the stoppage at New Orleans was not the act of his government, but rather the result of a misunderstanding by the intendant of the terms of the right of deposit. Therefore, the editors declared, "it will appear that the arguments, made use of in the late debates in the Senate, for involving the country in war, were entirely without foundation." Louis André PICHON saw Irujo on 11 Mch. and wrote to Manuel de Salcedo to point out that Spanish authorities should do nothing to alter Louisiana's relationship with the United States before France took control of the colony. Pichon's message to Salcedo was included with the dispatches from Irujo to the Spanish officials at New Orleans that Madison forwarded on the 11th (*National Intelligencer*, 14 Mch.; Madison, *Papers, Sec. of State Ser.*, 4:413; Madison to TJ, 10 Mch.).

WRITTEN ASSURANCE: Livingston reported to Madison in November that he had been frustrated in attempts to get a guarantee from the French government that the provisions of the existing treaty between the United States and Spain would remain in force after the transfer of Louisiana to French control. When pressed, Talleyrand told Livingston that a formal declaration would have to wait until Bonaparte returned to Paris from an inspection tour in the north of France (Madison, *Papers*, *Sec. of State Ser.*, 4:110-11, 115; Vol. 38:589n).

UNDERTAKE TO PRESCRIBE MEASURES: in coded passages in his letter of 20 Dec. and a POSTSCRIPT dated the 23d, Livingston stated that he had circumvented Talleyrand to bring his proposals directly to Bonaparte's attention (see also Livingston to TJ, 12 Mch.). Livingston gave no details of those memorials to the first consul, indicating that he would write more fully when he had a reliable means of conveying sensitive information. He stated cryptically, however, that his propositions were having an effect because they had "*alarmed*" Bonaparte (here and below, text that Livingston put in code is in italics). RATHER THAN A HOPE OF SUCCESSFUL NEGOCIATION: in the postscript of 23 Dec., Livingston advised Madison to "*Set on foot a negotiation for fixing our bounds with Britain but by no means conclude til you hear from me that all hope here is lost.*" Writing partly in the clear and partly in code, he declared: "Do not absolutely despair tho you may have no great reason to hope *should New Orleans be possessed by a small force*" (Madison, *Papers*, *Sec. of State Ser.*, 4:204).

Among the CONFIDENTIAL THINGS that Livingston did not encode in the letter of 20 Dec. and its postscript were comments relating to the ownership of Florida, which were in proximity to a remark about favorable "prospects of attaining the object." "I have made so many Converts," he wrote in clear text, "that I would wish, in case favorable circumstances should arise, to know how to act. If left to myself I may go beyond the mark." He also opined "that the storm in England will blow over for the present" and the peace in Europe "will not be lasting." Livingston began the 20 Dec. letter with the supposition that he would send it to Rouen "without being certain of finding the ship there by which I hope to send it." By the time he added the postscript on 23 Dec., he found he could send the letter "by the way of England" with Anthony Merry, who had been serving as the interim BRITISH MINISTER to France (same, 203-4; Vol. 38:588n).

In his dispatch of 23 Nov., O'Brien recommended that TJ send a SEPARATE LETTER to Mustafa Baba rather than answering through the U.S. consul. O'Brien sent a triplicate of his dispatch to Paris, asking Livingston "to note The Contents" and send the document on to Washington. Livingston forwarded it to Madison with his letter of 20 Dec. (Madison, *Papers*, *Sec. of State Ser.*, 4:136, 418n).

Earlier in 1802, O'Brien had prepared a "Correct list of the Terrible marine of the Potent Algerines," which provided American navy commanders a detailed description of the size and composition of the naval forces of Algiers. The list included a main force of 15 warships consisting of frigates, xebecs, polacres, schooners, and a brig, as well as about 50 gunboats and 200 coasting vessels. A militia force of 50,000 could also be raised "with difficulty" (MS in DLC: TJ Papers, 232:41547, undated, in an unidentified hand, endorsed by TJ: "Algiers. force of in 1802. by Capt. McNiel to which add a fine 44. gun frigate take from the Portuguese"; NDBW, 2:71-3; Madison, *Papers, Sec. of State Ser.*, 3:452n).

[1] Preceding four words interlined.

From Thomas Munroe

SIR, Washington 14th. March 1803

I recd., on the 10th Instant, the Letter which you did me the honor to write from Colo Wrens on the 7th—We are proceeding with diligence in our operations on Pennsylvania Avenue according to your directions. It seems to be a very general opinion here that without the trees are boxed, or otherwise protected from the horses and cattle a great many, if not all of them will be bark'd and destroyed—several instances have been pointed out to me where they were planted last year, and all destroyed—A man near the Avenue says he had twenty or thirty destroyed by a neighbours horse in one night—I should not myself suppose that we should lose more in that way than we could easily replace—Do you, Sir, think that a coat of white-wash, which I am told they give to the young trees in the English Deer parks would have any good effect, or be adviseable as a protection against cattle? A person who thinks boxing absolutely necessary says each tree will cost One dollar, when compleated, that is, the tree itself, planting, boxing, painting the box, and doing every thing else relating to it.—

The Stakes to tie the trees to, which it is said will probably cost nearly as much as the trees, wou'd as is said, be unnecessary, if boxes were used, but the expense of boxing would I imagine be at least double.—

Dr Thornton, Mr King and myself have conversed on the manner of laying off the lines and planting the trees—The three modes illustrated by the enclosed sections were suggested—I mentioned the plan No. 3 as the one which I believed you had designed, and would, I thought, adopt, but as no inconvenience would arise from the delay of submitting the other two plans to you I got Mr King to make the sketch—The row on each side the footways nearest the Houses[1] which we are proceeding in will at all events be right and conformable to either plan—I shall get the trees from Mount Vernon, and Genl Masons Island & I expect from the samples I have seen, they will be of a good size, price twelve & a half Cents each. Gen Mason is one of those who think they will not do without boxes.

I have just recd the enclosed letter from the Committee Appointed at a meeting of the Contributors to the Theatre contemplated to be built here, They are very anxious, on Acct. of the building season having arrived, to receive an answer so soon as the convenience of the President and the important subjects of his consideration will admit—The spot solicited is that coloured yellow in the space called "Bank square" in the sketch herewith sent.—Perhaps part of the public ground on the south side of the Avenue nearly opposite would suit as well, or better as a grant of the site asked for may be objectionable[2] on the ground of its having been generally supposed to be designed[3] for another purpose.—I have taken the liberty of forwarding herewith a plan of the City as it is possible you might not have one at Monticello.

I Have the Honor to be with perfect respect & Consideration Sir, Yr mo Ob Servt THOMAS MUNROE

RC (DLC); at foot of text: "President of the United States"; endorsed by TJ as received 18 Mch. and so recorded in SJL. Dft (DNA: RG 42, LRDLS). Enclosures: (1) Nicholas King to Munroe, Surveyor's Office, 12 Mch. 1803, enclosing four section drawings of Pennsylvania Avenue for the president, so that "his decision may be obtained on the distances to be observed in setting out the lines of trees between the Presidents House & Capitol"; section No. 1 shows the avenue in its current state, without trees, labeling the present gravel road, six-foot wide stone pavements, and ditches; section No. 2 shows the landscape plan considered "when Dr. Thornton was with us," which divides the avenue into two 33-foot carriage ways bisected with a 30-foot gravel carriage and horse way down the center; two double rows of trees separate the center way from the carriage ways, while a single row of trees separates the carriage ways from 13-foot brick pavements on each side of the avenue; King's objections to this plan include both the number of trees and the number of carriage ways, "none of them wide enough to permit a great intercourse—and allow a facility of turning"; section No. 3 includes a single, 80-foot carriage way with a 10-foot gravel foot way on either side flanked by double rows of trees 12 feet apart; in this plan, King believes that the width of the carriage way is more proportional to the avenue and that the two rows of trees on each side "will give a greater strength of coloring, and afford more shade"; the gravel foot way would be used by pedestrians passing a considerable distance along the avenue, although King adds that "the absolute necessity of such a walk may be doubted"; section No. 4 is similar to section No. 2, except that the two carriage ways have been widened to 47 feet and the central way narrowed into a 15-foot gravel horse way shaded by two single rows of trees planted 18 feet apart; King notes that this removes the great objection to section No. 2, namely the narrowness of the carriage ways, although planting trees at present "would injure the existing road, and make it too narrow for Carriages to turn in"; King has commenced running lines on each side of Pennsylvania Avenue, nearest the houses, so "that the work may be progressing until the Presidents determination on the most proper distances for the interior rows is known" (RC in DLC; addressed: "Thos. Munroe Esq. Superintendent of the City of Washington"; note by TJ in margin to the right of section No. 2: "adopted. but leaving out the 2 middle rows of trees"). (2) Daniel Carroll and others to Munroe, Washington, 14 Mch. 1803, stating that at a 12 Mch. meeting to raise a subscription for erecting a theater in Washington, a committee was formed to enquire if Munroe could allot them "a part of the Square, usually known by the appellation of a site for the Bank on Pennsylvania Avenue, or some other public Square as near the centre Market as possible"; the committee are informed that the desired square "is not a fixed appropriation" and that if a bank is ever established there, "the remainder, after granting our request, will be amply sufficient for the purpose"; in a postscript, the committee ask that their request be communicated to the president if Munroe does not think himself authorized to grant it (same; in an unidentified hand, signed by Carroll, John P. Van Ness, William Duane, W. M. Duncanson, and William Brent; addressed "Thomas Munroe Esq Superintendent of the City of Washington"; with note in Munroe's hand on verso of address sheet: "Memo. What is intended to be meant by *the site especially known by the appellation of the Bank Sq.* is the public space directly east of Sq 491, being the nearest thereto"). Other enclosures not found.

COLO WRENS: on his most recent journey from Washington to Monticello, TJ lodged the night of 7 Mch. at the Fairfax County tavern of James Wren (MB, 2:1094; Vol. 33:508n).

GENL. MASONS ISLAND: located in the Potomac River across from Georgetown, Mason's Island was owned by Georgetown merchant John Mason and was known for its elegant residence and the elaborate landscapes and gardens designed by gardener David Hepburn. Also called Analostan Island, it was renamed

Theodore Roosevelt Island in the twentieth century (Mary E. Curry, "Theodore Roosevelt Island: A Broken Link to Early Washington, D.C. History," RCHS, 71-72 [1971-72], 14-33).

Writing Munroe from Washington on 12 Apr. 1803, William M. Duncanson asked the superintendent to present the president his proposal to enclose the Mall "west of 7th. Street, turning along 15th. Street and terminating in the Potomack." Duncanson wished to cultivate the land "to raise nurseries of trees suited for the Mall or the Streets of the City, or in clover, garden stuffs, or such like." Inhabitants would retain "free egress & regress," but only on foot since horses could destroy any trees and shrubs. Since Mall improvements remained under the president's control, Duncanson assumes that he would be reimbursed for the value of the fence whenever the president chose to resume control of the property (RC in DLC).

[1] Preceding three words interlined.

[2] Munroe first wrote "or better in case a grant of the other site asked for should be rejected," before altering the text to read as above.

[3] Word interlined in place of "destined."

From S. Smith & Buchanan

Sir — Balto March 14. 1803

We have the honor, to hand you herewith, a statement of the Expences, on two Casks Wine received for you by the Ship Adelaide from Lisbon, & forwarded by us this day, agreeably to your desire, to Messrs. Gibson & Jefferson of Richmond—Mr Jarvis, by whom the Wine was addressed to us, has neither mentioned, nor authorised us to receive, the Cost of the Wine—

We have the honor to be Sir Your obedt Servts

S Smith & Buchanan

Amot. duties on two Casks Wine	36.55
Portage into Store	50
freight from Lisbon	5.12
Portage to the Packet	25
	$42.42

March 21st—We have reason to believe that a Letter written by us to a House in London on the same day as the preceding, was by mistake addressed to you, as we have only just now discovered that the present Letter was not regularly forwarded—if we have committed such mistake, we pray you to excuse us— SS & B

RC (MHi); endorsed by TJ as received 4 Apr. and so recorded in SJL.

In his account of wines purchased while he was president, TJ recorded paying William JARVIS $98.17 for the two half-pipes of Oeiras wine (MB, 2:1115).

From Jonathan Trumbull, Jr.

Sir — Connecticut Lebanon 14th Mar: 1803

I have been honored with your Excellency's Letter of Febry last—covering a Report of a Committee relative to the Militia Institution of the UStates,—and shall take care to have them placed before the Legislature of this State, at their approaching Session in May next—

With high respect & regard I have the Honor to be Sir Your Obet Servant

Jona Trumbull

RC (PHi); at foot of text: "President of the UStates"; endorsed by TJ as received 25 Mch. and so recorded in SJL with notation "W"; also endorsed by TJ: "to be filed in War office."

Scion of one of Connecticut's most prominent families, Jonathan Trumbull, Jr. (1740-1809), was George Washington's military secretary during the American Revolution and served in Congress from 1789 to 1796. A Federalist, Trumbull became governor of Connecticut in 1798 and retained the office until his death (ANB).

LETTER OF FEBRY LAST: Circular to the Governors of the States, 25 Feb. 1803.

From John Warner

Sir, — Wilmington March 14th 1803

I take the liberty to enclose for your perusal a number of the "Federal Ark," a paper lately removed from Dover to this place. It is generally believed that no paragraph of a low political nature, more particularly, is ever inserted in it without the approbation of the Collector of this port; this number may serve as a specimen of the manner in which this paper is conducted;—perhaps none on the continent, as far as the abilities of *all its editors* combined could contrive, has been more filled with misrepresentations and falsehood.

I am very respectfully Your Friend

John Warner

RC (DLC); endorsed by TJ as received 21 Mch. and so recorded in SJL; also endorsed by TJ: "Mc.lane." Enclosure: see below.

ENCLOSE FOR YOUR PERUSAL: the issue of *The Federal Ark* has not been identified. During his 1802 election campaign, Caesar A. Rodney informed TJ of the new Federalist publication at Dover. The first issue of the biweekly newspaper was published in Wilmington on 28 Feb. 1803 (Vol. 38:456).

COLLECTOR OF THIS PORT: Allen McLane. On 8 Feb., Warner and Wilmington merchant James Brobson wrote TJ recommending Nehemiah Tilton in place of McLane. The 28 Feb., 7 and 12 Mch. issues of *The Federal Ark* presented articles and documents supporting McLane against the "Office-Hunters" and attacking Tilton.

From George Jefferson

Dear Sir Richmond 15th. Mar: 1803

I duly received your favor of the 5th. inclosing 1000$, with which I have taken up your dft in favor of Craven Peyton for that sum. the box you mention after the most shameful neglect was sent to Norfolk to be forwarded on to Washington. I hope it has before this arrived there.

The iron from Phila. has arrived. the Wine from Baltimore has not.

I am Dear Sir Yr. Very humble servt. Geo. Jefferson

RC (MHi); at foot of text: "Thos. Jefferson esqr."; endorsed by TJ as received 18 Mch. and so recorded in SJL.

For the shipments of iron and wine, see TJ to Jones & Howell, 6 Feb.; S. Smith & Buchanan to TJ, 14 Mch.

From Levi Lincoln

Sir Washington March 15th 1803

As the accompanying, from their conciseness, will consume but eight, or ten minutes in their perusal; and as it may be useful to see Specimens of the *old* spirit exhibited on an interesting occasion, in a new shape, by *young*, & *old* hands, I take the liberty to forward them. There may be danger of too much heat, of the sacred glow bursting into a flame from the fuel with which it may be fed. In Massachusetts, hitherto, the evil has been the other way—A bold, constant spirited, & well directed exposure of the old, and explanation of the new order of things, will attach the people of that portion of the Union to their Government, & prostrate, by rendering obnoxious, the opposition. I believe the late removals, there, will have a salutary effect—Some of my letters state the measure, as desirable, & expected. All, agree that Government, is to look to its friends, & not to its enemies for support. The former appear to be more for acting, & more *awake* than they have been. One of, the most animating, and best composed songs, I have ever noticed, on a similar occasion, was made for, & sung at the Worcester celebration. at least, such I think is its character. But you know, Sir, I pretend to neither judgment or taste, but feeling only, in such things—Genl. Dearborn, has taken it, to his Italien musician to obtain an[1] appropriate & national tune for it, if possible—It was sung in the tune of J— & Liberty—

A frigate presenting herself, at the mouth of the Eastern branch, is this moment firing her salute, She is probably the one which was expected from the Mediterranian. Coll Burr & Morris have left the city; they remained near a week after Congress adjourned, The former is now at Alexandria, on his way to the Southward. Tracy is still here, or was two days since—Nothing important has occurred since your absence, excepting the dispatches from New Orleans to the Spanish minister, which you will have received before this reaches you—This is as seasonable as it will be mortifying to the war champions—

I am Sir most respectfully your obt Sevt LEVI LINCOLN

RC (DLC); at head of text: "The President of the United States"; endorsed by TJ as received 21 Mch. and so recorded in SJL. Enclosures: (1) probably the 9 Mch. issue of the Worcester *National Aegis*, describing Worcester's daylong celebration of the anniversary of TJ's inauguration on 4 Mch., beginning at sunrise with a 17-gun salute and tolling of the bells; at noon 200 people proceeded to the South Meeting House escorted by the Worcester Company of Artillery to hear an address by Levi Lincoln, Jr., evincing "a perfect sympathy of feeling, between the Orator and his audience," followed by the "Patriotic Ode"; dinner in the hall that customarily holds all guests for the 4th of July celebration on this day was not large enough, with the inhabitants of Worcester cheerfully yielding "to the accomodation of their Republican friends from the neighboring towns"; a grand finale brought appropriate toasts, cheers, songs, and gun salutes. (2) Levi Lincoln, Jr., *Address: Pronounced at Worcester, (Mass.) March 4th, 1803* (Worcester, 1803; Shaw-Shoemaker, No. 4526).

INTERESTING OCCASION: Lincoln informed TJ of preparations for the 4 Mch. celebration at Worcester in his letter to the president of 25 Feb.

William C. White wrote the "Patriotic Ode" for the CELEBRATION. Consisting of eight stanzas and a chorus, the second stanza reads:

"Yet louder, louder, strike the string!
And Faction's envious ear annoy!
'Tis Monticello's sage you sing!
Sweep, sweep, the thrilling chords of joy!"

The entire song was printed in the 9 Mch. issue of the Worcester *National Aegis*. It was sung to the tune of "Jefferson and Liberty."

The U.S. FRIGATE *Constellation* arrived at the Washington Navy Yard on 15 Mch. after a 40-day voyage from Gibraltar (*Washington Federalist*, 16 Mch.; Georgetown *Olio*, 18 Mch. 1803).

Vice President BURR planned to see John Taylor of Caroline on his journey to visit his daughter in South Carolina after the close of the congressional session. On 8 Apr., Burr wrote from Columbia, South Carolina, that he had been away from Washington for three weeks. By the end of May, he was back in New York City (Kline, *Burr*, 2:764-5, 769, 772-3).

DISPATCHES FROM NEW ORLEANS: see Madison to TJ, 10 Mch.

[1]MS: "&."

From Robert Patterson

SIR Philadelphia March 15th. 1803.

I have been honoured with your favour of the 2d. and thank you for your confidence, which I will never abuse—I am preparing a set of astronomical formulæ for Mr. L. and will, with the greatest pleasure, render him every assistance in my power—I take the liberty of subjoining the formula which I commonly use for computing the longitude from the common lunar observation, illustrated by an example—The other formulæ for computing the time, alts. &c are all expressed in the same manner, viz. by the common algebraic signs; which renders the process extremely easy even to boys or common sailors of but moderate capacities.

Example

Suppose the apparent angular distance of the sun & moon's nearest limbs (by taking the mean of a set of observations) to be 110°.2'.30" the app. Alt of ☉'s lower limb measuring 20°.40' and that of ☽'s lower limb 35°.24' height of the eye 18 feet, estimated Greenwich time Sept. 18th. 1798 about 6 hours p.m. time at place of observation, allowing for error of watch, or computed from the sun's alt. & lat. of place 4 h. 20 m 30 s p.m. apparent time. Reqd. the longitude of the place of observation, from the merid. of Greenwich.

Solution

From the app. alts. of the lower limbs of ☉ & ☽ find the app. alts. of their centers by subtracting the dip corresponding to the height of the eye, and adding the app. semidiameters: Also from the app. dist. of limbs find the app. dist. of centers by adding the semidiameters. The longitude may then be computed by the following formula; in which the capital letters represent the corresponding arches in the adjoining column; & the small letters, the logarithmic functions of these arches. Where the small letter is omitted, the arch is found from the log. funct. The logs. need not be taken out to more than 4 decimal places, and to the nearest minute only of their corresponding arches except in the case of proportional logs. Where an ambiguous sign [occurs][1] as ± or ± (expressing the sum or difference) the one or the other is to be used as directed in the explanatory note to which the number in the margin refers

		☉	☽	
° ' "		° ' "	° ' "	
110. 2. 30		20. 40. 00	35. 24. 00	
15. 59		3. 18	3. 18	dip
15. 20		20 36. 42	35. 20. 42	
110. 33. 49	app. dist. Cents	15. 59	15. 20	semi. diam
		20. 52. 41	35 36 2	App. Alt of Cents

Explanatory notes

1. Add when C is greater than B otherwise subtract
2 Subtract when C is greater than B otherwise add

3 Subtract when either H or I exceeds 90°, or when H is greater than I, otherwise add.

4 Add when either H or I exceeds 90°, or when H is less than I, otherwise subt.

5 In Tab. 13 (reg. tab.) under the nearest degree to Q at top find two numbers, one opp. the nearest min. to ☽'s corr. of alt. found in tab. 8, and the other opp. the nearest min. to 1st. corr. (N) and the diff. of these two numbers will be the 3d corr. This corr. may generally be omitted

6 Add when Q is less than 90°. otherwise sub.

7 These are to be found in N.A. from p. 8h. to p. 11th. of the month, and the sun or star from which the moons dist. was obsd taking out the two distances which are next greater, & next less than the true dist. (S) calling that the *preceding* dist. which comes first in the order of time, and the other the *folling*[2] dist.

8. The Gr. time and time at place of ob. must both be reckoned from the same n[. . .][3]

9. When Y is greater than Z the long. is W. otherwise it is E—and when the long. comes out more than 12 hours or 180°. subt. it from 24h or 360° & change it name

Formula

	App. dist. of cents.	A	110.33.49			
	☽'s app. alt	B	35.36	cosec	b	10.2350
	☉ or ✳'s app. alt	C	20.53			
	$\frac{1}{2}\overline{B+C}$	D	28.14	tan	d	9.7299
	$C \sim D$	E	7.21	cot	e	10.8894
	$\frac{1}{2}A$	F	55.17	tan	f	10.1593
	$d+e+f-20$	G	80.33	tan	–	10.7786
1	$F \pm G$	H	25.16			
2	$F \mp G$	I	135.50	tan	i	9.9874
	☽'s hor. par. N.A. page 7.	K	55.42	pr lg	k	.5994
	$b+i+k-20$	L	27. 8	pr lg	–	.8218
	Refr. of I (considd as an Alt) Tab. I. (reg. tables)	M	59			
	$L-M$ = 1st. corr.	N	26. 9			
3	$A \pm N$	O	110. 7.40			
	Refr. of H for ✳, refr-par for ☉ = 2d Corr	P	1.54			
4	$O \pm P$	Q	110. 9.34			

5	Corr. from Tab. 13th = 3d Corr	R	4			
6	Q ± R = true dist. of cents	S	110. 9.30			
7	Preceding dist. in N.A.	T	110. 2.21			
7	Following dist. in N.A	U	111.27.47			
	T ~ S	V	7. 9	pr lg	v	1.4010
	T ~ U	W	1.25.26	pr lg	w	3236
	v - w	X	15. 4	pr lg	–	1.0774
8	Hour above T, in N.A, + X = true Green. time	Y	6.15. 4			
8	Time at pl. of obs.	Z	4.20.30			
9	Y ~ Z = Long. in time	A	1.54.34			
9	A ÷ 4 = Long. in degrees &c	B	28°.38½'	West.		

Note, the logarithmetical part of the operation may, with sufficient accuracy be wrought on Gunters scale thus

1 Extend the compasses from Tang E to Tang D, and that extt. will reach from Tang. F to Tang. G.

2 Extend from Tang. I to sine B and that extent will reach (on the line of Numbers) from K to L

3 Extend (on the line of Numbers) from W to 180^{m} and that extent will reach from V to X

I am, Sir, with the most perfect respect & esteem, your obedient Servant

RT. PATTERSON

RC (DLC); endorsed by TJ as received 4 Apr. and so recorded in SJL with notation "lunar obsvns."

SET OF ASTRONOMICAL FORMULÆ: using a blank copy book, Patterson set out five problems to explicate astronomical observations and calculations for Meriwether Lewis. For each problem, Patterson gave a numbered set of directions, followed by an example that demonstrated a solution from hypothetical data. The problem explained in the letter printed above was a version of the fifth one in the notebook, "To find the Longitude by Lunar observation." The other problems in the notebook involved computations of latitude, time, and altitudes of celestial bodies (MS notebook in MoHi; for additional description, see Moulton, *Journals of the Lewis & Clark Expedition*, 2:542, 564-5).

Patterson used astronomical symbols for SUN (☉), moon (☽), and star (✳).

N.A.: *Nautical Almanac.*

Gunter's SCALE, a predecessor of the slide rule, had proportional markings that enabled a user with a pair of dividers—the COMPASSES mentioned by Patterson—to make logarithmic calculations (Florian Cajori, "On the History of Gunter's Scale and the Slide Rule during the Seventeenth

Century," *University of California Publications in Mathematics*, 1 [1920], 187-209).

[1] Patterson wrote off the edge of the paper.

[2] That is, "following."

[3] Patterson wrote off the edge of the paper.

From John Vaughan

D SIR Philad. March 15. 1803

The enclosed Accot. of a Method of preserving ship Bread from Weavils, I have extracted from Tilloc's Philosophical Magazine for Decr. last—& I concieve it sufficiently important to trouble you with it—

When our ships bring salt petre from the East Indies they sell the Bags for a low price, for the sake of the Nitre which [...] be extracted from them by boiling them, possibly they might hereafter be purchased to carry bread in—or the Bags made for the purpose of carrying bread, be boiled, as was the Case with the Bag in question—To avoid *Rats* the Bags might be put into Puncheons or tight trimed bread rooms.

I remain with the greatest respect D sir. Your obt. Servant

JN VAUGHAN

RC (DLC); torn; addressed: "The President of the United States Washington or Monticello"; franked; postmarked 16 Mch.; endorsed by TJ as received 25 Mch. and so recorded in SJL. Enclosure: Extract, titled "On the Weavil in Sea Bread," describing the accidental discovery of a means of protecting sea bread from weevils during long voyages; this problem has remained unsolved until now despite premiums offered for a solution; in the case that has now come to notice, a bag that fell into "a cauldron of liquid nitre" at a powder mill was dipped in cold water, allowed to dry, and then used to store sea biscuits on a long trip from England to the West Indies and back; when the bag was opened after nine months, as supplies ran low and weevils ruined other bread on the ship, the captain to his "great Surprise" found that the biscuits in the bag were "perfectly sound" and free of insects (Tr in same; in Vaughan's hand; from *Philosophical Magazine*, 14 [1802-1803], 286).

From James Currie

Richmond Virginia
DR SIR: March 16th. 1803

I take the liberty by this, of doing myself the honor of introducing to your acquaintance the Honble. Captain John Murray of the Royal British Navy, a son of the Earl of Dunmore, whom you will find, perfectly deserving of those Civilities & polite attentions (for which you have ever been remarkable, to Respectable Strangers) & to which I beg leave & take the pleasure to recommend him; 'tis not improbable he may impart to you some communication, in regard to some matters that nearly concern him, in which Event I have impressed him to expect any information or advice (if necessary—) in your power that might with propriety be expected or wished for

I remain Dr Sir with the most Sincere Esteem & great regard Your most Obedt. Hble. Servt JAMES CURRIE

RC (MHi); at foot of text: "His Excelly Thomas Jefferson Esqr"; endorsed by TJ as received 19 Apr. "by Capt Murray" and so recorded in SJL.

JOHN MURRAY consulted with a number of Americans in an effort to secure land claims acquired by his father while royal governor of New York and Virginia (Julius Goebel, Jr., and others, eds., *The Law Practice of Alexander Hamilton: Documents and Commentary*, 5 vols. [New York, 1964-81], 1:263-4; Madison, *Papers, Sec. of State Ser.*, 4:20-1n; DNB, s.v. "Murray, John, fourth earl of Dunmore"). In February, he solicited the views of one of his contacts, the Virginian Ralph Wormeley, and forwarded them to Robert Hobart, the British Secretary of State for War and the Colonies. In his letter, Wormeley blasted TJ's subversion of the Washington and Adams administrations and his affection for France, particularly his failure to reprobate the "monster Robespierre," but concluded that given France's uncertain intentions with regard to Louisiana, TJ was "prepared now to draw the chords of Amity and Alliance" with Great Britain. Should France rebuff James Monroe's efforts to secure free navigation of the Mississippi, Monroe's orders were "to repair to London, and to propose a treaty of alliance offensive and defensive" between Great Britain and the United States. "The President," Wormeley continued, "is a man of good sense, and now having a commanding Horizontal view of all our political affairs, can form a better judgement of them, than when he was in a less elevated situation, and, has certainly overcome and banished those prejudices which were wont to dim the eyesight of his judgement" (Ralph Wormeley to John Murray, undated, Dupl in Centre for Buckinghamshire Studies: Archives of the Earls of Buckinghamshire; enclosed in Murray to Robert Hobart, 1 Mch. 1803, RC in same).

From John Page

DEAR SIR Richmond March the 16th. 1803

I take the Liberty of introducing to your acquaintance and Civilities the Honorable Captain John Murray of his Britanic Majesty's Navy, third Son of the Earl of Dunmore.

He has been several weeks here, and seems worthy of the polite Attention which has been paid him.

I confess I am happy to hear that our Countrymen, where ever he has been, have exhibited a Conduct towards him, which can not fail to reflect honor on their Character.

I am with the highest Respect your obedient Servant

JOHN PAGE

RC (DLC); endorsed by TJ as received 19 Apr. "by Capt Murray" and so recorded in SJL.

From John Warner

SIR   Wilmington March 16th 1803

As further establishment of the facts stated in my communication of the 14th Inst, I take the liberty to enclose two more numbers of the "Federal Ark." I have reason to believe the Collector, perhaps from the Post master of this place, knows that a number of this paper has been sent to You in consequence of which the first paragraph under the Wilmington head is inserted. The intent is obvious.

I am very Respectfully Your Friend   JOHN WARNER

RC (DLC); endorsed by TJ as received 25 Mch. and so recorded in SJL. Enclosures: see below.

COLLECTOR: Allen McLane. POST MASTER OF THIS PLACE: Joseph Bringhurst, a Republican, who took office in January 1802 (Stets, *Postmasters*, 106; Latrobe, *Correspondence*, 2:7n).

The initial paragraph UNDER THE WILMINGTON HEAD of the 16 Mch. issue of the *Federal Ark* reads: "The Office-Hunting Gentry *must excuse us in refusing a place to their* hypocritical declamation—*their designs are seen through, and will in future be guarded against*." Under the same heading in the 12 Mch. issue of the newspaper it was charged that Hezekiah Niles, Warner, and several others had promised to use all of their influence "official, as well as secret" to have Nehemiah Tilton appointed collector and Isaac Hendrickson his deputy if the two, who were city officers, supported the effort to obtain public monies for the "Extension of the Market-House in a direction" that would increase the value of their property by 50 percent.

To Henry Dearborn

March 17. 1803. Monticello

Th: Jefferson [presents] his friendly [. . .] the Secretary at War and sends him the [. . .] Governors Page [. . .] in his office.

PrC (DLC); faint. Recorded in SJL with notation "lres from Govr Page & Saquiricia." Enclosures: (1) John Page to TJ, 2 Mch. 1803. (2) "Saquiricia" to TJ, 15 Feb. 1803 (recorded in SJL as received from Windsor, North Carolina, on 16 Mch. with notation "W," but not found). (3) probably John Lambert to TJ, 3 Mch. 1803 (recorded in SJL as received from Trenton on 16 Mch. with notation "W," but not found).

From Gideon Granger

Dear Sir, Washington, March. 17. 1803.

The extraordinary productions in the enclosed paper under the signatures of "A Western American" & "Americus" appear to be calculated to produce so much mischief, that I thought it my duty to transmit it for your perusal.

I am at present confined by an inflamation upon the kidnies; and am Sir most respectfully Your Friend

And Humble Servant— Gidn Granger

RC (DLC); in an unidentified hand, signed by Granger; at foot of text: "The President of the United States."; endorsed by TJ as received 21 Mch. and so recorded in SJL. Enclosure: see below.

extraordinary productions: the 2 Mch. issue of James M. Bradford's *Guardian of Freedom*, published at Frankfort, Kentucky, included two letters—one signed "A Western American," the other "Americus"—both critical of the administration's handling of the suspension of the right of deposit at New Orleans. The first letter, attributed to Francis Flournoy, was designed "to open the eyes of every Western American, to the unfriendly views and conduct of Eastern America towards us." The eastern states designed their policies to keep the West in a servile state, but the interests of France and Spain, he contended, would go hand in hand with "Western America." It was to the advantage of both countries to promote the commercial prosperity of the West. The writer urged that the states of Ohio, Kentucky, and Tennessee and the territories of Indiana and Mississippi send "spirited remonstrances" to Congress calling for independence. If the "petitions be spurned," he noted, let us "erect ourselves into an independent distinct republic," looking to France for aid, if necessary. In the second letter, "Americus," writing to Kentucky senator John Breckinridge, supported the president's goal "to effect an arrangement, which shall place our rights of navigation and deposit, beyond the power, or the caprice of any officer." This could only be done by acquiring territory on the banks of the Mississippi. "If the United States do not hold the country," he asserted, "we shall remain subject to the power and caprice of those who do hold it." The land could be acquired through cession or conquest. "Americus" questioned the appointment of Monroe as an envoy to France and Spain while ministers were already in residence there. He did not believe France would sell New Orleans, a location so important to Louisiana. "But if the president verily believes she will, and for a price, which he is prepared to give, then he is consistent, in sending Monroe to make the bargain, if Monroe, is a better broker than Livingston, or Pinkney." The writer, however, thought "conquest" was the only means by which an "effectual arrangement" would be made. He questioned: "What is there in the tone of the President's administration calculated to command the respect, or extort the concession of Buonaparte? Has he finished the six seventy-four gun ships? has he a force ready to take possession of Orleans, if it is not ceded to us? No." (Baltimore *Federal Gazette*, 28 Mch. 1803; Arthur Preston Whitaker, *The Mississippi Question, 1795-1803: A Study in Trade, Politics, and Diplomacy* [New York, 1934], 220-1).

To Lewis Harvie

Dear Sir Monticello Mar. [17. 03.]

Your favor is duly recieved and I am happy to learn that [it will] be convenient for you [. . .] my [family] prop[ose]d; [. . .] the [. . .] of Capt. Lewis [. . .] [your same views]; for I would not wish [. . .] to [be employed]. but [with] a view to your [. . .] I intended to be back to Washington by the 1st of April. I fear however I have in that allowed myself too little time for the business which brought me here. still I do not altogether despair of accomplishing it, but under this uncertainty I think you had better await a letter which I will write you either on my actual[1] departure hence or my arrival at Washington holding yourself in readiness to move on short warning. present my friendly respects to Colo. & mrs Harvie and accept yourself my affectionate salutations. Th: Jefferson

PrC (DLC); faint; at foot of text: "Lewis Harvie esqr."; endorsed by TJ in ink on verso.

TJ expected Meriwether LEWIS to return briefly to Washington before departing for the West, at which point Harvie would assume the duties of secretary (TJ to Lewis Harvie, 22 Apr.).

[1] Word interlined.

To James Madison

Dear Sir Monticello Mar. 17. 1803.

Your's of the 10th. is recieved and I now inclose a letter to the Secretary of the navy, which be pleased to seal & deliver after perusal. I think not a moment should be lost in forwarding the stores to Algiers, as it is of importance to keep those powers quiet. might it not be useful to propose to the Dey with a year's annuity in stores, to recieve another year's in money? the answer from the Intendant of New Orleans was not unexpected to me; and I question whether any thing moves him but the shipment to Spain. Accept my affectionate salutations. Th: Jefferson

RC (Mrs. James A. Reed, Kansas City, Missouri, 1962); at foot of text: "The Secretary of State"; endorsed. PrC (DLC). Enclosure: TJ to Robert Smith, 17 Mch.

From James Madison

Dear Sir Washington Mar. 17. 1803

In the inclosed Intelligencer you will find the letter from Pichon to the Govr. of Louisiana. Having been written without reference to its publication, it is less carefully fitted than Yrujo's for the contemplated impression; and in connection with that presents some points for sophistical comments, which are made rather more, than less salient by the reflections of the Editor. The letter will however be useful in several respects, particularly in rescuing France from the odium thrown on her suspected agency.

There are voluminous communications from the Mediterranean but in general of old date. The inclosed letter from the Bey of Tunis, of which a copy was some time ago recd. claims attention. Eaton says he dreads the consequence of a refusal, yet takes for granted that it will as it ought to take place. If an account recd. last night from Kirkpatrick be true, which appears to be authentic, Algiers will probably become more managiable. He writes from Malaga, on Feby. 1. that the French Consul there, had advice from his colleague at Barcelona, that a vessel had just arrived there with despatches for the French Govt. informing it of a declaration of war by the Dey Algiers, and that the despatches were gone on by Express to Paris. In general our affairs were considered in Mediterranean as tending the wrong way. All agree that peace with Tripoli was for a long time in our power & almost on our own terms; and lament that the crisis is probably past. For the present it seems essential that the gun carriages shd. go to Morroco; the stipulated stores to Algiers, and a complaisant refusal of the Frigate, to Tunis. With respect to Tripoli, we must wait for communications from Morris & Cathcart. I have written to Lear to sound him on the subject of taking Cathcart's place at Algiers.

The other inclosed letter has just been put into my hands by Mr. Pichon.

With respectful attachment always yours James Madison

RC (DLC); endorsed by TJ as received from the State Department on 21 Mch. and "Pichon. Bey Tunis. Tripoli. Marroco" and so recorded in SJL. Enclosures: see below.

On 16 Mch., the *National Intelligencer* printed, in English, Louis André Pichon's letter of the 11th to Manuel de Salcedo. Pichon declared that the interests of the French government were "implicated" in the events at New Orleans and argued that even if the intendant had acted without instructions from Spain in abolishing the right of deposit, Salcedo was not free of responsibility. Advocating that the Spanish crown surely wanted to maintain peace as a matter of course, Pichon implied that if Salcedo did not intercede and the situation ended in armed conflict, blame would fall on him as governor. In comments appended to the letter, the EDITOR asked readers to bear in mind "that it is *possible*" the crisis was in fact the result of policy—if misguided—on the part of higher authorities. The governments of Spain and France must recognize that the interests of both countries "would be deeply injured by the necessary, the inevitable effect of a deliberative invasion of our rights on the Mississippi." Americans along the seaboard and west of the Appalachians were in agreement on that point, the editor insisted: "There is, and can be but one opinion in America; and there is but one sentiment" (Madison to TJ, 14 Mch.).

The letter to TJ from Hammuda, the BEY OF TUNIS, who suggested that the United States show its respect for him through the gift of a 36-gun frigate, was dated 8 Sep. 1802 (Vol. 38:365-8). Writing to Madison on 12 Sep., William EATON advised that the bey and his ministers expected the request to be denied and would use the refusal as justification for a more adversarial position toward the United States (same, 367n).

ALGIERS: Mustafa Baba declared war on France in January, but then postponed to allow time for the French consul to receive instructions from Paris. At issue were the dey's demands for increases in presents, an unpaid loan taken out some years before by the Directory, and the role of France as guarantor of the treaty between Denmark and Algiers. When word came that the French government was preparing a shipment of presents, Mustafa did not pursue his threat to initiate hostilities. William Kirkpatrick was the U.S. consul at Malaga, Spain (Madison, *Papers*, *Sec. of State Ser.*, 4:242-3, 299, 463, 469).

Madison's letter asking Tobias LEAR to become the consul at Algiers has not been found. Mustafa Baba had written to TJ in October protesting the appointment of James Leander Cathcart to the position (same, 428, 429n; Vol. 38:509-10).

The OTHER INCLOSED LETTER may have been one from Pichon to Madison of 17 Mch. requesting credentials for Gérard Cazeaux as vice commissary for commercial relations at Portsmouth, New Hampshire (Madison, *Papers*, *Sec. of State Ser.*, 4:428, 429n, 431). TJ signed an exequatur for Cazeaux on 5 Apr. (FC in Lb in DNA: RG 59, Exequaturs).

Notes on Composition Ornaments

Andrews George

Mar. 17. 1803. the composition ornaments arrive for the fireplace of the Chamber, a [b]it like those of the entablature of the room.

---

for the pediments of the windows & arches of the Dining room & Tea-room

	metops		roses	
for 6. windows	18	+	18	= 36
1. double arch	12	+	12	= 24
1. single do.	6	+	6	= 12
	36	+	36	= 72

to wit. 36. metops of the size of those i[n th]e parlour

36. roses to lie in 6. I. square not in the frize of the inside window of the dining room the metops & roses will be confined to $5\frac{1}{4}$ I height, that being the height of the frize; & as the frize is $64\frac{3}{4}$ I. long the triglyphs, metops & roses will be disposed as follows

from the end of the frize to center of 1st. triglyph	3.$\frac{1}{2}$
6. metops & triglyphs @ 9$\frac{5}{8}$	57.$\frac{3}{4}$
from center of east[1] triglyph to end of frize	3 $\frac{1}{2}$
	64 $\frac{3}{4}$

note the triglyph is 3$\frac{1}{2}$ I. wide
the spaces for the metops will be 6$\frac{1}{8}$ I wide

---

over the arches & the windows of the tea room, there are to be no pediments, but only frize boards to tack curtains to. these frize boards of the arches will be 11. f. 3 I. long, & 6. I. wide

the frize-boards of the windows of the tea room will be 5. f. long & 6. I. wide

---

for the parlour these are the ornaments compleat for the Corinthian cornice round the room, also as follows for the windows & door

4. windows, 3 sets of ornaments & a metop extra[2] for each.
2. doors 4 sets of do. & a metop extra for each
[fire]place 3 sets of do & a metop extra
making in all 23. sets & 7. metops extra.

---

the following therefore gives a view of the whole ornaments for the windows, doors & arches of the Parlour Dining room & tea room. viz.

23. sets of ornaments (same as for frize of the parlour, for parlour
43. metops, to wit 7. for the parlour & 36. Ding & Tea rooms
36. roses for the Dining & Tea rooms.

MS (ViU); entirely in TJ's hand; written on verso of Statement of Account with George Andrews, 22 Feb. 1803; blurred.

For TJ's order with George Andrews for the COMPOSITION ORNAMENTS that adorned several rooms in Monticello, see Vol. 39:98-9n, 563-4.

[1] Word interlined.

[2] Preceding three words and ampersand interlined.

To Robert Smith

DEAR SIR Monticello Mar. 17. 1803.

I have recieved a letter from the Secy. of state informing me that the Dey of Algiers refuses to [accept?] the money offered him in commutation for the naval stores [due] him and consequently it becomes necessary to send the stores immediately. as it is [certainly?] better for the public that the purchase of naval stores should [be in?] the hands of one set of agents, not only to avoid employing [double sets] but their bidding on one another, and I understand it would not be disagreeable to you to undertake the procuring & forwarding these supplies. I must therefore ask the favor of you to do it, and hereby give you full authority for the purpose. the list of stores you will of course recieve from the Secretary of state, and take his advice on any particulars on which you may be at a loss. Accept my friendly salutations & assurances of great respect & esteem.

TH: JEFFERSON

PrC (DLC); faint; at foot of text: "The Secretary of the Navy." Recorded in SJL with notation "stores for Algiers." Enclosed in TJ to Madison, 17 Mch.

LETTER FROM THE SECY. OF STATE: Madison to TJ, 10 Mch. 1803.

From Robert Smith

SIR, Washington Mar. 17., 1803.

The Constellation Capt Murray is arrived and is now in the Eastern Branch. Her crew will be discharged immediately.

As nothing but a formidable force will effect an honorable peace with Tripoli and repress the dispositions of the other Barbary powers to hostility, would it not be adviseable to send immediately to the Medn either the Constitution now lying at Boston or the Philad now lying at Philad—Either of these Ships Could be in the Mediterranean in the Month of May.

Most respectfully I am Sir, Your Obed Servt RT SMITH

RC (DLC); endorsed by TJ as received from the Navy Department on 21 Mch. and "Murray. Tripoli" and so recorded in SJL.

Petition of Peter Veitch, with Jefferson's Order

TO HIS EXCELLENCY THE PRESIDENT OF THE UNITED STATES Alexa. 17th. March 1803

The Petition of Peter Veitch of Alexandria County Humbly Sheweth that during the year 1801, he was presented by a Grand Jury for the body of this County for retailing Spirituous Liquors without Licence, on which presentment Judgment and Execution has since been had, in favour of the United States; which including the costs of Prosecution amounts to Ninety eight dollars eighty five cents—which said

Sum, your petitioner is utterly unable to pay—and ruin and distress will be the inevitable fate of your petitioner, if your Excellency in tender Consideration does not remit the fine and Costs above staded Your petitioner begs leave to state that he is now far advanced in life and his means of procuring a livelihood very limited as he spent the early part of his life in the revolutionary Army which he entered at an early period remained in his Country's Service until the disbanding of the Army That his ignorance as to the time and manner of renewing his licence subjected him to the rigour of the Law and not a disposition to evade or elude its forms—your Petitioner as in duty Bound will ever pray &c PETER VEITCH

his × mark

District of Columbia
Alexandria County—[Sc]

The above named Peter Veitch personally appeared before me the Subscriber one of the United States Justices for the County aforesaid and made Oath that the facts Stated in the foregoing petition are true and Correct. Given under my hand this 19th. day of March 1803—

A FAW

We the Subscribers do hereby Certify that we believe the facts stated in the foregoing petition to be true—That Mr. Veitch is poor and far advanced in life but an honest and Industrious man and of good Character and do recommend his Case to the President as one entitled to mitigation and relief

Alexandria 17th. March 1803. A FAW

[*Order by TJ:*]

a pardon to be issued

TH: JEFFERSON
Apr. 6. 1803.

MS (DNA: RG 59, GPR); in a clerk's hand, signed by Abraham Faw and with Veitch's mark; with certificate signed by Faw and 24 others, including Cleon Moore, who added, "has known the petitioner ever since the year 1772, in the Character of an Honest Man & knew him in the Revolutionary War"; another signer noted Veitch was at the battle of Trenton and was a good soldier.

In a 7 Apr. 1803 opinion on the above case, U.S. attorney John Thomson Mason describes Peter Veitch as "a very poor aged and infirm man" of good character who served his country well during the American Revolution. Mason doubts that Veitch retains sufficient strength to work and deems him "an unoffensive man" and "worthy of Compassion." Recalling his trial, Mason states that Veitch was prosecuted for two offenses simultaneously, one for retailing liquor without a license and another for assaulting one Joseph Bowling. Bowling, "a stout strapping athletic young man," was the witness in both cases. Veitch was convicted on both charges and was able to pay the judgment for the assault, amounting to about $30. Mason was surprised by the verdict in the assault case, but states that Veitch was undoubtedly guilty of illegally retailing liquor, although he could not determine if this was due to ignorance or mistake as stated in Veitch's petition. Regarding Bowling, Mason considers Veitch's accuser to be "a man of very bad character" (DNA: RG 59, GPR). TJ pardoned Veitch on 8 Apr. 1803 (Lb in same).

To John Page

My dear friend Monticello Mar. 18. 1803

Your favor of the 2d. found me here, where I am for a few days[1] only. being an answer to mine it would not have needed an acknolegement but that I owe you a letter on an event which gave your country great satisfaction & to none more than to myself: I mean your appointment to the chair of the state. Mr. Olsen the Danish minister, having intended a visit to Richmond soon after your election, I availed myself of an introductory letter by him to express to you my sincere congratulations: but giving up at length[2] his intention, he returned me the letter the day before I left Washington. this is my apology for so late an expression of the pleasure I felt on this honourable testimony from our countrymen in your favor. a life of good length, spent in doing good, in faithful services to the public, and with rigorous adherence to the principles of free government through all the terrors of early & latter times, has merited from your country a 'well done, good and faithful servant.' we are now both drawing towards the end of the career of life as well as of honour. we began together, and probably shall end nearly together. we have both been drawn from our natural passion for study & tranquility, by times which took from us the freedom of choice: times however which, planting a new world with the seeds of just government, will produce a remarkeable aera in the history of mankind. it was incumbent on those therefore who fell into them, to give up every favorite pursuit, and lay the shoulder to the work of the day.—brought as near us as you now are, may we not hope to see you here? I shall be at home in August & September. Richmond is then unhealthy. could not mrs Page & yourself make it agreeable to come & spend a part of them at least with us. you have another old friend too in the neighborhood to tempt[3] you, and tho' he & I have unhappily fallen out by the way, yet both cherish your friendship and neither says with Achilles 'my friend must hate the man who injures me.' present me respectfully to mrs Page, and accept assurances of affectionate friendship and respect.

Th: Jefferson

RC (MWA); addressed: "John Page Governor of Virginia Richmond"; franked; endorsed by Page as received 25 Mch. "on my return to Richmd from Mannsfield." PrC (DLC). FC (DLC); entirely in TJ's hand.

ANOTHER OLD FRIEND: presumably John Walker.

MY FRIEND MUST HATE: Alexander Pope's translation of the *Iliad*, 9.728 (LCB, 87).

[1]In PrC, TJ wrote "fortnight" over "few days" in ink. FC: "fortnight."
[2]FC: "afterwards."
[3]FC: "attract."

From Alexander Wolcott

SIR Middletown (Con) March 18. 1803

I have taken the liberty of detaining the letter of Mr Edwards that accompanies this, until I had an oportunity of conferring with Mr Kirby on the subject of letter. Mr Kirby's letter will express to you his opinion on the same subject. I beg you to believe Sir, that any other man whose claims were equal, or nearly equal to those of my brother should, by me, have been prefered to him—but, all things considered, I feel myself compelled by reason, and justice, to unite with the other Gentlemen in recommending him for the office of Surveyor of the Port of Saybrook, in case a removal of the present Surveyor should be thought expedient.

In stating the circumstances which are thought to demand a removal, I will not dwell on the peculiar party bitterness of the present Surveyor, nor on the influence that his office gives him in his neighbourhood, (he having the distribution of certain subordinate employments which I shall presently explain,) nor on the influence, which he also derives from his office, over the minds of Master, and crews of vessels on board which he is employed—which class of men is, with us, by no means an unimportant one—and which influence has, as is universally understood, been exerted to the utmost, to excite prejudice, and discontent against the present administration of our general government. His removal would, on their accounts, be universally[1] acceptable to republicans here. Another circumstance, which has lately come to my knowledge, I will take the liberty to state particularly, and at the same time, with as much brevity as I am able.

It has been the practice in this, as I presume it has in every other district, for the Collector to employ, under general appointments, such number of Inspectors, or Tidewaiters as he finds proportionate to the business of the district. It frequently happens however, that at certain periods, a greater number of vessels arrive, and consequently a greater number of Inspectors are required than have received this general appointment; in this case the Collector makes a special appointment for the occasion. Owing to the peculiar situation of this district, it has been found necessary to devolve this power of appointing these special Inspectors on some person residing at the mouth of Connecticut-River. It has hitherto been entrusted to the Surveyor of the Port of Saybrook. Now Sir, it appears that in some, and I have reason to believe that if it were thought necessary to investigate the business, it would turn out that, in all instances, he has made those appointments on the express condition that he should share, in a certain proportion, in the wages of the Inspector, and that some men, who have refused to enter into such stipulations, have, on that account, been refused the employment—that the proportion which the Surveyor has thus reserved to himself as he has himself declared, never been less [than] fifty cents, and sometimes as high as a dollar for each day that the Inspector has been employed.

The fact of his having received, in some instances, part of the wages of the Inspectors, can be proved by the oaths of the Inspectors themselves if required, indeed, so far as I can learn, it is a thing of public notoriety in his neighbourhood.

These facts I have thought it my duty to communicate, but it would not become me to super add any comments.

Have the goodness Sir, to accept assurances of my perfect respect

ALEX WOLCOTT

RC (DNA: RG 59, LAR); torn; addressed: "His Excellency Thomas Jefferson President of the United States Washington"; endorsed by TJ as received 4 Apr. and "George Wolcott to be Surveyor of Saybrook vice Dickinson" and so recorded in SJL; also endorsed by TJ: "enquire of mr Granger." Enclosure: Pierpont Edwards to TJ, 25 Feb.

Alexander Wolcott (1758-1828), son of Dr. Alexander and Mary Richards Wolcott, was born in Windsor, Connecticut. He graduated from Yale College in 1778 and studied and practiced law. In 1785, he married Frances Burbank and settled in Middletown. He served as a Republican leader in the Connecticut General Assembly from 1796 to 1801. After the election of 1800, he was one of the Connecticut Republicans the administration consulted on appointments, and, in July 1801 the president named him collector at Middletown, a position he held until his death. In that capacity, he endorsed and firmly enforced the Embargo Act of 1807. On 4 Feb. 1811, Madison nominated Wolcott as associate justice of the Supreme Court. Levi Lincoln, who had recently declined the appointment after being confirmed by the Senate, supported Wolcott, but the Senate rejected his nomination on 13 Feb. by a vote of 9 to 24. Federalists strongly opposed him because of his vigorous support of the embargo; several Republican senators agreed that he did not have the legal and judicial expertise required for the office. Wolcott remained in politics and participated in the 1818 state constitutional convention. In 1828, he was remembered as the "father and founder of the Jeffersonian school of politics" in Connecticut (Wolcott's interim commission in NN: Lee Kohns Memorial Collection, dated 28 July 1801, signed by TJ and countersigned by Madison; Middletown *American Sentinel*, 2 July 1828; *West's Encyclopedia of American Law*, 12 vols. [Minneapolis, 1998], 10:364-5; Madison, *Papers, Pres. Ser.*, 3:57-8, 126-7, 165-6, 338-9; JEP, 2:165-7; Vol. 33:232, 588, 627; Vol. 34:94n, 130, 131n, 341-2; Vol. 35:486).

Ephraim KIRBY'S LETTER to TJ is dated 14 Mch.

[1]MS: "unversally."

To James Madison

DEAR SIR Monticello Mar. 19. 1803.

I wrote you on the 17th. since which yours of the 14th. is recieved, and I now return the letters of Mr. Livingston & O'Brien. I hope the game mr Livingston says he is playing is a candid & honourable one. besides an unwillingness to accept any advantage which should have been obtained by other means, no other means can probably succeed there. an American contending by stratagem against those exercised in it from their cradle would undoubtedly be outwitted by them. in such a field and for such an actor nothing but plain direct honesty can be either honourable or advantageous. I am in hopes the stores for Algiers will be sent off without delay, so as to stop the growling of that dog. when shall we get rid of Obrien? what says Colo. Lear? as to the 10,000. barrels of powder, if he refuses money for the annuity of the present year & would take that instead of naval stores, it would be well. certainly on so slight a *verbal* intimation no answer can be expected from the hand of the president in writing. mr Smith having observed that it would be much cheaper to have the guncarriages for the emperor of Marocco made in his vicinity, and that, made according to his directions, they would probably be more acceptable, than those we should send at hazard, I promised to speak to you on the subject, & thought I had done so. will you and he be so good as to conclude & do what is best? if the money be put into Simson's hands, perhaps the emperor would prefer taking it & having the gun carriages made or not made as he would prefer. Accept my affectionate salutations.

TH: JEFFERSON

P.S. I send you also a letter of Colo. Monroe for perusal, and have to add that Edward Turner of Kentucky is to be commissioned immediately as Register of the land office at Natchez.

RC (DLC: Madison Papers, Rives Collection); at foot of text: "The Secretary of State"; endorsed by Madison. Recorded in SJL with notation "Barbary affairs." PrC (DLC). Enclosures: (1) Robert R. Livingston to Madison, 20 Dec. (Enclosure No. 1 listed at Madison to TJ, 14 Mch.). (2) Richard O'Brien to Madison,

23 Nov. (Enclosure No. 2 listed at same). (3) James Monroe to TJ, 7 Mch.

MR SMITH HAVING OBSERVED: see Robert Smith to TJ, 12 Mch.

To Robert Smith

DEAR SIR Monticello Mar. 19. 1803.

I wrote you on the 17th. on the subject of the stores for Algiers, since which your's of the 12th. is recieved. I thought I had spoken to mr Madison on the day of my departure on the subject of the gun carriages for the emperor of Marocco. I now write to him respecting them. I presume the date of the enlistment of the crews of our frigates in the Mediterranean should decide which of them shall remain there, unless the Commodore can out of the whole enlist one or two crews for whatever longer time you think best, suppose two years.

I am sorry for the resolution Capt Tingey has taken, because I think him a good officer. but our course is a plain one. we should decide what we think a reasonable allowance (until the legislature shall think proper to do it.) what you proposed to him appears to me reasonable. perhaps, if the British have such a post, we might find their rule a proper one, for in naval matters we can follow no better model. having fixed our allowance we must not raise or lower it for particular characters. besides the embarrassment that would occasion, it would [cover] partialities, for which we should offer no cover: and there is neither safety nor honesty but in the doing the public business by general rules without regard to [persons?]. having made up your mind as to sum, if Capt Tingey will not accept of it, then the office does not suit him, and [he declines?] as is the common case, and I shall be sorry for it, because I [. . .] that I think him a good officer. you will of course have another to [. . .], and the utmost attention should be paid to fitness of character, for indeed the office is of extreme importance. no place requires more vigilance, activity & skill. Accept my affectionate salutations. TH: JEFFERSON

PrC (DLC); faint; at foot of text: "The Secretary of the Navy." Recorded in SJL with notation "Barbary Affairs. Tingey."

I NOW WRITE TO HIM: TJ to Madison, 19 Mch.

Writing Thomas TINGEY on 26 Mch., Smith informed him of the president's opinion that the allowance proposed was reasonable "and that he laments that, unwilling to accept such compensation, you have resolved to resign." Writing again on 7 Apr., Smith accepted Tingey's resignation as superintendent of the Washington Navy Yard and requested that he deliver an inventory of all public property in his possession to Captain John Cassin (FCs in Lb in DNA: RG 45, MLS). Tingey, however, seems to have been retained as a fiscal agent. In March 1804, Congress revised the Peace Establishment Act of 1801 and authorized the president to attach a captain of the navy to superintend the Washington Navy Yard, with said officer receiving the pay and emoluments of a captain commanding a squadron on separate service. TJ reappointed Tingey a captain in the navy in November 1804 and he remained superintendent of the facility until his death in 1829 (ANB; U.S. Statutes at Large, 2:207; Henry B. Hibben, *Navy-Yard. Washington. History from Organization, 1799 to Present Date* [Washington, D.C., 1890], 26).

To Albert Gallatin

DEAR SIR Monticello Mar. 20. 1803.

Your's of the 14th. is recieved and I have written to mr Madison to issue a commission to Edward Turner of Kentuckey to be Register of the land office at Natchez. a commission has issued to Trist vice Carmichael. Thompson and Watson may await my return. I now inclose the power for transferring the 2500. D. to the disposal of the Secretary at war.

I do not find in my library any thing which can throw light on the geography of the Rio Norte. I do not believe that in modern times any thing has been added to the information given as to that river in early times. of this information Mitchell had the benefit. his map was made under public patronage & with all the information that could procure him. that it was made with great care we know from what is laid down of those Western parts with which we have lately become acquainted. certainly we find his map much nearer the truth than could have been expected considering when it was made. hence I conclude that his delineation of the Rio Norte is more to be credited than any other, not excepting Danville & Delisle. Accept my best affections. TH: JEFFERSON

RC (NHi: Gallatin Papers); addressed: "Albert Gallatin Secretary of the Treasury Washington"; franked; postmarked Charlottesville, 21 Mch.; endorsed. PrC (DLC). Recorded in SJL with notation "Register Natchez. Missouri." Enclosure not found.

The 1755 map by John MITCHELL provided detailed information of the British colonies on the Atlantic coast and of the Ohio River settlements and drainage. His map, however, did not extend to the Pacific Ocean or include new information on lands west of the Mississippi River. PUBLIC PATRONAGE: Mitchell's draft map, completed in 1750 after he had emigrated from Virginia and settled in London, came to the attention of members of the Board of Trade and Plantations, who oversaw the American colonies. Impressed with his cartographic work, the board gave Mitchell access to all of their records so that he could make a more complete map. The board asked colonial governors and others to send new surveys to London. They asked the Hudson's Bay Company, for example, to send "as exact an Account as you can of the Limits and Boundaries of the Territory granted" to them "together with a Chart or Map thereof, and all the best Accounts and Vouchers you can obtain." The historical and geographical report from Virginia, compiled by Joshua Fry, included a map drawn by him with the assistance of Peter Jefferson, TJ's father. Between 1750 and 1755, the board spent £104 on maps and charts for Mitchell's use (Edmund Berkeley and Dorothy Smith Berkeley, *Dr. John Mitchell: The Man Who Made the Map of North America* [Chapel Hill, 1974], 85-7, 175-81, 194-7, 204 [illus.], 213; John Logan Allen, *Passage through the Garden: Lewis and Clark and the Image of the American Northwest* [Urbana, Ill., 1975], 118-19; John Mitchell, *A Map of the British and French Dominions in North America, with the Roads, Distances, Limits, and Extent of the Settlements* [London, 1755]). Robert King used the map by Guillaume de L'Isle (DELISLE) as his source for the Rio Norte (Gary E. Moulton, ed., *Atlas of the Lewis & Clark Expedition* [Lincoln, Neb., 1983], plate 2).

To John Brown

Monticello Mar. 21. 1803.

Th: Jefferson presents his friendly salutations to mr Brown. he recieved a letter and some nuts from the lady to whom the inclosed is an answer. being entirely unacquainted with her as far as he recollects, he incloses it open to mr Brown with a request that he will be so good as to seal & have it delivered if no circumstance unknown to Th: Jefferson would render it improper; or better in the judgment of mr Brown that it should not be delivered. his best respects are tendered to mrs Brown.

PrC (DLC); endorsed by TJ in ink on verso. Enclosure: TJ to Elize Winn, 21 Mch.

HE RECIEVED A LETTER: Elize Winn to TJ, 20 Feb.

From Thomas Cooper

DEAR SIR/ Lancaster March 21. 1803

Dr Hunter on his return from Washington to Philadelphia told me that unknowing of my application to you for a midshipman's birth in the service of the U. States for my Son, he had mentioned him to you as having behaved with Courage on the recapture of Dr Hunters Vessel from the British; but that in a subsequent conversation with Mr Duane, he found that my son instead of being put down second on the list of Vacancies was entered low on the list: & that objections had been made to his Sobriety, which Dr Hunter was good enough to say he would have repelled had he known of my intentions at the time of his conversation with you. I am glad he did not: for charges of insobriety during the latter part of his residence in Philada., might very justly have been made. But, it is the Insobriety arising not from a love of liquor but a love of Company, & such as I sincerely believe wd. not influence him in another Situation, & may fairly be attributed to the too common folly of mere Youth; & never out of the Society of Officers, either of the Army or Navy.

Be this as it may, I write now to request of you information necessary to his welfare and to my peace of mind about him; and I hope that notwithstanding the pressure of more important business on your time, you will excuse the trouble given to you by the anxiety of one of your sincerest well wishers.

If there is a prospect of his being appointed soon, (within half a Year for instance) the appointment will be of Service to him, and will be a relief to me: if not, if he is to remain on the list indefinitely, and this secret objection is to operate without the means of removing it, your kindness will eventually be no slight misfortune to both myself and my son. If he could obtain the birth he wishes for, I beleive he would be emulous to deserve it: but idleness and incertainty will be ruin to him. I beg of you therefore my dear Sir to forgive me for requesting, that you would enable me to know the Determination of the Navy department as early as possible, directed to Northumberland.

Believe me very sincerely & respectfully your friend

Thomas Cooper

RC (DNA: RG 59, LAR); endorsed by TJ as received 4 Apr. and "Cooper Thos. to be midshipman" and so recorded in SJL.

MY APPLICATION: see TJ to Cooper, 29 Nov. 1802.

RECAPTURE OF DR HUNTERS VESSEL: after the British captured George Hunter's ship, the *Mary Ann*, in the Caribbean and carried it to Jamaica, the vessel was released and then repossessed two more times by privateers (Madison, *Papers, Sec. of State*, 4:548-50, 5:573-4).

For the CHARGES OF INSOBRIETY and the appointment of Thomas Cooper, Jr., see Cooper to TJ, 18 Dec. 1802.

From Albert Gallatin

Dear Sir Washington 21 March 1803

I enclose the only letters of any importance which I have received since you left the city. The answer to that from Mr Thornton is also enclosed. To Mr Muhlenberg I answered generally that I would approve what he might think best to be done respecting the inspectors. I foresee a schism in Pennsylvania; the most thinking part of the community will not submit to the decree of partial ward or township meetings; and yet the violent party will have a strong hold on public opinion in representing that those who resist them must be considered as the friends of Jackson & Mcpherson. I have not heard whether they mean to address you, but hope they may not; and this incident will, at all events, render the question of removals still more delicate & difficult.

I had a long conversation with Capn. Murray of the Constellation; he says that at any time from March to the latter end of September whilst he was on the Tripoli station, peace might have been obtained for five thousand dollars, and that the opportunity has been lost by the delays of Morris in the vicinity of Gibraltar and in going up the Mediterranean, but that he is much afraid that now, that they are no longer at war with Sweden, matters accommodated with France, & no further danger apprehended by the Bashaw from his brother, a peace cannot be obtained but upon very extravagant terms. The refusal of a passport to the Morocco provision ship he considers as ridiculous; as it could not affect the state of affairs in relation to Tripoli, and those uncivilized States cannot understand the refined theory of the law of nations & of the duties of neutrals: he adds that there was not, when he left Europe any danger to be apprehended from Morocco; the only source of uneasiness being the non-arrival of the gun-carriages.

The late accounts from Algiers & Tunis appear unpleasant. No time, it Seems, should be lost in sending the stores to Algiers; and the appointment of a proper character in the Mediterranean to have the superintendence of the Barbary affairs appears indispensible. Will you be able to find such one? I feel more uneasy about the state of affairs in that quarter than[1] in relation to the Louisiana business. You did not mention whether Mr Briggs would accept the appointment of surveyor at Natchez.

With sincere respect & attachment Your obedt. Servt.

Albert Gallatin

RC (DLC); at foot of text: "Thomas Jefferson President of the United States"; endorsed by TJ as received from the Treasury Department on 25 Mch. and "Thornton's lre concerng. customs Michillim. Muhlenberg's Inspectors. Murray & Morris: Barbary affairs. Briggs" and so recorded in SJL. Enclosure: Peter Muhlenberg to Gallatin, Philadelphia, 17 Mch. 1803, requesting advice and direction on continuing Joseph Wharton as customs inspector, noting that he had previously informed the Treasury secretary that Wharton "was nominally—& not in reality" carrying out the duties of an inspector; Wharton's "situation" is generally known and he has been continued solely on the word of Muhlenberg's predecessor, George Latimer, who claims that he "stated the matter fully to you" and received your approbation; if Gallatin is still of that opinion, the collector will continue Wharton in office "without assigning any reasons for so doing," but because of pressure in another quarter, "some of the Inspectors, who are particularly obnoxious," must be removed; Muhlenberg directs Gallatin's attention to the newspapers and the stir caused "in the City, relative to continuing in Office, Men of a certain description"; while resolutions passed by the meetings have been chiefly leveled against William Jones, the collector comes in for "a full share, not only of blame, but abuse"; knowing the source of this protest, Muhlenberg pledges he will not be forced into measures which are "injurious to my Country & the Government" (RC in Gallatin, *Papers*, 8:209; ASP, *Miscellaneous*, 1:271). Other enclosures not found.

The letter from Edward THORNTON to the Treasury secretary and Gallatin's response have not been found, but according to TJ's endorsement Thornton's letter related to "customs" at Michilimackinac. On 16 Mch., Gallatin wrote David Duncan, the collector at the port, that as long as a custom house was not established at the falls at St. Mary's "goods passing towards and through Lake Superior need not be attended to." If Duncan, before receiving instructions, had "seized any merchandize the property of either of the North West Companies, which may have been landed and stored on the American side of the Straights," Gallatin authorized and directed him "to restore the same." Duncan was instructed, however, to collect duties on merchandise sold by the company while in storage (Gallatin, *Papers*, 8:205).

For the letter from Philadelphia customs collector Peter MUHLENBERG, see the enclosure described above. Muhlenberg wrote in response to the meetings of "democratic republican citizens" being held in private homes in Philadelphia wards. The first gathering, held at the house of Alexander Moore in the South Ward on 9 Mch., chose Joseph Scott as chairman and passed five resolutions. The first noted that Federalists holding federal office in Pennsylvania "being hostile to republican principles, and unfriendly to the present administration," were "highly obnoxious to the people." The second charged that attempts were being made to "mislead" the president into thinking that support for removing the Federalists from office was confined to a small minority of Republicans, particularly "interested individuals." The third resolution recommended that "democratic republican citizens" throughout the commonwealth hold meetings and appoint committees to take proper measures for transmitting memorials to the president declaring their "real sentiment." The fourth called for the appointment of a committee of three to meet with similar committees from the different wards to prepare the memorials. They also determined that their proceedings should be published in the *Aurora*. Another assembly pronounced that Republican officials who criticized the protests were "deserving of the most pointed censure and no longer worthy of their confidence." Numerous ward meetings held throughout Philadelphia in the coming weeks culminated with an address to the president in mid-July (Philadelphia *Aurora*, 11, 16, 17, 23, 31 Mch., 2, 11, 13 Apr. 1803; Address from the Philadelphia Ward Committees to TJ, [before 17 July 1803]). THOSE WHO RESIST THEM: on 30 Mch., Alexander J. Dallas described the ward meetings as a "nuisance," which would bring discredit to Republican interests. The participation of John Barker in the proceedings proved that the clamor proceeded from "interested Candidates" for office. "The meetings are composed of very few indeed," Dallas noted, "and the only real mischief to be apprehended, is the disgust excited in the minds of men like Capt. Jones." Republican congressman William Jones, Dallas's close friend, openly opposed the proscription of all Federalists as a test of one's commitment to Jeffersonian Republicanism (Gallatin, *Papers*, 8:239; Andrew Shankman, *Crucible of American Democracy: The Struggle to Fuse Egalitarianism & Capitalism in Jeffersonian Pennsylvania* [Lawrence, Kans., 2004], 98-9; Joseph H. Nicholson to TJ, 10 May 1803). FRIENDS OF JACKSON & MCPHERSON: that is, Federalists William Jackson and William McPherson, surveyor and naval officer, respectively, at the Philadelphia customs office (Vol. 34:428n; Vol. 36: 182n, 183n).

For the peace settlement between Tripoli and SWEDEN, see Vol. 39:192, 195n. NO FURTHER DANGER: Ahmad Qaramanli, brother of Yusuf Qaramanli, the Pasha of Tripoli, finally accepted an appointment at Derna, a province in eastern Libya, in August 1802 (Kola Folayan, "Tripoli and the War with the U.S.A., 1801-5," *Journal of African History*, 13 [1972], 263). See also Topics for Consultation with Heads of Departments, printed at 10 Feb.

REFUSAL OF A PASSPORT: see TJ to Madison, 9 Aug. and Gallatin to TJ, 20 Aug. 1802.

LATE ACCOUNTS: see Madison to TJ, 17 Mch.

[1]MS: "that."

From James Madison

DEAR SIR Washington Mar. 21. 1803

A letter from Hulings of Feby. 15. says that at that date the Intendant had not revoked the interruption of the deposit; but had from regard to the wants of the Colony, opened the market to flour & other provisions brought down the Mississippi; the articles being subject to a duty of 6 perCt. if consumed there, and to the usual export duty, (I believe 12 perCt) if sent as an indulgence in Spanish bottoms to Places within the lawful trade of the Colony. It is *possible* that this may be a retrograde step of the Intendant masked by his pride under the policy of a colonial regulation. It appears that the forbearance of that Officer to conform to the presumed object of Yrujo's first letters, had produced a general belief at N. Orleans that orders from the Spanish Govt had led to the violation of our right.

Eaton writes from Tunis late in Decr. that the Bey had not only renewed his demand of the Frigate; but had raked together all his old claims of Oxen Cattle &c and that his Minister insisted on the gold-mounted fusil in addition to the silver one recd. He complains of the vis inertia of our marine, anticipates evils, and decides on not passing another summer there. He signifies that he shall consult with Morris & Cathcart, in case of their appearing before Tunis, on the expediency of his giving the Bey the slip; apprehending that he may not be permitted by the Bey to leave that place. It will be necessary therefore to provide immediately a successor to him as well as to OBrien.

In consequence of my letter to Mr. Lear, he came over the day before yesterday. He is willing to take an appt. at Algiers, with a salary of $4000, but will require 6 weeks or two months, to prepare for embarkation.

With respectful attachment always Yrs. JAMES MADISON

Jarvis has pushed with great vigor & success the admission of our flour to the Portuguese Market, and the removal of the quarantine from our vessels. The result will be found in the Natl. intelligencer of this day, & his management will appear when you see his letter just recd. which is of Feby. 9.

RC (DLC); endorsed by TJ as received from the State Department on 25 Mch. and "N. Orleans. Tunis. Tripoli. Jarvis" and so recorded in SJL.

From New Orleans, William E. HULINGS sent a copy of a 5 Feb. proclamation by Juan Ventura Morales that allowed shippers from U.S. territories to land flour, salted meat, and other foodstuffs. Citing a royal ordinance of 1794, the intendant decreed that the goods would be subject to a six percent duty. Any of those provisions that were reshipped out of New Orleans would be subject to export regulations and duties. The "pretty general" opinion in the city, according to Hulings, was that Morales was generally too well informed and too aware of the consequences of his actions to have barred the right of deposit "without high authority" (Madison, *Papers*, *Sec. of State Ser.*, 4:312, 322-3; *National Intelligencer*, 21 Mch.).

In 1800, Hammuda Pasha had prepared a list of expensive personal items that he required in return for his confirmation of the treaty between TUNIS and the United States. Fulfilling the list had taken a long time because some of the pieces, including firearms, had to be custom-made in England. In a dispatch to Madison dated 20 Dec., William Eaton reported that Hammuda's prime minister, Yusuf Sahib-at-Taba, was making a false claim that a double-barreled fowling piece with gold mountings was supposed to be part of the gift. The Tunisians also renewed a request for some bulls, cows, and a pair of large oxen that Eaton had promised to obtain for them in 1801 (Madison, *Papers*, *Sec. of State Ser.*, 1:82; 4:51, 206-8; King, *Life*, 3:246-7; Vol. 36:667-8n).

HE COMPLAINS: Eaton contended that the lack of activity by the U.S. squadron against Tripoli weakened his position in resisting Hammuda's demands. The Tunisians distrusted him, and if he was no longer effective, his position could be filled by anyone "whose fidelity can be relied on, and who is capable of writing an intelligible letter." He hoped to find some "stratagem" to leave Tunis and return to the United States—"*I cannot serve another summer in this station!*" he declared (Madison, *Papers*, *Sec. of State Ser.*, 4:207).

VIS INERTIA: force of inertia.

In response to a memorial pressed by William JARVIS, the U.S. consul at Lisbon, in favor of the admission of FLOUR from the United States into Portugal, Prince Regent João had ordered an inspector to compare bread made from American flour with bread made from other flour. The report of that trial, Jarvis informed Madison in a dispatch dated 9 Feb., convinced a majority of the prince regent's ministers that American flour should be allowed into the Portuguese market. The government placed a duty on the commodity, but Jarvis, who had computed that flour would command a higher price than wheat, be less expensive to ship, and be exempt from duties on grain, deemed the special impost a "trifle." The prince regent also halted restrictions that had subjected vessels arriving from some American cities to a QUARANTINE. Under the new order, ships and cargo from the United States that showed no evidence of contagious disease would be allowed immediate entry into Portuguese harbors (same, 19-20, 196-7, 306, 313-15; *National Intelligencer*, 21 Mch.).

To Thomas Munroe

DEAR SIR Monticello Mar. 21. 1803.

Your letter of the 14th. was recieved on the 18th. and this goes by the return of the first post, that which brought it not affording time for an answer. No. 2. in the draught mr King was so kind as to send me is exactly what Dr. Thornton explained to me as the original design except that he did not mention the two middle rows of trees, but only the two outer ones on each side: and, omitting the two middle rows, I think this the best design. it will then stand thus.

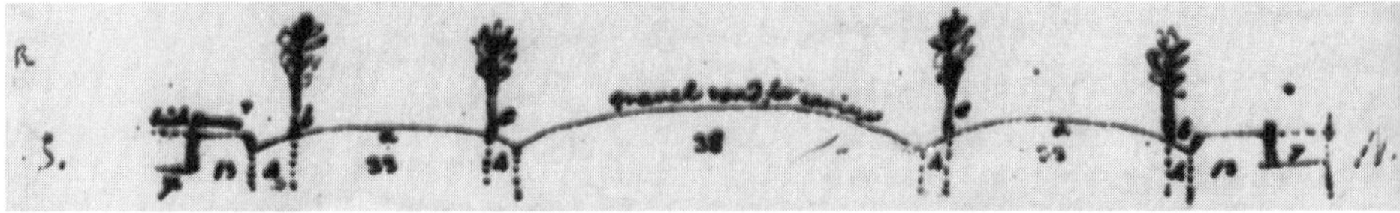

one reason of preference is that this agrees with the present disposition of the Pensylvania avenue. it will allow us also next autumn either to plant our oaks elms &c in the same lines with the Lombardy poplars, giving to these trees of large growth a distance suitable to their size, or we may plant them midway at a.a. so as to make a shaded Mall of 41. f. breadth, or pass a canal along the middle at a.a. at a future day, or a gravel walk, or any thing we please. as you have already planted the rows b.b. you will therefore be pleased to plant c.c. at 33. f. distance from b.b. or at 4. f. distance from the gutters. the stakes may be omitted, and as my return will be so soon, the boxing or other guard may then be the subject of consultation.

Until the organisation of the district of Columbia, when a better directory for the city than the President of the US. will probably be provided, I am unwilling to do any thing which will bear delay, and especially to change any original destination of the public grounds. and as I shall be with you within one week after you recieve this, the object of the committee for the Theatre shall be considered immediately on my return. be pleased to mention this to them and to accept my friendly salutations. Th: Jefferson

PrC (DLC); at foot of text: "Mr. Munroe."

An undated note in TJ's papers, probably from William THORNTON, provides information on Alexandria gardener John Ehlers, whose nursery near Spring Garden sold LOMBARDY POPLARS, apple trees, and seeds. The note states that Ehlers previously worked for George Washington and was recently in partnership with Thornton's gardener (MS in MHi, undated, endorsed by TJ; Alexandria *Times; and District of Columbia Daily Advertiser*, 9 Jan. 1802; Washington, *Papers, Pres. Ser.*, 3:64-5n; Miller, *Alexandria Artisans*, 1:124).

From Volney

Monsieur le President des Etats Unis

Paris 30 Ventose an XI
21 Mars

Je profite de l'occasion de Mr. Curwen de Philadelphie qui retourne chez lui par Norfolk, pour Vous adresser un exemplaire de la nouvelle traduction angloise de mes Ruines qui a enfin paru. Le paquet sera remis à Mr. Le Dr. thornton à Washington avec recommandation de Vous le faire parvenir. J'attache un grand prix à ce que ce travail obtienne Votre approbation et que sa publication Vous soit agréable. Votre ordre pour annuller des feuilles Manuscrites a été ponctuellement executé. Je crains que deja mon envoy actuel n'ait été prevenu par celui de l'editeur qui a fait passer Mille à 1200 copies à Newyork; mais Mr. Stone ne m'a delivré les Miennes que 3 Semaines après son expedition.

Ce sont là dailleurs de bien petits interets auprés de ceux qui Vous entourent et dont Vous êtes le foyer. Nous Voyons avec anxiété les evenemens possibles qui se préparent; Si la guerre a lieu, et tot ou tard une disposition constante d'irritation la determinera, elle causera dans le monde politique et moral des changemens plus grands et plus prompts que l'on ne veut ici le Croire ou le prévoir. On parle d'excluze de l'Europe un grand peuple; mais il pourrait arriver en revanche que l'Europe fut exclue des deux indes. Spectateur solitaire et presqu'infirme de passions que je ne partage point, et de Mouvemens tragiques qui M'affligent, mon rôle est de Souhaiter la paix publique, et de faire des Voeux constans pour le bonheur particulier des hommes qui comme Vous, Monsieur, placent le[1] leur à faire celui de la pauvre humanité. Agréez Mon respectueux attachement

Volney

EDITORS' TRANSLATION

Mr. President of the United States, — Paris, 30 Ventose Year 11, 21 Mch. 1803

By kind opportunity of Mr. Curwen of Philadelphia, who is returning home via Norfolk, I am sending you a copy of the new English translation of my *Ruines*, which has finally come out. The package will be entrusted to Dr. Thornton in Washington with a request that he transmit it to you. I give great weight to having this work meet your approval and to its publication pleasing you. Your order to cancel the handwritten pages was immediately carried out. I fear that my current shipment may have been preempted by that of the editor, who sent 1,000 to 1,200 copies to New York. But Mr. Stone did not deliver my copies until three weeks after they were sent.

These matters are of small interest compared to those that surround you and of which you are the focus. We look anxiously at the events that may loom ahead. If war takes place, and sooner or later the situation of constant irritation will provoke one, it will cause greater and swifter changes in the political and moral world than people here want to believe or foresee. They talk about excluding a great people from Europe, but the reverse could happen: that Europe will be excluded from the two Indies. As a lone and almost helpless spectator of passions I do not share and tragic movements that afflict me, my role is to wish for civic peace, to make constant vows for the personal happiness of men who, like you, Sir, devote theirs to the happiness of frail humanity.

Accept my respectful devotion.

VOLNEY

RC (DLC); at head of text: "Mr jefferson"; endorsed by TJ as received 11 June and so recorded in SJL.

Joseph CURWEN also carried several of Robert R. Livingston's dispatches to Madison (Madison, *Papers*, *Sec. of State Ser.*, 4:332n, 386n, 412n, 432n, 448n).

NOUVELLE TRADUCTION ANGLOISE: the translation, in two volumes titled *A New Translation of Volney's Ruins; or Meditations on the Revolution of Empires. Made Under the Inspection of the Author*, was published in Paris with an 1802 imprint.

Volney wrote hastily to William THORNTON on 21 Mch., informing him that he was sending five copies of the *New Translation*. One copy was for Thornton, and Volney asked him to see that TJ, Madison, Aaron Burr, and Louis André Pichon received the others (DLC: William Thornton Papers).

POUR ANNULLER DES FEUILLES MANUSCRITES: much of the new translation of Volney's *Ruines* was TJ's work. Joel Barlow completed the task in Paris. When Volney asked what he should do with TJ's portion of the manuscript when it was no longer needed by the printers, TJ replied, in April 1802, "it is desired that it may be burnt." TJ retained copies of those chapters in his own papers (Vol. 33:341-2n; Vol. 34:438, 440; Vol. 37:295, 297n).

Although his name does not appear on the book's title page, John Hurford STONE printed the *New Translation* and, as Volney mentioned again in his letter of 10 May, Stone was the "*editeur*" who oversaw the production and distribution of the work. Stone cooperated with the book's publisher, the firm of Levrault Frères, on other projects as well (Madeleine B. Stern, "The English Press in Paris and Its Successors, 1793-1852," *Papers of the Bibliographical Society of America*, 74 [1980], 336-9).

[1]Word supplied.

To Benjamin Waterhouse

Monticello Mar. 21. 1803.

Th: Jefferson returns his acknolegements to Doctr. Waterhouse for his letter of the lst. inst. & the book accompanying it, which he recieved & will have the pleasure of perusing here, where he is on a visit of a fortnight, engaged in the rural operations of the season. the small pox having got into a neighborhood about 30. miles from this, he was enabled yesterday, with some vaccine matter he brought from Washington, to inoculate a large deputation of persons from that neighborhood, and thus to communicate the blessing for which they are indebted to Dr. Waterhouse. he prays him to accept his friendly salutations & assurances of great respect.

PrC (DLC); endorsed by TJ in ink on verso.

To Elize Winn

Monticello March 21. 1803

Th: Jefferson returns his thanks to mrs Winn for the Paccan nuts she was so kind as to send him; which being recieved here, and in the season for planting, he has immediately committed to the earth. he makes his acknolegements also for the flattering terms in which she is pleased to speak of his political conduct; terms far beyond it's actual merit. he sincerely desires to direct the affairs of his country to the best advantage of all; and asks for it no reward but the approbation of his fellow citizens. he recieves it therefore on this, as on every other occasion, with a just sensibility, & prays her to accept his respectful salutations and best wishes

PrC (DLC); endorsed by TJ in ink on verso. Enclosed in TJ to John Brown, 21 Mch.

SO KIND AS TO SEND HIM: see Elize Winn to TJ, 20 Feb.

From John Brightthought

SIRS) Baltimore March the, 22d 1803

to you that are interested in the public Welfare of your Country Whose greattest Ambition is to reas larning and genious to its greatest perfection and whose prinsiples is to reward merrit and incurage the Arts of Manufacturing our own Country produce in All its Various branches A Spechely this Branch of Business that is At A low ebb in our Country Namely Manufacturing of Cotton And printting Calligoe, which we have to pay yourope Twenty five per Cent more than we Can do it for, therefore We Can With equal Skill And ingenuwity bring Calico printing to as great prefection her as in Any part of yourope And do it Cheeper for Which purpose I have invented A New machine for prenting Calico to go By Water hand or Any other powar And Will print With more exactness And will preimpress the Collars on more even then Can be done by hand And will print At the rate of Seven hundred And twenty yeards in Twelve ours with the Assistance of one man.

much more might be Said on the principals of this Machine But suffise,d to say it will An Orrigenate every Moshion Necessary to A Execute the Business to profection. I have modled this Machine in Minature and found it to Answer the purpose I intended it for thinking it would be a benifit to the public At Large, I thought it my Deuty to let my intentions be known first to the honourable gentlemen that is Apointed to Conduct the Affaires of our Country And on Whose Connduct Depends Such. I shall leave the hole of this business to the impartial Judgment of the members of this house of Congres. if this plan is Worthy of Atenshion pleas to rite to Baltimore for farder information. Derect your Letter to your humble Servant

JOHN BRIGHTTHOUGHT

T:J president of the U:S pleas to read this to the house of representives.

RC (DLC); with postscript on verso of address sheet; addressed: "To His Excellency the President of the U.S."; franked; postmarked 15 Mch.; endorsed by TJ as a letter of 22 Mch. received the 21st and so recorded in SJL.

From Thomas S. Cavender

SIR Milton 22nd March 1803

As I believe you to be a republican and Gentleman I believe you will not consider Poverty as a barrier I have taken the liberty to inform you that when I Preached that Superstitious Trinitarian Doctrine I had friends and Money at will, but Since I have Preached as a Unitarian and Republican I have not only Suffered for want of friends but Suffered for want of common Subsistence and Still mean So to do before I give up a rational doctrine and republican Principal. And as Such Suffer me Sir to inform you by letter as my heart was too big to do it in person that my Situation through a wound in defence of my Country last War And the Death of my horse this Summer five Hundred miles from home has Placed me in a distressed Situation and as there is a few freethinking Republicans who is now Contributing to my wants at Present and recommend me to make my case Known to you which I have done. Should you think Proper to contribute any thing for my Present wants you will Please enclose it in a letter directed to me by the bearer hereof. Whether you do or do not I remain your real friend and humble Servant untill you depart from the republican Principles which I hope you never will.—The Surgeons have Promised to bestow their labours on me I paying for the medecine and my Boarding and Says they will make a Perfect cure of my leg and this being the case I hope I will Still be able to pursue my duty in opposition to what I believe to be errors in Justification of religious truth, and at the Same time Still continue to warn my fellow Citizens to be always upon their guard in defense of their rights and liberties.

with due respect I remain yr ob sr. THOMAS S CAVENDER.

RC (MHi); addressed: "Thomas Jefferson Esquire President of the United States"; endorsed by TJ as received 22 Mch. and so recorded in SJL.

LIBERTY TO INFORM YOU: see Cavender to TJ, 25 Dec. 1802. In his financial memoranda under 22 Mch., TJ recorded that he contributed $10 "in charity" to Cavender (MB, 2:1095).

To James Madison

DEAR SIR Monticello Mar. 22. 1803.

Yours of the 17th is recieved. I concur in your ideas that the request from the Bey of Tunis of a frigate of 36. guns should be complaisantly refused. I think the greatest dispatch should be used in sending either the guncarriages or money to Simpson for the emperor of Marocco, and the stores to Algiers; &, if you approve it, the powder *on account*: or perhaps it would be better to authorise the purchase of it in Europe on the Dey's agreeing to recieve it on account. we must keep these two powers friendly by a steady course of justice aided occasionally with liberality. mr Smith has suggested the sending another frigate. but no new fact justifies a change of plan. our misfortune has been that our vessels have been employed in particular convoys, instead of a close blockade equivalent to universal convoy. I suppose Murray may be for sending more ships there. every officer in the navy, & every merchant in the US. would be for that: because they see but one object, themselves.—I see the federalists find one paper in Kentucky into which they can get what they write either here or there. Bradford's Guardian of freedom of Mar. 4. has a piece recommending immediate separation. a cool calculation of interest however would shew that Eastern America would not be the greatest sufferer by that folly. Accept my affectionate salutations.

TH: JEFFERSON

RC (DLC: Madison Papers); at foot of text: "The Secretary of State." PrC (DLC).

ANOTHER FRIGATE: see Robert Smith to TJ, 17 Mch.

See Gideon Granger to TJ, 17 Mch., for the letter calling for IMMEDIATE SEPARATION.

From Isaac Tichenor

SIR, Bennington March 22d. 1803

In compliance with your request of the 25th. of last month, I herewith enclose a Return of the Militia of this State—It will give me pleasure to communicate to our Legislature the Sentiments and principles expressed in your address on the Subject of our Militia—And you may be assured, that my official & personal influence will be exerted, to render the Militia of this State, a sure & conspicuous part of our "national defense"

With due Respect & Esteem I am Your Excellency's Most Obt. Servt.

Isaac Tichenor

RC (PHi); addressed: "The President of the United States City of Washington"; endorsed by TJ as received 4 Apr. and so recorded in SJL. Enclosure not found.

New Jersey native Isaac Tichenor (1754-1838) graduated from the College of New Jersey in 1775, then moved to upstate New York to study law. He later settled in Bennington, Vermont, where he became an influential political leader and played a key role in securing statehood for Vermont in 1791. A Federalist, Tichenor held a number of state offices during the 1780s and 1790s before his election to the United States Senate in 1796. He resigned the following year to become governor of Vermont, retaining the office until 1807 despite Republican majorities in the legislature after 1801. He briefly regained the office in 1808, due in large part to the unpopularity of TJ's embargo in the state, but lost a reelection bid the following year. He served again in the Senate from 1815 until 1821, when he retired from public life (ANB; *Biog. Dir. Cong.*; Richard A. Harrison, *Princetonians, 1769-1775: A Biographical Dictionary* [Princeton, 1980], 528-36).

YOUR REQUEST OF THE 25TH. OF LAST MONTH: Tichenor laid a copy of TJ's 25 Feb. circular letter regarding the militia before the Vermont legislature on 15 Oct. In his message to the assembly the preceding day, Tichenor reminded legislators that the militia "must be well armed and equipped," which required legislative support. "Our safety and freedom essentially depend on this class of our fellow citizens," he added. "It is our highest interest as a nation to engraft the character of the soldier on the citizen, and to cherish that spirit which gave us independence. It will be a sure and cheap defence" (*Journals of the General Assembly of the State of Vermont, At Their Session, Begun and Holden at Westminster, in the County of Windham, on Thursday, the Thirteenth Day of October, A.D. One Thousand Eight Hundred and Three* [Windsor, Vt., 1804], 16, 25-6).

From Anonymous

Missisippi territory March 23th. 1803

We the Cetticences of this territory, the liberty to trouble your Excelince to read these few lines the thing that imboldinges us is from your well known Philinthrophy it is natural for subjects to Pettion their suverion & as much natural for children to Petition their father when agrieved or in want our Grevence At this time is Great Jacibine Plots & Spanish intrigue awats us Daly our sincere wishes & Petitions is that your viglence & Care may be over us daliy every Day affords us knew alarms from the seccret & Prievets letters that daylie Comes from faddrel Goveremment Plots of Subtilliy are a Carring on by the old torreyes the right of theire title are Jacobines their whole

Study seemes to be to Deprive us of all scocal right But we Live in hopes that your Excelency will do every indevour to secoure our rights as far as it may Be in your Power we hope that from your aloustrous mereit of charecor in this Quarter of the world all we wish for is to let us have our Little improvements their is a Large Number of us scettled on improvements & we wish, to get them at the hand of faddrel Goverement it are not our wiheses to fall under the hands of specllators or Jacobines if it should Be our unhappy fate to fall into therer hands hard must be our fate all the old Jacobine set are in Commision here & if the Case should be that the land office is estiblished in the Green faimly scenacribes rules will be the misehures Prescribed & schreradrck machicks & Abendiggo will Be our fate we hope youl consider that we liy far from the mother states & srounded by the savag on three Quarters & a martum Power on the other & if our charter should not Be esteblished on Equatable terms the unhappy fat there is a Number of us must seek our rescidence else there many have fraighted thier hear that are not able to Go back to the mother states & are Determined to Go to the republicken Goverment or the spinards & if this should be the case & any ammositys or ombrages take Place unhappy must be the Concequance as we are far from any sucker many monscripts from this territoy many of them Comes from thoses that wishes Proffit & honour But have no merit others wish to hold their antidated tittles your Luster shines every wher in Missisippi only by the antydated titles & the Disbandied officers & Lecke boys Discharged off[. . .] from Geting their Bread & met at the Publick Expence

We ad No more at this time But due obdience & hopes your Lourles may be always Crouned with olives

Three hundred & ode of us would ascribe But it would Be trouble unnecessary to read its Become Commen for Missisippi to be annomios in subscribing

We have like to forgot to mention your Excelency Numbers of these antidated titels have been survayed By lantren & Candel others by moonshine But is Certain that Numbers of them have been survayed without any appointed Surveyer.

RC (DLC); frayed at margin; addressed: "To the fedriel Scity To his Excelency Mr Thomas Jefferson Prescident of the united states"; franked; postmarked Nashville, 28 June; endorsed by TJ as an anonymous letter and "lands" and so recorded in SJL at 10 July; also endorsed by TJ: "postmark Nashville."

GREEN FAIMLY: brothers Thomas Marston Green and Abner Green and their brother-in-law Cato West constituted an influential faction in Mississippi politics, and were rumored to be deeply interested in the territory's land claims (Dunbar Rowland, *Encyclopedia of Mississippi History*, 2 vols. [Madison, Wis., 1907], 1:796-8; *Terr. Papers*, 5:191n; Matthew Clay to TJ, 28 Feb. 1803; Isaac Briggs to TJ, 8 Sep. 1803).

SCENACRIBES RULES: that is, Sennacherib, the Assyrian king who plundered much of Judah and forced its king, Hezekiah, to pay a sizeable tribute of gold and silver (2 Kings 18:13-16).

SCHRERADRCK MACHICKS & ABENDIGGO: that is, Shadrach, Meshach, and Abednego. In the Old Testament, King Nebuchadnezzar of Babylon had the three men bound and thrown into a fiery furnace for refusing to worship a golden image made by the king (Daniel 3:1-21).

From Abraham Hargis

Cape Henlopen Light House
March 23 1803

HONOURED SIR

when I troubled you before with some lines on publick business, I did not expect to have troubled you with any more as I presume you have enough to employ all your time—But Sir necessity being the mother of invenshan & Self preservation the first Law of nature—I hope you will pardon my preasent address—as I am persuaded that my salary is lower than the labour deserves & lower than any other office in the Union that is attended with as much labour & expence. distant from the City 150 miles the markets here as high as at the city. distant from any inhabitent 3 miles on a sand bank that will not prodoose any thing for the support of man or beast the business Requires 2 hands & to pay a hand & support a family on 333—$\frac{33}{100}$ dols I find verry hard—ad to this that I have not Recd. my Salary (small as it is) as I should have done agreeable to contract. I was to Receeve it quarterly & I contracted debdtes payable at the same times—but insted of Receeveing my pay last faul was told that no money was in hand I have Recd. but one settlement in two years have Recd. six months sallery a fue days since & am informd the other is Redy tho the onnessesarie expence I have been put to by this detenshan has sunk half of the Sum I Recd. was obliged to pay intrest & detenshan money in the city to Msrs Baker & Commyges Harvy & Worth Allebone & Wittmore & was obliged to borrow money on Great advance from Mr. Thos. Latimore to enable me to leave the City by refering to whome you asertain the facts & in this county two Judgments of 20 dols. each obtaind aganst me the facts you may get from Governor Hall or Ceser A: Rodney Esqr these thing subjects me to disagreeable feelings for I was never cald before a court or Majestreet before on a debdt of My own creating—when I was appointed to keep the Light House I had 346—$\frac{33}{100}$ dols & some Pircusets I have not now as I informd in my last & at the time I was appointed keeper of the Light House articles of liveing was nearly as low as they ever ware Since the Revelution not above half the sum they have generly been since—When the Light House was Ceeded to the United states my salary was lowerd because it was said to be higher than any other on the Continent & Just right it has to be so—for it is the most ill convenant of any. neither fish Oisters or any such thing to be had without more trouble & expence that in the city. & no other Light House that I am acquainted with but has most of those advantages—When your Excellency comes to consider these thing & that I served during the War in the service of my Country (as my emasceated constitution & broken bones often causes me to Remember) I hope you will see the propriety of alowing a reasonable compensation for my labour which is all I want for in this world I want but little nor shall I want that little long—

My enimees is in hope I shall be forsed to sell my Property to pay my debdts & if so I cannot support my family on my Preasent salary Consequently must leave Sussex tho this I am determind not to do till I see an other State election which will determin our Presidentel Election as it Respects Deleware for one active person in Deleware is worth a hundred in Pensylvania—

May the Blessing of God Rest on you the wisdom of the highest guide your administration Prays Your onworthy servt.

ABRM. HARGIS

NB the cisterns leaks much I think fifty gals pr year is lost by leakage & I kno no way of Preventing it but to line the cisterns with lead which may be easily done & I think will save the Expence in 3 years—

ABRM. HARGIS

RC (DNA: RG 26, MLR); addressed: "His Excellency Thos. Jefferson President of the United States City of Washington"; franked; postmarked "Lewes Town, Dela.," 30 Mch.; endorsed by TJ as received 6 Apr. and so recorded in SJL.

TROUBLED YOU BEFORE: see Hargis to TJ, 26 May 1802.

To Levi Lincoln

DEAR SIR Monticello Mar. 23. 1803.

I now return you the papers recieved in yours of the 15th. inst. with thanks for the perusal, and sincere congratulations on the pleasure you must experience from the possession of a son whose talents afford a prospect not less comfortable to his family than promising to his country. amid the dreary prospect of a rising generation committed from their infancy to the education of bigotted & monarchical priests (for in their hands are nearly all the youth of the US.) it is a comfort to see some[1] individuals rising by the native force of their genius & virtue above the slavish precepts of their tutors, and shewing that among those to whom we are to deliver over the freedom & happiness of our country, there will not be wanting some advocates at least for the rights & dignity of man. I hail with sanctimonious reverence old Massachusets, recovering, like Samson, her shorn locks, grasping the pillars to which she has been chained, and overturning the fabric & the Philistines together. god bless you & make you happy.

Th: Jefferson

RC (MWA); at foot of text: "Levi Lincoln esq." PrC (DLC).

RECOVERING, LIKE SAMSON: see Judges 16:22-30.

[1]TJ here canceled "examples."

To William Short

Dear Sir Monticello Mar. 23. 1803

Your's of the 10th. came to hand two days ago only. I will carry with me to Washington the whole bundle of your papers, so as to be able to put into your hands any particulars of them. I informed you in my last that in the first week of this month 500. D. would be left in mr Barnes's hands for you, and the same sum monthly until the whole of my balance should be paid up. I am disabled from doing more during the present year by an unlucky circumstance. about 18. months ago I was offered 4. shares out of 10. of a tract of land adjoining me, on which was a valuable mill seat, the only rival to mine which can be on this river. I bought without sufficient consideration, with a view to bring the other shares under my power which I expected would be falling in, one by one in the course of 8. or 10. years. but contrary to all expectation they were offered for sale last summer. I authorised a friend going to Kentucky, where the parties reside, to purchase, taking a sufficient credit, which he expected could have been had. but he was induced to purchase it on paiments all to be made this year. it was on a view of this (which takes from me 6000. D.) that I informed you I could pay you only 500. D. a month. I shall endeavor to sell it immediately if possible: and if I can, the whole of your paiment can be accomplished in a little more than a twelvemonth from this time: if I cannot sell it, 6 months more will be requisite to accomplish

the whole; because I can begin with the next year to pay 1000. D. a month.
with respect to the settlement of the account I am perfectly satisfied with the principles, & the calculation you have made on them. the error you have detected in an early part of it can be corrected by laying interest on it, and entering it with it's interest at the foot of the account. since the date of the account I rendered you there are only some rents recieved by me, and some small disbursements to be added. my stay here (being now only of 4. or 5. days) is so short and my occupations so pressing that I shall be better able to attend to this matter at Washington than here. in the mean time be so good as to send me a copy of your statement of the account to Jan. 1. 1800. which you mention as the point of time to which you have brought it.

Mr. Lilly will make no more leases of your land but from year to year. some years hence; no doubt, 10. or even 12. D. an acre may be got for your lands, by the natural progression of price. but at present no such sum can be got, unless for very small & chosen spots, which being taken out, the residue will not sell at all. there is at present a sensible check in the price of lands, proceeding from the low prices of produce, consequent on the peace. I do not know that 8. D. could be immediately got for your's: tho' I suppose that by advertising, the purchaser or purchasers might offer at that. this, with the rents, would give you 20. percent per annum on your money. Henderson, who gave you false ideas on this subject, is an unprincipled creature, not worth a dollar in the world. Altho' you speak of going from Philadelphia to Kentucky direct, I do not surrender the hope of seeing you in Washington. at any rate, on your return, I shall count on seeing you either there or at Monticello. accept my friendly salutations & assurances of constant & affectionate esteem.

TH: JEFFERSON

P.S. since writing the above, mr Durrett your tenant has called on me and offers to take all the lands above the road, which is $\frac{4}{5}$ of the whole at 8. D. paying $\frac{1}{3}$ on delivery, and the remaining $\frac{2}{3}$ at two equal & annual instalments, & mortgaging the land itself as security. he supposed delivery would not be made till the end of this year, when a year's rent would be to be paid in addition. he wishes an answer. I think the part below the road can be readily sold for 10. D.

RC (DLC: William Short Papers); at foot of first page: "Mr. Short"; endorsed by Short as received 2 Apr.

FRIEND GOING TO KENTUCKY: Craven Peyton.

For Short's CALCULATION of TJ's debt to him, see Vol. 38:469n.

From Benjamin Vaughan

DEAR SIR, March 24, 1803.

In the travels of Tournefort, Vol. 1. 4to. edition, there are two chapters containing the description of Constantinople; & in one of them is a brief statement, that the Turkish *gallies* are there housed. Whether they are kept in wet or dry dock's, I forget; for I now write remote from my books.—In Snodgrass's folio letter to Mr. Dundas, printed some years since, you will find that the *building* of men of war is recommended to be performed under sheds; in correspondence to which are the reports made to parliament on these subjects. I know that Sir John Call was strenously in favor of this; & I think that the practice has been *partially* tried, though wood is not very cheap among the English.

If the violent counsels of some men were followed respecting New Orleans, not only the evils of war would be introduced for a people, whose continuance with the U.S. is somewhat contingent; and the obstructions to the Missisippi would merely change their form, the blockade being converted from one by land, to one by sea; but the French might patch up their quarrels with their refractory negroes in the islands, and introduce these into the vicinity of the slave colonies of the U.S. When they have evacuated their islands of these troublesome inmates, they may spare corresponding detachments of white troops. The latter will probably soon become so distasted with their present service; (which is without hope, without plunder, without glory; & to the certain loss of life by disease, as well as against that love of liberty which still beats so high in some of them, that they are sent there to extinguish it;) I say, they may become so distasted, as not only to refuse to act in the islands; but even shew symptoms of making common cause with the blacks; so as to make this almost the only brilliant ending of the negro-war left for Bonaparte. He will be proud of thus healing an evil by a stratagem to turn to his benefit & fame; for certain it is, that he now holds the wolf by the ears, and knows not whether to loose it, or how to keep it.

Rather than follow the rash advisers for the U.S., it would be wiser in the last resort, to station hulks or floating stages or even proper vessels at the river's mouth, to receive the descending produce.

Certain it is too, that the Spaniards are the most censurable in this business; & if upon them any evil is to fall, it is pretty clear that the genius of American enterprize will seek their gold mines. Would not the prudent form for the first of such expeditions be the following? To send forward a detachment of cavalry & mounted infantry; to fix by lot, or ballot, or the orders of a superior, who, & who alone, shall attend to plunder; to designate publicly, if not the proportions of the spoil, yet at least the precautions to secure it against embezzlement; to let the rest of the detachment keep the most rigorous guard; and to meet the party on their return with a body designed to support their retreat. Profound secrecy must attend every part of such a project.[1]

The Spaniards seem of late years not to have acted upon any of the principles common to the human understanding. A superior power seems to have bewildered their intellects. They are at once the prey, the scoff, & the tools of others, & when their moment comes, whether in Europe or America, they will probably break up at once.—As to the Western States of the Union, whether in unison or in opposition with the Spaniards, they are likely to be among the instruments of their fall in America. Believe me, my dear sir, Your attached & respectful friend & servant.

RC (DLC); in Benjamin Vaughan's hand; endorsed by TJ as from John Vaughan received from Hallowell, Maine, on 14 Apr. and so recorded in SJL; TJ corrected Vaughan's first name in the endorsement but not in SJL.

The French botanist Joseph Pitton de TOURNEFORT traveled in the Levant from 1700 to 1702. In his posthumously published account of the journey, he related that the Ottoman sultan's oared gallies were kept in "Barge-Houses" in Constantinople (Joseph Pitton de Tournefort, *A Voyage into the Levant: Perform'd by Command of the Late* French *King*, 2 vols. [London, 1718], 1:373; DSB).

SNODGRASS'S FOLIO LETTER: replying to a set of queries from Great Britain's commissioners of the land revenue, who collected information about the utilization of forests, the surveyor of shipping of the East India Company recommended in 1791 that ships be built on slips under SHEDS or roofs to protect them from the elements. SIR JOHN CALL, a former chief engineer of the East India Company, was one of the commissioners (*Letter from Gabriel Snodgrass, Esq. to the Right Honorable Henry Dundas ... on the Mode of Improving the Navy of Great Britain* [London, 1797], 22-3; DNB).

Later in the year TJ received more information from Vaughan about roofed enclosures for ships. Vaughan copied extracts of two passages from an account of travels in Russia and western Asia by Dr. John Cook. In one passage Cook described a modest wooden palace used by Peter the Great in St. Petersburg. The first boat built for the czar in that city had been placed next to the house and "a shade of timber" erected to protect the building and the vessel. The other passage described two dry docks constructed in Russia using dikes, locks, and sluices. In one of those locations wooden shades protected warships that had been "laid up on dry ground." Vaughan noted that Cook was mentioned in the *Travels of Jonas Hanway, Esq. through Russia into Persia* and James Lind's *Treatise of the Scurvy*. TJ received the extracts without any cover letter or identifying information but inferred that the unsigned, undated document had come from Vaughan (MS in DLC: TJ Papers, 130:22538, 2 p. in Vaughan's hand, endorsed by TJ as received 7 Oct. 1803, "supposed" from Vaughan, and so recorded in SJL with notation "being anon."; John Cook, *Voyages and Travels through the Russian Empire, Tartary, and Part of the Kingdom of Persia*, 2 vols. [Edinburgh, 1770], 1:14-15, 192).

[1] Sentence interlined.

To James Walker

SIR — Monticello Mar. 25. 1803.

I find it to be the opinion of mr Lilly that having hired an extraordinary force for the year he shall be able to compleat the canal for my mill this summer. I have contracted with mr Hope to build the mill houses for both the small & large mills. the smaller one he will begin immediately. I must therefore ask of you to come over without delay and mark out the site of both. if you come before Tuesday I shall be at home, if afterwards apply to mr Lilly my manager here who will send for mr Hope and both of them will attend you on the ground. Accept my best wishes. TH: JEFFERSON

PrC (MHi); at foot of text: "Mr. Walker"; endorsed by TJ in ink on verso.

CANAL FOR MY MILL: see Vol. 38:438.

To George Jefferson

DEAR SIR — Monticello Mar. 26. 1803.

On recurring to my papers here, I find I had overlooked an order of Moran & Mattox for £16–8–9=54.70½ D paid by me to John H. Craven, and consequently that my order sent you in favor of Moran Feb. 8. was that much over the balance due from me to him. if therefore he has not drawn all his money from you, be so good as to consider this as a counterdemand of 54.70½. D part of which you had been desired to pay him, and stop it for me in your hands. otherwise I shall probably lose it. Accept my affectionate salutations.

TH: JEFFERSON

PrC (MHi); at foot of text: "Mr. George Jefferson"; endorsed by TJ in ink on verso.

On this day, TJ recorded in SJL sending a letter to "Mattox & Moran." The letter has not been found.

To John B. Magruder

SIR — Monticello Mar. 26. 1803.

I recieved your note informing me of your mistake between the beech and birch. still however I must ask the favor of you to exert yourself and get for me all the beech you can, in breadths of 3½ Inches & of 7. Inches, and to do it immediately and give me information as soon as done. Accept my best wishes. TH: JEFFERSON

PrC (MHi); at foot of text: "Mr. Magruder"; endorsed by TJ in ink on verso.

John Bowie Magruder (d. 1815) moved to Virginia from Prince George's County, Maryland, in 1792. He purchased property along the Rivanna River between Albemarle and Fluvanna counties and began building a dam and gristmill there in 1796. Within three years, he expanded his operation under the name Union Mills. Magruder provided TJ with wood plank, probably for mill construction at Shadwell. According to his financial accounts, TJ directed payments for plank to Magruder of $104.54 on 20 Aug. 1802 and of $44.57 on 7 Feb. 1803, but later disagreed with him over prices charged. Magruder and his son-in-law purchased the Shadwell mills from the Jefferson estate in 1829 (Woods, *Albemarle*, 260-2; MB, 2:1079, 1092; RS, 4:420-1; Vol. 38: 423, 449; TJ to Magruder, 23 Sep. 1804, 14 Nov. 1805).

YOUR NOTE: a letter from Magruder to TJ, recorded in SJL as received on 19 Mch., has not been found.

TJ also used BEECH for the floor of the parlor at Monticello; see TJ to James Dinsmore, 18 May.

To Albert Gallatin

DEAR SIR Monticello Mar. 28. 1803.

Yours of the 21st. came to hand on the 25th. I now return the letters of Thornton & Muhlenberg with entire approbation of your answers. I am in all cases for liberal conduct towards other nations, believing that the practice of the same friendly feelings & generous dispositions which attach individuals in private life will attach societies on the large scale, which are composed of individuals. I have for some time believed that Commodore Morris's conduct would require investigation. his progress from Gibraltar has been astonishing.[1] I know of but one supposition which can cover him; that is that he has so far mistaken the object of his mission as to spend his time in convoying. I do not know the fact. we gave great latitude to his discretion, believing he had an ambition to distinguish himself and unwilling to check it by positive instructions.—I have for some time been satisfied a schism was taking place in Pensylvania, between the moderates & high-flyers. the same will take place in Congress whenever a proper head for the latter shall start up. and we must expect division of the same kind in other states as soon as the republicans shall be so strong as to fear no other enemy. I hope those of Philadelphia will not address on the subject of removals. it would be a delicate operation indeed.—Briggs reserved till my return to decide. but he will accept. I had hoped to be with you by the 1st. of April: but I now apprehend it will be that date before I can leave this place, without leaving the objects of my visit unaccomplished. the thermometer is at 29°. with us this morning. the peach trees in blossom for a week past. Accept affectionate salutations TH: JEFFERSON

RC (NHi: Gallatin Papers); at foot of text: "The Secretary of the Treasury"; endorsed. PrC (DLC). Recorded in SJL with notation "Thornton. Muhlenbg. Barbary. Pensva." Enclosures: see Gallatin to TJ, 21 Mch.

For the INSTRUCTIONS to Richard V. Morris during the summer of 1802, see Vol. 38:223, 235-6, 265-6, 304-6, 328.

[1]Preceding three words interlined.

From William Bache

DEAR SIR. New Orleans March 29 1803.

I arrived at this place on the 27th. of this month and finding the government occupied in the reception of Mr Laussat, Colonial Prefect, who had arrived two days before, I delay'd presenting myself to the Governor by the advice of Mr Hulings Mr Clarke being absent on a visit to the Natchez. Mr Hulings, tho he has been in possession of a copy of Mr Clarkes letter to the Secy of the Treasury of August last from New York, does not know upon what grounds Mr Clarke premises that the Spanish government will permit a Hospital establishment at New Orleans. I propose to day to present my respects to Govr Salcedo to know upon what footing the business is to rest until the Final cession of this country to France, of which I will give you the earliest advice. What will be the conduct of the New Masters becomes more problematical every day. Being detained by contrary winds some days at the Balise I had an opportunity of some conversation with Citoyen Laussot, and had his assurances of the Pacific inclinations of the French Government towards the United States and of the conciliatory sentiments of the Officers of the present Mission. How far this may accord with the real sentiments of the French Government I am not competent to decide, for he has all the suavity of manners of a French courtier, and I am allways a little inclined to distrust the unofficial assertions of men who have been brought up in the vortex of diplomacy.

I have forwarded to you his proclamation to the Lousianais; by which you will see that he understands both flattering the Power that made & that which is to preside over him. This proclamation tho bearing date the 6th. Germinal has certainly been prepared in France; besides there is not a press in this place capable of executing the work. It appears capable of any construction that the French Government may please to make hereafter; and it is sincerely to be wished that they may not think themselves bound to wipe off the remaining *blemishes of their history* by extending their possessions to their antient Limits in this country. A sentiment which appears to be inculcated in the Proclamation.

I learn this evening from Mr Fulton; an american who formerly was commisioned by Genet, who has been with Genl Victor at the battle of Marengo &c now holds the rank of Major; that Genl. Victor was to have left Helveot Sluys about the same time that the Prefet left france. This information I had also from the Prefet & that he was only to bring with him 3600 men. He is daily expected as it is now 70 days since the embarcation of the Prefect. Major Fulton also stated that it was their intention to establish a strong military Post on the Luisiana side on the nearest high ground above the Natches, to complete which 600 men were to be dispatch'd immediately upon the arrival of the Troops. Perhaps little credit is to be placed in the accuracy of his information both from his being an American and a little inclined to talk. The Illianois was also stated as an object of great military attention. One circumstance which he mentioned & which is very strange if true is, that the Prefect has given formal notice this day to the Intendant, that tho it was not his intention to take *final* possession of the country until the arrival of the commander in chief; yet that the Intendant must hold himself in readiness to give up the functions of his office tomorrow after which all commercial regulations were to be made by the french. He further stated that many of the officers were already appointed. It is however difficult to credit that part of the functions are to be carried on by the Spanish & part by the French.

That portion of the Etat major which arrived with the Prefect evince some activity in investigating the state of internal defence. They have already examined into the state of the fortifications and arsenal. They are men well calculated for the defence of this country as they have all served their Military apprenticeship in Holland and Egypt; but if they have in veiw offensive measures they must learn to fight in Woods as well as in Mud.

There are upwards of 50 american vessels in the river some of which will find a difficulty in obtaining cargoes, as cotton descends but slowly, and flour is at six dollars a Barrel. Permit me to apologise for troubling you with matters which are not my concern and receive my anxious wishes for your health & happiness

William Bache.

I have been since informed that the new post up the river was to be erected at little meadows; as high up as 36°. 10.—

RC (DLC); endorsed by TJ as received 2 May and so recorded in SJL.

Pierre Clément LAUSSAT, the prefect of the French colony of Louisiana, reached New Orleans on 26 Mch. On his arrival he met Governor Manuel de Salcedo and high military and civil officers of the Spanish colonial government. The municipal government received him in a ceremony the next day (Pierre Clément Laussat, *Memoirs of My Life*, trans. Sister Agnes-Josephine Pastwa, ed. Robert D. Bush [Baton Rouge, La., 1978], 17).

For Daniel Clark's 16 Aug. 1802 letter to Gallatin about the intended HOSPITAL for American seamen at New Orleans, see Vol. 38:255-6.

Balize (BALISE) was an outpost near the mouth of the Mississippi River. Marked by a flag tower that was visible from the Gulf of Mexico, the settlement consisted of a small garrison of soldiers, some pilots' residences, and a customs station. Sailing from Balize to New Orleans sometimes took weeks due to unfavorable winds. The French prefect was able to proceed upriver in boats rowed by sailors (E. Wilson Lyon, *Louisiana in French Diplomacy, 1759-1804* [Norman, Okla., 1974], 29; Laussat, *Memoirs of my Life*, 12-17; Michaël Garnier, *Bonaparte et la Louisiane* [Paris, 1992], 87-9).

A PROCLAMATION by Laussat, written in French and addressed to the people of Louisiana—the *Louisianais*—was dated 6 Germinal Year 11, which was 27 Mch. Lamenting the severence of the colony from France in 1763 as a shameful act of the old regime and the result of a disgraceful peace settlement, Laussat avowed that the abandoned inhabitants of the colony had never lost courage and, in return, never been forgotten by the people of France. As soon as the French could do so after recovering their national glory, he proclaimed, they had turned their attention back to Louisiana. FLATTERING THE POWER to which Laussat owed his appointment, the proclamation extolled Bonaparte's leadership and declared that the first consul controlled the destinies of France and Louisiana. Laussat also noted the accomplishments of General Victor, who was to be the *capitaine général* of the colony. CAPABLE OF EXECUTING THE WORK: Laussat issued the proclamation as a printed broadside. An elaborate ornamental rule separated the columns of the text. The date was inserted by hand in a blank in the printed document, perhaps reinforcing Bache's supposition that the prefect brought the printed copies of the proclamation with him. WIPE OFF THE REMAINING BLEMISHES: Bonaparte's goals, according to Laussat's declaration, included putting France back on its proper foundations, removing stains from the nation's history ("laver toutes les taches de ses Annales"), and restoring the full extent of its geographical LIMITS. While acknowledging the overall benevolence of Spain's administration of Louisiana, Laussat's address to the *Louisianais* offended Salcedo by decrying the actions of General Alejandro O'Reilly, who had decisively restored Spain's authority in 1769 after French inhabitants drove out the colony's first Spanish governor. The *National Intelligencer* published an English translation of the prefect's proclamation a few days after TJ received Bache's letter (*Proclamation au nom de la République française*, 6 Germinal Year 11, Shaw-Shoemaker, No. 4559; Garnier, *Bonaparte et la Louisiane*, 81-3, 90-3; Laussat, *Memoirs of My Life*, 18; Gilbert C. Din, ed., *The Spanish Presence in Louisiana, 1763-1803*, vol. 2 of *The Louisiana Purchase Bicentennial Series in Louisiana History* [Lafayette, La., 1996], 74-6, 124-5, 370-1; Madison, *Papers*, *Sec. of State Ser.*, 4:551; *National Intelligencer*, 6 May 1803).

For Samuel FULTON, see John Brown to TJ, 26 Nov. 1802.

DAILY EXPECTED: Laussat was unaware that Victor's expeditionary force for Louisiana had been kept in the harbor at Helvoët Sluys in the Netherlands, first by ice, then by the increased tension between Britain and France. In April, after more delays, Bonaparte canceled the orders for the flotilla's departure. Laussat could not assume authority in New Orleans until either the *capitaine général* or new instructions arrived. Juan Ventura Morales did not GIVE UP THE FUNCTIONS of the intendant's office until the Spanish formally ceded Louisiana to France in

November 1803 (Lyon, *Louisiana in French Diplomacy*, 134-44; Laussat, *Memoirs of My Life*, 20; Garnier, *Bonaparte et la Louisiane*, 91, 103, 113, 149, 173-7; Din, ed., *Spanish Presence*, 118-19).

Four French army officers traveled to New Orleans with the prefect's advance party, including two senior officers of the general staff, or ETAT MAJOR, of Victor's expeditionary force: the chief engineer, Major Antoine Joseph Vinache, and the adjutant general, General Charles André Burthe d'Annelet. A bitter dispute that arose between Laussat and Burthe before they left France continued in Louisiana, where they could not cooperate in making arrangements for the army's expected arrival (Robert D. Bush, "Civilian versus Military Prerogatives in Napoleonic Louisiana: The Laussat-Burthe Affair, 1803," *Revue de Louisiane*, 6 [1977], 45-58; Garnier, *Bonaparte et la Louisiane*, 72-4; Laussat, *Memoirs of My Life*, 21, 42-7, 84-5; Madison, *Papers*, *Sec. of State Ser.*, 4:551-2; 5:552).

From Joseph Clay

SIR Philadelphia 29th March 1803

I have been informed that Mr. John Harrison of this City has been named to you as a person proper to fill the vacancy in the Commission of Bankrupts, occasioned by the death of Mr. Vancleve. I know of no gentleman in Philadelphia whose appointment would in my opinion give more satisfaction, not only to the Republicans generally, but also to the present Commissioners.

Mr. Harrison's character is irreproachable; his talents are good; and his connexions are such as will give his nomination peculiar propriety. Under these impressions I have no hesitation in saying that his appointment will confer pleasure on many of your friends and will be considered a favor personally done to

Your most obedt. Servt. JOSEPH CLAY

RC (DNA: RG 59, LAR); at foot of text: "The President of the United States"; endorsed by TJ as received 4 Apr. and "Harrison John to be Commr. bkrpt vice Vancleve" and so recorded in SJL.

For the previous recommendation of JOHN HARRISON as bankruptcy commissioner, see Michael Leib to TJ, 1 Mch. 1803. PRESENT COMMISSIONERS: Clay, Alexander J. Dallas, Mahlon Dickerson, John Sergeant, and Thomas Cumpston (Vol. 37:577-8, 698, 709).

To Robert Smith

DEAR SIR Monticello Mar. 29. 1803.

I recieved yesterday your's of the 17th. suggesting the sending into the Mediterranean the Constitution or the Philadelphia to overawe the Barbary powers. our plan of keeping one or two frigates there with 4. schooners was concluded on great & general consideration, on the supposition that war with Tripoli alone would go on. your letter suggests no new fact changing the state of things. I cannot say therefore that I am ready to approve a change of our plan without further facts, or considerations which have not yet occurred. but I shall be with you within a week after your reciept of this, and will be ready to take the subject into consideration & consultation. in the mean time I think it better that no step should be taken on a change of hypothesis. my last letter recommended dispatch in sending to Algiers a year's stipulation of stores, & I proposed to the Secretary of state a supply of powder *on account* asked by the Dey, *as is said*, as a gift: as also the furnishing Simpson with money for the gun carriages destined for Marocco. both these powers are as quiet as usual. so we may say is Tunis, tho' she is asking a frigate, for if we consider those powers as quiet only when asking nothing that time will never come. it is not their system. I have never believed in any effect from a shew of force to those powers. they know they cannot meet us with force any more than they could France, Spain or England. their system is a war of little expence to them[1] which must put the great nations to a greater expence than the presents which would buy it off. yet nothing but the warring on them at times will keep the demand of presents within bounds. the important thing for us now is to dispatch our small vessels. Accept my affectionate salutations.

Th: Jefferson

PrC (DLC); in ink at foot of text: "Secy. of the Navy." Recorded in SJL with notation "Barbary."

MY LAST LETTER: TJ to Smith, 19 Mch., although TJ may be referring to his letter to Smith of 17 Mch.

I PROPOSED TO THE SECRETARY OF STATE: TJ to Madison, 19 Mch.

[1] Preceding two words interlined.

From "A Democrat"

Northampton County ES. Va.
30th. March 1803.

Mr President,

It is with great respect I offer to your patronage the following lines; In doing this I recognize the right you have to every tribute that a nation can pay to Patriotic virtue. You took your position at a very critical period and while your exertions had baffled the hopes of all foreign invaders, you were not inattentive to the domestic right of your Country. The spirit excited in you have communicated to all parties and professions within our teritories and you have effectually seconded an enlightened Legislature in restoreing your Fellow Citizens to Civil, religious, and commercial liberty; so quick a change from a languishing hectic state to a robust Constitution, has perhaps no parallel and it is the more completely happy as it was brought about without any recourse to the severe remedy administered in the cure of our former distempers. Instructed by experience and illumed by philosophy, you have discovered that for our political salvation, our creed of civil faith is sufficient, and that a deviation from that and that alone is the proper object of political penalties and civil excommunications. This wisdom which has drawn on you the attention of all Europe, forms an Epocha in History. Under a Legislature of Patriots our constitution collecting fresh vigour from the recent renewal of old privaliges must bring forward all the advantages derived from our Soil, and Climate as well as from our happy situation. Under your Guardianship that Constitution cannot be annoyed by extraneous power; nor undermined by domestic treachery and in such a train of things our prosperity will bring additional security to that of her sister Country with which we are connected by the strongest ties in our station and joyn in the gratitude due you from your countrymen of every description. Thus should I continue were not the limits of a letter which are consecrated to the expressions of friendship too circumscribed.

It is with a real though a very melancholly pleasure that I have had the presumption to give you some account of the behaviour of those nefarious and malicious Calumniators of the republican faction, the Federalists. You will recollect that Mr Bassett has lately been on this peninsula; there was an unlucky [in]stance took place relative to his vote in adding the two [counties?] to this district. Mr. Bt. did not recollect how he voted and consequently made a mistake. the Zealots you may well suppose would be glad even to invent much less to propogate any story to his disadvantage but in my humble oppinion they could not find any that I thought would wear the face of probability. I cannot say there is no vanity in making this assertion but I hope it is not a misplaced one; and this is a matter of fact which is easily cleared and ascertained. If my assertions were not founded on the basis of integrity why do they utter forth from their slanderous mouths those malicious falsehoods that are now circulating about Bassett, and I may with verity add of all the republican faction. Nothing gives them more satisfaction than to have the least iota of reason to censure you and your partizans; as a corroborating circumstance to this assertion I'll give you an instance. They have been exclaiming against the sending Monroe with 2000000$s to purchase the Navigation of the

Missisippi instead of using more spirited means. However flattering those assertions may appear I must nevertheless affirm them to be the sincere effusions of my intellectual faculties.

Let me mention before I conclude that were it possible I would have you arrest and develope that nefarious and mortal administration of the former whilst you would aid and urge forward that of the other I would call on United America to detect and abandon the fraud of the former and invite their unanimity to a cordial participation in the virtues of the other. Nothing more

I am respectfully your frend and fellow Citizen

A DEMOCRAT

RC (DLC); torn; addressed: "Thomas Jefferson esqr. President of the United States"; postmarked Northampton Courthouse, 5 Apr.; endorsed by TJ as received from "Anon." on 12 Apr. and "Eastern shore election" and so recorded in SJL.

Burwell BASSETT ran unsuccessfully to represent the district that included the eastern shore counties of Northampton and Accomack in the Eighth Congress. As a state senator the previous year, Bassett brought to the floor the bill that established Virginia's districts but voted against an unsuccessful amendment that would have placed the two counties in separate districts. In the 1790s, Northampton and Accomack had comprised a single district (*Acts Passed at a General Assembly of the Commonwealth of Virginia. Begun and Held at the Capitol, in the City of Richmond, on Monday, the Seventeenth Day of October, One Thousand Seven Hundred and Ninety One* [Richmond, 1791], 7; *Acts Passed at a General Assembly of the Commonwealth of Virginia: Begun and Held at the Capitol, in the City of Richmond, on Monday, the Seventh Day of December, One Thousand Eight Hundred and One* [Richmond, 1802], 17; *Journal of the Senate of the Commonwealth of Virginia. Begun and Held at the Capitol in the City of Richmond, on Monday the Seventh Day of December, One Thousand Eight Hundred and One* [Richmond, 1802], 70-1, 73; Dubin, *Congressional Elections*, 28; TJ to Gideon Granger, 8 May 1803).

From Gideon Fitz

SIR March 31 1803

I hope you will not think it strange that I have taken this way of communicating to you my situation, idieas & wishes at this time; when you come to know and consider the true cause why I have taken such measures or method it has been a thing impres'd on my mind for some considerable time and I still found it to increase. nature has bless'd me with so small a share of eloqunce or gift of speech that I always find it a hard task to communicate my idieas—notwithstanding they are so very few & so imperfect I always find myself much embarras't and at a great loss for words to express what I realley wish and with but little less difficulty I have prevaild on myself to undertake this method since I do not recollect a single instance of writing any letter that I did not regret after it was gone that I could not get it back to make some alteration or amendment but considering and being fully confident of your wisdom & unparralled goodness, I with but little hesitation have made the attempt—

First I must inform you of the many great difficulties I have in view and do not know by any means how to avoid therefore I find it hard to determin what is best to do I consider my constitution is but very weak & slender I have been sicly at times ever since my remembrance tho' I have been much more stout and healthy for this two or three years past I travelled out to Georgia and back in the fall of 1800 it did not seem to agree with me very well then tho it might now perhaps. Another great obstacle is that I do not know how I am to get provided to go I must undoubtedly depend upon my Father for assistance which I am apprehensive he will be backward to give I belive he is hardly willing that I should leave him so fare I have spent so much of my time & money in trying to improve myself in education since I have been to myself that I am now neither provided with horse or money to travel with improveing my mind by education and learning is one of the most delightfull sweet and agreeable idieas that has yet ever presented itself to my mind I have sometimes felt willing almost to risk even my life and fortune in the persuit yet it seems that a person ought and must in his youthfull days provide a subsistance and accommodations for old age which the length of his days does not admit of the loss of much time my condition and situation in life is continually bending my mind one way; and my strong inclinations and desires another thus am I continually tost to and fro between the waves of pleasure and pain I had also formed a design of providing so soon as I should be able some of the best books I could procure for the use and benefit of the younger children of both my relations and acquaintance that they may not labour under the same disadvantages that I have I believe some of them are great natural geniuses and if they had a chance of improvement might perhaps some day or other become usefull sitizens to society I find it is natural to the human mind in its early stage to take to itself some way or other to pass away life and the first impressions that are formed in the mind are always the most lasting and if in the way of vice hard to get shet of I think the sudy of learning to be the most effectual means to prevent this evil it seemes to me to be a plesant thing in all conditions of life and necessary to almost all persons whatsoever to the Carpenter it is necessary to be acquainted some what with the nature of Geometry and drawing in Architecture to the merchant it is necessary for Book keeping casting up his accompts and setling his affairs and even to the farmer and planter it is a pleasant thing to read good Geography's understand the maps know the situation of all the inhabitable parts of the globe and when they hear a place mentioned can refer to such Book as will give them a full satisfaction of all they could wish. Time will not admit me to go any farther at this time tho I have not mentioned a tenth part of what I could wish but from this hint I hope you will consider my case and tell me what you think is best for me to do I pray you not to think hard of my troubling you so much I do not know what to do for the best I am willing to leave it to your judgement and honour and whatever you think is best I will do I shall forever remember your Great kindness and good will for giving me the opportunity of comeing here and the chance of reading and improveing miself from your Books besides the trouble you have taken in shewing and explaining matters to me which I did not know of before all I can do is to declare to you that my intentions are good sincere and lasting And I am with most profound respect your friend and servant GIDEON FITZ

RC (MHi); at foot of text: "Tho. Jefferson P.U.S."; endorsed by TJ as received 31 Mch. and so recorded in SJL.

Gideon Fitz was the son of an Albemarle County "wheat-fan maker." According to TJ's account, while "living in the hollow of a mountain unknown to every body," Fitz somehow acquired books on surveying and mathematics and mastered them "without aid from any one." TJ invited Fitz to reside at Monticello in 1802, where he worked as a carpenter and surveyor. In exchange, Fitz received wages, room and board, and access to TJ's library. Impressed by the young man's intelligence and ability, TJ recommended him to Isaac Briggs for a surveyor's position in the Mississippi Territory, where Fitz moved to in 1804. The following year, TJ suggested Fitz to Albert Gallatin for a land office appointment, claiming that "no honester man lives" and that Fitz's "mathematical talents are good, and tho' this has been his particular line, his understanding & knolege of life fits him for other lines." Fitz went on to serve in a series of federal posts in the Mississippi and Orleans Territories, culminating with his appointment as surveyor of public lands south of Tennessee in 1831 (MB, 2:1082; JEP, 4:135, 158; RS, 1:215n, 650; Vol. 37:653, 654n; Vol. 38:329-30, 354, 356n; Isaac Briggs to TJ, 2 May 1803; Fitz to TJ, 17 Feb. 1804; TJ to Gallatin, 7 Aug. 1805).

TRAVELLED OUT TO GEORGIA: Thomas Mann Randolph recently attempted to engage Fitz in an unidentified undertaking, probably involving his long-contemplated plan to establish a cotton plantation in Georgia (Vol. 37:133-4; TJ to Thomas Mann Randolph, 17 Jan. 1803).

TELL ME WHAT YOU THINK IS BEST: a letter from TJ to Fitz, dated 20 Apr., is recorded in SJL but has not been found.

From Lafayette

Paris Germinal the 10th. 11th year.
[i.e. 31 Mch. 1803]

My dear Friend

this letter will be presented by General Bernadotte one of our first rate Generals, and most undaunted patriots. I know it is superfluous to introduce to you the man who by the éclat, the number, and the importance of his military atchievements, has so highly contributed to the successes and the glory of the late war. but I feel a heartfelt pleasure to think, and of course to say, that while the disinterestedness of his conduct had already marked him among the few, who have particularly been distinguished on this point, and while the generosity and frankness of his heart had made him a worthy object of confidence and friendship, he has at every period, and to the present hour, proved that no ambitious views with every temptation and facility to fulfill them, could make him deviate from his republican sentiments, nor from the conduct of a true friend of liberty.

I have thought my dear Sir, that to give you an Idea of the personal dispositions he carries with him this sincere sketch of his character could tell you more, than four pages of diplomatical reasoning—what his instructions are, I do not know, and I think that hitherto he himself knows very little about it. I am not at all in the secrets of government, and my disaprobation of the affair of Louisiana has been so early expressed that it should be an additional cause for my being excluded from any communication about it. yet it appears to me that the consul means to satisfy Mr. Livingston with respect to the treaty, and that, respecting the Louisiana affair, he Intends to take personally with you through General Bernadotte satisfactory arrangements. I wish it the most could I divest myself of my french feelings on the occasion I should still think it very dangerous for the united states to entangle themselves in any close connection with great Britain.

of this I am sure—that Bernadotte will do everything in his power to ciment the union between France and America, and that he knows how to feel for the honour and rights of a free Country. his lady accompanies him. I am sure your amiable daughters will be highly pleased with her acquaintance. she and Madame Joseph Bonaparte are sisters, and you may have observed that among government people, none has shewn himself so much disposed in favour of America as Joseph Bonaparte.

it is possible that before Bernadotte's departure, we may tell you more about the object of his mission. but Mr. Livingston will write to the last hour, and I my dear Sir I am dependent upon an accident which has rendered it impossible to write myself, and not very easy amidst my sufferings, and the attendance of surgeons to direct a correspondence. I have already been for five and fifty days under the pains of a broken *Phémurés-neck* and the operation of a new invented machine, I have still three weeks to remain uncomfortably on my back, but I now am sure to recover the use of my thigh without any lameness. as to the particulars of my misfortune and treatment, nobody can better give them than General Bernadotte who has been a most friendly visitor at my bedside.

I know my dear Sir how kindly you have interested yourself in my private concerns, for which I beg leave to express my most affectionate heartfelt acknowledgements. with the most entire grateful confidence, I refer myself to what you will think proper for your old constant friend.

with the highest respect, and most cordial affection, I am my dear sir yours

LAFAYETTE

RC (DLC); in a clerk's hand, signed by Lafayette; English date supplied; at foot of text: "Thomas Jefferson president of the United States"; endorsed by TJ as received 2 Oct. and so recorded in SJL.

Lafayette also wrote to Madison on this day with an expectation that Jean Baptiste BERNADOTTE would take the letter to the United States (Madison, *Papers*, *Sec. of State Ser.*, 4:468).

SATISFY MR. LIVINGSTON WITH RESPECT TO THE TREATY: see Madison to TJ, 14 Mch.

Bernadotte married Bernadine Eugénie Désirée Clary in 1798. She and Joseph Bonaparte's wife, Julie Clary Bonaparte, were SISTERS. Désirée Clary had once been engaged to Napoleon Bonaparte (Tulard, *Dictionnaire Napoléon*, 424-5; Jacques Henri-Robert, *Dictionnaire des diplomates de Napoléon: Histoire et dictionnaire du corps diplomatique consulaire et impérial* [Paris, 1990], 110; Vol. 33: 564).

ACCIDENT: slipping on ice, Lafayette had fractured his left femur near the hip. His physicians strapped his leg into a new MACHINE to gradually stretch the limb and realign the broken bone. The procedure did not work, leaving him with pain and LAMENESS for the rest of his life (Harlow Giles Unger, *Lafayette* [Hoboken, N.J., 2002], 333, 339; Madame de Corny to TJ, 15 Feb. 1803).

From Louis Pio

MONSIEUR LE PRÉSIDENT à Paris ... Mars 1803.

Permettez moi, que pour la quatrième ou cinquième fois je vous présente mes hommages respectueux et fasse Le Ciel au moins, que cette fois-ci ma Lettre Vous parvienne sous les yeux! Malgré quatorze années d'éloignement je conserve, et je conserverai toute ma vie ces mêmes sentimens que Vous même Vous m'avez inspirés. Vous Vous rappellerez[1] sans doute, monsieur, les premieres Leçons, que Vous m'avez données, de Liberté; elles n'ont pas été perdues, et Vous n'ignorez peut être pas ce que j'ai fait pour être Libre; mais le suis-je? Je joins ici un petit Extrait baptistaire de mon affranchissement. Aujourdhui reduit presque à La mendicité, car on me refuse tout emploi, je suis obligé de donner des leçons de Langue pour exister. Les années me pésent, et mon ame vieillit, *mea duodenum trepidavit aetas claudere Lustrum.* Je voudrais Vous voir encore, mais la mer immense m'effraye. Recevez donc, Monsieur, de loin tous mes voeux pour votre prospérité. Ce sont ceux pour la prospérité de la Nation, qui a le bonheur de Vous avoir pour Chef; et faites moi savoir, je Vous en supplie, par quelque moyen, si je puis m'honorer encore du titre de votre Ami. Vale Vir optime.

Votre trés dévoué Serviteur PIO

EDITORS' TRANSLATION

MISTER PRESIDENT, Paris, March 1803

Allow me, for the fourth or fifth time, to present my respectful homage. This time, at last, may heaven deign to have my letter reach you. Despite fourteen years of absence, I have, and I will forever have the sentiments you yourself inspired in me. You will undoubtedly remember, Sir, the first lessons you gave me on liberty. They have not been lost. Nor are you unaware, perhaps, of what I did to be free. But am I free? I am enclosing a small parish certificate of my enfranchisement. Today I am virtually reduced to begging, since all employment is refused. I am obliged to give language classes to subsist. The years weigh on me and my soul ages, *mea duodenum trepidavit aetas claudere Lustrum.* I would like to see you again, but the immense ocean terrifies me. Accept therefore, Sir, from afar, all my wishes for your prosperity. They are wishes for the prosperity of the nation that has the good fortune of having you for a leader. And let me know somehow, I beg you, if I may still honor myself with the title of your friend. *Vale Vir optime.*

Your very devoted servant, PIO

RC (DLC); ellipses in original; below dateline: "Rue St. honoré, prés S. Roch., maison du Libraire, no. 144" (Saint Honoré Street near the Church of Saint Roch, at the bookseller's shop, no. 144); endorsed by TJ as received 17 Aug. and so recorded in SJL. Enclosure not found, returned to Pio by TJ (see TJ to Pio, 31 Jan. 1804).

HOMMAGES RESPECTUEUX: a letter from Pio of 18 May 1797, received from Paris on 8 Sep. of that year, is recorded in SJL but has not been found. TJ and Pio became acquainted in 1784, when Pio was chargé d'affaires in Paris of the kingdom of Naples and TJ, Benjamin Franklin, and John Adams sought to negotiate treaties between the United States and various countries. TJ subsequently discussed with Pio his project for a multinational union against the Barbary states, and the two were friends the remainder of the time TJ was in France. In 1790, Pio received French citizenship from the commune of Paris and cut his ties with Naples. During the French Revolution he held positions in the ministry of foreign affairs and the bureau of war. He aligned himself with radical revolutionaries, made public accusations against several leaders, and survived being denounced himself. Before the revolution Pio had become a chevalier of a religious order, the Order of Saint Stephen (Albert Mathiez, "Le Chevalier Pio," *Annales révolutionnaires*,

11 [1919], 94-104; Albert Mathiez, *La Révolution et les Étrangers* [Paris, 1918], 105, 118, 126, 176; Vol. 7:424, 612-14; Vol. 8:309; Vol. 10:88, 561; Vol. 11:248, 255, 382; Vol. 16:47, 230-1; Vol. 20: 662-3).

In writing MEA DUODENUM TREPIDAVIT AETAS CLAUDERE LUSTRUM, Pio adapted a passage in which Horace lamented that he had turned 40 years of age: "cuius octavum trepidavit aetas claudere lustrum" (Horace, *Odes*, 2.4.23-4). In Pio's revision, 60 was the age that caused trepidation.

VALE VIR OPTIME: "farewell, best man."

[1]MS: "rappeller."

From William Short

New York, 2 Apr. 1803. Replying to TJ's letter of 23 Mch., he advises TJ not to sell the land the president recently purchased. He prefers waiting for TJ's payments to him, rather than causing regret. Before departing for Kentucky, Short will leave a power of attorney for his New York brokers, Lewis & Lawrence, who will receive payments and apply them on his behalf. He promises to send TJ a copy of his statement on the debt between them as soon as he can transcribe it. He wishes he could see the president, but a visit will have to wait for his return. It is possible, though barely, that he might choose to return to Europe by way of the Mississippi. He mentions John Durrett's offer for a portion of his Albemarle land and also a proposal to sell all of the land to John Wickham.

FC (DLC: Short Papers); 1 p.; entirely in Short's hand, consisting of an entry in his epistolary record. Recorded in SJL as received from New York on 7 Apr.

Short's stockbrokers Francis Lewis and Augustus H. Lawrence kept the firm's office at 40 Wall Street, New York (Joseph A. Scoville, *The Old Merchants of New York City*, 3d ser. [New York, 1865], 104; *Longworth's American Almanac, New York Register, and City Directory, for the Twenty Seventh Year of American Independence* [New York, 1802], 252).

John Wickham had expressed interest in Short's Albemarle land to George Jefferson, but Jefferson informed Short that Wickham would probably only purchase the property if he could "get it at less than its value" (George Jefferson to William Short, 10 Mch. 1803, in DLC: Short Papers).

From Justus Erich Bollmann

SIR, Philada. April 3d. 1803

I have duely received Your Excellency's Letter of the 4th of March and have forwarded by the Sloop Highland, Cap. Hand, to the address of Mr. Jams. Eakin, a Box of the Wine of Your Choice. Your Order for One gross of Bottles of Wine of the same Quality will be duely attended to.—

It is not in my Power to inform Your Excellency by which particular Name this Wine is designated or which is the Place of its Growth. But I have made Inquiries to that Effect and shall learn it in autumn. It is much to be regretted that the Navigation of the Danube is not open, for otherwise these Wines, as well as many other valuable Productions and Manufactures of Hungary and Austria might be imported into this Country by Way of the black Sea and the Mediteranean at very moderate Prices, but I think it is not improbable that the Turks will be soon obliged either to change their Policy or to quit Europe.

I have forwarded to Gen. Lafayette a Copy of the Law to which You allude in your letter and requested him to entrust me with his Powers to make the locations.

The February Packet has brought me a Letter from London which contains a Quotation of the Prices of the various kinds of meat &c. on the 11th of January last, which I take the liberty of mentioning to Your Excellency since it appears to me that such Prices must either effect an Increase of the Wages of Labour or a stock of Misery among the labouring Part of the Comunity which can hardly fail to produce in the Progress of Time political Effects of the utmost magnitude.

Beefstakes 1 sh. sterling pr. lb.
Fish. 2 sh. 3 sh. 4 sh. pr. lb. according to Quality
Fowles 4 sh 6d to 9 sh. *each*
Turkies 10 sh. to 25 sh. each.
Woodcocks 5 sh. each
Veal 1 sh to 1 sh. 6d.
Pork 11½ d—

I remain with great Respect Your Excellency's most obt. hble St.

J. ERICH BOLLMANN

RC (MHi); at foot of text: "The President of the United States"; endorsed by TJ as received 6 Apr. and so recorded in SJL.

In part of an act continuing military land grants, LAFAYETTE received 11,520 acres north of the Ohio River, above its confluence with the Kentucky River (U.S. Statutes at Large, 2:236).

From Albert Gallatin

SIR Treasury Department 4th April 1803

I have the honor to enclose the copy of a letter from Samuel Hay one of the commissioners for the direct tax in South Carolina. As the assessment is not yet completed in that State, and the principal cause of the delay has been the difficulty of finding gentlemen who would accept the office, the propriety of appointing the gentlemen recommended by Mr Hay is respectfully submitted.

I have the honor to be with great respect Sir Your most obedt. Servt.

ALBERT GALLATIN

RC (DLC); at foot of text: "The President of the United States"; endorsed by TJ as received from the Treasury Department on 5 Apr. and "Charles Jones Jenkins to be Commr. Direct tax S.C." and so recorded in SJL. Enclosure: Samuel Hay to Gallatin, Coosawhatchie, South Carolina, 17 Mch. 1803, submitting his resignation as Direct Tax commissioner for the state's fifth division, noting that his physician has prescribed "a European Voyage as absolutely necessary to the preservation of Life"; he recommends Charles Jones Jenkins, who lives in the neighborhood, is fully qualified, and will accept the position if offered; his appointment will keep the state from "procrastinating the business already too long procrastinated" (Tr in same).

An Adams appointee, SAMUEL HAY had served as commissioner since 1798. TJ recorded the appointment of Charles Jones Jenkins in place of Hay at 8 Apr. (see Appendix I). Jenkins's permanent commission was issued on 18 Nov. after his confirmation by the Senate (FC in Lb in DNA: RG 59, MPTPC; JEP, 1:297, 453, 455). For previous difficulties in finding candidates willing to accept the office of DIRECT TAX commissioner in South Carolina, see Vol. 34:136, 543; Vol. 36:625-6; and Vol. 37:189-90.

From Benjamin H. Latrobe

DEAR SIR, [4 Apr. 1803]

I arrived here about a fortnight ago, and have been so unwell since then, as not to be quite so forward in my report upon the state of the Capitol, and the necessary drawings as I could have wished. On this account, and because I believed that on your first arrival your time would be taking up by more important objects,—I have not yet waited upon you. Late this evening however, I will, with your permission, transmit to you my report, & some drawings, and if convenient, I will attend you at as early an hour as you may appoint tomorrow morning. Perhaps you may then have had time to read and consider my report.

When I left Philadelphia, Mrs. Latrobe was exceedingly unwell, and as she is in a situation to expect daily an increase of her family,—I am naturally anxious to return home as soon as possible,—& you would add to the obligations I owe to you,—if you could pay an early attention to the objects you have pleased to submit to me, so as to decide on what shall be done. I have already so prepared every thing, that the prelimary work may commence immediately & go on vigorously during my absence.—

I am with true respect Yrs. faithfully B H LATROBE

RC (DLC); undated; endorsed by TJ as received 4 Apr. and so recorded in SJL.

INCREASE OF HER FAMILY: the Latrobes' son, John Hazlehurst Boneval Latrobe, was born on 4 May (Latrobe, *Correspondence*, 1:289n).

From Benjamin H. Latrobe

Dear Sir, [4 Apr. 1803]

I herewith send you my report & the ground plan of the new wing. I fear I shall tire your patience, but I know not what I could have omitted.—

I am with true respect Yrs. faithfully B H Latrobe.

RC (DLC); undated; endorsed by TJ as received 4 Apr. and so recorded in SJL.

ENCLOSURE

Report on the Ground Plan of the Capitol's New Wing

Sir

Agreeably to your instructions I arrived at Washington on the 21st of March, and have since that time devoted my attention to the objects proposed by your letter of the 6th of March.

After having very carefully and minutely examined the present state of the Capitol as far as it has been completed, and the foundations of the South Wing, which it is proposed to carry forward this season, I now submit to you the following report,—in which, that my motives in the alterations I shall propose may be fully understood,—I shall be under the necessity of entering into the consideration of the general plan at some length.—I beg leave to add that the remarks to which I pray your attention, have been fully communicated and explained to——, the original author of the plan; a communication which I felt to be due to him, not only as a matter of politeness and ceremony, but as a just tribute of respect to his talents.

In considering the general plan of the Capitol the first remark that occurs is; that by the mode in which the exterior appearance has been connected with the internal arrangement,—a radical and incurable fault has been grafted upon the work, and made an essential part of it. The building has the appearance of a principal floor elevated upon a basement story.[1] But in the interior all this expectation is disappointed, the Porticoes lead only to the Galleries and committee rooms, and to get into the Halls of Legislation, it is necessary to descend a flight of stairs.—[2]

In the internal arrangement of the building another inconvenience results from this error. The grand Vestibule, the Senate chamber, and the Hall of the representatives present but one design. For though the vestibule is circular, the Senate chamber, a semiellipsis, and the Hall of representatives a full ellipsis, and though a variety may be produced by varying the detail of decoration,—the same principle remains,—viz, a high collonade upon a low arcade,—exhibiting a poverty of design, which is as little compatible with the talents of Doctor Thornton as it would have been necessary, had the principal Halls been upon a level with the floor of the Porticos.

To correct the error of landing one story too high is impossible in the present advanced state of the work. I shall therefore dismiss the subject.

The Senate chamber independently of its slight construction and the badness of workmanship is otherwise a handsome room, and should justice be done to the vestibule in the execution,—Europe will not be able to exhibit a more magnificent public Saloon.—It will be worthy of the intention of the building.

It is proposed that the Hall of conference shall be on the floor of the Porticos, which obviates every objection to that beautiful part of the plan; though a basement story will be lost.

I now come to the proposed Hall of representatives which in the original plan occupies with the stair case and a few committee rooms above the Galleries, 40 feet from the ground,—the whole of the South wing.

To this arrangement I think it my duty to state to you my objections, and

1., As they respect use and convenience.

For the commodious dispatch of business by the House of representatives it appears to me that the following appartments should be closely attached to the legislative Hall.—

1., Three or four committee rooms.—
2., A chamber for the Speaker in which he may transact such business with the members or others as does not require his sitting in the chair of the House.—
3., An office for the Clerk of the House.—
4., Offices of the engrossing clerks, 2 rooms.—
5., An apartment for the door keeper where he may assort and keep printed papers for delivery to the members distribute letters and preserve the articles belonging to his office.—
6., Another for subordinate officers of the House.—
7., Closets of convenience.—
8., Fire proof repositories of records.—
9., A lobby sufficient for the convenient retirement of a large number of members from the House, but not adapted to the purposes of a Gallery. The lobbies of the House of representatives and Senate, as hitherto used have been greviously complained against as serious nuisances,—and in the Senate the Vice President has given notice that he should not permit the introduction of strangers into the lobby as heretofore during the next session.—
10., A commodious gallery, not only overlooking the House,—but competely commanded by the view of the officers of the House, and accessible in such a manner that the members passing from one part of the building to another, shall never be interrupted by the persons entering or coming from the gallery.—

My objections to the plan proposed—originally—arise from the want of all these accommodations excepting only of such apartments as may be placed in the South East recess and in the projection between the legislative Hall and the conference room which must of necessity be badly lighted, or in the attic story above the gallery,—a situation remote and accessible only by a flight of 80 steps. Two only of these latter rooms are private, the two others being thoroughfares.—

It has always been understood that the upper story of the north wing would supply the apartments above enumerated,—But as the rooms on the Basement story contiguous to the Senate chamber will probably be appropriated to the use of that branch of the legislature, the upper stories alone will remain for the House of representatives, and a distance of at least 200 feet must be traversed to reach them. It will also be necessary that the members and officers of the House should pass through the people attending in the grand vestibule. This must be at all times unpleasant, and often highly inconvenient.—

I have already mentioned the inconvenience of a lobby calculated to serve the purposes of a gallery. The lobby which is proposed to surround the legislative Hall has all the inconveniences of a lobby within the walls of the House, without the advantage of being controuled by the view of officers of the House. Its size invites a croud, of which the intervening piers prevent the view,—and it is impossible to pass from the House without mingling with the persons in the lobby.

The gallery is inconvenient not only from its massy columns in front, but chiefly from the distance of the front seats from the edge of the area of the House, which unavoidably covers twenty feet of the floor from the sight of the persons in the first row of seats and still more from those behind.

2., As they respect safe practicability.—

The South wing of the Capitol consists of only two enclosures,—An external wall 65 feet high, and an internal enclosure consisting below of an elliptical arcade, and above of a range of 32 massy columns with their entablature. Between these two enclosures there is no possible bond or connection excepting the floor of the gallery, and that of the proposed committee rooms, which are to be lighted by the Attic windows.—Although it is not eligible in any case where it can be avoided, to carry up a wall so thin, so pierced with windows to so great a heighth without support by bond with internal walls or external projections, it would be in the present instance a still more daring attempt, when a domed roof of 90 feet span by 120 is to be carried, and all its lateral thrust resisted at the heighth of 60 feet from the ground.—My ideas on the safety of such a work are best explained by declaring that I want the courage necessary to embolden me to attempt it.

3., As they respect the taste of its architecture.—

It is impossible to deprive a series of 32 columns 25 feet in heighth of an effect singularly striking, and at first sight, pleasantly impressive; nor would the first effect produced be diminished by the frequency of looking at them, were the figure inclosed by the colonade an agreeable one in every point of view. But an ellipsis seen in perspective from any point not lying in one of its axes, has a distorted appearance, the parts on each side being of different figures. Nothing is so well known as that the eye judges of the forms and relative sizes of objects by the habit unconsciously acquired of reducing, their natural appearance in perspective, to orthographical projection. The eye is habituated to judge of circles and of rectilineal figures,—but ellipses occur seldom; no habit exists of judging of their lines perpetually varying in the principle of their progression, and they have always a distorted effect.—Experience proves the truth of this assertion, and therefore both architects and scene painters have substituted in their room parallelograms bounded by semicircles.—

This is a general objection to elliptical rooms. But another objection to the elliptical form of a colonade surmounted by a spheroidal dome occurs which is of more importance.—All the lines of the entablature, and of every other moulding of ever so small projection are lines belonging to parallel,—or to use an incorrect phrase, concentric ellipses. If the lines be accurately drawn, they become distorted in perspective by their having each a separate and different law of curvature, for the last of an infinite series of parallel ellipses is a straight line, equal to the distance of the foci. The bad effect of the attempt even at plain elliptical domes is well illustrated by the sky light of the stairs in the north wing of the Capitol.

If the cieling of the Hall be pannelled (the most beautiful mode of decoration) it will have the distorted effect of every other elliptical pannelled dome, of which in the first revival of arts a few have been attempted, for in each tier there will be only 4 pannels of equal forms and size.

The gallery and lobby have forms the most unpleasant.—The eye always judges of the form of a room by its cieling, for that is the only space in which the view can freely range. When it therefore becomes necessary to sacrifice the form of an apartment to more important arrangements, a cieling—ingeniously disposed—often hides the difficulty that has been encountered. But such an attempt would be vain, where the windows and their piers, considered relatively to the columns which form the opposite bound of the space, are disposed without the most distant reference to lines drawn either to the center, or to the foci, of the ellipsis. And that this is the case in the proposed plan, a slight inspection must evince.

Having spent several days in fruitless attempts to lay down a system of simple decoration for this apartment satisfactory to my habits of taste I have found myself wholly without the talents necessary to the task; and should be very unwilling to labor further in a field in which it is difficult to escape censure, and impossible to reap reputation.

4., As they respect expense.—

A very great expense ought to produce a permanent work:—and yet if the south wing be finished in the manner proposed the whole of the internal work, excepting the arcade, the colonade and its entablature must be of timber,—and of course liable to be destroyed by fire in a few hours: and the expense will be excessive.—

The columns may be either of Timber, cased with plank glued up; of timber frames, lathed and plaistered or stuccoed;—of bricks stuccoed;—of freestone plain or fluted;—or of Pennsylvanian marble.—Of all these materials the latter would probably be the most eligible, and the two first the least so. The columns of the senate room which are of Plaister upon frames are already tumbling to pieces. Brick columns stuccoed are extremely liable to injury, especially when exposed in a public gallery to the hands of a promiscuous croud.—Freestone columns therefore would perhaps, considering their smaller expense, with their permanence, be preferred to Marble, and I will proceed upon an idea of a freestone series of columns of the Corinthian or Attic order. Such a column would be 2 feet 6 inches in diameter and 25 high, the whole order being 30 feet, and could not be executed with their capitals, and placed, under 1200 dollars each column, including every expense. The Entablature 5 feet high, architrave frieze and enriched Cornice, would be a work requiring the most expert workmen, and the most watchful superintendence in the execution. The number of massy stones required would amount to at least 200, and the number of moulds to which they must be wrought would be double that number, for every projection would require a separate mould.—The *practical* difficulties attending the execution are incalculable. In a circle every stone fits every where, and the last stone which is set, is the only one the size of which is *not* arbitrary. But in an ellipsis each stone has its determined place from which if it be moved the smallest perceptible distance the line of curvature is destroyed, and the work spoiled.—To calculate the value of time, care, disappointment, and destruction of materials occasioned by this circumstance is impossible,—but at a moderate rate the Entablature supposing the architrave to carry the cieling of the gallery would cost 24.000 dollars.

32 columns at 1200 each are	$38.400
Entablature	24.000
	62.400.

As large as this amount appears, I believe that it would be found scarcely adequate to the completion of the work in a perfect and masterly manner.

5., I might also start objections to the fluttering and scanty light of that part of the room in which the legislative body must sit,—to the impossibility of warming the lobby and the gallery, and to the probable difficulty of speaking and hearing.

Under all these impressions of the imperfections of the plan of the South wing of the Capitol, and after having bestowed much time and study in a vain attempt to preserve its principal features, and to combine with them such accommodations for the use of the legislative body as seem absolutely indispensible,—I have thought it my duty to lay before you an arrangement entirely different from that proposed by the original plan.

This arrangement is explained in the plans and sections hereto annexed.—The form of the Hall is that of the ancient theatre (excedra),[3]—a form which the experience of ancient and modern times has established as the best for the purpose of speaking, seeing and hearing. The area of the Hall rather exceeds that of the elliptical design, and will hold with ease a body of 360 members, leaving sufficient room on the floor of the House. The principal entrance to this Hall will be from the grand vestibule, through a square lobby and colonade. On the south front will also be an entrance into the lobby behind the Speaker's chair. This lobby, intended for the retirement of members in order to confer with each other or to receive their friends, will be 80 feet in length, and can never be used as a gallery unless it should be thought proper to break the Wall into an arcade. This I presume will not be done, for if it be thought expedient that Ladies or particular friends of the members should be introduced on the floor of the House, there is ample room for them behind the last row of the seats, where a passage of 5 feet will be left open.

On the East and West fronts are the entrances to the public gallery by means of a stair case in each angle. This gallery,—while it commands a full view of the House facing the members,—is also under the compleat inspection of the officers of the House, whose place is at the north end of the Hall. On each side are also galleries, which may be either appropriated to public use, or reserved for the admission of particular persons.

In the north east angle of the wing is a commodious room appropriated to the clerk of the House, in which his chief clerk may sit, and in the third story above, the inferior and engrossing clerks may be accommodated. The stair case in the recess furnishes the communication with these apartments. At the north west angle is a room appropriated to the use of the Speaker.

In the second story of the east, and in the second and third stories of the West front are commodious committee rooms, to each of which is attached an office for the papers and documents belonging to the Committee. It would have been desirable to have attached to this wing, a greater number of Committee rooms,—but the size of the building forbids it, and should a greater number of committee rooms be wanted, they must be found in the North wing.—

By the necessary result of the general arrangement of the plan, there is an absolute want of light in all that part of the building which lies between the Wings and the center of the building. I have therefore appropriated it to a grand stair case,—to closets,—and to the offices of the door keeper and his assistants. The latter rooms will be lighted from the lower tier of arches of the House, the stair cases from the sky, and the closets by side lights from the staircase and from a small court which becomes necessary for light as well as domestic use,—for it must contain a pump or cistern, and a sink to take off water, and it is a great error in the general design of a building insulated in every side, and which has no cellar conveniences, that no open court of convenient dimensions exists within it.—

On the first floor, independently of the committee rooms, there will be,—a vestibule to the grand gallery, extending from the Stair case to the court, and lighted from the latter,—and a spacious repository of records over the offices of the doorkeeper, to which the access is from the vestibule, and the light from the stairs and open court.

The Hall of Representatives is lighted from the south front, and from a spacious lanthorn light in the center of the half dome.

The whole plan of the Wing as proposed is so arranged as to be capable of being vaulted in every part, and has been so adapted to the external elevation, that every apartment is perfectly symetrical.

I will beg leave to submit one observation on the expense which is *supposed* to attend vaulted buildings, as applicable to the present.—

The external walls are not altered:

The basement story of the internal enclosure is the same:

The internal enclosure above, contains 1.120 perch of stone work, which if executed with great precision and unusual care, and allowing for arches and nich heads, will cost not more than 5 dollars per perch say 5.600 dollars:

The colonade and entablature would cost at least 62.400 dollars,—the saving therefore will be at least 56.800 dollars in this respect:

The centering of the great dome will not be nearly equal in expense to the framing of a free roof of 120 feet by 96, but allowing it to be equal, no additional expense will arise in that article:

The vault and arches of the great Hall will contain less than 100.000 Bricks. As these bricks must be laid with unusual care, and at a great hight, and must probably be brought from Philadelphia so as to cost on the spot about 9 dollars per thousand,—I will estimate the expense of labor and all materials at 15 dollars per thousand instead of 13 dollars, the expense of the dome of the Bank of Pennsylvania.—at this estimate, the whole vault would cost 1.500 dollars,—which deducted from 56.800 still leaves a savings of 55.300 dollars. The expense of finishing in Stucco is in favor of the vault, as the whole expense of Blocking and Firring, and of all Laths and Nails, is saved.

As to the arches of the Basement story, they are so small in their dimensions, that they will exceed the expense of common well framed floors immaterially. But allowing 5.300 dollars for this excess of expense,—it is still clear that a saving of 50.000 dollars will be effected by the change of plan,—should the Colonade and Entablature be executed in stone; and if in the cheapest manner in timber, of at least 20.000 dollars.—

With these observations, I beg to submit to you the plans which accompany this letter.

I have now to state to you the measures which I have thought it necessary to pursue, in order to commence and prepare the work of the season.

Having understood that the foundation Walls of the South wing, which are carried up to the level at which the Work in freestone is to begin, had not been faithfully executed,—I caused them to be opened in several places, and on different levels, and find that they are on no account fit to bear the weight which is to be laid above them. The stones appear to have been loosely thrown between two thin external casings without mortar, and even without being made to bear upon each other. It is necessary therefore that the whole of this work should be taken down to the first offset; below which I am well informed that the work has been faithfully performed.

I have also caused the foundation Wall of the building in which the House of representatives sat during their last session, and which seems to have been intended for the permanent Basement of the elliptical Colonade,—to be opened in several places beneath the windows.—I have, in every instance discovered it to be of bad workmanship,—but in most of the places which I have examined, it consists also of small stones loosely thrown into a thin casing. I judge this wall to be wholly unfit to carry the weight of the colonade, and of the roof, and as the brick work, above, has been forced from 2 to 6 inches out of perpendicular by the roof,—I do not hesitate in declaring it to be my opinion that the whole building ought to be pulled down to the offset, even if the elliptical colonade be executed. And this must be done, not only on account of the wretched workmanship of the foundation walls, but because, with the best workmanship, no colonade carrying a heavy superstructure can be safely constructed unless its pressure be spread over the whole foundation by means of counter arches. The fissures in the walls of the south wing are entirely owing to the omission of such precaution.

In order that no delay might injure the progress of the work during your absence, I have,—with the concurrence of the Superintendant of the City,—proceeded to such measures as were of the first necessity.

The whole of the foundation Walls which must be pulled down consist of small stones. They are unfit for any purpose but to work up in the Wall with larger stone, and I have therefore contracted with Mr. Elliot, a respectable citizen, to furnish, at the price of $1.75 pr. Perch, 750 perch of large flat stone, none of which are to contain less than 3 feet on the surface, and to be from 5 to 9 inches thick. Mr. Elliot has already begun to deliver the stone. The wharfs at which materials were formerly delivered to the Commissioners being entirely out of repair, and the water in front rendered insufficient by the rubbish thrown into it, I have had the necessary repairs made to these wharves, and they are now fit to receive the rough stone, sand and other light materials. I have also repaired the bridge over the Canal, and mended the road from the upper wharf to the Pennsylvania avenue. The stone recovered in front of the wharves has amply repaid the expense of the work.

In respect to the work to be executed in cut stone, I find that it has hitherto been the custom to provide the stone to the Stonecutter, and to agree with him to cut and set it either by the day or by measurement. This method of doing the business is decidedly against the interest of the public.—All the risks are thrown upon the public,—of loss by labor in the quarry,—by false measurement,—by unsound stone,—by the danger of navigation,—and by faulty workmanship. Each of these operations requires separate and trusty agents;—the attention of the architect to the work is distracted by so many distant scenes of superintendance. If an expensive stone be so faulty in its workmanship as to be rejected,—though the workman lose his labor, the public lose the material. This was found to be the case, when on a trial, some tons of stones were proved to have been buried in the rubbish. Besides, in the œconomy of the material, waste cannot be avoided when the ease of the workman is often interested in cutting up a large block, when another, with somewhat more labor would have answered the purpose.

For these and many other reasons, I beg leave to recommend a contract with Mr. Blagden for the stone, cut ready to be set in the Wall, and I have prepared and delivered the terms of such a contract as I conceive to be for the interests of the work, to the Superintendant.—The stone work of the South wing, erected by Mr. Blagden, and his well known character, seem to authorize the expectation that so important a contract will be well executed by him.—

About 230 Tierces of New England lime have been purchased, which appears to be of a good quality.

In the supply of Scaffolding poles, ropes, sand plank and boards, no difficulty will occur.—There are several sets of good Blocks in the possession of the Superintendant, but two good hoisting Engines must be made.

I have now to report to you the state of the
North Wing of the Capitol.—

It is much to be feared that unless some openings be made to admit air into the Cellars, the Timbers of the floor will, in the course of a few years be consumed by what is termed the dry-rot.—This is the most dangerous of decays, because when it has once established itself in the Cellar story, it never fails to climb to the top of the House unperceived untill the surface of the woodwork is broken, or some material failure in the floors betrays it. For the dry-rot will consume a fixed and painted piece of wood work, untill a shell, one tenth of an inch thick remains, without injuring its appearance in the least. This species of rot almost always begins in unventilated cellars.—It is also on another account necessary that the Light and Air should be admitted to this part of the building. There is not any other means of warming the Senate chamber but by flues either to convey fire, or pipes to convey steam along the floor. The latter are the best, and now universally used in England in large apartments, as the fire flues have long been, in France and Holland.

On the state of repair of the Senate chamber and the necessity of warming it by some other means than those in use, I will report separately should you think it necessary.

The leakage of the roof, which has so much injured the Wall and Cielings of many parts of the house arises from the bad system of carrying off the water; from the bad quality of the lead used; from the joints of the sheets being soldered by which they appear to have been in many places torn; from the broken glass of the sky lights; and from the leakiness of the Cistern.

1., From the bad system of carrying off the Water.—

All the water is at present collected from evry gutter and discharged into one deep Cistern. After collecting in the gutters along the parapet, it is brought under the roofs, in many gutters, into the internal Area of the roof, so that the chance of leakage is greatly multiplied. It appears to me that the very great length of gutter, and the attempt to keep the roof as low as possible, has prevented a sufficient current being given to the Gutters. The aversion to Water pipes on the outside of buildings has been another cause of this erroneous mode of draining the roof. As, however the cistern appears to have no possible use, and there are corners of the buildings in which Water pipes may be advantageously brought down, I would suggest, as the only means of obtaining a water tight roof,—that the water from A to B be discharged through an external Water pipe at B, into a court yard which must be made in front of the brick part of the building now carried up, and which, though it was built to be pulled down again, ought to remain standing,—because, in the original design no light can be received from the West to this whole pile of handsome rooms and only a scanty light from the north from a window in the corner.

Besides, a court yard is absolutely necessary, *somewhere* for Privies, and other domestic purposes of Cleanliness, and I have in my plan provided for one for the South Wing.—All the space discharging the Water by this pipe is coloured *blue.*—

From A to C I propose to discharge the Water through an external pipe in the corner of the recess where it will be entirely hidden. The space supplying this water is coloured *yellow.*

From D to E I propose to discharge the Water through an external pipe in the other corner of the recess.—This space is coloured *red.*—

From F to G I propose to discharge the water into the present Waste pipe of the Cistern, which leads to a drain from the Cellar story.—This space is coloured *green.* All the shingling is remarkably good. It will be a great pity to desturb it, and yet I fear that it must not only be disturbed but destroyed, for I believe that all the gutters must be taken up,—because, though of lead, they are coated with tar and sand so as to prevent the possibility of seeing where they are faulty altho' nothing is more evident than that they are so.—When laid again, it must be with a much greater descent, and the roof will well admit of it.—

All the Gutters, at present passing under the roof, will become useless. Their lead will go some way towards paying the expense of the new arrangements.

2., Of the bad quality of the lead I have heard only from those who were present when it was laid. It must be examined when taken up.

3., Wherever the sheets have been soldered they must, if laid down again, be cut and groved together, with a good drip.—

4., Sky lights, unless made of thick Coach glass, with Metal frames, always leak. Even then they are great evils, for in summer they heat the house, and in winter they become darkened and often broken by the snow. But Lanthorn lights can always be made tight, their light is pleasant, in summer they can be opened and they cool the house, and in Winter they retain the advantage of a common sash. I propose therefore, as the only effectual method of curing the leaks arising from the Sky lights, to substitute in their room, Lanthorn lights,—that is, lights with upright Sashes and close tops. The sells of the sashes of the Lanthorn must be raised sufficiently to admit of a sloping roof to them instead of the flat, now existing. This will permanently cure leakage. I will remark at the same time that the Sky lights, as now built, are a disgrace to the architect and the workmen in their appearance, and ought to be altered if on no other account.

5., It is difficult to guess for what purpose the Cistern was intended, as it is not provided with any means of discharge.—Were it on the ground floor, or even in the Cellar story, and furnished with a good forcing pump, it could have been made exceedingly useful in case of fire. It is useless now even for the purposes of washing.—The leak in the Library has its rise from this cistern. It must be taken down, and perhaps placed below, and furnished with a forcing pump. The lead is valuable. The Waste pipe will act as a rain water pipe.

Submitting the above to your consideration—

I am, with respect—Your faithful humble Servant—

B Henry Latrobe

Washington City 4th April 1803.

MS (DLC); entirely in Latrobe's hand; at foot of text: "The President of the United States"; endorsed by TJ as received 4 Apr. and so recorded in SJL.

The GENERAL PLAN OF THE CAPITOL was a revision of William Thornton's original design, which had been deemed impracticable. While secretary of state, TJ had concurred with an altered design offered by Stephen Hallet, who retained Thornton's exterior elevation but changed elements of the interior plan. TJ later claimed credit for persuading Thornton to place the House chamber on the basement level (Dorothy Twohig, ed., *The Journal of the Proceedings of the President, 1793-1797* [Charlottesville, 1981], 198-99; Vol. 26:517-19; RS, 3: 555-6).

George BLAGDEN had already proposed a contract for the stonework of the South Wing to Thomas Munroe. He estimated the combined cost for free stone, black stone, and brick, along with the cutting and carving, to be about $18,000, and anticipated Latrobe's own condemnation of the South Wing's present foundation, deeming it unsafe "to erect a building of such magnitude thereon" (George Blagden to Thomas Munroe, 20 Dec. 1802, in DLC, endorsed by TJ: "Estimate S. wing of Capitol").

[1] Latrobe here canceled: "A magnificent flight of steps leads up to the Portico on the West front, and that towards the East, though placed upon an arcade has the effect of belonging to that floor.—"

[2] Latrobe here canceled: "On stating this remark to the author—he informed me that his first idea was that of a grand single story raised upon a basement sufficiently elevated to contain conveniently all the offices attached to the legislative bodies. On the floor of the principal story it was intended that the legislative bodies should hold their sittings. The access to this floor was to be by two grand flights of steps in the center of the East and West fronts. Reasons afterwards occurred by which he was induced to lower the altitude and diminish the diameters of his Columns: and in order that the general heighth of the building might not be thereby diminished, the Basement story was raised to one third of the whole heighth. As the diminished altitude of the principal story was no longer fitted to the high proportions of the Halls of the legislature, they were, without altering the features of the original ground plot,—let down to the level of the basement story.

On the East front the Portico, an entrance worthy of the grandest internal arrangements, being placed upon an arcade, is reduced to a mere balcony: if furnished with a flight of steps, such as it seems to demand, it will lead up to a narrow Gallery, from which the approach to the legislative Halls is by descending the internal stairs of the house. The same fault exists on the West front. The steps lead up a story too high."

[3] Preceding word and parentheses interlined.

From James B. Richardson

SIR, Charleston 4. April 1803.

The requisitions made by you in pursuance of the request from the House of Representatives of the United States have been received, and shall be duly attended to; all vigorous exertions shall be used to put this State in the best possible situation of defence by having the Militia diciplin'd and well armed, the latter of which they are deficient in, tho' the attention of the Legislature has been engaged on that subject, and considerable appropriations made for the purchase of arms, the greater part of which, has been expended in contracts, that I am in hourly expectation will be fullfil'd, which will then enable the state of South Carolina to be more formidable in defence, and the assertion of her infringed rights, which I flatter myself she will be ever willing and ready to do, against any power that may invade or oppress. I have directed the Adjutant General of the State to furnish you immediately with the return of Militia, their arms and accoutrements &c, and the State of the Arsenals and Magazine, in compliance with the Act of Congress on that subject, and in conformity with a copy of a return some time since received from the Secretary of War of the United States, which no doubt will be expeditiously transmitted you by that officer. With respect to the geographical divisions of the State, I cannot better at this time delineate, than by observing that it is divided into twenty six districts under a late judiciary regulation, six of which are situate on the Sea Coast, and in case of a war, would be subject to many ravages, as they are penetrable by small vessels, from their contiguous situation to Rivers and inlets; they are also more extensive in Territory than the interior or upper districts, and less in population, as upon the latter principle the division appears to have been founded. It is indeed to be desired that the violation of rights essential to our wellfare, and the infraction of treaty, may be found the unauthorised act of a subordinate agent, and not the leading measures of a System, in which case the negotiation presents a prospect of a peaceable redress of the injury, and I hope, will effectually provide against its repetition; for the continuation of peace to our Country is an object worthy of our best endeavors to retain; it is at all times desirable, but more especially so, when we are but just recover'd from the excessive depredations, sustained in the struggle for independence: yet those objects however desirable, the advantages however great, and the enjoyment however pleasing, must be lost to remembrance when their preservation is hazardous to the dignity and reputation of the nation which I assure you, of my prompt cooperation in any measures for its support.

With high considerations of respect and esteem I am
Sir Your most obedient JAMES B. RICHARDSON

RC (PHi); at foot of text: "Tho. Jefferson President of the United States"; endorsed by TJ as received 20 Apr. and so recorded in SJL with notation "W."

REQUISITIONS MADE BY YOU: Circular to the Governors of the States, 25 Feb. 1803.

ADJUTANT GENERAL OF THE STATE: Laurence Manning, who was also Richardson's brother-in-law (*S.C. Biographical Directory, House of Representatives*, 3:475-6). A militia return from Manning dated 10 June 1802 is recorded in SJL as received by TJ on 1 July of that year, but has not been found. A notation by TJ next to the entry recorded 35,785 total infantry and cavalry for the state, but only 13,000 firearms (Vol. 37:717).

For the circular letter from the SECRETARY OF WAR regarding annual militia returns by the states, see TJ to the House of Representatives, 5 Jan. 1803.

From Joseph Yznardi, Sr.

SIR— Cadiz 4th. April 1803—

I had the honour of writing you the 12th August ultimo, acquainting you of my safe arrival here, and my intentions of going up to Madrid from which place I am just return'd.

The advices given to the Secretary of State James Madison Esqr. concerning the Quarenteen been reduced to Twenty Days thro my personal acquaintance application to the Minister has no doubt been laid before you, and I am happy to see that my Sollicitations to the Court of Madrid has been attended with such benefit to our flagg—

I beg leave to assure you that my utmost exertions will always be govern'd by the Interest of that Country & to merit your full approbation in every respect.

Notwithstanding the reports of an approaching rupture between England & France, we still hope to enjoy the blessings of Peace, & that our trade may thereby encrease to the very utmost extent.

I have the honour to be with the most profound Respect—Sir. Your most obedt, humble servt. JOSEF YZNARDY

RC (DLC); in a clerk's hand, signed by Yznardi; at foot of text: "To the Honourable Thomas Jefferson—President of the United States of America—Washington"; endorsed by TJ as received 23 May and so recorded in SJL.

QUARENTEEN: the Spanish government had banned all ships arriving from Philadelphia. Vessels arriving from other ports in the United States were subject to a 40-day quarantine. Finding Charles Pinckney to be away from Madrid, Yznardi, as he wrote to Madison on 4 Apr., took the matter up with the Spanish MINISTER of state, Pedro Cevallos, and obtained some loosening of the restrictions. Yznardi continued to pursue the issue and informed Madison in a letter of 20 Apr. that the Spanish had lifted the quarantine for ships that had health certificates from Spanish consuls in the U.S. Ships without such certificates would be subject to only a brief quarantine (Madison, *Papers*, *Sec. of State Ser.*, 4:195, 477, 542; Vol. 37:675n).

From Edward Dowse

SIR, Dedham Massachusetts 5 April 1803

The extraordinary merit of this little treatise, which I now transmit to you, must be my apology, for the liberty I have taken in sending it. As its design (among other objects) is to promote the extension of civilization & Christian knowledge among the Aborigines of North-America, it seem'd to me to have a claim to your attention: at any rate, the Idea, hath struck me, that *you will find it of use*; and, perhaps, may see fit, to cause some copies of it to be reprinted, at your own charge, to distribute among our Indian missionaries. The gratification you find, in whatever is interesting to philanthropy, renders it unnecessary for me to glance at any advantage, which might result from such a measure, in silencing the voice of a calumniating opposition, on the score of your alleged indifference to the cause of religion.

You will please, Sir, to consider this, as the private* communication of a private friend, one who is sincerely attach'd to your person and administration, warm in your praises, and who wants nothing in your power to bestow. I am under the necessity, however, of making one stipulation, in regard to this pamphlet, which is, that you return it to me again, after keeping it, as short a time only, as you conveniently can, it being a borrow'd book, and I do not know that there is another copy of it, on this side of the Atlantic, certainly none within my reach.

Amidst the multifarious employment, which your high station imposes, I do not presume to trouble you, to write a line, accompanying the return of this book; let it be simply enveloped in a blank cover, and directed to me, at this place.

The Appendix to your "Notes on Virginia," of which, you did me the honour, soon after its publication, to inclose me a copy, I take this opportunity to thank you for; and beg you to accept the assurances of my profound respect. EDWARD DOWSE

*No person whatever is acquainted with it, or ever shall be.

RC (MHi); at foot of text: "Thomas Jefferson President of the United States"; endorsed by TJ as received 14 Apr. and so recorded in SJL. Enclosure: William Bennet, *The Excellence of Christian Morality: A Sermon, Preached Before the Society in Scotland for Propagating Christian Knowledge, at Their Anniversary Meeting, Thursday, 6th June 1799* (Edinburgh, 1800); see EG, 327n and TJ to Dowse, 19 Apr. 1803.

For the recipients of the APPENDIX to TJ's *Notes on the State of Virginia*, see Vol. 31:551-4.

From Jean Baptiste Emonnot

Paris 5 avril 1803.
MONSIEUR LE PRÉSIDENT 15 Germinal an XI.

La Société de Médecine de Paris, par L'organe de sa commission de Vaccine, à L'honneur de Vous offrir un resultat partiel de Ses recherches relatives à L'inoculation nouvelle et L'abrégé de Ses Correspondances chez presque toutes Les nations policées.

La Société Vous devait cet hommage à plus d'un titre, Monsieur Le Président, à vous qui par L'ascendant de vos Lumieres, non moins que par L'influence de votre Suprême autorité avez Si puissamment contribué à accréditer La vaccine chez cette heureuse portion de l'humanité commise à vos Soins.

Veuillez donc, Monsieur Le Président, agréer ce Léger don comme une expression de La gratitude publique et comme Le temoignage de notre Profond respect.

Pour La Société de Médecine de Paris

EMONNOT DM.
Secretaire de La commission de Vaccine
de la Société.

EDITORS' TRANSLATION

Paris, 5 Apr. 1803
MISTER PRESIDENT, 15 Germinal Year XI

The Society of Medicine of Paris, on behalf of its Commission on Vaccines, has the honor of presenting you with a partial result of its research concerning the new inoculations and a summary of its correspondence with almost all civilized countries.

The society owed you this honor on more grounds than one, Mister President, you who have so strongly contributed, by the power of your enlightened views, no less than by the influence of your supreme authority, to accrediting vaccine among that fortunate share of humankind entrusted to your care.

Please accept, Mister President, this small gift as an expression of public gratitude and a sign of our deep respect.

On behalf of the Society of Medicine of Paris.

EMONNOT M.D.
Secretary of the Society's
Commission on Vaccines

RC (DLC); at head of text: "La Société de Médecine de Paris Séant au Louvre A Monsieur Jefferson Président des états-Unis"; endorsed by TJ as received 2 Oct. and so recorded in SJL. Enclosure: see below.

Jean Baptiste Emonnot (1761-1823) had a doctorate in medicine from the University of Caen. He later served for a number of years as the president of the medical society in Paris, the SOCIÉTÉ DE MÉDECINE, which had been founded in

1796 (*Biographie universelle*, 12:448; Tulard, *Dictionnaire Napoléon*, 1157).

L'HONNEUR DE VOUS OFFRIR: Emonnot may have enclosed a report of the Comité Central de Vaccine that had been published several months earlier as a supplement to a medical journal. Beginning about 1800, doctors in Paris gave considerable attention to vaccination against smallpox and to preventive medicine in general ("Vaccine," *Journal de médecine, chirurgie, pharmacie, etc.*, 4 [1802], 389-400; Dora B. Weiner and Michael J. Sauter, "The City of Paris and the Rise of Clinical Medicine," *Osiris*, 2d ser., 18 [2003], 40).

From W. F. Harle

MR PRESIDENT [on or before 5 Apr. 1803]

I am an unfortunate young Man lately arrived from England—I came over to this Country, having first received a polite Education in one of the first seminaries of my native soil—What chiefly influenced me to take this step, was 1st because I imagined that a change of climate would greatly contribute to repair my constitution, which long study had somewhat injured—& 2dly. because I received intelligence from some member of the College, in which I was educated, that in the vicinity of Washington I should be received by some Gentlemen with great pleasure, have the expenses of my voyage defrayed & an annual pension of £75—I set sail in consequence in a vessel bound to New-York—The Captain's demands were forty Guineas—On making the land of *Liberty* I had not a greater sum than £10—which was scarcely sufficient to pay the expenses of my journey from New-York to Washington—At length I reached the City—But alas! how were my expectations frustrated, when I found that the reception I experienced, was quite in opposition to that which had been represented to me before my departure from Europe—

Mr President—for a young man to find himself in a foreign land without friends—without money, is a situation truly deplorable—but for a Person destitute of friends & money to experience ingratitude from those—whom he expected at least would treat him with civility, is a situation which cannot be conceived, unless by those who feel it—Such, Mr President, is my present unfortunate state—I am perhaps destined by Fate to suffer misfortunes—I know not—but I am certain at least that you are able & I feel myself convinced that you are willing to assist me in my deplorable condition—You have a noble & generous Heart—& since generosity resides in your Bosom, you cannot read my misfortunes, without feeling compassion.—I fly to you, because I know that you take delight in succouring the miserable—Cast on me, I beseech you, a propitious glance—

Mr President—

By the love of your Country—by all that is sacred & all that is dear to you give relief to an *unfortunate*—If such is your conduct, you will forever be dear to my heart—I shall love, reverence, & esteem you as a Father—and certainly with the greatest propriety—

To conclude

Mr President

I request, entreat & beseech you to pour into my throbbing bosom the balm of consolation by assisting me in a manner becoming you, the greatest ornament of a free, an independent Nation—

I am

Mr President

Your most humble but unfortunate Servant W F Harle

RC (MHi); undated; endorsed by TJ as received 5 Apr. 1803 and so recorded in SJL.

From Isaac Story

Most respected Sir, Marblehead, Ap. 5. 1803.

This leaves me in a state of private Independence; not having my authority as a Commissioner of Bankruptcy restored, nor receiving any other Commission from the source of Power, though my Nephew, Joseph Story, is the perticular mark of royal favor.

There has been but one Bankruptcy in this District, since the first appointment of Commissioners. And Judge Davis invested me with the power of acting, but I declined; because I had not been re-instated.

I am informed that these Commissions are confined to Merchants and Lawyers. No doubt, this is the general Establishment. But there have been some deviations; perticularly in the case of Mr. Burley and Doctor Kilham of this District.

I was not educated as a Merchant, but I have been largely concerned in money-transactions, by which I have arrived at my present state of Independence.

I was not brought up as a Lawyer, but I am well acquainted with the laws of my Country; and have sometimes been consulted, and my advice adopted.

And as to *figures*, I should yield the palm to very few. And as a demonstration, I inclose a geometrical illustration of the square-root, which I sent to the American Academy of Arts and Sciences in 1795.

I venerate the name of Washington; and have generally felt an esteem for Mr. Adams, on account of his public exertions in favor of America. I was conversant with him from a child; as he was often in my Father's office, as well [as] the Honble. James Otis, Governor Adams and Doctr. Cooper, great Liberty men.

But many of his public administrations I reprobated; while many acts of the present Government I admire. I rejoice in the Downfall of the Judiciary, and in the present System of Oeconomy. And should there be no Wars to cramp us, we shall soon be emancipated from the public debt, and be a flourishing people.

Whether I am publicly noticed or not, I shall always subscribe myself, yours with the homage of the utmost respect,

Isaac Story

N. B. As Mr. Story proposes to relinquish his appointment as Naval Officer in Salem and Beverly, it would no doubt be a gratification to him to see his Uncle in possession of it.

Printed in *Jefferson Correspondence, Bixby*, 99-100. Recorded in SJL as received 16 Apr. Enclosure: probably Story to Joseph Willard, president of Harvard College and vice president of the American Academy of Arts and Sciences, dated Marblehead, 17 Aug. 1795, enclosing "A geometrical illustration of the square-root or the grounds & reasons for the common process, which is used for the extraction of it" (MS in MiU-C; entirely in Story's hand).

For the revocation of Story's appointment as COMMISSIONER OF BANKRUPTCY, see Vol. 38:161-2, 179n, 216, 253, 266-7. The post had been offered to his nephew, JOSEPH STORY, whom TJ also nominated to be naval officer for Salem and Beverly in February 1803 (TJ to the Senate, 2 Feb. 1803).

From Pierre Samuel Du Pont de Nemours

Paris 16 Germinal An onze
6 Avril 1803

Monsieur le Président

Je continue d'esperer un heureux rapprochement entre nos deux Nations qui ne peuvent se dissimuler que c'est leur interêt réciproque.

Je l'espere d'autant plus que c'est le Général Bernadotte, véritable ami de toute liberté, qui est chargé de la Négociation.

Vous trouverez en lui un homme qui aime l'Amérique, les Américains, les principes de leur Gouvernement, les vôtres Monsieur; et qui rend à Votre Sagesse, à votre morale toute la justice que vous méritez. Vous y trouverez un loyal Frere d'armes de notre si cher et si malheureux La Fayette.

Je pense que Mr. Livingston vous aura dit que j'ai très activement employé mon Zêle pour les Etats unis. Et il n'a pas pû tout vous dire, car il y a des détails que je ne lui ai pas dit à lui même et que je ne pourrais confier qu'à vous.

Mais sans qu'on vous en parle vous connaissez assez mon coeur.

Vous savez donc que je ferai toujours, avec ou sans instruction, ce que je croirai le plus utile aux deux Pays.

Salut et profond respect. Du Pont (de Nemours)

EDITORS' TRANSLATION

Paris, 16 Germinal Year 11
6 Apr. 1803

Mister President,

I continue to hope for a happy rapprochement of our two nations, which cannot hide the fact that this is in their mutual interest.

I am all the more hopeful since it is General Bernadotte, true friend of all liberty, who is in charge of the negotiations.

In him you will find a man who loves America, Americans, the principles of their government, and your principles, Sir; a man who pays all the respect your wisdom and ethics deserve. You will find in him a loyal brother in arms of our very dear and unfortunate Lafayette.

I believe Mr. Livingston has told you that I have been zealous on behalf of the United States. And he could not tell you everything, since there are details I have not told him and can only confide in you.

Even if you have not been told, you are well acquainted with my intentions.

You know, therefore, that with or without instructions, I will always do what I believe is most useful to the two countries.

With greetings and deep respect. Du Pont (de Nemours)

RC (DLC); at head of text: "a Son Excellence Thomas Jefferson President des Etats-Unis"; endorsed by TJ as received 5 Sep. and so recorded in SJL. Enclosed in Du Pont to TJ, 27 June.

Although TJ wanted Du Pont to have independent discussions with the French government, that arrangement did not appeal to Robert R. LIVINGSTON; see Livingston's letter of 14 Apr. Livingston wrote to Madison on 24 Mch., "I cannot but hope that Something may be effected, tho' I fear Dupont de Nemours has given them with the best intentions Ideas that we Shall find it hard to eradicate, & impossible to yield to" (Madison, *Papers*, *Sec. of State Ser.*, 4:448; Vol. 37:333, 365-6, 418-19; TJ to Du Pont, 1 Feb.).

From William Hylton

Sir! Savana la mar Jamaica 6th Apr. 1803

When I felt it incumbent upon me to address your Excellency the 5th. ultimo. agreeably to the Copy inclosed—I considered the privelege of Shipping Molasses in American Bottoms, to be under an Act of Parliament. But I learnt immediately after, that it was under the

Governors proclamation, consequent of an Act, permitting certain enumerated articles to be exported in American vessells. The Substance, as to Right, was the same; and I have the satisfaction to inform your Excellency, that Mr. Ross, the Attorney General of the Island has given a clear opinion; confirming the Right and propriety of exporting the article objected to by the Collector at this port!

When part of the Western Army were disbanded, my Son Lieut. John Hylton, came to this Country from New Orleans; and was getting eligibly fixed here—But with the arduor of an American Soldier, upon the Reports of Hostilities, he intends to abandon his objects and persuits in this Country, and repair to offer his services under the Banner of the Spread Eagle!

I have the honor to be with high Consideration Your Excellencies very obt. hum. Sevt. WM. HYLTON

RC (DLC); at foot of text: "His Excellency Thomas Jefferson Esquire President &c. &c. United States of America"; endorsed by TJ as received 7 Apr. but recorded in SJL at 7 May. Enclosure: see Hylton to TJ, 5 Mch.

COLLECTOR AT THIS PORT: James Brown.

For JOHN HYLTON, who had been honorably discharged from the army on 1 June 1802, see Heitman, *Dictionary*, 1:561; Vol. 32:495; Vol. 33:464.

From Fulwar Skipwith

DEAR SIR Paris. 6 April 1803

The bearer of this Mr. Thos. L. Halsey, a Gentleman of very distinguished connexions in the State of Rhode Island informed me of his intention of waiting on you soon after his return to his native Country, and having expressed his design of soliciting a grade in the army of the U.S. is willing to charge himself with a letter of recommendation from me, with others from several of your friends in Europe, in order to be presented to you. I need not invoke my feelings of friendship & partiality to this young Gentleman to say that his mind, manners, and education have been equally highly cultivated, and that by his travels in Europe, he has lost nothing of his attachment to his own Country.

With great respect & esteem, I have the honor to be, Sir, Your Mo Ob Servt FULWAR SKIPWITH

RC (DLC); at foot of text: "Mr. Jefferson"; endorsed by TJ as received 8 Dec. and so recorded in SJL with notation "by mr Halsey."

Thomas L. HALSEY also carried a letter of recommendation from James Monroe to TJ, which he delivered with Skipwith's letter on 8 Dec. 1803 (Monroe to TJ, 28

Sep. 1803). He did not receive a military appointment, however, and was likewise unsuccessful in his application to be secretary of legation to Spain in 1804. In 1812, James Madison appointed him United States consul at Buenos Aires (DAB; Arthur Fenner to TJ, 28 May 1804; Theodore Foster to TJ, 1 June 1804).

To Thomas Munroe

SIR Washington Apr. 7. 1803.

The letter from the committee of subscribers to the theatre which I recieved from you on the 18th. Ult. has been the subject of enquiry & consideration since my return to this place. the theatre is proposed to be built by private individuals, it is to be their private property, for their own emolument, & may be conveyed to any other private individual. to cede to them public grounds for such a purpose[1] whether appropriated, or open spaces, would be a donation of it: and I do not find that the President has a power to make such a donation of the public lands: nor do I think they would be safe in building on such a donation, on account of it's invalidity. knowing, as I do, that this enterprise is undertaken with no view to their private benefit, but is really a sacrifice to advance the interest of the place, I am sorry that the accomodation desired cannot be obtained from the public, and that their funds are to be diminished either by a purchase of the site, or a ground rent for it. but I see no remedy. I have in two or three instances consented to the erection of buildings on public grounds, but with an explanation that whenever the grounds were wanted for the public, they would be resumed; and the buildings proposed have always been of such trifling value as to produce no repugnance towards a resumption from any sacrifice of the value of the building. Accept assurances of my esteem & respect. TH: JEFFERSON

PrC (DLC); at foot of text: "Mr. Thomas Munroe"; endorsed by TJ in ink on verso. Recorded in SJL with notation "theatre."

LETTER FROM THE COMMITTEE: see Munroe to TJ, 14 Mch. 1803.

Instead of on public grounds, the THEATRE would be built on land donated by John P. Van Ness in Square 349 at the intersection of 11th and C Streets Northwest. Named the Washington Theatre, it held its initial performance in November 1804. Never a financial success, it was damaged by fire in 1820 and sold two years later (*National Intelligencer*, 22 Apr. 1803; RCHS, 5 [1902], 68-77; TJ to Martha Jefferson Randolph, 3 Dec. 1804).

MY RETURN: TJ departed from Monticello on 31 Mch. and arrived in Washington on 3 Apr. His expenses for the journey totaled $18.98\frac{1}{2}$ (MB, 2:1096; TJ to Wilson Cary Nicholas, 11 Apr. 1803).

[1] Preceding four words interlined.

From James Turner

North Carolina
Sir Raleigh 7th. April 1803

In conformity to a Resolution of the Legislature, I have the honor of transmitting to You, A copy of the public Laws, passed at the last Session of the General Assembly of this State.

I have the honor to be Sir With high respect Your most obedient

J. Turner

RC (DLC); at foot of text: "The President of the United States"; endorsed by TJ as received 16 Apr. and so recorded in SJL. Enclosure: *Laws of North Carolina. At a General Assembly, Begun and Held at Raleigh, on the Fifteenth Day of November, in the Year of Our Lord One Thousand Eight Hundred and Two, and in the Twenty-seventh Year of the Independence of the Said State* (Raleigh, 1802; Shaw-Shoemaker, No. 2807).

A neighbor and close political associate of Nathaniel Macon, James Turner (1766-1824) was elected by his fellow legislators to fill an unexpired term as North Carolina's governor in 1802. He retained the office for three consecutive one-year terms before being elected to the United States Senate. There he supported initiatives of the Jefferson and Madison administrations, sometimes in conflict with Macon and other opponents of federal authority, until retiring due to poor health in 1816 (William S. Powell, ed., *Dictionary of North Carolina Biography*, 6 vols. [Chapel Hill, 1979-96], 6:65).

From Joseph Mathias Gérard de Rayneval

Paris ce vendredi 18. germ. an XI.
Monsieur 8. avril 1803.

Me flattant que Votre Excellence n'a pas oublié l'estime et l'amitié qu'elle a bien voulu m'accorder autrefois, je ne crains pas d'être importun en lui rappellant de nouveau ma reclamation auprès du Congrès. M. le général Bernadotte, notre Ministre plénipre., veut bien se charger, Monsieur, de la mettre sous vos yeux, et de plaider ma cause. Jose espérer d'avance, que vous l'écouterez avec intérêt, et avec la disposition de soutenir une demande qui est intimement liée à des services dont Votre Excellence a une parfaite connoissance. La nature de ces services m'inspire la confiance de penser que le gouvernement américain ne refusera point de prendre en considération le motif de laconcession faite à feu mon frere, et que ce motif le déterminera à ne point appliquer rigoureusement à ses héritiers la resolution relative aux Compagnies des ilinois et du Ouabash, mais à leur accorder une équitable indemnité. Je compte, Monsieur, sur votre puissante intervention, et vous prie d'avance d'en agréer mes remerciments, ainsi que l'assûrance du respectueux attachement avec lequel j'ai l'honneur d'etre,

Monsieur De Votre Excellce Le trés-humble et trés-obeisst Serviteur

GERARD DE RAYNEVAL

EDITORS' TRANSLATION

Paris, Friday, 18 Germinal Year 11
8 Apr. 1803

SIR,

Flattering myself that Your Excellency has not forgotten the esteem and friendship you kindly granted me in the past, I do not fear being importunate in reminding you again of my request before Congress. General Bernadotte, our minister plenipotentiary, is willing to take it on, Sir, to bring it to your attention and to plead my cause. I dare hope, in advance, that you will listen to him with interest, open to supporting a request that is intimately linked to services with which Your Excellency is very familiar. The nature of these services gives me the confidence to believe that the American government will not refuse to consider the rationale for the concession that was made to my late brother, and that this rationale will prompt it to decide not to be rigorous in applying to his heirs the resolution concerning the Illinois and Wabash companies, but to grant them a fair indemnity. I count on your powerful intervention, Sir, and ask you in advance to accept my thanks along with the assurance of the respectful attachment with which I have the honor of being

Your Excellency's very humble and obedient servant.

GERARD DE RAYNEVAL

RC (ViW: Tucker-Coleman Collection); endorsed by TJ as received 13 May 1805 and so recorded in SJL.

RECLAMATION: TJ, who had been acquainted with Gérard de Rayneval in Paris, had written him in March 1801 to explain that his efforts to obtain a tract of land granted to his brother years earlier by the Wabash Company would come to naught. The brother, Conrad Alexandre Gérard, since deceased, had been France's minister to the United States, and Gérard de Rayneval recruited influential individuals such as Pierre Samuel Du Pont de Nemours and Louis André Pichon to press the claim. The endeavor was "totally without foundation," TJ commented to Madison late in 1801 (Vol. 31:175-6; Vol. 32:384-5; Vol. 33:373-4; Vol. 36: 10-11).

To George Jefferson

DEAR SIR

Washington Apr. 8. 1803.

I inclose you a list of my Bedford crop of tobo. made the last year, partly brought down to Richmond, & partly soon to be there under your care. I have lately understood tobacco is looking up. I will thank you for information what can be got; and if 7. Doll. can be got, you may sell it immediately. the money will be wanting July 12. as on that day I have to pay at your counting house a note of 1300. D. to Craven

Peyton on order. I wrote to you to stop £16–8–9 of the orders formerly given on you in favor of Moran, if not already drawn out of your hands. if it is, I shall lose it.

I must ask the favor of you to buy me 150. fine hams. if mr Macon's are to be had, they have been found excellent. they are to be forwarded here. I just learn that the two hogsheads of wine are sent off from Baltimore for Richmond. be pleased to send them up by the boats in which David Higginbotham is concerned. I believe they are conducted by Johnson Roe. I have agreed with Higginbotham to carry up every thing for me, as he undertakes to be responsible for the fidelity of his boatmen, and carries cheaper than the others. I have reserved a right to send by others any particular matter very pressing when he has no boats down. accept my affectionate salutations.

TH: JEFFERSON

PrC (MHi); at foot of text: "Mr. George Jefferson"; endorsed by TJ in ink on verso. Recorded in SJL with notation "tobo. wine. Higginb's boat." Enclosure not found, but see below.

Excluding the amount of the CROP deducted by his overseer Burgess Griffin, TJ recorded the production of 45,139 pounds of tobacco at Poplar Forest in 1802 (MB, 2:1095).

I WROTE TO YOU: TJ to George Jefferson, 26 Mch.

For the HOGSHEADS OF WINE, see S. Smith & Buchanan to TJ, 14 Mch.

Navy Department: Summaries of Dispatches from the Voyages of the *Constellation* and the *Chesapeake*

[on or before 8 Apr. 1803]

Capt. Murray. Constellation
1802

14 March — Off Cape Henlopen

30 April — Off Malaga—shall proceed to Carthagena & endeavour to procure Anchors—if unsuccessful then shall proceed to Toulon—thence off Tripoli.

7 May — Has procured an Anchor at Gibraltar.

1 June — Tunis Bay. Took on board at Gibraltar Presents for the Bey, sent by Mr King—on his way stopped at Algiers, & had an interview with Mr OBrien—found all quiet there—just taking his departure for the coast of Tripoli.

5 July. — Off Tripoli—has been off Tripoli since the 7 June.

30 — ". — " — " has been nearly two months in sight of Tripoli—The Boston left that station 26 June for Malta.

14 Augt. At sea, on his way to Malta for a temporary supply

22 — " At Malta—just departing for Tripoli.

18 Septr. At Naples. "after cruising again off Tripoli for some time & meeting with a heavy blow, in which I found no small difficulty in beating off the Coast, & finding it of no avail to remain there any longer, I resolved to make a short cruise off Cape Bon—off which place I fell in with the Swedish Admiral & communicated to him the substance of my interview with the Bashaw of Tripoli. He has again gone to keep up the blockade a short time longer, & then means to turn his whole attention to convoying in cooperation with our ships—He advised me to proceed to Naples to collect all the Swedish & Amn. Vessels from thence Westerly to Gibraltar, & to return with such Vessels as are bound up the Straights, which is the plan I had previously adopted, for the Tripolitan Galleys are now out—4 sailed about the 20th. ult, & two were on the eve of departure, which I have been on the look out for off Cape Bon—the only place We can have a chance of meeting with them."

1802

7 Novr. Off Malaga

21 — " Do—has had heavy blows since he left Toulon—sprung his foremast & foreyard.

23 — " Off Malaga—Saw the Secys letter to Commre. Morris of 23 Octr 1802 requiring his return to America. shall proceed on his return accordingly.

20 Decr. Gibraltar Bay. So far on his way to the United States.

Arrived at Washington March 1803.[1]

Commodore Morris. Chesapeake.

1802

27 April. Off Cape Henry.

25 May. arrived at Gibraltar—Mainmast sprung—

14 June. At Gibraltar—Mainmast completed, does not conceive himself justified in leaving that station, till the arrival of the Adams.

20 June. Off Tangier—had not then seen Mr Simpson

26 June.	Informs of the Emperor of Morocco having ordered Mr. Simpson from his dominions—& that Mr. Simpson was at Gibraltar.
17 August.	The Adams had arrived—Commre. Morris states that he shall proceed up the Mediterranean touching at Leghorn, taking under convoy 20 sail of American & Swedish Vessels.
12 October.	Arrived in Leghorn Bay. "Our passage was extremely prolonged by calms & Easterly Winds." Bowsprit rotten—requires fishing—shall proceed off Tripoli.
30 November.	At Malta. The Bowsprit of the Chesapeake in a much worse condition that was expected—decayed more than 5 inches in—& the rot extended 35 feet. procured a fish at Malta.—
	Ordered the Constellation on the 15th October to Toulon from Leghorn—to repair—then to go to Gibraltar for provisions—thence to Malta.

MS (DLC: TJ Papers, 130:22552, 22561); undated; probably in Charles W. Goldsborough's hand; first sheet endorsed by TJ: "Murray. Capt."; second sheet endorsed by TJ as received from the Navy Department on 8 Apr. 1803 and "Morris. Murray."

The above summaries were compiled from dispatches sent to the Navy Department by Alexander MURRAY and Richard V. MORRIS between March and December 1802. They were presumably made in preparation for TJ's 8 Apr. cabinet meeting, in which Morris's ineffectiveness as commander of the Mediterranean squadron was the lead topic of discussion (NDBW, 2:85, 137, 139, 146, 163, 173, 182-3, 185, 192-3, 217-19, 234-5, 236-7, 246-7, 277-9, 296-7, 310-11, 318-19, 327, 332, 336; Christopher McKee, *Edward Preble: A Naval Biography, 1761-1807* [Annapolis, 1972], 113; Notes on a Cabinet Meeting, 8 Apr. 1803).

[1] First sheet ends here.

Notes on a Cabinet Meeting

1803. Apr. 8. present 4. Secretaries & Atty Genl.

1. is there sufficient ground to recall Morris & institute enquiry into his conduct. unanim. not.
2. shall Morris be ordd home in the returng vessel, & leave some other officer to command? unanim. not.
3. shall the return of the Chesapeake & Adams be countermanded till the 4. small vessels arrive? unanim. not. will be too [long?]
4. shall we buy peace of Tripoli? unan. yes.

5. by a sum in gross or a tribute? Gall. Dearb. Lincoln for both.[1] Mad. Smith for sum in gross & promise of renewing presents at [terms?] Dearb. 50. & 8,000 Lincoln 30. & 15,000. Mad. 10. & 5000. with some margin Gall 20. & 10. Smith 50. and 10.

Great Britain. if refusg our rights by France, forces us to overtures to England as an ally? on what conditions?

1. not to make a separate peace?
2. to let her take Louisiana?
3. commercial privileges?

} all reject the 2d & 3d. condns. Dearborne & Lincoln reject the 1st. the others agree to the 1st.

agreed to instruct our ministers, as soon as they find that no arrangement can be made with France, to use all possible procrastinations with them, and in the mean time enter into conferences with the British govmt thro' their ambassador at Paris to fix principles of alliance, and leave us in peace till Congress meets, & prevent war till next spring.

MS (DLC: TJ Papers, 112:19297); entirely in TJ's hand; follows, on same sheet, Notes on a Cabinet Meeting of 21 Oct. 1802; portions obscured by tape.

GROUND TO RECALL MORRIS: for TJ's dissatisfaction with Commodore Richard V. Morris, see Gallatin to TJ, 21 Mch., TJ to Gallatin, 28 Mch., and the Navy Department's summaries of dispatches, [on or before 8 Apr.].

BUY PEACE OF TRIPOLI: according to instructions that Madison gave James L. Cathcart a year earlier, even "the smallest contribution" to the bey of Tripoli "as the price of peace" was out of the question. In a new directive dated 9 Apr., the secretary of state informed Cathcart that "the President has thought proper" to revise the original instructions. Yusuf Qaramanli was "no longer under the domestic distresses which at one time humbled his pretensions." The United States was the only country that had not acceded to the bey's demands. A "concurrent policy of all civilized nations" could have forced the "barbarians" to alter their conduct, wrote Madison. The costs of the United States fulfilling that goal on its own—"not only without the co-operation of a single other power, but in opposition to the example of all, and at a period in different respects critical" to U.S. affairs—were too high. Cathcart was "accordingly authorized by the President," the new instructions stated, to agree to give Qaramanli $20,000 outright plus "8 or ten thousand dollars a year" thereafter. If Cathcart could persuade the Tripolitans to accept lesser amounts, "you will of course avail yourself of the opportunity. But no enlargement of them towards the example of other nations," Madison instructed, "will be admissible, especially, if at the date of the negotiations, none of our Citizens should be in captivity." The "periodical payments" must be payable in money, not in goods or stores, and made at two-year intervals rather than annually. If possible, any agreement about presents should be covered by "a private promise and understanding" rather than by treaty (Madison, *Papers*, *Sec. of State Ser.*, 3:135; 4:494-5; Vol. 38:277n).

OVERTURES TO ENGLAND: in a long, encoded passage in a communication to

James Monroe and Robert R. Livingston dated 18 Apr., Madison advised that if the French "should be found to meditate hostilities or to have formed projects which constrain the United States to resort to hostilities," the American diplomats must open discussions with the British government. Despite the "just repugnance" Americans felt for alliances with any of the contending powers of Europe, the "advantages to be derived from the cooperation of Great Britain" against France were "too obvious and too important" to overlook. To form a pact with the United States, the British might want "a stipulation that neither of the parties shall make peace or truce without the consent of the other." Such a condition would be reasonable, Madison conceded, but in return the Americans should try to obtain a statement of British objectives for the coalition, to protect the United States against an open-ended commitment. If the British pressed for new commercial advantages, the U.S. negotiators could say that Britons would have most favored nation status for trading in any ports along the Mississippi that should come into American jurisdiction. Should trade concessions became "an essential condition," the terms of the alliance could include a guarantee that British subjects would have, for "about ten years," the same commercial privileges as American citizens in those newly acquired Mississippi Valley ports. The United States was not, however, "to be bound to the exclusion of the trade of any particular nations or nation." Livingston and Monroe must reject any demand for "a mutual guaranty of the existing possessions or of the conquests to be made by the parties." Such a provision was "of no value to the United States," it would have the effect of "entangling" the U.S. in Britain's "frequent wars," and it could generate conflict between Britain and the United States. Finally, Madison warned, it was likely that the British would ask for all or part of "the country on the west side of the Mississippi understood to be ceded by Spain to France." The "evils" that would accompany British acquisition of any of that territory were "obvious." In addition to being "extremely displeasing to our western citizens," a British foothold in that region would alarm Spain and France and prolong the conflict with France. "Should this pretension therefore be pressed," the secretary of state instructed, "it must be resisted as altogether repugnant to the sentiments and the sound policy of the United States." What Monroe and Livingston could offer instead was that France would not be allowed to control any part of the trans-Mississippi territory from which the British were excluded. It was "manifestly desirable," Madison advised, that the United States not go to war with France until the alliance with Great Britain was in place and "legislative and other provisions can be made here." For the measures that TJ and Madison took to give Monroe or Livingston the authority to negotiate an agreement in Britain, see Preparations to Negotiate an Alliance with Great Britain, 18 Apr. (Madison, *Papers*, *Sec. of State Ser.*, 4:527-9).

[1] Word interlined in place of "tribute."

To Thomas Cooper

DEAR SIR Washington Apr. 9. 1803.

Your favor of Mar. 21. was recieved here on the 4th. inst. the warrant to your son as midshipman had been suspended for enquiry on a suggestion of too great a propensity in him to drink. no information has been recieved, but your's is sufficient. it is sufficient that you are apprised of it, and state the nature of the case yourself. his warrant was therefore signed two days ago, and has been, or will be forwarded from the navy office. I have no doubt you will apprise him that such a doubt having been once excited, more circumspection & regularity will on that account be necessary from him, than from others; and that, were it to be strengthened, he would find himself in a cul de sac, without explanation. my friendly respect for you calls for this candor, because no circumstance of connection could permit an inattention to public duty in matters of appointment; & because also, being put on his guard, he will feel a stronger inclination to dissipate all doubt by a regularity of deportment.—we have nothing very interesting from Europe. in June we may expect to percieve which way the wind sets at Paris: and on this will depend the future course & character of our nation. it is hard that the will of a single individual, & at such a distance, should be sufficient to force a nation out of it's pacific path & character. Accept my friendly salutations & great respect.

TH: JEFFERSON

PrC (DLC); at foot of text: "Thomas Cooper esq."; endorsed by TJ in ink on verso.

On 6 Apr., Robert Smith sent Thomas Cooper, Jr., a midshipman's WARRANT along with a copy of the naval rules and regulations and a blank oath of allegiance (FC in Lb in DNA: RG 45, LSO).

From Robert W. Cosbrough

SIR George Town 9th. April 1803

The peculiar situation in which I stand at this Period, is the only apology I can offer for such an intrusion, as the present—Your own sensibility will conceive it such, when I can assure you Sir that I came into this Country in *1794* & prior to the last twelve Months, was so successful as a Broker in N. York, that I gain'd a little Fortune of about *$12,000.* all of which, in consequence of misfortune in Trade I have been deprived of & am at this Moment, with a Wife & Child & not a Dollar for their, or my own support.

I have been in habits of Friendship and intimacy for some years with The Hon'ble De Witt Clinton, Mr. Le Fevre of the City, & the Hon'ble Mr. Galatins, Father in Law, to whom I can refer for the truth of this assertion.

The purport therefore, Sir, of my thus addressing you, is, that I have an humble hope, you'll please take into Consideration my present necessity, & if there is a Vacancy in any of the Public Offices, *not otherwise promised*, should you think me deserving the most subordinate, as a Clerk therein, you will have the goodness to recommend me—It will tend to the relief of a mind laboring for some time under the pressure of misfortune, & "now deprived of every thing save" this "last hope"—

I am Sir With all possible respect Your very Obedt. St.

R. W. Cosbrough

RC (DLC); endorsed by TJ as received 9 Apr. and "for office" and so recorded in SJL.

Robert W. Cosbrough was listed as an accountant in the New York City directory printed in 1797 and subsequently as a broker. He was last listed in the directory printed in 1802 (*Longworth's American Almanack, New-York Register, and City Directory, for the Twenty-Second Year of American Independence* [New York, 1797], 153; *Longworth's City Directory* [New York, 1799], 196; *Longworth's City Directory* [New York, 1802], 176).

Albert Gallatin's FATHER IN LAW was James Nicholson, a Republican leader in New York City (Vol. 31:556-7n; Vol. 35: 235n, 283-4).

To Nicolas Gouin Dufief

Washington Apr. 9. 1803.

Th: Jefferson asks the favor of mr Dufief to procure for him the following books.

Pensees de Pascal

Dr. Priestley's Harmony of the evangelists in Greek. 4. vols.

the same Harmony in English with notes & paraphrase. 4to.

Dr. Priestley being in Philadelphia can probably inform mr Dufief if there be any depot of his works at any particular book-shop in Philadelphia.

he presents him his salutations & respects.

PrC (DLC); endorsed by TJ in ink on verso. Recorded in SJL with notation "Pascal. Priestley."

The *Pensées* of Blaise PASCAL, a work that discussed rational proofs of Christianity, first appeared in print in 1670. English translations, one of which was titled *Thoughts on Religion*, were also available (Sowerby, No. 1516; Daniel Clifford Fouke, "Argument in Pascal's Pensées," *History of Philosophy Quarterly*, 6 [1989], 57-68).

Joseph PRIESTLEY's *A Harmony of the Evangelists, in Greek; To Which are Prefixed, Critical Dissertations in English* (London, 1777) and *A Harmony of the Evangelists in English: With Critical Dissertations, an Occasional Paraphrase, and Notes for the Use of the Unlearned* (London, 1780) arranged the New Testament gospels in chronological order (DNB; Sowerby, No. 1492).

From Albert Gallatin

Sir, Treasury Department April 9: 1803.

I have the honor to enclose a copy of a letter from the Treasurer of the United States, relative to the proclamation contemplated by the Act of the 8: May 1792: and the effect of which will be to prevent thereafter any other copper coin passing current than cents and half cents.

It appears by the enclosed statement that more than fifty six thousand dollars had been received in the Treasury, in cents and half cents, as early as the 31: March 1800; notwithstanding which the proclamation was forgotten. Under those circumstances the Treasurer having thought it his duty to apply for specific instructions, I beg leave to lay the subject before you; in order to know whether you perceive any objection to his giving immediately the notice required by the law.—

I have the honor to be, very respectfully, Sir, Your obed. Servant

ALBERT GALLATIN

RC (DLC); in a clerk's hand, signed by Gallatin; at foot of text: "The President of the United States"; endorsed by TJ as received from the Treasury Department on 9 Apr. and "Copper coin" and so recorded in SJL. Enclosures: (1) Thomas Tudor Tucker to Gallatin, 4 Apr. 1803, observing that the 8 May 1792 Act that provides "for a copper coinage" requires that public notice be given when the Treasury receives from the Mint "in Cents and half Cents," a sum not less than $50,000; the Treasury received this sum before Tucker's appointment, but no notice was given; he requests instructions on how to proceed (Tr in same). (2) Statement of "Account of Cents and half Cents received into the Treasury from the Mint; to the 1st. January 1803," dated 8 Apr. 1803, from the Register's Office, being a list of 44 warrants, with dates and sums for each, drawn in favor of the treasurer of the United States on the treasurer of the Mint from 31 Mch. 1793 to 31 Dec. 1802, totaling $107,495.19 (MS in same; in a clerk's hand, signed by Joseph Nourse).

PROCLAMATION: the 8 May 1792 "Act to provide for a Copper Coinage" noted that six months after the U.S. Treasury received "a sum not less than" $50,000 in cents and half cents from the U.S. Mint, the Treasurer of the United States was to place an announcement in two newspapers at the seat of government that "no copper coins or pieces whatsoever, except the said cents and half cents, shall pass current as money, or shall be paid, or offered to be paid or received in payment for any debt." A fine of $10 and forfeiture would be imposed on those attempting to use other copper coins or pieces in financial transactions (U.S. Statutes at Large, 1:284). In his 1 Jan. 1802 annual report, Director of the Mint Elias Boudinot had also expressed concern that the public announcement required by the 1792 Act had not been made (Vol. 36: 604n).

To Joseph Priestley

DEAR SIR Washington Apr. 9. 1803.

While on a short visit lately to Monticello, I recieved from you a copy of your comparative view of Socrates & Jesus, and I avail myself of the first moment of leisure after my return to acknolege the pleasure I had in the perusal of it, and the desire it excited to see you take up the subject on a more extensive scale. in consequence of some conversations with Dr. Rush in the years 1798.99. I had promised some day to write him a letter giving him my view of the Christian system. I have reflected often on it since, & even sketched the outlines in my own mind. I should first take a general view of the moral doctrines of the most remarkeable of the antient philosophers, of whose ethics we have sufficient information to make an estimate: say of Pythagoras, Epicurus, Epictetus, Socrates, Cicero, Seneca, Antoninus. I should do justice to the branches of morality they have treated well but point out the importance of those in which they are deficient. I should then take a view of the deism, and ethics of the Jews, and shew in what a degraded state they were, and the necessity they presented of a reformation. I should proceed to a view of the life, character, & doctrines of Jesus, who sensible of the incorrectness of their ideas of the deity, and of morality, endeavored to bring them to the principles of a pure deism, and juster notions of the attributes of god, to reform their moral doctrines[1] to the standard of reason, justice, & philanthropy, and to inculcate the belief of a future state. this view would purposely omit the question of his divinity & even of his inspiration. to do him justice it would be necessary to remark the disadvantages his doctrines have to encounter, not having been committed to writing by himself, but by the most unlettered of men, by memory, long after they had heard them from him; when much was forgotten, much misunderstood, & presented in very paradoxical shapes. yet such are the fragments remaining as to shew a master workman, and that his system of morality was the most benevolent & sublime probably that has been ever taught; and eminently more perfect than those of any of the antient philosophers. his character & doctrines have recieved still greater injury from those who pretend to be his special disciples, and who have disfigured and sophisticated his actions & precepts, from views of personal interest, so as to induce the unthinking part of mankind to throw off the whole system in disgust, and to pass sentence as an imposter on the most innocent, the most benevolent the most eloquent and sublime character that ever has been exhibited to man.—this is the outline; but I have not the time, & still less the information which the subject needs. it will therefore rest with me in contemplation only. you are the person who of all others would do it best, and most promptly. you have all the materials at hand, and you put together with ease. I wish you could be induced to extend your late work to the whole subject.—I have not heard particularly what is the state of your health: but as it has been equal to the journey to Philadelphia, perhaps it might encourage the curiosity you must feel to see for once this place, which nature has formed on a beautiful scale, and circumstances destine for a great one. as yet we are but a cluster of villages: we cannot offer you the learned society of Philadelphia; but you will have that of a few characters whom you esteem, & a bed & hearty welcome with one who will rejoice in every opportunity of testifying to you his high veneration & affectionate attachment. TH: JEFFERSON

PrC (DLC); at foot of first page: "Doctr. Priestley."

TJ received a COPY of Priestley's pamphlet *Socrates and Jesus Compared* (Sowerby, No. 1661), which Priestley had published during a recent visit to Philadelphia. The structure and ideas of the pamphlet were similar to what TJ outlined above (Edgar F. Smith, *Priestley in America, 1794-1804* [Philadelphia, 1920], 155-8; Benjamin Rush to TJ, 12 Mch.).

SOME CONVERSATIONS WITH DR. RUSH: see Vol. 32:110-12, 166-9. Priestley copied and sent this letter to his close friend and religious ally Theophilus Lindsey, and in 1812 it was included in the appendix of an appreciative volume on Lindsey by Unitarian minister Thomas Belsham. Also included in the appendix was Priestley's cover letter, which informed Lindsey that TJ was "generally considered as an unbeliever: if so, however, he cannot be far from us, and I hope in the way to be not only almost, but altogether what we are." Having received a copy of the volume, John Adams informed TJ of the letter's inclusion, causing TJ to worry that "it's publication will gratify the priesthood with new occasion of repeating their Comminations against me" (Thomas Belsham, *Memoirs of the Late Reverend Theophilus Lindsey, M.A.* [London, 1812], 417-19; EG, 327-9; RS, 6:145-6, 193).

[1]TJ here canceled "and bring them."

To Joseph T. Scott

SIR Washington Apr. 9. 1803.

I informed you in my letter of Mar. 6. of the measure I had taken to answer the object of your's of Feb. 25. I now inclose you two accounts of the family of General Washington from persons intimately acquainted with them and entirely to be relied on, and tender you my best wishes & respects. TH: JEFFERSON

PrC (DLC); at foot of text: "Mr. Joseph Scott"; endorsed by TJ in ink on verso. Enclosures not found, but see below.

Daniel Carroll Brent, to whom TJ had written on 6 Mch. on Scott's behalf, sought information from his friend Alexander Spotswood, who enclosed material relevant to Scott's proposed biography of GENERAL WASHINGTON and also offered to share letters his grandfather had written while serving as lieutenant governor of Virginia. Spotswood was married to George Washington's niece Elizabeth Washington (Alexander Spotswood to Daniel Carroll Brent, 16 Mch., in MHi, endorsed by TJ; Washington, *Papers, Pres. Ser.*, 15:389n).

From Robert Smith

SIR, Navy Dep. Ap. 9. 1803

As the Governor of Massachussetts has in a letter to the Secretary at War renewed his application respecting the Cannon and other Stores Obtained from that State in the year 1798, I consider it proper to send to you the enclosed Copies of letters, which will give you a view of the part of the Case for which this Department has been responsible.

The Books and papers of this Department have been carefully examined and I cannot find that the demand and refusal have ever been made as stated in the resolutions of the Legislature of that State. Neither is it presumeable that the Government of the United States would have refused to return the Cannon as, it seems, they were not fit for a Man of War and could not be used in the frigate Constitution for which they had been borrowed.

With great respect, I have the honor to be Sir, Your Ob. Ser

RT SMITH

RC (DLC); at foot of text: "The President"; endorsed by TJ as received from the Navy Department on 9 Apr. and "Massachusets cannon" and so recorded in SJL. Enclosures: (1) Secretary of War James McHenry to the Governor of Massachusetts, 30 May 1798, stating that the failure of a contract has left the frigate *Constitution* at Boston in need of cannon for its upper battery; McHenry has learned that Castle Island in Boston harbor has nineteen 18-pound cannon available and that Captain Samuel Nicholson wishes to obtain them for his ship; McHenry asks for "a loan" of 14 or 16 of these and in return offers "either to return the same Guns as soon as others can be provided for the frigate, or to replace them with Guns equally good," and also to order the same number of 32-pound cannon from Providence for use in defending Boston harbor; McHenry also asks the governor to furnish a suitable quantity of 18-pound shot, for which "the United States will punctually & promptly return an equal quantity." (2) Henry Jackson, navy agent at Boston, to McHenry, 7 June 1798, stating that he has been informed by James Warren that the 18-pound cannon requested from Massachusetts for use on the *Constitution* "are really the property of the United States"; the cannon were imported from France during the American Revolution for a vessel then being constructed and were delivered to Samuel Hodgdon, the commissary of military stores; application has been made to the governor of Massachusetts for the cannon and Jackson is certain that "he will cordially loan them" according to McHenry's request. (3) Extract of a letter from Jackson to McHenry, 11 June 1798, informing him that the governor of Massachusetts has given Jackson an order "for the Loan of 16 eighteen pound cannon laying at Castle Island, for the use of the frigate Constitution." (4) Robert Smith to Samuel Brown, 10 Dec. 1801, informing him that the state of Massachusetts has applied to the Navy Department "for repayment of some Cannon and Shot" that it loaned to the United States during the fitting out of the *Constitution*; Smith encloses a letter from Amasa Davis, the quartermaster general for Massachusetts, to Major Daniel Jackson, along with copies of the original vouchers given by former navy agent Henry Jackson for the articles received; Smith asks Brown to look into the matter and ascertain if remuneration has been made for the loan or any part of it; if not, Brown is to inquire if the original guns can be returned or if new guns would be preferable; Brown is also to see if he has enough suitable shot in store to return as well; Smith suggests that Captain Nicholson can provide information regarding the receipt and employment of the cannon and shot; in a postscript, Smith adds that the state will need to supply the original vouchers prior to any settlement. (5) Brown to Smith, 25 Jan. 1802, stating that he has made the necessary inquiries, but cannot find that any remuneration has been made for the cannon and shot; the cannon were too heavy for use in the *Constitution* and were therefore moved to the old Boston navy yard, where they remain; Brown wrote to Quartermaster Davis to inform him that he was ready to return the articles in question, but Davis was unwilling to receive them and instead hopes "to oblige the United States to pay for them in cash" agreeable to the appraisement he received from Daniel Jackson; as Brown understands it, the pretext for the refusal is that "the articles were not returned when asked for at some past period"; Brown believes he has sufficient shot to discharge that part of the loan, and that canister can be had from the *Constitution*. (6) Smith to Caleb Strong, 18 July 1802, enclosing a copy of McHenry's letter to the governor of Massachusetts of 30 May 1798, and pointing out that it contained a proposition "not of a purchase but merely of a loan" and that the cannon and shot could not have been delivered by the state or received by the navy agent at Boston on any other terms; Smith states that in his letter to Samuel Brown of 10 Dec. 1801, he authorized the navy agent to deliver the articles to the proper officer of the state; by Brown's reply of 25 Jan. 1802, Smith was informed that the state quartermaster general was unwilling to receive the cannon and shot, hoping instead that the United States would pay cash for them; believing that McHenry's letter will convince Strong that the transaction was a loan and not a purchase, Smith hopes that the governor will "authorise the proper Officer to receive the cannon and Shot" and adds that he has "repeated my instructions to the Navy Agent to deliver them" (Trs in same).

For previous efforts by Governor Caleb Strong to secure payment for ordnance and stores provided by Massachusetts to the United States in 1798, see Vol. 38:63-4, 340-1, 350. Strong's 5 Apr. 1803 LETTER TO THE SECRETARY AT WAR has not been found, but it enclosed a 5 Mch. resolution by the Massachusetts legislature authorizing the governor to propose referring the claim to the U.S. circuit court in Massachusetts. If the United States refused the suggestion, then Strong was to accept "any reasonable proposals which the government of the United States may offer as a substitute" and to secure a final settlement on the most advantageous terms possible. In his 16 Apr. reply to Strong, Henry Dearborn repeated his earlier position that the United States could only be held responsible for such articles that were deemed either necessary for the defense of Boston or actually used by the federal garrison. Dearborn had previously stated that the value placed by Massachusetts on the articles in question was far too high and suggested that they instead be appraised by a third party. Dearborn now proposes that Captain Nehemiah Freeman, the commander at Fort Independence, join with an artillery officer from Boston to determine a just valuation. Regarding the cannon and shot loaned to the navy, Dearborn has been informed that the secretary of the navy has written Strong on the subject "and will take the necessary measures for adjusting the business" (*Resolves, &c. of the General Court of Massachusetts. Begun and Held at Boston, on Wednesday, the Twenty-Sixth Day of May, Anno Domini, 1802, and Continued by Adjournment to Tuesday, March 8, 1803* [Boston, 1803], 64-5; Dearborn to Strong, 16 Apr. 1803, Lb in DNA: RG 107, MLS).

From "An Observer"

SIR New York [before 10] April 1803

It is observed that frost stops the progress of the malignant or yellow fever Is it not probable that the frosty air of an ice house would have the same effect upon a person in that disease

AN OBSERVER

RC (DLC); partially dated; endorsed by TJ as received from "Anon." on 10 Apr. and "yellow fever" and so recorded in SJL.

The same correspondent, writing from New York under the pseudonym "An Old Woman," addressed TJ again on the subject on 8 July 1804.

To Albert Gallatin

TH:J. TO MR GALLATIN. Apr. 10. 1803.

It appears that on the 31st. Mar. 1800. a paiment of cents & half cents was made into the treasury, which raised the whole amount paid in to more than 50,000. D. and that the Treasurer ought then *forthwith* to have announced it in the gazettes. consequently it ought, now that the omission is first percieved, to be *forthwith* announced. nevertheless, as the continuance of the mint is uncertain, &, if put down, the excluding other coppers might be inconvenient, I should think it better to delay the annunciation till the middle or last of next month, that Congress may have time to interpose before the expiration of the 6. months allowed the copper circulation, after the annunciation. when announced also, to avoid the appearance of blaming our predecessors within whose time the omission happened, I would not specify the date when the sum of 50,000. D. had been paid in, but say 'and whereas it appears that a sum *not less than 50,000. D.* has been paid by the Director of the mint into the treasury before this time' &c.

PrC (DLC). Recorded in SJL with notation "copper coin."

DELAY THE ANNUNCIATION: Thomas T. Tucker issued the notice on 15 Aug., declaring, "And whereas it appears by the books of this office, that more than fifty-thousand dollars in cents and halfcents have been so paid into the Treasury. I now therefore, in obedience to the said act, do hereby give public notice of the same" (*National Intelligencer*, 22 Aug.; *Alexandria Expositor, and the Columbian Advertiser*, 22 Aug.; *Washington Federalist*, 31 Aug. 1803).

OUR PREDECESSORS: Samuel Meredith, the first Treasurer of the United States, resigned in late 1801 and was succeeded by Tucker (Vol. 33:670, 678; Vol. 35:172, 530-1).

From John Bacon

Honored Sir, Stockbridge April 11. 1803

I recollect that during the last session of Congress, I transmitted to you two letters which I recd from Mr Sergeant, Missionary to a tribe of Indians in the State of New York, and that you did me the honor to request a continuation of those communications, from time to time, as I should receive them. The letters which I then transmitted to you were the first of the kind which I had recd from that quarter. Since my return to this place I have recd another from the same hand, which I shall here inclose. Previous to, and during our late revolutionary war, the tribe to which Mr Sergeant is missionary, resided in this town.—You are probably, in some measure acquainted with the character of Hendrick. He is reputed to be a man of talents and discernment, and, I believe, of integrity.

Our political prospects in this Commonwealth, it is believed, are not less favorable than they have been for two years past. I have not recd information respecting the votes that were given in on monday last for Governor, Lieut Governor, Counsellors and Senators, in distant parts of the state. It is expected, however, that there is a majority in favor of those who are called *federalists*. In this district, I believe there is no reason to doubt but that there is a decent majority in favor of *democratial republicanism*. I do not consider the number of votes given for Governor, or even for Counsellors and Senators, as an accurate criterion by which to judge of the real state of political sentiment with us. Mr Strong's *personal* popularity is such as has, apparently, considerable influence on the votes which are given for all public officers who are elected by the same men, and at the same time, with the Governor.

It seems to have been rather unhappy that letters written from Washington by citizens of this state had not been received by our friends then in Boston, at an earlier period.—Different arrangements had been previously contemplated by them, and the system so far advanced that it was judged most prudent to proceed as they had first proposed.

I am, with sentiments of high respect, Your obedient humble Servant, John Bacon

RC (DLC); at foot of text: "The President of the United States"; endorsed by TJ as received 20 Apr. and so recorded in SJL. Enclosure not found.

For the two letters related to the Stockbridge Mohican Indians, see TJ to Henry Dearborn, 15 Feb. While serving as vice president, TJ had met with Hendrick Aupaumut, the sachem of the Stockbridge Mohicans (Vol. 30:249).

In planning for the 1803 state elections, Massachusetts Republicans differed on whom to nominate for governor and whether they should make a full effort to unseat Caleb Strong, the incumbent Federalist. Strong won easily, having even received the endorsement of BOSTON Republicans, and carried the other state offices and many senate districts with him. When the legislature convened on 25 May, Federalists retained a healthy majority of about 50 votes in the house of representatives, though the Boston *Gazetteer*, a Republican sheet, noted that Republicans had increased their tally from 71 to 73 seats (Boston *New-England Palladium*, 8 Apr. 1803; *Boston Gazette*, 12 May 1803; Boston *Gazetteer*, 28 May 1803; Paul Goodman, *The Democratic-Republicans of Massachusetts: Politics in a Young Republic* [Cambridge, Mass., 1964], 129).

From William Benson

City of Washington 11th. April 1803

William Benson, of the State of Virginia, formerly a private in Blands Regiment, during the revolutionary war, respectfully shews,

That he faithfully servd the United States, during the period of his enlistment.—and that he made application to the General Assembly of Virginia to be paid for his services—by them he was refered to the Congress of the United States—That he repaired here at the last session for the purpose, and was led to believe the business would be closed—but thro' the hury and pressure of business, it was laid over till the next session—

That he is unable to get home, without some pecuniary assistance, and humbly solicits aid in that behalf from you, and he hopes that at the next session he shall receive his pay for his services faithfully rendered—

W. BENSON

RC (DLC); addressed: "Thomas Jefferson Esqr. President of United States"; endorsed by TJ as received 12 Apr. and so recorded in SJL.

In October, William Benson's claim for service with the Continental Army, as well as those of several other individuals whose cases had been LAID OVER, was tabled permanently (*Report of the Committee of Revisal and Unfinished Business, on Such Matters of Business As Were Depending and Undetermined at the Last Session* [Washington, D.C., 1803], 8; Shaw-Shoemaker, No. 5447).

From Josiah Meigs

University of Georgia,
MR. PRESIDENT JEFFERSON, Athens, April 11, 1803.—

I know not whether this address may not be judged impertinent; but I cannot refrain from expressing to you, personally, the grateful sentiments which your public conduct has excited in my breast. For thirty years I have been an attentive observer of that progress of Mind which has produced such great and beneficial effects as I have witnessed. When I consider the magnitude & difficulty of the task of directing the affairs of a great nation, even in the most favourable circumstances, I feel it a sort of duty to assure you, personally, of the sentiments which I entertain of high approbation of your public conduct.—

May the Author of Mind, & the bestower of happiness to the Universe protect & prosper all your labours and efforts for the preservation of public right, & public liberty, civil & religious.

With sentiments of the highest Esteem, and with the greatest respect, I am, Yours, J MEIGS

RC (DLC); endorsed by TJ as received 11 May and so recorded in SJL.

Born in Middletown, Connecticut, son of Return Meigs, a hatter, Josiah Meigs (1757-1822) graduated from Yale College in 1778 and several years later returned as a tutor of mathematics, natural philosophy, and astronomy. He also studied law and in 1783 was admitted to the bar. In 1794, Meigs was appointed professor of mathematics and natural philosophy at Yale, but he was soon threatened with dismissal for his zealous support of Jefferson and his political views. In 1800, he accepted an invitation from Abraham Baldwin, who had served as his mentor at Yale, to become a professor at the newly established college at Athens, Georgia. The next year Meigs became president of the new institution, which became the University of Georgia. He established an innovative curriculum, with an emphasis upon mathematics and science. Meigs resigned the presidency of the college in 1810 because of conflicts with the Federalist trustees and local citizens. In 1812, President Madison appointed him Surveyor General Northwest of the Ohio. Two years later Meigs moved to Washington as commissioner of the General Land Office. He served as a founding trustee of Columbian College, which became George Washington University. He was serving as professor of natural philosophy at the college at the time of his death (ANB; Malcolm J. Rohrbough, *The Land Office Business: The Settlement and Administration of American Public Lands, 1789-1837* [New York, 1968], 55-6, 69, 71-4).

To Wilson Cary Nicholas

TH: JEFFERSON TO W. C. NICHOLAS. Apr. 11. 1803.

I wrote you a letter from Gordon's on the 31st. of March, which having been on a particular subject, I am anxious to know that it has got safely to your hands. be so good as by return of post to say you have recieved it whenever you shall have recieved it.—nothing interesting from France. affectionate salutations.

PrC (MHi); endorsed by TJ in ink on verso.

TJ's LETTER FROM GORDON's Tavern, written during the first stop on his trip back to Washington, is recorded in SJL but has not been found (MB, 2:1096). PARTICULAR SUBJECT: see TJ to John Walker, 13 Apr. and Nicholas to TJ, 14 Apr.

From DeWitt Clinton

DEAR SIR New York 12 April 1803.

I take the liberty of communicating to you a transaction—for which communication I am sure no apology is necessary, when I assure you that my object is to prevent any injury to the republican interest or at least to one of its most worthy advocates in this State. I will state the circumstances as briefly as possible.—

Genl. Lamb Collector of this Port was a defaulter upwards of 120.000 Dollars—His securities are responsible for 50.000.—The two who were prosecuted by the Govt. were Col. Henry Rutgers one of the most respectable opulent and meritorious republicans in the State—The other Mr. Alexander Robertson a federalist[1]—Lamb in addition to the conveyance of a large tract of land to his sureties acknowledged a judgment to them for their further indemnification—The sureties were prosecuted—Robertson repaired to Philadelphia and made an agreement to the following effect with the Treasury Department, Mr Oliver Wolcott being then Secry.—The sureties would give up their judgment against Lamb and permit all the property not conveyed to them to be sold and applied to the satisfaction of the debt due to the U.S. over & above the 50.000 Dollars.—if there was any residuum it should be applied as far it went to extinguish it and the sureties should be liable for the remainder—A sale accordingly took place—The amount unknown—as Giles the Marshal has not accounted. The sureties have paid 25.000 Dollars to the U.S. and they now wish to have the amount of the sales by Giles ascertained and the surplus if any allowed to them or they will be content to waive this and pay the whole at a certain period if time is given. In the mean time Mr. Livingston the District Atty. says that he has positive instructions from the Govt. to proceed against them—and they threaten if the Govt. abandons their agreement to have recourse to their Judgment vs. Lamb & resell the lands. In this situation Col. Rutgers would go on immediately to Washington and settle the business with the Treasury—but his presence *at this juncture* is indispensable in this place. He will either assume to pay the balance in four years without interest & give approved security or will go on to Washington in June and come to some final understanding. The claim of the U.S. is perfectly secure—The pressuring Rutgers totally inexpedient—as no man has purer views & more means.

My object in writing is to get a direction to the District Atty. to arrest the proceedings until June when Rutgers will proceed to Washington if necessary—I know that in making this application I call your attention to a subject foreign in some measure from the business of your office—but it is really important in *more senses than one*, as time will satisfactorily evince. If you express a wish merely to the Comptroller (as I presume Mr. Gallatin is absent) without assigning any other than a general reason or referring to my application, it will be sufficient—and if you favor me with a line in immediate reply, it will be deemed a favor.—

Great efforts are made to divide the republicans at the approaching election—but they cannot Succeed—

With great respect I am your obedt servt.

DeWitt Clinton

RC (DLC); at foot of text: "The President of the U.S."; endorsed by TJ as received 14 Apr. and so recorded in SJL.

Governor George Clinton appointed John LAMB collector of customs at New York in 1784 and he continued in office under the Federal government in 1789. He was dismissed in April 1797 after the discovery of a large shortfall in his accounts, reportedly due to embezzlement by his deputy, who fled to Europe. The government charged that Lamb owed $150,000, while Lamb estimated his debt at $127,952.99. HIS SECURITIES: Henry Rutgers, Alexander Robertson, Melancton Smith, and Marinus Willett served as Lamb's sureties for up to $50,000, the amount prescribed by law. In 1799, U.S. District Attorney Richard Harison brought suit against Lamb, Rutgers, and Robertson to recover the money. Smith died in 1798 and there is no evidence that Willett was included in the suit. Lamb died in 1800. Rutgers, Robertson, and Willett unsuccessfully petitioned Congress in 1801 to release them from their obligation "in consideration of their having delivered up all the property of the said Collector to, and for the use and benefit of, the United States."

SURETIES HAVE PAID: on 16 Dec. 1802, Rutgers paid $25,000 to the U.S. Treasury on his and Robertson's behalf. He requested a delay in the final discharge of the bond, noting an agreement between Robertson and Comptroller John Steele in April 1800 that linked the final payment to the sale of Lamb's land. Until all of the land was sold, it was not clear what they owed. In his 16 Dec. letter to Gallatin, Rutgers guaranteed the rest of the payment as soon as the balance was ascertained. Gallatin referred the letter to Gabriel Duvall, the comptroller. POSITIVE INSTRUCTIONS: on 15 Mch. 1803, the U.S. District Court for the Southern District of New York found in favor of the U.S. in the Lamb suit, resulting in an effort by Edward Livingston to settle the account. In 1807, Rutgers was again writing the Treasury Department seeking a record of the sales from Lamb's estate. Rutgers and Robertson settled with the government the next year (Syrett, *Hamilton*, 24:390-1; Kline, *Burr*, 1:291, 296-7; 2:696n; Gallatin, *Papers*, 7:820; 14:418; ANB, s.v. "Lamb, John").

HIS PRESENCE AT THIS JUNCTURE IS INDISPENSABLE: Rutgers, toasted as "a firm republican—the poor man's friend," was endorsed as a Republican candidate for the state assembly in the upcoming 24 Apr. election. He had served in the New York assembly in 1802 but not in 1803. On the day Clinton wrote this letter, Rutgers chaired a party meeting of the Seventh Ward. All nine Republican candidates from New York City won seats in the assembly (New York *American Citizen*, 15, 21 Apr. 1803; New York *Chronicle Express*, 2 May; Newark, N.J., *Centinel of Freedom*, 3 May 1803; *Republican Watch-Tower*, 9 July 1803; *Journal of the Assembly of the State of New-York: At Their Twenty-Fifth Session* [Albany, 1802], 3; *Journal of the Assembly of the State of New-York: At Their Twenty-Sixth Session* [Albany, 1803], 3).

[1]Preceding two words interlined.

From Theophilus Harris

Sir, Alexandria April. 12th. 1803

It gives me no small satisfaction to have the honour of forwarding to you a Cask of Ale sent by Messrs. Bakewell of Newhaven Connecticut to me for your use, which they beg of you to have the goodness to accept—May I, Sir, be allowed on this occasion to observe that this act affords me peculiar pleasure because I view it, tho' trifling in itself, as an act of homage paid to those principles which I have ever been proud to advocate, and of which you have always rank'd as a distinguish'd supporter—Permit me Sir to take this opportunity of expressing my best wishes for your happiness, and to have the honour of Subscribeing myself with all due respect

Sir, Your most obedient Servant Theophilus Harris

RC (MHi); endorsed by TJ as received 12 Apr. and so recorded in SJL.

A native of Wales, Theophilus Harris (1769-1841) emigrated to the United States from England in 1794 with his wife, Mary. He ran a wet and dry goods shop in Alexandria, Virginia, from 1796 to at least 1798, and advertised the sale of porter and brown stout in early April 1803. Sometime around 1805, perhaps after the death of his wife, he moved to Philadelphia. There he purchased farm land in Lower Dublin from Baptist minister Samuel Jones and eventually married his widowed daughter, Sarah Jones Henderson. Harris was active in civil and religious affairs, becoming a director of the Philadelphia Bank and the Philadelphia Society for the Encouragement of Domestic Manufactures as well as a justice of the peace and clergy member of the Philadelphia Baptist Association (John Hammond Moore, "Theophilus Harris's Thoughts on Emigrating to America in 1793," WMQ, 3d ser., 36 [1979], 602-14; Hywel M. Davies, *Transatlantic Brethren: Rev. Samuel Jones (1735-1814) and His Friends: Baptists in Wales, Pennsylvania, and Beyond* [Bethlehem, Pa., 1995], 261-2; Miller, *Alexandria Artisans*, 1:189; *Constitution of the Philadelphia Society for the Encouragement of Domestic Manufactures* [Philadelphia, 1806; Shaw-Shoemaker, No. 11157], 10; *Journal of the Senate of the Commonwealth of Pennsylvania, which Commenced at Lancaster, the Second Day of December, in the Year of Our Lord, One Thousand Eight Hundred and Six* [Lancaster, 1806], 153; *Alexandria Expositor*, 1 Apr. 1803; *Paxton's Philadelphia Directory and Register, for 1819* [Philadelphia, 1819], xcii).

For the CASK OF ALE sent from the Bakewell brewery, see Vol. 39:478-9.

From William Short

New York, 12 Apr. 1803. He reports that his letter of 2 Apr. was delayed but now encloses the account that TJ requested. He mentions some transactions carried out by John Barnes. He informs TJ that the first $500 payment can be sent to him in Philadelphia. Short refers to John Wickham's interest in purchasing his Albemarle land, for which he seeks $10 an acre. He will be advertising the sale but is reluctant to ask Thomas Mann Randolph to act as his representative, preferring instead to ask Gabriel Lilly. He could supply

Lilly with a power of attorney to conduct the sale. He would rather keep the title to his land than issue a mortgage.

FC (DLC: Short Papers); 1 p.; entirely in Short's hand, being an entry in his epistolary record. Recorded in SJL as received 14 Apr.

Drafting Instructions for Meriwether Lewis

I. FROM JAMES MADISON, [BEFORE 13 APR. 1803?]

II. FROM ALBERT GALLATIN, [ON OR BEFORE 13 APR. 1803]

III. FROM LEVI LINCOLN, 17 APR. 1803

IV. INSTRUCTIONS FOR MERIWETHER LEWIS, 20 JUNE 1803

EDITORIAL NOTE

A brief, undated set of four comments jotted in pencil by James Madison is the earliest evidence of Jefferson's drafting of official instructions to Meriwether Lewis for the expedition to the Pacific (Document I). Due to an alteration that Jefferson made in his endorsement on that document, the date of its receipt is not clear but could be as early as 12 or 13 Apr. Jefferson's practice, shown by his composition of annual messages to Congress and in accordance with the customary seniority of the executive departments, put Madison first in the consultative chain. Albert Gallatin would be second, and the president received Gallatin's remarks about the draft on 13 Apr. (Document II). The attorney general commented on the draft on the 17th (Document III). Between Gallatin's review and Levi Lincoln's the secretaries of war and navy must have seen the draft, although no written comments about it by Henry Dearborn or Robert Smith have been found. Jefferson noted the receipt of Gallatin's comments in his epistolary record, but not those by Madison or Lincoln.

Madison's notes, though extremely concise, touched on topics ranging from the statement of the expedition's mission to natural history. Lincoln, as he tended to do with Jefferson's draft annual messages to Congress (see Vol. 39:17, 29-30), wondered how the administration's "perverse" political opponents might manipulate the occasion to influence public opinion. He made recommendations for collection of particular categories of information about Native Americans and advised that Lewis be prepared to vaccinate members of his party against smallpox (a suggestion Jefferson expanded, asking Lewis to instruct Indians about vaccination). Lincoln also made an important suggestion, discussed below, about framing Lewis's discretion to continue or abandon the enterprise in the face of danger. Gallatin's thoughts on the draft instructions had the broadest sweep: anticipating that "the future destinies of the Missouri country are of vast importance to the United States" and that the country Lewis would explore "will be settled by the people of the U. States," the Treasury secretary recommended activities that the president could not have mentioned in official instructions for Lewis. These included the collection of strategic information about Spanish military posts and an assessment of how British access to the Missouri River region from Canada might be blocked. As Gallatin knew from his compilation of cartographic information for Nicholas King's map (see Gallatin to TJ, 14 Mch.), geographical knowledge about the interior of the continent was scarce. In his response to the draft orders he suggested the acquisition of information about the extent of the Missouri River watershed, the topography of the region between that river and Hudson Bay, mountains that might separate the watersheds of the Missouri and the Rio Grande, and the suitability of the trans-Mississippi region for agriculture and the support of "a large population." Jefferson incorporated several of Gallatin's ambitious desiderata into the instructions but recognized that Lewis, to fulfill the mission of finding a route to the western sea, could only collect information about the vast regions to the north and south of his path "by enquiry" and as opportunity offered.

The manuscript the cabinet considered has not been found. The earliest surviving draft (see notes to Document IV) has the appearance not of a composition draft but of a fair copy with alterations, and it incorporates suggestions from Madison, Gallatin, and Lincoln. This second stage of the text was probably the "rough draught" that Jefferson sent to Lewis on 27 Apr., when Lewis was in Pennsylvania making preparations (TJ to Lewis, 27 Apr.). It is uncertain if Jefferson made the significant additions and changes that are now visible on that manuscript, including the insertion of two substantial paragraphs, before or after he sent the draft to Lewis.

Jefferson waited to sign and date the document until Lewis was about to set off on the expedition. The copy he sent Lewis on 27 Apr. caused some confusion when Lewis read in it that instruments for celestial observations "have been already provided." Jefferson had to explain that the statement was anticipatory (see their letters at 14 and 16 May). By the president's request, Lewis had some of the Philadelphia savants—Robert Patterson, Caspar Wistar, Benjamin Rush, and Benjamin Smith Barton—look over the instructions during May. They all, Lewis reported, approved of the document "very highly." There is no record that Jefferson incorporated any comments from them in his final alterations to the text (TJ to Lewis, 27 Apr.; Lewis to TJ, 29 May). He probably made the final copy in June when Lewis was back in Washington (Document IV). On 20 June, Jefferson added datelines and his signature to both the intermediate draft and the final version.

For almost twenty years, perhaps longer, the notion of dispatching an exploring party overland to the Pacific Coast had been in Jefferson's mind. Late in 1783, prompted by word that a subscription had been raised in England for such a purpose, he talked "in a feeble way" with others, perhaps fellow members of Congress, about initiating an expedition. The prospects of finding resources for such an exploration were so slim that it seemed almost "not worth asking the question," but Jefferson sounded out George Rogers Clark about leading the mission and received some observations from Clark in return. "Large parties will never answer the purpose," the veteran of frontier campaigns advised, for they would "allarm the Indian Nations." Clark suggested sending only three or four men, who "must learn the Language of the distant Nations they pass through, the Geography of their Country, antient Speech or Tradition, passing as men tracing the steps of our four Fathers wishing to know from whence we came." The cost of such a small expedition would be "very Trifling" and "worthey the attention of Congress," Clark thought (Donald Jackson, *Thomas Jefferson & the Stony Mountains: Exploring the West from Monticello* [Urbana, Ill., 1981], 42-3; Vol. 6:371; Vol. 15: 609-10). By the spring of 1792 the outlook for funding an enterprise had improved, and Jefferson, who was then a vice president of the American Philosophical Society, began to investigate prospects of forming a subscription to raise 1,000 guineas for an expedition to the Pacific by way of the Missouri River. The botanist André Michaux was probably aware of those discussions when, in December of that year, he proposed to make such an exploration with the society's assistance (APS, *Proceedings*, 22, pt. 3 [1884], 201; Vol. 25:75-7).

Jefferson took a primary role in working out the details of Michaux's proposed expedition and soliciting pledges. When Michaux asked David Rittenhouse, the president of the APS, for some guidelines for the journey, the society named Rittenhouse, Jefferson, Rush, Wistar, William Smith, and John Ewing a committee to "frame Instructions for his observance." Jefferson drafted the directive for Michaux, and although the French scientist did not carry through with the expedition to the Pacific, his instructions of April 1793 were similar to what Jefferson prepared for Lewis a decade later (see notes to Document IV). Jefferson asked Michaux, as he did Lewis, to go up the Missouri, find the most direct route to a river that drained to the Pacific, and follow that stream to the ocean. Michaux's instructions said nothing about making observations for latitude and longitude, but he was, like Lewis, to take note of soils, terrain, plants, animals, and the region's human inhabitants. Similar injunctions for preserving the accrued data—making duplicate records, some of them on birch bark, and sending copies back by sea as soon as the explorer reached the ocean—appeared in both sets of instructions. In each case also, Jefferson acknowledged that his directions, prepared in advance of such a trek through a huge and poorly understood expanse of the continent, could not cover every contingency (APS, *Proceedings*, 22, pt. 3 [1884], 211, 215-16; Vol. 25:77-84, 527, 530-1, 624-6).

"It is strongly recommended to you to expose yourself in no case to unnecessary dangers, whether such as might affect your health or your personal safety," Jefferson wrote in the 1793 directive for Michaux (same, 625-6). Ten years on, he gave more attention to safety in the directions for Lewis. In the draft he circulated to the cabinet, he ordered Lewis to retreat if he encountered—as we learn from Lincoln's comments—"certain destruction" (Document III). Heeding Lincoln's warning that the intrepid captain was "much more likely, in case of difficulty, to push too far, than to recede too soon," Jefferson changed the condition from "certain" to "probable" destruction. To make his meaning absolutely clear, he added that "we wish you to err on the side of your safety, and to bring back your party safe." He also gave the explorer the option of returning to the United States by sea if a return by land seemed "eminently dangerous" (Document IV).

In a change he made in the second stage of the drafting process, Jefferson observed that Lewis's party might gain "security" if they could send some young Indians to the U.S. for education. He also added the last full paragraph of the instructions, which provided for the creation of a chain of command to protect against the "total failure of the enterprize" should Lewis die during the expedition. Originally, Jefferson probably ended the manuscript with the succinct conclusion: "to which I have only to add my sincere prayers for your safe return" (see Document IV, notes 9 and 13). He struck through that clause and instead finished with the paragraph about succession of command. Perhaps he and Lewis discussed that subject in June, after Lewis had completed much of the preparation for the journey and was about to set off for Pittsburgh. On 19 June, the day before Jefferson dated and signed the instructions, Lewis wrote a confidential letter to his friend William Clark, "with the privity of the President, who expresses an anxious wish that you would consent to join me in this enterprise." Jefferson was offering Clark a captain's commission, Lewis explained, and "your situation if joined with me in this mission will in all respects be precisely such as my own" (Jackson, *Lewis and Clark*, 1:57-60; 2:571-2). The president had drafted and revised the orders for Lewis with the supposition that he would be the only commissioned officer on the expedition. The "anxious wish" that Lewis mentioned in the letter to Clark was born of the same concerns that prompted the injunctions about safety and the final paragraph. Lewis left Washington for Harpers Ferry and Pittsburgh, to make final preparations to proceed on his journey, on 5 July. Jefferson did not see Clark's affirmative response until 6 Aug., too late to change the instructions to allow for shared leadership (Lewis to TJ, 8 July; TJ to Caesar A. Rodney, 13 July; Clark to TJ, 24 July).

I. From James Madison

[before 13 Apr. 1803?]

(1.) Quer. if the laws give any authority at present beyond the limits of the U.S.?

2 "This Mission having reference to the Comerce"—may repell, more than the expression used, the criticism of illicit *principal* objects of the measure.

3 "including the fish"

4. if practicable he might note occasionally the variations of the Needle.

RC (DLC: TJ Papers, 181:22591); entirely in Madison's hand, in pencil; undated; endorsed by TJ as received from the State Department with notation "mr Madison's notes on the instrns to Capt Lewis"; date of receipt in endorsement overwritten and illegible, possibly 12 or 13 Apr.

Madison probably keyed his remarks to numbers he wrote on the now-missing early draft of the instructions. TJ cited exploration as the object of the MISSION—albeit "for the purposes of commerce" (Document IV).

INCLUDING THE FISH: Madison may have been suggesting an addition to the part of the instructions that concerns natural history. The finished instructions refer only to "the animals of the country generally" (same).

VARIATIONS OF THE NEEDLE: see notes to Document IV.

II. From Albert Gallatin

Dear Sir [on or before 13 Apr. 1803]

I perceive nothing in the enclosed which should in my opinion require alteration. perhaps something might be added.

The present aspect of affairs may, ere long, render it necessary that we should, by taking immediate possession, prevent G.B. from doing the same. Hence a perfect knowledge of the posts, establishments & force kept by Spain in upper Louisiana, and also of the most proper station to occupy, for the purpose of preventing effectually the occupying of any part of the Missouri country by G.B., seems important. With that view the present communications of the British with the Missouri, either from the Mississipi, or, which is still more in point, from the waters emptying in Lake Winnipec & generally in Hudson bay, should be well ascertained, as well as the mode in which a small but sufficient force could best be conveyed to the most proper point from whence to prevent any attempt from Lake Winnipec.

But whatever may be the issue of the present difficulties, the future destinies of the Missouri country are of vast importance to the United States, it being perhaps the only large tract of country, and certainly the *first* which lying out of the boundaries of the Union will be settled by the people of the U. States. The precise extent, therefore, of the country drained by all the waters emptying into that river, and consequently the length & directions of all the principal branches ought to be, as far as practicable, ascertained as well as that particular branch which may be followed for the purpose of examining the communications with the Pacific Ocean. That tract of country is bounded on the north by the Waters of Hudson's bay, the extent of which southwardly is tolerably ascertained by Mackenzie & others; Westwardly by the Waters of the Columbia & other rivers emptying into the Pacific, which it is the principal object of this voyage to explore; and southwardly, it is presumed by the waters of Rio Norte. How far these extend Northwardly & confine the waters of the Missouri it is important to know, as their position would generally determine the[1] extent of territory watered by the Missouri. It is presumable, from analogy that the Waters of Hudson's bay which interlock with the many northerly streams of the Missouri are divided from them by elevated lands interspersed with lakes, but not by any regular chain of mountains. By the same analogy; (for within the United States & known parts of North America the spring of[2] every river north of 42° Latitude issues from a lake, and south of 41° from a mountain;) it is probable that the northern branches of the Rio Norte are separated from the southern streams of the Kansas & Missouri rivers by a chain of mountains running westwardly till it unites with the chain which divides the waters of Missouri & other rivers from those emptying into the Pacific. Hence it is presumable that the distance of that east & west[3] chain from the Missouri will generally show the extent of country watered by this river. And although Cn. L. going westwardly towards his main object may not personally become acquainted with the country lying south of his track, yet so far as he may collect information on that subject & also on the communications with the Rio Norte or other southern rivers if any others, which is not probable, interlocks with the Missouri, it would be a desirable object. The great object to ascertain is whether from its extent & fertility that country is[4] Susceptible of a large population, in the same measure as the corresponding tract on the Ohio. Besides the general opinion which may be formed of its fertility, some more specific instructions on the signs of the soil might be given—the two principal of which are the *prevailing* species of timber whether oak—beech—or pine—or barren, and the evenness or mountainous & rocky situation of the lands. Those two circumstances do generally determine in America the quantity of soil fit for cultivation in any one large tract of country; for I presume there are no swamps in that part of the world. But several more signs might be added to which the traveller should pay attention.

I think C. L. ought to take, on the Spanish side of the Illinois settlement, some person who had navigated the Missouri[5] as high as possible & it might not be amiss to try to winter with the traders *from that quarter* who go to the farthest tribe of Indians in the proper direction. A boat or canoe might be hired there (at the Illinois) to carry up to that spot a sufficient quantity of flour to enable him to winter there with comfort so that his hands should be fresh & in good spirits in the spring.

Respectfully Your obt. Servt. ALBERT GALLATIN

RC (DLC); undated; endorsed by TJ as received from the Treasury Department on 13 Apr. and "Missouri" and so recorded in SJL.

BY THE SAME ANALOGY: for TJ's inclusion in the instructions of some of Gallatin's geographical queries, see the notes to Document IV.

[1] Gallatin here canceled "quantity."

[2] Preceding eight words and ampersand interlined.

[3] Preceding two words and ampersand interlined.

[4] Gallatin here canceled "likely."

[5] Word written over "Mississipi."

III. From Levi Lincoln

SIR Washington April 17 1803

From the perusal, & reperusal of your Instructions for Capt. Lewis nothing of importance has suggested itself to my mind which has not been particularly attended to.

I consider the enterprise of national consequence, and, to a degree, personally hazardous, to the projectors, & individual adventurers. In the perverse, hostile, and maligent state of the opposition, with their facility, of imposing on the public mind, & producing excitements, every measure originating with the executive will be attacked, with a virulence in proportion, to the patriotism of the motive, the wisdom of the means, & the probable utility of its execution. The greatest success, will but stop that mouth of clamor, which must be met with the merits of the projection, in case of its falure, or serious disaster. In this view of the subject may not some new aspects be usefully, given to the undertaking, and others made more prominent? Would it not be well, to those particulars which have a principal reference to oppening & promoting, a knowledge of the country, friendship & trade with its inhabitants, and their improvements in the arts of husbandry, to add more explicitly those articles which have for their object the improvement of the mind, & the preservation of the body—Such, as, the ideas the various tribes, or nations possess of a supreme being, their worship, their religion, the agency it has in their respective Govets in war, & in peace; its influence on their manners—their actions which are crimes agt. their society, & the punishments—Their ideas of property, & the tenures by which they claim it—& also the probability of impressing their minds with a sense of an *improved religion* & morality & the means by which it could be effected—Besides religion & morality making a very important article in the history of all countries as an object of attention, If the enterprise appears to be, an attempt to advance them, it will by many people, on that account, be justified, however calamitous the issue—

Would it not be well also to mention the diseases incident to various climates, situations, and seasons; the age most liable to them, the method of treating them, the medicinal articles applied, the age which is considered as old, & the manner of life most condusive to it &c? If any plants or roots of uncommon virtues as medicine should be found, would it not be an object to procure the seed?—

As Capt Lewis may have in his company, some who have not had the small pox, would it not be best to carry some of the matter for the kinepox with him?

From my ideas of Capt. Lewis he will be much more likely, in case of difficulty, to push too far, than to recede too soon—Would it not be well to change the term, '*certain* destruction' into *probable* destruction, & to add,—That those dangers are never to be encountered, which vigilance precaution & attention can secure against, at a reasonable expence—

The foregoing ideas, indigested, and unimportant in themselves as most of them are,[1] I communicate them for your inspection, without reserve—

I have always understood that Storys deficiency was not so much from the want of strength of intellect, as the want of discretion, & correctness of morals—

I am Sir most respectfully your most obt Servt

LEVI LINCOLN

RC (DLC); at head of text: "The President of the United States"; endorsed by TJ as received 18 Apr. and "Capt L's instrns."

KINEPOX: Lincoln's remarks indicate that TJ did not have anything about vaccination in his early draft of the instructions. TJ took up Lincoln's suggestion and included a passage on that subject. While Lincoln's recommendation was for Lewis to be ready to vaccinate members of his party as the expedition assembled, TJ asked Lewis to disseminate vaccine among Native Americans and instruct them in administering it (Document IV).

[1] Lincoln here canceled "assuming to me."

IV. Instructions for Meriwether Lewis

To Meriwether Lewis esquire, Captain of the 1st Regiment of infantry of the United States of America.

Your situation as Secretary of the President of the United States[1] has made you acquainted with the objects of my confidential message of Jan. 18. 1803. to the legislature: you have seen the act they passed, which, tho' expressed in general terms, was meant to sanction those objects, and you are appointed to carry them into execution.

Instruments for ascertaining by celestial observations the geography of the country thro' which you will pass, have been already provided. light articles for barter, & presents among the Indians, arms for your attendants, say for from 10. to 12. men, boats, tents, & other travelling apparatus, with ammunition, medecine, surgical instruments & provisions you will have prepared with such aids as the Secretary at War can yield in his department; & from him also you will recieve authority to engage among our troops, by voluntary agreement, the number of attendants abovementioned, over whom you, as their commanding officer, are invested with all the powers the laws give in such a case.

As your movements while within the limits of the US. will be better directed by occasional communications, adapted to circumstances as they arise, they will not be noticed here. what follows will respect your proceedings after your departure from the US.

Your mission has been communicated to the Ministers here from France, Spain, & Great Britain, and through them to their governments: and such assurances given them as to it's objects, as we trust will satisfy them. the country of Louisiana having been ceded by Spain to France,[2] the passport you have from the Minister of France, the representative of the present sovereign of the country, will be a protection with[3] all it's subjects: and that from the Minister of England will entitle you to the friendly aid of any traders of that allegiance with whom you may happen to meet.

The object of your mission is to explore the Missouri river, & such principal stream of it, as, by it's course & communication with the waters of the Pacific ocean,[4] may offer the most direct & practicable water communication across this continent, for the purposes of commerce.

Beginning at the mouth of the Missouri, you will take[5] observations of latitude & longitude, at all remarkeable points on the river, & especially at the mouths of rivers, at rapids, at islands & other places & objects distinguished by such natural marks & characters of a durable kind, as that they may with certainty be recognised hereafter. the courses of the river between these points of observation may be supplied by the compass, the log-line & by time, corrected by the observations themselves. the variations of the compass too, in different places, should be noticed.

The interesting points of the portage between the heads of the Missouri & the water offering the best communication with the Pacific ocean, should also be fixed by observation, & the course of that water to the ocean, in the same manner as that of the Missouri.

Your observations are to be taken with great pains & accuracy, to be entered distinctly, & intelligibly for others as well as yourself, to comprehend all the elements necessary, with the aid of the usual tables, to fix the latitude and longitude of the places at which they were taken, & are to be rendered to the war office, for the purpose of having the calculations made concurrently by proper persons within the US. several copies of these, as well as of your other notes, should be made at leisure times, & put into the care of the most trustworthy of your attendants, to guard, by multiplying them, against the accidental losses to which they will be exposed. a further guard would be that one of these copies be written[6] on the paper of the birch, as less liable to injury from damp than common paper.

The commerce which may be carried on with the people inhabiting the line you will pursue, renders a knolege of those people important. you will therefore endeavor to make yourself acquainted, as far as a diligent pursuit of your journey shall admit,

with the names of the nations & their numbers;

the extent & limits of their possessions;

their relations with other tribes or nations;

their language, traditions, monuments;

their ordinary occupations in agriculture, fishing, hunting, war, arts, & the implements for these;

their food, clothing, & domestic accomodations;

the diseases prevalent among them, & the remedies they use;

moral & physical circumstances which distinguish them from the tribes we know;

peculiarities in their laws, customs & dispositions;

and articles of commerce they may need, or furnish, & to what extent.

And, considering the interest which every nation has in extending & strengthening the authority of reason & justice among the people around them, it will be useful to acquire what knolege you can of the state of morality, religion & information among them; as it may better enable those who endeavor to civilize & instruct them, to adapt their measures to the existing notions & practices of those on whom they are to operate.

Other objects worthy of notice will be

the soil & face of the country, it's growth & vegetable productions, especially those not of the US.

the animals of the country generally, & especially those not known in the US.

the remains & accounts of any which may be deemed rare or extinct;

the mineral productions of every kind: but more particularly metals, limestone, pit-coal, & saltpetre; salines & mineral waters, noting the temperature of the last, & such circumstances as may indicate their character.

Volcanic appearances;

climate as characterized by the thermometer, by the proportion of rainy, cloudy, & clear days, by lightening, hail, snow, ice, by the access & recess of frost, by the winds prevailing at different seasons, the dates at which particular plants put forth their flower, or leaf, time of appearance of particular birds, reptiles or insects.

Altho' your route will be along the channel[7] of the Missouri, yet you will endeavor to inform yourself, by enquiry, of the character & extent of the country watered by it's branches; & especially on it's Southern side. the North river or Rio Bravo which runs into the gulph of Mexico, and the North river, or Rio colorado which runs into the gulph of California are understood to be the principal streams heading opposite to the waters of the Missouri, and running Southwardly. whether the dividing grounds between the Missouri & them are mountains or flat lands, what are their distance from the Missouri, the character of the intermediate country, and the people inhabiting it, are worthy of particular enquiry. the Northern waters of the Missouri are less to be enquired after, because they have been ascertained to a considerable degree, and are still in a course of ascertainment by English traders & travellers. but if you can learn any thing certain of the most Northern source of the Missisipi, & of it's position relative to the lake of the woods, it will be interesting to us. some account too of the path of the Canadian traders, from the Missisipi, at the mouth of the Ouisconsin river, to where it strikes the Missouri, and of the soil & rivers in it's course,[8] is desireable.

In all your intercourse with the natives treat them in the most friendly & conciliatory manner which their own conduct will admit; allay all jealousies as to the object of your journey, satisfy them of it's innocence, make them acquainted with the position, extent, character, peaceable & commercial dispositions of the US. of our wish to be neighborly, friendly & useful to them, & of our dispositions to a commercial intercourse with them; confer with them on the points most convenient as mutual emporiums, & the articles of most desireable interchange for them & us. if a few of their influential chiefs, within practicable distance, wish to visit us, arrange such a visit with them, & furnish them with authority to call on our officers, on their entering the US. to have them conveyed to this place at the public expence. if any of them should wish to have some of their young people brought up with us, & taught such arts as may be useful to them, we will recieve, instruct & take care of them. such a mission, whether of influential chiefs, or of young people, would give some security to your own party.[9] carry with you some matter of the kine-pox; inform those of them with whom you may be, of it's efficacy as a preservative from the small pox; and instruct & encourage them in the use of it. this may be especially done wherever you winter.

As it is impossible for us to foresee in what manner you will be recieved by those people, whether with hospitality or hostility, so is it impossible to prescribe the exact degree of perseverance with which you are to pursue your journey. we value too much the lives of citizens to offer them to probable destruction. your numbers will be sufficient to secure you against the unauthorised opposition of individuals, or of small parties: but if a superior force, authorised or not authorised, by a nation, should be arrayed against your further passage, & inflexibly determined to arrest it, you must decline it's further pursuit, and return. in the loss of yourselves, we should lose also the information you will have acquired. by returning safely with that, you may enable us to renew the essay with better calculated means. to your own discretion therefore must be left the degree of danger you may risk, & the point at which you should decline, only saying we wish you to err on the side of your safety, & to bring back your party safe, even if it be with less information.

As far up the Missouri as the white settlements extend, an intercourse will probably be found to exist between them and the Spanish posts at St. Louis, opposite Cahokia, or St. Genevieve opposite Kaskaskia. from still further up the river, the traders may furnish a conveyance for letters. beyond that you may perhaps be able to engage Indians to bring letters for the government to Cahokia or Kaskaskia, on promising that they shall there recieve such special compensation as you shall have stipulated with them. avail yourself of these means to communicate to us, at seasonable intervals, a copy of your journal, notes & observations of every kind, putting into cypher whatever might do injury if betrayed.

Should you reach the Pacific ocean, inform yourself of the circumstances which may decide whether the furs of those parts may not be collected as advantageously at the head of the Missouri (convenient as is supposed to the waters of the Colorado, & Oregan or Columbia) as at Nootka sound or any other point of that coast; & that trade be consequently conducted through the Missouri & U.S. more beneficially than by the circumnavigation now practised.[10]

On your arrival on that coast, endeavor to learn if there be any port within your reach frequented by the sea-vessels of any nation, and to send two of your trusty people back by sea, in such way as shall appear[11] practicable, with a copy of your notes. and should you be of opinion that the return of your party by the way they went will be eminently dangerous, then ship the whole, & return by sea, by the way of Cape Horn, or the Cape of good Hope, as you shall be able. as you will be without money, clothes or provisions, you must endeavor to use the credit of the US. to obtain them; for which purpose open letters of credit shall be furnished you, authorising you to draw on the Executive of the US. or any of it's officers, in any part of the world, on which draughts can be disposed of, and to apply with our recommendations to the Consuls, agents, merchants or citizens of any nation with which we have intercourse, assuring them in our name that any aids they may furnish you, shall be honorably repaid, and on demand. Our consuls Thomas Hewes at Batavia in Java, William Buchanan at the isles of France and Bourbon, & John Elmslie at the Cape of good hope will be able to supply your necessities by draughts on us.[12]

Should you find it safe to return by the way you go, after sending two of your party round by sea, or with your whole party, if no conveyance by sea can be found, do so; making such observations on your return, as may serve to supply, correct or confirm those made on your outward journey.

On re-entering the US. and reaching a place of safety, discharge any of your attendants who may desire & deserve it, procuring for them immediate paiment of all arrears of pay & cloathing which may have incurred since their departure; and assure them that they shall be recommended to the liberality of the legislature for the grant of a souldier's portion of land each, as proposed in my message to Congress: & repair yourself with your papers to the seat of government.[13]

To provide, on the accident of your death, against anarchy, dispersion & the consequent danger to your party, and total failure of the enterprise, you are hereby authorised, by any instrument signed & written in your own hand, to name the person among them who shall succeed to the command on your decease, & by like instruments to change the nomination from time to time, as further experience of the characters accompanying you shall point out superior fitness: and all the powers & authorities given to yourself are, in the event of your death, transferred to & vested in the successor so named, with further power to him, & his successors in like manner to name each his successor, who, on the death of his predecessor, shall be invested with all the powers & authorities given to yourself.

Given under my hand at the city of Washington this 20th. day of June 1803

TH: JEFFERSON
Pr. US. of America

PrC (DLC); dateline and signature added in ink; TJ's corrections of copying errors have not been noted. Dft (DLC: TJ Papers, 199:35393-4); probably written by 27 Apr. (see TJ to Lewis of that date); at foot of text: "Given under my hand at the city of Washington this 20th. day of June 1803. Th:J. Pr. US of A.";

notation by TJ at head of text: "Copd. where inserted in it's proper place as to date." Recorded in SJL with notation "instrns."

ALREADY PROVIDED: see Lewis to TJ, 14 May, and TJ's reply two days later.

For the PASSPORT, see Louis André Pichon to TJ, 4 Mch.

OBJECT OF YOUR MISSION: in the instructions for André Michaux in 1793, TJ wrote that "the chief objects of your journey are to find the shortest and most convenient route of communication between the US. and the Pacific ocean, within the temperate latitudes, and to learn such particulars as can be obtained of the country through which it passes, it's productions, inhabitants and other interesting circumstances." For those instructions, which appear in this series at 30 Apr. 1793, see Vol. 25:624-6.

Madison advised giving COMMERCE a primary role in the statement of objectives; see Document I.

Madison's remarks imply that the early draft did not include the instruction about noting VARIATIONS OF THE COMPASS and that TJ added it at Madison's suggestion.

RENDERED TO THE WAR OFFICE: see Andrew Ellicott to TJ, 6 Mch., for the CALCULATIONS to be performed on Lewis's astronomical data after his return.

PAPER OF THE BIRCH: in his instructions for Michaux, TJ suggested writing the "most important" notes on animal skin and putting "further details" on birch bark, which was durable against wetness and other accidents and "may not excite suspicions among the Indians."

PEOPLE INHABITING THE LINE YOU WILL PURSUE: the requests for information about DISEASES, remedies, MORALITY, and religion of Native Americans are likely the results of Lincoln's suggestions. In 1793, TJ wanted Michaux to take note of "the names, numbers, and dwellings of the inhabitants, and such particularities as you can learn of their history, connection with each other, languages, manners, state of society and of the arts and commerce among them." TJ also asked Michaux to collect information about the SOIL and "general face" of the country through which he was to pass, along with its rivers, mountains, and "productions animal, vegetable, and mineral so far as they may be new to us and may also be useful or very curious."

ANIMALS OF THE COUNTRY: Madison in his comments on the early draft may have suggested adding fishes to this category. DEEMED RARE OR EXTINCT: Michaux's instructions asked him to look for signs of mammoths and llamas.

ALTHO' YOUR ROUTE WILL BE ALONG THE CHANNEL: TJ probably introduced this paragraph—a limited exposition of some of the questions about the continent's interior posed by the secretary of the Treasury—in response to Gallatin's comments on the earlier draft. The directive for Michaux did not address these larger geographical issues.

KINE-POX: a suggestion from Lincoln prompted TJ to include the passage about vaccination (Document III).

IMPOSSIBLE FOR US TO FORESEE: "Ignorance of the country thro' which you are to pass and confidence in your judgment, zeal, and discretion," TJ had advised Michaux, "prevent the society from attempting more minute instructions."

PROBABLE DESTRUCTION: TJ's original phrasing, which he altered on Lincoln's advice, was "certain destruction" (see Document III).

WE SHOULD LOSE ALSO THE INFORMATION: TJ's directions for Michaux also placed an emphasis on safety, "not merely as your personal concern, but as the injunction of Science in general which expects it's enlargement from your enquiries."

In 1793, TJ expected Michaux to begin at KASKASKIA and proceed west to strike the Missouri River above the Spanish settlements, "that you may avoid the risk of being stopped."

CYPHER: see Cipher for Meriwether Lewis, [April 1803?].

OREGAN OR COLUMBIA: "by the latest maps," TJ wrote in the directions for Michaux, it appeared "as if a river called Oregan interlocked with the Missouri for a considerable distance, and entered the Pacific ocean, not far Southward of Nootka sound. But the Society are aware that these maps are not to be trusted so far as to be the ground of any positive instruction to you. They therefore only mention the fact, leaving to yourself to verify it, or to follow such other as you shall find to be the real truth."

ON YOUR ARRIVAL ON THAT COAST: Michaux's instructions called for him to send copies of his papers by sea after reaching the coast. TJ did not give Michaux the explicit option of returning by sea. Michaux was to go back by the way he had come "or such other route, as you shall think likely to fulfill with most satisfaction and certainty the objects of your mission."

LETTERS OF CREDIT: see TJ to Lewis, 4 July.

In his confidential message to Congress on 18 Jan., TJ anticipated that each member of the expedition could expect a PORTION OF LAND as compensation (first message of TJ to the Senate and the House of Representatives, 18 Jan.).

[1] Preceding nine words interlined in Dft.

[2] Here in Dft TJ canceled "& possession by this time probably [. . .]."

[3] Word interlined in Dft in place of "against."

[4] Here in Dft TJ interlined "whether the Columbia, Oregan, Colorado or any other river."

[5] Here in Dft TJ canceled "careful."

[6] TJ interlined this word, which is lacking in Dft. Sentence interlined in Dft.

[7] Word interlined in Dft in place of "bed."

[8] In Dft TJ first wrote "rivers it traverses" before altering the phrase to read as above. In Dft he interlined this sentence in place of "Two copies of your notes at least, & as many more as leisure will admit, should be made & confided to the care of the most trusty individuals of your attendants," which he wrote as the start of a paragraph.

[9] Sentence interlined in Dft.

[10] Preceding two paragraphs inserted in margin of Dft.

[11] Preceding two words interlined in Dft in place of "they shall judge."

[12] Sentence interlined in Dft.

[13] In Dft TJ here canceled "to which I have only to add my sincere prayers for your safe return."

From Nicolas Gouin Dufief

MONSIEUR, ce 13 avril 1803

Le Dr. Priestley était parti depuis plusieurs jours, pour se rendre à sa terre, lorsque j'ai reçu l'honneur de la vôtre du 9. Avril—Je suis d'autant plus fâché ce cette circonstance qu'aucun des Libraires de Philadelphia, ne peut me procurer ceux de ses ouvrages que vous demandez—Je tâcherai de découvrir quelques particuliers qui peuvent les avoir et ferai mon possible alors pour vous les obtenir, ainsi que les pensées de Pascal dont je n'ai pour le moment aucun exemplaire dans mon magazin—

Agréez l'assurance de mon profond respect N. G. DUFIEF

EDITORS' TRANSLATION

SIR, 13 Apr. 1803

Dr. Priestley had left for his home several days before I had the honor of receiving your letter of the 9th. I am all the more vexed by this circumstance because none of the Philadelphia bookstores is able to obtain the works of his that you requested. I will try to find individuals who might have them, and will do my best to obtain them for you, along with Pascal's *Pensées*, of which I do not have a single copy in my store.

Accept the assurance of my deep respect. N. G. DUFIEF

RC (DLC); at foot of text: "Ths Jefferson, Président des Etats-Unis"; endorsed by TJ as received 16 Apr. and so recorded in SJL.

From Bernard Smith

SIR Washington April 13. 1803.

Although I have not the honor to be personally acquainted with your Excellency, yet as I know that you are accessible to any of your fellow-citizens I shall take the liberty to address a few lines to you.

Levi Lincoln Esqr. to whom I had a Letter of introduction, did me the honor to recommend me to your Excellency, as a person capable of filling some subordinate Office under the government. Mr. Lincoln informs me that altho', you was disposed to serve me, it was not then in your power. This same gentlemen has likewise had the goodness to make application in my behalf to the Gentlemen who are at the head of the departments, but without sucess, as he was informed that there was no vacancies in the public Offices. and although many of those persons employed there, particularly the Clerks are the avowed partizans of a faction hostile to the government, it was not considered advisable to make any removals.

I will not presume to say how far it is politic or just to retain such persons in Office, when their places could easily be supplied by persons who are the friends of the administration. Your Excellency who so justly merits the confidence of the Republicans in this Country, was pleased to observe, in your answer to a remonstrance from the Merchants of New Haven—"If a due participation of office is a matter of right, how are vacancies to be obtained? Those by death are few, by resignation none. Can any other mode than by removal be proposed? This is a painful office: but this is my duty, and I meet it as such"—

Although I have ever been uniform in my politics, and indefatigable in my exertions in the republican cause, and which is well known to most of the destinguished patriots of my native state (N.J.), still I never before had the vanity nor the presumption to aspire after any office, nor should I now make application for one, where it not that my family on account of various misfortunes which they have recently experienced are unable to assist me in going into business at this time. Thus situated I concluded by the advice of my republican friends to repair to this place in hopes of obtaining some subordinate office under the government. and altho, I have been here for some time, and am concious of Mr. Lincoln's wishes to serve me I have not as yet been able to succeed. Persuaded as I am of your Excellency's justice and magnanimity, I have taken the liberty to make known to you my situation, and humbly solicit your high patronage; and should it be in your Excellency's power to serve me on this occasion, permit me to assure you that it will ever be held in grateful remembrance both by myself and all my friends, and the summit of my ambition will always be to merit your confidence.

I have taken the liberty to forward to your Excellency an Oration which I deliver'd on the death of Genr. Washington, and likewise a few numbers of the New Jersey "Centinel" in which are contained (under the signature of "Brutus") some writings of mine in defence of the administration.

If your Excellency should honor me with a few lines, please to direct it to me at my lodgings at Mrs. Sweeney's nearly opposite the Bank.

I have the honor to be very respectfully, Your Excellencey's Most obdt. & very Humle. Servt. BERNARD SMITH JUNR.

RC (DNA: RG 59, LAR); addressed: "His Excellency Thomas Jefferson Esqr. President of the United States. City of Washington"; endorsed by TJ "a clerkship" and so recorded in SJL at 13 Apr. Enclosures: see below.

Born in Morris County, New Jersey, Bernard Smith (1776-1835) actively supported the Republican cause in the state beginning in the late 1790s, reporting and writing pieces for the Newark *Centinel of Freedom* signed "Brutus." He served as a clerk in the State Department from 1804 until his appointment as postmaster at New Brunswick in 1810 and as surveyor and inspector of the revenue in 1812. He held those positions until 1819, when he returned to Washington as a New Jersey congressman. He served only one term, during which he voted to remove restrictions on slavery in the Missouri bill, an unpopular stand with his constituents. In 1821, President Monroe appointed Smith register of the land office at Little Rock, in Arkansas Territory, a position he held until his death. He also served as secretary to the territorial governor from 1825 to 1828 and as a subagent to the Quapaw Indians until their removal (*Biog. Dir. Cong.*; Madison, *Papers, Sec. of State Ser.*, 7:81, 346n; 8:131n, 178, 339; *Pres. Ser.*, 2:164; JEP, 2:270, 272; Carl E. Prince, *New Jersey's Jeffersonian Republicans: The Genesis of an Early Party Machine, 1789-1817* [Chapel Hill, 1964], 46n; Walter R. Fee, *The Transition from Aristocracy to Democracy in New Jersey, 1789-1829* [Somerville, N.J., 1933], 241-2; Stets, *Postmasters*, 169; Newark *Centinel of Freedom*, 10 July, 18 Sep., 30 Oct. 1798; 16 July 1799; *Daily National Intelligencer*, 12 Aug. 1835; RS, 3:510-11).

YOUR ANSWER TO A REMONSTRANCE: see Vol. 34:554-8.

Smith's ORATION on the death of Washington has not been found, but articles in the *Centinel of Freedom* signed BRUTUS extend from 3 Apr. 1798 to 18 Jan. 1803. In 1798, "Brutus," critical of the Adams administration, observed: "It is not from France that you are in danger—it is from the influence Britain is daily acquiring here, that our danger comes.—A stamp tax, land tax &c. are already the blessed fruits of following their foot-steps. A sedition bill is on the carpet." Brutus urged New Jersey voters to send Republican John Condit to Congress as "the true patriot and able defender of his country's rights, liberties, and independence." He applauded the election of Condit, Aaron Kitchell, and James Linn in the fall of 1798 with a piece entitled "Republicanism Triumphant: or, The British Faction out-done." In October 1798, "Brutus" also submitted a tribute to the memory of Benjamin F. Bache. In July 1800, he argued that prosecutions under the Sedition Act violated the Constitution and perverted justice. The courts had become "engines of oppression, and weapons of party vengeance." He described the election of Jefferson as the "pivot upon which turns the destinies of our country, our liberty." In a letter dated 26 Jan. 1801, "Brutus" warned against the "daring attempt to overset the free choice of the people in the late Elections." In his last piece dated Morris County, 12 Jan. 1803, he applauded the beneficial changes brought about by the Jefferson administration, including the relief from "obnoxious taxes" and the payment of $8,000,000 in principal and interest on the public debt, with a $4,500,000 surplus yet in the Treasury brought about through prudence and economy. Republicans still had to be on guard for the opposition party was "indefatigable in their opposition to every measure of the government" and resorted to calumny and misrepresentation. By "inventing the most infamous lies," they have attempted "to injure the character of our worthy chief magistrate." Scurrility and personal abuse were the order of the day. Smith called on Republicans to be vigilant. Should this faction ever succeed in their intrigues, "then may the *patriots of America* put on the *mantle of mourning*, and bid *adieu* to the *Constitution* and *liberties* of their *Country*" (Newark *Centinel of Freedom*, 3, 10 Apr., 10 July, 18 Sep., 9, 30 Oct. 1798; 29 July 1800; 3 Feb. 1801; 18 Jan. 1803). For several pieces written by Smith while a clerk in the State Department, using the signature "Franklin," see the *National Intelligencer*, 10 and 15 Oct. 1804 (Madison, *Papers, Sec. of State Ser.*, 8:339).

From John Smith

SIR New Orleans April the 13th 1803

Having been at this place for some days, I find every thing remaing in Statuco—The Intendant positively refuses to restore to us the Deposit—And it is commonly said to be in conformity to some secret instructions which he has received from the Court at Madrid

He certainly has something to protect him of the kind, or he would not dare to persist. He possesses more information & ability then all the Spanish officers of this Port put together And I do not think that one of his acquaintance here believes that he makes one solitary step as a public officer unauthorised—Many of his most intimate friends declare that he is friendly to the United States, And wishes with many more, the Americans had possession of this Country, for which they now have a sufficient cause for at least making the attempt

The french Prefect has made many flattering professions to the Americans at this place but this is calculated to enveigle them—To soften them down into supineness, or destroy them by faction—The french will here carry fire in there Bosom, & in due time will discover the flame—The consequences of their coming here is sincerely to be deprecated—And indeed is dreaded with horrow by both the Spanish & Americans at this moment—It will be matter of consolation if our Minister should succeed in the object of opening a negociation for the east side of the Mississippi River—The western Country from her Geographical, commercial & political situation has become an object of importance & loudly calls for this acquisition of Territory If the French should settle it, a war will be the inevitable consequence—

It is reported here that the French army destined for this place are ordered to St. Domingo—Mr. Hewling no doubt will state the particulars I beg pardon for this intrusion on your time

I am Sir with consideration & respect Your most obedient Servt

JOHN SMITH

RC (DLC); addressed: "Thomas Jefferson President of the United States City Washington"; postmarked Natchez, 26 Apr.; endorsed by TJ as received 22 May and so recorded in SJL with notation "of Ohio."

IN STATUCO: perhaps an attempt to render *in statu quo*, meaning in the same state or condition (OED).

MR. HEWLING: William E. Hulings.

To John Walker

SIR— Washington. Apl. 13. 1803—

Your letter of the fourth did not come to hand 'till last night—it covered a copy of that of May 15th 1788—which I had only hastily read in the hands of Genl. Lee—

I think its miscarriage unfortunate; as, had I received it I should without hesitation have made it my first object to have called on you on my return to this country, & to have come to an understanding as to the course we were to pursue, as was the object of the letter. time, silence, & the circumstances growing out of them have unfavorably affected the case—With respect to the newspapers, 'tho the silencing them would be very desirable yet it would be as difficult if not desperate. however if Callender & Coleman & Caldwell can be silenced, the others are but copyers or answerers of them. Wayne, Relf, Russel, have not pretended to original information. but these people slander for their bread, & as long as customers can be found who will read & relish & pay for their lies, they will fabricate them for the market. As for the antagonist presses; I have with conscientious exactness avoided the smallest interference with them, further than to have public documents published in them. the present occasion however will justify my using the intermediation of friends to direct the discretion of those of them of the principal circulation. with respect to the Bee which you particularly mention, I know not the editor & scarcely ever see his paper. but through a friend who knows him I can have a total silence recommended to him, probably with effect. through the same channel the Aurora & American Citizen may probably be induced to silence. these are the only papers of considerable circulation on that side: & if their antagonists can be brought to be silent, they can have no reason not to be so. however my best endeavors shall be used by these & all other means to consign this unfortunate matter to all the oblivion of which it is susceptible. I certainly could have no objection to your shewing my letter to Mr. Nicholas to the ladies of your family. My greatest anxieties are for their tranquility—I salute them & yourself with respect—

TH: JEFFERSON

Tr (NHi: Gilder Lehrman Collection at the Gilder Lehrman Institute of American History); in an unidentified hand; at foot of text: "John Walker esq."; two attestations at foot of text, the first in Bishop James Madison's hand and signed by him: "I certify this to be a true Copy from the Original—J Madison Bp of the Pr. Ep. Church in Virginia Apl. 10th 1806," the second in John Marshall's hand and signed by him: "A true copy from the original shown me by Mr. Walker, which I believe to be with handwriting of Mr. Jefferson J Marshall C.J. of the US. May 13th. 1806"; endorsed: "(Copy) Thomas Jefferson to John Walker April 13, 1803."

YOUR LETTER: Walker's correspondence of 4 Apr. 1803, recorded in SJL as received on the 12th, has not been found. According to SJL, TJ wrote Walker on 29 and 30 Mch. and Walker responded with one from his home at Belvoir on 30 Mch., received by TJ the same day. All are missing. Neither the original nor the copy of the 15 May 1788 letter, written while TJ was in France, has been found. Only the index to SJL is extant for 1788 and the Walker correspondence is not listed there. Some time after TJ's departure for Paris, Elizabeth Moore Walker informed her husband that TJ, his classmate, friend, neighbor, and groomsman in 1764, had made improper advances toward her, beginning in 1768. She had not informed her husband earlier, fearing a duel or other repercussions. John Walker later noted that after learning of the unsolicited overtures, he on numerous occasions wrote TJ demanding an explanation, but no letters have been found. A change in the tenor of the surviving correspondence between the two, that is, Walker to TJ, 4 Feb. 1786, and TJ to Walker, 7 Feb. 1790, was noted by the Editors (see Vol. 9:251-2; Vol. 11:194n; Vol. 16:156-7). For the history of the "Walker Affair," including the charges that became public in 1805, which indicated that TJ's attempts to seduce Elizabeth Walker extended from 1768 to 1779, see Jon Kukla, *Mr. Jefferson's Women* (New York, 2007), 41-63 and Appendix A and Malone, *Jefferson*, 1:447-51, 4:216-19. To his friends, TJ responded in 1805 by pleading guilty to only one charge, that when "young and single I offered love to a handsome lady" (TJ to Robert Smith, 1 July 1805).

HANDS OF GENL. LEE: in 1793, Henry Lee married Ann Hill Carter, Elizabeth Walker's niece. Lee, who as a Federalist congressman in 1801 supported Burr for president when the deadlocked election passed to the House of Representatives, served as a mediator between Walker and TJ, making several visits to Monticello during the years of controversy, which lasted until the death of the Walkers in 1809 (Malone, *Jefferson*, 1:447-8; Syrett, *Hamilton*, 25:331, 26:140-2; RS, 1:276-9, 499n).

In October 1802, James T. CALLENDER brought the charges of TJ's misconduct toward his neighbor's wife before the wider public through pieces in the Richmond *Recorder* (Vol. 38:37n). Callender's article of 13 Oct. headed "Mrs. Walker," described several attempts of "a certain great Personage" to injure the virtue of "a Lady in Albemarle county." The *Boston Gazette* reprinted the piece on 11 Nov. Callender noted that he was not the first to expose the affair. He referred to an article that appeared in the 21 Sep. issue of the *Bee* and was reprinted in the Richmond *Examiner*. It described efforts by Connecticut Federalists to disgrace the president by spreading an untrue story about TJ and a neighbor, who left his family under the "care of Mr. Jefferson" while he was away. During his absence, according to the report, "Mr. J. attempted to seduce his lady, and when he conceived himself sufficiently ingratiated into her favor he made an attack on her virtue, but was resisted by Mrs. W. and repulsed by her with a pair of scissors; that on Mr. Walker's return he called on Mr. Jefferson for satisfaction," and at that point "Mr. J. begged his pardon, and wrote him a letter confessing and apologising for his criminal intentions." This letter was said to be in the hands of William COLEMAN, editor of the *New-York Evening Post*, "who had possessed it a considerable time." Callender noted in February 1803 that John Walker had recently visited Richmond and showed "a celebrated correspondence" to several people who advised him to postpone publication until the next election, explaining that "the horrible infamy of the contents of a part of this correspondence might have its edge blunted in 18 months of newspaper repercussion." Callender, however, promised that "the letters will be printed, first or last, there can be no question." The piece was reprinted in the *New-York Evening Post* on 16 Feb. but Elias B. CALDWELL of the *Washington Federalist* did not cover the story at this time. John Russell and James Cutler printed it in the *Boston Gazette* on 21 Feb., but it did not appear in Benjamin Russell's *Columbian Centinel* (Pasley, *Tyranny of Printers*, 144-5, 233, 240-1; Brigham, *American Newspapers*, 1:277, 303; 2:913, 949).

FRIEND WHO KNOWS HIM: perhaps Gideon Granger. TJ used Granger to subscribe to Charles Holt's Hudson *Bee* (MB, 2:1123). The press was not silenced immediately. On 25 June, the *Gazette of the United States* printed a piece noting that "some democratick paper at the southward, deeming it necessary to say something of Mr. Jefferson's felonious attempt to seduce the wife of his friend, took certain unwarrantable liberties with the character of Mrs. Walker, and insinuated that her reputation was not perfectly free from blemish. Mr. Walker immediately wrote to Mr. Jefferson that he must silence the democratick presses upon that subject, and intimated what would be the consequence of neglecting to do so." A piece from the Richmond *Examiner* was reprinted by James Cheetham in the New York AMERICAN CITIZEN on 1 July, reporting that Henry Lee had carried a "challenge to the President of the United States from Mr. John Walker of Albemarle." According to SJL, a letter from Walker to TJ of 3 July was received by the president on the 6th. The next day TJ responded, but neither letter has been found.

NO OBJECTION: TJ perhaps permitted Walker to show the correspondence to John Nicholas, the Federalist Albemarle County clerk, who referred to the "unpleasant affair between W, J, & L" in correspondence with Alexander Hamilton in August 1803. He noted that "in consequence of the late infamous & foolish publications" in the Richmond *Examiner*, all "will certainly come out at full length now." Nicholas assured Hamilton that Walker and Lee were "holding the *great man* in a very unpleasant situation. They have both written to him & demanded certain things; which, I suppose, he will not comply with—and of course you may guess the rest. But this flagrant breach of *pretended* private friendship, you may depend forms but a small link in the great chain of deformity & vice" (Syrett, *Hamilton*, 26:140-1).

From Henry Dearborn

War Department
Sir, April 14, 1803

I have the honor to propose the following persons for appointments in the Army of the United States (Viz)

Henry B. Jackson	to be	2d Lieut. of Artillerists
Samuel W. Sayre		Ensign of the 2d Regt of Infty
Louis C. Bayly		ditto
William P. Clyma		ditto
Julius F. Heileman		Cadet of Artillerists
William McRea		Ditto
Sandwich		Surgeons Mate

Accept Sir the assurances &c

FC (Lb in DNA: RG 107, LSP).

On 14 April, Dearborn informed Henry B. JACKSON, Samuel W. SAYRE, Louis C. BAYLY, William P. CLYMA, Julius F. HEILEMAN, William McRee (MCREA), and Thomas K. SANDWICH that the president had approved their respective appointments (FCs in Lb in DNA: RG 107, LSMA; Dearborn to Sandwich, 1 June 1803, in same). Jackson and Bayly resigned within months, however, and only Sayre and Clyma were included in TJ's list of military nominations sent to the Senate on 18 Nov. 1803 (Heitman, *Dictionary*, 1:201, 312, 520, 567, 682, 863; JEP, 1:458).

From John Wayles Eppes

Dear Sir, Bermuda Hundred Apl. 14th.

I arrived at Monticello the day after you set out for Washington. Had I supposed you would have delayed your journey I should certainly have returned earlier—

Mr. Hancocke promised to forward your shrub & if you have not already heard from him you may calculate on hearing in a few days—

I attended the Albemarle election the result of which you have[1] heard—Cabbell is extremely irritated at the opposition & said while in Albemarle "that he thought it but a midling thing in the old President (after his lying two nights on his blanket to make him President) to set up his son in law in opposition to him"—

You were kind enough to say that the 400 dollars should be paid whenever my wants required—I have engaged to pay some money early in May & if you can between this time & the 4th. of May remit it to me in bank notes to this place it will be acceptable—

I left Maria at Monticello in good health on Saturday last—Francis has passed well through the measles—The election in Chesterfield the first county in my district is over—[1] I lost but 9 votes & near 600 polld—

accept for your health & happiness my warmest wishes. Yours sincerely JNO: W: EPPES

RC (ViU: Edgehill-Randolph Papers); closing quotation mark supplied; endorsed by TJ as received 23 Apr. and so recorded in SJL.

Mr. Hancocke of Petersburg supplied TJ with SHRUB and syrup of punch (TJ to George Jefferson, 12 May).

In 1803, Samuel Jordan Cabell ran in the ALBEMARLE ELECTION for his fifth term representing Virginia's fourteenth district in Congress. He was unexpectedly opposed by Thomas Mann Randolph. Cabell pledged to challenge the results, but never offered sufficient proof of any irregularity at the polls. In February 1801, during the deadlocked presidential contest in the House of Representatives, he was said to have spent TWO NIGHTS sleeping on a cot there throughout the voting (DVB, 2:494-5; Thomas Mann Randolph to TJ, 29 Apr.).

KIND ENOUGH TO SAY: see TJ to Eppes, 24 Apr.

Eppes won ELECTION IN CHESTERFIELD and assumed the seat vacated by William Branch Giles. Eppes represented Virginia's Sixteenth District for the Eighth through Eleventh and Thirteenth Congresses (*Biog. Dir. Cong.*).

[1] Eppes here canceled "doubtless."

From John Foncin

MONSIEUR Philadelphie 14 Avril 1803.

Le president des etats unis m'ayant honoré du Brevet cy inclus,[1] pour elever les fortifications necessaires à la defense du port de Boston, j'ai construit le fort independence à la Satisfaction des citoyens de cette Ville. Cet Ouvrage etant achevé, et aprés un travail assidû de quatre années tant à Baltimore qu'à Boston, j'ai Sollicité la permission de venir à philadelphie, et cette grace m'a eté accordée, d'aprés la lettre cy jointe[2] du Secretaire de la Guerre en datte du 5. aoust.

Etant ainsi continué au Service, j'ai achevé pendant l'hyver les dispositions de defense pour le port de Boston; j'ai envoyé au Secretaire de la Guerre differentes Observations relatives au Service, et j'ai reçû ma paye Sans aucune difficulté. Mais tandis que j'employois de la meilleure foy le resultat de mon experience dans l'art des fortifications pour être de plus en plus utile à une contrée que j'eusse Voulû Servir toute ma vie, quelle a eté ma Surprise, lorsque Sans aucune information prealable j'ai eté privé de ma paye depuis le 1er. decembre, en consequence de la lettre cy jointe[3] de Mr. Simmons. J'ai délors cessé mes fonctions d'ingenieur au Service des etats unis. Mais j'ai inutilement reclamé ce qui m'etoit dû depuis le 1er. decembre jusqu'au 12. fevrier; ce dernier jour etant celuy ou j'ai reçû quoique indirectement le premier avis de la Volonté du Secret. de la Guerre. Seroit-il donc possible que Moi qui ai travaillé avec une Si constante activité pour construire Sans interruption les forts de Baltimore et de Boston, Moi qui ai reçû les temoignages les plus flatteurs des citoyens de ces deux Villes (comme on peut le voir par l'article de la chronicle independente cy jointe) et des Membres du Congrés qui ont Visité mes travaux, Seroit il possible, dis-je, que je Serois privé des appointements de deux mois et 12 jours.

Je n'ai il est Vray rien à objecter lorsque le Secretaire de la Guerre Veut annuller mon brevêt du president des etats unis; mais au moins devois—je être informé en positive termes que je n'etois plus employé et dés lors je Serois retourné dans ma patrie.

On ne peut d'ailleurs alleguer que j'ai fini l'ouvrage entier confié à mes Soins. Le Brevet dont j'ai eté honoré comprend la defense generale du port et de la ville de Boston; et le fort independence n'est qu'une partie des dispositions. De l'aveu des Generaux et autres militaires qui ont Visité cette place, il est reconnû comme indispensable de Batir un fort, ou au moins la redoute dont j'ai envoyé le plan au Secretaire de la Guerre sur Governor's island.

La lettre cy jointe[4] en datte du 16. mars par laquelle le Secretaire de la Guerre desire m'employer de nouveau, mais en me considerant comme hors du Service depuis mon arrivée à Philadelphie, Sembleroit detruire la permission qu'il m'avoit donnée. Mais, dans ce Cas, il faudroit Supposer qu'elle a un effet retroactif, ce qui ne peut être. Je n'ai pû Voir Sans une extrême Sensibilité cette Severe interruption de mes Services, dans l'instant ou j'avois lieu d'attendre une recompense.

Ainsi, Monsieur, m'abandonnant tout entier à Votre impartiale justice, je prends la liberté de vous adresser (en vous priant de me les renvoyer) les Originaux des titres Sur lesquels je m'appuye, afin que Vous n'ayés aucun doute Sur ma bonne foy. Si Votre decision m'est favorable, je desirerois beaucoup recevoir ce qui m'est dû avant mon Depart pour france; ayant arreté mon passage Sur le Navire New Jersey (appartenant à Mr. Plumestade) qui partira dans quinze jours pour anvers.

Excusés, Monsieur, Si je vous écris dans ma langue naturelle. C'est une decence que je dois observer à Votre egard, pour ne point me Servir d'expressions impropres. Je Suis Monsieur avec le plus profond respect Votre trés humble et trés obeissant Serviteur

John Foncin

La Somme que je reclame est de 258. Dollars $\frac{89}{100}$.

P.S. Comme il Sera toujours flatteur à mon esprit que mes Services ayent eté approuvé par le president des etats unis de qui j'ai eu l'honneur d'avoir reçû deux brevets, je joins ici la derniere Lettre[5] en datte du 27 juillet que j'ai reçûe à Boston, sans parler de plusieurs autres par lesquelles le Secretaire de la guerre m'a donné les temoignages les plus autentiques de Sa Satisfaction.

EDITORS' TRANSLATION

Sir, Philadelphia, 14 Apr. 1803

The President of the United States having honored me with the enclosed commission to erect the fortifications necessary to defend Boston harbor, I built Fort Independence to the satisfaction of the citizens of that city. When that work was completed, and after four years of assiduous efforts in both Baltimore and Boston, I requested permission to come to Philadelphia. That favor was granted to me by the enclosed letter from the Secretary of War, dated August 5.

Because he had thus prolonged my service, I worked during the winter to complete preparations for the defense of Boston harbor. I sent the Secretary of War different observations concerning the project and received my salary with no problem. But while I devoted my expertise in the art of fortifications so as to be more and more useful to a country I would have wished to serve for the rest of my life, imagine my surprise when, with no prior notice, I was deprived of my salary beginning on December 1, based on the enclosed letter from Mr. Simmons. As of that date, my role as engineer in the service of the United States has been terminated. But I have asked in vain for the salary that was owed to me from December 1 until February 12, the date when I received, albeit indirectly, the first notification of Secretary of War's decision. Is it possible that I, who worked so assiduously and without interruption to build the forts of Baltimore and Boston, who received the most favorable testimonials from the citizens of these two cities (as evidenced by the enclosed article from the *Independent Chronicle*), and from the members of Congress who visited my project, is it possible, I ask, that I could be deprived of wages for two months and twelve days?

I have no objection to the Secretary of War's cancelling my commission from the President of the United States. But at least I should have been specifically informed that I was no longer employed. At that point, I would have returned to my country.

One cannot allege that I completed the entire task entrusted to me. The commission with which I was honored included the general defense of the port and the city of Boston, and Fort Independence is only part of this project. According to the generals and other military men who visited the site, it is indispensable to build a fort, or at least the redoubt on Governor's Island for which I sent plans to the Secretary of War.

The enclosed letter, dated March 16, in which the Secretary of War seeks to re-employ me, while considering me off-duty since my arrival in Philadelphia, seems to contradict the authorization he gave me. In this case, one would need to assume that my appointment is retroactive, which cannot be the case.

I could not help being deeply affected by this abrupt termination of my work, just when I was in a position to expect compensation.

Entrusting myself entirely to your impartial justice, Sir, I thus take the liberty of sending you the originals of the documents on which I am basing my case (with a request that you return them to me), so you will have no doubt about my good faith. If your decision is favorable, I would like very much to receive what is due to me before my departure for France. I have booked passage on the ship *New Jersey* (belonging to Mr. Plumstead) which leaves for Antwerp in two weeks.

Pardon me, Sir, for writing in my native language. I do so because of the deference I owe you, to avoid using any improper expressions. With the deepest respect, Sir, I am your very humble and obedient servant.

John Foncin

The sum I am requesting is $258.89.

P.S. Since I shall always be flattered that my work was approved by the president of the United States, from whom I have the honor of receiving two commissions, I am enclosing the last letter I received in Boston, dated July 27, one of several in which the secretary of war expressed his most genuine satisfaction.

RC (PHi); Foncin identified most of the enclosures by numbers in the margin (see notes 1-5 below); endorsed by TJ as received 16 Apr. and so recorded in SJL. Enclosures: (1) Dearborn to Foncin, 27 July 1802 (Foncin's "No. 5"), acknowledging a letter about progress on fortifications at Castle Island; the "success that has attended your labors is evidence for you that they were directed with judgement and pursued with energy" (FC in Lb in DNA: RG 107, MLS). (2) Dearborn to Foncin, 5 Aug. 1802 (Foncin's "No. 2"), granting him permission to visit Philadelphia whenever his presence is not required for the work at Fort Independence (FC in Lb in same, misdated 5 July). (3) Dearborn to Foncin, 16 Mch. 1803 (Foncin's "No. 4"), requesting him to accompany Jonathan Williams to North Carolina "for the purpose of settling a question between the United States and a Gentleman who contracted to erect a fortification near Wilmington in sd. State"; he will be given the pay of a colonel, plus stage hire and $1.25 per day for expenses; "You will not consider yourself as having been in the service of the United States after your arrival at Philadelphia the last Autumn—but must consider the pay already received as in full for all services up to that time" (FC in Lb in same). (4) Probably "Fort-Independence on Castle-Island," an essay by "Lucius Sempronius" in the Boston *Independent Chronicle*, 19 Aug. 1802; so "perfect is the plan" of the fortification, the author writes, "and so complete the workmanship, that the American when he passes this Fortification, may contemplate it with a *noble pride*"; the "immense labor necessary to complete the works has been performed in less than 18 months," Sempronius asserts, "and at an expence not amounting to two hundred thousand dollars, little more than what it cost this town for its Alms-House, or the state for the noble Building near Beacon-hill"; extolling the talents required to envision and create such a fortress on the irregular topography of the island, the writer proclaims that it is "but justice to the character of an amiable and worthy man, publicly to declare, that if it had been possible to have made a selection from the whole catalogue of Engineers, no one probably would have given greater satisfaction, or deserved more from the citizens of this metropolis, than Colonel John Foncin." Other enclosures not found.

John (Jean) Foncin was a French-born military engineer who began working on the design and construction of U.S. fortifications during John Adams's presidential administration. In the early planning for a school to train artillerists and engineers at West Point, Foncin drew one of the proposed designs for the building. Samuel Dexter suggested him as head mathematics instructor for the cadets, but Adams wanted the position to go to an American. After succeeding Louis de Tousard as the engineer in charge of fortifications under construction at Baltimore, Foncin made a new design for what became Fort McHenry. In 1803, disappointed in his efforts to obtain a permanent position with the War Department, Foncin left the United States for France. He returned later in the year with endorsements from the Marquis de Lafayette and other influential individuals. He sought employment, possibly in Louisiana, from TJ and Dearborn, and renewed the request several times. In 1808, Dearborn offered him a position overseeing defensive works near New Orleans. Foncin accepted, went to Louisiana, but then decided he did not want the job. The secretary of war, forced to find another engineer and to cope with the delays brought on by the resignation, found Foncin's behavior "unaccountable." Foncin, however, resumed his imploring. In a newspaper advertisement in Philadelphia in the fall of 1807, he offered himself as an instructor of "the science of fortifications," mathematics as it applied to military science, and the French language. He was, he declared in that solicitation, the engineer "who built Fort McHenry at Baltimore, Fort Independence at Boston, and finished Fort Mifflin near Philadelphia" (Theodore J. Crackel, *Mr. Jefferson's Army: Political and Social Reform of the Military Establishment, 1801-1809* [New York, 1987], 56; Sidney Forman, "Why the United States Military Academy was Established in 1802," *Military Affairs*, 29 [1965], 24; Scott Scheads, *Fort McHenry* [Baltimore, 1995], 6-7; Syrett, *Hamilton*, 26:168-9; *Aurora*, 13 Oct. 1807; Foncin to the War Department, 28 Oct., 8 Dec. 1803, 9 Feb. 1804, 26 May 1806, 23 July 1807, 10, 21 Feb. 1808, 20 Mch., 25 Apr., 4 May 1809, recorded in DNA: RG 107, RLRMS; Foncin to TJ, 28 Oct. 1803, not found but recorded in SJL as received from New York on 30 Oct. with notation "emploimt. Louisa"; Madame de Corny to TJ, 15 Aug.; Du Pont de Nemours to TJ, 15 Aug.; Jean Baptiste Ternant to TJ, 18 Aug.; Lafayette to TJ, 1 Sep. 1803; Dearborn to TJ, 24 Oct. 1808).

When TJ took office as president, Foncin was carrying out plans for the completion of FORT INDEPENDENCE on Castle Island in Boston Harbor. Dearborn ordered an inspection of the project before allowing Foncin to proceed. As the work went on, the secretary of war cautioned the engineer that his expenditures were exceeding his estimates. In December 1802, the War Department suspended "any further expense at Fort Independence." According to Dearborn, Foncin's estimate, made when work on the fortifications was well under way, came to approximately $38,000, but expenditures, when Dearborn suspended the work, had reached nearly $60,000. William SIMMONS was the accountant for the War Department (Dearborn to Foncin, 26 Mch., 23 Apr. 1801, 14 June, 22 Dec. 1802, 25 Mch. 1803, in DNA: RG 107, MLS; Foncin to War Department, 14 Nov., 17 Dec. 1802, recorded in DNA: RG 107, RLRMS; Vol. 34:81-2, 85n; Vol. 37:197n, 529n).

EN DATTE DU 16. MARS: when Dearborn contacted Jonathan Williams in March 1803 about the trip to North Carolina (see Enclosure No. 3 listed above), he stated that Foncin would be assisting him—"provided he will consent to go." Foncin declined the offer, stating that he had expected to have long-term employment. If Foncin thought his earlier work "laid the Government under an obligation to give you a permanent appointment," Dearborn declared in response, "I regret that there had not been a better understanding on the subject previous to your engagements." Observing that "you claim great merit for your services," Dearborn noted that the estimate for Castle Island "was so incorrect as to prove either a want of candour or judgement" (Dearborn to Williams, 16 Mch. 1803, in DNA: RG 107, LSMA; Foncin to Dearborn, 21 Mch. 1803, recorded in DNA: RG 107, RLRMS; Dearborn to Foncin, 25 Mch. 1803, in DNA: RG 107, MLS).

George Plumstead (PLUMESTADE) was a Philadelphia merchant (James Robinson, *The Philadelphia Directory, City and County Register, for 1802* [Philadelphia, 1801], 194).

[1] In margin: "No. 1."
[2] In margin: "No. 2."
[3] In margin: "No. 3."
[4] In margin: "No. 4."
[5] In margin: "No. 5."

To Hammuda Pasha, Bey of Tunis

GREAT AND GOOD FRIEND,

Your letter of September the 8th of the last year has been lately received by me, and I observe with pleasure that the Stores and jewels sent you on our part have given entire satisfaction, and that you preserve for our nation those sentiments of friendship which we wish to cultivate and continue: and it is further intimated that the present of a frigate of 36 guns would at this time be acceptable. Altho' circumstances[1] do not permit us to add this to the proofs of our friendship for you,[2] yet we propose on this occasion to give you a testimony of the good will we bear you in a way which we hope may be acceptable, and which will be explained to our Consul, whom we shall appoint as Successor to Mr William Eaton.

We continue to recommend to your hospitality such of our vessels of war as may have occasion to enter your harbours for safety or supply, as well as our Merchant vessels resorting to them for purposes of commerce with your subjects, or on other necessary emergencies: and repeating to you assurances of our desire to improve the harmony so happily subsisting between us by rendering you all the good offices which our distance and other circumstances permit, I pray God, Great and Good Friend, to have you always in his safe and holy keeping.

Done at the City of Washington this fourteenth day of April in the year of our Lord one thousand Eight hundred and three[3]

TH: JEFFERSON

FC (Lb in DNA: RG 59, Credences); in a clerk's hand; at head of text: "Thomas Jefferson, President of the United States of America, To the Most Illustrious and most Magnificent Prince, the Bey of Tunis"; below signature: "By the President, James Madison Secretary of State." Tr (NN: Cathcart Collection); in James L. Cathcart's hand, in Italian (see below). PrC (DLC); a Dft, signed "Th:J."; at head of text: "To the Bey of Tunis &c"; without emendations, but text varies from later version (see notes 1 and 2 below).

TESTIMONY OF THE GOOD WILL: on 9 Apr., with the same letter in which Madison gave James Leander Cathcart new instructions for negotiations with Tripoli, the secretary of state sent the consul a commission to succeed William Eaton at Tunis. "It is foreseen that the Bey of Tunis will expect to receive periodical payments in like manner as the Bashaw of Tripoli," Madison wrote, "and we are prepared to arrange them." He explained that "we wish at once to manifest our good will and liberality to the Regency, to give him an interest in preserving peace, and to regulate at a fixed rate what is now so uncertain as its demands." Making an arrangement with Tunis would also establish a precedent for negotiations with Tripoli on the question of presents, Madison indicated. The payments to Tunis were not to exceed $10,000 per annum, payable in money, "biennially if it can be so settled." Cathcart could offer a one-time "Consular present" not to exceed the customary amount, "about 4,000 Dollars" (Madison, *Papers*, *Sec. of State Ser.*, 4:495).

EXPLAINED TO OUR CONSUL: Madison wrote to Eaton on 14 Apr., indicating that Mustafa Baba's refusal to accept Cathcart as consul to Algiers had presented an opportunity to appoint Cathcart to the post at Tunis and comply with Eaton's wish to resign. Madison informed Eaton that Cathcart would present TJ's letter to Hammuda Pasha and that it would mention "certain testimonies of our good will." Cathcart rather than Eaton would convey the details of that "gratuitous concession" to the bey, Madison explained, so that "the good humour it ought to produce" would benefit the new consul (same, 517). Cathcart's rendering of TJ's letter into the Italian language reflects historic commercial ties between North Africa and Italy, and in particular the role of the *Grana*, Jewish mercantile families that migrated to Tunis from Leghorn. Some of the *Grana* acted as financial brokers for the Tunisian regime and as intermediaries in diplomatic relations (Kenneth J. Perkins, *Historical Dictionary of Tunisia* [Metuchen, N.J., 1989], 55-6, 68).

[1] PrC: "existing circumstances."

[2] In PrC remainder of paragraph reads: "yet we shall certainly take care to avail ourselves from time to time of such future occasions as may arise of renewing the testimonies of the good will we bear you, in such a way as shall be acceptable."

[3] PrC: "Done at Washington this 14th. day of April 1803 &c."

To Jones & Howell

GENTLEMEN Washington Apr. 14. 1803.

Your two last bills for iron furnished were for 278. Dollars falling due this month, & 47. D 45c due the next month, I now inclose you the amount of both, towit a 50. dollar Pensva bank bill and a check of the branch bank here on the bank of the US. for 275.45 D. making in the whole 325. D 45c which I hope will get safe to hand.

In the first week of the ensuing month be pleased to ship to the address of Gibson & Jefferson Richmond, for me, 2. tons of nail rod assorted as usual from 6 d to 20. d. inclusive, a quarter ton of half crown rods, and a quarter ton of hoop iron Inch & quarter wide, so that the paiment may fall due the first week of August. Accept my best wishes TH: JEFFERSON

Dr.	D	Cr.	D c
	278.		275.45
	47.45		50.
	325.45		325.45

PrC (MHi); at foot of text: "Messrs. Jones & Howell"; endorsed by TJ in ink on verso. Recorded in SJL with notation "278 + 47.45. also ord. for 2. t. rod $\frac{1}{4}$ t. 30 d. $\frac{1}{4}$ t. hoop $1\frac{1}{4}$ I."

TWO LAST BILLS: probably the letter from Jones & Howell of 4 Jan., recorded in SJL as received 8 Jan., and a letter of 12 Feb., recorded in SJL as received 19 Feb. with the notation "47.45." Neither letter has been found.

From Robert R. Livingston

DEAR SIR Paris 14. April 1803

Mr. Monroe delivered me your very friendly Letter of the 3d. of Feby. the night before last immediately upon his arrival here—I wish it was in my power to give a more full answer to it, than the hurry of the present moment affords me. For the last three weeks I have been in continual agitation, the days were to the last degree important. It was necessary to seek information thro' every possible channel, it was[1] equally necessary to endeavour to turn that information to advantage. How far I have done this you will be able to[2] judge from the dispatches that accompany this—When I cast my eye upon the Map, and consider the vast and rich Country that lays before us, when I look forward one hundred years & see that Country improved & settled by Millions who will either be ranged in hostile array against us, or enlisted under our banners as we now decide. I think the weal, or woe of our[3] Country lays in our hands, & depends upon the determination of a moment—I have not seen Mr. Monroe Since last night having been continually[4] engaged since, I trust however that we shall concur in opinion, & that your administration will be distinguished, by the acquisition of a territory not less valuable to us than half the United States—That we shall be freed from European controversies, & that we shall rest in the physical impossibility of having an enemy at our doors;—which could not be the case if the mississippi was our boundary, the region on the other side is too inviting to be unsettled, & whoever is the sovereign our own people, as well as the inhabitants of Europe, would flock to it[5]—Tho' the coming of Mr. Monroe has put a little check to my opperations, & afforded a pretence for delays here, yet I am persuaded that the measure was a prudent one, as it respected the crisis in our own Country, and as it added an able counseller to your agent here—So important and weighty is the matter before us, that I rejoice in the aid of a friend, in whose patriotism & judgement I have the highest confidence—Tho' not being presented he cannot officially appear as yet in the present negotiation—I shall do nothing but with his full approbation, & in a few days I hope he may engage officially—Not a moment is to be lost, least a change should take place in the situation of Europe, in the present dispositions of the first Consul, or least he should go, as he proposes in a few days to Brussells, before any thing is concluded—I have agreed with Mr. Monroe that it will be best for the present not to deliver your letter to Dupond—he has no interest that can in any wise serve us, and his warm imagination hurries him into plans that may hurt us—The only person with whom he converses freely is one that interferes but little in great political arrangements, & as he delivers his plans to him without any previous consultation with me, tho' as we are upon the best terms, he shews them to me afterwards—they are more calculated to promote the views of France, than of our Country, & were[6] they fortified by a letter expressive of so much confidence in him as yours discovers, they would[7] have a dangerous weight—You will pardon the liberty we have taken,[8] we trust that were you on the spot you would think as we do, when our negotiations have taken some decided complection we will deliver the Letter—The reflection contained in Mr. Ross'es speach on the subject of the distribution of two millions of dollars[9] in bribes has been much noticed here, as you find by my letter to Mr. Madison—it naturally leads to a belief that some such hint has been given by me—I think it not improbable that Clark, or some other person may have said or written this—it is very extraordinary that Clark who was but ten days here, & in a rank, & character, that admitted him into no society about the Court should have presumed to fathom the secrets of the most secret cabinet of Europe—I am very sorry that you have made no appointment for England; as a war is almost certain you want a man of Talents, address, & character there—your political, & commercial concerns will call for the utmost attention—I have written to endeavour[10] to persuade Mr. King to remain some time longer at least 'till we close our negotiation here, as it may be well to be backed there if necessary—I broke off here to call on Mr. Monroe & have some conversation with him relative to the communication of Mr. Marbois—& to take him to Mr. Talleyrands, agreeably to appointment—I there saw our commission for the first time, which I find contrary to my expectation, in making him Envoy extraordinary, gives him a step above me—but this is of little moment[11] as our powers are similar, but what astonished me was to find that the commission limits our power to treat for territory on the East side of the Mississippi,[12] so that if they are scrupulous, all our hopes of treating for this immense Country must vanish into air—I shall have no difficulty in going on since my old commission will bear me out—Mr. Monroe will not refuse to act under his commission—the fear is that they will scruple here when our powers are examined—I find too that Mr. Monroe has one title in the commission & another in his letter of credence, in which letter also, the titles of the first Consul are mistaken—

At three OClock Mr. Monroe was presented by me to the Minister who received us very graciously, we found Mr. Marbois there, he told me that he had just been communicating to the Minister, what had passed between us last night and added that he wished that I would enable him, to meet the proposition of the first Consul on this subject, I told him they were too wide of our mark, and our means—I asked the Minister to obtain the earliest day for the presentation of Mr. Monroe, as it was important that we should enter upon our mission as soon as possible, he assured me, he would speak to the first Consul on the subject that night so that I am in hopes he will be presented on sunday, tho' it has been usual only to present on the 15th of each month—Lord Witworth and others have been kept a whole month in waiting—Talleyrand added that even before the presentation some person would probably be indicated with whom we might treat—This person will of course be Marbois; Thus you find us fairly afloat, & if our commission does not set us aground, I hope we shall make a noble harbour, you[13] must not however be surprised if the ships charges run high—

War you may consider as morally certain, tho' the sword may yet be suspended some days—I thank you Sir for your very polite & friendly expressions, with which you conclude your letter—I think with you that much of the happiness of our Country will depend upon the success of our mission, now particularly that so great a field is opened upon us—our zeal & attention to the object, I believe you may have the utmost reliance upon, & if we fail it will not be from the want of the most earnest desire to serve our Country, but from mistaken views of what will have that happy effect—Be assured my Dear Sir of the interest I take in your happiness, & the honor of your administration which has given to our Country the most splendid consideration in Europe, as well as real happiness at home[14]

Believe me to be Dear Sir with the highest Respect & Esteem your Obt. Hube Sert

Robt R Livingston

Dupl (DLC); in a clerk's hand, signed by Livingston; at head of text: "Duplicate"; at foot of text: "Thomas Jefferson Esqr. President of the U: States"; endorsed by TJ as received 9 June and so recorded in SJL. RC (DLC); in the same clerk's hand, signed by Livingston; concluding portion in Livingston's hand (see note 14 below); endorsed by TJ as received 24 Aug. and so recorded in SJL.

James MONROE landed at Le Havre on 8 Apr. and got to Paris on the 12th (Madison, *Papers*, *Sec. of State Ser.*, 4:520).

Livingston sent Madison DISPATCHES dated 11 and 13 Apr. (same, 500-2, 511-15).

ACQUISITION OF A TERRITORY: in one of his dispatches, Livingston reported that Talleyrand had suddenly asked, in a meeting on 11 Apr., "whether we wished to have the whole of Louisiana." Livingston replied "no, that our wishes extended only to New Orleans & the Floridas," although he added that he thought it would be wise for the French to cede the territory north of the Arkansas River to the United States, as he had suggested in a memorandum for Bonaparte, thereby creating a buffer between lower Louisiana and the British in Canada. Talleyrand dismissed that prospect, pointing out that there was no reason for France to keep lower Louisiana without New Orleans. He pressed Livingston to think about the prospect of buying all of Louisiana and to come up with a figure for a purchase price. Although the foreign minister claimed "that he did not speak from authority"—the "idea" of selling all of Louisiana had simply "struck him," he avowed—Bonaparte had by 11 Apr. decided to sell the entire colony to the United States (same, 500-1; François Barbé de Marbois, *Histoire de la Louisiane: et de la cession de cette colonie par la France aux États-Unis de l'Amérique septentionale* [Paris, 1829], 285-98; Alexander DeConde, *This Affair of Louisiana* [New York, 1976], 162-4; note to Document I of Livingston to TJ, 12 Mch.).

Monroe was not PRESENTED to the first consul until an official reception at the Louvre on 1 May, after most of the negotiation for the sale of Louisiana was over. Livingston excluded his colleague from the initial discussions about the purchase, and Monroe learned from Fulwar Skipwith that, as Monroe put it in a letter to Madison that he decided not to send, Livingston "regretted his misfortune in my arrival, since it took from him the credit of having brot. every thing to a proper conclusion without my aid." On the day after Monroe's arrival in Paris, however, Talleyrand indicated that a delay in the envoy's presentation of credentials would not be an impediment. According to Monroe, the foreign minister said that someone "would be designated to treat with us, with whom we might communicate before I was presented." As the negotiations with François Barbé de Marbois developed, Monroe was involved, including one conference held at his sickbed so that he would not be excluded. "It is proper for me to inform you," he wrote to Madison in May, "that the most difficult vexatious and embarrassing part of my labour has been with my associate" (Monroe to Madison, 15 Apr., not sent, and Monroe, "Journal or note of proceedings relative to mission to France & negotiation," 27 Apr.-[May] 1803, both in DLC: Monroe Papers; Madison, *Papers, Sec. of State Ser.*, 4:521-3, 612-14).

LETTER TO DUPOND: TJ to Pierre Samuel Du Pont de Nemours, 1 Feb. ONLY PERSON WITH WHOM HE CONVERSES FREELY: see Du Pont to TJ, 3 Mch., concerning Du Pont's contacts with the French government.

MR. ROSS'ES SPEACH: news of James Ross's February speech and motion in the Senate urging that New Orleans be taken by force had reached France through London newspapers. Livingston, who sent Ross's motion to Talleyrand as soon as he received it himself, believed that the threat of an American seizure of New Orleans, along with the possibility that Great Britain would never allow the Floridas to come under French control, convinced Bonaparte to offer Louisiana to the United States. According to Barbé de Marbois's account of the meetings in which he learned of the first consul's decision, however, Bonaparte felt sure that a renewal of war with Britain had become inevitable, and with war would come a British invasion of Louisiana. If he was going to lose the colony, Bonaparte reasoned, it was better for it to go to the United States than to Britain (Madison, *Papers, Sec. of State Ser.*, 4:501, 512-13; Barbé de Marbois, *Histoire de la Louisiane*, 286-7; TJ to Thomas McKean, 19 Feb.).

TWO MILLIONS OF DOLLARS IN BRIBES: in his speech in the Senate on 14 Feb., Ross dismissed the idea that it would be possible to buy New Orleans and said: "Sell, sir! for how much? Why sir, although there is no information before this

House, of any terms, yet I have seen it stated in the newspapers, that those who now pretend to claim that country may be persuaded to sell, by giving two million of dollars to certain influential persons about the Court." Two million dollars was the amount of the appropriation in the secret bill for the purchase of New Orleans and the Floridas that the House of Representatives had passed and sent to the Senate on the day that Ross began his speech. Senator Robert Wright of Maryland interrupted Ross, charging that he had touched on "confidential information." Aaron Burr, in the chair as presiding officer, ordered the galleries cleared of spectators, and the Senate went into closed session. When Ross resumed his address two days later he did not refer to the alleged bribery money, but his remarks on the 14th and Wright's protest appeared in the published record of the Senate's debates of that day. NOTICED: Bonaparte was aware of the published comments about bribery, Livingston learned from Barbé de Marbois (JEP, 1:443; New York *Daily Advertiser*, 26 Feb.; Madison, *Papers*, *Sec. of State Ser.*, 4:512-13; TJ to Monroe, 25 Feb.).

In November, Daniel CLARK spent about two weeks in Paris. As he and Fulwar Skipwith reported to Madison, he met with General Victor and Pierre Clément Laussat about the expeditionary force for Louisiana (Madison, *Papers*, *Sec. of State Ser.*, 4:110, 129, 218).

Livingston had written to Rufus KING, he reported to Madison, "pressing him to stay 'till a successor is appointed. The moment is so critical that we cannot justify being without a Minister in England, he is a very useful one." "Thro' the whole of this business," Monroe wrote to Madison in May, Livingston "has kept up a correspondence with Mr. King" (same, 501, 613).

COMMUNICATION OF MR. MARBOIS: Livingston and Talleyrand saw each other again on 12 Apr., but Talleyrand was unable to get Livingston to talk about a possible price for Louisiana. Later that day, Barbé de Marbois dropped by Livingston's house and arranged to meet with him at the Treasury offices late that night. It was no secret that Livingston had an uncomfortable relationship with Talleyrand, but the American, as Bonaparte was aware, claimed "personal friendship" for Barbé de Marbois, who had been a diplomat in the United States years earlier. The two, as Livingston remarked in his 13 Apr. dispatch to Madison, were accustomed to having "free conversations," and in that late-night meeting at Marbois's offices they had a long talk about the amount of money that would constitute an acceptable offer for the purchase of the colony (same, 77-9, 81n, 511-14; Vol. 34: xli-xlii, 423-4).

See the joint COMMISSION for Monroe and Livingston at 12 Jan. (Vol. 39:320-1). For Madison's explanation of the envoys' titles, see Madison, *Papers, Sec. of State Ser.*, 5:236-7. LIMITS OUR POWER: Livingston lamented in a letter to Madison also that the commission said nothing about negotiating for land west of the Mississippi. "You will recollect," he declared, writing partly in code, "that I had been long preparing this Government to yield us the country above the arkansas." When TJ sent Monroe to France, however, he did not know that Livingston had made a proposal involving land west of the Mississippi—for Livingston did not inform the president and the secretary of state of the proposition until 18 Feb., in a letter to Madison, and he did not send them a copy of the memorandum he had submitted to Bonaparte until after the negotiations for Louisiana were concluded (same, 4:329, 525, 592, 594-5n).

For the LETTER OF CREDENCE that TJ addressed to Bonaparte for Monroe, see above in this series at 11 Feb.

PRESENTED BY ME TO THE MINISTER: Livingston took Monroe to see Talleyrand on the 13th. Talleyrand, Monroe reported to Madison, "said that the first Consul was much gratified by the disposition which our Government had shewn, in the Circumstances which produced the present Mission, and had also expressed himself in Terms very favorable to my Colleague and myself" (Madison, *Papers*, *Sec. of State Ser.*, 4:520).

PROPOSITION OF THE FIRST CONSUL: in the late-night meeting at the Treasury office, Barbé de Marbois told Livingston that Bonaparte had put a price of 100 million francs on Louisiana. The United States would also have to assume the outstanding claims of American citizens against France, which Livingston thought could add another 25 million francs. (Barbé de Marbois professed to share Livingston's shock at the figures, saying that he himself found the sums "exorbitant," but that was a tactic: when the first consul instructed him to negotiate the sale of Louisiana, the price he named was 50 million francs.) When Barbé de Marbois, as Talleyrand had done, pressed Livingston to name a figure, Livingston demurred but asked Marbois to "oblige me by telling me what he thought to be reasonable." Barbé de Marbois's answer was 60 million francs, plus another 20 million for the claims. A few days earlier in April, the French government had confirmed the franc, which had first been promulgated in 1795, as the official currency. The franc was close in value to the older livre tournois (same, 512-13; Barbé de Marbois, *Histoire de la Louisiane*, 299; Tulard, *Dictionnaire Napoléon*, 757; Miller, *Treaties*, 2:514).

POLITE & FRIENDLY EXPRESSIONS: at the end of his letter of 3 Feb., TJ told Livingston: "the future destinies of our country hang on the event of this negotiation, and I am sure they could not be placed in more able or more zealous hands. on our parts we shall be satisfied that what you do not effect cannot be effected."

[1] RC: "and it was."

[2] RC: "you will judge."

[3] RC: "my."

[4] RC: "constantly."

[5] Paragraph break here in RC.

[6] MS: "where." RC: "were."

[7] MS: "woud.," the copyist having run out of room on the line. RC: "would."

[8] RC: "liberty we take, but."

[9] Preceding two words lacking in RC.

[10] Preceding two words lacking in RC.

[11] RC: "importance."

[12] RC: "*East* side of the River Mississippi."

[13] RC: "we."

[14] RC concludes in Livingston's hand: "Excuse my using my son's pen. I was compelled to risk the opportunity or neglect a very important conference—Yours most respectfully RR Livingston."

From Louis Philippe Gallot de Lormerie

Washington City avril 1803.
[on or before 14 Apr.]

MONSIEUR LE PRESIDENT

Lorsque la Voix du Peuple des Etats unis vous a apellé au Poste Eminent de premier Magistrat de ce Vaste Empire, J'ai Eu Lhonneur de vous Ecrire pour vous féliçiter sur cet Evénement important. N'aÿant eté depuis honoré d'aucune réponse de Votre part j'ignore si ce Silence a Eté Causé par vos nombreuses Occupations, ou parceque quelqun vous auroit indisposé contre moi; car en toute autre occasion, même depuis que je suis dans ces Etats vous m'avés toujours favorisé de Réponses a mes Lettres. quoi qu'il en soit cette incertitude m'a privé de L'honneur d'aller vous Presenter ici mon Respect avant d'avoir celui de vous en prevenir. Jose dire avoir Eté assés heureux pour conserver L Estime de ceux qui m'ont bien connu, notamment des hommes d'Etat qui reprèsentent en ce Paÿs la Nation française. M. Pichon, m'a fait Lhonneur de me Visiter deux fois pendant mon court sèjour en cette Ville et de me reçevoir et inviter chés lui plusieurs fois. M. De L Etombe qui l'a precèdé m'a Ecrit de france il ÿ a quelque tems une Lettre pleine de témoignâges d'Estime et d'attachement. (Lettre que j'ai ici dans mon Portefeuille.) Ces Preuves sont suffisantes pour me Justifier a vos ÿeux si la Calomnie qui n'Epargne pas même les hommes les plus respectables m'a attaqué.

Les circonstances ne m'aÿant pas permis de tirer Encor aucun Parti ni même d'aller voir les terres que j'ai achetées en votre presençe et par votre intervention a Paris En 1787 et paÿees au C. Blackden; aÿant en outre Perdu 12 Mil dollars Environ avec la maison Swannwick a Phila. Je me suis dècidé a tirer parti d'objets que mon Goût pour les arts me rendoient Agréables mais qui dans une situation mèdiocre ne me conviennent plus. Jai donc importé dans cette ville comme le siège du Gouvernement le Centre de L'instruction publique quinz pieces de Tapesseries donc 10 au moins sont tres dignes de L'attention d'un amateur Eclairé tel que vous. Jaÿ Lhonneur de vous en remettre une notice Cy Jointe.

Les sujects historiques surtout peuvent orner une Gallerie des Arts, Bibliotheque &c ou Appartements. Elles conviendroient aussi comme Modèles pour une Ecole Gratuite de Dessin etant de la Composition du Celebre Le Brun et trés bien Executées d'après les tableaux de sa Main.

Les Paÿsâges du fameux Boucher sont tres Agréables et ces Piéces en Genèral sont d'une si belle Exècution que M. La Trobe, (bon juge) en a Eté Etonne et m'a dit, (de lui même) qu'il vous en feroit part.

Je prens la Liberté de vous inviter pour en bien Juger a venir les voir ètant plaçées, et ce seroit ajouter beaucoup a la faveur que vous me ferés si vous le pouvés convenablement aujourdhui ou deman, aÿant attendu Longtems votre Arrivée icÿ, et si vous avés la Bonte de me faire savoir L'heure qui vous sera Agrèable, Persuadé qu'elles vous conviendront tres probablement soit pour vous, soit pour une institution publique. Jaÿ Lhonneur dEtre avec un sincère et profond Respect Monsieur le President Votre tres humble et tres Devoué Serviteur LORMERIE

P.S J'ai appris depuis peu avec beaucoup de peine que M. De la faÿette auquel je dois Lhonneur de votre connoissançe, s'est cassé la cuisse cet hiver En sortant de Chés le Ministre de la Marine a Paris.

Notiçe des Piéces historiques de la Composition du Celebre Le Brun et des Paÿsâges du fameux Boucher et autres des premières Manufactures de françe. Savoir

quatre Pièçes histoire du Général Romain Scipio, nommé L'Africain, par le celébre Le Brun Ensemble £ 450–
quatre Paÿsâges superbes representant plusieurs amusemens de la campagne et parties des maisons de plaisances, roÿales des Environs de paris par le même Ensble 350–
3 idem par le fameux Boucher Ensemble 250–
4 Piéces de LEcriture ançien & nouveau Testament Evaluées au plus bas prix (ainsi que les autres) a 40–35. 35.–25.) 135.–

At Stelle's hôtel Capitol's hill.

N:B Ces Pieces Peuvent orner une Galerie des arts, une Bibliothéque, des appartemens, un Lieu de repos dans un Parc &c comme en Angleterre.

2° elles peuvent procurer avec avantage La Rançon de plusieurs infortunès hommes de mer américains a Tripoli tunis et Alger ou les chefs Estiment a grand Prix ces ouvrâges de manufactures françaises que nos missionnaires rèdempteurs presentoient toujours avec avantage pour La Liberte des malheureux Captifs de toutes nations.

EDITORS' TRANSLATION

Mister President, Washington, [on or before 14] April 1803

When the voice of the people of the United States called you to the eminent position of first magistrate of this vast empire, I had the honor of writing to congratulate you on this important event. Not having been honored by a response from you, I do not know whether this silence was caused by your numerous occupations or because someone set you against me, since on all other occasions, even since I have been in the United States, you have always favored my letters with replies. Whatever the cause, this uncertainty has prevented me from having the honor of informing you in advance and presenting my respects to you in person. I dare say that I have been fortunate in maintaining the esteem of those who know me well, especially the statesmen who represent the French nation in this country. Mr. Pichon did me the honor of visiting twice during my short stay in this city and of hosting me several times at his house. Mr. Létombe, who preceded him, sent me a letter from France a while ago, with warm expressions of esteem and attachment. (I have the letter here in my portfolio.) These signs are sufficient to justify me in your eyes, if I have been attacked by the calumny that does not even spare good men.

Circumstances did not allow me to benefit from, or even to go and see, the land I purchased from Col. Blackden in Paris in 1787 in your presence and through your intervention. Having lost some twelve thousand dollars on the Swanwick house in Philadelphia, I decided to take advantage of objects that please my taste for the arts but no longer befit my modest situation. I therefore brought to Washington, as the government seat and center of public education, fifteen tapestries. At least ten of them merit the attention of an enlightened connoisseur like yourself. I have the honor of sending you the enclosed notice.

The historical motifs in particular could adorn an art gallery, a library, or a home. Since they were designed by the famous Le Brun and were very well executed from his original paintings, they would also be suitable as models in a public drawing school.

The landscapes by the famous Boucher are beautiful, and the tapestries are so well made that Mr. Latrobe (a good judge) was stunned and said (of his own initiative) that he would tell you so.

I take the liberty of inviting you to see them hung so you can judge for yourself. It would add much to the favor you would do me if you could come today or tomorrow, since I have been waiting a long time for your arrival. Would you be kind enough to let me know the time that is best for you? I am convinced they will suit you, either for yourself or for a public institution.

With deep and sincere respect, I have the honor, Mister President, of being your very humble and devoted servant. LORMERIE

P.S. I recently learned, with much distress, that M. de Lafayette, to whom I owe the honor of meeting you, broke his hip this winter coming out of the home of the minister of the navy in Paris.

Notice of historical works by the eminent Le Brun and of landscapes by the famous Boucher and others by the foremost manufactories in France. To wit:

Four historic scenes depicting the Roman general Scipio, called "the African," by the famous Le Brun. The set:	£ 450.00
Four superb landscapes representing various country pastimes and pleasures at the royal country houses around Paris, by the same artist. The set:	350.00
Three more similar landscapes by the famous Boucher. The set:	250.00
Four biblical scenes from the Old and New Testaments, which (like the others) have been appraised at the lowest rate. 40; 35; 35; 25.	135.00

At Stelle's Hotel, Capitol Hill

N.B. These works can decorate an art gallery, library, home, or a country manor, etc., as in England.

2. They can also be useful in providing ransom for several ill-fated American sailors in Tripoli, Tunis, and Algiers, whose leaders prize these works from French ateliers. Our missionaries always offered them, with success, to free miserable captives from all nations.

RC (DLC); partially dated; addressed: "H.E. Ths Jefferson President of the united states Washington city"; endorsed by TJ as received 14 Apr. and so recorded in SJL. Enclosure: Notice of items for sale in Philadelphia, undated; includes a "Collection of Elegant Paintings, By the Best Masters of the french italian, English, flemish, and Hollander schools," a variety of "Superb Engravings" by the "most Eminent Artists" of Rome, France, and England, and original drawings; an "Assorted Library" of works in English, French, and Latin by "the Best authors," plus maps and atlases; items of "Needle Wrought Tapestry with figures, Landscapes &c" in various sizes, "Suitable for Carpets &c Verÿ Ornamental"; and "Sundry other Articles of taste and utility not particularised"; inquiries should be addressed to Henry Meyer (MS in DLC: TJ Papers, 131:22649; in Lormerie's hand; at head of text: "For Sale at No. 134 north 3d st Philadelphia").

DE VOUS ECRIRE: Lormerie had written to TJ in May 1801 (Vol. 34:203-4).

TJ had witnessed the deed when Lormerie, in Paris in 1787, purchased a tract of land in the United States from Colonel Samuel BLACKDEN (Vol. 11:486, 519; Vol. 12:601-2; Vol. 14:359-60).

PIECES DE TAPESSERIES: unable to sell any of his land, Lormerie in 1801 had attempted to interest TJ in purchasing some tapestries with public funds for use as presents to Barbary Coast rulers. Charles LE BRUN, who also acquired the position of first painter to Louis XIV, became director of the Gobelins tapestry works in Paris in 1663. In the 18th century, François BOUCHER had a long affiliation with the Gobelins shop and with the tapestry factory at Beauvais. The workshops produced tapestries from Le Brun's and Boucher's paintings, and the artists also made original designs for the weavers. Advertising his tapestries for sale in Washington, Lormerie called Le Brun "one of the first painters that ever lived in Europe" and declared that the weavings were of a quality suitable for a museum or an art school (Christa C. Mayer Thurman and Koenraad Brosens, "'Autumn and Winter': Two Gobelins Tapestries after Charles Le Brun," *Art Institute of Chicago Museum Studies*, 32 [2006], 65-8; Edith Appleton Standen, "Renaissance to Modern Tapestries in the Metropolitan Museum of Art," *Metropolitan Museum of Art Bulletin*, new ser., 44 [1987], 6, 41, 44; "Tapisseries de la Manufacture des Gobelins [1662-1913]," *Lotus Magazine*, 6 [1915], 253-76; *National Intelligencer*, 15 Apr.; Vol. 34:203-4).

To Louis Philippe Gallot de Lormerie

Apr. 14. 1803.

Th: Jefferson presents his compliments to M. de L'ormerie & hopes he will do him the justice to ascribe to the indispensable calls of the public affairs the impossibility of answering letters of private correspondence not relating to business. he knows of no institution in these states where the objects described in M. de Lormerie's letter might be sought after, unless in a private one lately established in New York. nothing of that kind is within the present views of the United states. Th: Jefferson however will avail himself of the permission of M. de Lormerie to satisfy his own curiosity by calling to see them, either to day or tomorrow, between the hours of one and two. he prays him to accept his salutations.

PrC (DLC); endorsed by TJ in ink on verso.

From Wilson Cary Nicholas

Dear Sir Warren. Apl. 14. 1803

It gives me the most sincere pleasure to have it in my power to congratulate you upon the amicable termination of an affair that must have given you great uneasiness. I am sure it ought to be the wish of all parties that it shou'd be consigned to eternal oblivion. permit me however to say that the honorable manner in which you have uniformly asserted the innocence of the lady, and all the circumstances taken together, wou'd have made this business as little injurious to you as it is possible a tale of that sort cou'd be. anticipating this adjustment, I had before I received your letter, taken the liberty to suggest to Messrs. Randolph Eppes & Carr, that the utmost reserve ought to be observed by your personal friends in speaking of Mrs. — that no pretence shou'd be given for the publication of your letter, this I did without communicating to them that I had any particular information upon the subject—those Gentn. at once saw the propriety of what I recommended, and I am sure will pursue that course, and if they do it is impossible that any man can be mad enough to hold you in any degree responsible for what can be said by others. Be assured Sir, that every thing shall be done by me to give full effect to your wishes upon this subject. in doing this care shou'd be taken not to give publicity to the story, and not to commit you unnecessarily, or subject you to inconvenience from the want of honor or good faith in others—if the business is finally adjusted why shou'd not the letter be given up, or at least be placed in the hands of some common friend? at present there are very few people who give any credit to what has been said about that affair. I shall see Mr. Randolph on Monday next at Amherst Court house, when I will shew him your letter in confidence, I shall do this with a full conviction that it will be approved by you and that it will do good. I am the more induced to do this by my being obliged to go immediately to Kentucky, which will put it out of my power to use the exertions that I wou'd otherwise do to check the conversation of particular people upon this subject. In doing it I am conscious that I take a liberty with you that I am not strictly justifiable in doing—I do it because I believe it may do you service, and can not possibly do harm, and because I think you will approve of it. It seems to be the general opinion that Mr. Randolph will be elected, I sincerely wish it, there is a general dissatisfaction with Cabell, most of the people who vote for him wish he had retired. When I was in Washington I was disposed to have asked you for an appointment in the Mississippi territory for my brother George's oldest son,

I did not do it, from a doubt of his entire fitness, he is a man of good sense and irreproachable character as to sobriety and morals, but unfortunately not much cultivated, owing to mere caprice in his father; I am induced to mention him to you now, by having heard that a Mr. Turner is likely to obtain one of the most important of those appointments, Turner I know well and am confident Robert Carter Nicholas is a man of superior understanding, and cou'd discharge the duties of any office that Mr. Turner is fit for. It wou'd be a want of candour in me not to inform you that Mr. Turner is a respectable worthy young man. If the appointments are not all made, and you cou'd confide it to me to decide after I got to Kentucky, I will write you not only my opinion of my nephew, but the opinions of others who know him better than I do. My impression is that he cou'd procure recommendations from the most respectable people in that country. I do not recollect the offices that were created by the law of the last Session, but I think it probable that the law will reach Lexington by the time I get there, which I expect will be the first of May.

I am Dear Sir with the highest respect & regard Your humble Servt.

WILSON C. NICHOLAS

RC (DNA: RG 59, LAR); endorsed by TJ as received 19 Apr. and "Nicholas Ro. C. to office" and so recorded in SJL.

THE LADY: Elizabeth Moore Walker (see TJ to John Walker, 13 Apr.).

I RECEIVED YOUR LETTER: that of 31 Mch., now missing (see TJ to Nicholas, 11 Apr.). PUBLICATION OF YOUR LETTER: see TJ to John Walker, 13 Apr.

For the appointment of Edward TURNER, see Gallatin to TJ, 14 Mch.

To S. Smith & Buchanan

GENTLEMEN Washington April 14. 1803.

Agreeably to the tenor of your letter of Mar. 14. recieved only the 4th. inst. I now inclose you a note of the branch bank here on that of Baltimore for 42.42 D for the freight from Lisbon, duties & porterage of two casks of wine sent for me by mr Jarvis. should he inform you of the cost &c. due him you will oblige me by communicating it. Accept my salutations.

TH: JEFFERSON

PrC (MHi); at foot of text: "Messrs. Smith & Buchanan"; endorsed by TJ in ink on verso.

Two days later, the firm of S. Smith & Buchanan wrote TJ, acknowledging "receipt of your letter dated 14th Inst., & inclosing a Check for forty two dollars & forty two Cents, in full for the Expenses paid by us on two Casks Wine forwarded to our care by Mr Jarvis from Lisbon" (RC in MHi; endorsed by TJ as received 17 Apr. and so recorded in SJL).

To William, Benjamin, and W. L. Bakewell

Gentlemen Washington Apr. 15. 1803.

Your letter of Feb. 8. came to my hands only a few days ago and yesterday the barrel of ale therein mentioned was delivered here. I am to return you thanks in the first place for the indulgence with which you view my character & administration, and the dispositions you express in favor of those political principles which have made this country what it is, & the abandonment of which, whenever it shall take place, will be the signal that it is then to become what other countries are. between these two states of being our countrymen have a right to chuse, and when they chuse the latter, I shall be no longer qualified to lead them to it. I am next to thank you for the specimen presented of your manufacture. in these cases the intention is the essential circumstance which is pleasing, and this intention will I trust lead you to increase the gratification to me by letting me know the price which should be paid for it: that will place me more at my ease, & make me more contented with myself: it is from the heart, & not the hands, of my fellow citizens that I wish evidences of their satisfaction. in expectation of your adding this to your favor I salute you with my friendly respects. Th: Jefferson

PrC (DLC); at foot of text: "Messrs. Wm. Benj. & W. L. Bakewell. Newhaven"; endorsed by TJ in ink on verso.

For the conveyance of the barrel of malt liquor from the Bakewell brewery, see Theophilus Harris to TJ, 12 Apr.

From Seth Hunt

Sir, Keene April 15th. 1803

It has been suggested to me that a Minister Plenipotentiary, is shortly to be appointed to succeed Mr King at the Court of St. James, should that appointment take place and a Secritary to the Embassy be required, I request the favour of beeing considered as a Candidate & should feel myself highly distinguished in beeing selected by the Executive for that sittuation—should I be found upon enquiry, to possess the requisite quallifications—For a particular Knowledge of my Character I beg leave to refer the President to my friends (at the seat of Govt) the Secty. at War, the Atty. Genl and the Post Master Genl—to all of whom I have this day written soliciting their interest with the President in obtaining for me the *only place*, in the gift of the administration for which I have at present the least desire—In making my present application, I feel myself peculiarly sittuated—I am a young man, without the popularity of a name—I stand *politically* alone, unaided by the influence of a long list of relatives & unsupported except it should be, by the interest of a few *Political friends*—My family Connections in Massachusetts & New Hampshire are numerous, respectable & influential—upon their friendship & support in the *ordinary* concerns of life, I can ever most confidently rely, but in my political relations, they are lost to me—they are as tho they did not exist, for they were the friends of the last administration and they are the opponents of the present—but permit me Sir, to hope that this circumstance, will opperate as no objection in the mind of the President, to the granting of my request.—My *claims* to Executive Patronage, rest solely upon my own merit (if I have any) they are founded in an ardent attachment to the Present Administration and in an early, faithfull and undeviating adhereance to Republican principles and Measures; in the worst of times and in opposition to the opinions and wishes of every relation—and I flatter myself that *they* will be found sufficient, to justify the President in granting my prayer—With the highest Esteem & veneration for the Presidents private & publick Character and a sincere and ardent devotion to the Goverment under his wise & happy administration—

I remain most Respectfully The Presidents very obt Servt

SETH HUNT

RC (DNA: RG 59, LAR); at head of text: "The President of the United States"; endorsed by TJ as received 22 Apr. and "to be Secy. of legation" and so recorded in SJL.

Seth Hunt (ca. 1780-1846), the son of Seth Hunt of Northampton, Massachusetts, became a minor, yet controversial, political figure in New Hampshire and the Louisiana Territory. A former law student and failed Boston trader, he enjoyed the political patronage of Gideon Granger and Henry Dearborn and became affiliated with the *Political Observatory*, a Republican newspaper established at Walpole, New Hampshire, in late 1803. His writings and efforts "to assist in revolutionizing the State" earned him the enmity of New England Federalists. In early 1804, TJ considered Hunt for a western appointment, which Albert Gallatin advised against after learning that Hunt was deemed so "obnoxious to all our southern friends" and to the eastern Federalists that he worried the Senate would never confirm him. Dearborn, however, supported Hunt, and TJ appointed him commandant of Ste. Genevieve district in Louisiana. Hunt's tenure was short and turbulent, marked by his remarkably hostile relationship with Governor James Wilkinson that culminated in his arrest and removal from office by late 1805. He afterward engaged in a variety of business enterprises, including a trans-Atlantic dry goods venture with lead mine entrepreneur Moses Austin. He eventually returned to New Hampshire where he resided until his death (T. B. Wyman, Jr., *Genealogy of the Name and Family of Hunt* [Boston, 1862-63], 186, 193; Hanover, N.H., *Dartmouth Gazette*, 30 Mch. 1804; *Terr. Papers*, 13:204-18, 240-2, 290-7, 445-6; David B. Gracy II, *Moses Austin, His Life* [San Antonio, Tex., 1987], 99-102, 106-8, 122, 124, 128; Keene *New-Hampshire Sentinel*, 15 Apr. 1846; Gallatin to TJ, 11 May 1804; Dearborn to TJ, 1 June 1804).

To Edmund J. Lee, Cuthbert Powell, and Archibald McClean

GENTLEMEN Washington Apr. 15. 1803.

Agreeably to the request in your letter of Dec. 30. when at Monticello the last month, I examined my collection of the Virginia laws and found in it those below mentioned which [related] to Alexandria &[1] were not noted in your catalogue of those you possess. I delivered the volumes, with the list of the acts to a person who will copy them carefully & forward them to me. when recieved they shall be immediately sent to you. Accept my respectful salutations.

TH: JEFFERSON

1752. c. 37. An act for allowing fairs to be kept in the town of Alexandria.

1755. c. 15. An act reviving an act intitled 'an act for allowing fairs &c.'

1762. c. 25. An act for enlarging the town of Alexandria in the county of Fairfax.

1764. c. 10. An act for encouraging the settlement of the towns of Alexandria & Falmouth and for other purposes therein mentioned.

1772. c. 52. An act to encourage the further settlement of the town of Alexandria in the county of Fairfax.

PrC (ViW: Tucker-Coleman Collection); blurred; at foot of text: "Messrs. Lee, Powell & Mc.lean"; endorsed by TJ in ink on verso.

Edmund Jennings Lee (1772-1843), an attorney; Cuthbert Powell (1775-1849), a merchant in King's Street; and Archibald McClean, a schoolmaster and merchant, were all active in Alexandria's local government in 1803. During the decade, Lee, who married his cousin Sarah Lee, daughter of Richard Henry Lee, served as a member and then president of the city council. From 1802 to 1803, he was recorder of the council. In 1815, he became mayor of Alexandria. He acted as clerk of the U.S. Circuit Court from 1818 to 1837. TJ appointed Powell justice of the peace for Alexandria County in 1801 and renewed the appointment in 1807. He was married to Catherine Simms, daughter of Alexandria collector Charles Simms. Powell served as a director of the Alexandria Library Company and as an officer of the Sun Fire Company in 1803. In 1806, he became a city councilman and in 1808 mayor of Alexandria. He moved to Loudoun County and served in the Virginia Assembly, as a senator from 1815 to 1819 and as a delegate from 1828 to 1829. He became a Virginia congressman in 1841, serving one term. McClean served as an Alexandria councilman from 1802 to 1803 and was elected to supervise elections in the First Ward in 1804. His father-in-law, David Jones, a Baptist minister in Chester County, Pennsylvania, wrote TJ recommending McClean as collector at the port of Alexandria in case of Simms's removal. McClean also wrote TJ about the appointment in 1802. McClean and Lee, in early 1804, served on the committee that prepared a memorial to Congress seeking changes in Alexandria's charter of incorporation (Miller, *Alexandria Artisans*, 1:xxviii-xxxii, 268, 308; 2:50, 304; Alexandria *Times; and District of Co-*

lumbia Daily Advertiser, 18 May, 22 July 1802; *Alexandria Advertiser and Commercial Intelligencer*, 3 Feb. 1802; 22 Feb., 30 Mch. 1803; *Alexandria Daily Advertiser*, 11 Jan., 9, 29 Feb. 1804; Washington, *Diaries*, 6:258n; commission in Lb in DNA: RG 59, MPTPC; Vol. 33:123-4, 674; Vol. 34:492; Vol. 36:314-17, 326, 335; Vol. 37:154).

According to SJL, TJ received the LETTER OF 30 Dec. from Lee, Powell, and McClean at Alexandria on 1 Jan. TJ responded the next day. On 9 Jan., according to SJL, TJ received another letter from them dated the 8th. All three letters are missing.

For TJ's COLLECTION OF THE VIRGINIA LAWS and his efforts to organize and make them accessible to the public, see Vol. 28:319, 332, 569, 581-91.

[1]Preceding three words and ampersand interlined.

From Louis Philippe Gallot de Lormerie

MONSIEUR LE PRÉSIDENT Washington city 15. avril 1803.

L'introduction dans les Etats unis des Arts qui peuvent seuls Civiliser les Mœurs, Consoler les hommes de la méchançeté humaine, et prévenir ou Guèrir les maux inseparables de la Vie soçiale, semblent appartenir a votre Administration. Vous savés trés bien qu'on les a Calomniés; mais qu'on a Confondu L'abus avec Lusage. L Art du Dessin ètant la Bâse de toute Perfection, même dans les métiers peut produire, au sein de Votre Nation, des amèliorations importantes. Les hollandais peuple 1°. pecheur et Navig. 2° commerçant trés Econome, 3° sage Calculateur, Les hollandais dis je ont apperçu dès le siécle de Loüis XIV qu'ils pouroient avec les tableaux qui Sortoient de françe alors *Créer une Branche de Commerce Conséquente.* Ils les ont donc achetés recueillis, et ont fait des Profits immenses aprés quelques années. Le Goût de ces Productions admirables a Contribué beaucoup a Ralentir et Enfin a Dètruire cet Esprit de *Spéculation* excessif qui Dispersoit les Capitaux comme les vents Dispersent les nuâges et les *abÿment dans L'Oçéan.* Ce Goût les a fixés et des Richesses d'abord fictives sont devenues rèelles. Plusieurs Collections se sont vendues et ont offert, chaque souvent, un Capital de 3 a cinq cent mille florins.

La Superbe Gallerie de Scipio que j'ai Lhonneur de vous offrir, ne poura jamais se retrouver ici a un prix aussi modique, et ce seroit un Bienfait qui Distingueroit pour toujours votre Administration si dans une des salles du Capitole, ou *chés vous* elle etoit offerte comme Modéle aux Elèves pour la Peinture de L'histoire. La Noblesse de la Composition, la Pureté du Dessin, L Elegance des formes et la Beauté de L Ensemble, ont Obtenu et obtiendront pour ces 4 Piéces L'Admiration Genérale.

Les quatre autres Charmants Paÿsâges orneroient Elegamment une *summer house* ou autre appartment comme de beaux Tableaux a Monticello. Dans L hiver elles pouroient Encor Etre trés utiles dans Votre Maison de *fèderal City* ou au mileuu des frimats elles vous offriroient Le spectacle Dèliçieux des fleurs et des arbres toujours Verds et des situations riches de St. Cloud &c qui vous rapelleroient des souvenirs agrèables.

Je n'insisterois cependant pas a vous les offrir, si une Circonstance que j'ai oublié de vous mentionner hier lorsque j'ai eu Lhonneur de vous reçevoir ne m'y obigeoit. au Tribunal de la Vertu, la Probité doit Triomphér. Mon Desir de paÿer Exactement en votre Paÿs comme dans le mien m'a porté seul a faire cette importation. Je ne dois que deux cent vingt dollars a une maison de Philadie. pour objets que j'ai achetés dElle et qui montent a 920 dollars sur lesquels J'en ai payés 700. Ces objets sont chés moi invendus et par Eux je dois rèaliser un Benéfice. C'est une industrie honnête qu'il me faut Exerçer jusqu'a ce que j'aie [Encore] recouvré quelques fonds dEurope et realisé mes terres. Vous savés que par Partialité pour votre Paÿs J'ai placé vingt mille dollars que je n'ai pas Encore realisés.... J Espere que Vous ne me refuserés pas de m'aider en achetant ou les 4 Charmans paÿsâges qui Egalent les plus beaux tableaux pour 250. dollars qui sont reellement une Bagatelle pour vous. Ces Pieces cousues deux a deux pouroient au moins vous fournir deux trés Grands et beaux Tapis a bon marcheé.

Je vous offre Egalement les 4 Superbes Pieces de Scipio a 450. A votre Choix on ne poura qu'applaudir a Vos Vües d humanité et d'utilité Publique qui vous auront Engagé a les acquérir.

J Espere qu'en faveur de L'ancienne Connoissance que m'a procuré le Marquis De La faÿette vous ne me refuserés pas d'acheter pour une aussi *modique Somme* et, afin de vous prouver la Verité de ce que J'ai Lhonneur de vous annoncer cÿ dessus soit que vous Preniés ces 4 ou ces 8 pièces Je Chargerai *demain* par M Granger maitre general de la Poste aux Lettres Deux cens vingt dollars pour M. Robert Ralston respectable maison a Philadelphia; et Desormais je ne vous importunerai plus d'aucune affaire Semblable.

Je vous communiquerai seulement, si vous Le trouvés bon, un Memoire sur des *Moÿens de sureté publique dans vos Etats*, plus adaptés encor au Local, que ceux que vous approuvâtes de moi En 1787. par votre Lettre dattée 6 Juillet a Paris, susdite année, et que vous trouvates calculés pour *remplir cet Objet important*. Jaÿ Lhonneur dEtre avec un sincère et profond Respect

Monsieur, Votre trés humble & trés Devoué serviteur

Lormerie

EDITORS' TRANSLATION

Mister President, Washington, 15 Apr. 1803

Only the arts can civilize human behavior, console men for human cruelty, and prevent or heal the evils that are inseparable from life in society. Introducing the arts into the United States is part of your administration. As you well know, the arts have been calumniated, but that is because people have mistaken abuse for use. Drawing is the foundation of all perfection, even in crafts. The arts could bring about significant improvements at the heart of your nation. The Dutch, a population of fishermen and sailors, thrifty businessmen and wise accountants, recognized as early as the century of Louis XIV that they could create an important branch of commerce with the paintings that were emerging from France. They thus purchased and collected them and made enormous profits in a few years. The taste for these admirable works greatly contributed to slowing and finally destroying the excessive spirit of speculation that disperses capital the way the wind disperses clouds and drowns them in the sea. Taste stabilized the Dutch; wealth that was initially virtual became real. Several collections were sold, each one generating a capital of three hundred to five hundred thousand florins.

The superb collection of Scipio tapestries that I have the honor of offering you will never again be found in America at so modest a price. If it could provide students with a model for historical painting, either in one of the rooms of the Capitol or at your home, your administration would be known forever for this benefaction. The nobility of the composition, the purity of the design, the elegance of the form and the beauty of the ensemble have earned, and will continue to earn, universal admiration for these four works.

The four charming landscapes, like the beautiful paintings at Monticello, would be elegant adornments for a summer house or other home. In the winter they could also be useful in your home in the federal city where, with frost outside, they would provide you the delicious spectacle of flowers and trees that are always green as well as exquisite views of St Cloud, etc., that would remind you of happy memories.

I would not insist on offering them to you, however, if I were not obliged to do so by a circumstance that I forgot to mention yesterday when I had the honor of welcoming you. In the Tribunal of Virtue, honesty must triumph. My only motivation is my desire to pay exactly the same in your country as in my own. I owe $220 to a shop in Philadelphia for works that I bought there, totaling $920, toward which I paid $700. These works are unsold, at my house, and I must make a profit on them. This is honest business that I must undertake until I have received funds from Europe and sold my land. You know that, out of partiality to your country, I invested $20,000 that I have not yet recovered. I hope you will not refuse to help me out by buying the four charming landscapes which are as beautiful as the most exquisite paintings. They cost $250, which is just a trifle for you. If these tapestries were sewn together, two by two, you would have at least two very large, beautiful rugs for a reasonable price.

I am also offering you the four superb Scipio works for $450. Everyone who saw your purchases would applaud the spirit of humanity and public good that inspired you to acquire them.

Based on our long acquaintance, initiated by the Marquis de Lafayette, you will not refuse to make a purchase for such a modest price. To prove the truth of what I have the honor of announcing above, if you take either four or eight works, I will send $220 tomorrow to Mr. Robert Ralston, a respectable Philadelphia shopkeeper, through the postmaster general, Mr. Granger. Henceforth, I will not bother you with any other similar affair.

I will merely send you, if you wish, my text about the means of ensuring security in your states which is better suited to local conditions than my previous one, which you approved in 1787 by your letter from Paris dated July 6 of that year, and which you found suitable for filling this important function.

With deep and profound respect, Sir, I have the honor of being your very humble and devoted servant. LORMERIE

RC (DLC); one word uncertain due to overwriting; ellipses in original; addressed: "H.E Ths Jefferson President of the united States federal city"; endorsed by TJ as received 15 Apr. and so recorded in SJL.

VOTRE LETTRE DATTÉE 6 JUILLET A PARIS: in Paris in the summer of 1787, Lormerie gave TJ an essay on means of improving public safety in the United States—"*moijens d'opérer la sureté publique dans les états unis.*" According to TJ's reply on 6 July of that year, the *memoire*, which has not been found, made suggestions "well calculated to remedy the evil of public robbers and unsafe highroads." TJ explained, however, that "it is a happy truth for us, Sir, that these evils do not exist, and never did exist in our part of America." The only cases of "robbery on the highroad" in the United States that TJ recalled ever hearing about occurred when deserters from the British army "infested" New York City and Philadelphia for a period after the withdrawal of British forces from those cities (Vol. 11:528, 554-5).

From Philip Mazzei

Pisa, 15 Aprile, 1803.

Dopo la mia dei 6 xbre 1800 (che Ella ricevè) Le scrissi il 5 Febb., il 2 e il 30 Luglio, il 28 7bre, e il 15 9bre 1801. Il 28 7bre Le mandai in un sacchettino dei noccioli di pesche di varie qualità. Al principio Apr. 1802 mi pervennero da Milano coll'istesso corriere le 2 sue dei 29 Ap. 1800, e dei 17 Marzo 1801. Le risposi subito il 10 Aprile, sul punto della mia partenza per Pietroburgo; Le scrissi da Venezia il 17 do. e[1] il 15 Febb. passato Le resi conto del do. mio viaggio, del mio ritorno qui, Le inclusi una lettera del nostro comune e buono Amico Piattoli, e Le mandai 2 miei Opuscoli, uno sulla

EDITORS' TRANSLATION

Pisa, 15 April, 1803.

After my letter of 6 December 1800 (which you received), I wrote you on 5 Feb., 2 and 30 July, 28 September, and 15 November 1801. On 28 September I sent you a little bag containing some peach pits of different varieties. At the beginning of April 1802 I received via Milan with the same delivery your two letters dated 29 April 1800 and 17 March 1801. I replied right away on 10 April, when I was about to leave for Petersburg; I wrote you from Venice on the 17th of the said month and on 15 Feb. of this year. I gave you an account of that trip and of my return here; I also attached a letter from our common and good friend Piattoli, and I sent along my two little works, one on

Dft (Archivio Filippo Mazzei, Pisa, Italy); part of a conjoined series of Mazzei's drafts of letters to TJ, where it follows Mazzei's letter of 15 Feb. 1803 (see Margherita Marchione and Barbara B. Oberg, eds., *Philip Mazzei: The Comprehensive Microform Edition of his Papers*, 9 reels [Millwood, N.Y., 1981], 5:418); incomplete. RC recorded in SJL as received from Pisa on 17 Aug. 1803, but not found.

OPUSCOLI: for Mazzei's two pamphlets, *Reflections on the Nature of Money and Exchange* and *Reflections on the Evils of Beggary and the Means of Avoiding Them*, see enclosures at Mazzei to TJ, 15 Feb. (Vol. 39:540n).

[1]Mazzei here canceled "l'ultimamia."

From Thomas Munroe

Superintendants office
Washington April 15th 1803

SIR

From the Presidents message to Congress of the 24th January last, concerning the affairs of this City, and also from Conversations which I had with some of the Members of the Committee to whom that Message was referred, I had no doubt that the Act of Congress, passed in consequence thereof, entitled "An Act concerning the City of Washington"[1] was intended to be retrospective to the 1st. June last as to the several Items of expense mentioned in the 3d. Section of the said Act, they being expenses incidental to, and coexistent with the Office or duties of the Superintendant[2] and necessarily incurred under the Act of the proceding Session intituled "An Act to abolish the board of Commissioners in the City of Washington and for other purposes" by which the necessary provision for the Institution was omitted to be made.—It would however appear on reading the first mentioned Act that such retrospective provision is not only one month short as to the Superintendants Salary but is so doubtful as to a retrospective operation at all with regard to the other articles of expenditure mentioned in the aforesaid third section that, perhaps, it may create a difficulty in the passage of my accounts at the Treasury for Monies necessarily paid away for those purposes, prior to the date of the Law. If such a Construction be the true one it will be useless for me to offer Vouchers for those disbursements at the Treasury, as it will require an Act of Congress to authorise their allowance—altho' the novelty and unimportance of the subject, and the hurry of business in the house when the Law passed and not an objection to passing it pursuant to the presidents Message was, I doubt not, the sole Cause of the Irregularity or imperfection of its provisions.[3] Not expecting that the provision which Congress might deem proper to make on this subject must necessarily pass thro' all the formalities and be governed by all the rules of the Treasury of the U.S. I had supposed the appropriation clause unnecessary as the Money is to be paid out of the City funds, and not from the Treasury, and that a declaration of the amount to be allowed for the several purposes would have been quite sufficient—. I have taken the Liberty of communicating these Circumstances to you, Sir, and to pray of you such advice or direction as you may deem proper, and be pleased to give

I have the honor to be with the greatest respect Yr. Mo obdt Servt.

THOMAS MUNROE

I enclose a Copy of the message, also a Copy of the Law, which I shall be glad to get again

RC (DLC); postscript written on separate sheet; at foot of text: "President of the U.S."; endorsed by TJ as received 16 Apr. and so recorded in SJL. Enclosures: (1) TJ to the Senate and the House of Representatives, 24 Jan. 1803. (2) "An Act concerning the City of Washington," 3 Mch. 1803 (U.S. Statutes at Large, 2:235-6).

Section three of AN ACT CONCERNING THE CITY OF WASHINGTON included an appropriation for the salary of the superintendent for 1803 and "for six months of the preceding year," that is, to 1 July 1802. The same section also appropriated funds for clerk hire, surveyor's wages, and other expenses, but without stipulating a retrospective period for which the said appropriation could be applied. The 1 May 1802 ACT TO ABOLISH THE BOARD OF COMMISSIONERS that created the office of superintendent had gone into effect on 1 June 1802 (U.S. Statutes at Large, 2:175-8, 235-6).

[1] Closing quotation mark supplied by Editors.

[2] Preceding ten words interlined.

[3] Preceding five words interlined.

To William Short

DEAR SIR Washington Apr. 15. 1803.

Your favor of the 2d. was recd on the 7th. & that of the 12th. last night. as you had informed mr Barnes not to write to you to New York after the 4th. and me, that you would notify[1] me of your arrival in Philadelphia, I was awaiting that to answer your letter. I now do it at hazard & shall address it to you at Philadelphia to be kept in the post office till called for.

I have not time at this moment to examine the statement inclosed in yours, but the principles being right I have no doubt the result is so. before your return from Kentucky I will go through it, & furnish the subsequent supplementary articles, which relate chiefly to the rent, as far as it has been recieved. the principal tenant is now under suit for his arrearages. when at Monticello, where the tenants papers are kept for settlement, I will make out an exact statement of all their accounts for you. with respect to the balance due you from me you may make all your calculations & orders on a rigorous paiment of 500. D. monthly, for the 1st. year from Mar. 4. last, and such a monthly paiment afterwards as shall compleatly extinguish the whole by the end of the 2d. year, say Mar. 4. 1805. In the sale of your lands such a purchaser as mr Wickham would be greatly preferable to a mere planter. the latter considers the term of paiment as only fixing the paiment of interest, & that for the principal he has a legal right to withold it till legally compelled. suits then for the most part must be counted on. mr Randolph sets out for Georgia next month, so cannot be useful to you in the sale of your lands. Lilly can shew them, but I think Price would be a better hand, as being on the spot, better acquainted with them, & a very honest man. he would very readily do it, at your request. mr Barnes expected you would chuse to recieve the April 500. D. in Philadelphia, & has been waiting to know your arrival there to send you a check of the bank of the US. here on their bank there for that sum. I will consult with him whether it will be best to hazard it *poste restante*. as I hardly think you can be back from Kentucky before August, I shall hope to recieve you on your return at Monticello, where I shall pass the months of Aug. & September. in the mean time accept my best wishes for your health and a pleasant journey, and assurances of my affectionate esteem.

TH: JEFFERSON

RC (DLC: Short Papers); at foot of text: "W. Short"; endorsed by Short as received at Philadelphia on 3 May and "ansd. May 3—shall wait until I get his answer & mention my preference to have the check sent here—ansr. at present only that part of his letter."

[1]Preceding two words interlined in place of "write to."

From Edward Tiffin

SIR Chillicothe "Ohio" April 15th. 1803

Inclosed you will receive a certified copy of some Resolutions which passed the General Assembly of this State, and which I have been requested to forward to you.

with due respect I have the honor to be Sir your obt Servt

EDWARD TIFFIN

RC (DLC); at foot of text: "The President of the United States"; endorsed by TJ as received 10 May and so recorded in SJL. Enclosure: Resolutions of the Ohio General Assembly, 16 Apr. 1803, declaring their satisfaction with the measures taken by Congress in relation to navigation of the Mississippi River, which demonstrate that the United States, while disposed toward peace, is "determined to vindicate their rights"; the legislature also has "full confidence" that the present administration will pursue measures that will "best secure the rights and interests of the western states" regarding the Mississippi and will cooperate fully with the national government "in support of their rights and interests"; the governor is requested to forward a copy of the resolutions to the president of the United States (*Acts of the State of Ohio, First Session of the General Assembly, Held Under the Constitution of the State, A.D. One Thousand Eight Hundred and Three* [Chillicothe, 1803], 149).

To Louis Philippe Gallot de Lormerie

Apr. 16. 1803.

Th: Jefferson presents his compliments to M. de Lormerie, and regrets that it is not in his power to accept the proposals he is so kind as to make him on the subject of his tapestry. circumstances in his own situation render it neither prudent nor practicable on his own private account, nor has he any authority to do it for the public. he is in hopes some of the rich persons in & near the great cities who are building & furnishing splendid houses will find an accomodation to themselves as well as M. de Lormerie in making the acquisition. he presents him his salutations & respect.

PrC (DLC); endorsed by TJ in ink on verso.

From Isaac Coffin

Dear Sir, Nantucket April the: 17th: 1803.

I take the Liberty to Address a few Lines to you to enquire after your welfare I had the Honour to be Introduced to your Excellency last February by my Friend Doctor Logan when I was at the City of Washington with a Petition to Congress from our Town; I have been again Elected a Senator in our State Legislature for this County—My Friend Matthew Barney one of the Society Called Quakers a Respectable Merchant of our Town being bound on to the City of Washington on Business, I take the Liberty to Recommend him to your Cordial esteem, any advice you may think fit to give him Respecting his

Business will be Esteemed a favour granted to: Dear Sir, your most Obedient Servant

ISAAC COFFIN

RC (DLC); at foot of text: "His Excellency Thomas Jefferson Esqr: President of the United States"; endorsed by TJ. Recorded in SJL as received 29 Apr.

Isaac Coffin (1764-1842), a native of Nantucket Island in Massachusetts and member of the Society of Friends, began serving in the state senate in 1798, one of only two Republicans in that body. He continued to be elected by large majorities and in 1805 was unanimously chosen by the state legislature to also serve on the nine-member advisory council to the governor. In 1808, Coffin was appointed judge of probate for the county of Nantucket, a position he held until his death (*Vital Records of Nantucket Massachusetts to the Year 1850*, 5 vols. [Boston, 1925-28], 1:282; 5:160; Boston *Independent Chronicle*, 14 Apr. 1803, 6 June 1805; *Salem Register*, 9 May 1803; Boston *Democrat*, 18 Apr. 1804; *Newburyport Herald*, 6 May 1807; *New-Bedford Mercury*, 18 Mch., 20 May 1808, 4 Feb., 4 Mch. 1842; Coffin to TJ, 13 Apr. 1804, 16 Feb. 1805).

Appointed by the town meeting at Nantucket, Coffin brought a PETITION TO CONGRESS, which was presented and read in the House of Representatives on 11 Feb. The petitioners requested congressional aid to open a channel near the harbor at Nantucket "for the accommodation and safety" of the large ships used in "that most valuable branch of business, the whale fishery." To help defray the expense, the petitioners requested, for a limited time, the use of the revenues collected by the federal government at the port. The petition was referred to the Committee of Commerce and Manufactures. On 16 Feb., Samuel Smith reported that although aid could not be granted in the manner requested, the committee was "strongly impressed with the great importance of the whale fishery to the United States" and thought it "highly worthy of the attention of the Government." It was too late in the session to give the subject the attention its great importance demanded but "to procure every information necessary to a fair investigation of the subject at the next session," the committee resolved "That the Secretary of the Treasury be authorized to employ proper and intelligent persons to take a survey of the harbor in the island of Nantucket, and the bar and shoals near the same, as far as may be requisite, and to report their opinion as to the measures necessary to secure a sufficient channel for loaded ships destined for that port, with an estimate of the probable expense" (JHR, 4:335, 343-4; ASP, *Commerce and Navigation*, 1:526-7). For the report on the survey of the harbor at Nantucket presented to Congress on 27 Oct., see ASP, *Commerce and Navigation*, 1:533-5.

From Anonymous

GREAT SIR [on or before 18 Apr. 1803]

Supposing the Muse requested to be informed, of the Presidents Birth day—Would She not justly be Spurned at, for obtruding Herself—On the other hand, the muse will be concious she merited such treatment, And will not dare to think hard—but still, While you protect her Liberty, will determine to be greatfull—application was made at the office of the aurora for the above, and a very polite promise recived, last november, but no information—the personage left their adress at that office—

RC (DLC); undated; endorsed by TJ as received 18 Apr. and "my birth-day."

For other undated letters TJ received from this author under the pseudonym "The Voice of A Sybil," "A Sybilline Voice," and "A Sybill Leafe," see Vol. 35:575-6; Vol. 37:458-9; Vol. 38:430.

From Andrew Ellicott

Dear Sir Lancaster April 18th. 1803

A few days ago I received a letter from Mr. John Vaughan from which the following is an extract, "I am desired by a person in the District of Maine Kennebeck River, to enquire as soon as may be of Mr. Ellicott the cost of a Box, with the sextant, and portable horizon, and a place for an Arnold watch, (such as Mr. Ellicott describes in the 5th. Vol. of the Phil: Trants.,) we have the Watch, and wish for the rest made under the inspection of Mr. E. if possible if it can be done reasonably in order to settle longitudes, and latitudes, in this country."—

I immediately replied to Mr. Vaughan's letter, and undertook to have the apparatus for an artificial, or portable horizon, made in this place under my own inspection.—

Notwithstanding the manner in which this business is covered, I feel a strong presumption that the apparatus is for Captn. Lewis, and under this impression I have enclosed a few remarks for his use.

I expect shortly to have a work out of the press on which I have been engaged for some time, and which has been much longer delayed than I intended, owing to the little time I have to spare from manual labour, and the duties of my office.—As soon as this work is handed to the Publick I intend publishing a small treatise on practical astronomy as connected with geography, for the use of such persons as may be exploring our extensive western regions, and capable of making the necessary observations.—

In a few weeks I shall have another communication ready for the national Institute, a body of men, from whom I have received much more attention than from any in my own country.—The celebrated la Lande is dead, he has not perhaps left an equal behind:—he sent me his works shortly after I came to this place:—Delambre has likewise promised me a large work on which he has been long employed, it will be published this summer.—

My new pendulum, which was the work of five sundays, exceeds my warmest expectations.

I am Sir, with sentiments of great esteem, your sincere friend and Hbl: Servt. ANDW; ELLICOTT.

RC (DLC); at foot of text: "Thomas Jefferson, President of the United States"; endorsed by TJ as received 20 Apr. and so recorded in SJL. PrC (DLC: Ellicott Papers).

The PERSON IN THE DISTRICT OF MAINE was Benjamin Vaughan, who lived in Hallowell, Maine, and preferred to communicate with the outside world indirectly, through his brother John in Philadelphia. Benjamin Vaughan, who had studied medicine as a young man, was interested in scientific subjects and in 1801 had advised TJ about obtaining a telescope from London (ANB; Vol. 33:304, 305n; Vol. 34:272, 434, 436n; Vol. 35:605).

For Ellicott's brief description, published in the *Transactions* of the American Philosophical Society, of a BOX to hold a SEXTANT, an artificial HORIZON, and a WATCH, see the note to his letter to TJ of 6 Mch.

WORK OUT OF THE PRESS: Ellicott's account of the survey of the southern boundary of the United States, published by Thomas Dobson, appeared late in the summer. Ellicott dated the preface 22 July (*The Journal of Andrew Ellicott, Late Commissioner on Behalf of the United States ... for Determining the Boundary between the United States and the Possessions of His Catholic Majesty in America* [Philadelphia, 1803], vii; *Poulson's American Daily Advertiser*, 10 Sep.).

LA LANDE IS DEAD: although newspaper reports named Joseph Jérôme Le Français de Lalande as a victim of an epidemic in Paris, the astronomer was still alive. He died in 1807 (New York *Daily Advertiser*, 5 Apr.; Tulard, *Dictionnaire Napoléon*, 1022).

ENCLOSURE

Remarks on Observations with a Sextant

By a practice of more than twenty years, I have constantly found water preferable to any other fluid for an artificial, or portable horizon.—The reflection of the Sun from the water it is true, will be fainter than that from the specula, unless the Telescope of the Sextant be directed nearly off the foliated part of the horizon speculum.—This direction can be easily given to it, by a screw for that purpose, and which carries the Telescope parallel to the plane of the Sextant.—

Altho the meridian altitude of the sun, when it exceeds 60.°, cannot be taken with a Sextant from the artificial horizon; yet the latitude may be accurately determined by using the altitude of the sun, and the horary angles formed in taking equal altitudes to ascertain the error, and rate of going of either a clock, or watch.—This method I have constantly used when the meridional altitude of the sun exceeded 60.°, and am convinced from a long experience, that the latitude may be deduced from such observations nearly, if not quite as accurately, as from the sun's meridional altitude:—By many trials made at this place, the latitude in no case, differs so much as half a minute from that settled by the Zenith Sector.—

The equal altitudes ought always to be taken at least two hours before, and after noon.—

If the distance of the moon, from the sun, be taken immediately before the morning equal altitudes, or after those of the afternoon, or both if the position of the moon will permit, every requisite for determining with accuracy both the latitude, and longitude, will be had.

I do not find that this method has been practised by any person but myself, the theory has however been long understood.—

After the forenoon equal altitudes have been taken, the sextant should be carefully laid away, and the index not moved, till the afternoon ones are taken, and if the latitude is to be deduced from the observations, the altitude must be carefully counted off, but if the time only is wanted, the degrees, minutes, and seconds of altitude are of no importance.

It is rather better to have the vessel which contains the water for the artificial horizon unconnected with the talk, or isinglass cover, because the wind is sometimes so violent, as to shake the cover, and consequently if the two parts are connected, an undulatory motion will be communicated to the water.

It will be a necessary precaution, to have the Chronometer, with its case, tied up in a bladder when not in use,—it will prevent its being injured if by accident, it should be thrown in the water by the overturning of a canoe, or other accident. A.E.—

MS (DLC: TJ Papers, 130:22461); in Ellicott's hand, undated.

TALK, OR ISINGLASS: Ellicott recommended using thin sheets of talc or mica (sometimes called isinglass) for the cover of an artificial horizon apparatus (APS, *Transactions*, 5 [1802], 207; OED).

From George Jefferson

DEAR SIR Richmond 18th. Apl. 1803

I found on my return home after an absence of several weeks, that your quarterly account had not as usual been forwarded. You will now find it inclosed, observing a balance in favor of G. & J. of £29.16.6

The amount which you had directed to be paid to Moran, had been paid to his order a few days previous to the receipt of your letter giving information of the error in his account. it was paid to a Mr. Irvine, to whom we immediately wrote, requesting that if he had merely received it for Moran's use, he would endeavour to retain the sum mentioned by you in his hands. we have not yet heard from him.

We have procured from Mr. Macon, and forwarded to Norfolk, to be sent on to Washington, nine dozen hams, which we hope may prove good. I shall endeavour to procure four dozen more, but am not certain that I shall be able to get such as I can rely upon; if I cannot, I shall decline it.

I have just seen Lewis Harvie, who requested that I would inform you he has been for some time expecting to hear from you. he begs that you will let him know as soon as possible when you wish him to be with you.

I am Dear Sir Your Very humble servt. GEO. JEFFERSON

RC (MHi); at foot of text: "Thomas Jefferson esqr."; endorsed by TJ as received 21 Apr. and so recorded in SJL. Enclosure not found.

YOUR LETTER: TJ to George Jefferson, 26 Mch.

To João, Prince Regent of Portugal

GREAT AND GOOD FRIEND,

I have received your letter of the 26. of October last in which your Royal Highness has been pleased to communicate to me, that the Princess of Brazil, your much loved Spouse, had that day happily increased your Royal Family by the birth of a Son. Participating in all the events which may increase your happiness, we offer you on this joyous occasion our sincere congratulations, and we pray you to be assured at the same time of our desire to cherish and improve the good correspondence which so happily prevails between the two nations.

May the Lord have you, Great and Good friend in his safe and holy keeping.

Written at the City of Washington the 18th. day of April in the year of our Lord one thousand eight hundred and three.

TH: JEFFERSON

FC (Lb in DNA: RG 59, Credences); in a clerk's hand; at head of text: "Thomas Jefferson, President of the United States of America. To His Royal Highness, the Prince Regent of Portugal, and of the two Algarves, on this side and on that of the sea; in Africa, of Guinea, and of the conquest, Navigation and commerce of Ethiopia, Arabia, Persia and of India &ca."; below signature: "By the President" and "James Madison Secretary of State." Not recorded in SJL.

From John Millar

Shepherd Street May Fair
April[1] 18th. 1803

SIR

In the year 1797 having occasion to investigate the means of subuing and preventing Contagious Fevers, that which had proved so fatal to the Citizens of Philadelphia, became of course, a subject of consideration. The Book was sent to Dr Rush by Mr Perry and I have observed that he had in some subsequent publications retracted some opinions he formerly held on that subject, and with great pleasure I have observed that the rage of that destructive pestilence has since been restrained.

I humbly submit to your consideration a Copy of that work, and if it has, formerly, or should, in future, contribute, in any degree to the safety and preservation of the worthy Citizens of Philadelphia, I shall esteem it the best reward of my Labours. With the highest respect and Esteem, I have the Honour to be

Your Excellencys most Obedient & most Humble Servant

JOHN MILLAR

RC (MHi); endorsed by TJ as a letter of 18 Apr. 1804 received 14 May 1804 and so recorded in SJL. Enclosure: Millar's *Observations on the Change of Public Opinion in Religion, Politics, and Medicine; on the Conduct of the War; on the Prevailing Diseases in Great Britain; and on Medical Arrangements in the Army and Navy*, 2 vols. (London, [1803]); Sowerby, No. 928.

Born in Scotland, John Millar (1733-1805) trained as a doctor at the University of Edinburgh and earned positive attention for his work *Observations on the Asthma and on the Hooping Cough* (London, 1769). In 1774, he was named physician at the Westminster General Dispensary in London, where he became an active member of the city's recently established medical society (DNB).

Millar was an outspoken critic of intensive purgation and venesection in the treatment of CONTAGIOUS FEVERS, advising instead the use of Peruvian bark, an opinion squarely at odds with the practice developed by Benjamin RUSH during Philadelphia's yellow fever epidemic of 1793 and to which Rush remained committed throughout his career (Paul E. Kopperman, "'Venerate the Lancet': Benjamin Rush's Yellow Fever Therapy in Context," *Bulletin of the History of Medicine*, 78 [2004], 553, 572-4; *The British Critic, and Quarterly Theological Review*, 25 [1805], 411-13).

Given the time necessary for transporting something from London to Washington, it is unlikely that Millar misdated the letter. London publications, nevertheless, did not begin to take notice of *Observations on the Change of Public Opinion in Religion, Politics, and Medicine* until near the end of 1804, when *The Monthly Magazine; or, British Register* included it among its list of new publications. One reviewer chastised the work, which appears to have compiled several of Millar's writings, some previously published, for its many attacks on individuals who Millar believed had either ignored or plagiarized his findings (*The British Critic*, 411).

[1]Month written over an illegible word.

Preparations to Negotiate an Alliance with Great Britain

I. COMMISSION FOR MINISTER PLENIPOTENTIARY TO GREAT BRITAIN, 18 APR. 1803

II. TO GEORGE III, KING OF GREAT BRITAIN, 18 APR. 1803

III. TO NAPOLEON BONAPARTE, 18 APR. 1803

IV. COMMISSION FOR MINISTER PLENIPOTENTIARY TO FRANCE, 18 APR. 1803

V. TO NAPOLEON BONAPARTE, 19 APR. 1803

VI. TO CHARLOTTE, QUEEN OF GREAT BRITAIN, 20 APR. 1803

EDITORIAL NOTE

On 8 Apr., the president posed a question to the four heads of departments and the attorney general: was it time to make "overtures to England" to ensure American access to the Mississippi River waterway? The French government had not given Robert R. Livingston assurance that the 1795 treaty between the United States and Spain—particularly those sections that pertained to American commerce along the Mississippi—would remain in effect after France took control of Louisiana. It was essential for the United States to "know at once whether we can acquire N. Orleans or not," Jefferson had declared earlier, and Madison viewed the negotiations over New Orleans as "a test" of the still unknown intentions of Bonaparte's government. Writing to Livingston early in February about the decision to send James Monroe to France, the president gave notice that "should we fail in this object of the mission, a further one will be superadded for the other side of the channel." Months earlier in letters to Livingston and Pierre Samuel Du Pont de Nemours, Jefferson signaled that a failure by France to satisfy American concerns would likely prompt the formation of a military pact between the United States and Great Britain. In the cabinet meeting on 8 Apr., the president and his advisers decided that if Livingston and Monroe found themselves stymied in the effort to get New Orleans, they should "enter into conferences with the British govmt" to work out "principles of alliance" (Vol. 37:264-5, 333, 418-19; Vol. 39:444-6; Madison to TJ, 14 Mch.; Notes on a Cabinet Meeting, 8 Apr.).

If a pact with Great Britain became necessary, Jefferson and Madison hoped that Monroe and Livingston could make the overture through Charles Whitworth, the British minister to France. Approaching Whitworth in Paris would be "less likely to alarm and stimulate the French government," Madison advised the envoys, "and to raise the pretensions of the British government than the repairing of either of you to London." Madison cautioned that if relations between France and the United States started to break down over the New Orleans problem, the departure of Monroe or Livingston for Britain might be taken as "a signal of rupture," which could force the United States to commit to an alliance with Britain prematurely and on unfavorable terms. To let the American diplomats start talking to Whitworth without attracting attention, Madison drew up a letter that, "without the formality of a commission," authorized Livingston and Monroe "to open a confidential communication with the Ministers of the British Government, and to confer freely and fully on the precautions and provisions best adapted to the Crisis" (Madison, *Papers*, *Sec. of State Ser.*, 4:528, 529-30, 533).

Although Jefferson and Madison hoped that discussions with Whitworth in Paris might buy time and let them craft a coalition on the best terms for the United States—"leave us in peace till Congress meets, & prevent war till next spring," as Jefferson wrote in his notes of the cabinet meeting on 8 Apr.—they knew that "the pressure of the crisis" might require direct negotiations in Britain. Should that happen, they did not want their representatives to have to wait for new authorization. To give Monroe and Livingston power to act in any of a potential variety of situations, the president and secretary of state prepared a set of blank documents—three identical sets, in fact, all signed and bearing the seal of the United States, to ensure against accidents in transit. Madison, in coded instructions that were also painstakingly made out in triplicate, explained how the papers should be employed (same, 527-32).

First were a commission and a letter of credence for a minister plenipotentiary to Great Britain (Documents I and II below). Monroe's name, Madison indicated, was to go in the blanks of those documents "unless his mission to France should have an issue likely to be disagreeable to Great Britain." In that case, Livingston would be the one to go to London. To cover that possibility, the packet of documents included a letter of leave, giving Livingston a means of resigning his position in Paris (Document III), along with a commission and letter of credence for a minister plenipotentiary to France (Documents IV and V), which would let Monroe occupy that post as Livingston departed (Madison, *Papers*, *Sec. of State Ser.*, 4:529).

A final document took the form of a second letter of credence for a minister plenipotentiary to Britain (Document VI). Briefer than the one addressed to George III (Document II), this letter was directed to his wife, Queen Charlotte. Bearing a date of 20 Apr., the letter to the queen may have been an afterthought. George III had suffered a debilitating episode of delirium in February and March 1801, and George W. Erving, writing from London the following February, reported to Madison that the monarch, "tho perhaps not actually crazy," was "so near it, that any considerable irritation may subject him to relapse." During the king's bout with derangement in 1788 and 1789, Charlotte had maintained control over the royal household and resisted efforts to establish a regency. If George should become incapacitated again, Erving predicted, Charlotte "will have at least her share" of power. Jefferson and Madison, unable to know what circumstances an American envoy might find on his arrival in Britain, apparently thought it best to provide Livingston and Monroe with a letter to the queen in addition to the one for her husband (DNB, s.v. "Charlotte," "George III"; Madison, *Papers*, *Sec. of State Ser.*, 2:444; John Ehrman, *The Younger Pitt: The Consuming Struggle* [London, 1996], 525-8; Ida Macalpine and Richard Hunter, *George III and the Mad-Business* [London, 1969], 111-30).

The president and secretary of state could do little beyond furnishing their diplomats with the tools, in the form of the blank letters and commissions, to make an arrangement with the British against France. "The price which she may attach to her cooperation," Madison advised with regard to Britain, "cannot be foreseen and therefore cannot be the subject of full and precise instructions." If Britain and France were once again at war when his instructions arrived, he advised, the French would surely try to reach an accommodation with the United States and a union with Britain would be unnecessary—or, if required, could be crafted on terms favorable to the U.S. "Whatever *connection* indeed, may be *eventually formed* with *Great Britain* in *reference* to *war*," Madison admonished (he had the words in italics put into code), "the *policy* of the *United States* requires that it be as *little entangling* as the nature of the case will permit" (Madison, *Papers*, *Sec. of State Ser.*, 4:528, 530).

Madison's instructions for the diplomatic advance to Britain were dated 18 Apr. He added to them two days later, reporting the restoration of the right of deposit at New Orleans along with a supposition that the cession of Louisiana from Spain to France had either been canceled or would be much delayed. "However this may be," he wrote to Monroe and Livingston, the new circumstances should not "slacken the negociations for the greater security and the enlargement" of American rights on the Mississippi. Those negotiations, in the form of bargaining for Louisiana, were going forward in Paris before Jefferson signed the blank documents for Livingston and Monroe. Just after they concluded the agreements for the purchase of Louisiana, the envoys learned from Rufus King that the British government was contemplating a seizure of New Orleans. The pair quickly informed King that the territory was coming into the possession of the United States. There would be no need to initiate a coalition with Great Britain to wrest New Orleans from France (same, 531-2, 605, 606n; Bradford Perkins, "England and the Louisiana Question," *Huntington Library Quarterly*, 18 [1955], 288-92).

Nevertheless, neither the documents nor the discretionary power that accompanied them went entirely unused. In June, after they received the instructions, commissions, and letters of credence, Monroe and Livingston decided that Monroe should "proceed immediately to England"—not to work out a now-unneeded alliance, but because King's resignation as minister to Britain would leave the United States unrepresented at the Court of St. James's just as Britain and France tumbled back into a state of war. The two diplomats were unsure from Madison's orders if it was all right for one of them to go to England as a new minister in residence, or if the commission for a minister plenipotentiary was to be used only "on the contingency" of a negotiation for a military alliance. They convinced themselves that it would be "conformable to the presidents intention" for Monroe to cross the English Channel and fill the vacancy left by King. Accordingly, Monroe, who had been expecting to go to Spain to haggle for West Florida, utilized the blank commission and letters of credence to become the U.S. minister to Great Britain (see notes to Documents I, II, and VI). He assured the secretary of state that he was no longer needed in Paris and that his departure for London would not impair relations between the United States and France (Madison, *Papers*, *Sec. of State Ser.*, 5:6, 12-13, 103-4, 120, 169, 244).

Livingston had declared his intention not to remain as minister in Paris beyond the spring of 1804, but he waited for the president to name a successor and did not employ the letter of leave included in the packet with the blank documents. When Jefferson appointed John Armstrong as minister to France in June 1804, the secretary of state informed Livingston that "it has been thought proper to transmit a fresh letter of leave to be used in preference to" the one of April 1803 (same, 6:446; 7:395; Livingston to TJ, 12 Mch.).

I. Commission for Minister Plenipotentiary to Great Britain

Thomas Jefferson, President of the United States of America,
To   Greeting:

Reposing especial Trust and Confidence in Your Integrity, Prudence and Ability I have appointed[1] you the said   Minister Plenipotentiary for the United States of America at the Court of His Britannic Majesty, authorizing you hereby to do and perform all such matters and things as to the said place or office do appertain, or as may be duly given you in charge hereafter, and the said office to Hold and exercise during the pleasure of the President of the United States for the time being, and until the end of the next Session of the Senate of the United States, and no longer.

In Testimony whereof, I have caused these Letters to be made Patent, and the Seal of the United States to be hereunto affixed.

Given under my Hand at the City of Washington the eighteenth day of April in the year of our Lord one thousand Eight hundred and three; and of the Independence of the United States of America the Twenty Seventh

TH: JEFFERSON

MS (Roger W. Barrett, Chicago, 1947); in a clerk's hand except day of month, which Madison inserted in a blank, and signatures; below signature: "By the President," followed by Madison's signature as secretary of state; with seal of the United States; Monroe's full name was later inserted in both blanks in text by a clerk. Dupl (PHC); in a clerk's hand except signatures; at head of text: "(Duplicate)"; with seal. Tripl (PWW); in a clerk's hand except signatures; at head of text: "(Triplicate)"; with seal. FC (Lb in DNA: RG 59, Credences); in a clerk's hand, with Monroe's name inserted in blanks.

[1] Dupl, Tripl, and FC: "do appoint."

II. To George III, King of Great Britain

GREAT AND GOOD FRIEND,

I have made choice of   one of our distinguished citizens to reside near your Majesty, in the quality of Minister Plenipotentiary of the United States of America. He is well informed of the relative interests of the two Countries, and of our sincere desire to cultivate and strengthen the friendship and good correspondence between us; and from a knowledge of his fidelity, probity and good conduct, I have entire confidence that he will render himself acceptable to your Majesty, by his constant endeavours to preserve and advance the interest and happiness of both nations. I therefore request your Majesty to receive him favourably and to give full credence to whatever he shall say to you on the part of the United States; and most of all when he shall assure you of their friendship and wishes for your prosperity: and I pray God to have your Majesty in his safe and holy keeping.

Written at the City of Washington the Eighteenth day of April in the year of our Lord one thousand Eight hundred and three.

TH: JEFFERSON

Tripl (PHC); in a clerk's hand except signatures; at head of text: "(Triplicate)"; below signature: "By the President," followed by Madison's signature as secretary of state; addressed: "To Our Great and Good Friend His Britannic Majesty"; with seal of the United States. Dupl (NHi: Robert R. Livingston Papers); in a clerk's hand except signatures; at head of text: "(Duplicate)"; with seal. FC (Lb in DNA: RG 59, Credences); in a clerk's hand, with Monroe's name inserted in blank.

III. To Napoleon Bonaparte

CITIZEN FIRST CONSUL,

Circumstances rendering it expedient that Robert R. Livingston who has for some time past resided with you as our Minister Plenipotentiary should be in a situation to render other services to his Country, we have authorized him to take his leave of you, embracing that occasion to assure you of our friendship and sincere desire to preserve and strengthen the harmony and good understanding between the two nations. We are persuaded that he will do this in the manner most expressive of these sentiments and of the respect and sincerity with which they are offered.

We pray God to keep you, Citizen First Consul, under his safe and holy protection.

Written at the City of Washington, the Eighteenth day of April in the year of our Lord one thousand Eight hundred and three.

TH: JEFFERSON

RC (PHC); in a clerk's hand except signatures; below signature: "By the President," followed by Madison's signature as secretary of state; addressed: "To the First Consul of the French Republic"; with seal of the United States. Dupl (Christie's

Catalogue, Item No. 171, New York City, 26 Jan. 1996); in a clerk's hand except signatures; at head of text: "(Duplicate)"; with seal. FC (Lb in DNA: RG 59, Credences); in a clerk's hand.

IV. Commission for Minister Plenipotentiary to France

Thomas Jefferson, President of the United States of America,
To Greeting:

Reposing especial Trust and Confidence in Your Integrity, Prudence and Ability I have appointed[1] you the said Minister Plenipotentiary of the United States of America to the Republic of France, authorizing you hereby to do and perform all such matters and things as to the said place or office do appertain, or as may be duly given you in charge hereafter, and the said office to Hold and exercise, during the pleasure of the President of the United States, for the time being, and until the end of the next Session of the Senate of the United States, and no longer.

In Testimony whereof, I have caused the Seal of the United States to be hereunto affixed.

Given under my Hand, at the City of Washington the eighteenth day of April in the year of our Lord one thousand Eight hundred and three; and of the Independence of the United States of America the Twenty Seventh. TH: JEFFERSON

MS (NHi: Robert R. Livingston Papers); in a clerk's hand except day of month, which Madison inserted in a blank, and signatures; below signature: "By the President," followed by Madison's signature as secretary of state; with seal of the United States. Dupl (same); in a clerk's hand except signatures; at head of text: "(Duplicate)"; with seal. Tripl (PHC); in a clerk's hand except signatures; at head of text: "(Triplicate)"; with seal. FC (Lb in DNA: RG 59, Credences); in a clerk's hand.

[1]Dupl, Tripl, and FC: "do appoint."

V. To Napoleon Bonaparte

CITIZEN FIRST CONSUL,

I have made choice of [1] one of our distinguished Citizens, to reside near the French Republic in quality of Minister Plenipotentiary of the United States of America. He is well apprized of the friendship which we bear to your Republic, and of our desire to cultivate the harmony and good correspondence so happily subsisting between us. From a knowledge of his fidelity, probity and good conduct, I have entire confidence that he will render himself acceptable to you, and give effect to our desire of preserving and advancing on all occasions the interest and happiness of the two Nations. I beseech you, therefore, Citizen First Consul, to give full credence to whatever he shall say on the part of the United States, and most of all when he shall assure you of our friendship and wishes for the prosperity of the French Republic: and I pray God to have you, Citizen First Consul, in his safe and holy keeping.

Written at the City of Washington, the Nineteenth day of April in the year of our Lord one thousand Eight hundred and three.

TH: JEFFERSON

RC (DLC: Monroe Papers); in a clerk's hand except signatures; below signature: "By the President," followed by Madison's signature as secretary of state; addressed in Jacob Wagner's hand: "To the First Consul of the French Republic"; with seal of the United States. Dupl (PHC); in a clerk's hand except signatures; at head of text: "(Duplicate)"; with seal. FC (Lb in DNA: RG 59, Credences); in a clerk's hand.

[1]In RC, Dupl, and FC, clerks inserted Monroe's name in the blank. In FC his name was later canceled.

VI. To Charlotte, Queen of Great Britain

MADAM OUR GOOD FRIEND

I have named   Minister Plenipotentiary of the United States of America to your Royal consort. My knowledge of his good qualities gives me full confidence that he will so conduct himself, as to merit your esteem. I pray therefore, that you yield entire credence to the assurances, which he will bear to you of our friendship; and that God may always have you, Madam, our Good friend, in his holy keeping.

Written at the City of Washington the Twentieth of April in the year of our Lord one thousand Eight hundred and three.

TH: JEFFERSON

Tripl (PHC); in a clerk's hand except signatures; at head of text: "(Triplicate)"; below signature: "By the President," followed by Madison's signature as secretary of state; with seal of the United States; addressed: "To Our Good Friend The Queen of England." RC (Sotheby's Catalogue, Item No. 276, New York City, 25 Nov. 1997); in a clerk's hand except signatures; with seal. FC (Lb in DNA: RG 59, Credences); in a clerk's hand, with Monroe's name inserted in blank.

Charlotte (1744-1818) married George III in 1761, when she was a princess of the duchy of Mecklenburg-Strelitz. Although the letter printed above was addressed to her as the queen of England, as of 1 Jan. 1801 she was queen of the United Kingdom of Great Britain and Ireland (DNB; John Ehrman, *The Younger Pitt: The Consuming Struggle* [London, 1996], 194).

From Hugh Williamson

SIR New York 18th April 1803

Some days ago a gentleman from Rhode Island Mr Forster who was making some enquiries concerning Florida told me that he had heard you speaking to a gentleman from New Orleans concerning the prospects of making the Iberville navigable. As the navigation of our western waters is become an object of great concern to every man who has the entiriety & prosperity of the United States at heart I deem it a duty to give you such informations respecting the Iberville as have occasionally been handed to me.

Before the revolution war I corresponded with a Doctor Lorimer of West Florida a good botanist and a man of learning; at my nomination he was chosen a member of the philosophical society in Philada: By him I was introduced to a British engineer who had served some years in Florida and whom I frequently conversed with. From that gentleman I obtained complete drafts of the River Ohio & Mobille, of which Genl Knox, when secy at war took a copy. Conversing with that gentleman and with another engineer who served also in west Florida I was told that after the cession of the Floridas to great Britain attempts were made to render the Iberville navigable, but they proved ineffectual through the ignorance and obstinacy of the commanding officer. That gentleman conceiving that art must yield in all cases to nature conceived that the original passage of the water was the best possible passage, therefore a frigate or sloop of war was sent up the Mississippi to the entrance of the Iberville and workmen were employed to cut away the logs that appeared very numerous in the channel when the waters were out. He presumed that when the logs were removed the current would deepen the channel as formerly at Point Coupe. That Officer did not consider that the Iberville was in fact an Eddy or refluent water which could never have much force and that it would necessarily be choaked again by logs the first time the waters were high. Supposing the course of the Missisippi to be due South the direction of the Iberville, if it was a proper debouchement of the Mississippi, like those of the Ganges or the Nile, should be South East southerly, but the course is North East nearly or to the northward of East as you will find by any correct Map. My informant alledged to me as a thing not to be questioned that if the labourers had begun a new canal several miles above the entrance of the Iberville & had cut it in a South Easterly direction to the river Amité at or below the mouth of the Iberville the navigation might at a small expence have been thrown into the Lake Ponchartrain. The outlet of that lake or sound is not deep but the depth of water would doubtless be increased on the present bar by throwing more water into the sound. I do not recollect the distance between the rivers Mississippi and Amité but I know that from frequent conversations on the subject my mind was fully convinced that a navigable cut might be effected with certainty and at a moderate expence from the Mississippi to the Lake. Although at the time to which I refer I had not the same solicitude as at present concerning the navigation of the Mississippi, I viewed the island of New Orleans as a great impediment and heartily wished that the river Mississippi or a good part of it could be induced to run to the Eastward of New Orleans.

Wishing a prosperous issue to your negotiations in favour of the commerce of our western bretheren I am

with the utmost respect Your most obedient and very humble Servant
Hu Williamson

RC (DLC); at foot of text: "Thomas Jefferson Esqr Presdt of the U:S:"; endorsed by TJ as received 20 Apr. and so recorded in SJL.

mr forster: possibly Senator Theodore Foster of Rhode Island.

The iberville River, or Bayou Manchac, runs almost directly east from the Mississippi River south of present-day Baton Rouge to the Amite River. The latter waterway runs east of and roughly parallel to the Mississippi. During the 1760s, the British attempted unsuccessfully to employ the Iberville and Amite as a means to connect Lake Pontchartrain with the Mississippi and thereby avoid French and Spanish controlled New Orleans and the tedious navigation of the lower part of the river. The Iberville and lower Amite also formed part of the boundary between West Florida and Louisiana (Douglas Stewart Brown, "The Iberville Canal Project: Its Relation to Anglo-French Commercial Rivalry in the Mississippi Valley, 1763-1775," *Mississippi Valley Historical Review*, 32 [1946], 491-516; Mary Ann Sternberg, *Winding Through Time: The Forgotten History and Present-Day Peril of Bayou Manchac* [Baton Rouge, 2007], 2, 39-48).

Dr. John lorimer had sent Williamson descriptions of the natural resources, climate, and geography of West Florida, some of which were published by the American Philosophical Society. He was elected a member in 1769 (aps, *Transactions*, 1 [1771], xviii, 250-4; aps, *Proceedings*, 22, pt. 3 [1884], 35).

To Edward Dowse

Dear Sir Washington Apr. 19. 1803.

I now return the sermon you were so kind as to inclose me, having perused it with attention. the reprinting it[1] by me, as you have proposed, would very readily be ascribed to hypocritical affectation, by those who, when they cannot blame our acts, have recourse to the expedient of imputing them to bad motives. this is a resource which can never fail them; because there is no act, however virtuous, for which ingenuity may not find some bad motive. I must also add that tho' I concur with the author in considering the moral precepts of Jesus, as more pure, correct, & sublime than those of the antient philosophers, yet I do not concur with him in the mode of proving it. he thinks it necessary to libel and decry the doctrines of the philosophers. but a man must be blinded indeed by prejudice, who can deny them a great degree of merit. I give them their just due, & yet maintain that the morality of Jesus, as taught by himself & freed from the corruptions of later times, is far superior. their philosophy went chiefly to the government of our passions, so far as respected ourselves, & the procuring our own tranquility. on our duties to others they were short & deficient. they extended their cares[2] scarcely beyond our kindred & friends individually, & our country in the abstract. Jesus embraced, with charity & philanthropy, our neighbors, our countrymen, & the whole family of mankind. they confined themselves to actions: he pressed his scrutinies into the region of our thoughts, & called for purity at the fountain head. In a pamphlet lately published in Philadelphia by Dr. Priestly, he has treated, with more justice & skill than mr Bennet, a small portion of this subject. his is a comparative view of Socrates only with Jesus. I have urged him to take up the subject on a broader scale.

Every word which goes from me, whether verbally or in writing, becomes the subject of so much malignant distortion, & perverted construction, that I am obliged to caution my friends against admitting the possibility of my letters getting into the public papers, or a copy of them to be taken under any degree of confidence. the present one is perhaps of a tenor to silence some calumniators. but I never will, by any word or act, bow to the shrine of intolerance, or admit a right of enquiry into the religious opinions of others. on the contrary we are bound, you, I, & every one, to make common cause, even with error itself, to maintain the common right of freedom of conscience. we ought with one heart and one hand to hew down the daring and dangerous efforts of those who would seduce the public opinion to substitute itself into that tyranny over religious faith which the laws have so justly abdicated. for this reason, were my opinions up to the standard of those who arrogate the right of questioning them, I would not countenance that arrogance by descending to an explanation. Accept my friendly salutations & high esteem.

Th: Jefferson

PrC (DLC); at foot of first page: "Edward Dowse esq."

SERMON YOU WERE SO KIND AS TO INCLOSE ME: see Dowse to TJ, 5 Apr.

[1] TJ here canceled "with."
[2] Preceding two words interlined.

From Benjamin H. Latrobe

DEAR SIR Philadelphia April 19th. 1803

In order to save the postage of the enclosed packet, containing the drawings & sections of the foundation Walls of the S. Wing of the Capitol,—I have taken the liberty of addressing it to you, and if there be no impropriety in my giving you the trouble I should beg leave to send further packets by the same means, as most of them will be very heavy.—

As soon as I can move my family I shall return to Washington,—or even sooner, if my presence be required. I am with the truest respect

Your faithful hble Servt B HENRY LATROBE

RC (DLC); endorsed by TJ as received 22 Apr. and so recorded in SJL. Enclosure: Latrobe to John Lenthall, 19 Apr. (DLC: Latrobe Papers; Latrobe, *Correspondence*, 1:288n).

To Thomas Munroe

SIR Washington Apr. 19. 1803.

I inclose you the Attorney general's opinion on so much of the act concerning the city of Washington as relates to the monies allowed to it's officers. you will percieve that he thinks the appropriation for yourself the only one[1] limited to a particular period of time, viz from July 1. 1802. to Dec. 31. 1803 that the time for which the other appropriations are made is undefined, and the monies[2] therefore applicable to the services they remunerate at whatever time these shall have been, or shall be, rendered; to pay debts where the services have been already performed, as well as to place a sum in hand for future services. it is the intention of a statute which is to be regarded, and that may be sought not only in the words, but in matter out of the statute, & especially when the words are not against the construction, but merely indefinite. Accept my salutations. TH: JEFFERSON

RC (DLC: Digges-L'Enfant-Morgan Papers); at foot of text: "Mr. Munroe." PrC (DLC); endorsed by TJ in ink on verso. Enclosure not found.

ACT CONCERNING THE CITY OF WASHINGTON: see Munroe to TJ, 15 Apr.

[1] TJ here canceled "strictly."
[2] Preceding two words interlined.

From Charles Willson Peale

DEAR SIR Museum April 19th. 1803.

At last I have received Letters from my Sons in London—their neglect of writing, as I expected, was in part caused by an unwillingness to give me uneasiness at their want of success in their exhibition—but having lowered the price of 2/6 to one shilling for each Visitor, their income is greatly increased; nearly tribled, and some Gentleman who had visited their Room twice since the date of their letters, tell me they are crowd'd so much that some Lady complaining of being *squeesed*, it is waggishly said that *all London will now go there.*

Rembrandt has written two pieces for the Philosophical Magazine, with one of them is anexed a Plate to shew the difference between the head of the Mammoth and the Elephant. He has turned the Tusks downward, giving his reasons for thinking such should be their position, if placed as the Elephants their great curviture and twist over the head would render them less useful in defence. but his best reason is drawn from a pr of Tusks that we dug up that had their ends very much worn, which could not have happened to the uppermost side. I hope you may have seen or will shortly see the late numbers of this Magazine.

Rembrandt supposes it might be an amphibious animal, and a Mr. Pownal has a piece in the same Magazine for the month of January, he is inclined also to think it amphibious.

But neither of them has noticed what I consider a strong trait in favour of such an opinion, which is the great length of Cartilage that has been attached to the ends of the ribs necessary to give the body a proportionate size. This extraordinary length, giving the Animal the power of expanding and contracting the body, more especially necessary in animals going under water.

You might ask as Doctr Wistar did, *how I know that the cartilage should be so much longer than in common Animals*—

Two points being assertained, no doubt can arise on the remainder—begining with the front part of the Sternum to attach the Ribs, by attaching to it the first and 2d pair of Ribs in their proper place with as little cartilage as shall accord with the form of those first ribs, consequently all the differences of lengths in the other Ribs must be made up by Cartilage.

When I first put up this Skeleton I was[1] pleased with the nice and accurate fitting of Bone to Bone, it delighted me to shew them close togather. Without having any subject to follow, it is not to be wondered at, if the skeleton should be deficient in the manner of connecting some of the bones—and finding it more like the general structure of the Elephant than any other Animal I knew, naturally led me to make that imitation, and my numerous Visitors approved the work faulty as it was. Mounting it a second time, having exercised my judgement, find it a wonderful Animal, possessing other differences from the Elephant besides those enumerated by my Son Rembrandt.

The lengthened neck, which might very properly be made still longer by thicker cartilage, with a very little bend of the fore-legs, the Animal with his strong and long lips might come close to the ground, and which the present position of those enormous tusks does not much oppose; their curve turning more outwardly than down, except at their points.

The measurement of this Skeleton as it now stands, are from the front of the Tusks to the tail in a strait line 19 feet 5½ Ins:, Along the Tusks in the curve, the temporal bones and along the curveture of back in the part where the spinal marrow should be, to the end of the tail 30 feet 6 Inches.[2] From the ground out side of the fore-legs over the Blades and the highest vertebræ spines, from side to side 25 feet 6 Inches. The perpendicular heigth 11 feet 10 In. behind at the hips 9 feet 1 Inch high.

From the upper part of the sternum or breast bone to the underside of the Vertebræ 4 feet 3 Inches. Between the Humerus at the upper part from leg to leg 2 feet 7 Inches, at the bottom of ditto 2 feet 4 Inches, and at the bottom of the Radius across 2 feet one Inch. Between the hind Legs from the head of one Femur to the other 2 feet, at the bottom of ditto 21 Inches. between the Tibia's at the bottom 19 Inches.

The length of the Head 3 feet 3 Inches. greatest width behind, at the holes communicating to the internal part of the Ears, 2 feet 8 Inches. width at the front of the Temporal bones 2 feet 4 Inches. width of the Atlass including the Spines 1 foot 4 Inches. Length of the 4th. Vertebræ of the back with its spine 2 feet 4 Inches. Width of the last lumber Vertebræ independant of its Spines 7 Inches. Length of front Rib 2 feet 3 Inches. width at the bottom where the Cartilage joins it 9 Inches. Length of the 5th. Rib 3 f. 6 Inches and width at 10 or 12 Inches from its head 4 Inches. Length of the 10th. or longest rib 4 feet 2 Inches. Length of the Humerus, or upper bone of the fore leg 3 feet 2½ Inches. Circumference at the Head 3 feet 3 Inches. Ditto at the middle or smallest part 1 f. 6 Inches; Ditto at the lower end 2 feet 8 Inches. Length of the *Ulna*, or lower bone of the fore leg 2 feet 9 Inches. Ditto of the *radius*, or lessor bone of ditto 2 feet 5 Inches. Circumference of the *Ulna* and Radius togather, at the largest part above 3 feet 4 Inches. Ditto at the middle or smallest part 1 f. 7½ Inches. Ditto below 2 feet 8 Inches. Length of the *Femur*, or thigh bone 3 feet 8 Inches. Circumference at the head 2 feet 5 Inches. Ditto at the middle or smallest part 1 f. 5½ Inches. Ditto at the lowest end 2 feet 8 Inches. Length of the *Tibia* 2 feet 2¾. Fibula 2 feet 1½ Ins. Circumference of the Tibia and Fibula or lower bones of the hind Leg at their heads 2 feet 4 Inches. ditto at the middle 1 foot 6½ In. Ditto below, next the foot 2 feet 2 Ins. Ditto of the Patella, or knee pan, which is nearly round 1 f. 6 Inches. Length of the Tusks 11 feet. Circumference near the root 1 f. 11 Inches. Length of the first and largest of the Phalanges of the fore foot 7 Inches, greatest width 4 In. The largest grinder weighs 6 pounds. The front or smallest Grinders are very much worn; even through the Enamel.

A Tusk belonging to these bones I lent to Rembrandt to exhibit with his Skeleton, on the end which joined the head is a ridge length-ways of the thickness of my finger, and no part of the upper Jaw in my possession has the cavity to receive this ridge. It has exactly half of the diameter of each socket. The Farmers draging out the head with those enormous Tusks in the mud, broke them to pieces.
It would have been fortunate had that part been left for me to uncover, no part of it would then have been lost. Fortune may yet favor me with a cranium from some other quarter, the only important part wanting in my Skeleton.

I should be glad to know our prospect of those Bones found in the Salt Petre cave in Green bryar County Virginia, which you have so obligingly given your aid to procure for me. I have some hope, that if it is not the Megalonyx, it may aid Us to greater knowledge of the Mammoth.

Your regard and aid to Arts and Science, ought to attach to you all engenious good men. By your counsels may America long enjoy peace with the means of extending useful knowledge and improvments, in Agriculture, Arts, and Manufacories of every kind, and that you may have health and length of days is the ardent wish of your friend

C W Peale

RC (DLC); at foot of text: "To His excellency Thomas Jefferson"; endorsed by TJ as received 26 Apr. and so recorded in SJL. PoC (PPAmP: Peale-Sellers Papers).

For the EXHIBITION of a mastodon skeleton in England by Peale's sons Rembrandt and Rubens, see Vol. 37:423; Vol. 38:592, 593n; Vol. 39:144-5, 306-7.

The TWO PIECES by Rembrandt Peale appeared in the November and December 1802 issues of the PHILOSOPHICAL MAGAZINE of London. He titled the articles, respectively, "A Short Account of the Mammoth" and "On the Differences which Exist between the Heads of the Mammoth and Elephant." As he explained in the essays and showed in an illustration that compared the jaws and tusks of a mastodon with those of a modern elephant, he had concluded that a mastodon's curved tusks must have pointed DOWNWARD (*Philosophical Magazine*, 14 [1802-1803], 162-9, 228-9, plate 5).

A MR. POWNAL: Thomas Pownall, the English statesman, author, and former colonial governor of Massachusetts, wrote to Alexander Tilloch, editor of the *Philosophical Magazine*, from his country house in Bedfordshire to say that Rembrandt Peale's description of the "mammoth" in the publication had raised doubts in his mind. Two visits to the exhibition to examine the skeleton, however, convinced him that the young man's conclusions about the animal were correct. Pownall reasoned that the mastodon was a sea animal from an epoch when the Earth was "an *aqueous planet*." The magazine called Pownall "Governor" but misprinted his first initial, which may have caused some confusion about his identity. TJ owned several of Pownall's books (same, 332-7; DNB; Sowerby, Nos. 659, 3054, 3064, 3065; Vol. 13:651).

MEASUREMENT OF THIS SKELETON: Peale's measurements were probably of the mastodon skeleton he had on display in Philadelphia. His son's "Short Account of the Mammoth" included a table of dimensions of the specimen on exhibit in London (*Philosophical Magazine*, 14 [1802-1803], 168-9).

For the report of large bones in a CAVE in Greenbrier County, see Vol. 38:591-3, 634-5, and Peale to TJ, 12 Dec. 1802.

[1] Peale here canceled "unwilling."

[2] Peale first wrote "27 feet 9 Inches" before altering the figures to read as above.

Petition from Citizens of Portland, Maine

[before 20 Apr. 1803]

The subscribers, citizens of the town of Portland in the District of Maine, respectfully represent,

That they have understood from unquestionable authority that Nathaniel F. Fosdick Esqr. late Collector of the United States for the District of Portland & Falmouth, has been removed from office:—that there has been such a mistake in the name of the person who was probably intended to be the Successor of Mr Fosdick, that he will doubtless[1] not incline to assume the duties of the office, untill this mistake has been rectified, or a new nomination shall have taken place.—The subscribers therefore take this method to express to you their sentiments upon this subject, in the hope, that as they are perfectly sincere, they will be the less obtrusive.

Mr Fosdick was elected to the office of Naval officer of this port, by the Legislature of this state, prior to adoption of the Constitution of the United States.—He was annually elected to the same office, in the same manner, untill the final organization of the federal Government, when he was appointed to the office of Collector, by the then President Washington; which office he has continued to hold untill the time of his late removal.—

Being intirely uninformed as to the reasons for which Mr Fosdick has been removed; and being equally with himself ignorant of the accusations (if any) which have been made against him, it cannot be expected either from him or us that they can be repelled; but we take the liberty to assure you, and that from a constant course of experience & observation since he has been in office,

That he has not been excelled by any officer in the department to which he belongs, for his *correctness, intelligence, industry, punctuality* and *official integrity.*

That since the Executive part of the Government, has devolved on you, he has conducted himself both in his language, and general deportment with perfect *decency prudence* & *respect*; and in such a manner, as the most zealous admirer of your character and administration, would deem proper, and even faultless.—

That whatever representations or calumnies may have been conveyed to you respecting him, we are ready to pledge ourselves that when they shall be made known, he will have it in his power to remove and refute them.—

That we hold sacred the sentiment[2] founded in immutable justice, and the peculiar and appropriate principles of a republican and free Government, that it is the right of every man to meet his accusers face to face;—or at least that he may know who they are, and of what they accuse him, before he is condemned; and that a proper oppertunity should be given to defend himself.—

That we have reason to conjecture (and from the secret nature of the Communications against Mr Fosdick, we can do no more than conjecture) that certain individuals in our vicinity, who have undertaken to furnish information to the Government and its servants, have been actuated more from private interest and prejudice, than the principles of publick justice; and that some of them have sought the removal and ruin of Mr Fosdick from motives peculiarly malignant, and such as all honest men will be disposed to reprobate.

That there are strong reasons to apprehend that his removal has been Occasioned by a misrepresentation of a particular instance of official duty, in which we believe he conducted with uprightness and delicacy; and which on the part of the delinquents respected a most violent and outrageous attack upon the laws of Government.

That for many years after Mr Fosdick held the office, the proceeds of it were inadequate to the support of his family—

That the private character of Mr Fosdick, is that of a man not merely just and honest in his dealings; but remarkable for his *generosity* & *hospitality.*—

That he has a large and expensive family under his care; the greater part of whom are the objects of his benevolence; the circumstances of whom from motives of delicacy to him we forbear to particularize.—

That Mr Ilsley, the Gentlemen probably intended as the Successor of Mr Fosdick, is a young man with a small family, who now holds an office from the Citizens of this County, which places him in an easy and eligable situation.—

We therefore earnestly request, that Mr Fosdick may be restored to his office; and that as a just and reasonable preliminary to such a measure, an impartial enquiry may be made into his official conduct, if it should be thought necessary.

MS (DNA: RG 59, LAR, 4:0326-30); undated; in an unidentified hand, signed by Daniel Davis and 25 others; at head of text: "To the President of the United States"; endorsed by TJ as received 20 Apr. and "Portland petn. Fosdyck to be continued" and so recorded in SJL.

Federalist partisan Daniel Davis, a former state senator who resigned as U.S. attorney for the district of Maine in 1801 to become solicitor general of Massachusetts, was the primary author of this petition. Other signers included Lemuel Weeks, Daniel Cobb, James Neal, Daniel Tucker, Arthur McLellan, and Joseph H. Ingraham, holders of various town offices, and Ebenezer Mayo and Edward Oxnard, inspectors at the port. Mayo also served as a collector of internal revenue in Massachusetts (ASP, *Miscellaneous*, 1:265, 280; *Jenks's Portland Gazette*, 20 May 1799; 9 Mch., 17 Aug. 1801; 29 Mch. 1802; Brookfield, Mass., *Political Repository*, 10 Feb. 1801; Vol. 33:219, 520-1, 668, 670, 677; Vol. 34:682n; Vol. 36:319, 323, 331).

A critical comment on the removal of NATHANIEL F. FOSDICK appeared in the Boston *Columbian Centinel* on 23 Mch. Rumors of Fosdick's imminent removal led Peleg Wadsworth to write Gallatin in January 1803 defending the collector's record. He enclosed a letter from Fosdick that Gallatin showed the president (Enclosure No. 4, described at Gallatin to TJ, 18 Jan. 1803). Levi Lincoln urged Fosdick's removal, noting that his correspondents had characterized the Portland collector as "very bitter and open mouthed." TJ also had seen a letter from William Wilson at Portland advocating Fosdick's removal (Lincoln to TJ, 6, 13 Dec. 1802; 30 Jan. 1803).

MISTAKE IN THE NAME: on 2 Feb., TJ nominated "Isaac Illsley, junr." as collector in place of Fosdick "removed." Davis wrote Gallatin on 5 Apr. that there was "no such person" by that name in Portland. On 20 Apr.—the day TJ received the petition above—he entered on his personal list, the appointment of Isaac Ilsley "vice Isaac Illsley, junr. by misnomer." In his nominations to the Senate on 11 Nov., TJ appointed Isaac Ilsley, "being the same person intended, but misnamed, in a former nomination for the same post to the Senate" (Davis to Gallatin, in DNA: RG 59, LAR, 4:0322; Appendix I: List of Appointments; TJ to the Senate, 2 Feb., 11 Nov. 1803). For support of Ilsley by James Deering and others, see Lincoln to TJ, 30 Jan. Ilsley was also recommended as a candidate for bankruptcy commissioner (Vol. 39:612n).

MISREPRESENTATION OF A PARTICULAR INSTANCE OF OFFICIAL DUTY: in his 5 Apr. letter to the Treasury secretary, Davis detailed the charges brought against John Deering for smuggling 45 bags of coffee in the brig *Ranger* in the summer of 1800. After the coffee was confiscated,

Deering was accused of leading an expedition to forcibly remove it from storage at Fort Sumner. In the process the building where the coffee was being held was partially destroyed. The coffee was taken to an island in Portland harbor owned by the Deering family and then disappeared. The collector "spared neither trouble nor expence to discover the authors of this felony." As U.S. attorney, Davis brought suit against Deering and his accomplices. Deering's friends used their influence to have the charges of stealing the coffee and destroying state property reduced. An agreement was reached that the indictment for stealing would be dismissed, when a quantity of coffee equal to that taken was received by the marshal. Davis argued that it was through Fosdick's leniency that Deering was "exonerated from the penalties of an odious crime" and kept from being "convicted & rendered infamous." Davis noted that James Deering, a respectable Portland merchant and cousin of the "delinquent," had threatened the removal of Fosdick. He was being aided by U.S. Navy Captain Edward Preble, James Deering's brother-in-law. Davis had also heard that William Wilson "of the army" had "calumniated" against Fosdick. Isaac Ilsley, the person probably intended as Fosdick's successor, was also James Deering's brother-in-law. Deering was "considered to be the *secret concealed* author of Mr Fosdicks removal" (Davis to Gallatin, 5 Apr. 1803, in DNA: RG 59, LAR, 4:0321-5; postmarked Portland, 10 Apr.; endorsed by TJ: "Fosdyck. not to be removed").

HOLDS AN OFFICE: Ilsley resigned as Register of Deeds in Cumberland County after his appointment as collector (Boston *New-England Palladium*, 28 Feb. 1804).

[1] MS: "doubless."
[2] Interlined in place of "principle."

To Isaac Briggs

DEAR SIR Washington Apr. 20. 1803.

The writer of the inclosed letter, James Dinsmore, is an excellent young man from Philadelphia, who has lived in my family as a house-joiner 5. or 6. years. I have great confidence in his recommendations making due allowance for the connection in this case. of his brother John Dinsmore I know nothing. but as he resides near the Natchez, should you have occasion for him, you can learn his character there. I pray you not to understand this as a sollicitation, but merely for information of those who would be willing to be employed under you, should you need. you will probably also think it just in a reasonable degree[1] to prefer inhabitants of the state itself, as the states generally think is right, rather than to import all those you employ from other states. Accept my salutations and best wishes.

TH: JEFFERSON

PrC (DLC); at foot of text: "Mr. Isaac Briggs"; endorsed by TJ in ink on verso. Enclosure: James Dinsmore to TJ, 15 Apr. 1803, recorded in SJL as received from Monticello on 19 Apr. with notation "John Dinsmore. Natchez. to be surveyor," but not found.

[1] Preceding four words interlined.

From William C. C. Claiborne

SIR, Near Natchez April 20th, 1803.

I have been honored with the receipt of your *Letter* of the 25th. Ultimo, together with a *Report* of a Committee of Congress, which accompanyed *it*.

So far as may depend upon my Agency, no exertions shall be wanting to carry into effect in this Territory, the Militia System adopted by the National Legislature, "and in a manner the best calculated to insure such a degree of military discipline and knowledge of tactics, as will, under the auspices of a benign Providence, render the Militia a sure and permanent bulwark of National Defence."

I sincerely hope, that the wise and pacific Measures which have been adopted, to obtain a redress of the injuries we lately received on the Missisippi, may be attended with success, but should we be disappointed in this reasonable expectation, I doubt not but the Strength of the Nation will enable the Government "to do with promptitude and effect whatever a regard to Justice, and our future Security may require."—

The enclosed Return which was made to me on this day, by the Brigade Major and Inspector of the Militia, will present to you, the Military strength of this Territory.

With every sentiment of Esteem & Respect I have the honor to be Sir, Your mo: obt Sevt WILLIAM C. C. CLAIBORNE

RC (PHi); at foot of text: "His Excellency The President of the United States"; endorsed by TJ as received 16 May and so recorded in SJL. Tr (MsJS). Enclosure not found.

LETTER OF THE 25TH. ULTIMO: Circular to the Governors of the States, 25 Feb. 1803.

From Meriwether Lewis

SIR, Lancaster Apl. 20th. 1803.

With a view to forward as much as possible the preparations which must necessarily be made in the Western country previous to my final departure,[1] as also to prevent the delay, which would attatch to their being made after my arrival in that quarter, I have taken the following measures, which I hope will meet your approbation; they appear to me to be as complete as my present view of the subject will admit my making them, and I trust the result will prove as favorable as wished for.—

I have writen triplicates to Mr: John Conner accepting his services as an Interpreter; he is the young man I recollect mentioning to you as having proffered his services to accompany me: to him I have communicated the real extent and objects of my mission, but with strict injunctions to secresy. He is directed to bring with him two Indians, provided he can engage such as perfectly answer the description given him. I have informed him of the Military posts at which I shall touch on the Ohio and Mississippi rivers, and the probable time of my arrival at each, leaving it discretionary with himself to meet me at either: in these letters are inclosed triplicates, addressed to the Commandants of those posts, recommending Mr. Conner to their good offices, and requesting for him every aid in their power to bestow, should he be in want of assistance to enable him to get forward in due time. The circumstance of Mr. Conner's residence being at the Delleware Town on White river, and distant of course from any post office, induced me to give these letters different conveyances, which I did by inclosing them by different mails to three gentlemen of my acquaintance in that country, two of whom, Capts. Mc,Clelland & Hamilton, live within twenty seven miles of the town; they are requested, and I am confident will find the means of conveying the letters to him; the other with a similar request was inclosed to Capt. Findley of Cincinnatti, in whose exertions tho' more distant, I have equal confidence.—

I have also written to Majr. Mac Rea, the Commandant of South West Point, and to several officers of my acquaintance who constitute that garrison, stating to them that my destination was up the Mississippi for the purpose of accomplishing the objects, which we agreed on as most proper to be declared publicly:[2] the qualifications of the men are mentioned, and they are requested to look out in time for such volunteers as will answer that description; the inducements for those persons engaging in this service were also stated. The garrison of South West Point must form my first resourse for the scelection of my party, which I shall afterwards change as circumstances may seem to recommend; and with a view to this change, I have written in a similar manner to the officers commanding the posts of Massac, Kaskaskais and Illinois, the posts at which I shall touch previous to ascending the Missourie, and subsequent to my departure from S.W. Point. the men in every instance are to be engaged conditionally, or subject to my approval or otherwise.—

I have also written to Dr. Dickson, at Nashville, and requested him to contract in my behalf with some confidential boat-builder at that place, to prepare a boat for me as soon as possible, and to purchase a large light wooden canoe: for this purpose I inclosed the Dr. 50. Dollars, which sum I did not concieve equal by any means to the purchase of the two vessels, but supposed it sufficient for the purchase of the canoe, and to answer also as a small advance to the boat-builder: a discription of these vessels was given. The objects of my mission are stated to him as beforementioned to the several officers.—

I have also written to Genl. Irwine of Philadelphia, requesting that he will have in a state of prepareation some articles which are necessary for me, and which will be most difficult to obtain, or may take the greates length of time in their prepareation.—

My detention at Harper's Ferry was unavoidable for one month, a period much greater than could reasonably have been calculated on; my greatest difficulty was the frame of the canoe, which could not be completed without my personal attention to such portion of it as would enable the workmen to understand the design perfectly; other inducements seemed with equal force to urge my waiting the issue of a full experiment, arising as well from a wish to incur no expence unnecessarily, as from an unwillingness to risk any calculation on the advantages of this canoe in which hereafter I might possibly be deceived; experiment was necessary also to determine it's dementions: I therefore resolved to give[3] it a fair trial, and accordingly prepared two sections of it with the same materials, of which they must of necessity be composed when completed for servise on my voyage; they were of two disciptions, the one curved, or in the shape necessary for the stem and stern, the other simicilindrical, or in the form of those sections which constitute the body of the canoe. The experiment and it's result wer as follow.

Dementions.

Curved Section.	F. I.	*Simicilindrical Section.*	F. I.
Length of Keel from junction of section to commencement of curve	1. 2	Length of Keel	4. 6
		ditto Beam	4. 10
		Debth of Hole	2. 2
Length of curve	4. 5	Note—The curve of the body of the canoe was formed by a suspended cord.—	
Width of broad end	4. 10		
Debth of Do. Do.	2. 2		

Weight of the materials.

Curved Section	lbs.	*Simicilindrical Section*	
Iron	22.	Iron	22
Hide	25	Hide	30
Wood	10	Wood	12
Bark	21	Bark	25
Total	78	Total	89

Competent to a

Burthen of	850. lbs.	Burthen of	920. lbs.

Necessary to be transported by land.

Iron and Hide of Curved Section	47.
Iron and Hide of Simicilindrical do.	52. = 99. lbs.
Burthen of Curved Section	850.
Do. Do. Simicilindrical	920. = 1,770. lbs.

Thus the weight of this vessel competent to the burthen of 1,770 lbs. amounts to no more than 99 lbs.—the bark and wood, when it becomes necessary to transport the vessel to any considerable distance, may be discarded; as those articles are reaidily obtained for the purposes of this canoe, at all seasons of the year, and in every quarter of the country, which is tolerably furnished with forest trees. When these sections were united they appeared to acquire an additional strength and firmness, and I am confident that in cases of emergency they would be competent to 150 lbs. more than the burthen already stated.—Altho' the weight of the articles employed in the construction of a canoe on this plan, have considerably exceeded the estimate I had previously made, yet they do not weigh more than those which form a bark canoe of equal dementions, and in my opinion is much preferable to it in many respects; it is much stronger, will carry it's burthen with equal ease, and greater security; and when the Bark and wood are discarded, will be much lighter, and can be transported with more safety and ease. I was induced from the result of this experiment to direct the iron frame of the canoe to be completed.—

My Rifles, Tomahawks & knives are preparing at Harper's Ferry, and are already in a state of forwardness that leaves me little doubt of their being in readiness in due time.—

I arrived at this place yesterday, called on Mr. Ellicot, and have this day commenced, under his direction, my observations &c, to perfect myself in the use and application of the instruments. Mr. Ellicot is extreemly friendly and attentive, and I am confident is disposed to render me every aid in his power: he thinks it will be necessary I should remain here ten or twelve days.—

Being fully impressed with the necessity of seting out as early as possible, you may rest assured that not a moment shall be lost in making the necessary preperations. I still think it practicable to reach the mouth of the Missourie by the 1st. of August.—

I am Sir, with much esteem and regard Your Most Obt. Servt.

MERIWETHER LEWIS.

RC (DLC); at foot of text: "The President of the U. States"; endorsed by TJ as received 25 Apr. and so recorded in SJL.

PREPARATIONS: Lewis had set off from Washington in mid-March to obtain equipment and materials from the armory at Harpers Ferry and in Philadelphia. He carried orders dated 14 Mch. from the War Department's chief clerk, Joshua Wingate, Jr., to Joseph Perkin, the superintendent of the Harpers Ferry arsenal, who was to see to the manufacture of "such arms & Iron work" as Lewis might want; to William Irvine, the superintendent of military stores at Philadelphia, for "Articles from the public Stores"; and to Israel Whelen, the purveyor of public supplies in that city, for the purchase of items that Lewis could not obtain from Irvine (Jackson, *Lewis and Clark*, 1:75-6; Merritt Roe Smith, *Harpers Ferry Armory and the New Technology: The Challenge of Change* [Ithaca, N.Y., 1977], 37; Gallatin to TJ, 14 Mch.).

For JOHN CONNER of Indiana Territory, see his letter to TJ of 10 Jan. 1803. Conner had written to Lewis in February about going on the western expedition as an interpreter. Lewis offered him $300 in pay, plus provisions and clothing. In September, after William Clark was able to make contact with him, Conner declined, saying that he did not have time to arrange his affairs to make the journey and that the pay was too low—$5,000 would be a more proper figure for his services, he avowed. Conner, Clark noted, did not speak any languages from west of the Mississippi anyway, and Lewis agreed that the trader "has decieved me very much" (Jackson, *Lewis and Clark*, 1:116, 118-19, 123, 125).

MC,CLELLAND: Robert McClellan had been a scout for the army in the Northwest Territory in the 1790s. He later went on trading expeditions up the Missouri River and into the Pacific Northwest. Lewis also knew John McClallen, a captain of artillery in the regular army, but McClallen was on active service and not in the location mentioned by Lewis (same, 41n, 203; Moulton, *Journals of the Lewis & Clark Expedition*, 8:358n, 363, 364n; Dearborn to McClellan, 9 Nov. 1802, 25 Mch. 1803, Dearborn to Thomas H. Cushing, 9 Nov. 1802, in DNA: RG 107, LSMA).

A Captain HAMILTON served as an interpreter in the Northwest Territory in 1799. He was perhaps John Hamilton, who lived in that region and a few years later was probably trading in Indiana Territory (*Terr. Papers*, 3:68, 158; 7:370; Jackson, *Lewis and Clark*, 1:41).

FINDLEY OF CINCINNATTI: probably James Findlay, who at the time was receiver of public monies at Cincinnati (same, 41n, 127; Dearborn to Findlay, 5 Apr. 1803, in DNA: RG 107, MLS; Vol. 38:110n).

VOLUNTEERS: in the spring of 1803, one company of artillerists and two companies of infantry made up the garrison at Southwest Point. Massac had one company of infantry, Kaskaskia one artillery company and one of infantry. The army had not yet built a new post intended for one company at the mouth of the Illinois River. In July, Henry Dearborn directed the officers at the posts to find suitable candidates for Lewis. "If any non-commissioned officer or private in your Company should be disposed to join Capt. Lewis, whose characters for sobriety, integrity and other necessary qualifications render them suitable for such service," Dearborn wrote, "you will detach them accordingly." Soldiers from Southwest Point, Massac, and Kaskaskia became members of Lewis's expedition (Dearborn to William Irvine, 7 Mch. 1803, in DNA: RG 107, LSMA; Jackson, *Lewis and Clark*, 1:102-4; Moulton, *Journals of the Lewis & Clark Expedition*, 2:139n, 510; note to Topics for Consultation with Heads of Departments, [on or after 10 Feb. 1803]).

Lewis wanted a keeled BOAT at least 60 feet in length, "light" and "strong" in construction, with a carrying capacity of eight tons. He had to have it built in Pittsburgh rather than Nashville, and it was not ready until the end of August. The finished boat, as Clark later described it to Nicholas Biddle, was open in the midsection with decking at the bow and stern. It was powered by a square sail and 22 oars. Lewis also needed a large WOODEN CANOE (Jackson, *Lewis and Clark*, 1:73,

99; 2:497, 534; Lewis to TJ, 22 July, 8 Sep.).

FRAME OF THE CANOE: at Lewis's request the metalworkers at Harpers Ferry built a portable iron frame that when assembled could be covered with animal HIDE to become what Lewis later called "a perogue of skins" or "leather boat." He expected to fabricate crosspieces of WOOD when he put the watercraft together and to find BARK and pine pitch to seal the seams. According to his plan, assembly would require "a few hours," but when he and members of the expedition began to construct the vessel from elk and bison skins above the falls of the Missouri River in June 1805, the labor stretched on for days. They could not find pitch, and a substitute sealer that Lewis concocted from tallow and charcoal did not keep the joints between the hides watertight. "I therefore relinquished all further hope of my favorite boat," Lewis recorded in his journal on 9 July 1805. He "bid a dieu" to the iron frame and left it behind as the expedition continued upriver (Jackson, *Lewis and Clark*, 1:73, 233; Moulton, *Journals of the Lewis & Clark Expedition*, 4:149, 323-4, 336, 343-4, 349-50, 354, 359, 363, 366, 368-9; Lewis to TJ, 7 Apr. 1805).

To outfit the expedition Lewis desired 15 RIFLES, 24 pipe TOMAHAWKS, and 24 large KNIVES. He also expected to take an additional 36 pipe tomahawks from Harpers Ferry and a number of knives as presents to Indians. He obtained other items from Harpers Ferry as well, including barbed fish gigs for use as presents (Jackson, *Lewis and Clark*, 1:70, 72, 73).

[1] MS: "departue."
[2] Preceding seven words interlined.
[3] MS: "gve."

From Pierce Butler

DEAR SIR Charleston April 21. 1803

The inclosed letter must plead my apology for troubling you—I know Mr. Fitzpatrick to be a good, and prudent Man, who may be made useful in a Young Country—He is possessed of good property—

I have the honor to be with great Consideration Yr Most Obedt

P. BUTLER

RC (DNA: RG 59, LAR); endorsed by TJ as received 3 June and "Fitzpatrick Thos. to office in Missipi" and so recorded in SJL. Enclosure not found, but see below.

TJ received two additional letters on 3 June from South Carolina recommending Thomas FITZPATRICK for office, one from Thomas Sumter, Sr., dated April from Stateburg, and another from Wade Hampton, dated 13 May from Charleston. TJ recorded both entries in SJL with the notation "Fitzpatrick to office," but neither has been found. In November 1804, Fitzpatrick received an appointment as register for the land office in Adams County, Mississippi Territory (JEP, 1:472).

To Albert Gallatin

TH:J. TO MR GALLATIN Apr. 21. 1803.

The act of Congress 1789. c. 9. assumes on the General government the maintenance & repair of all lighthouses, beacons, buoys & public piers then existing, and provides for the building a new lighthouse. this was done under the authority given by the constitution 'to regulate commerce,' was contested at the time as not within the meaning of these terms, & yielded to only on the urgent necessity of the case. the act of 1802. c. 20. §. 8. for repairing & erecting public piers in the Delaware does not take any new ground, it is in strict conformity with the act of 1789. while we pursue then the construction of the legislature that the repairing & erecting lighthouses, beacons, buoys & piers, is authorised as belonging to the regulation of commerce, we must take care not to go ahead of them, and strain the meaning of the terms still further to the clearing out the channels of all the rivers &c of the US. the removing a sunken vessel is not the repairing of a pier.

How far the authority 'to levy taxes to provide for the common defence' & that 'for providing and maintaining a navy' may authorise the removing obstructions in a river or harbour, is a question not involved in the present case.

RC (NHi: Gallatin Papers); addressed: "The Secretary of the Treasury." PrC (DLC). Recorded in SJL with notation "piers."

The act of Congress approved on 7 Aug. 1789 called for the erection of a NEW LIGHTHOUSE near the entrance of Chesapeake Bay (U.S. Statutes at Large, 1:53-4). CONTESTED AT THE TIME: see TJ to Gallatin, 13 Oct. 1802. For the appropriation of $30,000 for PUBLIC PIERS IN THE DELAWARE, see Vol. 37:667; Vol. 38:488-9.

To Benjamin Rush

DEAR SIR Washington April 21. 1803.

In some of the delightful conversations with you, in the evenings of 1798. 99. which[1] served as an Anodyne to the afflictions of the crisis through which our country was then labouring, the Christian religion was sometimes our topic: and I then promised you that, one day or other, I would give you my views of it. they are the result of a life of enquiry & reflection, and very different from that Anti-Christian system, imputed to me by those who know nothing of my opinions. to the corruptions of Christianity, I am indeed opposed; but not to the genuine precepts of Jesus himself. I am a Christian, in the only sense in which he wished any one to be; sincerely attached to his doctrines, in preference to all others; ascribing to himself every human[2] excellence, & believing he never claimed any other. at the short[3] intervals, since these conversations, when I could justifiably abstract my mind from public affairs,[4] this subject has been under my contemplation. but the more I considered it, the more it expanded beyond the measure of either my time or information. in the moment of my late departure from Monticello,[5] I recieved from Doctr. Priestly his little treatise of 'Socrates & Jesus compared.' this being a section of the general view I had taken of the field, it became a subject of reflection, while on the road, and unoccupied otherwise. the result was, to arrange in my mind a Syllabus, or Outline, of such an Estimate of the comparative merits of Christianity, as I wished to see executed, by some one of more leisure and information for the task than myself. this I now send you, as the only discharge of my promise I can probably ever execute. and, in confiding it to you, I know it will not be exposed to the malignant perversions of those who make[6] every word from me a text for new misrepresentations & calumnies. I am moreover averse to the communication of my religious tenets to the public; because it would countenance the presumption of those who have endeavored to draw them before that tribunal, and to seduce public opinion to erect itself into that Inquisition over the rights of[7] conscience, which the laws have so justly proscribed. it behoves every man, who values liberty of conscience for himself, to resist invasions of it in the case of others;[8] or their case may, by change of circumstances, become his own. it behoves him too, in his own case, to give no example of concession, betraying the common right of independant opinion, by answering questions of faith, which the laws have left between god & himself. Accept my affectionate salutations.

TH: JEFFERSON

RC (ViU); at foot of text: "Doctr. Benjamin Rush"; enclosed in TJ to Benjamin Rush, 23 Apr. PrC (DLC: TJ Papers, 131:22622). Tr (same, 131:22620); entirely in TJ's hand; at foot of text: "Doctr. Benjamin Rush"; probably enclosed in TJ to Henry Dearborn, [23 Apr.], and in Dearborn to TJ, [4 May]. Tr (same, 131:22617); entirely in TJ's hand; at foot of text: "Doctr. Benjamin Rush"; probably enclosed in TJ to Levi Lincoln, [23 Apr.], and in Lincoln to TJ, 24 Apr.; also probably enclosed in TJ to John Adams, 22 Aug. 1813, and in Adams to TJ, 14 Sep. 1813. Tr (MHi); entirely in TJ's hand; at head of text: "To Doctr. Benjamin Rush;" probably enclosed in TJ to Martha Jefferson Randolph, 25 Apr. Tr (NBuHi); entirely in TJ's hand; at foot of text: "To mr ____"; lacks place in dateline, complimentary closing, and signature; enclosed in TJ to Francis Adrian Van der Kemp, 25 Apr. 1816. Tr (ViW); in Ellen Wayles Randolph's hand; enclosed in TJ to William Short, 13 Apr. 1820. Enclosed also in TJ to Mary Jefferson Eppes, 25 Apr. 1803.

For an additional transcript and other information, see EG, 331-6.

[1]TJ first wrote "and" but then overwrote "which." Trs in DLC and MHi read "and which" or "& which," while Tr in NBuHi lacks the entire phrase beginning with "which" and ending with "labouring."

[2]Word underscored in the first Tr in DLC and Tr in MHi.

[3]Tr in NBuHi lacks preceding word, as well as the comma after "intervals."

[4]In Tr in NBuHi, TJ wrote "abstract my self from other affairs."

[5]In Tr in NBuHi, TJ wrote "setting out on a late journey" instead of preceding five words.

[6] In Tr in NBuHi, the remainder of the sentence reads, "of every word on the subject of religion, a text for misrepresentations and calumnies."

[7] In Tr in NBuHi, TJ here wrote and then canceled "private."

[8] Tr in NBuHi lacks remainder of sentence.

ENCLOSURE

Doctrines of Jesus Compared with Others

Syllabus of an Estimate of the merit of the doctrines of Jesus, compared with those of others.

In a comparative view of the Ethics of the enlightened nations of antiquity, of the Jews, and of Jesus, no notice should be taken of the corruptions of reason, among the antients, to wit, the idolatry & superstition of their vulgar, Nor of the corruptions of Christianity by the over[1] learned among it's professors.

Let a just view be taken of the moral principles inculcated by the most esteemed of the sects of antt. philosophy, or of their individuals; particularly Pythagoras, Socrates, Epicurus, Cicero, Epictetus, Seneca, Antoninus.

I. Philosophers.

1. Their precepts related chiefly to ourselves, and the government of those passions which, unrestrained, would disturb our tranquility of mind.* in this branch of Philosophy they were really great.
2. In developing our duties to others, they were short and defective. they embraced indeed the circles of kindred & friends; and inculcated patriotism, or the love of our country in the aggregate, as a primary obligation: towards our neighbors & countrymen, they taught justice, but scarcely viewed them as within the circle of benevolence. still less have they inculcated peace, charity, & love to our fellow men, or embraced, with benevolence, the whole family of mankind.

II. Jews.

1. Their system was Deism, that is, the belief of one only god. but their ideas of him, & of his attributes, were degrading & injurious.

* To explain, I will exhibit the heads of Seneca's & Cicero's philosophical works, the most extensive of any we have recieved from the antients. of 10. heads in Seneca, 7. relate to ourselves, to wit, de irâ, Consolatio, de tranquilitate, de constantiâ sapientis, de otio sapientis, de vitâ beatâ, de brevitate vitae. 2. relate to others, de clementia, de beneficiis. & 1. relates to the government of the world, de providentiâ. of 11. tracts of Cicero, 5 respect ourselves, viz. de finibus, Tusculana, Academica, Paradoxa, de Senectute. 1. de officiis, partly to ourselves, partly to others. 1. de amicitiâ, relates to others: and 4. are on different subjects, to wit, de naturâ deorum, de divinatione, de fato, Somnium Scipionis.

2. their Ethics were not only imperfect, but often irreconcileable with the sound dictates of reason & morality, as they respect intercourse with those around us: & repulsive, & anti-social, as respecting other nations. they needed reformation therefore in an eminent degree.

III. Jesus. In this state of things among the Jews, Jesus appeared. his parentage was obscure, his condition poor, his education null, his natural endowments great, his life correct & innocent; he was meek, benevolent, patient, firm, disinterested, & of the sublimest eloquence.

The disadvantages under which his doctrines appear are remarkeable.

1. like Socrates & Epictetus, he wrote nothing himself.
2. but he had not, like them, a Xenophon or an Arrian to write for him.[2] on the contrary, all the learned of his country, entrenched in it's power & riches, were opposed to him, lest his labours should undermine their advantages: and the committing to writing his life & doctrines, fell on the most unlettered, & ignorant of men:[3] who wrote too from memory, & not till long after the transactions had passed.
3. according to the ordinary fate of those who attempt to enlighten and reform mankind, he fell an early victim to the jealousy & combination of the altar and the throne; at about 33. years of age,[4] his reason having not yet attained the maximum of it's energy, nor the course of his preaching, which was but of about 3. years,[5] presented occasions for developing a compleat system of morals.[6]
4. Hence the doctrines which he really delivered were defective as a whole. and fragments only of what he did deliver have come to us, mutilated, mistated, & often unintelligible.
5. they have been still more disfigured by the corruptions of schismatising followers, who have found an interest in sophisticating & perverting the simple doctrines he taught, by engrafting on them the mysticisms of a Graecian Sophist,[7] frittering them into subtleties, & obscuring them with jargon, until they have caused good men to reject the whole in disgust, & to view Jesus himself as an impostor.

Notwithstanding these disadvantages, a system of morals is presented to us, which, if filled up in the true style and spirit of the rich fragments he left us, would be the most perfect and sublime that has ever been taught by man.

The question of his being a member of the god-head, or in direct communication with it, claimed for him by some of his followers, and denied by others, is foreign to the present view, which is merely an estimate of the intrinsic merit of his doctrines.

1. He corrected the Deism of the Jews, confirming them in their belief of one only god, and giving them juster notions of his attributes and government.
2. His moral doctrines relating to kindred & friends were more pure & perfect, than those of the most correct of the philosophers, and greatly more so than those of the Jews.

and they went far beyond both in inculcating universal philanthropy, not only to kindred and friends, to neighbors and countrymen, but to all mankind, gathering all into one family, under the bonds of love, charity, peace, common wants, and common aids. a developement of this head will evince the peculiar superiority of the system of Jesus over all others.

3. the precepts of Philosophy, & of the Hebrew code, laid hold of actions only. he pushed his scrutinies into the heart of man; erected his tribunal in the region of his thoughts, and purified the waters at the fountain head.
4. he taught, emphatically, the doctrine of a future state: which was either doubted or disbelieved by the Jews: and wielded it with efficacy, as an important incentive, supplementary to the other motives to moral conduct.

MS (ViU); entirely in TJ's hand. PrC (DLC: TJ Papers, 131:22623-4). Tr (same, 131:22621); entirely in TJ's hand. Tr (same, 131:22618); entirely in TJ's hand. Tr (MHi); entirely in TJ's hand. Tr (NBuHi); entirely in TJ's hand. Tr (ViW); in Ellen Wayles Randolph's hand. Tr (MHi: Adams Papers); in Ellen Wayles Randolph's hand; enclosed in TJ to John Adams, 12 Oct. 1813. Other Trs and MS enclosed as recorded in letter above.

TJ wrote his SYLLABUS sometime after 9 Apr., when he wrote Joseph Priestley to praise Priestley's pamphlet *Socrates and Jesus Compared*, which provided TJ the intellectual framework for his efforts to compare the moral teachings of Jesus with those of other ancient western authorities. He guarded the syllabus carefully, making sure to share it and the letter in which it was enclosed only with people he could trust, and often requesting its prompt return (see TJ to Henry Dearborn and Levi Lincoln, [23 Apr.]; TJ to Lincoln, 26 Apr.; TJ to Thomas Cooper, 24 Feb. 1804; TJ to Joseph Priestley, Jr., 27 Dec. 1804; RS, 6:160-1, 439-40).

[1] Word interlined.

[2] In the first Tr in DLC and in the Tr in MHi, TJ interlined, "I name not Plato, who only used the name of Socrates to cover the whimsies of his own brain."

[3] In the first Tr in DLC, TJ altered the preceding phrase to read "fell on unlettered, & ignorant men" (see Dearborn to TJ, [4 May]).

[4] TJ wrote the preceding five words and numeral over erased and illegible text.

[5] In the first Tr in DLC and in the Tr in MHi, TJ altered the preceding phrase to read "of 3. years at most."

[6] In the second Tr in DLC and in the Trs in NBuHi, MHi: Adams Papers, and ViW, TJ wrote "moral duties" instead of "morals."

[7] In the Tr in MHi, TJ here added "(Plato)."

To DeWitt Clinton

Dear Sir Washington Apr. 22. 1803.

Your's of the 12th. was recieved in due time, and I had immediately a consultation with mr G. on the subject. he explained to me the circumstances, with which I had only been partially acquainted before, and as he shewed every disposition for indulgence which his position would admit, I engaged him to write to you, as he could better explain his views of the case than I could. to that then I must refer you for answer in this particular, with an assurance as to myself that so far as my agency may be proper, a desire not to injure any one, but especially an innocent security, will be limited only by the imperious dictates of duty.

I have not before acknoleged your's of Mar. 3. the first case therein mentioned involved the transfer of which you will recollect I spoke to you the session before. you know this has awaited the winding up a former business. mr G. seems to think it may now take place without delay; but promises to examine more particularly & to inform me. with respect to the[1] second case, mr S. appointed by my predecessor, I will observe that there are facts, and points in character, which being known before appointment would be good cause for refusing it, but which happening or becoming known afterwards, would not be deemed sufficient to remove from office one who is in possession. undoubtedly there are crimes of such a hue as to be a cause of immediate removal, even before a conviction by jury, & tho not relating to office. yet in cases below this it would not be expedient for us to undertake the office of Censor morum over the public agents. it is best to leave them to the law in other things[2] while their official acts are regular. in the case alluded to, the connection with my predecessor would give room for imputations which would be seized with avidity.—to the letter of the Marquis d'Yrujo, already published, I am happy to add official assurance that in the instrument of cession of Louisiana to France was this clause 'Saving the rights acquired by other powers in virtue of treaties made with them by Spain.' that government shews itself very sensible of our pacific & friendly dispositions manifested by our late forbearance on the irregular conduct of her officer. Accept my friendly salutations & assurances of great esteem & respect. Th: Jefferson

RC (NNC); addressed: "The honble Dewitt Clinton New York"; franked and postmarked; endorsed by Clinton. PrC (DLC).

mr g.: Albert Gallatin.

your's of mar. 3: Clinton's letter of 3 Mch., recorded in SJL as received the same day with notation "removal Ludlow.

Rogers. Smith," has not been found. The Navy Department accepted Daniel Ludlow's resignation as Navy agent at New York in November 1803. The TRANSFER of Samuel Osgood from Supervisor of the Internal Revenue for the District of New York to naval officer at the port in place of Richard Rogers took place on 10 May (NDBW, 3:241; Vol. 34:126-7; Vol. 37: 148-9; TJ to Madison, 10 May). INFORM ME: see Memorandum from Albert Gallatin, printed at 9 May.

MR S.: William Stephens Smith, who was nominated as surveyor and inspector of the district of New York by his father-in-law John Adams in 1800. CENSOR MORUM: that is, moral censor. The CASE ALLUDED TO was probably that covered in the New York City newspapers, in which Smith was accused of extorting money from Robert Troup to delay a legal action against Troup's business associate Ephraim Hart, owner of the ship *Huron*, which was seized by port authorities. Smith had not repaid the money as promised. James Cheetham led the attack against Smith in the *American Citizen*, calling for his removal from office, as one who "tarnishes the lustre of the government." Cheetham charged: "We put it to the country, we ask the Executive whether *such a man* ought to be continued in office!" (Kline, *Burr*, 2:761-3; New York *American Citizen*, 14 Jan. 1803).

LETTER OF THE MARQUIS D'YRUJO: a Spanish naval brig had arrived at Baltimore with express dispatches for Carlos Martínez de Irujo, who wrote to Madison on 19 Apr. to report that his government was restoring the right of deposit at New Orleans. Irujo asked Madison to inform the president and to forward an order to Juan Ventura Morales for the reopening of New Orleans until the Spanish and United States governments could agree on another location for the place of deposit. The *National Intelligencer* published a translation of Irujo's letter in a special issue on the 19th and again in the regular issue of the following day. Other newspapers reprinted the item (Baltimore *Federal Gazette*, 19 Apr.; *National Intelligencer*, 20 Apr.; *Albany Gazette*, 28 Apr.; Burlington *Vermont Centinel*, 5 May; Madison, *Papers*, *Sec. of State Ser.*, 4:535, 545).

Irujo wrote to Madison again on 20 Apr. to give OFFICIAL ASSURANCE that the terms of the retrocession of Louisiana to France affirmed treaties made during Spain's possession of the colony. Pedro Cevallos had given Charles Pinckney a similar declaration on 31 Mch. The clause appeared in Article 3 of the secret treaty of San Ildefonso of October 1800. Irujo assured Madison that the clause would protect the rights of the United States to a place of deposit on the lower Mississippi and to navigation on the river as specified in the 1795 treaty between Spain and the United States (same, 471-2n, 542; Parry, *Consolidated Treaty Series*, 55:375-8).

[1] TJ here canceled "other case."
[2] Preceding three words interlined.

To Hammuda Pasha, Bey of Tunis

ILLUSTRIOUS FRIEND,

Mr. Eaton, who has resided at Tunis for some time past, in the character of our Consul, having requested leave to return home to visit his family and to attend to his affairs, I have yielded to his request and appointed Mr. James Leander Cathcart to fill the vacancy which will be left. Mr Cathcart, who possesses such good qualities, as I hope will recommend him to your notice and esteem, is charged to testify to you the continuance of our friendship and to give you the proofs of it which are usual on such occasions. In return I pray you to treat him with kindness and confidence, placing entire reliance on what he shall say to you on our behalf especially when he shall repeat the assurances of our good will towards you.

Written at the City of Washington, the twenty Second day of April 1803.

Th: Jefferson

FC (Lb in DNA: RG 59, Credences); in a clerk's hand; at head of text: "Thomas Jefferson, President of the United States of America To the Most Illustrious and most Magnificent Prince, the Bey of Tunis, the abode of happiness"; below signature: "By the President, James Madison Secretary of State." Tr (NN: Cathcart Collection); in James L. Cathcart's hand, in Italian; endorsed by Cathcart. Enclosed in Madison to Cathcart, 9 Apr. (Madison, *Papers*, *Sec. of State Ser.*, 4:496n). Not recorded in SJL.

To Lewis Harvie

Dear Sir Washington Apr. 22. 1803.

Since my return to this place I have been in the daily expectation that the stage of the day would bring back Capt Lewis, and that then within a few days he would set out on his Missisipi expedition. it was only the day before yesterday I learned that he had been detained at Harper's ferry a month instead of a week, and that he is probably but about this time arriving at Philadelphia, where his stay is uncertain, tho' probably 1, 2, or 3 weeks, after which he will return here for some days only. this at least is the present view I have of his movements. I have delayed writing to you, because my great regard for Capt Lewis made me unwilling to shew a haste to fill his place before he was gone, & to counteract also a malignant & unfounded report that I was parting with him from dissatisfaction, a thing impossible either from his conduct or my dispositions towards him. I shall probably recieve a letter from him on his arrival at Philadelphia, informing me when he expects to be back here, and will have the pleasure of communicating to you the earliest conjecture I can form myself for your government. it cannot now be many days. You will have seen the letter of the Spanish minister, which we have forwarded to N. Orleans with an order from Spain to take off immediately the suspension of our right of deposit. to this I can add that we have formal assurances that the treaty of cession of Louisiana to France contained this clause 'Saving the rights acquired by other powers in virtue of treaties made with them by Spain.' that cession is probably not yet finally settled between those powers, which has occasioned an unwillingness in them to say any thing of it to others. Spain has been very sensible of our friendly forbearance, and of our dispositions towards her, on the late occasion, and to manifest her sense of it has broken through the reserve which circumstances had laid her under with respect to the cession of Louisiana. Accept my affectionate salutations & assurances of esteem & respect. TH: JEFFERSON

PrC (DLC); at foot of text: "L. Harvie esq."

A REPORT about a journey Meriwether Lewis was to take to the southwest, the purpose of which was "supposed to be political" appeared in March (*Alexandria Expositor, and the Columbian Advertiser*, 16 Mch. 1803; *Poulson's American Daily Advertiser*, 24 Mch. 1803).

To Wilson Cary Nicholas

DEAR SIR Washington Apr. 22. 1803.

Your's of the 14th. is recieved, and every thing you have done in the affair therein mentioned meets my approbation & thanks. I reserve details until I can see you. the offices filled & to be filled under the Missisipi law, are a Register for the Eastern & another for the Western district at 500. D. a year. a Reciever of public monies for each district. two Commissioners for each district at 2000. D. a year; a Surveyor at 1500. D. who appoints two clerks at 1000. D. and all his own under-surveyors. Edward L. Turner was appointed Register of the Western district on great recommendation. Isaac Briggs of Maryland, a quaker, & obscure man (Secretary of the new Agricultural society of the US.) was appointed Surveyor, on my personal knolege that in virtuous[1] worth he was equal, and in the special qualifications for the office superior, to any other man in the US. he is now setting out for his destination. the offices of Commissioners you know must be given to men of special qualifications, wherein law knolege would be sought for tho' not quite indispensably. these appointments will wait awhile. I should certainly think it a duty to give to any son of your brothers a preference over other candidates of only equal qualifications to serve the public. I am apprehensive he might not like the Registry of the Eastern district. mr Gallatin says you spoke of a deputy surveyor's place. for this a letter from yourself directed to 'Isaac Briggs Surveyor of the Missisipi territory, at Natchez' would probably be sufficient; but if desired by you, it shall be strengthened by one from me. I shall expect the information you promise of what you think would suit him & what he would suit.—In addition to the letter of the Marquis de Casa-Yrujo, which you will have seen, we have official assurances from him that the instrument of cession of Louisiana to France had this clause 'Saving the rights acquired by other powers in virtue of treaties made with them by Spain.' that government has been very sensible of our friendly forbearance & dispositions manifested on the late misconduct of her officer, and expresses it with frankness. an order to him to restore the deposit immediately was inclosed to Yrujo, & went on by our express by land to N. Orleans. the infraction, without having occasioned much loss, will probably have had fortunate effects. Accept my affectionate salutations and assurances of great esteem & respect.

TH: JEFFERSON

RC (MoSHi: Jefferson Papers); at foot of text: "W. C. Nicholas"; endorsed. PrC (same); endorsed by TJ in ink on verso.

The law allowed the land office REGISTER for each district $500 for service as one of the three land commissioners for the district. As register he received the same fees and compensation as his counterparts in land offices north of the Ohio River and $.25 for entering each certificate granted by the commissioners (U.S. Statutes at Large, 2:234).

[1] Interlined in place of "personal."

To Henry Dearborn and Levi Lincoln

[23 Apr. 1803]

A promise to a friend sometime ago, executed but lately, has placed my religious creed on paper. I am desirous it should be perused by three or four particular friends, with whom tho' I never desired to make a mystery of it, yet no occasion has happened to occur of explaining it to them. it is communicated for their personal satisfaction, & to enable them to judge of the truth or falsehood of the libels published on that subject. when read, the return of the paper with this cover is asked.

TH: JEFFERSON

RC (DLC); undated; unaddressed. Not recorded in SJL. Enclosure: Trs of TJ to Benjamin Rush, 21 Apr., and enclosure.

THREE OR FOUR PARTICULAR FRIENDS: TJ enclosed transcripts of his letter to Rush and the "Syllabus of an Estimate of the merit of the doctrines of Jesus" to Lincoln and Dearborn, both of whom returned their copies, Lincoln on 24 April, and Dearborn on 4 May. TJ likely retained these transcripts in his files (see notes to TJ to Rush, 21 Apr.). There is no evidence that he shared transcripts with any other members of his cabinet.

From John Goddard

SIR Portsmouth NH April 23d 1803

In obedience to your pleasure made known to me a short time since by Mr Cutts of the US. Legislature, I beg leave to observe, that the address communicated through him recommending Mr Steele as a candidate for the office of district Judge for this district was dictated, as I believe by no other motive than a sincere regard for the republican cause, the honor of your administration & the general interests of their fellow citizens.—The subscribers thereto have ever been on terms of friendship (external at least) with the Gentleman who in the usual course would succeed to the appointment, and deeply regretted the necessity of transgressing the bounds which private citizens in ordinary cases should prescribe to themselves.—Such is the prevalence of aristocratic federalism among the Gentlemen of the law in this district, that two of them only, who are in other respects qualified can, on political grounds, have any pretensions to any important office while our Government is administered on republican principles—Vizt Mr. Sherburne now district Attorney and Mr Steele Clerk of the district Court.—From a concurrence of causes the former has become extremely unpopular & no less so with his friends and *family connexions* than with others. The objections to him are of a *moral* as well as political nature, and he is considered by those who were his best friends, too destitute of principle to be entrusted with any important office from which he cannot be easily removed. To the moral or political character of Mr. Steele it is presumed there can be no exceptions, & in point of professional talents he is by no means second to Mr Sherburne. He was not indeed the earliest convert to republicanism, but for upwards of three years past has openly advocated right principles in which I believe he has been firm & consistent. Should he be appointed to the office in view, it would undoubtedly meet the approbation of *all* the friends of Government here—if others should censure it could only be for the sake of uniformity.

Circumstanced as I am an acquaintance and neighbour of Mr Sherburne, it has been with much reluctance and from a sense of duty only, that I have been thus explicit, should it have any effect in promoting the respectability of Government and the due execution of the laws in this district, I shall be compensated for the many unpleasant sensations experienced on this occasion.—

With sentiments of high respect, for your public and private character, & best wishes for the success of your administration I have the honor to be Yr Most obedient Servant JOHN GODDARD

RC (DNA: RG 59, LAR); at head of text: "To Thomas Jefferson Esquire President of the United States"; endorsed by TJ as received 1 May and "Steele to be appd Distr. judge of N.H." and so recorded in SJL.

Born in Brookline, Massachusetts, John Goddard (1756-1829) graduated from Harvard College in 1777 and moved to Portsmouth, where he studied medicine. He turned away from his medical practice and became a successful hardware merchant. Goddard served as a Jeffersonian Republican in the state legislature, leading the drive for the incorporation of the New Hampshire Union Bank when it was being blocked by the Federalists. As recommended by New Hampshire Republicans, TJ in 1802 appointed him a commissioner of bankruptcy. As an elector, Goddard cast his vote for Jefferson in 1804. Opposed to the War of 1812, he helped organize the Peace party ticket and as a presidential elector in 1812 voted for DeWitt Clinton. He served many years as an officer of the Union Bank and was frequently placed on local committees to settle "disputed matters of business." He also served with Daniel Webster on the select committee that reformed New Hampshire's criminal code. William Plumer described Goddard as "a man of handsome talents, good address, loquacious, & jesuitical" (Lynn Warren Turner, *The Ninth State: New Hampshire's Formative Years* [Chapel Hill, 1983], 150, 178-82, 200, 276-8, 302; Madison, *Papers, Sec. of State Ser.*, 6:11n; *Portsmouth Oracle*, 22 Oct. 1803; *New-Hampshire Gazette*, 4 Dec. 1804; *Portsmouth Journal and Rockingham Gazette*, 19 Dec. 1829, 9 Jan. 1830; Vol. 37: 462-3, 621-2, 703).

For the previous communication RECOMMENDING Jonathan STEELE as district judge, see Clement Storer and Others to TJ, 10 Feb. The subscribers included Storer, Goddard, Elijah Hall, Edward and Charles Cutts, and John McClintock.

John S. SHERBURNE was one of those who recommended Goddard as bankruptcy commissioner (Vol. 37:703).

FAMILY CONNEXIONS: John Langdon was Sherburne's brother-in-law (Turner, *Ninth State*, 114).

To Benjamin H. Latrobe

DEAR SIR Washington Apr. 23. 1803.

Your letter for mr Lenthall was recieved last night & will be delivered this morning. thinking the demolition did not go on with spirit enough I sent for him 2. days ago. he assures me the foundation will be down this week, and the rebuilding begin on Monday. from that day to the end of September, by which time the stone work to the top of the basement[1] should be compleat, we have 23. weeks. I should like to know the number of perch of stone work to be laid to the top of the basement, to divide that on the 23. weeks, and to have a weekly[2] report from your agent of the number of perch laid each week, that, in your absence, I may be quite secure that the due progress is kept up.—I presume you are providing sheet iron for both buildings, the covering of which had better be done as early as possible, in order if any leak should appear, that it may be secured before winter. will you be so good as to order [. . .] [on 120 to 150] panes of window glass 28. I. by $18\frac{5}{8}$ I. for the President's house. glass of that size you know must have a due thickness. Donath in Philadelphia imports Bohemian glass from Hamburg, such as is used in all the first-rate buildings in Europe (England excepted) he furnished all for my house at about 21. or 22. cents the square foot. but this glass being twice as large as mine, should be of superior thickness, & consequently superior price by the square foot.—could not a file of necessaries be placed under each wing of the Capitol, with a deep [sewer?] underneath of [rapid descent?],[3] and the cistern be made, by a syphon, to discharge itself through that, in a torrent, whenever it should be filled by a rain? this would be an advantageous disposition of the external water pipes, while the internal might be reserved for [fire] or [ice?] [. . .].[4] the defectiveness of the pipes of this house is rotting it fast at the waterclosets. strong pipes will be wanting, and the water must be taken out from the cistern, not at the bottom, but at the side by a syphon going to the bottom, but capable of being turned within the body of the[5] water, so as to place it's mouth at any depth we please.—my building arrangements at home require the sheets of iron bespoke of you to leave Philadelphia early in May.—not knowing if Capt Lewis is arrived in Phila, I inclose a letter for him, & ask the favor of you to have it delivered to him on his arrival. mr Patterson, Doctors Wistar, Barton & Rush, will know when he arrives. accept my friendly salutations. TH: JEFFERSON

PrC (DLC); blurred; at foot of text: "Mr. Latrobe"; endorsed by TJ in ink on verso. Enclosure: TJ to Meriwether Lewis, 23 Apr.

Latrobe enclosed instructions and sketches for John LENTHALL, his foreman at the Capitol, in his letter to TJ of 19 Apr.

[1] Preceding six words interlined.
[2] Word interlined.
[3] Preceding three words interlined.
[4] Preceding three words interlined.
[5] Preceding three words interlined.

To Meriwether Lewis

DEAR SIR Washington Apr. 23. 1803.

I have not been able to hear any thing of you since Mar. 7. till two or three days ago, Lieutt. Wilson told me you would leave Frederic the 18th. inst. & that you had been detained till then at Harper's ferry, where Capt Murray also told me he had seen you. I have no doubt you have used every possible exertion to get off, and therefore we have only to lament what cannot be helped, as the delay of a month now may lose a year in the end.—will you be so good as to call on Doctr. Bollman with my compliments & pay him for some wine sent me? I suppose it will be about 12. Doll. but it must be whatever he says. I will also thank you to purchase for me a Leopard or tyger's skin, such as the covers of our saddles were cut out of. in North 3d. street & North 4th. street a few doors only from Market street there used to be a considerable furrier's store in each. at one of them it was that I saw a robe of what they called the Peruvian sheep, and I took to be of the Lama or Vigogna. it was made up of several skins, & was of the price of 12. D. if there be such a thing there now, you can either observe & report it to me, or if you think it good (for I have almost forgot it) I would take it at once. let me hear from you on your reciept of this, and inform me of your prospect of getting off. I have letters here for you from your friends in Albemarle. Accept my affectionate salutations. TH: JEFFERSON

PrC (DLC); at foot of text: "Capt M. Lewis."; endorsed by TJ in ink on verso.

James WILSON, a first lieutenant in the Corps of Engineers, was in transit from West Point, New York, to Norfolk (Dearborn to Wilson, 13 Apr. 1802, 21 Apr. 1803, Dearborn to Jonathan Williams, 16 Mch. 1803, in DNA: RG 107, LSMA; Wilson to War Department, 25 Aug. 1802, 14 May 1803, recorded in same, RLRMS; Heitman, *Dictionary*, 1:1046).

TJ saw John MURRAY on 19 Apr., when Murray gave him letters of introduction from James Currie and John Page; see Currie's and Page's letters at 16 Mch.

VIGOGNA: vicuña.

From John F. Mercer

DEAR SIR Annapolis, April 23rd. 1803

I have been frequently flatterd with the expectation of seeing you at Annapolis or West River, & I had as frequently indulged the hope of paying my respects to you at the City—circumstances not under my controul have hitherto prevented my gratifying my own wishes on this subject.—

On my way to Virginia I hope to see you in Washington on the 28th. when I may offer you what I believe is unnecessary a renewal of my assurances of the highest respect & personal esteem with which

I am your friend & Svt. JOHN F. MERCER

RC (MHi); endorsed by TJ as received 26 Apr. and so recorded in SJL with notation "Govr. Annapolis."

EXPECTATION OF SEEING YOU: Vol. 38:85.

To Benjamin Rush

DEAR SIR Washington Apr. 23. 1803.

Your friendly letter of Mar. 12. was recieved in due time and with a due sense of it's value. I shall with confidence avail myself of it's general prescription, and of the special should the state of my health alter for the worse. at present it wears a promising aspect.

At length I send you a letter, long due, and even now but a sketch of what I wished to make it. but your candour will find my just excuse in the indispensable occupations of my public duties. I communicate a copy of the Syllabus to Dr. Priestley in the hope he will extend his work of Socrates & Jesus compared. he views a part of the subject differently from myself: but in the main object of my syllabus we go perfectly together. Accept my affectionate salutations & assurances of great respect. TH: JEFFERSON

RC (DLC); at foot of text: "Doctr. Benjamin Rush." PrC (DLC); endorsed by TJ in ink on verso. Enclosure: TJ to Rush, 21 Apr., and enclosure.

To Samuel Harrison Smith and Margaret Bayard Smith

Th: Jefferson requests the favour of *mr and mrs Smith*—to dine with him *on Tuesday next (26th.)*—at half after three, *and any friends who may be with them.*

Apr. 23. 1803:

The favour of an answer is asked.

RC (DLC: J. Henley Smith Papers); printed form, with blanks filled by TJ reproduced in italics; addressed by TJ: "Mr. Samuel H. Smith"; endorsed by Smith.

To John Wayles Eppes

DEAR SIR Washington Apr. 24. 1803.

Your's of the 14th. came to hand last night, and I am glad it was written before mine of the 13th. could have been recieved, because that might have delayed the expression of your convenience. the 400. D. shall be remitted to G. Jefferson the first week in May for you. I remit it there because it appears that the conveyance by post between that place & you is too tardy & unsafe to be relied on. your's of the

14th. for instance was 9. days on the way, 2 only of which were from Richmond here, and a week from you to Richmond. am I right in directing my letters to you by the way of City point?—I have never heard from Monticello or Edgehill since I left them, except verbally by P. Carr who with mrs Carr is gone on to Baltimore. Accept my affectionate salutations.

TH: JEFFERSON

PrC (CSmH); at foot of text: "J. W. Eppes"; endorsed by TJ in ink on verso.

MINE OF THE 13TH.: TJ's letter to Eppes of 13 Apr., recorded in SJL as "written at Washington," has not been found.

SHALL BE REMITTED TO G. JEFFERSON: see TJ to George Jefferson and TJ to Eppes, both 12 May.

To George Jefferson

DEAR SIR Washington Apr. 24. 1803.

Will you be so good as to procure from old mr Collins or any other faithful seedsman 1. gallon of earliest Frame peas and 2. gallons of Dwarf marrow fats and send them addressed to Gabriel Lilly at Monticello.

I have recd yours of the 18th. informing me that you have sent on 9. doz. hams. on conferring with my steward I find he has now on hand 4. doz. which with the 9. doz. coming on he thinks will be enough. if you should have obtained the other 4. doz. you proposed to order from another quarter, let them come on; but if not too late to revoke the order, they may be countermanded. in the 1st. week of the next month I will make a remittance to cover every thing, as well as some new draughts then to be made.—I shall be glad to hear from you on the subject of my tobo. Accept affectionate salutations.

TH: JEFFERSON

PrC (MHi); at foot of text: "Mr. George Jefferson"; endorsed by TJ in ink on verso. Recorded in SJL with notation "peas. hams."

From Levi Lincoln

SIR Washington April 24th 1803.

I have been gratified by the reading of the abstract of those Ethical and religious doctrines, which by peculiar indulgence have been submitted to my perusal. Accept, Sir, of my sincere thanks, for this token of confidence & attention, to me so personally pleasing & flattering. It was impossible, from the examination to repress the wish of having a copy of the valuable compendium. Supposing you might be induced to grant this favor, subject to your injunctions, or to his discretion, with whom you had intrusted its possession for the purpose of reading, & being determined to ask for it, I have presumed on the consent, & copied the Syllabus, without names—If there is neither indelicacy, or any kind of objection or impropriety, in your mind, to the retention of this copy & I can perceive none, by anticipating the indulgence, I shall have but saved you the trouble of refurnishing an original for copying, at some future opportunity. If there is an objection, this copy shall be instantly destroyd and its having been taken, will have been only the most effectual mode of impressing its contents on the memory of the reader—and in either case, the liberty I have taken it is respectfully hoped, will be considered[1] as not exceeding an implied permission—

The unasked for representations & solicitations of the friends to Mr Fosdic, and their ideas of the propriety of a disclosure of any communications which may have been made, & of the persons making them, for the purpose of impeaching these, & trying & defending him, when his removal required, nor implied, no alledged charge, is proof of their erroneous views, federal feelings, and perverse reasonings, in reference to the measures of the present administration—These letter writers, excepting Davis, who has always been considered as a man of very warm politicks, are not particularly known to me: Genl. Dearborn can probably tell if there is a single republican among them. I presume Fosdick's decorous demeanor towards the Genl. Govt. and his friends's sense of it, is similar to what we have frequent specimens of, in the New England States—

The enclosed letter from Crowinshield, shews the situation of the navy office in Salem—will it not be best to postpone another appointment untill you hear further on the subject. As the old collector will continue to discharge the duties of that office no particular inconvenience will take place—In my letter to Crowninshield on this subject—He is asked, if Pickman continued his official duties?—What effect the proposed removal had had?—If it was still his, Crowninsd's—& the opinion of the enlightened republicans, that the removal was necessary, & would be for the public interest?—and, finally, he was requested to consult with the most respectable supporters of the Govt. and agree on some good character for the office, the best who could be induced to accept it—An answer will probably be received in a few days—

I am Sir with perfect respect your obt Sert LEVI LINCOLN

RC (DLC); at head of text: "The Presidt. of the U.S."; endorsed by TJ as received 25 Apr. and so recorded in SJL. Enclosure not found.

SUBMITTED TO MY PERUSAL: see TJ to Henry Dearborn and Levi Lincoln, printed at 23 Apr.

UNASKED FOR REPRESENTATIONS: see Petition from Citizens of Portland, Maine, [before 20 Apr. 1803]. FRIENDS of Nathaniel F. Fosdick were undoubtedly behind efforts to hold up the confirmation of his replacement, Isaac Ilsley, when Uriah Tracy, on behalf of the Senate committee, requested letters from the executive regarding the appointment (see Gallatin to TJ, [9 Feb. 1803]; TJ to Gallatin, 10 Feb.).

Upon the recommendations of Lincoln and Jacob CROWNINSHIELD, TJ, on 2 Feb., nominated Joseph Story as naval officer for Salem, Massachusetts, in place of William PICKMAN. On 19 Apr., Gallatin informed Madison that Story had declined the position and returned the commission (Madison, *Papers, Sec. of State Ser.*, 4:504n; Lincoln to TJ, 13 Dec. 1802; TJ to the Senate, 2 Feb. 1803; TJ to Gallatin, 10 Feb.).

[1]MS: "consided."

To Joseph Priestley

DEAR SIR Washington Apr. 24. 1803.

I have heard that you have left Philadelphia, and altho' it was not said for what place, yet I presume for Northumberland, and consequently that we are not to have the pleasure of seeing you here. I am almost persuaded that were you to try the difference between 41.° and 38.° of latitude you would find the genial effects of the latter towards that happiness which arises from sensation, and which produces that which is moral also, so superior to what it is in the former, as to court you to a Southern residence, & to surmount all the obstacles opposed to it. I confess I concur with my friend mr Rittenhouse in wondering that men should ever settle in a Northern climate, as long as there is room for them in a Southern one. but of all things, I have been the most astonished at the location our friend, mr B. Vaughan made of himself; because I consider man not only as an animal of a warm climate, but as social also, meaning by society that which is assorted to his own mind.

In my letter of Apr. 9. I gave you the substance of a view I had taken of the morality taught by the antient philosophers & by Jesus. the subject being in my mind, I committed to writing a syllabus of it, as I would treat it had I time or information sufficient, and sent it to Dr. Rush in performance of the promise I had formerly made him. tho' this differs no otherwise from my letter to you than in being more full & formal, yet I send you a copy of it. there is a point or two in which you & I probably differ. but the wonder would be that any two persons should see in the same point of view all the parts of an extensive subject. I did not know that any comparative view of these schemes of morality had been taken till I saw your tract on Socrates & Jesus, & learnt from that that a mr Toulmin had written a dissertation in the same way. but I am sure he has left enough of the field to employ your pen advantageously. Accept my sincere prayers for your health and life, and assurances of my affectionate esteem & respect.

TH: JEFFERSON

PrC (DLC); at foot of text: "Dr. Priestley." Enclosure: TJ to Rush, 21 Apr., and enclosure.

Benjamin VAUGHAN had moved from Europe to Maine in 1797 (Vol. 33:305n).

Priestley dedicated his TRACT, *Socrates and Jesus Compared*, to Joshua TOULMIN, an English Unitarian minister who in 1785 had published in London *Dissertations on the Internal Evidences and Excellence of Christianity: And on the Character of Christ, Compared with That of Some Other Celebrated Founders of Religion or Philosophy*.

To Samuel J. Cabell

[25 Apr. 1803]

I have [. . .] have been instrumental [. . .] Randolph my son in law, with you, [. . .]. I assure you on my honour it is without foundation. the first idea I ever had of his offering himself was on my arrival at his house the 11th. of March, when he had already been acting some days in it, & when probably it was known to yourself, and the only conversation I ever had with him on the subject was one in which I endeavored to prepare him by calculation for a failure. had I believed that the abandonment of his own affairs, & his engaging in public life would contribute to his interest or happiness, there would have been nothing unnatural or unreasonable in my wishing him to do so but having a very different opinion there was no motive for me to depart from my ordinary rule of not intermedling in any election, still less in a case where my long regard for you would certainly have dissuaded me. knowing nothing of the event of the election, I am urged to this explanation by no earthly motive but that of preventing your having any false impression on the subject, which would be to me a matter of real concern.

In addition to the orders from the government of Spain to the Intendant of New Orleans to restore instantly our right of deposit, as you have seen by the letter of the Marquis Yrujo we have received official assurance that in the instrument of cession of Louisiana to France is a clause with these words 'Saving the rights acquired by other powers in virtue of treaties made with them by Spain' which shews that neither power proposed to disturb our rights. Accept my friendly salutations and assurances of great esteem & respect.

TH: JEFFERSON

PrC (DLC); damaged, including dateline; at foot of text: "Colo. Saml. J. Cab[ell]"; endorsed by TJ in ink on verso. Recorded in SJL as a letter of 25 Apr.

MY LONG REGARD FOR YOU: in 1795, TJ opposed Cabell's congressional candidacy, blasting Cabell's "low practices," which appealed to "the unthinking who merchandize their votes for grog," and in 1799, he unsuccessfully advanced James Monroe as a replacement (Vol. 28:292; Cabell to TJ, 19 Feb.).

From Henry Dearborn

War Department
April 25. 1803.

SIR,

I have the honor to propose John Livingston for the appointment of 2d. Lieut. in the Corp's of Artillerists, to take rank as such from and after the 30th. day of the present month.

Accept Sir, the assurances &c. H. D.

FC (Lb in DNA: RG 107, LSP).

JOHN LIVINGSTON was among the military nominations TJ sent to the Senate in his message of 18 Nov. 1803. For his earlier appointment as a cadet, see Vol. 37:553.

To Mary Jefferson Eppes

MY DEAR MARIA Washington Apr. 25. 1803.

A promise made to a friend some years ago, but executed only lately, has placed my religious creed on paper. I have thought it just that my family, by possessing this, should be enabled to estimate the libels published against me on this, as on every other possible subject. I have written to Philadelphia for Dr. Priestley's history of the corruptions of Christianity, which I will send you, & recommend to an attentive perusal, because it establishes the groundwork of my view of this subject.

In a letter from mr Eppes dated at the Hundred Apr. 14. he informed me Francis had got well through his measles; but he does not say what your movements are to be. my chief anxiety is that you should be back to Monticello by the end of June. I shall advise Martha to get back from here by the middle of July, because the sickly season really commences here by that time, altho' the members of the government venture to remain till the last week of that month.—mr and mrs P. Carr staid with me 5. or 6. days on their way to Baltimore. I think they propose to return in June. Nelly Carr continues in ill health. I believe they expect about the same time to get back to Dunlora. I wrote to mr Eppes yesterday. be assured of my most affectionate and tender love to yourself, and kiss Francis for me. my cordial salutations to the family of Eppington when you see them. Adieu.

Th: Jefferson

RC (Irene Hallam, Davenport, Florida, 1947); at foot of text: "Mrs. Eppes." PrC (ViU: Edgehill-Randolph Papers); endorsed by TJ in ink on verso. Enclosure: TJ to Benjamin Rush, 21 Apr. and enclosure.

TJ repeatedly read and often recommended Joseph Priestley's two-volume HISTORY OF THE CORRUPTIONS OF CHRISTIANITY, first published in Birmingham in 1782, and always considered the work "a favorite" (Sowerby, Nos. 1525, 1526; Vol. 32:179; TJ to Henry Fry, 17 June 1804). Philadelphia bookseller Nicolas Gouin Dufief helped TJ obtain other Priestley titles; see TJ to Dufief, 9 Apr. and Dufief's reply of the 13th.

From John Page

Rosewell April 25th. 1803

Your letter, my dear and much respected Friend, was handed to me at Richmond, after 9 O'Clock at night, at the instant of my return from my sad visit to my dying Brother.

I should have acknowledged the receipt of it on the following Morning, had I not been so much indisposed, by taking cold in walking the night of my Journey over much of wet bad roads, to be scarcely able to perform the duties of my office. I then resolved that I would express the high pleasure it gave me, on my return home, whither I was immediately to set out, to bring up my Wife Family & Furniture, & where I supposed I should have more leisure to find expressions suitable to the occasion, & adequate to my feelings.

But on my arrival here, & to this very day, I could find not an hour for retirement; as my Children immediately collected themselves & Friends together to take leave of me, & to celebrate their Sister's wedding, when they found that I could not accommodate them in Richmond.

Accept then my Friend, of this long detail of Facts, as an Apology for my long delay in acknowledging the receipt of your highly valued letter.—The leisure I wanted to enable me to find suitable Expressions, I now plainly see time itself could not furnish, even if my talents as a writer, were not so unequall to my Sensibility. I had experienced a sufficient Proof of your Friendship in the lucrative Office which you bestowed on me, and in the delicate manner in which you had inclined my preference to it. But proud as I am of the friendship of such a Man as you are, I will confess that my pride is encreased by your approbation of my public character.

Your Congratulations on my late Appointment are truly grateful to my proud feelings; and render the Office dear to me indeed; as it has held me up to the world, as having deserved well of my country, & has furnished me with your invaluable testimony in support of that opinion. I rejoice that I was not elected, till I had the Proof of your inclination to reward my Services more substantially, & till I could have the Congratulations of the most exalted, & most deservedly exalted Character, I will not say in the United States, but upon earth. I do not flatter you my dear Jefferson, your Country thinks as I do, & the world will confirm what I say. And it is but Justice to your Character & Feelings, that one who has known your Talents & worth from your early Youth, & has seen with delight & Admiration the happy application of them, through a long series of Years, to the support of Civil & religious liberty, & to the Establishment of the glorious Independence of the United States, should declare to you, as he has repeatedly to the world his high Sense of your meritorious Services.

I have one advantage in delaying my acknowledgements respecting your Letter till now, & that is, that I can now add Mrs. Page's Thanks to mine, & desire as I do your Acceptance of them. If possible, Our Obligations are encreased by your friendly invitation to Monticello. And greatly are you indeared to us by the benevolent & amiable expressions used respecting your Neighbour our Friend. But we want no inducements of that sort to visit you. We could with pleasure spend the time you propose at Monticello, with you, were it in an Island inhabited by yourself & Family alone.

Curses on the Tongue of Slander! Perdition seize the wretches who would open the Scars of wounded Friendship, to gratify private resentment & party Spirit.

I can only say at present that if in our power we will with great pleasure wait on you.

I am with the highest respect & Esteem dear Sir Your most obedient humble Servant JOHN PAGE

RC (DLC); endorsed by TJ as received 3 May and so recorded in SJL.

YOUR LETTER: TJ to John Page, 18 Mch.

To Martha Jefferson Randolph

MY DEAR MARTHA Washington Apr. 25. 1803.

A promise made to a friend some years ago, but executed only lately, has placed my religious creed on paper. I have thought it just that my family, by possessing this, should be enabled to estimate the libels published against me on this, as on every other possible subject. I have written to Philadelphia for Doctr. Priestley's history of the corruptions of Christianity, which I will send you, & recommend to an attentive perusal, because it establishes the groundwork of my view of this subject.

I have not had a line from Monticello or Edgehill since I parted with you. P. Carr, & mrs Carr, who staid with me 5. or 6. days, told me Cornelia had got happily through her measles, & that Ellen had not taken them. but what has become of Anne? I thought I had her promise to write once a week, at least the words 'all's well.' It is now time for you to let me know when you expect to be able to set out for Washington, and whether your own carriage can bring you half way. I think my Chickasaws, if drove moderately, will bring you well that far. mr Lilly knows you will want them, & can add a fourth. I think that by changing horses half way, you will come with more comfort. I have no gentleman to send for your escort. finding here a beautiful blue Casimir, waterproof, and thinking it will be particularly à propòs for mr Randolph as a travelling coat for his journey, I have taken enough for that purpose, and will send it to mr Benson, postmaster at Fredericksbg to be forwarded by Abrahams, & hope it will be recieved in time. mr & mrs Madison will set out for Orange about the last day of the month. they will stay there but a week.—I write to Maria to-day, but supposing her at the Hundred, according to what she told me of her movements, I send my letter there.—I wish you to come on as early as possible: because tho' the members of the government remain here to the last week in July, yet the sickly season commences in fact by the middle of that month: and it would not be safe for you to keep the children here longer than that, lest any one of them being taken sick early, might detain the whole here till the season of general danger, & perhaps through it. kiss the children for me. present me affectionately to mr Randolph, & accept yourself assurances of my constant & tenderest love.

TH: JEFFERSON

RC (DLC); at foot of text: "Mrs. Randolph." PrC (MHi); endorsed by TJ in ink on verso. Enclosure: TJ to Benjamin Rush, 21 Apr., and enclosure.

From Joseph Turner

SIR Brunswick, Georgia, 25th. April, 1803

I have received from the Comptroller of the Treasury two Commissions with your signature annexed to each, conferring on me the office of Collector of the Customs, & Inspector of the Revenue for the District of Brunswick.

Permit me, Sir, to assure you that I shall exert myself not to disappoint the confidence which you have been pleased to repose in me; that I am happy in the opportunity which now presents itself of executing the duties of these offices under *your* superintendence; under the auspices of our chief Magistrate, who, by the propriety & wisdom of his administration deserves the confidence, & commands the respect, the admiration of the people over whom he presides, & whose welfare, whose happiness, he contemplates with unceasing attention.

It will be my highest ambition to merit your approbation.

I am, Sir, with the utmost deference & respect Your obliged, humble servant JH. TURNER

RC (MoSHi: Jefferson Papers); at foot of text: "The President of the United States"; endorsed by TJ as received 16 May and so recorded in SJL.

The appointment of Joseph Turner was confirmed by the Senate on 15 Nov. 1803. He continued in office at Brunswick, Georgia, throughout TJ's presidency. His duties included providing and supervising the contract for the erection of the lighthouse on St. Simons Island (Gallatin, *Papers*, 18:884; 19:30; 20:457, 464; 48:172-4, 196-7; JEP, 1:454, 455; TJ to the Senate, 11 Nov. 1803). For Turner's appointment, see also Gallatin to TJ, 14 Mch.

From James Warren

SIR, Plymouth (Mass:) April 25th. 1803

You have gratified me exceedingly by appointing my son the Collector of this district.—You have fixed him in our vicinity, where at our period of life, we wanted his care and assiduities. You have done one of my family the honour to hold an office under a man whose person and Administration we all respect,—and have given him an Oppertunity to indulge with more effect his inclination to serve the cause of republicanism.—Will you permit me to thank you for this, & to assure you with confidence of his correctness and attention in the office, and of his fidelity to the revenue.

You have gratified every republican, every honest and even moderate man, by dismissing an Officer, whose conduct has long disgraced the Government.—You have broken by his dismission the principal bond of union which has enabled a virulent set of federalists here, to do mischief.—That Officer has always combined with them to slander your character and oppose your measures,—and by his ignorance, his indolence, his subserviency to the party, and consequently his connivance, has injured the revenue to an amount, the detail of which would appear to any one not on the spot, exaggerated.—

The event of our State Elections has not been so favourable as I wished and expected,—but I think it more owing to the want of attention in the republicans, than the want of principle in the people;—and indeed I have the additional pleasure of supposing it in some measure owing to the increased confidence in the General Government.—Like mariners who have just escaped shipwreck, by the unskilfulness of one pilot, and have been moored in security by the wisdom of another, they for a time think little of any new dangers.—

I congratulate you on the successful settlement of the New Orleans business.—I enjoy the confusion of your enemies and the triumph of your friends on this and many other occasions.—May the blessings of heaven & the applause of your country, reward your virtues!—I am, Sir, with the greatest esteem and respect,

Your sincere Friend & Hble. Servant JAS. WARREN

RC (DLC); in Mercy Warren's hand, signed by James Warren; at foot of text: "Thomas Jefferson Esqr."; endorsed by TJ as received 7 May and so recorded in SJL.

Warren advocated on behalf of his SON, Henry, whom TJ appointed in place of William Watson as COLLECTOR at Plymouth in March 1803; see Vol. 35:221-3n.

For the Massachusetts STATE ELECTIONS, see John Bacon to TJ, 11 Apr.

Statement of Account with Thomas Carpenter

1802.	Thomas Jefferson Esq.	
October 14th.	To Thomas Carpenter	Dr.
	To a fine flannel under waistcoat	$2.25
Decr. 1.	To 4 suits of winter Clothes (Livery) @ 28 $	112.
	To a Blue waterproof Coat Steele Buttons &c.	21.50
	To a Buff Waist—shawl pattern, pearl Buttons	8.25
	To a dove coloured Do —— Do ——	8.25
	To a pr of Chorded Breeches	6.50
	To an embroidered Cassimere waistcoat	7.50
	To a pr of Cassimere Breeches Buff	7.75
	To a pr of black Do ——	7.50

		Buttoning a Coat and 18 Gilt Buttons	1.50
	13.	3½ yds of waterproof Cloth @ 7 $	24.50
		To a Cloak of Superfine Coating for Mrs. Randolph	15.
	20	To a Surtout of waterproof Cloth & apron for Mr R.	30.50
		To a Do —— Do. Capt Lewis	30.50
Febry	1	4½ yds waterproof Cassimere	13.50
		To a pr of ribbed Sheravaloes	5.50
		To a pr of Do. Breeches	6.
		Facing a waistcoat with velvet	2.25
April	26	To a Superfine Waterproof Cassimere Coat Steele Buttons and Silk Sleeve Lynings	21.75
			$ 332.50
		June 13 By cash of mr Barnes before this day	*150.*
			182.50

servts. *112*
self *124.*
family *96.50*
332.50

MS (MHi); in Carpenter's hand, words and figures in italics later added by TJ; endorsed by TJ: "Carpenter Thos. Acct. 1802. Oct. 14 1803. Apr. 26."

SHERAVALOES: sherryvallies, or overalls, were breeches of thick velvet or leather, buttoned on the outside of each leg and typically worn over knee breeches (OED; Linda R. Baumgarten, "Jefferson's Clothing," *Magazine Antiques*, 144 [1993], 104).

On 6 July 1803, TJ ordered John Barnes to pay the balance on Carpenter's account for $332.50 "after taking credit for such part thereof as he has already paid" (MS in ViU; in TJ's hand and signed by him; at foot of text: "Mr. John Barnes"; with receipt in Barnes's hand acknowledging whole amount for $332.50, with payment on 12 May for $50 and on 10 June for $150 ℔ note, for a balance due of $132.50, also noting 60 days at 6 July with receipt of payment on that date; signed by Carpenter; endorsed by Barnes on verso).

To Levi Lincoln

Apr. 26. 1803.

Th: Jefferson with his compliments to mr Lincoln returns him mr Crowninshield's letter. the appointmt. of a substitute for mr Story shall await further information.—he has not been at all moved to doubt the propriety of Fosdyck's removal.

Mr. Lincoln is perfectly free to retain the copy of the Syllabus, & to make any use of it his discretion would approve, confident as Th:J. is that his discretion would not permit him to let it be copied lest it should get into print. in the latter case Th:J. would become the butt of every set of disquisitions which every priest would undertake to write on every tenet it expresses. their object is not truth, but matter whereon to write against Th:J. and this Synopsis would furnish matter for repeating in new forms all the volumes of divinity which are now mouldering on the shelves from which they should never more be taken. Th:J. would thank mr L. not to put his name on the paper in filing it away, lest in case of accident to mr L. it should get out.

PrC (DLC).

CROWNINSHIELD'S LETTER: see Lincoln to TJ, 24 Apr.

From George Jefferson

DEAR SIR — Richmond 27th. Apl. 1803

I have to acknowledge the receipt of your favor of the 24th. and to inform you that only four Hhds of your Tobacco have yet come down. I think it probable that if it were now here, it would command 7$:—the current price however is only about 33/. there being a much greater difference made this year on account of the quality than was ever known.

I imagine that you must know it could not be sold before it comes down, except at a disadvantage, and of course that you did not intend the attempt should be made.

Be so good as to inform me if you have heard any thing particular of the quality. I think I have understood that it is better this year than common.

The seeds you mention shall be forwarded.

I am Dear Sir Yr. very humble servt. — GEO. JEFFERSON

RC (MHi); at foot of text: "Thomas Jefferson esqr."; endorsed by TJ as received 1 May and so recorded in SJL; also endorsed by TJ:

"tobo good
bill ladg. groceries
syrup punch
<*boxes composn. raisins*>
clock."

To Meriwether Lewis

DEAR SIR — Washington April 27. 1803.

Your's of the 20th from Lancaster was recieved the night before last. not having heard from you since the time of my leaving Washington, I had written to you on the 23d. and lodged it in Philadelphia.

you will therefore probably recieve that & this together. I inclose you a copy of the rough draught of instructions I have prepared for you, that you may have time to consider them, & to propose any modifications which may occur to yourself as useful. your destination being known to mr Patterson, Doctrs. Wistar, Rush & Barton, these instructions may be submitted to their perusal. a considerable portion of them being within the field of the Philosophical society, which once undertook the same mission, I think it my duty to consult some of it's members, limiting the communication by the necessity of secrecy in a good degree. these gentlemen will suggest any additions they will think useful, as has been before asked of them.—we have recieved information that Connor cultivates in the first degree the patronage of the British government; to which he values ours as only secondary. as it is possible however that his passion for this expedition may overrule that for the British, and as I do not see that the British agents will necessarily be disposed to counterwork us, I think Connor's qualifications make it desireable to engage him, and that the communication to him will be as useful, as it was certainly proper under our former impression of him. the idea that you are going to explore the Missisipi has been generally given out: it satisfies public curiosity, and masks sufficiently the real destination. I shall be glad to hear from you, as soon after your arrival at Philadelphia as you can form an idea when you will leave, & when be [here.] accept assurances of my constant & sincere affection. TH: JEFFERSON

PrC (DLC); torn; at foot of text: "Capt M. Lewis"; endorsed by TJ in ink on verso. Enclosure: see Drafting Instructions for Meriwether Lewis, at 13 Apr.

TJ wrote to Robert PATTERSON about Lewis's expedition on 2 Mch., Caspar WISTAR and Benjamin RUSH on 28 Feb., and Benjamin Smith BARTON on 27 Feb.

ONCE UNDERTOOK THE SAME MISSION: that is, the proposed expedition of André Michaux (see Drafting Instructions for Meriwether Lewis, 13 Apr.).

CONSULT SOME OF IT'S MEMBERS: for example, Isaac Briggs (see 1 Mch.), Andrew Ellicott (6 Mch. and 18 Apr.), and John Garnett (TJ to Lewis, 30 Apr.).

From Meriwether Lewis

SIR, Lancaster Aprile 27th. 1803.

Mr. Joseph Ellicott, being about to visit the City of Washington I have taken the liberty of introducing him to your acquaintance—he is a brother of Mr. Andrew Ellicott, your old friend and acquaintance of this place; a judge, and resident of the western part of the State of New York—he is a good republican, and a man of good information and reputation.—

I am with much respect Your Obt. & very Humble Sert.

M. LEWIS.

RC (DLC); at foot of text: "The President of the United States"; endorsed by TJ. Recorded in SJL as received 30 Apr.

Andrew Ellicott's brother JOSEPH was the land agent of the Holland Land Company (Vol. 32:549n; Vol. 38:344n).

From Nathaniel Ingraham

MOST HONOURED SUR Bristol April the 28 AD 1803

I am the Poor and humbel Petitioner that has sant on two Petitions for my 'Relf and Eant heaired Eany thing from thim Nor from your honour most honoured Sur. Sur I am Poor and Eant Nothing to Suport me and my famly on Most honoured Sur I Eant marster of Eany trade to Supoort me and my famly With I humbly Badg that you: Sur Will send me Sum relf If not Sur I and my famly must Sufer in a Criston land If I Sur Was in a furing Curnty and a Prisner With the trippooling I Should have Sum Suport from their Chif but Sur heir I am and Eant had Eany Suport from no one and God Only Noes Wheir It is a Coming from Sur but grant me the Lebty of going about the town to Work for my Suport for hear Sur their is Nothing hear to Suport me and my famly With in this Prisen but the beear Worls Sur I humbelly Wish to have a frue Lins from your honour to Let me No If thier is Eany time Sat for my Relf this Sur Is the Secont that I have Sant to your honour and I hope Sur that I shant have a Cashon to Sand No mor

I am your most humbel Servent NATHANIEL INGRAHAM

RC (DLC); addressed: "To the President of the United States"; franked; postmarked 3 May. Recorded in SJL as received 8 May.

TWO PETITIONS: for earlier correspondence regarding a pardon for Rhode Island mariner Nathaniel Ingraham, who had been tried and convicted for engaging in the slave trade, see Vol. 37:199-200, 648 and Vol. 39:399-401. For the pardon request from his wife, Mary Ingraham, which TJ recorded in SJL as received the same day as the petition above, see Vol. 38:606.

TRIPPOOLING: presumably Ingraham means Tripolitans.

From Philip Norborne Nicholas

DEAR SIR, Richmond April 28th 1803.

I wrote to the Secretary of State some time ago and mentioned that Mr William Duval of this city had been induced to resign his office of commissioner of bankruptcy just previous to the elections for the

Assembly for which he was a candidate at the solicitation of the republicans here[1] & to which he was ineligible from his holding a commission under the general Government, and that it would be convenient to Mr Duval & acceptable to the Republicans here if the administration should see no impropriety in his reappointment.
I believe Mr Duval discharged the duties of the office with great fidelity and to the satisfaction of those concerned. & I could wish to see him in the same situation. If the administration should feel any difficulty as to the reappointment of Major Duval from the peculiar circumstances of the case, I would beg leave to mention that I believe Peyton Randolph would accept the appointment. I believe he is known to you Sir & that he is every way both from ability & discretion qualified for the proper discharge of the duties of the office. But I would by no means wish the latter gentleman to be thought of unless the administration should feel any difficulty in the reappointment of Major Duvall which would be agreable to us here because it is convenient to him & he is qualified for the office. I hope you will excuse the liberty I have taken on this subject and believe me with every consideration of sincere regard & friendship

PHILIP NORBORNE NICHOLAS

P.S. I am informed by the Secretary to the Commissioners of bankruptcy that there is great want of another commissioner & I imagine from Mr Duvalls having acted on all the cases which have occured here that his being reappointed would from that circumstance contribute to facilitate the business very much. There are a great number of cases which are in this situation.

RC (DNA: RG 59, LAR); addressed: "Thomas Jefferson Esqr. President of U States. Washington"; franked and postmarked; endorsed by TJ as received 1 May and "Duvall to be reappd Commr. bkrptcy" and so recorded in SJL.

Nicholas WROTE TO THE SECRETARY OF STATE on 14 Apr. at "the Solicitation" of a number of Richmond Republicans, who had induced WILLIAM DUVAL to resign as bankruptcy commissioner and run as their delegate to the assembly. The Republicans lost the election "by a few votes only" and were "very desirous" to have their candidate reappointed to office (RC in same; endorsed by TJ: "Duvall to be reappointed Commr. bkrptcy"). TJ also saw the letter that DuVal wrote Madison on 8 Apr., resigning his office (RC in same; endorsed by TJ: "Duval Wm. to mr Madison. resigng. as Commr. bkrptcy"). TJ reappointed DuVal with a commission dated 3 June (list of commissions in Lb in DNA: RG 59, MPTPC; Vol. 37: 710; Appendix I: List of Appointments).

SECRETARY TO THE COMMISSIONERS OF BANKRUPTCY: Robert Brooke (Richmond *Virginia Argus*, 1 Jan., 16 Feb. 1803).

[1] Preceding four words interlined.

From Joseph T. Scott

Sir, Philada. Apl. 28th. 1803

Being indisposed for several days I was prevented from acknowledging the receipt of yours of the 9th. containing two papers of information.

Accept I pray you the assurances of my personal esteem for your very polite and kind attention to my request.

I expect to have, in a short time, the life of Washington in the press.

With sentiments of great respect I am Sir your most obt. Sert.

Joseph Scott

RC (DLC); torn; at foot of text: "President of the [. . .] States"; endorsed by TJ as received 1 May and so recorded in SJL.

From John Vaughan

D sir Philada April 28. 1803

Vaccination is becoming every day more current amongst us
in order to assist in removing prejudice where any still remains the enclosed has been published here, & proves a powerful agent
I take the liberty of enclosing a few to you knowing how much Interest you have taken in its adoption, & being indebted to you for its introduction here,

I remain with respect D sir Your ob. Servant Jn Vaughan

RC (DLC); addressed: "Thomas Jefferson President of the United States Washington City"; franked and postmarked. Recorded in SJL as received 1 May. Enclosure: *A Comparative view of the Natural Small-Pox, Inoculated Small-Pox, and Vaccination in their effects on Individuals and Society*, a broadside printed by Jane Aitken in Philadelphia, dated 25 Apr.; comparing in three columns the potential physical effects of smallpox, smallpox inoculation, and vaccination, concluding that contracting smallpox is equivalent to "attempting to cross a large and rapid stream by swimming, when one in six perish," that inoculation using smallpox is equivalent to "passing the river in a boat subject to accidents, where one in 300 perish, and one in 40 suffer partially," and that vaccination with cowpox is equivalent to "passing over a safe bridge"; presenting also a statement of 12 Apr. by 50 physicians of Philadelphia, including Benjamin Rush, Caspar Wistar, John Redman Coxe, and Benjamin Smith Barton, declaring it "a duty thus publicly to declare our opinion" that cowpox vaccination is a safe and "certain preventive" of smallpox, and they recommend it for general use; with a statement by the board of managers of the Philadelphia Dispensary that the institution's attending and consulting physicians, after 18 months' experience with cowpox vaccination and finding it to be "mild, unattended with danger, and a full security against the Small-Pox," wish the procedure to be made available through the Dispensary; accordingly, the managers announce that doctors will perform cowpox vaccination there daily; "the poor of the city" are encouraged "to embrace the means now offered of preserving themselves and families from a dangerous and loathsome disease" (Shaw-Shoemaker, No. 3998).

EVERY DAY MORE CURRENT: the 12 Apr. statement by the Philadelphia physicians also appeared in newspapers there and elsewhere. Benjamin Rush and others founded the Philadelphia Dispensary, the first free medical clinic in the United States, in 1786. Dispensaries in American cities took on a primary role in the vaccination of urban populations (*Gazette of the United States*, 19 Apr.; Richmond *Virginia Argus*, 27 Apr.; L. H. Butterfield, ed., *Letters of Benjamin Rush*, 2 vols. [Princeton, 1951], 1:448n; Charles E. Rosenberg, "Social Class and Medical Care in Nineteenth-Century America: The Rise and Fall of the Dispensary," *Journal of the History of Medicine and Allied Sciences*, 29 [1974], 32-54).

From James Ash, with Jefferson's Note

SIR Baltimore 29th. April 1803

The proposals, which I had the honor to transmit you some time ago, for "The American Law of Merchants," have been returned with your Signature."

Agreeably to the conditions, be pleased to transmit me the advance therein required; because I consider my character pledged for the return of every Cent, if the undertaking should not be sufficiently encouraged, to authorize the publication, and reward my labor. Besides my present necessities, from Judicial persecution, which will be reasonably explained to my fellow Citizens, require every aid to forward the Work Contemplated; and it is trusted, whatever defects it may Contain, will be attributed to inability, and not to the want of zeal and faithful endeavours in the execution.

I have the honor to be Sir, Yr: mo: ob: Hble: Servt:

JAMES ASH

[*Note by TJ*:]

May 11. inclosd. 5. D. to author at Baltimore.

RC (MHi); at foot of text: "Thomas Jefferson, President, of the United States"; endorsed by TJ as received 1 May and so recorded in SJL.

SOME TIME AGO: see Ash to TJ, 7 Feb.

According to his financial memoranda of 11 May, TJ remitted a $5 ADVANCE for the book (MB, 2:1100). On 14 May, Ash acknowledged receipt of payment with "his compliments" to TJ and noted: "Received from the President of the United States, by Mail, Five Dollars," being in full, "for one Copy of The American Law of merchants, to be 'sent to press whenever there is a sufficient fund to defray the expence of printing'" (RC in MHi; endorsed by TJ as received from Baltimore on 17 May and so recorded in SJL).

From Craven Peyton

DEAR SIR Milton 29th. Apl. 1803

On my coming to this place to day I was much surprised to find Mr. Issack Millar & John Henderson engaged in leveling the Mill-seat and from what Henderson informd. Millar he actually offard him One Thousand Dollars for his interest. as I was informd. in consequence of what I said to Millar he appeared to be back ward, himself & Mr. Meriweathar are about to be concerned in the purchase. the plan they are now about to persue is to establish an Ordar of Court Monday Next which I shall oppose and at all events have it posponed untill I receave instructions from you how to act Henderson is a Man of so base principles I railey wish you woud. purchase those two lotts. howevar if you think him in your way. Any instructions which you may think propar to give shall be strictly attended to. Majr. Randolph is elected for this district.

with much Esteem Yr. Obt. C PEYTON

RC (ViU); endorsed by TJ as received 1 May and so recorded in SJL.

MUCH SURPRISED: TJ had his own plans for mills on the Rivanna River. The toll mill, built by Peter Jefferson and later destroyed in a freshet, was not rebuilt until 1803. TJ had also been planning a large manufacturing mill since 1793 and contracted with James Walker and Michael Hope for the layout of the site (Betts, *Farm Book*, 341-3; Vol. 38:429-30, 438; TJ to Walker, 25 Mch. 1803).

For Peyton's earlier concerns about JOHN HENDERSON, see Peyton to TJ, 13 Nov. 1802.

From Joseph Prentis

DEAR SIR, wmsburg 29 April 1803.

On my return to this place I was delayed in my Journey a day, with a view to procure that information which was contemplated, when I had the pleasure of seeing you last. Subsequent communications however appeared to me so to have paved the way to conciliation, that it would have been highly improper to have introduced the subject in the way proposed, and consequently silence was imposed on me. The Letters that have passed thro the means of the military character who visited you before you left Monticello, I firmly believe will prove the source of relief to the person to whom they were addressed, and the impression made on his mind, as to the object of certain persons in exciting improper sentiments toward you, is at the moment a correct one. To some of his friends I stated the necessity of using their influence to counter act similar efforts, and I hope they will be able if it be necessary to provide an antidote to this person—

The last letter you received had not been answered when I saw Mr W. the expectation of an answer I endeavoured to lessen, by stating, that the subject of it, did not seem to require it. I rathar however think that it was expected, and the way to reconciliation being opened, I feel such solicitude for its progression, that you will pardon the suggestion on my part. Since my departure however, circumstances may have already occurred which have been satisfactory. I am Dr Sir with sentiments of unfeigned Esteem yr Friend JP.

PS. May I beg you to present my affection to Mr Madison.

RC (ViW: Tucker-Coleman Collection); endorsed by TJ as received from Joseph Prentis on 5 May and so recorded in SJL.

Joseph Prentis and TJ served together in the Virginia House of Delegates from 1776 to 1778. Prentis was on the Executive Council during most of TJ's years as governor. He was elected judge of the General Court in 1788, a position he held until his death in 1809 (Washington, *Papers, Pres. Ser.*, 14:89n; Leonard, *General Assembly*, 122-3, 125, 127, 131, 158; Vol. 3:564; Vol. 5:383; Vol. 6:89).

PLEASURE OF SEEING YOU LAST: Prentis visited Monticello after TJ's arrival there in March and evidently agreed to serve as one of TJ's liaisons with John Walker (TJ to Prentis, 6 May). General Henry Lee was the MILITARY CHARACTER who visited Monticello as Walker's liaison. TJ did not receive Walker's LAST LETTER of 4 Apr. (now missing) until the 12th. For TJ's reply, see TJ to Walker, 13 Apr.

From Thomas Mann Randolph

DEAR SIR, Monticello April 29. 1803.

My struggle with Colo. Cabell has terminated in my favor for the present, after nine days continuance; but the majority is so small, only 13 in the whole District, that I may perhaps yet, if he should resolve to contest my election, lose my seat. My belief at this moment is that he has more bad votes than myself but it is founded on a scrutiny of the Amherst polls only, which I had examined by fit men while there. Those of Albemarle, and Fluvanna, I have not had time yet to look into: if not worse, than report now makes them, I shall still maintain a small majority.—My absence has kept Martha and the children here till now: we go over on Sunday and Mr Eppes & Maria with us, to remain some time, I hope, for his election is concluded. A smart indisposition kept him from going to Amelia.

Lillie requests me to repeat some information allready forwarded you, respecting matters within his department of your affairs.—Captain Hudson asks $\frac{1}{4}$\$ for [180][1] Cub. inchs. of his Cherrie logs, calculating them by the Cubic contents & not the plank they may yield, refusing the ordinary allowance for the Sand-track: this is his last price, from which he declares he will not depart.—Rives & Co. in Milton, have given John Perrie credit for 112. £ due them from him, and take credit with John Craven by his consent, he demanding the same of you.—Lillie suspects you gave him by mistake a 5$ Bank Note of Alexa., instead of a 50$, which you intended; for he has such a note, has recieved no such from any one for a great length of time, and cannot account for 45$ in any way. He did not take the note you gave him from the paper he wraped it in, till he was about to change it & then to his astonishment found only a 5$. note. He begs you to consult your minutes of such things, & inform him, that he may try yet to satisfy himself if his present belief is not just.—I was at Poplar forest a few days since. The Negroes are healthy, and feel as happy as while under Clarke. The plantations have allready assumed a different face.—I expect to be disappointed entirely now in my Georgia scheme and even in the trip there. I am inclined at present to dispose of such of the Negroes, destined to settle in Georgia according to my late scheme, as are of bad character, either here or there, and to reserve the others for improvements. I mention this that you may know I shall be at home to take care of the Children, if you should yet desire Martha to come to Washington; though your own return being now not very distant I have a hope you may not be so anxious for it; though I am ready to forward the[2] journey & shall part with her cheerfully. With true attachment yr. &c TH: M: RANDOLPH.

RC (ViU: Edgehill-Randolph Papers); endorsed by TJ as received 4 May and so recorded in SJL.

CAPTAIN HUDSON: probably Charles Hudson, an officer in the Albemarle militia (Woods, *Albemarle*, 373).

[1] Numerals overwritten and blurred are supplied from TJ to Randolph, 5 May.

[2] MS: "he."

To John Bacon

DEAR SIR Washington Apr. 30. 1803.

Your favor of the 11th. has been recieved, & I thank you for the communication on Indian affairs. I observe what you say on the aspect of your elections. altho' federalism appears to have boasted prematurely of it's gains, yet it does not appear to have yielded as we might have expected to the evidence either of their reason or their senses. two facts are certainly as true as irreconcileable. the people of Massachusets love economy & freedom civil & religious. the present legislature & executive functionaries endeavor to practice economy,

& to strengthen civil & religious freedom. yet they are disapproved by the people of Massachusets. it cannot be that these had rather give up principles than men. however the riddle is to be solved, our duty is plain; to administer their interests faithfully and to overcome evil with good.

You have seen that the government of Spain has instantly redressed the infraction of treaty by her intendent at New Orleans; and that, by a reasonable and peaceable process, we have obtained in 4. months, what would have cost us 7. years of war, 100,000 human lives, 100. millions of additional debt besides ten hundred millions lost by the want of market for our produce, or depredations on[1] it in seeking markets, and the general demoralising of our citizens which war occasions. I have the satisfaction to add that we have recieved official information that in the instrument of cession of Louisiana by Spain to France, is this clause 'Saving the rights acquired by other powers in virtue of treaties made with them by Spain.' although I am not sanguine in obtaining a cession of New Orleans for money, yet I am confident in the policy of putting off the day of contention for it, till we are stronger in ourselves, & stronger in allies; but especially till we shall have planted such a population on the Missisipi as will be able to do their own business, without the necessity of marching men from the shores of the Atlantic 1500. or 2000. miles thither, to perish by fatigue & change of climate. Accept my friendly salutations & assurances of high respect. TH: JEFFERSON

P.S. I inclose you a pamphlet.

PrC (DLC); at foot of text: "John Bacon esq." Enclosure: possibly *A Vindication of the Measures of the Present Administration* by Gideon Granger (see John Langdon to TJ, 8 May).

[1] Preceding two words interlined in place of two illegible, canceled words.

To Justus Erich Bollmann

SIR Washington Apr. 30. 1803.

Understanding that you were withdrawing from the business in which you have been engaged, but not informed as to your future views, I take the liberty of mentioning to you that there is at present no Consul of the US. at Rotterdam, and that I should name you to that office with a perfect satisfaction that it's functions would be performed by you usefully for the public. you know that no salaries are annexed to those offices, & that the fees are inconsiderable. yet I have observed that no office is more sought after, which I presume proceeds from the incidental business which it brings to a person engaged in a mercantile line. whether this may be within your views, is not for me to say; but I avail myself with satisfaction of this occasion of being useful to you, should the appointment be acceptable.

The box of Hungary wine, which you were so good as to forward, has been safely recieved, and Capt Lewis, my secretary, who will be in Philadelphia in a few days, will call on you, and discharge it's amount. Accept my salutations & assurances of respect.

TH: JEFFERSON

PrC (DLC); at foot of text: "Doctr. J. Erich Bollman"; endorsed by TJ in ink on verso.

Bollmann's mercantile BUSINESS had recently failed (Benjamin H. Latrobe to TJ, 13 Mch.).

John Henderson Deed to Craven Peyton

This Indenture, made this Thirtieth day of April in the year of our Lord one thousand eight hundred and three: Between John Henderson and Ann B. Henderson his wife, of the County of Albemarle of the one part, and Craven Peyton of the said County of the other part, Witnesseth, that the said John Henderson, and Ann B. his wife, for and in consideration of the sum of One Hundred and forty pounds Current money of Virginia to them in hand Paid by the said Craven Peyton, before the sealing and delivery of these presents, the receipt of which they doth hereby acknowledge: Hath Given Granted, Bargained, and sold, and by these presents doth give grant bargain and sell unto the said Craven Peyton, his heirs and assigns forever, the following Lands, lying and being in the County of Albemarle, which were drawn by the said John Henderson as a legatee of Bennett Henderson dec'd at a division of said Bennett Hendersons lands, as will appear by the returns made by the Commissioners, who were appointed by the County Court of Albemarle, to divide said Lands, to wit, Lot No. 1. in the back lands Containing One Hundred and two Acres, and Lot No. 9. in the lower field Containing six acres and one quarter Acres,—be the same, more or less.

To have and to hold the Lands, herein before specified, unto the said Craven Peyton, his heirs and assigns forever, and the said John Henderson and Ann B. his wife, do by these presents, warrant and agree, with the said Craven Peyton, that they will warrant, and for ever, defend, a good and sufficient, title in fee simple, in the aforesaid

Lands, free and clear from the claim, or claims, of all and every person or Persons, whatsoever, unto the said Craven Peyton, his heirs and assigns forever,—

In Testimony whereof the said John Henderson, and Ann B. his wife have herewith set their hands and affixed their seals, the day and Year first within written

JNO HENDERSON
NANCY HENDERSON

Signed Sealed and delivered in presence of }
RICHARD ANDERSON
RICHD JOHNSON
DAVID ANDERSON
WILL. CLARKSON

MS (ViU); in a clerk's hand, signed by all, with hand-drawn facsimile seals beside Henderson signatures; attested by John Nicholas, clerk, as recorded in "Albemarle February Court 1804," noting that the indenture of bargain and sale was produced and acknowledged by John Henderson and his wife Nancy "she being first privily examined as the Law directs"; endorsed:

" Henderson
to } Deed
Peyton
February 7th. 1804.
Acknowledged wifes
Relinquishment taken &
to be Recorded";

endorsed by Peyton:

" Deed
Henderson
to
Peyton";

endorsed by TJ:

" John Henderson to Craven Peyton } 1803. Apr. 30.
140. £
No. 1. back lands 102. as.
" 9. lower field $6\frac{1}{4}$ as.
$108\frac{1}{4}$ acres."

Tr (Albemarle County Deed Book No. 14); certified and ordered to be recorded by Nicholas at the Albemarle Court, February 1804.

For TJ's record of payment to John Henderson for the SUM of £140 for $108\frac{1}{4}$ acres, see Vol. 38:621-2n.

To Meriwether Lewis

TH: JEFFERSON TO CAPT. LEWIS Washington Apr. 30. 1803

I think we spoke together of your carrying some steel or cast iron[1] corn mills to give to the Indians or to trade with them, as well as for your own use. lest however I should be mistaken, I mention them now. I make no doubt you have consulted with mr Ellicot as to the best instruments to carry. I would wish that nothing which passed between us here should prevent your following his advice, which is certainly the best. should a timepiece be requisite, it is probable mr Garnet can furnish you one. neither Ellicot nor Garnet have given me their opinion on the substituting a meridian at land, instead of observations of time, for ascertaining longitude by the lunar motions. I presume therefore it will not answer. accept my affectionate salutations.

PrC (DLC); endorsed by TJ in ink on verso.

CORN MILLS: an iron mill for grinding corn was on Lewis's list of needs for camp equipage. The purveyor's office in Philadelphia bought one mill for that purpose for $9 and two others for the stock of presents for $20. The implement for the expedition's use weighed 20 pounds and the two others weighed a total of about 53 pounds (Jackson, *Lewis and Clark*, 1:71, 84, 94, 95).

TJ had thought that if Lewis used a theodolite or universal equatorial instrument he would not need a precision TIMEPIECE such as a chronometer to make observations for longitude (Silvio A. Bedini, *Thomas Jefferson: Statesman of Science* [New York, 1990], 344-6).

MR GARNET: John Garnett's cousin, Horatio Gates, called him "a Man of much Science." A wealthy resident of New Brunswick, New Jersey, who was born in England, Garnett made celestial observations, edited and published nautical almanacs and astronomical tables, was a scientific farmer, and wrote papers on astronomical methods, mathematics, and windmill technology. The American Philosophical Society elected him to membership in July 1802 and awarded him a gold medal in 1807 for innovations in navigational charts (same, 341-2; John C. Greene, *American Science in the Age of Jefferson* [Ames, Iowa, 1984], 141-2, 147; William H. Benedict, *New Brunswick in History* [New Brunswick, N.J., 1925], 53, 134-6; APS, *Proceedings*, 22, pt. 3 [1884], 311, 326, 344, 376, 400; APS, *Transactions*, 6 [1809], 303-18, 391-8; Vol. 30: 110; Vol. 36:50-1; Robert Patterson to TJ, 7 Feb. 1807, in DLC).

[1] Preceding four words interlined.

From John Francis Vacher

Bottle Hill near Morristown N. Jersey
30th April 1803

SIR

It ought not to be within the Sphere of a private Individual, to adress the first Magistrate of a Country; Let it even be as free, as ours is at present. but when this individual is influenced by no other motive, but by that which may contribute in the least to the honor, to the happiness of a Community, of an Empire, of the whole of the human Race. then inspired with Such sentiments, he cannot become blamable; and may venture in decent expressions, to ask a feasable thing: Should he not ever in his endeavours Succeed in forwarding and compleating a work; extracts of which Your Excellency will find here annex't for his perusal: this thing being out of the line of the duty attach't to a Government, where a man ought then to act with the utmost candor; even if it could be obtain'd from inferior Powers. Yet a well placed delicacy as to free him-self from the least suspicion; he the undersigned thinks him-self and impress't with respect towards

Your Excellency in observing this line of conduct, bound to apologize for breaking upon Your Excellency's immense labour.

The author has endeavour'd to have had the first canto of this work printed; and to have presented the Copy of it which first fell under his hand, to Your Excellency, not only as a due homage to his Magistracy, but Yet as he is able by his Science to appreciate the worth of the undertaking. but difficulties presenting them-selves, the author must wait such a time as he may find a more favorable opportunity. therefore however disagreeable he thinks, it may be to Your Excellency, to read a manuscript. Yet it's better to present it under this form to Shew cause for his request, than to Shew nothing at all.

It is not from this day the author influenced by the cause in which he embark't early, that he conceived to venture him-self in this laborious carrier. but as providence does not pour his munificence with Such bountiful a hand as to bestow riches, natural Gifts, virtue, and that Gentleness which render a man the admiration of the world, and the ornament of his nature then he or those who possess but part of those Qualifications, Satisfyed with such a Share Providence granted him or them, ought to apply it Soon or late or when possible, to forward the happiness of human nature.

America has produced a poem of this kind. an anonimous french writer whom I think if one is allow'd to Judge by the Similarity of the Stile, (the famous Count de Mirabeau) gave out also *l'amerique delivrée*, and dedicated to John Adams Esqr whilst he was embassador to the united provinces. Those two authors Seem to have agreed in several points, as they were both beating the Same path at the Same time, to have hurried the business; left out many of the principal actors who figur'd on the Stage of our revolution, and Slided on the characters of Some of those they retained with the rapidity of the lightning, which in being the Soul of the epopee ought I believe neither be too long, but ought not to be too short. the french production particularly; and with Such unaccountable a negligence both in the want from time to time of the Sublimity of Stile, Such a work requires; and the rules of Poetry these last above all (what he mentions in his preface) as to make one believe that the grandeur of the american revolution has been Sacrificed to the altar of hurry and that one half of that work cannot be possibly wrote by the author *des lettres a Sophie in de l'adresses aux bataves*. &.c.

Unities in a work of the kind ought to be observed. 1777 is that of time; Still-water; Saratoga; that of place, the capture of Genl Burgoine with his whole army as the most proper Subject which presents it-self during our glorious Struggle, forms that of action, & has therefore given the poem the title of Gatiade.

order in a Poem ought to be attended to as well as Unities, & it is this desire which makes the object of this application: the present the honble Secretary at war knows me from the campaign 1777 under Genl Gates, I might have taken the liberty to have ask't this favor of him. the honble Doctr william Eustis one of my benefactors from 1776 had the kindness in the course of the last Session to offer me his influence, So that I might obtain my request, but the course of a Session he Said, was improper for Such an application, on account of the crowd of business. therefore, I thought it would be fairer to make my application to the Supreme power, So that there could be no mistrust in what an individual desired to do with documents.

Finally the object of this, amounts to no more than that your Excellency may have the kindness to order the Secretary at war that he may cause a return of the Generals, field officers, and captains, regiment by regiment; and State by State of the revolutionary army for the Year *1777* and the number of Brigades English had against america with the names of their respective chiefs and Send the Same to the underSigned?

May he that rules with Such a Sublimity, millions of worlds! for the honor and happiness of this keep Your Excellency to the longest term nature can favor man with

I am with respect of Your Excellency Your Excellency's most obedient and very humble Servant JOHN F. VACHER

RC (DLC); at foot of text: "His Excellency T. Jefferson Esqr President of the U. States"; endorsed by TJ as received 3 May and so recorded in SJL. Enclosure not found.

INFLUENCED BY THE CAUSE: a native of France, where he received his medical education, Vacher served as a surgeon in the Fourth New York regiment from February 1777 to 1 Jan. 1781. He wrote TJ in 1790 seeking a position as a translator in the State Department (Washington, *Papers, Rev. War Ser.*, 14:474n; Vol. 16:309-10).

ANONIMOUS FRENCH WRITER: perhaps a reference to "R," the author of *L'Amériquiade*, the epic poem on the American Revolution published in Philadelphia and Amsterdam in 1780 (John L. Brown, "Revolution and the Muse: The American War of Independence in Contemporary French Poetry," WMQ, 3d ser., 41 [1984], 600n). L. de Chavannes de la Giraudière DEDICATED *L'Amérique délivrée: Esquisse d'un poëme sur l'Indépendance de l'Amérique* to JOHN ADAMS. Published in two volumes in Amsterdam in 1783, it is noted as the most ambitious of the French epics on the American Revolution (same, 592-3, 596-600). LETTRES A SOPHIE: a four-volume edition of Mirabeau's letters to Sophie de Monnier while in prison entitled *Lettres originales de Mirabeau, écrites du donjon de Vincennes, pendant les années 1777, 78, 79 et 80; contenant tous les détails sur sa vie privée, ses malheurs, et ses amours avec Sophie Ruffei, marquise de Monnier* was published in Paris in 1792. TJ owned Mirabeau's *Aux*

Bataves sur le Stathouderat (see Sowerby, No. 2415).

In March 1804, TJ received a list of REVOLUTIONARY ARMY officers from Dearborn, which he immediately forwarded to Vacher (Dearborn to TJ, 22 Mch.; TJ to Vacher, 23 Mch.; Vacher to TJ, 3 Apr. 1804).

To Hugh Williamson

DEAR SIR Washington Apr. 30. 1803.

I thank you for the information on the subject of the navigation of the Iberville contained in your's of the 18th. in running the late line between the Choctaws and us, we found the Amit to be about 50. miles from the Missisipi where that line crossed it, which was but a little Northward of our Southern boundary. for the present we have a respite on that subject, Spain having without delay restored our infracted right, & assured us it is expressly saved by the instrument of her cession of Louisiana to France. altho' I do not count with confidence on obtaining N. Orleans from France for money, yet I am confident in the policy of putting off the day of contention for it, till we have lessened the embarrasments of debt accumulated instead of being discharged by our predecessors, till we attain more of that strength which is growing on us so rapidly, & especially till we have planted a population on the Missisipi itself, sufficient to do it's own work, without marching men 1500. miles from the Atlantic shores to perish by fatigue and unfriendly climates. this will soon take place. in the mean time we have obtained by a peaceable appeal[1] to justice, in 4. months, what we should not have obtained under 7. years of war, the loss of 100,000. lives, an hundred millions of additional debt, many hundred millions worth of produce & property lost for want of market, or in seeking it, & that demoralisation which war superinduces on the human mind. to have seised N. Orleans as our federal Maniacs wished, would only have changed the character & extent of the blockade of our Western commerce. it would have produced a blockade by[2] superior naval force of the navigation of the river as well as of the entrance into N. Orleans, instead of a paper blockade from N. Orleans alone, while the river remained open. and I am persuaded that had not the deposit been so quickly restored, we should have found soon that it would be better now to ascend the river to Natchez, in order to be clear of the embarrasments, plunderings & irritations at N. Orleans, & to fatten by the benefits of the depot a city & citizens of our own, rather than those of a foreign nation. Accept my friendly & respectful salutations. TH: JEFFERSON

P.S. the water line of the Iberville, Amite, & L. Ponchartrain, becoming a boundary between France & Spain, we have a double chance of an acknolegement of our right to use it, on the same ground of natural right on which we claim the navigation of the Mobile & other rivers heading in our territory & running thro' the Floridas.[3]

RC (Public Library of New South Wales, Sydney, Australia, 1945); addressed: "Doctr. Hugh Williamson near New York"; franked and postmarked. PrC (DLC).

For the LATE LINE BETWEEN THE CHOCTAWS and the United States, as specified by the treaty signed at Fort Adams on 17 Dec. 1801, see Vol. 37:51-2.

[1]TJ first wrote "an appeal" before altering text to read as above.

[2]TJ here canceled "vessels of."

[3]Postscript interlined in left margin perpendicular to text.

Cipher for Meriwether Lewis

I. DRAFT CIPHER TABLE, [APRIL 1803?]

II. CIPHER TABLE, [APRIL 1803?]

EDITORIAL NOTE

In his instructions for the expedition to the Pacific, Jefferson anticipated that Meriwether Lewis might find opportunity to send dispatches back by way of western army posts, "putting into cypher whatever might do injury if betrayed" (see Document IV of the group of documents on drafting instructions for Lewis, at 13 Apr. above). Two undated manuscripts, in Jefferson's handwriting and among his papers at the Library of Congress, record the cipher he worked up for Lewis. Jefferson put no heading on either manuscript, but in one of them he enciphered a hypothetical message that he could speculate might someday come from Lewis, beginning "I am at the head of the Missouri" (see Document I below). Jefferson endorsed the other paper as a "Cypher establd. with Captain Lewis" (Document II). In that endorsement he also identified "Artichokes" as a key for the cipher. That word forms a direct connection between the manuscripts, for in Document I, "artichoke" was the key (he used "antipodes" in Document II). Document I records the first stage of his work on the cipher, shown by unused columns on the right side of the table, his labored effort to explain the method, and his first practice exercise using no key word. Document II is a neatly written manuscript, made after he had developed the system to his liking.

He noted in the endorsement to Document II that he *established* ("establd.") the cipher with Lewis. They must have discussed it in person, for the subject of the cipher did not come up in the letters they exchanged during the spring of 1803 while Lewis was in Harpers Ferry, Lancaster, and Philadelphia making preparations for the expedition. Perhaps Jefferson drew up the method in April, when he drafted the instructions for the journey and included the reference to a cipher. If he "established" it with Lewis in person, however, they could not have done so until Lewis returned to Washington in June, and it is possible that Jefferson prepared the cipher as late as that month.

The tableau-style cipher system that Jefferson drew up for Lewis dated from the sixteenth century (Weber, *United States Diplomatic Codes*, 10-12; David Kahn, *The Codebreakers: The Story of Secret Writing*, rev. ed. [New York, 1996], 133-7, 145-51). The letters of the alphabet appear in order in each row, but the position of the letters shifts from row to row. (Jefferson included the ampersand as, in effect, a 27th letter of the alphabet.) In his first trial of the cipher, at the top of the grid he numbered the columns, leaving the one on the far left unnumbered (see Document I). The user would work through the intended message letter by letter, finding the first letter in the column on the left and reading across to the column numbered "1," then finding the second letter in the left column and reading across to column 2, and so on. On reaching the 27th letter of the message, the user would begin again with column 1. Jefferson experimentally encrypted a passage that was 27 letters long, "the man whose mind on virtue bent," to get the result "ujh qft epxbp yvas dd maknpa zcmu." He followed that exercise with a brief set of directions.

He revised the instructions to incorporate the usage of a key word, a device that was, like the form of the cipher itself, well established (Kahn, *Codebreakers*, 148). Now instead of finding the numbered column to match the letter's position in the message, he decided on a key word—"artichoke"—and aligned the letters of the message to be encoded with the letters of the key, repeating the key word as many times as necessary to complete the message. Going then to the cipher table, he found each letter of the message in the left-hand column as before, located the corresponding letter of the key word along the bottom row of the table, and at the intersection of the appropriate row and column found the letter needed for the encryption. As a demonstration, he aligned the first two words of his test passage ("the man") with the first six letters of "artichoke," then from the table found the encryption "u z y v d v." To try the method with a longer passage, which would require repetition of the key word, he experimented at the foot of Document I with the imagined message from Lewis: "I am at the head of the Missouri. all well, and the Indians so far, friendly." Lewis echoed that demonstration passage when, on his arrival at Pittsburgh on 15 July, he cheerfully wrote the president to announce—not in cipher—"so far and *all is well*."

For the fair copy of the cipher, Jefferson, now assuming that a key word would always be employed, did not number the columns (Document II). Instead he added an alphabetical row at the top of the table, to be used to find the letters of the key word. With "antipodes" as his key this time, he enciphered the phrase he had used in the draft ("the man whose mind ..."). He also added a new feature, digits alongside the first ten rows of the chart. This element allowed the user to code numerals. To encipher "18," as shown by an example he gave in the document, one would align the two digits with the first two letters of the key word—*a* and *n* in the case of "antipodes"—and then find the intersections of the numeral 1 row with the "a" column and the numeral 8 row with the "n" column. The result was the letters *b* and *v*, which—as Jefferson demonstrated but did not explain—should be underlined to indicate that they stood for numbers, not letters of the alphabet.

In his instructions for the cipher, Jefferson did not discuss his criteria for the selection of key words. "Artichoke" and "antipodes," however, are each nine letters long and no letter appears more than once in either word. Employing either word as the key therefore utilizes nine columns of the cipher table, whereas a word such as "attention," also nine letters long, would use only six columns. Making "artichoke" plural, as he did in the endorsement to Document II, expands to ten the number of columns put into service. Ease of recollection may be one reason he chose to experiment with key words beginning with the letter *a*, or perhaps he consulted an alphabetically ordered word list, such as Samuel Johnson's *Dictionary of the English Language*, and early in his quest found words that met his criteria.

The distinctive phrase that Jefferson enciphered as a practice exercise in each document—"the man whose mind on virtue bent"—was the first line of an interpretation by the poet Thomas Blacklock of an ode by Horace. Although Jefferson was probably not familiar with Blacklock's poetry, he knew very well the work in which the ode first appeared: David Hume's history of Britain. In a volume first published in 1757, Hume recounted the story of Cornelis de Witt of the Netherlands, who in 1672 was falsely accused of plotting against the stadtholder and, under torture, maintained his innocence by repeatedly reciting the ode in Latin. In a footnote, Hume, who at the time was Blacklock's friend and benefactor, included an English translation that he had solicited from the poet. Blacklock's three verses begin:

"The man, whose mind on virtue bent,
Pursues some greatly good intent,
With undiverted aim,
Serene, beholds the angry crowd;
Nor can their clamors, fierce and loud,
His stubborn honor tame."

The verse was quoted a few times (including praise by Oliver Goldsmith) but was likely not very widely known. Jefferson had long acquaintance with Hume's *History*, though, purchasing his first set of the volumes in 1764. Although he came to denounce Hume as an "Apologist" of first the Stuarts, and then of their many predecessors on the English throne going back to Saxon and Norman times, he acknowledged the powerful "charms of stile" that made the philosopher's prose dangerously beguiling to unsuspecting readers. Jefferson had once been vulnerable himself: "I remember well the enthusiasm with which I devoured it when young," he recalled of the *History* in 1810. Perhaps he found the ode's opening line to be a practical exercise for his cipher in 1803 because it uses 15 different letters, more than half the alphabet. It is 27 letters in length, which conveniently required him to utilize every column of the table in his first practice and to begin again with column 1. But what really led him to choose that passage, rather than some other phrase that could serve the purpose, is not known. About a year earlier, he used the Lord's Prayer and an address from the first Continental Congress as exercises using the cipher invented by Robert Patterson (David Hume, *The History of Great Britain. Vol. II. Containing the Commonwealth, and the Reigns of Charles II. and James II.* [London, 1757], 224-5; Hume, *The History of Great Britain. Vol. II*, 2d ed. [London, 1759], 224; Ernest Campbell Mossner, *The Forgotten Hume: Le bon David* [New York, 1943], 18-37; DNB; H. Trevor Colbourn, *The Lamp of Experience: Whig History and the Intellectual Origins of the American Revolution* [Chapel Hill, 1965], 158-9, 177-81, 217; John M. Werner, "David Hume and America," *Journal of the History of Ideas*, 33 [1972], 454-6; *London Magazine*, 40 [1771], 538; *The Miscellaneous Works of Oliver Goldsmith, M.B. A New Edition*, 4 vols. [London, 1801], 4:406-7; Maarten Prak, *The Dutch Republic in the Seventeenth Century: The Golden Age*, trans. Diane Webb [Cambridge, 2005], 53; LCB, 167-9; Sowerby, No. 370; RS, 3:5; Vol. 37:275-81).

If Lewis ever implemented the cipher, no documents in which he did so have been found. Jefferson may have expected him to encrypt communications only in the event of extraordinary circumstances. The contingency foreseen in the instructions, that Lewis might recruit Native Americans as couriers to take dispatches to Cahokia or Kaskaskia, did not arise. The last documents that Lewis and William Clark sent from Fort Mandan in April 1805, before they continued up the Missouri River, they left in plain text and put in the care of the crew that returned downriver to St. Louis in the expedition's keelboat. Lewis did not write to the president again until September 1806, after he reached St. Louis on his return journey (Jackson, *Lewis and Clark*, 1:231-42, 317-25).

I. Draft Cipher Table

[April 1803?]

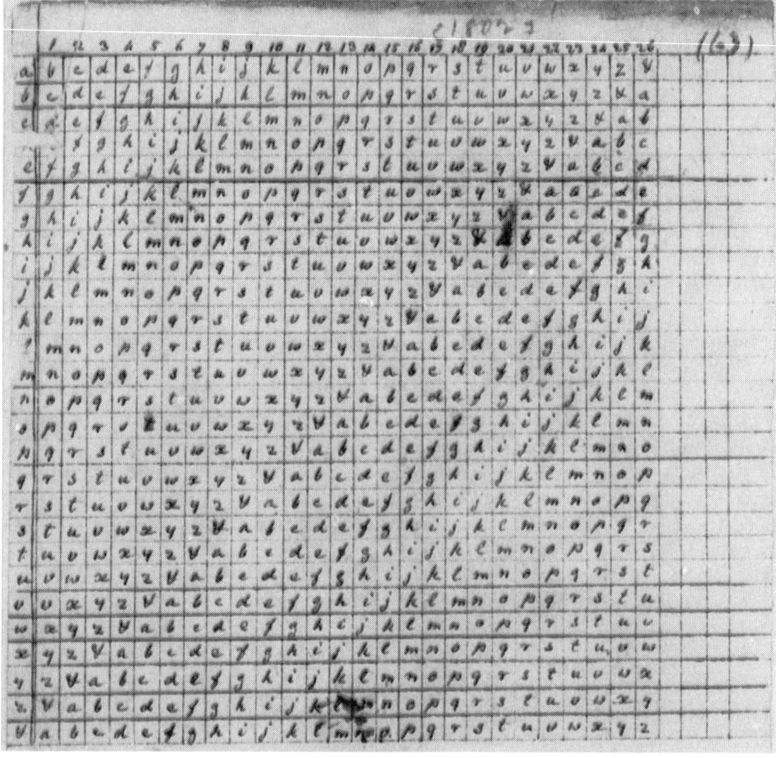

	1	2	3	4	5	6	7	8	9	10	11	12	13	14	15	16	17	18	19	20	21	22	23	24	25	26
a	b	c	d	e	f	g	h	i	j	k	l	m	n	o	p	q	r	s	t	u	v	w	x	y	z	&
b	c	d	e	f	g	h	i	j	k	l	m	n	o	p	q	r	s	t	u	v	w	x	y	z	&	a
c	d	e	f	g	h	i	j	k	l	m	n	o	p	q	r	s	t	u	v	w	x	y	z	&	a	b
		f	g	h	i	j	k	l	m	n	o	p	q	r	s	t	u	v	w	x	y	z	&	a	b	c
e	f	g	h	i	j	k	l	m	n	o	p	q	r	s	t	u	v	w	x	y	z	&	a	b	c	d
f	g	h	i	j	k	l	m	n	o	p	q	r	s	t	u	v	w	x	y	z	&	a	b	c	d	e
g	h	i	j	k	l	m	n	o	p	q	r	s	t	u	v	w	x	y	z	&	a	b	c	d	e	f
h	i	j	k	l	m	n	o	p	q	r	s	t	u	v	w	x	y	z	&	a	b	c	d	e	f	g
i	j	k	l	m	n	o	p	q	r	s	t	u	v	w	x	y	z	&	a	b	c	d	e	f	g	h
j	k	l	m	n	o	p	q	r	s	t	u	v	w	x	y	z	&	a	b	c	d	e	f	g	h	i
k	l	m	n	o	p	q	r	s	t	u	v	w	x	y	z	&	a	b	c	d	e	f	g	h	i	j
l	m	n	o	p	q	r	s	t	u	v	w	x	y	z	&	a	b	c	d	e	f	g	h	i	j	k
m	n	o	p	q	r	s	t	u	v	w	x	y	z	&	a	b	c	d	e	f	g	h	i	j	k	l
n	o	p	q	r	s	t	u	v	w	x	y	z	&	a	b	c	d	e	f	g	h	i	j	k	l	m
o	p	q	r	s	t	u	v	w	x	y	z	&	a	b	c	d	e	f	g	h	i	j	k	l	m	n
p	q	r	s	t	u	v	w	x	y	z	&	a	b	c	d	e	f	g	h	i	j	k	l	m	n	o
q	r	s	t	u	v	w	x	y	z	&	a	b	c	d	e	f	g	h	i	j	k	l	m	n	o	p
r	s	t	u	v	w	x	y	z	&	a	b	c	d	e	f	g	h	i	j	k	l	m	n	o	p	q
s	t	u	v	w	x	y	z	&	a	b	c	d	e	f	g	h	i	j	k	l	m	n	o	p	q	r
t	u	v	w	x	y	z	&	a	b	c	d	e	f	g	h	i	j	k	l	m	n	o	p	q	r	s
u	v	w	x	y	z	&	a	b	c	d	e	f	g	h	i	j	k	l	m	n	o	p	q	r	s	t
v	w	x	y	z	&	a	b	c	d	e	f	g	h	i	j	k	l	m	n	o	p	q	r	s	t	u
w	x	y	z	&	a	b	c	d	e	f	g	h	i	j	k	l	m	n	o	p	q	r	s	t	u	v
x	y	z	&	a	b	c	d	e	f	g	h	i	j	k	l	m	n	o	p	q	r	s	t	u	v	w
y	z	&	a	b	c	d	e	f	g	h	i	j	k	l	m	n	o	p	q	r	s	t	u	v	w	x
z	&	a	b	c	d	e	f	g	h	i	j	k	l	m	n	o	p	q	r	s	t	u	v	w	x	y
&	a	b	c	d	e	f	g	h	i	j	k	l	m	n	o	p	q	r	s	t	u	v	w	x	y	z

The	man	whose	mind	on	virtue	bent
ujh	qft	epxbp	yvas	dd	maknpa	zcmu

the equivalent of the 1st. lre is taken from the 1st. col.
of the 2d from the 2d
of the 3d from the 3d.
and so on to the 26th. and then begin again with the 1st. 2d. &c.

---

or instead of using them in the regular numerical order, have a key word, suppose 'artichoke' and finding the letter to be cyphered [t], in the 1st. vertical column, seek it's equivalent in the column <*under*> over *a*[1] in the last horizontal line &c so on as follows

t in the 1st. vertical over	a in the last horizontal, which is	u
h	r	z
e	t	y
m	i	v
a	c	d
n	h	v

I a m a t t h e h e a d o f t h e M i s s o u r i.
a r t i c h o k e a r t i c h o k e a r t i c h
j s f j w a w p m f s x x i a w p r j j l x x z

a l l w e l l, a n d t h e I n d i a n s s o f a r, f r i e n d l y
o k e a r t i c h o k e a r t i c h o k e a r t i c h o k e a r t
p w q x w e u d v s d m f & g m l i b e x p x u & i z x p s e e r

then copy fair thus.
jsfjwawpmfsxxiawprjjlxxzpwqxweudvsdmf&gmlibexpxu&izxpseer

MS (DLC: TJ Papers, 128:22136); undated; entirely in TJ's hand, including brackets.

THEN COPY FAIR THUS: eliminating the spaces between the words of the encoded message made it more difficult for someone to break the cipher (Kahn, *Codebreakers*, 149-50). When TJ matched the text of his demonstration message to his key word "artichoke," he overlooked the final letter of the word "Missouri." Correcting the mistake would have required redoing one step, and perhaps both steps, of the encryption process for more than half the message. Instead, he omitted that letter from his encipherment.

[1] TJ here canceled "to wit *t* the next letter *h* under the 17th. vertical column *r* (it is y) the next *e* under *t* (it is *x*) the next *m* under *i* (it is *u*) the next *a* under *c* (it is *e*) the next *n* under *h* (it is *v*) &c," followed on a new line by "the man," canceled, and "in the bottom line viz u," also canceled.

II. Cipher Table

[April 1803?]

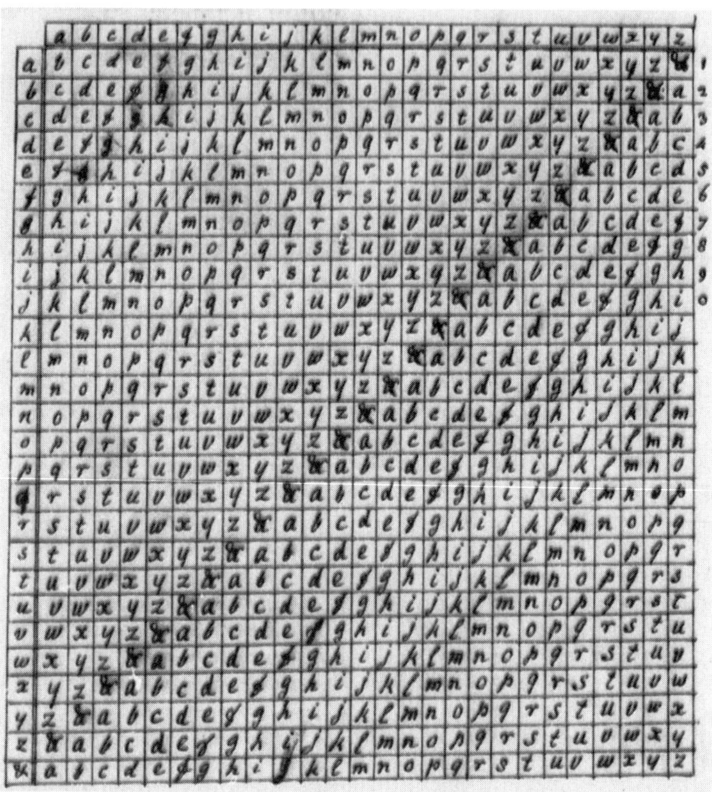

	a	b	c	d	e	f	g	h	i	j	k	l	m	n	o	p	q	r	s	t	u	v	w	x	y	z	
a	b	c	d	e	f	g	h	i	j	k	l	m	n	o	p	q	r	s	t	u	v	w	x	y	z	&	1
b	c	d	e	f	g	h	i	j	k	l	m	n	o	p	q	r	s	t	u	v	w	x	y	z	&	a	2
c	d	e	f	g	h	i	j	k	l	m	n	o	p	q	r	s	t	u	v	w	x	y	z	&	a	b	3
d	e	f	g	h	i	j	k	l	m	n	o	p	q	r	s	t	u	v	w	x	y	z	&	a	b	c	4
e	f	g	h	i	j	k	l	m	n	o	p	q	r	s	t	u	v	w	x	y	z	&	a	b	c	d	5
f	g	h	i	j	k	l	m	n	o	p	q	r	s	t	u	v	w	x	y	z	&	a	b	c	d	e	6
g	h	i	j	k	l	m	n	o	p	q	r	s	t	u	v	w	x	y	z	&	a	b	c	d	e	f	7
h	i	j	k	l	m	n	o	p	q	r	s	t	u	v	w	x	y	z	&	a	b	c	d	e	f	g	8
i	j	k	l	m	n	o	p	q	r	s	t	u	v	w	x	y	z	&	a	b	c	d	e	f	g	h	9
j	k	l	m	n	o	p	q	r	s	t	u	v	w	x	y	z	&	a	b	c	d	e	f	g	h	i	0
k	l	m	n	o	p	q	r	s	t	u	v	w	x	y	z	&	a	b	c	d	e	f	g	h	i	j	
l	m	n	o	p	q	r	s	t	u	v	w	x	y	z	&	a	b	c	d	e	f	g	h	i	j	k	
m	n	o	p	q	r	s	t	u	v	w	x	y	z	&	a	b	c	d	e	f	g	h	i	j	k	l	
n	o	p	q	r	s	t	u	v	w	x	y	z	&	a	b	c	d	e	f	g	h	i	j	k	l	m	
o	p	q	r	s	t	u	v	w	x	y	z	&	a	b	c	d	e	f	g	h	i	j	k	l	m	n	
p	q	r	s	t	u	v	w	x	y	z	&	a	b	c	d	e	f	g	h	i	j	k	l	m	n	o	
q	r	s	t	u	v	w	x	y	z	&	a	b	c	d	e	f	g	h	i	j	k	l	m	n	o	p	
r	s	t	u	v	w	x	y	z	&	a	b	c	d	e	f	g	h	i	j	k	l	m	n	o	p	q	
s	t	u	v	w	x	y	z	&	a	b	c	d	e	f	g	h	i	j	k	l	m	n	o	p	q	r	
t	u	v	w	x	y	z	&	a	b	c	d	e	f	g	h	i	j	k	l	m	n	o	p	q	r	s	
u	v	w	x	y	z	&	a	b	c	d	e	f	g	h	i	j	k	l	m	n	o	p	q	r	s	t	
v	w	x	y	z	&	a	b	c	d	e	f	g	h	i	j	k	l	m	n	o	p	q	r	s	t	u	
w	x	y	z	&	a	b	c	d	e	f	g	h	i	j	k	l	m	n	o	p	q	r	s	t	u	v	
x	y	z	&	a	b	c	d	e	f	g	h	i	j	k	l	m	n	o	p	q	r	s	t	u	v	w	
y	z	&	a	b	c	d	e	f	g	h	i	j	k	l	m	n	o	p	q	r	s	t	u	v	w	x	
z	&	a	b	c	d	e	f	g	h	i	j	k	l	m	n	o	p	q	r	s	t	u	v	w	x	y	
&	a	b	c	d	e	f	g	h	i	j	k	l	m	n	o	p	q	r	s	t	u	v	w	x	y	z	

suppose the key word to be 'antipodes'

write it thus. a n t i p o d e s a n t i p o d e s a n t i p o d e s
to be cyphered t h e m a n w h o s e m i n d o n v i r t u e b e n t
u v y v q b & m g t s f r c s s s n j e m c u q i t m

then copy out the cyphered line thus. uvyvqb&mgtsfrcsssnjemcuqitm

---

numbers are thus. 18. is b v. 1798 is thus b u b q

---

the method is this.

look for t. in the 1st. vertical column, & a in the 1st horizontal one. gives u

h	n	v
e	t	y
m	i	v
a	p	q
n	o	b

MS (DLC: TJ Papers, 131:22608); undated; entirely in TJ's hand; endorsed by him: "Cypher establd. with Captain Lewis" and "key. Artichokes."

COPY OUT THE CYPHERED LINE THUS: the final letters of the encipherment should be *s* and *l* rather than *t* and *m*.

From Isaac Briggs

MY DEAR FRIEND, Philadelphia, 2nd. of the 5th. Mo. 1803

Thy letter, dated 20th. of April, I received yesterday. I have had several applications for employment under me, to which my standing answer has been, that I shall make no appointments until I arrive at the scene of operation, and that those who wish a clerkship or deputyship must make their application to me there, where evidence of their suitableness, in all respects, will be my standard and only rule of preference.

Perhaps, if John Dinsmore have this hint it may answer his purpose. I should be glad to see Gideon Fitz there, no recommendation, in addition to what I have heard and seen, will be necessary for him. Poor Claiborne, I wish he could go there! he told me that the loan of $100 would be sufficient; but he appears to have a spirit too independent to solicit much, and I am at present not able to help him.

I have procured a clock for thee with a neat black walnut case: the whole including box and packing will be about $70. Benjamin Ferris, No. 17 North Second Street, Philadelphia, will transmit it according to thy order, immediately on his receiving it.

Henry Voight is engaged in making for me a portable transit—I hope in the course of ten days it will be finished, as this alone detains me. I have made an application to Andrew Ellicott for his Transit, but he absolutely refuses to sell it.

I have drawn up a proposition, in writing, to the American Philosophical Society to consent to the removal of their Observatory Transit to the City of Washington to be used under thy direction.

Accept assurances of my esteem and gratitude,

ISAAC BRIGGS.

RC (DLC); at foot of text: "Thomas Jefferson Pr. U.S."; endorsed by TJ as received 4 May and so recorded in SJL.

Richard CLAIBORNE previously sought an appointment in the Mississippi Territory and had asked Meriwether Lewis to bring his request to the attention of the president (Claiborne to Lewis, 9 Jan. 1803, RC in DNA: RG 59, LAR; endorsed by TJ: "Claiborne Richd. office. Missipi.").

For the CLOCK TJ acquired from BENJAMIN FERRIS, see TJ to Ferris, 8 June 1803 and Ferris to TJ, 20 June 1803.

At the 6 May 1803 meeting of the AMERICAN PHILOSOPHICAL SOCIETY, Briggs asked that the society "consent to the removal of the Transit Instrument to the city of Washington." The request was referred to a committee consisting of Robert Patterson, Jonathan Bayard Smith, and John Vaughan. Reporting on 17 June, the committee explained that the society "have only the use of a Transit Instrument, but possess no property therein" (APS, *Proceedings*, 22, pt. 3 [1884], 337-8).

From Henry Dearborn

SIR, War Department May 2d. 1803

I have the honor to propose Docr. R. Chew for Surgeons Mate, and Wm. P. Graham for second Lieut. of the Corps of Artillerists in the service of the United States.

I have the honor to be &c.

FC (Lb in DNA: RG 107, LSP).

Richard CHEW was among the military nominations TJ sent to the Senate in his message of 18 Nov. 1803. William P. GRAHAM resigned his commission in October 1803 (Heitman, *Dictionary*, 1:298, 469).

From Nicolas Gouin Dufief

MONSIEUR, Philadelphie ce 2 de Mai—1803

Vous trouverez ci-inclus l'ouvrage de Pascal; j'espère pouvoir vous procurer aussi celui du Dr. Priestley. Après avoir tenté plusieurs moyens infructueux, à Philadelphie & à N. York, je viens de m'aviser du seul qui me reste peut-être pour réussir, & dans quelques Jours je saurai s'il faut y renoncer pour le présent—Je me rappelle que vous désiriez, l'année passée, d'avoir les divers ouvrages de Cuvier. J'ai dans ce moment son *Tableau élémentaire de l'Histoire naturelle des animaux*, gros vol relié 8vo de 700 pages, avec planches—prix 2-50—Il vous sera adressé aussitôt, s'il vous convient—

Je vous Salue avec le profond respect qui vous est dû

N. G. DUFIEF

P.S. à ajouter au Mémoire Transmis il y a quelque tems	
Lettres de Pascal—2. vol. petit format	2 .25
(ouvrage omis)	
Les petits Moralistes—3 vol Do.	1 .25
	3 .50

EDITORS' TRANSLATION

SIR, Philadelphia, 2 May 1803

Enclosed you will find the Pascal book. I hope I can also procure Dr. Priestley's. After several unsuccessful attempts in Philadelphia and New York, I have just thought of the only other promising possibility. In a few days I will know whether or not we have to give up hope on that project for now.

I remember that last year you sought to acquire various works by Cuvier. I now have his *Tableau élémentaire de l'Histoire naturelle des animaux*. It is a large, bound 700-page octavo volume with illustrations. The price is 2.50. If this suits you, it can be sent immediately.

I greet you with the profound respect you deserve. N. G. DUFIEF

P.S. Addition to the previous bill	
Pascal's *Letters*, 2 volumes, small format	2 .25
(omitted from the mailing)	
Les Petits Moralistes, 3 volumes ditto	1 .25
	3 .50

RC (DLC); at foot of text: "Le President des Etats-Unis"; endorsed by TJ as received 4 May and so recorded in SJL.

In March 1802, TJ asked Dufief to acquire several titles from France, including the *Leçons d'Anatomie Comparée* of Georges CUVIER. TJ also expressed a wish to have any other works by Cuvier "in the anatomical line" (Vol. 37:114, 115n). Cuvier's TABLEAU ÉLÉMENTAIRE DE L'HISTOIRE NATURELLE DES ANIMAUX was published in Paris in 1798 (Sowerby, No. 1020).

LETTRES DE PASCAL: that is, the *Pensées*; see TJ to Dufief, 5 May.

MORALISTES: included in TJ's request of March 1802 were volumes of the *Collection des moralistes anciens* of Pierre Charles Lévesque; see Vol. 37:113, 114n; Dufief to TJ, 25 Jan. 1803; TJ to Dufief, 4 Feb.

From Robert R. Livingston

DEAR SIR Paris 2 May 1803

Having just heard of a vessel going from Havre I give you this hasty letter merely to inform you that it is now understood that war is inevitable & that within a few days. Yesterday I presented Mr. Monroe to the first consul at his levee where he publicly declared that the terms demanded by Britain were totally inadmissable. Lord Wetworth did not attend the Levee & this day has asked his pasports.

Mr. Monroe has been extreamly sick ever since the third day of his arrival, but within the last three days is so much recruted that he is able to go out. Our affairs you may consider as compleatly finished they are arranged & we shall probably sign tomorrow *New Orleans as it now is and as it was when France possessed it and Louisiana are ours and* subject to subsequent treaties upon my construction which I think we shall be able to support by the old french carts *the river perdigo is our Eastern boundary we* have mentioned that this is the construction we put on it so that there will be no deception should we claim it in treating with Spain—You will have a large sum to pay *Eleven millions* two hundred & fifty thousand dollars besides what is due to our own citizens which, principal & interest, under the restrictions to which we have confined it can not exceed four millions but except for what you pay them you will only create a 6 pr Ct Stock redeemable after fifteen years by instalments. Our creditors will be fully rectified & I trust the acquisition we have made will be satisfactory to our country tho in obtaining it we have exceeded our powers. this is the point to which my unwearied labours have tended ever since I have been here because I forsaw that anything short of this would be insufficient to save us at some future day from rivalry & that the fine country above the Akransa in the hands of England or france with the favorable terms they might hold out to settlers could not fail to depopulate our western territory—It is now in your power to open or shut the door & at all events Bet settlers will be citizens & not enemies. At my arrival I found strong prejudices against both our nation, & government, & the most exagerated opinion of the importance of Louisiana. I have been happy enough to change the sentiment with respect to both or rather as it regards the first we owe it to your wise & prudent measures & to the pictures your messages have drawn of the prosperity of our country. At present be assured that we stand here not only with this government, but with those of other nations as a very high and respectable friend, the spirited conduct of all parties on the subject of New Orleans has also had a good effect. Mr King writes me that he will go the middle of the month, having stayed at my request to see the turn things might take—We shall loose in him a very able minister & one particularly useful as he is a favorite of the King & much in the confidence of the present ministers. the difference of our political sentiments has not prevented a cordial cooperation in our measures where necessary.

I flatter myself that in the course of two days Mr Monroe & myself (who have happily agreed in every point) will be able to send the treaties & our joint letter to the secretary of State—as this may reach you earlier you may consider this information as sufficiently authentic to justify your calling together the senate. I am

Dear Sir with the most respectful consideration Your Most Obt hum: Servt R R LIVINGSTON

RC (DLC); at foot of text: "Thomas Jefferson Esqr president of the United States"; at head of text: "private"; portions in same code as Livingston used on 12 Mch., with interlinear decipherment by TJ (in italics); endorsed by TJ as received 13 July and so recorded in SJL. Enclosed in John Mitchell to TJ, 9 May.

WAR IS INEVITABLE: during April in a succession of meetings between Charles Whitworth, Talleyrand, and in some cases Joseph Bonaparte, the French and British governments failed to come to agreement over issues that included Britain's continuing occupation of Malta, French troops in Holland, the annexation of Piedmont by France, and French interference in the governance of Switzerland. On instructions from Lord Hawkesbury, Whitworth presented an ultimatum on 27 Apr. and declared that he would leave Paris on 2 May. A counterproposal from Talleyrand delayed Whitworth's departure, but there was no progress in negotiation and the British ambassador left Paris on the 12th. Britain commenced a naval war against France by an order in council of 16 May and made a formal declaration of war two days later. On the 20th, the first consul announced the war in a message to the *Sénat* (Grainger, *Amiens Truce*, 178-94; Michel Poniatowski, *Talleyrand et le Consulat* [Paris, 1986], 752-64; Thierry Lentz, *Le Grand Consulat, 1799-1804* [Paris, 1999], 468-9).

After Livingston presented MONROE to Bonaparte at the reception for the diplomatic corps at the Louvre palace on 1 May, Monroe and the FIRST CONSUL had a brief conversation in French in which Bonaparte said he was glad to see Monroe. They spoke again after dinner, when Bonaparte asked Monroe about TJ's age and family, the population and public buildings of Washington, and other subjects. Soon after his arrival in Paris, Monroe had met with Joseph Bonaparte, who said that he would continue to "promote our views with his brother" (Madison, *Papers, Sec. of State Ser.*, 4:613; Monroe, "Journal or note of proceedings relative to mission to France & negotiation," 27 Apr.-[May] 1803, in DLC: Monroe Papers).

At the LEVEE on 1 May, the first consul in comments to Russian and Prussian diplomats expressed his dissatisfaction with the terms presented by the British and declared that Britain underestimated France (Grainger, *Amiens Truce*, 188-9).

EXTREAMLY SICK: early in the negotiations over Louisiana, Monroe was suffering from a back injury that Fulwar Skipwith described as "as violent an attack of the Rumatism as I ever witnessed." Monroe later informed Madison that the malady, which was "very severe for 48. hours," did not impede the negotiations (Ammon, *Monroe*, 212; Madison, *Papers, Sec. of State Ser.*, 4:565n; 5:295).

NEW ORLEANS ... AND LOUISIANA ARE OURS: in the discussions continuing from mid-April, François Barbé de Marbois would not budge from the figure of 60 million francs plus assumption by the U.S. of claims against Frence by American citizens. Nor would the French consider selling only part of Louisiana for a reduced price. Barbé de Marbois pressed for full payment within a year, but Monroe and Livingston won agreement for the United States to give France shares of six percent stock for $11,250,000 (the equivalent of 60 million francs). Semiannual interest payments were to begin soon after the United States took possession of Louisiana, but no payment of principal would be due for 15 years. The United States would also pay up to 20 million francs (about $3,750,000) for the claims. The purchase agreement consisted of three instruments: a treaty for the cession of Louisiana to the United States, a convention for the payment to France, and another convention for the resolution of the debts. The pacts were officially dated 30 Apr., the day on which the parties agreed to the terms, although the papers were not signed until several days later (same, 4:525-6, 538-9, 601-4, 610; Miller,

Treaties, 2:498-505, 512-23; Alexander DeConde, *This Affair of Louisiana* [New York, 1976], 171-2).

OLD FRENCH CARTS: that is, *cartes* (maps). The treaty for the conveyance of Louisiana to the United States did not specify the boundaries of the colony but quoted the treaty of San Ildefonso, which said that Louisiana as Spain ceded it to France had the same limits as when France originally possessed it. Livingston argued that the colony's eastern boundary was at the Perdido (PERDIGO) River, which would put much of West Florida within the bounds of Louisiana (same, 169-71, 213-14; J. C. A. Stagg, *Borderlines in Borderlands: James Madison and the Spanish-American Frontier, 1776-1821* [New Haven, 2009], 39-41; Madison, *Papers*, *Sec. of State Ser.*, 4:329, 600; Miller, *Treaties*, 2:499).

Rufus KING had closed his household in London and shipped his effects by 8 Apr., but delayed his departure as relations between Britain and France deteriorated. He left London on 18 May and sailed for the U.S. on the 21st (King, *Life*, 4:243; Madison, *Papers*, *Sec. of State Ser.*, 5:113).

SEND THE TREATIES: Livingston and Monroe dispatched the treaty and conventions with a letter to Madison dated 13 May (same, 4:601; 5:5).

To Craven Peyton

DEAR SIR Washington May 2. 1803.

Your favor of Apr. 29. came to hand last night. having left at Monticello the plat of the partition of Henderson's land, I do not from memory recollect the position of John & Charles Henderson's 4. acres very accurately;[1] but think I recollect enough to say it is impossible for him to build a mill on them, and bring water to it without drawing his canal through lands not his, and which no court can give him authority to do. besides, if he is opposed, by an application for an order of court to build a mill, by the proprietor of the residue of the tract, it is impossible the rights of the general[2] proprietor should not prevail against him. surely the right of building a mill cannot belong to the owner of 4. acres rather than to the owner of the whole tract. on this ground, and in this way I think he should be opposed. and as it is impossible we should not obtain the right in preference to him, his 4. acres will then be reduced to be of no more value than so much of any other lands, & he may be bought out on reasonable terms. I would therefore wish you to employ mr Carr to petition for leave to build a mill on the scite which fell to me. it had still better be in your name. should they propose to avail themselves of the canal of the old mill, I will give orders for the immediate removal of every stone in the dam, so as to put an end to that expectation. otherwise I do not wish to disturb the dam till my own mill needs the water. I should be glad you could prevent mr Meriwether & mr Millar from getting themselves into a matter which will certainly be a losing one to them; and which I presume they would not meddle with if they were apprised that there is no chance of their using the water in the old dam, nor of drawing a canal through the lands above or below. I will thank you to keep me advised of what is done in this business. Accept my friendly salutations & respects. TH: JEFFERSON

RC (NHi: Gilder Lehrman Collection at the Gilder Lehrman Institute of American History); addressed: "Mr. Craven Peyton near Milton"; franked and postmarked. PrC (ViU); endorsed by TJ in ink on verso.

For the PLAT OF THE PARTITION of land originally owned by Bennett Henderson and detailed in the apportionment of 1 Oct. 1801, see Vol. 35:xlvi-viii, 382 (illus.). CHARLES HENDERSON's lot No. 1 in the upper field partition, which Peyton had previously purchased for TJ, consisted of $4\frac{1}{2}$ acres and was adjacent to Elizabeth Henderson's lands that contained the Henderson mill and dam. In the narrow strip of land below the town of Milton and between the Rivanna River that had been divided into two-acre partitions, Charles had drawn lot No. 8 and John lot No. 10, the latter of which abutted his mother's dower lands. John began building a 380-foot-long canal from the Rivanna to his mill seat, and claimed that his mother had granted him this permission in November 1801, ten months before the sale of her Albermarle County lands to Peyton. He suggested that nothing in his mother's contract of 18 Sep. 1802 could be construed as interfering with his right to run a canal to the present Henderson mill (Robert Haggard, "Thomas Jefferson v. The Heirs of Bennett Henderson, 1795–1818: A Case Study in Caveat Emptor," *Magazine of Albemarle County History*, 63 [2005], 9-11; Boynton Merrill, Jr., *Jefferson's Nephews: A Frontier Tragedy* [Princeton, 1976], 66-7; Vol. 38:578-9).

[1] Preceding two words interlined.
[2] Word interlined.

Abstracts of Warrants from Robert Smith

Navy Department
May 2d. 1803

Abstract of Warrants drawn on the Treasurer by the Secretary of the navy for navy purposes, shewing also the balance on hand for the week ending the 30th. day of april 1803—

Date	no.	In whose favor & for what purpose		amot. of Warrants	amot of Deposits & Balance
1803		Balance from last report			121,982.95
apl. 26	2120	Alexr. Kerr assignee of Keith Spence—	Pay &c. m.c.	145 00	
"	2121/1119	E & A. Winchester Boston m.c.		507 23	
"	2122/1120	Charles McLaughlin agt. for Saml. Houston	Pay &c navy	81 62	

27 2123/1121	Octavus A. Page	do	65 10	
" 2124	Henry Foxall—74 Gun Ships		2000 00	
" 2125/1122	William C Jenckes, Contingent		200 00	
" 2126/1123	William Duncanson, Pay &c.		9 30	
28 2127/1124	William Dyer	Marine Corps	314 25	
" 2128/1125	Michael Reynolds	do	396 71	
29 2129	Danl. Olcott. Hartford Cont. Provisions		2,200 00	
" 2130/1126	James Huie	Pay &c navy	50 71	
30 2131	Thomas Tingey	Pay &c	5,500 00	
" 2132/1127	John Steele	Repairs of Vessels	848 94	
" 2133/1128	George W. Spotswood. Pay &c		111 60	
	Balance on hand		109552.49	
	Drs.		121,982 95	121,982 95

Rt Smith

MS (DLC); in a clerk's hand, signed by Smith; endorsed by TJ as received from the Navy Department and "Apr. 30. 1803. Warrants."

JOHN STEELE was the master carpenter and surveyor at the Washington Navy Yard (ASP, *Claims*, 1:378; NDBW, 3:283).

Notes on the Consular Convention of 1788

1803. May 3.

Notes on the subject of the Consular convention between the US. & France.

In 1784. a convention was entered into between Dr. Franklin & the Count de Vergennes concerning Consuls. it contained many things absolutely inadmissible by the laws of the several states, & inconsistent with their genius & character. Dr. Franklin not being a lawyer, & the projet offered by the Ct. de Vergennes being a copy of the conventions which were established between France & the despotic states on the Continent (for with England they never had one) he seems to have supposed it a formula established by universal experience, & not to have suspected that it might contain matters inconsistent with the principles of a free people. he returned to America soon after the signature of it. Congress recieved it with the deepest concern. they honoured Dr. Franklin; they were attached to the French nation; but they could not relinquish fundamental principles. they declined ratifying it, & sent it back with new powers & instructions to mr Jefferson who had succeeded Dr. Franklin at Paris. the most objectionable matters were the privileges & exemptions given to the Consuls, & their powers over persons of their nation, establishing a jurisdiction independent of that of the nation in which it was exercised, & uncontrouleable by it. the French government valued these, because they then apprehended a very extensive emigration from France to the US. which this convention enabled them to controul. it was therefore with the utmost reluctance, & inch by inch, that they could be induced to relinquish these conditions. the following changes however were effected by the Convention of 1788.

The clauses of the convention of 1784. cloathing Consuls with the privileges of the laws of Nations were struck out, & they were expressly subjected, in their persons and property, to the laws of the land.

The giving the right of Sanctuary to their houses, was reduced to a protection of their chancery room & it's papers.

Their coercive powers over passengers were taken away; and over those whom they might have termed deserters of their nation were restrained to deserted seamen only.

The clause allowing them to arrest & send back vessels was struck out, & instead of it they were allowed to exercise a police over the ships of their nation generally.

So was that which declared the indelibility of the character of subject, and the explanation & extension of the 11th. article of the treaty of Amity.

The innovations in the laws of evidence were done away.

And the Convention, from being perpetual, was limited to 12. years.

Altho' strong endeavors were used to do away some other disagreeable articles, yet it was found that more could not be done without disturbing the good humour which Congress wished so much to preserve, and the limitation obtained for the continuance of the Convention ensured our getting finally rid of the whole. Congress therefore satisfied with having so far amended their situation, ratified the Convention of 1788. without hesitation.

PrC (DLC); dated in ink; at foot of first page in ink: "Wingate Mr." Recorded in SJL as a communication to "Wingate mr."

The CONSULAR CONVENTION of 1788 had become an issue during the April elections in Massachusetts. Opponents of Jonathan Mason, a Federalist candidate for a seat in the state senate, accused him of having harmed American interests when, as a U.S. senator in February 1801, he voted with the majority to remove the second article of the Convention of 1800 before ratifying that document. The second article provided for negotiations to settle Americans' claims against France, but also anticipated talks about restoring the 1778 treaty of alliance, the treaty of amity and commerce of that year, and the 1788 consular convention. The *Palladium* of Boston defended the abrogation of the treaty of alliance and the consular convention, declaring that the latter was TJ's creation "in a moment of blind confidence and ardent fondness for *France*." The "unparalleled" consular convention, the newspapers's editors contended, "provided for a French Judiciary in every State, independent of the authority of our Government or Courts. The pretensions of the French Consuls, and the embarrassment they created, are well remembered" (*New-England Palladium*, 29 Mch., 1 Apr.; Miller, *Treaties*, 2:458-9; Vol. 33:22n). TJ may have prepared these notes about the creation of the consular convention for Joshua Wingate, Jr., the chief clerk of the War Department, who was Henry Dearborn's son-in-law. In correspondence with TJ, Dearborn referred to his daughter as Mrs. Wingate, and Joshua Wingate was the person TJ was most likely to refer to as simply Mr. Wingate, with no first name, as he did in recording this document. Wingate, the son of a prominent resident of Hallowell, Maine, and the grandson of former New Hampshire congressman Paine Wingate, later entered politics in Maine (William H. Smith, "Gen. Henry Dearborn: A Genealogical Sketch," *Maine Historical and Genealogical Recorder*, 3 [1886], 6-7; Vol. 36:200n; Vol. 38:296-7n; Dearborn to TJ, 28 Aug. 1803, two letters; Thomas Paine to TJ, 25 Jan. 1805).

When John Jay, as secretary for foreign affairs, asked TJ in 1786 to negotiate a revision of the 1784 consular convention that Congress had DECLINED to ratify, TJ first requested new INSTRUCTIONS, which Jay sent in July 1787. After completing the negotiations in November 1788, TJ sent Jay the new convention along with printed copies of a side-by-side comparison of its articles with those of the rejected 1784 convention (Vol. 10: 430-1; Vol. 11:31, 627-9; Vol. 14:xxxiv, 56-8, 66-92, 121-6, 178n).

CHANGES HOWEVER WERE EFFECTED: the earlier convention would have given consular officials "a full and entire immunity for their person, their papers and their houses." The 1788 convention gave immunity only to "their chancery and the papers which shall be therein contained." The new agreement also had a clause making consuls subject to THE LAWS OF THE LAND "as the natives are," a provision not found in the earlier instrument. Under the convention of 1784, consuls would have had the power to arrest passengers as well as DESERTED SEAMEN and to sequester or send back VESSELS. The 1788 convention allowed for the arrest of deserters, but not of passengers, and had no provision for the seizure or sending back of ships (JCC, 31:727, 732; Miller, *Treaties*, 2:230, 237).

INDELIBILITY OF THE CHARACTER OF SUBJECT: an article of the unratified convention declared that persons of either nation "shall not lose, for any cause whatever, in the respective domains and states, the quality of subjects of the country of which they originally were, conformably to the eleventh article of the treaty of amity and commerce" of 1778. That article of the treaty, which concerned the status of individuals living in the other country's jurisdiction, stated that nothing in the treaty would alter "the laws made or that may be made hereafter in France against Emigrations, which shall remain in all their Force and Vigour" (JCC, 31: 734-5; Miller, *Treaties*, 2:11-12).

INNOVATIONS IN THE LAWS OF EVIDENCE: under the unratified convention, if a consul wanted deserters seized, "no tribunals, judges and officers whatsoever, shall in any manner whatever take cognizance of the complaints which the said sailors and deserters may make." To get custody of deserters under the 1788 convention, consuls must "address themselves to the courts, judges, and officers competent, and shall demand the said deserters in writing, proving by an exhibition of the registers of the vessel or ship's roll that those men were part of the said crews" (JCC, 31:732-3; Miller, *Treaties*, 2:237-8).

The 1788 convention was to be in force for 12 YEARS from the exchange of ratifications. The 1784 convention contained no limitation on its term. The Senate ratified the new convention in July 1789 (same, 241, 242; JCC, 31:735).

From Justus Erich Bollmann

SIR Philada. May 4th. 1803

I have duely received Your Excellency's Letter of the 30th. of April. I have read it with sincere Emotions of Gratitude and the Impression it has made upon me will be the more permanent since this Proof of Your kind Disposition towards me is the first Circumstance which seems to interrupt a long Chain of adverse Occurrences.

There are many Reasons why a Change of Scene would be agreable to me and if I were alone I would accept of Your Excellency's obliging Offer without a moment's Hesitation. But I have Two little Girls, the One Two and a Half the other One Year old, who engross all my Affections, and from whom I feel myself the more insepirable since They are the dear Representatives of a Woman of great Qualities, with whom, after a long and mutual Contention with many Difficulties, I lived a Life of exquisite Happiness, and whom I lost a Twelve Months ago in Consequence of a puerperul Fever, unknown and neglected by Her Physicians for a considerable Time. Besides, I have become so totally destitute of means by an inevitable Surrender of all my Property that I hardly know I could face the previous Expences attending the offered Situation. My Share in the manufacturing Concern, which I have created here with Mr. Latrobe's assistance, and which promisses fair to become of considerable Importance will be sold shortly. If I can succeed to get it purchased by a Friend who will agree to let the Management of it, for an adequate Consideration, remain in my Hands I think I ought to stay here. Should I fail in this, as I very possibly may, it would then become an Object to make the Respectability of the Situation You offer me a means of future Employment and Success. I could therefore wish that this Prospect were to remain open to me for Two or Three Weeks if it can be left so without Inconvenience.

I beg Your Excellency to excuse my having entered into some Details respecting myself and to consider the Candour of my Reply as a

Proof that I feel myself highly honoured with the received Mark of Your Confidence.

I remain with great Respect Your Excellency's most obt. St.

J. Erich Bollmann

RC (DLC); at foot of text: "The President of the United States"; endorsed by TJ as received 6 May and "Consulship Rotterdam" and so recorded in SJL.

From DeWitt Clinton

Dear Sir New York 4 May 1803

I have great satisfaction in informing you that the late election in this State has been attended with unexampled success. Out of ten Senators, the federalists in all probability will not have one and out of one hundred representatives, their numbers will not exceed fifteen. The relative strength of parties will stand thus.—

	Repub:	Fed:
In the Senate	26	6
In the Assembly	85	15

We have not as yet *all* the official returns, but from the best information, the foregoing estimate may be relied on. Federalism as it is termed was of course never at a lower ebb: This proud ascendency we shall maintain at the next election in defiance of every obstacle. We have labored under many difficulties in this City[1] arising from a variety of sources which it will be in our power in a great measure to control before the next election—our majority will undoubtedly be encreased by that time. The mal-contents generally speaking did all they could to injure us—Their number does not exceed one hundred and their influence is perfectly trifling. Our Legislature embraces more ability and weight than the last and I have no doubt but that such wise measures will be pursued by them, as will confine federalism to two or three Counties, composed of persons[2] on the estate of Mr Van Rensselaer and emigrants from the Eastward deluded by their lawyers and Clergy.

If the arrangement you allude to in your letter respecting the custom house here could take place soon, it would much enhance the favor in the estimation of the person receiving it.

We are agitated with a report of an European War which comes via Boston.

With much respect I am Yours most Sincerely

DeWitt Clinton

RC (DLC); at foot of text: "The President of the U.S."; endorsed by TJ as received 6 May and so recorded in SJL.

TJ received another description of the LATE ELECTION in New York. On 30 Apr., Gallatin sent the president an extract of the letter he had just received from James Nicholson, his father-in-law, dated 28 Apr. Nicholson reported: "This is the last day of holding the election. By the report of the general committee last evening, the republican ticket was upwards of 700 votes ahead: you know that those calculations though not certain are made in such manner that they have not heretofore in any one instance greatly erred. The other party had great confidence in our divisions proceeding from Col. Burr's friends leaving us; this has no doubt injured us, but very short of what the other party expected. The heads of both parties are extremely active, none more than Hamilton. It is generally expected that this evening at the close of the polls we will have a majority of one thousand votes" (Tr in DLC; in Gallatin's hand; undated; at head of text: "Extract of a letter from Mr Nicholson to A. Gallatin dated New York 28th April"; endorsed by TJ as received from Gallatin on 30 Apr. and so recorded in SJL). For the campaign in New York City, see also Clinton to TJ, 12 Apr.

MAL-CONTENTS: that is, the Burrites.

Stephen VAN RENSSELAER, the eighth patroon of the Manor of Rensselaerwyck, a vast estate in Rensselaer and Albany counties, received rents and tithes perpetually from his tenants under the Dutch patroon system. In 1783, he married Margaret Schuyler, younger sister of Alexander Hamilton's wife, Elizabeth. In this election, Republicans for the first time swept Rensselaer County sending five members to the state assembly, but all six Federalist candidates won in Albany County. The final tally gave 17 assembly seats to the Federalists (ANB; Syrett, *Hamilton*, 26:467; *Albany Register*, 1 July 1803). For counties with EMIGRANTS FROM THE EASTWARD who elected Federalists, see Gideon Granger to TJ, 6 May.

YOUR LETTER: TJ to Clinton, 22 Apr.

PERSON RECEIVING IT: Samuel Osgood (same).

On 4 May, the New York *American Citizen* carried a report VIA BOSTON from a vessel that sailed from England on 26 Mch. "that WAR was just declared between England and France, and that there was no doubt of its truth."

[1] Preceding three words interlined.
[2] Preceding two words interlined.

From Henry Dearborn

SIR [4 May 1803]

please to accept my perticular thanks for the perusal you have afforded me of your remarks on religion,—as they will probably at some future day be laid before the public, permit me Sir, to suggest a small deviation from the mode of expression you have used in one sentance.—insted of saying the Committing to writing his life and doctrines fell on the most unlettered and ignorant of men, would it not be as well to say,—fell on men of but little litterary information. as you will not mistake my motive for suggesting the alteration, you will the more readily pardon the liberty I have taken.

with the most respectfull consederation I am Sir Your Huml. Servt.

H. DEARBORN

RC (DLC); undated; endorsed by TJ as a letter of 4 May received the same day and so recorded in SJL. Enclosure: TJ to Benjamin Rush, 21 Apr., and enclosure.

In one of the transcripts he made of his REMARKS ON RELIGION, TJ altered the phrase that worried Dearborn to read "fell on unlettered and ignorant men" (see enclosure to TJ to Benjamin Rush, 21 Apr.).

To Victor Marie du Pont

DEAR SIR Washington May 4. 1803.

Mr. Dupont your father informed me he should have occasion to remit considerable sums of money from France to the US. the small matter for which I have occasion cannot be proposed as a convenience to him, but to myself alone. I wish to place 400. Dollars in Paris for the purchase of some wine, and know not how to remit it there. if it be convenient for you to give me your draught on your father for the equivalent of that sum in money of France, I shall be obliged to you for it; and for that purpose now inclose you four bills of the U.S. bank of this place of one hundred dollars each. to wit Nos. 4000. 4045. 5818. 5864. should you know of any vessel bound to any port of France direct, I would thank you for the information, for the conveyance of my letters. Accept my friendly salutations & respect.

TH: JEFFERSON

RC (ViU); addressed: "Mr. Dupont at New York"; franked and postmarked; endorsed by du Pont. PrC (DLC); endorsed by TJ in ink on verso. Enclosures not found, but see below.

YOUR FATHER INFORMED ME: in a letter written in August 1802 and received by TJ in October, Pierre Samuel Du Pont de Nemours indicated that his bank in Paris could handle remittances from the United States made in the form of deposits to the firm his son managed in New York City (Vol. 38:227-9).

FOUR BILLS OF THE U.S. BANK: in his financial memoranda TJ recorded that he received $400 from John Barnes on 3 May and sent it to du Pont the next day to purchase a bill of exchange (MB, 2:1098).

To Fulwar Skipwith

DEAR SIR Washington May 4. 1803.

I am about to ask from you the execution of a troublesome commission, without being able to encourage it's undertaking by an assurance that it may not be repeated hereafter. the meanness of quality, as well as extravagance of price of the French wines which can be purchased in this country have determined me to seek them in the spot where they grow. when in France I visited all the remarkeable wine cantons, went into the vineyards & cellars of those whose crops were of the first quality, noted their names, quantities and prices, and after my return to Paris took my supplies regularly from the owner of the best vineyard, whose interest for the character of his wine ensured his fidelity as to quality & price. the wines of Champagne can be best got by the way of Paris, where the agency of a friend becomes necessary. this agency I take the liberty of solliciting from you. the following were the places, persons & quantities for Champagne of the first quality when I was there in 1788.

at Aij. Monsr. Dorsay made 1100. pieces, M. le Duc 400. M. de Villermont 300. M. Janson 250.

at Auvillaij the Benedictines made 1000. pieces, & l'Abbatiale 1100.

at Pierrij M. Casotte made 500. pieces, de la Motte 300. de Failli 300. Hoquart 200. les Seminaristes 150

at Verzis Verzennis, the property of the Marquis de Silleri, were made the wines called de Silleri.

of all these however the wines of Aij made in M. Dorsay's vineyard, were the best; and from him I always afterwards took my supplies. his homme d'affaires was then a Monsr. Louis, & I paid always from 3.^{tt} to 3^{tt}-10s the bottle for the best, & of the best years. I am told wines have considerably risen since that. M. Dorsay lived in Paris during winter, I believe on the Quai D'orsay. I think there is little reason to doubt that the culture of so great a property & of such established reputation has been kept up in perfection. but this presumption is submitted to the controul of your information & enquiry, my object being to get the best, & only from an old customer of preference, if his wines maintain their relative excellence. I would wish 400. bottles of the white champagne, non-mousseux, of the best year now on hand. for which purpose I shall inclose herein a bill of exchange for 400. Dollars, which not being yet recieved, shall be explained in a postscript. the package of the wine on the spot should be recommended to be made with great care, and some attention is requisite on their passage from Aij to Havre that they may not be exposed to a hot sun. at Havre be so good as to address them to mr Barnet our Consul, if there, & if not then to M. de la Motte, either of whom will take the charge off your hands at that place. it is essential that they should leave Havre by the middle of July, or they will not be here in time to save me from the necessity of buying here bad & dear. consequently there will be no time to lose after you recieve this letter. The wines of Burgundy would be very desireable, and there are three kinds of their red wines Chambertin, Voujeau & Veaune, and one of their whites, Monrachet which under favorable circumstances will bear transportation, but always with risk of being spoiled if exposed, on the way, to either great heat or cold, as I have known by experience since I returned to America. unless the Champagnes have risen in price more than I am informed, there may be something left of my bill which I should like to recieve in Chambertin & Monrachet in equal and ever so small[1] quantities, if you can take the trouble of getting it for me, merely as an experiment. if it succeeds I may ask a quantity the next year. it should leave it's cellars in Chambertin & Monrachet about the beginning of October and come through without delay at either Paris or Havre. there was living at Beaune near Chambertin & Monrachet, a tonnelier named Parent, who being a taster & bottler of wines by trade was my conductor thro' the vineyards and cellars of the Cote, & ever after my wine broker & correspondent. I inclose you the last letter I recieved from him, by which you will see that, if living, he will execute for me faithfully any order you may be so good as to send him. the only wines of 1st. quality made at Monrachet, were in the vineyards of M. de Clermont, and of the Marquis de Sarsnet of Dijon. I shall be happy to recieve a line of information as soon as the Champagne is under way. Epernay the center of the wine villages is but a day's journey from Paris.—we are just now learning from a message of the British king to parliament that war with France is probable. Accept my friendly salutations, & assurances of great esteem. TH: JEFFERSON

P.S. the bill inclosed is for 2100.tt from V. duPont de Nemours & co. on Messrs. duPont de Nemours pere et fils et co. Banqrs. rue de Montholon No. 300. dated May 7. 1803. at 60. days sight.

RC (H. W. Lende, Jr., San Antonio, Texas, 1988); at foot of first page: "Fulwar Skipwith esq."; endorsed. PrC (DLC); endorsed by TJ in ink on verso. Dupl (John G. Herndon, Haverford, Pennsylvania, 1944); endorsed. Recorded in SJL with notation "3.plicates by Dupont, Dufief, & Burrell. for Champagne & Burgundy." Enclosures: (1) Probably M. Parent to TJ, 24 July 1790, recorded in SJL as received 20 Nov. 1790 but not found. (2) Bill of exchange for Du Pont de Nemours, Père, Fils & Cie., Paris, 7 May 1803, for 2,100 francs payable at 60 days from sight (MS with H. W. Lende, Jr., San Antonio, Texas, 1988, being a printed form, with blanks filled by Victor Marie du Pont and signed by him, in French, noted as first; Quadruplicate in DLC). Enclosed in TJ to Victor Marie du Pont, 10 May. See also Nicolas Gouin Dufief to TJ, 15 May; Charles Burrall to TJ, 20 May.

PIECES: a commonly used term for measuring quantities of wine, brandy, and ale, particularly in France. During his tours of different wine producing regions of France, TJ had determined that a piece was equivalent to 200 to 250 bottles (OED; Vol. 11:417; Vol. 13:30).

TJ recorded in his financial memoranda on 9 May receiving from Victor DUPONT the bill of exchange "for the 400. D. sent him ante May 4. and inclosed by triplicates to Fulwar Skipwith in a letter written May 4. for wines" (MB, 2:1100).

[1]Preceding four words interlined.

Statement of Interest Account with John Barnes

Interest account between J. Barnes & Th: Jefferson from 1801. Mar. 4. to 1803. May 4.

1801.		Monthly balance	Int. of month at 6.p.Ct.
	Mar. 4.	316.485	1.58
	Apr. 4.	316.40	1.58
in favr Th:J.	May 4. June 4. July 4.		
	Aug. 4.	1815.41	9.07
	Sep. 4.	29.69	.15
	30.	1814.	9.07
	Nov. 4.	3071.98	15.36
	Dec. 4.	2656.99	13.28
1802.			
	Jan. 4.	5689.97	28.45
	Feb. 4.	5646.87	28.23
	Mar. 4.	4361.705	21.81
	Apr. 4.	4398.805	21.99
	30.	5446.	27.23
	May 31.	5757.50	28.79
	July 4.	3341.50	16.71
	Aug. 4.	3651.60	18.26
	Sep. 4	1569.915	7.85
	Oct.4 favr. Th:J		
	Nov. 4.	805.70	4.03
	Dec. 4.	1368.70	6.84
1803.			
	Jan. 4.	2268.50	11.34
	Feb. 4	2937.	14.68
	Mar. 4.	3030.	15.15
	Apr. 4.	3874.	19.37
	May 4.	3239.50	16.20
			337.02

Articles of discount between those dates paid by Th:J. extracted from the accounts.

		D
1801.	July 25.	10.50
	Oct. 9.	21.
	Dec. 3.	7.
1802.	Jan. 1.	5.35
	8.	10.70
	May 5.	21.
	July 14.	21.
		96.55

The above discounts being so much interest paid to the bank, is of course a deduction from the interest which would otherwise have been payable to mr Barnes.

The interest is carried out in the first instance at 6. pr. cent because a month's interest at 6. pr. cent is so easily noted, to wit, by carrying the dot 2. figures back,

thus	3.16485	and then
halving it thus	1.58	which gives int. of a month @6. pr. cent; &
adding $\frac{1}{6}$	.26	gives int. of
a month at	1.84	7. pr. cent.

or (which is the same thing) add the articles of 6. per cent, and, by a

add $\frac{1}{6}$ to make 7.p.c.	56.17	single operation, lay $\frac{1}{6}$ on the whole
	393.19	
deduct discts. paid	96.55	
	296.64	

MS (CSmH); entirely in TJ's hand.

To Nicolas Gouin Dufief

DEAR SIR   Washington May 5. 1803.

I recieved yesterday evening the Pensées de Pascal, and am particularly pleased with the edition, being fond of those which are small & handy & particularly the petit formats. I shall be glad to recieve the work of Cuvier. perhaps it may be the very one which I asked for the last year under the title of his Comparative anatomy, doubting whether that was the title. but it is enough that it is his, & on anatomy. I suppose Jombert's works in Architecture & the Geoponica Bassi, then also mentioned, were not to be had. I shall be glad if you succeed in getting the Greek & English Harmonies of Dr. Priestly. I state below some other works of his, which, if to be had, I should be glad to recieve. I fear you have thought me tardy in remitting the amount of my bill. as long ago as the first of March I sent the money by Capt Lewis my secretary, who then expected to be in Philada in 3. weeks. he has been detained greatly beyond his expectations, & I imagine arrived in Philadelphia about the 1st. inst. if you will let him know the amount of the additional articles, he will pay the whole together. I find that I omitted in due time to make you my acknolegements for the precious reliques of Doctr. Franklin, which you were so obliging as to spare from your particular collection. not only the intrinsic value of whatever came from him, but my particular affection for him extend the measure of my obligations to you for this kindness. I salute you with my esteem & best wishes

TH: JEFFERSON

Institutes of natural & revealed religion 2. v. 8vo.
a History of the early opinions concerning Jesus Christ. 4. v. 8vo.
Disquisitions relating to matter & spirit.
Sequel to the Disquisitions.
} by Dr. Priestly.

PrC (DLC); at foot of text: "M. Dufief."; endorsed by TJ in ink on verso.

COMPARATIVE ANATOMY: see Dufief to TJ, 2 May.

In March 1802, TJ had asked Dufief to find volumes 5 and 6 of Charles Antoine JOMBERT'S *Bibliothèque portative d'architecture*, not knowing that those volumes had been projected but never completed. At the same time TJ asked for the GEOPONICA, a compilation of information about Greek agriculture (Vol. 37: 114-15).

OTHER WORKS OF HIS: Joseph Priestley's *Institutes of Natural and Revealed Religion* first appeared in three volumes published in London in 1772. Dufief found a copy of a two-volume third edition, published in London in 1794, for TJ (Sowerby, No. 1524). Priestley's *An History of Early Opinions Concerning Jesus Christ, Compiled from Original Writers* was published in London in 1786 in four volumes (Sowerby, No. 1527). In September, Dufief was still looking for Priestley's *Disquisitions Relating to Matter and Spirit*, published in London in 1777, and its "sequel," which may have been *The Doctrine of Philosophical Necessity Illustrated, Being an Appendix to the Disquisitions Relating to Matter and Spirit*, also printed in London that year (Dufief to TJ, 12 Sep. 1803).

For two pamphlets containing marginal notes by Benjamin FRANKLIN that Dufief sent to TJ earlier in the year, see the correspondence between them of 31 Jan., 4, 14 Feb.

To Albert Gallatin

Thursday morning [5 May 1803?]

Th Jefferson asks the favor of a consultation with the heads of Departments on Saturday at 11 OClock—

RC (NHi: Gallatin Papers); partially dated; addressed: "The Secretary of the Treasury." Not recorded in SJL.

CONSULTATION: see Notes on a Cabinet Meeting, 7 May. According to TJ's notes, cabinet meetings were held on 10 other Saturdays between 16 July 1803 and 25 Feb. 1809. He may have issued this notice to Gallatin before any of those meetings.

To Thomas Mann Randolph

DEAR SIR Washington May 5. 1803.

Your's of the 29th. came to hand last night only, so it has loitered a post somewhere. I am sorry you have succeeded by so small a majority in your election. the danger is that as in Albemarle you had 5 times as many good votes as your competitor, you may also have had 5. times as many bad ones; & the trial will be before judges $\frac{1}{3}$ or $\frac{1}{4}$ of whom will be predetermined against you, so that a few impartial votes joining them will endanger you. I accede to the accomodation of £112. credited by Rives to J. Perry, by Perry to me, by myself to Craven, & by him to Rives. four debts are thus paid by a stroke of a pen. Lilly's finding a 5. Dollar bill instead of a 50. D. one in his paper solves an enigma which had puzzled us much here. about a fortnight after I returned here, I found a 50. D. bill in my pocketbook which I was sure ought not to be there. I carried it immediately to mr Barnes and insisted he must have given it me by mistake for a 5. D. he examined his books & his cash, he found them agree, & said he could not have made such a mistake. I put the bill into his hands however till he should examine better & on sight of it he recollected the bill from a particular circumstance, and that he had furnished it to me on my departure for Monticello, & had duly charged it to me. I then concluded I must have miscredited my money on leaving Monticello, as I did not intend to bring away such a sum over & above my expences. it never occurred that in the morning of my departure I had paid mr Lilly (as I supposed) 50. D. and might in my hurry have given him a 5. D. bill instead of a 50. D. yet this must have been the case, and the puzzle is explained all round. I shall accordingly account to him for the 45. D. mr Hudson you say asks 25. cents for 180. cubic inches of cherry. taking off $\frac{1}{5}$ for the saw, this is 25. cents for 144. cubic inches, or 1. square foot, consequently 250. D. or £75. the thousand. I have never given more than £10. but might, under a pressure, have gone to £15. or 50. D. the thousand. good mahogany costs 22. cents the square foot here, & I suppose the same at Richmond, transportation from thence to Monticello would be not quite 2. cents a foot. from mr Hudson's it would be about the same. his cherry is therefore 3. cents a foot dearer than Mahogany, which costs 6. times as much as cherry with us, & 10. times as much at Philadelphia, where wild cherry is about the price of good pine, that is to say 20. to 25. D. the thousand. mr Hudson's must therefore be declined, and mr Dinsmore must finish his rooms without the floors, leaving them till we can supply ourselves with cherry at the usual price, or Mahogany if we must go to an extraordinary one. You recollect my mentioning to you confidentially the purchase I had made of about half the shares in an adjoining tract of land. I have since got the whole except 4. acres some distance below the mill, which remain to J.H. altho' no water can be drawn from above the falls or present dam[1] but through the upper part of[2] my purchase, and at the position of these 4. acres a sufficient fall below the present dam is not yet acquired for a mill, which consequently can only be in the lower part of my purchase, yet I learn from mr Peyton that J. Henderson is proposing to sell these 4. acres as a mill seat to Isaac Miller & Wm. Meriwether who are to give him 1000. D. for them, and an order of court was to be immediately applied for to build a mill there. he must have practised some gross deception on those gentlemen, as it is incomprehensible how they could imagine[3] a mill could be built there. it must be by a dam raising the water to the height of the falls above. but besides that this would be too little, it would overflow the existing mill, which still remains the property of the family, unsold to any body. such a dam must injure your seat on the opposite side. as I have thought it best that mr Peyton should still appear the ostensible purchaser, I have recommended to him to apply, as owner of the whole tract (except the 4. as.) for an order of court to build a mill on the lower place to which he can draw a canal from the falls or present dam, round J. Henderson's 4. acres & without touching them, or injuring the present mill, or your seat. for he can have 12. or 15. f. fall without any dam, even after the present dam is pulled down. I have no conception but that his claim to the right of building a mill would be preferred. as you are interested in this matter, would it not be well for you to act in concert with mr Peyton, to whom you can mention my having communicated it to you, and who will be glad to have you to consult with in my absence. I have paid mr Peyton already 3106.50 D am to pay him July 12. 1300. D and shall still owe 1200. with a deduction of about 350. D. for rents. the whole cost will have been a little over 5600. D. the present mill & the 4. acres not being included. I count that when an order of court in favor of my lower place shall be obtained to the suppression of all pretensions to a mill on his 4. acres, they may be bought at the ordinary price of land; & that when the present dam is taken down, the present mill may be bought for the price of the irons & scantling.

Altho' the cotton estates in Georgia are certainly profitable, yet I doubt whether it would be profiteable to you on the whole to scatter your property so much. to the pecuniary inconveniences too must be added those of an annual journey, long absences from your family, and risk to your own health. on the whole therefore I am glad you decline it.

With respect to Martha's visit, I could not possibly propose or consent to it, if it were to separate the family. I could not, to gratify myself, wish to do what I know must produce both pain & injury to them. the time of her stay too, from that at which she could arrive here, would be short, as it ought not to go much into the month of July from considerations of health. my time here too is so totally engrossed by business that I should have but very small portions of the 24. hours to enjoy their society. I remit this satisfaction therefore till I can have it at Monticello, and till the meeting of Congress here. I have invited Govr. Page & family to pass as much as they can of Aug. & Sep. with us at Monticello, and he gives me hopes he will. we were affectionate friends & inseparable companions in youth, and have always preserved our feelings with mutual fidelity to each other through the stormy times into which we were thrown. I am little acquainted with mrs Page, but believe she is a rational & agreeable person in society. my letters since I came here have been of Apr. 13. to you, Apr. 25. to Martha, Apr. 13. & 24. to mr Eppes & Apr. 25. to Maria. their letters went to City point. your's of last night is the first I have recieved from Monticello. from mr Eppes I have recieved one. if they are with you present to them & to Martha and accept for yourself assurances of my affectionate & constant attachments.

Th: Jefferson

P.S. the ground on which war is expected to be renewed between Gr. Br. & France is much more serious and difficult than the public suppose. I believe it almost inevitable. I have recieved T. Eston's letter for Shadwell have informed him of the stated terms & offered the accomodation he asked in the buildings without [. . .] [rent] for what they will cost me. I presume he will accept.

RC (DLC); torn; at foot of first page: "T M Randolph"; endorsed by Randolph as received 9 May.

Craven PEYTON informed TJ of John Henderson's plan to sell his mill seat in a letter of 29 Apr.

TJ's letters of 13 Apr. to Randolph and to John Wayles EPPES were recorded in SJL but have not been found.

[1]Preceding three words interlined.
[2]Preceding four words interlined.
[3]Preceding three words interlined.

From Benjamin Rush

Dear Sir, Philadelphia May 5th: 1803.

I was made very happy by learning from your letter of the 23rd of April that your disease is less troublesome than formerly. As I know you have no faith in the *principles* of our Science, I shall from time to time combat your prejudices, and your disease (should it continue) by means of *facts*. Ever since I began the practice of medicine, I have kept common place books, in which I have recorded the results of the observations of my patients & friends upon the causes—symptoms & cure of diseases. From these Sources, I think I have derived much useful knowledge.—In the course of the last month I have added to my stock of facts upon the Diarrhœa the history of the following Cases.—

1 A gentleman of great worth Mr George Clymer informed me a few days ago, that he had been afflicted occasionally for fifteen years with a bowel complaint, and that it had yeilded to his wearing muslin Shirts only, for the last two years of his life.

2 An old nurse whom I met a few weeks ago in a sick room, told me She had been cured of a Diarrhœa of three years continuance by

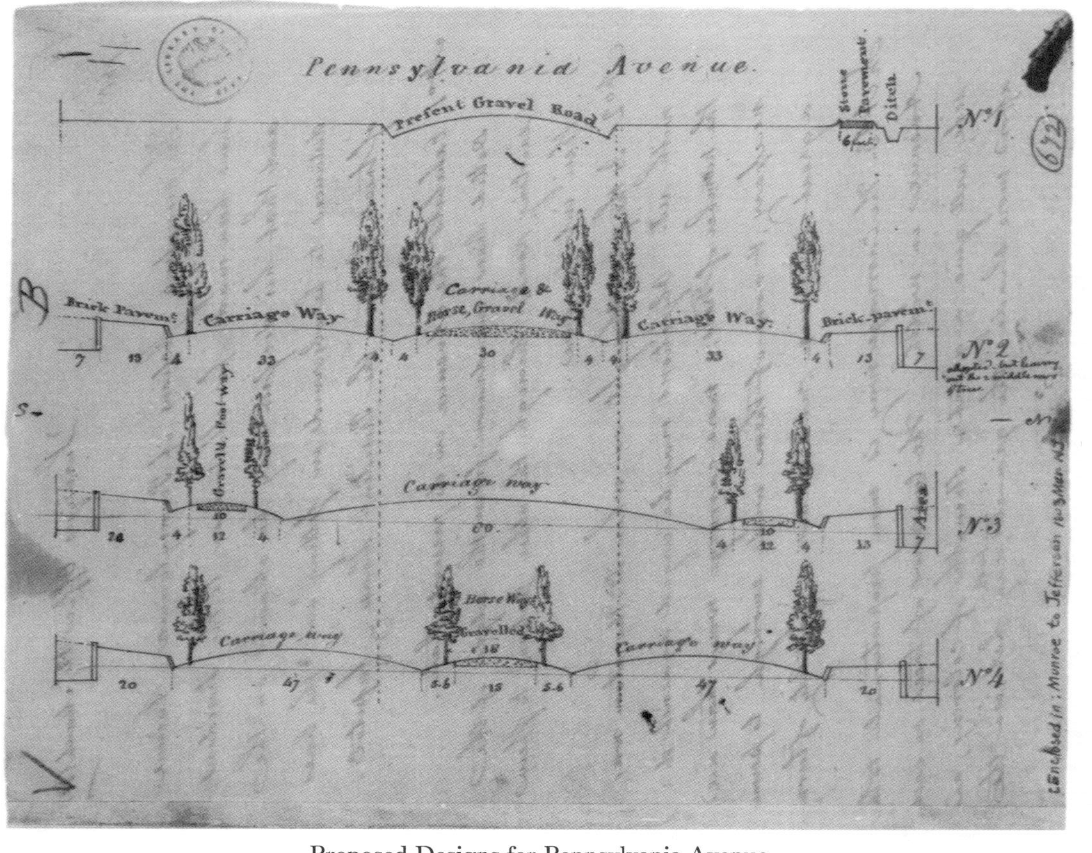

Proposed Designs for Pennsylvania Avenue

Robert R. Livingston

James Monroe

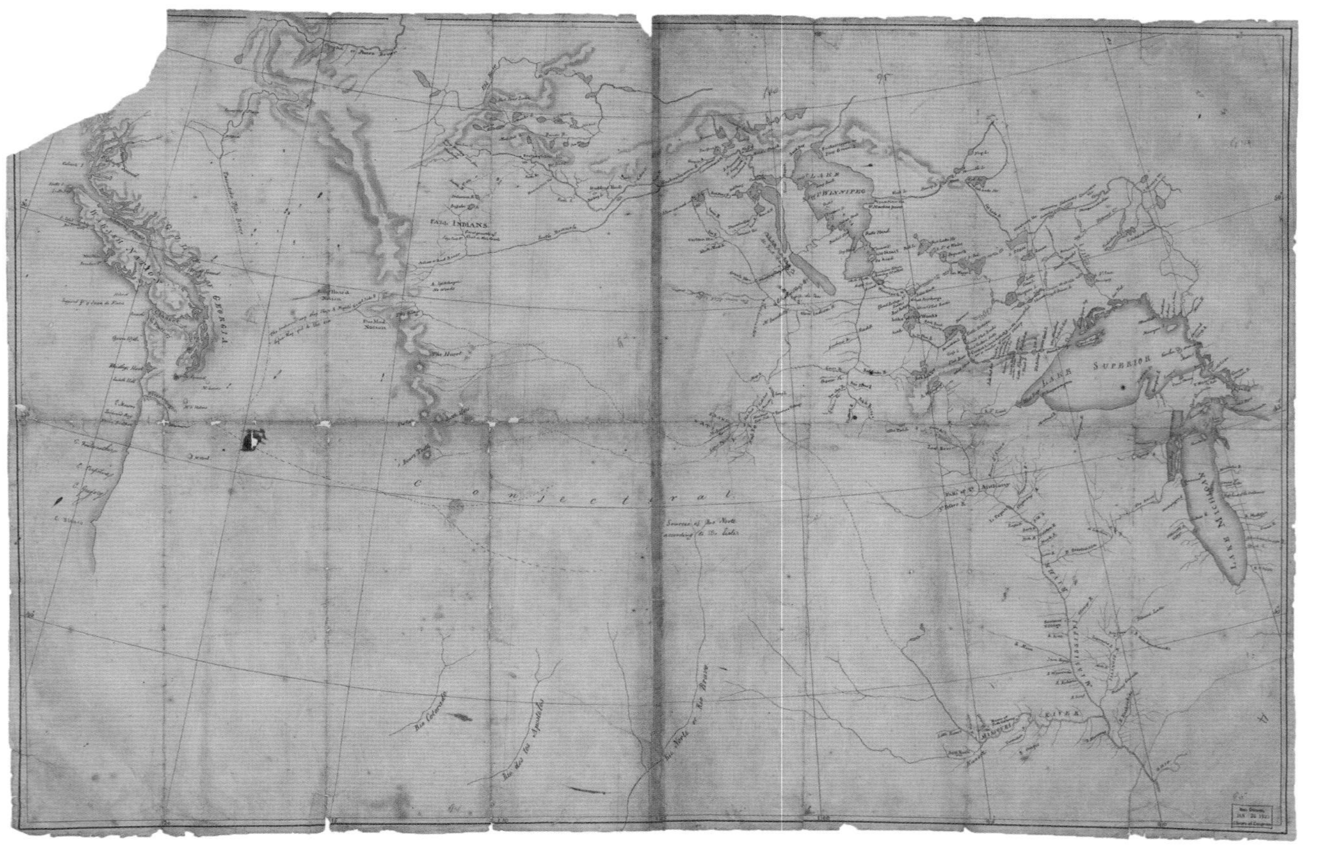

Map by Nicholas King

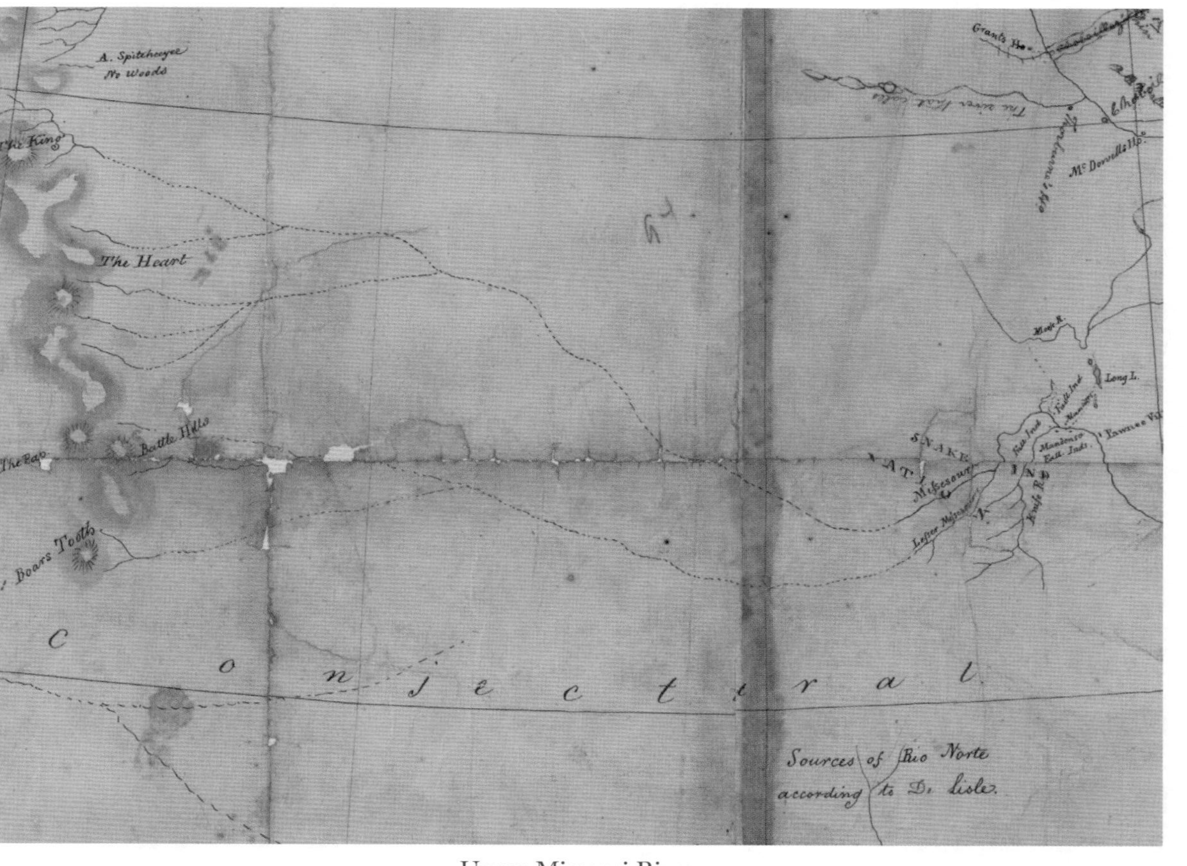

Upper Missouri River

Thomas Jefferson

Encyclopedie methodique 67. Livraisons. 15

Agriculture, Tome, 3e. et Tome 4. 1re partie	3 Vol.
Amusemens, depuis page 560 jusqua 900 on fournit le tome entier	2. in 1.
Antiquités Tome, 4e, 2e partie et tome 5 entier	3.
Architecture, Tome 2e. 1re partie	1.
Art militaire, Tome 4,	2.
Beaux arts, Tome 2e. 2e partie	1.
Botanique, Tome 4e	2.
Chirurgie, Tome 2. 2e partie	1.
Geographie, Ancienne. 3e partie Tome 3.. 2de partie	1.
Histoire, Tome 5e. 2 partie	1.
Histoire, naturelle, Tome 7 entier	2.
Manufacture, Tome 2e 2e partie, et tome 3e 2de partie	2.
Medicine, Tome, 3e* 2e partie tome †4.5.6.7 entier.	9.
Philosophie, Tome 2e & 3 entier	4.
Art Aratoire,	1.
Chasse,	1.
Jeux,	2.
Pêches,	1.
Phisique, 1 Tome entier	2. in 1.
Systeme, Anatomique 1 Tome entier,	2 in 1
Chimie, Tome 2 et 3 entire,	4. in 2
Geograhie Phisique	2.
Planches,	
Botanique Tome 4 à 9,	6.
Chirurgie,	1.
Pêchez,	1.
Histoire naturelle XVIII. Partie, Insectes - XIX. Partie - Coquilles	2.
Idem des‡ vers XXI. Partie	2. – des Vers
Art aratoire	1
Volumes	62 £. 535.

*I had it before

†the 1st part of Tome 4 still to come, & I had it before

I have now 67 livraisons complete, and Médicine Tome III. 2de partie duplicate to be returned.

22829

60. parts in 58. volumes

they sent me Tome III. 2d partie, which I had before, & charged without sending it Tome IV. partie 1re which I had before

Invoice for Encyclopédie Méthodique

U.S. Cent

drawing the breasts of a woman (who had lost her child) and Swallowing her milk. The Cure in this case was accidental—for she did not expect it. It was effected in a single month. Cows milk may be made to partake of the qualities of women's milk by adding a little Sugar to it.

I have read your Creed with great attention, and was much pleased to find you are by no means so heterodox as you have been supposed to be by your enemies. I do not think with you in your account of the character and mission of the Author of our Religion, and my opinions are the result of a long & patient investigation of that Subject. You shall receive my creed shortly. In the mean while we will agree, to disagree. From the slender influence which Opinions in Religion have upon morals, and from the bad practices of many people, who have graduated themselves at the highest point on the scale of orthodoxy, I have long ceased to consider principles of any kind as the criterion of disposition and conduct, & much less of our future acceptance at the bar of the supreme Judge of the World.

The prevalence of a narrow Spirit in our country with respect to principles, to which you allude, shall induce me faithfully to comply with your request by not communicating the contents of your creed even to your friends.

ADieu! my Dear Sir. May the Ruler of nations direct, and prosper you in all your duties and enterprizes in the present difficult & awful posture of human Affairs!

From your sincere *Old* friend BENJN: RUSH

PS: I am sorry to inform you that your friend Mr: Mason is in the lowest stage of a general Dropsy under Dr Reynolds & my Care. He has precipitated danger by his long, rapid[1] and debilitating ride to our city.

RC (DLC); endorsed by TJ as received 7 May and so recorded in SJL.

[1] Word interlined.

From John Wayles Eppes

DEAR SIR, Edge-hill May 6th. 1803

We received last Evening three letters from you—One to Maria & two to myself—I have been kept in albemarle first by a fever which continued five or 6 days and afterwards by the indisposition of Maria who without our being able to assign any reason for it has had her former bad luck & experienced a mishap—She is now I hope well & we shall set out on Tuesday for the Hundred—I have endeavoured since her sickness to prevail on her to give up the trip down the Country altogether but neither my influence or her Sisters could obtain her consent—

Mr. Randolph[1] is elected by 13 votes to the great Mortification of Cabbell—In his electioneering campaign he was in Bedford and had an opportunity of seeing the land which has been laid off there for Maria—He says the survey contains 900 acres and that 356 of it is prime Tobacco land—If his idea of it is correct I imagine it must be equal in value to Lego for which I would gladly exchange with you—Or if you suppose Lego more valuable I will only take such part of it as you may deem equal in value to the Bedford Land—I know of but one objection which you can make to the exchange To wit, The Land at Lego being already cleared would rent & yield immediate income—In order to obviate this objection I am willing to pay as boot in the exchange the price of clearing as much land in Bedford as will make a Rent equal to the rent of Lego—The pleasure which I anticipate from living near you prevents my offering in lieu of this; exchanging Pant-ops for land in Bedford—Two reasons induce me to wish very much that the exchange may be agreeable to you—The 1st. That it would enable me immediately to move up my hands from below & rent out my plantation there & 2dly. That Lego joined to Pantops would give a farm sufficiently large to afford occupation which I know from experience a small one does not—If you can admit the idea of exchanging you may make your own Terms—As I am willing to swap even—or to have the two tracts valued and pay you the difference in money—Or to pay whatever difference you may yourself fix as you are as well acquainted with the two tracts as any other[2] person—I will moreover oblige myself to complete the road thro' Lego to join yours from Shadwell within the next year—accept for your health & happiness the best wishes of

Yours sincerely JNO: W: EPPES

RC (MHi); addressed: "Thomas Jefferson President of the United States Washington"; franked and postmarked; endorsed by TJ as received 8 May and so recorded in SJL.

THREE LETTERS: TJ to Mary Jefferson Eppes, 25 Apr.; TJ to John Wayles Eppes, 13 (not found) and 24 Apr.

For Eppes's desire to sell or exchange the BEDFORD LAND that TJ had given his daughters, see Vol. 37:448-9.

[1] MS: "Randolp."

[2] Word interlined.

From Gideon Granger

DR SIR. New York May 6th. 1803.

I arrived here yesterday noon having taken time to ascertain the State of Things in the Several States. you are so near Maryland that any remarks are unnecessary. In Delaware the unhappy divisions among our friends will give additional Strength to Our Enemies and we may set down that *Tory State lost.* The fretful turbulent Disposition which has manifested itself in Pha. originated in some degree from a Sufficient cause which I will explain when I return a reunion will take place and in the Issue it will be useful. I had a long conversation with Tench Cox and can truly say I admire him both for Talents, conduct and Manners—Their Resolves will be so tempered as to remove most of the unpleasant feelings which have been experienced. The State of New Jersey is interesting. In joint meeting the whole number is 52—of these the Republicans have 24 certain and the Tories 19. A Sharp contest exists respecting the remaining 9. From a display of a variety of facts I have been convinced we shall Succeed in Huntingdon County which gives us 29. Our paper in that County has increased 600 in 6 mths. by fair Subscription and all our friends are confident of 300 majority—The Clerk of the various republican meetings says there will be a majority of at least 500. The Other remaining County is Gloucester in that there is certainly a majority of Republicans—but unfortunately a misunderstanding subsists between two Influential Characters, which if not removed will, as it has done, give the Tories a majority—both of these Counties have lately elected a republican Court of Free holders—The first has 11—agt. 9—the last 14–6—I believe we may calculate on that State. Our Triumph in this State is the greatest we have ever had. There are 30 Counties. from the best Information now to be procured. we have carried 25 Counties & 2 agt. 1 in the 26th. The Conduct of this One is [doubtful?]. In two Counties (Albany & Oneida) [they] have carried 9 members & in the latter we have *one.* Two Counties are very doubtful (Chenango & Ontario) my own opinion is from a knowledge of the settlements. They will be divided—we are certain in this state of 83 agt. 17. and it will probably be 86 agt. 14. In the Senatorial elections we have carried every Member but One and it is believed that One also, but that is uncertain—The probable state of the Senate will be 26 agt. 6—we are certain of 25. agt. 7.—

In Rhode Island we have carried an increased majority of 2 in the House. And every Other Officer—Gov: Lt. Gov. 10 Counsellors. Treasurer. [. . .] &c. without opposition.

With great Esteem Your friend GIDN GRANGER

RC (DLC); torn; addressed: "The President of the United States"; endorsed by TJ as received 13 May and so recorded in SJL.

DIVISIONS AMONG OUR FRIENDS: Democratic-Republicans in Wilmington and New Castle were divided over the erection of a bridge in Wilmington. Articles on both sides of the issue appeared in the Wilmington *Mirror of the Times.* In a letter dated 23 Apr., "A Kent County Democrat" noted that they had a sheriff to elect and it was important for the Democrats to elect him. He warned: "If you divide, it will only be as it has been heretofore; your Sheriff lost by your own divisions. Such bickerings between brother democrats, are unpleasant and such in my opinion deserve pointed censure" (*Mirror of the Times, & General Advertiser*, 6 Apr., 4, 7 May 1803; James Brobson and John Warner to TJ, 8 Feb.). For other divisions, see Thomas Mendenhall to TJ, 12 Feb. and Caesar A. Rodney to TJ, 7 July.

THEIR RESOLVES: for the resolutions passed by the ward meetings in Philadelphia, see Gallatin to TJ, 21 Mch.

The 1802 elections in NEW JERSEY resulted in 26 Federalists and 26 Republicans convening at the JOINT MEETING of the legislature, causing a deadlock in the selection of a governor and U.S. Senator (see Granger to TJ, 30 Oct. 1802). HUNTINGDON: that is, Hunterdon County. OUR PAPER: the Trenton *True American*, edited by James J. Wilson, who also served as clerk at the December 1802 meeting of Trenton Republicans and has been characterized as "the county's leading political professional." In January 1803, Wilson wrote a friend that the subscription list for the *True American* had "been for several months continually and rapidly increasing." In the fall election, Republicans gained three seats in Hunterdon and four in Gloucester giving the party complete control in the two counties and a majority of 14 in the joint meeting of the legislature (*True American*, 3 Jan. 1803; Newark *Centinel of Freedom*, 8 Nov. 1803; Pasley, *Tyranny of Printers*, 323-5; Carl E. Prince, *New Jersey's Jeffersonian Republicans: The Genesis of an Early Party Machine, 1789-1817* [Chapel Hill, 1967], 88-91; Walter R. Fee, *The Transition from Aristocracy to Democracy in New Jersey, 1789-1829* [Somerville, N.J., 1933], 124, 136-7).

TRIUMPH IN THIS STATE: for the New York election results, see also DeWitt Clinton to TJ, 4 May. By the final returns, the Federalists swept ONEIDA County sending four delegates to the assembly to join the Federalists elected in Albany County. CHENANGO County divided its votes and elected two Republicans and two Federalists. Onondaga County did the same, electing one candidate from each party. The counties of Genesee and ONTARIO, voting as one unit, chose three Federalists. New York Republicans prevailed in all of the 1803 SENATE races, giving them a majority of 20 in the senate in 1804 (*Albany Register*, 1 July 1803; *Journal of the Assembly, of the State of New-York, at Their Twenty-Seventh Session, Begun and Held at the City of Albany, the Thirty-First Day of January, 1804* [Albany, 1804], 3-4).

On 21 May, the Republican newspaper in RHODE ISLAND reported that in the general assembly all 10 senators and 50 out of the 70 representatives were Republican. COUNSELLORS: Granger probably refers to the state senators, who in Rhode Island were known as "Assistants" until 1799. The Republican officers elected included the attorney general (Newport *Rhode-Island Republican*, 23 Apr., 21 May; Michael J. Dubin, *Party Affiliations in the State Legislatures: A Year by Year Summary, 1796-2006* [Jefferson, N.C., 2007], 162-4).

To Joseph Prentis

DEAR SIR Washington May 6. 1803.

Your favor of the 29th. was recieved last night. what followed after I had the pleasure of seeing you at Monticello, so compleatly covered the whole ground of difference, as to supersede the partial affect of the letter I gave you. altho' I have no doubt that an affair of five & thirty years standing, explained 15. years ago & dormant ever since, must have been so suddenly excited by party [enmity] in others towards me, and by a desire in them to make an honest man, with far different views, an instrument of their personal & party vengeance, without any regard to his happiness, which they have [mortified] by their publications. yet I must say in justice to the gentleman alluded to in your letter, & who was the sole intermediary of the accomodation, that he shewed a sincere desire to affect that accomodation, and carefully avoided the producing difficulties by the *manner* of asking, where the *matter* presented none. he only desired that I would say in a letter addressed to his friend, what I had said before to another, & then repeated to him verbally. the letter last written to me, & alluded to in your letter, was answered by me without delay, but suffered some accidental delay by the post. I have seen, Sir, with a just sensibility the friendly & well intended interest you have been so good as to take in this business, and acknolege it with sincerity. desirous that no vestige of it may remain on earth to be raised up hereafter, I will pray you to burn now this letter, as I hope in time will be done with every other which has been written on the subject. the difference is understood to be finally closed: but nothing has been said about future intercourse. that must depend on the feelings of the other party solely. Accept my friendly salutations & assurances of high respect & esteem. TH: JEFFERSON

PrC (ViW: Tucker-Coleman Collection); blurred; at foot of text: "The honble Joseph Prentis"; endorsed by TJ in ink on verso.

LETTER I GAVE YOU: not identified, but TJ's missing March 1803 correspondence with John Walker is noted at TJ to Walker, 13 Apr.

GENTLEMAN ALLUDED TO: Henry Lee.

ANSWERED BY ME: TJ to Walker, 13 Apr.

To William Short

Dear Sir Washington May 6. 1803.

Your's of the 3d. was recieved last night. the uncertainty where you were has alone prevented mr Barnes from remitting to you the April 500. D. I have this morning informed him you were in Philadelphia, and it is probable he will defer writing to you till Tuesday (10th.) because on Monday he will draw the May 500. and remit both together. remember you are to inform us to whom these monthly remittances are to be made, and you may take your measures on them with the same certainty as if they were in the bank.

War between England and France is, by our advices, inevitable, and is probably commenced. it is no longer the treaty of Amiens that is in question. England considers that treaty as made & to be continued only 'rebus sic stantibus' as when it was made: that France has been enlarging itself more rapidly in peace than war; and that this enlargement calls for revisal and a new settlement of the affairs of Europe. it offers negociation for this purpose. Buonaparte does not wish war; but he must see that if he once begins to give back, all his new plumage will be plucked out of him. in that case he could not stand his ground at home. the insulting language in his public statements, and in his conversations with Ld. Whitworth seems to have stimulated the British mind to immediate action.—we have recieved from Spain official assurance that in the instrument of cession of Louisiana is this clause 'Saving the rights acquired by other powers in virtue of treaties made with them by Spain' and expressions of great sensibility for our friendly conduct on the late act of her intendant: so that our purpose will be effected peaceably in four months, whereas had we followed the wicked impulse of the federal leaders in Congress & the seaport towns, we should have had N. Orleans blocked up by superior naval force during 7. years of war, have lost 100,000 lives &[1] added 100. millions to our debt. I do not believe the federal prophets foresaw the war between England & France. if they did, they still misjudged, because we can probably obtain for our neutrality what they preferred acquiring by war. accept my friendly salutations and affectionate attachment.

RC (NjMoHP); at foot of text: "Mr. Short."

Short recorded his letter of the 3d to TJ in his epistolary journal but noted that he "forgot to extract from" it (FC in DLC: Short Papers).

rebus sic stantibus: matters so standing, that is, the treaty was to be in force only if the circumstances involved in its negotiation remained the same (Garner, *Black's Law Dictionary*, 1295).

[1] MS: "& and."

From Jean Chas

MONSIEUR LE PRÉSIDENT. paris 17 floreal L'an 11. [7 May 1803]

daignés accepter quelques exemplaires du parallele de bonaparte avec charlemagne. L'amour de la verité, et du bien public m'ont dicté cet ouvrage.

il y a deja quelque tems que j'ai eu Lhonneur de vous envoyer Le tableau historique et politique des operations civiles et militaires de bonaparte, et trente exemplaires de L'histoire de La revolution de L'amerique Septentrionale. j'ignore si mes depeches vous ont eté remises.

je m'occupe d'une seconde edition de L'histoire de La revolution des etats unis. je vous prie, monsieur Le president d'en accepter La dedicace. cet ouvrage merite de paroitre Sous vos auspices. il est honorable pour moi d'offrir a L'admiration publique L'histoire d'un peuple dont je respecte Les vertus, et admire Le courage. vous etes digne, monsieur Le president, d'etre Le chef d'une nation qui promet d'heureuses et brillantes destinées.

recevés avec bonté, monsieur Le president Les assurances de mon profond respect.

J CHAS

EDITORS' TRANSLATION

MISTER PRESIDENT, Paris, 17 Floreal Year 11 [7 May 1803]

Please accept these copies of my *Parallèle de Bonaparte avec Charlemagne*, a work that was dictated by my love of truth and the public good.

Some time ago, I had the honor of sending you the *Tableau historique et politique des opérations militaires et civiles de Bonaparte* and thirty copies of the *Histoire politique et philosophique de la révolution de l'Amérique septentrionale*. I do not know whether you received them.

I am now working on a second edition of the history of the American Revolution, and seek your permission, Mr. President, to dedicate the book to you. It is worthy of being published under your auspices. I am honored to hold up for public admiration the history of a people whose virtues I respect and whose courage I admire. You are worthy, Mr. President, of leading a nation that looks ahead to such an auspicious, brilliant destiny.

Receive with kindness, Mr. President, the assurance of my profound respect.

J CHAS

RC (DLC); English date supplied; below signature: "rue du bout du monde n. 184"; endorsed by TJ as received 15 July and so recorded in SJL.

Bonaparte encouraged comparisons to CHARLEMAGNE and the Frankish Empire, had a medal struck in the emperor's honor, and later in 1803 had a statue of him erected in Paris. Chas's brief *Parallèle de Bonaparte avec Charlemagne* was printed in Paris in 1803. Chas had previously sent TJ his earlier work on the first consul, *Sur Bonaparte* (Thierry Lentz, *Le Grand Consulat, 1799-1804* [Paris, 1999], 261, 456; Grainger, *Amiens Truce*, 181;

Leo Gershoy, *The French Revolution and Napoleon* [Englewood Cliffs, N.J., 1964], 379; Vol. 33:516, 517).

TJ received Chas's TABLEAU in February 1802 and had the book bound later in the year (Vol. 36:95-6; Vol. 38:483, 484n).

L'HISTOIRE: Chas sent TJ a copy of his work on the American Revolution, the *Histoire politique et philosophique de la révolution de l'Amérique septentrionale*, in the spring of 1801. TJ acknowledged receiving the book in a letter to Chas in September of that year (Vol. 33:515-17; Vol. 35:203-4).

D'EN ACCEPTER LA DEDICACE: TJ did not reply to this letter, which was the last correspondence between them.

From Victor Marie du Pont

MONSIEUR LE PRESIDENT New York 7 may 1803.

Je recois la lettre dont vous m'avez honoré en date du 4 Courrant et je m'empresse de vous envoyer la traite que vous desirez sur Paris—Toute la famille dans l'un et l'autre hemisphere sera toujours reconnaissante lorsque vous lui fournirez l'occasion de faire quelque chose qui vous soit agreable. Les nouvelles de guerre ont un peu suspendu les expeditions par france les assureurs, n'ayant point encore determiné leur prime pour ce nouvel ordre de choses. mais je ne doute pas que d'ici a 15 jours il ne s'en presente quelqu'une, plusieurs se preparant—J'aurai l'honneur de vous prevenir d'avance de leur depart, & je vous prie de vouloir bien agréer l'offre de mes plus devoués services et l'hommage de mon respect— V. DU PONT

EDITORS' TRANSLATION

MISTER PRESIDENT, New York, 7 May 1803

I have received the letter of 4 May with which you honored me and I hasten to send the draft you asked to be drawn on Paris. The entire family on both hemispheres will always be grateful when you provide us with the opportunity of doing something that pleases you.

News of the war has somewhat halted shipments from France, since the insurers have not yet determined their costs in this new situation. But I do not doubt that one will present itself in the next two weeks, since there are several in preparation. I will be honored to inform you in advance of their departure.

Please accept this offer of my most devoted service and respectful homage.

V. DU PONT

RC (DLC); endorsed by TJ as received 9 May and so recorded in SJL. Enclosure: Enclosure No. 2 listed at TJ to Fulwar Skipwith, 4 May.

From Andrew Gregg

Dear Sir Aaronsburg—7th. May 1803

Mr. Edward Lynch of the City of Philadelphia wishes an Appointment in the Land Office in the Mississippi Territory, and has requested me to mention his Name to you for that Purpose. This I can do with Confidence because I beleive him very adequate to such an Appointment. He has for some Years past been engaged in Commerce, but the greatest Part of his Time since he was capable of Business was spent in the Office of the Surveyor General of this State. While Mr. Lukens held the Office of Surveyor General, the Business of that Department was almost entirely under the Direction of Mr. Lynch, and at the Death of the former he was within one or two Votes of being appointed his Successor, so well had he conducted himself in the Estimation of the supreme executive Council of the State, in whom the Power of making that Appointment was then vested. He is a practical Surveyor, as well as an Adept in the official Details of Land Business, and it is thro' a strong Predilection for Business of that Kind in Preference to Commerce that he now offers himself a Candidate for an Appointment in the Mississippi Land Office. My long personal Acquaintance with Mr. Lynch induces me not only to express my Beleif of his Capacity, but also my earnest Wish that he may succeed in his Application.

With the most sincere Esteem I have the Honor to subscribe myself your Friend & huml. svt. Andrew Gregg

RC (DNA: RG 59, LAR); at foot of text: "Thomas Jefferson Esqr."; endorsed by TJ as received 21 May and "Lynch Edwd. to be empld. in land office Misipi" and so recorded in SJL. Enclosed in Edward Lynch to TJ, 17 May.

Born in Carlisle, Pennsylvania, Andrew Gregg (1755-1835) worked as a tutor in Philadelphia and storekeeper in Dauphin County before taking up farming in Centre County, Pennsylvania. Elected as a representative to the Second Congress, he served eight consecutive terms. A staunch Republican at the national level, he aligned with the faction in Pennsylvania that supported Governor Thomas McKean instead of more democratically inclined leaders such as William Duane and Michael Leib. Defeated for reelection in 1806, he subsequently became the United States Senate candidate preferred by McKean's supporters. He served one term in the Senate from 1807 to 1813. Becoming a banker in Centre County, he later served as secretary of the Commonwealth but in 1823 lost a race for governor and retired to his farm (ANB; Higginbotham, *Pennsylvania Politics*, 58, 131-3).

Report from John Lenthall

Amount of the Rough stone work to the South wing of The Capitol from April 30th to May 7th 1803

Foundations of 13 Piers up to the offset. to which the Walls were pulled down	2350	Perches 173
Work done above the offset on the West Front including the Voids of the Arches as solid work	1933	

for B H Latrobe Surveyor

Jno Lenthall

MS (DLC); in Lenthall's hand and signed by him; addressed: "Prest. U.S."; endorsed by TJ: "Capitol. work Apr. 30. to May 7. 1803."

John Lenthall (d. 1808) was born in Chesterfield, England, and trained as a carpenter. About 1793, he moved to the United States, becoming one of the early residents of the Federal City. He married Jane King, the daughter of Robert King, Sr., then the chief surveyor for the City of Washington, and eventually became friends with Benjamin Henry Latrobe, who hired him as clerk, or chief foreman, of the public works. Latrobe's long absences from Washington required Lenthall to assume management over most aspects of the project. On 19 Sep. 1808, Lenthall was crushed to death when the vault of the court room in the north wing of the Capitol collapsed. In a eulogy composed the following day, Latrobe described Lenthall as "a perfect master" of his trade and praised his "benevolence of heart," while also noting Lenthall's "reserved exterior" and "rigid adherence to his own principles and opinions which nothing could bend" (*National Intelligencer*, 23 Sep. 1808; Latrobe, *Correspondence*, 1:256n; Benjamin H. Latrobe to TJ, 23 Sep. 1808).

As a measurement for stone, PERCHES were understood to equal $16\frac{1}{2}$ feet in length, 18 inches in height, and 12 inches in thickness (OED; Carl R. Lounsbury, *An Illustrated Glossary of Early Southern Architecture and Landscape* [New York, 1994], 267). After consulting with Lenthall, TJ had asked Latrobe in his letter of 23 Apr. to have Lenthall report on the perches of stonework laid every week.

Notes on a Cabinet Meeting

1803.

May. 7. Present 4. Secretaries & Atty Genl. on the supposition that war between England & France is commenced, or whenever it shall commence.

1. shall we issue a Proclamation of neutrality? unanimously not. it's object as to our citizens is unnecessary, to wit, the informg. them that they are to observe the duties of neutrality, because the late instance is so recent as to be in their minds. as to foreign nations, it will be assuring them of our neutrality without price, whereas France

may be willing to give N. Orleans for it. and England to engage a just & respectful conduct.

2. Sea letters to be given even on the present apparent probability of war.
3. Customhouse officers to attend to the having our seamen furnishd with certif. of citizenship in bonâ fide cases.
4. New Orleans. altho' no specific opinion is asked, because premature till we hear from our ministers, see the complexion & probable course & duration of the war, yet the opinion seems to be that we must[1] avail ourselves of this war to get it. whether[2] if negocian fails, we shall take it directly, or encourage a decln of independce. & then enter into alliance &c. we have time enough to consider. we all deprecate Gr. Br's taking possn of it. we all agree we should not commit ourselves by a convention with France, accepting merely our right of deposit, or any improvement of it short of the sovereignty of the island of N. Orleans, or a portion sufficient for a town to be located by ourselves.

MS (DLC: TJ Papers, 131:22677); entirely in TJ's hand; on same sheet as his notes on cabinet consultations of 16 July, 4 Oct. 1803, 18 Feb., 26 May, 8 Oct. 1804, 8 July, 12, 19 Nov. 1805.

LATE INSTANCE: George Washington's neutrality proclamation of 22 Apr. 1793 declared that the United States would "pursue a conduct friendly and impartial" toward Great Britain, its allies, and France. The document warned citizens against committing or aiding hostilities against any of the warring nations or carrying contraband articles to any of them. A primary aim of the proclamation was to forestall the arming of American privateers, and TJ joined the other members of Washington's cabinet in support of the declaration of neutrality although there was a division of opinion over the status of the relationship between the United States and France (Washington, *Papers*, *Pres. Ser.*, 12:472-4; Vol. 25:518, 541, 568-71, 597-619, 665-8).

Gallatin sent batches of printed SEA LETTERS to customs collectors on 11 June. Each form bore TJ's and Madison's signatures and was to be filled out by a collector to certify that a vessel was American owned. TJ had decided in December that the United States would not issue sea letters, which were also called ship passports, unless war broke out (allowing an exception, as was customary, for ships bound on voyages beyond the Cape of Good Hope). Gallatin instructed the collectors not to issue sea letters before 25 June unless they were "morally certain" that France and Britain had gone to war (Gallatin to Robert Purviance and to Thomas de Mattos Johnson, 11 June, in Gallatin, *Papers*, 8:413, 429; Vol. 25: 167n, 642-3, 645-8, 680-2; Gallatin to TJ, 6 Dec.; TJ to Gallatin, 7, 25 Dec.; sea letter for ship *May Flower*, 8 Sep. 1803, in DNA: RG 76, French Spoliations, MR).

See Gallatin to TJ, 6 July, for the certificates of CITIZENSHIP for mariners.

AVAIL OURSELVES OF THIS WAR: writing to Robert R. Livingston about various subjects on 25 May, Madison declared: "We are still ignorant of the result of the armed negotiations between Great Britain and France. Should it be war, or should the uncertainty of the result, be spun out, the crisis may be favorable to our rights and our just objects, and the President assures himself that the proper use will be made of it." Three days later Madison wrote to Livingston and Monroe in cipher: "The crisis presented by this jealous and hostile attitude of those rival powers has doubtless been seen in its bearings on the arrangements contemplated in your commission and instructions and it is hoped (tho we have not yet heard) that the arrival of Mr. Monroe will have taken place in time to give full advantage to the means of turning the actual state of things to the just benefit of the United States." The situation "authorizes us to expect better terms than your original instructions allow," he added (Madison, *Papers*, *Sec. of State Ser.*, 5:33, 39).

DEPRECATE GR. BR'S TAKING POSSN: by the time Madison wrote to the diplomats on the 28th, he and TJ had learned from Rufus King that the British, if they seized New Orleans, expected to turn it over to the United States. Madison confided to Monroe and Livingston that the president, impressed by the frankness with which Prime Minister Henry Addington had revealed Britain's intentions to King, now wanted "as little concession as possible" made to France "on points disagreeable to Great Britain." In particular, if the French kept possession of one bank of the Mississippi, they should not be allowed to claim a right to exclude British ships from the river. The secretary of state also outlined arguments to justify the transfer of captured territory from a belligerent nation to a neutral country in wartime, in case a cession of New Orleans from Britain to the United States should come to pass (same, 39-40).

PORTION SUFFICIENT FOR A TOWN: Madison informed Livingston and Monroe that the president did not want them to enter into any convention with France "that will not secure to the United States the jurisdiction of a reasonable district on some convenient part of the banks of the Mississippi" (same, 39).

[1]TJ here canceled "not."
[2]TJ here canceled "by."

From Joseph Priestley

DEAR SIR, Northumberland May 7. 1803

I have now to acknowledge the receipt of two of your valuable letters, one of them directed to me at Philadelphia, and the other to this place. They give me the more pleasure as I perceive by them that you are not so much occupied by public business, but that you are at leisure for speculation of a different and higher nature, and that you do not think unfavourably of my late tract on the *comparison of Socrates and Jesus*. Your flattering invitation to enter farther into the comparison of Jesus with other philosophers, I cannot, at least at present, attend to, tho I should be glad if you, or some other person, would take it up.

With respect to one part of your letter to Dr Rush, which I thank you for sending me, you will allow me to express some surprize (tho it is not very extraordinary that, educated, and situated, as different men are, they should see any subject in different lights) that you should be of opinion, that Jesus never laid claim to a divine mission.

It is an opinion that I do not remember ever to have heard before. By this means you, no doubt, make *him* to have been no imposter, but then you make many others to have been such, who yet appear to have been men of great integrity and piety; and who, besides having no advantage to expect from any scheme of an imposture, must have been less qualified to carry it on. If Mahomet could not be classed with impostors, is it at all probable that his immediate followers, who must then have been such, could have established his religion, as those of Jesus did his; and his disciples had originally as much ambition and jealousy as those of Mahomet, and yet they all pretended to act by authority from him. How came so many persons, hundreds in the first instance, and thousands presently after, to believe that Jesus *did* pretend to a divine mission, and to be satisfied, by some means or other, that his pretensions were well founded. What could have induced any Jew to abandon his favourite idea of their Messiah being a temporal prince, and to receive in that character one who disclaimed all worldly power? With respect to natural ability, or advantage of any other kind, the apostles, at least Paul, were upon a level with Jesus; and yet they all submitted to him as their leader, and as much after he was dead, as while he was living.—How came the Gnostics, the philosophers of the age, who despised the apostles as illiterate men, to admit the supposed high claims of Jesus, tho equally illiterate? There must have been a wonderful power of imposing upon mankind somewhere, and for no probable or rational end that we can discover, and this appears to me to be as great a miracle as any that is ascribed to Jesus; whereas the supposition that Jesus had a divine mission, and that he gave sufficient evidence of it solves every difficulty. It accounts for his superior knowledge and all the authority that he assumed, and makes the whole of the subsequent history consistent and natural, which no other hypothesis does. Without this the question of the people of Nazareth where Jesus was brought up, remains unsolved, *Whence has this man this wisdom*?

But I ask pardon for writing in this manner, and by no means wish to draw you into a controversy, or a correspondence on the subject; but suggest the hints for your private consideration.

I think myself greatly honoured by your repeated kind invitations, but fear that my health will not admit of my availing myself of them.

With the truest attachment, I am yours sincerely,

J PRIESTLEY

RC (DLC); endorsed by TJ as received 12 May and so recorded in SJL.

VALUABLE LETTERS: TJ to Priestley, 9 and 24 Apr.

To Justus Erich Bollmann

May 8. 1803. Washington.

Th: Jefferson presents his salutations to Dr. Bollman and informs him that the appointment proposed to him may wait a month or two.

PrC (DLC); endorsed by TJ in ink on verso.

APPOINTMENT PROPOSED: see TJ to Bollmann, 30 Apr.

To Gideon Granger

DEAR SIR Washington May. 8. 1803.

I promised to inform you of the result of the Virginia elections. one only has issued differently from what I expected; that is the Eastern shore district. the 2. Eastern shore counties were almost in the entire mass a body of tories during the revolutionary war, among whom we were obliged to station a regiment or two to keep them in order. they have never lost that spirit. they have now given 735. federal votes & 55 republican. there being some division in the Western shore counties of the residue of the district, the federal candidate has carried it by a majority of about 150. out of about 1920. votes given in the whole district say 1000. against 900. Brent's case you know. Sprigg lost it against Stephenson, a Fed, by a majority not yet known[1] [. . .], but it is [. . .]. he had been living in the state but one year, unfortunately had attached interest enough to him to be able to prevent Lawrence Washington (nephew of the General and) a good republican, who could otherwise have been elected with certainty. Holmes, where the Feds counted to carry their man, got 1000. against 473. Jackson, where they had been very sure also carried his by about 200. we have therefore 3. black sheep in our flock of 22.—Monroe's appointment was known at Paris Feb. 24. he may be expected to have arrived there the middle of Apr. in the Journal des defenseurs (the special paper of Buonaparte, edited by his secretary) is a pretty long tirade against those, whom they call Anglomen, in the US. for endeavoring to irritate our citizens against France by pretending that the act of the Intendant of N. Orleans was dictated by France; and quoting with approbation the republican papers which proved that the body of our nation had seen through the wicked design 'de ces feuilles excitratices,' (these inflamatory papers.) the ground of war between England & France is much deeper & more irremoveable than the public are aware. I consider it as next to impossible that they should compromise the real differences. Accept my affectionate & respectful salutations.

TH: JEFFERSON

PrC (DLC); blurred; at foot of text: "Gideon Granger esq."

For Republican Burwell Bassett's campaign in the EASTERN SHORE COUNTIES, part of the newly reorganized twelfth congressional district, see "A Democrat" to TJ, 30 Mch. In the end, Thomas Griffin, the FEDERAL CANDIDATE, reportedly won by 33 votes, 1089 to 1056. BRENT'S CASE: Joseph Lewis, Jr., defeated the incumbent Republican Richard Brent in the district composed of Fairfax, Loudoun, and Prince William counties. Republican over confidence leading to a poor turnout in Prince William County was cited as the cause of Brent's defeat (*New-York Gazette*, 18 Apr.; *Gazette of the United States*, 16 May; Madison, *Papers, Sec. of State Ser.*, 4:541; Vol. 32:460n).

Federalists accused Maryland native Osburn SPRIGG, a Hampshire County delegate in the Virginia assembly from 1800 to 1803, of forming the second congressional district in a way that "would secure his election to the next Congress." The opposition described him as "a thorough going Jeffersonian" who believed "that Tom Paine was inspired to write the 'Age of Reason.'" James STEPHENSON defeated Sprigg by 131 votes, 984 to 853. NEPHEW OF THE GENERAL: son of George Washington's brother Samuel, Lawrence A. Washington served in the Virginia Senate from 1801 to 1803 (Leonard, *General Assembly*, 220, 224, 226, 228, 230; Madison, *Papers, Sec. of State Ser.*, 1:122-3; Dubin, *Congressional Elections*, 28; Hartford *Connecticut Courant*, 11 May 1803; Vol. 35:228-9n).

Incumbent Republican David HOLMES defeated Isaac Vanmeter by 1,134 to 477 votes, respectively. Republican John G. JACKSON, who represented Harrison County in the house of delegates from 1798 to 1801, defeated Thomas Wilson, the state senator representing Monongalia, Harrison, and other counties in 1803 (Dubin, *Congressional Elections*, 28; Leonard, *General Assembly*, 212, 216, 220, 230, 234; Vol. 36:492n).

[1]Remainder of sentence interlined.

From John Langdon

DEAR SR. Portsmouth May 8th. 1803

I pray you to accept my acknowledgement, for the papers sent me. I received last week a *pamphlet* which is consider'd of great importance, it is now rangg. thro' the News papers, and will be republished here. We have reports every day that War has been declared between France and great Britain; let this be as it may, I hope America will remain at peace, which will give us great advantages. Our New Orleans Business has been happily settled, a little too soon for the British and American factions, that there has been an understanding between them, on the Declaration of War, I have no doubt.

I have the honor to be with the greatest, respect, Dear Sr. most, sincerely your's

JOHN LANGDON

RC (DLC); at foot of text: "President of US."; endorsed by TJ as received 16 May and so recorded in SJL.

The PAMPHLET mentioned by Langdon was probably *A Vindication of the Measures of the Present Administration*, a vigorous defense of TJ's policies written by Gideon Granger under the pseudonym Algernon Sidney. The three-part essay first appeared in Samuel H. Smith's *National Intelligencer* on 15, 18, and 22

Apr. 1803 and was reprinted in newspapers across the country. Smith soon after collected the articles into a pamphlet and additional versions were subsequently published in Portsmouth, New Hampshire; Hartford, Connecticut; Wilmington, Delaware; and Trenton, New Jersey. TJ apparently sent copies of the essays to various political friends, including William C. C. Claiborne and probably Thomas Worthington and John Bacon (ANB, s.v. "Granger, Gideon"; Shaw-Shoemaker, Nos. 4301-5; Sowerby, No. 3301; TJ to John Bacon, 30 Apr. 1803; Thomas Worthington to TJ, 23 May 1803; William C. C. Claiborne to TJ, 30 May 1803).

From William Bakewell

SIR New Haven 9th. May 1803

Your esteemed favor would have been answered immediately, but for the absence of two of our firm. It was not with any pecuniary view that we sent the Malt liquor, perhaps a little vanity might combine with our principal motive, which was to shew that we who have lived under the English Government, (during that Parliament, which in the words of Mr. Fox, "added more to the burthens, & took more from the liberties of the people than any of its predecessors,") can duly appreciate the value of a Constitution, which as now *practically administered*, would have been deemed a Utopian romance, but that mankind may "read *this* history in a nations eyes."—

If, Sir, motives of delicacy in your public situation, render it unpleasant to you to accept even the value of ten dollars, (which is the price of a barrl of this Ale,) please to defer the matter till we hear from a person in Baltimore whom we desired to settle our accot for Mr Smith's National Intelligencer. Was it not trespassing on your time, we would solicit a few lines of information relative to the state of Virginia, which did not enter into the plan of your "notes." Since our last we have been induced to change our views, & propose (one of us at least) to purchase & cultivate a Farm in such part of the U States as appears most eligible. In the communications to the English board of agriculture, Mr Strictland speaks highly of the climate & soil near the blue ridge in Virginia. Genl Washington in his letters to A. Young, recommends the country near the Potowmac. We have heard much in praise of the Shenadoah valley, but are told the price of land is much higher than that of equal quality in other parts of the state. Could you spare a few minutes from your more important concerns, to say what part unites in the greatest degree a good soil, a temperate & healthy climate, & if possible a near water conveyance & some society of the better kind; you would do us a service infinitely beyond the trivial matter in question.

Had we known any one on whose judgment we could have depended, we would not have troubled you with this inquiry, & hope you will excuse the liberty we have taken on this occasion—With sentiments of the highest esteem, I remain for Self and Partners, Sir, Your obedt Servt

Wm Bakewell

RC (DLC); addressed: "The President of the United States Washington City"; franked; postmarked 10 May; endorsed by TJ as received 13 May and so recorded in SJL.

your esteemed favor: TJ to William, Benjamin, and W. L. Bakewell, 15 Apr.

English politician and orator Charles James fox remarked in his address to the electors of Westminster on 21 May 1796, that the last Parliament had "added more to the burthens, and taken away more from the rights of the subject, than any Parliament ever did in the annals of our history" (*Jordan's Complete Collection of All the Addresses and Speeches of the Hon. C. J. Fox, Sir A. Gardner, and J. H. Tooke, Esq. at the Late Interesting Contest for Westminster*, 3d ed. [London, 1796], 5-6).

history in a nations eyes: "And read their history in a nation's eyes" from the 16th stanza of Thomas Gray's "Elegy in a Country Churchyard."

our last: William, Benjamin, and W. L. Bakewell to TJ, 8 Feb. 1803.

purchase & cultivate a farm: Bakewell moved with his family in the fall of 1803 to the Fatland Ford farm near Norristown, Pennsylvania (Arlene Palmer, *Artistry and Innovation in Pittsburgh Glass, 1808-1882: From Bakewell & Ensell to Bakewell, Pears & Co.* [Pittsburgh, 2004], 17).

William Strickland (strictland), a Yorkshire agriculturalist and naturalist, wrote an assessment of American farming practices after a tour of the United States in 1794 and 1795 that included a visit to Monticello. His findings, *Observations on the Agriculture of the United States of America*, including sections on Virginia climate and soil, were published in London in 1801, in response to queries posed to him by the British Board of Agriculture (Sowerby, No. 819; Vol. 28: 372n).

George washington exchanged several letters with English agricultural reformer Arthur young about animal husbandry and the sanguine prospects for farming near the Potomac River. Bakewell may have been familiar with Washington's letter of 5 Dec. 1791, published in London in 1801 in *Letters from His Excellency General Washington, to Arthur Young, Esq. F.R.S.: Containing an Account of His Husbandry, with a Map of His Farm; His Opinions on Various Questions in Agriculture; and Many Particulars of the Rural Economy of the United States.* TJ had forwarded his own "Notes on Virginia Lands" to Washington for Young in 1791 (Washington, *Papers, Pres. Ser.*, 8:431-2, 9:253-7; Vol. 20: 716-7; Vol. 24:98-9n).

To Christopher Ellery

Dear Sir

Washington May 9. 1803.

I have lately recieved a letter from Ingraham, who is in prison under a ca. sa. on a judgment for 14000. dollars & costs, one moiety (I presume) to the US. for having been the master of a vessel which brought from Africa a cargo of the natives of that country to be sold in slavery. he petitions for a pardon, as does his wife also on behalf of herself, her children & his mother. his situation,[1] so far as respects himself, merits no commiseration: that[2] of his wife, children & mother, suffering for want of his aid, does: so also does the condition of the unhappy human beings whom he forcibly brought away from their native country, & whose wives, children & parents are now suffering for want of their aid & comfort. between these two sets of suffering beings whom his crimes have placed in that condition, we are to apportion our commiseration. I presume his conviction was under the act of 1794. c. 11. which inflicts pecuniary punishment only, without imprisonment. as that punishment was sometimes[3] evaded by the insolvency of the offenders, the legislature in 1800. added, for subsequent cases, imprisonment not exceeding 2. years. Ingraham's case is exactly such an one as the law of 1800[4] intended to meet; and tho' it could not be retrospective, yet if it's measure be just now, it would have been just then, and consequently we shall act according to the views of the legislature, by restricting his imprisonment to their maximum of 2 years, instead of letting it be perpetual as the law of 94. under which he was convicted, would make it, in his case of insolvency. he must remain therefore the two years in prison: & at the end of that term I would wish a statement by the Judges & District attorney, who acted in the cause, of such facts as are material, & of their judgment on them, recommending him, or not, at their discretion, to pardon at the end of 2. years or any other term they think will be sufficient to operate as a terror to others meditating the same crime, without losing just attention to the sufferings of his family. this of course can only respect the moiety of the US. The interest you took in this case during the last congress has encouraged me to hope you would lend your instrumentality to the bringing it to a close, which would gratify me, so far as it could be done without abusing the power of pardon, confided to the discretion of the Executive to be used in cases, which tho' within the words, are not within the intention of the law. the law certainly did not intend perpetual imprisonment. Accept my friendly salutations and high respect.

Th: Jefferson

RC (NBLiHi); addressed: "The honble Christopher Ellery Newport, Rhode island"; franked and postmarked; endorsed. PrC (DLC).

letter from ingraham: Nathaniel Ingraham to TJ, 28 Apr. 1803. as does his wife: Mary Ingraham to TJ, 30 Oct. 1802.

For the terms of the act of 1794 and law of 1800 regarding the slave trade, see U.S. Statutes at Large, 1:347-9, 2:70-1 and Vol. 39:399-401.

interest you took in this case: see Ellery to TJ, 27 Jan. 1803.

[1] Word interlined in place of "sufferings."

[2] Word altered from "those."

[3] Word interlined.

[4] Preceding word and year interlined.

Memorandum from Albert Gallatin

[9 May 1803]

House—Master of the revenue cutter at New London vice Hindmen—
Note—The commission denotes neither the name of the cutter nor the station; it should be sent from the Comptroller's office to the Collector of New London with notice that it is intended to supercede Hindmen

Osgood—Naval officer for the district of New York vice Rogers
Sam. Ward do. for the do of Salem— Story
Jeremiah Bennet junr. collector of customs for the district of Bridgetown—vice Elmer and also inspector of the revenue for the port of Bridgetown in the district of Bridgetown

MS (DLC: TJ Papers, 132:22774); entirely in Gallatin's hand; undated; endorsed by Gallatin: "Denomination of offices"; endorsed by TJ as received from the Treasury Department on [9] May and "removals" and so recorded in SJL.

Shortly after TJ took office, George HOUSE wrote Madison claiming that he rightly deserved to be captain of the New London revenue cutter instead of Elisha Hinman, who received the appointment during the Adams administration only because he was a Federalist (Vol. 34: 357n). On 29 Jan. 1803, Nicoll Fosdick, a bankruptcy commissioner, and nine other New London Republicans petitioned Gallatin to appoint House, declaring that the change "would be consistant with sound policy, and conducive of publick good." They noted that Hinman was not the best qualified for the office, "but on the contrary it is well known that his advanced age, increasing infirmities, together with the superanuated state of his mind, give Cap. House a decided superiority." Gallatin sent the petition to TJ with the note: "From other quarters Captn. Hinman has been represented to me as incapacitated by age & inattention to his duty.—Albert Gallatin" (RC in DNA: RG 59, LAR, 5:0316-18; Vol. 37: 704, 708). Gallatin also forwarded a 10 Mch. letter from Nathan Post who, with Fosdick and John Cahoone, had conducted a survey of Long Island Sound in 1802 using the revenue cutter commanded by Hinman. Post described the poor condition of the cutter, including "Large holes in her sails." He characterized Hinman "as worn out with old age his, Politicks full of Pison" (RC in DNA: RG 59, LAR, 5:0374-5, endorsed by TJ: "House v. Hindman. Post's lre to mr Gallatin"; Vol. 38:491n). Hinman defended his right to retain office in a letter to TJ of 16 Nov. 1801. Gideon Granger also forwarded TJ arguments against Hinman's removal (Vol. 36:292).

On 10 Nov. 1802, Samuel WARD applied to TJ for a position at the port of Salem (Vol. 38:660-1). Upon learning that Joseph Story would not agree to serve as naval officer there, Ward wrote James Sullivan on 7 Apr. 1803, requesting that he use his influence with the president "that I may be appointed to that office." Fourteen Salem residents, described as "respectable and friendly to the present administration," endorsed the request. Sullivan forwarded the letter to James Madison on 11 Apr. and gave his personal recommendation of Ward, noting "I have known him as a magistrate and military officer when much depended on his exertions, and when many who would now gladly take offices were skulking from public danger" (RC in DNA: RG 59, LAR; endorsed by TJ: "Ward Saml. to be Naval officer of Salem vice Story"). Fearing that his previous applications and recommendations had not been received in Washington, Ward wrote Gideon Granger on 16 May reviewing the correspondence and assuring the postmaster general that his appointment would be "agreeable to all the Republicans of the Town" including Salem collector William R. Lee, with whom he had been "intimately acquainted for nearly forty years" (RC in same; endorsed by TJ: "Ward Saml. to mr Granger. to be naval officer of Salem"). TJ saw one other application for naval officer. On 6 May, William Carlton of the *Salem Register* wrote Samuel H. Smith describing the persecution he had experienced from Federalists after he opposed Timothy Pickering's candidacy for Congress. Carlton noted: "I think there is no one in this quarter who has been more buffetted in the political tempest than I have. If I deserve reward, I shall be grateful for it—if not, I am content—But it would be extremely agreeable to 500 Citizens of this town, that I should be noticed, particularly noticed, by the Gen. Govt., as I have been so particularly noticed by the cancorous enemies of that Government" (RC in DNA: RG 59, LAR; endorsed by TJ: "Carlton Wm. Salem. May 6. 03. to S. H. Smith. to be Naval officer Salem"). For the efforts of the Massachusetts Federalists to silence Carlton and his newspaper, see Vol. 39:150-1, 154n.

JEREMIAH BENNET JUNR.: on 3 Mch., New Jersey congressman Ebenezer Elmer recommended Bennett for the position at Bridgeton, New Jersey, in case Eli Elmer, his cousin, was removed (RC in DNA: RG 59, LAR; endorsed by TJ: "Bennet, Jeremiah, junr. to be Collector of the district of Bridgetown N.J. Elmer's lre to mr Gallatin"; Gallatin to TJ, 3 Jan.).

From John Mitchell

SIR Havre 9h. May 1803

I have now the Honor to cover you a Letter from Mr. Livingston and take Advantage of the Occasion to solisit the favor of your Confirming the appointment our Ministers at Paris have made in nameing Me to the Commercial Agency for this place.

It is now two years past since I solisited this appointment, and I believe in conformity to my request Mr. Monroe Mr. McKean Govr. of Pennsylvania and some other of my friends did recomend me. to the latter I have been known almost from My Infancy—to the former for many years and perticularly so While he was at Paris also to Genl. S. Smyth & Mr. T. Paine throughout the Whole of our Revolution and to this time. to them and the Commercial interest of Philada. I venture to refer for my Character—'tho the Confidence placed in me by Mr. Livingston in sending Me his despatches to forward ever since my being established here—and now appointing Me Agent for the U.S. will alone I flatter myself be a suffitient recomendation for your favor to Confirm the appointment

I feel Confident of giveing satisfaction to our Goverment as well as the Commercial interest of our Country—my best endeavours shall be Used to merit your Confidence and favor—and with the most perfect respect—I beg leave for to subscribe my self—Sir,

Your very Obedient and Very Humble Servant

JOHN MITCHELL

RC (DNA: RG 59, LAR); addressed: "Thomas Jefferson Esqe President of the United States of America Washington"; franked; postmarked Philadelphia, 11 July; endorsed by TJ as received 13 July and so recorded in SJL. Enclosure: Robert R. Livingston to TJ, 2 May.

John Mitchell was originally from Philadelphia. In the fall of 1803, TJ gave him a commission as vice commercial agent at Le Havre and the Senate confirmed the appointment on 15 Dec. Mitchell was back in the United States by August 1808, when he solicited another nomination from TJ. In 1811, Mitchell received an appointment as consul at Santiago, Cuba, but the Spanish government refused to allow any foreign officials on the island. In the War of 1812, he was agent for Americans held prisoner at Halifax (JEP, 1:459, 460; Madison, *Papers*, *Sec. of State Ser.*, 2:140; 5:475; *Pres. Ser.*, 5:612n; 6:529n, 644n; Preston, *Catalogue*, 1:215, 240; Mitchell to TJ, 5 Aug. 1808).

APPOINTMENT OUR MINISTERS AT PARIS HAVE MADE: Mitchell began acting as vice commercial agent at Le Havre in the fall of 1802. He had applied for the consular position there in 1800. John Adams named him to be commercial agent at Ostend instead, to which the Senate consented on 24 Feb. 1801. TJ considered that nomination a midnight appointment, withheld the commission, and named someone else to the post. TJ was aware that Mitchell wanted the place at Le Havre, but in June 1801 made Peter Dobell the commercial agent and F. C. A. Delamotte the vice agent for that port. Dobell never took up residence at Le Havre, finally determining in 1802 to resign the position, and the French government declined to accept Delamotte's appointment because he was a French citizen. Mitchell, who received endorsement from Robert R. Livingston and James Monroe to continue performing the duties of the office temporarily, wrote to Madison and Gallatin as well as to TJ to solicit the permanent appointment as commercial agent. He had made an arrangement with Isaac Cox Barnet, to whom TJ and Madison had finally offered a choice of Antwerp or Le Havre. Barnet agreed to take the consular post at Antwerp if Mitchell received a commission for Le Havre (Mitchell to John Marshall, [April 1800], in DNA: RG 59, LAR, endorsed by TJ: "John Mitchell to be Consul at Havre or elsewhere in France"; Mitchell to Gallatin, 8 May 1803, in same, endorsed by TJ; Marshall, *Papers*, 4:212; JEP, 1:382, 385; Madison, *Papers*, *Sec. of State Ser.*, 3:469; 4:426, 563-4, 584; 5:105-6, 475; Vol. 33:173n, 557n, 666, 672, 677; Vol. 36:470-1; Vol. 38:59-60, 295-6, 309-10, 377-8).

Mitchell went to France in 1795 with a letter of introduction to MONROE, who was U.S. minister in Paris, from Secretary of State Edmund Randolph. Mitchell renewed their former acquaintance when Monroe landed at Le Havre in April 1803 (Preston, *Catalogue*, 1:44; Madison, *Papers*, *Sec. of State Ser.*, 4:499).

Thomas MCKEAN wrote to TJ on 25 July about Mitchell's application. That letter, which is recorded in SJL as received from Philadelphia on 1 Aug., has not been found. Writing to Gallatin on 8 May, Mitchell referred to McKean as an old friend (Mitchell to Gallatin, 8 May, in DNA: RG 59, LAR).

SENDING ME HIS DESPATCHES: Livingston had begun to send his letters to the State Department through Mitchell at Le Havre (Madison, *Papers*, *Sec. of State Ser.*, 4:386n).

Notes on Nathaniel Ingraham's Case

[ca. 9 May 1803]

Ingraham's case for carrying on the slave trade.

1801. Feb. action of q.t. institd. by J. W. Leonard

Nov. verdict & jdmt[1] for 14,000 D. & costs. does not appear that any term of imprismt entered into the quantum of punmt adjudged.

act of 1794. c.11. §.4. inflicts 200. D. for every slave, by qui tam.

1800. c.51. respects slave trade betw. foreign ports, or in forn. vesls.

the conviction then has probably been under act of 94. which punished pecuniarily only, & not by imprismt.

the act of 1800. inflicted imprismt. maximum 2. years, in addition to pecuniary.

as the pecuniary punmt of 94. is evaded by the offender having no property, it seems right that he suffer the equivalent punmt by imprisonmt which the legislature found it necessary to provide, to prevent that very evasion by poverty which would now have takn place, that is, 2. y. imprisonmt.

he must therefore suffer the imprismt of 2. y. which the law has declared to be[2] not too high a measure, even when accompand by pecuniary forfeitures. & at the end of that term (Nov. 1803) let him apply to the judges & Atty of distr. who were in the cause for their statement & opn on his character, conduct, & all the circumstances of the transaction & whether in their judgment a sufficient punmt has been inflicted, or what longer term of imprisonmt will be proper as a terror to others meditating the crime of which he has been convicted.[3] the condition of the offender merits no commiseration that of his wife, children & parents suffering for want of his aid, does: so also does the condition of the unhappy people whom he brought away from their native country, and whose[4] wives, children & parents are[5] now suffering for want of their aid & comfort.

see my lre to mr Ellery May 9. 1803.

MS (DLC: TJ Papers, 129:22262); undated; entirely in TJ's hand; written on verso of Christopher Ellery to TJ, 27 Jan. 1803.

ACTION OF Q.T.: that is, a qui tam action or "An action brought under a statute that allows a private person to sue for a penalty, part of which the government or some specified institution will receive" (Garner, *Black's Law Dictionary*, 1282). Under the terms of the 1794 statute regarding the slave trade, the pecuniary penalties against those convicted under the law were divided between the United States and the person or persons that sued for and prosecuted the case in federal court (U.S. Statutes at Large, 1:349).

[1] TJ here canceled "£."
[2] TJ here canceled "the proper."
[3] TJ first wrote "the crime which is the subject of this law," then altered the text to read as above.
[4] Preceding two words interlined in place of "their."
[5] Word interlined.

From Robert Smith

Navy depmt.
May 9. 1803

Sir,

I have the honor to present for your approbation,

Pascal Paoli Peck, of Rhode Island,
James Marshall of Virginia, &
Robert Gamble of Pensya.

to be Midshipmen in the Navy.—

Mr. Peck is highly recommended by Governor Fenner and others; Mr. Marshall, by Colonels Taylor & New, and Mr. Gamble, by Capt. Jones, Mr. Muhlenburgh, Mr. Beckley and other Gentlemen of Phila.—

Should you approve of these nominations, the enclosed warrants will require your signature.—

With high Consideration, I am Sir; yr mo: ob: Servt.

Rt Smith

RC (DLC); in a clerk's hand, signed by Smith; at foot of text: "The President"; endorsed by TJ as received from the Navy Department on 9 May and "Midshipmen" and so recorded in SJL. FC (Lb in DNA: RG 45, LSP).

Pascal Paoli peck, James marshall, and Robert gamble would each see extensive service as midshipmen in the Mediterranean. Peck participated in the attack on Derna in 1805, Marshall served on board the frigates *Essex* and *Constitution*, and Gamble was taken prisoner following the capture of the *Philadelphia* by Tripoli in October 1803 (ndbw, *Register*, 19-20, 35, 42).

To Isaac Cox Barnet

Sir Washington May 10. 1803.

I have asked the favor of mr Skipwith, our Consul at Paris to procure & forward me some wines from Champagne & Burgundy which I have specially pointed out to him. I have desired him to dispatch those of Champagne immediately, because they will be pressingly wanting, but not to forward those of Burgundy till autumn because they cannot stand either the heat of a summer transportation or cold of a winter one. as they must descend the Seine to Havre I have taken the liberty of desiring him to address them to your care. [. . .] you would be so good as to procure them the speediest conveyance you can either to Alexandria, Baltimore, Philadelphia, or New York it will be safest to address them to the custom house officer of the place where they shall be landed 'to be forwarded by him to Washington.' while they are waiting a passage at Havre, they will need the precaution of being stored in a good cellar & not a warehouse. whatever post or other expences may attend this will be paid you by mr Skipwith or by myself to any person in the US. with whom you are connected, as shall best suit yourself. apologising for the trouble I am thus giving you I pray you to accept my salutations & assurances of respect.

TH: JEFFERSON

PrC (DLC); torn; at foot of text: "Mr. Isaac Coxe Barnet"; endorsed by TJ in ink on verso. Enclosed in TJ to Charles Burrall, 10 May (see Burrall to TJ, 20 May).

FAVOR: TJ to Fulwar Skipwith, 4 May.

To Victor Marie du Pont

Washington May 10. 1803.

Th: Jefferson presents his salutations to M. duPont is thankful to him for the accomodation of his bill of exchange, and offers of notice when there shall be a conveyance. to save him this trouble he gives him that of recieving his letter to mr Skipwith and forwarding it by any conveyance he approves.

RC (DeGH). Enclosure: TJ to Fulwar Skipwith, 4 May.

To Gabriel Duvall

[10 May 1803]

Th: Jefferson presents his salutations to mr Duval and informs him that in conformity with the report of the Secretary of the Treasury he has directed a commission to be made out for George House to be master of the revenue cutter at New London in Connecticut vice   Hindman, who is superceded

PrC (DLC); undated, but pressed on same sheet as TJ's memorandum to Madison, 10 May; at foot of text: "The Comptroller of the Treasury." Not recorded in SJL.

REPORT OF THE SECRETARY: see Gallatin's memorandum to TJ printed at 9 May. HINDMAN: that is, Elisha Hinman (same).

To Christopher Ellery

DEAR SIR Washington May 10. 1803.

William Martin, keeper of the lighthouse in the district of Newport is dead, and mr Ellery the collector names two persons either of which he deems fit for a successor, to wit, Philip Caswell, son-in-law to the decedent & who has actually been the keeper of it, and Benjamin Remington of Conanicut, an old sea-captain of between 60. and 70. years of age. the age of the latter, if not now, will shortly be an objection, & nothing is said of the politics of either. considering that the republican description of our citizens has not yet nearly obtained that share in the public offices to which they are entitled, & from which they were so long excluded, such an one of equal qualifications for the public service, ought to be preferred to a federal competitor. will you be so good as to inform me who, on the whole, you think most proper to be appointed, not letting the enquiry in the mean time become public? Accept my friendly & respectful salutations.

TH: JEFFERSON

Caswell seems to have some claim from possession, if his politics should not give a preference to another as well qualified.

PrC (DLC); at foot of text: "The honble Mr Ellery"; endorsed by TJ in ink on verso.

WILLIAM MARTIN died on 23 Apr. at age 81. Newport collector William Ellery wrote Gallatin a week later informing him of the event and noted that Martin's son-in-law PHILIP CASWELL, who was caring for the lighthouse at the time of Martin's death, had agreed to continue until the president appointed a new keeper. Ellery described Caswell as a young man of good character who would keep the lighthouse "carefully and honestly." He was a weaver by trade. BENJAMIN REMINGTON was the only other applicant. He lived on Conanicut Island, where the lighthouse was situated, and cultivated a few acres of land. He knew the lighthouse and "would keep it well" (Gallatin, *Papers*, 8:338; *Newport Mercury*, 3 May 1803).

According to SJL, TJ received Christopher Ellery's reply of 23 May on the 29th, but it has not been found. TJ noted in SJL "Philip Caswell to keep lighthouse."

To William Jarvis

SIR Washington May 10. 1803.

Your favors of Aug. 10. & Oct. 25. were both recieved, the last not till Jan. 6. some time after which the two half pipes of Oeyras arrived at Baltimore, which you were so kind as to procure for me. they have been forwarded by messrs. Smith & Buchanan to Monticello at my desire. I percieve by the sample sent me, in the phial, the truth of your observation, that the wines of that name are no longer of their antient quality, at least not of the quality of what I tasted at the Chevalier de [Freyres]. the objection is just what you mention, a too great sweetness, which tho' age will lessen, it will never reduce to the dryness we esteem here. as this was meant but for an experiment, I must recur to the wine called Termo, with which mr Bulkeley used to supply me, and which I preferred out of many samples of the dry wines of Portugal which he sent me. I will therefore ask the favor of you to send me a pipe of it. I paid messrs. Smith & Buchanan the freight, duties &c. of the two half pipes of Oeyras[1] but they informed me they were neither authorised to recieve, nor informed of, the amount of the wine itself. You must be so good then as to draw on me for that, & the amount of the pipe of Termo conjointly, & your bill shall be paid at short sight, and as this will inform me of the cost at Lisbon I will hereafter remit in advance for what I shall desire. the pipe should be put into an outer cask to prevent frauds, & sent to Norfolk or Richmond of preference. should no vessel offer for either of these ports, it may be sent to Baltimore, Philadelphia or New York, addressed to the Collector of the customs of the port where landed, to be forwarded by them to Richmond.—the privilege you have obtained for our flour gives great & just satisfaction to our country, of which you have deserved well for this benefit. Accept my friendly salutations & assurances of esteem. TH: JEFFERSON

P.S. I do not know whether it is the practice at Lisbon [to put brandy] into the wines, I would [wish none] in [mine]. a good cellar keeps the wine [better] than brandy, which [effects] the [. . .] and makes it too strong.

PrC (MHi); blurred; postscript written along left margin; at foot of text: "William Jarvis esq."; endorsed by TJ in ink on verso. Recorded in SJL with notation "for Termo."

For Jarvis's successful lobbying for the admission of American FLOUR into the Portuguese market, see James Madison to TJ, 21 Mch.

[1] Preceding two words interlined.

Memorandum to James Madison

Commissions to be issued to

Samuel Ward of Massachusets to be Naval officer for the district of Salem in Massachusets.

Samuel Osgood of New York to be Naval officer for the district of New York

Jeremiah Bennet junr. of New Jersey.[1] to be Collector of customs for the district[2] and Inspector of the revenue for the port of Bridgetown in New Jersey

George House of Connecticut to be Master of a revenue cutter.[3]

TH: JEFFERSON
May 10. 1803.

MS (MH); entirely in TJ's hand; with check marks later added by a clerk to the left of each entry; addressed: "The Secretary of State." PrC (DLC); pressed on same sheet as TJ to Gabriel Duvall, [10 May]; lacks check marks.

[1] Preceding three words and period interlined.

[2] Preceding three words interlined.

[3] TJ here canceled "at New London in Connecticut."

From Joseph H. Nicholson

SIR Chesterfield May 10. 1803

I beg Leave to enclose you a Letter which I received a few Days past from Capt. Jones of Philada. In this I have no Authority from him, but as it may throw some light on a Transaction with which I believe you are already partially acquainted, I have no Doubt he will pardon me. It will discover to you the Reason why you did not receive from the Pennsylvania Delegation, a written Communication, which I understood you were induced to expect.

It is a Circumstance of real Regret, that many of our Friends have discovered so strong an anxiety for office, as to afford too much reason to believe that this was their leading Motive in desiring a Change of administration. Whenever the Views of such Men are developed, Disgrace and Disappointment ought to follow them. As far as my Knowledge extends, I am persuaded the public are satisfied with the Course that has been pursued in Relation to offices, and that it ought not to be abandoned at the will of a few unprincipled Demagogues—

I would not have taken the Liberty of offering these Remarks, but for a Belief that you would be gratified at hearing the Opinions of Men who feel a Pleasure in avowing themselves personally and politically your Friends.

After perusing Capt. Jones's Letter, I will beg the Favor to have it returned to me, and remain Sir Most respectfully Yr. Ob. Servt.

JOSEPH H. NICHOLSON

RC (DLC); endorsed by TJ as received 12 May and so recorded in SJL. Enclosure not found.

William JONES was angered by fellow congressman Michael Leib's efforts to make banishing all Federalists from public office a test of commitment to the Republican Party. In February 1803, Jones, Andrew Gregg, Robert Brown, John Smilie, John A. Hanna, and Isaac Van Horne, Republican members of the PENNSYLVANIA DELEGATION to Congress, drafted and signed a letter to TJ in which they denied that they were dissatisfied with the president because he had failed to dismiss all Federalists from office. They asserted that the calls for removals were restricted to a small minority of their constituents, particularly to those interested in office. Three other Republican congressmen—Leib, William Hoge, and Joseph Hiester—refused to sign the letter. In an effort to gain their approval, a second draft was drawn up. After Leib declined to sign it as well and took a copy of the original letter to Philadelphia for use in organizing ward meetings, the initial signers decided against sending either letter (Raymond Walters, Jr., *Albert Gallatin: Jeffersonian Financier and Diplomat* [New York, 1957], 159-60; Higginbotham, *Pennsylvania Politics*, 58-9; Andrew Shankman, *Crucible of American Democracy: The Struggle to Fuse Egalitarianism & Capitalism in Jeffersonian Pennsylvania* [Lawrence, Kans., 2004], 98-9; William Jones and Others to TJ, 12 Feb. 1803, Dfts in PHi). For both drafts of the letter, dated 12 and 14 Feb., see the *Aurora*, 6 Aug. 1805. For the ward meetings held in Philadelphia demanding the removal of all Federalists from public office, see Gallatin to TJ, 21 Mch. In March, Jones, who had left Washington before Leib failed to sign the revised letter, wrote Virginia congressman John Randolph: "I am now more than ever convinced of the propriety and necessity of that address to the President, and regret as well as all the respectable independant republicans with whom I have conversed, that the original letter was not sent to the President when the faithless 'prevaricator' refused to sign the substitute" (William Jones to John Randolph, 19 Mch. 1803, in PHi).

From Volney

MONSIEUR LE PRÉSIDENT paris 20 floreal an xi. 10 Mai 1803

Votre lettre du 6 fevrier dernier me fut remise il y a quelques jours par Mr. Mounroe avec les deux volumes dont Vous avez eu la bonté de l'accompagner; celui des transactions est arrivé à tems pour me donner des idées nouvelles sur la topographie des florides; quant a l'autre qui enseigne les règles de l'art important de delibérer, cela est désormais considéré comme *livre revolutionaire*, tant nous nous sommes deja amendés.

Je profitai, il ya environ six semaines de l'occasion de Mr. Curwen de philadelphie pour vous adresser un Exemplaire de la Nouvelle traduction de mes Ruines. Mr. Curwen a bien Voulu se charger d'un paquet entier pour divers amis, et me promettre que s'il ne Vous trouvait point à *Ouachin'ton'*, il remettrait votre *Copie* au dr. Thornton avec recommandation speciale de vous l'envoyer. il a dû s'embarquer à Bordeaux du 5 au 10 Avril pour Norfolk.

D'autre part, l'editeur, Mr. Stone, en a fait passer un millier d'exemplaires à Newyork des la fin de mars; il en agardé encore quelques Cents ici; Moi même j'en conserve quelques-uns, afin, si le

Votre s'égarait, de pouvoir le remplacer: ainsi l'existence de ce livre est desormais assurée.

Dans ma Courte lettre par Mr. Curwen, j'ai eu lhonneur de Vous accuser la reception de la Vôtre en date du 20 avril 1802. elle me parvint à Spa où je m'étais rendu pour la funeste maladie dont je suis attaqué et que je n'ai encore pû guerir, quoique depuis quelque tems j'aye quelques lueurs d'Esperance. Mais pour les réaliser il faudra renoncer à tout travail assidu et sérieux, et passer désormais l'hyver en climat très different de paris puisque j'ai besoin d'un air sec, constant, et chaud. un Medecin instruit pourra vous satisfaire si vous desirez de savoir ce qu'est un Catarrhe glaireux Sur La Vessie.

Vous me demandiez quelque livre sur l'Egypte; Celui de Mr. Denon a paru avec beaucoup de Succès; mais il a trois volumes in 12 de texte, et dans l'in folio qui Coute 15 guinées, et dont on netrouve plus de Copies, Le Volume de planches joint à celui du texte est un *Atlas*, *immaniable*. Mr. Mounroe m'a annoncé une Explication de Vos intentions à cet egard.

Le Mien, sur le *climat* et le *Sol* des Etats unis s'imprime, erest à la 5e feuille: ce sera un Volume de 450 à 500 pages; il contiendra bien peu de chose sur la situation politique et morale, si même il en contient aucune; il faudrait dire trop ou trop peu. j'y joindrai un Curieux vocabulaire du langage Miâmis que je dressai en 1797 à philadelphie pendant 2 mois sous la dictée de Votre interprète Wells, et de *Petite tortue*. à cette occasion je forme le Vœu que Vous donniez des ordres pour que L'on recueille un échantillon de chacune des langues des diverses tribus sauvages de Votre Continent: il serait digne du congres detablir pour cet objet trois ou quatre places d'interpretes afin d'empêcher la perte absolue de Cette Espece de monument historique, le plus Certain et le plus instructif de tous sur l'origine et L'affinité des diverses Nations. en 100 ans peut-être, plusieurs tribus actuelles auront totalement disparu, en emportant avec elles des chaînons essentiels de la filiation générale. j'adresse aussi dans Mon livre au gouvernement americain L'invitation de faire dresser un procès Verbal Exact du *Statu quo* de la chute du Niagara, afin de servir par la Suite de terme de Comparaison à ses progrés ultérieurs.

Le Courier qui Vous transmettra Cette lettre, Vous porte je Crois dimportantes et agréables nouvelles sur l'affaire du Missi-sipi. Le 1er consul me dit, à ma derniere Visite que l'affaire etait Conclue; et personne ne vous en fera, de ce pays-ci, des complimens plus sinceres que Moi; dés longtems, Monsieur, Vous avez connu mes opinions á cet égard; je les ai maintenues ici avec quelque Mérite, puis qu'elles

Mont Valu des Calomnies, et selon le dictionaire de ce tems, *de la défaveur.* aujourdhui j'ai la satisfaction de voir que les Evenemens ecoulés depuis la paix ont si parfaitement repondu à la marche que j'avais predite, lors du depart du Gl. Le Clerc, que l'on croirait que j'avais lû le livre du destin. à cette epoque j'osai dire a qui il etait utile et hardi de le dire, qu'il fallait faire par sagesse, et avec mesure et precaution, ce que la nature des choses ferait très prochainement avec necessité et Violence: quil fallait abandonner des possessions lointaines onereuses, illusoires, impossibles á garder, parcequ'un Ennemi superieur en occupait les routes; et que, lors meme que l'on reussirait à retablir par force un systeme dont le Vice venait de se demontrer, la faculté quavait cet ennemi de tout paralyser par une nouvelle guerre rendait de telles possessions illusoires, qu'il fallait encore moins se brouiller avec un tiers, ami ou Neutre en occupant l'une des issues naturelles de sa maison; surtout quand cette *issue* n'apportait que des depenses actuelles et des Esperances plus qu'Equivoques: que la Vraie puissance consistait à ne pas se dilater au delá de sa sphere d'activité; et que maintenant puisque l'on etait une puissance Continentale, il fallait se borner á cette solide preponderance; et que sans sortir de la Mediterranée l'on avait de quoi remplir tous les besoins et Meme tout le luxe des possessions coloniales et des productions des deux indes &c. je fus alors Consideré comme un rêveur *philosophique*, ce qui maintenant est la perfection du ridicule et de l'absurdité. Vous Voyez si le tems m'a vengé, et si nous en sommes à regretter la perte de tant d'hommes, de richesses, de tems &c. La guerre, selon mon horoscope, Va serallumer; et parce qu'elle est autant de passion que de *necessité* (pour Notre adverse) elle sera d'une longueur et d une Conséquence revolutionnaire que l'on ne me parait pas assez sentir et calculer. Celui des deux athlétes qui est maitre de la mer, pourra bien comme il En menace, être Exclus du continent de L'Europe; mais il excluza encore plus Certainement son adverse et ses alliés du continent des deux ameriques. peut être trois ou quatre Campagnes suffiront-elles à provoquer, a etablir L'independance des Empires de Montezume et de Manco-Copac; et alors, adieu l'empire d'isabelle, adieu les galions et les piastres, dont le cours derivé ira alimenter les Manufactures de Manchester, de Birmingham, et rendre a la Banque ses moyens d'echanges en *hard-money.* Delá une réaction sur le continent de l'Europe dont les effets contrarieront pour le moins des speculations trop confiantes, surtout quand chaque jour developpe des realités qui dissipent à l'interieur les illusions de la credulité. Mais placé, comme Vous lêtes, en un poste d'oú Vous pouvez entendre et Voir le pour et le contre, dont il N'est desormais permis de Voir ici qu'une coté, Vous jugez Mieux que je ne le puis faire de l'avenir politique qui se prepare. Le parti que vous avez pris dans cette circonstance d'aquerir par moyens Consacrés chez les Nations Ceque la Votre eut pû obtenir par force ou astuce, vous prepare une reconnaissance qui s'augmentera chaque jour. Heureux le pays où les principes de gouvernement sont l'œconomie du Sang, et de l'argent, la moderation dans les depenses privées et publiques, le respect et l'amour de la justice, et sinon l'estime du moins la compassion de la pauvre espece humaine, et de cette portion appellée peuple, que l'on ne meprise tant que pour avoir ledroit de l'ecraser. pauvre Europe! theatre de carnage et jouet de Conquérans! Vous connaissez, Monsieur, Les sentimens inalterables de mon respect et de Mon attachement. VOLNEY

EDITORS' TRANSLATION

Paris, 20 Floreal Year 11.
10 May 1803

MISTER PRESIDENT,

A few days ago, Mr. Monroe gave me your letter of February 6 and the two books you were kind enough to send me. The one on transactions arrived in time to give me new ideas about the topography of the Floridas. The other, providing rules for the important art of deliberation, is henceforth considered a *revolutionary book*, given how much change our society has already undergone.

About six weeks ago, I entrusted to Mr. Curwen of Philadelphia a copy of the new translation of my *Ruins*. He graciously agreed to take a whole box for various friends and promised that if he did not find you in Washington, he would give your copy to Dr. Thornton with a special request to send it to you. He was to have left Bordeaux for Norfolk between April 5th and 10th.

Mr. Stone, the publisher, also sent a thousand copies to New York at the end of March. He kept a few hundred copies here, and I have a few myself so I can replace yours if it was lost. The survival of the book is thus assured.

In my short letter via Mr. Curwen, I had the honor of acknowledging yours of 20 Apr. 1802. It reached me in Spa where I was being treated for the deadly illness that afflicts me. I am still not recovered, although I have had some glimmers of hope lately. To fulfill them, I will have to renounce all serious, assiduous work and spend winters in a climate very different from that of Paris, since I need daily dry, warm air. A knowledgeable doctor can enlighten you if you wish to know more about bladder inflammation.

You asked me for a book about Egypt. Mr. Denon's was published to great acclaim, but it is in three volumes in duodecimo. The infolio version costs 15 guineas and is no longer available. The volume that combines plates and text is like an *Atlas*, unwieldy to handle. Mr. Monroe says he will communicate your intentions about this.

My book about the *climate* and *soil* of the United States, 450-500 pages, is in press. They are up to the fifth leaf. It contains little, if anything, about politics and ethics, since one would have to say either too much or too little. It includes a curious dictionary of the Miami language, as dictated by your interpreter, Wells, and Little Turtle, that I assembled during two months in Philadelphia in 1797.

My wish is that you could collect samples of all the languages of the various indigenous tribes on your continent. It would be a worthy project for Congress to create three or four positions for interpreters, to prevent the irrevocable loss of this kind of historic treasure, which is the most authentic and revealing information about the origin of nations and affinities among them. In a hundred years, several of these tribes may have disappeared entirely, taking with them essential links to the human filiation.

In my book I also invite the American government to do a precise report on the current state of Niagara Falls that can serve as a basis for future comparisons.

The messenger who is bringing you this letter is, I believe, bringing you important and welcome news about the Mississippi affair. The First Consul told me, on my last visit, that the case had been resolved. No one in this country will offer more sincere compliments than I do. You have long known my opinions, Sir, on this subject. They earned me calumny here, and, in contemporary parlance, "disfavor," but I persevered, to my credit. Today I have the satisfaction of seeing that what has occurred since the peace treaty so perfectly mirrors the predictions I made at General Leclerc's departure that one might believe I had read the book of destiny. At that time, I dared say to whomever it was bold and useful to tell, that it was necessary to carry out with wisdom, moderation, and prudence what the nature of things would otherwise soon do inevitably and violently. It was necessary to abandon faraway, burdensome possessions that were illusory and impossible to retain because a superior enemy was in the way. Even if we succeeded in forcefully restoring a system whose evil had just been manifest, the enemy's capacity to paralyze everything with a new war made such possessions illusory. It was all the more necessary not to antagonize a third party, ally or neutral, by occupying one of the normal exits from his house, especially since this *exit* provided nothing but expense and more-than-equivocal hope. True power consists in not dispersing oneself outside one's sphere of activity. Since we are a continental power, we should now limit ourselves to a strong presence here. Without leaving the Mediterranean, we have enough to meet all needs and even all the luxuries of colonial possession and production in the two Indies, etc. At the time, I was considered a philosophical dreamer, which is now perfectly ridiculous and absurd. As you can see, time has avenged me. If we begin to regret the loss of so many men, riches, time, etc., I predict that there will be another war. And since war is as much about passion as about necessity (to our misfortune), it will last longer and have more disruptive consequences than people seem to realize or measure. Of the two rivals the one that rules the sea might well, as seems ominous, be excluded from the European continent. But it will even more certainly exclude its enemy and that country's allies from the American continent. The empires of Montezuma and Manco Capac could be provoked by two or three battles to establish their independence. At that point, farewell to the empire of Isabella; farewell to the galleons and piasters, which would be redirected to enrich the factories of Manchester and Birmingham, and thereby allow banks to use hard currency. A reaction would then ensue on the European continent which would interfere, at the very least, with overly confident speculation, especially when every day the illusions of credulity are unveiled. Since from your vantage point you can see and hear the pros and cons, while we can see only one side, you can judge better than I the political future that is in store. The decision you made to acquire by time-honored means what your country could have obtained by force or ruse will reap ever-growing gratitude. What a fortunate country whose principles of government include the sparing of lives and money, moderation in public and private spending, love and respect for justice, as well as compassion, if not esteem, for the poor human race, and for that portion of the human race that is the common people, whom one treats with contempt only to have the right to crush them. Poor Europe! A theater of carnage and a plaything of conquerors!

You know, Sir, my unwavering feelings of respect and devotion.

VOLNEY

RC (DLC); at head of text: "Mr jefferson"; endorsed by TJ as received 5 Sep. and so recorded in SJL.

DEUX VOLUMES: TJ had sent Volney the latest volume of American Philosophical Society *Transactions* and TJ's *Manual of Parliamentary Practice* (TJ to Nicolas Gouin Dufief, 4 Feb.; TJ to Volney, 6 Feb.). TOPOGRAPHIE DES FLORIDES: the *Transactions* included Andrew Ellicott's "Astronomical, and Thermometrical Observations" from the survey of the southern boundary of the U.S. (APS, *Transactions*, 5 [1802], 203-311).

UN MILLIER D'EXEMPLAIRES À NEW-YORK: later in May, the *New Translation of Volney's Ruins* began to appear in advertisements in New York City (*Morning Chronicle*, 20 May).

COURTE LETTRE PAR MR. CURWEN: Volney to TJ, 21 Mch.

Volney's doctors sent him to SPA in Belgium for several weeks in the summer of 1802. The chronic inflammation of the bladder from which he suffered could be very painful and he was becoming more reclusive, due in part to his malady (Jean Gaulmier, *L'Idéologue Volney, 1757–1820: Contribution à l'Histoire de l'Orientalisme en France* [Geneva, 1980], 483, 490-5).

QUELQUE LIVRE SUR L'EGYPTE: in his 20 Apr. 1802 letter, after thanking Volney for sending a model of the Great Pyramid, TJ asked for a recommendation of a book "giving a general view of Egypt, it's inhabitants and antiquities." In 1801, Volney sent TJ a prospectus for Vivant Denon's *Voyage dans la Basse et la Haute Égypte*, which was published the next year (Vol. 34:454; Vol. 37:295).

SUR LE CLIMAT ET LE SOL DES ETATS UNIS: publication of Volney's *Tableau du Climat et du Sol des États-Unis d'Amérique* was complete by November 1803. He based the two-volume work on information he collected during the time he spent in the United States from the fall of 1795 to the spring of 1798. VOCABULAIRE: at the end of the *Tableau* Volney included a word list of the language of the Miami Indians, which he had collected in Philadelphia, probably in the early months of 1798. He compiled the list by using one of TJ's blank vocabulary forms and interviewing Little Turtle and William WELLS, who was the Miami leader's translator and son-in-law. Volney visited NIAGARA Falls and devoted a chapter of his book to it. In his call for an official report on the falls, he noted that the time for such a study was opportune, with a friend of learning, "un ami des sciences et des arts," at the head of the U.S. government (Volney, *Tableau du Climat et du Sol des États-Unis d'Amérique*, 2 vols. [Paris, 1803], 1:119-20n; 2:525-32; Vol. 28:525-6; Vol. 30:82n, 393; Vol. 36:284n; Volney to TJ, 26 Nov. 1803).

EMPIRES DE MONTEZUME ET DE MANCO-COPAC: that is, Mexico and South America.

From Hugh Williamson

SIR New York 10th: May 1803.

Your's of 30th ult: conveys the most agreeable information for which I give you my cordial thanks. I had suspected and I think it is generally believed that East and West Florida had been ceded to France as appendages of Louisiana. It was even asserted that the French had already taken possession of St: Augustine and I confess that I had painful presages from the circumstance of our fellow citizens in Georgia coming in contact with such restless intrigueing neighbours. It is said to be a maxim in France that the crown cannot, even by treaty, alienate any part of the empire. If Louisiana (undescribed) had been ceded to France by her late treaty with Spain, one might easily discover that under the flexible & dilatable term Louisiana Bonaparte might, in a future day, have claimed much territory to the eastward of the Messissippi. The circumstance of the Iberville Amite & L. Ponchartrain being the described boundary in the late treaty of cession and all our rights according to treaties with Spain being saved by the said late Treaty has fully removed my greatest apprehensions.

I am nevertheless perfectly of your opinion that a place of deposit, without our own territory, should not if possible be resorted to. To avail ourselves of such a place, except as a meer temporary expedient, is contrary to all commercial or oeconomical maxims. He must be little versed in history who does not know that great cities are created by the meer Depôt of commerce who does not know that the splendid Palmira arose from the bosom of a sandy desart by this advantage alone. I think the exports from Asia to Europe by land were small when compared with the future exports of a great and fertile country that is watered by a thousand branches of the river Ohio. The depôt of this commerce will infallibly create a great & powerful city, a city that should not be nourished for the benefit of a rival nation, lest we should nourish a serpent whose bite may be fatal. Such a city, in a few years, would be able to laugh at our pretences to a right of free deposit. So far am I from wishing that we should make use of New Orleans as a perpetual place of deposit, that I would gladly hear of its being absolutely neglected and forsaken by our citizens, provided we could substitute a position within our own territories not more unhealthy & fit for the site of a City. A Project that was suggested to me many years ago by a western gentleman, I deem visionary viz "to cut a navigable canal from the great bend of the Tennessee to the head of the river Mobille." He alledged that the freshes in a few years would increase that canal so as to make it a chief vent of the River Tennessee. When I consider that the head of Bear River is near the head of Mobille & that Bear river runs to the northward, I conclude that the source of those two rivers is upon ground too high to be cut through, but that is not the case with the ground between the Mississippi and the River Amite. It is confessedly mud or sand & perfectly level. Such a cut is doubtless practicable and the navigation of the lake much less tedious than ascending the Mississippi from its mouth. If the Spaniard could be induced to give us West Florida, which can never be of any use to him, we should be effectually relieved. We might effect a clear passage to the Sea of which one side at least would be our own. By our own commerce we should build a city inhabited by our own citizens and we should not be hourly endangered by embargos and other vexations. In a word, Belgrade upon the Danube is not, in my estimation, more obnoxious to the Germans than New Orleans must be to our fellow citizens on the western waters, provided they cannot arrive at the ocean without passing by a long and narrow river through the possessions of France. Forgive this long digression, I sat down to thank you for grateful intelligence but my pen has run away with my prudence. I have been writing on a subject you understand much better.

As to the late proposition that was made in Congress viz the taking immediate possession of New Orleans by an armed force, I had always regarded it as one of the cases in which the common order of appearances was reversed. Men are frequently more wicked but seldom less wicked than they pretend. But such as I hoped was the case with Ross & Co: It was hardly to be seriously believed that any civilised men were so perfectly lost to prudence, so prodigal of blood & treasure as to involve the United States in war with two great nations meerly because an officer of little respectability at 3000 miles distance from his court, probably without authority and meerly with the hope of making money by mercantile speculations and the fall of produce, had interrupted our commerce. I have long observed that our species is not correctly defined "animal rationale." It is an animal guided by passion & that in many cases less discreetly than other animals are guided by instinct. A full blooded oppositionist in most cases is prepared to afferm that two and two are not equal to four.

I am with the utmost consideration & respect Your most obedient and very humble Servant HU WILLIAMSON

RC (DLC); at foot of text: "Thomas Jefferson Esqr President of the U:S:"; endorsed by TJ as received 12 May and so recorded in SJL.

To Joseph Yznardi, Sr.

DEAR SIR Washington May 10. 1803.

Among the wines you were so kind as to furnish me the one called in your letter Xeres sin color (pale Sherry) has most particularly attached my taste to it. I now drink nothing else, and am apprehensive that if I should fail in the means of getting it, it will be a privation which I shall feel sensibly once a day. while you live I am sure I shall be able to get it pure & good, and in the event of my surviving you, you must in the mean time inform me of the vineyard, & the owner of it, where the best crop is made, so that I may have it purchased directly on the spot where it's quality is sure. for the present I will ask you to send me annually a pipe of it, old & fine. your bill on me for the amount of the first pipe shall be paid at short sight, and as this will inform me of the cost at Cadiz, it shall afterwards be remitted in advance.

I am in hopes your health has been re-established since your return to your native country, and, taking an interest in it, I shall be glad to learn it from yourself. Accept my friendly salutations and assurances of my great esteem & respect. TH: JEFFERSON

P.S. The wine should always be in a double cask. Norfolk or Richmond are the most convenient ports for me & they may be addressed to the Collector of the customs of the place to be forwarded to *my order*.

PrC (DLC); at foot of text: "Don Joseph Yznardi"; endorsed by TJ in ink on verso. Recorded in SJL with notation "for pale Sherry."

XERES SIN COLOR: TJ received from Yznardi in February 1802 three half-pipes of what Yznardi then termed "Natural Sherry" (Vol. 33:362; Vol. 36:482-3, 572-3).

From James Burnham

SIR, Beverly May 11, 1803

Mr. Cutler has informed me that you intimated a wish, to purchase some Ticking in the course of the Summer ensuing. I have sent some to Mr Lewis Deblois of Washington for Sale, & among them two pieces of superfine, about enough for five beds, which I have directed him not to sell until you have seen them.—I have also sent a piece of coarse printed cotton, designed for the wear of laboring people & servants; and considering the price of it (altho' it may seem high) I believe it will be found, in point of durability, to be equal to any article of clothing in the Country, and on the whole cheaper—Should you think well of it, I should be gratified by your giving a few yards of it a trial, on some of your Domestics—

I am Sir respectfully your obdt Sert. JAMES BURNHAM

RC (MHi); at head of text: "Thomas Jefferson Esqr."; endorsed by TJ as received 16 May and so recorded in SJL.

Manasseh CUTLER showed some of Burnham's textile samples to TJ on the previous New Year's Day (see Vol. 39: 525-6). On 24 May, LEWIS DEBLOIS issued an invoice for $79.59 for TJ's purchase of 70¾ yards of "Superfine Bed Tick from James Burnhams Manufactory in Beverly." On 13 June, TJ added to the invoice an order that John "Barnes will be pleased to pay this." Deblois wrote below TJ's order the following day, "Recd. of Mr. John Barnes Seventy nine dollars & fifty nine Cents in full of the above amount" (MS in CSmH; in Lewis Deblois's hand and signed by him; with order on Barnes in TJ's hand and signed by him; endorsed by Barnes). TJ recorded the transaction in his financial memoranda on 13 June (MB, 2:1102).

From Pierre Samuel Du Pont de Nemours

Paris 22 Floréal 11
(12 May 1803.)

MONSIEUR LE PRÉSIDENT,

Permettez moi de féliciter les Etats Unis et Vous sur la Sagesse avec laquelle, résistant à la guerre qui aurait jetté votre Nation dans les bras d'un Allié redoutable, vous avez acquis sans répandre de sang un Pays décuple en étendue et en fertilité de celui même que vous désiriez.

Vous êtes surs à présent, non seulement du débouché nécessaire à vos Etats de l'Ouest, mais de les étendre sans difficulté en raison du progrès des lumieres et de celui des travaux utiles, et de ne pouvoir jamais être cernés par aucune Puissance, comme il n'eut pas eté impossible que vous le fussiez si la Louisiane et le Canada eussent appartenu soit à la même Nation, soit à des Nations passagerement coalisées.

Dans l'état actuel, la Louisiane pompera le Canada par l'attrait de son climat plus doux, et par celui que trouveront les habitans à former dans votre confédération un Etat libre lorsque leur population sera suffisamment nombreuse.

Et j'espere que vous trouverez qu'il est assez doux d'avoir une Nation Française à gouverner quand les principes de guerre et de corruption sont éloignés d'elle.

Notre sensibilité, notre activité, notre gayté, notre ardeur, ne feront point un mauvais mélange pour vos entreprises, ni par la suite dans votre Congrès avec la gravité, la profondeur et le sens de votre ancien Peuple anglais, allemand, hollandais et suisse.

Ces deux dernieres Nations, dont une partie parle français seront au nombre de celles qui recruteront la Louisiane. Et, si j'ôsais à parler de mon plaisir, de mon bonheur personnel dans ce grand événement, je vous dirais que ce m'est une extrême consolation de voir unir à Votre chere et respectable République une Nation dont je sais bien la Langue, dont je connais bien les mœurs, chez laquelle je pourrai mieux concourir à vos vues, et trouver, non pas seulement un asyle comme un pauvre Mortel abandonné, mais employer mes derniers jours dans les travaux d'instruction et de civilisation qui ont occupé ma vie en Europe, d'abord avec tant de justes espérances et en suite avec si peu de succès.

J'aurai l'avantage de vous revoir; et ce qui vient d'arriver à la Louisiane en est avec le sentiment qui m'attache à vous un gage triplement certain. Mais ce ne pourra être aussitôt que je le désirerais.

J'ai plusieurs devoirs à remplir avant de disposer definitivement de ma vie. L'accommodement entre nos deux Nations n'en était qu'un.

Je n'exposerai point les manuscrits de Mr. Turgot à repasser une troisieme fois l'Atlantique. Il faut qu'avant de quitter la France j'en aie publié, tout ce qu'il eut désiré qu'on en publiât.

Il faut encore que j'aie augmenté autant qu'il sera possible mes moyens de vous bien servir quand je retournerai chez vous. Car ce que j'ai dans la tête et dans le cœur ne se fait pas avec de petits moyens, et la richesse est aussi une puissance pour l'homme qui veut être bon avec quelque grandeur.

Vous y pouvez contribuer en Amérique par votre bienveillance pour mes enfans; et à Paris en y chargeant ma maison de Banque et de Commerce d'acquitter les arrérages de vos *Stocks* qui sont dus à des Français et à des Suisses, comme aussi de négocier les emprunts que vous pourriez avoir à faire, si vos ressources intérieures ne suffisent pas à vos payemens.

Lorsque j'aurai mis ce travail en parfaite marche, et publié les œuvres de mon excellent Ami, et fait encore quelque chose d'utile à la France que je ne veux pas quitter en ingrat, je laisserai, toujours sous mon nom et ma garantie, diriger ce que vous m'aurez confié d'operations de banque en Europe à un Associé complettement sûr, et je rapporterai ma personne, mon travail, mes efforts au seul Pays libre de l'Univers, au seul qui puisse esperer d'être désormais l'exemple du monde.

Je vous dis ici le secret des Secrets de mon cœur, que je ne pourrais laisser connaitre en France sans y perdre toute possibilité de bien faire.

Ne croyez donc pas que j'aie changé d'opinion ou de plan, quand même vous me verriez accepter quelques fonctions qui sembleraient me fixer loin de vos climats. Il est possible que je devienne Sénateur français, et impossible que je cesse d'être Républicain d'Amérique.

En me voyant ainsi tailler devant moi des besognes de longue haleine, mon illustre Ami, ne vous inquietez pas de mon âge. J'ai encore de la vie pour le nombre d'années qu'il me faut; vous en pouvez juger par mes projets même: et le Vin généreux s'améliore en vieillissant.

Salut, attachement, reconnaissance et respect.

Du Pont (de Nemours)

J'ajoute encore un mot qui ne choquera pas vos principes.

Il devient plus nécessaire que jamais d'organiser l'éducation de votre Peuple, et de maniere qu'elle lui rende dès l'enfance l'esprit de conquête odieux. Il faut qu'on s'accoutume à regarder avec horreur et mépris, comme un brigand, celui qui songerait à marcher en armes chez une autre Nation pour s'emparer de son Pays.

Repoussez ainsi, sans en parler formellement, la tentation que le Mexique donnerait à des Aventuriers politiques.

Si jamais les Etats unis s'abaissaient à le conquérir, tous les vices et tous les malheurs en reflueraient sur eux. Les uns se croiraient assez riches pour achetter la liberté de leurs Freres. Les autres émigreraient pour la terre d'argent. Vos Agriculteurs quitteraient leurs champs fertiles et salubres pour le sol infécond et mal sain des mines. Votre Peuple s'écoulerait, se fondrait. Et l'on dirait sur les débris de vos fermes: *Là fut une Nation heureuse et riche qu'une sote avidité appauvrit et perdit.*

EDITORS' TRANSLATION

Paris, 22 Floreal Year 11
(12 May 1803)

Mister President,

Allow me to congratulate you and the United States for the wisdom with which you resisted a war that would have thrown your country into the arms of a formidable ally; as a result acquired, without bloodshed, a country ten times larger and richer than the one you wished for.

Now you have ensured, not only a necessary waterway for your western states, but a feasible means of expanding these states, given the progress of science and industry. Thus you will never be surrounded by another power, as you might have been if Louisiana and Canada had belonged to the same country, or to a temporary coalition of nations.

Now Louisiana will draw inhabitants away from Canada because of its milder weather and the political climate they will find when their population is sufficiently large to allow them to create a free state in your confederation.

I hope you will take pleasure in governing a French nation that has been freed from the principles of war and corruption.

Our spirit, energy, optimism, and ardor will contribute to your projects, and, ultimately to your Congress, alongside the seriousness, depth, and sensibility of your citizens of English, German, Dutch, and Swiss origin.

These two latter countries, which are partly French-speaking, will be among those that recruit population for Louisiana. If I dared evoke my own pleasure, my personal happiness at this great event, I would tell you that it is a great consolation for me to see your cherished, eminent republic united with a nation whose language and customs I know. In this landscape I can better contribute to your plans and not only find refuge as a poor, abandoned mortal, but use my final days in the service of teaching and civilization, as I have spent my time in Europe, with so much legitimate hope at the beginning and so little success now.

I will also have the advantage of seeing you again. What has just happened to Louisiana is a thrice-certain pledge of the sentiments by which I am attached to you. But I cannot yet satisfy my desire. I have several obligations to fulfill before I can make definitive plans for my life. The understanding between our two countries was only one of these obligations.

I will not take the risk of having Mr. Turgot's manuscripts cross the Atlantic a third time. Before leaving France, I must publish all that he wished to see published.

I must also enhance, as much as possible, my capacity to serve you well when I return to your country. What I have in heart and mind cannot be done with modest means; wealth is also a quality for a man who wants to be good on a large scale.

You can help me in America by your benevolence toward my children, and in Paris by asking my banking and trading company to make the payments that are due to French and Swiss creditors and to negotiate whatever loans might be necessary, if your finances are not sufficient to cover the payments.

When I have put all this in place, published the works of my excellent friend, and done something else useful for France, which I do not want to leave as an ingrate, I will delegate your financial transactions to an absolutely trustworthy associate, who will act in my name and with my guarantee. Then I will bring myself, my work and my efforts to the only free country in the universe, the only one that can aspire, henceforth, to be an example for the world.

Here I am sharing the most hidden secrets of my heart which I could not reveal in France without giving up all possibility of doing good.

If you see me accepting positions that would seem to keep me far from your soil, do not imagine that my thinking or planning have changed. I may become a French senator, but I will never cease being an American republican.

When you see me undertaking long-term projects, my illustrious friend, do not worry about my age. There are still enough years in my lifetime. You can judge by the projects themselves. And good wine improves with age.

Greetings, devotion, gratitude and respect.

Du Pont (de Nemours)

I am adding a few words that will not shock your principles.

It is becoming more necessary than ever to organize the education of your people, and in a way that renders the spirit of conquest odious to them from childhood. We must accustom them to view with horror and disdain, as a brigand, someone who would contemplate invading another nation to seize its land.

Repel, in this way, without specifically mentioning it, the temptation that Mexico might offer to political adventurers.

If the United States should ever stoop to conquer it, all evils and misfortunes would befall your country. Some would feel rich enough to buy the liberty of their brothers. Others would emigrate to the Land of Silver. Your farmers would leave their fertile, healthy fields for sterile, unhealthy mines. Your people would fall apart, dissolve. And it would be said, on the remains of your farms: *there was once a rich, happy nation, that became impoverished and lost by foolish greed.*

RC (DLC); at head of text: "A Son Excellence Thomas Jefferson, Président des Etats Unis"; endorsed by TJ as received 14 July and so recorded in SJL.

Du Pont had taken with him, from France to the United States and back again, the correspondence and manuscripts of Anne Robert Jacques TURGOT. Du Pont prepared an edition of the political economist's *Œuvres* in nine volumes published in Paris from 1809 to 1811 (Ambrose Saricks, *Pierre Samuel Du Pont de Nemours* [Lawrence, Kans., 1965], 314-16; Vol. 36:132n).

SÉNATEUR FRANÇAIS: Du Pont hoped —ultimately in vain—that Bonaparte would give him a seat in the *Sénat* (Saricks, *Du Pont*, 301-2).

To John Wayles Eppes

DEAR SIR   Washington May 12. 1803.

Your's of the 6th. is recieved. I have not yet heard any thing from mr Hancocke respecting the syrup of punch. I remit monies to G. Jefferson by this post, out of which he will answer the 400 D. for which I now inclose you an order.

If the proposition you make of the exchange of the lands in Bedford for Lego, involved no further consequence, the difficulties would be lessened. but a principle of just equality would oblige me then to make a like exchange with mr Randolph, to whom it would certainly be as desireable to have his lands close around him. this would strip me at home, and the operation would end in transferring my concerns from thence to Bedford, at a time of life when I am becoming less able to take long journies to look after them, & more anxious to gather all my cares around me into as contracted a circle as I can. but both your object & mine can be effected substantially in another form. you propose to have the lands in Bedford cleared so as to yield a rent equivalent to that of Lego. take Lego then as a tenant, & reimburse yourself the rent by clearing & leasing the lands in

Bedford. I should have no objections to the recieving the rent from your tenant there, & my overseer should always be charged to overlook the conduct of the tenant as if it were my own. the conditions too, as to the mode of cultivating Lego, which would be exacted of another tenant, should be relaxed for you, so as to permit you to give it the same course of culture with your own adjoining farm. if this will suit you, you may take immediate possession of Lego, and begin it's culture or preparation. no rent shall be required for the present or the ensuing year, as well in consideration that the place is so much out of order, as to give you time to have the lands in Bedford opened and as I must have a road along the river side, & the farm ought moreover to have a fence on the river, I will make it the next winter, you maintaining it afterwards. Petty occupies a part of the tract adjoining Shadwell, and, had he complied with the conditions of[1] his lease, would have had a right for some time to come; but he has complied with no part, & I had meditated to exercise my right of re-entry this fall. in the mean time it would be better to say nothing of it, to give him any such suspicion. present my tenderest love to my ever dear Maria. I hope she will return soon to Monticello, where Lilly, & Craven & the cellars will furnish you as if I were there. Accept yourself assurances of my affectionate attachment.

TH: JEFFERSON

RC (Stanley Neyhart, Brooklyn, New York, 1948); at foot of text: "J. W. Eppes." PrC (ViU: Edgehill-Randolph Papers); endorsed by TJ in ink on verso. Enclosure not found.

James PETTY leased part of TJ's Lego land (MB, 2:1107; Vol. 34:595).

[1]Preceding three words interlined.

To George Jefferson

DEAR SIR Washington May 12. 1803.

Your's of Apr. 27. was recieved in due time. I have recieved general information only from my overseer that the tobacco of the last year was of good quality, but he did not say how it was in comparison with other years; the idea impressed on me was that it was better than usual. I wrote immediately to him to hasten it down, as it is essential to me to provide out of it to meet my note of 1300. D. payable at your counting house July 12. I inclose you a bill of lading of some groceries which left this place about the 8th. to be forwarded to Monticello. they went by the Schooner Active capt Scott J. No. 1. 2. 4. 5. 6. 7. being six barrels & casks, and No. 3. a box of oil. mr Hancocke of Petersburg was to send me two barrels of Syrup of punch or Center, one for Monticello & one for this place. I know not whether he will send both to you, or only the one for Monticello. should he send both, be so good as to forward one here. in the course of a month or so a clock will be sent from Philadelphia to your address to be forwarded to Monticello. it must go by water, and should it not be so cased as to be waterproof, I will gladly incur the expence of covering the part containing the works with oil cloth, as the rains, while in an open boat would destroy it. I inclose you 750 Dollars, and draw on you this day for 400. in favor of J. W. Eppes. Accept my affectionate salutations.

TH: JEFFERSON

PrC (MHi); at foot of text: "Mr. G. Jefferson"; endorsed by TJ in ink on verso. Recorded in SJL with notation "400. D. for J.W.E. 350. for himself. groceries. lemonade. clock." Enclosures not found.

A letter of 23 Mch. from TJ's Poplar Forest OVERSEER Burgess Griffin, recorded in SJL as received 28 Mch., has not been found. A letter of 31 Mch. from TJ to Griffin has also not been found.

For the CLOCK that TJ was obtaining, see Isaac Briggs to TJ, 2 May.

From Rufus King

SIR London May 12. 1803

I have not been able to obtain the consent of the Sierra Leone Company to receive the Slaves which the State of Virginia might be willing to send to that settlement. My Correspondence on this Subject has been closed by a Letter from the Chairman Mr. Thornton which states that the Company are in Treaty with Government to receive the Colony under its exclusive control.

The fact I understand to be that the Negroes who have been sent thither are so refractory and ungovernable, and the expense and trouble of maintaining the settlement so great, that the Company have determined to abandon their plan, and the application to Government is with the view of disembarrassing themselves of the Settlement.

With perfect Respect—I have the honour to be, Sir, Your obedt: & faithful Servt

RUFUS KING

RC (DLC); in a clerk's hand, signed by King; at foot of text: "His Excellency Thomas Jefferson &c &c &c"; endorsed by TJ as received 4 July, but recorded in SJL as received 3 July. FC (NHi: Rufus King Papers). Enclosures: (1) King to William Wilberforce, Randalls Park estate, Surrey, 8 Jan.; asks Wilberforce to speak to his neighbor, Henry Thornton, about the application "to send certain of our Negroes to Sierra Leone"; King does not believe that "the Presumption, that our Negroes are all of the same idle and disorderly character, as those who joined the English army in America, and who afterwards were abandoned to and infected by the vices of a succession of Garrison Towns," has any basis, but proposes that the Sierra Leone Company allow "a limited number" of blacks from the United

States to be settled in the colony "by way of experiment"; the people to be sent would fall into two categories, the first being slaves "manumitted by their Masters," a group that would "include our most meritorious Slaves"; the second category would consist of slaves "detected in attempts to excite Insurrections among their fellow Slaves"; this second group would not include "the idle and the vicious," who would lack "sufficient influence over their associates to become Leaders in Schemes of Insurrection"; King notes that "occasional good offices, and Tokens of regard" will be beneficial to good relations between Great Britain and the United States (Tr in DLC; in a clerk's hand; at head of text: "Copies" and "Mr. King to Mr. Wilberforce"). (2) King to Henry Thornton, London, 30 Apr., reminding him of the application for permission for the state of Virginia to send to Sierra Leone emancipated slaves, "together with those whose residence in virginia might prove injurious to the subordination of its Slaves" (Tr in same; in a clerk's hand; at head of text: "Mr. King to Mr. Thornton"). (3) Thornton to King, London, 10 May, informing him that talks are under way for a transfer of the colony from the company to the British government; the company's directors advise King to contact the secretary or undersecretary for war and the colonies for an answer to the Virginia proposition (Tr in same; in a clerk's hand; at head of text: "Mr. Thornton to Mr. King").

MY CORRESPONDENCE: King did not enclose a copy of the reply that William Wilberforce wrote him on 11 Jan., in which Wilberforce said that he would impress on "Mr. A."—Henry Addington, the prime minister—"the extreme Importance of cultivating that friendship betwn. the two countries so desirable, on all accounts, for both." Wilberforce reported that he would try to take the matter up with Lord Hawkesbury also, but he was "not on the same *confidential* terms" with Hawkesbury as he was with Addington (King, *Life*, 4:206-7).

Henry THORNTON was chairman of the Court of Directors of the Sierra Leone Company. Wilberforce represented Yorkshire in the House of Commons. The two of them were founders of the company in 1791. Although in 1803 the company's directors and Parliament considered transferring the colony to the crown's control, an act for that purpose did not pass until 1807 (Michael J. Turner, "The Limits of Abolition: Government, Saints and the 'African Question,' c. 1780-1820," *English Historical Review*, 112 [1997], 319-57; DNB; Vol. 38:473-6).

From John H. Barney

SR. George Town 13th. May 1803

I have the Honour of sending herewith two Books which I reced. from my brother Joshua Barney some few days since, as also a Letter accompaing them.

Yr. Ob. St. JNO. H. BARNEY

RC (MHi); at head of text: "Thos. Jefferson President of the U.S."; endorsed by TJ as received 13 May and so recorded in SJL. Enclosure: probably John Dawson to TJ, 4 Mch.

Upon his retirement from the French naval service, JOSHUA BARNEY tended to his lapsed commercial ventures in Baltimore. He dined with TJ on 23 Oct. 1802, shortly after his return from France (Mary Barney, ed., *A Biographical Memoir of the Late Commodore Joshua Barney* [Boston, 1832], 233-7; Vol. 34:261n).

To Henry Dearborn

TH:J. TO GENL. DEARBORNE May 13. 1803.

I am much pleased with both the ideas suggested by Lyons, viz. 1. to proceed from Knoxville direct through the Cherokee Creek & Choctaw[1] country to Natchez. 2. to encourage individuals to make terms with the Indians on their private account for establishing farms along the line at every 15. or 30. or 45. miles distance as can be obtained. but instead of going from Knoxville to Natchez in a strait line, it might be[2] better to go down the Tennissee to our Trading post, because [that] must be a settled country; then to run a strait line, by compass to Fort Confederation, & from thence to Natchez: or better perhaps a strait line at once from the Trading post to Natchez, on the presumption that Fort Confederation is but a temporary establishment, & ought not therefore to affect a permanent road. leave need only be asked of the Indians to open a horsepath at first. a waggon way will grow out of that in due time, taking advantage of occurrences to gain it. could not Freeman be employed in running & marking the strait line, when he shall have finished at Vincennes? it is possible however that the road from Knoxville down the Tennissee may be very hilly; this is generally the case on rivers[3] unless a[4] road can be carried along the bank. should it be too hilly, the strait line might be preferable, as it seems to lead along the ridge dividing the waters of the Tennissee and head waters of the Alabama. the best *carriage* road would be along the ridge between the head waters of the Tennissee & Alabama, & thence along the ridge between the head waters of the Yazoo & Big black. but this would be circuitous, and only desireable when the intercourse by waggons & other carriages shall become considerable. I wish we had a survey of the Yazoo, with a view to our acquiring the country between that & the Missisipi.

PrC (DLC); blurred. Recorded in SJL with notation "road to Natchez."

SUGGESTED BY LYONS: possibly Matthew Lyon, whose many western business interests included contracts with the War Department and postal service (Aleine Austin, *Matthew Lyon: "New Man" of the Democratic Revolution, 1749-1822* [University Park, Pa., 1981], 133-4).

Located on the upper Tombigbee River in present-day Alabama, FORT CONFEDERATION was abandoned by Spain as part of the Pinckney Treaty. The outpost was the site of the conference and treaty signing between the Choctaws and James Wilkinson in October 1802 (James P. Pate, "The Fort of the Confederation: The Spanish on the Upper Tombigbee," *Alabama Historical Quarterly*, 44 [1982], 171-86; ASP, *Indian Affairs*, 1:682; TJ to the Senate, 7 Jan. 1803).

Thomas FREEMAN was in charge of surveying the boundary of the Vincennes tract in the Indiana Territory (*Indiana Magazine of History*, 12 [1916], 1-15; *Terr. Papers*, 7:54-5).

[1]Preceding two words and ampersand interlined.

[2]Preceding three words interlined in place of canceled words.

[3]Preceding two words interlined.

[4]Word interlined in place of "the."

From Gideon Granger, with Jefferson's Note

DR SIR. Suffield May 13th. 1803.

I have the pleasure to acknowledge the receipt of yours of the 8th. and in return to communicate Intelligence no less pleasing. yesterday our Legislature assembled at the City of Hartford. The Votes for Govr. were—for Trumbull something over 14,300. for Kirby 7,848. last year Trumbull had over eleven Thousand and Kirby 4,523. The Increase of votes in our favor Since the last Struggle is 3,325. and exceeding the increase of federal votes in proportion a little short of 2,200. votes. I cannot be precise as my Letters are circulating amongst Our Citizens for their encouragement. party runs excessively high here—evry thing is said and done by the Tories. the Republicans Keep themselves cool & active. They are now aranging for the next Struggle. Their Spirit is good—but they are warm for removals. I inclose you the Copy of a petition which was this day presented to the Legislature. The Legislature of Rhode Island Mr. Ellery has just informd. me takes very strong ground.

Your sincere friend GIDN GRANGER

[*Note by TJ*:]

this year, of 100 parts of the whole voters we had 35 parts—they 65
last year of 100. parts of the whole voters we had 29 parts they 71
our increase then is in the ratio of 29:35
6:7

RC (DLC); note by TJ written in left margin; endorsed by TJ as received 19 May and so recorded in SJL. Enclosure not found, but see TJ to Granger, 20 May.

There were fewer Republicans in the LEGISLATURE that assembled at HARTFORD in May 1803. A year earlier, the Connecticut House included 55 Republicans and 136 Federalists. At the fall 1802 assembly at New Haven, the number of Republicans had increased to 66. In 1803, the total number of representatives in the Connecticut House increased to 193, but the number of Republicans declined to 48 versus 145 Federalists. The Republicans did much better in the fall 1803 election, increasing their number to 63 (Michael J. Dubin, *Party Affiliations in the State Legislatures: A Year by Year Summary, 1796-2006* [Jefferson, N.C., 2007], 32-3).

VOTES FOR GOVR.: Jonathan Trumbull received 14,375 votes in 1803 compared with 11,398 in 1802. Ephraim Kirby's percentage of the votes increased from 28.4 in 1802 to 35.3 in 1803 (Michael J. Dubin, *United States Gubernatorial Elections, 1776-1860: The Official Results by State and County* [Jefferson, N.C., 2003], 17; Norwich *Connecticut Centinel*, 17 May; Newport *Rhode-Island Republican*, 28 May 1803).

From Lacépède

à paris, le 23. floréal, an. 11.—
13. may 1803.

MONSIEUR LE PRÉSIDENT

Je m'empresse d'avoir l'honneur de vous remercier de la lettre que vous avez bien voulu me faire parvenir par M. Monroe. Cette lettre, Monsieur le président, est une marque de votre estime et parconséquent un titre très honorable pour moi. Je la conserverai, d ailleurs, comme un monument pour l'histoire. Il est si rare de voir le premier magistrat d'une grande nation, allier les lumières et les soins qu'exige le bonheur de ses concitoyens, aux vastes connoissances et aux travaux d'un philosophe célèbre.

On ne se trompe jamais lorsqu'on prédit qu'une grande et utile entreprise sera exécutée par une nation libre et que gouverne un chef digne d'elle. J'ai donc appris sans surprise, mais avec beaucoup de satisfaction, par le premier article de votre lettre, que vous allez faire reconnoître les sources du missouri, et chercher une rivière qui voisine dans son origine, de l'origine du missouri, porte ses eaux dans le grand océan boréal. Cette rivière que vous desirez pourroit bien être celle de *colombia* que M. gray votre compatriote a découverte en 1788 ou en 1789. M. brougthen, l'un des compagnons du Capitaine vancover, l'a remontée pendant cent *milles*, en décembre 1792. Il s'est arrêté à une pointe qu'il a nommée *vancover*, et qui est située au 45me degré 27. minutes de latitude septentrionale, et au 237me degré 50. minutes de longitude orientale, à compter du méridien de londres. Dans cet endroit, la rivière *colombia*, a encore un quart de mille de largeur, et sa profondeur varie entre 12. et trente six pieds anglois. Elle est donc à la pointe vancover encore loin de sa source; et cependant on voit de cette pointe, le mont *hood*, à la distance d'une vingtaine de lieues; or ce mont hood, pourroit bien être une dépendance des *stony mountains* dont M. fiedler a vu le commencement vers le 40me degré de latitude boréale; et les sources du missouri doivent être dans ces *stony mountains*, entre le 40me et le 45me degrés. Si votre nation peut établir une communication facile par des rivières, des canaux, et de courts *portages*, entre new yorck, par exemple, et la ville que l'on bâtiroit à l'embouchure de la colombia, quelle route pour le commerce de l'europe, de l'asie, et de l'amérique, dont les productions septentrionales arriveroient à cette route par les grands lacs et le mississipi supérieur pendant que les productions méridionales du nouveau continent, y parviendroient par le mississipi inférieur, et par cette rivière du nord du nouveau mexique, dont la source est voisine du 40me degré! Quels grands moyens de civilisation, que ces communications nouvelles!

Quelque soit, cependant, le succès du voyage que vous faites faire, il sera extrèmement utile aux progrès de l'industrie, des sciences, et particulièrement de l'histoire naturelle. Puissent vos concitoyens, par la sagesse de leurs choix, conserver à jamais leur liberté, leur gouvernement, et la paix! Jusques à présent, le mouvement des lumières, est d'orient en occident. Les habitants des états unis, s'ils ne se refusent pas à leur destinée, arrêteront un jour ce mouvement, et le rendront rétrograde.

Buffon est mort sans avoir pu faire usage du présent très précieux que vous lui aviez fait au sujet des animaux d'amérique qu'il avoit rapportés à l'espèce du renne, à celle du chevreuil, et à celle du cougar.

Le 5me et dernier volume de mon histoire des poissons va paroitre. J'écris maintenant celle des cétacées. L'avantage qu'a l'institut national de vous compter parmi ses membres, me fait espérer que vous voudrez bien me permettre de vous faire hommage d'un exemplaire de ces divers ouvrages.

Si ma santé n'avoit pas été entièrement dérangée par le malheur affreux que j'ai eu l'hiver dernier, de perdre une épouse chérie et des plus dignes de l'être, je formerois le projet d'aller un jour, dans votre continent, voir votre jeune nature, votre heureuse nation, et son digne magistrat suprême; mais le bonheur n'est plus fait pour moi.

agréez, Monsieur le président, l'expression de ma tendre admiration, de ma vive reconnoissance, et de mon respect.

B. G. É. L. LACEPÈDE

EDITORS' TRANSLATION

Paris, 23 Floreal Year 11.
13 May 1803

MISTER PRESIDENT,

I hasten to have the honor of thanking you for the letter you kindly entrusted to Mr. Monroe. It is a sign of your esteem, Mister President, and I am most honored. In fact, I shall keep it, like a monument for posterity. It is so rare to see the leader of a great nation who combines the intelligence and care that are necessary for the welfare of his citizens with the vast knowledge and scholarship of an eminent philosopher.

One never errs in predicting that great and useful things will be accomplished by a nation that is free and is governed by a leader who is worthy of that nation. I was therefore not surprised, although very happy, to learn from the first point in your letter that you are going to call for exploration of the source of the Missouri and look for another river, whose source is near the Missouri's but which flows into the great northern sea. The river you seek might well be the Columbia that your compatriot Mr. Gray discovered in 1788 or 1789. Mr. Broughton, one of Captain Vancouver's companions, navigated it northward for a hundred miles in December 1792. He stopped at a place he called Vancouver, located at latitude 45° 27′ N and longitude 237°

50′ E, starting from the London meridian. In this place, the Columbia river is still a quarter of a mile wide. Its depth varies from 12 to 36 English feet. Vancouver Point is thus still far from its source, and yet, from this place one can see Mount Hood, at a distance of about twenty leagues. Mount Hood might well be part of the Stony Mountains that Mr. Fidler began to see near 40° N. The source of the Missouri must be in those Stony Mountains, between the 40th and 45th parallels. If your country can establish easy communication between New York, for example, and a city founded on the mouth of the Columbia, using rivers, canals, and short portages, imagine what a route this would be for European, Asian, and American commerce. Products from the north would reach it from the Great Lakes and upper Mississippi while goods from the south of the new continent would arrive from the lower Mississippi and from the river in northern New Mexico whose source is close to the 40th parallel. What a great boon for civilization these new routes would be!

Whatever the outcome of the exploration you are commissioning, it will be extremely useful for the progress of industry, science, and, especially, natural history. May your fellow citizens, by the wisdom of their decisions, forever preserve their liberty, their government, and peace! Until now, the movement of enlightenment has been from east to west. Unless the inhabitants of the United States reject their destiny, they will one day check this movement and reverse it.

Buffon died without having been able to use the precious gift you gave him about the animals of America, which he was able to compare to the reindeer, the roe deer, and the cougar.

The fifth and final volume of my history of fish is about to come out. I am now writing a history of cetaceans. Knowing that the National Institute has the good fortune of counting you among its members gives me hope that you will allow me to honor you with a copy of these books.

If my health had not been completely undermined by the terrible misfortune I suffered last winter, losing the beloved wife who was so worthy of my love, I would make plans to visit your continent some day, to see your young nature, your happy country, and its worthy leader; but such happiness is not to be my fate.

Accept, Mister President, the expression of my warm admiration, my deep gratitude and my respect.
B. G. É. L. LACEPÈDE

RC (DLC); endorsed by TJ as received 14 July and so recorded in SJL.

LETTRE: TJ to Lacépède, 24 Feb. 1803.

On the Pacific Coast in May 1792, the *Columbia Rediviva*, a merchant vessel from Boston on a fur-trading voyage under the command of Robert GRAY, became the first ship to negotiate the sand bars and currents at the mouth of what Gray, in honor of his ship, named Columbia's River. Gray had made an earlier voyage to the Northwest Coast (DAB; J. Richard Nokes, *Columbia's River: The Voyages of Robert Gray, 1787-1793* [Tacoma, Wash., 1991], 14, 180-91).

L'UN DES COMPAGNONS DU CAPITAINE VANCOVER: later in 1792, William Robert Broughton, who commanded the brig *Chatham* on George Vancouver's exploration of the Northwest Coast for Great Britain, entered the estuary of the Columbia and investigated the lower course of the river by boat (same, 193; DNB).

M. FIEDLER: on behalf of the Hudson's Bay Company, Peter Fidler mapped the region from the North Saskatchewan River southwest to the foothills of the

Rocky Mountains in 1792 and 1793 (*Dictionary of Canadian Biography*, 15 vols. to date [Toronto, 1966-], 6:249).

See TJ's letter to Lacépède, 24 Feb., for TJ's interactions with the Comte de BUFFON about differences between American and Eurasian animals.

POISSONS: the fifth volume of Lacépède's *Histoire naturelle* of fish appeared in 1803. His volume on whales—CÉTACÉES—was published the following year.

UNE ÉPOUSE CHÉRIE: Lacépède had married Anne Huberte Charlotte Jubé Gauthier, a widow, in 1795 (*Dictionnaire*, 18:1476).

From James Lyon

May 13. 1803.

J. Lyon presents his respects to the president and takes the liberty of enclosing *a letter and an address "to the public"*; to shew what is doing (and what is necessary to be done) towards the accomplishment of an object which it is conceived must be in some measure interesting to every citizen.

RC (DLC); endorsed by TJ as received 13 May and so recorded in SJL. Enclosures: (1) Lyon to the Public, dated Washington, D.C., 1 May 1803, encouraging proposals for a contract for carrying the mail in stage coaches from Richmond, Virginia, to Lexington, Kentucky, beginning on 1 Apr. 1804, and seeking "public spirited individuals" to subscribe and provide premiums to underwrite the contract (printed copy in same; unsigned). (2) Address to the Public, providing estimates for first-year expenses to establish a line of stage coaches, including the "capital necessary to be expended" and the "support for the line one year" for the sum of $21,610; also announcing a premium, to be paid by subscribers, to the person who shall establish the stage line within 15 months of the notice (broadside in same; undated).

To J. P. G. Muhlenberg

DEAR SIR Washington May. 13. 1803.

There being no means of conveying foreign letters from this port, and your position being supposed advantageous for that, I take the liberty of availing myself of your friendship to ask you to give conveyance to the inclosed letters by such vessels bound to Cadiz and Lisbon direct, as may occur at your office. be so good as to excuse this trouble & to accept my friendly salutations. TH: JEFFERSON

PrC (DLC); at foot of text: "Genl. Muhlenberg"; endorsed by TJ in ink on verso. Enclosures: (1) TJ to William Jarvis, 10 May. (2) TJ to Joseph Yznardi, Sr., 10 May.

YOUR POSITION: Muhlenberg was collector of customs at Philadelphia (Muhlenberg to TJ, 7 Feb. 1803).

To Joseph H. Nicholson

Dear Sir Washington May 13. 1803.

I return you the letter of Capt Jones, with thanks for the perusal. while it is well to have an eye on our enemy's camp, it is not amiss to keep one for the movements in our own. I have no doubt that the agitation of the public mind on the continuance of tories in office, is excited in some degree by those who want to get in themselves. however the mass of those affected by it[1] can have no views of that kind. it is composed of such of our friends as have a warm sense of the former intolerance, and present bitterness of our adversaries and they are not without excuse. while it is best for our own tranquility to see and hear with apathy the atrocious calumnies of the presses which our enemies[2] support for the purposes of calumny, it is what they have no right to expect; nor can we consider the indignation they excite in others[3] as unjust, or strongly censure those whose temperament is not proof against it. nor are they protected in their places by any right they have to more than a just proportion of them, & still less by their own examples while in power: but by considerations respecting the tranquility of the public mind. this tranquility seems necessary to predispose the candid part of our fellow-citizens who have erred & strayed from their ways, to return again to them, and to consolidate once more[4] that union of will, without which the nation will not stand firm against foreign force & intrigue. on the subject of the particular schism at Philadelphia, a well informed friend says, 'the fretful turbulent disposition which has manifested itself in Phila. originated in some degree from a sufficient cause, which I will explain when I see you. a reunion will take place, & in the issue it will be useful. their resolves will be so tempered as to remove most of the unpleasant feelings which have been experienced.' I shall certainly be glad to recieve the explanation and modification of their proceedings; for they were taking a form which could not be approved on true principles. we laid down our line of proceedings on mature enquiry & consideration in 1801. and have not departed from it. some removals, to wit 16. to the end of our 1st. session of Congress[5] were made on political principle alone, in very urgent cases: and we determined to make no more but for delinquency, or active & bitter opposition to the order of things which the public will had established. on this last ground 9. were removed from the end of the 1st. to the end of the 2d. session of Congress; and one since that. so that 16. only have been removed in the whole for political principle, that is to say to make room for some participation for the republicans who had been systematically excluded from office. I do not include the midnight appointments. these were a mere fraud not suffered to go into effect. pursuing our object of harmonising all good people of whatever description, we shall steadily adhere to our rule, and it is with sincere pleasure I learn that it is approved by the more moderate part of our friends.

We have recieved official information that in the instrument of cession of Louisiana to France were these words, 'Saving the rights acquired by other powers in virtue of treaties made with them by Spain'; and cordial acknolegements from this power for our temperate forbearance under the misconduct of her officer. the French prefect too has assured Governor Claiborne that if the Suspension is not removed before he takes place, he will then remove it. but the Spanish Intendant has before this day recieved the positive order of his government to do it, sent here by a vessel of war, & forwarded by us to Natchez.

Altho' there is probably no truth in the stories of war actually commenced, yet I believe it inevitable. England insists on a remodification of the affairs of Europe, so much changed by Buonaparte since the treaty of Amiens. so that we may soon expect to hear of hostilities.—you must have heard of the extraordinary charge of Chace to the grand jury at Baltimore. ought this seditious & official attack on the principles of our constitution, and on the proceedings of a state, to go unpunished? and to whom so pointedly as yourself will the public look for the necessary measures? I ask these questions for your consideration. for myself, it is better that I should not interfere. Accept my friendly salutations and assurances of great esteem & respect.

TH: JEFFERSON

RC (Herbert R. Strauss, Chicago, Illinois, 1957); addressed: "Joseph H. Nicholson esq. Chesterfield near Centreville Maryld."; franked and postmarked; endorsed by Nicholson. PrC (DLC).

LETTER OF CAPT JONES: see Nicholson to TJ, 10 May.

WELL INFORMED FRIEND: TJ quotes from Gideon Granger's letter of 6 May, which he had received this day.

For the lists of appointments and removals prepared by TJ at the end of the congressional sessions in 1802 and 1803, categorizing the removals to include those dismissed ON POLITICAL PRINCIPLE to make room for Republican participation, see Vol. 33:668-74. For changes in TJ's categorization of removals in 1803, see Noble E. Cunningham, Jr., *The Jeffersonian Republicans in Power, Party Operations, 1801-1809* (Chapel Hill, 1963), 60-3.

FRENCH PREFECT: Pierre Clément Laussat (William Bache to TJ, 29 Mch.).

On 2 May, Supreme Court Justice Samuel Chase delivered a charge to the GRAND JURY meeting at Baltimore. Referring to the repeal of the Judiciary Act of 1801, he declared: "The independence of the national Judiciary is already shaken to its foundation, and the virtue of the people alone can restore it." On the state level, he deplored changes in the Maryland constitution that established universal suffrage. He believed the change would "certainly and rapidly destroy all protection to property, and all security to personal liberty," noting "our republican constitution will sink into a mobocracy, the worst of all possible governments." Although he did not attack the president by name, he charged that the "modern doctrines by our late reformers, that all men in a state of society are entitled to enjoy equal liberty and equal rights" had "brought this mighty mischief upon us." Chase observed "that there could be no rights of man in a state of nature previous to the institution of society; and that liberty, properly speaking, could not exist in a state of nature." In fact, "state of nature," he challenged, was "a creature of the imagination only, although great names" sanctioned "a contrary opinion" (*Annals*, 14:673-6; *National Intelligencer*, 20 May). Nicholson consulted with Nathaniel Macon in the summer of 1803 on taking NECESSARY MEASURES against Chase. Macon discouraged Nicholson from leading the effort to have Chase removed, since the Maryland congressman would be considered a likely appointee to an open seat on the court. In January 1804, it was John Randolph who brought a resolution before the House of Representatives calling for an inquiry into Chase's conduct (Malone, *Jefferson*, 4: 464-9; James Haw and others, *Stormy Patriot: The Life of Samuel Chase* [Baltimore, 1980], 214-18; Richard E. Ellis, *The Jeffersonian Crisis: Courts and Politics in the Young Republic* [New York, 1971], 79-81).

[1]TJ here reworked "the" to "those" and interlined the preceding three words in place of "nation."

[2]Preceding two words interlined in place of "they."

[3]Preceding two words interlined.

[4]Preceding two words interlined in place of "again."

[5]Preceding passage beginning at "to wit" interlined in place of "not exceeding 20. or 30."

From Richard Claiborne

SIR Alexandria 14. May—'3

I take a pleasure in informing you that my experiments here, of the Duck's Foot Paddle, as far as the single stroke, have been attended with entire success,—and I am about to experience the contributions of my acquaintances and other gentlemen of Alexandria, to enable me to prosecute the invention to the double stroke. In the mean time I have another machine going on under the patronage of the Potomak Company, for propelling boats by the setting poles, which I trust will be successful, also.

I have not time to write to Mr. Madison, Genl. Dearborn, Mr. Granger, Mr. Tucker, and Capt. Tingey, to whom, with yourself, I am under obligations. For you Sir, and these gentlemen, I entertain the highest respect; and it will be my highest gratification to find, in the event of my productions, that you are not disappointed.

R CLAIBORNE

RC (DLC); endorsed by TJ as received 16 May and so recorded in SJL.

During the spring, Claiborne conducted four EXPERIMENTS crossing the Potomac at Alexandria in boats propelled by his PADDLE, which TJ had experienced firsthand the previous summer. Claiborne's demonstrations garnered some national attention, and the *Alexandria*

Expositor praised the invention as well as the patriotism of those local citizens who had subscribed to Claiborne's efforts (New York *American Citizen*, 20 May 1803; *Alexandria Expositor, and the Columbian Advertiser*, 27 May 1803; Vol. 38:271-2).

Report from John Lenthall

Rough Stone work done at the Capitol
from 7th May to 14th

Foundations of seven Piers flushed to the offset and a new founded wall in the recess on The East Front	1460	230 perches
Work above the offset on the South Front, incuding the Piers of the internal Arches.—The 7 Arches, as solded[1] work.	$ 4242	

for B H Latrobe

JNO LENTHALL

MS (DLC); partially dated; in Lenthall's hand and signed by him; endorsed by TJ: "Capitol. return of work. May 14. 1803."

[1]Thus in MS.

From Meriwether Lewis

DEAR SIR, Philadelpia, May 14th. 1803.

In your instructions to me you mention that the instruments for ascertaining by celestial observations the geography of the country through which I shall pass, *have been already provided*: I shall not therefore purchase any articles of that discription untill I hear further from you on this subject. Will you be so good as to inform me what instruments have been provided? and where they are?—it may be possible that some instrument has been omitted, which Mr. Patterson, Mr. Ellicott and those gentlemen to whom you have referred me in this place, may deem necessary for me, and if so the deficiency can be supplyed in time.—

Mr. Patterson and Mr. Ellicott both disapprove of the Theodolite as applicable to my purposes; they think it a delicate instrument, difficult of transportation, and one that would be very liable to get out of order; they also state that in it's application to any observations for obtaining the Longitude, it would be liable to many objections, and to much more inacuracy than the Sextant—The instruments these gentlemen recommend, and which indeed they think indispensibly necessary, are, two Sextants, (one of which, must be constructed for the *back observation*,) an artificial Horizon or two; a good Arnald's watch or Chronometer, a Surveyor's Compass with a ball and socket and two pole chain, and a set of plotting instruments.—By means of the Sextant fixed for the back observation and an artificial Horizon also constructed for the purpose, the meridian altitude of the Sun may always be taken, altho it should even exceed eighty degrees: for this valuable problem I am indebted to Mr. Patterson.—

As a perfect knolege of the time will be of the first importance in all my Astronomical observations, it is necessary that the time-keeper intended for this expedition should be put in the best possible order, if therefore Sir, one has been procured for me, and you are not perfectly assured of her being in good order, it would be best perhaps to send her to me by some safe hand (should any such conveyance offer in time); Mr. Voit could then clean her, and Mr. Ellicott has promised to regulate her, which, I believe he has the means of doing just now, more perfectly than it can be done any where else in the UStates.—

I cannot yet say what day it will be in my power to leave this place.—Your different orders have been attended to, and the result you shall have in a day or two.—

I am Sir, with every sentiment of gratitude and respect—

Your most Obt. & very Humble Servt.

MERIWETHER LEWIS

RC (DLC); at foot of text: "The President of the UStates"; endorsed by TJ as received 16 May and so recorded in SJL.

INSTRUCTIONS: see Drafting Instructions for Meriwether Lewis at 13 Apr. and TJ to Lewis, 27 Apr.

GOOD ARNALD'S WATCH: see Andrew Ellicott to TJ, 6 Mch.

From Nicolas Gouin Dufief

MONSIEUR, Philadelphia. May. 15. 1803.

D'après les informations que j'ai prises des principaux negocians de cette ville, il parait certain qu'il ne partira point de Bâtimens pour France d'ici à un mois au moins—Et comme deux occasions se présentent à la fois pour Hambourg, j'ai cru qu'il vaudrait mieux profiter d'une des deux pour y envoyer la lettre que vous m'avez confiée que d'attendre peut-être inutilement pendant longtems—

Hambourg étant hors du territoire Français, il faut nécessairement que quelqu'un se charge dans cette ville d'affranchir la lettre à la poste—Il m'est venu naturellement à l'idée, de l'adresser au consul des Etats-unis qui se fera un devoir et un vrai plaisir de l'envoyer par la premiere occasion—Vous trouverez ci jointe la lettre que je lui ai écrite à ce Sujet—Quand vous Jugerez convenable d'ecrire en Europe, par la voie de Philadelphie, je serai toujours charmé d'être chargé d'y faire tenir vos lettres—

Je Suis avec la plus respectueuse estime Votre très dévoué Serviteur N. G. Dufief

EDITORS' TRANSLATION

Sir, Philadelphia, 15 May 1803

According to information I have obtained from the leading merchants in this city, it appears that no ships will be leaving for France for a least a month. Since two possibilities have presented themselves simultaneously for Hamburg, I thought it was better to take advantage of one of those to send the letter you entrusted to me, rather than waiting a long time, perhaps in vain.

Since Hamburg is outside French territory, someone there will have to take responsibility for mailing the letter. Naturally, I thought of the United States consul who would willingly take on the responsibility of sending it by the earliest possible means. Enclosed you will find a copy of my letter to him. Any time you wish to write to Europe via Philadelphia, I will be happy to be entrusted with your letters.

With respectful esteem, I am your very devoted servant.

N. G. Dufief

RC (DLC); at foot of text: "The President of the United States"; endorsed by TJ as received 17 May and so recorded in SJL. Enclosure: Dufief to the U.S. consul at Hamburg (i.e., John Murray Forbes), 15 May, enclosing a letter from TJ to Fulwar Skipwith that TJ on 10 May asked Dufief to forward to Paris (Tr in same, written in Dufief's hand below signature of letter printed above; for the letter to Skipwith, see 4 May; no letter to Dufief of 10 May has been found or is recorded in SJL; for Forbes's appointment as consul, see Vol. 36:608-9).

From DeWitt Clinton

Dear Sir Newtown 16 May 1803

Major Fairlie a respectable Citizen of this State will write to you in behalf of his brother-in-law William Yates who is a Lt. in the Army. The situation of this young Gentleman's Health is such as will render it necessary for him to resign if the order for him to repair to Tenessee shall be persisted in: After apologising to you for this intrusion upon your valuable time, permit me to add that your compliance with the wishes of Major Fairlie will confer a very great favor upon a worthy family who have done much & suffered much in the republican cause and will relieve the afflictions of a widowed mother, who feels the greatest anxiety on this occasion

With the most respectful attachment I am your obedt. servt.

DEWITT CLINTON

RC (PHi); at foot of text: "The President of the U.S."; endorsed by TJ as a letter of 1 May and so recorded in SJL at 19 May with notation "W."

WILL WRITE TO YOU: see James Fairlie to TJ, 17 May 1803.

To Meriwether Lewis

DEAR SIR Washington May 16. 1803.

Your's of the 14th: is this moment recieved, & I hasten to answer it by return of post, that no time may be lost. the copy of instructions sent you are only a rough draught for consideration. they will not be signed or *dated* till your departure. presuming you would procure all the necessary instruments at Philadelphia, which is a principal object of your journey there, the instructions say that the necessary instruments '*have been* provided,' which will be true when they recieve their ultimate form, date & signature, tho' nothing was provided at the time of writing the rough draught. this will serve to correct the expression which has been misunderstood, and to let you know you are relied on to provide every thing for yourself.—with respect to the theodolite, I wish you to be governed entirely by the advice of mr Patterson & mr Ellicott: as also as to the time piece & whatever else they think best. mr Garnett told us he had some good ones still on hand; which I remind you of, lest you should not be able to get one in Philadelphia. Accept my affectionate salutations.

TH: JEFFERSON

PrC (DLC); at foot of text: "Capt Meriwether Lewis"; endorsed by TJ in ink on verso.

From John F. Mercer

SIR In Council May 16 1803

I have submitted to the Council the result of the conversation which I had the honor of holding with you on the Application which the Executive of Maryland were directed to make to you on the subject of the Stock of this State in the British Funds.—I have stated to them the Measures which you have directed in conformity with the views and wishes of this Legislature in which they have expressed their entire concurrence, but as it will be their duty to communicate their proceedings under these Resolutions to the Legislature at their next Session, they would be gratified by being furnished with a Copy of the Letter which you have caused to be written to Mr. William Pinkney on this subject, if no wise inconsistent with the rules you may have established on similar subjects.

I have also communicated to the Council the result of my application to you respecting this State's Claim on the United States for Arms and Military Stores furnished during the Western Insurrection, as well as the substance of a personal conference I had with the Secretary at War to whom you had referred this subject.—they appear impressed with an opinion that the Secretary has given a force to some expressions of a Letter of Mr. McHenry, the late Minister, to this Executive, which they had not themselves discovered, but which in every view can in no wise affect the justice and legality of the demand.—If however there shall exist objections to this Claim on the part of the Executive of the United States, they hope to be furnished with them, in order that they may communicate them to the Legislature of their State, who will no doubt resort to some mode that may remove the doubts, or present the demand in some form that may be more acceptable.

I cannot close this letter without praying you to receive my warm acknowledgements, in which the Council have expressed their entire concurrence, for the interest you have at all times taken in the attainment of that Justice which has so long been withheld from the State and more especially for your prompt attention to their late application.

With perfect respect & devotion I have the honor to be, Sir Your Most obedient Serv.

John F. Mercer

FC (MdAA: Letterbooks of Governor and Council); in a clerk's hand; at foot of text: "The President of the United States." Recorded in SJL as received from Annapolis on 17 May.

The date and place of Mercer's conversation with TJ are unknown, but Mercer had written recently that he hoped to see TJ in Washington on 28 Apr. (Mercer to TJ, 23 Apr. 1803).

stock of this state in the british funds: for the ongoing efforts by the state of Maryland to gain control of funds invested in the Bank of England before the American Revolution, see Vol. 23:589, 609n; Vol. 37:547-8. On 31 Dec. 1802, the Maryland legislature passed a joint resolution authorizing the governor and council to seek the assistance of the president in the matter (Jacob M. Price, "The Maryland Bank Stock Case: British-American Financial and Political Relations Before and After the American Revolution," in Aubrey C. Land, Lois Green Carr, and Edward C. Papenfuse, eds., *Law, Society, and Politics in Early Maryland* [Baltimore, 1977], 25).

On 3 May 1803, James Madison wrote WILLIAM PINKNEY, one of the American claims commissioners in London, and enclosed a power authorizing him to negotiate the transfer of the Bank of England stock to the state of Maryland in place of Rufus King, who had recently resigned as the American minister to Great Britain. Citing Pinkney's intimate acquaintance with the subject and his Maryland citizenship, Madison informed him that the "President therefore invests you with powers for this purpose," and instructed him to apply to the ministry and courts "in such manner as may be judged proper & effectual for terminating the claim of the state and for receiving a transfer of the stock for its use." Agreeable to Mercer's request, Madison sent him copies of the power and instructions on 19 May, adding that the originals would be sent to London as soon as the governor sent him "the communications you may think necessary to add to Mr. Pinkney" (Madison, *Papers, Sec. of State Ser.*, 4:568-9; 5:15).

CLAIM ON THE UNITED STATES FOR ARMS: in an address to the Maryland legislature on 10 Nov. 1802, Mercer suggested that the shortage of arms for the state militia could be offset in part by an arrangement with the United States regarding "an unsatisfied claim for military supplies furnished during the western insurrection" (Baltimore *American and Commercial Daily Advertiser*, 10 Nov. 1802). The date and substance of his application to TJ and conference with Dearborn on the subject are not known, but see Dearborn to TJ, [on or before 28 May 1803].

From Joseph Sansom

Philada. 5th. Mo. 16th. 1803

With all the respect due to thy public character, I take the liberty to address thee on a subject familiar to a Man of taste and virtu:

When I was in Europe I caught the usual passion of Travellers to possess some of the interesting objects of art with which that part of the World abounds; and had formed the Plan of a Private Cabinet; but my views and avocations have changed since my return; and I have among other things a small Collection of Models of the principal Roman Antiquities in the South of France, which I could wish to dispose of to thee, in the hope of their being kept together as elegant companions of thy philosophic retirement, or suitable appendages to the public Museums or Drawing Rooms at Washington.

They consist of

The Amphitheatre of Nismes, on a scale that makes it no more than 19 inches long by 32½ high; yet the inimitable Artist has contrived to represent the most intricate cells, passages, and stairways, throughout the complicated interior, as well as the majestic simplicity of the front.

The Maison Quarrée, 18 inches long by 9 & ½ high.

The Pont du Gard 24 inches long by 4 & ½ high.

A circular tomb at Aix, three stories high, of singular beauty, 7 & ½ diameter by 23 high.

A tomb near Vienne on the Rhone 4 & ½ square by 17 high.

They are all represented with astonishing accuracy, in that state of ruin they are now in, which only tends to increase their picturesque effect, the Maison Quarrée excepted, the actual preservation of which renders it unnecessary to exhibit it otherwise than in its pristine perfection.

I forbear a more particular description as these celebrated Edifices are well known to thee, tho' I must do the Models the justice to say that they are wrought with a degree of beauty and exactness that none but such as have seen the perfect specimens of art preserved in European Cabinets can form an idea of without seeing them.

I bought them of the Artist himself, Therondel, a Citizen of Nismes, who seems to have been born with a peculiar faculty to illustrate, as they deserve, the superb Monuments of Antiquity in his native place. He had so far injured his sight by years of labour upon the minuter parts of these objects that he considered it impossible ever to make a similar model of the Maison Quarrée, the foliated modillions on the cornish of which require a glass to be distinctly seen.

He happened to be exhibiting them in Paris at the time I was there, and the state of his Family requiring his return to Nismes, with pecuniary supplies, he sold them to me for a sum far below the value of so much ingenious labour.

I now the take the liberty to offer them to thee, at the cost, and subscribe myself,

with all due consideration, as well as personal esteem, Thy respectful Friend JOSEPH SANSOM

P.S. They would be shewn to any Person whose opinion [. . .] choose to have, or a more particular description would be given, if required. In case of purchase they could be sent to order, with perfect safety, as they are secured for transportation in separate boxes.

RC (DLC); torn; addressed: "Thomas Jefferson Esquire President of the United States Washington"; postmarked 20 May; endorsed by TJ as received 22 May and so recorded in SJL.

Pennsylvania Quaker Joseph Sansom (1767-1826) was the brother and business partner of prosperous Philadelphia merchant and East India trader William Sansom. Self-described as a merchant, Joseph Sansom used his resources to further interests in literature, travel, and the arts. As an amateur artist, he mastered the silhouette profile, producing his "physiognomical sketches" of "remarkable persons" from 1790 to 1792. He recorded portions of his three-year tour abroad in *Letters from Europe during a Tour Through Switzerland and Italy, in the Years 1801 and 1802*, published in Philadelphia in 1805. The following year, he was elected to the American Philosophical Society and, in 1808, contributed to it his mineral collections and Roman relics (Elva Tooker, *Nathan Trotter, Philadelphia Merchant, 1787-1853* [Cambridge, Mass., 1955], 39-42, 237; Charles Coleman Sellers, "Joseph Sansom, Philadelphia Silhouettist," PMHB, 88 [1964], 395-401; APS, *Transactions*, new ser., 42, pt. 1 [1952], 190).

THERONDEL advanced the small-scale museum concept by creating exact cardboard replicas of monuments as they existed "in a state of ruination" such as the obelisk at Arles, the Pont du Gard, and the amphitheater at Nîmes. He exhibited them in Paris in 1801 at the Cabinet Thérondel, 904 rue de la Loi, near the Passage Duchesne (Jeremy D. Popkin and Richard H. Popkin, eds., *The Abbé Grégoire and His World* [Dordrecht, Netherlands, 2000], 154-5).

After his return from Europe, Sansom wrote a letter to "The President & Members of the American Philosophical Society" requesting the acceptance of a plaster of Paris bust of Benjamin Franklin made by the elder John Flaxman of London after the original by the French sculptor, Houdon. Sansom noted that, "The resemblance will speak for itself. It was taken from the Life, during his residence at the Court of France" (RC in PPAmP, endorsed as received on 21 Jan. 1803 and "Donation of Bust of Dr. Franklin"; *Bulletin of the City Art Museum of St. Louis*, 21 [1936], 52).

From William Short

May 16 [1803]

Jeffn.—ansr. his last—mention my lands—shall request Mr. G. Jeff. to advertise them—shall endeavour to return to Virgia. Springs—uncertain if I shall find him at Mont. if [so shd.] be happy to see him there once more—Taylor to recieve the 500 a month—as to the political part of his letter—always my opinion on this subject—founded on my knowlege of the Spa. Govt—happy in the result—do not give credit to the idea of purchasing to the left bank [&c if] it [exacts] and it may [. . .], contrary to my expectation—beyond the most sanguine

FC (DLC: Short Papers); blurred; partially dated; entirely in Short's hand, consisting of an entry in his epistolary record. Recorded in SJL as received from Philadelphia on 18 May.

HIS LAST: TJ to Short, 6 May.

From Robert Smith

Nav Dep
16 May 1803

SIR!

The accompanying statement No 2—exhibits a view of the exact state of the Navy appropriations on this day.

Presuming that it will be agreeable to you, I shall in future lay before you, similar statements weekly.

I have the honor to be with the greatest respect & esteem, Sir, yr mo ob st

RT SMITH

RC (DLC); in a clerk's hand, signed by Smith; at foot of text: "President United States"; endorsed by TJ as received from the Navy Department on 16 May and "Appropriations" and so recorded in SJL. FC (Lb in DNA: RG 45, LSP). Enclosure not found.

For previous examples of WEEKLY returns received by TJ from the Navy Department, see Abstract of Warrants from Robert Smith, 28 Feb. 1803 and 2 May 1803.

From Anonymous

SIR [17 May 1803]

It seems right to me to give you the following information, because altho' my authority is only hearsay [such however as I rely very much in] you will be able to judge correctly of its truth.

Mr: W. is said to be making the use of your letters, which the most malignant cunning can suggest; including that written in F. and one or more, of a late correspondence. They are shewn to federalists almost indiscriminately, whose business seems to be to prepare the public for their publication. An itinerant cancer doctor, lately with Mr: W, has seen them all, and is the missionary at Richmond, for infusing artful ideas to your prejudice. They have been shewn to a friend of yours, and great address used by Mr: W. to impress a charge of falsehood against you, from your having pretermited an Enquiry concerning the coldness between you, by relating the protest of an order, given by Mr: W. on you for a Sum of money. It is believed by some, that certain discussions between you & Mr: W. concerning stoping the presses on each side, as to the subject, are an artifice to increase the mass of publication. As you observe (as is said) in a letter to Mr: W., himself & his side, could do this at any time—the republican presses, being mearly defensive. And it is believed, that this whole mass will certainly appear at a critical time, if the missionaries shall encourage its publication. That you might close your correspondence with W. with an Eye to such an event, was my reason for giving you this information, through which I have sprinkled such circumstances, as might enable you to judge of its probability. Having no motive but public good & private justice for writing this, my name is only withheld to obstruct curiosity, if it should assail the letter. Accept, Sir, my highest respect.

RC (DLC); undated; brackets in original, perhaps added by TJ; addressed: "The President of the United States Washington"; franked; postmarked: "Port Royal 17 May"; endorsed by TJ as received from "Anon. postmark Portroyal" on 20 May and so recorded in SJL.

MR: W.: John Walker (see TJ to Walker, 13 Apr.). F.: France.

COLDNESS BETWEEN YOU: see TJ to Walker, 7 Feb. 1790. For TJ's plans to keep the subject out of the newspapers, see his LETTER TO Walker of 13 Apr.

From Isaac Briggs

MY DEAR FRIEND, Sharon, 17th. of the 5th. Month 1803

Permit me to introduce to thee my youngest brother, Joseph Briggs, who is going with me to the Mississippi Territory, and whom I mean to employ as a clerk.

I enclose a copy of a letter which I wrote to thee from Philadelphia, lest the original should have miscarried.

I must have misunderstood Henry Voight, or he must have deceived himself, in the probable time when my Transit Instrument would be finished; as he advanced in the work, the period of its completion seemed to be removed to a distance far beyond my expectation. Upon his informing me that it would probably require several months to complete it, I immediately packed up the remainder of my outfit, and had it put into a waggon, which left Philadelphia, on the 12th. instant, for Pittsburg, where I intend to arrive as soon as it—I shall leave home on the 23rd. instant.

Henry Voight is to send my Portable Transit and a Chronometer, immediately when finished, by sea, to Natchez.

I saw Captain M. Lewis, in Philadelphia, on the 10th. & 11th. instants.

Permit me to repeat assurances of my esteem and respect, and that I am Thy friend, ISAAC BRIGGS.

RC (DLC); at foot of text: "Thomas Jefferson, President U.S."; endorsed by TJ as received 19 May and so recorded in SJL. Enclosure: Briggs to TJ, 2 May 1803.

From James Fairlie

SIR/ New York 17 May 1803

Lieut: William Yates—of the Artillery is ordered by the War Department, to proceed to Tenessee with Captn: Izard's company—

Application has been made to the Secretary at War, to dispense with that order, on Accot of certain family circumstances, as well as the bad state of this young Gentleman's Health.

As the last hope on this Occasion Sir, I have presumed to request your interference in his favor—

If it is impossible that the order can be countermanded in Season to reach Richmond, before the Company leaves that place, knowing as I do the impossibility of Mr. Yates's being able to proceed on that Service—I must entreat that his Resignation, which is this day forwarded to the War Office may be accepted

My extreem Solisitude on this occasion (which is of no common kind) in behalf of a Relation I hope Sir will be accepted by you as some appology for thus intruding on your time upon a Subject which you may deem of a trifling nature, but which is very Interest[ing] to me

I am with the greatest Respe[ct] Sir your most Obedient Serv[ant]

JA: FAIRLIE

RC (PHi); torn; at foot of text: "The President of the United States"; endorsed by TJ as received 19 May and so recorded in SJL with notation "W."

James Fairlie (1757-1830) served as an aide-de-camp to Baron von Steuben during the American Revolution. He married Maria Yates, daughter of the chief justice of the New York Supreme Court, and became clerk to that court in 1796. TJ appointed him a commissioner of bankruptcy for New York in 1802. He also served in the New York legislature and as a director of the Manhattan Company (Geddeth Smith, *Thomas Abthorpe Cooper: America's Premier Tragedian* [Madison, N.J., 1996], 160; Kline, *Burr*, 1:374; New York *Evening Post*, 9 Dec. 1803; New York *Spectator*, 16 Oct. 1830; Vol. 37:402-3, 516, 698).

The 14 May request by Lieutenant WILLIAM YATES not to travel with his company to Tennessee was denied. Replying on 20 May, Henry Dearborn admonished Yates by stating that "it would appear that you as well as many other Officers of the Army consider a Military Commission as a convenience, and that when Military duty in any degree interferes with private concerns, the service is no longer an object worthy of attention." Yates would not be discharged, Dearborn continued, until he had "performed the duties on which you have been ordered." If poor health prevented him from marching, Yates would be considered on furlough until he recovered (FC in Lb in DNA: RG 107, LSMA). Writing from Tennessee in 1805, Yates twice solicited a furlough from duty before resigning his commission in November 1806 (DNA: RG 107, RLRMS; Dearborn to TJ, 30 May 1807).

From Samuel L. Holmes

DEAR SIR, Brooklyn, May 17th 1803

For some time past I have been endeavouring to find out some method by which I might obtain Learning At length I have (as I knew not of any so likely method by which I could acquire it) to write to you.

Sir—In the first place I will give you a short detail of the Circumstances of myself and then the reasons which induced me to take the Liberty of writing to you.

1stly. My Father is poor; and is my only parent thats is living, he is old and is now I expect among the Indians there sent by the Baptist Misionary Society of New-York He has given me but a little Learning, though as much as he possibly could afford. At twelve years of age I was bound an apprentice to the Printing business, wher I still remain.

2dly. But Learning is my object, the sole cause of this letter, and what renders me unhappy because I cannot attain it. Finally, (I do consent) it is to ask the boon of you. Excuse me dear Sir if what I am saying is wrong. If Fortune will but smile when You receive these few simple lines (simple, for perfection cannot be expected from a boy of only 14 years of age, with no more Learning than barely to read and write.) then will I call myself the happiest of beings, but if not—why I suppose I must bear it with patience as Job did when he felt the rod yet blessed God.—That this request may succeed, will from this time to the time I shall receive an answer (for do please to write a few words in return, if not I shall be more wretched than ever) be most earnestly prayed for—O God Interfere!

Dear Sir if you will but consider that my relations are poor and not able to go as it such a request, and knew my thirst for Learning you would not think my asking it of you strange. I cannot ask you in any grand style which perhaps might be rather more agreeable to you, for I am yet too young—And again I repeat it, if I have said any thing improper please to forgive me—What more can I say?—why my dear sir, no more than the Glorious words Learning. Learning the greatest blesing, the only ornament and jewel of man's life—and to conclude that I remain now Your unhappy, but when at the arrival of the answer with the transporting Consent!—Then your happy O ever happy Friend and

Humble Servant SAMUEL L. HOLMES

P.S.—Please to excuse me for the manner in which this Letter is wrote as the time I had to write it in was in the working hours—Please to write a few words in return and direct to

SAMUEL L. HOLMES
at
Mr. Thomas Kirks Printing Office
Brooklyn Long Island

RC (MHi); addressed: "His Excellency Thomas Jefferson President of the United States of America at the City of Washington"; franked; postmarked New York 19 May; endorsed by TJ as received 21 May and so recorded in SJL.

Samuel L. Holmes (ca. 1788-1853) became a high school teacher in Bedford, New York, and, in 1842, a member of the state assembly. From 1848 until his death, he was superintendent of Brooklyn public schools (*Brooklyn Eagle*, 20 May 1853; *New York Times*, 21 May 1853).

THOMAS KIRKS PRINTING OFFICE: Irish native Thomas Kirk established Brooklyn's first newspaper, *The Courier, and New-York and Long Island Advertiser*, in 1799, and published it until 13 Jan. 1803. Kirk was also proprietor of a circulating library and bookstore. In 1816, Kirk established the first Sunday school in Brooklyn at his printing office, where he offered reading and writing as part of the curriculum. He helped create, in 1823, the Apprentices Library Association, a free reading library for the apprentices of Brooklyn, and awarded prizes to boys who were its regular readers (Marguerite V. Doggett, *Long Island Printing, 1791-1830* [Brooklyn, 1979], 29-32; Brigham, *American Newspapers*, 1:555).

From John Irvin

Lancaster Fairfield County S. Ohio
17th. May 1803

Dear Sir

On perusing a Law of the last session of Congress, I observed that provisions were made for establishing a Land Office at the Town of Zaneville. should a Register not be appointed to that Office, I beg leave to offer myself as a candidate, and should it be concieved proper to confer that office on my self, it shall be my constant care, and greatest Pleasure, to discharge the duties appertaining to the same, with that Assiduity, and Punctuality, which the importance of the institution requires

Except, Sir, the high Esteem of Your Humble Servant

John Irvin

RC (DNA: RG 59, LAR); endorsed by TJ as received 7 July and "to be Register at Zaneville" and so recorded in SJL.

John Irvin (d. 1828) was the son of Presbyterian minister William Irvin of Albemarle County, Virginia. He immigrated to the west like several of his brothers, two of whom became successful judges and politicians in Ohio and another in Wisconsin. John, however, returned to Albemarle, where he became a county magistrate (Woods, *Albemarle*, 232-4; William Irvin to TJ, 2 July 1803).

LAW OF THE LAST SESSION: on 3 Mch. 1803, as part of an act regarding land grants, Congress authorized the establishment of a land office at Zanesville, Ohio, and the appointment of a register and receiver for the same (U.S. Statutes at Large, 2:236-7).

From Lafayette

My dear Sir — Paris 27th. Floréal 17. Mai 1803.

In the Joy of my heart I congratulate you on the happy arrangement which has Lately taken place—The occupation of Louisiana by the French Governement was big with Evils—I doubly felt them—Now I see for the United States noble boundaries, and for that Vast Country the insurance of Liberty and republican Union—How happy I am in that transaction I want Words to Express

With respectful and heartfelt Gratitude I have heard from Mr. Munroe what the Congress of the United States have been pleased to do in my behalf nor am I insensible of my new obligations to the president—This bountiful Gift at the Same time it is highly useful I consider as most honourable to me—To you, my dear Sir, with all the confidence of friendship, I wholly refer myself and upon you I gratefully depend for what is farther to be done in this affair—No official Account having Yet reached me my Letter of Thanks must necessarily be differed

I have met with a Sad accident, the breaking of my Thigh, at the *Col du femur* it has[1] been more compleatly mended than perhaps any fracture of the Kind, but I have paid it dear—the application of a new machine has left me very deep Wounds, besides the great sufferings I have undergone—My Situation does not yet allow much writing—But I wanted to express to you my Joy on the grand affair and my Gratitude, both to Congress and to you, for the honourable bountiful mark of Kindness I have received—

Present my affectionate Compliments to your family to Madisson, M. Dawson and all other friends—With the most grateful Sense of what you have done and of your friendly Concern for me, with every Sentiment of high respect and affectionate friendship I am my dear Sir

for ever Yours LAFAYETTE

My Wife, and Children beg to be remembered to you And So does Mad. de Tessé at whose house I lay untill I can be transported, first to her Country seat near Paris, then to my happy Rural retirements of La grange.

Dupl (DLC); in a clerk's hand, signed by Lafayette; at head of text: "duplicate"; endorsed by TJ as received 24 Aug. and so recorded in SJL. RC (DLC).

TO DO IN MY BEHALF: an act of 3 Mch. on military bounty lands authorized the secretary of war to issue Lafayette land warrants for 11,520 acres (U.S. Statutes at Large, 2:236).

COL DU FEMUR: the neck of the femur.

[1]MS: "as." RC: "Has."

From Edward Lynch

SIR Philada. May 17th. 1803

Not having the honor of being personally known to you and being desirous to offer myself a Candidate for an Appointment in the Land Office established by an Act of Congress of the last Session "Regulating the grants of lands &ca. South of the State of Tennassee"

I beg leave to lay before you the inclosed letter of introduction from Andrew Gregg Esqr.—

Should this Application be in time and so fortunate as to be honor'd with your approbation, I flatter myself I can procure such corroborative Testimonials of Character as will be perfectly satisfactory, together with any security that may be required—For more particular information I take the liberty of referring to Albert Gallatine Esqr. and am most Respectfully

Sir Your Obedt. Servt. EDWD. LYNCH

RC (DNA: RG 59, LAR); at foot of text: "Thomas Jefferson Esqr. Presidt. of the United States"; endorsed by TJ as received 21 May and "to be empld under land law Missipi" and so recorded in SJL. Enclosure: Andrew Gregg to TJ, 7 May.

During the 1780s, Edward Lynch (d. 1818) worked as the chief clerk to Pennsylvania's surveyor general. He remained a surveyor for a short time but eventually became a merchant. In 1797, he ran for a seat in Philadelphia's Common Council. For about the last 10 years of his life, he was in the insurance business in Philadelphia (*Philadelphia Gazette*, 9 Oct. 1797, 6 Oct. 1800; *Poulson's American Daily Advertiser*, 3 Mch. 1818; *The Philadelphia Directory, by Francis White* [Philadelphia, 1785], 45; Clement Biddle, *The Philadelphia Directory* [Philadelphia, 1791], 79; James Hardie, *The Philadelphia Directory and Register* [Philadelphia, 1794], 94; James Robinson, *The Philadelphia Directory, for 1810* [Philadelphia, 1810], 175; John Adems Paxton, *The Philadelphia Directory, for 1818* [Philadelphia, 1818]).

For the ACT OF CONGRESS providing for the disposal of lands in Mississippi Territory, see U.S. Statutes at Large, 2: 229-35.

From "A Republican"

SIR N York 17th. May 1803

That you are a damned Scoundrel is the opinion of your former friend but present ennemy a REPUBLICAN

If you can justify yourself please to write me what reason you had for getting Jno. Burnet turned out of the Post Office at Newark & address yr letter to Jno. H Williams Junr: New York

RC (DLC); addressed: "His Exleny Thomas Jefferson Prest. of the United States Washington City with request to forward this immediately being of *importance*"; franked; postmarked 4 June; endorsed by TJ as a letter of 17 May received 6 June and "Anon. care of John H. Williams N.Y." and "John Burnet P.M. Newark" and so recorded in SJL with notation "postmark New York."

On 12 May, James Cheetham's *American Citizen* announced the appointment of Samuel Hay as postmaster at Newark in place of John BURNET, who, according to the notice, had "long been in the habit of *stopping* or *destroying* republican papers in his office." On 13 May, the *New-York Gazette* reported the removal, noting that Burnet, one of the oldest postmasters in the United States, was a Revolutionary War veteran who cared for the post office when it was not profitable to do so. "He nursed and tended it in its growth" and now another was "appointed to reap the harvest." To the credit of the postmaster general, the report noted, there could be no objection to the appointment of Hay "on the score of private reputation or public services." Other Federalist newspapers reprinted this article under the headline "Another removal." On 17 May, the *New-York Herald* printed a more virulent account of the dismissal, citing it as another example of the persecution of Federalists by the administration. Gideon Granger, "the servile instrument of an unworthy passion," had dismissed Burnet "one of our brave revolutionary officers" to "reward a good democrat." On the same day, the Newark *Centinel of Freedom* defended Hay as "a mercantile gentleman, an old revolutionary officer, and a good accountant" who would "perform the duties of the office with impartiality, fidelity and dispatch." On 31 May, the Hudson *Bee* also defended the Hay appointment against the "cry" of the Federalists, especially pointing out his service as a Revolutionary War officer (New York *Spectator*, 14 May; *New-York Herald*, 14, 17 May; Baltimore *Federal Gazette*, 17 May; *Albany Centinel*, 17 May; Hartford *Connecticut Courant*, 18 May).

John H. WILLIAMS was printer of the *Newark Gazette and New-Jersey Advertiser* from 1798 to 1799 (Brigham, *American Newspapers*, 1:510).

From Henry Dearborn

SIR, War Department May 18th. 1803.

I have the honor to propose Doctor Joseph Macrary for a Surgeons Mate in the Army of the United States.

Accept Sir, the assurances &c.

FC (Lb in DNA: RG 107, LSP).

MACRARY: probably Joseph McCreery (Macrery) of Delaware, who had been recommended to TJ in 1802 for appointment to the marine hospital at New Orleans. Upon receiving his commission, he was ordered to Washington in the Mississippi Territory, where he resigned in October 1803 (Heitman, *Dictionary*, 1: 661; Dearborn to McCreery, 19 May, 7 Nov. 1803, in DNA: RG 107, LSMA; Vol. 37:247-9, 350-1).

To James Dinsmore

DEAR SIR Washington May 18. 1803.

Yours of the 1st. & 9th. have been recieved, and the last has much relieved me as to the last box or boxes of Composition ornament. it was impossible to think of taking mr Hudson's cherry, for which he asked five times what has ever been given within my knolege. I hope mr Meriwether's will suffice for the parlour, and we must take time for the rest. I am told there is great difference in point of beauty & value between the wild cherry which grows in the low grounds & in high lands. we must attend to this.

I do not recollect that I had given you drawings for the fireplace of the parlour. I believe I had not. I therefore have prepared some which I now inclose. Accept my best wishes TH: JEFFERSON

RC (NjP: Andre De Coppet Collection); at foot of text: "Mr. Dinsmore."

A letter from Dinsmore of 1 May, recorded in SJL as received 8 May, and one of 9 May, recorded in SJL as received 11 May, have not been found.

For TJ's emphatic rejection of Charles HUDSON'S CHERRY, which was intended for the parlor floor, see TJ to Thomas Mann Randolph, 5 May. There is no record of a purchase from William D. Meriwether, though Meriwether did produce lumber at his mills. In November 1802, TJ asked Thomas Mann Randolph to acquire some wild cherry stocks from the nearby Birdwood estate (RS, 1:74; TJ to Thomas Mann Randolph, 25 Nov. 1802). Monticello's parlor floor, notable for its parquet design, consisted of 10-inch squares of cherry framed by two-inch-wide slats of beech. TJ acquired some beech from John B. Magruder in March, and in August he paid Hancock Allen for sawing some pine and beech wood. As late as September 1804, the floor remained unfinished (McLaughlin, *Jefferson and Monticello*, 315-16; MB, 2:1105; TJ to John B. Magruder, 26 Mch.; Notes on Work to be Done by James Dinsmore, and Notes on Work to be Done by James Dinsmore and John Hemings, both 24 Sep. 1804).

E N C L O S U R E

Drawing of the Fireplace for Monticello's Parlor

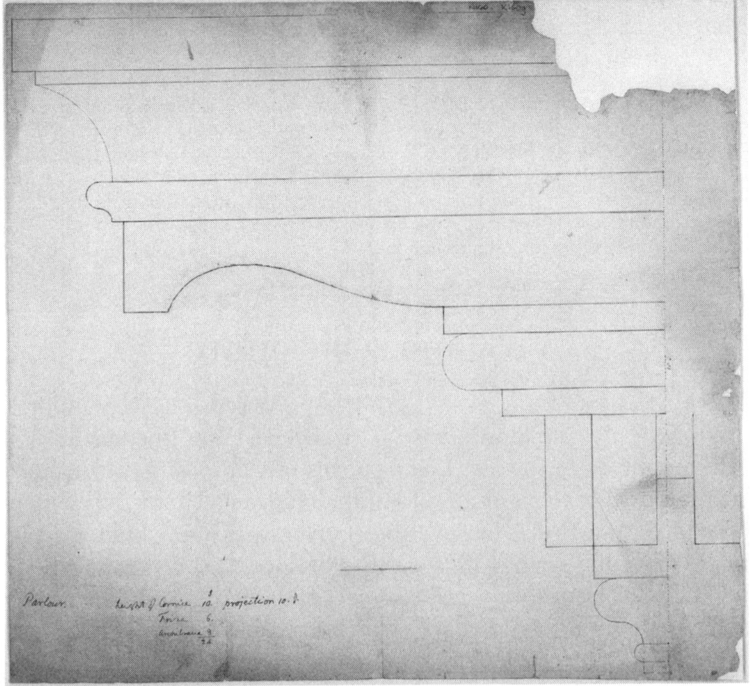

MS (MHi); undated; entirely in TJ's hand; see Nichols, *Architectural Drawings*, No. 160.

Although the Editors cannnot be completely certain that this sketch was among those enclosed by TJ, the above drawing matches almost exactly the design that Dinsmore executed. A cruder sketch illustrating a front view of a fireplace may be one of the other drawings that TJ sent Dinsmore (MS in same; Nichols, *Architectural Drawings*, No. 571).

From John A. Houseman

HONORABLE SIR, Washington May 18th. 1803

The confidence I take in presenting these few lines to your view, will, I hope be excused by the cause that enforces me to it.

I have a Sister by name Sally Houseman living in your House. She has been ill used by one of your Domesticks (Abraham Golden) and knocked prostrate on the floor; and that without any assault from her side. Since she hath no Friend nearer related than myself she Disclosed the same to me, consulting me what to do in such a case. I advised her rather than litigate the matter to submit the same to your Honour. As I, Honourable, Sir, am highly grieved at the insult offered and done to my Sister, I thought proper to petition as a Brother for her Person. The design of this is not you will presume to reap satisfaction, but wholly directed to preserve in future peace and tranquility; without which it is impossible to live consoled. I desire, Honourable Sir, your Protection in behalf of my sister. Your humble and obedient Servant and Petitioner JOHN A HOUSEMAN

RC (MHi); endorsed by TJ as received 19 May and so recorded in SJL.

SALLY HOUSEMAN was a resident washerwoman in the President's House. ABRAHAM GOLDEN was a footman and a personal servant of Meriwether Lewis and his successor. In his personal financial memoranda, TJ recorded on 9 May that he had paid servants' wages through 4 May, of $7 to Houseman and $14 to Golden (Gaulding). TJ later remarked to his son-in-law that while at Washington, he preferred white servants "who when they misbehave can be exchanged" (Lucia Stanton, "'A Well-Ordered Household': Domestic Servants in Jefferson's White House," *White House History*, 17 [2006], 8-9; MB, 2:1100; Vol. 35:395n; TJ to John Wayles Eppes, 7 Aug. 1804).

From James Monroe

DEAR SIR Paris May 18. 1803.

In my communications to Mr. Madison publick & private which you would see, I have been so full, that it seemed as if I shod. only trouble you by a repetition of the same ideas in writing you. I most earnestly hope that what is done here, and may be done in Spain, will not only prove an ample vindication of the measures of yr. administration during the last Session of Congress, when contrasted with the rash and extravigant projects that were opposed to them, but lay the solid foundation of great and permanent happiness to our country. To have contributed in any degree to carry into effect those measures, and justify the wisdom and benevolence of the policy which dictated them, if the result is approved, will always be a source of much delight to me. Since the conclusion of the business with France, I have doubted much whether it wod. be best for me to remain here till I heard the result of the deliberations in the U States on what is already done, or proceed directly to Spain to treat for the Floridas; and after much reflection have decided in favor of the latter opinion. It is the only question which remains to be settled with these powers, which interests our future peace and tranquility; the present appears, to be a favorable moment for the settlement of it, and I trust it may be done on terms which will not be embarrassing to our finances. After extricating ourselves from the danger of war we have nothing to attend to, but our interior concerns, & among others to our finances. With our revenue and such immense resources in land, we may easily discharge all our debts in a reasonable time, without bringing more land to market than wod. command a good price, or be consistent with a slow and gradual extention of our settlements, founded on the progressive state of our population. I shall sit out for Spain in a week or ten days, and hope to be back in three or four months at most. I leave my family at St. Germain in my absence, where my daughter is at school. After a long negotiation or the appearance of it, war seems to be declared between Engld. & France. Where it will end or what its effect will be is uncertain. I have no doubt that it will tend in its consequences to improve the condition of our country in its wealth, independance of Europe, and in the character of our government. Both these powers see as I presume that our growth & prosperity are inevitable, and that it is for their interest respectively to stand well with us. The adjustment of the affr. of Louisiana with France, & of the Floridas, if it can be done with Spain will contribute much to the advancement of our credit in Europe. It is to be feared that the question of neutral rights which is certain to be again discussed, may give us much trouble. It is to be expected that Engld. will adhere to her doctrine, and probable that it may be opposed by Russia & the other neutral powers, to the north. To direct our course with advantage in reference to that question, and the parties connected with it, will require all the moderation & wisdom of our government. I am persuaded that a systematic plan of fortifying our seaports ought to be adopted; that it wod. be grateful to our citizens interested cannot be doubted; that it would produce an useful effect abroad is certain.

From every thing I can learn the doctrine of dry docks is at best doubtful, and that ships suffer more in fresh water by all the causes which produce decay than in salt is the opinion of all that I have conversed with. On these points I will write you hereafter. I send this by the way of Engld., deeming it the safest route at present. I have attended to the delivery of all your letters here, in a mode and at times which I thought most adviseable in reference to all circumstances which merited attention. A Mr. Chas who has a letter from you in terms of complement, who says he was acquainted with you formerly, has sent out to you 30. copies of his history of our revolution, & other works, after many pressing applications has obtained of me 150[tt]. on acct. of those remittances to you. He is I presume an honest man but worried me so much, that in giving the money I got no credit by it, being irritated by his importunities, and doubt whether I have not made him my enemy, by asking by what authority he sent you books &ca. I am dear sir very sincerely your friend & servt

JAS. MONROE

PS. Mr. Skipwith is desirous of an appointment at New Orleans, if the treaty is approved and a govt. organised there. His views are directed to the office of Collector for which he is well qualified. He has served long & faithfully here, and I believe without any improv'ment of his fortune. Having known the direct & upright line of his conduct, through a period of great political embarrassment, I own I feel much interest in his future establishment.

RC (DLC); endorsed by TJ as received 5 Sep. and so recorded in SJL.

Since his arrival in France, Monroe had written to MADISON six times as an individual, including a letter of 18 May, and twice as co-signer with Robert R. Livingston (Madison, *Papers*, *Sec. of State Ser.*, 4:497-8, 520-3, 538-9, 601-6, 610-15; 5:4-7, 12-13).

Monroe's daughter Eliza had reentered the fashionable school at ST. GERMAIN-en-Laye that she had attended several years earlier. The site of a former royal château west of Paris, St. Germain was a popular locale among Americans in France, including TJ, who went there on an excursion with Maria Cosway (Ammon, *Monroe*, 138-9, 207, 237; Howard C. Rice, Jr., *Thomas Jefferson's Paris* [Princeton, 1976], 11, 111; Vol. 10:445-6; Vol. 29: 164).

MR. CHAS WHO HAS A LETTER FROM YOU: TJ had written to Jean Chas in September 1801 (Vol. 35:203-4). BY WHAT AUTHORITY HE SENT YOU BOOKS: TJ repaid Monroe the 150 livres early in 1804, explaining that although Monroe could not have known otherwise, there was no reason for Chas to send him a supply of books and he had not received them (TJ to Monroe, 8 Jan. 1804).

Fulwar SKIPWITH had gone to France with Monroe in 1794 as secretary of legation. After Skipwith became U.S. consul in Paris, Monroe had to refute accusations that the two of them had engaged in illicit financial dealings. Federalists also attacked Skipwith when he petitioned Congress for the reimbursement of advances he had made from his own funds (Ammon, *Monroe*, 116; Vol. 29:165n; Vol. 30:222, 246, 247n, 272).

From Nicolas Gouin Dufief

MONSIEUR, May 19. 1803—

Le petit Livret que vous trouverez ci inclus m'a été donné, & moi je l'envoye à celui à qui il doit naturellement appartenir. L'homme de Goût qui a fait la collection intéressante qui s'y trouve, a voulu qu'on dise de son travail *Finis coronat opus*, en placant ce qu'il y a de meilleur à la fin.

C'est en y lisant la traduction d'une partie d'un Sublime Discours, sur lequel tout ce qui pense en Europe & en Amérique est de la même opinion que moi, que les quatre vers que j'ai pris la liberté de mettre au bas du portrait de l'Auteur, se sont présentés à mon esprit—Ils expriment bien faiblement ce que j'ai toujours senti en lisant l'Original qui étincelle de toutes les beautés d'une langue féconde & énergique, & qui renferme le Code éternel des Législateurs, qui voudront établir le bonheur des Individus & des Nations, sur la base inébranlable de la Morale & de la bonne-foi publique. Un jeune Médecin de la Virginie, qui partage mon enthousiasme pour l'Auteur & pour ses ouvrages, a voulu traduire mon Quatrain. Il s'en est acquitté avec tant de facilité & de plaisir que j'ai cru devoir y Joindre sa traduction—Monsieur le Capitaine Lewis, votre Secrétaire, S'est donné la peine de passer chez moi, & de me remettre une petite Somme, dont je n'étais nullement pressé—

Je vous remercie de votre attention à laquelle rien ne Saurait échapper—

Vous recevrez par le *Sloop Hiland*, Priestley's institutes, his early opinions, & un Ouvrage de Cuvier qui n'est point le même que son Anatomie comparée; ainsi nous Gagnons à cela un bon ouvrage de plus.

Je ne perds point de vue les autres livres que j'espere toujours vous procurer.

Votre lettre n'est point encore partie: je ne la mettrai dans le sac aux lettres, à la Bourse, que la veille du départ du Navire qui doit s'effectuer vers la fin de cette semaine. J'aurai alors l'honneur de vous en prévenir.

Je vous réitere, avec empressement, mes offres de service pour les choses auxquelles je pourrais vous être bon, à Philadelphie, & même à New-York, où j'ai un Correspondant sûr & diligent—

J'ai l'honneur d'être, Monsieur, avec Les Sentimens que nous vous devons tous, & ceux que je vous dois en particulier.

Votre très dévoué Serviteur N. G. DUFIEF

EDITORS' TRANSLATION

Sir, May 19. 1803—

The small book you will find enclosed was given to me; I am sending it to the person to whom it should rightfully belong. The man of taste who assembled this interesting collection placed the best at the end, in hopes that one would say of his work: *Finis coronat opus.*

While reading in translation a passage of a sublime discourse, about which all thinking people in Europe and America concur, four verses came to my mind. I took the liberty of placing them below the author's portrait. They express very poorly what I have always felt in reading the original which sparkles with all the beauty of a rich, strong language and contains the eternal law of legislators who seek to base the happiness of individuals and nations on the unshakeable foundation of morality and civic trust. A young doctor from Virginia, who shares my enthusiasm for the author and his works, was willing to translate my quatrain. He did so with such ease and pleasure that I feel obliged to enclose his translation.

Your secretary, Captain Lewis, took the trouble to visit and give me a small sum for which I was in no hurry. Thank you for your attentiveness which lets nothing escape.

On the sloop *Hiland* you will receive Priestley's *Institutes*, his early opinions, and a work by Cuvier which is not the same as his comparative anatomy. We thus gain another good work.

I have not forgotten the other books I still hope to procure for you.

Your letter has not yet been sent. I will put it in the letter bag at the exchange on the eve of the ship's departure which is supposed to take place toward the end of this week. Then I will have the honor of informing you that it is done.

I hasten to repeat my offer to help in any way I can be useful to you, in Philadelphia and even in New York, where I have a reliable, diligent correspondent.

Sir, with the sentiments we all owe you and those I personally owe you, I have the honor of being your most devoted servant. N. G. Dufief

RC (DLC); at foot of text: "Le Président des Etats-Unis d'Amérique"; endorsed by TJ as received 21 May and so recorded in SJL. Enclosure not identified.

FINIS CORONAT OPUS: the end crowns the work.

With this letter Dufief probably sent a bill of lading that John Hand, the master of the HILAND, signed at Philadelphia on 18 May: "I John Hand, Master of the Sloop Hiland, do certify that Mr. N. G. Dufief, has shipped on board of the said vessel a Bundle of Books, directed to Ths. Jefferson President of the U.S.—and which I promise to deliver or to have delivered to the same.—(the dangers of the sea excepted)" (MS in DLC; in a clerk's hand, signed by Hand). Hand and the *Hiland* made frequent voyages between Philadelphia and Alexandria, Georgetown, and Washington, and had previously transported items for TJ (*Alexandria Advertiser*, 1 Jan., 3 June; *Poulson's American Daily Advertiser*, 21 Jan., 19 Mch., 21 May; Vol. 36:689, 691, 693).

VOTRE LETTRE: TJ to Fulwar Skipwith, 4 May; see Dufief to TJ, 15 May.

BOURSE: ships' letter bags were left at the Merchants' Coffee House in Philadelphia's City Tavern to collect mail prior to transatlantic voyages. The coffee house was the home of the Board of Brokers—the city's stock exchange—and of a variety of other commercial activities, including insurance brokerage, meetings of corporations, real estate auctions, and sales of ships (*Poulson's American Daily Advertiser*, 7 Mch., 8, 13 Apr.; *Gazette of the United States*, 18 Mch., 24 May, 7, 10 June; Philadelphia *Aurora*, 16 Nov. 1803; Robert C. Smith, "A Portuguese Naturalist in Philadelphia, 1799," PMHB, 78 [1954], 86; Thomas C. Chochran, "Philadelphia: The American Industrial Center, 1750-1850," PMHB, 106 [1982], 327).

From James Wallace

259 Broadway N.Y.
Newyork May 19th. 1803.

SIR

Having but lately arrived in this Country, and therefore being a stranger to most of its customs as well as to its Inhabitants; and having through propensity of Genius made Mathematics my pursuit for some time back, I have, I believe, happened to discover some new hints, relative to Natural Philosophy: which might be of considerable advantage in this Science no less than in Natural & Supernatural Religion: which from my humble situation, I am unable to pursue, with pleasure to myself, or advantage to the Subject. I thought I could not communicate those principles, to any one so adequate to Judge, or whose Judgment when delivered would tend so much to establish the reputation, and induce me to prosecute these Enquiries, as far as my limitted circumstances would permit, as the Author of the Notes on Virginia: As I am confident, from the many proofs of Philanthrophy that are manifest in that work, as well as in all your Excellencys Acts; this Essay will meet with that indulgence, which men cultivating Science in all parts of the World, are willing to extend to each other.

Before I proceed it may not be improper to mention the accidence which gave these thoughts a being.—

Having since my arrival in this Country, met with "Paines Age of Reason," which I have read with attention, and being unable to answer many of the objections there set forth against Christianity, I resolved to make a candid enquiry, and as strict, as the powers of my mind, aided by every assistance I could procure, was able to perform: as I could not from the Sublime Morality set forth in the Bible, hastily abandon the Doctrine, this resolution I began immediately to carry into effect, by examining some of the hints relative to Natural Philosophy, which are to be met with in this Book; as it was from these hints that I presumed to form my Judgment, being convinced that truth will always be found consistent with itself; and also determined if I should find these parts manifestly false, to yield to Mr Paines Objections.—

Hence the Writings of St. Paul, being in Nat. Science the best informed of the Apostles, and as he witnesses the whole doctrine of the New Testament first claimed my particular attention, and those passages which Mr. Paine terms the Jargon of a Conjuror chiefly attracted my notice. One of those passages being that which first expanded my Ideas with respect to the System of the World, I take the liberty to mention here. "There are also" Says St. Paul, "*Bodies* Celestial Bodies and bodies Terrestrial, but the glory of the Celestial is One, and the glory of the Terrestrial is another. there is one glory of the Sun and another glory of the moon, and another glory of the Stars for one Star differs from another Star in Glory." 1st. Cor. Ch. 15. This seems to me a full description of the System of the Universe, for he says that all the Stars receive their light from One Body, and that the Planets Receive their light from the *Stars* Sun; and his saying that one Star differs from another Star in glory, shews that one Star receives more light from this body than another, and consequently must be nearer to it. and Gravity being essential to matter, as Sir Isaac Newton has Demonstrated, these Stars [&c.] must perform their Revolutions round this Body, which must therefore be the Center of the Universe.

Being convinced that Paul could not come at this System, from all the Philosophy that was Known in his time, which if found true, will not only give us an amazing Idea of the wonderful works of God; but invincibly prove that St. Paul was divinely inspired, this being Once admitted, the doctrine of Christianity must rest upon a foundation, never to be Shaken and the chief objection, that its doctrines are not all agreeable to Natural Philosophy, removed—

That I could go some length in Demonstrating this System the following hints may shew, but to undertake to perform it in my present circumstance would perhaps be as vain an attempt, as that of the Giants of Old, who endeavoured to throw Mount Ossa upon Pelion, and Olympus upon Ossa. For it cant be expected I could proceed, when my circumstances will not allow me, at present, to buy the few Books I want to finish my studies in Nat. Philosophy, which I almost just began: and when I have no time to spare, Save what little I must take from the Ordinary hours of Sleep. being employed as teacher of Mathematics &c. in an Academy in Newyork, where I have rather too much to do, but not being here much more than half a year my Salary is but Small—tho' it is since I have commenced this employment, I happened to meet with the "Age of Reason," and to make my Remarks on the above System—

In the various Branches of Mathematics being pretty well informed. and at a time which did not much favour these Studies, having without the assistance of any man, Save thro' the Medium of a few Books, got over most of the difficulties generally complained of in them: I applyed myself to practise Land Surveying with Success, but my natural bent for Science encreasing, I thought my native country too unfavourable a Spot for prosecuting my enquiries with any advantage or encouragement, and accordingly resolved to adopt the well Known Maxim "Where Liberty dwells, there is my country," here every man who acknowledges the rights of a rational being, ought to bring his mite of Knowledge or experience, to encrease the rising Glory of this happy People.

Impressed with these Ideas, I have ventured to lay before your Excellency the above Remarks, and shall now proceed to mention some of the principles upon which I think the truth of the above System is founded.—It is well Known that heat expands, and Cold condenses the Atmosphere: it is equally as well Known, that the rays of light are small bodies, projected with an incredible Velocity; and therefore their Actions on Matter must be exceeding great, as is manifest from the Nature of heat; for the greatest friction is scarcely able to burn Some Bodies, and yet the Rays of light collected in a small space, will not only burn, but melt Glass &c. and reduce to Ashes the hardest Bodies—Now the part of the Atmosphere over which the Sun is perpendicular, or that which has been but a few Minutes from under its direct influence, being most rarified, afford a freeer passage for the Rays to pass thro', consequently, thro' this rarified Medium, their action, whether of repulsion or attraction, must be greater than thro' the medium, which is equally near the perpendicular, but has not at as yet been under the Direct influence of the Sun, and therefore a motion of the Earth must ensue. this being premised—

If we consider the Earth at rest, its plain that the rays at every Side of the perpendicular, and equally distant from it, will have equal effects and that no motion (I mean on its Axis) will ensue, but conceiving the Almighty in the beginning to impress such a motion on it then by the above mode of reasoning this motion will be continued by the difference of the Actions of the rays of light, to enter into details concerning these Actions, and how they are likewise the cause of the Planets periodical revolutions in their Orbits, also of the Figure of the Earth taken notice of by St. Pierre in a work entitled the "Studies of Nature" published in france in 1784, and translated & published in London in 1795, would far exceed the bounds of a Letter Moreover as they depend on Experiments which I am (at least as yet) unable to make, on Optical principles not fully handled (in my opinion) by any Author, that I Know of, and on tedious calculations which the Subtilty of Fluxions are hardly able to Surmount—but I shall mention A few more conclusions

This being so with Respect to the Earth it must be the case with respect to all the Planets, which as far as we can make observations on them, are surrounded with an Atmosphere, and consequently must have a motion on their Axis, which observations likewise Shew: but with respect to the Secondary Planets, having no motion on their Axis, but Keeping the same Side always turned to their primaries; it is plain they can have no atmosphere. As is the case with the Moon and consequently that their density must be greater than that of their Primary. also, from the greater Action of the Rays of light—which Newton has demonstrated to be the case with Respect to the Earth and Moon—from these instances it may, I believe, without further Demonstration be infered, that light is the Cause of Gravity, motion, &C in Bodies, and of all those Phaenomena which Newton takes notice of at the end of his General Scholium, Book the 3d. of his Principia.—Newton has likewise demonstrated, that the nearer any of the Planets are to the Sun, the density of them are proportionably encreased; tho' the Sun which is the fountain of light to this System, is less dense (Newton) than the Earth; this may shew that the matter of it is different from Terrestrial Bodies.—What must our Ideas then be of those beings who inhabit the Planets, Saturn or Herschell, and doubtless others that are more Remote, which are almost deprived both of light and heat—when it is considered, that every being is fitted by providence for the part of the creation allotted for his existance, and that the Body of man is composed of the Earth which he inhabits, this appears still clearer in the various Species of Animals which are fitted for the different Climates of this little Globe, as is fully noticed in Notes on Virginia. All these instances loudly proclaim the hand of an allwise and powerful God, who regulates every atom of the Universe—But if we extend our Ideas beyond this Solar system, to trace the Phaenomena thence occuring, its necessary after what is here laid down, to begin with the Sun, which has likewise an Atmosphere and also a motion on its Axis regularly performed, from whence then can this motion Arise? it cant be from the Irregular Actions of the Planets, nor (I believe) from the joint influence of the Stars. and that it cant have a motion in itself without some external (and regular) cause is I think manifest; it must, therefore, proceed from some certain Body, which the Sun respects as its Center, and round which it must revolve, and from which it receives light motion &c. from this it might, with some reason, be concluded, that there must be some beings inhabiting the Sun, who equally enjoy the influence of this Body, as man equally enjoys day and night by the rotation of the Earth on its Axis—And as the Stars are of the Same nature with the Sun, the same reasoning may be extended to them, moreover the nicety of modern observations goes a great way to shew, that they have really a motion, and probably from some optical Instruments which chance may discover. we shall be clearly convinced of these matters—and I conjecture from their different colours, that they must have an atmosphere, as the brightness of an Object is the same at all distances from the Eye, if none of the rays be stopt by the Way by means of any Medium through which they pass, and that this atmosphere varies, as the light which passes thro' it varies; or that the Atmosphere which surrounds these Stars, must be of different densities.

The Planets being more perfect the nearer the approach the Neighbourhood of the Sun, there is nothing more reasonable to allow, than that the nearer the Stars are to this Body, the more perfect they must be. Now As the Sun is greater than all the Bodies put together which Regard him as their Center, which is also true with respect to the Primary planets and their Secondaries, what Idea can be formed of the Magnitude and perfection of this Body, which Occupies the Center of the Universe & round which all the heavenly Bodies Revolve.

To enlarge a little more on this subject would be a pleasant task, but I must confine myself at present to these outlines, fearing to trespass too much on your time—

Yet I cant help reflecting, how I must
From this delightful clime now wander back,
Into this lower World so distant far!
And so obscure, but fate ordains it
And I must Obey.

If it be allowed, that those Stars which with respect to the Sun may be called inferior, or more properly interior Stars, are more perfect than the Sun, as I think it cannot be denied; it must be allowed likewise, that those which are exterior are less perfect, and consequently, the planets which Revolve round them, (if any,) than those in similiar situations which revolve round the Sun, and those Stars again which are more Remote, less perfect than the next nearest; and so on to the extremity of the Universe—

The Philosophers may find here a curious fund for speculation, in considering besides the nature &C. of these Bodies, the condition of the beings which inhabit them. but if the distance can be conceived infinite, then matter looses every active principle which it derives from light, and becomes what the Poets describe a frightful Chaos (Milton's Par L. B. 2) The Idea I cant pursue any farther, but shall leave to those Philosophers, who are not fond of allowing that any space should be left unoccupied, to determine, whether God in his goodness, could consign any beings over to those Regions of Eternal Misery.

There are many passages which have occured to me, in the Bible, to this purpose; a few of which I shall take the Liberty to insert.—In the Book of Job, Chap. 38. we Read.—"Have the Gates of death been opened unto thee, or hast thou Seen the doors of the Shadow of Death. Hast thou perceivest the breath of the Earth, declare if thou canst it all, Where is the way" (that is providing he has seen it) "where light dwelleth and as for darkness, where is the way thereof: hast thou entered into the treasures of the Snow, or hast thou seen the treasures of the hail which, I have reserved against the time of trouble, against the day of battle and War" And again Chap 18, speaking of the Wicked "He shall be driven from light into darkness, & chased Out of the World; Surely such are the dwellings of the Wicked, and this is the place of him who Knoweth not God" and St. Matthew Chap 23 "Then said the King to the servants, bind him hand and foot and take him away, and cast him into Outer darkness, there shall be weeping and gnashing of teeth. for many are called, but few are Chosen."

These passages I have selected to prove, that the Bible contains more Philosophy, than man, in this life, can ever pretend to—

These hints may likewise show, what despised Irishmen might do, if they had the Advantage of those Seminaries of Learning, which admit none but the great and opulent.—I cant but look back to my native country, once the Seat of Arts and learning, but now in Slavery and oppression fallen, perhaps to rise no more.

If these hints claim any degree of Merit or patronage, I should be happy to have Your excellencys opinion on them. As I might then labour to bring them to some perfection, and add my little Stock to the common fund, for the improvement of these Sciences, in a Country, which in all probability, from the Revolutions which learning has taken on the old continent, and the principles of the Constitution of the United States; will become the principal seat of Knowledge & Science, and give these Arts, their greatest perfection—

France indeed, is now doing a great deal in this way. for the English "monthly review" has mentioned two Authors the one on Fluxions, and the other on Physical Astronomy; that will do more honor to France, than the Victories of their most renowned Generals. Will Columbia then not signalize herself in these laudable pursuits? or must france & England unrivalled, bear the Palm alone—

Should these remarks appear but crudely digested, or improperly Set forth, Your Excellency will I hope excuse them, and feel rather disposed to indulge a poor Foreigner, and pardon his liberty in troubling you with these matters, and attribute these faults to his youth, his inexperience, & want of the necessary Qualifications; to any thing, rather than want of due Respect for a man, who is so high in the estimation of Mankind.—and by merit alone thus favoured—

With great and Sincere Esteem I respectfully subscribe myself Sir Your most obedient and most humble Servant.

James Wallace.

RC (DLC); torn; at head of text: "To the President Of the United States of America"; endorsed by TJ as received 21 May and so recorded in SJL.

After emigrating as a teenager from Ireland, James Wallace (d. 1850) taught for a few years in New York before becoming an instructor of mathematics at Georgetown College in the District of Columbia. There, he entered the order of the Society of Jesus. He returned to New York in 1809 to become professor of mathematics and astronomy at the New-York Literary Institution, a recently formed Jesuit-run academy that after four years' operation the Church decided not to sustain. While in New York, he published a well-regarded astronomy textbook, *A New Treatise on the Use of the Globes, and Practical Astronomy; or a Comprehensive View of the System of the World*. He was recalled to Georgetown in 1813 as the chair in mathematics and astronomy and remained there until being sent as a missionary to South Carolina in 1818. A couple of years later he took a position as the professor of mathematics and natural philosophy at South Carolina College in Columbia, an action which prompted his expulsion from the Jesuit order. He remained a Catholic priest, serving posts in South Carolina until his death (Shaw-Shoemaker, No. 27419; Robert Emmett Curran, *The Bicentennial History of Georgetown University: From Academy to University, 1789-1889*, Vol. 1 [Washington, D.C., 1993], 70-1, 81, 90; *New-York Commercial Advertiser*, 2 May 1810; New Haven *Columbian Register*, 15 Jan. 1851; *National Intelligencer*, 6 Feb. 1851).

JARGON OF THE CONJUROR: critiquing 1 Corinthians 15:39-41, part of Paul's defense of the concept of the resurrection, Thomas Paine characterized Paul as someone "who picks up phrases he does not understand, to confound the credulous people who come to have their fortune told. Priests and conjurors are of the same trade" (Thomas Paine, *Age of Reason. Part the Second* [London, 1796], 73).

In Homer's *Odyssey*, 11.305-20, young GIANTS Otus and Ephialtes hoped to scale the heavens and challenge the gods by piling MOUNT OSSA on Olympus, and Pelion on Ossa.

HERSCHELL: that is, Uranus, which was discovered by British astronomer William Herschel (DNB).

FLUXIONS: the term used by Newton for what modern mathematicians understand as differential calculus (OED).

In the second book of John MILTON's *Paradise Lost*, Satan travels to the newly created Earth across "a dark, Illimitable ocean, without bound, Without dimension, where length, breadth, and height, And time and place are lost," and where

Night and Chaos "hold Eternal anarchy" (2.891-6).

The passage from MATTHEW appears at 22:13-14.

The MONTHLY REVIEW was an English periodical that TJ had long collected (Sowerby, No. 4721; Vol. 37:564n). Wallace may have been alluding to a two-part review the journal published in 1800 of Silvestre François Lacroix's *Traité du calcul différentiel et du calcul intégral* (Paris, 1797-1800), a three-volume reference work on developments in calculus during the eighteenth century. The review discussed a number of mathematicians, both English and French, who had pointed out flaws in Newton's concept of fluxions. In its second part, the review argued that many of the recent advances in integral calculus had derived from efforts to resolve problems associated with the science of PHYSICAL ASTRONOMY (*The Monthly Review; or, Literary Journal*, 31 [1800], 493-505; 32 [1800], 485-95; João Caramalho Domingues, *Lacroix and the Calculus* [Basel, Switzerland, 2008], 1, 16).

From Stephen R. Bradley

SIR Westminster May 20th. 1803

I have Just learnt that James Elliot has resigned as a Commissioner of Bankruptcy and to my surprise that he has recommended his Brother to succeed him—The recommendation of his Brother is an injudicious one, his brother I understand is a young man reading law as a Clerk in an office and has removed to live in the State but a Very Short time I am convinced his appointment would be viewed unfavourably by the best friends to the Government—I will take the liberty to Recommend *Samuel Knight* Esqr. to be appointed *vice* James Elliot he has been a firm Republican through the whole reign of Terror was Chief Justice of our Supreme Court for Several Years and was left out by the Federalists when the Government was in their hands, Since which he has never been replaced he is an able Lawyer and well calculated to Discharge the Duties of that office lives in the Same town with Mr Elliot resigned I wish for the sake of the Government he might obtain

With the highest respect except the Homage of

STEPHEN R BRADLEY

RC (DNA: RG 59, LAR); at head of text: "The President of the United States"; endorsed by TJ as received 30 May and "Knight Saml. to be Commr. bkrptcy v. James Elliott resd." and so recorded in SJL.

On 25 Mch., James Elliot wrote the secretary of state, submitting his resignation as a Vermont bankruptcy commissioner and recommending his BROTHER Samuel, who had recently moved from Salem, Massachusetts, to Guilford, Vermont, in his place (Vol. 38:515n; Vol. 39:97-8n). For James Elliot's subsequent recommendation of SAMUEL KNIGHT for the position, see the enclosure described at Gideon Granger to TJ, 30 May. Knight received the appointment with a commission dated 16 June (list of commissions in Lb in DNA: RG 59, MPTPC).

To Isaac Briggs

DEAR SIR Washington May 20. 1803.

I thank you for your attention to the commission respecting the clock, and will immediately remit the money to mr Ferris with directions how to forward the clock. I inclose you part of a letter from mr Fitz, (the residue I tore off & retained as relating to something else.) I write him this day that you will recieve his queries but in the moment of your departure when you will not have time to answer them, even if you had information sufficient; but that it will be much better for you to write to him after you shall have arrived at your destination, and had time to look about and form a judgment of the place & business. if you can do this I shall be obliged to you. Fitz not being a man of robust health, ought not to set out till October. I informed James Dinsmore that you would make no appointments till you get to the place, & will there see his brother. he desired me to return you his thanks, & to express his wish which was only that his brother should have an opportunity of being examined by you, & recieved *if qualified*, which he is confident in. with respect to Claiborne I have before gone as far in relieving his distresses as justice to others equally distressed & pressing will admit; and my means will answer, which are pressed to their uttermost bearing. as the salary annexed to my office looks large in every man's eye, it draws the attention of the needy in every part of the Union and increases the demands of aid, far beyond the proportion of means it furnishes to satisfy them.[1] I am obliged therefore to proceed by rule, & not to give to one the share of another. but I am glad to inform you that by a letter from Claiborne he has succeeded so far in his boat-experiment as to excite an interest for him in Alexandria, where they are making up a sum to enable him to make a fair experiment, and doubtless something more. I wish you a pleasant journey and a safe arrival at your destination. I will write by post to Govr. Claiborne to inform him of your coming. Accept my friendly salutations & assurances of esteem.

TH: JEFFERSON

PrC (DLC); at foot of text: "Mr. Isaac Briggs"; endorsed by TJ in ink on verso. Enclosure not identified, but see below.

LETTER FROM MR FITZ: a letter of 2 May from Gideon Fitz is recorded in SJL as received 8 May from Monticello, but has not been found. TJ's reply to Fitz is recorded at 20 May, but likewise has not been found.

I INFORMED JAMES DINSMORE: letters from TJ to Dinsmore are recorded in SJL at 20 and 22 Apr., but neither has been found. For correspondence regarding a position for John Dinsmore, see TJ to Briggs, 20 Apr. and Briggs to TJ, 2 May.

A LETTER FROM CLAIBORNE: Richard Claiborne to TJ, 14 May.

[1] Word interlined.

From Charles Burrall

SIR, Baltimore May 20, 1803

I have the honor to acknowledge the receipt of your Note of the 10th Inst, covering two letters, one for Mr Skipwith, & the other for Mr Barnet both of which I forwarded by the Brig Henry, Capt Sherman that sailed on the 12th Inst for Bourdeaux. There being no prospect of a conveyance direct for Havre, I thought it advisable to send both letters by Capt Sherman.—

I am Sir with great respect your obedient servant

CHAS: BURRALL

RC (MHi); at foot of text: "The President of the United States"; endorsed by TJ as received 21 May and so recorded in SJL with notation "lre to Skipw. went May 12. to Bord."; also endorsed by TJ: "that my lres to Skipwith & Barnet went by a vessel which sailed May 12. for Bordeaux. may be in Paris in 6. weeks, viz June 22."

TJ did not record his NOTE of 10 May to the Baltimore postmaster in SJL and it has not been found (Vol. 33:427n). The letters FORWARDED were TJ to Fulwar Skipwith, 4 May, and TJ to Isaac Cox Barnet, 10 May.

To Peter Freneau

DEAR SIR Washington May 20. 1803.

I recieved last night from Paris the inclosed small parcel of Egyptian rice. I am not informed of it's merit: but your's being the state where that can be best tried, I take the liberty of consigning it to your care, that we may be availed of whatever good it may offer.

The New York election no doubt attracted your attention from the inflated hopes of the Federalists. from a concurrence of circumstances they had been drawn out with all their boldness. one source of their delusion was that they were so desirous of war themselves that they really believed the nation desired it. never was defeat more compleat. in Jersey it is confidently believed we shall have 29. members out of 52 which constitute both houses. in Massachusets we have gained 3. Senators more than we had last year, and it is believed that in the elections of representatives now going on, we shall gain also. in Connecticut we have lost greatly in their house of representatives: yet in the whole body of the people we have unquestionably gained, as is proved by the votes for Governor. last year the votes for Trumbull & Kirby were 11,000 to 4523. this year they are 14,300 to 7848. so that the last year, of 100. parts of the whole voters the federalists had 71. and the republicans 29. this year, of 100. parts of the whole voters the federalists had 65. and the republicans 35. we have advanced then from 29 to 35 or $\frac{1}{6}$ while they have fallen from 71. to 65 or $\frac{1}{11}$. in New Hampshire they appear to have been more stationary. Delaware is entirely equivocal & uncertain. on the whole there is no doubt of republicanism gaining the entire ascendancy in New England within a moderate term[1] & consolidating the union into one homogeneous mass. in Philadelphia some heats have been excited against the leaving any federalists in office. but these are softening down to moderation, while in the other[2] states generally the course which has been pursued, altho' thought to have gone too far into removal, is acquiesced in & on the whole approved. we laid it down as a principle, in the beginning, that the federalists had a right to a participation of office proportioned to their numbers. they in fact possessed all. we removed a few in marked cases. we determined to remove all others who should take an active & bitter part against the order of things established by the public will. removals for this cause & for other delinquencies, resignations & deaths have nearly given us our full proportion of office in all the states except Massachusets. I speak of those offices only which are given by the President himself. the subordinate ones are left to their principals. at present therefore, as from[3] an early period of the administration, political principle, unless producing active opposition, is not a ground of removal, altho' it is as yet a bar to appointment, until the just proportion is fully restored.

A letter begun with a view to cover a few seeds, & to say a word about elections, has led to a length not at first contemplated. desirous however that the principles of our proceedings should be understood, I explain them to no one more willingly than yourself, because I am sure you will use them with prudence & sincerity for the information & satisfaction of others when occasions may lead you to an expression of sentiment. should it be the means of giving me the advantage of recieving communications sometimes from you on the political state of things in your quarter, it will contribute to that information so desireable to myself & so necessary to enable me to do what is best for the public interest. I pray you to accept my salutations and assurances of esteem & respect. TH: JEFFERSON

RC (PWacD: Feinstone Collection, on deposit PPAmP); at foot of first page: "Mr. Freneau"; endorsed. PrC (DLC).

Republicans in the 40-member Massachusetts Senate remained constant in 1803 at 12 SENATORS. In 1804, the party gained two senators. Two years later, Republicans controlled both houses (Michael J. Dubin, *Party Affiliations in the State Legislatures: A Year by Year Summary, 1796-2006* [Jefferson, N.C., 2007], 90-1). For the election in Massachusetts, see also John Bacon to TJ, 11 Apr.

[1] Preceding four words interlined.
[2] Word interlined.
[3] TJ here canceled "the beginning."

To Gideon Granger

DEAR SIR Washington May 20. 1803.

I recieved last night yours of the 13th. and rejoice that in some forms, tho' not in all, republicanism shows progress in Connecticut. as Clerical bondage is the root of the evil, I have more hopes, from the petition you inclosed me, of seeing that loosened, than from any other agency. the lawyers, the other pillar of federalism, are from the nature of their calling so ready to take either side, that as soon as they see as much, or perhaps more money to be got on one side than the other, they will tack over. the clergy are unwilling to exchange the certain resource of legal compulsion for the uncertain one of their own merit & industry. altho' the solidity & duration of republicanism in these states is so certain, that I would [...] give one dollar to ensure it's ascendancy during our lives, yet the three federal states of New England withdrawn from their affections to the constituted authorities, form a stock on which the feeble branches of federalism in the other states engraft themselves, nourish their malcontent habits, & keep open the bleeding wounds of society. their recognition therefore of their own principles in those from whom they have been persuaded to separate is desirable as well to harmonize as to consolidate the strength of the Union. it is possible my letter may have led you into an error in which I may have been myself. it is now said by the federalists that another tory Lewis is elected in opposition to Moore. and they make it probable by stating the fact that another republican candidate took from Moore 400. votes, which gave a majority of 200. to Lewis when Moore would otherwise have had a majority of 200. if this be true, we shall have 4. federalists out of 22. in Congress. this is the more curious as in our legislature we shall have but 15. out of 200. but the fact is that there is so little federalism in Virginia that it is not feared, nor attended to, nor a principle of voting. what little we have is in the string of presbyterian counties in the valley between the blue ridge & North mountain where the clergy are as bitter as they are in Connecticut. our advices from Paris & London are to the last of March. war, tho' deprecated by Buonaparte, will hardly be avoided. Accept my friendly salutations & respects. TH: JEFFERSON

PrC (DLC); torn; at foot of text: "Gideon Granger esq."

Election results for Virginia's fifth congressional district indicated that Thomas

LEWIS, Federalist, received 1,004 votes; former Republican congressman Andrew MOORE, 832; and John Woodward, a delegate representing Monroe County in the Virginia Assembly and identified as a Federalist, 423. On 18 May, several newspapers reported that Moore had experienced "*foul play*" in one or two counties and that Lewis was not "legally elected." On 17 Oct., however, Lewis was sworn in as a member of Congress. Almost a month later, Moore petitioned the House, complaining of the "undue election and return of Thomas Lewis." The complaint was submitted to the Committee on Elections, along with other depositions, papers, and petitions from Kanawha, Greenbrier, Rockbridge, and Augusta counties during the following weeks. On 5 Mch. 1804, the House supported the election committee's findings that after deducting the "unqualified votes from the respective polls," Moore had received the highest number of votes and was duly elected. Moore took his seat in the House the same day (Richmond *Virginia Argus*, 18 May; *National Intelligencer*, 18 May; Leonard, *General Assembly*, 224; Dubin, *Congressional Elections*, 28; JHR, 4:401-3, 442, 452, 509, 617-19). For the 1 Mch. report of the Committee on Elections and subsequent debate, see *Annals*, 13:1082-6, 1089-92. For Moore's career, see Vol. 35:26n.

NORTH MOUNTAIN: that is, "one of the ridges of the Alleghany Mountains, which extends through Virginia and Pennsylvania" (Jedidiah Morse, *The American Gazetteer*, 2d ed. [Charlestown, Mass., 1804]). For TJ's definition, see *Notes*, ed. Peden, 20.

To Josiah Meigs

DEAR SIR Washington May 20. 1803.

Your friendly letter of April 11. was not recieved till the 11th. of this month. the approbation which you are pleased to express of my efforts in the public cause are highly acceptable. the concurrence of our fellow citizens of understanding & good principles being more than a countervail with me for all the dirty ribaldry & falsehoods with which the tory papers are constantly filled. we are giving a fair course to the experiment whether an honest government can stand against the licentiousness of the press. a fair one I call it; because we do not deter them by prosecutions given under those laws against libels established by the states, whose authority to establish such is always affirmed to be exclusive of that of the general government. I believe we shall succeed in the experiment, & that it will appear that the people will consider the acts of the government which they see & feel, no better or worse than the unceasing falsehoods which they read. it is with great pleasure I learn that the college of Georgia is under your care. science is indisputably necessary for the support of a republican government, & it is to the middle & Southern states we must look for support until the [stock &?] chains in which the New England states are bound, can be broken or lightened. this shall be done in time. two of those states are with us. in Massachusets we continue to gain, & even in Connecticut, where we have lost in the house of representatives, we have gained in the mass of people. in 1802. Trumbull & Kirby had 11,000. and 4523 votes, to wit of every 100. Trumbull had 71. Kirby 29. in 1803. the votes are 14,300 and 7848, to wit of every 100. Trumbull has 65. & Kirby 35. the people of that country move slowly but steadily. I pray you to accept my salutations & assurances of great esteem & respect.

TH: JEFFERSON

PrC (DLC); blurred; at foot of text: "J. Meigs. esq" Recorded in SJL with notation "Athens Georgia."

To Anne Cary Randolph

Washington May 20. 1803.

It is very long, my dear Anne, since I have recieved a letter from you. when was it? in the mean time verses have been accumulating till I find it necessary to get them off my hands without further waiting. with them I send an A.B.C. for miss Cornelia, & she must pay you a kiss for it on my account. the little recipe about charcoal is worth your Mama's notice. we had peas here on Tuesday the 17th. & every day since. we had then also full grown cucumbers: but I suppose they had been forced. what sort of weather had you from the 4th. to the 10th. here we had frost, ice & snow, & great damage in the gardens & orchards. how stands the fruit with you in the neighborhood & at Monticello? and particularly the peaches, as they are what will be in season when I come home. the figs also, have they been hurt? you must mount Midas & ride over to Monticello to inform yourself, or collect the information from good authority & let me have it by next post. tell your papa that I delivered waterproof blue Casimir for a coat for him to mr Madison a fortnight ago. he has been expecting to set out every day. he will forward it by the rider from Orange court house whenever he does go. present my tenderest affections to your Mama, and accept my kisses for yourself & the little ones. to your papa health and attachment.

TH: JEFFERSON

PrC (MHi); at foot of text: "Miss Anne C. Randolph"; endorsed by TJ in ink on verso. Enclosures not identified.

WHEN WAS IT: see Anne Cary Randolph to TJ, [before 24 Feb. 1803].

From Henry Dearborn

SIR [21 May 1803]

I enclose Govr. Claiborns letter on the subject of a Brigadier Genl. may it not be prudent to consult Govr. Claiborn on the effect which the appointment of his brother as Majr. Genl. would probably have in the Territory, previous to making any appointment of Genl. officers.

H. DEARBORN

RC (DLC); undated; endorsed by TJ as received from the War Department on 21 May 1803 and "Brigadr. Genl. for Missipi" and so recorded in SJL. Enclosure not found.

Claiborne had previously recommended HIS BROTHER, Ferdinand L. Claiborne, a former captain in the U.S. Army, to be surveyor general of the Mississippi Territory (Heitman, *Dictionary*, 1:302; Dunbar Rowland, *Encyclopedia of Mississippi History*, 2 vols. [Madison, Wis., 1907], 1:423-4; Vol. 39:158-9).

Report from John Lenthall

Rough Stone & Brick work done to the south wing of
The Capitol from May 16 to 21st

Stone work on the West front, and the return Racks, North end of do, and in the Arches up to the Cellar window sills, on the south front,

about 2314 Cubic feet or 93 perches

Brick Work

7 Beds or soffeits of Reversed Arches, on the South front, prepared with strong Gravel cement, and the Arches turned to support the piers, and 7 smaller do within the larger ones to support the Jambs of the openings containing, together, about 14,000 Bricks

for B H Latrobe JNO LENTHALL

MS (DLC); partially dated; in Lenthall's hand and signed by him; addressed: "P. U.S.A."; endorsed by TJ: "Capitol May 21. 1803."

To Jared Mansfield

SIR Washington May 21. 1803.

You will be sensible of the reasons why the subject of this letter is desired to be entirely confidential for a time. Mr. Putnam the present Surveyor General in the Northern quarter is totally incompetent to the office he holds. the errors which he has committed in laying off the townships, not having been able to run parallel East & West lines, so that those of the several townships do not meet by considerable distances, have fixed an indelible blot on the map of the US. some of the sections consequently containing more & some less than they ought to contain, disputes with the US. are engendered without end. the purchasers of the sections having a surplus refusing to pay for it, & those of the defective ones demanding reimbursement. it has cost Congress a great deal of time at several of their former sessions to endeavor to rectify this, but it has been found impossible, & the removal of the blunderer has been sorely and generally desired. we have been wanting also from that officer, accurate determinations by astronomical observations of several points & lines in our geography very interesting to us. mr Ellicott has furnished us an accurate survey of the Missisipi from it's mouth to that of the Ohio, and an accurate determination of the most important points of lake Erie. we wish to have the South end of Lake Michigan, the West end of lake Superior (say the mouth of St. Louis) and Michillimacinac determined, as also a continuation of the course of the Missisipi from the mouth of the Ohio to the falls of St. Anthony, about Lat. 45.° but mr Putnam is incompetent & it would have been[1] in vain to set him about it. I am happy in possessing satisfactory proof of your being[2] entirely master of this subject, and therefore in proposing to you to undertake the office. the salary is 2000. D. a year, with allowance for 2. clerks at 500. & 450. D. a year. a good deal of new surveying is now to be begun, & it is important to have an immediate change or we shall have the same blunders continued. the ascertaining the geographical points above-mentioned, not being immediately pressing, must always be accomodated to the necessities of the ordinary business. the survey[3] of the portion of the Missisipi above mentioned would be best done while the river is frozen, when it could be run with a compass & chain & corrected at proper intervals by celestial observations. the length of the line between 5. and 600. miles. all instruments & assistance necessary would be furnished by the US. the immediate business however to be entered on is the laying off the townships & sections. if you accept the office, as I hope you will, it would be necessary for you to come here about the 1st. of June, when mr Gallatin will put you in possession of all the information necessary. several days reading in his office will be requisite. your expences to, at, & from this place back to your present position shall be defrayed. you would of course have your ordinary residence at either Chillicothe or

Cincinnati. within a reasonable time before your departure for either of those places, no public inconvenience can arise from this appointment being made known. Accept my respectful salutations.

TH: JEFFERSON

RC (NHi: Gilder Lehrman Collection at the Gilder Lehrman Institute of American History); at foot of first page: "Mr. Mansfield." PrC (DLC). Recorded in SJL at 20 May.

Connecticut native Jared Mansfield (1759-1830) was the author of *Essays, Mathematical and Physical*, one of the first books of mathematical research written by a native American. First published in 1801, it brought Mansfield to the attention of TJ, who helped convey the work to a wider audience. In 1802, Mansfield was appointed a captain of engineers and became a mathematics instructor at West Point. Appointed surveyor general of the United States in 1803, Mansfield held the position until 1812, when he resigned and returned to West Point as a professor of natural and experimental philosophy (DAB; Vol. 37:131-2, 251).

Long among the most prominent Federalists in the Northwest Territory, Rufus PUTNAM of Marietta had been appointed surveyor general by his friend George Washington in 1796 (Andrew R. L. Cayton, *The Frontier Republic: Ideology and Politics in the Ohio Country, 1780-1825* [Kent, Ohio, 1986], 47-50).

[1] TJ first wrote "it has been" before altering the text to read as above.

[2] Word interlined.

[3] Word interlined in place of "map."

From John Mitchell

SIR

Havre 21 May 1803

I had the honor of addressing You the 9h. instant solisiting to be Confirmed in Appointment of Commercial Agent for this place.—Which I beg leave to repeat.

It affords Me great pleasure that My first official Act should be the sending on Mr. Hughes charged with despatches of such importance to My Country;—and am very happy that Under your Administration so great an Aquisition has been Made to the United States.—and a Treaty concluded that Will afford such universal satisfaction

Most sinceerly do I congratulate You and beg leave to Assure you that I am with Most perfect respect

Sir, Your very Obd Servt.

JOHN MITCHELL

RC (DNA: RG 59, LAR); at head of text: "Thomas Jefferson Esqr President of the United States of America"; endorsed by TJ as received 14 July with added notation "to be Consul at Havre" and so recorded in SJL.

DESPATCHES OF SUCH IMPORTANCE: Monroe and Livingston originally expected J. P. P. Derieux to carry the signed original of the Louisiana treaty and conventions to the United States. Learning that George A. Hughes of Baltimore could depart from Le Havre sooner than Derieux would from Bordeaux, the diplomats gave the papers to Hughes on 13 May and sent word ahead to Mitchell asking him to arrange passage for the courier. Hughes sailed on 23 May and delivered the papers in Washington on

14 July. As a precaution due to the rupture in relations between Britain and France, Livingston and Monroe also dispatched copies to London with Joseph Reed, Jr., asking him to send them on from there. Derieux took a second official set of copies via Bordeaux as first planned (Madison, *Papers*, *Sec. of State Ser.*, 4: 606, 617; 5:5, 12, 23, 28, 47, 66, 98, 238).

From H. B. Scudamore

Brockley Hall Lewisham.
21st. May 1803.

Sir,

In the Infant state of a Country like yours, it is the duty of every well disposed person to promote its welfare, and prosperity.—Impressed with every good wish for the happiness of America, I herewith transmit you a plan of my own, (among many others,) which the Government of this Country have in contemplation to adopt, and which appears to me to be of great importance to a nation like yours, possessing a vast district of territory.

Should you approve of it, and think me entitled to a handsome remuneration for the [pur]pose of residing among you, and carrying it [into] complete execution, it will give me real comfort in thus rendering my feeble but most hearty assistance. I have the honor to be most respectfully

Sir, Your most obedt. hble Servt. H B Scudamore.

RC (MoSHi: Jefferson Papers); torn; at foot of text: "To the care of Messrs Blandford and Scocet Inner Temple London"; addressed: "Thomas Jefferson Esqr. President of the United States Washington America"; postmarked 24 May; endorsed by TJ as received 15 Aug. and so recorded in SJL.

ENCLOSURE

Plan for a National Registry Office

Plan for establishing an Office in the City of Washington, for Registering Real and personal property.

To secure public and private property, it is submited warrants its adoption.

Plan.

That there be established a Register office for the Inrollment (by Memorial and Affidavit) of all Real and Personal property, the latter above a limited Sum, stating its real and annual value or not as may be thought proper, and regulating the fees of Office accordingly.

That the Real property be Alphabetically arranged in Books for each State, and the personal property according to the Names and additions of the owners, to which they, and their agents, may have free access, to read, copy, and take extracts, on payment of certain Fees to be fixed.

That in the same office, may be established a Register, for Baptisms, Marriages, and Burials.

That the Clergymen of the respective Parishes in each State, shall annually transmit accurate Copies of the Registers, mentioning the number of Men, Women, Boys, and Girls, in each Parish, and to furnish the Registers complete to the present time.

That a sufficient number of Books be opened for each State, and the Parish Registers Alphabetically, correctly, and fairly, inserted therein, and that Certificates of Baptisms, Marriages, and Burials, granted by the Office, (for which certain Fees to be fixed shall be paid,) be deemed good Evidence in Law, and Equity.

That there be a Register, Deputy Registers, and a sufficient number of Clerks, to transact the Business of the Office.

Observations.

By Registering of Property it is submited, that it will be secured in the event of Title Deeds or Securities being lost, burnt, or destroyed, fraud prevented by false Deeds, and a considerable saving of expence in transfering property.

By it, if Government should ever have occasion, a considerable source of Revenue may be secured without inconveniencing the Rich, or oppressing the poor, by Stamp duties, and by increasing the Fees of Office for Registering, Searching, Copying, and Extracting.

By the plan of consolidating the Parish Registers into one Office they will be preserved, (of which Great Britain shows a sad instance of neglect,) and the exact population of the nation annually, and accurately ascertained. To the public it must be a great accommodation, and a considerable saving of expence in making out Titles to Estates, Pedigrees, Searching Parish Registers, and obtaining Certificates, while at any time a considerable source of Revenue may be secured to Government, by Stamp Certificates, and by enlarging the Fees for Searches, Copies, and Extracts.—

MS (MoSHi: Jefferson Papers); in Scudamore's hand; undated.

To Samuel Harrison Smith

TH:J. TO MR SMITH [21 May 1803]

Can mr Smith furnish Th:J. with a copy of the laws of the last session as far as they are printed? the difficulty of collecting them from the newspapers endangers omissions & errors in their execution.

Mr. Granger informs me that the election in Connecticut in 1802. gave Trumbull 11,000 some odd votes & Kirby 4,523. and that of the present year has given Trumbull 14,300. & Kirby 7848.

then in 1802 of every 100. votes the federalists had 71. & the republicans 29.

& in 1803. of every 100. votes the federalists had 65. & the republicans 35. so that the latter have advanced from 29. to 35. and the former sunk from 71. to 65 in the hundred. would it not be worth presenting to the public in this concise view, to let them see that tho' from causes we do not understand, we have lost ground in their H. of Representatives, yet we have unquestionably gained in the mass of the people? and that Connecticut is advancing slowly to a reunion of sentiment with her sister states.

RC (DLC: J. Henley Smith Papers); undated; addressed: "Mr. Saml. H. Smith"; endorsed by Smith as a letter of 21 May "attended to May 23. 1803." Not recorded in SJL.

MR. GRANGER INFORMS ME: see Gideon Granger to TJ, 13 May. For a report on the ELECTION IN CONNECTICUT using the information provided by TJ above, see the *National Intelligencer*, 23 May.

From Lafayette

MY DEAR SIR Paris 2 prairial, May the 22d 1803

Altho' the Affair for Which I presume to Adress You Has Been Recommended and Elucidated by the Governement of this Country, and altho' My friends the Heirs Beaumarchais Are Giving an Account of the Business, Which to Mr Munroe Has Appeared Satisfactory, and Will, I think, Equally Satisfy Mr Livingston, I feel Myself, on two Accounts, Impelled to Unite My private Voice to those public Authorities—The one is that *delaRue* Whom You Have known My Aid de Camp Has Married Beaumarchais's only daughter, that paternal debts Being Compensated there Remains only for them to live Upon what they are to Get from their American transactions, and that the other person Concerned in the Affair is General *Mathieu dumas* Whose Services in the Cause of the United States, as a Staff officer in Rochambeau's Army Have Been Highly Useful and Distinguished, Whom You Have known as one of My Best Companion in the National Guards, and Who after Many Honourable Vicissitudes of a public life, Has Made the last Campaign as *Chef d'Etat Major* to Macdonald's Army, and is Now foremost Among the Counsellors of State, Having Ever Been Equally Remarkable By His talents in the Cabinet, in the field, and in public Assemblies.

An other Motive for My Intrusion in this Business, Besides the interest I shall Ever feel for those first transactions of our Glorious Revolution (and Beaumarchais's Wit and Activity was no doubt Very Useful) is to Be found in My Respectful Concern for the Memory of *franklin*. it Has Been Most Unjustly Attacked, and the More discussions and Explanations there Will Be in Beaumarchais's affair, the

More light Will Be thrown on the dark Insinuations which Have Lately Envelopped the tomb of one of the Greatest and Best of Men.

Gal. Bernadotte Has Received from this Governement a Letter Relative to the Affairs of Beaumarchais wherein the Minister of Exterior Relations makes *a positive declaration* Respecting the Million—This Instruction to Bernadotte Will no doubt Be a Matter of Communication Between Him and the Governement of the United States

Under those Circumstances it Seems to Me Very desirable that a good definitive Arrangement Be devised and settled—I Have told you the personal friendly Motives I Have to Wish it, and I therefore flatter Myself You Will find No Impropriety, in My Expressing, By a private Letter to You, My Sentiments on the Occasion—With the Highest Regard and Most Constant Affection I Have the Honour to Be

Your obliged friend LAFAYETTE

RC (DLC); endorsed by TJ, date of receipt torn; recorded in SJL as received 25 Sep. Dupl (DLC); in a clerk's hand, signed by Lafayette; at head of text: "duplicate"; endorsed by TJ as received 13 May 1805 and so recorded in SJL. Enclosed in John A. Chevallié to TJ, 16 Sep. 1803.

For the claim by the heirs of Pierre Augustin Caron de BEAUMARCHAIS for reimbursement for the assistance he had provided to the United States during the American Revolution, see Vol. 32:252. Louis André Toussaint DELARUE married Eugénie Beaumarchais in 1796. GENERAL MATHIEU DUMAS was Delarue's brother-in-law (Brian N. Morton and Donald C. Spinelli, *Beaumarchais and the American Revolution* [Lanham, Md., 2003], 303). CHEF D'ETAT MAJOR: chief of staff.

MACDONALD'S ARMY: in 1800, General Étienne Jacques Joseph Alexandre Macdonald took command of the *armée de Grisons*, formerly called the *armée de réserve*. After serving under Macdonald, Dumas was an ambassador and a councillor of state (Tulard, *Dictionnaire Napoléon*, 1106; *Dictionnaire*, 12:140).

MINISTER OF EXTERIOR RELATIONS: Talleyrand.

The primary obstacle to the payment of the Beaumarchais claim was an inability to account for a MILLION livres tournois expended in 1776; see Vol. 32:252n.

From Thomas Mann Randolph

DEAR SIR, Edgehill May 22. 1803.

I suspect I omitted to acknowledge your letter preceding that of 5th. inst. I received it on my return from Amherst and did with it, & in regard to Martha as you directed. With respect to others no occasion of any kind has occurred since, for me to do any thing; & perhaps never may, that subject having ceased I believe to afford discourse to the malignant, as well as the idle and inquisitive. Should it again arise I shall with the warmth my zeal inspires represent to those disposed to agitate it the danger they incurr of being charged with baseness or folly for reviving & propagating a story engendered itself by hatred and begeting the misery of individuals who are never heard of in good or in evil. Nothing farther.

The actual event of my contest with Colo. Cabell is, of all possible, the most disagreeable to me. If it had terminated unfavorably to me, as I expected at the commencement of it, and again as soon as I went into Amherst, I should not have felt the smallest mortification and should have escaped a heavy anxiety which the consciousness of wanting the qualities and acquirements necessary for passing through with honour, now makes me feel. I knew well when I determined on the undertaking that if I succeeded I should enlarge my circle of thought and action far beyond my power to fill, but I thought it possible by industry, in time, to travel through it without disgrace and I even hoped I might at last move in it so as to give some satisfaction.

RC (DLC); endorsed by Randolph as a letter of 2 May.

A LETTER from TJ to Randolph was recorded in SJL under the date of 13 Apr. but has not been found. It likely related to the SUBJECT of charges recently circulated that TJ had made improper advances on Elizabeth Moore Walker, wife of his former friend and classmate John Walker (see TJ to John Walker, 13 Apr.).

To William C. C. Claiborne

SIR Washington May 23. 1803.

I have duly recieved the memorial and petition of the House of Representatives of the Missisipi territory, praying that measures may be adopted for procuring to the citizens of the US. settled on the navigable rivers running into the bay of Mexico the free navigation of those rivers to & from the ocean. early in the last year, having recieved an application from the inhabitants themselves, instructions were given to our Minister in Spain to represent to it's government the importance to us of a free passage through those rivers, on principles similar to those on which a like right had been established on the Missisipi. the subject was resumed in the instructions to our joint ministers lately appointed to the same government: and the House of Representatives may rest assured that I consider an innocent and free passage along those waters as so necessary to the use of our territories on them, that nothing will be wanting on my part to their ultimate attainment. praying you to make this communication to the House of Representatives at their next meeting, I tender you assurances of my high consideration & respect. TH: JEFFERSON

RC (NNPM); at foot of text: "Governr. Claiborne." PrC (DLC). Enclosed in TJ to Claiborne, 24 May.

See 12 Mch. for the MEMORIAL AND PETITION from the Mississippi territorial legislators. On 15 Feb. 1802, the U.S. House of Representatives received a memorial from INHABITANTS of the territory's Washington County asking for the establishment of ports of entry and delivery on the Tombigbee and Alabama Rivers. Madison sent a copy of that memorial to the U.S. MINISTER IN SPAIN, Charles Pinckney, on 30 Mch. 1802. Passage along rivers that originated in U.S. territory and flowed through Spanish possessions to reach the Gulf of Mexico was not guaranteed by treaty, and Madison asked Pinckney to take the matter up with the Spanish government (Madison, *Papers*, *Sec. of State Ser.*, 3:86-7, 88n).

TO OUR JOINT MINISTERS: the United States "have a just claim to the use of the Rivers which pass from their Territories thro' the Floridas," Madison wrote in instructions to Robert R. Livingston and Monroe dated 2 Mch. 1803. "They found their claim," he stated, "on like principles with those which supported their claim to the use of the Mississipi" (same, 4: 368-9).

In an undated memorandum, Madison made notes of instances in which the question of navigation of rivers that emptied into the Gulf had come up in his correspondence with the U.S. ministers to Spain and France. As he indicated on that list, Madison on 25 Sep. 1801 "observed to Mr. Pinkney as a motive for acquiring the Floridas, that they contain the mouths of rivers of the greatest importance to the U. States"; on 28 Sep. of that year, "the same motive given to Mr. Livingston, in case the Floridas sd. belong to France." In those communications to Pinckney and Livingston, Madison mentioned the Mobile River in particular (see same, 2:131, 145). As a final entry in the list, Madison noted his letter to Pinckney of 30 Mch. 1802: "Mr. P. instructed on the subject of the Memorial from the Inhabts. of the waters rung. into the Gulph." There is no evidence that TJ saw the memorandum, which Madison may have drawn up for his own use (MS in ViW; undated and unsigned; entirely in Madison's hand).

From Henry Dearborn

SIR, War Department May 23d. 1803.

I have the honor to propose for your approbation, the following persons for promotion.

Lieut. Col. Thomas Hunt of the 1st. Regt. of Infty. to be promoted to the rank of Colonel (vice) Colonel John F. Hamtramck, deceased.

Major Jacob Kingsbury of the 2d. Regt. of Infty. to be promoted to Lieut. Col. of the 1st. Regt. of Infty. (vice) Lieut. Col. Hunt promoted.

Capt. Thomas Pasteur of the 1st. Regt. of Infty. to be promoted Major of the 2d Regt. of Infty. (vice) Major Kingsbury promoted.

1st. Lieut. John Whipple of the 1st. Regt. of Infty. to be promoted to Capt. in sd. Regt. (vice) Capt. Thomas Pasteur, promoted.

Ensign William Richardson of the 1st. Regt. of Infty. to be promoted to 2d. Lieut. in said Regt. (vice) 2d. Lieut. Alexr. McComb Jnr. transferred to the Corps of Engineers—

Accept, Sir, the assurance &c.

FC (Lb in DNA: RG 107, LSP); in a clerk's hand.

The above recommendations were all included in TJ's list of appointments and promotions sent to the Senate on 18 Nov. 1803.

To Benjamin H. Latrobe

May 23. [1803] Washington.

Th: Jefferson presents his salutations to mr Latrobe, and recommends to him, in passing through Baltimore, to examine the covering on the flat part of Genl. Smith's house. it is with sheet iron in gutturs, is the first & only example yet executed, and may furnish us, by the manner of it's execution, information both as to what succeeds, and as to what may not succeed & therefore is to be avoided, if any thing about it does not succeed. Genl. Smith will also be so good as to inform mr Latrobe how it answers. if the stage should not stop long enough in Baltimore to admit this examination, it would still be worth while that mr Latrobe should sacrifice a day to it, considering the importance of a succesful operation on the Capitol & President's house. health and good will.

PrC (DLC); partially dated; endorsed by TJ in ink on verso as a letter of "May 23. 03."

Samuel Smith designed a house for his use in Baltimore that was completed in 1796, and Montebello, an estate just northeast of the city that was completed about four years later (Lawrence Hall Fowler, "Montebello, Maryland," *Architectural Review*, 16 [1909], 145-8).

From Thomas Worthington

SIR Chilicothe May 23rd 1803

The day before yesterday I wrote you from Lancaster on the Hockhocking and informed you of the murder of a white man by the indians in the neighbourhood of this place—I gave you the report as I recd it from the post-rider—It was in part correct and part exaggerated—The circumstances so far as we can collect them are these—A Captain Herod who lived about 12 miles from me had some dispute with an indian or Indians—He was found on friday last[1] about sundown shot through the body and scalped near his house—When found he was not dead and could only state before he did die that he had recd the injury from indians—The report at first was very alarming We were informed that a large body of Indians well armed were in the neighbourhood and had killed several families This part of the report is not true It appears entirely probable that not more than one or two Indians at most have done the injury and that from personal revenge—Several parties have been out for two days past in search of the murderer—and have not yet returned—That part of the treaty with the Indians permitting them to hunt in our ground is attended with many evil consequences and will I fear ultimately produce serious effects—They encamp within the frontier settlements Obtain whisky and do many[2] injuries to our citizens by stealing their horses and other property which provokes revenge—I hope this affair will blow over without any thing more serious—I beg you will accept my thanks for the pamphlet you were so good as enclose to me—I am much pleased with it and shall have it published in the sioto gazette The organization of our state government has been so far attended with much harmony and satisfaction Our citizens generally have the most perfect confidence in the administration of the genl Government—so that our situation is a pleasing one Accept my very sincere wishes for your health and happiness and believe me with the highest respect and esteem Sir Your obt St. T. WORTHINGTON

RC (DLC); at foot of text: "The President of the U States"; endorsed by TJ as received 2 June and so recorded in SJL.

I WROTE YOU FROM LANCASTER: Worthington to TJ, 21 May 1803, is recorded in SJL as received from Lancaster on 31 May, but has not been found.

MURDER OF A WHITE MAN: news regarding the murder of militia captain Thomas Herrod (Herod) appeared in newspapers across the county and largely coincided with the details provided by Worthington. Initial reports from Chillicothe of a large party of Shawnees in the vicinity were later retracted, however, after militia parties found the Indians in the vicinity knew nothing of the murder and denounced its perpetrators. A few days later, however, a party of white men shot and killed a lone Indian, an elderly Shawnee named Wawilaway, whom they deemed suspicious after questioning him about Herrod's death. A council of Wyandot and Mingo Indians, held at the head of Mad River on 23 and 28 May, denounced the murders and declared their willingness to help find and deliver up the guilty parties. Governor Edward Tiffin lauded the council's actions and hoped their example would serve to "deter the inconsiderate both of your people and ours, from committing acts of hostility which may endanger the peace and happiness of both sides." Subsequent newspaper accounts suggested that Herrod's killer was most likely a white man, "with whom he had been at variance for some time." The actual murderer, however, was never positively identified (*Terr. Papers*, 3:520, 532; *Poulson's American Daily Advertiser*, 8, 11 June 1803; *Bartgis's Republican Gazette*, 17 June 1803; Fredericktown, Md., *Hornet*, 21 June 1803; New York *Daily Advertiser*, 23 June 1803; Lyle S. Evans, *A Standard History of Ross County, Ohio*, 2 vols. [Chicago, 1917], 1:390-1; W. P. Strickland, ed., *Autobiography of Rev. James B. Finley; Or, Pioneer Life in the West* [Cincinnati, 1853], 135-42).

TREATY WITH THE INDIANS: that is, the 1795 treaty of Greenville, article seven of which permitted the Indians to hunt on ceded lands, "so long as they demean themselves peaceably, and offer no injury to the people of the United States" (Parry, *Consolidated Treaty Series*, 52:442).

PAMPHLET: *A Vindication of the Measures of the Present Administration* (see John Langdon to TJ, 8 May). It was reprinted in the 28 May, 4 June, and 18 June editions of the *Scioto Gazette*.

[1] Word interlined.
[2] MS: "may."

From Daniel Carroll, Daniel Brent, and Charles Minifie

SIR, Washington, May 24th. 1803

The Eastern Branch Bridge Company, incorporated by law, is now engaged in the erection of a Bridge from the intersection of Pennsylvania and Kentucky Avenues at the Branch, to the Land of Mathew Wigfield on the opposite Shore, with the best prospect of a completion of the work by the last of the Summer. Under these circumstances, we trust, Sir, you will concur with us in opinion that the improvement of Pennsylvania Avenue to this point, will contribute greatly to the convenience and accommodation of the City, from the facility that it will give to travelling & to the transportation of articles coming and going across the Bridge—and that under this view of the subject, you will not be averse to the application of any public Monies that may be under your controul, which can with propriety be so used, to this object. We take the liberty, therefore, respectfully to ask the favor of you to take this subject into consideration, and to give such Directions in the case as you shall think proper.

We are, with Sentiments of very high respect, Sir, Yr. Mo: Obt Servants.

DANL. CARROLL of Dudn
DANL BRENT.
CHA MINIFIE
} Directors the Eastern Branch Bridge Co.

RC (DLC); in an unidentified hand, signed by all; torn; at foot of text: "The President of the United States"; endorsed by TJ as received "May [...]." Recorded in SJL as received on 25 May.

The EASTERN BRANCH BRIDGE COMPANY was chartered by the Maryland legislature in 1795 with a capital of $45,000. Subscriptions were not completed until 1801 and the company did not commence collecting tolls until January 1804. The bridge was destroyed by American forces in August 1814 (Baltimore *Federal Gazette*, 9 Jan. 1796, 9 June 1801; *National Intelligencer*, 4 May 1801, 2 May 1803, 9 Jan. 1804; JS, 5:529; U.S. Statutes at Large, 6:152).

To William C. C. Claiborne

Dear Sir Washington May 24. 1803

The within being for communication to your H. of Representatives when it meets, I inclose it in this which is of a private character. the former I think had better be kept up until the meeting of the Representatives, lest it should have any effect on the present critical state of things beyond the Atlantic, altho' I have indeavored to make it as inoffensive there as was compatible with the giving an answer to the Representatives. pending a negociation, and with a jealous power, small matters may excite alarm, & repugnance to what we are claiming. I consider war between France & England as unavoidable. the former is much averse to it: but the latter sees her own existence to depend on a remodification of the face of Europe, over which France has extended it's sway much farther since, then before the treaty of Amiens. that instrument is therefore considered as insufficient for the general security, in fact as virtually subverted by the subsequent usurpations of Buonaparte on the powers of Europe. a remodification is therefore required by England, & evidently cannot be agreed to by Buonaparte, whose power resting on the transcendent opinion entertained of him, would sink with that on any retrograde movement. in this conflict our neutrality will be cheaply purchased by a cession of the island of N. Orleans & the Floridas, because, taking part in the war, we could so certainly sieze & securely hold them and more.[1] and although it would be unwise in us to let such an opportunity pass by of obtaining this necessary accession to our territory, even[2] by force, if not obtaineable otherwise, yet it is infinitely more desireable to obtain it with the blessing of neutrality rather than the curse of war. as a means of increasing the security, & providing a protection for our lower possessions on the Missisipi, I think it also all important to press on the Indians, as steadily and strenuously as they can bear, the extension of our purchases on the Missisipi from the Yazoo upwards: and to encourage a settlement along the whole length of that river, that it may possess on it's own banks the means of defending itself, & present as strong a frontier on our Western, as we have on our Eastern border. we have therefore recommended to Genl. Wilkinson, taking on the Tombigbee only as much as will cover our actual settlements, to transfer the purchase from the Choctaws to their lands Westward of the Big black, rather than the fork of Tombickbee and Alabama, which has been offered by them in order to pay their debt to Panton & Leslie. I have confident expectations of purchasing this summer a good breadth on the Missisipi from the mouth of the Illinois down to the mouth of Ohio, which would settle immediately & thickly; & we should then have between that settlement and the lower one, only the uninhabited lands of the Chickasaws on the Missipi., on which we could be working at both ends.—you will be sensible that the preceding views, as well those which respect the European powers as the Indians, are such as should not be formally declared, but be held as a rule of action to govern the conduct of those within whose agency they lie; and it is for this reason that instead of having it said to you in an official letter, committed to records which are open to many, I have thought it better that you should learn my views from a private & confidential letter, and be enabled to act upon them yourself and guide others into them.—the elections which have taken place this spring, prove that the spirit of republicanism has repossessed the whole mass of our country from Connecticut Southwardly & Westwardly. the three New England states of N.H. Mass. and Connecticut alone hold out. in these tho' we have not gained the last year as much as we expected, yet we are gaining steadily & sensibly. in Massachusets we have gained 3. Senators more than we had the last year, & it is believed our gain in the lower house will be in proportion.[3] in Connecticut we have rather lost in their legislature, but in the mass of the people where we had, on the election of Governor the last year[4] but 29. republican out of every 100. votes, we this year have 35. of every 100. with the phalanx of priests & lawyers against us, republicanism works up slowly in that quarter.[5] but in a year or two more we shall have a majority even in Massachusets. in the next H. of R. there will be about [150?] federal and [100?] republican members.[6] be assured that, excepting in this North Eastern & your South Western corner of the Union, Monarchism, which has been so falsely miscalled federalism, is dead & buried, and no day of resurrection will ever dawn upon that: that it[7] has retired to the two extreme & opposite angles of our land, from whence it will have ultimately & shortly to take it's final flight.—while speaking of the Indians I omitted to mention that I think it would be good policy in us to take by the hand those of them[8] who have emigrated from ours to the other side of the Missisipi, to furnish them generously with arms, ammunition, & other essentials, with a view to render a situation there desireable to those they have left behind, to [toll] them in this way across the Missisipi, and thus prepare in time[9] an eligible retreat for the whole. we have not as yet however begun to act on this. I believe a considerable number from all the four Southern tribes, have settled between the St Francis & Akanza, but mostly from the Cherokees. I presume that with a view to this object we ought to establish a factory on the Eastern bank of the Missisipi, where it would be most convenient for them to come and trade. we have an idea of running a path in a direct line from Knoxville to Natchez, believing it would save 200. miles in the carriage of our mail. the consent of the Indians will be necessary, and it will be very important to get individuals among them to take each a white man into partnership and to establish at every 15. miles a house of entertainment & a farm for it's support. the profits of this would soon reconcile the Indians to the practice & extend it, and render the public use of the road as much an object of desire as it is now of fear; & such a horsepath would soon, with their consent, become a waggon road. I have appointed Isaac Briggs of Maryland surveyor of the lands South of Tennissee. he is a quaker, a sound republican, & of a pure & unspotted character. in point of science in astronomy, geometry & mathematics he stands in a line with mr Ellicot, & second to no man in the US. he set out yesterday for his destination, and I recommend him to your particular patronage. the candour[10] modesty and simplicity of his manners cannot fail to gain your esteem. for the offices of surveyor, men of the first order of science in astronomy & mathematics are essentially necessary. I am about appointing a similar character for the Northwestern department, & charging him with determining by celestial observations the longitude & latitude of several interesting points of lakes Michigan and Superior, and an accurate survey of the Missisipi from St. Anthony's falls to the mouth of Ohio, correcting his admeasurements by observations of longitude & latitude. from your quarter mr Briggs will be expected to take accurate observations of such interesting points as mr Ellicot has omitted: so that it will not be long before we shall possess an accurate map of the outlines of the US.—Your country is so abundant in every thing which is good, that one does not know what there is here, of that description, which you have not, and which could be offered in exchange for a barrel of fresh paccans every autumn. yet I will venture to propose such an exchange, taking information of the article most acceptable from hence, either from yourself or such others as can inform me. I pray you to accept my friendly salutations & assurances of great esteem & respect.

Th: Jefferson

PrC (DLC); blurred; at foot of first page: "Govr. Claiborne." Enclosure: TJ to Claiborne, 23 May 1803.

For the proposed road FROM KNOXVILLE TO NATCHEZ, see TJ to Dearborn, 13 May.

SIMILAR CHARACTER FOR THE NORTH-WESTERN DEPARTMENT: Jared Mansfield (see TJ to Mansfield, 21 May).

[1] Preceding two words interlined.
[2] Word interlined.

[3] Preceding two words interlined in place of "as great."

[4] Preceding three words interlined.

[5] Preceding three words interlined.

[6] Preceding sentence interlined.

[7] TJ here canceled "has been [. . .]d to the."

[8] Preceding two words interlined in place of "Indians."

[9] Preceding two words interlined.

[10] Word interlined.

From Chauncy Hall

SIR May 24th AD1803

it is betwen hope and Despare that I take my Pen to Present the following plan and reasons for a Perpetual motion I almost give up all hopes of Seing it accompished when I Consider how many men of Great Education and fortunes Sufficient to try all the experiments that they thought reasonable and have not brought it to perfection

and further when I think of my own Situation being brought up in the Country and by a Parent that was a farmer and not willing to give me any more than a Small Education and not haveing had but a little assistance and am not able to go through the Expence of the following Experriment without the Assistance of Some friend and not knowing any that Could do the work I have been reddy to through of all further thoughts about it

but when I Consider the works of Nature and find how reasonable all the opperations move and in what Equal preportions and how many great inventions have been found by Simple Experriments

I am encouraged to give the following reasons whitch I do believe will make a Perpetual Motion on whitch the Calculation of Longitude may be made as Simple and easy as the Calculation of Lattitude for whitch I give you the following reasons

I think that all Motions are made by Attraction and opposition and that these two Powers are Equal and in impregnateing the power of Magnet into Steel they are both given and being Equal I believe that the following Plan will bring them both to force round a Circle in one Direction for the North end will oppose the North end and the South end will oppose the South end

but the North end will Attract the South and the South will Draw the North

therefore I have Set forty Eight Magnetts as they incline to Each other with the North end as in the plan believeing that the power Lyes acrost them when So connected more than Lengthways

and thirteen Nedles with the North end out

the two Circles on whitch the Magnetts are Set are to be of a bigness and put into a frame the one part a perpendicular over the other and the Nedles to be put into a Wheel and Set between them then I find that there will be one that will be one nedle[1] held at both ends as the first by the full Strength of the Magnetts that are above and below it but the Second and third and forth and so round[2] are attracted and Drawing against it and on the other hand they are all opposed and forced the same way and if there Can be Power enough to take off the first I Cannot find why it will not move

I do believe that this Number would be Sufficient

but the Numbers may be in increased according to the proportion of the Circle and that this Number of Magnetts must not Cover more than one thirteenth part of the Circle or there will be more than one Nedle held at a time

and there Must not be any iron or Steel in the machine[3] for it will Counteract the Attraction but it will pass through all Materials that will take heat although I have not been able to try the experriment Yet I do believe that Live quick Silver will Set bounds to the Attraction without hurting it

then if the Magnetts and Nedles ware inclosed on both Side it would prevent all Counter attractions

it would be a great Satisfaction to me for to Se this Experriment tryed but I have Spent a Considerable part of the time that I had for myself in trying Experriments on this and other Inventions and find that I Cannot procede any further at the present although I have other great Inventions in view

therefore I humbly Submit this to You hopeing that my Sincerity may be an excuse though it Should not answer the Expectation and Should take it as a great favor if You would write to me the opinion that You or any other jentleman that You please to Lay this before may form Concerning it

therefore I Subscribe myself Your humble Servant

Chauncy Hall

of Merriden in Wallingford State of Connecticut

RC (MHi); at head of text: "Mr Jefferson"; endorsed by TJ as received 30 May and so recorded in SJL.

Chauncy Hall (ca. 1780-1863) was a prolific, if largely unsuccessful, inventor from Meriden, Connecticut. He secured three patents for his work, including a "diving dress," a straw cutting machine, and wire fencing, and petitioned Congress for several more in the ensuing decades. Hall wrote TJ three more times regarding his ideas on perpetual motion, but never received a reply (Madison, *Papers, Pres. Ser.*, 3:439; *List of Patents*, 88, 298; JS, 15:72, 19:159, 28:474, 29:68, 30:93, 197; JHR, 44:529; New Haven *Columbian Register*, 31 Oct. 1863; Hall to TJ, 4 Oct. 1804, 20 Dec. 1805, 23 May 1806).

[1] Preceding two words interlined.
[2] Preceding three words interlined.
[3] Preceding three words interlined.

From Gideon Granger

DR. SIR Suffield May 25. 1803.

I take the liberty to inclose a petition addressed to my care and also a Letter I have recd. from Saml Ward Esq. I have no acquaint[ance] with mr. Ward and therefore can say nothing on that Subject. The Petition is Subscribed by some very respectable People. This day the Legislature of Massachusetts assemble from what I have heard. I believe When the House is formed The Tories will have but little to boast Of.

Your Affectionate [friend] GIDN. GRANGER

RC (DLC); torn; endorsed by TJ as received 30 May and so recorded in SJL. Enclosure: Samuel Ward to Granger, Salem, 16 May 1803, renewing his application for office since his letters from an earlier solicitation apparently miscarried, including one to Granger of 11 Nov. 1802, of which he encloses a copy; observing that Joseph Story has declined to serve as naval officer at Salem, he now applies for that position; he has already requested that James Sullivan use his influence with the president, but he has heard nothing; he is anxious "having a large & promising Family and but small means for their support, nor any thing to hope for from the unrelenting Federalists"; he assures Granger that his appointment will be agreeable to "all the Republicans of the Town," including William R. Lee, collector at the port, whom he has known for 40 years (RC in DNA: RG 59, LAR; endorsed by TJ: "Ward Saml. to mr Granger to be naval officer of Salem").

TJ viewed another application by Samuel WARD, who had written James Sullivan on 7 Apr., requesting that he use his influence with the president "regarding the appointment." Ward annexed a petition signed by Joseph Sprague and 13 other inhabitants of Salem. On 11 Apr., Sullivan enclosed the letter to Madison with his own recommendation. He had served with Ward in the Massachusetts legislature for several years during the "late revolutionary war." He continued: "I have known him as a magistrate and military officer when much depended on his exertions, and when many who would now gladly take offices were skulking from public danger." Sullivan requested that Madison communicate the contents to the president and do whatever he could to serve Ward's interest. He also noted that those who signed Ward's letter were "respectable and friendly to the present administration" (RCs in DNA: RG 59, LAR; endorsed by TJ: "Ward Saml. to be Naval officer of Salem vice Story"). For an earlier petition for office, see Ward to TJ, 10 Nov. 1802.

ENCLOSURE

Petition of Samuel Huntington and Others

[before 25 Apr. 1803]

The undersignd. Inhabitants of The State of Ohio beg leave to Represent that at the Mouth of Cuyahoga River (the Boundary line between the Settlements in the County of Trumbull and the lands where the Indian Title is yet Unextinguished) there are Annually large Assemblages of Indians Cheifly Ottowas Wyandotts Shawanoes Chipawas & Senecas Amounting from three hundred to five hundred. that it is the practice of those Indians to meet in the fall of the Year at Cleaveland a Town Situated within the County of Trumbull where Sd. River Emptyes into Lake Erie from whence they Proceed to their winters Hunt up Said river & the Other Adjacent Streams and Return again in the Spring with their Skins Sugar and Oil which they barter for goods with The Merchants of that place and Factors sent there from Detroit & Other places that their Trade has become of Considerable Consequence & would prove Highly usefull To both parties were it not for the Disputes and disorders that necessarily result from the want of an efficient force or of Some person Authorised to Interfere upon Certain Occasions. Constant Complaints are made by the Indians of The Incroachments of Our people in getting Grindstones from Quarries on their Side the Line this They apprehend justifies them in Stealing Our horses Cattle & Corn The unauthorised retakeing of These by Individual force on theire own ground furnishes a theme of reiterated Complaint. & the well known Customs of the Indians to make reprisals from any of The supposd. agressors often Exposes the Innocent to Suffer for the misdemeanors of the Guilty—When Complaints have been made by the Indians they have been Referd to the Superintendant of Indian affairs. the Distance of his residence has been so great that they have always Considered Even a Successfull application to him as amounting to the Same thing as a Denial of redress—and our own people for the Same reason have Chosen to pursue the Indians to their Own Towns and Take at any risque from their very Cabins their Stolen property by force. many disorders and Even Murder is Sometimes Committed under Our Doors at their meeting in the Spring & the Civil Authority has felt itself two weak to interpose for the Establishment of Tranquility or the Execution of Justice. their Numbers at such Times gives them Confidence and the Dispersed situation of our Frontier Settlements render it Impossible to Calculate on Our Safety in case of a Sudden or unexpected Contest with them—Most or all of these difficulties it is believed woud. be Removed by the appointment of a Superintendant of Indian affairs or Indian agent to Reside at Cleaveland—a Discription of Officers known to the Indians to whom they would look up with a Certainty of haveing their Greivances redressd. & to whoom our Own people might apply without the danger or Trouble of Carving out the measure of Justice they think due to themselves—The undersignd. further beg leave to suggest that in their Opinion there is no place within the United States that has not an Indian agent, where their is so much Necessity for one being the Dividing line between a rapidly populateing Country and Indian lands Inhabited by numerous Tribes long accustomed to hunt in the Neighbourhood of the Cuyahoga & to Dispose of their goods to the Traders at its mouth and they apprehend that the

Appointment of Such Officer woud Tend to promote peace & good understanding between the people of this part of The State & their Indian Neighbours by Distroying in their Infancy all Causes of dissension and in this way prove Highly benificial to the United States as well as to those parts more Immediately Connected with Our Vicinity the undersignors from the Above mentioned Circumstances are Induced to request the President to appoint Such Superintendant or agent of Indian Affairs & with Such powers & Authority as he Shall Deem proper and Competant to effect the Object of his Appointment and They beg leave to Recomend for the Office Majr. Amos Spafford a Citizen of Said Cleaveland a man whose Constant Residence there & whose Acquaintance with the Indians & their Affairs & whose talents & Experience they believe will Qualify him to discharge it with fidelity & To universal acceptation

SAML HUNTINGTON
AMOS LUSK
JOSEPH BADGER
DAVID HUDSON
HEMAN OVIATT
GEORGE KILBORN
LEWIS DAY
REUBEN HAMMON
ELIJAH WADSWORTH
ABIJAH PECK
MATTHEW STEELE

MS (PHi); undated, but see below; in an unidentified hand, signed by all; at head of text: "To the President of the United States"; endorsed by TJ as received 30 May and "Amos Spafford to be Indn agent" and so recorded in SJL; also endorsed by TJ: "refd to Secy. at war."

Samuel Huntington (1765-1817) descended from a prominent Connecticut family, which included his uncle and mentor, Samuel Huntington, a signer of the Declaration of Independence and former governor of the state. As a young attorney, he immigrated to the Northwest Territory in 1801 and quickly rose to political prominence, serving in the Ohio constitutional convention and first state legislature before receiving an appointment to the Ohio supreme court in 1803. TJ nominated him for a Michigan Territorial judgeship in 1805, but he declined the office. Although a professed Republican, Huntington's political views were flexible and somewhat ambiguous. He was elected governor of Ohio in 1808, defeating Thomas Worthington with the support of conservative Republicans and Federalists. Losing a close election to Worthington for the U.S. Senate in 1810, Huntington won another term in the state legislature in 1811 before retiring from politics (DAB; Jeffrey P. Brown, "Samuel Huntington: A Connecticut Aristocrat on the Ohio Frontier," *Ohio History*, 89 [1980], 420-38).

On 25 Apr., Huntington wrote Granger and enclosed the petition, above, which had been circulating for some time. On 23 Mch., Huntington wrote Elijah Wadsworth, the postmaster at Canfield, Ohio, noting that he was "sorry to find no more encouragement" given to the "petition for Indian Agent—an establishment which would be very useful to our County besides bringing in considerable money." On 25 May, Granger informed Huntington that he had transmitted the document to the president and would himself "pay evry proper attention to it" when he returned to Washington ("Letters from the Samuel Huntington Correspondence, 1800-1812," in Western Reserve Historical Society, *Annual Report for 1914-1915* [Cleveland, 1915], 84-5).

As a surveyor for the Connecticut Land Company in 1796, AMOS SPAFFORD produced one of the first maps of the town of

Cleveland, Ohio. He later became a prominent early resident of northern Ohio and was appointed collector of the Miami district by James Madison in 1809 (William Ganson Rose, *Cleveland: The Making of a City* [Cleveland, 1950], 24, 28, 40, 43, 44, 48-50, 56, 60; JEP, 2:134-5).

From William Lee

American Agency Bordeaux
May 25th 1803—

I have the honour to enclose for the perusal of the President of the United States an interesting paper just published in this City—

William Lee

RC (DLC); endorsed by TJ as received 1 Aug. and so recorded in SJL. Enclosure not found, but see below.

The PAPER has not been identified, but may have related to recruitment of sailors to serve on privateers. Lee was soon faced with that problem as numbers of American seamen began to desert their ships in Bordeaux to join privateers. Other news from the port that Lee might have passed along included a halting of the payment of bills of credit that had been issued to pay for Victoire Emmanuel Leclerc's preparations for his Saint-Domingue expedition; a rise in the prices of some commodities; and a battle fought a few miles from the city between young men and military impressment squads (Madison, *Papers, Sec. of State Ser.*, 5:89, 126-7; Norwich *Connecticut Centinel*, 26 July; New York *Evening Post*, 28 July; New York *Daily Advertiser*, 29 July; New Bedford *Columbian Courier*, 5 Aug.).

To Joseph Sansom

Sir — Washington May 25. 1803.

Your favor of the 16th. was duly recieved and I thank you for the attention of the offer you are pleased to make in it. there has been a time of life when it would have been very tempting, but I have too little of it left now to merit gratifications expensive and short lived. objects of the kind too which you mention are a century ahead of the taste of our fellow citizens who, very happily in my opinion, have not yet extended their views of luxury beyond the directly useful. a society has been formed in New York for establishing a museum of the fine arts, & they have lately imported some casts, & have sent a first rate painter to Europe to procure other objects for it. those you mention are exactly within their plan & would very probably be taken by them. I do not know who is at the head of the institution: but mr E. Livingston is concerned in it. perhaps too, were you to drop me a line of the prices, I might in the intercourse of society find some one who would be glad of them, things of this sort being often the subject of conversation in society. I shall with pleasure be[1] the channel of accomodating two persons, the one wishing[2] to part with & the other to acquire such objects. Accept my best wishes & respects.

TH: JEFFERSON

PrC (DLC); at foot of text: "Mr. Joseph Sansom"; endorsed by TJ in ink on verso.

Aaron Burr recommended his beneficiary and PAINTER, John Vanderlyn, to evaluate and purchase statues and replicas of the Old Masters for the Society of Fine Arts. Vanderlyn, who studied under Gilbert Stuart and had refined his artistic talents abroad, became its purchasing agent in Italy and France (ANB).

Edward LIVINGSTON was the recently elected president of the New-York Academy of the Fine Arts; see Livingston to TJ, 19 Jan.

[1]TJ here canceled "instrumental in being."

[2]TJ first wrote "one who wishes" before altering the text to read as above.

From Robert R. Livingston

DEAR SIR Paris 26 May 1803

You will receive by this conveyance the ratification of our treaties. I shall feel some anxiety considering how much we have taken upon ourselves beyond our powers to learn that this transaction meets your approbation. Here every body is loud in its commendation & we are supposed to have made a more important acquisition for our country than the purchase of Germany would be for france. Since the ratification I have openly declared to the ministers that we include west florida & I trust that you will take possession to Mobile. As to east florida it is at least doubtful with me how far it would be wise to acquire it as yet if (as I believe) Spain should be disposed to part with it. It is an extensive & desolate waste with so many harbours & inlets that I fear it would cost us some trouble to prevent its being the abode of adventurers & freebooters. It may also be important to us to have some spanish ports in the gulph to keep up the communication between us & the Spanish Colonies & if, which we may easily do, we obtain the navigation of the river Apalachecoles perhaps it would be best to leave to Spain the expence of guarding it and paying the Indians. War as you have learned has broken out here with extream animosity on both sides. France has been very anxious to avoid it, but England was so determined on it that she has seized the weakest pretences for violating the treaty of Amiens. The general sentiment of the corps diplomatique is against her—Nothing having happened since the signature of the treaty which was not well known at the time & the offer of Russia not only to guarantee but to garrison Malta which the british ministry have concealed in their communications to parliment has put them very much in the wrong. I send you a copy of the french manifesto this with the papers sent the secretary of State you will find very interesting. The moderation of the first consul has united this nation, & I have no doubt that some desperate measure will be attempted against England. The granting letters of Marque & the seizure of french & batavian vessels in British ports prior to a declaration of war or even to a discussion on its subject has excited here the highest degree of resentment all the British in France are put in arrest to the number of many hundreds & are sent on their parols as prisoners of war to fontainbleu they are to be retained till they are exchanged against persons taken in Britain contrary to the law of nations among this number is Mr. Talbot Lord Witworths secretary who was left here after his departure & went yesterday only from Paris but was arrested on his way. You may judge by this that no measures will be kept in future by either of these incensed rivals. The merchants both of france & Batavia will be ruined but it is impossible to say that the blow may not be returned & carried to the vitals of Britain. The paper credit has for some time past been shaken an invasion would at least tear up this by the roots. I mentioned to you in my letter of march last a wish to leave this in the autumn but I find such an aversion among the American creditors here to part with me till their affairs are finally arranged, & indeed the treaty & the present state of Europe calls for so much attention & so many matters may arise that can not be so well executed by any person who has not been here long enough to make himself acquainted with both persons & things, that if you have not made any other arrangment I will continue my residence to the next spring by which time I presume that all great points will be settled. If you should have any temporary call to England that would afford me an opportunity or a pretence to vissit it for a few days I would execute it with pleasure. Tho I think yr affairs there will require that Mr. Kings place be immediately filled by a resident minister. Mr. Munroe talks of going directly to Spain, but I presume when he finally determines he will inform you of his intention. This is a favourable moment to press Batavia on the subject of the West india duty she exacts from us & it is very important that it be immediately settled. If you will send me full powers I think I can arrange it with the batavian Ambassadour to have full powers sent to him so that the bussiness may be finished here. Genl Bernadotte is still at Rockfort where he has been near two months the frigate designed for him having been sent to the west indies & no other yet prepared. I have not been able to get Pougens to fulfill your commission tho I have arranged the prices with him, nothing is more difficult than to do any sort of bussiness with merchants or tradesmen here, I shall again send to him to know when he means to execute your orders. I have a set of the proceedings of the national institute for you which I shall send by the first safe opportunity to Norfolk.

I pray you to believe that I am dear Sir with the most respectful attatchment Your Most Obt hum: Servt

ROBT R LIVINGSTON

Mr Talbot is released—inclosed is a letter written at Mr Munroes request containing a sketch of my reasons for supposing Mobile included in our purchase.

RC (DLC); at foot of text: "Thomas Jefferson Esqr president of the U.S:"; endorsed by TJ as received 24 Aug. and so recorded in SJL, as a letter of 24 May. Enclosure: Livingston to Monroe, 23 May, concerning "the extent of the Louisiana cession to the East"; "I trust I Shall leave no doubt upon your mind," he writes, "that it extends to the River Perdigo & of course includes the whole of west Florida"; the first French settlements at Mobile and Biloxi were included within what was then termed Louisiana; only after the left bank of the Mississippi was ceded to Great Britain in 1763 did the name West Florida come into use for that area to distinguish it from the Spanish settlements to the east; maps showed either the Perdido River or Mobile to be the boundary between Louisiana and West Florida; Spain has ceded Louisana to France with the same bounds that the province had while previously under French control, as confirmed by letters from the Spanish government to Charles Pinckney, and during the negotiations with Livingston and Monroe, Barbé de Marbois and Talleyrand did not contradict Livingston's assertions that Louisiana includes Mobile; José Nicolás de Azara has agreed with that interpretation also; Livingston could perhaps strengthen the argument by consulting more documents and maps, "but I do not believe the question will be contested, & the only object of this is to induce you to agree with me that it will be proper for our Government to demand, & if disputed to take the possession at least as far as Mobile"; they need not "probe this business to the bottom unless any future circumstance Should render it proper" (Tr in same; in a clerk's hand with an insertion by Livingston).

The French RATIFICATION of the Louisiana treaty and conventions was dated 22 May and signed by Bonaparte, Talleyrand, Barbé de Marbois, and Hugues Bernard Maret, who, as the secretary of state, promulgated laws and decrees (Michaël Garnier, *Bonaparte et la Louisiane* [Paris, 1992], 144; Tulard, *Dictionnaire Napoléon*, 1138; Vol. 36:188).

INCLUDE WEST FLORIDA: before he received Livingston's letter of the 23d, Monroe began his own examination of the limits of Louisiana on the east side of the Mississippi River. Disagreeing with Livingston's view that it was not necessary "to probe this business to the bottom," Monroe considered it his "first duty" to establish the bounds of Louisiana "by reference to all the authentic documents to wh. access could be had" and to be sure of any information or opinions he and Livingston transmitted to the U.S. government about West Florida (Monroe to Livingston, undated, in DLC: Monroe Papers; endorsed by Monroe "not sent"). Monroe prepared an undated memorandum on the subject, which he sent to Madison on 7 June, and TJ received a copy through the State Department. Monroe examined the language of the treaty of San Ildefonso between Spain and France in October 1800 and the recent cession of the province from France to the United States. He then cited international agreements that pertained to West Florida and Louisiana: a secret convention between

France and Spain of 3 Nov. 1762; the treaty of 10 Feb. 1763 signed by France, Britain, Spain, and Portugal, along with preliminary articles dated 3 Nov. 1762; a 3 Sep. 1783 treaty between Spain and Great Britain; and the 1795 treaty between the United States and Spain. He found that Louisiana and West Florida had been administered as a single entity by Spain and France. He paid particular attention to the agreements of 1762 and 1763 to satisfy himself that West Florida had not been separated from Louisiana while in the possession of France. "Indeed I think that the doctrine is too clear to admit of any doubt," he informed Madison (MS in DLC: TJ Papers, 132:22814-19, in a clerk's hand, endorsed by TJ: "on the cession of W. Florida," endorsed by Jacob Wagner: "enclosed in Mr Monroe's letter of June 7th 1803"; printed, from a copy in DNA: RG 59, DD, in Madison, *Papers*, *Sec. of State Ser.*, 5:72-7; FC in DLC: Monroe Papers).

Bonaparte had attempted to involve RUSSIA in the issue of the continuing British occupation of MALTA. The British government, however, had been working to improve relations with the Russians, and Emperor Alexander did not immediately agree to mediate the Malta disagreement. He finally did so in April, but news of that decision did not reach London until mid-May, too late to avert the breach between Britain and France (Grainger, *Amiens Truce*, 189, 193, 204, 205).

FRENCH MANIFESTO: Livingston probably sent a copy of Bonaparte's 20 May message announcing the probable onset of war. The message blamed the breach on the British government and said little about the points of contention. The first consul also released papers from the recent negotiations between the two countries, including the final statement of terms from the French, which Talleyrand completed just after Charles Whitworth had left Paris and was en route back to England. That document, although it was more detailed than Bonaparte's message, said nothing about most of the issues that were of concern to the British. American newspapers used the term "manifesto" for both Talleyrand's statement of terms and the first consul's war message (same, 190-1, 194; New York *Morning Chronicle*, 13 July; Georgetown *Washington Federalist*, 15 July; Baltimore *Republican*, 18 July; Amherst, N.H., *Farmer's Cabinet*, 4 Aug.).

Orders by the British Admiralty and Privy Council on 15 and 16 May called for the detention of merchant vessels and warships of France and the Batavian Republic, at sea or in port, and authorized LETTERS OF MARQUE (Grainger, *Amiens Truce*, 192; William Laird Clowes, *The Royal Navy: A History from the Earliest Times to the Present*, 7 vols. [London, 1897–1903; repr. 1996–97], 5:47).

A few days before Livingston wrote the letter printed above, Bonaparte issued an order for the ARREST as prisoners of war of all British naval and army officers in France, and all men enrolled in Britain's militia. Officials took into custody not just male Britons of military age, but also women and children, and briefly detained James TALBOT, the first secretary of the British legation, at Calais (Grainger, *Amiens Truce*, 152, 200-1).

LETTER OF MARCH LAST: Livingston to TJ, 12 Mch.

For the Dutch WEST INDIA Company duties charged on American goods shipped to the Batavian Republic, see Vol. 38:586, 589n.

Memorandum from John Barnes

Memdm Geo Town 27th May 1803

In J Barnes's estimates on his Monthly Balances, in Order to Ascertain a reasonable Compensation of 6 ℔ Cent. in Conformity, to the Presidents request, JB have endeavoured, nearly as the several Accts. & Statemts. here Annexed will admit—(allowing for some few, irregularities—making—as well for—as against, the Actual—or exact, debits & Credits.)—that, comparing the total Amt charged say $311 50 on the several Monthly Balances—with the Average—in the gross Amt. of Balances—say, $308.10. So nearly corrisponding, that JB. flatters himself—will be found pretty Correct, up to the 8 May and ending 8th June. differing only $340 in favor of the Average estimate.—

Summary Estimate, On the Presidents Monthly Balances Compared with the Average on their gross Amt.

Mar. 31. 1801	to 30t Jany 1802.	for 10 Mos. on	$16,260.95.	℔ a/c	$89. "
Jany. 30 1802.	to 10t Jany. 1803	for 12 Mos. on	32,326.66.	do	158.50
" 10. 1803	to 8 May	for 4 Mos. on	13 031. "	do	64. "
		for 26 Mos.	61,618.61		311.50

NB the Average on $61,618. for 26 Mos. say $2370 a 11.85 ℔ Mo. is 308.10
differs only. 3.40.

Errors Excepted. J Barnes.

RC (ViU); endorsed by Barnes: "Estimate of the Presidents Monthly Statements and Balances—from 31 March 1801. to—8 May, and Ending 8 June—1803 with 6 ℔ Ct Int thereon Amotg to $311 50."

ENCLOSURES

I

Statement of Interest Account with John Barnes, 31 March 1801-30 January 1802

Sketch of the Apparent Monthly Balances, on the Presidents a/c with J Barnes, will Appear from the Annexed Statemts. Commencing, viz.

1801				1801	Monthly	Int. a 6 ℔ Ct.
Mar 31.	To Amt. of a/ rendered page	7"	1450.17.	Mar 31.	1450.17.	7"
Apr 25	do do	59"	826.51½	Apr 25.	826.51½	4"
May 26	do do	"	2180.28.			
			4456.96½			
May 7	By Warrt. deducted	59	4000 "			
			456.96½			
June 4	To Amot. of a/c rendd		737.93½			
" 30	To do do		2062.10.			
			3257. "			
June 8	By Warrt. deducted		2000 "	June 30th	1257.	6—"
			1257 "			

July 25	To Amt. of a/c rendered		2298.38			
" 6	To Colo. Cary		1500.			
			5055.38			
" 6	By 2 Warrts for	2000.				
" 16	By $1000 distd [a 5 pr]	989.50	2989.50	July 25.	2065.88	
			2065.88	say for [3] Mos.		20—"
to July 28th. 29 & 30 Augst [&] to Sepr. 30	To Amot. as ꝑ a/	3748.12				
	Sep. 17. Cash for Note					
	16 July	1000 "	4748.12			
			6814. "			
Sepr 7.	By Warrt.	4000 "				
17.	By G & Jeffn.	1000 "	5000. "	Sepr 30th	1814	9—"
			1814			
from 1st Octr to 5 Novr	To Amot of a/c	80	5237.46			
			7051.46.			
Octr. 7	By Warrt. (80)	2000				
9	By Capt Lewis's Note	2000	4000	Octr 9th.	3051.46	15—"
			3051.46			
Novr 7	By Warrt. (81)	2000				
9	By Capt Lewis's Note	1000	3000			
			51.46.	Novr 9.	51.46	
to Decr 4.	To Amot of 3 a/c	1605.26.				
9	To Bank for Note 9 Or	2000	3605.26.			
			3656.72			
7	By Warrt. (81) deducted		2000 —	Decr 9	1656.72.	8.
9	To Balance Card. forwd		$1656.72.		12,173.20½	69"
to 31	To Amot of a/c rendered addl.		1226.28			
			2883.			
decr 10.	By Mr McEwan on WS a/c dedt		1800			
1802			1083			
to Jany 30.	To Amt of a/c (117) rendd. [p.]		6276.22			
			7359.22			
Jany 9.	By Warrt. deductd.	2000.				
	By T. Carpenter a/	12.67	2012.67.			
	Note...this Balance of is Carried to a New Acct. of Balances—		$5346.55.			

But in order to Ascertain the real Balance on said a/c to the 9th Jany. it will be Necessary, to Annex the following particulars...Viz

decr. 10th By McEwans on WS a/- 1800.

9.	deduct Bale. due	1656.72	143.28	due the Prest.		
31.	To amt. of a/c	1226.28				
	from which deduct	143.28				
	as above	1083.				
to Jany 9	To disburmt 5017.42	5017.42				
		6100.42.				
Jany 9	from which deduct	2012.67.				
do	due leaves	4087.75	due J.B.	Jany 9th.	4087.75.	20"
from do						
to Jany 30	To aditional due a/c					
	1258.80.	1258.80				
	& on above is $6276.22	5346.55				
				on	16,260.95	for 89
Jany. 30	which said Bale. of $5346.55.					
	is Card. to a New a/c of Balances—					

Errors & Omissions Excepted

John Barnes
Geo: Town 27th May 1803.

MS (ViU); entirely in Barnes's hand; with several illegible abbreviations and numerals; ellipses in original.

by warrt. deducted: starting at 7 May 1801 in this statement of account and continuing through the ensuing two statements at approximately one-month intervals, the warrants recorded by Barnes are the installments TJ received from the Treasury Department on his $25,000 annual salary as president. Treasury statements of these payments for the periods 5 May 1801 to 8 Mch. 1802 and 14 Apr. 1802 to 7 Mch. 1803 are in DNA: RG 217, MTA.

colo. cary: that is, Edward Carrington, the supervisor of the revenue for Virginia. The $1,500 draft on Carrington was used primarily to reimburse John Wayles Eppes for horses he purchased on TJ's behalf in 1801 (mb, 2:1037, 1045-6; Vol. 34:521).

by g & jeffn: on 12 Sep. 1801, TJ directed George Jefferson to remit immediately $1,000 to Barnes. TJ informed Barnes of the transaction the same day, explaining that "I am afraid my arrearages are inconvenient to you" (mb, 2: 1050; Vol. 35:270, 275-6).

by capt lewis's note: for Meriwether Lewis's notes on the Bank of Columbia that were credited to TJ's account with Barnes, see Vol. 36:77-8, 695-7; Vol. 37:439-40.

ws: William Short. For the $1,800 credited to TJ from Short's account with Barnes, see Vol. 36:697.

by t. carpenter: for the reimbursement of $12.67 received from tailor Thomas Carpenter, see Vol. 36:698.

II

Statement of Interest Account with John Barnes, 30 January 1802-10 January 1803

Sketch of the Apparent, Monthly Balances—Advances in the Presidents a/c with J Barnes will Appear from the Annexed Statem. Commencing

1802				1802	Monthly Int. a 6 ℔ Ct	
Jany 30.	To Amt of a/- rendd. ℔ leds.	117.	5346.55.			
Feby 8.	By Warrt. deducted	"	2000.	Feby. 8th	3346.55.	16 50.

to Mar 4	To Amt includg Errors & Advances		7361.70			
Mar 6.	By Warrt deducted		3000 —	Mar 6.	4361.70.	21.50.
to 31	To Amt of a/c	(125)	6213.30			
Aprl 16	By warrt deducted		2000 —	Aprl 16.	4213.30	21. .
Aprl 30	To Amt. of a/-	(125)	5446.			
May 1 & 10	By Warrt &c. deducted		2002.50	May 10th.	3443.50	17. .
to 31.	To Amt. of a/c	(125)	5757.50			
June 8.	By Warrt deducted		2000 —	June 8.	3757.50	18.50.
to 30	To Amt. of a/c	(144)	5341.50.			
July 6	By Warrt. deducted		2000 —	July 6	3341.50.	16.50
to 31	To Amt. of a/c	(144.)	5651.60			
Aug. 13	By Warrt deducted		2000 —	Augt. 13	3651.60	18. .
to 31	To Amt. of a/c	(144.)	4267.91½			
Sepr. 13	By Warrt deducted		2500 —	Sepr. 13.	1767.91½	8.50.
to 30	To Amt. of a/c	(146.)	2019.			
Oct. 11.	By Warrt deducted		2000 —	Octr 11th	19.—	
to 27	To Amt. of a/c	(146)	2984.70			
7 Oct. & Nov. 8	By do. a/- deducted		2198.	Nov. 8	786.70	3.50.
Novr. 30	To Amt. of a/c	(146)	3368.70.			
decr. 6.	By Warrt deducted		2000 —	Decr. 6	1368.70.	6.50.
to 31	To Amot. of a/c	(146)	4261.70.			
1803				1803		
Jany. 10.	By Warrt deducted		2000 —	Jany. 10.	2268.70.	11. .
					$32,326.66.	158.50
Jany. 10	which said Balance is Carried to a New a/c of Balances—Errors & Omissions Excepted—		$2268.70			

John Barnes
Geo: Town 27 May 1803.

MS (ViU); entirely in Barnes's hand; endorsed by Barnes: "Int. on Monthly Statements from 30 Jany. 1802. to 10 Jany. 1803. $158.50."

III

Statement of Interest Account with John Barnes, 10 January-8 May 1803

Sketch of Apparent Monthly Balances on The Presidents a/c with J Barnes, will Appear from the Annexed Statemt. Commencing Viz

				Monthly Int. a 6 ℔ Ct.
1803			1803.	
Jany. 10.	To amt. of a/c rendered (46) $2268.70 shd be	2268.50		
to 31.	To additional expenditures	2668.50.		
		4937.		

Feby 7.	By Warrant deducted	2000.	Feby 7th	2937.	14.—
to 27	To Amt. of a/c rendered	5530.			
Mar 7.	By Warrt deducted	2500.	Mar 7th	3030.	15.
to 30	To Amt of a/c rendered	5874.50.			
Apl 11 & 12	By Warrt & $50.	2050.	Aprl 11.	3824.50.	19.
to 31.	To Amt. of a/c rendered	5239.50.			
May 8	By Warrant deducted	2000.	May 8.	3239.50.	16.
				$13,031.	$64.

which said Balance of $3239.50 is Card.
to a New a/c Balns
Errors & Omissions Excepted.

John Barnes
Geo. Town 27 May 1803.

MS (ViU); entirely in Barnes's hand; endorsed by Barnes: "Int. on Mothy. Statements from 10th. Jany to 8th. May 1803 $64."

From Robert Smith

Navy depmt.
May 27. 1803

Sir,

I enclose six blank warrants which it is intended to fill up with the names of the following young Gentlemen for Midshipmen

George W. Barker	recommended by Mr. Gregg
John Quynn	Mr. Duvall & others
John R. Sherwood	Jacob Gibson & others—
John Nevitt	R. Bowie & others—
John Pettigrew	Docr. Bullus & others
Thos. Baldwin jr.	Ben. Austin & others—

Should you approve of these appointments, the enclosed warrants will require your Signature.—

I have the honor to be, with high respect, Sir, yr mo: ob: Servt.

Rt Smith

RC (DLC); in a clerk's hand, signed by Smith; at foot of text: "The President"; endorsed by TJ as received from the Navy Department and "Midshipmen" and so recorded in SJL at 27 May. FC (Lb in DNA: RG 45, LSP).

On 30 May, Smith sent warrants for midshipmen to George W. barker of Pennsylvania; John quynn, John R. sherwood, and John nevitt of Maryland; John pettigrew of Washington, D.C.; and Thomas baldwin, Jr., of Massachusetts. Barker, however, refused to accept his warrant and returned it to the Navy Department (FC in Lb in DNA: RG 45, LSO).

To Daniel Carroll, Daniel Brent, and Charles Minifie

GENTLEMEN Washington May 28. 1803.

I have recieved your letter of the 24th. proposing the application of any public monies that may be under my controul, & which could with propriety be so used to the improvement of the Pensylvania avenue from the capitol to the bridge now to be built over the Eastern branch. the funds of the city formerly applicable to such objects, are now appropriated by law to the reimbursement of the monies lent by the US. to the Commissioners. the only remaining fund under my direction, which has any relation to the city, is the sum of 50,000. D. appropriated by a law of the last session to 'such repairs or alterations in the capitol & other public buildings as may be necessary &c. and also for keeping in repair the *highway between* the capitol & other public buildings.' these are the words of the law, and you will be sensible that they are descriptive of the Pensylvania avenue between the capitol & the public buildings on the President's square exactly, and of no other highways[1] and so they were expressly explained to me by the member who moved the insertion of these words, and by others. sincerely desirous of promoting the interests of the city and of Georgetown (for their contiguity & other circumstances identify them in their relations to the government) I should have been happy to have it in my power to improve their communications with each other & with the country round about them: but no such power has been given to me. Accept assurances of my great respect & consideration.

TH: JEFFERSON

PrC (DLC); at foot of text:
Danl. Carrol of Dudn.
Dan. Brent
Chas. Minifie
} esquires. Directors of the Eastern branch bridge co.

LAW OF THE LAST SESSION: "An Act concerning the City of Washington," passed by Congress on 3 Mch. TJ quotes from section five of the act (U.S. Statutes at Large, 2:235-6).

MEMBER WHO MOVED THE INSERTION: William Eustis (*Annals*, 12:608).

[1] Word interlined.

Memorandum from Henry Dearborn, with Jefferson's Notes

[on or before 28 May 1803]

the papers exhibited by Govr. Mercer relating to the demand made by the State of Maryland, on the U.S. for muskets &c, furnish no evidence of an ingagement on the part of the U.S. to be responsible for any other Arms &c except what should be furnished to the Virginia militia—the only question of consequence to be decided, is, whether the United States shall, (under all the circumstances of the case) account with the State of Maryland for the whole deficiency of Arms &c delivered to the Maryland, as well as the Virginia Militia.

[*Notes by TJ*:]

Notes. there can be no doubt we are bound to replace to Maryland the arms they furnished the Virginia militia.

whether we are bound to replace those furnished at our request to their own militia & lost, depends on the general question whether a state is bound to furnish arms, ammunition &c. as well as men?

if they are, as it is a duty which cannot be fulfilled by the states which have not armed their militia, it will fall unjustly on those which have armed them, & therefore *can* comply with their duty.

if the militia bring their state arms, they will be of different calibers, qualities &c.

on the whole it seems to me more convenient & equal that the US. should furnish arms to all.

and that it is advantageous to encourage the states to lend us in distress, by a ready replacement of what they lend.

MS (DLC); undated; in Dearborn's hand, with notes by TJ at foot of text; endorsed by TJ as received from the War Department on 28 May and "Maryland arms" and so recorded in SJL.

Writing Maryland governor John F. MERCER on 11 June, Dearborn informs him of his inability to find evidence of an engagement by the United States to replace any arms or equipment "excepting those deliver'd to the Militia of Virginia, the number of which cannot by me be ascertained from any document which has come to my Knowledge." Maryland appears to have furnished 2,000 troops and 3,341 arms and accoutrements, so the number supplied to Virginia probably did not much exceed 1,000, most of which were presumably returned at the end of the campaign. Since the United States supplied 1,000 arms and 545 tents to Maryland, Dearborn believes a balance is "undoubtedly" due by the state to the United States, unless "the proper authority," which Dearborn presumes to be Congress, decides that the United States should be held accountable for all the arms and accoutrements delivered to the Maryland and Virginia militias. In the latter case, Dearborn thinks "a small balance" will be due to Maryland after deducting the value of the tents. The military storekeeper can probably ascertain the number of arms supplied to the Virginia militia and the number returned. Dearborn finds it difficult to understand "how so great a proportion of the arms & accoutrements could have been lost in the course of two or three months" and deems the failure to hold each man accountable for returning the equipment he received to be "among the many extraordinary circumstances of the expedition." Maryland's claim involves a question of "considerable importance," that is, whether the states or the federal government are to arm the militia when called into service. Therefore, Dearborn believes it best to let Congress decide and recommends that the claim be laid before them at their next session. The resolution of the issue, Dearborn feels, "will fix a principle by which the Executives of the General and the respective State Governments will in future be governed, relative to the arming the Militia when called into actual service" (FC in Lb in DNA: RG 107, MLS).

To Lewis Harvie

DEAR SIR Washington May 28. 1803.

The motives explained to you in my letter of April 22. have induced me to [meet] for myself[1] the inconveniencies of wanting a secretary, and, I fear, to derange for you also your plan of reading, two months beyond the time I had expected. the time of Capt. Lewis's return from Philadelphia and consequently of his departure from hence, being still uncertain, tho' daily possible, I take the liberty of proposing to you to come on so soon as your own convenience will permit. should you desire to bring on any thing too bulky for the stage, there are vessels which ply constantly between Richmond & Alexandria & this place, by which they will come safely.

Advices from Europe to Apr. 24. shew war to be almost inevitable between France & Great Britain. it's plan will make a greater change on the face of the globe than even the late war has done; and will have effects on us of so complicated an aspect as to defy calculation. if our citizens will yield to neither the hopes nor fears with which the malcontents among us will endeavor to agitate them, our course will be a safe one. but to make the best of it will require calmness and confidence on their part, on ours to[2] preserve the advantages of neutrality as long as possible, and if forced to relinquish them, to obtain such improvements of our situation as may lay the foundation for future & further prosperities. be so good as to present my friendly salutations to Colo. & mrs Harvie & to accept yourself assurance of my affections & best wishes. TH: JEFFERSON

PrC (DLC); blurred; at foot of text: "Lewis Harvie esq."

Harvie took up his post as the president's secretary on 6 June (MB, 2:1101).

[1] Preceding two words interlined.
[2] TJ here canceled "keep."

Report from John Lenthall

Rough Stone and Brick work done to the south Wing of the Capitol May 23d to 28th 1803

	feet	
West front, including Voids of 5 Arches & Rack'd returns	888	96 Perches
four Arches prepared for the Bricks, and 2800 laid in do		
South front, Stone Work in the Arches	138	
6 Cellar Window stools set in do—		
East front, Stone Work, Voids as before included—	1351	

for B H Latrobe

JNO LENTHALL

MS (DLC); in Lenthall's hand and signed by him; addressed: "P. USA."; endorsed by TJ: "Capitol May 28. 1803."

From Jackson Browne

Hartford Connecticut
May 29th 1803

SIR

Inclosed; I have the Honor of Transmitting for your Excellency's Perusal—A Letter from my Friend Mr Gideon Granger.

If "through the Medium of his Intercession" I shou'd prove so fortunate—as to Obtain your Patronage—I, shall "in future" exert my Utmost Endeavors to render myself Deserving of it.—By a Strict Adherence to your Instructions—and a Prompt and Faithful Discharge—of the Duties Attached to my Appointment.

With Sentiments of the most Profound Respect—I Remain Your Excellency's most Humble Sevt.

JACKSON BROWNE

RC (DNA: RG 59, LAR); at foot of text: "His Excellency The President"; endorsed by TJ as received 2 June and "to be Consul at Tripoli" and so recorded in SJL. Enclosure: Granger to TJ, 27 May, recorded in SJL as received from Suffield on 2 June with notation "in favr. Jackson Browne," but not found.

Jackson Browne (d. 1804) had been recommended for a consular appointment by Pierpont Edwards and Alexander J. Dallas in 1801. For his career, see Vol. 35:259-60. He died while in Barbados (Hartford *American Mercury*, 6 Dec. 1804).

TJ saw another application for a consulship in the Barbary states. John P. Ripley, a Philadelphia attorney, wrote Madison on 27 May offering his services. Ripley noted that Timothy Pickering had assured him of the consulship at Tunis in 1797, but it was given to William Eaton (RC in DNA: RG 59, LAR; endorsed by TJ: "to be Consul in Barbary" and "he is federal").

From Meriwether Lewis

Dear Sir, Philadelphia May 29th. 1803.

I have at length so far succeeded in making the necessary preparations for my intended journey as to be enabled to fix on the sixth or seventh of June as the probable time of my departure for Washington. All the article have been either procured, or are in such state of forwardness in the hands of the workmen as to induce me to hope that my stay here after that period will be unnecessary; indeed it is probable that I might set out by the middle of this week, was it not for a wish to attend Mr. Patterson a few days longer; this, Mr. Patteson recommends; he has been extreemly obliging to me since my arrival here, but his avocations for the last ten days have been such, as rendered it impossible for him to afford me the benefit of his instructions; in the mean time I have employed myself in attending more immediately to the objects of my equipment, and am now more at leasure to pursue with effect the subjects to which, he may think proper to direct my attention.

Agreeably to your instructions the draught of your orders prepared for my government, has been submitted to Mr. Patterson, and to Drs. Rush Barton & Wister; they approve of them very highly: Dr. Rush has favored me with some abstract queries under the several heads of *Physical History*, *medicine*, *Morals* and *Religeon* of the Indians, which I have no doubt will be servicable in directing my inquiries among that people: Drs. Barton and Wister have each promised[1] to contribute in like manner any thing, which may suggest itself to them as being of any importance in furthering the objects of this expedition. Dr. Barton has sometimes flattered me with the pleasure of his company as far as the Illinois; this event would be extreemly pleasing to me for many reasons; I fear the Dr. will not carry his design into effect; he tells me that his health has been pretty good latterly, and that he is determined to travel in some direction two or three months during the ensuing summer and autumn.—

I paid Mr. Dufief 74$. and Dr. Bolman 18$. I have also purchased a Vigogna Blanket, of which I hope you will approve; it is about the size of a common three point Blanket, the skins appear to be too thin for rough service, tho' it is a very pretty thing; it is the best I could find, the price was 10$.—The Tiger's skin you requested I have not been able to procure, those I have seen appear to be too small for your purpose, perhaps they may be had in Baltimore if so, I will get one at that place—The 2 pole chain & 2 pair of fleecy socks have also been procured. I recieved your watch this morning from Mr. Voigt, who tells me shee is well regulated and in perfect order. Mr. Whitney has not yet repared your sextant tho' it was put into his hands immediately on my arrival; he has promised however, after repeated applications, that it shall be ready tomorrow evening: he seemed unwilling to undertake the alteration you wished in the brass Sextant stand, I therefore declined having the alteration made; I was further induced to this resolution from the opinion of Mr. Ellicott, who thought that the ball & socket would be reather a disadvantage than otherwise, and that in every event he concieved the advantages of the ball and socket would not be equivalent to the expence attending the alteration.—

I have writen again to Dr. Dickson at Nashville, (from whom I have not yet heard) on the subject of my boat and canoe. I have recieved an answer from Majr. Mac Rea, Comdr. at S.W. Point: his report is reather unfavorable to my wishes: he tells me that out of twenty men who have volunteered their services to accompany me, not more than three or four do by any means possess the necessary qualifications for this expedition, or who answer the discription which I had given him; this however I must endeavour to remedy by taking with me from that place a sufficient number of the best of them to man my boat, and if possible scelect others of a better discription as I pass the Garrisons of Massac, Kaskaskais & Illinois.—

You will recieve herewith inclosed some sketches taken from Vancouver's survey of the Western Coast of North America; they were taken in a haisty manner, but I believe they will be found sufficiently accurate to be of service in composing the map, which Mr. Gallatin was so good as to promise he would have projected and compleated for me— Will you be so obliging Sir, as to mention to Mr. Gallatin, that I have not been able to procure Danvill's map—The maps attatched to Vancouver's voyage cannot be procured seperately from that work, which is both too costly, and too weighty, for me either to[2] purchase or carry.—

I have the honor to be with the most sincere esteem & attatchment—Your Obt. Servt. MERIWETHER LEWIS.

RC (DLC); at foot of text: "The President of the UStates"; endorsed by TJ as received 1 June.

Benjamin Rush prepared a set of QUERIES for Lewis as a means of collecting information about American Indians. Rush grouped the questions, which he dated 17 May, into three categories: physical history and medicine, morals, and religion. Among the questions were: "What are the *acute* diseases of the Indians?"; queries about diet; "What are their vices?"; whether suicide was common, and "ever from love?"; "What Affinity between their religious Ceremonies & those of the Jews?"; and "How do they dispose of their dead, and with what Ceremonies do they inter them?" Rush's "Questions to Merryweather Lewis" are printed in Jackson, *Lewis and Clark*, 1: 50-1, and George W. Corner, ed., *The Autobiography of Benjamin Rush: His "Travels Through Life" together with his* Commonplace Book *for 1789-1813* (Princeton, 1948), 265-6.

VIGOGNA: vicuña; see TJ to Lewis, 23 Apr. By the latter part of the 18th century, woolen blankets with short bars or "points" woven into one edge to indicate size were a standard trade item of the Hudson's Bay Company. A THREE POINT BLANKET had about three square yards of material, roughly six feet long and four and a half feet wide. Native Americans often used that size blanket as a robe, draped over the shoulders or wrapped around the body (Harold Tichenor, *The Blanket: An Illustrated History of the Hudson's Bay Point Blanket* [Toronto, 2002], 11-12, 14-15, 29, 36, 38).

The WATCH that Henry VOIGT worked on for TJ may have been a silver one with a second hand that Voigt charged 62½ cents to clean. Voigt also cleaned and adjusted a gold chronometer that Lewis purchased in Philadelphia for the western expedition for $250. Lewis asked Andrew Ellicott to regulate that timepiece. From Voigt, Lewis obtained a new mahogany box, probably for the chronometer, and a universal joint. From Thomas WHITNEY, Lewis bought instruments for the expedition totaling $162.20 (Jackson, *Lewis and Clark*, 1:51, 78, 88, 91; Vol. 37:598-9).

WRITEN AGAIN TO DR. DICKSON: see Lewis to TJ, 20 Apr.

VANCOUVER'S SURVEY: George Vancouver, *A Voyage of Discovery to the North Pacific Ocean, and Round the World; in Which the Coast of North-West America Has Been Carefully Examined and Accurately Surveyed*, which first appeared in a three-volume edition published in London in 1798. Editions of the work were hard to obtain in the United States, and expensive; see Vol. 39:20-1, 24n.

[1] MS: "pomised."

[2] Lewis here canceled "think."

To James Oldham

SIR Washington May 29. 1803

On the 26th. inst. there were shipped from Philadelphia 2 boxes of sheet iron for the terras, bent & painted ready to be laid. these contain 39. sheets only. for the terras it will take

96. sheets in the whole and
20. do. for the 8. gutturs of the porticos & piazzas
3. do. for the gutturs where the roof joins the walls of the dome room
119 in the whole.

so that about a third only of the whole is shipped; this will cover about 25. f. in length of the terras. the rest are promised as fast as they can be prepared. I am informed however that these sheets are not in one piece each, but in two put together with a tuck thus consequently you must observe to put the proper end uppermost. I will direct them, as soon as they have 60. sheets more ready, to send them off, that the terras may be compleated. those for the gutturs of the porticos &c [ma]y come last.

I have this day calculated the number of pannels &c of the ballustrade, & find [th]ere will be 26. pannels of from 5. to 6. ballusters each, 8 pilasters of 2f—6I and 24. do. of 2. feet breadth each. the thickness of the pilasters double that of the balluster. this will take in the whole 136. ballusters, but say 150. but this is on the supposition the ballusters are 5. I. thick, as I *believe* they are, for I have no note of them here, and am not very certain in my recollection of them. if they are smaller or larger, they will take more or fewer exactly in proportion to the error I commit in estimating their size: for instance if they are only 4. I. diameter, then it will take 5. for every 4. of my estimate, that is to say 188 instead of 150.

I think it would be better to use these first sheets over the hall, leaving the two ends of the terras to be done last: because these will compleatly cover the hall, so that the work in it may be begun. Accept my best wishes TH: JEFFERSON

P.S. on second thoughts I will direct the sheets to be forwarded in parcels of 30. as fast as done, because each 30. will finish one end of the terras, the middle part being covered with those now sent.

RC (MHi: Frothingham Papers); torn; addressed: "Mr. James Oldham Monticello near Milton"; franked; postmarked 30 May.

Benjamin Henry Latrobe was supplying TJ with SHEET IRON (Vol. 39:257n). A letter of 26 May from Latrobe, recorded in SJL as received 28 May, has not been found.

TJ designed a BALLUSTRADE running along the top of Monticello's exterior walls, where they joined the lower portion of the roof. Undated design notes in his hand reflected the calculations above, with 33 balusters divided into 6 panels on the west and south angles, 35 balusters divided into 7 panels on the east and north angles, and 8 pilasters on each side. For some time, workmen at Monticello had been producing balusters with a lathe, but the project took a number of years to complete, and TJ may have modified some of his calculations. At the bottom of his notes he appended on 17 Sep. 1805, "the ballusters on actual measurement are 30. I. high & $5\frac{3}{4}$ I. diam. or square. the spaces between them may be <*3. I. to avoid* [. . .] *or even* $3\frac{1}{2}$ *I.*> the half of the diameter." A sketch of the cap and base of the balustrade, accompanied by some design notes on the balusters, also indicated that each would have a diameter of $5\frac{3}{4}$ inches, separated from one another by half as much space (McLaughlin, *Jefferson and Monticello*, 265-6; "Monticello: notebook of improvements" [1804-1807], in MHi; "Monticello: architectural detail [top of house], [1803]," in same; Nichols, *Architectural Drawings*, Nos. 159 and 171; Vol. 39:99n).

From James Cheetham

SIR New-York 30th May 1803.

Agreeably to your request I have kept for you and have now bound in blue boards, a file of the "Watch Tower" for the year ending in May 1803: will you be so obliging as to inform me by what Conveyance you wish it to be transmitted?

We are blest, sir, with an unusual degree of tranquillity; little of party spirit is to be seen in this City, except among those who on account of a Certain Controversy will neither wholly withdraw from, nor Cordially unite with, us. These, although few in number, are exceedingly rancorous: they Cannot, however, do us essential injury.

In the Assembly of this State the federal party will Certainly not have more, and in all probability they will have less[1] than 15: the whole number is 100. In the senate their whole number will not exceed *Six*: the Senate Consists of 32.

If that wisdom which has hither to characterized your administration shall be Continued unto us, the federal party Can have no hopes of re-ascending to power. The reduction of our taxes and the diminution of the public debt, are arguments which the worst reasoner in the union Can Justly appreciate.

With very great respect I am, Sir, Your obt servt.

JAMES CHEETHAM

RC (DLC); at foot of text: "His Excellency Thomas Jefferson President of the United States"; endorsed by TJ as received 2 June and so recorded in SJL.

YOUR REQUEST: see TJ to Cheetham, 23 Apr. 1802.

For news of the New York ASSEMBLY and SENATE elections, see DeWitt Clinton to TJ, 4 May, and Granger to TJ, 6 May.

[1] Preceding eight words interlined.

From William C. C. Claiborne

DEAR SIR, Near Natchez, May 30th. 1803.

In my last Letter, I anticipated the resignation of Mr. *Seth Lewis*, the Chief Justice of this Territory;—I was yesterday informed by *that Gentleman*, that his resignation had actually been forwarded.

If Judge Jackson of Tennessee (the Gentleman I named to you in my last Letter) should not be offer'ed the Appointment of a Judge for this Territory, or be unwilling to accept, permit me Sir, to suggest the propriety of selecting *another Character of Law Talents*, from some one of the States;—If however, you should deem it advisable to make the appointment within the Territory, I will ask the liberty to mention a Mr. George Poindexter as a deserving young Man, and whose Law Information is very respectable.—I have understood, that a Mr. Abner L. Duncan has been recommended as Mr. Lewis's Successor.—I do not think this information is correct, should[1] it however be so, I feel it my duty to state, that Mr. Duncan's Talents as a Lawyer are not more than equal to Mediocrity, and that he is *unworthy of your Confidence.*—

I have not heard of any appointments under the Land Law; It would I think be most satisfactory, if the Surveyor General, Commissioners and Registers were *not* selected from among the Citizens of this District, and I do also believe that this mode of appointment, would be most beneficial to the public service; There are indeed Sir, but *few men* of Talents in this quarter, and these *few* are either mediately or immediately interested in the existing Titles for Land.—

Finding in the Land Law, that an office is to be opened, "at such place in the County of Adams, as shall be designated by the President," I will take the liberty to mention the Town of Washington (our present Seat of Government) as the most elligible position; It's situation is healthy, and central to the population of this Division of the Territory;—As to the most eligible position for the Office in Washington County, I cannot particularly say, but I will venture to recommend either the *place* where the County Courts are holden, or at (or near) *Fort Stoddart*, perhaps the latter position will be best.—

The Pamphlet signed Algernon Sidney, which you did me the honor to enclose me, I have read with great satisfaction;—The writer has done Justice to the Government, and must carry Conviction to every Candid and Rational Reader;—The pamphlet will be reprinted at Natchez, and generally circulated.

I enclose you the prospectus of a News-paper, contemplated to be printed at Natchez, the intended Editor is without printing Materials or pecuniary Resources, but I hope, he will receive sufficient private support, to enable him to prosecute his Design.—A Republican paper has long been wanting in this *District.*—In *no part of the Union*, are the Citizens less informed of the principles of our Government, and (generally speaking) involved in as much mental Ignorance;—The Federalists availing themselves of that Credulity, which invariably attaches to Ignorance, have nearly deluged this District with the *New-York Herald*, and the Calumnies circulated thro' the Medium of *that paper*, have made some unfortunate *impressions*;—*these* however, I trust will be removed, when the people are better informed.—

The Port of New-Orleans is open, and I hope it will never more be shut against us.—The well disposed part of your Constituents, rejoice at the restoration of the Deposit, & thank the Government for averting from their Country the Calamities of War.—The French Prefect continues at Orleans, but without authority, and of Victor & his Army, there is no late Intelligence.

It appears from the late papers, that *War* between England and France would speedily ensue;—on the score of humanity, an event of *this kind*, is to be regreted, yet for my Country's Interest, it might (probably) be desirable—Perhaps it would enable Mr. Monroe to obtain (with the more facility) from France and Spain, such concessions on the Missisippi, "as a regard to Justice, and our future security may require."—

With assurances of my very sincere & respectful Attachment, I remain Dr Sir, Your affectionate friend & Hb Sevt

WILLIAM C. C. CLAIBORNE

RC (DLC); at foot of text: "Tho Jefferson Esqr. President of the U. States"; endorsed by TJ as received 26 June and so recorded in SJL; also endorsed by TJ: "Town of Washington for the Adams land office Fort Stoddert for the Washington office." Enclosure not found.

MY LAST LETTER: the Editors have found no communications from Claiborne to TJ since his last extant letter of 20 Apr., nor are any recorded in SJL.

On 16 Apr. 1803, SETH LEWIS informed James Madison of his determination to resign as chief justice of the Mississippi Territory, to take effect on 15 May, and asked the secretary to inform the president of his decision. He had been appointed in 1800 (RC in DNA: RG 59, RD, endorsed by TJ: "Lewis Seth to mr Madison. resigns office of judge of Missipi"; Madison, *Papers, Sec. of State Ser.*, 4:523; Vol. 37:4n).

JUDGE JACKSON: presumably Andrew Jackson, who served as a judge of the Tennessee superior court from 1798 to 1804 (ANB).

Virginia lawyer GEORGE POINDEXTER arrived in Natchez in 1802 and was appointed attorney general of the Mississippi Territory by Claiborne the following year. He went on to a distinguished, if sometimes tempestuous, political career that included service as a congressman, federal judge, governor, and U.S. Senator (ANB). In 1805, he became involved in a quarrel with leading Natchez attorney ABNER L. DUNCAN (Richard Aubrey McLemore, ed., *A History of Mississippi*, 2 vols. [Hattiesburg, Miss., 1973], 1:238). A letter from Poindexter to TJ, dated Washington, Mississippi Territory, 30 May 1803, is recorded in SJL as received 3 July and "to be judge Missipi," but has not been found.

PAMPHLET SIGNED ALGERNON SIDNEY: *A Vindication of the Measures of the Present Administration* (see John Langdon to TJ, 8 May).

Established in 1802 and possessing a national circulation, the NEW-YORK HERALD was the semiweekly edition of the *New-York Evening Post*, the influential Federalist newspaper edited by William Coleman and associated with Alexander Hamilton (DAB, s.v. "Coleman, William"; Brigham, *American Newspapers*, 1:631, 649; Syrett, *Hamilton*, 26:2).

AS A REGARD TO JUSTICE: Claiborne quotes from TJ's Circular Letter to the Governors of the States, 25 Feb. 1803.

[1]MS: "shoul."

From Samuel R. Demaree

HONORABLE SIR, Harrodsburgh (Kenty) May 30th 1803.

Believing information from all quarters absolutely necessary to a proper managment of duties which, you will readily acknowledge, are too extensive & intricate for any man to execute fully,—I trust you will pardon me for tendering a few observations relative to the Mississippi, Floridas & Louisiana. This, being a matter of great moment to the western country, considerably agitates the minds of the inhabitants. The world concedes that we have a right to the navigation of the river; and nearly all of us agree that we must possess those territories. Our reasons are—their proximity to the U.S.—their intinsic value—their peculiar situation with regard to our commerce. I would observe tho', if proximity be a *just* reason why we *must* acquire those places, any nation in Europe or Asia may *justly* claim these continents & contend for Africa. The same & more might be said of the next reason; viz. *intinsic value.* If we must possess them for the advantage of our commerce, the inhabitants of the heads of the Rhine & Danube &c. have the same right to drive away those from the banks and mouths[1] of these rivers. Self-interest reasons without regard to justice. I am however in favor of the acquisition. But how are these countries to be acquired? Here we are divided:—some say by conquest—others by purchace. The advocates of force (whose temerity is at least equal to their knowledge or humanity) urge, on the one hand, the facility of the enterprize by arms—on the other, the expensiveness of a purchace. The friends of purchace argue the expence of equipping & provisioning a single army during one campaign—The hazard of a long war, (as we cannot claim exclusive expertness in discipline or in arms): in which case the pecuniary expence will almost certainly exceed the price of purchace, besides the corruption of the armies—the danger of disaster—the loss of lives—& every evil. Should we suceed well in taking those countries, yet an army would be needed to guard them from other nations. Here agan are expence & evil incalculable. I think natural calamities are fully sufficient to render life uncomfortable—add factitious evils & we make life intolerable. We ought not therefore to hazard all these evils together with the probability of redoubled expence, which may produce only shame & misery, for the possibility of saving a little money. Add to these the uncertain tenure of conquered countries, and I am clearly for an honest purchace; or no more than a free navigation of the river—an acquisition with peace or not at all.

Being unable to farm I have spent some of my time in books—Scarce can I open the historic page but one calamity follows another in quick succession. I have looked for the cause—I find *ignorance* & *pride*, both increased by *flattery*, are the common parents of oppression. Allow me to make one more observation. The great Washington, being decieved signed the British Treaty—died leaving only half his glory. Adams took "the Spirit of Despotism" for his guide—& alas! ruined himself & his country.—What if Jefferson too should fall? What a stab to representative Government! I cannot bear the thought—I pray it may never happen. But I have intruded perhaps too long. I desire to subscribe myself, with great defference

Your fellow Citizen SAM. R. DEMAREE

RC (DLC); addressed: "Hon. Thomas Jefferson President of U.S."; franked; endorsed by TJ as received 16 June and so recorded in SJL.

[1]MS: "moths."

From Gideon Granger

DR SIR. May 30. 1803

The Inclosed is from Eliot who ran down Morris—he is a worthy man. Yours of the 20th. is recd. I am on the wing for Boston—

Yours Sincerely GIDN GRANGER

RC (DLC); at foot of text: "The President." Recorded in SJL as received 4 June. Enclosure: James Elliot to Granger, Brattleboro, 24 May 1803, noting two vacancies for bankruptcy commissioner in his district of Vermont, one due to his resignation, the other to Oliver Gallup's declining to serve; Elliot recommends Samuel Knight, former chief justice of the state, who has indicated he will serve; Knight is "old, but still capable of business, and venerable in the decline of life; and is a very ardent republican" who has suffered under "federal persecution" (RC in DNA: RG 59, LAR; with note in TJ's hand in margin: "Oliver Gallup was appd v. Elliott his nonacceptance then only leaves the same single vacancy"; endorsed by TJ: "Elliott James. to mr Granger. Knight Saml. to be commr. bkrptcy v. Elliott resd.").

James Elliot (ELIOT) succeeded Federalist congressman Lewis R. MORRIS (*Biog. Dir. Cong.*; Vol. 33:16, 17n).

From Thomas Eston Randolph

DEAR SIR Richmond 30th May 1803

I would have replied to your much esteem'd favor of the 3d. inst. immediately—but having had the offer of a valuable property at Jenito—I thought it advisable first to view it—indeed I was on my way there at the time I received your letter—with respect to a lease of Shadwell—the terms mention'd by you are what I expected—the situation is desirable—and the improvemts. you proposed to make to the buildings would render them sufficiently commodious for my family—and I lament that I cannot now avail myself of the opportunity to remove to a neighbourhood which for many reasons is so desirable—for the present however I am compell'd to decline it—my engagements with my tenant at Dungeoness render my frequent attendance there indispensable having undertaken to do the repairs with my own people and being disappointed in obtaining a proper person to overlook them—and have in consequence rented a house convenient thereto—For the very friendly intentions expressed in your letter Mrs. Randolph and myself most cordially thank you—we offer our affectionate regards—and I am with perfect esteem your obliged friend

THOS. ESTON RANDOLPH

RC (MHi); endorsed by TJ as received 2 June and so recorded in SJL.

Thomas Eston Randolph (1767-1842) from Bristol, England, was the eldest son of TJ's uncle William Randolph. In 1795, he married Jane Cary Randolph, the sister of TJ's son-in-law, Thomas Mann Randolph. By the end of 1803, they lived at Glenmore, across the Rivanna River from Milton, and purchased the surrounding land in 1805. He became an Albemarle County magistrate in 1807. Around 1810, he sold Glenmore and the family moved to Ashton, which adjoined TJ's Pouncey's property. From July 1814 until his move to Florida in 1829, he leased TJ's manufacturing mill at Shadwell, at first in partnership with Thomas Mann Randolph, and later with Daniel Colcaster. Financial failures forced him to sell his ancestral home of Dungeness as well as all his slaves. Once settled in Florida, he grew active in civic life and became a federal marshal for the Middle Florida district in 1831. His daughter, Mary Cleland Randolph, married TJ's grandson, Francis Wayles Eppes. In April 1836, he and Eppes were among a group of men who petitioned Congress, albeit unsuccessfully, for the establishment of an institution of higher learning in the Tallahassee area (Woods, *Albemarle*, 303; Cynthia A. Kierner, "'The Dark and Dense Cloud Perpetually Lowering over Us': Gender and the Decline of the Gentry in Postrevolutionary Virginia," *Journal of the Early Republic*, 20 [2000], 193; MB, 2:1156n, 1310n; JS, 25:447; JEP, 4:178, 193; RS, 1:488n; Vol. 1:410n; Vol. 35:507-8).

FAVOR OF THE 3D. INST.: TJ to Randolph, 3 May, is recorded in SJL but has not been found. Randolph to TJ, 28 Apr., recorded in SJL as written from Richmond and received on 1 May, has also not been found.

Genito (JENITO) was a small village on the Appomattox River in Powhatan County (*Journal of the House of Delegates of the Commonwealth of Virginia, Begun and Held at the Capitol in the City of Richmond, on Monday, the Fifth Day of December Eighteen Hundred and Thirty One* [Richmond, 1831], 174).

Dungeness (DUNGEONESS), the Randolph family estate in Goochland County where TJ's parents married in 1739, was confiscated by the British in 1779 and passed to Thomas Randolph, who later deeded it to his nephew Thomas Eston Randolph (Vol. 1:408-10; Vol. 27:676n).

From Thomas Mann Randolph

Dear Sir, Edgehill May 30. 1803

Your favor of the 5th. instant arrived regularly, and I made the communications from it intended for Monticello, without delay. An accident happened in the nailery at Lillies on Friday last which presented[1] a shocking prospect at first but promises now an issue very different from the dismal end at first expected. The boy Cary, irritated at some little trick from Brown, who hid part of his nail rod to teaze him, but restored it as soon as he found him angry, took a most barbarous revenge; approaching him by stealth he struck him with his whole strength upon the skull, very near the longitudinal suture, on the left side, midway between the horizontal & perpendicular faces of the skull bone, when the body is erect. The skull yielded to the face of the hammer in its whole circumference but was driven in only about $\frac{2}{3}$ of it, bending the other part & fracturing no where else. The instantaneous suspension of life did not continue longer than a minute: for an hour no damage was suspected but at the end of that time violent convulsions took place which were quickly succeeded by Coma & its usual symptoms, the leaden eye and apoplectic stupor:[2] the patient was sensible of what was done to him and answered reasonably yet to my astonishment when the pressure was removed had no recollection at all of any circumstance from the blow to that moment. Wardlaw & myself arriving nearly at the same time I acted as his assistant in the operation which he performed by means of the trephine (the saw which works both ways or with the motion of the wrist only) with the greatest boldness, steadiness and skill. The boy is as well as we could have expected today, and will, no doubt I think, in a month, be as well as ever. The other, I committed to jail till Browns fate is determined.

Martha is in perfect health: so is all the family indeed. She is considerably advanced in pregnancy: on that account chiefly I am pleased with your relinguishing her visit to you this summer for the stage carriages all jolt severely, and perhaps as late as the end of July she might have been incommoded by the journey back.—I have not had an opportunity of consulting with Mr. Peyton since I recieved your letter nor can I learn from Henderson what the true ground of his claim to the Mill seat is, but his explanations have not been satisfactory, I believe, to Meriwether & Miller for they have made proposals to me to purchase the whole, or half, of my seat in North Milton, which I am now considering. There is nine feet fall, from the foot of Hendersons Dam to the spot they deem best for the mill house, & the water can be taken out with ease by stoping the sluices of the great fall, which you know is about 60 yards below that Dam. Is it necessary to you to reduce the water entirely down to the old level at the Dam? If so I fear those sluices cannot be stoped, for there is no fall between the foot of it and that place. I have some idea that there was some check of the water at the present dam before it was erected and while your Mill worked: if so *that* will be sufficient for us; for it could not have been larger than one or one and a half foot, that being the descent at the smallest falls in the river, near it, above & below. I must trouble you to give me that information, also to say candidly what you conceive the effect on your improvement may be of their establishment, as to rivalry and consequent diminution of your rent. They say they can have a toll mill by October if we bargain. I will not part with the whole of mine but the half would be a just compromise between my own interests & those of my successors. I have no hope of being able to improve myself, but can furnish them a considerable quota in labor at the seasons when my force employed in banking at Varina ought to be withdrawn to avoid sickness and on account of cold; and they offer to improve in partnership with me. I shall apply to the next Court for an order but shall do nothing with them till I hear from you. With the most sincere attachment yr. &c

TH: M. RANDOLPH

RC (ViU: Edgehill-Randolph Papers); endorsed by TJ as received 2 June and so recorded in SJL.

BROWN Colbert eventually recovered from his fractured skull and, after negotiating a sale to the owner of his wife, achieved his emancipation and died in Liberia (Annette Gordon-Reed, *The Hemingses of Monticello: An American Family* [New York, 2008], 580; MB, 2:1174).

Randolph owned several lots, including a warehouse, in NORTH MILTON, a village on the north bank of the Rivanna River that the Virginia General Assembly had incorporated from 50 acres of Randolph's land during the 1800-1801 session (*Acts Passed at a General Assembly of the Commonwealth of Virginia Begun and Held at the Capitol, in the City of Richmond, on Monday, the First Day of December, One Thousand Eight Hundred* [Richmond, 1801], 18; William H. Gaines, *Thomas Mann Randolph: Jefferson's Son-in-Law* [Baton Rouge, 1966], 78n).

[1] MS: "pesented."
[2] MS: "stutor."

From Stephen Cathalan, Jr.

DEAR SIR Marseilles the 31st. May 1803

on the 1st. Inst. I was honored with your most Gracious Favor of the 7th. Last February, which became a day of Joy & happiness for me and all my Family; When I had perused it's Contents, I assembled them all in my old Father's Bed room, & charged my Daughter to read and make a faith full Translation of it to him, to my Mother, & wife; Since She has spent Three years at the English nuns, Rue des Fossés Snt. victor at Paris, where she entered for her education by the advise of the most unfortunate & Respectable Dutchess of Orleans, she speaks & writes english perhaps better than I do;—she is Proud, but very Gratefull, for having obtained from you, Sir, the honorable & Flatering tittle and expression of your Young Friend;—she is not yet a mater Familias, tho' she is in the 19th. year of age, because it is now very Difficult to meet in this part of the Globe, with a young man of a good morality Education & Talents,—many Proposals for marrying her are made to us, but we don't like, in Genal., nor the cy-devant nobility, nor the new entittled or *enrichés*;—we should preffer a young reputed Merchant of Talents, tho' not very Rich, but we have So many instances of Faillures or heavy Losses, in Trade, that the best would be for her a good Farmer on his own State;—I must confess to her Commendation, she is not as our Young French Misses, so witty, Gay & Dissipated, but has much of the English or american Manners, habits, good common sense, & understanding, being very Studious; her recreations are, my country house on the sea shore, or her Piano, singing with a Charming voice favorite Italian French or English songs;—she is gone, 15 Days ago, to Montpellier with her Mother, who is afflicted with an athsmatic Disorder, for the Benefit of her health;—my Good old Father, tho' at 86 years of age and afflicted with his Gout, keeps up still his spirits & Good head,—my Mother who has overpassed 80, enjoys of the best health; all in chorus & Individualy joins me in begging you to accept our sincere acknowledgments of everlasting & Respectfull Gratitude, for your honble. Recollection, & kind expressions of your Precious Friendship towards all of us & me particularly, in Delaying of taking any measure respecting this office, untill I have had time enough to remove the obstacles that were opposed by this Governt.—renewing, you my assurances that should I Despair of the Success, I should Readily beg you to appoint a successor in my stead; but with great Pleasure I can advance that the late occurence of *Two French Natives* Lately appointed agents for Russia, & Naples, *for this same Port of Marseilles*, who on the Demand of their respective Embassadors, have obtained their exequatur, gives me *now* the most sanguine hopes I will succeed, moreso since I have Learned a few Days ago that our Minister extraordy. Jas. Monroe Esqr. has fully succeeded in the honorable Mission, you was so kind as to confide me the Particulars, to the mutual advantage of Both Nations, to the honor of the united States, which will add to the Illustration of your Political & *Truly*

Philosophical Life, so much Precious at the head of that Paternal Government, as it will Preserve for the Future, an everlasting Peace and Friendship between France, & america;—Mr. Livingston having from the Beggining, had a negative answer from Mr. Talleyrand on *his verbal* demand of my exequatur, declined to make any further sollicitations in my behalf, ever since the acknowlegdment of these Two French Natives, unless he should receive from the Secretary of State instructions for that Purpose;—he returned me then my Commission, & a new Memorial I had made for the Minister of Foreign Relations, advising me to sollicit it direct or thro' my Friends; of Course my Commission and memorial which was delivered to this minister has remained There, & it has been wrote to me, I would obtain it, if now, & according to the usual form it should be demanded by the Minister Plenipy. of the U. States Resident at Paris;—I have in the interim begged Mr. Monroe with whom I have the honor to be Personally acquainted; sending him a Copy of my memorial, and of the Paragraph of your Letter to me on that subject, to sound the Ground, in speaking in my favor & if obstacles are Removed, to engage Mr. Livingston to make the necessary Demand, & I hope I will not be long now witht. a favorable answer from him;—there is the actual situation of that matter; but I continue more than ever, to be acknowledged here by the French authorities, who have the greatest Confidence in my Certificates to american Citizens, in this late unfortunate Circumstce. of war between France & england.

Please to excuse me for this Long & too Tedious Detail, on my Self and family, but your Goodness has perhaps too much prompted me to enter into it.

on Receipt of your Letter, I have been Eager to Collect the Sundries Productions, you asked of me for your own use;—some of them were out of the season rather too far advanced towards the summer to thin till november next to Send you any; There is neither now in Town any Good fresh Maccaroni of Naples, nor fresh viandes de Patte, pour les Potages; but I have wrote to Consul wollaston to procure me the nicest & best made by the nons of Genoa, with some fresh Maccaroni if there are any such as I wish for you, which I will put in to Jars.

The other articles, I have Shipped on Board the american Ship fair american John Spear Master, bound to Cette & Boston, as pr. Bill of Loading & the Invoice hereunto Inclosed; to the Consignation of the collector of the Customs at Boston; the whole amounting to *f*667—as to the white Wine of hermitage I wrote to the mayor of Tains, inclosing the copy of the Paragraph of your Letter on that subject; he answered me a civil Letter, offering me for that Purpose the services of his house of Commerce Messrs. Jourdan & fils, who supplies the high nobility of england, but I observing they did not Bear the names of the owners of the vineyard you mention to me, I have Lessened the quantity you wish for to 50 Bottles, which cost *f*4– pr. Bottle, and I Ordered them to send direct by the River Rhosne to cette where I hope they may be now arived & in time to be shipped on Board the same vessel, otherwise they would be on another one, since on the Loading there Bound to new York; as to the small amount of these articles and further ones I will ship in novber. next, you may whenever you will think Convenient, cause it to be reimburced to me in Paris on my Receipt for your account; you be I hope at time Of having tasted the hermitage & if satisfied of it's quality, I will then on your orders send you a Larger quantity.

allow me to renew you my best tender of Services in anything you may Command me;

I have the honor to be with the utmost Respect and Gratitude Dear Sir Your most humble & Devoted Servant

STEPHEN CATHALAN JUNR.

RC (DLC); at foot of first page: "The honorable Thos. Jefferson Esqre. President"; endorsed by TJ as received 17 Aug. and so recorded in SJL. Enclosures not found, but see below.

TJ had recently replaced Frederick Hyde WOLLASTON as the U.S. consul for GENOA. The State Department had received no word from Wollaston since 1800, and on 18 May TJ received a letter from DeWitt Clinton recommending John M. Goetschius. Two days later, TJ signed a commission for Goetschius to take the post at Genoa (Madison, *Papers, Sec. of State Ser.*, 6:99; commission, 20 May, in DNA: RG 59, PTCC; Clinton to TJ, 10 May, not found, recorded in SJL as received 18 May with notation "mr Goetschius. Sacket harb."; TJ to the Senate, 11 Nov.).

Cathalan sent ten containers to TJ aboard the FAIR AMERICAN: three cases holding a total of 72 bottles of olive oil; a case with 40 square bottles of olives; a case containing 12 bottles of capers, three bottles of anchovies, and one bottle of stuffed olives in oil; two cases containing a total of 48 bottles of preserved fruit in brandy; a jar holding 62 pounds (Marseilles weight) of dried and glazed fruit; a jar with 44 pounds of dates; and a jar containing 89 pounds of "Sundry Sorts of Almonds." In a letter to the COLLECTOR of customs at Boston, Benjamin Lincoln, Cathalan asked that the goods be forwarded to the president and, although he presumed that no duties would be collected on "Such triffling matters" intended for TJ's "own use," he included an invoice of the shipment. The *Fair American* arrived in Boston early in August (Cathalan to collector, 19 May, in DNA: RG 36, Boston; *New-England Palladium*, 5 Aug.).

The 50 bottles of HERMITAGE wine did not reach Sète in time to be shipped with the foodstuffs. Instead, at Cathalan's request a Sète firm sent the wine on the *Pyomingo*, which reached New York by 11 Aug. (Walsh & Cie. to collector of customs at New York, 9 June 1803, in MHi, enclosed in David Gelston to TJ, 12 Aug.; New York *Daily Advertiser*, 11 Aug.).

From George Jefferson

Dear Sir Richmond 31st. May 1803

The last of your Tobacco, excepting the light hogshead, which I suppose will not come to us arrived to day. I am very apprehensive that the heavy rains we have lately had may have injured it. I have been making some little inquiry to day, and am doubtful whether the price of seven dollars can be now obtained without opening it, or at least a few Hhds.—the noise which was made by M. & F. respecting the crop they purchased for Jackson & Wharton, I suspect must have injured the credit of yr. crops. Richard, likewise, who purchased the last crop for the same persons, I am inclined to think has been of no service to them; he says it turned out but tolerably,—yet appears anxious to get the present crop.

Although I disapprove of the practice of opening Tobacco generally, yet under existing circumstances I think it will be advisable to open a few hhds. of yours.—I shall however wait your orders. The current price of transient Hhds is now 33/.—that of good known crops about 40/. yet a few particular Hhds of *prime* quality, and which it was supposed would suit particular markets, have sold even as high as 50/.!

I am Dear Sir Your Very humble servt. Geo. Jefferson

RC (MHi); at foot of text: "Thos. Jefferson esqr."; endorsed by TJ as received 3 June and so recorded in SJL.

In late 1800, the Richmond firm McMurdo & Fisher purchased TJ's tobacco crop on behalf of the Philadelphia concern of JACKSON & WHARTON and subsequently forwarded the latter firm's report on the crop's poor quality. John Richard was Jackson & Wharton's buyer for TJ's LAST CROP (Vol. 32:516, 545-7; Vol. 38: 430). Richard, who was frequently identified as Richards, moved to Richmond from Philadelphia, where he had handled a number of transactions on behalf of John Barnes and TJ (Vol. 32:64; Vol. 33:289n; Vol. 35:11, 225).

From Wilson Cary Nicholas

Dear Sir Lexington May 31. 1803

I had not the pleasure of receiving your favour of the 22d. of Apl. until the day before yesterday. Be pleased Sir to accept my most cordial thanks for the very friendly attention that you have paid to my letter, asking an appointment for the son of my brother and be assured that I wou'd not in his case, or any other propose any person to you for an office, where I believed there was a possibility of injury to the public service, or that the appointment wou'd give justifiable ground of dissatisfaction in any part of this State. Since I came here

I have taken pains to inform my self as to the character and qualifications of R. C. Nicholas. I can now inform you that he is a man of unquestionable good character as to morals, and I think possesses an excellent understanding. I have endeavoured to ascertain the opinion that is entertained of him by the respectable part of the people in this State who know him, I believe they woud subscribe to the character that I have given of him. I have lately read the missisipi law and attended particularly to the duties assigned to the different officers that are to be appointed under it, and feel a full confidence that R.C.N. is competent to discharge all the duties assigned to the commissioner, with credit to himself and advantage to the public and individuals who are interested. When I ask this office for my nephew I beg you to be assured, I neither wish nor expect that he shou'd receive the appointment, if any other persons shou'd be in nomination for it, of superior qualifications. I have taken great pains to ascertain the real feelings of the people here about the New Orleans business, it is with great pleasure that I assure you that a vast majority of the people are perfectly satisfied with the measures that you have taken, but there is a general opinion that the restoration of the right of deposit only, will be very far short of what their interest requires and they most anxiously hope that their rights will be enlarged in some way or other. you will no doubt see in a Frankfort paper a most infamous letter from T. Davis to the people of this state. I expect to leave this place for virginia in two days.

I am Dear Sir with the greatest respect Your friend & humble Servant W. C. Nicholas

RC (DNA: RG 59, LAR); endorsed by TJ "Nicholas Rob. C. to be Commr. Missipi" and so recorded in SJL at 14 June. Enclosures: (1) Joseph H. Daveiss to Wilson Cary Nicholas, Lexington, 27 May, endorsing Robert Carter Nicholas, a personal acquaintance, as a man of integrity, "very clear understanding," and a remarkable "power of judgment" (RC in same). (2) Recommendation by Harry Innes, 30 May, noting that for over a decade he was a friend of the late George Nicholas; he has formed an opinion of the talents of his children and considers R. C. Nicholas "a young man of strict integrity & possessing strong mental faculties & great firmness" (MS in same; in Innes's hand and signed by him). (3) Certificate of Thomas Todd, 30 May 1803, acknowledging his "great intimacy" with the family of George Nicholas since 1789 and certifying that the eldest son, R. C. Nicholas, "has ever been considered as a young man of strict integrity, possessing strong mental faculties & great firmness" (MS in same; in Todd's hand and signed by him). (4) John A. Seitz and James Morrison to W. C. Nicholas, 31 May 1803; in response to Nicholas's inquiries, the bankruptcy commissioners, without hesitation, recommend R. C. Nicholas as a "Gentleman possessed of Considerable talents, a sound & correct Judgment & unquestionable integrity"; any position he consents to hold will be executed "to the satisfaction of his friends & to his own credit" (RC in same, perhaps in Morrison's hand, signed by both; Vol. 37:402).

OPINION THAT IS ENTERTAINED OF HIM: Nicholas probably enclosed in this letter the testimonies in favor of his nephew described above. TJ received one other recommendation, dated 12 June and signed by Kentucky judges George Muter, Benjamin Sebastian, and Caleb Wallace. It certified that Robert C. Nicholas was "generally considered as a young man of strict integrity, possessing strong mental faculties & great firmness" (MS in DNA: RG 59, LAR, in an unidentified hand, signed by all; Madison, *Papers*, 1: 239n; Madison, *Papers, Sec. of State Ser.*, 4:252n; 7:93n).

INFAMOUS LETTER: in a 15 May letter to his Kentucky constituents, Thomas T. Davis announced his retirement from elected office. In his review of events of the last session of Congress, Davis expressed his displeasure with the administration's handling of the closure of the right of deposit at New Orleans. He did not favor sending an envoy to Europe, declaring that "a weak nation must beg for its rights but a strong one ought to demand them." He thought the closure was an act of the Spanish court, not of the local intendant, and that U.S. troops should have been immediately dispatched to take possession of the port. If the intendant was responsible for the action, Davis argued, the court of Spain could not blame the U.S. for resisting "with *manly firmness*, any unauthorised aggression on our national rights." If it was an act of the Spanish court, the U.S. had a duty to protect its "citizens in the enjoyment of a right secured to them by treaty." Davis asserted that New Orleans "and the adjacent country must belong to the United States, or the fruit of the people in the western country will always be in the power of the foreign nation holding that port." The U.S. Treasury "could well afford the support of the army necessary to conquer the country, and western men a plenty would execute the enterprise." If the French gained possession of that country, Davis protested, hopes of the U.S. ever obtaining it were very faint. He concluded: "I believe we have let the golden opportunity pass by, without reaping the benefits it offered us." At the next election, Davis hoped Kentucky would elect "independent men" who would firmly contend for the rights of the western people and "view with becoming jealousy the growing influence of the great states of New-York and Virginia." *Poulson's American Daily Advertiser* reprinted Davis's letter from the Frankfort *Palladium* on 20 June.

From William Bache

DEAR SIR. June 1st. 1803. New Orleans.

It was not until the first week in may that I was permitted to exercise my functions in this place, since which time I have been fully employed. From the annexed list you will be able to judge the insufficiency of the late appropriation as an adequate releif for the sick even during the four sickly months of the year. May is deem'd here a healthy month, and yet in the last three weeks of that month 18 objects of charity have offered & had the knowledge of the institution been more general, in all probability there would have been more applications.

If the grand object of the Preservation of our fellow citizens is to be gone into in its fullest extent something more than medical assistance will be found absolutely necessary. The sick boatman must have a retreat from the scorching heat of the sun, & the penetrating dews of the night and the Sailor in cases of contagion should not remain on board Ship. If in these cases rescourse is had to lodging houses more expence will accrue in two months than a hospital would cost in one year. such are the enormous charges of tavern keepers & nurses. The following is the list of patients & their diseases &c.

John Mitchell—	New england,	shippg.	Luxatio.	well.
Henry Botts.	Philadelphia.	Do.	Rheumats.	well
James Neunan.	——	Do.	Scarlatina	well
John Smith	New York.	Do.	Syphilis—	well
Paul Sanbourn	Do—	Do.	Peripneumn.	well
Robt. Milligan black.	Do.	Do.	Abscess—	well
Wm Giles black	Do—	Do.	Syphilis—	
Joseph Newman—	Do—	Do.	Syphilis—	
name not known.	Kentucky.	boats.	diarrhœa—	dead
Nicholas Reed—	Pennsylvania	Do.	Feb: Bil. rem.	well
—— White—	Do—	Do—	Do—	Do—
Pat. Maloy—	Do—	Do—	Do—	Do—
John ——	Do—	Do—	Do—	Do—
Wm Smith—	Do—	Do—	Syphilis—	—
John Pine.	Kentucky—	Do—	Anasarca	—
Joseph Bridgham	—	boats—	diarrhœa.	well
Saml. Chapin—	Pennsylvania	Do.	Feb. bil: rem.	well
Saml. Kertright	Do—	Do—	Do—	Do—

As nothing can be done further in the business untill the next session Mr Clarke in conjunction with Mr Hulings and myself will prepare a plan the better adapted to the circumstances of this place, & which will require some thought & leisure, but which we will forward for your consideration before the expiration of summer. accept of my grateful & res[pectful] considerations William Bache

Mr Dayton & young Dearborn arriv'd here yesterday after a delay at Natchez of two or three days.

RC (DLC); torn; addressed: "Thomas Jefferson. President of the U.S. Washington City"; franked; postmarked New York, 6 July; endorsed by TJ as received 9 July and so recorded in SJL.

EXERCISE MY FUNCTIONS: that is, begin work as the doctor for the marine hospital at New Orleans (Vol. 37:619-20; Bache to TJ, 29 Mch.).

Luxation or LUXATIO was a dislocated joint (Robley Dunglison, *A Dictionary of Medical Science*, 6th ed. [Philadelphia, 1846], 457-8).

RHEUMATS.: rheumatismus, here probably meaning rheumatic fever (same, 652-3).

PERIPNEUMN.: peripneumonia, a term for pneumonia (same, 593).

FEB: BIL. REM.: that is, *febris biliosa remittens*, bilious remittent fever—probably malaria (Erwin H. Ackerknecht, *Malaria in the Upper Mississippi Valley, 1760-1900* [Baltimore, 1945], 6; George M. Sternberg, *Malaria and Malarial Diseases* [New York, 1884], 211-12, 224; Dr. Mouat, "Observations on Diseases at Bangalore," *Madras Quarterly Medical Journal*, 2 [1840], 1-3; Dunglison, *Dictionary of Medical Science*, 315, 647).

Jonathan DAYTON, who had been involved in controversial land speculation schemes, spent about six weeks in New Orleans. He traveled there via the Ohio and Mississippi Rivers and returned to the United States by sea (Madison, *Papers, Sec. of State Ser.*, 5:226; Kline, *Burr*, 2:798n; New York *American Citizen*, 29 July; *Alexandria Expositor*, 5 Aug.; *Poulson's American Daily Advertiser*, 13 Aug.; ANB).

From John Hollins

SIR Balto. 1st. June 1803

I had the honor to address you yesterday at the request of our esteemed friend Mr P. Carr, in which was enclosed a letter for his Bro. informing of the alarming indisposition of P.C. & requesting his Bro. S.C. to visit Baltimore, all which I now confirm; & sorry indeed am I to add, that in my opinion, appearances are still more unfavourable to a speedy recovery. The Doctors, Brown & Littlejohn, concluded last evening to put a Blister on each leg, what effect they have, or may produce, I cannot pretend to say, but Mrs. Hollins, who has been up with him all Night, says he rested badly with a regular succession from fever to chill, & so on.

Mrs. C. appears much alarmed, indeed poor Woman I fear she has too much cause for it.

I have used this freedom in some degree to ease my mind, believing at the same time the intrusion I give will not be thot. too officious—

JNO. HOLLINS

RC (MHi); endorsed by TJ as received 1 June.

A letter of the previous day from Hollins, recorded in SJL as received from Baltimore that same day, has not been found. Hollins was a brother-in-law of TJ's nephew Peter CARR (Vol. 38:18-19, 632n).

S.C.: Samuel Carr.

To Levi Lincoln

TH:J. TO MR LINCOLN. June 1 1803.

On reading a paragraph in the N.Y. Evening post, I took up my pen to write a squib on it; but the subject ran away with me till I found I had written a treatise. it is one on which I have a great desire to reconcile the parties among the republicans, & the paragraph in the post seemed to offer an occasion of taking just ground, & introducing a public discussion of it, on which I have no doubt the opinion of all candid men would settle together with that of the executive. the interest I take in the question made me willing to hazard a few lines for the press, altho' I have thro' life[1] scrupulously refrained from it; insomuch that this is but the second instance of my being willing to depart from my rule. I have written it under the character of a Massachusets citizen, with a view to it's appearing in a paper there; the Chronicle I suppose is most read, but how to get it there, divested of the evidence of my handwriting? think of this if you please; correct the paper also to make it what it should be, & we will talk of it the first time we meet. friendly salutations, & religious silence about it.

P.S. it probably requires considerable pruning to adopt it to the character and feelings of a Massachusets writer. of this you can judge best, and will be so good as to perform the operation with severity.

RC (DLC). PrC (DLC); lacks postscript.

BUT THE SECOND INSTANCE: TJ may have thought of his piece on Connecticut politics printed by Samuel H. Smith as a recent departure from the rule (see Noble E. Cunningham, Jr., *The Jeffersonian Republicans in Power, Party Operations, 1801-1809* [Chapel Hill, 1963], 256; TJ to Smith, 21 May).

DIVESTED OF THE EVIDENCE OF MY HANDWRITING: Lincoln undoubtedly made a copy of TJ's essay, which he then submitted to the Boston *Independent Chronicle* for publication, but it has not been found. No notice of the piece was taken after its appearance in the 27 June issue, indicating that TJ's authorship was not suspected at the time. Lincoln returned TJ's manuscript; both the original and press copy are in TJ's papers (see Enclosure below). For other examples of TJ using an amanuensis to keep his authorship a secret, see Vol. 29:491-3 and Vol. 30:529-35, 549n.

Instead of CONSIDERABLE PRUNING, a concluding paragraph was added to TJ's essay (see note 18 at Enclosure printed below). Perhaps Lincoln and TJ composed it together, but no evidence has been found to indicate TJ's involvement.

[1] TJ here canceled "carefully."

ENCLOSURE

"Fair play"

Federalism returning to reason, tho not to good manners.[1] no matter. decency will come in turn, when outrages on it are found to reflect only on those who commit them.

The symptom[2] of returning reason to those pitiable maniacs is the following paragraph in the N. York Evening post of May 24. where, speaking of the removal of mr Rogers the naval officer, a revolutionary tory, an Englishman & not even a citizen, till the expectation of office suggested to him the expediency of becoming one; & of the appointment of mr Osgood, a member of the Old Congress & President of it's board of treasury, & Postmaster general under the administration of Genl Washington, mr Coleman says 'the democrats have not long since had the impudence & *contempt of truth* to declare, that, notwithstanding the removals, the federalists hold still a greater number of offices than they do themselves. in answer to which we have sometimes replied that, in point of value there was no comparison, & that every office of any value, *in this city* at least, if not in the US. except one, had been transferred to the Jeffersonian sect, & that one is now gone.' and then he goes on with his usual scurrilities against the chief magistrate of his country, which shall not be here repeated; and with references to the President's reply to the New Haven remonstrance. I remember that in that reply it was asked 'Whether it is political intolerance for the majority to claim *a proportionate share* in the direction of the public affairs? and, if a *due participation* of office is a matter of right, how it is to be obtained but by some removals, when nearly the whole offices of the US. are monopolised by a particular political sect?'[3] the reasonableness of this claim to a *due proportion* of office was felt by every candid man at the first blush. but it did not accord with the feelings of federalists. nothing but a continuance in their monopoly of office could satisfy them: and, on the removal of the first individual, the whole band opened on the violation of their sanctuary of office, as if a general sweep had been made of every federalist within it's pale. after much uproar however repeated on every single removal, not finding in the President that want of nerve which with atheism, hypocrisy, malice &c &c &c they have so liberally lent him, but that, on the contrary, regardless of their barking, he proceeded steadily towards his object of restoring to the excluded republicans some participation in office; they find it expedient to lower their tone a little. they can now bear to talk themselves of an *equal number*, instead of a monopoly, of offices. this is well, as a first symptom; & we hope, in the progress of convalescence, they will become able to bear the idea of a *due proportion*. on this ground we are ready to compromise with them: and I ask what is their due proportion? I suppose the relative numbers of the two parties will be thought to fix it; & that, judging from the elections, we over-rate the federalists at one third or fourth of the whole mass of our citizens. in a few states, say New Hampsh. Massachus. & Connecticut, they have a greater proportion; but in the others much less. by mr Coleman's expression 'that every office in this city [New York] is transferred to the Jeffersonian sect,' it seems expected that the distribution of office, in every town & county taken by itself,[4] is to be in proportion to it's party division. this is impossible. it is questionable whether the scale of proportion can ever be known & preserved in individual states, and whether we must not be contented with considering all the states as forming a single mass. I am not qualified to say, taking the state of New York by itself, how it's parties are proportioned either in numbers or offices. but I think it probable that, if mr Coleman will extend his views beyond the limits of the city, thro' the whole state, he will find his brethren possessing much more than their *due share* of office. I invite him to this examination, & doubt not the republicans of New York will attend to his statements, & correct them if erroneous. confining myself to my own state, that I may speak only of what I know, I can assure mr Coleman we are far below our *just proportion*. the Roll of offices published by Congress at their session before the last, informs me that in the revenue department alone of Massachusets, there are 183. officers; of whom 33. are appointed by the President. of these he has removed 7. either on the principle of participation, or because they were active, bitter and indecent opposers of the existing legislature & Executive. I will name them that I may be corrected if I am wrong, not meaning wilfully to mistate any thing. they were, Lee of Penobscot, Head of Waldoboro', Tuck & Whittermore of Gloucester, Tyng of Newburyport, Fosdyck[5] of Portland, & Pickman of Salem. there have been two or three other removals in this state, but we have understood they were[6] for misconduct. in Boston alone are about 30 revenue officers, dependant on the collector, who, with the Naval officer, surveyor & revenue inspectors, recieve under the general government between 40. & 50,000 D. a year the whole weight of whose numbers, patronage & connections is actively exerted in opposition to that government, & renders the issue of the Boston election always doubtful; when, if shifted into the scale which is in support of the government, there would no longer be any question, and Boston, one of the great cities of the US. would arrange herself, at her proper post, under the banners of the union. and at the head of this massive phalanx is a character, otherwise respectable & meritorious;[7] but certainly not so when leading processions & joining in dinners, where toasts the most insulting and outrageous against the president personally & other constituted authorities, & calculated to excite seditious combinations[8] against the authority of the Union, are drank with riotous acclamations within, & announced with the roar of cannon without. if mr Coleman counts the[9] continuance of this gentleman in office among the proofs of the intolerance of the President, I can furnish him more such. In the judiciary department we had imagined that, the judges being federal, republican attornies & marshals would be appointed to mollify in the execution what is rigorously decreed; & that republicans might find in our courts some of that protection which flows from fellow-feeling, while their opponents enjoy that which the laws are made to pronounce. in some of the states this has been done. but here I see mr Bradford[10] still holding the office of marshal, to execute federally what the judges shall federally decree: an office too of great patronage & influence in this state, & acting with all it's dependencies heavily in our elections. while in the expressions of my opinion I yield sincere respect to the authorities of my country, due to their own worth, as well as to the will of the nation establishing them, yet I am free to declare my opinion, that they are wrong in retaining this person[11] in office. I respect his private character; but his political bias unfits him for qualifying that of the court. In the post-offices of Massachusets are about 200 officers. I know not how many may have been removed by the Postmaster Genl. but judging by the sound in the federal papers, which is never below truth, I should conjecture a very small proportion indeed. it should be observed too that these offices are solely within the gift & removal of the Post Mast. Genl. the President & Senate having nothing to do with them.

Hitherto I have spoken of the federalists as if they were a homogeneous body. but this is not the truth. under that name lurks the heretical sect of monarchists. afraid to wear their own name, they creep under the mantle of federalism, & the federalists, like sheep, permit the fox to take shelter among them, when pursued by the dogs. these men have no right to office. if a monarchist be in office any where, & it be known to the President, the oath he has taken to support the constitution, imperiously requires the instantaneous dismission of such officer; & I should hold the President highly criminal if he permitted such to remain. to appoint a monarchist to conduct the affairs of a republic, is like appointing an Atheist to the priesthood. but as to the real federalists, I take them to my bosom as brothers: I view them as honest men, friends to the present constitution. our difference has been about measures only, which now having past away, should no longer divide us. it was, how we should treat France for the injuries offered us? they thought the occasion called for armies & navies, that we should burthen ourselves with taxes, & our posterity with debts at exorbitant interest: that we should pass alien & sedition laws, punishing men with exile without trial by jury, & usurping the regulation of the press, exclusively belonging to the state governments.[12] we thought some of these measures inexpedient, others unconstitutional. they however were the majority, they carried their opinions into effect, & we submitted. the measures themselves are now done with, except the debts contracted, which we are honestly proceeding to pay off. why then should we longer be opposed to each other? I confess myself of opinion that this portion of our fellow-citizens should have a just participation of office, and am far from concurring with those who advocate a general sweep, without discriminating between federalist & monarchist. should not these recollect their own complaints against the late administration for proscribing them from all public trust? and shall we now be so inconsistent as to act ourselves on the very principle we then so highly condemned? to countenance the anti-social[13] doctrine that a minority has no rights? never let *us* do wrong, because our opponents did so. let us, rather, by doing right, shew them what they ought to have done, & establish into a rule[14] the dictates of reason & conscience, rather than of the angry passions. if the federalists will amalgamate with us on these terms, let us recieve them, and once more unite our country into one mass. but, as they seem to hold off with a remarkeable repugnance, I agree that in the mean time both justice & safety require a due proportion of office in republican hands. whether it is best to effect this by a single stroke, or to await the operation of deaths, resignations, & removals for delinquency, for virulent[15] opposition, & for monarchism, I am not satisfied: but am willing to leave it to the constitutional authorities, who, tho' they proceed slower than I had expected, yet are probably better judges than I am of the comparative merits of the two methods. the course they seem to have preferred tends more perhaps to allay the passions which so unpleasantly divide & disquiet us: & trusted, as they are, with the care of the public happiness, they are bound so to modify jarring principles as to effect that happiness as far as the state of things will admit. this seems too to be a fair ground of compromise between the extremes of opinion, even among republicans, some of whom think there should be a general removal, & others none at all. the latter opinion, I am told, is much entertained in the Southern states. Still I think it will be useful[16] to go into the examination of the question which party holds an overproportion of office? and I therefore again invite mr Coleman to take the field for the state of New York, not doubting but some champion there will enter the lists for the opposite interest.[17] in my own state the fact is too obvious that I believe no federalist here will undertake to question it. should such an one however appear, he will certainly find persons able & ready to confront him with facts.[18]

FAIR PLAY

MS (DLC); entirely in TJ's hand; undated; square brackets in original. PrC (DLC). Printed in the Boston *Independent Chronicle*, 27 June, with changes in capitalization, expansion of ampersands and abbreviations, and minor variations in punctuation; for other changes, including the addition of a final paragraph above the signature, see below.

On 12 July, the Springfield, Massachusetts, *Republican Spy* reprinted "Fair Play" from the Boston *Independent Chronicle*, but the essay was not widely reprinted in other newspapers during July 1803.

PARAGRAPH IN THE N. YORK EVENING POST: TJ quoted from the editorial captioned, "*Another Proof of Mr. Jefferson's Sincerity*." The words emphasized by TJ in the quote from the *Evening Post* were not italicized in the newspaper (*New-York Evening Post*, 24 May 1803).

REPLY TO THE NEW HAVEN REMONSTRANCE: see Vol. 34:554-8.

For the 1802 ROLL OF OFFICES, see ASP, *Miscellaneous*, 1:260-319, and Vol. 36:568-71.

TJ categorized his removals in lists he compiled in 1802 and 1803 with the PRINCIPLE OF PARTICIPATION for Republicans as one of the major "classes." In his chronological list of appointments, TJ noted that John Lee, Joshua Head, and Nathaniel F. Fosdick were removed for being "delinquent." William Watson, collector at Plymouth, was "removed for malconduct" and Republican Samuel R. Gerry, at Marblehead, for delinquency (Vol. 33:668-74, 677; Vol. 38:682; Vol. 39: Appendix I).

As the collector of customs, Benjamin Lincoln was HEAD OF THE MASSIVE PHALANX at Boston (ASP, *Miscellaneous*, 1:263).

In May 1801, TJ and the cabinet decided not to remove Samuel BRADFORD as U.S. marshal for the district of Massachusetts (Vol. 34:129-30; Vol. 38:613n). For opposition to Bradford, see Vol. 38: 662.

[1] In the *Independent Chronicle* the text to this point is rendered in italics and used as the title of the essay on "Politics. For the Chronicle."

[2] TJ first wrote "symptoms" and then canceled the final "s." *Independent Chronicle*: "symptoms."

[3] Opening single quotation mark supplied by Editors. TJ used only phrases from his reply to the New Haven merchants (see Vol. 34:555-6). The *Independent Chronicle* does not put the passage in quotes.

[4] Preceding three words interlined in MS.

[5] *Independent Chronicle*: "Fosdick."

[6] Preceding two words altered by TJ from "it was." *Independent Chronicle* lacks "they were."

[7] *Independent Chronicle*: "otherwise meritorious."

[8] *Independent Chronicle*: "seditions and combinations."

[9] TJ here canceled "toleration."

[10] The *Independent Chronicle* reads "But in others I see them" in place of "here I see mr Bradford." TJ interlined "I see" in MS.

[11] *Independent Chronicle*: "such persons"; the pronouns in the next sentence are changed from singular to plural.

[12] Preceding five words rendered in italics in the *Independent Chronicle*.

[13] *Independent Chronicle*: "Aristocratical."

[14] Preceding four words interlined in place of "follow." *Independent Chronicle*: "establish a rule of."

[15] *Independent Chronicle*: "violent."

[16] *Independent Chronicle*: "well."

[17] MS: remaining two sentences and signature written perpendicular to text in right margin.

[18] The *Independent Chronicle* continues with a concluding paragraph: "This may be done in a manner conducive to the general good. The prosperity of our common country ought to be the object of all. Deficient and unfortunate must have been his information, or deep his prejudices, who has not perceived, prevailing and unequivocal expressions of the public will in favor of administering the General Government on its existing principles. Why then intemperate opposition? In vain will be the attempt to drive or seduce the people from measures meriting support from a superior utility already experienced. In vain is the effort to destroy their increasing confidence in the tried ability and patriotism of the present Executive, or in the steady exertions of the present Legisla-

ture. Republicans thus entrenched, should be doubly solicitous to set examples of magnanimity, worthy themselves, and the cause they are engaged in. If there are federalists, whose feelings still prompt them to abuse and oppose the General Government, we urge them to consideration, to review the motives by which they are actuated, and the effects of such conduct on the national happiness. If distrust, seditions, and perpetuated discords in society, are abhorrent to their wishes, as they are destructive in their nature: If private animosity is as ungrateful as it is individually baneful, they will exhibit, if not the zeal of an attachment, if not the complacency of a cordial acquiescence, yet, certainly the patience and decency of a submission to the Constituted Authorities of their Country."

From Samuel Smith

SIR/ 6. O'Clock. 1 June 1803

I have this Moment left Mr. Carr, he is Something easier, the Blisters on his Back & Ankles have raised & are painful,—from appearances I Should expect he would recover,—but the Doctors do not believe it possible that he can.—The Mouth of the Bladder they Say is Stopped—my hope arises from a Small discharge of Urine this afternoon.—I need not Say that every possible attention has been given to his Case—he Scarcely appears to expect a Recovery, and has in Consequence made his Will this Morning—It will be for you to prepare his Mother for the Event, the attack has been sudden & violent from its Commencement—On Thursday he dined with me, and retired perfectly well, in the Night he was Seized, and chills & fever followed Successively—I hope his Brother is now on his Way—his appearance would afford Comfort—I am Sir

Your friend & Obedt. Servt. S. SMITH

RC (DLC); endorsed by TJ as received from Baltimore on 2 June and so recorded in SJL.

THURSDAY: that is, 26 May.

From Samuel Carr

DEAR SIR Baltimore 12 Oclock. June 2d 1803

With pleasure I hasten to inform you that my brother is much better than when Mr Hollins wrote you. I have conversed with Doctors Brown & Little John who attend him, and are of opinion that, tho' much better, he is still not out of danger. He has had a suppression of urine for nearly a week untill yesterday morning, when he was much relieved, by a copious discharge, or he could not in the opinion of his physicians have survived twelve hours. This evening his unfavorable symptoms have much abated except a hickup which is troublesome and distressing. My anxiety and hopes induce me to believe that in a few days he will be out of danger.

with sentiments of sincere attachment and esteem I remain Dr Sir Yr friend. & servt. SAMUEL CARR

RC (DLC); endorsed by TJ as received 3 June and so recorded in SJL. Probably enclosed in TJ to Thomas Mann Randolph, 4 June.

From Robert R. Livingston

DEAR SIR Paris 2d June 1803 midnight

Mr Monroe having undertaken to write our Joint letter on the subject of Louisiana I should confine mine to the Secretary of State[1] to objects that relate only to my individual Department, but I must communicate to you in the utmost confidence a circumstance that has just come to my knowledge & that must be known only to yourself & Mr Madisson because it will influence your measures.—You know that the ratifications have been delivered & that we were to send them directly to you, we have accordingly applied for a passport for Mr Jay the bearer.—to our note on this subject we received no answer I called this day on Mr Talleyrand to accelerate it; he was at St Cloud I called on the Minister of the Treasury. he was there also. I called again this night & am just[2] returned *they have been these two days past in Council and principally basting Mr. Marbois on the subject of the Treaty for it seems that the Consul is less pleased with it since the ratification than before and I [am]*[3] *persuaded that if he could conveniently get off he would, he insists that our whole debt does not exceed*[4] *four millions and that we have got twenty, that the delivering the ratifications to us was contrary to all form and that they must be recalled and given to Mr Pichon to exchange*[5] *and to this I believe we must consent as it is certainly regular tho' we shall first keep copies of the ratifications he insists that if the Stock is not delivered in the [time]*[6] *prescribed the Treaty is void* that as it is not to be created till after the delivery of the territory a party among us may create delays in taking possession &c *he insists upon writing to Pichon not to deliver them but upon a certainty that we will create the Stock &c and upon giving him certain discretionary powers &c in short he appears to wish the thing undone and he will not be sorry to see an opposition to its ratification with us or such a delay [as]*[7] *will render it void* I told you in a letter to Mr Madisson how & why the negotiation *was put into the hands of Mr Marbois This has not been forgiven by …*[8] *and I doubt not that every possible objection and*[9] *insinuation has been made use of to disgust the first Consul with it. To appease him in some measure Mr Marbois* has engaged to write a letter to us stating that it is understood that if the treaty is not complied within the time prescribed that it will be void—I have told him, that nothing we can write will change the treaty[10] that a non compliance on our part if unnecessary or done with bad faith might render it void. but that an accidental non complyance would not defeat it and I strongly objected to writing any thing upon the subject *he was very much distressed at what had passed and told me that he had done every thing for us & that we must not sacrifice him you will see his letter and our answer he promised to send it tomorrow we will take care that the answer shall occasion no change in the Treaty which indeed is impossible it should, but we must as far as we can soothe the youthful Conqueror whose will knows no resistance* I will add nothing to this, Mr Monroe I presume will so frame our joint letter as to give you every necessary information[11]—You see the object of this is to guard you[12] against any *delays but*[13] *above all against any change in the form of the ratification for be assured that the slightest pretence will be seized to undo the work* the first Consul had expressed much resentment at the change made in the former Convention when ratified and makes it a principal objection to having been induced to send the ratification before you had agreed to ratify it & will give[14] *express direction to Mr Pichon not to deliver the ratifications in case you make the slightest alteration it is necessary you should know this. it is equally necessary that those who oppose the administration should not know it as it will be a trump card in their hands. I really pity Marbois* Instead of delivering an order they now talk of sending a special messenger, a Commissary to surrender the country, but I hope we shall induce them to change this resolution & give orders to Mr Pichon—

As it was near midnight when I left the treasury I have not been able to communicate with Mr Monroe on this subject or to tell him of the unexpected difficulties that have intervened, & as we are anxious to send off Mr Jay to morrow if they can be removed, & I have to write to Mr Madisson & we are[15] to adjust these matters with Mr Marbois, & with Mr Talleyrand and to sollicit a flag of truce[16]—the morrow will be fully occupied so that I cannot defer writing till I have seen him, & indeed I am under engagements that no official letter shall be written on[17] this subject, & with difficulty have obtained permission to mention it to you[18]—

I am Dear Sir, with much respect and esteem Your most obt hum: Servt

Robt R Livingston

Dr Sir

I mentioned to you in one of my former letters a wish to leave this this summer but as things are now circumstanced I think it best to remain at my station till the spring unless you shd order otherwise[19]

RC (DLC); in a clerk's hand, signed by Livingston, who added postscript, "duplicate" at head of text, and below signature: "Thomas Jefferson Esqr President US:A"; portions in same code as in Livingston's letter of 12 Mch.; text in italics is TJ's interlinear decipherment, and his corrections of significant coding anomalies are noted below; endorsed by TJ as received 17 Aug. and so recorded in SJL. RC (DLC); in Livingston's hand except coded passages inserted by clerk in gaps left by Livingston; not deciphered; at head of text: "private & confidential"; endorsed by TJ as received 24 Aug. Dupl (DNA: RG 59, Duplicate Dispatches); in a clerk's hand, signed by Livingston; at head of text: "Duplicate"; at foot of text in Livingston's hand: "Thomas Jefferson Esqr prest the United States" in place of canceled "The honble James Madison Esqr"; lacks postscript; coded passages not deciphered; notation by TJ at foot of text: "to be filed in Secy. of state's office"; endorsed by Jacob Wagner as received 30 Sep. Enclosed in TJ to Madison, 18 Aug. 1803.

Livingston's and Monroe's JOINT LETTER to Madison was dated 7 June (Madison, *Papers*, *Sec. of State Ser.*, 5:66-72).

MINE TO THE SECRETARY OF STATE: Livingston wrote to Madison on 3 June, responding to requests from the secretary of state that he press the case of John Rodgers and William Davidson over their detention at Cap-Français, protest the forcing of American ships to transport blacks from the island of Guadeloupe, and pursue other matters with the French government (same, 4:304-5, 344; 5:52-4; Vol. 37:427-8).

YOU KNOW: a dispatch from Monroe to Madison on 23 May announced that the American envoys had received the French ratifications of the Louisiana treaty and conventions from François Barbé de Marbois the day before; see also Livingston to TJ, 26 May (Madison, *Papers*, *Sec. of State Ser.*, 5:24-5). Although the treaty and two conventions were interdependent, the French government ratified each of them individually (Miller, *Treaties*, 2: 505-6).

Livingston and Monroe chose Peter Augustus JAY, a son of John Jay, to be the courier for the ratifications (Madison, *Papers*, *Sec. of State Ser.*, 5:47, 71).

MINISTER OF THE TREASURY: Barbé de Marbois.

IN A LETTER TO MR MADISSON: Livingston reported in a dispatch to Madison of 13 Apr. that Barbé de Marbois had taken on the negotiations over Louisiana (same, 4:511-15; Livingston to TJ, 14 Apr.).

HIS LETTER AND OUR ANSWER: according to the terms of the convention covering the financial payment for the cession, the United States was to issue the stock within three months of the exchange of ratifications and the transfer of possession of Louisiana. In a letter to Livingston and Monroe, Barbé de Marbois argued that the three-month term would start with the exchange of ratifications, not the transfer of possession, and that failure to comply with the deadline would void the convention. In reply, the American diplomats stated that it was the "duty" of the United States "to carry into effect the provisions of the treaty and conventions in the times therein specified," and the French should not bring up the matter of consequences unless the U.S. failed to meet its responsibility. Barbé de Marbois told the Americans that in Bonaparte's opinion the taking of possession of Louisiana by the United States could be delayed indefinitely if Spain was slow in giving up the colony, if the British took control of it before the United States had possession, or by other circumstances. In their joint letter to Madison of 7 June, Monroe and Livingston expressed an opinion that the first consul might have become dissatisfied with the financial terms of the cession and hoped, by setting the deadline at three months from the exchange of ratifications, to nullify the transaction. In an undated postscript, Livingston reported that the French government "of its own accord" had officially withdrawn Barbé de Marbois's letter and returned the Americans' response to it, but had not changed its position regarding the potential voiding of the convention (Miller, *Treaties*, 2:514; Madison, *Papers*, *Sec. of State Ser.*, 5: 67-8, 70-1, 71n).

GUARD AGAINST ANY DELAYS: "It is our earnest wish and advice if the treaties are approved by the president," Monroe and Livingston declared in the joint letter, "that he convene the Congress to provide the funds for an immediate compliance with them." Also, although it was Pichon's responsibility to send the bonds when they were ready, Livingston and Monroe recommended that a U.S. naval vessel be used to take the certificates to France to avoid delay. "We cannot too strongly impress an idea," the envoys wrote, "if our conduct is approved, of the most prompt execution of the stipulations to be performed on our part, and of a course of proceeding which leaves nothing to chance, by giving any cause of complaint" to the French (same, 68-9).

CHANGE MADE IN THE FORMER CONVENTION WHEN RATIFIED: according to Barbé de Marbois, Bonaparte considered his country's ratification of the Louisiana treaty and conventions to be subject to change until the United States ratified the documents. Citing the precedent of the Convention of 1800, which the U.S. Senate had ratified only after removing one article and adding a limit of duration, Bonaparte threatened to append conditions to his ratification of the Louisiana sale (same, 67; Vol. 33:22n).

GIVE ORDERS TO MR PICHON: on 6 June, Denis Decrès, the minister of marine and the colonies, signed instructions to Pichon for the transfer of Louisiana. Once ratifications had been exchanged, the chargé was to see that possession of the colony was ceded from Spain to France and immediately from France to the United States. Instructions from Talleyrand of 7 June authorized Pichon to proceed with the exchange of ratifications. He was to add to the official record two clauses, one stating that the United States must fulfill its obligations even if the British should occupy Louisiana, the other declaring that the treaty and conventions would become null if the U.S. did not follow the financial terms specified in those agreements. The French government put the instructions from the ministers, which were in cipher, and the ratification documents into an envelope that Livingston and Monroe gave to Jay, who was to convey it to Madison for transmittal to Pichon. The packet also included a letter from Talleyrand to Madison confirming the French ratification and one from Barbé de Marbois, as finance minister, to Gallatin, enclosing a copy of a contract of 12 Floréal (2 May) between the French government and two banking firms, Francis Baring & Company of London and Hope & Company of Amsterdam. That agreement had been made in consultation with Livingston and Monroe, who wanted to ensure that the price of the stock issued for the purchase of Louisiana would not drop from open trading in the United States or Europe. In the contract, the Baring and Hope firms agreed to buy all of the stock from France. Baring & Company had become bankers in London for U.S. government transactions, and that firm had long-standing business and personal connections to Hope & Company, which could make payments in France. The American envoys enclosed a copy of the contract in their 7 June joint letter to Madison. Jay, who also carried Livingston's and Monroe's dispatches and copies of the French ratifications, traveled on the *Oliver Ellsworth*, which sailed from Le Havre on 23 June and stopped at Rochelle on the west coast of France before crossing the Atlantic. The ship, boarded twice en route by British privateers and once by a Royal Navy frigate, arrived in New York on 18 Aug. (Madison, *Papers*, *Sec. of State Ser.*, 4:509, 534; 5:47n, 55, 66-8, 70, 71, 81, 89, 98, 105, 123, 251, 294, 355-7, 365, 386; J. E. Winston and R. W. Colomb, "How the Louisiana Purchase was Financed," *Louisiana Historical Quarterly*, 12 [1929], 189-237; Ralph W. Hidy, *The House of Baring in American Trade and Finance: English Merchant*

Bankers at Work, 1763-1861 [Cambridge, Mass., 1949], 31-4; Martin G. Buist, *At Spes Non Fracta: Hope & Co. 1770-1815, Merchant Bankers and Diplomats at Work* [The Hague, 1974], 39, 40, 53-4, 57-8; King, *Life*, 4:223-4; New York *Evening Post*, 19 Aug.).

[1] 2d RC: "mine to Mr Madison."

[2] In place of this word 2d RC has "this moment."

[3] This word, omitted by Livingston's clerk in the coded passage of the RC, has been supplied from the code in the 2d RC and Dupl.

[4] In accordance with the code in the MS, TJ first wrote "sent" (code 379). He corrected it to "exceed" (code 1379); Weber, *United States Diplomatic Codes*, 469, 475. The word was coded correctly in the Dupl, incorrectly in the 2d RC.

[5] In accordance with the code in the MS, TJ first wrote "Europe change" (codes 1375 and 21). He corrected that to "exchange" (codes 1377 and 21); Weber, *United States Diplomatic Codes*, 475. 2d RC and Dupl both contain the coding error.

[6] TJ's brackets. "Time" (code 843) is his substitution for "to" (code 849) in MS (Weber, *United States Diplomatic Codes*, 472). 2d RC and Dupl both contain the error.

[7] TJ's brackets. As coded in MS, the word (code 1627) would be "ay" instead of "as" (code 1657). Dupl contains the error; 2d RC has code 1327, "der" (Weber, *United States Diplomatic Codes*, 475, 477).

[8] This ellipsis also appears in 2d RC and Dupl.

[9] Word coded correctly in MS (code 1667), but TJ first wrote "that" before correcting himself (Weber, *United States Diplomatic Codes*, 477).

[10] Dupl: "nothing we can write will avail."

[11] Preceding nine words are in code in 2d RC and Dupl.

[12] Word lacking in 2d RC and Dupl.

[13] TJ first wrote "that" and then substituted "but," although "and" (code 1667) was the correct word (Weber, *United States Diplomatic Codes*, 477).

[14] Preceding eight words and ampersand lacking in 2d RC.

[15] MS: "let." Dupl: "we are to adjust these matters"; 2d RC: "we must adjust the business."

[16] 2d RC: "obtain passports."

[17] 2d RC: "shall enter into."

[18] 2d RC: "to state it thus fully to you." 2d RC concludes: "The french troops have entered Hanover & are by this time I believe in full possession—I have the honor to be Dear Sir With the most respectful consideration Your Most Obt hum: servt."

[19] 2d RC postscript: "PS. I wrote a few days ago informing you my williness to remain here till the spring as I believe the present state of things may render it necessary to await the return of your ratification & to adjust difficulties on the subject of the debts &c. after which it will be too late to sail."

From Charles Willson Peale

Dear Sir Museum June 2d. 1803.

After a long silence Rembrandt again communicates to me, dated London March 28th.—1803. "*The best news I can tell you*, is that we are all well from, Influenza, coughs & colds, and feel the balmy breath of Spring; Nothing but a tempory Fog obscures the morning Sun, our Parlour fire is extinguished, the buds are bursting & the fragrant Hyacinth is drest in all her gaiety: such a pleasing change on the face of Nature in unnatural London almost[1] compels us to be happy!

The worst news I can tell you is that from present appearances, the Exhibitional income will not afford us the means of leaving London. Had we landed in November & opened in December, I have no doubt but that it would have done something handsome. My debt, at this moment to Mr. Vaughan for the rent of the Room &c amounts to *350 Dollars more* than I am in possession of. Gladly would I hide this[2] picture from your sight, but unless you see it you cannot excuse my deficiences in writing—perhaps I may look with too serious an eye to this adverse cloud, but I certainly have done more to deserve success since I have been here than I ever thought I could—every nerve has been strained and every Cel in my brain has been racked. I really believe had I continued to exhibit in America & sold it there, I should have money enough to purchase a Home and to have enabled me to spend a few months in London & Paris with great advantage." again, "Much as Bones may tend to strengthen & exhilerate when properly treated in a *Digester*, yet hung on a London Gallows (that is a Gallows in London) they afford but a *Tyburn* kind of comfort! for Fortune has not touched them with her wand."

My other Son (Rubens) writes me, "that Rembrandt has began a Portrait of the celebrated Bloomfield the author of *Farmers Boy*, and will begin the likeness's of Sir Joseph Banks and the celebrated Mr. Erskin the Lawyer."

Rembrandt says, "some evenings since I was present at Mr. Pepys (a Scientific Citizen who has a private Laboratory where every Monday his particular friends are invited to converse or experiment) when he exhibited some brilliant experiments in Galvanism; the Battery consisted of 60 double plates of Copper & Zinc soldered togather 6 Inches square (180 square feet) fitted into a trough and each rendered water tight so as not to suffer the liquid to flow between them—2 Gallons of water & 2 quarts of nitric Acid were mixed & put between them. Moveable wires connected the first and last troughs & the effects were truely astonishing, Charcoal of Box was instantly in a red heat, wires and leaves of Gold, Silver, Platina lead, Tin, Iron &c were instantly, inflamed, melted & Calcined—these effects lasted three hours—Something wonderful will certainly be discovered by means of this extraordinary agent.

Wars and rumours of wars, have lately much alarmed the good folk here, I have felt no uneasiness, not being willing to persuade myself either nation would foolishly rush into the folly again. Still all is a mystery & the mighty Politicians heart still palpitates.

But I believe something is to be apprehended betwixt America & France. Avert it heaven!"

I have given extracts of the most interesting parts of my Sons letters—I wish Rembrandt had been more particular—had given me some account of what prospects he had of selling the Skeleton in London, or whether he might not dispose of it to the Paris Museum reserving the exhibition of it for a stated period, as Mr. Roume proposed to the National Institute. If he should try to visit Paris, perhaps our Ministers or Consuls might render them some services in the necessary pasports of his Packing Cases from London to Paris—The countenance of a Public officer is often of greater import than Money.

I shall write to Mr. Vaughan to inform him that I will pay the Principal part of what is due to him if Rembrandt draws on me.

I hope Rembrandt will not want friends to aid him if it is known that he is in want.

I have made for him a Portable Physiognotrace of Mr. Hawkins invention which I will send by Mr Hawkins who has now taken his passage for England in a Vessel which is to sail about the 18th.—

Mr. Hawkins intends to visit Paris soon after his arrival in England. His object is to make some profit by his improvements of Musical Instruments.

He requests me to ask your favor of recommendations to some of your corrispondants in that City.

I send Enclosed some profiles, presuming it is not necessary to say of whom. The correctness of likeness given by this engenious invention, brings considerable numbers of Visitors to my Museum. very probable Rembrandt if he now had one it might help to carry him through his difficulties.

I am with much esteem your friend C W PEALE

RC (DLC); at foot of text: "His Excellency Thomas Jefferson Esqr."; endorsed by TJ as received 4 June and so recorded in SJL. PoC (PPAmP: Peale-Sellers Papers). Enclosures not found.

Rembrandt and Rubens Peale became indebted to the London merchant and philanthropist William VAUGHAN at the outset of their visit to Britain, when he loaned them money to pay customs duties on their mastodon bones. Vaughan, a brother of Benjamin and John Vaughan, was a member of the Royal Society and other learned societies (Peale, *Papers*, v. 2, pt. 1:467, 485; DNB; Vol. 35:699n).

The DIGESTER was a pressure cooker invented by Denis Papin in the 1670s. The elder Peale had incorporated such devices into his designs for kitchens (OED; H. W. Robinson, "Denis Papin [1647-1712]," *Notes and Records of the Royal Society of London*, 5 [1947], 47-50; Vol. 33:222, 224n).

Public executions had formerly taken place at TYBURN Hill in London (Peale, *Papers*, v. 2, pt. 1:534n).

The portraits by Rembrandt Peale were of the poet Robert BLOOMFIELD, Joseph Banks, and Thomas Erskine. William Hasledine PEPYS was a surgical instrument maker and inventor (same, 534-5n).

CHARCOAL OF BOX: chemists put charcoal made from boxwood to various uses in the laboratory (J. G. Children, "An Account of Some Experiments with a

Large Voltaic Battery," in Royal Society of London, *Philosophical Transactions*, 105 [1815], 369; *Palmer's New Catalogue of Chemical and Philosophical Apparatus*, 2d ed. with supplement [London, 1839], 43).

In Rembrandt Peale's report from London, the MIGHTY politician was William Pitt (Peale, *Papers*, v. 2, pt. 1:535n).

PARIS MUSEUM: after viewing the mastodon skeleton on display in Philadelphia, Philippe Rose ROUME urged that the elder Peale be made a corresponding member of the National Institute and that the French government purchase, for the Muséum d'Histoire Naturelle in Paris, the skeleton that his sons had taken across the Atlantic for exhibition (same, 535n; *Philosophical Magazine*, 13 [1802], 206-8; Tulard, *Dictionnaire Napoléon*, 1212; Vol. 37:566n).

I SHALL WRITE TO MR. VAUGHAN: Peale wrote to William Vaughan on 4 June, saying that by curtailing expenditures at his museum he could let Rembrandt draw on him for $200, half at 60 days' sight and half at 30 days' sight. In a letter to his father dated 20 July, Rubens Peale reported that Rembrandt had settled their account with Vaughan as the brothers closed their exhibit in London and moved the skeleton to Reading (Peale, *Papers*, v. 2, pt. 1:535-6, 584-5).

[1] MS: "almosts."
[2] MS: "his."

From Samuel Smith

SIR/ Baltimore 2d. June 1803

When I paid my respects yesterday I had no great expectation that I should now have the pleasure to say that Mr. Carr's Illness had taken a favorable turn—He has had a free Discharge & I am in hopes is now out of Danger—The Doctors do not yet give very positive favorable Opinion but being relieved from the Suppression his Strong Constitution will Soon defeat his Fever—I think I never have Seen a Man apparently worse than he was yesterday—I am

with Sincere friendship Your Obed Servt. S. SMITH

RC (DLC); endorsed by TJ as received 3 June and so recorded in SJL. Probably enclosed in TJ to Thomas Mann Randolph, 4 June.

From Reuben Harvey

RESPECTED FRIEND Cork 3rd. June 1803

Altho' I have retired from business these several Years, being advanced in Age, I am notwithstanding induced through a long continued regard for the United States of America, to represent to thee the great injury which your Commerce now suffers on this Coast by the pressing of Men from every American Vessel that is met by British Ships of War. In general there are two or more taken, out of each Vessel, & the Juno from Norfolk—which touch'd here on her Voyage to Liverpool lost five—As I am ignorant of the Treatys existing between Great Britain & America I cannot pretend to say by what authority the British Officers press your Seamen, therefore shall not presume to make any remarks on the occasion more than to say that your Trade will suffer much if something be not settled by the respective Governments of both Countrys, with respect to what Men shall be liable to be impress'd from American Ships—The American Consul at London has been recently acquainted with the above mention'd Matter. I had the favour of receiving the thanks of Congress dated in June 1783 for my attention & service to American Prisoners in that War

With sincere esteem I remain thy real friend

Reuben Harvey Senr.

RC (DLC); at foot of text: "Thos. Jefferson Esqr. President of Congress"; endorsed by TJ as received 15 Aug. and so recorded in SJL.

During the American Revolution, Quaker merchant Reuben Harvey (1734-1808) worked diligently for the relief of distressed American prisoners held at Kinsale, Ireland. His efforts earned him the thanks of George Washington and Congress. When Washington was president, Harvey sent him information detailing abuses committed by British authorities against American vessels and their crews at Cork (Sheldon S. Cohen, *British Supporters of the American Revolution, 1775-1783: The Role of the 'Middling-level' Activists* [Woodbridge, Eng., 2004], 83-105; Washington, *Papers, Pres. Ser.*, 15: 316-19, 610-11).

AMERICAN CONSUL AT LONDON: George W. Erving.

To Thomas Mann Randolph

Dear Sir Washington June 3. 1803. Friday

I am sorry to have to inform you of the dangerous situation of our friend Peter Carr at mr Hollins's at Baltimore. yesterday was sennight he was taken suddenly & violently ill. gravel entered certainly into the complaint, but whether something bilious was not also a part of it seems doubtful. on Tuesday I recieved from mr Hollins the first information of his illness & danger, & his wish to see Sam Carr. I immediately dispatched an express into the country for him. he came here in the evening when the arrival of a letter of that morning's date from mr Hollins informed us he was worse, & that blisters were applied. Sam set off yesterday morning and in the evening I recieved a letter from Genl. Smith dated 6. aclock the evening before (Wednesday) that the blisters on his back & ankles had raised & were painful. from appearances, he said, he should expect he would recover, but the Doctors do not believe it possible that he can. the mouth of the bladder they say is stopped. 'my hope, he sais, arises from a small discharge of urine this afternoon. he scarcely appears to expect a recovery and has in consequence made his will this morning.' I must pray you to prepare my sister by information of his being very seriously ill, & that Sam is gone on to him: this should be without delay; because the next post will certainly bring you the issue whether favourable or unfavourable. it will be 5. days before another post. my tenderest love to my dear Martha & affectionate salutations to yourself.

P.S. I recieved last night a letter from T. Eston Randolph. he has taken a place near Dungeoness, so declines Shadwell.

RC (DLC); at foot of text: "T M Randolph"; endorsed by Randolph as received 10 June.

To Thomas Mann Randolph

DEAR SIR Washington June 3. 1803.

My previous letter of this day's date (now gone to the post office) gave you information of mr Carr's situation to June 1. 6 aclock P.M. a letter from mr Hollins, 12 hours later, (yesterday morning) who had sat up with him the preceding night, says he was better, & he began to have hopes he might recover. Adieu. TH: JEFFERSON

RC (PWacD: Feinstone Collection, on deposit PPAmP); at foot of text: "T M Randolph." PrC (CSmH); endorsed by TJ in ink on verso.

The letter from John HOLLINS was not recorded in SJL and has not been found.

From John Armstrong

SIR/ Cincinnati June 4th. 1803

your letter thro Madam L. F. Felix was answered some time since, and in compliance with her request I beg leave to forward the inclosed for your perusal and consideration, if the Land Located by me for your friend does not meet the approbation of that Lady, it is no fault of mine as a Locator—the lines of those small tracts not being run at the time the Locations were made, it was imposible for me to give a correct description of those perticular Lots—I hazard nothing in saying, my information as to the fraction or quarter in which they lie is correct speaking of the quarter Township Generally, and if the inclosed Plat made by actual survey does not correspond with the one handed by your Excellency, the fault must lie with the Public surveyers and not with me—may I intrude on your time so far as to ask a line in answer to this and my former letter on the subject of this Land, Perhaps Mr Smith the Surveyor expects his fees paid thro me—

I have the honer to be with due consideration your Excellencys most Obt. Servt. JOHN ARMSTRONG

RC (MHi); at head of text: "To the President of the United States"; endorsed by TJ as received 28 June and so recorded in SJL. Enclosures: (1) Samuel Smith to Armstrong, Franklin County, Ohio, 29 Apr. 1803, sending a draft of the land he surveyed for Louise Françoise Felix, which does not agree with her plat; Felix complains that the land is only second rate in quality, that a hill and two surrounding springs marked on her plat cannot be found, and that a "run" marked on her plat was found to be a "fine spring which arises fifteen or twenty poles below her line"; Smith has provided Felix and her agent, Philippe Reibelt ("Mr. Rible"), a copy of his survey, "which they are determined to send to the President"; Felix and Reibelt want Armstrong to write the president regarding the business, "& if he says they may take it for the Land they will rest secure"; they also request that Armstrong send TJ the bill for surveying, "as he is to replace the Money to them as agent for Col. Kosciuszko"; Smith suggested to Felix and Reibelt that they purchase 300 acres from Armstrong and "Mr Milzes," which they intend to do as well as an additional 400 adjoining acres; in a postscript, Smith adds that Felix and Reibelt request that Armstrong send the draft as well as the bill to TJ (same; addressed: "John Armstrong Esq. Columbia Cincinnati Post office"; postmarked Chillicothe, 26 May; notation by TJ on address sheet: "T.K. guarantees the existence, the situation, the title, contents, & possession"). (2) Plat of 500 acres of land, dated Franklin County, Ohio, 28 Apr. 1803, surveyed by Smith for Felix, "being Lots No. 4, 7, 10, 18, & 19, of Fractional section No. 2 in Township No 2 & Range 19," which were located for Tadeusz Kosciuszko (MS in same).

YOUR LETTER: TJ to Armstrong, 21 Dec. 1802, which related to land in Ohio sold by Tadeusz Kosciuszko to Louise Françoise Felix (see Philippe Reibelt to TJ, 30 Nov. 1802). The answer to it was probably Armstrong to TJ, 23 Apr. 1803, recorded in SJL as received 10 May from Cincinnati, but not found.

YOUR FRIEND: Tadeusz Kosciuszko (Vol. 31:560-1).

From Joseph Barnes

Paris june 4th 1803—

When I had the pleasure of addressing Mr Jefferson from Leghorn Decemr. 20th 1802—I expected Long since to have been personally at my Post in Sicily; I flatter myself however, tho' a succession of unforeseen occurrences in closing my concerns especially in Leghorn have caused my detention, yet, as it has given me the opportunity of proceeding here from Marseilles, and having interviews with our Ministers Mr Livingston, and Mr Monroe, on objects of the United States, that *good* may *result* from it.

Soon after the date of my Last, I proceed'd to Naples presented my Commission & got it Acknowledged by the King; having in a previous interview with General Acton, who is prime Minister, (& in effect King) suggest'd the *necessity* of some *Commercial Arrangements* beteween the United States & His Sicilian Majesty, from the rapid increase, and very advantageous Commerce of the U.S. to the Sicilian States, and that the *heavy* duties & indeed prohibitions in the Ports of France & Spain must cause a still greater increase. He observed, being persuaded of the same, that he should communicate with His Majesty & open the way; in consequence, in his Letter Acknowledging me as consul of the U.S. in Sicily, he observes, that his Majesty will with much pleasure receive any person whom the U.S. may appoint, as Minister Plenepotentiary and bearing proper procreation or powers to enter into a Treaty of commercial relations immediately with the U.S.—a second Copy of which Letter I have the pleasure of transmitting herewith to the President, for his information, the first copy I sent thro' the means of Mr Mazzei from Leghorn.—From the knowledge I have of the Commerce & the principal commercial men of the two Sicilies; from my interest with the chief Bankers & Officers of State, as suggest'd in my Last Letter, Mr Jefferson will judge whether these advantages would not enable me to effect more than any one coming directly out unacquainted with the same, exclusive of the *high gratification* it would afford me, were I authorized.—

While I congratulate Mr Jefferson, and felicitate myself & fellow citizens on the very *important* event of the *Acquisition* of *Louisiana*, which I hope will enable us to preserve our *Great Political Maxim* of *Peace* and *friendship* with the *whole World*, the Convention of which Mr jay, who will have the pleasure of presenting this, takes with him; Yet for the sake of *humanity* I *regret* the *renewal of hostilities* between France & England; which have commenced with so much *Acrimony* on both sides that the consequences are incalculable—The English commenced by the Capture of two Vessels previous to a declaration of War,! & the French by having made prisoners of War of all the English within their territory! having sent an Army to take possession of Hanover,* shut the Elbe & the Weser against the English, and most Likely Lay Hamburg & Bremen under contribution—Another Army is order'd to Naples & Sicily; the Latter however no doubt the English will prevent—In fine, the French will cause all the Ports of France, Holland, Italy & probably of Portigal & Spain to be shut against the English, and the presumption is, the English will declare all those Ports in a State of Blockage, which will be very detrimental

* Tis suggest'd they will make prisoners of War of all the Hanoverians in Mass!! above 16 & under 60 years—

to our commercial interest; however I flatter myself Neither England nor France will attempt to *Commit* the *Spoilations* they did the Last War, contrary to the rights of Neutrality & usage of Nations.

Boneparte being much exasperated against the English, & having no effective alternative other than an *invasion* of England, the presumption is he will make the attempt—time however must demonstrate.—

Under present circumstances, I shall proceed in a few days by way of Leghorn & Naples for Sicily, to take my post for the protection of the persons & property of my fellow Citizens personally there.—

Tis probable Mr Jefferson will have reced. Letters from Mr Mazzei with my inclosure. consequently he will have noticed the name of a very good friend of mine, and true friend to Liberty, Mr Newton, whose services have & may pave the way to any thing in reason with the Neapolitan Govt. we may wish: and, whose intimate knowledge & acquaintance with some of the first British Characters, at present in the Medeterranean, address, judgment & exertions may assist most essentially in securing us against any Evils in those parts of the World, more I need not suggest—Being a true friend to Liberty, he is consequently a friend to the United States—we have had various concerns together, & indeed been scarcely separate since I have been in Europe: he is not influenced by pecuniary interest, but is ambitious of success in whatever he undertakes; &, in fact, his talents & exertions generally ensure success. He purpos'd returning to England & from thence to America, however thro' my persuasion, sensible of the advantages he may be of to my Country, he is induced to remain in Sicily. Mr. Mazzei having no doubt fully Explain'd it would be needless for me to repeat, however, should it meet the Ideas of Mr Jefferson to *Authorize me*, jointly with Mr Mazzei & Mr Newton, to negotiate a Treaty of Commercial relations with His Sicilian Majesty, as well as a Convention relative to, and for the more effectual resistance of the Barbary Powers, and protection of our commerce in the Medeterranean, I am fully persuaded every expectation would be answer'd—The matter may, should it be deem'd requisite, be subject to the Sanction of our Ministers at Paris & Madrid.—The more formidable we can appear with the Least expense, the better, and more effectual will be our efforts.—By attacking the Neapolitans on certain considerations, they would pay the presumtion is $\frac{2}{3}$rds the expense; therefore two or 3 Frigates and 12 or 15 Schooners, if required, would *not* cast more to our share than the expense we are at, at present, and our object so much more effectually promoted; which may be continued 'at pleasure' till those Barbarians May be brot. to the considerations & conditions of civilized Nations.—

Impress'd as I am, I should do injustice to my feelings were I not again to congratulate my fellow citizens & felicitate myself on the happy events which have result'd from the *influence* of Mr *Jefferson* since his presidency—having *caused* the repeal of all the oppressive internal taxes, Viz, the *Excise* &c the *vexatious* (& indeed unconstitional) *Seditious* & *Alien* Bills; dissolved many supernumerary judges, & in fine made a saving notwithstanding of upwards of one & a half Million of Dollars! in the appropriations of the Last year!! the presumption therefore is, the good citizens of the U.S., the great mass of whom would generally *Act right* were they *not deceived*, will be so *fully satisfied who* are their *true friends* that hereafter there will be but Little opposition, consequently but *one party*, that of the People—which added to the continued success of the administration of Mr. Jefferson & the prosperity of the U.S. are amongst my first wishes—begging the indulgence of Mr Jefferson for the Length of this Letter—

I have the honor to remain with every consideration & respect his obedt. Sert. J: BARNES

P.S. Mr Jay, as well as others, if necessary, can state the Late *inattention* & improper conduct of Mr Mathiew at Naples, who has suggest'd to myself & others that his office of consul of the U.S. is no object to him—

I consider it my duty also to suggest, that the person appointed at Malta, recommended by Mr Cathcart is not capable of rendering the services he ought, being a native of Malta, not speaking any English, nor respected Even in his situation by the English; exclusive of which, I was told by reputable person in Malta that he is *agent* for the *Tripolians*, our enemies!!

There are moreover the Seven United Islands, call'd the Ragusian Republic, to which an appointment would be of considerable Service to our Commerce.

I have never suggest'd to my friend Mr Newton any Idea of reward from the U.S. knowing he has, & will do all in his power from friendship for me, & his Love of rational Liberty: Nevertheless, should Mr Jefferson think proper, I am sensible my friend Mr N. would Accept an appoint to the office of consul in either Malta or said United Islands—

RC (DLC); addressed: "H.E. Thomas Jefferson President of the United States Washington"; endorsed by TJ as received 24 Aug. and so recorded in SJL. Enclosure: Sir John Francis Edward Acton to Barnes, from Caserta, 17 Jan. 1803, acknowledging Barnes's credentials and stating that the king would welcome any overture by an envoy plenipotentiary or other authorized representative to establish a commercial relationship with the United States (Tr in DLC: TJ Papers, 129:22220; in a clerk's hand, in Italian, on letterhead of the U.S. consulate at Leghorn; with attestation by Thomas Appleton; sealed).

KING: Ferdinand IV of Naples, who (as Ferdinand III) was also monarch of the Two Sicilies (Desmond Gregory, *Napoleon's Italy* [Madison, N.J., 2001], 17; Vol. 38:18n).

An English baronet born in France, ACTON first entered the service of Naples in 1778. By 1789, he was minister of the navy, minister of war, and minister of foreign affairs (DNB).

The copy of Acton's letter that Barnes asked Philip MAZZEI to forward was probably enclosed in a letter from Mazzei to TJ of 20 May, which is recorded in SJL as received from Leghorn on 17 Aug. but has not been found; see also TJ to Madison, 18 Aug. 1803.

By 13 May, Bonaparte had begun preparations to seize the electorate of HANOVER, which was controlled by the British royal family. On the 26th, French troops entered the electorate from the Batavian Republic. By capitulations of 3 June and 5 July, Hanover surrendered and its military forces, which had shown almost no resistance to the invaders, were broken up. ANOTHER ARMY on orders from the first consul moved to occupy ports in the kingdom of Naples (Grainger, *Amiens Truce*, 194-7; Parry, *Consolidated Treaty Series*, 57:135-40).

E. J. NEWTON, originally from England, was Barnes's business partner and vice consul (Madison, *Papers, Sec. of State Ser.*, 6:554n; 8:79, 80n; Miriam Allen Deford, "An American Murder Mystery," *Prairie Schooner*, 22 [1948], 284-7).

TJ named Joseph Pulis as U.S. consul at MALTA in an interim appointment in July 1801. After confirmation by the Senate in January 1802, TJ signed a new commission for Pulis (commissions, 1 July 1801 and 26 Jan. 1802, in DNA: RG 59, PTCC; Vol. 33:676; Vol. 36:320, 332). Pulis wrote to TJ in October 1801, thanking him for the appointment, noting that the government on Malta had accepted his credentials, and declaring that he would zealously serve the interests of the United States. He had a relationship with the bey of Tripoli, he observed, and would be willing to meet with the bey if TJ desired. He forwarded news from Egypt and a report that Tripoli had no corsairs at sea. Pulis also wrote to Madison on 25 Oct. 1801 (RC in DNA: RG 59, CD, in French, at head of text: "Monsieur l'honorable president," endorsed by TJ as received 29 Apr. 1802 and so recorded in SJL, also endorsed for the State Department; Madison, *Papers, Sec. of State Ser.*, 2:204).

SEVEN UNITED ISLANDS, CALL'D THE RAGUSIAN REPUBLIC: Barnes was conflating two entities, both of which were called republics and were located to the east of the Italian peninsula. An article of the 1797 Treaty of Campoformio gave France sovereignty over islands in the Ionian Sea that had previously been ruled by Venice. Three years later, an arrangement between Russia and the Ottoman Empire, with approval from France, created the Septinsular Republic, or Republic of the Seven United Islands, which encompassed Corfu and six other isles. The Dubrovnik or Ragusan Republic was a neutral, sea-trading city-state on the eastern side of the Adriatic Sea with a long history of independence. The Campoformio pact between France and Austria gave Austria control over Dalmatia, which adjoined Dubrovnik on the north, but did not interfere with the Dubrovnik Republic (Parry, *Consolidated Treaty Series*, 54:160; Tulard, *Dictionnaire Napoléon*, 937-8; Francis W. Carter, *Dubrovnik [Ragusa]: A Classic City-state* [London, 1972], 44, 439-42).

To George Jefferson

Dear Sir Washington June 4. 1803.

I recieved last night your favor of May 31. and leave to your own judgment entirely what is best to be done with my tobo. the danger of the rains having injured it may be a good reason for examining it so far as to be satisfied on that score. by sending it to Philadelphia I can always have a dollar more than is given for any crop that goes there; but it is troublesome sending it, and I wish moreover to secure the paiment of my note the 12th. of next month for 1300. D. perhaps you may find it more eligible, if offers are dull, to sell only as much as will raise the 1300. D. and reserve the rest for better offers. all this is left to yourself.—we are sending off from Albemarle 18. barrels of fish for myself, and 4. or 5. for Sam Carr, to be forwarded. Accept my affectionate salutations. Th: Jefferson

P.S. 2 boxes of sheet iron were lately sent from Philadelphia to your address. I would wish them to be forwarded to Monticello without delay, as they are to cover a part of the house now very much exposed & suffering.

PrC (MHi); at foot of text: "Mr. George Jefferson"; endorsed by TJ in ink on verso.

On an invoice of 20 May from William Lyles to Samuel carr for the sale and transport to Alexandria of 18 barrels of herring for £27.11.3, or $73.50, TJ added on 1 June an order on John Barnes "to pay the above to mr Carr" (MS in ViU; invoice in William Lyles's hand and signed by him, acknowledging payment; order in TJ's hand and signed by him; endorsed by Barnes as paid on 2 June). See mb, 2:1101.

From Lafayette

Auteuïl 15th floreal [i.e. Prairial]

My dear Sir June the 4th. 1803

I Hope You will Have Received My Joyfull Congratulations on the Happy, Thrice Happy Arrangement for Louisiana, as Well as my Thankfull Aknowledgements for the Honourable Bounty of Congress in my Behalf and for the kind part You Have Been pleased to take in this Equally flattering and advantageous favour.

These Lines shall be Consecrated to The Memory of a departed friend of ours General *Chastelux*—The inclosed Letter from His Widow, and the Note which Accompagnies it will Let You know Her particular Case, and the Hope she Has Some Thing Might Be Made of it for the Sake of Her Son a very promising Youth—I am Sure You

Will Be So kind as to Make the Enquiry, and if there was Some thing to be done, that Your patronage would not be Wanting

I write this by Mr. Mery, a french Citizen, St. domingo planter, who is Going to the West indias By Way of philadelphia and Has Been Recommended to Me by Her Cousin, Madame d'Astorg, whom You Have often Seen at the Hôtel La Rochefoucauld.

I am Here, with my Wife, Son, daughter in law, and New Born little grand daughter taking Care of my Wounds, and Stretching My Rusted Articulations untill I can Return to my Beloved Rural Abode at *La Grange*.

With Every Sentiment of Respect, Gratitude, and Affection I am my dear Sir Your Constant friend LAFAYETTE

RC (DLC). Recorded in SJL as received 24 Aug. Dupl (same); in a clerk's hand, signed by Lafayette; dated 15 Prairial and 4 June; at head of text: "duplicate"; addressed: "Thomas Jefferson Esq. President of the United States" with notation "2a"; notation of forwarding, signed by John Mitchell; franked; postmarked New York, 30 Aug., with note by a postmaster: "Milton Va." Enclosures: (1) Madame de Chastellux to TJ, 5 June. (2) Memorandum, undated and unsigned, stating that Lord Baltimore received a grant from Charles I that made Baltimore and his heirs proprietors of the lands north of the Potomac River that became the province of Maryland; that the proprietor's lands and privileges were bound by entail and should have passed to two female members of the family who married two brothers of the Plunkett family of Ireland; the property and titles went instead to illegitimate descendants of Lord Baltimore; the land and privileges were sequestered by Maryland during the American Revolution, after which those illegitimate heirs received a large indemnification from Great Britain; Madame de Chastellux is the great-granddaughter of one of the legitimate female heirs who should have received the lands and titles; her son Alfred, the only child of General Chastellux, is the only legitimate direct descendant of Lord Baltimore and can by right claim the indemnification made for the property seized by the state of Maryland; he also has a claim, not by right but by favor, to some compensation for his father's assistance to the United States as an officer in the French army during the American War for Independence (MS in DLC: TJ Papers, 132:22804, in a clerk's hand; MS in same, 132:22807, in a clerk's hand); see also Madame de Chastellux to TJ, 5 June and 30 June.

MADAME D'ASTORG was a close friend of the Duchesse de La Rochefoucauld (Doina Pasca Harsanyi, ed., *Lettres de la Duchesse de La Rochefoucauld à William Short* [Paris, 2001], 255; George Green Shackelford, *Jefferson's Adoptive Son: The Life of William Short, 1759-1848* [Lexington, Ky., 1993], 61, 64, 130).

NEW BORN LITTLE GRAND DAUGHTER: Natalie Renée Émilie du Motier de Lafayette, born 22 May (Arnaud Chaffanjon, *La Fayette et sa descendance* [Paris, 1976], 171).

To Thomas Mann Randolph

Washington
TH:J. TO T M RANDOLPH. Saturday morng. June 4. 1803.
I wrote you two letters yesterday by the direct post. in the evening I recieved the two now inclosed, and altho' I do not know that sending them by Richmond they can get to you sooner than if sent by our next post of Wednesday, yet I take that chance, to lessen the anxiety of yesterday's accounts. affectionate salutations

RC (DLC); endorsed by Randolph as received 10 June. Recorded in SJL with notation "no copy kept. P. Carr's situation." Enclosures: probably Samuel Carr to TJ and Samuel Smith to TJ, both 2 June.

From Madame de Chastellux

DEAR SIR Paris June the 5th. 1803.

The remembrance of your friendship for the father of my Child, and the very kind letter you was so good as to write to me some years past at a moment I addressed you in favo'r of my dr. Boy emboldens me to claim your protection again, if you are of opinion that I can apply to the States of Maryland for an indemnification as being the direct & legal descendant of Lord Baltimore: my right which I readily & joyfully make up to my Son can be sufficiently ascertained, but I shall not go to that trouble & expence untill you have approved of my laying down before the States, those claims, which acquire I think more strength from resting upon the Child of one who was so entirely devoted to America; & to you I can say My dr. Sir that my poor Boy is to the full as unfortunate as Monsieur de Grasse's family, as he must lose very nearly the whole of the small property he had to expect, it being in the hands of his cousin who is an Emigrant: this circumstance makes me wish still more ardently that attention should be paid to the application I am inclined to make, if countenanced by Monsieur de Chastellux friends, & Should it be attended to by the States of Maryland how satisfactory & flattering it would be to think, that the provision of my child, should be granted in consideration of his Father's services, to that country which after his own was dearest to him! general la fayette who is the best of relations and warmest of friends wishes eagerly we may succeed, and as he writes upon the same subject, I shall only add that I beg as a favo'r My dr. Sir you will allow Monsieur Petry prime secretary to the french Legacy to consult you upon this head: he was entirely devoted to my husband, & sincerely wishes to serve his son.

Believe me I entreat you with unfeigned affection and profound esteem

My dr. Sir Your most obedient humble Servant

PLUNKETT CHASTELLUX

RC (DLC); endorsed by TJ as received 24 Aug. and so recorded in SJL. Enclosed in Lafayette to TJ, 4 June.

SO GOOD AS TO WRITE TO ME: in 1795, when her son was six years old, Madame de Chastellux wrote to TJ about prospects of receiving compensation from the United States. At her request TJ involved George Washington in the question, and he also consulted Madison. They all agreed that Madame de Chastellux's deceased husband's service in the French army during the American Revolution did not merit a financial award from Congress. TJ and the Marquis de Chastellux had become acquainted in Virginia—Chastellux visited Monticello in April 1782—and continued the friendship when TJ became minister to France. In a letter to Madame de Chastellux of 10 July 1796, TJ reported that there was no likelihood of aid from the U.S. government. He acknowledged the "very sincere esteem" he had felt for her husband, whose death in 1788 "was one of the events which the most sensibly afflicted" TJ during his time in Paris (Howard C. Rice, ed. and trans., *Travels in North America in the Years 1780, 1781 and 1782 by the Marquis de Chastellux*, 2 vols. [Chapel Hill, 1963], 2:390-6; Vol. 6:190-1; Vol. 28:343-4, 463-4, 498, 542, 613; Vol. 29:7, 144-5, 312-13).

An act of Congress in 1795 granted $4,000 to the Comte DE GRASSE's daughters. TJ, Washington, and Madison rued the precedent established by that appropriation. Congress increased the award in 1798, adding an annuity of $400 for each of the four daughters for five years. To Madame de Chastellux, TJ explained that the payment to the French admiral's heirs was based "on circumstances peculiar to the case, and excluding the general principle" (Vol. 28:498, 500n, 613; Vol. 29:7, 144-5; Vol. 33:519n).

Jean Baptiste PETRY, who had previously held consular positions in South Carolina and Philadelphia, had been appointed secretary of the French legation in the United States (Madison, *Papers, Sec. of State Ser.*, 4:502, 521, 539; 8:382; Syrett, *Hamilton*, 15:609n; 18:236; Vol. 28:27).

I ENTREAT YOU: writing to Lafayette about various subjects on 31 Jan. 1804 and declaring that he did not have time to write to Madame de Chastellux, TJ advised that if the British government made a mistake in its indemnification of Lord Baltimore's heirs, she should seek redress from Britain, not Maryland. Madame de Chastellux's son Alfred, the Comte de Chastellux, pursued a career in government and military service (Rice, ed., *Travels in North America*, 1:22, 23).

Commissioners of Bankruptcy: List of Candidates

[on or before 5 June 1803]

Jacob I. Cohen
William Hull
Wm. Vaughan for Portland

———

Worcester. Samuel Flagg
Abraham Lincoln
Francis Blake

MS (DNA: RG 59, LAR, 2:0414); undated but see Lincoln to TJ, at this date, below; entirely in TJ's hand.

In October 1802, James Monroe recommended JACOB I. COHEN as bankruptcy commissioner at Richmond. William VAUGHAN of PORTLAND sought appointment as marshal for the district of Maine in 1793, but no solicitations or recommendations on his behalf in 1802 or 1803 have been found (Vol. 25:316-17n; Vol. 38:529-30).

WORCESTER: Levi Lincoln wrote the three names listed here on a scrap of paper now found with other recommendations (MS in DNA: RG 59, LAR, 2: 0415). All three named by Lincoln were appointed with commissions dated 16 June (list of commissions in Lb in DNA: RG 59, MPTPC).

From Levi Lincoln

SIR [on or before 5 June 1803]

The names, agt Worcester, in the memorandum were intended for commissioners of bankruptcy;—*Vaughan* I think was designed to supply the place of one who had not accepted, *Cohen*, I have no recollection of—Hull was named, altho the commission was considered as full, to quiet his feelings, which appeared to have been very much hurt, from an idea of his having been neglected—As the commissioners, in Boston, are now organised & are acting, without him: I doubt whether it Would be best to make that appointment—I think it would not satisfy him, & something better may be done for him hereafter—

most respectfully yours LEVI LINCOLN

RC (DNA: RG 59, LAR, 2:0417-18); undated; at foot of text: "President of U.S."; endorsed by TJ as received 5 June and so recorded in SJL; also endorsed by TJ: "Commrs. bkrptcy Worcester."

MEMORANDUM: see document printed immediately above. No cover letter was found with TJ's list.

HULL WAS NAMED: William Hull was not included on TJ's lists of candidates and appointees for bankruptcy commissioner and his name does not appear on the State Department's list of commissions for that office. TJ appointed him governor of Michigan Territory in early 1805 (list of commissions in Lb in DNA: RG 59, MPTPC; commission dated 1 Mch. 1805, in same; Vol. 37:703-11).

To James Monroe

1400. 621. 1410. 327. 251. 569. 1402. 640. 146. 1486. 1445. 956. 530. 43. 954. 1399. 1006. 1436. 1379 1576. 1372. 1501. 1436. 981. 167. 996. 548. 604. 805. 809. 1046. 377. 1401. 1513. 1274. 1067. 1440. 569. 663. 981. 818. 1443. 270. 1315. 1440. 627. 1310. 219. 179. 1337. 520. 1440. 1225. 271. 569. 1549. 925. 1153. 569. 341. 801. 1501.

126. 1550. 94. 352. 879. 569. 177. 1507. 1042. 1102. 439. 271. 1440. 1513. 1410. 451.

THOMAS JEFFERSON TO JAMES MONROE. June 5. 1803.
the cannister of tea is for my friend Made. de Corny. I address it to you for delivery[1] because it may be prohibited. It goes to another port to find a conveyance, therefore no letter to her accompanies it. Adieu

PrC (DLC); endorsed by TJ in ink on verso. Recorded in SJL with notation "9¾ ℔ imperial tea for Made. de Corny," but perhaps not sent (see below).

The appearance of the PrC suggests that TJ letterpressed two separate documents onto one sheet: on the bottom, the brief message to Monroe, and on the top, the text rendered in code as TJ intended to send it. As decoded, allowing for interchangeability of i and j and of u and v, the message would read: "tho mas je fer son to ja mes mon ro june 5 eighteen hundred three this can is ter of te a is for my fri end mad dam de cor ny I ad dre s it to you for del iv ery because it may be pro hi bit ed it go es to an other port to fin d a convey ance therefore no letter to her ac com pa ni es it ad ie u." The code was one that Madison sent to Monroe in February 1803 before Monroe departed for France. Madison and Monroe used it in their diplomatic correspondence, and various U.S. diplomats and agents employed it until 1866. Robert R. Livingston did not adopt the code and continued to use the one he had taken with him to France (Madison, *Papers*, *Sec. of State Ser.*, 4:352; Weber, *United States Diplomatic Codes*, 154-7, 185-8, 201, 203, 207-10, 216-19, 478-89).

Madame DE CORNY asked TJ to send her some tea in her letter of 15 Feb., which reached TJ on 2 May. He had already acquired the canister of "fine tea" before he received her request. Despite his intention to send it to her in June, he did not FIND A CONVEYANCE until November, when the schooner *Citizen* departed on a transatlantic voyage on public service, carrying gun carriages to Morocco and stopping along the way at L'Orient to deliver the ratification of the Louisiana Purchase treaty. The tea reached a delighted and grateful Madame de Corny by early February 1804 (Madison, *Papers*, *Sec. of State Ser.*, 5:593; NDBW, 3:297; TJ to Madame de Corny, 1 Nov. 1803; TJ to Livingston, 4 Nov.; Livingston to TJ, 11 Jan. 1804; Madame de Corny to TJ, 2 Feb.).

[1] Preceding two words interlined.

From François Navoni

MONSIEUR Cailleri le 5. juin 1803.

Je me suis avec empressement fait un devoir de vous humilier deux de mes lettres datées 30. 7mbre., et 4. Xmbre. passés les quels j'avois remis a Marseille les ayant raccomandées pour sa promte expedition, et j'ai eté deja averti qu'elles furent acheminées par Battiment.

Comme jusqu'a present je n'ai pas encore eté honnoré de reponse aux dittes Lettres, de rechef, et par la meme voye de Marseille j'avance la presente pour confirmer les dites deux deja rèmises, que de me recommander a Sa protection, ainsi qu'a tout le Gouvernement pour meriter une reponse avec le Brevet de confirme de l'honneur qu'il a voulu me partager le nommé Monsr. le Commandeur Morris, ainsi que toutes les instructions necessaires pour me mettre au Service, et pour attester dans le même tems les empressements que j'ai eù pour la Nation en qualité de Consul Garant depuis 1769. comme fidellement je l'ai representé avec la mienne 30. 7mbre.

Egalement je n'ai pas manqué de remettre une notte en detail du Sel de nos Salines, et un'autre egalement remise avec mes offres a cete Chambre du Commerce affin qu'ils soyent instruits de ce que ici pourroient charger les Battiments Ameriquains, et les Marchandises qu'ils pourroient aporter ici pour charger du Sel, etoit un article tréz avantageu pour les Etats.

Je continue mes Correspondences avec Leurs Consuls de Genes, Livourne, Naples, Marseille, Tunis, touts mes bons Amis, et dernierement tant celui de Livourne Monsr. Appleton, que celui de Naples Monsr. Mattieus m'assurent de m'addresser des Navires pour les Charger de Sel, comme en son tems je me fairois un devoir de les favoriser.

Dernierement parvinrent dans ces Mers deux fregates, et un Brick de la Nation qui Croisoient pour les Tripolins, et ayant parlementé avec un Battiment qui venoit de Malte, dans le même tems m'ont honnoré de m'envoyer des Compliments; et qu'au plus tot mouilleront dans cette Rade pour prendre des provisions, comme des nouvelles, si l'occasion se presente je fairai comme plusieurs autre fois j'ai practiqué, tant vis avis de Monsr. Ammekenil, que de Monsr. Morris, et ceux de leur Suitte.

Dans la même occasion que j'ai Ecrit a Monsr. le Presidant je n'ai pas manqué d'Ecrire a Monsr. le Secretaire d'Etât, et de même de me raccomander a me procurer le Brevet, comme je n'en doute point, que pour honnorer au nommè Commandeur Morris, m'honnoreront les Etats unis selon mes desirs.

Pardon Monsr. le Presidant de ma liberté, elle pour Sa bonté me doit considerer en service, et que j'ai eté toujôurs attaché a la Nation dans touts les occasions, qui se sont presentées, et je continuerai toujours avec la meme fidelité, et empressement, et desirant une favorable reponse avec ses ordres precieux, avec le plus humble respect, et obbeissance Je suis Monsieur Votre Le Trés Humble Trés obbeissant et Fidele Serviteur et Sujet.

François de Navoni
Agent.

EDITORS' TRANSLATION

MISTER PRESIDENT, Cagliari, 5 June 1803

I took it upon myself to send you two letters, via Marseilles, dated 30 September and 4 November, and I was told they were dispatched by ship.

Since I have not had the honor of a reply to these letters, I am writing again, also via Marseilles, to confirm the previous letters, to ask for your protection, and to request a reply from the government. I am enclosing the certificate Commander Morris gave me, with all the necessary instructions for my service, and certifying my work on behalf of your country in my capacity as consul guarantor since 1769, as described in my letter of 30 September.

I have also included a detailed price list concerning salt from our salt ponds as well as another one I prepared for the chamber of commerce, detailing prices for American ships and the merchandise they could trade for salt. This trade would be very advantageous to the States.

I continue my correspondence with the consuls in Genoa, Leghorn, Naples, Marseilles, and Tunis, all of whom are good friends. Recently both Mr. Appleton of Leghorn and Mr. Mathieu of Naples have promised to send ships to embark salt. In return, I will help them when the occasion arises.

Not long ago two frigates arrived in these waters, as did a brig that was sailing on behalf of Tripoli. After I negotiated with a ship from Malta, they honored me with compliments, and will anchor here to take on supplies. For them and for any other ships, I will do what I have for Mr. McNeill, Mr. Morris, their officers, and others.

When I wrote to the president, I also wrote to the secretary of state, requesting the license, since I do not doubt that, to honor Commander Morris, the United States will honor my wish.

Forgive my taking this liberty, Mister President. Please consider me to be at your service. I have always served your nation in every circumstance, and will continue to do so with the same zeal and fidelity. Awaiting a favorable reply and your precious orders, I am, Sir, with the most humble respect and obedience, your very humble, very obedient servant and subject.

FRANÇOIS DE NAVONI
Agent

RC (DNA: RG 59, LAR); at head of text: "François Navoni Consul Garant des Etats Unis de l'Amerique, et honnoré par Monsr. le Commandeur Morris du titre d'Agent de la meme, dans tout ce Royaume de Sardaigne A Monsieur Le premier President des Etats Unis de L'Amerique residant a Wasingthon"; endorsed by TJ as received 13 Oct. and "to be Consul at Cagliari" and so recorded in SJL.

François Navoni, a count, was a member of a prosperous merchant family of Cagliari, on the southern coast of Sardinia. The family had ties to Genoa (Pasquale Tola, *Dizionario biografico degli uomini illustri di Sardegna*, ed. Manlio Brigaglia, 3 vols. [Turin, 1837-38; repr. Nuoro, Italy, 2001], 3:24-5; Francesco d'Austria-Este, *Descrizione Della Sardegna [1812]*, ed. Giorgio Bardanzellu [Cagliari, 1993], 266; Navoni to TJ, 6 July 1806, in DNA: RG 59, LAR; Navoni to TJ, 30 Nov. 1807, in DLC).

LETTRES: no letter from Navoni of 4 Dec. 1802 has been found or is recorded in SJL. In his letter of 30 Sep. 1802 from Cagliari, as in the one printed above, he called himself *consul garant* (consul guarantor) and indicated that he corresponded with American consuls in the Mediterranean region. He hoped to be made consul general of the United States in the kingdom of Sardinia. The previous April, when Daniel McNeill stopped on his way between Toulon and Naples, Navoni offered to assist him in any way possible. Navoni also communicated with William Eaton about provisions for the U.S. frigates. In September, Richard Morris and a convoy of merchant ships bound for Leghorn arrived. Navoni entertained Morris and presented him to the viceroy. Navoni gave the captains of the ships in the convoy information about the salt available from the royal salines on Sardinia. Learning that Navoni handled consular duties for Denmark, Holland, and France, Morris on 27 Sep. made him provisional agent for U.S. affairs in the kingdom. Navoni enclosed a list of types and prices of salt available from the royal salines (RC in DNA: RG 59, CD, Cagliari; at head of text: "François de Navoni Consul Garant des Etats Unis de l'Amerique destiné en absence de consul dans ce Royaume de Sardaigne A Monsieur Le premier President de l'Assemblée Resident a Wasintong"; endorsed by TJ as received 16 Feb. 1803 and so recorded in SJL).

DANS CETTE RADE: France had seized the other primary possessions of the House of Savoy—Piedmont, Savoy, and Nice—but allowed the dynasty to retain the throne of Sardinia. The king beginning in 1802 was Victor Emmanuel (Tulard, *Dictionnaire Napoléon*, 1332-3; Vol. 35:714, 715n).

MONSR. AMMEKENIL: Daniel McNeill.

A MONSR. LE SECRETAIRE D'ETÂT: to Madison, also on 5 June, Navoni wrote a letter similar to the one to TJ. He also wrote to the secretary of state on 30 Sep. and 4 Dec. 1802, the latter of which has not been found (Madison, *Papers*, *Sec. of State Ser.*, 3:605; 5:62).

To Christian VII, King of Denmark

GREAT AND GOOD FRIEND

Mr. Blicherolsen your Minister Resident with the United States, having communicated his purpose of making, under your permission, a voyage to his country, I make it an occasion of expressing the satisfaction which his estimable qualities and the use he has made of them in the exercise of his functions, have inspired: and at the same time of assuring your Majesty of the perfect reciprocity in the United States, of the kindly sentiments contained in the letter of which your worthy Minister was the bearer. It is their sincere disposition to promote all the relations with the Danish Nation which may foster such sentiments, and which are prescribed by a mutual interest; and it is not doubted that, on this subject, the knowledge which Mr. Blicherolsen acquired by his residence, will render him, a just interpreter. I pray God to have you Great and Good Friend in his holy keeping.

Written at the City of Washington the sixth day of June in the year of our Lord one thousand eight hundred and three.

TH: JEFFERSON

FC in Lb (DNA: RG 59, Credences); in a clerk's hand; at head of text: "Thomas Jefferson President of the United States of America To His Majesty the King of Denmark, Norway, the Vandals and the Goths, Duke of Sleswic, Holstein, Stormar Ditmarsh and Odenburg &ca."; at foot of text: "To Our Great & Good

Friend His Danish Majesty"; below signature: "By the President James Madison, Secretary of State."

Christian VII (1749-1808) assumed the throne in 1766, but severe mental problems impaired his ability to rule. Beginning in 1772, a form of regency governed Denmark, and from 1784, Christian's son Frederick, the crown prince, ruled in all but name. Christian was the son of King Frederick V of Denmark and Queen Louisa, who was a daughter of George II of England (Svend Cedergreen Bech, ed., *Dansk Biografisk Leksikon*, 3d ed., 16 vols. [Copenhagen, 1979-84], 3:316-18; Thomas Munck, "Absolute Monarchy in Later Eighteenth-Century Denmark: Centralized Reform, Public Expectations, and the Copenhagen Press," *Historical Journal*, 41 [1998], 201-24; DNB, s.v. "Anne, princess royal [1709-59]").

Peder Blicher Olsen had been serving as both MINISTER and consul general. He informed Madison on 3 June that the king had granted him a leave of absence to go home to Denmark. He indicated also that his government had appointed Peder Pedersen, who had not yet arrived in the United States, to take over as consul general, and Pedersen was to act as chargé d'affaires for diplomatic relations during Blicher Olsen's absence (Madison, *Papers*, *Sec. of State Ser.*, 5:55, 327, 363; Vol. 35:162, 163n; Vol. 39:206).

Christian's LETTER of credence for Peder Blicher Olsen was dated 16 Jan. 1801 (Vol. 34:451n; Vol. 35:111n).

PRESCRIBED BY A MUTUAL INTEREST: Madison wrote to Blicher Olsen on 6 June, enclosing TJ's letter to the king and reiterating "all the sentiments it contains." Madison lauded what he saw in Blicher Olsen as "a just tendency to strengthen the friendly ties between two nations which have every motive to cultivate a perfect harmony, and to render their intercourse more and more liberal and useful" (Madison, *Papers*, *Sec. of State Ser.*, 5:62).

From Thomas McKean

SIR, Philadelphia June 6th. 1803.

This will be handed to your Excellency by the Reverend Mr; Gideon Blackburn, who has been appointed by the General Assembly of Presbyterians in the United States, at their late session in this City; a Missionary to the Cheerokee nation of Indians; for the purpose of instructing them in the ways of civilized life and in piety.

This Gentleman is a native of Cumberland County in Pennsylvania, but has resided the last ten years in Tennessee, near to the Cheerokees, among whom he is now going. His constituents are anxious for the success of his mission, and I have been applied to for his introduction to the President of the United States, in order that he may obtain his countenance and approbation; as he would not enter upon this business without the knowledge and consent of the Government, being a zealous Republican and a Friend to the present administration.

A letter from Your Excellency to Colo. Benjamin Hawkins Superintendant of Indian affairs, or a Certificate, signifying your approbation of or consent to this mission of the General Assembly, is what, I understand, is hoped and expected.

Accept, Sir, a tender of my best services, and an assurance of my attachment.

THOS M:KEAN

RC (DLC); in a clerk's hand, signed by McKean; at foot of text: "His Excellency Thomas Jefferson Esquire Presidt. of U.S."; endorsed by TJ as received 1 July "by revd Gideon Blackburn" and so recorded in SJL, where TJ mistakenly wrote "by revd Gideon Granger." Dft (PHi); in McKean's hand, signed and endorsed by him.

COUNTENANCE AND APPROBATION: Henry Dearborn wrote to Return Jonathan Meigs on 1 July to report TJ's determination "that in conformity with the intentions of the Government respecting the melioration of the present situation of our Indian Neighbours," the government would aid Gideon Blackburn in the establishment of a school for Cherokee children. Dearborn authorized Meigs, as the agent for the Cherokees, to help the Presbyterian minister find a suitable location and build a schoolhouse. The secretary of war anticipated that the government's expenditures for the first six months of the endeavor would amount to perhaps $300. Dearborn advised Blackburn, who had financial support from private individuals as well as the Presbyterian General Assembly, that he could have "no claim on the United States, for compensation for your services, other than what may from time to time be deemed advisable, in addition to what you may receive from the Society with whom you are connected or from individuals." Cherokee leaders consented to the establishment of the school, which opened in February 1804. When Blackburn suggested that an increase of resources would enable him to establish schools for all Indian nations, Dearborn replied that although the initial success with the Cherokees was "highly pleasing," there were too many people, "both in and out of Congress, who possess unfriendly dispositions towards the Natives," and a broader enterprise could not be undertaken. In 1807, Blackburn informed TJ of the progress of young Cherokees in learning to read and write the English language (Dearborn to Meigs, 1 July, and to Blackburn, 1 July 1803, 12 Jan. 1804, in DNA: RG 75, LSIA; William G. McLoughlin, *Cherokees and Missionaries, 1789-1839* [New Haven, 1984], 56-7; Blackburn to TJ, 11 Sep. 1807, in DNA: RG 107, LRUS).

From John P. Whitwell and Andrew Oliver, Jr.

Boston 6th June 1803

We, the Subscribers, citizens of the Town of Boston, with the greatest deference, and respect, humbly beg leave to enclose a Copy of a Letter from ourselves to the Secretary of the Navy; and to solicit thereto, the momentary attention and interference of the Chief Magistrate of the Union; whose exalted Character, whether Moral, Political, or Literary, we have ever beheld with the highest attachment & veneration. The ground of this application rests upon the commonly receiv'd maxim, That the Inhabitants of a City, possess a superior claim to the emoluments arising from the outfit of a Public Vessel where She may happen to be Station'd or constructed.—

The grievance specified in the enclos'd may at first appear to be merely personal and interested; but, we are at liberty to State as the belief of others, whose opinions are more influential than our own, that similar deviations from established customs might serve to excite, the regret of the well-wishers to the present policy; and the open exultation of its political opponents—

With due reflection, and adequate respect, we subscribe ourselves, Your Servts. & political adherents

John P. Whitwell
Andrew Oliver Junr

RC (MiU-C); at head of text: "To Thomas Jefferson, President of the United States"; endorsed by TJ as received 12 June and so recorded in SJL. Enclosure: Whitwell and Oliver to Robert Smith, dated Boston, 4 June 1803, identifying themselves as "extensive Importers of Drugs and Medicines from England, Holland, Mediterranean, and most parts of Europe and Asia"; due to their "political principles," the authors never obtained the patronage of previous administrations; they "heard with a great degree of exultation a projected Naval Armament from this Post," and subsequently made applications to the navy agent in Boston, Samuel Brown, to supply medicines, which were supported by Charles Jarvis and Benjamin Austin; as a result, Whitwell and Oliver received "every assurance that anticipation cou'd suggest, or promises bestow" from Brown; these expectations, however, were frustrated when they received news that prior arrangements had been made at Washington; the authors will not dwell on the unprecedented nature of this measure, or on the losses they sustained, but rather emphasize their just pretensions to government patronage; Whitwell and Oliver have long been loyal Republicans, they have paid nearly $10,000 in duties to the government, and have lately been "great losers by Bills of Exchange"; nevertheless, they claim to be able to supply medicines at half the cost of any that have heretofore been furnished; they ask Smith to consider their case and, if it is not too late, to "countermand any orders your disposition may dictate, or judgment conceive will ultimately prove beneficial to the existing Government, or the common Interests of the United States"; they note in a postscript that they were promised the business by the Boston navy agent almost 12 months ago (Printed in *Jefferson Correspondence, Bixby*, 101-2).

Writing Whitwell and Oliver on 13 June 1803, SECRETARY OF THE NAVY Robert Smith acknowledged receipt of their 4 June letter and explained that procuring medical supplies in the ports where vessels were outfitted had caused considerable "inconveniencies & losses." Under Smith's new arrangements, when vessels arrived in any United States port, their medical chests and instruments are removed and sent to Washington, "where all the medicines that are good are taken out and carefully preserved & the instruments are kept in order so as to be ready for immediate use." When chests were allowed to remain in vessels, it was found that the remaining medicines were lost and the instruments became rusty and "in many instances entirely unfit for future use" (FC in Lb in DNA: RG 45, MLS).

To Victor Marie du Pont

Dear Sir Washington June 7. 1803

Your kindness on a former occasion has emboldened me to trouble you again for a draught on Paris of the value of 200. Dollars, for which sum I inclose you a check on the New York branch bank. my apology is that it shall be the last time *for the present year*, and that I am really so helpless in things of this kind that like other helpless beings I throw myself on the charity of the benevolent. Accept my best wishes & respectful salutations. TH: JEFFERSON

RC (DeGH); addressed: "M. Victor Dupont New York"; franked and postmarked; endorsed by du Pont. PrC (DLC); endorsed by TJ in ink on verso. Recorded in SJL with notation "200. D."

To Albert Gallatin

TH:J. TO MR GALLATIN June 7. 1803.

The bearer hereof is mr Mansfield, to be appointed Surveyor vice Putnam. he is come to get whatever information you think necessary to have communicated to him for the proper discharge of his duties. he is informed that when the other duties of his office will admit, he is to make a survey of the Missisipi, & to fix certain geographical points such as the South end of Lake Michigan, the West end of Lake Superior &c he will remain here to read & examine whatever you think proper for him. affectionate salutations.

RC (NHi: Gallatin Papers); endorsed. Not recorded in SJL.

On 14 July, Jared MANSFIELD wrote Gallatin that he had spent considerable time since his return to West Point considering "the subjects you were pleased to lay before me, & of the means of prosecuting the business with honor to myself, & advantage to the public." He enclosed a list of instruments he needed to carry out his duties, including "A Description of Astronomical Instruments to be purchased in Europe." He requested Gallatin's advice on procuring them (Gallatin, *Papers*, 8:536-9). For another account of the meeting, see Mansfield to TJ, 7 July.

HE IS INFORMED: see TJ to Mansfield, 21 May.

From Frederick Harris

SIR Charlottesville 7th. June 1803

Not knowing whether Mr. Mirriwether Lewis has left the City of Washington or not, have taken the liberty of inclosing a letter of importance to him under cover of one to you—If Mr. Lewis has left Washington you would conferr a singular favor on me by forwarding the inclosed letter to him, by post, & by writing me by post to Charlottesville the place of his destination & where I may direct to him, as also whether he has left any agent in or about the city of Washington or else where—I am informed by his brother Mr. Reuben Lewis that it is unknown to him whether Mr. M. Lewis, has left Washington or not, or if he has whether he has left an agent to transact his business in his absence—My presuming to address you Sir, is owing to my being intirely unacquainted with any person in the city of Washington except Mr. M. Lewis, and knowing also that he has been a member of your family for some time past; These circumstances I hope sir will plead my excuse for troubling you, in a matter of no moment to yourself but of importance to a person unknown to yourself, & can be truly stiled

Your friend & ob. sert. FREDERICK HARRIS

RC (DLC); endorsed by TJ as received 12 June and so recorded in SJL. Enclosure not found.

Frederick Harris (1780-1842) of Louisa County, Virginia, later invested in canal and railroad development, owned real estate, a store, and slaves, and became a county political leader. He participated in the founding of the Virginia Society for Promoting Agriculture in 1811 (Malcolm H. Harris, *History of Louisa County, Virginia* [Richmond, 1936], 130, 146-8, 351; Mrs. William B. Ardery, "Harris of Louisa County," VMHB, 36 [1928], 254-7; *Daily National Intelligencer*, 21 Nov. 1827; *Alexandria Gazette*, 28 July 1828; *Richmond Enquirer*, 24 Mch. 1829, 27 July 1832; Charles W. Turner, "Virginia State Agricultural Societies 1811-1860," *Agricultural History*, 38 [1964], 167; John Edmund Stealey III, "The Responsibilities and Liabilities of the Bailee of Slave Labor in Virginia," *American Journal of Legal History*, 12 [1968], 345).

When Meriwether Lewis became TJ's secretary in 1801, he gave his younger brother REUBEN a power of attorney over his personal estate (Thomas C. Danisi and John C. Jackson, *Meriwether Lewis* [Amherst, N.Y., 2009], 40).

From Robert Smith

Navy depmt
June 7, 1803

SIR,

A number of Boatswains, Gunners, Carpenters and Sailmakers are wanting for the Squadron now preparing for the Mediterranean. I therefore enclose 20 blank warrants to which I have the honor to request your Signature.—

with high respect, I am Sir yr. ob: Servt. RT SMITH

RC (DLC); in a clerk's hand, signed by Smith; at foot of text: "The President"; endorsed by TJ as received from the Navy Department and "boatswains &c." FC (Lb in DNA: RG 45, LSP).

The SQUADRON NOW PREPARING FOR THE MEDITERRANEAN, to be commanded by Edward Preble, included the frigates *Constitution* and *Philadelphia*, the brigs *Siren* and *Argus*, and the schooners *Nautilus* and *Vixen*. They would be joined by the schooner *Enterprize*, which was still in the Mediterranean (NDBW, 2:411, 457).

To Benjamin Ferris

SIR Washington June 8. 1803.

Mr. Isaac Briggs informed me by letter that he had purchased for me, from you a clock and that the price of it including box & packing would be about seventy dollars. I now inclose you that sum, and will thank you to have it well packed & secure against rain, and sent by a vessel bound to Richmond addressed to the care of Messrs. Gibson & Jefferson merchants of that place. they will pay the freight. should the sum not be exact it may be [rectified] on your information to me. be so good as to send me the bill of lading when put on board that I may be enabled to apprize messrs. Gibson & Jefferson of the shipment. Accept my best wishes. TH: JEFFERSON

P.S. should you be at a loss to find a vessel bound to Richmond, messrs. Jones and Howell [iron dealers], & correspondents of mine, who are in the habit of making shipments to that place, will be able to inform you.

PrC (DLC); faint; at foot of text: "Mr. Benjamin Ferris clockmaker No. 17 N 2d street Philadelphia"; endorsed by TJ in ink on verso. Recorded in SJL with notation "70. D. for clock."

A native of Wilmington, Delaware, Benjamin Ferris (1780-1867) moved during his youth to Philadelphia and apprenticed as a watchmaker. Although successful, he abandoned the trade in 1813 and returned to Wilmington, where he worked as a conveyancer and eventually became the city surveyor. A self-educated man with a particular interest in history, he published in 1846 in Wilmington, *A History of the Original Settlements on the Delaware, from Its Discovery by Hudson to the Colonization under William Penn*, for which he acquired a working knowledge of Swedish. Prominent among area Quakers, he took an active role in defending the Friends from interdenominational attacks. When the Friends split into Orthodox and Hicksite movements, Ferris became one of the leading advocates of the more liberal, Hicksite side ("Benjamin Ferris," *Papers of the Historical Society of Delaware*, 37 [1903]; Robert W. Doherty, "A Response to Orthodoxy: The Hicksite Movement in the Society of Friends," PMHB, 90 [1966], 240-1).

ISAAC BRIGGS informed TJ of the clock order in a letter of 2 May. A tall case clock with a simple, unornamented design, it likely was used in Monticello's kitchen (Susan R. Stein, *The Worlds of Thomas Jefferson at Monticello* [New York, 1993], 378-9).

From Elijah Griffiths

DEAR SIR, Philadelphia June 8th. 1803

Professional pursuits have absorbed so much of my attention, since the last Presidential election, that I have been a very superficial observer of the political affairs of our country. Knowing the just views, & upright intentions of the Executive of the Union; I rested in the hope, that the adverse party, had the policy, if not the justice, to estimate properly, that lenity which was extended to them, by the General Government; but in this I have been mistaken. In calculating future events, we would sometimes be saved from error, by recuring to the past; the political events that succeeded to the American revolution, are still fresh in every mans memory; the conciliatory and republican espirit of the Whigs, gave the Tories an ascendancy which they never lost till 1800; it was that generous spirit that cost us so many painful struggles to wrest our constitution out of the hands of it's worst enemies. Regardless of the mild, & conciliatory measures of the Federal government; the antirepublican presses announce the most hostile dispositions toward the head, & members, of that Government. Another growing evil begins to present itself, discontent among our own people; in some cases very likely from disappointed expectations, and in other cases from seeing men in power, still leagued with a party, whose professed object, is the overthrow of the administration; & the restoration of the reign of terror. Is there a remedy for these evils? I think there is; Shall I instance the political conditions of Pennsylvania, Jersy, & New York, since 1799. When Mr McKean was first elected, his majority was 5000 votes; he immediately broke the antirepublican phalanx, by discharging them all from office. Did he increas the opposition, or abuse? No, the measure was full, their efforts were idle repetition, and their clamors died in empty murmurs at his feet: his next majority exceeded 30,000 votes, he is now respected by the men, who, once boldly insulted him.

New York has pursued a policy like that of Pennsylvania; both states are highly republican, their Government's respected, & likely to remain so. The republicans of Jersey, by much exertion raised Genl. Bloomfield to the Governmental chair; his political opponents were retained in office, their opposition to him at the next election, could not have been more virulent, had he discharged the whole party from public trust; and their means certainly would have been much less efficient.

I have been assured by some inteligent Gentlemen of Delawar State, that the retention of fœderalists in office in that state, has thrown a damp on the exertions of many active men, & will opperate so as to retain Delawar long under the influence of that party. I am far from wishing to see displacements for [the] accommodation of idle office hunters; but were t[he of]fices filled by reputable republicans, would not the hopes & cabals of expectants be at an end, & will they cease till that is the case? I may add, moderation is a virtue few are capable of estimating according to its worth; and few possess in a more eminent degree than yourself. Be assured Dr. Sir, the above has been dictated by candour & disinterestedness; I have no wish for public employment, nor any friend seeking promotion, that I know of. That God may grant You wisdom, & strength, in the discharge of the arduous duties of your Station, with much domestic hapiness, is the prayer of your friend & Humble. Servt.

E. GRIFFITHS
No 96 north 3d Street

RC (DLC); torn; at foot of text: "Thomas Jefferson Esqr."; endorsed by TJ as received 15 June and so recorded in SJL.

PROFESSIONAL PURSUITS: for Griffiths's medical career in Philadelphia and the publication of his dissertation in 1804, see Vol. 31:152n.

From John Isaac Hawkins

SIR/ Philadelphia June 8th. 1803

I take the liberty to request as a favor you will permit the bearer Mr. Uri K. Hill to take your likeness in Profile with one of my Patent Physiognotraces, and would also ask leave to Publish copies of the same, here & in Europe.

Mr. Hill is a Pupil of Nature, whom I have lately met with in travelling thro' the New England states. with her instruction he has composed several beautiful pieces of Music in a peculiar stile, and plays with much taste on various musical instruments, particularly the violin, of which he bids fair to become a master. I flatter myself you would be pleased with his performances as a specimen of the force[1] of native american genius.

I expect to sail for England in about two weeks one of my first objects will be to set forward a manufactory of Claviols; will send the first perfect one to your order.

I am Sir Your Hbl Sevt

JOHN I. HAWKINS

RC (MHi); at foot of text: "Thomas Jefferson Esqr."; endorsed by TJ as received 14 June and so recorded in SJL with notation "by mr Hill."

After he left Georgetown in 1803, 22-year-old URI K. HILL took his Hawkins physiognotrace to New York City and New England. Hawkins had given him the use of the patented invention to help pay his debts, and Hill advertised profile likenesses "taken in gold, on glass, for seven Dollars each, or cut in paper for fifty Cents" from a machine known to "excel all others in accuracy." He had less success as a profilist than he did in advancing his musical, engraving, and publishing career. Hill's published music included *The Vermont Harmony* in 1801 and *The Sacred Minstrel, No. 1,* in 1806. He advertised his vocal and instrumental schools and concerts in Hartford and Boston and solicited subscriptions to a proposed quarterly publication, *American Musical Museum.* He was briefly in debtors prison in Rutland, Vermont, in

1804 (Randolph, Vt., *Weekly Wanderer*, 27 Feb. 1802; *Rutland Herald*, 12 May 1804; Boston *Repertory*, 10 Oct. 1806, 10 Apr. 1810; *Boston Gazette*, 13 Mch. 1806; Peter Benes, "Machine-Assisted Portrait and Profile Imaging in New England after 1803," in *Painting and Portrait Making in the American Northeast*, published as *Dublin Seminar for New England Folklife Annual Proceedings*, 19 [1994], 138-9; Ellen G. Miles, "1803—The Year of the Physiognotrace," in same, 135-6).

For Hawkins's PATENT PHYSIOGNOTRACES, see Vol. 39:306-7, 383-4.

[1]Preceding three words interlined.

To George Jefferson

DEAR SIR Washington June 8. 1803.

I inclose you the manifests of my tobacco which I had not recieved till last night. they agree with the list I sent you, except omitting the light hhd of 700. ℔ which I presume has been retained above. the amount is 44,439. ℔ Accept my affectionate salutations.

TH: JEFFERSON

PrC (MHi); at foot of text: "Mr. George Jefferson"; endorsed by TJ in ink on verso. Recorded in SJL with notation "manifests 44,439 ℔ tobo." Enclosure not found.

The MANIFESTS were enclosed by TJ's overseer Burgess Griffin in a letter of 27 May, recorded in SJL as received from Poplar Forest on 7 June, but not found.

From Martin Kinsley and Others

SIR Castine June 8th. 1803.

We the underwritten inhabitants of the District of Maine and in the vicinity of Frenchmans Bay haveing been informed that Meletiah Jordan Esqr: Collector of that Port is likely to be removed from his Office; would with great deference introduce to your notice Paul Dudley Sargent Esqr of Sullivan within the Port to fill the vacancy if there should be one, we can recommend as a Gentleman fully qualify'd to fill that Office, firmly attached to You and the present Administration, and through the whole of the Revolution and to this Day a steady Republican and has served his Country in the Field, the Legislature & the Judiciary with integrity and fidelity for thirty years past—With profound Respect

We are Sir Your Most Obedient And Most Humble Servs:

MARTIN KINSLEY.
JEREH. WARDWELL
WILLIAM VINAL
OLIVER MANN

RC (DNA: RG 59, LAR); probably in Kinsley's hand, signed by all; at head of text: "Thomas Jefferson Esqr. President of the United States"; endorsed by TJ as received 17 June and "Sargeant, Paul Dudley, to be collector Frenchman's bay. Maine. v. Meletiah Jordan" and so recorded in SJL; also noted by TJ on verso: "he is a federalist, a very weak man & merely a tool. he is now quiet & submissive."

A native of Bridgewater, Massachusetts, Martin Kinsley (1754-1835) graduated from Harvard in 1778, studied medicine, and served as a purveyor of supplies during the Revolution. He moved to Hampden, Maine, in 1797. Kinsley served in the Massachusetts state government as a representative intermittently between 1787 and 1806, in the executive council in 1810 and 1811, and in the senate in 1814. In 1818, he was elected to Congress, serving one term from 1819 to 1821. In 1803, he became postmaster at Hampden. Jeremiah Wardwell of Penobscot, William Vinal of Vinalhaven, and Dr. Oliver Mann of Castine served, along with Kinsley, as state representatives in 1803. Wardwell and Mann had served together as selectmen at Penobscot in 1793 and 1794, before Castine was established as a separate town (*Biog. Dir. Cong.*; Stets, *Postmasters*, 129; Boston *Independent Chronicle*, 28 May-1 June 1801; Boston *Republican Gazetteer*, 9 June 1802; Boston *Columbian Centinel*, 15 June 1803; George A. Wheeler, *History of Castine, Penobscot and Brooksville, Maine* [Cornwall, N.Y., 1923], 60-2, 66, 185, 327).

In 1801, the Treasury Department considered complaints against Melatiah JORDAN, collector at Frenchman's Bay. Jordan charged that PAUL DUDLEY SARGENT had instigated the investigation because he sought the collectorship. Jordan, a Federalist, remained in office until his death in 1818. According to SJL, on 9 June 1803 Jacob Crowninshield and others also wrote TJ recommending Sargent for the collectorship at Frenchman's Bay. The letter, received by TJ on 17 June, has not been found (John A. Peters, "Memoir of Col. Melatiah Jordan, of Ellsworth, Maine," *Bangor Historical Magazine*, 4 [1888-89], 66, 68; Vol. 35: 726). For Sargent's earlier interest in the collectorship at Penobscot, see Vol. 35: 227, 229-30n.

To James Oldham

SIR Washington June 8. 1803.

Yours of the 3d. was recieved last night. would not riven pine slabs make a better moveable cover for the plaistered part of the house, than linen? if slabs 10. f. long and 2. f. apart were first laid cross ways thus  horizontally and then others nailed up & down close, & breaking joints and the nails clinched on the under side, it would hang together strongly, and might be laid on, & laid by in pannels very handily. if pannels 10. f. wide would be too unhandy, they might be only 8. or 6. f. wide. I think this would be best. linen would soon be stolen. however if there be no other way effectual but linen, mr Lilly must get that for you, for we must not permit the plaistering to get wet on any account.

With respect to help, if Lewis be not sufficient, I must get you to consult with mr Lilly, who will endeavor to assist you, on better terms for me than giving mr Perry a dollar a day for a hand which he talks of asking. I could get the best housejoiner here to go for much less than that: but it seems not worth while for a mere job, & especially as a coarse hand I imagine will do. Accept my best wishes.

TH: JEFFERSON

RC (William Tatcher, Philadelphia, Pennsylvania, 1951); addressed: "Mr. James Oldham Monticello near Milton"; franked and postmarked.

Oldham's letter OF THE 3D., recorded in SJL as received 7 June, has not been found. A letter of 12 May from Oldham, recorded as received 16 May, and TJ's response of 18 May have also not been found. A letter of 13 June, recorded in SJL as received from Oldham on 16 June, is also missing.

A letter of 3 June from John PERRY, recorded in SJL as received from Shadwell on 7 June, has not been found.

From Craven Peyton

DEAR SIR Stump Island June 8. 1803

Nothing was done at May Court. M. Carr and Barber was employed. my instructions to them was to have the business put of untill the next Court. I attended Monday last; but Nelson who appears for Henderson did nothing. M. Carr thought it ought to come before the quarterly Court at which your instructions shall be executed. when Meriweather & Millar was leaveling the Mill seat I expressed my centiments to Henderson so fully and endeavoured to impress on their minds the fraudulent intentions of Henderson. I have not since heard any thing of their bargaining. shoud. you approve and will authorise me, at any time his dam shall be taken down or at least he might be foarced into just measures. the pappers which I was to of forward to you some of them M. Carr was in want of. shoud. you wish the ballance they shall be forwarded

with great Respt Yr. Mst. Obt. C PEYTON

RC (ViU); endorsed by TJ as received 12 June and so recorded in SJL.

From Nicholas N. Quackenbush

Albany (State of New York)
SIR— June 8th. 1803

In the close of the last winter the Council of Appointment of this State was pleased to appoint me to an office which by the constitution of this State incapacitates me during my continuance therein from holding any other—Having accepted this appointment—I am therefore obliged to, and hereby do, resign the office of General Commissioner of Bankruptcy with which I have been Honored by you—

Immediately after my acceptance of the appointment under this State, I forwarded my resignation to you by a friend, but as he shortly afterwards died (as I have lately heard) I therefore expect that it has not been delivered—

I am with the most perfect respect Sir Your Obliged and most Obedient Humble Servant NICHS. N. QUACKENBUSH

RC (DNA: RG 59, LAR); at foot of text: "The president of the United States"; endorsed by TJ as received 16 June and so recorded in SJL; also endorsed by TJ: "resigns as Commr. bkrptcy."

Nicholas N. Quackenbush (1764-1823) was a Republican attorney in Albany, a Federalist stronghold. Following DeWitt Clinton's recommendation, TJ appointed him bankruptcy commissioner in June 1802. He unsuccessfully ran for the state senate in 1805 as a Clintonian Republican (Joel Munsell, *The Annals of Albany*, 10 vols. [Albany, 1850-59], 8:87; *Albany Register*, 2, 9 Apr. 1805; Lansingburgh *Farmers' Register*, 2 Apr. 1805; New York *Morning Chronicle*, 14 May 1805; New York *Spectator*, 4 Feb. 1823; Vol. 37:514-15).

In January 1803, the New York COUNCIL OF APPOINTMENT named Quackenbush "first judge of the county of Albany." On 17 June, DeWitt Clinton wrote Madison recommending Abraham Ten Eyck as "a very proper successor" to Quackenbush. TJ immediately made the appointment (RC in DNA: RG 59, LAR, endorsed by TJ: "Tenwyck Abraham. to be Commr bkrptcy Albany"; list of commissions in Lb in DNA: RG 59, MPTPC; *Albany Gazette*, 20 Jan. 1803). In the same letter, Clinton supported Frederick Jenkins as commercial agent at Le Havre (see Rensselaer Havens to TJ, 25 June 1803).

To Thomas Mann Randolph

DEAR SIR Washington June 8. 1803.

Your's of May 30. has been recieved. should Brown recover so that the law shall inflict no punishment on Cary, it will be necessary for me to make an example of him in terrorem to others, in order to maintain the police so rigorously necessary among the nailboys. there are generally negro purchasers from Georgia passing about the state, to one of whom I would rather he should be sold than to any other person. if none such offers, if he could be sold in any other quarter so distant as never more to be heard of among us, it would to the others be as if he were put out of the way by death. I should regard price but little in comparison with so distant an exile of him as to cut him off compleatly from ever again being heard of. I have written this to mr Lilly and will thank you to advise & aid him in procuring a sale. in the mean time let him remain in jail at my expence, & under orders not to permit him to see or speak to any person whatever.

With respect to the sale of the moiety of your mill seat, I shall willingly do any thing that may give it value, with only a single reservation that we do nothing which may communicate value to Henderson's lots & mill, so as to render them saleable. if by reducing them to the only value they *now* have, that of mere soil, I can once buy them in, I shall willingly communicate to your situation whatever shall be necessary to make it a good one. I shall be at home in 7. weeks from this time. would they not give you, till I come, time to consider, in the expectation that you would thereby get the site improved & more worth their acquisition? I could then see with you in what manner a benefit could be given to your site without being communicated to Henderson's, which would for ever put it out of my power to get rid of him as to the rivalry, I do not in the least wish to avoid that. the neighborhood will gain by having more than one mill, and I desire no advantage but from the intrinsic merits of my position. I should indeed be glad to have my toll mill up a season before another, merely to learn people the way to it. but this I am in hopes Lilly will enable me to effect. my tender love to my dear Martha & the little ones, & affectionate esteem to yourself. TH: JEFFERSON

P.S. I have reserved for a P.S. to mention that the last news from P. Carr was 24. hours later than what I sent you viâ Richmond. he had continued to get better; & I consider their subsequent silence as unequivocal evidence that all is going well.

RC (DLC); endorsed by Randolph as received 10 June.

By a Virginia LAW of 1765, slaves accused of manslaughter against other slaves were expected to face criminal prosecution, not just the informal punishment of slaveholders (William Waller Hening, ed., *The Statutes at Large; Being a Collection of All the Laws of Virginia*, 13 vols. [1809-23], 8:139; Philip Schwarz, "Forging the Shackles: The Development of Virginia's Criminial Code for Slaves," in David J. Bodenhamer and James W. Ely, Jr., eds., *Ambivalent Legacy: A Legal History of the South* [Jackson, Miss., 1984], 134).

A letter from TJ to Gabriel LILLY, recorded this day in SJL with the notation "120. D. for Chisolm," has not been found. The payment for Hugh Chisholm, a bricklayer and plasterer, closed a balance dating from the previous September (MB, 2:950, 1081, 1102).

SENT YOU VIÂ RICHMOND: TJ to Randolph, 4 June.

From Edward Thornton

Wednesday Noon. [8 June 1803]

Mr Thornton presents his respectful compliments to the President, and proposes to have the honour of waiting on him this evening for the purpose of receiving his orders.—

In the mean time he begs to inform him that Mr Parkyns was some months ago at Halifax in Nova Scotia, where he had resided for a year or two before: but from Mr T.'s having received no answer to several letters addressed to him, he concludes that Mr Parkyns returned to England on the death of his father.

RC (MHi); partially dated; endorsed by TJ as a letter of 8 June 1803.

MR PARKYNS: probably English landscape artist and designer George Isham Parkyns, with whom TJ corresponded in 1800. TJ admired Parkyns's work and tried unsuccessfully to secure his advice on landscaping at Monticello. Around 1800, Parkyns created a series of landscape images of Halifax, Nova Scotia, and its environs (*Collections of the Nova Scotia Historical Society*, 18 [1914], 110; Vol. 31:446-7; TJ to Philippe Reibelt, 24 Dec. 1804, 19 Oct. 1805, 12 Aug. 1807; TJ to William Hamilton, July 1806).

Petition of James Carroll, with Jefferson's Order

[on or before 9 June 1803]

The Petition of James Carroll of the City of Washington, Blacksmith.

Most humbly sheweth,

That at a circuit court of the District of Columbia held in the City of Washington in December one thousand eight hundred and one, he was Indicted for an Assault on the body of Daniel McGinnis, for which the Court fined him in the sum of Twenty dollars and costs of suit; and that at same court he was Indicted for an Assault on the body of John Veach, for which the Court fined him in the sum of twenty dollars and costs of suit, for which he now stands committed.

That the motive which urged him to these breaches of the Law, arose from the said McGinnis and Veach's having previously beaten and abused John Galloway with whom your Petitioner then wrought at Journeywork.

Your Petitioner therefore most humbly prays, that you will be pleased to remit the fines and costs of suit aforesaid; and thereby enable him to apply his labor to the maintenance and support of himself and Wife.

and he as in duty bound will pray &c. JAMES CARROLL

It has been represented to me that the petitioner is very poor and totally unable to pay his fines and costs—and that he has been in close confinement for several months. If such are the facts, although to the best of my recollection the assault and battery was very violent and clearly proved, yet from motives of humanity to his family, as well as economy to the United States, I respectfully recommend a remission of his fines and Costs.

W. CRANCH
June 9th. 1803

For reasons Similar to these which Mr Cranch has expressed I Concur with him in the recommendation which He has made

W KILTY

[*Order by TJ*:]
let a pardon issue as to the *fine* to the US.

TH: JEFFERSON
June 16. 1803.

MS (DNA: RG 59, GPR); undated; in an unidentified hand, signed by Carroll; TJ's order written on verso below recommendations written and signed by William Cranch and William Kilty; at head of text: "To the President of the United States."

Carroll sent TJ a nearly identical PETITION for pardon the previous summer, but which specified that MCGINNIS and VEACH were black and that GALLOWAY was white (Vol. 38:43). An undated affidavit signed by Elisha Lanham and 27 others recommended Carroll as a proper object for pardon, knowing him to be "a sober, honest and industrious man." Individual affidavits in Carroll's favor by Daniel Carroll Brent, Uriah Forrest, and John W. Pratt were added at the bottom of the same sheet (MS in DNA: RG 59, GPR). On 16 June, TJ pardoned Carroll for his two fines (FC in Lb in same).

To Arnold Oelrichs in the Name of Lewis Harvie

SIR Washington June 9. 1803.

The President of the US. had recieved in due time your letter of Sep. 14. 1801. and lately that of Dec. 28. 1802. and he was informed by the officer of the customs[1] in Philadelphia of the reciept of certain boxes there addressed to him containing busts. as it is inconsistent with the law he has laid down for himself to accept presents while in public office, he meant to have given this answer to the letter of explanation of mr Twisler of Baltimore which yours gave him reason to expect. no such letter having come to hand, he gave instructions to the officer of the customs on his application some time ago, to consider the boxes not as addressed to him but to Mr. Twisler & subject to his orders. he desires me to assure you he is as sensible of your kind intentions as if he could have availed himself of them, and he is satisfied they will lead you to approve the rule of conduct which his duty to the public & to himself requires him to pursue. I am &c

LEWIS HARVIE
secretary to the Presidt of the US.

Dft (DLC); entirely in TJ's hand; month and day interlined in dateline in place of canceled "Apr."; at head of text: "Copy of a letter to be written by <*Capt. Lewis*> mr Harvie to Mr. Arnold Oelrichs at Bremen"; TJ inserted Harvie's name for the signature in place of canceled "M.L."; endorsed by TJ with notation "written to him in the name of mr Harvie." Not recorded in SJL.

INFORMED BY THE OFFICER OF THE CUSTOMS: George Latimer notified TJ in November 1801 that the shipment from Oelrichs had arrived in Philadelphia (Vol. 35:741; Vol. 36:19).

TWISLER OF BALTIMORE: James Zwisler (Vol. 36:19n).

[1] TJ first wrote "by the custom house" before altering the phrase to read as above.

From Charles Pougens

Paris, Quai Voltaire, No. 10.
ce 20 Prairial an xi.
9 Juin 1803. (V. style.)

MONSIEUR

J'ai l'honneur de vous confirmer toutes mes précédentes et de vous donner avis que, conformément à vos ordres, Je viens d'expédier deux caisses sous la marque JFP. No. 1. et 2. ci joint facture. J'ai établi les prix les plus doux possible et ménagé vos intérêts comme les miens propres. La note des parties manquantes à votre Encyclopédie méthodique était si claire que J'ai pu les réunir toutes et vous en faire expedition. Vous trouverez ci bas, Monsieur, 1o. Note de quelques articles qui feront l'objet d'une troisieme caisse. J'ai déduit les motifs pour les quels ils ne se trouvent pas dans ces deux premières. 2o. Note des articles que je ne vous fournis pas avec causes motivées.

Croyez, Monsieur, à mon zèle inaltérable. Il est proportionné à ma haute admiration pour votre personne.

Ci inclus prospectus d'un ouvrage périodique qui a rendu quelques services aux sciences et aux lettres. L'Estimable redacteur de l'Aurora en a déja parlé dans sa feuille. J'ai fait pour la 4e. année des changemens assez considérables au plan de ce journal. Vous trouverez aussi dans cette lettre le programme de mon Dictionnaire Etymologique et raisonné de la langue française au quel je travaille depuis près de vingt quatre ans. J'ai l'honneur d'être avec respect, Monsieur Votre très humble et très obeissant Serviteur POUGENS

Articles qui doivent former la Caisse No. 3.—

Ouvrage très cher lorsqu'on le demande dans les boutiques J'en attends sous quinze jours un exemplaire dans la vente des livres du feu Prince Monaco.—	Corps universel diplomatique par Dumont 8 vol fol

J'en attends à pris honnête dans une vente qui doit avoir lieu très incessamnent.	Code de l'humanité par felice
même réponse que ci dessus. Cet ouvrage est très rare à Paris	Dictionnaire de l'Academie Royale de Madrid.
Je n'ai trouvé à Paris que l'Edition in 4o et je voulais pour vous l'Edit. de Florence. J'ai écrit à mon correspondant. Si cet envoi tardait Je vous enverrais mon propre exemplaire, ce que j'eusse déjà fait s'il eût été mieux conditionné.	Dictrio. dell'Academia della Crusca

N.B. Si le hazard d'une vente me fesait trouver quelques uns des articles ci bas cottés Je les joindrais à la susdite Caisse

Articles demandés par Mr Jefferson et qu'on n'a pu encore trouves.

Introuvable à moins du hazard d'une vente	Essai historique et chronologique de l'abbé Berlié
Idem.	Abrégé chronologique de l'histoire ancienne avant Jesus Christ
Epuisé et peu estimé	Dictionnaire historique et bibliographique by Ladvocat 4 vol in 12
On imprime cet ouvrage à Lyon en 12 vol 8o	Dictionnaire historique par une société de Gens de lettres 9 vol 8o
Rare. Attendre le hazard d'une vente.	Abrégé chronologique de l'histoire de Pologne par l'abbé Coyer
inconnu Nous ne connaisson que le droit des gens.	Watel Questions du droit Naturel
Lequel des ouvrages de Muratori? faut-il vous envoyer les antiquités, les annales, les écrivains d'Italie? Je n'ai osé prendre sur moi.	Muratori
Introuvable	Shardü Leges Rhodiorum
Idem.	Us et coutumes de la mer par Clairac
Idem.	Heineccie scriptores de Jure maritimo
Continuation de recherces	Wadin œuvres sur les lois maritimes dont les titres sont inconnus

Idem	Arithmetique de Playfair 4o imprimé à Paris en 1787 ou environ
Idem	Table des vivans de Susmick
introuvable à Paris. J'ai écrit à Londres à mon correspondant Mr Aug. Gameau Albermarle street No 51 Piccadilly qui peut vous bien servir pour toutes demandes de livres anglais	Scapulæ Lexicon Edit. de Londres
Continuation de recherches.	Heiderici Lexicon 4o

EDITORS' TRANSLATION

Paris, 10 Quai Voltaire
20 Prairial Year 11.
9 June 1803 (Old Style)

SIR,

I have the honor of confirming my earlier letters and informing you that, per your order, I have just sent two cases designated JFP No. 1 and 2. The invoice is enclosed. I set the prices as moderately as possible and considered your interest as if it were my own. The notes concerning the missing volumes from your *Encyclopédie méthodique* were so clear that I was able to gather and send all of them. Below you will find, Sir: 1. A few titles that will be sent in a third case with the reasons why they are not in the first two. 2. A list of the books I cannot locate along with the explanations.

Be sure of my unwavering zeal, Sir. It is proportionate to my deep admiration for you.

Enclosed is the prospectus for a periodical that has served the arts and sciences. The *Aurora*'s esteemed editor has already discussed it in his paper. For the fourth year, I have made considerable changes in the format of this journal.

With this letter you will also find the outline of my etymological and systematic dictionary of the French language on which I have been working for almost 24 years.

I have the honor of being your respectful, very humble, and very obedient servant.

POUGENS

Contents of Case No. 3

This work is very expensive in shops. I am waiting for a copy to come up at the book sale of the late Prince of Monaco in the next two weeks.	*Corps universel diplomatique* by Dumont. 8 volumes in folio.
I am waiting to acquire this at a fair price in a sale that is supposed to take place very soon.	*Code de l'humanité* by Felice.
As above. This work is very rare in Paris.	Dictionary of the royal academy of Madrid.

I wanted you to have the Florence edition, but have found only the in-quarto in Paris. I have written to my correspondent. If there is a delay, I will send you my own copy, which I would have done earlier if it had been in better condition.	Dictionary of the academy of Crusca.

N.B. If I have the good fortune of finding some of the titles listed below, I will add them to the case.

Books requested by Mr. Jefferson that we have not yet located

Impossible to obtain, unless I am lucky enough to come upon it at a book sale.	*Essai historique et chronologique* by the Abbé Berlié.
Same.	*Abrégé chronologique de l'histoire ancienne … avant Jesus Christ.*
Out of print and not highly regarded.	*Dictionnaire historique et bibliographique* by Ladvocat, 4 volumes in duodecimo.
This work is published in Lyon in 12 volumes octavo.	*Dictionnaire historique* by a society of men of letters, 9 volumes octavo.
Rare. We must await the good fortune of finding it in a book sale.	Chronological summary of the history of Poland by the Abbé Coyer.
Unknown. I only know his *Droit des gens*.	Vattel, *Questions de droit naturel.*
Which of Muratori's works should I send you? The *Antiquités*, the *Annales*, or the *Ecrivains d'Italie*? I dare not take it upon myself to choose.	Muratori.
Impossible to find.	Schardius, *Leges Rhodiorum.*
Same.	*Us et coustumes de la mer* by Cleirac.
Same.	Heineccius, *Scriptores de Jure Nautico.*
I am still searching.	Valin, works on maritime law (titles unknown).
Same.	Playfair, *Arithmétique*, in quarto, printed in Paris in 1787 or thereabouts.
Same.	Life table by Süssmilch.
Cannot be found in Paris. I wrote to my London correspondent, Mr. Auguste Gameau, 51 Albemarle Street, Picadilly, who can help you with requests for English books.	Scapula, *Lexicon*, London edition.
Still searching.	Hederich, *Lexicon*, in quarto.

RC (DLC); in a clerk's hand, signed by Pougens; on printed letterhead, including dateline with blanks for date filled by clerk; at head of text, printed: "Charles Pougens, Membre de l'Institut National de France, Imprimeur-Libraire, à" continuing in clerk's hand: "Monsieur Jefferson président du Congrès et associé Etranger de l'Institut"; endorsed by TJ as received 28 Sep. and so recorded in SJL. Enclosures: (1) Invoice of books for the Library of Congress, not found.

(2) Notice of *Bibliothèque française*, not found (see below). (3) Syllabus of Pougens's *Dictionnaire*, not found (see below). Enclosed in Pougens to Robert R. Livingston, 8 June (see Livingston to TJ, 11 June).

JE VIENS D'EXPÉDIER DEUX CAISSES: the two containers held books that Pougens had acquired for the congressional library, plus installments of the *Encyclopédie méthodique* that TJ, in a letter to the bookseller dated 5 Feb. 1803, had requested for his personal collection. For the titles wanted from Paris for the Library of Congress, see Vol. 37:229-33 and Vol. 38:76-7. The books in Pougens's shipment intended for the congressional collection cost 1,866 livres, or $345.55 according to the rate TJ later used to calculate his portion of the costs (TJ to John Beckley, 6 Mch. 1806). Pougens sent the two cases to the American consul at Le Havre for shipment to the United States (undated invoice of packing and freight charges totaling 87.15.3 livres, MS in DLC: TJ Papers, 133:23073, in a clerk's hand, endorsed by Robert R. Livingston; John Mitchell to Pougens, 24 July, RC in DLC, which was enclosed in Pougens to Livingston, 26 July, RC in same, a brief covering note endorsed by Livingston).

D'UN OUVRAGE PÉRIODIQUE: Pougens recruited scholars and writers to review books on an array of subjects for the *Bibliothèque française*, a monthly periodical he began in 1800. William Duane, in hopes of securing subscriptions to the periodical or orders for French books, devoted part of a column of the AURORA to a description of the *Bibliothèque française* in June 1802 (Philadelphia *Aurora*, 8 June 1802; *Mémoires et Souvenirs de Charles de Pougens ... commencés par lui et continués par Mme Louise B. de Saint-Léon* [Paris, 1834], 243-4).

DICTIONNAIRE ETYMOLOGIQUE: Pougens labored for years compiling etymologies from several languages for a scholarly work on the French language to be organized alphabetically on the model of Samuel Johnson's dictionary. He was able to put into print only a single specimen volume in 1819 that included words beginning with the letters A through C. He envisioned the work as having three components, a *Trésor* of word origins in six volumes, a three-volume abridgment of the *Trésor*, and a four-volume *Dictionnaire grammatical raisonné* (Charles Pougens, *Trésor des origines et dictionnaire grammatical raisonné de la langue française. Specimen* [Paris, 1819], v-xiv; A. V. Arnault and others, *Biographie nouvelle des contemporains, ou dictionnaire historique et raisonné de tous les hommes qui, depuis la Révolution Française, ont acquis de la célébrité*, 20 vols. [Paris, 1820-25], 17:50, 52-3).

ENCLOSURE

Invoice for Encyclopédie Méthodique, with Jefferson's Notes

Encyclopedie methodique 67 Livraisons.

✓	Agriculture, Tome, 3me. et Tome 4me. 1re partie	3. Vol.
✓	Amusemens, depuis page 560 jusqua 900 on fournit le tome entier	2. *in 1.*
✓	Antiquités Tome, 4me. 2me partie et tome 5 entier	3.
✓	Architecture, Tome 2me. 1re partie	1.
✓	Art militaire, Tome 4,	2.
✓	Beaux arts, Tome 2me. 2me partie	1.
✓	Botanique, Tome 4me	2.
✓	Chirurgie, Tome 2me. 2me partie	1.
✓	Geographie, Ancienne.[1] *Tome 3. 2nde partie*	1.

✓	Histoire, Tome 5me. 2 partie	1.
✓	Histoire, Naturelle, Tome 7 entier	2.
✓	Manufacture, Tome 2me. 2me partie, et tome 3d *2de*[2] partie	2.
	Medicine, Tome, 3d.[3] 2me partie tome[4] 4. 5. 6. 7 entier.	9.
✓	Philosophie, Tome 2me & 3 entier	4.
✓	Art Aratoire,	1.
✓	Chasse,	1.
✓	Jeux,	2.
✓	Pêches,	1.
✓	Phisique. 1 Tome entier	2. *in 1.*
✓	Systeme, Anatomique 1 Tome entier,	2. *in 1.*
✓	Chimie, Tome 2 et 3 entier,	4. in 2
✓	Geographie Phisique	2.
	Planches,	
✓	Botanique, Tome 4 à 9,	6.
✓	Chirurgie,	1.
✓	Pêches,	1.
✓	Histoire naturelle *XXIII. Partie, Insectes—XIX. Partie—Coquilles*	2.
	Idem, des vert.[5] *XXI. Partie. Mollusques.*	2.—*des Vers*
✓	Art Aratoire	1.
	Volumes	62 £.535.

[*In TJ's hand perpendicularly in margin*:]

I have now 67. livraisons complete, and Medecine. Tome III. 2me partie duplicate to be returned.

[*In TJ's hand at foot of text*:]

60. parts in 55. volumes.

<*wanting Medecine Tome 4. Partie 1re. to fill up between Bluet. & Capillaire de Montpelier.*

Planches. Histoire Naturelle [*XVIII.*] *partie des Vers*>

they sent me Tome III. 2d partie, which I had before, & charged without sending it Tome IV. partie 1re. which I had before

MS (DLC); in a clerk's hand, undated; with checkmarks by TJ in pencil; notations by him within the body of the list, also in pencil, are in italics; his notations in margin and at foot of text are in ink, and his cancellations within them are shown as <*italics*>.

DEPUIS PAGE 560 JUSQUA 900 ON FOURNIT LE TOME ENTIER: that is, from page 560 to 900, completing the volume.

The 535 livres equaled $98.98 (TJ to John Beckley, 6 Mch. 1806). For the serial publication of the *Encyclopédie méthodique* in parts called livraisons, with illustrative plates (PLANCHES) issued separately, and for TJ's desire to bring his set of the large work up to date, see his letter to Pougens of 5 Feb.

[1]TJ here canceled the clerk's "3me partie."

[2]"2de" is TJ's substitution in pencil for the clerk's "pe." (for *première,* "first").

[3]In margin, keyed here by an asterisk, TJ wrote "I had it before."

[4]In margin, keyed here by a dagger, TJ wrote "the 1st. part of Tome 4. did not come, & I had it before."

[5]In margin, keyed to this word by a double dagger, TJ wrote and canceled "partie des Vers. did not come" and wrote "there came only 1. partie. Mollusques."

From John Vaughan

D SIR 9 June 1803

I enclose a letter recieved by a young friend of mine from the hands of the writer, to whom he went particularly recommended; he has a packet for D Thornton which contains something for yourself—I Have spoken to Capt Lewis, who politely takes charge of it.—My friend had many conversations with the writer of the letter who was very free in his remarks, upon the ideas of the leading men in that Country.—who thought lightly of this Country, that when possessed of N.O. they would have a considerable hold upon us—"There are amongst us who dream of Universal empire" "If a war does take place & England & America are induced to join, we shall loose our Ultramarine possessions but they will not believe me" Several expressions dropped which shewed dissatisfaction with head quarters, & it appears it had even proceeded to misunderstanding—but it appeared also that the views of the Chief were not such, as had in view any real intention of being particularly friendly to us but rather the Contrary—Your information no doubt is more complete than any my friend can give, he left the place on 31 March, & if a further detail would be of any service he would readily give it—

The Phil: Socy. goes on with rather more animation, we have at last resolved to publish a 6th Vol. the work will Very shortly go to press—Communications now made would be peculiarly important, & not delayed in publication—We have recd several valuable presents of Books from the Different European Societies to whom we had sent ours—The Edinburg Societies have merely acknowledged the receipt—from the Italian Society no reply—We Sent ours to the Care of Count Castiglioni or in Case of his Death requested Mess. Grant Sibbald & Balfour of Leghorn to attend to the distribution—

Mr Thomas Leiper has been trying experiments upon Pounded & Ground Lime Stone as manure without burning the effect promises to be equal to Plaister of Paris—with this & Mr Livingstons Communication of the effect of Pyrites will be a valuable addition to our Stock of manures

A Connecticut Agricultural Socy. have published the result of their proceedings—The Information they collect from the Members being chiefly communicated orally & recorded by the Secy. appears to command in an easy manner all that the Members know—A Committee afterwards Collect & publish—If I can procure a Copy, I shall have the pleasure of Sendg you one—as the plan is useful. It appears by some of the Communications, that a large quantity of lime or plaister

Or a large quantity of Farm Yard Manure are not so productive as a much smaller portion of each United—I remain

With the greatest respect D sir, Your friend & servt

JN VAUGHAN

RC (DLC); endorsed by TJ as received 11 June and so recorded in SJL. Enclosure not found.

Vaughan's YOUNG FRIEND was Joseph Curwen, who had recently returned from France; see Volney to TJ, 21 Mch. and 10 May.

6TH VOL.: in May, the American Philosophical Society accepted a proposal from Jane Aitken to publish the next volume of the society's *Transactions* at her own expense. She agreed to give 100 copies to the society (APS, *Proceedings*, 22, pt. 3 [1884], 337).

VALUABLE PRESENTS OF BOOKS: acting as librarian for the APS, Vaughan sought to carry out a 1799 initiative to reinvigorate or establish regular exchanges of publications with learned associations in other countries. From mid-1802 to mid-1803, the APS had formed such connections with societies in Prussia, Sweden, Ireland, Spain, Russia, and the Batavian Republic, as well as the National Institute of France, the Literary and Philosophical Society of Manchester, England, and, in London, the Society of Antiquaries, the Royal Institution, the Royal Society, and the Linnean Society. The Royal Society of Edinburgh and the Society of Antiquaries in that city had ACKNOWLEDGED THE RECEIPT of volumes of the *Transactions* of the APS without sending their collections of papers in return (same, 282-3, 327-8, 331-2, 334-5, 337-9; APS, *Transactions*, 6 [1809], ix-x).

As Vaughan informed TJ in December 1801, the APS library lacked recent volumes of the transactions of several ITALIAN organizations (Vol. 36:236-8). Vaughan and TJ were acquainted with Luigi CASTIGLIONI, who devoted much of his time to the study of botany. The APS elected him to membership during a two-year sojourn he made to the United States in the 1780s. William Short visited Castiglioni in Milan in 1788 (ANB; Antonio Pace, "The American Philosophical Society and Italy," APS, *Proceedings*, 90 [1946], 392-7; Vol. 14:41-2; Vol. 24:787).

GRANT, Sibbald & Balfour, a Scottish mercantile firm at Leghorn, had commercial connections to the United States (Kenneth Wiggins Porter, ed., *The Jacksons and the Lees: Two Generations of Massachusetts Merchants, 1765-1844*, 2 vols. [New York, 1937], 1:512-14, 518-24).

For Robert R. Livingston's reporting on the use of burned PYRITES as fertilizer in Europe, which TJ passed along to the APS, see Livingston's letter to TJ of 26 Nov. 1802.

The APS had received a copy of printed *Transactions* of the CONNECTICUT Society for Promoting Agriculture. Rather than solicit formal essays, the Connecticut association posed a set of queries about agricultural practices and printed its members' responses, some of which were only a few sentences long. One series of questions concerned the use of various materials as fertilizer (APS, *Proceedings*, 22, pt. 3 [1884], 338; *Transactions of the Society, for Promoting Agriculture in the State of Connecticut* [New Haven, 1802], 4-15).

From William Dunbar

DEAR SIR Natchez 10th. June 1803

I am honored with yours of the 3d March. My unconfirmed state of health suffered some retardment from my attendance on the Legislature: its new position chosen by the late assembly, altho' tollerable in our climate for a summer Session, was found to be, during a very cold winter, without comfort or even common accommodation: my sufferings demanded considerable repose; want of bodily health induces habits of indolence upon the mind, and I am but just returning to my favorite amusements; I never the less enjoy the flattering prospect of returning health. My Sketch towards a history of the Missisippi therefore remains unfinished, but as the Whole has been long in the form of notes & memorandums, I shall be able soon to connect it so as to be fit to transmit.

You have done me the favor to communicate your ideas respecting the politicks of our Country; it was not my intention to introduce this Subject into any communications from me, knowing that your Governor and General here must keep you apprised of every event meriting notice: to those Gentlemen I have always communicated every intelligence (of any importance) which my acquaintance and correspondence with New Orleans may have brought early to my knowledge, with a view that it might be conveyed to you.

The reasons you assign for negotiating in preference to going to war, must be completely satisfactory to every unprejudiced person, if the object in view be solely the restoration of the deposit. Of the few persons in this Country who reflect, the greater part contemplate another object which they conceive to be of immense magnitude and which at a future day will powerfully operate upon the happiness of this great Continent. The french—an ambitious, enterprising and warlike people are preparing to scatter their myriads over these countries. we are informed that 30 thousand persons in france had obtained passports to migrate to the Missisippi, exclusive of those composing Genl. Victor's expedition. They will create a great Nation speaking a different language from ours. It is true we consist of millions and they only of thousands, but a few years of uninterrupted prosperity will multiply them into a great people, sufficient for their own defence and capable of annoying the Neighbours. The West Valley of the Missisippi is greatly more fertile by nature than that on the side of the United States: that Country is undisturbed by those ferocious Savages who have with so much constancy and firmness retarded the progress of Civilised population on our Side. If then with every favorable circumstance, the French shall advance only in the known ratio of two to one in twenty years, their present population in Louisiana which we shall call only 60 thousand, will in 200 years, amount to more than 60 millions: it must be allowed that the uncommon Supplies of men to be expected from Europe must greatly anticipate the hour when those people will become formidable. We shall thus have in one and the same Country, two great rival Nations speaking different languages; and experience has demonstrated that the rivalry of Nations is little short of a State of perpetual hostility; the immense number of fine navigable rivers furnished by our Country, so far from constituting natural boundaries become the natural bonds and connection of the People; and if hostilely disposed, greatly facilitate their reciprocal incursions; it would seem that immense Chains of rugged, barren & inhospitable Mountains are the most perfect boundaries and barriers in Nature.—How desireable—to preserve the whole of the Valley of the Missisippi for the spread of the people of the United States; who might in the progress of one Century, plant the fine Western Valley of the Missisippi with many millions of industrious inhabitants, speaking the same language with ourselves: it ought not to be objected, that this object is too remote to merit the contemplation of the present moment; it may be considered comparatively as at hand. Those who do not chuse to penetrate so far into futurity, are greatly alarmed by a danger which they conceive to be pressing. It is not doubted that the french Govt. has for some time fostered principles extremely innimical to the Govt. and general prosperity of the United States. By arts which they have reduced to a System their successful progress in Europe has been wonderful; they acquire by their superior talents and facinating address an ascendancy over the minds of a great part of a People, whose Govt. they intend to annihilate: their project becoming mature, the foreign Govt. must tamely submit to the *mediatory* mandates of the great Nation, or if blind to the progress of french principles they attempt to rouse the people in defence of their Country, they fall an easy conquest to the superiority of french arms, the people receiving with open arms their pretended deliverers. There is no doubt, the french will attempt to play the same game with us. From the present good disposition of the mass of the people of the Western States, towards their own Govt. and a general detestation of french principles, a superficial observer might draw arguments unfavorable to any impression to be made upon us by the french; but who shall say, what influence a series of favors, indulgencies and immunities, with a crafty, conciliatory well directed conduct, may effect? the trade of france, no doubt, will be open to the Western people, their Commerce upon the Ocean will receive protection from the Navy of france, & no return will be exacted beyond what is paid by the 'Soi disant' Citizens of france. In due time the well chosen emissaries of our *Sister Republic* (who will not be sparing in the almighty influence of the precious metals) will create a party among the least virtuous but most clamorous of our Citizens;

a false idea (already afloat) will be industriously inculcated that the interests of the Eastern and Western United States are opposed, and that an entire Separation will advance the prosperity of the Latter; by those and a thousand other wiles and stratagems, the integrity of our union will be attacked; with what success, time only will demonstrate: but I must confess, when I observe with what facility and indifference, many of our native Americans talk of flinging aside their allegiance and becoming the willing subjects of a despotic Government, I tremble. It may be said that those will still continue to be Americans and will in due time facilitate the acquisition of the Country. Such was my own opinion under the inactive and lethargic Govt. of Spain; but we cannot dissemble that our quondam friends (in the event of a war) will be but a few among the many, when mingled with the numerous & warlike bands of the french, and will be compelled to present the bayonet against the breasts of their fathers and brothers, or should their new Masters doubt of their fidelity (which is highly probable) they will be degraded into the rank of hewers of wood and drawers of water for the army, and thus throw an additional weight into the Scale of the Enemy, which a spirit truely patriotic ought to have preserved to ourselves. But how such mighty evils are to be prevented, must be left to the contemplation of the Sages of our Country. We cannot allege that we possess any right derived from the ordinary principles of human Justice or the law of Nations to inhibit the completion of a Contract made by two independent nations. But is there not a law in our favor superior to all others, the Divine law of Self-preservation? But even upon this principle, Violence is unjustifiable untill fair and honorable negotiation shall have failed.

We observe that an idea has gained ground in the U.S. that a Subaltern Intendant has dared to infract a solemn treaty between two Nations, without the positive command of his Court: this thought has not failed to excite a smile here among those who are intimately acquainted with Spanish polity and who know the precision of Conduct which pervades its departments, for of all Govts. certainly the Spanish is one of the most regular, methodical and correct; the rule of conduct of the principal officers is delineated so clearly, that they cannot deviate but with a certainty of punishment, unless sheltered under powerful protection. The only doubt among the few who have penetrated a little the secret, is whether the act has been done with or without the knowledge of the french Government; for my own part, I have believed, in consequence of several private reasons, particularly the information of some old friends near the Cabinet at New Orleans, that the transaction was brought forward without the privity of the Chief Consul: the idea I have formed & which I conceive to be upon solid ground, is, that the Spanish Govt. tremblingly alive to their own danger from the transplantation of a Colony or rather an army of rapacious frenchmen in the vicinity of their rich mexican possessions, have made a feeble attempt by the apparent insult of suspending the deposit, to stimulate the Americans to step forward for their relief: this being a matter of peculiar delicacy, putting to risk, the very existence of the Spanish Monarchy, it became necessary to conduct the measure with such profound privacy that it should be impossible for the french Govt. ever to penetrate the secret; a speedy revolution might have been the immediate consequence of the discovery. My ideas have been long since communicated to Genl. Wilkinson: it is scarsely supposeable that the Governor of New Orleans could tamely suffer his own dignity to be so far wounded as to permit an officer subaltern to himself, (& whose power extends only to the regulation of Commerce) to infract by an unauthorised act, a solemn treaty with a foreign nation, respecting which the Governor himself is the sole external organ. Governor Salcedo tells Govr. Claiborne in very obscure, I may,[1] mysterious language; that he was himself opposed to the Intendant's decree untill that officer presented to his view, the propriety of acting with circumspection and prudence, in order that they might be prepared against possible events which might spring from revolving occurrences; or words to that effect: those expressions do not in any sense apply to the continuance or suspension of the deposit, nor can we interpret them upon any other principle, but from the existence of some violent alarm in the minds of the Spanish Officers. Immediately after the promulgation of the Intendant's decree, suspending the deposit; a great anxiety became evident in the minds of Govr. & Intendant, to dispatch a Confidential express to the Spanish minister near the U.S. and the first Clerk of the Secretary's office was chosen for the purpose, but after some reflection he declined being engaged in the service: a Mr. Power was afterwards applied to, and he asked (I think) 2000 dollars; the Govr. thought the sum too much, and while they continued to deliberate, the Express pilot-boat sent by the Marquis d'Yrujo arrived at New Orleans. Whether the Govt. at New Orleans transmitted the secret they wished to communicate, by the return of the Pilot-boat, or found it then too late, time perhaps may discover.—I will add one more circumstance which is perhaps a corroboration of my idea. It has been a policy of the Spanish Govt. to send occasionally into their Colonies, persons vested with supreme power to enquire into and remedy such evils and abuses as spring from the malversation of their officers: no such

Dictatorial officer had ever appeared in Louisiana, yet at the moment when the Country was forever to be lost to Spain and when She could not be much interested in the existence of any abuses real or pretended within the Province, an Officer of the above description makes his appearance in New Orleans: he arrived (as customary) incog; he was extremely intimate with the Intendant, and I believe lived in his house; after remaining unknown a short time, he proclaimed his pretended Mission and exercised his authority in one or two slight cases, and soon after departed: it is difficult not to believe that this person was entrusted with a commission of the most private nature, widely different from that of the very unnecessary character with which he seemed to be alone invested: a short time after his departure the proclamation of the Intendant was issued. The late order of the Spanish Court, tho' apparently militating against the above idea, proves nothing but the imbecility and pusilanimity of that Govt. which cedes to every passing impulse. Disimulation has ever been a favorite engine in Spanish politicks, and when we reflect upon the depressed Situation of the Spanish Monarchy, goaded by the Govt. of france; the apparent inconsistencies which mingle in the transactions respecting the Suspension and restoration of the deposit are easily reconciled.

It is time I should apologise for having detained you so long, but my excuse must be found in my motive, which is a desire to inform you of a few circumstances which may hereafter throw some light upon present and future transactions. Politicks are not a favorite subject with me & I shall probably not introduce it again into our Correspondence, unless in the view of communicating something which may be important for you to know.

With the highest Consideration I have the honor to be Your Obedient Servant

William Dunbar

RC (DLC); endorsed by TJ as received 17 July and so recorded in SJL.

Dunbar was a member of the territorial LEGISLATURE (Dunbar to TJ, 5 Jan. 1803).

NEW POSITION: political considerations had prompted the transfer of the territorial government from Natchez to the small settlement of Washington several miles to the north (Robert V. Haynes, *The Mississippi Territory and the Southwest Frontier, 1795-1817* [Lexington, Ky., 2010], 206).

SOI DISANT: so-called.

The FIRST CLERK OF THE SECRETARY'S OFFICE was Peter Pedesclaux, who since 1788 had been clerk notary for the colony of Louisiana and clerk of the cabildo government of New Orleans (Pedesclaux memorial, April 1804, enclosed in William C. C. Claiborne to TJ, 27 Apr. 1804). Thomas POWER, a naturalized Spanish subject originally from England, occasionally acted as a confidential agent or performed other services for the Spanish colonial government (James Ripley Jacobs, *Tarnished Warrior: Major-General James Wilkinson* [New York, 1938], 150-1, 163-6, 181; Charles Gayarré, *History of Louisiana*, 3d ed., 4 vols. [New Orleans, 1885], 3:345-6; Jack D. L. Holmes, "The Marqués de Casa-Calvo, Nicolás deFiniels, and the 1805 Spanish Expedition through East Texas and Louisiana," *Southwestern Historical Quarterly*, 69 [1966], 326, 331; Vol. 31:468, 469n).

SHORT TIME AFTER: for the instructions from Spain that prompted Juan Ventura Morales to revoke the right of deposit at New Orleans, see Arthur Preston Whitaker, *The Mississippi Question, 1795-1803: A Study in Trade, Politics, and Diplomacy* (New York, 1934), 190-4.

LATE ORDER OF THE SPANISH COURT: see TJ to DeWitt Clinton, 22 Apr.

[1]Thus in MS.

From George Logan

DEAR SIR Stenton June 10th. 1803

My apprehensions respecting our late valuable friend Mason have been realised; his Family whilst sensible of his loss, have less occasion to lament the event of his death from home, as every attention of eminent Physicians and sincere friends was given to him. I only regret that on his arrival in Philadelphia, he did not immediately come to Stenton.

The proceedings of some men in Philadelphia intended to influence the official conduct of yourself & of the Governor of this State, are condemned by our best republican characters. Should events of this kind not be checked by a proper degree of firmness on the part of our executive magistrates we may expect that the same spirit will in a short time dictate the proceedings of our Legislatures

It is proposed to address a public Letter to you on the subject of removals from office—should this be the case I trust you will give them a public answer, honorable to yourself as first magistrate of a free Nation

The combinations & intrigues of a few desperate men destroyed the fair prospect of liberty in france, after having by the most sanguine prosecutions removed some of the best men in their Country. *I do know* that some active fœderal characters look forward to a similar termination to the american revolution. On my seeing you at Washington I will take the liberty of speaking to you more fully on this subject.

Mrs. Logan presents her best respects

I am your obliged Friend GEO: LOGAN

RC (DLC); at foot of text: "Thos. Jefferson"; endorsed by TJ as received 15 June and so recorded in SJL.

LATE VALUABLE FRIEND: Senator Stevens Thomson Mason died late on 9 May, a week after he arrived in Philadelphia. His funeral was held the next day with William White, bishop of the Protestant Episcopal Church, presiding. According to the *Aurora*, the funeral procession was led by the militia unit commanded by General John Shee "with reversed arms, in advance of the whole." Governor Mc-

From Albert Gallatin

Dear Sir June 11th 1803

By a law of last session Beaufort in North Carolina, which was formerly a port of delivery attached to the district of New Bern, is made a district (or distinct port of entry & delivery) from and after the last day of June next. Heretofore the officer of the port was a surveyor with a salary of 150 dollars. His office will cease of course, and a collector must be appointed. The two candidates are Benjamin Cheney the present surveyor, & Bryan Hellen formerly deputy of Colo. Easton the former surveyor, on whose death, in 1802, Mr Cheney was appointed. At that time Cheney & Hellen were candidates for the office of surveyor, & Cheney was appointed on the recommendation of Mr Spaight which remains in your hands. Mr Stanley had recommended both. The recommendation then made in favor of Hellen is now transmitted underlined *Old.* At present Mr Cheney applies for the new office as a matter of course, and sends no recommendations. Mr Hellen sends very strong recommendations. The papers are all enclosed for your decision. From their letters Mr Hellen seems best qualified.

By the same law Easton in the district of Oxford, Maryland—and Tiverton in the district of Newport R. I. are made ports of delivery after the sd. 30th day of June next and a surveyor must be appointed for each with a salary of 200 dollars.

For the office at Easton, there are two candidates vizt. Charles Gibson and John Harwood. Their recommendations are enclosed. I presume that the first will be the object of your choice.

Each officer is to have two commissions vizt.

For Beaufort

1. Collector of the district of Beaufort
2. Inspector of the revenue for the port of Beaufort in the district of Beaufort

For Easton

1. Surveyor of the port of Easton in the district of Oxford
2. Inspector of the revenue for the port do. in the district of do.

For Tiverton

1. Surveyor of the port of Tiverton in the district of Newport
2. Inspector of the revenue for the port of do. in the district of do.

But for the office in that last port—*Tiverton*, I have received no recommendations; but I presume you have. You will perceive that the commissions cannot be delayed any longer. I continue very unwell or would have called on you this morning.

With respect & attachment Your obedt. Servt.

ALBERT GALLATIN

RC (DLC); at foot of text: "The President of the United States"; endorsed by TJ as received from the Treasury Department and
"Collectr. & Inspector Beaufort N.C.
Cheney & Hellen
Surveyr. & Inspectr. Easton Maryld.
Harwood & Gibson
do. of Tiverton R.I."
and recorded in SJL as received 11 June with notation "Collector of Beaufort & Surveyors of Easton & Tiverton." Enclosures: (1) John Stanly to Gallatin, 15 Mch. 1802, enclosing a recommendation for Brian Hellen as surveyor signed by 15 merchants at the port of Beaufort (see Vol. 37:11n). (2) Benjamin Cheney to Gallatin, Beaufort, 1 Apr. 1803, understanding that Beaufort has been made a port of entry and that a collector is to be appointed, he, as the present surveyor, applies for the new position (RC in DNA: RG 59, LAR; endorsed by TJ: "Cheney Benj. to mr Gallatin. to be Collector of Beaufort N.C."). (3) Brian Hellen to Gallatin, Beaufort, 23 Apr. 1803, applying for the collectorship at Beaufort and enclosing testimonials to his character; if appointed, he promises to discharge the duties honestly and to the best of his abilities (RC in same; endorsed by TJ: "Hellen Brian to be Collector of Beaufort N.C."; probably enclosing Nos. 4, 5, and 6, below). (4) Residents of Beaufort to Gallatin, recommending Hellen as better qualified than any other to be collector of customs because as deputy for many years he has carried out all of the duties of surveyor "to the general Satisfaction of all parties"; with great pleasure they note that Hellen "has been uniformly a friend to the principles of Republican government, and Warmly attached to the present Administration" (MS in same; undated; in an unidentified hand; signed by Joel Henry, Jacob Henry, and 38 others; probably enclosed in No. 3, above). (5) Owners of vessels and residents of Beaufort, North Carolina, to Gallatin, recommending the appointment of Hellen as customs collector at the port, noting that as deputy surveyor he has been performing the duties of inspector and surveyor with "Ability and integrity"; Cheney, the present surveyor, lives a distance from Beaufort and if he receives the appointment, it will be "a mere sinecure" with the duties continuing to be performed by Hellen, his deputy; Hellen is a friend to Republican principles and "firmly *attached* to the present Administration" (MS in same; undated; in an unidentified hand, signed by William Fisher, Jr., and 17 others; endorsed by TJ; probably enclosed in No. 3, above). (6) Inhabitants of New Bern, North Carolina, to Gallatin, undated, recommending Hellen as collector at Beaufort because he is "a man of good moral character integrity and ability and they have confidence that the duties of this office if committed to his care will be discharged to the Satisfaction of the Government and its Citizens" (MS in same, in an unidentified hand, signed by John Stanly, bankruptcy commissioners William Blackledge and Edward Harris, and 30 others, endorsed by TJ: "Hellen Bryan to be Collectr. Beaufort," probably enclosed in No. 3, above; Vol. 37:710; Vol. 38:644n). (7) Jacob Gibson to Gallatin, Talbot County, Maryland, undated, but encloses Nos. 8 and 9, below, recommending Charles Gibson as surveyor at the new port of delivery at Easton; Jacob Gibson identifies William Hayward as a state senator and notes that those who recommend John Harwood, the only competitor for the position, are Federalists, with the exception of one or two Republicans who did not know that Charles Gibson was applying for the position (RC in same; endorsed by TJ: "Gibson Jacob to mr Gallatin Gibson Charles to be Survr. Easton"). (8) William Hayward to Gallatin, Talbot County, 21 Apr. 1803, recommending Charles Gibson as a young man of good character with "talents and integrity fitted for the appointment" (RC in same; endorsed by TJ; enclosed in No. 7, above). (9) Joseph H. Nicholson to Gallatin, Wye House, 22 Apr. 1803, recommending Gibson, "a Democrat" of good character and "in every Respect equal" to the appointment as surveyor at

Easton; he notes that John Harwood, the other applicant, is a "clever man, and would do extremly well; but he is a Federalist" (RC in same; endorsed by TJ; enclosed in No. 7, above). (10) Robert Wright to Gallatin, Chester Town, Maryland, 27 Apr. 1803, joins Joseph H. Nicholson and other Republicans at Easton in recommending Charles Gibson as surveyor; he notes that Harwood, Gibson's competitor, "has been a pretty high toned federal" while Gibson, "always correct in his politics" is also better qualified; Wright fears that the "few republicans in office under the federal Government, and the non removal of many truly noxious to the people" will make it difficult to obtain support for the president from "some of our best friends" who object "'that he has got the Office he wished, and that he leaves the people to be insulted by petty federal'" officers; Wright seeks the removal of one "*old Tory*" in his county who "is bitterly opposed to every Measure of the present Administration" and recommends the appointment of Edward Markland who would be "agreeable to the *real* Friends of the Administration" (RC in same; endorsed by TJ). (11) John Scott to Robert Smith, Easton, Maryland, 22 Apr. 1803, recommending John Harwood, a man of "understanding and integrity," as surveyor at Easton; although his "politics are federal," he is a moderate Federalist who has "never been in any other manner offensive" (RC in same, endorsed by TJ: "Harwood John. to be Surveyr Easton. John Scott to Robt. Smith"). (12) Inhabitants of Easton and Talbot County, Maryland, to Gallatin, undated, recommending John Harwood as surveyor at the newly designated port of delivery at Easton, noting that he will execute the office "with integrity and to the satisfaction of the People (MS in same; in an unidentified hand, signed by Samuel Nichols and 26 others, including merchants and traders of Easton; perhaps enclosed in No. 11, above).

LAW OF LAST SESSION: for the 3 Mch. 1803 legislation on collection districts, see U.S. Statutes at Large, 2:228-9 and Augustus B. Woodward to TJ, 4 Mch.

Richard Dobbs SPAIGHT recommended Benjamin Cheney as surveyor at Beaufort in February 1802 (see Vol. 37:10). For John Stanly's recommendation of both Cheney and Brian Hellen, see Vol. 37:10-11n. TRANSMITTED UNDERLINED OLD: on a scrap of paper that Gallatin sent to TJ with Enclosure No. 1, above, the Treasury secretary wrote: "Note—Mr Stanley recommendd both Mr Hellen and Mr Cheney—The last gentlemen was appointed—His recommendations are with the President——*Old* recommendation in favr. of Mr Hellen for office of surveyor A.G." (MS in DNA: RG 59, LAR, 5:0244; written on address sheet to "The Secretary"; at head of text, in a clerk's hand: "March 15. 1802, Hon John Stanley, enclosing recommendn. fav of Brian Hellen for Surveyor of Beaufort. No Carola"). Gallatin attached another note with the later, VERY STRONG RECOMMENDATIONS for Hellen (see enclosures Nos. 3 through 6, above): "Recommendation in favor of Brian Hellen for the office of 'Collector of the *district* of Beaufort' in North Carolina, established by the law of 2d March 1803 *Note* A commission of inspector of the revenue for the *port* of Beaufort should accompany that of collector for the district.—A.G." (MS in same, 5:0249; in Gallatin's hand).

OFFICE IN THAT LAST PORT—TIVERTON: according to SJL, TJ received two letters recommending Thomas Durfee as surveyor at Tiverton, Rhode Island. The first was from Senator Christopher Ellery, dated 28 Feb. and received by TJ the same day; the other came from Congressman Joseph Stanton, Jr., also dated 28 Feb., received by TJ on 1 Mch. Neither has been found.

Report from John Lenthall

Rough Stone and Brick work done to the South Wing of the Capitol from 28th May to 11th June 1803

– West front –

The Voids of 5 Reversed arches filled up, the Cellar window stools set & the Cellar windows taken up to level of the Arches which amt. to about 1000 Cubic feet

Bricks laid in the Reversed Arches about	9160
do in the Internal Arches	4728
	13888

— South front —

Voids of 5 Arches taken up from the Cellar Window stools to the level of the arches, excluding the extra labor of the Quoins and fluing Jambs of Cellar Windows—377

Bricks laid in 5 Internal Arches	4,572

— East front —

The Walls taken up to the level of the Arches. The Beds of the Arches prepared to receive the Bricks, and the Voids filled up to the tops of the Cellar Window stools, Window stools set &c, Amot. about 4467 feet

Bricks laid in Reversed Arches	11,964
do in the Internal Arches, about $\frac{2}{3}$ of which only is done—say	3100
	15,064

Stone	5844 Cubic feet or
Bricks laid about 33,000	236 Perches

for B H Latrobe

Jno Lenthall

MS (DLC); in Lenthall's hand and signed by him; endorsed by TJ: "Capitol June 11. 1803."

quoins are the external angles of walls, more commonly referred to as cornerstones. A quoin might also refer to the stones or bricks that form the angle (OED).

From Robert R. Livingston

Dear Sir Paris 11th. June 1803

Having very latly writen to you this is merely to inform you that our mutual friend Mr. Skipwith being now the father of a family is desirous of removing to Louisiana. His knowledge of the french language the religion of his family & his amiable manner fit him in a peculiar manner for conciliating the affections of the people of that country to our government, and should you distribute that country into separate governments I think he would from his long services merrit one of them or the collection of one of the ports. But you know him too well to render any particular recommendation necessary.

Hanover is in the hands of the french. The army prisoners on parol & the duke of Cambridge who was to share the fate of his Majestys hanoverian subjects has made his escape in time—Genl. Bernadotte has returned to Paris—After the plan of treating in America for New Orleans was relinquished nothing sufficiently Important remained to Justify the sending a man of his rank Mr. Laussat (the consul of New Orleans) will probably succeed him—Your Books are packed & will be forwarded by Pugens in a few days. I mentioned to you in one of my late letters that I find that it will be necessary for me in consequence of the late arrangements & the wishes of the Americans here to remain till the next spring at this place which I am ready to do unless you have made some other arrangement. I have the honor to be Dear Sir

With the most respectful attatchment Your Most Obt hme. Servt

ROBT R LIVINGSTON

RC (DLC); at foot of text: "Thomas Jefferson Esq president of the United States"; endorsed by TJ as received 17 Aug. and so recorded in SJL. Enclosure: Charles Pougens to Livingston, 19 Prairial (8 June), informing him that the books are ready to go to Le Havre and enclosing his letter to TJ (9 June); the total price for the two cases is 2,446 livres; Pougens appends a list of those titles he obtained for less than the expected cost, for a savings of 215 livres (MS in DLC: TJ Papers, 132:22823; in a clerk's hand, signed by Pougens; on same printed letterhead as Pougens to TJ, 9 June; at head of text in clerk's hand: "Monsieur Livingston Ambassadeur des Etats unis d'Amérique"; endorsed by Livingston). Enclosed in TJ to Madison, 18 Aug. 1803.

FATHER OF A FAMILY: Fulwar Skipwith had married a French citizen, Evalina Barlié van den Clooster, in 1802. They had two children by 1805 (Henry Bartholomew Cox, *The Parisian American: Fulwar Skipwith of Virginia* [Washington, D.C., 1964], 98).

Twenty-nine-year-old Prince Adolphus Frederick, the DUKE OF CAMBRIDGE and youngest son of King George and Queen Charlotte of Great Britain, had been an officer with Hanoverian troops in the 1790s and was his father's representative in the electorate when the French invaded in May 1803. A British ship took him to safety in England (DNB; Grainger, *Amiens Truce*, 194-5).

From Benjamin Rush

Dear Sir, Philadelphia June 11th: 1803.

I have endeavoured to fulfil your Wishes by furnishing Mr Lewis with some inquiries relative to the natural history of the Indians. The enclosed letter contains a few short directions for the preservation of his health, As well as the health of the persons Under his Command.

His mission is truly interesting. I shall wait with great solicitude for its issue. Mr: Lewis appears admirably qualified for it. May its Advantages prove no less honourable to your Administration, than to the interests of Science!

The enclosed letter from Mr Sumpter contains some new Views of the present military arrangements of France & Great Britain. You need not return it.

From Dear Sir yours very respectfully & sincerely

Benjn: Rush

RC (NjP: Rush Family Papers); at foot of text: "Thos Jefferson Esqr:"; endorsed by TJ as received 16 June and so recorded in SJL. Enclosure: Thomas Sumter, Jr., to Rush, Paris, 25 Mch. 1803; he sends a copy of a treatise by a French chemist on "the means of disinfecting bad air"; he also states his opinion that war may help restore Britain's commerce and influence; war will also weaken the naval strength of France, Spain, and Holland, which they need to strike at Britain but which can only be strengthened during peace; the central issue in the previous conflict, he observes, was "between the principles of Republicanism & Monarchy," a question that "interested all the powers of Europe"; the new war will not be on that basis and other countries may stay out of the fray to let Britain and France, which are becoming like Carthage and Rome, "both exhaust their power"; however, "Ambition & folly have so much more to do with these matters, between Nations, than wisdom or justice, that it is possible the conflagration may again become general"; Sumter will soon go to London "to embark for Charleston" (RC in same).

For the queries that Rush drew up for Meriwether Lewis concerning indians, see Lewis to TJ, 29 May.

ENCLOSURE

Rush's Directions to Meriwether Lewis for Preserving Health

June 11. 1803.

Dr. Rush to Capt. Lewis. for preserving his health.

1. when you feel the least indisposition, do not attempt to overcome it by labour or marching. *rest* in a horizontal posture.—also fasting and diluting drinks for a day or two will generally prevent an attack of fever. to these preventatives of disease may be added a gentle sweat obtained by warm drinks, or gently opening the bowels by means of one, two, or more of the purging pills.

2. Unusual costiveness is often a sign of approaching disease. when you feel it take one or more of the purging pills.

3. want of appetite is likewise a sign of approaching indisposition. it should be obviated by the same remedy.

4. in difficult & laborious enterprizes & marches, *eating sparingly* will enable you to bear them with less fatigue & less danger to your health.

5. flannel should be worn constantly next to the skin, especially in wet weather.

6. the less spirit you use the better. after being *wetted* or *much* fatigued, or *long* exposed to the night air, it should be taken in an *undiluted* state. 3 tablespoonfuls taken in this way will be more useful in preventing sickness, than half a pint mixed with water.

7. molasses or sugar & water with a few drops of the acid of vitriol will make a pleasant & wholsome drink with your meals.

8. after having had your feet much chilled, it will be useful to wash them with a little spirit.

9. washing the feet every morning in *cold* water, will conduce very much to fortify them against the action of cold.

10. after long marches, or much fatigue from any cause, you will be more refreshed by *lying down* in a horizontal posture for two hours, than by resting a much longer time in any other position of the body.

11. shoes made without heels, by affording *equal* action to all the muscles of the legs, will enable you to march with less fatigue, than shoes made in the ordinary way.

Tr (DLC: 132:22841); entirely in TJ's hand and endorsed by him: "Health. Rush's rules for preserving." FC (PPAmP), in Rush's commonplace book, printed in George W. Corner, ed., *The Autobiography of Benjamin Rush: His "Travels Through Life" together with his* Commonplace Book *for 1789-1813* (Princeton, 1948), 267; see Jackson, *Lewis and Clark*, 1:55n.

The original manuscript of Rush's guidelines has not been found. TJ probably made this copy before LEWIS, who was in Washington by 19 June, took the original with him when he left the capital on 5 July (editorial note to Drafting Instructions for Meriwether Lewis, at 13 Apr.; TJ to Thomas Mann Randolph, 5 July).

PURGING PILLS: among the pharmaceutical supplies for Lewis's western expedition were 600 "Bilious Pills to Order of B. Rush" (Jackson, *Lewis and Clark*, 1:80).

SPIRIT: the provisions gathered for the expedition included 30 gallons of strong rectified wine spirits "such as is used for the Indian trade" (same, 72, 88).

Several pounds of white VITRIOL (sulfuric acid) powder and a quarter pound of elixir of vitriol were in the medical supplies (same, 74, 80).

From "J. G. D."

MR. PRESIDENT. June 13th 1803—

I have no doubt, but Your curiosity will be considerably awaken'd at the reception of an epistle of so singular a nature as the following; especially from one who does not, nor cannot hope to enjoy the pleasure of Your acquaintance:—and, before I proceed any further, it may be necessary to observe, that this letter is of importance to none but myself; And if there should be any thing amiss, in the method I have adopted in the conveyance, or, in the *familiarity* of the stile, it is oweing intirely to my want of better information, which I am convinced, Your goodness will readily pardon.

My intention in so doing, Mr President, is, to inform You, that I wish, by Your kind[1] permission, to be favour'd with an opportunity of requesting of You, verbally,[2] a particular favour,—and such an one as I could not presume to ask of any other gentleman in the United States:—and, I do assure You, Mr. President, that nothing less, than the most exalted opinion of Your generosity could have embolden'd me to trouble You in this way, or any other[3] especily with out an *introduction.*

Before I conclude, I would beg leave to inform You that I am a resident of Alexa, Virginia) and in my sircumstances considerably limited, but have, nothwithstanding, the honor of being known to, and respected by, some of Your best, tho probably, unknown friends in that place

If the above should meet Your approbation, Your petitioner (who has the honor of standing at Your gate) will expect to recieve from You, a verbal message, through the medium of the bearer hereof informing him when, & where he may have the honor of making known to You, the request above alluded to.

I am, Mr President, With very great, And unfeigned respect, Your most humble, And most obedient Servant, J. G. D—.

RC (DLC); endorsed by TJ as received from "Anonymous" on 13 June and "for money" and so recorded in SJL.

"J. G. D." may have been Joseph G. Daffin of Maryland who married Betsey Cooke of Alexandria in 1799. A man by this name from Caroline County, Maryland, apparently suffered financial difficulties and appeared as an insolvent debtor in county court in November 1805 (Alexandria *Columbian Mirror*, 9 Nov. 1799; Easton, Md., *Republican Star*, 16 Sep. 1806; Virgil Maxcy, ed., *The Laws of Maryland, with the Charter, The Bill of Rights, The Constitution of the State, and Its Alterations, The Declaration of Independence, and the Constitution of the United States, and Its Amendments*, 3 vols. [Baltimore, 1811], 3:269-70).

[1] Word interlined.
[2] MS: "vervally."
[3] Preceding three words interlined.

To George Jefferson

Th: Jefferson to
mr George Jefferson Washington June 13. 03

Will you be so good as to procure for me from the clerk of the high court of Chancery a copy of the decree of Jefferson v. Henderson which was given by mr Wythe three or four years ago, and inclose it to me? as I have occasion immediately for an authentic copy. I am in hopes your business will permit you to come and pass some time with us at Monticello in August or September, where we shall all be very happy to see you. affectionate salutations.

PrC (MHi); endorsed by TJ in ink on verso. Recorded in SJL with notation "decree v. Henderson."

For the DECREE, see Vol. 31:208. TJ's need for an AUTHENTIC COPY derived from the application he and Craven Peyton filed with the county court for permission to develop a mill seat that would have rendered useless the mill seat still controlled by John Henderson (Robert Haggard, "Thomas Jefferson v. The Heirs of Bennett Henderson, 1795-1818: A Case Study in Caveat Emptor," *Magazine of Albemarle County History*, 63 [2005], 9-12; TJ to Craven Peyton, 2 May; Thomas Mann Randolph to TJ, 30 May; TJ to Thomas Mann Randolph, 8 June).

From Bishop James Madison

Dear Sir June 13. 1803 Williamsburg

Being appointed by the Executive of this State, in Conjunction with two other Gentlemen, Mr J. Taylor, & Mr Venable, to collect all necessary Information relative to the Claim, which In Maryland has, of late, seriously revived, upon a part of the Territory of Virginia; & finding in your Notes on Virga. P. 363 Papers mentioned, particularly—1. "Survey & Report of the Commissioners appointed on the Part of the Crown to settle the Line between the Crown & Lord Fairfax—2. Report of the Council &c. & 3. Order of the King in Council confirming the said Report &c.—I take the Liberty to inquire of you, as the best Source to which I can apply.—where Copies of those Papers can be had; or, whether they can be procured without sending to London for them. I would not give you this Trouble, were I not perfectly assured of your Readiness to aid us with those Lights upon this Subject, which you may possess.

The Pretensions of Maryland are, surely, most extraordinary; but the Legislature of this State, very properly, determined to repel them by decent Reasons.

As all the Maps of Virginia describe Ld. Fairfax's Boundary by a Line beginning at the first Fountain of *N*. Branch of the Potowmac, the Inference is, that such description is conformable to the Order of the King in Council. It is probable, that Fry's & Jefferson's Map, on which Fairfax's Line was first drawn, is accurate in that Respect. If so, they must have possessed Copies of the Proceedings in G. Britain relative to the Lines; but I know not whether they now exist; if they do, I have conjectured, they would, most probably, be in your Possession.—If they are not to be had in America, would it not be adviseable to send to London for them?

To enter into a Discussion with Maryland as to the strict geographical Meaning of the Terms, "first Fountain," upon which she grounds her Claim, would be both tedious & fruitless;—whatever Reason might be urged, would scarcely operate so as to produce Conviction.

The Map in your Notes, as well as the Map of Fry & Jefferson make the Source of the So. Branch the most western. I should have no objection, this Fall, to ascertain the respective Longitude of the 3 Sources; but perhaps, the Expd. would militate more powerfully against us, than for us.—

I am, Dr Sir, With the sincerest Respect & Esteem, Yr Friend & Sevt J MADISON

RC (DLC); at foot of text: "Thos Jefferson Esqr Pr U.S—"; endorsed by TJ as received 18 June and so recorded in SJL.

For the boundary CLAIM dispute between Maryland and Virginia, see Vol. 38:325-6, 336-8.

FRY'S & JEFFERSON'S MAP: the map of Virginia and Maryland prepared in 1751 by TJ's father, Peter Jefferson, and surveyor Joshua Fry (Vol. 28:302).

MAP IN YOUR NOTES: the map TJ included in his *Notes on the State of Virginia* was engraved by Samuel J. Neele of London and was based primarily on the Fry-Jefferson map (*Notes*, ed. Peden, xviii; Vol. 10:621-2).

From Thomas Munroe

SIR Suptds Office, W. 13 June 1803

The St. of Maryld has since 19 Decr 91, sold to a considerable amot., lands within the City of Washington wch. she had become possess'd of under her acts of confiscation.

Amongst other sales was one of about 56 A. @ £50 ℔ A. to James Williams & U. Forrest who passed their bond for the amount, the Agt. of the State at the time of the Sale entering into the enclosed agreemt. mark'd A.—

It appears that about 45 A. of the before mentioned 56 A. have been appropriated to public purposes, it being within the Mall, for which Mr. Williams (to whom Mr. Forrest assign'd his int.) now claims for the State or himself £25 ℔ A, the Sums stipulated in the Deeds of trust to be paid to the original proprieters for public appropriations—one of the deeds of trust is also enclosed, marked B.—

It is at present doubtful as appears by a report of the Surveyor marked C. whether a part or the whole of the land sold as aforesaid to Williams & Forrest, will not be taken away or included within older Surveys by Carroll Burns &c.—But if the State's right to the number of acres sold by her agent is admitted to have been good,[1] prior to the passing of the act of her legislature on the aforesaid 19th Decr. 91 Chap. 45, entituled "an Act concerning the territory of Columbia & the City of Washington" was not that right transferred or relinquished by the said act, to the governmt. of the U.S., or was the *jurisdiction* only thereby ceded?—If *the right of property in the Soil* owned by the State was transferred or relinquished, could the state afterwards sell that soil to individuals? but in case it is considered she retained the right to sell such part thereof as should be laid off into building lots, had she also the right to sell or demand of the City funds £25 ℔ A. for the part which might be appropriated for public uses? or does the Act of Assembly, or agreement before recited, or any other circumstance, distinguish one part from the other as to the right of Sale?—

The deep interest which Maryld had in the establishmt. of the permanent[2] Seat of the general governmt. within her territory & which induced her to make a donation of $72,000, towards the erection of the public buildings would authorize the presumption that she meant to give her small possessions of soil also—As The presidt. by an Act of Congress had authority to accept & sell it & apply the money like other donations of land or money, but it is still more presumable she meant to give such part of her soil as might be wanted for public purposes, for a refusal to do so, & a demand of payment for it, would exhibit the inconsistency of making a donation with one hand & taking back part of it with the other.—The rights of property of *individuals* in the soil are clearly & expressly reserved, by the 2nd Sect. of the before recited act of assembly but no such reservation is made of the State's right—It is true the 3rd Sect. subjects the land belonging to the State to certain conditions which were necessary to enable the Commrs. to act on it in common with other land in the City, but this 3rd. Sect. it is contended amounts to as full a reservation of the State's right of property in the Soil as is made by the preceding Sect. of individual rights, notwithstanding the great difference of the language of the two Sectns, the former of which relinquishes the Soil of the State in full & absolute right as well as exclusive jurisdiction.—I have taken the liberty of stating these circumstances to you, sir, & respectfully solicit your directions before I answer the letters of Mr. Williams & the Treasr. of the State of Md. which I have received on the subject.

I have the honor to be with the greatest respect Sir, yr. mo. obt. Svt.

T. M

The papers enclos'd being originals I beg the favor of a return of them to file in the office

FC (DNA: RG 42, LRDLS); at foot of text: "President of U.S." Recorded in SJL as received 15 June. Enclosures not found, but see below.

Writing JAMES WILLIAMS on 27 June, Munroe stated that he had requested the city surveyor to examine the boundaries of his land claim in the District of Columbia. The surveyor found that the property sold to Williams by the state of Maryland lay within surveys previously claimed by Daniel Carroll of Duddington and the heirs of David Burnes. A portion of the land was under water and occupied by the bed of Tiber Creek or a proposed canal, and the attorney general believed it should not be paid for as appropriated ground. The city of Washington had already compensated Carroll and Burnes for the same lands claimed by Williams or the state of Maryland, observed Munroe, which rendered a legal decision regarding the claim necessary before a refund could be compelled from Carroll and Burnes's heirs or the right of Williams and the state to payment could be established. Munroe believed that Maryland had given up all rights to the land by its act of 19 Dec. 1791, which ceded to the United States the portion of the District of Columbia that lay within the state. Nevertheless, he closed by stating that "no objection, however, on this ground is now made by me to the States right to receive payment for all the land Appropriated to public use to which she can make good her title agt. the claims of Caroll Burns & others" (FC in same).

[1]Munroe first wrote "to be good" before altering the passage to read as above.

[2]Word interlined.

From John Wayles Eppes

DEAR SIR, Bermuda-Hundred June: 14. 1803.

Your letter of the 12th. of May arrived here while Maria and myself were on a visit to my Sister Walker the first we have been able to make since her marriage—We were detained there 13. days by rain—

As it will not be long before we shall meet—Lego & the arrangement proposed by you shall be the subject of conversation—The idea of occasioning personal inconvenience to you would induce me to abandon any project calculated solely for my own benefit—There is a part of Lego which would be to me a valuable acquisition & will give me more room near the Top of the Mountain—If you would sell this part it would obviate the objection as to Mr Randolph—As whatever objection there might be to a swap in a fair purchase I should stand on the same footing with any other citizen—I had mentioned to Mr Randolph the first propositions I made to you & he was clearly of opinion that they would be acceeded to—If you would sell this which would include I imagine about 200 acres I would take it at a valuation & in lieu of paying you rent pay interest on the purchase from its date until I could make the payment—This would be more convenient to me than paying up the whole purchase at once—however if it is necessary that the payment should be made I can raise the money & put down the whole—

We have got the Hessian Fly I believe in our Wheat—I have lost I imagine $\frac{1}{3}$ of my crop here—I enclose you a specimen of the Fly in three stages & will thank you to examine them & inform me whether you suppose it to be the real Hessian Fly—

Marias health is pretty good—We shall leave this place on the 10th. of July for the Green Springs where we shall wait your return to Monticello

Accept for your health my warmest wishes

I am yours sincerely JNO: W: EPPES

P.S.

The crops in charles city are entirely destroyed with the Fly—

RC (ViU: Edgehill-Randolph Papers); addressed: "Thomas Jefferson President of the United States Washington"; franked; postmarked Richmond, 16 June; endorsed by TJ as received 18 June and so recorded in SJL. Enclosure: see below.

MY SISTER WALKER: Eppes's younger sister, Elizabeth, married Dr. David Walker, a physician from Petersburg. She died at Eppington on 9 Dec. 1805 (John Frederick Dorman, *Ancestors and Descendants of Francis Epes I of Virginia*, 2 vols. [Petersburg, Va., 1992-99], 2:399).

FIRST PROPOSITIONS I MADE TO YOU: see Eppes to TJ, 6 May, and TJ to Eppes, 12 May.

TJ had a long-standing interest in the HESSIAN FLY. He had previously been chairman of a committee of the American Philosophical Society that systematically studied the insect and its infestation throughout the states. SPECIMEN collection and investigation were a principal motivation for his northern journey with Madison in 1791. TJ's own concerns about a southern blight grew as he reported to his son-in-law in 1801 that wheat fields near Washington suffered damage from the fly (Vol. 20:445-9, 461-2n; Vol. 23:430-2; Vol. 24:xli; Vol. 35:678).

From Albert Gallatin, with Jefferson's Note

Dear Sir 14 June 1803

I enclose a representation against the naval officer of Wilmington; together with a letter from the collector to whom I had communicated the grounds of complaint.

Those grounds being general, & no charge specified except that of absence which is not supported by the evidence of Mr Bloodworth, the regular course would be an admonition to Mr Walker to be attentive & correct, without harshness & too strict adherence to punctilios. Indeed it is not improbable that his fault may be a rigid performance of his duty. But the circumstance which seems to deserve most attention is his holding the office of clerk of the district court which renders it his interest, on account of his fee as clerk, to institute suits as naval officer upon every petty infraction or omission of the numerous & complex provisions of the revenue laws. Ought the two offices be considered as incompatible?

With respectful attachment Your obedt. Servt.

Albert Gallatin

[*Note by TJ:*]

Walker to be admonished that those who are compelled by law to come to a public office have a right to be treated with temper attention[1] and complaisance. interest teaches this to the private[2] shopkeeper, reason & duty should do it to the public officer: that a continued course of harsh & rude conduct to those who come on business[3] is good cause of removal.

that the intention of a law is that which is to be carried into effect, & it is to be found not by a rigorous adherence to the letter of a single word or expression but in it's general object and all it's provisions & expressions taken together; the object[4] and that he should be the more on his guard against a multiplication of suits for[5] ignorance, more probably than fraud, lest it should be imputed to the interest which his other office gives him[6] in increasing the business of his court.

the object of the law in the cases complained of is to punish fraud, not ignorance, and he should be the more &c.

RC (DLC); on one folded sheet with TJ's note on verso of address, below endorsement; addressed: "The President"; endorsed by TJ as received from the Treasury Department on 14 June and "Walker navl officer of Wilmington. complaint agt." and so recorded in SJL. Enclosures not found.

John Adams appointed Carleton Walker NAVAL OFFICER at Wilmington, North Carolina, in December 1800. Walker was also clerk of the federal district court that met in Wilmington. TJ appointed Timothy Bloodworth COLLECTOR of the port in early 1802 (Raleigh *Star*, 16 Feb. 1809; Vol. 35:467-8, 469n; Vol. 36:488).

WALKER TO BE ADMONISHED: TJ used his thoughts noted here as a partial draft for his letter to Gallatin of 15 June.

[1] Word interlined.

[2] Word interlined.

[3] Preceding six words interlined.

[4] Preceding two words interlined.

[5] Word interlined in place of "in cases of."

[6] Preceding six words interlined by TJ in place of "he has."

To William Lee

SIR Washington June 14. 1803.

I have to thank you for the sample of Medoc wine which you were so kind as to send me, and which I found very good. I liked it the better as it seemed not to have been brandied, a species of adulteration so disagreeable and so common. when I was at Bordeaux in 1787. I took great pains to make myself acquainted with the good wines, went to every vineyard & cellar of note, learned the names of the proprietors of those of 1st. 2d. or 3d. quality, the character of their wines, quantities & prices. the result was, as to the red wines, that passing over the 4. crops, I found the wine of Madame de Rozan of Margault to be so nearly equal to those of the Chateau Margault, as to be scarcely distinguishable when tried together, & not at all when tried separately; while the price was a great deal less. of the white wines, I preferred the Sauterne, and found those of M. de Salus the best. I therefore afterwards at Paris & Philadelphia drew my supplies of wine from Made. de Rozan & M. de Salus, who delivered them bottled & packed to my correspondent & recieved the price from them. I understand that these two proprietors are still living on their estates, and I have therefore a partiality for them in returning to them as an old customer, and a confidence they will serve me with whatever they have best, & ready for drinking. I take the liberty therefore of inclosing you a bill of M. Victor Dupont on the house of Dupont de Nemours pere et fils et co. banquiers Rue Montholon No. 300. à Paris for 200. Dollars, say 1050.tt which I will pray you to vest in the two wines above mentioned, about an equal *quantity* of each, as far as the sum will cover, naming me to Made. de Rozan & M. de Salus as an ancient customer whom they may perhaps recollect. I should be glad to have the wines shipped from Bordeaux in the latter part of August at latest, or they will not be here in time to save me from the necessity of buying in the country. Norfolk, Alexandria[1] Baltimore, Philadelphia or New York are proper ports to address them to the last however the least so,[2] & a line from you to the Collector of the customs[3] of whatever place they come to will induce him to notify me to take necessary steps for having them forwarded. I pray you to excuse the liberty I am taking & to accept my salutations & assurances of respect & esteem. TH: JEFFERSON

PrC (MHi); at foot of text: "William Lee esq. Bordeaux"; endorsed by TJ in ink on verso. Recorded in SJL with notation "1050^{tt}." Enclosure not found. Enclosed in TJ to Robert Purviance, 14 June.

[1] Word interlined.

[2] Preceding six words interlined.

[3] TJ first wrote "customshouse officer" before altering the text to read as above.

To Craven Peyton

DEAR SIR Washington June 14. 1803

Your favor of the 10th. is at hand particular circumstances relative to mr Randolph's mill seat had obliged me to communicate to him confidentially the interest I had acquired in the opposite one. I have therefore referred to him to consider with respect to his own as well as my interests whether it will be necessary to take down Henderson's dam before I come home, and if he thinks proper to have it done. I have also desired him to advise with you if necessary as to the [...]ings preventing mr Henderson from annexing to his [...] a right to a mill which belongs so much more justly to the whole tract. I shall be at home myself the last week of July, before which it seems probable the court will not have decided on the right. accept my best wishes & friendly salutations TH: JEFFERSON

PrC (ViU); blurred; at foot of text: "Mr. C. Peyton"; endorsed by TJ in ink on verso.

Peyton's FAVOR OF THE 10TH has not been found and is not recorded in SJL. For TJ's communication with Thomas Mann Randolph on the Henderson dam, see TJ to Randolph, 14 June.

To Robert Purviance

Washington June 14. 1803.

Th: Jefferson with his compliments to mr Purviance asks the favor of him to give the inclosed letter a passage in any vessel bound from his port to any port of France, but to Bordeaux of preference, if one be bound thither; and to accept his salutations.

RC (NN); addressed: "Mr. Robert Purviance Collector of the customs Baltimore"; franked and postmarked; endorsed by Purviance. Enclosure: TJ to William Lee, 14 June, and enclosure.

Robert Purviance (1733-1806) emigrated from Ireland and was living in Baltimore by the 1760s. There, he became a merchant with his brother Samuel Purviance. During the Revolution, the two engaged in privateering on the patriot side, and they later speculated in western lands. Wartime losses, perhaps compounded by liberal contributions to the Revolution, forced the brothers into bankruptcy during the 1780s, and in 1788 Samuel Purviance was captured and likely killed by Indians on the frontier. Despite being characterized as the lesser-skilled, junior partner in his mercantile business, Robert Purviance successfully applied for the post of naval officer at the port of Baltimore in 1789. He became collector in 1794 and, although a committed Federalist, retained the post until his death (New York *People's Friend & Daily Advertiser*, 15 Oct. 1806; Washington, *Papers, Pres. Ser.*, 2:332-3; Vol. 35:444-5).

To Thomas Mann Randolph

DEAR SIR Washington June 14. 1803.

In a letter of May 2. to mr Peyton I had said to him that if Henderson, counting on the indulgence I have used in leaving his dam hitherto, should propose to sell his 4. acres as a mill seat, I would immediately direct mr Lilly to take down the dam, and I desired mr Peyton to employ counsel & obtain an order for a mill on my part of the lands, but still to act in his own name & keep me out of sight. he writes me that the matter is in court, and will perhaps be decided next month, and proposes the demolition of the dam. the inconvenience this would be to the neighborhood as well as the wish to reserve the necessary accomodation for your seat, makes me averse to it. my object is only to prevent Henderson's giving an artificial value to his 4. acres at my expence. I must therefore get you, who are on the spot, and can decide as circumstances shall arise, to advise mr Peyton in the conduct of the business, so as to prevent Henderson from an order & to obtain one in his own name for me: and if you find this can be done by abating the dam, & cannot be done without it, then to direct mr Lilly to take it down. if every thing can be kept in statu quo till I come home, it would be well: but that may be difficult because I am not to be named as interested in it. if I could get Henderson ousted, so that the whole of the falls from the Secretary's ford to the recommencement of still water below Milton should be ours, I should very willingly give to each position the advantages necessary for it. I inclose you a copy of Binns's pamphlet on Plaister of Paris.—we have reason to expect a favorable result from Monroe's mission. my constant love to my dear Martha & the little ones and affectionate salutations to yourself. TH: JEFFERSON

P.S. not a word concerning P. Carr since my last to you, which I consider as certain proof of his recovery. S. Carr is not yet returned.

RC (DLC); at foot of text: "T M Randolph"; endorsed by Randolph as received 27 June. Enclosure: John A. Binns, *A Treatise on Practical Farming; Embracing Particularly the Following Subjects, viz. The Use of Plaister of Paris, with Directions for Using It; and General Observations on the Use of Other Manures. On Deep Ploughing; Thick Sowing of Grain; Method of Preventing Fruit Trees from Decaying, and Farming in General* (Frederick, Md., 1803; Sowerby, No. 721).

HE WRITES ME: Craven Peyton to TJ, 8 June.

Randolph was entertaining an offer from Isaac Miller and William D. Meriwether for a portion of his land in North Milton on which they hoped to erect a mill. TJ did not object to mills operating on EACH POSITION, that is, both sides of the Rivanna, but he could not tolerate a mill operating on Henderson's property in competition with his proposed mill (Randolph to TJ, 30 May; TJ to Randolph, 8 June).

TJ thought highly enough of John A. BINNS's "Loudoun System" of using gypsum plaster as a fertilizer to obtain multiple copies of Binns's pamphlet, at least four of which he forwarded to friends and relations (see also TJ to John Wayles Eppes, 19 June; TJ to John Sinclair, 30 June; and TJ to William Strickland, 30 June). He may have purchased the pamphlets through his Alexandria contact Francis Peyton, who at some point sent TJ a receipt of 12 June for eight pamphlets purchased from the firm of R. & W. P. Richardson for $2.58 (MS in DLC: TJ Papers, 132:22845; in an unknown hand). On 24 Nov., TJ recorded in his financial memoranda paying $2 to "Col. Peyton for Binn's pamphlets" (MB, 2:1112).

From Madame de Corny

le 15 juin 1803

jespere mon cher monsieur que vous aurez recu une lettre de moi ecritte en fevrier, et remise a M. charles wilkes qui partoit pour langleterre. Il ma tant promis detre fidel a sa promesse que je ne doute point que Cette lettre ne vous soit remise dans son tems. Mde monroé ma fait un plaisir bien sensible en me donnant de vos nouvelles. toute preuve de votre souvenir me sera toujours bien agreable et je vous prie au milieu de vos affaires importantes de me donner quelques instans. cette marque damitie sera payée par une amitie bien sincere.
je vous demande en grace de donner tout ce que vous pouvez de bonté et de protection au capitaine americain appellé Ledet. c'est une personne qui meritte sous tous les rapports et a laquelle je prend linteret que reclame ces Excellentes qualites.
il me seroit bien doux au retour de M. Ledet de savoir de luy que vous avez eu egard a ma recommandation. et jaimerois a pouvoir vous en temoigner ma reconnoissance
jaurai lhonneur de vous ecrire par Mde monroé et je me permettrai quelques details sur ma maniere de vivre. pour me justifier aupres de

vous detre separee de la Societe dont vous me recommandez lusage je vous ai parlé dun accident qui ma forcee de rester chez moi depuis 10 mois. on me fait esperer que le soleil me guerira par sa seul influence. jen attend les bons effets sans y croire absolument

recevez monsieur lassurance dun attachement bien sincere et qui durera toute ma vie. DE CORNY

EDITORS' TRANSLATION

15 June 1803

I hope, my dear sir, that you received my letter, written in February and entrusted to Mr. Charles Wilkes who was leaving for England. He made so many promises to be faithful to his promise that I have no doubt the letter was given to you in due course. Mrs. Monroe brought me much pleasure by giving me news of you. Any sign from you will always please me and I beg you to give me a few moments amid your important business. This token of friendship will be repaid with my very sincere friendship.

I ask you to please accord whatever kindness and protection you can to the American captain Ledet. He is worthy of admiration in all ways and his excellent qualities warrant the attention I have taken in him. I would be very happy if Mr. Ledet could tell me, on his return, that you heeded my recommendation. And I would like to be able to show you my gratitude.

I will have the honor of sending you a letter with Mrs. Monroe, sharing some details about my life to explain why I have been isolated from the company whose enjoyment you recommended to me. I told you about the accident that has forced me to remain home for the past ten months. People tell me to hope that the sun will be enough to heal me. I await its good effects without being totally convinced.

Receive, Sir, the assurance of my sincere and lifelong attachment.

DE CORNY

RC (DLC); endorsed by TJ as received 10 Oct. 1803 and so recorded in SJL. Enclosed in Joseph Ledet to TJ, 25 Aug. (see below).

EN FEVRIER: Madame de Corny last wrote to TJ on 15 Feb. Charles WILKES, the cashier of the Bank of New York, was in Paris that month. He must have forwarded her letter rather than carrying it across the Atlantic himself, for he returned by way of the British Isles and did not arrive back in the United States until the middle of August, more than three months after TJ received the 15 Feb. missive from Madame de Corny (New York *Evening Post*, 18 Apr.; New York *Commercial Advertiser*, 17 Aug.).

As master of the merchant brig *Washington*, Joseph M. LEDET made transatlantic voyages to and from New York (*New-York Gazette*, 19 Mch. 1804; New York *American Citizen*, 12 Apr. 1804; New York *Mercantile Advertiser*, 27 Apr. 1804). On 25 Aug. 1803, he wrote to TJ from London: "Sir, I have the honour to forward you inclosed a letter from Madame De Corny, which I kept untill this time, expecting to go soon to America & to deliver it myself into your hands; but business has prevented me to effectuate that design. You will please to excuse, Sir, my sending it to you with the cover cut open, but I did it myself at Calais, to prevent it to be read by the French Comissary to whom the searching officer wanted to carry it; as it is not permitted to carry over a sealed letter. Give me leave, Sir, to suscribe myself with the greatest regard & consideration Your Excellency's most Humble & Obedient Servant" (RC in ViW: Tucker-Coleman Collection; at head of text: "His Excellency Thomas Jefferson Esqre. President of the United States of America"; endorsed by TJ as received 10 Oct. 1803 and so recorded in SJL).

To Albert Gallatin

TH:J. TO MR GALLATIN ON WALKER'S CASE. June 15. 1803.

Those who are compelled by law to come to a public office have a right to be treated there with temper, attention & complaisance. interest teaches this to the private shopkeeper; reason & duty should do it to the public officer; and a continued course of harsh & rude conduct to those who come on business, will be good cause of removal. in the construction of a law, he should understand that it's intention constitutes the real law, which is to be found not in a rigorous adherence to the letter of a single word or expression, but in it's general object, & all it's provisions & expressions taken together. the object of the law in the cases complained of, is to punish fraud, not ignorance; and he should be the more on his guard against a multiplication of suits for ignorance, more probably than fraud, lest it should be imputed to the interest which his other office gives him in increasing the business of his court.

These are some of the considerations which I think should be presented to him by way of admonition. but has he been heard, or should he not be asked for explanations of his conduct? perhaps as the charges are of a general nature, and he could not prove a negative, this might be an useless protraction of the matter: and I rather suppose it would. you will decide on the whole according to your discretion.

RC (NHi: Gallatin Papers); endorsed. PrC (DLC).

WALKER'S CASE: see Gallatin's letter to TJ at 14 June, along with TJ's note, which serves as a partial draft for his response here.

From Albert Gallatin

DEAR SIR June 16th 1803

I enclose a sketch of the conditions on which the salt springs on Wabash may be offered—also T. Coxe's answer respecting the purveyorship. Please to examine the conditions of the lease & to suggest alterations. I will call tomorrow, in order to explain the reasons of some of them & receive your decision, after which I will make an official report.

I received last night a private letter from New York, in which E. Livingston's defalcation is spoken of as a matter of public notoriety in that city. I suspected as much from the last letter from Gelston & answered rather angrily. His letters & copy of my last answer are enclosed. The copy of mine of the 21st April I cannot find; it was short but very explicit. A resignation or removal must unavoidably follow; and I apprehend an explosion. But, at all events, a successor should be immediately provided. Will you have any objection to write to D. W. Clinton or shall I do it? I would prefer that he should be requested to mention the names of two or three persons; and he must be told that talents & legal knowledge sufficient to defend the suits of the U. States & integrity that may hereafter secure us against any danger or even imputation of want of caution, are absolutely necessary. I think no time ought to be lost; and if we had a successor ready I would propose an immediate appointment; for by the law every bond unpaid must on the day after it has become due be lodged in hands of the dist. attorney and no day passes without several being there placed.

With sincere respect & attachment Your obedt. Servt.

ALBERT GALLATIN

RC (DLC); addressed: "The President"; endorsed by TJ as received from the Treasury Department on 16 "Jan." and "salt springs. T. Coxe E. Livingston" and so recorded in SJL but at 16 June. Enclosures not found.

SALT SPRINGS ON WABASH: at TJ's urging, on 3 Mch. Congress appropriated $3,000 for the establishment of salt works at the Wabash site (see TJ to the Senate and the House of Representatives, 18 Jan., second letter).

In July 1802, Israel Whelen informed Gallatin of his plans to resign the PURVEYORSHIP in the coming year. At that time, both the Treasury secretary and the president agreed that Tench Coxe should be offered the position. After some hesitation, Coxe accepted the appointment and took office as purveyor of public supplies in August 1803 (Jacob E. Cooke, *Tench Coxe and the Early Republic* [Chapel Hill, 1978], 404-5, 415; Vol. 38:122, 123n, 156; Gallatin to TJ, 21 June, first letter).

OFFICIAL REPORT: see Gallatin to TJ, 22 June.

For LIVINGSTON'S DEFALCATION, see Vol. 38:122, 123n. In July 1802, Gallatin wrote TJ that he had evidence that Edward Livingston was recovering monies from bonds put in suit "& not paying the same to the Collector" (same).

OR SHALL I DO IT: Gallatin wrote DeWitt Clinton a confidential letter on 17 June, explaining that Livingston, the district attorney, had "on various occasions neglected to pay over, the proceeds of impost bonds which he had recovered." As a consequence, credit had been refused at the custom house to persons who had actually paid their bonds. Livingston had not provided David Gelston, the collector, with "a precise account of the situation of bonds put in suit," although he had been "repeatedly pressed to state it." Livingston's conduct, Gallatin asserted, was due either to "extreme carelessness or to a misapplication of the public monies." In either case, he could not continue in office. Even if an investigation indicated that what had taken place "was owing to want of arrangement & to neglect; yet, as all bonds remaining unpaid must, by law, be placed in his hands, and as dist. attornies give no security, the same danger would be perpetually incurred & might lead to an ultimate loss of money." Gallatin invited Clinton to provide the names of two or three lawyers qualified for the office, in whom "a perfect reliance" could be placed as to their "integrity & correctness in money affairs." Although the office was worth only $1,000 to $1,500, it required "no inconsiderable share of talents" and "a great portion of the attorney's attention." Gallatin also proposed that Clinton, if his relationship with Livingston allowed, go to him and explain the situation. The administration wanted to avoid an "explosion," but public duty demanded that Livingston give "an immediate statement of his accounts & a prompt payment of any balance" in his hands. A "regard to his own character & to his future prospects," Gallatin observed, "may induce him to do this quietly and without exposing himself to public animadversion; and, provided that the same effect shall be produced, that mode will be the most pleasing to me." Finally, Gallatin asked Clinton to consult with Gelston, share parts of the letter with him, and advise him on the steps he should take "to bring Mr L. to an account." Gallatin had already written to the collector "confidentially but very peremptorily, to act immediately" on the subject (Gallatin, *Papers*, 8:446).

From George Jefferson

DEAR SIR Richmond 16th. June 1803

Your favor of the 8th. inclosing manifests for 29 Hhds Tobacco was duly received.

The Tobacco is not yet sold. the price at which I hold it is 7½$—I have received no offer for it, but have been told by several persons that they should be glad to purchase it if I would take a more reasonable price. I think I could now get 7$—but as the last advices from Europe are more favorable than they have been for several years past, I think there will be no danger in holding it until towards the 12th. of July, when you wish to make the payment you mention.—

I inclose you a copy of the decree requested in yours of the 13th.

I am Dear Sir Yr. Very humble Servt. GEO. JEFFERSON

RC (MHi); at foot of text: "Thos. Jefferson esqr."; endorsed by TJ as received 18 June and so recorded in SJL. Enclosure: Virginia High Court of Chancery decree of 1 Oct. 1799 in the case between TJ and the Henderson heirs (see Vol. 31:208); enclosed in TJ to Thomas Mann Randolph, 22 June.

Notes on the Movements of the Mediterranean Squadron

[on or before 16 June 1803]

1802,
Nov. 3. sailed from Leghorn. took under convoy vessel bd. to Palermo
11. entered Palermo.
15. sailed for Malta.
20. arrived there. had to repair Bowsprit.
Dec. 7. bowsprit got in. but crew sickly with Influenza.
25. left Malta.
26. went into Syracuse to see if provns cheapr than Malta. dearer.
1803. Jan. 1. sailed for Malta.
4. arrived there. found there the J. Adams & New York. the John Adams leaky. repaired by 25th. & all the provns brot by Rogers from Gibr. distribd eqly amg ships[1] sent Enterprize to take Imperial vessel with Tripoline cargo.

on the 29th. sent the Enterprize to Tunis.

30. sailed for coast of Tripoli, to offer peace, or burn cruizers in the bay
eleven days heavy gale. Chesapeake labored. provns short.
Feb. 10. got into[2] Malta, with the John Adams.

on the 11th. the New York came in also.

19. sailed for Tunis.
22. arrived there. if Murray hd. brot provns, cd have destroyed the cruizers of Tripoli. bt wd nt hve attemptd. it till Equinox.

Cathcart's proposals to Tripoli were rejected.

probability of the Bashaw's bror making succesful attempt[3]

Mar. 19. arrived at Algiers
arrived at Gibraltar.
30. writes to Secy. of navy. the John Adams & Adams shall convoy.

the New York shall proceed direct (whither?) if no Amer. vessel wants convoy the Enterprize shall be employed to best advge (how?)

Apr. 6. writes a 2d lre by Chesapeak.

MS (DLC: TJ Papers, 131:22651); undated; entirely in TJ's hand.

TJ's notes summarize Commodore Richard V. Morris's 30 Mch. 1803 dispatch from the Mediterranean to the secretary of the navy. A report by Morris of 6 Apr. has not been found. The dispatches were carried to the United States by the frigate *Chesapeake*, under the command of James Barron. Departing Gibraltar on 6 Apr., the *Chesapeake* arrived at Norfolk around 18 May and was at the Washington Navy Yard by 3 June (Georgetown, D.C., *Olio*, 19 May 1803; *Poulson's American Daily Advertiser*, 26 May 1803; *National Intelligencer*, 3 June 1803; Christopher McKee, *Edward Preble: A Naval Biography, 1761-1807* [Annapolis, 1972], 112-14).

[1] Remainder of entry interlined.

[2] TJ here canceled "Tunis."

[3] TJ here canceled "while at Malta, sent Enterprise who took Imperl bott. wth Tripoline [gds]."

To Robert Smith

DEAR SIR Washington June 16. 1803.

I learn from Capt Tingey that the Philadelphia will probably not sail till August, and the frigate at Boston is expected to be still later. the Nautilus we are told is on the point of sailing. on consultation with the heads of department here, I am of opinion, and suggest it for your consideration, that an order of recall to Capt Morris should go by the Nautilus. from his inactivity hitherto, I have no expectation that any thing will be done against Tripoli by the frigates in the Mediterranean while under his command. if he is recalled by the Nautilus, and the command devolves on the others, we shall gain six weeks at least in the best season, for whatever they can effect in that time against the enemy. I think he may be permitted to come back in his own frigate, the other two with the Nautilus & Enterprize being equal to any operation to which the port of Tripoli is open. if you think with me, be so good as to send orders accordingly. if you think there are any strong reasons against it, be so good as to communicate them for consideration, and in the mean time to delay the Nautilus. should she have left Baltimore, letters would probably reach her at Norfolk by post. Accept my affectionate salutations & assurances of esteem & respect. TH: JEFFERSON

PrC (DLC); at foot of text: "The Secretary of the Navy at Baltimore." Recorded in SJL with notation "Morris."

FRIGATE AT BOSTON: the *Constitution* (Smith to TJ, 7 June 1803).

To James Cheetham

SIR Washington June 17 1803

I have deferred answering your letter of May 30. until I could find the means of having paiment made in New York for the volume of the Watch tower therein mentioned. mr Barnes tells me he has an account with mr Charles Ludlow of New York, on which some little balance will perhaps be due, and authorises me to say he will pay for that as well as what I am now to add. I have understood there is to be had in New York an 8vo. edition of Mc.kenzie's travels with the same maps which are in the 4to. edition. I will thank you to procure it for me. the American 8vo. edition is defective in it's maps, and the English 4to. edition is too large & cumbersome. I think I have seen[1] advertized in some paper that an edition of Arrowsmith's map of the US. has been published at New York. I shall be glad to recieve either that or the English one if to be had there. the latter would be preferred because I know the engraving is superiorly well done. be so good as to deliver these articles to mr Ludlow who will pay for & forward them to me. accept my best wishes. TH: JEFFERSON

PrC (DLC); at foot of text: "Mr. Cheetham"; endorsed by TJ in ink on verso. Enclosed in TJ to Charles Ludlow, 17 June.

8VO EDITION OF MC.KENZIE'S TRAVELS: Cheetham sent TJ the octavo edition of Alexander Mackenzie's *Voyages from Montreal, on the River St. Laurence, through the Continent of North America, to the Frozen and Pacific Oceans; In the Years 1789 and 1793*, published in London in 1802. The edition was advertised in Cheetham's *Republican Watch-Tower* for $3.50 (*Republican Watch-Tower*, 22 Jan., 12 Mch. 1803; Sowerby, No. 4087; Cheetham's account statement enclosed in Charles Ludlow to TJ, 24 June). For a description of McKenzie's publication and the AMERICAN edition that TJ considered DEFECTIVE, see Vol. 37:435n, 565-6.

TJ received the 1802 London edition of ARROWSMITH'S *Map Exhibiting All the New Discoveries in the Interior Parts of North America* engraved on four sheets. It was considered "the most accurate representation to date of the land west of the Mississippi" (Susan R. Stein, *The Worlds of Thomas Jefferson at Monticello* [New York, 1993], 393; Sowerby, No. 3846; Vol. 32:69n). For Nicholas King's use of the 1802 Arrowsmith engravings in the preparation of his map for Meriwether Lewis, see Gallatin to TJ, 14 Mch. 1803.

[1]MS: "see."

From Peter Freneau

DEAR SIR, Charleston, June 17th, 1803.

The Letter you did me the honor to write enclosing a small parcel of Egyptian Rice I have received. as soon after it came to hand, as possible, I divided it amongst several Gentlemen who will give it a fair trial. One of them informed me that it is a rice not unknown in this State, that it is not of so good a quality as the rice that is now raised here, which he thinks is the best that is known and is fully proved to be so by its bringing a higher price in Europe than that which is brought from The Levant, and East Indies. It is his opinion that no rice of a better quality than that we possess can be introduced into the Country if it requires water in its cultivation, but if there is a species which will grow without water, like wheat, Barley, Rye &c. its introduction would be a great acquisition, but this, he thinks, will not soon be found tho' it has been often asserted that there is such a grain in China, some of it was to have been sent here by the late Mr Van Bram, who had made mention of it when he resided here, as he afterwards went to China, and did not send any, it is probable that he was mistaken. From the paper which contained the rice you sent it appears that it grows in water, as it is marked "sous l'eau" However let the results of the experiments now making on it be promising or otherwise, they shall be made known to you,—Your attention to serve this State requires my most sincere Thanks.

The Elections in New York have exceeded my most sanguine expectations. their result must have given a severe shock to the prime mover of the federal faction there as it has to his followers here.—I feel confident that at the approaching elections in New Jersey Republicanism will triumph, the leading federalists of that state have so shamefully imposed on the people that it is impossible they can be so blind as to be led by them any longer—

I have no hopes of Connecticut, and but little of Massachusetts, I therefore, with submission differ from your better judgment, when you say "there is no doubt of Republicanism gaining the entire ascendency in New England within a moderate term." while the Clergy continue to hold the sway they now possess in those states, I see little prospect of amendment. for my part I shall expect nothing so shall not be disappointed.

I am perfectly satisfied with the conduct that has been pursued in regard to removals from office and am fully convinced that the principle laid down was a good one, but the Government has had to do with an undeserving[1] set, for tho' the federalists have been treated with unheard of lenity yet they cannot refrain from abuse—and they persist in it with such obstinacy as to entitle them to little favor. The federalists now appear to me a desperate faction so far gone in wickedness that if by the measure they could obtain revenge on those who dismissed them from power, they would not stop at destroying our independence and even restore us to the hated Monarchy from which we were separated at the expence of so much blood and treasure.—As to the few in office here I do not think it would be of any use to make a change, it is the opinion of some men, in whose judgement at times I confide, that if the Collector was removed it would be the means of the republicans carrying the elections in this City; but of this I am by no means certain.

I feel highly honor'd at the trouble you have taken to explain to me the principles the Government has proceeded on, and in your expressing a wish that it may lead to some communications on the political state of things in this quarter, from me. these, Sir, as far as I am able, you may rest assured shall be made, but if from the circumscribed sphere I act in, or for want of abilities, they should appear trivial you will have the goodness to believe they are made with sincerity and a desire to be useful—

I believe this State to be strong in Republicanism, taking it as a whole, but in this City the federalists are rather more numerous than the Republicans, this I ascribe to the number[2] of Scotch and English men we have in it, who have become Citizens, and on all occasions shew their attachment to the Country from whence they came. the federalists cling to these men, for without them they would be nothing. Federalism also prevails in Beaufort, but not in the District so called, I think that our next elections will make a change there in our favor, There is also a little knot of Federalists at Orangeburgh, but they cannot carry an election there.—Georgetown & Cheraws have a majority of republicans, Huger would not have attained his election for Congress if there had been a decent man to oppose to him—in those Districts—

The Federalists finding last year that their cause was desperate fell upon a plan of establishing a News paper here, in hopes by it to raise themselves, they purchased a press and Types in Philadelphia and began their Career in January last, Hamilton, it is said, sent them on a Man who calls himself Carpenter, who is now employed in writing for them, but his name does not appear, One Andrews is the ostensible Editor but he is a poor tool. Carpenter has abilities, but they are such as have done no injury to Republicans. at least this is my firm opinion for, I find that many of the moderate federalists are displeased at his productions. The paper gets very little support from the public and I am told its Contrivers[3] begin to find the expences are too heavy to be borne in the[4] way they are, that is by a few.—When the paper appeared it was the opinion of Mr Williams, my partner, and myself that we should take no notice of it unless it began an attack, we concluded that it woud not rise into notice if it was not opposed, I am still of opinion that we thought right, tho' many of my friends think differently. a few weeks will determine who was right, I believe it will not exist beyond october. if it does other measures must be resorted to.

I take the liberty to inclose you a paragraph which first made appearance in the paper called the Patriot, printed at Baltimore. I do it to shew the impropriety of Editors medling when they are uninformed. there is scarcely a word of truth in it. of course it has done more injury here than all Carpenter's writings. Burr did not travel with Tracy nor Genl Pinckney, and the President of the Senate has been attending Court in this City for many weeks past as a Lawyer. I know that Mr B. has little or no acquaintance with Genl P. in short Sir, the whole is a misrepresentation. John Rutledge did travel for some weeks with Tracy, but with such a Conductor little would be done by the latter, who in my opinion is not a fit person to make converts. He is now here and is in a poor state of health, this is the ostensible reason for his being here, but I am told that he cannot return to Connecticut as he owes three or four thousand Dollars which he cannot pay.—Rutledge has no longer any weight in this Country, he looses ground daily. I may be mistaken but I do not believe Genl P's journey to Boston was undertaken from political Motives, He had built a House and laid his plans to reside this summer on an island he has near Beaufort, but his wife was taken so ill that her Physicians declared if she was not removed to a Northern Climate she could exist but a short time, she was at the point of death when she left this—No doubt while he is there the federalists will pay him great attention but I do not believe they will support him with their Votes as they did heretofore, they then thought that he could carry this state to their party, they were convinced he could not and they have no grounds for believing he will ever be able to do it in future.[5] He does not possess a disposition to gain popularity, He appears to me to have been so much mortified at the ill success that attended his presidential attempt as not yet to have forgotten it; hence he keeps aloof and is seldom seen in the streets. his brother is equally reserved,—If paragraphs of the nature of the one I inclose appear frequently they will be of more service to the enemy[6] then any lye the federalists can invent, you can scarcely believe what work they are making with it, every person in the streets for two days past is asked, have you seen it? See what lies the Demo's are deceiving the people with.—It appears to me that it should be our study to expose all their deceptions and not to meddle with their journeys or private parties, it gives them a consequence they would not possess if let alone. No man that knows General P. would take him for a great man, if he is left to himself[7] he can do no harm.—I beg your pardon Sir for mentioning this subject to you, but perhaps a hint from you may put a stop to such absurd things.

I fear I have now troubled you too long, I therefore repeat my thanks for your most friendly Letter and by that you will believe me to be, with the most perfect regard and respect,

Dear Sir, Your Most obedient & Very humble Servant;

PETER FRENEAU

Perhaps it is wrong to add any thing to a letter which of itself is too long, but I take the liberty to add, that the Wise procedure of the Government respecting the affair of the depot at New Orleans has made it popular with every thinking man in this state, it has fairly beat down the Federalists, their clamours now are truly pitiful and beneath notice.—We have an arrival this day from France. the accounts by it lead us to believe that War has commenced between England and France, we rely on your wisdom to keep this dreadful scourge from us, I know we shall not be disappointed. Letters by this Vessel stated that Mr Munro has purchased Louisiana, but I give no Credit to the report.—One fellow in the Courier of this day has made you a writer for the National Intelligencer, what absurdities will they not descend to?—As to that paper I think it is of no consequence, it is certainly loosing what little hold it first had on the public, Carpenter is, I am told, intoxicated every night.—should he ever become dangerous here he will be noticed.—

RC (DLC); endorsed by TJ as received 1 July and so recorded in SJL. Enclosure: see below.

For the LETTER enclosing the EGYPTIAN RICE, see TJ to Freneau, 20 May. LATE MR. VAN BRAM: after spending 15 years with the Dutch East India Company, including travels to China, Andreas Everardus van Braam Houckgeest emigrated to the United States, settling as a merchant in Charleston with an interest in planting. He was described by David Ramsay in 1787 as a "Gentleman of reputation much esteemed by his lately adopted country." In the early 1790s, he returned to China, again employed by the Dutch East India Company, and from 1794 to 1795 took part in the Dutch embassy to the Chinese court. He died in 1801 (Philip M. Hamer and others, eds., *The Papers of Henry Laurens*, 16 vols. [Columbia, S.C., 1968-2003], 16:672-4; Vol. 11:283, 295). SOUS L'EAU: that is, "under water."

James Simons was the COLLECTOR at Charleston. For recent efforts to have him replaced, see Vol. 38:534-5 and Vol. 39: 364-6.

The first issue of the *Charleston Courier* appeared on 10 Jan. 1803. In 1806, after he returned to New York, Stephen Cullen CARPENTER described himself as "once a Proprietor, and, for three years, sole Editor" of the Charleston newspaper. Federalist Loring ANDREWS, a journalist at the Albany *Centinel* from 1797 to 1801, published the *Charleston Courier* from 1803 to 1805. David Rogerson WILLIAMS, Freneau's partner at the daily Charleston *City Gazette* and the weekly *Carolina Gazette* since 1801, went on to become a congressman and then governor of South Carolina (Pasley, *Tyranny of Printers*, 262-3; Brigham, *American Newspapers*, 2:1024, 1025-6, 1029, 1370, 1389).

INCLOSE YOU A PARAGRAPH: on 31 May, Samuel McCrea and Samuel Kennedy of the Baltimore *American Patriot* published a piece under the headline "Federal Movements," which asserted that Federalists were pursuing "some plan of operation," not yet fully developed, that in all probability would lead to the "explosion of some deep intrigue." According to the report, Burr, while visiting South Carolina, traveled to almost every part of the state accompanied by Uriah Tracy, Charles C. Pinckney, the president of the South Carolina Senate, and several other leading Federalists. The "whole party" had then gone to Boston. After reflecting on the "intriguing character of the Vice-President," the "ambition of General Pinckney," and the fact that the Massachusetts General Assembly was meeting in Boston, the Baltimore newspaper noted, "it leaves a strong suspicion, that *politics*, and not recreation, is the object of this jaunt." Realizing that he could "never again be elected by the democrats," Burr's only recourse was "to throw himself entirely on the federalists." Although the "northern people are suspicious and doubtful" of Burr, Pinckney's "*personal* recommendation" would "have no small effect in the work of reconciliation." The *Gazette of the United States* quoted the paragraph on 3 June, sarcastically commenting on its inaccuracies. The article from the Philadelphia newspaper was reprinted in the *Charleston Courier* on 17 June.

PRESIDENT OF THE SENATE: Federalist attorney and planter John Ward (*S.C. Biographical Directory, Senate*, 3:1673-4, 1829; Vol. 32:265; Vol. 35:102n). On 5 June, former Congressman JOHN RUTLEDGE, Jr., and his family arrived in New York City on their way to Connecticut, where they planned to spend the summer. Rutledge attended and was toasted at the 4th of July celebration at Hartford (*New-York Evening Post*, 6 June; Hartford *Connecticut Courant*, 15 June; *Gazette of the United States*, 11 July). HE IS NOW HERE: Tracy remained in Charleston until 20 June when he and South Carolina congressman Thomas Lowndes sailed in a vessel bound for New York. The *Charleston Courier* used his departure to point out the fabrications "cooked up" by the Baltimore "Jacobin" newspaper reporting that Tracy had gone to Boston with Burr and Pinckney. Tracy had come to Charleston for his health, the Federalist paper reported, and his residence in the city had "proved very beneficial." GENL P'S JOURNEY TO BOSTON: Charles C. Pinckney resided at Newton and visited many of his political friends in the summer of 1803. At the behest of his Federalist supporters, he received an honorary doctor of laws degree at the 31 Aug. commencement at Harvard College. He then toured the district of Maine with his wife and two daughters. He left Newburyport on 12 Sep. "escorted by the clergy, public officers and the principal citizens of the town" (Frances Leigh Williams, *A Founding Family: The Pinckneys of South Carolina* [New York, 1978], 321; *Newburyport Herald*, 13 Sep.; Keene *New Hampshire Sentinel*, 17 Sep.; *Charleston Courier*, 22 Sep.; *Salem Gazette*, 27 Sep. 1803).

[1] MS: "underserving."
[2] MS: "mumber."
[3] Interlined in place of "supporters."
[4] MS: "they."
[5] Preceding two words interlined.
[6] Preceding three words interlined.
[7] Preceding two words interlined in place of "alone."

To Charles Ludlow

SIR Washington June 17. 1803.

Having occasion to have a small matter paid to mr Cheetham for the articles mentioned in the inclosed letter to him, and having no pecuniary connections in New York, mr Barnes authorises me to hope you will be so good as to make paiment for them, and to debit it to him in an account existing between you. under these circumstances I take the liberty of inclosing the within, open, that you may be apprised of the extent of the trouble I propose to you, which goes to the forwarding to me the articles to be recieved from mr Cheetham, by the stage, under my address: and to ask the favor of you to stick a wafer in the letter to mr Cheetham, handing it on to him, and letting him know you will pay his bill. hoping you will excuse the liberty I take, I pray you to accept my salutations & assurances of respect.

TH: JEFFERSON

RC (NjMoHP); addressed: "Mr. Charles Ludlow New York"; franked and postmarked; endorsed by Ludlow as answered 24 June. PrC (MHi); endorsed by TJ in ink on verso. Enclosure: TJ to James Cheetham, 17 June 1803.

New York merchant Charles Ludlow (1765-1814) resided at 18 Wall Street. With the support of Clintonian Republicans, TJ appointed him commissioner of bankruptcy in early 1803. He was elected director of the New York branch of the Bank of the United States for the first time on 31 Jan. 1803 and continued serving as a director of the New-York Insurance Company. Ludlow served for many years as John Barnes's friend and business agent in New York (*Longworth's American Almanac, New-York Register, and City-Directory* [New York, 1803], 199; *New-York Gazette and General Advertiser*, 10 Jan. 1801, 5 Feb. 1803; *Republican Watch-Tower*, 17 Jan. 1801; New York *Commercial Advertiser*, 11 Jan. 1806; New York *Mercantile Advertiser*, 12 Dec. 1814; RS, 3:524; Vol. 37:308, 439, 572; Vol. 39:299-300, 612).

To Caesar A. Rodney

DEAR SIR Washington June 17. 1803.

The inclosed is put under cover to you, because I do not know to what particular place to address it. it proposes to the person to whom it is addressed to be a Commissioner of the land office either in the Eastern or Western district of the Missisipi state (temporary offices) and if the latter should be preferred, to add to it the appointment of judge there, vacant by a late resignation. I shall be happy if they are accepted.

I owe you an answer to a letter long since recieved and which constant emploiment has prevented my answering. it was on the subject of Colo. Mc.lane. you will recollect that when Govr. Hall & yourself were here, I mentioned that he stood on the ground of all others, liable to be removed if he should be active in opposition to the present order of things: and you both expressed entire satisfaction that it should rest on that ground, as it would restrain[1] him from electioneering or disarm him of official influence if he should become active. soon after this he wrote a letter the expressions of which were susceptible of being construed into a willingness to resign if permitted to stay in a given time. This was immediately noticed, & he was informed he should be indulged in time,[2] as I informed you by letter at the time. but he instantly replied that his meaning in the letter had been quite misunderstood & that he never had meant to offer a resignation. we could not therefore persist in imputing to him an intention to resign contrary to his own express declaration, and his case resumed the same ground on which it had been before and on which all others stood, to wit, a tenure depending on future conduct. the deaths, resignations, and removals for malversation or active hostility to the constituted authorities, have now nearly reduced the participation of office to a just state, so far as respects those offices in my immediate gift, and will ere long give us our just measure. how it is in subordinate offices I know not, as I do not interfere with them. that there should be a general sweep is too contrary to our own declarations on the exclusive principles of the preceding administration. if it was wrong for them to exclude their opponents from all office, it would be equally wrong for us to do it. I have no doubt of the pressure on you on the subject of removal. but few persons care about it; but these few feel strongly. the principles and measures of conducting the affairs of the nation are what is chiefly interesting to the[3] nation at large. who are the subordinate agents, provided the business is well done, is of less concern with them. a candid attention to the rights of the minority is a sacred duty, and I am not of opinion that the majority of our country wish them to be violated, or would fail to disapprove it.

We have reason to consider as certain the information in the papers that the deposit at New Orleans was restored on the 17th. of May. it was in consequence of an express order from the king of Spain sent to us by a vessel of war, and delivered by our Messenger in N. Orleans on the 12th. or 13th. of May. we hourly expect official information of it. believing certainly that war between France & England is inevitable, I have considerable confidence it will be the means of giving us all the security we can wish on the Missisipi, even if the other motives to do this should have not[4] been listened to. Accept my wishes for your health & happiness & assurances of my esteem & attachment.

Th: Jefferson

RC (CtY); at foot of first page: "Caesar A. Rodney esq." PrC (DLC). Enclosure: TJ to Thomas Rodney, 17 June 1803. Enclosed in TJ to Joseph Bringhurst, 17 June (not recorded in SJL and not found, but see Bringhurst to TJ, 8 July).

I OWE YOU AN ANSWER: TJ may be referring to Rodney's letter of 19 June

1802, that was almost entirely devoted to a discussion of removal policies, especially as they applied to Allen McLane. For Rodney's plans to visit Washington with David HALL, see Vol. 37:387.

HE WROTE A LETTER: for the description of McLane's letter to the Treasury secretary, interpreted as an offer to resign, see Vol. 38:639n. I INFORMED YOU: TJ to Rodney, 28 Nov. 1802.

The 17 June issue of the *National Intelligencer* included news of the restoration of the right of DEPOSIT AT NEW ORLEANS on 17 May. A translation of the 1 Mch. dispatch from Pedro Cevallos, the Spanish secretary of state, to Juan Ventura Morales, which included the EXPRESS ORDER FROM THE KING OF SPAIN to permit the right of deposit, appeared in the *National Intelligencer* on 22 June. The translation concluded with Morales's 17 May proclamation officially lifting the ban (Madison, *Papers, Sec. of State Ser.*, 4:535; TJ to DeWitt Clinton, 22 Apr. 1803).

[1] Word interlined in place of "oblige."

[2] Remainder of sentence interlined.

[3] TJ altered "them" to "the" and interlined the remainder of the sentence.

[4] Word interlined.

To Thomas Rodney

SIR Washington June 17. 1803.

From what passed between mr Nicholson & myself last winter, I have presumed it possible you might be willing to undertake soon a distant service for the US. the act of the last session of Congress regulating grants of lands South of the Tennissee, authorises me to appoint two Commissioners for the territory West of Pearl river & two for that East of the same river. they are to meet on the 1st. day of December next and not to adjourn before the 1st. of April ensuing. it is believed that within that term the business of the Eastern district will be finished, but that the Western will require a couple of years. 2000. D. are allowed for the whole service whether long or short. I should be happy to avail the public of your services in either whichever you shall chuse. the resignation of one of the judges of the Missisipi territory leaves a vacancy to be filled there. the salary is 800. D. a year, and I should be glad if you could undertake that also. I mention it now, as in conjunction with the office of Commissioner, it might be a reason with you for preferring the Western district. I will ask an answer from you as soon as you shall have had time to consider and decide on it. accept my respectful salutations & assurances of esteem.

TH: JEFFERSON

PrC (DLC); at foot of text: "Thomas Rodney esq." Not recorded in SJL. Enclosed in TJ to Caesar A. Rodney, 17 June.

LAST WINTER: see TJ to Joseph H. Nicholson, 1 Mch.

For the RESIGNATION of Seth Lewis, ONE OF THE JUDGES, see William C. C. Claiborne to TJ, 30 May.

From Robert Smith

Sir, Baltimore June 17, 1803

I think with you that Morris ought to be recalled by the Nautilus. And I will send orders accordingly. The permitting him to return in his own frigate is a great indulgence. I have no expectation that any thing of importance will be effected by the Squadron now out.

With great respect I am Sir Your Ob. Ser. Rt Smith

RC (DLC); endorsed by TJ as received from the Navy Department on 18 June and so recorded in SJL with notation "Morris's return."

From Samuel Smith

State of Connecticut
Friend Thomas Jefferson/ Salisbury June 17: 1803

I take the Liberty as one of thy wellwishers to address Thee thy Enemies assert that thou art a Deist and thy Friends that thou art a Christian, but thy conduct demonstrates to me that thou art suitable for the office that thou fillest, as I look not at Names but actions. our beloved Saviour says that a Tree is known by its Fruit which is truly Philosophical and consequently agreable to that Religion whose foundation is Wisdom, supported by Truth, As I observ'd that I look at actions. And as the Auther of our Religion declares that his Kingdom is not of this World therefore his Servants cannot fight, of consequence the fomenters of Warrs are not Christians in practice, and the makers of Peace are, and as I am a professor of Christianity I cannot help Joyning the Latter, As a believer in the Scriptures I of consequence must be a believer of the Prophesys, which demonstrates to me that those who are the fomenters of Warrs, belong to that beastly power mentioned in the Seventh Chapter of Daniel, who had Iron Teeth and stamp'd the residue under his feet, (that is destroy'd the remaining Liberty) this appears to be the Roman Power, and made its appearance in many forms of Government but all dispotick after the first, which despotism destroy'd the remaining Liberty of Man. The first Imperial and Terminating in Kingly power or a union of Church and State which took the whole, binding soul and Body in one Mass of Tyrany, the Imperial was a great despotism but only bound the body, but the last give a finishing Stroke Stamped the residue under the feet of its power which last was an Image of the first but more affectual, as the first was a Tyranny of Armed Men, or supported by such, the last was a two fold Army of Priests and soldiers both, one Chaining the Soul in Eclesiastical Fetters, the other Chaining them by the outward Sword and each supported by the other, a riveted despotism, and consequently might well be said as aforesaid he stamped the residue under his feet, and in this situation was Urope at the time of the American revolution, and their Despots sent over their Minions to each to establish their power which was so order'd by the ruler of the Universe that out of their evil designs good should spring as the French Officers and Men by that means tasted the Sweets of Liberty and communicated it to their Bretheren which sow'd the seeds of the French Revolution which Brought on that great Earthquake mention'd in 11 chaptr: of the Revelation by St. John which shook Despotism to its Center, in which Seven Thousand Men or names of Men where destroy'd in France or in other words all the priviled'd Orders, from the King to the lowest Priest, and as it was founded as aforesaid on the Union of Church and State it spread itself to different parts of Urope who combin'd in the support of its Cause, destroying what they the despots had accummulated in their repositorys the Churches, and the Priests Coffers, which alarm'd the whole Fraternity as they expected their church was discover'd (which Sodom Signifies) and their more than Egyptian Bondage broke, as it was not only outward but inward as aforesaid, as they expected that this two fold cord could not be broke, as they had the horns of a Lamb but the Voise of a Dragon, and on this foundation they built their happyness but it would not stand the Fire of Truth and Love, and so they suffer'd Loss, i.e. their Church and state Union for a Little season, but reviv'd for a little season that its fall may be the greater, for we find agreable to the aforesaid Chapt: that the first war is past and the second cometh quickly, and then the Seventh Angel will sound i.e. the Spirit of truth will sound through the Angels or Ministers of the Seventh church, or Universal Church, who will proclaim that the Kingdoms of this World are become the Kingdoms of God and of his Christ that is that, the true Bride or Church is reconcil'd to her husband, and that this obomination of dissolation has ceased, the old Whore of Babylon or unnatural connnection is broke; she, that is, the Whore that rid on the aforesaid beastly power, that made herself Scarlet by Bloody measures or by plunging the outward Sword into the Bowels of the true Church is fallen from the emmince which she had placed herself on, the Church and state Conection being so shatter'd that they which stand afar of weep and Wail because of her fall, i.e. as far of as America, Pittying those poor Christian Ministers or Clergymen which they used to pray for the downfall of, and runing out against that Government which they were Zealous to Establish, but the first war is past but the second cometh quikly, even that war that altho' it wears a triple Crown, must fall to the ground, in Urope its supported by Kings Lords and Priests and in America by Priests, Lawyers and Judges, but she must,—or her Power must be cast into the midst of the Sea, or into many Waters as many Waters are many People, so the power must revert back to the People, and that Union of Church and State be no more found. oh the Lamentation, the Dying groans that was heard in Congress, and now in the three Federal States of Connecticut, Massachusets and New Hampshire, the rig[...] men weep and howl, this great City is fallen is fallen, She that abounds in Gold Silver and precious Stones and fine dinners and Slaves and [Souls?] of Men, and in Horses and Chariots her merchandise is discover'd to be Dross and Dung of no Value, the people assume their own Authority, they no longer are affraid of their greatest Enemys themselves, the Old Whore is Strip'd of her power, Lamentable times the Idlers must return to their Labour, and men trust in their God, and believe him to be good gratious and benevolent, now these Pulpit Trumpeters are hurl'd from their emminences wherein they used to Reproach his Benevolent Carracter, representing him to be more cruel then the worst of human Tyrants, the people of American or a Majority have agreed to come out from Amongst them and pertake no longer of her Abominations by which she Made desolate the inhabitants of the Earth, they had rather part with their Cash then the Lives of their fellow Men, they had rather purchase Naboth's Vineyard then Kill him for sake of it, they find that True honour consists in honesty and Love, they dont want to spend 5 millions to hire a parcel of Cutthroats when 2 million will Answer a better purpose, they know the difference between false and true honour, and are determin'd to Chuse for themselves, proceed my honest Friend in thy career of Justice and God will Bless thee, and cause all good Men to bless thee also, regard not their Blasphemy, who have blasphemed their God, stand forth as a Rock of Liberty and let their despotick waves beat, they can do no harm to the Righteous cause that thou and Millions espouseth, they are windy or lighter then Air, and came from the Prince of Darkness, God Laughs at their Calamity and Mocks at their Fear, because they have no foundation but in a false Immagination, but it will finally redound to their happyness, and then this false Aluminate false Mirror will cease to deceive, and then they will find that their Steady or Antient habits where destructive to the happiness of Man upon a General Scale, and when they are alluminated with the true Alumination they will find why thou wast so indifferent about Mens Opinions as thou meant to be a Friend to the whole without a respect to Opinions, as a Man may be a good Cityzen altho' he may be of a different Opinion from us, which thy friendly conduct to the Indians demonstrates, and the same Friendship will cause thee to extend thy benevolence to the poor Affricans when it shall be in thy Power, in expectation of which I remain thine unknown Friend

SAML SMITH

RC (MoSHi: Jefferson Papers); torn; addressed: "His Excellency Thomas Jefferson President of the United States of America at the City of Washington"; franked; endorsed by TJ as received 28 June and so recorded in SJL.

Samuel Smith (d. 1813) was born in Salem, Massachusetts. Raised a Quaker, he embraced at some point the doctrine of universalism, and by 1801, he was listed among 22 preachers recognized by the New England Convention of Universalists. Two years later, the Convention welcomed him formally into fellowship. He quickly fell out of favor with his coreligionists, who scorned his mystical bent and apparent lack of learning, and about five years before his death he converted to Methodism (*The Religious Inquirer and Gospel Anchor*, 13 [1834-35], 387-8, 390-1; Richard Eddy, *Universalism in America: A History*, 3d ed., 2 vols. [Boston, 1891-94], 2:5-6, 8-12).

In the biblical story, Naboth refuses to sell his small VINEYARD to Ahab, the King of Samaria. Ahab's wife Jezebel orchestrates Naboth's murder, thus allowing Ahab to take possession but prompting the prophet Elijah to curse him (1 Kings 21).

To John Barnes

DEAR SIR — Washington June 18. 1803.

Before the reciept of your letter this morning, I had taken an exact view of my affairs, and had found that the balance can not be lessened till after the next month. in August it can be lessened 8. or 900. D. in Sep. 11, or 1200, or say 2000. dollars in those two months, & 500. D. a month afterwards till it disappears. I had therefore prepared the letter which accompanies this for the president of the bank; should it be acceded to, I would wish you to call for whatever sums of money your convenience may require from time to time, only letting so much of your capital, as you can conveniently, remain, so that I may be whittling down the balance by degrees on one hand, and by degrees also be shifting parts of it into the bank. be so good as to consider this matter, & the letter and let me know your opinion on it. Accept my affectionate salutations.

TH: JEFFERSON

PrC (CSmH); at foot of text: "Mr. Barnes"; endorsed by TJ in ink on verso. Enclosure not found.

YOUR LETTER THIS MORNING: a letter from Barnes received 18 June has not been found, nor is one recorded in SJL.

From Justus Erich Bollmann

SIR, Philada. June 18th. 1803

I should have replied sooner to Your Excellency's letter of the 8th. of May last if I had not been desirous previously to see somewhat clearer with Regard to my own Situation. Permit me now to give You an Account of it and have the Goodness to consider my doing so not as arising from any improper Fordwardness but rather as the natural Result of the Conviction I feel of Your Kindness and good Will toward me.

I shall be legally freed from my Embarrassments on the 8th. of July next, but, to judge from my present Impressions, I shall never enjoy my former Tranquility of mind untill I have succeeded, if not to pay off the whole arrears due to my Creditors, at least to prove the Sincerity of my Intentions in this Respect by a handsome Payment on Account. I must therefore try to engage in Pursuits which not only may afford me a Subsistence, but also a Prospect of Emoluments increasing proportionably with my Application and the utmost Exertion of what little I may have acquired of Knowledge and Experience.—

With this View the manufacturing Concern, which I have several Times taken the liberty of mentioning to you, excited my first Attention. But it has, contrary to my Wish been purchased by my Relations, One of which, Mr. Wm. Cramond, a man of whom it is well known that he is too often guided by sordid Views towards his own Interest, has so well contrived to wound my Feelings by the most unhandsome Proceedings towards me during my late Misfortunes, that, as a man of Honour, I can hold no Interest in a Business in which He is concerned. I should besides, knowing the Difficulties attending this Business and the Insufficiency of the present Proprietors, have no Confidence in its Success unless the Whole were under my sole Management and Controul which under the present Circumstances it would be impossible to effect.

The next Idea seems to be to form a new commercial Establishment on a similar Plan as the former.—My House had earned upwards of $75,000 Commissions in 5 years which would have become the Basis of a solid Fortune if we had avoided Dependencies abroad and been less liberal with Our Name at home. The most valuable of Our European Connexions continue to be Our Friends notwithstanding Our misfortunes and the former Transactions with them could easily be renewed particularly in Case of a War in Europe. I have further the advantage of having acquired good Correspondents in most of the SeaPort Towns from Savannah to the Province of Maine, by means of which an important inland Commission Business could be set on Foot, a Branch now much neglected in this City or followed by People who have not sufficient Talents to do Justice to it.—Philada. also affords to an active Man many Opportunities of advantageous Purchases and Sales on the Spot, without being under the Necessity of suffering the Property to go out of Reach.

To realize the Idea of a new commercial Establishment confined to those Three Branches nothing is wanted but the loan of a Capital from 12 to 15.000 dollars at legal Interest, but, as a Security for which I have nothing to offer except the solemn Assurance that I should guard with the most scrupulous Care against exposing it to any Hazard!—Unfortunately this Security is but a very indifferent One in the Eyes of monied People, and those of this City in particular happen mostly to be Men whose minds are extremely contracted and totally incapable of generous Confidence. They will even confide least in Men dissimilar to themselves or their Superiors in Point of Education and Acquirements, for, as it requires Virtue to believe in Virtue, it requires superior Talents perhaps not to be afraid of Talents in others. I have therefore no Chance except with Gentlemen of Your Excellency's Stamp, and I candidly confess that this Conviction induces me to make to You this unreserved Statement of my Views and Wishes.

I might perhaps derive some Ressources from my Relations in Germany, but They have not seen me for these Seven Years past, and these Ressources besides would be long coming forward whilst it is of the utmost Importance to revive into commercial Activity during the Period that the Habits of Consideration and Confidence remain still active with the Public.

It is also possible that the Marquis Lafayette who is informed of my present Situation, may avail himself of the Grant of Land made to him by Congress to afford me some Assistance, particularly as I have never made any Use of an Annuity which he offered me Six Years ago in a very obliging Manner; but it would be imprudent to calculate on this Event.

Nothing therefore seems to be left but to await whether it is perhaps to Your Excellency that I am to be indebted for a useful and satisfactory Existence during the Rest of my life; and flattering myself that You will at any Rate receive this letter with Indulgence I remain with great Respect

Your Excellency's most obt. St. J. Erich Bollmann

P.S. I have still to mention that I shall have Occasion to go to Baltimore in the Course of next Week and intend to proceed to

Washington to have the Pleasure of paying my Respects to you personally.

RC (DLC); above postscript: "To the President of the United States"; endorsed by TJ as received 21 June and so recorded in SJL.

Erich and Lewis Bollmann's share of the rolling mill on the Schuylkill River was sold at auction to members of Erich Bollmann's deceased wife's family, with whom Bollmann did not get along. The family was connected to William CRAMOND by marriage and business (*Gazette of the United States*, 9 Apr. 1803; Fritz Redlich, "Notes and Documents: The Philadelphia Water Works in Relation to the Industrial Revolution in the United States," PMHB, 69 [1945], 249; Michael W. Fazio and Patrick A. Snadon, *The Domestic Architecture of Benjamin Henry Latrobe* [Baltimore, 2006], 267).

From Joseph Forster

[on or before 18 June 1803]

Reverendissime, Praesul, Domine,
ac Moecoenas
gratiossissime!

Your Excellence will excuse the bold presumption which I undertook by addressing myself to You. Before I acquaint Your Excellence, with the design, what induced me, to come thitherto, You will be desirious to know, who I am, and from whence I come from. Here my attestats explain it—

In short, I had the same fate, as Virgil, when he exclaimed: "Nos patriae fines, nos dulcia linquimus arva," whilst was caused the great revolution, of which Virgil gives this striking likeness.

Quippe ubi fas versum atque nefas, tot bella per orbem;
Tam multae scoelerum facies: non ullus aratro
Dignus honos: squallent abductis arva colonis
Et curvae rigidum falces conflantur in ensem.
Hinc movet Euphrates, illinc Germania bellum,
Vicinae ruptis inter se legibus urbes
Arma ferunt: saevit toto Mars impious orbe.

Among them unfortunate I was one, Vouchase, then Your regard and consider:—The story is short—but striking—My parents are dead, my house is burnt, & my property robb'd Desolate & destitute from every body:—then the maxim of Ovid saying

"Donec eris felix multos numerabis amicos,
Tempora si fuerint nubila solus eris"

I found, alas, too true;—I confirmed, to go into a country, which by fame & describtion is called, the earthly Paradies. And in fact, people, who has learnt, how to work, lives happier here, then in Europe, because they do not feel hard oppression from their superiors, & the iron hand of war.

But, alas, for me did not blossom yet in this American Eden a smile of fate;—grief & misery are my nossegays. But you, o Excellence! could change in a moment this tragicat scene. May this Proverb: Post nubila Phoebus be as true: as sunshine follows after a cloudy day; then when this storm of Misfortunes will not quite, I perish in Harm.—To You then, O Excellence, I make my Supplication, Your Excellencies help I implore, to put me into a place, where I may recover again from tossing of such a boisterous a storm; Employment is it, for what I Your Excellence most humble supplicate You. In Your Excellencies power is it, to make his Subjects happy or wretched. Pity the Sorrows of a poor wretched Accedent, who has no friends, who would speak for him, no recommendations, no inducements of Your bonty.

When I consider, that Your Excellence is surrounded with the most eminent heads of astonishing faculties, then my hope of acquiring some, decreases.

Then Your Excellence, do not want my Services, because they are either of a trifling consequence, or none at all.

When I shall be happy enough to sensuate Your Grace in acquiring some emploiment, it is only for to exercise Your magnificence, generosity, magnamity, & an endeavour, which is natural to You; to render people happy.

Upon such foundations emboldened I offer myself to Your service, & crave Your mercy for acquiring a comfortable life. Do not refuse me; then Tytus, whose name You have already acquired by Your Clemency,—refused none, and every one went smiling from his palace. Fame relates a unpartial hystory of the American Tytus of Your Excellence in American as well as in the remotest parts of Europe, Germany. Thus they say: Your Excellence Jefferson is no King, but he is greater, than any of the Kings. May God Almighty disclose Your tender heart, and You o Excellence, propitious look down on me from the hight, to which Your Excellence is raised.

Some Apprehensions may perhaps linger a gracious resolution on me, for I will allowe, that some base villains have abused Your clemency; but, most noble American Tytus, after having proved me, You will be convinced, that I do not belong under those base villains; whose heart is as black as Virgil describes a Monster in the Aeneid III V 658.

Monstrum horrendum, informe, ingens, cui lumen ademptum.

And I exclaim with Shakespeare.

Freeze, Freeze, thou bitter sky.
Thou doest not bite so nigh
As benefits forgot;
Tho' thou the waters warp
Thy sting is not so sharp.
As friend[1] rememberd not.

And indeed; In all the Catalogue of human imperfections, there is not one of a more execrable & diabolical hue, than the ungrateful man. Once more I crave Your mercy, invoke Your assistance, in yealding me a proper livelyhood, and implore Your favour which, when bestowed upon me, I never cease to forget it. with infinite thanksgiving, and I will endeavor with the utmost zeal to be

Your Excellence most humble and obedient Servant,

JOSSEPH FORSTER

RC (DLC: TJPapers, 133:22928-9; 178:31573); undated; endorsed by TJ as received 18 June and so recorded in SJL.

German printer Joseph Forster established *Der Pelican*, a quarto-size weekly German language newspaper in Philadelphia in 1805. The paper became a biweekly and, later in 1806, a triweekly printed in alternating columns of English, German, and French. In January 1807, when the paper appeared only in English and French, he established another newspaper, *Der Pelikan Edlere*, published only in German under the name "P.J. Forster." He was the proprietor of a New York edition of the *Pelican* as of October 1808. Forster became an accomplished book binder in New York for many years before returning to Philadelphia, advertising his talents there in 1832 (Brigham, *American Newspapers*, 1:678, 2:928; Douglas C. McMurtrie, "A Note on P. Joseph Forster, Pioneer Alabama Printer," *Alabama Historical Quarterly*, 5 [1943], 235-6; *Portland Advertiser*, 18 Sep. 1824; *Philadelphia Inquirer*, 26 Oct. 1832; Forster to TJ, 14 Sep. 1805).

REVERENDISSIME, PRAESUL, DOMINE, AC MOECOENAS GRATIOSSISSIME: loosely translated, "Most Reverend leader my Lord Maecenas." Maecenas, a Roman statesman from 8 B.C., was a generous patron of literature and art (*Encyclopedia Britannica*).

NOS PATRIAE FINES, NOS DULCIA LINQUIMUS ARVA: "I from my sweet fields, and home's familiar bounds, even now depart" (Virgil, *Eclogues*, 1.3.).

The stanza beginning, QUIPPE UBI FAS VERSUM ATQUE NEFAS, translates as "Here right and wrong are reversed: so many wars in the world, so many faces of evil: the plough not worthy of any honor, our lands neglected, robbed of farmers, and the curved pruning hooks beaten into solid blades. Here Germany, there Euphrates wages war: neighboring cities take up arms, breaking the laws that bound them: impious Mars rages through the world" (Virgil, *Georgics*, 1.505-11).

The two-line MAXIM OF OVID, loosely translated from Latin reads, "So long as you are secure you will count many friends; if your life becomes clouded you will be alone" (Ovid, *Tristia*, 1.9.5-6).

POST NUBILA PHOEBUS: "after the clouds, the sun."

The first-century Roman emperor, Titus (TYTUS) Flavius Vespasiamus, was known for his benevolence and concern for the welfare of his people (Vol. 34:635n).

MONSTRUM HORRENDUM, INFORME, INGENS, CUI LUMEN ADEMPTUM: "an immense, misshapen marvelous monster whose eye is out" (Virgil, *Aeneid*, 3.658).

Forster quoted from SHAKESPEARE, *As You Like It*, 2.7.

[1]MS: "friends."

From David Gelston

Sir, New York June 18th. 1803

The enclosed was this day received under cover from Mr Maury—your note of the 14th instant, covering a letter for Mr Lee at Bordeaux has also been received, the letter will go by the Ship Sophrona, Capt. Gillender, which will be the first American Ship for Bordeaux, and will sail in a few days—

I have the honor to be, very respectfully, Sir, your obedt. Servant

David Gelston

RC (MHi); at foot of text: "The President of the United States"; endorsed by TJ as received 20 June and so recorded in SJL. Enclosure not found.

There is no record of a note from TJ to Gelston on 14 June, but see TJ's letters of that day to William Lee and Robert Purviance.

From John Hankart

Respected Sir, City of Washington June 18th. 1803.

I take the liberty of addressing a few lines to you in consequence of the conversation that passed when I had the pleasure of being last in your Company. when speaking of the advantage of a Snuff Manufactory in this City, you remarked the Superior quality of your Tobacco.

since I had the pleasure of seeing you, I have my Mill at work, and have no doubt of a living.

I can get any quantity I want, of the common run of Tobacco, but am much in want of a Superior kind, which could I obtain; I am confident Sir, I could soon convince you; no Man is my Superior in that branch. I have had the pleasure, and I flatter myself with Credit, to serve your household with Snuff for a considerable time. and from the same kind of Tobacco, I think no Man can exceed me, but if I could obtain the favor of a few Hogsheads of the Superior kind, I would soon be able to show my abilities in that line to the Credit of this City. the request I have to make of your Excellency is; that you would indulge me with a tryal of your Tobacco, of that superior kind; by giving an order for Two, or Three Hogsheads; to your Agent in Richmond for that purpose: and I only wish for a reasonable indulgence respecting payment; which shall be punctual to the time engaged for.

If your Excellency would be inclined to oblige me so far, you will lay me under great obligations; and the additional price as mention'd by you, would be no object if it answers my expectations; and I have no doubt but it will leave me a permanent establishment. and if it should meet your approbation, the earlier I receive it, the more usefull.

I am, with great respect Your Excellencys, Most Obedt. h'ble. Servt. JOHN HANKART

P.S. you will confer a favor upon your humble Servant by your acceptance of the Bottle of Snuff now sent: the quality of which will be pleasing to all your friends. Major Lewis I believe to be a good judge of the Article.

RC (DLC); addressed: "His Excellency Thomas Jefferson President of the United States"; endorsed by TJ as received 27 June and so recorded in SJL.

John Hankart was a merchant in Baltimore during the 1780s but moved to Philadelphia, where he operated a tobacco factory for much of the 1790s. Along with Thomas Leiper and other like-minded manufacturers, he became an ardent opponent of the Washington administration's excise taxes and helped forge the nascent Republican opposition in Philadelphia. He left Philadelphia in 1797, perhaps to live in Europe, and was identified as a resident of Washington in January 1803, when he unsuccessfully petitioned Congress for relief from the excise taxes he had paid while conducting his tobacco business. He eventually settled in Pittsburgh, where he continued to manufacture tobacco and also served as the city's tobacco inspector (*Maryland Journal and Baltimore Advertiser*, 9 Mch. 1784; *Philadelphia Gazette & Universal Daily Advertiser*, 19 May 1797; JHR, 4: 264, 268; *The Honest Man's Extra Almanac for the City of Pittsburgh and the Surrounding Country* [Pittsburgh, 1812]; *The Pittsburgh Directory, for 1815* [Pittsburgh, 1815], 35; Roland M. Baumann, "Philadelphia's Manufacturers and the Excise Taxes of 1794: The Forging of the Jeffersonian Coalition," PMHB, 106 [1982], 15, 18-19; George Thornton Fleming, *History of Pittsburgh and Environs*, 4 vols. [New York, 1922], 2:61).

To Meriwether Jones

DEAR SIR Washington June 18. 1803.

Altho' I have made it a point to disregard the various calumnies by which the federalists have endeavored to wound republicanism through me, yet when a respectable man, as Gabriel Jones, comes forward and sets his name to facts candidly stated & calculated the more to raise false impressions as his facts are not Sound, I have thought it would not be amiss that a just statement should be made, in order to satisfy candid minds. I have therefore made the inclosed, thinking I could not do better than commit it to your friendship, to publish it in such form, with such alterations or abridgments as you think proper. whether too as an anonymous communication, or with a feigned name, or as the editor's own observations is left to yourself as you are sufficiently apprised of the utter impropriety of it's being in any form which should engage me in that field, or if you think it better to suppress it, I leave it to your judgment. There is no fact in it but what is stated by mr Jones, and the historical references are known to every one, and may most of them be verified by the journals of Congress or proceedings of the Virginia legislature. I pray you to accept assurances of my great esteem & best wishes.

TH: JEFFERSON

P.S. I will thank you to destroy the original & this letter.

PrC (DLC); at foot of text: "Mr. Meriwether Jones." Recorded in SJL with notation "G. Jones."

Meriwether Jones (1766-1806), a nephew of Martha Wayles Jefferson by marriage, was a member of the Virginia House of Delegates from Hanover County in 1792 and 1794. After leaving elected office, Jones became involved in partisan newspaper battles. He established two newspapers in Richmond, the strongly Republican *Examiner* from 1798 to 1803, and the short-lived *Press* in 1800, as well as the Norfolk *Commercial Register* from 1802 to 1803. Jones challenged Federalist printers and, according to his obituary, "frequently superintended his press with his pistols within his reach." Jones became public printer for Virginia in December 1798, but resigned in March 1804 when TJ named him state loan commissioner, a position he held until his death (Leonard, *General Assembly*, 188, 196; Brigham, *American Newspapers*, 2: 1124, 1139, 1141; JEP, 1:464, 465; *Federal Gazette & Baltimore Daily Advertiser*, 16 Apr. 1800; Richmond *Enquirer*, 22 Aug. 1806; New York *Republican Watch-Tower*, 2 Sep. 1806; Vol. 31:163-5n, 290n). For the 1802 newspaper war that erupted between Jones and his former employee James T. Callender, see Vol. 38:37-8n.

SETS HIS NAME TO FACTS: Gabriel Jones had a statement dated 17 Mch. 1803 printed in the *Virginia Gazette* regarding a loan he made to TJ in 1773 that was repaid in what he deemed to be depreciated currency (see notes to Enclosure printed below).

Jones decided to PUBLISH TJ's account, with only slight variation, in the Richmond *Examiner*, 25 June 1803. It was reprinted in the *National Intelligencer* on 1 July 1803. ANONYMOUS COMMUNICATION: in the newspapers the article was signed "Timoleon," alluding to the Greek statesman and general. For TJ's use of the press as an anonymous presidential mouthpiece, see Noble E. Cunningham, Jr., *The Jeffersonian Republicans in Power, Party Operations, 1801-1809* [Chapel Hill, 1963], 255-60.

ENCLOSURE

Money Transaction with Gabriel Jones

Mr Gabriel Jones has given to the public the statement of a pecuniary transaction of about 30. years ago, between the President & himself, with comments[1] of so angry a complection as to excite at once doubts in the mind of a candid reader that there must have been something more in the case than is there presented to his view. in truth the history of the times is so necessary to the explanation of the money transactions of the day that these cannot be understood without a recurrence to that and with this recurrence alone mr Jones's own facts will enable us to judge whether like many others he has not suffered his political antipathies to distort his estimate of characters whose '*honour, honesty & integrity*' proved to him in more dispassionate times himself acknowledges to have '*inspired him with the highest confidence.*'

Mr Jefferson on some emergency borrowed £50. of mr Jones who was in the habit of lending money on interest & gave his bond for repaiment.[2] this, mr Jones says was in autumn 1773. consequently about the period of the destruction of the tea in Boston, which was followed by Genl Gage's arrival in Boston[3] with an army and by other events in rapid succession which brought on the revolution, & suspended in a great degree the ordinary intercourse of business. this state of things, & the known habit of mr Jones of leaving his money at interest in good hands, may furnish the reasons why his £50. in this instance were not repaid so soon as contemplated. all the hard money of the US. was suddenly exported to procure arms ammunition and other necessaries for the times, and it's place was supplied by emissions of paper money bottomed on the faith of the nation. of this faith the whigs had no doubt, and the money maintained it's ground at par for a considerable time. and even when successive emissions, aided by the efforts of the disaffected, had begun to make an impression on it, the whigs were still confident it would be redeemed dollar for dollar, & therefore continued to recieve & pay it at par. in Jany. & May 1779. Congress by circular letters, encouraged their fellow citizens to maintain the credit of the paper; represented to them the false policy of 'asking enormous prices for the produce of their farms, when a little reflection might convince them that it was injurious to their interests, & to the general welfare;' and affirmed that the whole emissions (which as late as Sep. 3. 1779. they stated at less than 160. millions) might 'without public inconvenience or private distress be cancelled by taxes in a period so limited as must leave the possessor of the bills satisfied with his security.' such was the whig sentiment as late as Sep. 79. the offer of paiment by[4] mr Jefferson had been in April preceding. it was the only one [he] could offer for a paiment in hard money was then impossible. mr Jones not chusing to recieve it, sent it back to mr Jefferson, with his bond, under a blank cover: & mr Jefferson, not meaning to cancel the debt, returned the bond to mr Jones under a blank cover[5] also; the inference from which was plainly that mr Jefferson was willing, as mr Jones seemed to be, to let the matter lie over till there should be hard money to pay it. but mr Jones finds ground of crimination even in the mode of conveying the letter. yet he well knows that no cross posts existed at that day, & that indirect conveyance could alone be resorted to. the imputation he raises on this is as unjustifiable as it would be to impute to him a reciept of the letter in due time, & a willingness now to deny it. that he recieved it late is probable, because he says so; and that the delay was accidental is much more probable than the absurd manoeuvre which his passions impute to mr Jefferson. To shew further the public sense with respect to the revolutionary money, it may be noted that in the June following the date of this offer, mr Jefferson was chosen Governor of Virginia, & continued to June 1781.[6] during the whole of which time he recieved his salary at the rate of £1000 a year of the same money, the rate at which it had been fixed by law before any emission of paper. the legislature therefore considered the salary[7] as equivalent to what it called [itself] for two years after the transaction in question. It may be remembered that a letter of mr Jefferson's to the house of Farrell & Jones of England was published by their agent as an act of justice to him, from which it appeared that after this date he had recieved between 4. & 5000£ for lands sold in 1773. to pay the debt of his father in law, mr Wayles to that house. this fact, & the lands sold are known to many. they lie in the counties of Cumberland and Bedford. in Aug. 1780. Congress first had a table of depreciation established with reference to their new emission of 40. for 1. and in Aug. 1781. they extended it to Specie. by the retrospective information of that table we are now enabled to say that in Apr. 1779. paper money was to specie as 1. to 11. not as 1. to 20 as mr Jones suggests. but this was neither known, nor believed at the time by persons well affected [to the revolution]. it was not till the close of 1781. or beginning of 1782. that the Virginia legislature formally acknowledged a depreciation by establishing a scale for it. mr Jefferson went to Europe immediately after the peace; and his agent is known to have declared that the instructions he left were that this debt to mr Jones, principal & interest, should be the very first paid as soon as hard money could be obtained.

On the whole, if it was criminal in mr Jefferson to recieve that kind of money on which the event of the revolution depended, & to support it's credit, then let mr Jones arraign every whig in the union at the bar of his country as a criminal. few were more so, nor more to their own loss than mr Jefferson. if it was criminal for a whig to pay this money to those who like himself were willing to recieve it;[8] then was every whig a criminal. if it was just not to force it on those who were unwilling to recieve it, mr Jefferson exercised that justice. he took back the money when refused; returned his obligation for the debt, & paid it with interest in hard money, as soon as hard money reappeared in circulation.[9]

PrC (DLC); faint; with words in brackets supplied from newspaper. Printed in the *National Intelligencer*, 1 July 1803.

GABRIEL JONES submitted his STATEMENT of 17 Mch. 1803 to Augustine Davis, editor of the *Virginia Gazette, & General Advertiser* at Richmond, noting that he had seen imperfect, unauthorized accounts of his financial transaction with TJ in the Richmond *Recorder* and wished to present "a true state of the facts." The statement appeared in the *Alexandria Advertiser* on 3 June, the Richmond *Recorder* on 4 June, and quickly spread to other Federalist papers (*Gazette of the United States*, 7, 8 June; Baltimore *Federal Gazette*, 6 June; New York *Spectator*, 8 June; *Kennebec Gazette*, 23 June; Brigham, *American Newspapers*, 2:1146). James Cheetham's *American Citizen* printed a rebuttal on 9 June.

In his financial records, TJ noted that he BORROWED £50 from Gabriel Jones on 29 Sep. 1773 and GAVE HIS BOND for repayment (MB, 1:346).

ASKING ENORMOUS PRICES: this idea was expressed in a circular letter from Congress to the "Inhabitants of the United States of America," dated 26 May 1779, and published in the *Pennsylvania Packet* on 29 May. WITHOUT PUBLIC INCONVENIENCE: this passage is from a Congressional address adopted on 13 Jan. 1779 (Philadelphia *Pennsylvania Packet*, 21 Jan. 1779).

OFFER OF PAIMENT: in his statement, Gabriel Jones included TJ's letter to him of 29 Apr. 1779 (*Alexandria Advertiser and Commercial Intelligencer*, 3 June 1803; Vol. 2:260-1). TJ noted in his accounts at 28 Apr. 1779 that he had enclosed £64 to Gabriel Jones "principal & int. of money borrowed Sep. 29. 1773" (MB, 1:477). SENT IT BACK TO MR JEFFERSON: on 30 June 1779, TJ recorded in his financial records, "Recd. from Gabr. Jones the money sent him ante Apr. 28. viz. £64. with my bond. Note I consider myself still liable to pay it with interest when he shall be willing to accept it" (MB, 1:481). In his newspaper account,

Gabriel Jones described TJ's MODE OF CONVEYING THE LETTER, noting that a neighbor found the missive directed to Jones in the "sash of a window in a public house in Staunton" and delivered it to him on 29 Feb. 1780. It contained the bond, which was "considerably fretted, especially at the corners." Jones continued: "By whom that paper was forwarded, or how it found its way to the sash, where my obliging neighbor accidentally discovered it, I have never yet been able to learn: but, from the whole of the circumstances, I was induced to believe it might be intended, never to reach my hands" (*Alexandria Advertiser and Commercial Intelligencer*, 3 June 1803).

LETTER OF MR JEFFERSON'S TO THE HOUSE OF FARRELL & JONES: TJ was probably referring to his letter to William Jones, of 5 Jan. 1787, which was used in 1800 to refute charges that TJ had not paid his British debts. TJ provided the *Aurora* with anonymous comments when the letter was published there on 5 Apr. 1800 (Vol. 11:14-18; Vol. 31:210-11, 457-61).

HIS AGENT: Gabriel Jones observed that he received payment of principal and interest from Nicholas Lewis only "after sundry evasions, and repeated applications" (*Alexandria Advertiser and Commercial Intelligencer*, 3 June 1803).

[1] *National Intelligencer*: "commentaries."

[2] *National Intelligencer*: "payment."

[3] In the *National Intelligencer* "there" appears in place of "in Boston."

[4] *National Intelligencer* lacks preceding two words.

[5] *National Intelligencer* lacks preceding passage from "& mr Jefferson" to this point.

[6] *National Intelligencer*: "1801."

[7] *National Intelligencer*: "money."

[8] *National Intelligencer* lacks text from this point through "unwilling to receive it."

[9] Signed "TIMOLEON" in *National Intelligencer*.

Report from John Lenthall

Rough Stone & Brick work done to the
South Wing of the Capitol June 13th. to 18th. 1803

— South front —

	Cubc feet
Stone work excluding extra labor to the Cellar Windows—about	1695
Bricks laid in do about 1000	
— East front —	
Stone work &c, as above	713
Bricks laid in do—1500	2408
Perches	98
Whole Amt. of Bricks laid in the Reversed Arches	37,598
Whole Amt of Bricks in the internal Arches	14,964
Whole Tale	52,562
Customary allowance for wast. 10/100 say 6/100 =	3153
for B H Latrobe	55,715

JNO LENTHALL

NB there are 480 Bricks yet to lay, in the two large Reversed Arches, East and West fronts, included in the above Statement—

MS (DLC); in Lenthall's hand and signed by him; endorsed by TJ: "Capitol. June 18. 1803."

From Robert Patterson

SIR Philada. June 18th. 1803—

I recommended to Capt. Lewis, the use of a *statistical Table*, in which to set down his Astronomical observations, in the course of his intended expedition; as an expedient that would save a great deal of time, and be productive of many other obvious advantages. I had proposed to draw him out a sketch of such a table, but an unusual hurry of business prevented me, while he was in the city—I have now, however, fulfilled my promise—and transmit the inclosed for his inspection.

I have sent it under cover to you, Sir, lest Capt. Lewis may have proceeded on his tour; in which case, if you shall judge it worth his notice, you will have the trouble of forwarding it to him—

I am Sir with the highest respect & esteem—Your Obed. Servt.—

R. PATTERSON

RC (DLC); endorsed by TJ as received 21 June and so recorded in SJL. Enclosure: see below.

The blank frame of a STATISTICAL TABLE that Patterson drew up for Meriwether Lewis has not been found, but Lewis copied it for the notebook of astronomical problems and instructions he had received from the Philadelphia mathematician (see Patterson to TJ, 15 Mch.). The table, for recording the astronomical observations that Patterson wanted Lewis to make regularly, included columns for the place where an observation was made; the date; the apparent time, mean time, and time by the watch; the error of the watch against the mean time and the watch's daily gain or loss of time; the apparent altitude of the sun's center or its lower or upper edge (limb); the true altitude of the sun's center; the apparent altitude of the moon's center or edge; the true altitude of the moon's center; the error of the intrument employed for the observation; the name of the star used for an observation; the apparent altitude of the star; the apparent distance of the sun's or moon's edge; the apparent and true distances between the moon and the star; the longitude of the place of observation from Greenwich; the latitude; the magnetic azimuth of the sun or pole star, the true azimuth, and the variation of the magnetic needle; and notes relating to the observation (MS in MoHi, in astronomical notebook, in Lewis's hand).

From Robert Purviance

SIR, Baltimore June 18th 1803

Since I had the Honor to receive your note of the 14 Instant, enclosing a Letter for Mr. Lee, no opportunity by an American Vessel has offer'd for any Port in France, nor do I know of any will offer shortly. This being the case, I have taken the liberty to deliver it this day to Cap. Dalton Williams of the Ship Nancy belonging to this Port and bound for Corunna, to whom I have given particular directions to put it into the Post Office at that place (and if It was found necessary to pay Postage to do it) which I hope will meet your approbation

I have the Honor to be with the greatest respect Sir, Your Mo Obedent & huml. Serv. RT. PURVIANCE

RC (DLC); at foot of text: "The President of the U States"; endorsed by TJ as received from "Purviance Thos." on 19 June and so recorded in SJL.

To Robert Smith

TH: JEFFERSON TO
THE SECRETARY OF THE NAVY. June 18. 9. P.M. [1803]

I this moment recieve from mr Madison a communication of your letter of the 17th. proposing that Capt Morris shall come home in the Adams whose crew have served their time instead of the New York which has still some time to serve. the reasons are entirely good and I concur with you in the change. Affectionate salutations.

PrC (DLC); partially dated. Recorded in SJL with notation "Morris."

RECIEVE FROM MR MADISON: a letter from James Madison to TJ received 18 June has not been found, nor is one recorded in SJL. No communication from Smith to Madison of 17 June has been found, either.

In a letter to Richard V. MORRIS dated 21 June, Smith informed him that, upon its receipt, he was to consider himself suspended as commander of the Mediterranean squadron and of the frigate *New York*. Smith added that it was also "the command of the President" that Morris take charge of the frigate *Adams* and return without delay to the United States. Command of the squadron and of the *New York* was transferred to John Rodgers (NDBW, 2:457-8).

To James Taylor, Jr.

SIR Washington June 18. 1803.

Not having recieved an account of the cyder recieved the last winter, I have guessed at it's amount, and included it in the inclosed check on the bank at Norfolk for seven hundred and sixty six dollars, meant to pay for the two pipes of wine recieved in March, and to cover the cyder also. the small variation which may be between this conjectural and the real sum may be settled either now on your information or in the next wine account. Accept my respects & best wishes.

TH: JEFFERSON

PrC (MHi); at foot of text: "Mr. James Taylor Norfolk"; endorsed by TJ in ink on verso. Recorded in SJL with notation "766. D."

For the CYDER and wine, see Vol. 39: 556.

To John Wayles Eppes

DEAR SIR Washington June 19. 1803.

Yours of the 14th. came to hand last night. I am glad you are all well so far, but having terrible apprehensions of the Hundred after the warm weather sets in, I should have been better pleased to learn you would go to Monticello immediately from whence you could make your trip to the Louisa springs if necessary at your convenience. groceries & other necessaries for summer use at Monticello have been forwarded some time since. I shall leave this on the 25th. of July, and be there the 28th. the matter of Lego will be easily arranged viva voce when we understand better what will be convenient to each. I have examined your Hessian flies & find them very genuine on which I condole with you. a poor remedy is sowing so late as to die by the rust. the advantageous remedy is to sow no more wheat grounds than can be well manured, & sowing the yellow bearded wheat, the surplus grounds put into rye and clover.[1] they attack barley more readily than wheat. when they drive us to this, they are a great blessing. I have recieved a cask of mr Hancock's syrup of punch here, & another is gone to Monticello. not having recieved any note of the cost, I inclose you an order on Gibson & Jefferson[2] in favor of mr Hancock for the amount, which be so good as to enquire of him & hand on the order to him. I inclose you one of Binns's pamphlets on the use of plaister. it is bunglingly composed, but it is generally said his facts may be relied on. the important one is that from being poor he is become rich by it. my tenderest love attends my dearest Maria, for whom I am uneasy till I hear she has left the Hundred. should she be caught there by a fever coming on a little earlier than usual, it may prevent your getting away, for it would be less dangerous to continue than to travel with a fever. accept yourself my affectionate salutations & assurances of sincere attachment. TH: JEFFERSON

P.S. all were well at Edgehill May 30. and Patsy fattening for an Autumn exhibition.

RC (ViU); addressed: "John W. Eppes Bermuda Hundred." Enclosure: John Binns, *A Treatise on Practical Farming* (see enclosure listed at TJ to Thomas Mann Randolph, 14 June). Other enclosure not found.

[1] Preceding two words interlined.
[2] Interlined: "on Gibson & Jefferson."

From Charles W. Goldsborough

Navy depmt.
June 19. 1803

The President

The Secretary of the Navy has instructed me to submit to you the propriety of the enclosed Letter to Mr David Vallanzino, who, being considered a Tripolitan Subject and found on board the Vessel recently captured by Lieut Sterett, of the cargo of which he is part owner, was sent to this country in the frigate Chesapeake as a prisoner of war.

Ch W. Goldsborough

FC (Lb in DNA: RG 45, LSP). Enclosure: probably Robert Smith to David Valenzin, 17 June 1803, informing Valenzin that he was not considered a prisoner and was "at liberty to pursue your own Business"; if Valenzin wished to return to the Mediterranean, he would be allowed passage "in any one of our public Ships going thither" (FC in Lb in DNA: RG 45, MLS).

A Jewish merchant trading in the Mediterranean, David Valenzin (vallanzino) and his cargo were captured by the schooner *Enterprize* off Malta in January 1803. Commodore Richard V. Morris defended the action by claiming that the vessel was bound for Tripoli and that Valenzin was a Tripolitan citizen. Valenzin, however, asserted that he was a citizen of Venice and that the vessel carrying his cargo was bound for Djerba, not Tripoli. Valenzin's efforts to secure restitution were severely hampered by his destitute condition and his inability to speak English. He presented a petition to the House of Representatives in November 1803, which was debated for months by the Committee on Claims as it sought additional evidence in the case. Despairing of ever receiving compensation, Valenzin committed suicide in January 1804. The following March, Congress authorized payment of $2,665.70 to Valenzin's legal representatives and an additional $500 to reimburse individuals who had contributed to his support while in the United States (Baltimore *Republican, or Anti-Democrat*, 14 Jan. 1804; Boston *New-England Palladium*, 14 Feb. 1804; asp, *Claims*, 1:288-9, 292-6; ndbw, 2:364-5, 383-4; U.S. Statutes at Large, 6:54-5).

A letter from Valenzin to TJ, dated 24 Oct. 1803, is recorded in SJL as received from Washington on 26 Oct. with notation "N," but has not been found. Describing the letter in his November 1803 petition to the House of Representatives, Valenzin stated that he, "emboldened by the report of the great humanity and justice which characterize his excellency the President of the United States, addressed a letter to him, praying some *amelioration* of his unhappy condition: from that time to the present your petitioner has not had the honor of receiving any notice" (Baltimore *Republican, or Anti-Democrat*, 14 Jan. 1804).

To Bishop James Madison

Dear Sir Washington June 19. 1803

I recieved last night your favor of the 13th. with regard to the papers which respect the claim of Maryland to the South branch of Potomak, whose titles are particularly mentioned by you as extracted from the Notes on Virginia. I can say no more than is there said. the source from whence the papers are to be obtained is always stated there when known to myself. I think the Commissioners should procure the following papers.

1632.	June 20.	the grant of Maryland to Ld. Baltimore. probably in Hazard's collection.
1633.	July 3.	the petition of the planters of Virginia against the grant to Ld. Baltimore. perhaps in the Notes of the Representatives of Pensylvania.
	July 3.	the order [of Council thereon]. this is in the Notes of the Representatives of Pensylvania.
1649.	Sep. [18.]	Grant of Northern neck to Ld. Hopton & others. and [1656. Oct. 12.] Objections against this. 5 [Thurl. 482?]
1733.		the Petition of Ld. Fairfax for a commission to run the line between the Northern Neck & the [cross?].
1733.	Nov. 29.	Order of King & council on do.
1737.	Aug. 10.	Survey & report of the Commissioners of the crown thereon
	Aug. 11.	Survey & report of the Commissioners of Ld. Fairfax thereon
1738.	Dec. 21.	Order of reference of the surveys to the council of plantation affairs.
1745.	Apr. 6.	Report of the council for plantation affairs thereon.
	Apr. 11.	Order of the king & council confirming this report.

no doubt that all these papers on the petition of Ld. Fairfax for the establishment of his boundary are to be found in his land office. it is impossible they should not have been recorded & bound up in a book by themselves. should they be lost, they ought to be sought from England. I well remember to have heard my father explain the experiments & principles on which the Commissioners decided that the Northern was the principal branch of the Potomac. the very question now called up by Maryland was the one decided by these commissioners. I have a copy of their survey, which was engraved and struck off on a scale of 5. I. to the degree of latitude. it is exactly copied in Fry & Jefferson's map, Ld. Fairfax having furnished them from his land-office all the materials for the country between the Potomac & Rappahanoc. the degrees & minutes are laid down in the margins of this survey.

The proceedings on a suit in the Chancery of England between Lord Baltimore & Penn are interesting in this case. they are collected in the form of a preface to the Laws of Pensylvania, as they stood before the revolution. this volume ought to be procured. they took [place?] in 1680. & 1681. under this decree in Chancery Mason & Dixon were sent over to run a boundary between Pensylvania & Maryland from the Delaware to the meridian of the 1st. fountain of the Potomak, and did it with the more accuracy as they were at the same time employed by the royal society to measure a degree of longitude in the same parallel of latitude. it is impossible but that in these proceedings in Chancery will be found the most unequivocal acknolegements by Ld. Baltimore that the branch of the Potomak to the meridian of whose first fountain they run, was the branch bounding his claim. in the 58th. vol. of the Phil. transactions is the report of Mason & Dixon on their operations on this survey. probably that will give useful information. no doubt a compleat record of every paper in the chancery suit can be had from England. the case itself is reported, as to the law questions, in one of the Chancery reports. I believe it is Vezey, but cannot say certainly as I am writing here where I have neither books nor papers. the copies of surveys &c. furnished by Ld. Fairfax to Messrs. Fry & Jefferson were among my fathers papers when he died in 1757. and remained in my possession till they were burnt in the house at Shadwell in 1768. which was the 1st. fountain of the Potomak might have been doubtful in the beginning, but the doubt was settled, and the lines depending on it have been long since located & are attested 1. by the exercise of the rights of soil & jurisdiction by Virginia from the first settlement of the country, & 2. by the non-exercise of the same rights by Maryland, South of the North branch or West of the meridian of it's 1st. fountain. 3. by the proceedings in Chancery & the survey of Mason & Dixon thereon & acknolegements of Ld. Baltimore. 4. by the proceedings between the king & Ld. Fairfax & the survey [&] final decision thereon. tho' these are res inter alios actae, yet they are good historical testimony, and history is always competent evidence in disputes between nations. 5. the grant by the crown to Ld. Fairfax & proceedings on that were good or not good. if good on the principle that a subsequent grant could curtail or controul a preceding one, there the question is decided[1] by the grant to Ld. Fairfax and the actual location of it. if not good, on the contrary principle that a subsequent could not controul a preceding grant: then the grant of the crown to Lord Baltimore of what had been before granted to Virginia [. . .] and all Maryland belongs to us. if they urge that Virginia ceded the charter boundaries of Maryland[2] by her constitution, I answer that her intention as to the limits ceded cannot be departed from, if the claim is built on her cession. that in the relinquishment of her title to the state of Maryland, she meant it[3] according to the limits within which Maryland had ever, & then did exercise the rights of soil & jurisdiction, is known to every one who was concerned in the transaction. I drew the clause in the constitution, and know that I had no idea that any other claim was or would be thought of by Maryland. very many members of the convention are still living, and can attest that Maryland as laid down in the maps was the Maryland meant to be[4] ceded by Virginia. the decision of Congress on the Connecticut reserve has given great strength to the claims under the oldest grant.

I have with difficulty snatched a moment from other calls to answer your letter, and have most hastily sketched some general outlines, which may suggest to you some particulars in the investigation you are appointed to. I suspect that Colo. George Mason's papers must contain something valuable on this subject. he had long had it in his head, understood it intimately, and probably collected papers and made notes relative to it. but whether his representatives will take the trouble of making such a search among his papers as might be necessary must depend on the interest your committee can make with them. Accept my affectionate salutations and assurances of great esteem & respect.

TH: JEFFERSON

PrC (DLC); faint and torn; at foot of first page: "Bishop Madison." Recorded in SJL with notation "dispute with Maryld."

The proprietary GRANT by Charles I to Cecelius Calvert, the second Lord Baltimore, which created the colony of Maryland, sparked an immediate protest from colonists in Virginia and their representatives in London, but the Privy Council sustained the grant in an ORDER of 3 July 1633 (*Pennsylvania Archives*, 8th Ser., 8 vols. [Harrisburg, Pa., 1931], 1:iv-v).

The seven initial grantees of the NORTHERN NECK proprietary included Ralph HOPTON (Douglas Southall Freeman, *George Washington: A Biography*, 7 vols. [New York, 1948-57], 1:447-9).

In 1735, Virginia's lieutenant governor William Gooch named William Byrd II, John Robinson, and John Grymes, as COMMISSIONERS to represent the Crown's interest in determining whether the Northern Neck proprietary should be bounded by the southern or northern branch of the Rappahannock River and to oversee the development of surveys and maps of the proprietary's area. The proprietor, Thomas Fairfax, in turn named Charles Carter, William Beverley, and William Fairfax to act on his behalf. Both sets of commissioners submitted reports to the Privy Council, which referred the matter to the committee in charge of colonial affairs. This committee ruled in Fairfax's favor in 1745 and ordered the surveying of a western boundary line from the headwaters of the Rapidan River, southern branch of the Rappahannock, to the headwaters of the Potomac, which all parties assumed to be the springs of its northern branch. TJ's FATHER was part of the surveying team that established this boundary line, as was Joshua Fry, with whom Peter Jefferson later executed a map of Virginia (Freeman, *Washington*, 1:502-9; Fairfax Harrison, "The Northern Neck Maps of 1737-1747," WMQ, 2d ser., 4 [1924], 2-3, 8-9).

For the case in CHANCERY between the heirs of William Penn and Charles Calvert, the fifth Lord Baltimore, see Vol. 38: 338n.

RES INTER ALIOS ACTAE: or, a thing done between others. TJ refers here to the common law rule prohibiting the admission of collateral facts into evidence (Garner, *Black's Law Dictionary*, 1336).

TJ's second and third drafts of Virginia's Constitution included language that confirmed Virginia's cession of territory to Maryland, Pennsylvania, and the Carolinas, as reflected in the royal charters that had created those colonies. The final version of the Constitution kept this clause, while adding an assertion of navigation rights in the Potomac (Vol. 1:352-3, 362-3, 383).

For the act concerning the Western RESERVE, land immediately west of Pennsylvania that was claimed and controlled by Connecticut, see U.S. Statutes at Large, 2:56-7.

[1] Remainder of the sentence, including period, interlined.

[2] Preceding two words interlined.

[3] TJ here canceled "soil had been occupied."

[4] Preceding three words interlined.

From Thomas Newton, Jr.

SIR Norfolk June 19th. 1803

I now take the liberty of informing you that we have in this place but one Commissioner for Bankrupts Mr. Richd E. Lee having been elected to represent the Borough of Norfolk in the legislature is under the necessity of given up his commission or vacating his seat the former of which he prefers, and also of recommending for Commissioners Messrs Richard Henry Lee and John E Holt—Mr. Lee is a young man who has just commenced the practice of Law, he possesses talents and is very deserving[1]—Mr. Holt has been a Merchant but has for some time giving up Commerce—he is an intelligent man and a worthy Character—both the gentlemen are republicans and will accept of the appointments if you should think proper to confer Commissions. Mr. Nimmo who was some time ago appointed Commissioner has requested me to transmit his commission to the Secretary of State with his acknowledgements to you for the honor done him by the appointment. He has soliceted me to inform you that the reason which compelled him not to accept it was his holding a State office which he preferred Our Laws on that subject you are fully acquainted with. they do not permit an union of Federal & State offices in the same person.—

Accept Sir my best wishes for yr. health THO. NEWTON JR

RC (DNA: RG 59, LAR); at head of text: "Thos: Jefferson esqr"; endorsed by TJ as received 23 June and so recorded in SJL with notation "Commrs. bkrptcy"; also endorsed by TJ: "Lee Richd. H. Holt John E. } to be Commrs. bkrptcy Norfolk."

BUT ONE COMMISSIONER FOR BANKRUPTS: TJ's list of bankruptcy commissioners indicates that of the original July 1802 appointees at Norfolk, only Thomas Blanchard remained (Vol. 37:710; Vol. 38:27). Richard E. LEE, however, did not return his bankruptcy commission to Madison until 28 Oct. 1803. He then noted that he found it "inconvenient" to continue in the office any longer and gave several reasons for his decision, including "the extensive latitude for fraud, which the Bankrupt Law" afforded and "the obstacles," which were constantly thrown in the way, impeding "a complete discovery of the Bankrupts effects" (RC in DNA: RG 59, MLR, endorsed by TJ: "Lee Richd. E. to mr Madison. returns Commn of bkrptcy"; Madison, *Papers, Sec. of State Ser.*, 5:587-8).

On 24 June, the State Department issued commissions for RICHARD HENRY LEE and JOHN E HOLT. On his ongoing list of bankruptcy commissioners, TJ noted that Lee was appointed in place of James NIMMO and Holt in place of Richard Evers Lee (list of commissions in Lb in DNA: RG 59, MPTPC; Vol. 37:710). For Nimmo's appointment in November 1802, see Vol. 38:632-3, 634n, 677-8; Vol. 39: Appendix I.

[1]MS: "derserving."

From Benjamin Ferris

RESPECTED FRIEND Philada. 6th mo. 20th. 1803

Pursuant to the directions of Isaac Briggs I have completed a Clock for thee. he informed me that it was not in any degree for ornamental purposes and particularly requested that it might be made plain; The workmanship is good, and the regulation nearly perfected. I had the rod of the pendulum made of well seasoned Wood, it being less affected by the changes of the weather than either Brass or Steel.—I have had it well packed and I hope perfectly secure from the weather; It is shipped on board the schooner Success capt Tice bound to Richmond and directed to the care of Gibson & Jefferson of that place—When it arrives at its place of destination there will be nothing to do, but to take out the clock, hang on the weights and draw out a few small Nails which secures the pendulum binding it to the back of the case. Some attention will be necessary to have the Case fixed perpendicularly—

I received thine of the 8th instant inclosing 70 Dollars, which pays for the Clock, Case, Packing &c—for which I am with thanks thy obliged friend

BENJ. FERRIS

No 17 North 2nd St

RC (DLC); at foot of text: "Thomas Jefferson Presdt. U.S."; endorsed by TJ as received 22 June and so recorded in SJL.

To Edward Tiffin

Sir Washington June 20: 1803.

The resolution of the Genl. Assembly of Ohio expressing their satisfaction with the measures adopted by the National legislature, at their last session, in relation to the navigation of the Missisipi is a just tribute to the wisdom of those measures. it is worthy also the sound discernment with which that state disregarded the seductive suggestions of a supposed separate interest; and manifests dispositions to support the constitutional authority of the General government, of which the state legislatures will doubtless ever set the example. nothing can so effectually contribute to produce the greatest good of our country, as harmony and mutual confidence between the general & State authorities, & a conviction that local & general interests, well understood, can never be in opposition.

The confidence which they are also pleased to express in the administration of the General government, calls for my particular acknolegements. I have conscientiously pursued those measures which, on the best advice, seemed most likely to secure the rights & interests of the Western states in the navigation of the Missisipi. if these interests can be secured (and nothing yet forbids the hope) and our country saved from the havoc & desolations of war, from the burthens necessary to support it, & the consequent increase of the public debt, which would not fail in the end to absorb all the produce of our labor, and to overwhelm our liberties, I flatter myself that my fellow-citizens will be contented with the course pursued, and will countenance future endeavors to preserve their peace & prosperity. I pray you to accept assurances of my high respect & consideration.

Th: Jefferson

PrC (DLC); at foot of text: "Governor Tiffin."

resolution: see Tiffin to TJ, 15 Apr. 1803.

To Thomas Tingey

June 20. 1803.

Th: Jefferson presents his compliments to Capt Tingey, and having little acquaintance among the directors of the bank, asks the favor of him to consider the inclosed letter proposed to be written to the

President, as to the mode of keeping his account, should he open one with them on the departure of mr Barnes who has hitherto been his banker. if there be anything in it, which Capt Tingey knows to be against the laws of the institution, then Th:J. would not send it in. The whole difficulty is in permitting him to overdraw on emergencies without the form of giving a note which he believes is done by the banks sometimes because he knows it was done commonly by the bank of the US. with himself when he lived in Philadelphia. should Capt Tingey at any time be passing into this part of the city, Th:J. would thank him to call & tell him his opinion on the subject. he offers his friendly salutations.

PrC (MoSHi: Jefferson Papers); endorsed by TJ in ink on verso. Enclosure not found.

Tingey was one of the DIRECTORS OF THE BANK of the United States branch at Washington (*Washington Federalist*, 7 Feb. 1803).

From John Vinall

DEAR AND RESPECTABLE SIR, Boston June 20th 1803

It may appear presumption for an individual citizen, to take the freedom of addressing the first Majestrate of the United States, elevated to that exalted Station by the suffrages of a free and enlightned People. But your well known candor, respectable Sir, I trust will excuse the liberty which I have taken.

I address you, as the Patriot and framer of the glorious declaration of American Independence, who emancipated this Country from the Shackles of the British Monarchy; and, elevated Columbia to that high Rank which she holds among the most powerful Nations of the Earth. Heaven still smiles upon us—Heaven has not left us a prey to the intrigue and artifices of an unprincipled Faction among ourselves, who have been aiming, and are now using every mean in their power, to destroy the Union—pervert our free republican forms of Government and to erect upon its ruins a monarchical, Aristocratical Government.

The reign of terror is no more—persecution, and prosecution for republican principles, will no longer disgrace the Annals of America. The sovereign ruler of Events has placed you, sir at the head of the Union as the protector of religious as well as civil liberty.—Your inaugural Speech has resounded through the vast and extended Continent of the United States; and received with the greatest plaudits by an immense majority of the freemen whom you are called to govern.

Pardon me respectable sir, pardon the man who though he never had the pleasure of beholding your person, is intimately acquainted with your merit and virtues; not from News paper panegyrics, and fulsom Addresses; but, from the mouth of the Patriot Hancock, now, no more; and from other Patriots, your compeers, at that awful Crisis, when Congress boldly declared these, then british Colonies, to be free sovereign and independent States.

Permit me venerable Sir a persecuted citizen for my attachment to republican principles, to lay before you my situation; and to trouble you with the relation of some facts relevant to myself anterior to the fatal period of Feby 1800 which brought distress upon me and an innocent family.

Born in the Town of Boston, and educated in principles of sobriety—I received an education commensurate with my Parents circumstances, and afterwards followed a profession for many years calculated to promote the benefit of the Community.

In the year 1794 His Excellency Samuel Adams Esqr then Commander in chief of the State of Massachusetts honoured me with a Commission of Justice of the Peace for the County of Suffolk; and I was qualified according to the Constitution to exercise the functions of that office.—In three years afterwards I received from the same Gentleman another Commission of Justice of the Peace and of the Quorum, the duties of which Offices I performed until Feby 1800 when by a combination of malignant unprincipled enemies, aided by the evidence of false Witnesses, and some of the basest Characters I was removed from office.

Every Republican officer has in a greater or less degree suffered persecuton during and through the reign of *Terror* in this Country; but, my persecution has been singular; and, I can say with sincerety—"That false Witnesses have risen up against me, and laid to my charge things which I knew not of" But, previous to my persecution, and at the present moment, I feel that consciousness of having endeavoured to the best of my abilities, faithfully to support the Constitution and execute the Laws of my Country within the jurisdiction of a Majestrate, unbiassed by any party motives.

I am now a little turned of sixty years of Age—I have an infirm wife and a large family to support, and, the means which is left is but small and inconsiderable to provide for them and myself.—My friends have repeatedly advised me to lay my case before you, not doubting but some Office might be given me under the United States, which might enable me to pass more smoothly down the rugged path of Life.

For the last ten or twelve years of my Life I have applied myself closely to the study of Law, and the multeplicity of business while in Office has enabled me to bring it into practice.—If any vacancy should happen among the Commissioners of Bankruptcy in the Town of Boston or any other Office calculated for my abeleties—I should esteem it the greatest favour if I could be so happy as to be esteemed worthy of it by your Excellency: I can obtain the best recommendation from Gentlemen who have been acquainted with me and my conduct for many years past.

But, respectable Sir, I must apologize for the prolexity of this Letter, relying upon your candor to excuse that and every other defect.

With every consideration of the highest esteem & respect I beg leave to subscribe myself Your obedient, humble Servant

JOHN VINALL

RC (DNA: RG 59, LAR); endorsed by TJ as received 26 June and "to be Commr. loans" and so recorded in SJL.

John Vinall (1736-1823) spent his early career as a mathematics and writing teacher in Boston and Newburyport. He published *The Preceptor's Assistant, or Students' Guide: Being a Systematical Treatise of Arithmetic, both Vulgar and Decimal; Calculated for the Use of Schools, Counting Houses, and Private Families* in Boston in 1792. Two years later he became a Suffolk County justice of the peace. On 1 Mch. 1800, the Massachusetts General Court convicted and impeached him for "misconduct and maladministration in his office" specifically for "extortion, bribery and corruption." Although removed as a magistrate and disqualified from holding any future office of "honor, trust, or profit," in the commonwealth, Vinall continued to advertise his ability to draft wills and other legal documents. On 24 June 1806, the court remitted part of Vinall's sentence. He recovered all the privileges of a citizen, including the right to hold office, but was neither reinstated as justice of the peace nor released from the charges (Worcester *Massachusetts Spy*, 5, 12 Mch. 1800; Boston *Columbian Centinel*, 22 Mch. 1800; *Newburyport Herald*, 11 July 1806).

FALSE WITNESSES HAVE RISEN UP AGAINST ME: Psalm 35:11.

From Albert Gallatin

Tuesday 21. June 1803

The enclosed letter from the Collector of Presque Isle seems to render the organization of the district of Niagara, which is authorized by the last paragraph of the 5th Sect. of the Collection Law, (Vol. 4. page 288), necessary. A collector at Niagara & a surveyor on Buffaloe will be necessary. But the place is so remote that it is difficult to obtain recommendations. Oliver Phelps is the republican member of Congress for that district. A son of General Irvine is Indian agent on Buffaloe & might act as surveyor there if a collector could be obtained for Niagara.

The propriety of sending the within letter to Mr Thornton is submitted. Is it sufficiently civil?

With respect Your obedt. Servt. ALBERT GALLATIN

RC (DLC); addressed: "The President"; endorsed by TJ as received from the Treasury Department on 21 June and "Collector at Niagara. Surveyor at Buffalo. Irvine" and so recorded in SJL. Enclosures not found.

COLLECTOR OF PRESQUE ISLE: Thomas Forster (Vol. 36:428-9). Congress established the DISTRICT OF NIAGARA, extending from Lake Ontario and Lake Erie "and the rivers connected therewith" to the west bank of the Genesee River, in the 2 Mch. 1799 COLLECTION LAW. The president was authorized to appoint a collector at Niagara, the port of entry, and up to two surveyors at places designated by him (U.S. Statutes at Large, 1:627, 631). Callender Irvine served as the U.S. INDIAN AGENT to the Six Nations tribes (Vol. 38:274n). Gallatin's letter to Edward THORNTON has not been found but it probably concerned customs violations on the Great Lakes. For the custom house officers appointed for the Niagara district, see Gallatin to TJ, 11 Aug. 1803 (first letter).

From Albert Gallatin

DEAR SIR 21 June 1803

I enclose a letter from the Commissioner of the revenue respecting Mr Gordon's claim: as he gave a memorandum in writing, Mr G. should produce it.—also recommendations from Messrs. Bacon & Varnum in favor of Francis Carr for the office of Naval officer at Newbury port. The present incumbent is Jonathan Titcomb[1] of whom I know nothing—also a letter from Tench Coxe: his suggestions of a report proceeding from Messrs. Madison & Lewis are without foundation; but Capn. Lewis says that the Republicans in Philada. seem generally agreed that in case of the removal of either of the two custom house officers, he, Mr Coxe, is entitled to the preference. The salary of the naval officer (M'pherson) is 3,500 dollars, of the surveyor (Jackson) 3000, & of the purveyor only 2,000. I feel no hesitation in saying that on the grounds of public services, & capacity as well as on Account of his having been formerly removed, Mr Coxe's pretensions to the most lucrative of those offices which may be vacated appear well founded: personal predilection for him I have not & I do not know who would be the best person to appoint purveyor, if he was made Surveyor; but justice seemed to require that expression of my opinion in his favor on that point. There would, however, be an objection to his being substituted in lieu of Mr M'pherson which does not apply to his replacing Jackson: in the first instance the act of giving to a man who had left the Americans & joined the British, the office of him who had left the British to join the Americans would make too forcible a contrast. Yet, to me, the prefect of the Pretorian bands is much more obnoxious than the insignificant Jackson. As it will be necessary for me to answer Mr Coxe's letter, I wish to know your final determination respecting those Philadelphia offices, in order that my answer may be properly modified to meet your own intentions; it seems to me that if the surveyor's place is to be given to another person, it will be proper without entering into any confidential communications that I should inform Mr Coxe that he was altogether mistaken, & that you had not intended any other office for him than that of purveyor. It is proper at the same time that you should know that although this last office has a less salary affixed to it, perhaps because it is less laborious, it is more respectable, important, & responsible than that of surveyor. The surveyor is the head of the tide-waiters, inspectors & other out-doors inferior officers of the custom house, distributes them on board the vessels, recieves their reports, watches smuggling & other irregular proceedings &a; but not a single penny of public monies passes through his hands. The purveyor is by law the officer who should make all the purchases of clothing, stores &a. for the war & navy departments; and several hundred thousand dollars pass annually through his hands. He is practically employed principally by the Secretary of War; the navy department having, improperly in my opinion, continued to employ in Philada. agents (Harrison & Sterret) to whom a commission is paid for services which the purveyor ought to perform.—By conversing with Capn. Lewis you will receive every necessary information respecting public opinion & feeling in Philada.; and you will perceive that I cannot wish to communicate with any person there on the subject of removals & offices except with a full knowledge of your ultimate determination & even then not without some considerable reluctance. I think, however, that what is right in itself ought to be done without being deterred by the imputation that the ward-meetings have compelled the Executive to Act in a different way from what he intended; and the intemperance of some individuals will not prevent my communicating to you my impressions even when the result is favorable to their views as freely as if they had acted & spoken with perfect propriety.

Robert Hays Marshal of West Tenessee has drawn improperly on the Treasury for more than 2 thd. dollars. The bill was not paid & on a settlement of his accounts about one thousand dollars were found due to him. In order to apologize for his having drawn the two thousand he pretends now that a bill drawn more than a year ago by him on the Treasury in favor of Henning & Dixon, (who is I believe Dixon of Congress) endorsed by them to a respectable merchant in Philada. to whom it was paid by the Treasury, was a forgery. Should that be the case there will be no loss as the endorsers are perfectly responsible. But from comparing the hand writing, from the respectability of the parties & various other circumstances, I have not the least doubt of that his assertion being altogether false. This having led me to further enquiry, I find that he never writes any thing but his name & that sometimes under the visible effects of intoxication, that he renders his accounts irregularly & always in an incomplete manner, that he is incapable & has contracted such habits of intemperance as render it necessary that he should be removed. The only persons I know in West Tenessee are Mr Dixon the member of Congress & Andrew Jackson formerly a member: the two Senators live in East Tenessee which is a distinct district with a Marshal of its own. Where Mr Smith lives I do not positively know but believe in East Tenessee. Please to direct what shall be done & whether I may write to Messrs. Dixon & Jackson or to either of them for information of a proper successor.

With sincere respect & attachment Your obedt. Servt.

Albert Gallatin

RC (DLC); at foot of text: "The President"; endorsed by TJ as received from the Treasury Department on 22 June and "Gordon's claim.—Carr v. Titcomb. —Tenche Coxe. Jackson. Mc.pherson. Hayes Marshal of W. Tennissee" and so recorded in SJL. Enclosures: (1) John Bacon to Gallatin, 11 June 1803, from Boston, where he is attending the General Court; having learned that a vacancy is soon to occur in the surveyor's office at Newburyport, Bacon recommends Francis Carr of Haverhill, in Essex County, for the position; he personally attests to Carr as "a gentleman of integrity, system," and industry, who has adhered to "sound political sentiments" without rendering himself "either odious, or despicable" to those of opposite sentiments (RC in DNA: RG 59, LAR; endorsed by TJ: "Carr Francis to be Surveyor of Newbury port v. <*Jona. Titcomb*> Michael Hodge"). (2) Tench Coxe to Gallatin, Philadelphia, 16 June 1803, informing the Treasury secretary that he has heard that the purveyorship may be transferred to Washington, but the emoluments of the office will not allow him to move his family from Philadelphia; he has received information through reputable channels that Madison and Meriwether Lewis indicated "that the President had determined upon another change here in my favor," and they were not referring to the purveyor's office; Coxe saw Lewis several times and spent a day with him, but those "great public Subjects, which are not to be neglected at this time, were our only topics," he notes, "I never spoke to him of myself"; Coxe does not want his willingness to perform the duties of the purveyorship to prevent his appointment to a vacancy at the custom house in Philadelphia (RC in NHi: Gallatin Papers; at head of text: "private"). Other enclosures not found.

For an earlier endorsement of FRANCIS CARR as surveyor at Newburyport in place of Michael Hodge who was characterized as "violent against the administration," see Levi Lincoln to TJ, 13 Dec. 1802. John Bacon also recommended Carr as surveyor, not NAVAL OFFICER (see Enclosure No. 1, above). JONATHAN TITCOMB continued as naval officer until 1812, but TJ replaced Hodge in February 1809 (Washington, *Papers, Rev. War Ser.*, 16:260n; same, *Pres. Ser.*, 3:84; JEP, 2:107-8).

FORMERLY REMOVED: Coxe lost his position as commissioner of the revenue in December 1797. On 17 June 1801, TJ wrote Coxe explaining why he had not restored him to the position from which he had been "so unjustly removed" (Vol. 34:372, 447-8, 450n). JOINED THE BRITISH: for Coxe's attachment to the British cause during the American Revolution, see Jacob E. Cooke, *Tench Coxe and the Early Republic* [Chapel Hill, 1978], 25-43. PREFECT OF THE PRETORIAN BANDS: that is, militia commander of "McPherson's Blues" (Vol. 34:426-8; Vol. 37:539).

HARRISON & STERRET: that is, George Harrison, navy agent at Philadelphia since 1799, and Samuel Sterett, former Baltimore merchant, Maryland congressman from 1791 to 1793, and navy agent with his brother Joseph Sterett. After the failure of his business in Baltimore, Samuel Sterett moved to Philadelphia and established a partnership with Harrison. As the Philadelphia agent of Van Staphorst & Hubbard, TJ corresponded with Harrison & Sterett in 1796 (NDQW, Dec. 1800-Dec. 1801, 374-5; Syrett, *Hamilton*, 24:413n; Vol. 23:495; Vol. 29:106-7, 186, 212, 329, 458; Vol. 30:503).

As a member of Congress in 1797, Andrew Jackson used his influence to have ROBERT HAYS appointed marshal. Hays was married to Jane Donelson, sister of Jackson's wife, Rachel (Harold D. Moser and others, eds., *The Papers of Andrew Jackson*, 8 vols. [Knoxville, 1980-], 1:35n, 124). DIXON OF CONGRESS: William Dickson. TWO SENATORS: Joseph Anderson and William Cocke. MR SMITH: probably Daniel Smith, who attended the College of William and Mary and in 1784 moved to Cumberland County, in East Tennessee. He filled the state's vacancy in the U.S. Senate after Jackson resigned in 1798. In 1800, Smith sent TJ a "vocabulary of the Chickasaw language" (same, 1:16n, 259n; *Biog. Dir. Cong.*; Vol. 32:44, 134).

[1]TJ underlined "Jonathan Titcomb" and wrote "Michael Hodge" in the left margin.

From Louis Landais, with Jefferson's Note

Charleston June 21st 1803

Altho' I have been advised to publish every transactions, I was by some advised to inclose your Excellency the whole, as it was known well enough that I had been very ill treated, and that Justice & Satisfaction having been refused me, I resigned on account of it; and that My Parents calling me near to them in the W. indies, for business of importance I was very Justifiable in every thing.

As I am not at all averse to the Citizens of America, I would beg your Excellency to direct the Secretary of War to give me a Certificate that I had a Commissn., in the Service of the U.S. which I bore with dignity; and that Should I come back, as it is very probable in a short time, I might reclaim my title of Citizen of America. This Certificate, I beg your Excellency to direct to be inclosed to the Care of Guilliam Aertsen, State bank, Charleston, who shall forward it to me by the 1st. opportunity.

Your most obedt. Servt. LOUIS LANDAIS

[*Note by TJ*:]
refd to the Secy. at War.

TH: JEFFERSON
July 2. 03.

RC (PHi); TJ's note written below endorsement; endorsed by TJ. Recorded in SJL as received 1 July. Enclosure: Landais to TJ, undated, "publickly stating" his reasons for resigning his army commission; these revolved around his ongoing dispute with Captain Jonathan Robeson, which began shortly after Landais's transfer to Georgia in May 1801 and continued after both officers were ordered to South Carolina; Landais blames the origins of his "misunderstandings" on Robeson's wife, a "base, Malicious, designing Woman," and accuses both husband and wife of spreading false information about him and attacking his character behind his back; the quarrel escalated in March 1803, after Robeson denied Landais the use of the police to bring wood to his quarters and a sergeant overheard Landais exclaim to himself, "*dam* me what is the police for?"; the sergeant reported that Landais had damned Captain Robeson; confronted by Robeson, Landais denied the epithet was intended for him but added that "since you persist in it you may take it as you choose"; Robeson subsequently told Landais to "take your sword & follow me immediately"; Landais sent for "Captain Pain of the revenue cutter," who stood with him and convinced him not to participate in the duel, not out of cowardice, but because of his responsibility to his wife and infant child; Landais then wrote to Lieutenant Colonel Constant Freeman, acquainting him with the evening's transactions, lodging six charges against Robeson, and requesting that a regimental court martial be convened; Landais's charges against Robeson include abuse of authority, abusive language, disobedience of orders, embezzlement of public property, ungentlemanly conduct, and "Behaving in a manner unbecoming an Officer and a Gentleman"; after some delay, Freeman ordered the arrest of Robeson in April 1803, but released him the following month and permitted him to resume command of Fort Moultrie; Freeman further informed Landais that "there will not be any further bickerings" and that duty at the fort "will be done in harmony"; upon receiving Freeman's letter and learning that no court-martial would take place, Landais resigned his commission; for further details, Landais refers the president to the secretary of war, "to whom I have transmitted every transaction more detailed and sent vouchers to prove several of the charges" (same, at foot of text: "To the President of the United States"; Heitman, *Dictionary*, 1:836).

A native of France, Louis Landais was an artillery lieutenant stationed at Fort Moultrie near Charleston, South Carolina. A letter from him to TJ dated 8 Nov. 1802, recorded in SJL as received from Fort Moultrie on 20 Nov. with notation "W," has not been found. On 23 Nov., Henry Dearborn wrote Lieutenant Colonel Thomas H. Cushing, the adjutant and inspector of the army, enclosing Landais's letter to the president "in relation to the date of his commission, and the command of Fort Johnston in North Carolina." Dearborn declined to interfere in the matter and added that it would be "very desirable to put a stop to the frequent applications which are made to the President on subjects often in their nature frivolous, and many times such as do not properly appertain to his Executive functions" (FC in Lb in DNA: RG 107, LSMA; Heitman, *Dictionary*, 1:613; Vol. 38:689).

Notes on the Wabash Saline

[before 22 June 1803]

Notes of Wabash Salines.

on Saline creek which empties into Ohio 16. mi. below Wabash

the Saline is 16. miles up the creek, which is navigable, & 16. miles across from the nearest part of Wabash.

the bed or saline marsh is about 20. yards square.

it ought to be so worked as to make 100. bush. salt a day.

this would require boilers of 15,000. galls. contents. containg. 40. galls. each, they cost 20. D. each, delivd there. salt could be made for 1. dollar per bushel.

worked to this extent, they wd be worth 5000. to 10,000 D. a year to US.

4. miles square of land will furnish timber for 10. years.

by that time it will be reproduced in greater quantity of about 6. I. diam. which is the best size to use.

a few hundred yards below there is a stronger water, & also 6. miles above, in Indn. territory.

no coal nearer than White river.

MS (DLC: TJ Papers, 234:41888); undated, but see TJ to Gallatin, 22 June (first letter) and Gallatin to TJ, 22 June; entirely in TJ's hand.

To Justus Erich Bollmann

Sir Washington June 22. 1803.

Your favor of the 18th. is come to hand, and I am sorry you are not likely to get your affairs into the shape you have desired. I am the more so as it is not in my power to be useful to you in the way you propose. I will say to you with candour, that having two years ago purchased some land adjoining me, and extremely important to me for 6000 D. it has kept me in constant distress and remains still in part unpaid. I am sensible that I ought to reduce my scale of expence so as not only to keep myself more at ease but to be able to increase my means of assisting others. but it is a difficult operation. I fear the Marquis de la Fayette will be little able to assist you from the pittance remaining to him. I believe he is really poor. I shall be very happy to see you here, should your business bring you this far as you expect. accept my salutations & assurances of respect.

Th: Jefferson

PrC (DLC); at foot of text: "Doctr. Bollman"; endorsed by TJ in ink on verso.

The MARQUIS de Lafayette eventually gave Bollmann $6,000 in lieu of the annuity he had once promised (Fritz Redlich, "Eric Bollmann: Adventurer, Businessman, and Economic Writer," in *Essays in American Economic History: Eric Bollmann and Studies in Banking* [Ann Arbor, Mich., 1944], 18, 25).

To Albert Gallatin

TH:J. TO MR GALLATIN June 22. 1803.

The letter to Thornton is civil both in matter & manner, and entirely proper. I dare say Irvine will do very well as Surveyor at Buffalo. he seems so far to have conducted himself well as Indian agent.

I do not know Oliver Phelps's particular character, except that he has all the sagacity of a Connecticut man, and is attached to the little band. but I do not see that his recommendation need be distrusted on this account. I should think it best to write to him to recommend a Collector.

RC (NHi: Gallatin Papers); endorsed. PrC (DLC). Recorded in SJL with notation "Thornton.—Irvine—Phelps."

LETTER TO THORNTON: not found (see Gallatin to TJ, 21 June, second letter). A few days later, Gallatin sent TJ the following: "Be pleased to examine this letter which is intended for Mr Thornton, and to suggest the alterations which you may think proper. Respectfully Your obt. Servt. Albert Gallatin" (RC in DLC; undated; addressed: "The President of the United States"; endorsed by TJ as received from the Treasury Department on 28 June and "with copy of lre to Thornton on seisure of Mc.kenz's goods" and so recorded in SJL). The enclosed letter has not been found, but as TJ's endorsement indicates it probably had to do with the collection of duties and smuggling along the Canadian border (see Gallatin to TJ, 21 Mch.).

ATTACHED TO THE LITTLE BAND: at the urging of Albany Burrites, Oliver Phelps agreed to fill the ticket as Burr's running mate in the New York gubernatorial election of 1804 (Kline, *Burr*, 2:835).

To Albert Gallatin

TH:J. TO MR GALLATIN [22 June 1803]

Mr. Coxe may be informed with truth that the information he says he has recieved is entirely without foundation, no such resolution as he alludes to having ever been formed, and mr Madison & Capt Lewis too guarded to have ever spoken of it, had it been formed. but in truth a pretended rumor of removal is the common ground for application for an office.

With respect to Hays the Marshal of West Tennissee, I think both Jackson & Dickson should be written to. I have more confidence in the first than the last. it would be well to ask their opinion whether Hays' conduct & habits are such as to render it proper that he should be removed, & to recommend a successor.

On the whole I think Govr. Harrison had better send his contract here for ratification; the right to do so being previously reserved by him.

I have never heard any objection to Titcomb surveyor of Newbury port.

RC (NHi: Gallatin Papers); undated; addressed: "The Secretary of the Treasury." PrC (DLC). Recorded in SJL as a letter to the Treasury Department of 22 June with notation "Coxe—Hays—Govr Harrison salt springs."

COXE MAY BE INFORMED: see Gallatin to TJ, 21 June (first letter).

From Albert Gallatin

SIR, Treasury Department June 22d: 1803.

I have the honor to submit to your consideration a sketch of the conditions on which it seems that the Salt springs near the Wabash, lately ceded by the Indians, may be offered on lease.—

The object, in conformity to your instructions, is, besides a moderate rent in salt intended for the use of the Indians, to let the springs to the person who shall engage to manufacture the largest quantity of salt, and to sell it on the cheapest terms. Although the information obtained from Mr. Prince is not as complete as might have been desired, especially respecting the quantity of water afforded by the two springs; yet I believe, from all I have been able to collect, that they will be fully sufficient to employ kettles of greater aggregate contents than sixteen thousand gallons.—

I am informed that the Holston Springs owned by Mr. King, supply Kettles of the aggregate contents of 12,000 gallons, from which 180 bushels of salt are daily made; and as those springs contain about $\frac{2}{11}$ salt & $\frac{9}{11}$ fresh water, it would follow that the daily evaporation of water boiled in kettles containing 12,000 gallons, is equal to six thousand four hundred and eighty gallons.—Kettles of the contents of 16,000 gallons will therefore evaporate daily 8,640 gallons of fresh water; make, according to Mr. Prince's report that the Wabash Springs contain $\frac{2}{45}$ths salt, about fifty bushels of salt every day, and require from the springs a daily supply of nine thousand gallons; which is less than six gallons and an half per minute.

It is intended to transmit the proposals to the Governor of the Indiana Territory, and to have them printed in the News-papers of the

States of Ohio, Kentuckey, and Tenessee; but whether the Governor should be authorized to conclude the contract, or instructed to transmit the proposals, with his opinion, to this Department, for your determination, is submitted to your decision.

I have the honor to be, very respectfully, Sir, Your obedt. Servant

ALBERT GALLATIN

RC (DLC); in a clerk's hand, signed by Gallatin; at foot of text: "The President of the United States"; endorsed by TJ as received from the Treasury Department on 22 June and "Salt springs Wabash" and so recorded in SJL. Enclosure: see below.

Gallatin's SKETCH OF THE CONDITIONS for the lease of the Wabash salt springs has not been found but it probably differed little from the notice issued by the Treasury Department, dated 24 June, calling for proposals for the lease of the salines for three years beginning 1 Dec. 1803. No rent would be expected the first year of the lease, but after that the lessees were to pay 1,000 bushels equal to 50,000 pounds of "merchantable salt" each year to be delivered at set times. During the first year, they were to establish kettles for making salt with aggregate contents of at least 8,000 gallons to be increased to 15,000 during the second year and for the remainder of the lease. The U.S. would advance $2,500 to assist with the purchase of the "kettles, and erection of the works," the money to be repaid at the end of the lease with six percent interest from the end of the first year. The proposals were to include the quantity of salt to be produced annually and the price for which it would be sold. After the first year, they would provide the quantity of salt agreed upon "at a price not greater than that fixed" by the terms, with the U.S. reserving the right to purchase all of the salt manufactured at that price. The government sought to lease the spring to those who would "engage to sell the greatest quantity of salt at the lowest price." The lessees were required to post bond with approved security (printed in the Lexington *Kentucky Gazette*, 20 Sep. 1803).

In a letter of 26 Apr. 1803, William PRINCE, who had been sent by Governor Harrison to investigate the salt springs, reported that the water from the well along the Saline River was of excellent quality with "a bushel of good Salt" produced from 180 gallons. Prince noted that the well afforded sufficient water for 32 kettles of from 25 to 30 gallons each. He described another spring "equal in quality and quantity" about 150 yards away that was next to a spring of fresh water. Prince did not investigate the salt lick five miles away but observed "that the earth for a considerable distance around is strongly impregnated with Salt" (RC in DLC; endorsed as received from Vincennes on 17 May and "Making a Report relative to the Salt Spring on the Wabash"; endorsed by TJ as a letter "to Genl. Dearborne on the Salt springs. for mr Gallatin").

HOLSTON SPRINGS, a saline in western Virginia, was taken over by William KING in 1795. He established an efficient salt-making operation, with a warehouse and a wagon road from the salt works to the Holston River to transport the salt to eastern Tennessee (John A. Jakle, "Salt on the Ohio Valley Frontier, 1770-1820," *Annals of the Association of American Geographers*, 59 [1969], 708).

The Treasury Department notice called for the PROPOSALS to be sent to the GOVERNOR at Vincennes by 30 Sep. 1803. To stimulate participation, Gallatin encouraged those who were interested in leasing but thought the number of kettles specified more than they could establish to submit proposals, stating "the quantity, expressed in gallons of the contents, which they would agree to establish and keep up" (Lexington *Kentucky Gazette*, 20 Sep. 1803).

From J. P. G. Muhlenberg

Philadelphia June 22d. 1803—

The enclosed Letter, which I have the Honor to transmit To The President, was under cover directed to me, with the request that I should forward it—The Letters which The President was pleasd to direct to my care, and which were to be forwarded to different ports in Europe have been sent on, by what I deemd safe conveyances.

I have the Honor to be with perfect Respect Sir Your Most Obedt Servt.

P Muhlenberg

RC (DLC); at foot of text: "The President of the U.S."; endorsed by TJ as received 24 June and so recorded in SJL. Enclosure not identified.

For the letters directed to Muhlenberg's CARE, see TJ to Muhlenberg, 13 May.

To Thomas Mann Randolph

Th:J. to TMR. Washington June 22. 1803.

As possibly an authentic copy of the decree against Henderson may be wanted at the hearing of his & Peyton's applications for an order of court for a mill, I have procured one from Richmond & inclose it to you. you will observe the level to which it restores & confirms my right is that at which the water stood at *the confines between Henderson & myself*, before the erection of his dam. that is to say at the corner chesnut where our line terminates on the river, a little above the corner of his field on the river. of course it entitles me to remove every unfixed stone of the dam & to leave the ledge of fixed rock only, in it's natural state. this would not give sufficient fall for a mill at his 4. acres, but would give a plenty to the owner of the ground from thence to where the river makes still water. On this circumstance & the greater right of the owner of the whole tract rather than the owner of the 4. acres, I build my belief that the justice of the court will refuse Henderson an order, and give it to his competitor.

Every thing confirms that war between England and France cannot be avoided: and our last intelligence from both places gives us reason to believe we shall be able to make it the occasion of placing ourselves at ease on the Missisipi, and continuing at peace with both. I had a letter of the 14th. from mr Eppes mentioning that Maria's health was *pretty good*, that they should leave that place the 10th. of July for the Louisa springs, and meet me at Monticello the last of the month. my tender love to my dear Martha, & the little ones & affectionate attachment to yourself.

Th: Jefferson

RC (DLC); endorsed by Randolph as received 27 June. Enclosure: see enclosure listed at George Jefferson to TJ, 16 June.

From William C. C. Claiborne

DEAR SIR, Town of Washington June 23d. 1803

The State of things in New Orleans continue in uncertainty. The Prefect is yet in that City; but not in the exercise of authority.

A Vessel from Philadelphia, laden[1] with military Stores, and destined for Fort Adams is now in the Mississippi;—It is said, the Prefect requested the Spanish Government not to permit this Vessel to pass New-Orleans, & was answered, that the free navigation of the Mississippi, was secured to the *U. States* by Treaty, and that *their* Flag should not be interrupted.

It is also stated, (and I believe correctly) that there is no good understanding between the Prefect and the *Spanish Officers* at Orleans, and that the *latter* do not conceal their Chagrin at the Cession of Louisiana to France, and openly avow *their* friendly wishes for the Success of Mr. Monroe's Mission.—

In a former Letter, I expressed a wish, that you would permit me (in the Fall) to accompany Mrs Claiborne to Nashville—I must again renew this request, and ask leave of Absence for four or five Months, & if it should be granted me, I shall be enabled to pass a few Weeks with my friends in Tennessee, and to do myself the honor of paying my respects to you in person, at the City of Washington, in the course of the Winter.—

It is now Sir, near two years since I landed at Natchez, & since I have had one Days respite from arduous public Duties, which required great confinement to an office, and much fatigue and anxiety of Mind.—I must confess that since relaxation from Business would be highly agreeable to my feelings, and could not be otherwise than beneficial to my *Health*, which altho' not openly attacked, yet I find from the Warmth[2] of the Climate & Confinement, it is in some degree impaired.—

I think the duties of my office, may safely be committed to the Secretary for a few Months;—every thing is now tranquill in this quarter, and there is a prospect that it will remain so;—Should events however arise, which may make it necessary, I can remain at my post, or if absent, repair hither immediately.—

I pray you to accept my best wishes for your Individual, Domestic & public happiness, & believe me to be—

Dear Sir Your faithful friend & Mo. Obt. Servt.

WILLIAM C. C. CLAIBORNE

RC (DLC); at foot of text: "The President of the U. States"; endorsed by TJ as received 17 July and so recorded in SJL.

THE PREFECT: Pierre Clément Laussat. A FORMER LETTER: not found and apparently never received by TJ. See TJ to Claiborne, 18 July.

THE SECRETARY: Cato West (Albert Gallatin to TJ, 14 Mch. 1803).

[1]MS: "landen."
[2]MS: "Warmpth."

From Jean Jacques Dessalines

au quartier Général,
habitation de Frere,
Plaine du Cul de Sac,
23 Juin 1803.

MONSIEUR LE PRÉSIDENT,

La Goelette des Etats-Unis (La Fédérale, Capitaine Neheniah Barr) forcee d'entrer dans le port du Petit Goave par nos chaloupes en Croisiere, m'offre l'honneur de vous Instruire des évenemens survenus dans notre malheureuse Isle depuis l'arrivée des Français et de la revolution qu'y a Occasionné la tirannie de leur gouvernement Oppresseur.

Lassé de payer par l'effusion de tout notre sang le prix de notre aveugle fidelité à une métropole qui égorge ses enfans, le peuple de Saint Domingue, à l'éxemple des nations les plus sages, a secoué le Joug de la tirannie et juré l'expulsion de ses bourreaux.

Déjà nos campagnes sont Purgées de leur aspect; quelques Villes leur restent encore, mais n'offrent plus rien à leur avide Rapacité.

Le Commerce avec les états-Unis, Monsieur Le Président, présente aux immenses récoltes que nous avons en dépot et à celles plus riantes encore qui se préparent cette année, un débouché que nous reclamons des armateurs de votre Nation. Ses anciennes Relations avec St. Domingue ont dù la convaincre de la loyauté et de la bonne foi avec lesquelles ses bâtimens seront accueillis dans nos Ports.

Le Retour de la Goelette la Fédérale lui prouvera nos dispositions actuelles.

Veuillés, Monsieur Le Président, être persuadé de l'Empressement que je mettrai à Contribuer de toute l'autorité qui m'est Confiée à la sùreté des bâtimens des Etats-Unis et à l'avantage qu'ils retireont de nos échanges.

Agrées, Monsieur Le Président, l'expression de la plus haute Consideration pour Votre personne. DESSALINES

EDITORS' TRANSLATION

Headquarters, Frère plantation,
Cul-de-Sac plain
23 June 1803

Mister President,

The American schooner *The Federal*, under Captain Nehemiah Barr, forced by our patrol boats to enter the port of Petit-Goâve, provides me the honor of informing you of the events that have occurred on our unfortunate island since the arrival of the French and the revolution caused in France by the tyranny of their oppressive government.

The people of Saint-Domingue, tired of paying with our blood the price of our blind allegiance to a mother country that cuts her children's throats, and following the example of the wisest nations, have thrown off the yoke of tyranny and sworn to expel the torturers.

Our countryside is already purged of their sight. A few cities are still under their domination but have nothing further to offer to their avid rapacity.

Commerce with the United States, Mister President, offers a market for the huge harvests we have in storage and the even more abundant ones that are now growing. Your country's shippers are calling for it. Your nation's long-standing relations with Saint-Domingue are evidence of the loyalty and good faith that await your ships in our ports.

The return of the schooner *The Federal* will prove to your country our current disposition.

Please be sure, Mister President, of the eagerness with which I will exert all my authority for the safety of the United States' ships and the benefits they will reap from trading with us.

Accept, Mister President, the expression of my highest consideration.

Dessalines

RC (DLC); in a clerk's hand, signed by Dessalines; below dateline: "Jean Jacques Dessalines le Général en chef de l'armée de saint Domingue. À Monsieur Le Président du Congrès Des Etats-Unis d'amérique"; endorsed by TJ as received 14 Sep. and so recorded in SJL.

Jean Jacques Dessalines (1758?-1806) commanded the recently consolidated revolutionary armies of Saint-Domingue. Scholars dispute whether he was born in Africa and taken to Saint-Domingue as a slave or was born into slavery on the island. In the civil wars that began in 1791, he rose to the rank of general under Toussaint-Louverture. He acquired ownership or control of several plantations. His suppression of dissident groups among the insurgents, his execution of white prisoners and civilians on some occasions, and his destruction of roads, water sources, and cities in a scorched-earth strategy ordered by Toussaint to hinder the French army under Victoire Emmanuel Leclerc, earned him a reputation for brutality. After Toussaint submitted to the French, Dessalines served Leclerc, disarming the population and hunting down renegade rebel units. In the fall of 1802, however, Dessalines and other Saint-Dominguen officers deserted the French and began to rebuild the rebel forces. Following the withdrawal of the French army under the Vicomte de Rochambeau from Saint-Domingue in November 1803, Dessalines oversaw the issuing of declarations of independence for the nation of Haiti. He took the title of governor general for life, then in the fall of 1804 had himself crowned as emperor. Two years later he was killed in a coup d'etat (Philippe R. Girard, *The Slaves Who Defeated Napoléon: Toussaint Louverture and the Haitian War of Independence, 1801-1804* [Tuscaloosa, Ala., 2011], 16, 125-6, 136-7, 155-6, 200-2, 217-18, 248-9, 256, 311, 313-14; Laurent Dubois,

Avengers of the New World: The Story of the Haitian Revolution [Cambridge, Mass., 2004], 1, 193, 222, 266, 269-71, 275-6, 281-3, 287-9, 294, 297-8; Berthony Dupont, *Jean-Jacques Dessalines: Itinéraire d'un révolutionnaire* [Paris, 2006], 73-4; Tulard, *Dictionnaire Napoléon*, 599-600).

PLAINE DU CUL DE SAC: a fertile, irrigated area outside Port-au-Prince, the Cul-de-Sac plain escaped the devastation of war until 1803, when it became a primary zone of conflict between the insurgents and the French. Habitation Frère, the plantation where Dessalines established his headquarters, was later the home of the Haitian military academy (Thomas Madiou, *Histoire d'Haiti*, 8 vols. [Port-au-Prince, 1989], 3:41-9; Robert Debs Heinl, Jr., Nancy Gordon Heinl, and Michael Heinl, *Written in Blood: The Story of the Haitian People, 1492-1995* [Lanham, Md., 1996], 20, 111-12; Dubois, *Avengers of the New World*, 26-7).

Meriwether Lewis: Promissory Note

I promise to pay Thomas Jefferson his Heirs or Assigns, on demand, the sum of one hundred and three Dollars and ninety three Cents, for value recieved.—

June 23rd. 1803. $.103.93 MERIWETHER LEWIS.

MS (MHi); entirely in Lewis's hand; endorsement and later notations by TJ on verso:

"Lewis Meriwether

		D
Note of hand		
1803. June 23.		103.93
	Y M D	
1807. Aug. 1.	4 -1 -9	25.61
		129.54
by disbursemts. for me.		21.50
		108.04."

In 1810, when TJ brought this debt to the attention of one of the executors of Lewis's estate, he described it as "monies furnished" to Lewis "some time before he set out on his Western expedition" (RS, 2:294, 336).

From Cephas Carpenter

DEAR SIR— Moretown Vermont June 24th 1803

doubtless you will think it Strange to Receive A letter from one you never herd of nor Saw in the world & More So when you come to se what Subject it is on. I am A man that was bred up A farmer in Vermont. having A mind to Settle in the world I Moved in to A new town with About five hundred dollars which I had Acumilated by my own Industry the town being Very new & the want of Mills was Very much felt in this place I determined to undertake to Buil If noboddy Else would Acordingly in the Spring 78 I proceded on the business & by the first of November following I had Arected A Saw and grist mill on What is cauled Mad River on the 28th day of that Same Mongth Novb. there came the Largest flood Ever known by the oldest man on the River the water Ros 24 feet Rite up & cared Both of my mills Away before I had the Sattisfaction of Injoying them one Mongth & Landed me About five hundred dollars [bod?] far from being disscuraeged I Resolved to try to Extend My Credit & Rebuild Acordingly the next Spring I pressed my determanation Acordingly Rebuit Both By the forth of the next october & built them so Stout that water could not Inundate them in which possion I have Ben Ever Since But the grate Expence Incured by Building plunged me into debt About 2 thousand dollars for which I had to Mortgage the mills & Land I owened in this town & have on one [. . .] my family and Lesoned the demand to 1 thousand dollars the Mortgage now being Run out the man sese fit to Eject me off of the premises thinking to get the property that is worth 25 hundred dollars for two hundred the time that I must give them up will be the first of March next Which Must unadvoidly take place unless Some boddy interferes in my behalf—haveing always herd that you was A man that was posesed of Real benevolence Knowing the one thousand dollars never could make A blank in your property or frustate your happiness in the Lest I Must Come forred in this way to Request 10 or twelve hundred dollars of you I am confident When you come to Red this & consider that Sum Will Be mine of Makeing A man of business of Me & Make So Small A blank in your property you Will not hisetate to Send me the Money & point out Whether you will Make A present of it to me or Whether I must pay you at Some futer day Either of Which I shall happily Comply With.—it has Every be Reported in this Country that you was A man of Charity & had Extended the Arme of Charity far beyond your predesesors in office.

With high Consideration I Subscribe my Self Your Friend & humble Servent Cephas Carpenter

You will be plesed to put the bills in to A letter A direct it to the Subscriber here of at Moretown in Chittendon County to be Left at the post office, at Waterbury in Said County Where I Shall be Likely to get the Money Sone you Will not hissetate to Send the Money as this is Stated Acording to Real Fact & Honnestty & If you dont Send the Money I must unadvoidly be Come A bankrupt If you hisetate in the Lest About the honesty of these be plesed to wright me Whether I can have the Money If I Come down their C Carpenter

RC (DLC); two words illegible; addressed: "His Excellency Thomas Jefferson President of the united States of America to be directed to the Citty of Washington by the Male"; postmarked Montpelier, 2 July; endorsed by TJ as received 14 July and so recorded in SJL.

Cephas Carpenter, a farmer originally from Coventry, Connecticut, was one of the first inhabitants of Moretown, Vermont, in the early 1790s. He served as a justice of the peace for almost 40 years and as a representative from Chittenden County in the Vermont legislature (Windsor *Spooner's Vermont Journal*, 20 Oct. 1806; Annie I. Carpenter, *Carpenter and Allied Families: Genealogical and Biographical* [New York, 1930], 27-9; Leonard Deming, *Catalogue of the Principal Officers of Vermont, As Connected with Its Political History, From 1778 to 1851, with Some Biographical Notices, &c.* [Middlebury, Vt., 1851], 163).

From Charles Ludlow

SIR— New York. June 24th: 1803.

This acknowledges the receipt of your Excellency's Letter of the 17th: Instant with the one inclosed for Mr: Cheetham which delivered to him after sealing it, at the same time informed that I would pay his Bill for such Articles as he had sent before together with those [to be] procured. Mr: Cheetham having compleated the Order I now forward [by Stage] two packages and one long Box marked No. 1-2 & 3 addressed agreeably to request. The balance due Mr: Cheetham Amot: $22.\frac{93}{100}$ have paid him as pr Acct: inclosed and charged the same to Mr: John Barnes as you was pleased to direct—I shall always be happy to execute such further Commands as you may hereafter honor me with—

In the mean time I subscribe myself Your Excellency's Most Obed:. & very humb. servt: CHAS: LUDLOW

RC (MHi); torn, with words in brackets supplied from Dft; at head of text: "His Excellency Thomas Jefferson"; endorsed by TJ as received 26 June but recorded in SJL at the 25th. Dft (ViW).

ENCLOSURE

Statement of Account with James Cheetham

His Excellency Thomas Jefferson

1802	To the American Citizen	Dr.
Apr 26th }	To Cash paid postage	37
June 10	To Adams's Administration	2 –
	" News to May last 1 Year	8 –
	" pamphlets	1.31
Augt. 9	To An Antidote	25
	" An Exposition	37½
Sept. 8	To Woods Illuminati	37½
1803		
Feby. 24	To 1 of J.C.s Nine letters	50

Apl 1	To a Letter &c.		25
May 1	To 1 Years News		8 –
	" 1 Years Watch Towr		3 –
Apl 14	To the Evening post from Apl 22nd. 1802 " to Apl 22nd. 1803 1 Year		8 –
June 21	To Binding a file of the Watch Towr		3 –
	" 1 Copy of McKenzies Travels		3.50
	Arrowsmiths Map of the United States[1]		15 –
			$53:93
1802	Contra—Cr.		
June 11	By Cash	$11–	
1803			
Feby. 22	By Cash	20.	31 –
			$ 22.93

New=York June 22d. 1803

Recd. payment from Charles Ludlow Esq *James Cheetham*

MS (DLC); in a clerk's hand; receipt, rendered in italics, in Cheetham's hand and signed by him; endorsed by same clerk: "Mr. Charles Ludlow 18 Wall Street"; endorsed by TJ.

ADAMS'S ADMINISTRATION: for TJ's search for John Wood's *History of the Administration of John Adams* published in New York in 1802, see Sowerby, No. 506, and Vol. 36:228-9, 387, 472-80. NEWS TO MAY LAST: for TJ's order on Cheetham for newspapers, see Vol. 37:308.

AN ANTIDOTE: on 9 Aug. 1802, Cheetham issued *An Antidote to John Wood's Poison* (New York *American Citizen*, 9 Aug. 1802; *New-York Gazette*, 11 Aug. 1802; Kline, *Burr*, 2:727).

WOODS ILLUMINATI: that is, *A Full Exposition of the Clintonian Faction, and the Society of the Columbian Illuminati* published in Newark, New Jersey, shortly after *An Antidote*. Wood attacked Cheetham and derisively associated the Clintonians with the deistic movement and the creation of the Theistical Society of New York (same, 727-8; Sowerby, No. 3280).

J.C.S: James Cheetham's *Nine Letters on the Subject of Aaron Burr's Political Defection*, on the election of 1800 (New York, 1803; Sowerby, No. 3444; Vol. 38: 418n). A LETTER may refer to *A Letter Concerning The Ten Pound Court, in the City of New-York, Addressed to the State Legislature*, dated 15 Mch., and published by Denniston & Cheetham. On the title page, Cheetham wrote: "From James Cheetham to His Excellency Thomas Jefferson President of the United States" (see Sowerby, No. 3326).

[1]MS: "State."

From James Lyle

DEAR SIR Manchester June 24th. 1803

I was favord with yours of the 12th. of Septemr. last, acknowledging having received the statement of your affairs with our Company at June 1800; since that I received from Mr Clark Attorney, £29.12.0. & from Messrs. Gibson & Jefferson £300.—. Virga. Currency. I imagine Mr. Clark has furnished you with a statement of his collection, and the remittances made me from the Bonds you put under his care. Colo. Bollings bond will not come to your credit till paid, then the amount with the interest will be entred. I am doubtful the Estate cannot pay it soon. it owes our Comp'y a large debt, and as the Exors are endeavouring to pay off all the debts,—I am loath to distress them with a Law suit. Your bond to R. Harvee for £198.12.7¾ is in my hands assigned in May 1786. I think you told me, that part was paid, or that you had some discount to bring forward; I hope you got it rectified before Dick died, and the exact balance due asscertain'd, which I wish to know, his estate is largely in our debt.

I have to beg pardon for troubling you with this letter at a time when your mind must be greatly employed on important affairs of State, but the frequent urgency of our Company to have remittances must plead my excuse. I am with very great Regard

Dear Sir Your most hule Servt. JAMES LYLE

RC (MHi); at head of text: "His Excellency Thomas Jefferson"; endorsed by TJ as received 1 July and so recorded in SJL; later endorsed by TJ: "1803. Oct. 20. Jefferson. D. 500."

As part of a payment to Lyle's firm, Henderson, McCaul & COMPANY, TJ forwarded a bond in 1791 from his brother-in-law John Bolling. Richard Harvie (HARVEE) had been an agent for Kippen & Co., a previous incarnation of the firm (Vol. 22:198-9; Vol. 28:413-17; Vol. 32: 107).

From Amos Ogden

DEAR SIR Baltimore County Maryland June 24 1803

The trunk I send you Contains part of a stone (as you will see) which is one of the Greatest Curiositys of the kind (that I have seen) of natures works When the piece was separated from the whole lump the small hallow square was inaccessable and filld with red rust If the thing should be worthy your philosophical notice and are Charactors of natures history How has it happend that she has acted so partial in dissolving the once Containd substances of those hallow squares if Ever those hallow squares did Contain petrifaction as from their present Appearance they must have done, and layd as it wore hilter skelter without being Connected in form or regularity The overthrow of Mountains and the rending of rocks may happen from strong fits of Convulsions either by fire or water But in this Case it appears as if natures agent had whisperd an act of silent partiallity, The stone And Trunk I hope you will receive from a stranger & friend as a mark of his highest and best Opinion, To Call you grate good and wise would be to say what thousand have said with heart felt joy, Wonderful man who has put Millions to flight without sheding of human Blood or left a mark on record to make innocence weep that you may live long to Extend your system of Liberty Economy philanthophy and philosophy and reap the reward in the Bosom of your Well served Country. is my sincere prayer—

Accept sir my sincere Attachment AMOS OGDEN

RC (DLC); endorsed by TJ as received 1 July and so recorded in SJL.

Amos Ogden won election to the Maryland House of Delegates, representing Baltimore County, in the fall of 1805. Of his potential reelection to the seat the following year, a newspaper declared: "Surely the people of Baltimore County are not about to be duped again by that creature. A more insignificant person never went to the legislative body. And what did he effect for his constituents? Nothing!" Ogden was, according to the editor, an "ignorant and impertinent biped." He had been imprisoned for debt in 1787, although a few years later he owned slaves and had other assets (Baltimore *Maryland Journal*, 29 June 1787, 6 May 1791; Fredericktown, Md., *Republican Advocate*, 18 Oct. 1805, 20 June, 1 Aug. 1806; Baltimore *American and Commercial Daily Advertiser*, 11 Nov. 1805).

From Thomas Rodney

DEAR SIR Dover Delaware June 24th. 1803

Your favor of the 17th. Instant came safe to hand—I return you My thanks for the confidence you are pleased to place in me, and for the friendly politeness with which you Submit a Choice of Offices to my consideration—My own inclination favors an acceptance of the appointmts. proposed but it will be proper for me to Consult the Govr. of Our State and Some Other friends before I can Venture to return a final answer which I shall not delay imbracing the Earliest Opertunity of doing.

It has ever been My disposition to act where I could be most Servicable in preserving the Liberty, and promoting the welfare of the United States, but as the acceptance of any appointment Under the United States will vacate my Seat in the Supreme Court of this State, and as it will be difficult to supply my place I presume both my political and domestic friends will be reluctant to part with me.

Please to accept assurances of my very high respect and Esteem. Your most Obedient THOMAS RODNEY

RC (DNA: RG 59, LAR); endorsed by TJ as received 28 June and so recorded in SJL, but as a letter of "21" not "24" June.

VACATE MY SEAT: in December 1802, Governor David Hall appointed Rodney a justice of the state supreme court, which carried with it a judgeship on the appeals court (Dwight L. Smith and Ray Swick, eds., *A Journey through the West: Thomas Rodney's 1803 Journal from Delaware to the Mississippi Territory* [Athens, Ohio, 1997], 8, 205n).

To Benjamin Rush

TH: JEFFERSON TO DR. RUSH June 24. 1803. Washington.

I am thankful to you for your attentions to Capt Lewis while at Philadelphia and the useful counsels he recieved from you. he will set out in about 4. or 5. days, and expects to leave Kaskaskias about the 1st. of September. he will have two travelling months which will probably carry him 7. or 800. miles up the river for his winter quarters, from whence he will communicate to us, in the course of the winter his observations so far. he tells me you wish to see the inclosed pamphlet on longevity by Sr. John Sinclair, which you can return me at your leisure. Accept affectionate salutations.

PrC (DLC). Enclosure: Sir John Sinclair, *An Essay on Longevity* (London, 1802); see Vol. 37:537.

From Jonathan Williams

SIR. Philadelphia June 24 1803.

To depart from Washington without taking leave of you was extreemly unpleasant to me; but I found it impossible to separate the real motive of such a visit, from the apprehension of an imputed one, which, to those not well acquainted with me, would but illy accord with a decision of character, and the events of the day had placed me in a very delicate position.[1]

Being now out of the way of any such Suspicion, I think it my duty to return you my sincere thanks for the honourable marks you have, in many Instances, given of your good Opinion of me; It was, Sir, the friendly, and when I reflect on my own Merits, I must say partial manner in which these honours were bestowed, joined to the dignified nature of the duties assigned me, that produced in my mind a determination to devote the whole of my future Life to the Service of my Country. My disposition, Sir, has undergone no other change, than what a change of principles (or at least of my apprehension of them) imperiously direct; and I trust that the slightest consideration of the following Facts, will convince you that my resignation proceeded from nothing but the unpleasant beleif that I could not hold my Commission without humiliation and disgrace.

I was a major of Artillery, transferred into the Engineers, the new Commission bearing date with the old one: You will allow, Sir, that an Officer may *gain* Rank by a transfer, but he can never *lose* any, unless he consents to it, and then he would deserve none.—[2]I had formed my Opinion of the new Corps of Engineers upon the Act of Congress, and upon the military Rules of those Countries where *Corps du Genie* are known and acknowledged to be the most dignified of all other military Corps: It was upon these Grounds, that I made the Observations in my Report of the 14th of December last: It was natural for me to conclude that if my sense of the[3] Subject had been incorrect, the Secretary of War would then have told me so;[4] but not a Syllable was said, and at my Return to West Point in the Spring, I found myself in a State of humiliation not to be endured; myself and the whole Corps were in effect prisoners within Centinels every night; an armed Force, uncontrouled by me, being at the very place assigned by Act of Congress to be the Station of the Corps I commanded. It became necessary to act decisively, and that I might act with Caution, I called the next officer of the Corps, Major Wadsworth, to my Council. We together weighed the Law, we maturely considered those military principles which we believed to be uniformly admitted, and we particularly considered what we supposed to be the Object of the Institution of our Corps. Taking all these together we formed certain Points, which we take to be the Rights of Engineers, and we determined that the refusal of them would involve the establishment of opposite Principles under which we could not, as Officers of the Corps of Engineers, exist.[5]

These Points were put into the Secretary of Wars hands in April last, As I was then ordered on duty, it appeared to me indecorous to insist on an Answer 'till after my Duty was performed; but as soon as my Reports were given in, and I was declared to be free to return to my Post, I requested a decision on these Points. The answer was short, and in Substance this. "The Engineers cannot be intitled to any military command, they are like Brigade Majors."—That is, like Subalterns ordered on Special Duty.—I need not repeat what has since past, for my Letters have doubtless been laid before you; but in my own Justification I beg leave to State what the[6] Corps of Engineers in my Opinion ought to be, and what by the decision of the Secretary of War it at this moment is.[7]

It is in essence diametrically opposite to what Major Wadsworth and myself had stated.—We Stated 1st. That it was equal to any other Corps; it now appears to be inferior to all others. We Stated 2d. That West Point was its legal Station under the command of its chief; it now appears that a Serjeant at the head of his Guard, Stationed at West Point, is in a military point of view more respectable than any Officer of the Corps, for he is not responsible to its commander. We Stated 3d. That Officers of the Engineers have the same right to arrest any officer or Soldier of any other Corps for unmilitary conduct that Officers of other Corps have; It now appears that Officers of Engineers have no such right, whatever right other Officers may have; that is they cannot arrest, yet they may be arrested. We Stated 4th. that an Officer of Engineers ought not to be obliged to accept the Parole or Countersign from an inferior Officer; It now appears that an officer of Engineers must accept the Countersign from an inferior officer, or be put into the Guard House if he presumes to go from his Quarters after Tattoo. We Stated 5 That Officers of Engineers ought not to sit on a Court martial ordered by an Officer inferior to them in Rank. It now appears that an Officer of Engineers be his rank what it may, must Sit on a Court martial ordered by an Officer of another Corps however inferior.

I am not Sure that this Subject has been seen in so strong a light as I have Stated; but I notwithstanding believe it to be correctly Stated, and the consequences described appear to me infallible. I do not mean Sir to make any complaint, I only mean to justify myself in your Eyes for it would be a Source of great Pain to me if on quitting the Service, I felt an Apprehension that I had left on your mind an impression unfavourable to that coolness & propriety of conduct which I hope belongs to my Character.—

I have the honour to be With the greatest deference & respect Sir Your most faithfull & most obedient Servant JON WILLIAMS

RC (PHi); at foot of text: "The President of the United States"; endorsed by TJ as received 27 June and so recorded in SJL. Dft (InU: Jonathan Williams Manuscripts).

Williams submitted his RESIGNATION as lieutenant colonel of the Corps of Engineers and commander of the military academy at West Point to Henry Dearborn on 20 June. Replying the next day, Dearborn urged Williams to reconsider, suggesting that the decision "may have been the effect of impressions which had not been maturely considered." Dearborn added, however, that no change could take place "in the principles early established relative to the Command contended for," that is, that no military command should be attached to members of the Corps of Engineers. If Williams persisted in his opinion, "there will only remain the unpleasant alternative of accepting your resignation" (Dearborn to Williams, 21 June 1803, Dearborn to Decius Wadsworth, 21 June 1803, both in DNA: RG 107, LSMA). Williams would be reappointed lieutenant colonel of the Corps of Engineers in April 1805 (JEP, 2:23).

[1] In Dft, Williams here canceled "I was not apprehensive that you would have placed a construction upon the object of my visit different from its reality, because you have too long known me to have any doubts as to my real Character, but the world always forms its opinion by an ostensible act, without looking beyond the first impression."

[2] In Dft, Williams here canceled "On the 20th Instant the Secretary of War informed me that he considered an Engineer as he would consider a major of brigade; that is as a Subaltern Officer, ordered to perform certain duties during which he had a titular rank, while as commissioned officer he could be considered as a Subaltern only."

[3] MS: "of the of the."

[4] In Dft, Williams here canceled "for it ought not to have Supposed that I would be content with an equivocal State of things, but during the whole of the vacation."

[5] In Dft, Williams here canceled "The Secretary of War has not discussed these points with me although they have remained two months in his hands he has not shown me any mistake in them nor if I am in error has he given me."

[6] In Dft, Williams here canceled "Lt Col Commandant."

[7] In Dft, written in the margin perpendicular to the text as an author's note, Williams here canceled "*It should here be remembered that no military command has been contended for by the Engineers except at their proper Posts or Stations regularly on duty.—As a passing officer for the inspection or repairs of post no derangement of the Command previously established would be expected."

From Rensselaer Havens

SIR　　　　New York 25th June 1803

Under date of the 28th April last I receivd a Letter from my friend Mr. Frederick Jenkins at Havre de Grace, stating that the commercial Agency for the United States at that place was then exercised by deputation and that he was desirous of obtaining the appointment—to promote his wishes I have procured such Letters of recommendation as I am pursuaded will receive attention—and if the office be yet vacant and fairly open for a new appointment I flatter myself the Letter which I now have the honor to inclose from his Excellency Governor Clinton, together with those which have already been forwarded to the Hone James Maddison Secretary of State on this Subject will be Sufficient to procure Mr. Jenkins the appointment without personal application—

with the greatest respect I have the honor to be Your Excellenies obedient Svt.

RENSSELAER HAVENS

RC (DNA: RG 59, LAR); endorsed by TJ as received 29 June and "Jenkins Frederick to be Coml Agt Havre" and so recorded in SJL. Enclosure: George Clinton to TJ, 21 June, recorded in SJL as received 29 June with notation "Fred. Jenkins to be Coml. Agt. Havre" but not found.

Born on Shelter Island, New York, Rensselaer Havens (1773-1854) moved to New York City in the 1790s and opened a dry goods business. His older brother, Jonathan N. Havens, was a Republican congressman. Havens eventually became a partner with FREDERICK JENKINS in a shipping business, and during the War of 1812, the two outfitted several private brigs, including the *General Armstrong*, which was destroyed by the British in the neutral port of Fayal despite a spirited and celebrated defense. After the war, Havens, a lay leader in the Presbyterian Church, devoted much of his energy to philanthropic activities but also helped run an insurance company (*New York Evangelist*, 29 June 1854; Joseph A. Scoville, *The Old Merchants of New York City*, 1st ser. [New York, 1864], 359-61; ASP, *Claims*, 1:503-4; *Biog. Dir. Cong.*, s.v., "Havens, Jonathan Nicoll").

HAVRE DE GRACE: that is, Le Havre, France.

For letters on Jenkins's behalf sent to the SECRETARY OF STATE, see David Gelston to James Madison, 15 June (RC in

DNA: RG 59, LAR; endorsed by TJ: "Jenkins Frederic to be consul at Havre") and DeWitt Clinton to Madison, 17 June (RC in same; endorsed by TJ).

Report from John Lenthall

Rough Stone work done to the South
Wing of the Capitol June 20th to 25th 1803

All the walls of the three fronts and the inside piers and backings of the Arches raised to the commencement of the free Stone work, making together, about 102 Perches

for B H Latrobe
JNO. LENTHALL

MS (DLC); in Lenthall's hand and signed by him; endorsed by TJ: "Capitol report of work. June 20-25. 1803."

From David A. Ogden

SIR THOMAS JEFFERSON [on or before 25 June 1803]

You are a Clever Fellow.

D.A.O.

If you send an answer direct it to David A. Ogden No. 33 Broad Street New York

RC (DLC: TJ Papers, 141:24486-7); undated; addressed: "Sir Tom Jefferson"; endorsed by TJ as an anonymous letter "signed D. A. O." received 25 June 1803 and "nothing" and so recorded in SJL.

David A. Ogden (1770-1829), a native of New Jersey, became active in New York government as a lawyer and professional associate of Alexander Hamilton, a judge in the court of common pleas, and a member of the state assembly. He was implicated in endorsing Aaron Burr among the New York congressional delegation in the election of 1800. Ogden served as a one-term Federalist representative from New York to the Fifteenth Congress and as a commissioner to settle the boundary dispute between the United States and Canada. The New York city directories for 1802, 1803, and 1804, listed him as a "counsellor at law" residing at 33 Broad Street (*Biog. Dir. Cong.*; *Longworth's American Almanac, New-York Register, and City-Directory, for the Twenty Seventh Year of American Independence* [New York, 1802], 283; Kline, *Burr*, 1:487-90).

From Joseph Priestley

DEAR SIR Northumberland June 25. 1803.

As you were pleased to think favourably of my pamphlet intitled *Socrates and Jesus compared*, I take the liberty to send you a *defence* of it. My principal object, you will perceive, was to lay hold of the opportunity, given me by Mr. Blair Linn, to excite some attention to doctrines which I consider as of peculiar importance in the christian system, and which I do not find to have been discussed in this country.

The *Church History* is, I hope, by this time in the hands of the bookseller at Philadelphia, so that you will soon, if my directions have been attended to, receive a copy of the work which I have the honour to dedicate to you

With the greatest respect and attachment, I am, Dear Sir Yours sincerely
J PRIESTLEY

RC (DLC); endorsed by TJ as received 30 June and so recorded in SJL. Enclosure: *A Letter to the Reverend John Blair Linn, A. M. Pastor of the First Presbyterian Congregation in the City of Philadelphia. In Defence of the Pamphlet, Intitled, Socrates and Jesus Compared* (Northumberland, Pa., 1803; Sowerby, No. 1662).

In response to Priestley's recently published PAMPHLET, John BLAIR LINN, a Presbyterian minister in Philadelphia, published in that city a critique entitled *A Letter to Joseph Priestley, L.L.D. F.R.S. &c. &c. In Answer to His Performance, Entitled Socrates and Jesus Compared* (Shaw-Shoemaker, No. 4527).

DEDICATE TO YOU: for Priestley's dedication, see Vol. 37:593-5.

From John Sergeant of New Stockbridge

New Stockbridge in the vicinity of Oneida June 25th. 1803.

HONOURABLE SIR.

Mr Parish Subagent for Indian affairs of the six nations informes me that Mr Irvine the Superintendant having had no instructions from the war office to pay over to me the proportion of the Annuity coming to the Stockbridge Indians, he therefore don't feel himself authorised to do it untill further orders. By looking at Col: Pickerings Treaty with the six nations, your Excellency will find the Stockbridge Indians being in close connection with them. ever since that Treaty have always received their proportion which has hitherto been $354 a year but as their numbers have of late been increased to about 600 by the removal of a Tribe of Delawares from New Jersey in strick propriety the sum might also be increased. The above sum of $354 by a particular agreement between our Cheifs and the Secretary at War as I have also understood during the good pleasure of the President of the United States about five years since was agreed to be sent in money and paid to me to be laid out for the general publick benefit of the Tribe, since which it has always been done by the former Superintendant and generally been paid in Feb: every year.

I have been in advance between two and three hundred hundred dollars to promote their publick Intrest and am now suffering for want of my money.

Mr Parish is here and has satisfied himself with regard to expending the publick money. proposes to write immediately to the Secretary of War on the subject. This is therefore to request your Excellencys friendship to confer with Mr Darborn that the necessary orders and instructions be immediately forwarded whereby myself and Indians might obtain relief.

I have not received any communications from my people who are gone on the western Mission since the 10th. Jany. as they are not returned and from slight information believe they are visiting the Tribes on the Waters of the Missisipi. hope they will do much publick good. with due respect remain your Excellencys most humble servant JOHN SERGEANT.

RC (PHi); addressed: "To His Excellency Thomas Jefferson Esqr President Washington"; franked; postmarked Utica, N.Y., 29 June; endorsed by TJ as received 6 July and so recorded in SJL with notation "W."; also endorsed by TJ: "refd. to Secretary at War Th: Jefferson."

John Sergeant died in 1824 at the age of 77. He resided with the Stockbridge Mohicans on six square miles of land, called New Stockbridge, that adjoined the Oneida reservation in central New York. He and members of his family had gone there with the Mohicans in the 1780s, when the Indians moved from Stockbridge, Massachusetts, where Sergeant's father had been a missionary among them some years earlier. Sergeant was not an ordained minister, but was fluent in the Mohicans' language. He became the mission's schoolteacher at the age of 19 and later assumed his deceased father's role as missionary. After the American Revolution, when he could no longer rely on support from the British proselytizing society that had backed the mission, he sought aid for the Stockbridge Mohicans from other sources, including state governments and Congress (Patrick Frazier, *The Mohicans of Stockbridge* [Lincoln, Neb., 1992], 99-100, 190, 194-5, 205-6, 237-8; David J. Silverman, *Red Brethren: The Brothertown and Stockbridge Indians and the Problem of Race in Early America* [Ithaca, N.Y., 2010], 120-4; Jeremy Belknap and Jedidiah Morse, *Report on the Oneida, Stockbridge and Brotherton Indians, 1796*, Museum of the American Indian *Indian Notes and Monographs*, 54 [New York, 1955], 5-7; ANB; Stockbridge, Mass., *Berkshire Star*, 7 Oct. 1824).

In 1792, the U.S. government coupled the Stockbridge Mohicans with the Oneidas for ANNUITY payments. Two years later, after he negotiated a treaty with the Six Nations, Timothy Pickering signed a treaty that included some "very meritorious persons of the Stockbridge Indians" in a payment to the Oneidas and the Tuscaroras in recognition of their support for the United States during the Revolutionary War. Probably to support the argument that the people of New Stockbridge were to share in the Oneidas' annuities, when Sergeant corresponded with Dearborn about the issue early in 1804, he sent a copy of an address from James McHenry to the Mohicans (ASP, *Indian Affairs*, 1:232; Charles J. Kappler, comp. and ed., *Indian Affairs: Laws and Treaties*, 5 vols. [Washington, D.C., 1975], 2:34-9; Sergeant to Dearborn, received 10 Feb. 1804, recorded in DNA: RG 107, RLRMS).

NUMBERS HAVE OF LATE BEEN INCREASED: according to a 1796 report on the missionary activity among the Stockbridge Mohicans and the Oneidas, the New Stockbridge group then numbered about 300. Another 150 individuals made up the nearby Brothertown Indians, who, like the Stockbridge people, had relocated from the east to live on lands offered them by the Oneidas. Before they left Massachusetts, the Stockbridge Mohicans had invited a group of DELAWARES FROM NEW JERSEY to join them. In 1802, the New Jersey group moved to the Brothertown-New Stockbridge area (Belknap and Morse, *Report*, 6-7; Silverman, *Red Brethren*, 1, 76, 100, 159).

On 7 July 1803, the SECRETARY OF WAR wrote to Jasper Parrish, the recently appointed assistant agent for the Stockbridge Mohicans, the Oneidas, and some other groups in New York. Responding to a letter from Parrish dated 23 June and without mentioning Sergeant's letter to the president, Dearborn informed the agent that there should be no change to the customary payments to the Oneidas and the New Stockbridge community. Early in 1804, Sergeant advised the government that the New Stockbridge group had received only part of its annuity for 1803. Informing Parrish that a complaint had been received, Dearborn instructed the agent to pay the balance of the annuity "without delay" (Parrish to War Department, 23 June 1803, and Sergeant to the War Department, received 10 Feb., recorded in DNA: RG 107, RLRMS; Dearborn to Parrish, 7 July 1803, 11 Feb. 1804, and Dearborn to Sergeant, 11 Feb. 1804, in DNA: RG 75, LSIA; TJ to Farmer's Brother and Others, 14 Feb. 1803).

GONE ON THE WESTERN MISSION: in the spring of 1802, in response to a letter that Sergeant had written to Aaron Burr, Dearborn sent a blank pass to allow a few of the Stockbridge Mohicans to visit Indian nations in the Northwest Territory and Indiana Territory to promote the introduction of "the arts of civilization, the principles of morality and the cultivation of the social and friendly affections." The secretary of war also instructed commandants of western military posts to aid the travelers and furnish them with provisions. Hendrick Aupaumut led a group that visited settlements of the Miami and Delaware Indians on the White River in 1803. For the Mohicans, the trip was a means of exploring prospects of once again relocating farther westward. Sergeant wrote to TJ in January 1804, enclosing an address from Aupaumut about the visit to the western tribes. TJ passed Sergeant's letter along to the War Department with instructions to make "reasonable compensation" to the Indians of New Stockbridge for their efforts to reach out to other Indian nations. Dearborn authorized payment, through Sergeant, of $200 to the community and $50 to Aupaumut (Sergeant to TJ, 20 Jan. 1804, not found, recorded in SJL as received 9 Feb.; Dearborn to Sergeant, 20 Apr. 1802, 13 Feb. 1804, in DNA: RG 75, LSIA; Sergeant to the War Department, 16 Apr. 1804, recorded in DNA: RG 107, RLRMS; Silverman, *Red Brethren*, 151-2, 157-9).

From John Vaughan

DEAR SIR Philad: June 25. 1803

I enclose you a letter from the Dutch Commercial Resident Heinekin—The Commn. alluded to is a letter of 21. Oct. 1802 to the Socy. accompanying three Numbers of the Flora Batava, (we have now 6) executing by the order of the Batavn. Govt.—also by a list of which I have the pleasure of Enclosing a Copy, of plants, the Bat. Govt. desire to be procured under the direction of our Socy.—as those forwarded from Batram by Mr Heinekin had not Succeeded—

They offer in return to procure any of the plants to be found in Holland—

The names in the list are taken Chiefly from Lin: Systema Vegetabilium Ed. XV, Millers Gards. Dicty. Ayton, Hortus Kewensis—Michaux chênes D'amerique—Acy. of Boston Tr: 1 Vol. Cutler—They desire to be added any other Seeds or Plants which promise to be useful & suited to their Country & public use—requests them to be sent in the fall or Winter—Mention that many are from Virginia

For their plants which they can procure—they refer to D Gorter & S. J van Geuns—our Socy do not meet for 3 Weeks when the papers &c will be laid before them.—I hope that immediate attention will be paid to their request—

With 20 Vol Trans. of the Socy. of Arts Manuf & Commerce we recd a few copies of the Premiums also Rules & orders of the Socy of London—I enclose a copy of each—I also enclose a Copy of the proceedings of the Connecticut Agricultural Society of which I made mention in a late letter—of which I take the liberty of requesting your acceptance—Should either of the above suggest any Ideas useful to our Country—no person has so much in his power to give them a useful Currency

I remain with the greatest respect Your obt Sert & friend

JN VAUGHAN

PS.

Excuse the Liberty I take of enclosing a line for Capt Lewis as I do not know his adress—

RC (DLC); at foot of text: "Thos. Jefferson Esqr"; endorsed by TJ as received 27 June and so recorded in SJL. Enclosures: (1) Jan H. C. Heineken to TJ, at Philadelphia, 23 June, stating "The Secretary of the Executive Council for internal affairs of the Batavian Republick has transmitted to me the hourly going packet with the request to deliver it to the Institution" and "I embrace this opportunity to offer my best services in the promotion of Your usefull labours & have the honor to be with the highest consideration Your most obedt humbe Servt Jan: Hend Ch: Heineken" (RC in PPAmP; addressed: "Thomas Jefferson President of the American Philosophical Society"; endorsed by TJ as received 27 June and so recorded in SJL with notation "A.P.S."; endorsed for the American Philosophical Society as read at a meeting of 15 July). (2) List of plants wanted by the government of the Batavian Republic, not found. (3) *Abstract of the Premiums Offered, in 1800, by the Society Instituted at London for the Encouragement of Arts, Manufactures, and Commerce* (London, 1800). (4) *Rules and Orders of the Society Instituted at London, for the Encouragement of Arts, Manufactures, and Commerce* (London, 1802). (5) *Transactions of the Society, for Promoting Agriculture in the State of Connecticut* (New Haven, 1802). (6) Vaughan to Meriwether Lewis, not found.

The Council of the Interior of the Batavian Republic at The Hague sent the American Philosophical Society volumes of FLORA BATAVA, a serial publication of illustrations and descriptions of plants of the Netherlands. The council also sent *Flora Batava* to the American Academy of Arts and Sciences. At a meeting on 15 July, the APS asked Vaughan to confer with William Hamilton, who had horticultural collections at his estate near Philadelphia, about the LIST of plants and seeds the council desired. When Vaughan, in August, reported that Hamilton had declined to participate, the society asked Benjamin Smith Barton to oversee the acquisition of the requested items. Vaughan, the society's treasurer, was to advance funds for the project in anticipation of reimbursement from the Batavian Republic (APS, *Proceedings*, 22, pt. 3 [1884], 330, 339-41; Sarah S. Gibson, "Scientific Societies and Exchange: A Facet of the History of Scientific Communication," *Journal of Library History [1974-1987]*, 17 [1982], 156-7; Adriaan Jacob Barnouw and Bartholomeus Landheer, eds., *The Contribution of Holland to the Sciences* [New York, 1943], 333; *Memoirs of the American Academy of Arts and Sciences*, 2 [1804], 161; Vol. 31:535n).

TAKEN CHIEFLY FROM: the references cited by Vaughan were the *Systema Vegetabilium* of Linnaeus, Philip Miller's *Gardeners Dictionary*, William Aiton's *Hortus Kewensis*, André Michaux's *Histoire des chênes de l'Amerique*, and "An Account of Some of the Vegetable Productions, Naturally Growing in this Part of America, Botanically Arranged," by Manasseh Cutler, published in the *Memoirs of the American Academy of Arts and Sciences*, 1 (1783), 396-493.

David de GORTER, *Flora Belgica* (1767), and Stephanus Joannes van GEUNS, *Plantarum Belgii* (1788), were the sources mentioned for information about Dutch plants.

WITH 20 VOL TRANS.: the APS had recently received the first 20 volumes, dating from 1783 to 1802, of *Transactions of the Society, Instituted at London, for the Encouragement of Arts, Manufactures, and Commerce*, with a letter acknowledging the receipt of the four most recent volumes of the *Transactions* of the APS (APS, *Proceedings*, 22, pt. 3 [1884], 339).

LATE LETTER: Vaughan to TJ, 9 June.

From John Strode

Culpeper 26 June 1803

There are many and many Thousands as well as myself, (Good & Worthy Man) who Needeth not any Vindication of the Measures of the present administration, the Rectitude of its principles, purity of its motives & Energey of intellectual faculties form and complete a character whose fair resplendant fame will Reflect everlasting Lustre on the present Age; nor can malignancey however deep and inviterate in design ever be able to render it or any individual thereof a material injury, every attempt or stroke of that sort is meant (tho' indirectly) to wound the Sacred cause of freedom and Civil Liberty; and in that point of View is well understood by every good Republican—When facts are erroniously Stated, when Scurrilous abuse is founded on Vague assertion, & when Argument consists of invective; then, there is none among us, so remote and uninformed as not to know and determine by these criterions that the premisses are base and falacious.

I am Sir not unaware, with what diffidence and caution a man of my humble Situation ought to approach Your hand for a single moment to interupt either Your private Repose or attention to matters transcendantly important; but in this particular case, I consider it not Only the exercise of a Just Right but also an indispincible duty, to which through Zeal and fervency I am irresistably impell'd to acknowledge and manefest my Sentiments of the most decided approbation of "the Measures of the present Administration."

The foregoing Sentiments of my Heart were wrote on the Rect. of a Small pamphlet on the Subject, and hardly should have mustered sufficient presumption to Send them on, had not my friend Mr. Daniel P. Ramsey a Young Gentleman who had for some time served me in the quality of a Clerk, ask'd of me to say to the President what I knew of Him, for that He had a desire to enter Himself as a Midshipman on board some of the Commissiond Ships of the Navey of the United States. My Testimony in favour of this Young Gentleman; is, That I Consider Him inferiour to No man in point of Moral Rectitude, Honor and Bravery, a true Republican, Zealous for His Country Cause; and most undoubtedly Stands among that description of Men, which a Commander of perspicueity will soon discover and Select when Occasion Requires for hardy Deeds; Mr Ramsey does not Only possess those cardinal Virtues, but He also Writes a fine hand, understands Mercantile Accounts and has a mind capable of enlarged improvements; two things alone make against the promotion of this young man, that is He is extremely Modest & diffedent, and alas! He is poor!

Pray Sir withdraw not altogether from my poor family & humble Cot, the honor pleasure and pride which sometimes empassant we experienced. With all due regard

I am Worthy Sir Your most Obdt hble Servt

John Strode

RC (DLC); at foot of text: "Thomas Jefferson esqr. president of the United States"; endorsed by TJ as received 5 July and so recorded in SJL.

Strode was almost certainly referring to Gideon Granger's *A Vindication of the Measures of the Present Administration*, which was published as a PAMPHLET after appearing during the spring in the *National Intelligencer* (John Langdon to TJ, 8 May).

DANIEL P. RAMSEY received a midshipman's commission on 6 July (NDBW, *Register*, 44; Robert Smith to TJ, 6 July).

From Pierre Samuel Du Pont de Nemours

Monsieur le Président, Paris 8 Messidor 11 (27 Juin 1803.)

Je joins ici une lettre que j'avais donneè pour Votre Excellence au Général Bernadotte, et qu'il vient de me renvoyer depuis que la Négociation terminée sans lui, et la Guerre qui peut rendre utiles ses talens militaires, l'ont engagé, non sans regret, à renoncer à son Ambassade auprès de vous.

Celui qui lui suceede, Mr. de Laussat, a êté mon Collegue au Conseil des Anciens, quoiqu'il fut jeune encore. C'est un homme d'esprit, sage et doux. Je crois que vous en serez satisfait. Il êtait parti pour administrer cette même Louisiane qu'il sera chargé de vous remettre, et qui prospérera entre vos mains plus qu'elle n'aurait pu le faire dans celles d'aucune Puissance de l'Europe.

Cette acquisition, si peu esperée, faite par les Etats unis, si promptement, sous votre Présidence, est un des événemens qui m'ont causé en ma vie le plus de plaisir. Et le bonheur d'y avoir concouru jusqu'à un certain point sera toujours un de mes souvenirs les plus chers.

J'aime vos Républiques américaines, et la Philantropie sérieuse de votre grave Nation. Mais, condamneé, par l'impossibilité de bien apprendre la langue anglaise lorsque ce n'est plus dans la jeunesse qu'on l'étudie, à n'être jamais qu'une bête au milieu de vos Etats anglais, à n'y être aimé que de ma Famille, à n'y servir que mes enfans, il est naturel que l'introduction dans votre Corps fédéral d'une couple de Républiques Françaises, où je puis entendre, être entendu, aller aux choses sans m'user sur les mots, suivre encore les leçons de mes illustres Maitres Quesnay et Turgot, continuer d'être utile au Monde, me donne une satisfaction particuliere.

Mon Corps engraissera quelque partie de votre Amérique. Je voudrais que mon esprit l'eut servie.

Mais je vous ai marqué les raisons qui peuvent me retenir encore assez longtems.

J'en vois une nouvelle aujourd'hui dans l'occasion qui se présente de contribuer à l'adoption stable des bons Principes sur la navigation des Neutres. Et j'ai aussi d'autres devoirs que je ne puis secouer.

Que votre amitié m'aide dans tous les sens à les remplir.

C'en sera un grand moyen dont je serai très reconnaissant que de charger notre Maison de Banque à Paris, par l'entremise de celle de New York, du payement des Interêts des Stocks dus par votre Gouvernement aux Français et aux Suisses, et qui, attendu le Prix que vous payez en cette monnaie de l'acquisition de la Louisiane vont devenir bien plus considerables.

Cette mesure, que j'espere de votre Bonté, ne pourra qu'être agréable aussi aux Amis que j'ai dans le Gouvernement français.

Je vous prie d'en recevoir d'avance tous mes remerciemens.

Salut, reconnaissance, attachement, Zêle et respect.

Du Pont (de Nemours)

EDITORS' TRANSLATION

Mister President, Paris, 8 Messidor 11 (27 June 1803)

I am enclosing the letter I gave General Bernadotte on your behalf which he has just returned to me. Now that the negotiations have concluded without him and that the war can benefit from his military experience, he feels compelled to give up his role as emissary to you, although not without regret.

His successor, Mr. de Laussat, was my colleague on the Council of Elders, even though he was still young. He is intelligent, wise, and charming. I think you will be pleased with him. He had set out to administer the same Louisiana he is now entrusted with handing over to you. It will prosper more in your hands than in those of any European power.

This swift and unhoped-for acquisition by the United States, under your presidency, is one of the events that has given me the most pleasure in my lifetime. The happiness of having contributed to it in some measure will always be one of my most cherished memories.

I love your American republics and the sincere philanthropy of your earnest nation. Given the impossibility of mastering the English language when one is no longer young, condemned to being a fool amid your English states, loved only by my family, serving only my children, I take special and understandable satisfaction in the addition of a couple of French Republics to your federal body. There I can understand and be understood, go to the heart of things without the obstacle of language, follow the precepts of my illustrious teachers Quesnay and Turgot, and continue to be useful to the world.

My body will be buried somewhere in your America. I would like my mind to have served her.

I have already explained the reasons that will keep me here for quite some time.

A new one has arisen today: the opportunity to contribute to the lasting adoption of wise principles concerning navigation for neutral parties. I also have other obligations that I cannot shake off.

May your friendship help me, in all ways, to fulfill them.

One important way, for which I would be very grateful, is for you to ask our bank in Paris, through the intermediary of the one in New York, to pay the interest your government owes to the French and Swiss. Given the amount you are paying to purchase Louisiana, the sum is going to become even larger.

This measure, which I ask of your kindness, will also please my friends in the French government.

Accept in advance all my thanks.
Greetings, gratitude, devotion, ardor, and respect.

DU PONT (DE NEMOURS)

RC (DLC); at head of text: "A Son Excellence Thomas Jefferson. Président des Etats unis"; endorsed by TJ as received 5 Sep. and so recorded in SJL. Enclosure: Du Pont to TJ, 6 Apr.

Under the French constitution of the Year 3 (1795), a 250-member, elected CONSEIL DES ANCIENS (Council of Elders) reviewed all legislation proposed by the Council of Five Hundred, rejecting or approving each proposed law (John H. Stewart, *A Documentary Survey of the French Revolution* [New York, 1951], 584-8).

SUR LA NAVIGATION DES NEUTRES: as secretary of a newly formed Paris chamber of commerce, Du Pont tried to obtain the release of cargoes from neutral ships sequestered by the French government and was involved in the development of recommendations for a code of commercial law (Ambrose Saricks, *Pierre Samuel Du Pont de Nemours* [Lawrence, Kans., 1965], 316-18; Tulard, *Dictionnaire Napoléon*, 444).

Thomas Munroe's Account of Public Expenditures

Expenditures on the Capitol

1803				
April	For	Lime	596.17	
	"	Sand	100.80	
	"	Laborers & carters	75.30	
	"	Surveyor's Salary on accot.	141.66	
			———	913 93
May	"	Lumber	595 91	
	"	Lime	742.87	
	"	Laborers & carters	417.53	
	"	Masons	491.29	
	"	Carpenters	91.06	
	"	Bricks	126.	
	"	Pulling down old wall	229.80	
	"	Black Smith's work	20.02	
	"	Cleaning Well & repairing pump	45.	
	"	Surveyor's Salary on account	141.66	
	"	B H Latrobe's drafts for materials particulars not known	500.	
	"	Free stone & cutting it, on accot.	1,000.	
	"	Sundry small articles	65.10	
			———	4,466 24
June	"	Lime	334.11	

"	Lumber	134.83	
"	Sand	122.40	
"	Scaffold poles	415.63	
"	Bricks	207.94	
"	Free Stone & cutting it on Acct.	1000 —	
		———	2,214 91
		Ds	7,595 08

NB. Foundation stone pay rolls for June &c, estimated at about $1,700, not included in the above, no Accounts thereof having been rendered—

Expended on the High ways

In March 1803		for Trees	$76.33	
		Labour	55.83	132.16
April	"	for Trees	68.50	
		boxing Do	448.50	
		Labour & Carts	423.44	940.44
May	"	for Labour & Carts		330.70
			Ds:	1,403.30

27th June 1803
Thomas Munroe

MS (DLC); in Munroe's hand and signed by him; endorsed by TJ: "Capitol. Accounts 1803. Apr. May. part of June."

From Jacob Rinker

Washington, City Tavern,
Monday morning June 27th. 1803.

Sir,

General Isaac Zane by his last Will and Testamont left you a small Legacy (for the purpose in the said Will mentioned) I am one of the Executors acting under the said Will and am now ready to pay said legacy—must beg the favor of you to be so good and inform me when and where to waite on you to pay the same.—

With Sentiments of Respect I am your most Obedient Humble Servant
Jacob Rinker

RC (MHi); at foot of text: "Thomas Jefferson President of the United States"; endorsed by TJ as received 27 June and so recorded in SJL with notation "Zane's legacy."

The son of a Swiss immigrant, Jacob Rinker (1749-1827) served as an officer during the American Revolution. He resided near Conicville, in Shenandoah County, Virginia, where he was a county surveyor and magistrate (John W. Wayland, *A History of Shenandoah County, Virginia* [Strasburg, Va., 1927], 157-8, 556-8).

A close friend of TJ, ISAAC ZANE of Frederick County, Virginia, died in 1795 (MB, 1:429n; Vol. 2:175n; Vol. 36:520n).

To Jacob Rinker

SIR Washington June 27. 1803.

I had only heard generally that my late friend Genl. Zane had directed some mark of his friendship for me in his will; but what it was I never heard, nor does your letter mention particularly. but it is probable a commutation may be proposed, agreeable to both of us. Genl. Zane had a pair of Turkish pistols, with an antient kind of lock. they were entirely dismounted: he made me a present of one, and as I was then at his house on my way to Philadelphia, he asked of me to take the other with me & have it mounted for him. I took it with me: but being unexpectedly sent on from there to France where I staid 6. or 7. years, the pistol went with my baggage. it came back with my baggage in 1790, but I never had an opportunity of sending it to him before his death. it is rather a pity to break the pair by separating them, and if there should be no obstacle I shall be very willing to accept that as the mark of my friend's affection, in satisfaction of what he has been so kind as to propose. if it is convenient for you to call here, at any time before 1. oclock to-day, I shall be at home and glad to see you. I present my very respectful salutations.

TH: JEFFERSON

PrC (MHi); at foot of text: "Jacob Rinker esq"; endorsed by TJ in ink on verso with notation "Exr of Zane" and so recorded in SJL.

PAIR OF TURKISH PISTOLS: the pistol described here may have been the one mentioned by TJ in a letter written to Isaac Zane from Philadelphia on 8 Nov. 1783: "The pistol is not yet ready. I have put it into very good hands by the advice of Mr. Nancarro, but I am afraid they will be tedious, and it does not appear very certain to me that I shall not be obliged to leave it here." An inventory of TJ's baggage from France contained several pistols, including a pair of large pistols in a leather case, a pair of silver-plated pistols, a single pistol and case, and two separate pistol cases (Vol. 6:348; Vol. 18:36-7n).

To Benjamin Austin, Jr.

SIR Washington June 28. 1803.

I have to acknowledge the reciept, some time ago, of a volume from you, the papers of which I had before read as they appeared under the signature of Old South, and had read with uncommon satisfaction. a sacred devotion to the natural rights of man, and to the principles of representative government which offers the fairest chance of preserving them, with an intrepidity bidding defiance to every thing which was not *reason*, had already marked the author as one of the valuable advocates of human nature. it is with pleasure I offer my portion of the tribute due for your pure & disinterested exertions in the general behalf, and, with my thanks for the volume sent, I tender you the assurances of my high esteem & respect TH: JEFFERSON

PrC (DLC); at foot of text: "Benjamin Austin esq."

Benjamin Austin, Jr. (1752-1820), Boston-born Republican and brother of Jonathan Loring Austin, published a series of 13 letters in 1786 in the Boston *Independent Chronicle* and later included many of them in a pamphlet, *Observations on the Pernicious Practice of the Law*. Writing under the pseudonym "Honestus," he argued for simplification of the legal process by a greater reliance on judges and juries than on lawyers. In 1787, 1789 to 1794, and 1796, he served in the Massachusetts Senate where he had been an outspoken advocate of New England fisheries and influenced TJ's own report on the subject in 1791. Although part of the colonial Massachusetts mercantile elite, Austin espoused Jeffersonian republicanism and allied himself with the urban artisan population, advocating in newspaper essays written under the pseudonym "Old South" for such reforms as rotation in office and elimination of the national debt. In a recess appointment in 1803, TJ named Austin commissioner of loans for Massachusetts (ANB; DAB; JEP, 1:476; Vol. 19:148-51, Vol. 38: 124, 126n).

A VOLUME FROM YOU: Austin's *Constitutional Republicanism, in Opposition to Fallacious Federalism; as Published Occasionally in the Independent Chronicle, Under the Signature of Old-South* (Boston, 1803; Sowerby, No. 3534).

From Michael Bowyer

HONORABLE SIR. Sulphur Springs 28th. June 1803

Not before the 18th. of May did I recve your favour of the date Novr. 3d. 1802. Shortly afterwards I made the inquirey agreable to your request relative to those bones which have been found in a Salt-peter cave the property of A Mr. Pattin about 15 Miles distance from me. the claw & other bones will be eaquel to the information you have ricvd. within a few weeks past. Pattin informes me when didging in the cave a considerable distance from whare the claws & other bones was got nearly six foot under ground the back bone, as is Suposed of the same Species of animal of those formerly sent by Col. Stuurt. The Tube or hollow through the bone is Nearly three Inches diameter the bone is much dcayed. as is also the Claw and other parts of the bones yet when collected may be interesting in order to Assertain what prodigious animal of that Species it must have been. on the receipt of your favour I immediately made application to Mr. Pattin for the whole of the bones and if could have got them would with much pleasur complyd. with your request in sending Them on—but it Seems Mr. Pattin was & is under a promis to send them to Mr. Monrow the late governor. which he intends to do this fall with any other's that he may yet get in the cave in which he is working by that time, I doubt not but Mr. Monrow may intend them for you or Mr. Peals. that being the case I hope will fully answer your desire. it gives me grate satisfaction as it must also to every citizen of the United States to find the grate Zeal you so Ardently pursue in distributing infirmation & Knowledge amongst all the happy citizens over which you preside. That you may long live & injoy all the happiness this world can afford is the sencere wish of your most obedt. & Hble Sert—

Michl Bowyer

RC (MHi); at foot of text: "Thos. Jefferson Esqr."; endorsed by TJ as received 8 July.

same species: the megalonyx. In 1796, John Stuart sent TJ bones of that animal from a cave in Greenbrier County (Vol. 29:64-5, 152-3).

To John Hankart

Sir — Washington June 28. 1803.

I recieved yesterday only your favor of the 18th. my whole crop of tobo.[1] was put into the hands of my agent at Richmond (being about 45,000. ℔) who in his last letter informed me he was about to sell it at 7½ Dollars the hundred, and I presume it is actually sold, as I had desired it should be. were it still on hand I could not withdraw a few hogsheads from it without greatly injuring the sale of the residue; the purchasers always suspecting that the best hogsheads have been picked out for the first sale. mr Madison, the Secretary of state has now at Fredericksburg a very choice crop of tobacco of the same quality with mine. whether he has engaged it or not I do not know. Accept my salutations & respect

Th: Jefferson

PrC (DLC); at foot of text: "Mr. John Hankart"; endorsed by TJ in ink on verso.

[1]Preceding two words interlined.

Statement of Account with Henry Ingle, with Jefferson's Order

Washington 28 June 1803

Mr Thomas Jefferson

1802	To Henry Ingle	Dr
Decr 27	To 2 Peases $3\frac{1}{4}$ Oil Stone @ 80	2–60
Jany 14	To 1 Brass Pulley	0–25
March 8	To 2 Mahogany Coasters	10–00
Apr 23	To 6 Cubbart Locks @ 60	3–60
May 26	To 1 Pair Pinchers	0–40
	To 1 Pair Plyers	0–$37\frac{1}{2}$
	To $1\frac{1}{2}$ In Chisel	0–25
	To 4 Sprig Alls	0–25
	To 400 Sprigs & Nails @ 10	0–40
	To 2 Shinglin Hatchets @ 75	1–50
		\$19:$62\frac{1}{2}$

Recd Payment in full[1] HENRY INGLE

\$19:$62\frac{1}{2}$

[*Order by TJ:*]

Mr. Barnes will be pleased to pay the above sum of 19.$62\frac{1}{2}$ D

TH: JEFFERSON

MS (CSmH); statement in Ingle's hand, with date of payment added by John Barnes (see note below).

In his financial memoranda at 7 July 1803, TJ recorded giving Ingle an order on John Barnes for \$19.625 "for tools &c." (MB, 2:1104).

[1] John Barnes here added "(13 July)."

From William Kilty and John P. Van Ness

SIR June 28th. 1803

We have the honor to inform you that the Committee of arrangements for the celebration of the 4th. of July next, appointed by the Citizens of Washington have determined on a public dinner at Stelle's Hotel; and have directed us to request the favor of your company on the occasion at half after three OClock P.M—

We have very great pleasure in executing this commission; and shall be highly gratified if the man who was so instrumental in the accomplishment of our Independence, and who now presides in our

Councils shall find it agreeable & convenient to comply with the wishes of the Committee and the Citizens whom they represent, upon this subject—

We have the honor to be with the greatest respect your very hble. Servants

Wm. Kilty
John P. Van Ness

RC (MoSHi: Jefferson Papers); in Van Ness's hand, signed by Kilty and Van Ness; at foot of text: "The President of the U. States"; endorsed by TJ as received from Washington on 29 June and so recorded in SJL.

A former New York congressman, John P. Van Ness (1770-1846) became a resident of Washington, D.C., after accepting appointment as major of the District of Columbia militia in 1802. The next year, he was elected to the city council and became its president. He was mayor of Washington from 1830 to 1834. He also became a prominent banker (*Biog. Dir. Cong.*; *National Intelligencer*, 12 Dec. 1803). For Van Ness's family background and early career, see Vol. 36:82n.

Kilty and Van Ness were both part of a nine-person COMMITTEE OF ARRANGEMENTS. Other members included Mayor Robert Brent, Daniel Carroll of Dudington, who was president of the second chamber of the city council, William Ward Burrows, Thomas Munroe, John Cassin, Samuel Harrison Smith, and Thomas Tingey (*National Intelligencer*, 27 June, 12 Dec. 1803).

The Washington CELEBRATION OF THE 4TH. OF JULY included 18-gun salutes at sunrise and noon, an oration by Captain William O. Sprigg, and a parade of uniformed militia in front of the President's House. Between noon and two o'clock, a large gathering of ladies and gentlemen, including militia officers, city officials, heads of departments, and foreign ministers, waited on the president and enjoyed cake, punch, and wine. At half past three o'clock, about 100 people, "including the heads of department, foreign ministers, the officers of the general government, and strangers of distinction," met at Stelle's Hotel. Smith read the Declaration of Independence before the assembled diners. After dinner, 18 toasts, including one to TJ, were interspersed with patriotic songs and with entertainment provided by Burrows's "excellent band." The *National Intelligencer* reported that "in addition to the usual circumstances that endear the day to Americans, the deeply interesting intelligence of the cession of Louisiana, received the antecedent evening, excited the most lively joy" (*National Intelligencer*, 4, 6, 11 July; Margaret Bayard Smith, *The First Forty Years of Washington Society*, ed. Gaillard Hunt [New York, 1906], 38-9).

To Barnabas McShane

Sir

Washington June 28. 1803.

Genl. John Armstrong of Cincinnati having paid the sum of 4 D. 75c for a friend of mine at my request, he desires me to place it in your hands to his credit. I have no means of doing this but in an Alexandria bank bill of 5. D. which I am in hopes you will be able either to exchange or pay away.—Accept my best wishes.

Th: Jefferson

PrC (MHi); at foot of text: "Mr. Barnabas Mc.Shane. 43. N. 3d. street"; endorsed by TJ in ink on verso.

A native of Hunterdon County, New Jersey, Barnabas McShane (1747-1803) received a captain's commission in the Philadelphia militia during the American Revolution. After the war, he became a merchant, importer, and innkeeper in Philadelphia. In 1787, he purchased the Harp and Crown tavern at 43 North Third Street. A charter member of the local Hibernian Society, he died leaving an estate valued at $10,000 (Joseph R. Klett, ed., *Genealogies of New Jersey Families: From the Genealogical Magazine of New Jersey*, 2 vols. [Baltimore, 1996], 1:526; W. A. Newman Dorland, "The Second Troop Philadelphia City Cavalry," PMHB, 46 [1922], 363-4; Philadelphia *Independent Gazetteer*, 20 June 1788).

A FRIEND OF MINE: Tadeusz Kosciuszko. According to TJ's financial memoranda, on 28 June he enclosed $5 to McShane on order of Armstrong "to repay taxes of Genl. Kosciuzko's land." In 1800, Armstrong had purchased bounty lands in Franklin County, Ohio, on Kosciuszko's behalf, but two years later the Polish exile sold the land to Madame Louise Françoise Felix (MB, 2:1104; Vol. 31:560-1; Vol. 32:245; Vol. 39:202-3).

McShane replied to TJ on 2 July, acknowledging receipt of this letter and crediting the $5 enclosed to Armstrong whom he would advise of the "Rect. thereof By Next Post in your Name" (RC in MHi; endorsed by TJ as received 5 July and so recorded in SJL).

To James Mease

SIR Washington June 28. 1803.

I recieved lately the inclosed pamphlet from the Author at Lingen in Westphalia. not understanding the German myself, I submitted it to a gentleman who does, and he assures me it contains valuable matter on the subject of rendering wood incombustible, preventing the rot &c. as this might come within the plan of the Domestic Encyclopedia you are publishing, I have supposed it might be acceptable to you & therefore tender it with my salutations & assurances of respect.

TH: JEFFERSON

PrC (DLC); at foot of text: "Doctr. Maese"; endorsed by TJ in ink on verso. Enclosure: Johann Gotthilff Angerman, *Anweisung, wie das Holz zum Haus- und Schiffsbau so zubereitet werden könne, dass es vor Feuer, Faulniss und Wurmfrass...verwahrt bleibe: nebst einer Anweisung, wie Stroh-, Rohr- und Schindeldächer feuerfest...auszuführen, auch die Feueranstalten zu verbessern seyn* (Lingen, 1802; see Angerman to TJ, 20 Dec. 1802).

GENTLEMAN WHO DOES: see Jacob Wagner to TJ, 28 June 1803.

DOMESTIC ENCYCLOPEDIA: Mease's American edition of Anthony F. M. Willich's five volume, *Domestic Encyclopædia; or, A Dictionary of Facts, and Useful Knowledge*, was printed in Philadelphia in 1803-04 (Vol. 39:128).

To Daniel Trump

SIR Washington June 28. 1803.

At the desire of mr Oldham I inclose you sixty dollars, of the disposition of which he informs me he has before advised you. I avail myself of this occasion of offering you my best wishes.

TH: JEFFERSON

PrC (MHi); at foot of text: "Mr. Trump"; endorsed by TJ in ink on verso.

A letter of 24 June from James OLDHAM to TJ, recorded in SJL as received 25 June, has not been found, nor has TJ's response of 28 June. Another letter from Oldham, recorded in SJL as one of 8 July received 10 July, has also not been found. In his financial memoranda, TJ recorded on this day enclosing a payment of $60 to Trump "for James Oldham" (MB, 2: 1104).

To John Vaughan

DEAR SIR Washington June 28. 03.

I recieved last night your favor of the 25th. covering mr Heineken's letter & list, & the Rules & premiums of the London society of arts & manufactures, which being intended for the A. Philos. Society I now return, & ask their transmission to the Society through the same channel by which I recieved them. the premiums offered by that society are curious, as presenting a statement of the desiderata in the arts at the present moment. I retain the copy of the proceedings of the Connecticut Agricultural society according to your permission with thanks for the favor. their plan is new, and useful. a great deal will be said which would never have been written, and the finding a redacteur for so much of it exactly as is worthy of preservation was a happy idea. from the variety of witnesses to the same fact we derive a more satisfactory idea of it than from a more handsome statement by a single one. Accept my friendly salutations & respects.

TH: JEFFERSON

RC (PPAmP); at foot of text: "John Vaughan esq." PrC (DLC). Enclosures: see Vaughan to TJ, 25 June.

From Jacob Wagner

28 June 1803

J. Wagner has the honor to present his respects to the President and to return him the german letter and pamphlet sent to him on Saturday. The letter is complimentary from the author of the pamphlet,

Mr. Angerman of Lingen in Westphalia. The pamphlet proposes a method of securing wood for house and ship-building from fire, decay and the worm, by means of a solution of pot-ash, common salt, salmoniac and alum, in which it is to be soaked. 2nd. to render roofs of shingles, straw and reeds durable and uninflammable, the two latter by the application of a mixture of lime & pickle—& 3rd. to prevent fire-engines and reservoirs from freezing in cold weather, when they may be necessary for the extinguishment of fires, by adding a quantity of pickle to the water contained in them.

The above is a very concise summary of his inventions, which appear to J:W. to be judiciously formed and strikingly explained.

As Dr. Mease of Philada. is publishing a revised edition of the Domestic encyclopœdia, J:W. uses the presumption to suggest that it might be of service to that work, if the Dr. had the opportunity of incorporating in it such hints from the pamphlet as he might think worthy of selection.

RC (MoSHi: Jefferson Papers); endorsement damaged; addressed: "The President of the U.States"; endorsed by TJ as received 28 June and "[Angerm]an's pamphlet." For the enclosures, see TJ to James Mease, 28 June.

From Joseph Barnes

Paris june 29th. 1803—

I should not have troubled Mr Jefferson further 'till I arrived at my post, but in consequence of information of the Mal-conduct of some of the American pro-consuls in Sicily, especially the one at Palermo; against whom a protest I understand has been made and forwarded to the Owners of the Vessel; and being solicitous not merely to avoid censure but to merit the approbation of my country, I conceive it indispensible to suggest, that those acting as yet in the ports of Sicily are the Creatures of Mr Mathieu of Naples; who, having purchased their places it seems they wish'd to make the most of them even at the expense of those they ought to have protected; and who I permitted to remain in office merely because I did not conceive it expedient to make temporary appointments; consequently, I shall hasten to my consulate in order to remove those mercenary beings, and replace them by men of character and influence.

As the commerce of the United States will now become an object of great importance in the Medeterranian, Adriatic, and Levant, I need only remind Mr Jefferson, that should the powers suggest'd in my Last, by Mr. jay, be sent out, I would pledge myself that we should obtain in those parts of the Globe much more preponderance than we have reason to expect.

The two great powers who could interupt or frustrate our views being engaged in War, we should seize the Moment and extend our influence even to Constantinople itself, which maybe effected with Little difficulty & expense.

The British are in possession of Sicily, and the French of Naples, we should avail ourselves of their influence and power, and the imbecility of the Neapolitan Government, as far as expediency will admit, to effect our objects—To obtain the signature as far as concerns the Kingdom of Naples, a Little bribery may be requisite, however I would disburse it myself and trust to Mr Jefferson on seeing the advantages to reimburse me.

Mr Monroe, who I am happy to find is appointed to the British court, will be kind enough to forward this Letter for me—That the health of Mr Jefferson may permit him to continue in the office of first Magistrate 'till he shall have cause the *principles* of *Republicanism, Virtue & political Economy* to be *fixed* on such a firm basis as *never to be shaken*, and his happiness are amongst my first & most ardent wishes—

with the highest consideration & respect I have the honor to be Mr Jefferson your obedt. sert. J: BARNES

P.S.

Our ingenious countryman Mr Fulton, who Mr Jefferson knows Invented the diving Boat for the distruction of Vessels, & even fleets of War, has devised a plan by means thereof, by which all the Vessels [. . .] Piratical Barbarians may be effectually destroy[ed] should this be effected by us so young a Nation, it would give us great Eclat, especially as these Barbarian have hitherto baffled the efforts of the Most power Nations of Europe—Mr Fulton purposes sailing for America in the course of two months, and if his project meets the approbation of Mr Jefferson, he will, if authorized, proceed out and devote himself immediately to effect this *grand object*—I need not suggest Mr Jefferson may command my services to Act in cooperation with him if necessary—I have detain'd here ten days to see the effect of an experiment with a Boat by Mr Fulton, intend'd to Navigate the Missicippi, which will be made in a day or two—

RC (DNA: RG 59, CD, Palermo); torn; addressed: "H.E. Thomas Jefferson President of the United States of America Washington" and "pr favor of J. Monroe Eqr &c &c &c"; franked; postmarked New York, 15 Sep.; endorsed by TJ as received 25 Sep. and so recorded in SJL; also endorsed by Jacob Wagner.

POWERS SUGGEST'D IN MY LAST: see Barnes to TJ, 4 June.

In France, Robert FULTON made a prototype for a DIVING BOAT or submarine (Vol. 32:143, 144n; Vol. 37:482-3, 484-5n).

EXPERIMENT: Fulton had also gone into partnership with Robert R. Livingston, who was eager to promote the development of steam propulsion on the Hudson River. In May 1803, Fulton assembled a paddlewheel steamboat on the Seine River in Paris. A trial run had to be postponed when the vessel sank at the pier, perhaps due to sabotage, but the inventor recovered the machinery and successfully demonstrated the vessel in August before the public and members of the National Institute. Fulton, who had lived in France since 1797, declared his intention to return to the United States to build steamboats there, but instead went to Britain and did not return to America until 1806 (Cynthia Owen Philip, *Robert Fulton: A Biography* [New York, 1985], 120-6, 129-36, 139-52; ANB).

From Henry Dearborn

SIR, War Department June 29th: 1803.

I have the honor to propose _____ Rathburn, for a Cadet of Artilerist in the service of the U. States.

I have the honor to be &c.

FC (Lb in DNA: RG 107, LSP).

RATHBURN: that is, Samuel B. Rathbone of New York (Heitman, *Dictionary*, 1:817).

From James Fleming, Sr.

Middleton township Cumberland county
SIR State of Pennsylvania June 29th 1803

May it please your Excellency

Among the highest public rights I humbly allege free access and reciprocal intelligence, between the officers of government and their constituents must be of invaluable utillity. I hope sir, you will not be inattentive to a few general hints from one of the truest advocates for equal liberty and rightfull clemency, that ever walked the probationary paths of universal existance. I served in the militia and flying camp from the appearance of the British Army off New-York till after the capture of the Hessians at Trenton. My only brother being wounded in the battle on Long Island, was taken and starved to death in prison. I never flinched but served every tour the laws warned me to attend. In one up susquehanna we had a skirmish with the savages; by sea we were taken in the Minerva and confined in Jamaica. After the capture of Count De Grasse I returned in the Lively. The independence of the American republic being duly acknowledged, and new forces being required to protect the settlement of our Western Territories, I enlisted in the first regiment and marched in the expedition up Wabash at the same time of Harmars unfortunate assay up the Miamees, and remained at Vincennes till St Clair was defeated. After spending some time viewing the new improvements of the extensive purchases I returned to the vicinity of my native ground, and resuming the occupation of a country Schoolmaster my leisure hours produced food for meditation. And being always told that I was an orphan from my infancy; I found many depredations were committed by some near relations, who were entrusted with the executive distribution of my fathers property. Our minority happening to terminate about the time of the lowest ebb of depreciated Congress Money our guardians artfully endeavoured to make us believe that their defalcations were solely occasioned by the tender laws. Consanguineous ravages and other encroachments on widows houses were not the only plundering scenes I experienced, being employed by doubtful characters who were so often tampering with politics and provokingly sounding for sentiments, I made free to intimate that so many Tories and double headed Arnolds were creeping into our legislative councils, that it was high time to check their bare faced machinations by the same means that curbed the Tyrants of England. Divers being neither cold nor hot but rather inclining to the old plan of taxation under his Britannic Majesty or a cisatlantic King, the overbearing woud be Nobles and their fawning Minions found means by base Informers, to endeavour to make the temporary Rulers of the Land believe, that I was inimical to the Constitution of the United States. Thus the greedy Judas's perjured Peter's whited walls, devouring Hypocrates and murdering Jews called forth their ravenous Armies to suppress true hearted Patriots, for reproving in the gate, and not only *turned* aside the just, but murdered the innocent although the great Washington was highest in command. Such was the fury of those mighty Aristocrats who arrived into Carlisle on the first sabbath of october Anno Domini MDCCXCIV. The next morning they came galloping to my school at Coll. Ephraim Blaine's country seat Middlesex, and presented a pistol to my breast while a child was saying his lesson by my chair near to the door; and ordered me to step out into the centre of the Troop, charging the affrighted children to stay in the house. Leaving a few to guard me, the rest galloped off to an employers dwelling in full view and hearing of our little seminary, the family being industrious jermans were chiefly all out in the fields seeding, the old woman, two or three girls and a sick boy being at home; the youth stepped to the door and a pistol was instantly presented at him, the females all prayed them not to shoot, yet, while the unfortunate lad declared he was not the one they wanted, those desperate warriors let slip their lead through his body, which ended all his sublunary complaints before the day closed. The old man and two or three other sons came running to the house, but pistols were presented at them, with threats to be quiet while search was made for another son who in the interim went out of their way. The father of the dying child was even hindered from riding for a Doctor, till by repeated appealing they let him go on sending their nefarious pilot to keep him from alarming the neighbours. They took me before the States Attorney Mr. Ingersol, who talked to me about high treason, pettit treason, and other high crimes and misdemeanors. False witnesses were sought for and brought up to swear against me. I said very little having no other preparation than the prophecies of the Gospel afforded. Bail being mentioned, one of our graven images called an associate judge; he interfered and said I was a dangerous man and must be committed into prison. Thus I was hurried into the gloomy dungeon by a numerous gang of vagabonds bellowing blasphemous denunciations and vindictive imprecations for my destruction; calling themselves the only friends of order and good government. Night and day they[1] insulted me telling me I woud be hung on the whiskey pole which they said I helped to raise in the public square of the town, and then guilotined for a terrifying example to all insurgents. Our clergy man tried to comfort me, by persuasive injunctions to tell on others and save my self; but all their threatnings and canvassing did them no service. Collonel Hartley saw the iniquity of venting spite upon individuals who were not adequate to their fabricated allegations; as well as the foolishness of making a man an offender for a word at the instance of a persecuting Paul, therefore, I was turned out of Jail to follow my teaching with strict charges to keep better company, and to never say any thing against the powers that be. Thus I was obliged to live under the jeerings of a set of excise officers and haughty partisans, who soon prevailed on the chief Sachem to let the Brittish Lion keep a paw over our commerce, which gave great opportunity to the eastern Impostor to albionise our lukewarm citizens to comply with grosser acts of oppression. The best part of my days has been subjected by crosses and losses, for my attachment to truth and sound polity, while over grown rich gluttons, hypocritical pretenders and even the persecutors of republicans are continued in office and places of trust with cloying salaries and immense emoluments, that only enables them the more to undermine the happiness of the people. I have not only been put to unjust costs and enormous expences by those pests of society, but even robbed of the very wages promised for the time spent in the capacity of a soldier. The first depreciated to nothing the certificates were embezzled by the most aggravated conspiracy, and every idea of good faith staggered. My losses in every tour were double the wages, even if I had been paid honestly; my certificate from Coll J. F. Hamtramach shews I got but one years wages though I enlisted for three. I was ordered to sign receipts for something they called installments in the Captains hands, but special care was taken to keep the money out of my hands. And the sergeants said if I complained I woud get a hundred lashes. I was told that there was bills against me for all that was due to me; but I never could learn what cloak they cou,d be invented under as I never drank any distilled liquor nor used tobacco or any other luxury: and although we hardly ever got half the quantity of the rations we understood we were entitled to, even after the choice bits were culled for the officers; yet they treated us with the utmost rigour besides confining and flogging us for every triffling pretext. The confusion under Harmar and St Clair was certainly facilitated by such indifference, as the victory of Wayne so clearly testified under his superior arrangements. The peculations of public officers in conjunction with deceitful legislators, false imprisonment fees, and other incidental disbursements; besides unjust confinement and loss of time being very depressive; Yet since the principles of fredom humanity and justice appears once more triumphant over tyranny, terror, and delusion, I am in greater hopes of better ecomony and more safety. While partiality and intolerance reigned it woud have been too fool hardy to have went to law for a redress of grievances, even if I had had money to have Lawyers. My fellow prisoners had trouble enough defending themselves in different parts of the state among almost as great strangers to their own neighborhoods as if they had been taken over the seas for trial. I have never spoke to any of my acquaintances to speak for me; neither have I applied for any lucrative appointment for restitution, notwithstanding so many less capable and far less worthy have been so amply rewarded. My progenitors were the first settlers of Pennsylvania, who fled from the persecutions of great britain to seek some other country where both civil and religious priveleges might be more propitious. I was taught from the early periods of understanding, the baneful effects of depending upon monarchial establishments for righteous defence, or sacrificing the favour of god for the favour of wicked men. If the citizens of the state in which I have so long resided passes by my sufferings without taking any compensative notice; I cannot expect the citizens of the Union will be moved to consider them. I beg leave to conclude with my fervent prayers that you may be supported by that Deity in whom we all live move and have our being, and that the administration may still be improving, so that the virtuous may be protected from the power of the vicious; Vigilent friends of true liberty from the malice of railing enemies, as well as the harmless from the wiles of deception; and no officer entrusted with more than sufficient security may oblige him to perform.

I desire to be accounted worthy of your good opinion and particular friendship as well as the implicit integrity of a genuine patriot.

JAMES FLEMING SNR

RC (DLC); at foot of text: "Thomas Jefferson President of the United States"; endorsed by TJ as received 5 July and so recorded in SJL.

James Fleming owned a plantation $2\frac{1}{2}$ miles north of Carlisle, Pennsylvania, in Middleton Township (*Kline's Carlisle Weekly Gazette*, 2 Jan. 1807).

George Washington and Alexander Hamilton arrived in CARLISLE on 4 Oct. 1794 in response to violence in western Pennsylvania over opposition to the collection of the whiskey excise tax. Various, and sometimes contradictory, reports spread throughout the region, and federal forces sent to quell the unrest left two men dead. One account suggested that an innocent, sickly young boy was accidentally shot by a light horseman. Washington, who stayed at the home of Ephraim Blaine, assistant quartermaster general of the militia, instructed that the perpetrators of the crimes should be brought before the civil magistrate. Jared Ingersoll, attorney general of Pennsylvania, directed Jasper Yeates of the Supreme Court of Pennsylvania, to take depositions of the witnesses (Judith Ridner, *A Town In-Between: Carlisle, Pennsylvania, and the Early Mid-Atlantic Interior* [Philadelphia, 2010], 193-5; Syrett, *Hamilton*, 17:225, 262, 303, 316-17; Washington, *Diaries*, 6:170-7, 182-8).

[1]MS: "the."

From Madame de Chastellux

DEAR SIR — Paris june the 30th. 1803.

Your past kindness, those ties of friendship which existed between you & Monsieur de Chastellux, & our good friend General de la fayette's advice, induce me to sollicit your protection and interest in favo'r of My dr Boy. at the time I applied to you My dr. Sir you was so good as to promiss you would lend your helping hand if ever an opportunity offered of serving the Son of a friend: I then had imagined from the generosity of Congress to Count de Grace's family that something might be done for my Boy, but informed by you that this was a particular case I did not make bold to put in my claim: my situation however instead of improving has been growing worse & worse, & from my husbands family's Emigration his Childs property is as good as lost: under these painful circumstances you will easily conceive

My dr. Sir how happy I should feel, if my personnal rights could be any ways serviceable towards securing my poor Boy any sort of provision. you will after perusing the enclosed note be acquainted with his Situation which is very peculiar & I hope you will not only be of opinion that General la fayette who acts the part of a father to him might be favorably attended to by the States of Maryland if he made application in his behalf, but that you will use your influence, & join him in his generous and friendly endeavours, for these My dr. Sir I shall entertain Sanguine hopes of success, & to be indebted to you both for the independance of my Son, will be a great addition to my happiness: to contract obligations towards those we esteem & honno'r is very gratifying & it will be a truly felt satisfaction to unite the sentiment of gratitude to all those I have ever entertained for you My dr. Sir I request you will not doubt their Sincerity and believe me as Ever

My dr. Sir Your affectionate humble Servant

PLUNKETT CHASTELLUX

My right which I readily make up to my Son can be Sufficiently ascertained, but I shall not go to that expence, except you give your approbation to my laying down before the States of Maryland those claims which acquire I think more Strength from resting upon the Child of one who was so ardently devoted to America.

RC (DLC). Enclosure: copy of the memorandum listed as Enclosure No. 2 at Lafayette to TJ, 4 June (MS in DLC: TJ Papers, 132:22805; in Madame de Chastellux's hand). Enclosed in Lafayette to TJ, 4 July.

From Albert Gallatin

SIR Treasury Department June 30th. 1803.

I have the honor of enclosing a report of the commissioner of the revenue, by which it appears that the collection of the Direct Tax and of the Internal Revenues, has been so far completed in the States of New-Hampshire, Vermont, Rhode-Island, New-York, and New-Jersey, that the office of Supervisor may, in those several districts, be discontinued without injury to the public service. The following arrangements are, therefore submitted to your consideration.

1st. The office of Supervisor shall be immediately discontinued in the Districts abovementioned.

2. For the purpose of closing the business in the Districts of Vermont, New-York, Rhode-Island and New-Jersey, the duties of Su-

pervisor shall, in conformity to the provision made, for that purpose, last session be attached to the several following offices: Vizt.

in Vermont, to the office of Marshall:

in New-York, to the office of naval officer:

in Rhode-Island, to the office either of collector of Surveyor of some Port, or Marshal:

in New-Jersey, to the office of commr. of loans, Marshal, or surveyor of Brunswick.

3. To each of the four officers selected as aforesaid in the said districts, there shall be allowed for the ensuing quarter, in addition to such allowance for clerk-hire as shall be approved by the Secretary of the Treasury, the highest compensation provided in this case: vzt. at the rate of two hundred & fifty dollars a year.

It is expected that within a very short time, similar measures may be adopted in all the other states; North & South Carolina, Georgia, and Kentucky excepted.

The two last States, but especially Kentucky, are so much in arrears, that doubts may reasonably be entertained of the regularity & energy of the Supervisors. In the two Carolinas, every exertion has been made by those officers; and the delays in the assessment of the Direct Tax, are the only causes why the business is not terminated in those two states.

Whatever relates to the Internal revenues, is so far advanced in South Carolina, that, as the assessment of the Direct Tax is not yet completed, there is not at present any use for the Supervisor's Office; and the only reason why the office should not be discontinued, is that it would hereafter be impracticable to find an officer who would undertake the collection of the Direct Tax, for the consideration of two hundred and fifty dollars a year.—

I have the honor to be, very respectfully, Sir, Your obed. Servant

ALBERT GALLATIN

RC (DLC); in a clerk's hand, signed by Gallatin; at foot of text: "The President of the United States"; endorsed by TJ as received from the Treasury Department on 1 July and "Supervisors discontince" and so recorded in SJL; also endorsed by TJ: "N.H. R.I. Verm. N.Y. N.J." Enclosure: William Miller to Gallatin, Revenue Office, Treasury Department, 27 June 1803, recommending the discontinuance of the office of supervisor in New Hampshire, Rhode Island, Vermont, New York, New Jersey, and South Carolina, under the conditions of the report, noting that commissions and allowances in New York should remain in Samuel Osgood's hands, but as "proceedings in Vermont, Rhode Island & New Jersey, have been rather dilatory, it may be proper to designate some active officer in each of these Districts, to take charge" of the accounts that remain unsettled; supervisors of Massachusetts, Maryland, and Virginia "will require but a short period to complete their Collections" and may be able to render final accounts during the ensuing quarter; declining to say anything definitive about Pennsylvania, North Carolina, Georgia, Kentucky, and Tennessee, Miller observes, "much will depend on the future exertions of the Supervisors & Subordinate Officers"; and enclosing "A Statement relative to the Accounts of the Supervisors of the Revenue," with a summary of districts, including Connecticut and Delaware, where the offices have been suppresed after the resignation of the supervisors; in Pennsylvania, Miller notes, "the business which Mr Coxe has undertaken will occupy his attention for some months longer," and he will not be able to submit his final account until J. P. G. Muhlenberg's statement has been completed; although Miller has "repeatedly urged" the supervisor of Georgia to render his account, the last received was that of 30 Apr. 1801; accounts and remittances from Kentucky are also overdue as "Collections do not progress with alacrity," Miller contends, and the "attempts of the Officers to enforce Collection, appear to have been less strenuous or much less successful than in other districts" (Gallatin, *Papers*, 47:831-44; ASP, *Miscellaneous*, 1:280-8; Vol. 38:420, 482-3).

PROVISION MADE: the act of 3 Mch. 1803 gave the president the authority to transfer the duties of the office of supervisor to any other U.S. officer within the district. The designated officer would receive the same commissions as the supervisor was allowed, an allowance for clerk hire not to exceed that fixed by law and "such salary not exceeding" $250 per year, as the president "shall deem a sufficient compensation" (U.S. Statutes at Large, 2:243-4).

To J. P. G. Muhlenberg

DEAR SIR Washington June 30. 03.

I wrote you some time last summer on the subject of mr Barnes, and recieved with pleasure your answer in his favor. the winding up his affairs here has induced him to postpone his removal to Philadelphia until about Octob. tho' he has some thought of paying a short visit to it soon. I shall therefore take the liberty of again recommending him to you. tho' old he is very active, vigilant, & with his pen laborious. any thing on earth may be confided to his integrity. he understands accounts from habit, more than from genius and where he understands them he is very accurate. I do not think he would answer for letter writing, unless in cases of plain business. I write these minute things that you may know how to avail the public of the good qualities he has; as I have known him very long (upwards of 40. years) and very intimately and have a great regard for him. his age, tho' firm in his health, might occasion him to break down in a business of too much labour. I ought to add that his extreme good humour & indulgent disposition would not do where any rigorous conduct would be essential.

I thank you for your care of my letters mentioned in yours of the 22d. and tender you my friendly salutations & assurances of great respect and esteem. TH: JEFFERSON

PrC (DLC); at foot of text: "Genl. Muhlenberg"; endorsed by TJ in ink on verso.

I WROTE YOU: TJ to Muhlenberg, 10 Oct. 1802. YOUR ANSWER: Muhlenberg to TJ, 14 Oct. 1802.

To Sir John Sinclair

DEAR SIR Washington June 30. 1803.

It is so long since I have had the pleasure of writing to you, that it would be vain to look back to dates,[1] to connect the old & the new; yet I ought [not] to pass over my acknolegements to you for various publications recieved from time to time,[2] and with great satisfaction[3] & thankfulness. I send you a small[4] [one] in return, the work of a very unlettered farmer, yet valuable, as it relates plain[5] facts of importance to farmers. you will discover that mr Binns is an enthusiast for the use of gypsum. but there are two facts which prove he has a right to be so. 1. he began poor, & has made himself tolerably[6] rich by his farming alone. 2. the county of Loudon, in which he lives, had been so exhausted & wasted by bad husbandry, that it began to depopulate, the inhabitants going Southwardly in quest of better lands. Binn's success has stopped that emigration. it is now becoming [one] of the most productive counties of the state of Virginia, and the price given for th[ose] lands is multiplied manifold.

We are still uninformed here whether you are again at war. Buonaparte has produced such a state of things in Europe as it would seem difficult for him to relinquish in any sensible degree, and equally dangerous for Great Britain to suffer to go on, especially if accompanied by maritime preparations, on his part. the events which have taken place in France have lessened in the American mind the motives of interest which it felt[7] in that revolution, and it's amity towards that country now rests on it's love of peace &[8] commerce. we see at the same time with great[9] concern the position in which Great Britain is placed, and should be sincerely afflicted were any disaster to deprive mankind of the benefit of such a bulwark against the torrent which has for some time[10] been bearing down all before it. but her power & prowess [by] sea seem to render every thing safe in the end.[11] peace is our passion, & tho' wrongs might drive us from it, we prefer trying every[12] other just principle [of][13] right & safety before we would recur to war.

I hope your agricultural institution goes on with success. I consider you as the author of all the good it shall do.[14] a better idea has never been carried into practice. our Agricultural society has at length formed itself. like our American Philosophical society it is voluntary, & unconnected with the public, and is precisely an execution of the plan I formerly sketched to you. some state societies have been formed heretofore. the others will do the same. each state society names two of it's members of Congress to be their members in the Central society, which is of course together during the sessions of Congress. they are to select matter from the proceedings of the state societies & to publish it, so that their publications may be called l'esprit des societés d'agriculture &c. the central society was formed the last winter only so that it will be some time before they get under way. mr Madison, the Secretary of state was elected their President.

Recollecting with great satisfaction our friendly intercourse while I was in Europe,[15] I nourish the hope it still preserves a place in your mind, and with my salutations I pray you to accept assurances of my constant attachment and high respect. TH: JEFFERSON

PrC (DLC); margin frayed, with text in brackets supplied from Dft; at foot of first page: "Sir John Sinclair." Dft (DLC); undated. Tr (NjP); entire second paragraph underscored, with quotation marks at opening and close of paragraph and at beginning of each line; endorsed as received by Sinclair at Edinburgh on 19 Nov. 1803. Enclosure: John A. Binns, *A Treatise on Practical Farming* (see enclosure listed at TJ to Thomas Mann Randolph, 14 June). Enclosed in TJ to George W. Erving, 10 July. Tr enclosed in Sinclair to Lord Melville, 28 Nov. 1803, in which Sinclair writes from Charlotte Square: "I received, the other day, a very interesting communication from Mr Jefferson, President of the united States, and as the opinions of a person in his high situation, regarding the present state of European politics, must be interesting to the statesmen on this side of the water, I thought it right to send you a copy of it, which you may also communicate to mr Pitt" (RC in NjP).

PLEASURE OF WRITING TO YOU: TJ to Sinclair, 23 Mch. and 28 Apr. 1798. For the VARIOUS PUBLICATIONS TJ received from Sinclair, which he had not yet acknowledged, see Vol. 31:91; Vol. 32:13-14; Vol. 34:414; Vol. 37:536-7.

TJ carefully constructed this second paragraph, with his depiction of Great Britain as a beneficial BULWARK AGAINST the French TORRENT, as a way to convey diplomatic information that could be shared with British authorities, as Sinclair did by sending it to Lord Melville (see descriptive note and textual notes from Dft). TJ's 27 June 1790 letter to Benjamin Vaughan is an earlier example of his use of private correspondence as a vehicle for diplomatic communication (Vol. 16: viii-ix; 578-80).

OUR AGRICULTURAL SOCIETY: the American Board of Agriculture was established in February 1803, with Madison elected president and Isaac Briggs, secretary (*National Intelligencer*, 2 Mch. 1803; Vol. 37:172-3, 339-40).

OUR FRIENDLY INTERCOURSE: for Sinclair's recollection of his meeting and exchanges with TJ, see Vol. 9:405-6.

[1] In Dft TJ here canceled "as if to keep."

[2] Preceding two words interlined in Dft.

[3] Sentence ends here in Dft.

[4] Preceding two words interlined in Dft.

[5] Word interlined in Dft.

[6] Word interlined in Dft.

[7] Word interlined in Dft in place of "took."

[8] In PrC TJ here canceled "tranquility." Dft: "peace & commerce."

[9] Word interlined in Dft in place of "sincere."

[10] Preceding three words interlined in Dft. Tr lacks "for some time."

[11] Dft: preceding three words interlined.

[12] PrC: "ever."

[13] In Dft TJ first wrote "we prefer every other means of obtaining" before altering the preceding text to read as above. Tr: "prefer trying every just principle of."

[14] In Dft TJ here interlined "ours has at length established itself on the plan I mentioned to you &c." Dft lacks remainder of paragraph.

[15] In Dft TJ first began the sentence "recollecting myself with great satisfaction the friendly intercourse I had with you in Europe" before altering it to read as above.

To William Strickland

DEAR SIR Washington June 30. 1803.

It is long since I had the pleasure of hearing[1] from you, of which I take all the blame[2] on myself; acknoleging myself to be entirely the defaulter. with a mass generally before me which will not admit delay, I have suffered those things to lie too long[3] which might bear some postponement[4] without reproach. knowing your love of agriculture, and your skill in it, I could not pretermit the occasion of sending you the inclosed pamphlet on the use of Gypsum, by a mr Binns, a plain farmer, who understands handling his plough better than his pen. he is certainly somewhat of an enthusiast[5] in the use of this manure: but he has a right to be so. the result of his husbandry proves his confidence in it well founded, for from being poor, it has made him rich.[6] the county of Loudon, in which he lives,[7] exhausted & wasted by bad husbandry, has, from his example, become[8] the most productive one in Virginia: and it's lands, from being the lowest,.[9] sell at the highest prices. these facts speak more strongly for his pamphlet than a better arrangement & more polished phrases would have done. were I now a farmer I should surely adopt the gypsum. but when I found myself called from home for four years certain, perhaps for eight, I leased the farms in which I had begun the course of husbandry which you saw: obliging.[10] the tenant to continue the same. he does so in a good degree, and I have reason to be content with the result.

We see here with great concern the necessity which seems to have befallen you of renewing the war, in order to stop the torrent which is overwhelming the world.[11] the interest which my countrymen felt in the first stages of the French revolution has been done away by it's issue: and they no longer see the good of mankind as likely to flow from the successes of that nation. still enamoured however with peace & commerce,[12] we hope[13] to find the indulgence of them in the interest of both parties: and that doing no injustice ourselves, none will be offered us. we have important interests indeed to settle, but we would rather settle them by reason than an appeal to force.

It will always give me great pleasure to hear of your welfare and that of those dear to you: and it is with great sincerity that I assure you of my constant attachment, and great esteem & respect.

Th: Jefferson

PrC (DLC); at foot of first page: "William Strickland esq." Dft (DLC); undated; with calculations by TJ on verso. Enclosure: John A. Binns, *A Treatise on Practical Farming* (see enclosure listed at TJ to Thomas Mann Randolph, 14 June). Enclosed in TJ to George W. Erving, 10 July.

pleasure of hearing from you: Strickland to TJ, 16 July 1798. For TJ's last letter to the Yorkshire agriculturist, see Vol. 30:209-14.

you saw: Strickland visited TJ at Monticello in May 1795 (Vol. 28:371-3).

tenant: John H. Craven leased TJ's land at Monticello. When TJ resumed his agricultural pursuits as a retired president, he purchased and applied large quantities of gypsum annually to his land (rs, 2:197; Vol. 32:108-10, 163-6).

[1] In Dft TJ wrote "receiving a line" in place of preceding word.

[2] Dft: "cause."

[3] Preceding two words interlined in Dft.

[4] Word interlined in Dft in place of "delay."

[5] Dft: "somewhat enthusiastical."

[6] In Dft TJ here canceled "and his conviction" and "his [example]."

[7] Preceding four words interlined in Dft.

[8] Preceding five words interlined in Dft without punctuation in place of "to become a [. . .]."

[9] In Dft TJ first wrote "are become the highest priced" before altering the remainder of the sentence to read as above.

[10] Dft: "husbandry you saw, only obliging."

[11] In Dft preceding four words interlined in place of "seems to threaten a general deluge."

[12] In Dft preceding word interlined in place of "tranquility."

[13] In Dft TJ here canceled "we shall not."

From David Campbell

Dear Sir, Campbella July 1st. 1803—

Several reciprocal injuries done by individuals of the Cherokee Nation, and some of the Citizens of this State to each other, convince me that it is absolutely necessary to continue the millitary posts at South West Point and Tellico; that they may aid the Civil Authority to compel the parties to abstain from all offence, from all abuse, from all injury, and from every thing that may be of prejudice to each other.

This Millitary aid, I think necessary, because your experience, as well as mine, has sufficiently demonstrated to us, that it is impossible for the best regulated Government, or for the most vigilant chief Magistrate, such Sir, as I really know you to be, to model all the Actions of the Citizens, and to confine them to the strict rules of Law.

In civilized States, the mode to bring offenders against the Law of Nations to punishment, is pretty well systematized. Letters Rogatory, is an admirable institution amongst neighbouring States: But this regulation will not answer the Indian Tribes.

I like the stipulation in the fourth Article in addition to the Treaty of Holston, which authorises the deduction of fifty Dollars, from the Annuity of five thousand Dollars, for every horse which shall be stollen from the white Inhabitants by any Cherokee Indians, and not returned within three months.

May not this mode of redress, by implication, and fair Deduction be applyed, for any other stolen property?

I am lead to make those remarks, on account of a robery being committed, a few Days since, on one of the Citizens of the State of Tennessee, by an Indian as appeared to me by proof. The fellow was brought in Custody, to me. On Deliberation, I concluded there were but two legal modes of procuring redress. The one by the forms and rules of the Civil and Statute Laws.

The other agreeable to the Law of Nations and existing Treaties. I preferred the latter, as being more Summary, and as I thought, more congenial to the feelings of independant Nations, particularly the Indian Tribes, who know little or nothing about our System of jurisprudence.

I therefore released the Indian from Custody, taking the proof of the facts, by Affidavit, and refered the Case to the Agent, Col. Meigs, whose Zeal, prudence and Wisdom merit the highest Confidence.

Doctor Thomas J. Vandyke's appoint[ment] for So. Wt. Point. It may be, the S[ecretary] of War may not attend to this circum[stance] and in arranging the Troops from one post to another, may also order the Doctor to some other post. The Situation of his family and some other Circumstances would make a change at this time very inconvenient. As the public Interest will not be injured but really served by his remaining at So. Wt. point I know your friendship for me, will induce you to permit his remaining at his present post while the public Service will admit of it.

I have it in command from the Doctor, to inform you, should a War break out, or any other circumstance of moment require his Service in a different post he will be the first to obey your Order.

I am, Dear Sir, with great Respect Your Obt. Servt.

David Campbell

RC (DLC); torn; addressed: "His Excellency Thomas Jefferson President of the United States. City of Washington"; endorsed by TJ as received 24 Aug. and so recorded in SJL.

By a June 1794 treaty that supplemented the 1791 Treaty of HOLSTON between the United States and the Cherokee nation, if an Indian stole a horse "from the white inhabitants" and the animal was not returned within three months, $50 would be deducted from the Cherokees' annuity. A provision in the March 1802 "trade and intercourse" act empowered the president to deduct the value of stolen property from tribes' annuities (Charles J. Kappler, comp. and ed., *Indian Affairs: Laws and Treaties*, 5 vols. [Washington, D.C., 1975], 2:34; U.S. Statutes at Large, 2:144).

BROUGHT IN CUSTODY: Campbell was a judge of the Superior Court of Tennessee (Robert M. McBride and Dan M. Robison, *Biographical Directory of the Tennessee General Assembly*, 2 vols. [Nashville, 1975-79], 1:113).

On recommendations from Campbell and others, TJ in the spring of 1802 appointed THOMAS J. VANDYKE as surgeon's mate for the post at Southwest Point (Vol. 36:566-7; Vol. 37:144, 155, 156n).

From Thomas Rodney

DEAR SIR Dover July 1. 1803.

Upon consulting my friends, I found most of my connections very reluctant to my seperating from them at so great a distance, and to my resigning a permanent Station for such as may be but temporary; and many Political friends regret the Injury the Republican Interest here may sustain by my leaving the State, yet considering that my services may be of much greater National advantage in that Part of our Empire than here, most of them, tho reluctantly, acquiese in my determination to accept Your proposials, to act as one of the Judges for the Missisipi territory, and as one of the Commissioners for the district west of Pearl River—Since having formed this Resolution I begin to feel a more lively Interest in the prosperity of that particular part of our country and shall exert all my humble abilities with Integrity and fidility to promote its welfare—as I propose setting out on my Journey by the Middle of august perhaps it may be necessary for me in the meantime to wait on you at the seat of Government to receive Your Instructions and such authentic papers & Doquements as are necessary in Conducting the business there, unless they be already forwarded or you prefer forwarding them in some other way—

I beg leave here to mention that as my Journey will be pretty long, It would be very pleasing to have an agreeable Companion with me—A young Gentleman of good carrecter and promising abilities who studied the Law under my son C.A.R. and was admitted at our last supreme Court has proposed to go with me if he can obtain the appointment of Register or Clerk for Either of the Districts, but would prefer the one in which I may act as Commissioner. his Name is *William Shields*, and I am persuaded he would be a Valuable acquisition to [that] new part of Our Country.

My Intention is To go by the way of Fort Pitt and thence down the Ohio and Missisipi by water to the Natches unless you should think it more to the public Interest to take some other Road. Please to accept assurances of my very high respect and Esteem.

Your Most Obedient THOMAS RODNEY

RC (DNA: RG 59, LAR); torn; endorsed by TJ as received 5 July and so recorded in SJL.

WILLIAM SHIELDS, related to both the Rodney and Bayard families, accompanied Rodney to Mississippi Territory. His first office was as an assistant clerk to the Board of Land Commissioners. Appointed to the governor's staff in 1805, he went on to become prominent in the legislative and judicial history of Mississippi (Dwight L. Smith and Ray Swick, eds., *A Journey through the West: Thomas Rodney's 1803 Journal from Delaware to the Mississippi Territory* [Athens, Ohio, 1997], 17, 204n; Kline, *Burr*, 2:1013).

From Robert W. Cosbrough

SIR— Geo. Town 2d. July *1803*.

I am compell'd from dire necessity once more to beg your interference with the heads of Departments for any situation, however subordinate, as Clerk—I had the honor of relating to you, some time back, my distress'd state, and mentioned my intimacy, with the Hon. DeWitt Clinton & family &c; You advis'd me to apply to Mr. Galatin, which I did, but he told me there was no Vacancy at present—I am now reduced to that state, that I have not a shilling, nor know I whither to turn me—Mr. Mc.Laughlin has my Gold Watch which cost me forty four Guenias & Aparel to the Amt. of sixteen Gueneas, but I owe him *$250*—Having enjoy'd the sweets of plenty for years, such a reversal of Fortune, bears hard upon me, & unless I can obtain Employment, I must starve—In the humble hope of experiencing your Protection I remain

Sir With all possible respect Your Obt Servt.—

R. W. COSBROUGH

RC (DLC); at foot of text: "Thos. Jefferson Esqr. President U.S—"; endorsed by TJ as received 2 July and so recorded in SJL.

RELATING TO YOU, SOMETIME BACK: Cosbrough to TJ, 9 Apr.

I OWE HIM: perhaps Charles McLaughlin, who, in 1803, owned the Union Tavern in Georgetown, had an interest in stage lines, and served as secretary and treasurer of the Washington Jockey Club (*Washington Federalist*, 5 Oct. 1803; RCHS, 50 [1952], 15, 19, 37n; Vol. 37:50).

To Christopher Ellery

Dear Sir Washington July 2. 1803.

The business of Supervisor for Rhode island[1] being nearly finished it has become proper according to the provisions of the law to suppress the office and transfer the residuary duties of it to some other officer. as it has been thought that Newport has not had it's due share of office, I have thought of making the transfer to some one of the officers of the US. there. mr Nichols & mr Slocum are the only ones I know of. will you be so good as to inform me which is more capable of undertaking the winding up of this business? the best accountant would be the properest. or if there be any other officer of the US. that you think preferable, be so good as to name him. as the business is almost nothing so is the allowance fixed by law, being only at the rate of 250. D. a year. consequently it may be well to know they will[2] accept of it. yet it had better be kept in confidence till we decide on the arrangement. I am not quite certain we can await your answer, but if it be without delay we probably can. our annual vacation begins on the 25th. inst. when we shall every one go some where in quest of security to our health. I go then to Monticello, and the absence will be during the months of Aug. & September. we shall reassemble on the last day of September. Accept my salutations & assurances of great esteem & respect

Th: Jefferson

PrC (DLC); at foot of text: "the honble Christopher Ellery esq."; endorsed by TJ in ink on verso.

In 1802, TJ had appointed Walter NICHOLS and John SLOCUM, respectively, the naval officer and the surveyor at Newport, Rhode Island (Vol. 36:488; Vol. 37:348).

[1] Preceding three words interlined.

[2] Word interlined.

To Albert Gallatin

Th:J. to mr Gallatin July 2. 1803.

The arrangement you propose as to supervisors is approved. to wit

Vermont. the marshal to do the duties

New York. the Naval officer.

Rhode isld. either Nichols the Navl. officer of Newport, or Slocum the Surveyor. Newport has complained with reason that all general offices have been given to Providence, & none to Newport.

New Jersey. not to the loan officer. the Marshal or any other officer of late appointment. Th:J.

RC (NHi: Gallatin Papers); addressed: "Mr. Gallatin." PrC (DLC). Recorded in SJL with notation "Supervisors."

VERMONT. THE MARSHAL: John Willard (Willard to TJ, 11 Mch.).

Samuel Osgood was the recently appointed New York NAVAL OFFICER (Memorandum to James Madison, 10 May).

NOT TO THE LOAN OFFICER: James Ewing was New Jersey's commissioner of loans (Vol. 34:43n). TJ appointed Oliver Barnet MARSHAL when John Heard became collector at Perth Amboy in 1802 (Vol. 33:183-4, 670, 679; Vol. 37:356, 697).

From Albert Gallatin

DEAR SIR July 2d 1803

I enclose the letters received on the subject of E. Livingston. If Mr Gelston is right in supposing that the list dated 18th June has been paid to the dist. attorney there is a defalcation of at least that amount to witt thirty thousand dollars; besides which he may have received part of the bonds which had been put in suit whilst Mr Harrison was district attorney and has received some of the proceeds of the sales of Mr Lamb's (the late collector) estate. I would not be astonished if the whole deficiency exceeded forty thousand dollars. That is far greater than I had any idea of from Mr G.'s preceding letters; but his account is neither clear nor final. What may bring Mr L. here I do not understand; he can have no expectation of remaining in office under such circumstances. Mr Clinton's recommendation appears unexceptionable. Mr Sandford was, I believe, originally recommended by Gen. Smith of Long Island.

As Mr L. may be expected every moment, I will thank you to send back the papers when you shall have done with them, & to suggest whether any particular line of conduct must be followed with him.

From the recommendation of Nichols & Slocum, can any conjecture be formed which is the most active & has most capacity. If equal, the naval officer would be preferable to fill the duties of Supervisor. It must be observed that the present appointments will be considered rather as a burthen than as a favor.

With respect & attachment Your obedt. Servt.

ALBERT GALLATIN

RC (DLC); endorsed by TJ as received from the Treasury Department on 2 July and "E. Livingston—Sandford—Nichols—Slocum" and so recorded in SJL. Enclosures not found.

WHAT MAY BRING MR L. HERE: for Edward Livington's Washington visit, see Gallatin to TJ, 27 July.

In 1802, Nathan Sanford (SANDFORD) was recommended as bankruptcy commissioner by Congressman John SMITH. Both were from Long Island, New York (*Biog. Dir. Cong.*; Vol. 37:704).

From William Irvin

Worthy & Dear Sir, Albemarle 2d. July 1803.

If the Prayer of my Son's Letter, which encloses this, could meet your Approbation, I should be highly gratified. I must take it for granted that you have no Acquaintance with his Person, & perhaps as little with his Character. Prudence forbids my saying much in the Case: I would only beg Leave to say, that such is his Steadiness and Attention to Business, that I hope He would not disappoint the publick Confidence.

I am happy, Sir, that you preside over the Union, & still farther happy, should this Line find you enjoying Health of Body & Tranquility of Mind. With the unremitted Esteem of Thirty years, I have the Honour, Sir, to subscribe my self

Your cordial Friend, & very huml. Servant

William Irvin

RC (DNA: RG 59, LAR); endorsed by TJ as received 7 July and "John Irvin to be Register Zaneville" and so recorded in SJL.

William Irvin (1744-1809) was a Presbyterian minister in Albemarle County who became pastor of the Cove and Rockfish Churches. In 1776, the year his ties to the Rockfish Church dissolved, he favored religious disestablishment and signed the Petition of Dissenters in Albemarle and Amherst counties. He and his wife Elizabeth Holt Irvin had ten children, including a son, John, who became county magistrate (Woods, *Albemarle*, 232-4; Vol. 1:585-9).

my son's letter: John Irvin to TJ, 17 May.

Report from John Lenthall

Rough Stone Work at the South Wing of Capitol from June 27th to July 2d 1803

Backing up the Walls to the Ashler on the three fronts Amt. to about—105 Perches

— Cut Stone —

On the East Front 2 Courses 2 feet high

South do. $1\frac{1}{2}$ Couse at 12 inches each high

West do 1 Course at 12 Inchs high

for B H Latrobe

Jno. Lenthall

MS (DLC); in Lenthall's hand and signed by him; endorsed by TJ: "Capitol July 2. 03."

An ashlar (ashler) is a square hewn stone, ideal for building purposes (OED).

Notes on William Eaton's Accounts

I. DRAFT NOTES ON EATON'S ACCOUNTS, [2 JULY 1803]

II. NOTES ON EATON'S ACCOUNTS, [ON OR AFTER 2 JULY 1803]

EDITORIAL NOTE

In the spring of 1802, confronting an expenditure by William Eaton of $16,000 primarily for the charter of a vessel to carry dispatches to the United States, James Madison wrote to remind the consul that he must submit a full statement of his accounts. Eaton complied reluctantly, agreeing in November 1802 to send the information but contending that he could not always obtain receipts, even from the Tunisian government. He was uncomfortable, he said, submitting his financial charges for settlement if he could not be present to explain them. Writing in April 1803 to approve Eaton's request to leave his post at Tunis, Madison cautioned that as the consul's "pecuniary transactions have been spread over a number of years," settlement of his accounts would depend on the sufficiency of the documentation he submitted (Madison, *Papers*, *Sec. of State Ser.*, 1:78, 82n; 2:314; 3:202-3; 4:107, 517).

When he wrote in April, Madison did not know that the consul had already left Tunis. Eaton had made an abrupt departure, an event prompted by some of his financial transactions. He had paid out a large amount of money, about $23,000 by his reckoning, to finance the scheme to place Ahmad Qaramanli at the head of a rebel army against his brother, the bey of Tripoli. In addition, in 1801, Yusuf Sahib-at-Taba, Hammuda's chief minister, had demanded the use of the *Anna Maria*, a vessel chartered by the United States, for a voyage to obtain a cargo of oil. Yusuf made Eaton cover the costs of the cargo and the use of the ship beyond the term of its charter, then refused to reimburse him. Such large outlays of funds forced Eaton to borrow 34,000 Spanish dollars from Hammuda's commercial agent. When the Tunisians insisted on repayment of the loan in March 1803, Eaton used his own assets to cover part of the debt, and Richard V. Morris reluctantly authorized payment of $22,000 from U.S. funds for the remainder. The incident made relations between the Americans and the Tunisian regime so acrimonious that Hammuda insisted on Eaton's immediate departure. Morris detailed a surgeon from his squadron, George Davis, to remain in Tunis as temporary consul, and Eaton made his way to the United States by Leghorn and Gibraltar, arriving in Boston early in May. In June he appeared in Washington, where he could fulfill his wish to be available when his accounts were adjusted (same, 4:107, 390-2, 422n; 5:197; 6:328; NDBW, 2:352-5, 370, 374, 383-4; ASP, *Claims*, 1:299-307, 322, 337-41; Charles Prentiss, ed., *The Life of the Late Gen. William Eaton* [Brookfield, Mass., 1813], 242; Vol. 38:347n; Vol. 39:494-5n).

Richard Harrison, the Treasury's auditor, arranged Eaton's accounts into 14 categories or "heads" and sent a comprehensive statement, which has not been found, to the State Department on 27 June. The auditor asked Madison for "principles of settlement" to guide the review of Eaton's accounts, which were "the first of the kind that have been presented for examination at the Treasury"—the first set of accounts for a consular post in one of the Barbary states. Harrison asked in particular about Eaton's salary; about categories of expenditures to be allowed; whether vouchers were required for all types of expenditures; and whether "Stores & Merchandize" sent to Tunis were "considered as already accounted for, or whether they are to form a debit against the Agent" (Madison, *Papers*, *Sec. of State Ser.*, 5:126).

Madison responded on 1 July. In that reply to Harrison, Madison mentioned only the first, second, fourth, seventh, eighth, and fourteenth headings. The undated notes by Jefferson printed as Document II below, which the president evidently intended to augment, amend, and in some cases contradict what Madison had written to Harrison, refer to the first, second, fourth, seventh, and eighth headings. Document I below, dated 2 July in Jefferson's endorsement, appears to consist of notes for his own use and touches on two additional headings, the ninth and eleventh. Madison informed the auditor that most of the items in Eaton's accounts would be "subject to the ordinary rules of settlement, with respect to vouchers." One exception was the eighth heading of the accounts, which according to Madison's response to Harrison included a variety of gifts, some in the form of money. Although the presents might not be covered by individual receipts, the secretary of state declared, detailed documentation and "the best proof which circumstances permit" were required. Madison stated that the stores and merchandise that Harrison had asked about were chargeable to Eaton (same, 5:131-2).

Consuls in Barbary Coast states were the only U.S. consuls authorized by statute to receive salaries, an acknowledgment that their functions were more diplomatic than commercial. Other consuls could charge fees for their services but did not draw salaries (U.S. Statutes at Large, 1:255-6, 533). Jefferson noted that the rules for settling diplomats' accounts provided guidance for what to do with Barbary consuls' transactions (see Document II). He was in accord with an instruction from Madison to Harrison allowing Eaton a quarter of a year's salary for his expenses in returning to the United States, and he agreed also with Madison's reckoning that Eaton's salaried term of service ended with his eviction from Tunis by Hammuda. Eaton, however, also put in a charge for outfit, the allowance given a diplomat to set up his household-cum-legation. A U.S. minister in a foreign capital could receive as much as a year's salary for outfit. Madison favored allowing the charge—"under the first head of Mr. Eatons charge the outfit may be admitted," he informed Harrison—but Jefferson thought otherwise: "No outfit can be allowed." Eaton's request for payment for furniture met a similar response. Madison suggested that more information was necessary, advising Harrison that the furniture "must be accounted for," but Jefferson said no, the charges for furnishings should just be "disallowed." Both statesmen were inclined to reject Eaton's claims under the fourth heading, which according to Jefferson included "distributions of charity," although in this case Jefferson pondered the question while Madison simply deemed the expenditures "inadmissible." In his response to Harrison, Madison did not refer to expenses for horses and mules or for repairs and alterations to buildings, items that found a place in Jefferson's consideration (Documents I and II, below; Madison, *Papers*, *Sec. of State Ser.*, 5:131; Vol. 28:619n; Vol. 35:371n).

EDITORIAL NOTE

By 14 July, when Madison dated his instructions to Tobias Lear as consul general at Algiers, the president and the secretary of state had decided to allow consuls in North Africa the amount of a year's salary as an allowance for outfit. The "nature of the Office admits of and requires it," Madison explained to Richard O'Brien, who would be the next consul after Eaton to submit accounts. The allowance would also "enable the Treasury to strike out some charges in the Consular accounts, which are deemed inconvenient to be admitted, & at the same time are supposed to have been in a degree necessary to be disbursed." Lear was also to have house rent "on a moderate but decent scale," plus expenses for couriers, postage, printing, secretarial and translation services, and presents to officials as custom might demand. "There may be calls for Charitable donations," Madison advised the new consul general, "but it has been judged most consonant with principle and the public Interest, to refer them to the Consuls private account, and to free the Treasury from them. Should you find any usage requiring national Charities, you will be pleased to state them and their amount for Consideration" (Madison, *Papers*, *Sec. of State Ser.*, 5:177, 234-5).

Madison's answer to Harrison on 1 July indicates that Eaton's accounts included charges relating to the *Anna Maria* and also the *Gloria*, a vessel Eaton purchased, used for carrying dispatches and other purposes, and sold. Madison asked the auditor to move the charges for the *Gloria* from the seventh heading, where Harrison had put them, to the thirteenth heading and to classify them as relating to the Navy Department. To collect information about the account items for the *Anna Maria* and the *Gloria*, Madison made inquiries of George Davis and, later, Lear. When Robert Smith, with Jefferson's approbation, rejected Eaton's claim that the *Gloria* had in effect been part of the U.S. Navy, Madison and Jefferson thought they might be able to allow Eaton some payment for use of the ship as an "advice-boat" for carrying dispatches. Madison in his response to the auditor suspended "for enquiry and consideration" an item of $10,131.73 under Harrison's fourteenth heading, which involved a transaction between Eaton and Yusuf Sahib-at-Taba. Jefferson did not mention that charge or those relating to the *Anna Maria* and the *Gloria* in his notes (same, 5:131; 6:465-6, 515-16; 7:289-90; Vol. 38:367-8n; TJ to Eaton, 8 Feb. 1804).

The statement that Harrison sent to Madison on 27 June evidently contained a variety of miscellaneous charges under the second heading. Both sets of Jefferson's notes printed below show that he studied several of those entries in the accounts. The president in Document II echoed a request from Madison to Harrison for more information about the "contingencies" included in Eaton's submission. By January 1804, the auditor obtained more details from Eaton about the miscellaneous charges and sent Madison an abstract, which has not been found. After reviewing that statement, Madison authorized Harrison to allow charges for "Customary presents at public feasts, expences of horses & carriages, repairs of the house & appurtenances, hire of boats, porterage, postage, sums paid to Couriers, and small presents to Messengers coming on public business" (Madison, *Papers*, *Sec. of State Ser.*, 6:369, 465).

When he sent the revised statement of contingencies, Harrison also inquired about the entry for $10,131.73 that had been deferred. That charge, which Madison came to characterize as an extortion of funds from Eaton by the Tunisian chief minister, stemmed from an agreement by Eaton to pay $10,000 for the Tunisians' assistance in the plan to back Ahmad Qaramanli against his brother. The payment was supposed to depend on the successful toppling of Yusuf Qaramanli from the Tripolitan throne, and the money was to come from Ahmad, not the United States. However, when Eaton asked for reimbursement of the money he had put up for the cargo of the unauthorized voyage of the *Anna Maria*, Yusuf Sahib-at-Taba refused to turn over the funds, saying they were owed for the Tripolitan scheme. Jefferson and Madison decided that the executive branch had no authority to reimburse that money to Eaton. The president in lawyerlike fashion informed the ex-consul that it was a private matter, the chief minister having failed to pay a debt for a mercantile transaction: the United States could "lend their aid" to an effort to recover the money in Tunis, "but this is the utmost to which they are bound." Madison suggested that Congress might be able to provide some remedy where the executive branch could not, and Eaton prepared a long memorial to the House of Representatives. The Committee on Claims declined to move the matter forward, however. Eaton made a second attempt in 1806, when his unsettled claims encompassed charges relating to the *Anna Maria*, the *Gloria*, the chief minister's detention of funds, and Eaton's payment of ransom to free a Christian woman from slavery (same, 369, 508, 512, 515, 588; ASP, *Claims*, 1:299-307, 323-32; TJ to Eaton, 8 Feb. 1804).

I. Draft Notes on Eaton's Accounts

[2 July 1803]

Notes additional to those of the Secy. of state

2d. head.

<*382.52 totally inadmissible*>

51.28. we should determine whether we will keep the house in repair, alter it from time to time to the taste of the tenant. to this there is no end. we had better let the landlord keep in repair at a higher rent, & reject all occcasional alterations.

10. give credit for the horse, or reject the countervail

3.60. 6.50 1.56 .86 3.43 these are ordinary expences

10.92 4.12 19.89 7.93 60.68[1] repairs. alterations 14.57

114.57 expence for horses. 34.42 25.72

4th. head. all the articles should be explained. I do not see a single one which should be allowed primâ facie. charity is the duty of individuals & should come out of their own pocket. states allow no distributions of charity but by the act of their legislature because of the abuses it would lead to. our ministers[2] abroad are allowed no such charge.

7th. head. the articles of furniture shd. be disallowed, not accounted for. they furnish their own houses, & sell their furniture as they can.

8th. head. full explanations of every article, & affidavit

9th. head. is it possible the Bey should take duties on things imported for himself?

11th. who is Doctr. Shaw?

MS (DLC: 133:22935); undated; entirely in TJ's hand, including endorsement: "Departmt. State. Eaton's accts. July 2."

ALL THE ARTICLES SHOULD BE EXPLAINED: Madison, to Harrison on 1 July, had indicated that everything under the fourth heading was "inadmissible" (Madison, *Papers*, *Sec. of State Ser.*, 5:131).

DISALLOWED, NOT ACCOUNTED FOR: furniture charged under the seventh heading "must be accounted for," Madison had informed Harrison (same).

In 1799, Eaton paid John SHAW as vice consul and to carry dispatches to the United States. Shaw had gone to the Mediterranean as surgeon of a U.S. naval vessel (Charles Prentiss, ed., *The Life of the Late Gen. William Eaton* [Brookfield, Mass., 1813], 117-19; NDBW, 1:284, 369; Louis B. Wright and Julia H. Macleod, *The First Americans in North Africa: William Eaton's Struggle for a Vigorous Policy against the Barbary Pirates, 1799-1805* [Princeton, 1945], 58).

[1]TJ here canceled "ordinary expences."
[2]MS: "minister."

II. Notes on Eaton's Accounts

[on or after 2 July 1803]

Notes on mr Eaton's accounts, additional to those of the Secretary of state.

When we consider that this is the first of the Barbary accounts which comes to us for settlement, and that every article now allowed will be a precedent for futurity, we ought to reduce it to what is rigorously right. the rules of settlement of the accounts of our foreign ministers are generally applicable to those of the Barbary Consuls.

1st. Head. No outfit can be allowed.

the office of Consul is determined by the receipt of their recall, or by their departure. in the case of recall, a quarter's salary for their return is just: and it seems a good enough measure when they come away[1] by order of the Bey.

2d. the article of 382.52 inadmissible.

House rent. this is not allowed our foreign ministers. it therefore will be proper to consider what are the circumstances which give these consuls a better right to it.

repairs, alterations, & additions to the house, out houses &c. in my opinion totally inadmissible. as to external repairs the landlord does them every where, & the tenant the internal. as to alterations from time to time at the caprice or particular taste of the tenant, the next one will perhaps undo them, and there is no bottom to such an article of indulgence.[2] see articles 51.28/10.92/4.12/19.89/7.93 60.68/14.57.

the present in return for a present not admissible.

Carriage, mules & attendants to Bardo. are not these the ordinary expences, as are carriages &c. to Versailles, to Pardo, St. Ildefonso &c.[3] see articles 3.60/7./1.56/.86/3.43

horse & mule hire monthly forage for horses. barley field for do. } these are ordinary expences, as much as those of the table. the salary is to be employed in them.

Contingencies. a very heavy article. they should be detailed & sifted.

4th. Charities. no such article is allowed ministers, or any other public servt in a single instance. states never allow charities at the public expence, but on a special act of their legislature. charity is the duty of the individual & should be out of his own funds, as a portion of his ordinary expence. if it be allowed to give charities out of the pocket of another, the greatest abuses would follow.

7th. the houses of ministers are not furnished. they buy their own furniture, sell it as they can, & never bring it into the public account. the paiments for furniture were misapplications of the public monies, & ought to be disallowed.

8th. head. a particular explanation of every article should be given so as to enable us to have it enquired into by the successor.

MS (DLC: Madison Papers); undated, but after Document I; entirely in TJ's hand.

Madison had deemed HOUSE RENT, dragomans' pay, and contingencies to be allowable charges within the second heading of the accounts (Madison, *Papers, Sec. of State Ser.*, 5:131).

The BARDO was Hammuda's palace in Tunis (Vol. 33:591, 592n).

An estate called El PARDO outside Madrid and a palace at San ILDEFONSO in the province of Segovia were among the royal residences of the Spanish monarchs (Germán Bleiberg, ed., *Diccionario de Historia de España*, 2d ed., 3 vols. [Madrid, 1968-69], 3:560, 672, 674).

[1] TJ here canceled "without being recalled."

[2] Remainder of paragraph interlined.

[3] Remainder of paragraph interlined.

To Henri Peyroux de la Coudrèniere

DEAR SIR Washington July 3. 1803.

Since I had the pleasure of your acquaintance in Philadelphia in 1791. I had supposed you were returned to Europe. I have lately however been told that you preside at present at Ste Genevieve & St. Louis. I cannot therefore omit the satisfaction of writing to you by Capt. Lewis, an officer in our army, & for some time past my Secretary. as our former acquaintance was a mixt one of science and business, so is the occasion of renewing it. you know that the geography of the Missouri and the most convenient water communication from the head of that to the Pacific ocean is a desideratum not yet satisfied. since coming to the administration of the US. I have taken the earliest opportunity in my power to have that communication explored, and Capt. Lewis with a party of twelve or fifteen men is authorised to do it. his journey being merely literary, to inform us of the geography & natural history of the country, I have procured a passport for him & his party, from the Minister of France here, it being agreed between him & the Spanish minister, that the country having been ceded to France, her minister may most properly give the authority for the journey. this was the state of things when the passport was given, which was some time since. but before Capt. Lewis's actual departure we learn through a channel of unquestionable information that France has ceded the whole country of Louisiana to the US. by a treaty concluded in the first days of May. but for an object as innocent & useful as this I am sure you will not be scrupulous as to the authorities on which the journey is undertaken; & that you will give all the protection you can to Capt. Lewis & his party in going & returning. I have no doubt you can be particularly useful to him, and it is to sollicit your patronage that I trouble you with the present letter, praying you at the same time to accept my friendly salutations and assurances of my high respect & consideration

TH: JEFFERSON

PrC (DLC); at foot of text: "M. Peyroux Commandant of Upper Louisiana."

PLEASURE OF YOUR ACQUAINTANCE: Peyroux traveled to the United States from Upper Louisiana from 1792 to 1793 and visited Philadelphia during the trip (Vol. 29:133n).

TOLD THAT YOU PRESIDE: Peyroux was in charge of the post at Ste. Genevieve beginning in 1787, but colonial administrators transferred him to New Madrid in the late 1790s and demoted him from command there in May 1803. In St. Louis in December 1803, Meriwether Lewis gave the letter printed above to Charles Dehault Delassus, the Spanish lieutenant governor for Upper Louisiana, who sent a copy to Spanish officials in New Orleans (A. P. Nasatir, ed., *Before Lewis and Clark: Documents Illustrating the History of the Missouri, 1785-1804*, 2 vols. [St. Louis, 1952], 2:591n, 598, 719-21; Moulton, *Journals of the Lewis & Clark Expedition*, 1:5; Jackson, *Lewis and Clark*, 1:169).

From Harry Innes

D. SIR, Kentucky Frankfort July 4th. 1803

The bearer of this letter James Morrison Esqr. who is the Supervisor for the District of Ohio, being called to the City of Washington on business, & among other considerations contemplates making proposals to supply the troops stationed on the Mississippi & its branches.

Mr. Morrison deservedly stands high in the esteem of the people of this State. in saying this every thing is included which is necessary to recommend him as a gentleman of the first respectability among us & as such permit me sir, to recommend him to your acquaintance & civilities.

Mr. Morrison's place of residence & public character enables him to collect every information in the political line which may exist in this State; should you incline to make any inquiries in that way, he will answer them with pleasure, & on his representations you may implicitly rely.

With considerations of great respect, & sincere wishes for a continuence of your health & happiness

I am Dr. Sir your mo. ob. Servt. HARRY INNES

RC (DLC); at foot of text: "His Excy. Thomas Jefferson"; endorsed by TJ as received 25 July and so recorded in SJL with notation "(by mr Morrison)."

JAMES MORRISON was appointed supervisor for the district of Kentucky in 1797. TJ made him a commissioner of bankruptcy for the state in 1802 (JEP, 1:247; Vol. 37:710).

From Lafayette

My dear Sir Aulnay 4th July

On this Anniversary day of the immortal declaration of independance I am Happy of an Opportunity to Adress *You*—it is Some Consolation for My Having Been prevented, By the Remains of my Accident or rather its Cure, to Meet in paris My American fellow Citizens—inclosed You Will find the duplicate of a Letter from Madame de chastelux, and as Mine Have also Been Sent duplicate, I shall only Repeat the Expression of the High and Affectionate Regard I Have the Honore to Be With

Your old Constant friend Lafayette

RC (DLC); endorsed by TJ as received 26 Sep. and so recorded in SJL. Enclosure: Madame de Chastellux to TJ, 30 June.

To Meriwether Lewis

Washington. US. of America.
Dear Sir July 4. 1803.

In the journey which you are about to undertake for the discovery of the course and source of the Missisipi,[1] and of the most convenient water communication from thence to the Pacific ocean, your party being small,[2] it is to be expected that you will encounter considerable dangers from the Indian inhabitants.[3] should you escape those dangers and reach the Pacific ocean, you may find it imprudent to hazard a return the same way, and be forced to seek a passage round by sea, in such vessels as you may find on the Western coast. but you will be without money, without clothes, & other necessaries; as a sufficient supply cannot be carried with you from hence.[4] your resource in that case can only be in the credit of the US. for which purpose I hereby authorise you to draw on the Secretaries of State, of the Treasury, of War & of the Navy of the US. according as you may find your draughts will be most negociable, for the purpose of obtaining money or necessaries for yourself & your men: and I solemnly[5] pledge the faith of the United States that these draughts shall be[6] paid punctually at the date they are made payable. I also[7] ask of the Consuls, agents, merchants & citizens of any nation with which we have intercourse or amity to furnish you with those supplies which your necessities may call for, assuring them of honorable and prompt retribution. and our own Consuls[8] in foreign parts where you may happen to be, are hereby instructed & required to be aiding & assisting to you in whatsoever may be necessary for procuring your return back to the United States. And to give more entire satisfaction & confidence to those who may be disposed to aid you, I Thomas Jefferson, President of the United States of America, have written this letter of general credit for you with my own hand, and signed it with my name.

TH: JEFFERSON

RC (MoSHi: Clark Family Collection); at foot of text: "To Capt. Meriwether Lewis." PrC (DLC). Dft (same); date overwritten, probably "4" over "3"; unrelated financial notations by TJ on same sheet: "balance etc 4913," canceled; a notation relating to an order on John Barnes on 1 June to pay TJ's barber, Edward Frethy, $5 (MB, 2:1101; Vol. 34: 210; Vol. 36:693, 696, 697, 698); and "Daugherty," canceled. Recorded in SJL with notation "lre of credit."

[1]TJ first wrote "Missouri," then reformed it into "Missisipi." Dft: "Missouri."

[2]Here in Dft TJ canceled "you will of cou."

[3]Preceding four words interlined in Dft.

[4]In Dft TJ first wrote "it being impossible you can carry these from hence" before altering the clause to read as above.

[5]Word interlined in Dft in place of "hereby."

[6]Here in Dft TJ canceled "honorably."

[7]In Dft TJ first wrote "I hereby also invite and recommend."

[8]Here in Dft TJ canceled "within whose reach."

From Charles Murray

SIR! London 4th. July 1803.

I have the honour, by the direction of the Royal Jennerian Society for the Extermination of the Small pox, to entreat Your acceptance of the Society's Address and it's other publications.

The ardour already manifested in the United States in promoting the Vaccine Inoculation, and the progress which it has made there under Your Auspices, sufficiently evince Sir, that no inducements are wanting to engage You in this great cause of benevolence.

It cannot however but be satisfactory to You to be informed of the origin and Success of an Establishment which has received the most august Patronage in this Country, and from which, as it tends to systematize, and by every possible means encourage the diffusion of the new Practice, the greatest advantages may be expected.

With Sentiments of the highest Respect, I have the honour to be Sir! Your most devoted, and most humble Servant

CHARLES MURRAY
Secretary.

RC (ViW: Tucker-Coleman Collection); at foot of first page: "The President of the United States"; endorsed by TJ as received 5 Sep. and "Secy. of Royl

Jennerian society" and so recorded in SJL. Enclosure: *Address of the Royal Jennerian Society, for the Extermination of the Small-Pox, with the Plan, Regulations, and Instructions for Vaccine Inoculation* (London, 1803; Sowerby, No. 948).

Son of a prominent, philanthropic-minded physician and brother to another, Charles Murray (1768-1847) became a lawyer and devoted his energies to several relief organizations over the course of his life. Having developed a professional relationship with Edward Jenner, Murray became secretary to the board of directors of the Royal Jennerian Society, which sought to spread the use of cowpox vaccination in London. The Society disbanded over medical disagreements in 1809, but Murray remained close to Jenner and was named that year secretary of the Jenner-headed National Vaccine Establishment. He retained the position into the 1820s. Afterwards he became steward of a country estate near Plymouth (*Gentleman's Magazine*, new ser., 27, pt. 1 [1847], 554-6; "Report of the Select committee on the Vaccine Board, with the Minutes of Evidence, and an Appendix," London *Monthly Review*, 3d ser., 3 [1833], 437-8; Richard B. Fisher, *Edward Jenner, 1749-1823* [London, 1991], 138, 169-70, 199).

To Thomas Appleton

Sir Washington July 5. 1803.

Having occasion to have a communication made to Madame Teresa Ceracchi at Rome, & no correspondent there, I take the liberty of asking leave to do it through you. she is the widow of Ceracchi the Sculptor from Rome who lived sometime in Vienna, came over to Philadelphia, returned to Paris, there engaged in a conspiracy against the first Consul & was executed. his wife & family returned to Rome from whence I have recieved two letters painting her distresses & praying relief from Congress. she says in these that Ceracchi had been charged with the execution of a national monument to perpetuate the foundation of our republic, that he had made all his models in terra cotta, that this work was suspended, & he not paid for his labours, and she prays an indemnity from Congress. she is entirely mistaken in the facts, which were strictly as follows. Ceracchi came over to Philadelphia of his own accord, bringing letters of introduction from the Van Staphorsts of Amsterdam. his first request was that General Washington would permit him to take his bust. Genl. Washington having been fatigued by numerous applications from painters to sit for their drawing, into a determination never to sit again, it was with great difficulty he could be prevailed on to yield to Ceracchi's request. he did so at length, & an excellent bust was made of clay. he then employed himself at his lodgings in forming the model of a monument in honor of General Washington which he proposed to be employed by Congress to erect. it was a work of great genius, but so enormously beyond our habits of employing public money, that he was advised at once not to expect it, by those who best knew the American way of thinking on matters of expence. he persevered however in solliciting the members. by way of disposing them favorably he asked leave to take the busts of many of them in clay & did so. it is not improbable that some of these gentlemen from mere good nature, may have avoided damping his hopes of inducing Congress to engage him in the work, but there were others who constantly & carefully warned him against the delusion. but not being able to persuade himself of the truth he brought over his family. this involved him in deep expence. his finances began to fail and [his?] hopes. despair drove him almost to insanity. he quitted the country abruptly [in] the highest disgust, leaving debts to a considerable amount, and giving his creditors orders on 4. or 5. particular individuals whose busts or medallions he had [made] in marble or Alabaster, and had sent to them unsolicited as presents. paiments however were made for these to his creditors: and so ended his visit [to this] country. nothing like an engagement, nor nothing like an intention to employ him ever was entered into by any public authority: and under these circumstances it is impossible that Congress should make any allowance. [th]is is the true state of facts. it is proper she should understand it, that she may not be kept under ill-founded hopes. it is not proper for me however [to] engage in this correspondence; & I have therefore thought I might ask of you [to] write to her, and to say that the above is known here to be a true statement [of] facts, & that therefore your government cannot think themselves justifiable [in] granting her the relief she desires.

I think Ceracchi took as many as 20. busts of members, but most of them [...] obscure. whether he destroyed them when he got angry, I do not know. it is [hardly] probable he took the trouble of carrying or sending them to Rome. if he did, they [...] be of no value to his family, as the names are unknown there, and perhaps it might [...] some relief to them to convert them into money at some price. I learn that a bust [in] plaister is taken at Rome for about 1½ or 2 guineas. if the converting them into money at that price would be a relief to them, I would take the busts, & give [them] the money. yet I would not have them purchased in my name lest [the] family should mistake my motive. perhaps you may have some acquaintance in Rome who could enquire first whether such busts exist, and next whether they can be bought for that price. I know they have the bust in clay of Genl. Washington. I should be willing to give 10. or 15 guineas for that, which is 6. or 8 [times] the price at Rome.

Supposing that you are connected in commerce with some house in America to whom paiment could be made for you for the preceding object or [. . .] other, I would ask the favor of you, if that be the case, to send me one or two gross of the best Florence wine. I think the Montepulciano is generally deemed the best. if addressed to any port from New York to Norfolk inclusive, to the care of the collector of the customs of the place, it will be forwarded safely to me; and I imagine there must be vessels coming sometimes from Florence to that part of the United States. I am not much acquainted with the Montepulciano, (which is meant here by the term of Florence wine;) but I know it is not a sweet wine. these (sweet wines) you know are not esteemed in America.

Mr. Lear took leave yesterday, on his departure for Boston, where he goes in the Constitution frigate, bound to the Mediterranean, as Consul general at Algiers, in place of mr Obrien who has resigned. the Philadelphia will also sail in a few days for the same destination, and will be followed by two or three 16. gun vessels. Accept my salutations and assurances of esteem. TH: JEFFERSON

PrC (DLC); some text lost at edge of page; at foot of first page: "Thomas Appleton esq." Enclosed in TJ to George W. Erving, 10 July.

The TWO LETTERS from Therese Ceracchi were dated 3 and 21 Dec. 1802.

As Madison noted in instructions dated 14 July, the position that Tobias LEAR was to occupy at Algiers was CONSUL GENERAL rather than consul. Algiers had "influence" over Tunis and Tripoli, Madison explained, and Algiers also required the largest share of American expenditures. The consuls for Tripoli and Tunis were to report to the consul general as well as to the State Department. "In all cases of difficulty and urgency," Madison instructed, "they are to ask and follow your opinion, especially when the state of our affairs may require immediate decision" (Madison, *Papers*, *Sec. of State Ser.*, 5:175-9).

To Christopher Ellery

DEAR SIR Washington July 5. 03.

I must revoke my letter of the 2d. inst. mr Gallatin informs me the transfer of the office of Supervisor cannot wait, and that it will be much more proper to add it to the Marshal's office, because he is already possessed of the principal materials for finishing it, which would cost much time, trouble & expence to any other. you will therefore be so good as to consider this only as a proof of my wish to do justice to Newport, which cannot take place in the present instance.

I congratulate you on the better issue of our mode of warfare for N. Orleans & Louisiana than would have ensued mr Ross's plan. Salutations & esteem. TH: JEFFERSON

RC (NN); addressed: "The honble Christopher Ellery Newport R.I."; franked and postmarked. PrC (DLC); endorsed by TJ in ink on verso.

GALLATIN INFORMS ME: see Gallatin to TJ, 5 July 1803.

From Albert Gallatin

DEAR SIR Tuesday [5 July 1803]

If you have no objection, I would prefer transferring the Supervisor's duties in Rhode Island to the Marshal rather than to the naval officer of Newport.

Please to let me know as the other arrangements are made—

With respect Your obt. Servt. ALBERT GALLATIN

RC (DLC); partially dated; at foot of text: "The President"; endorsed by TJ as a letter of 5 July from the Treasury Department received the same day and so recorded in SJL with notation "supervisor R.I."; also endorsed by TJ: "Supervisorship R.I. added to Marshal."

The SUPERVISOR'S DUTIES were transferred to William Peck, whom TJ had reappointed marshal in December 1802 (Gallatin, *Papers*, 9:50-1; TJ to the Senate, 15 Dec. 1802).

To Thomas Mann Randolph

DEAR SIR Washington July 5. 1803.

On the evening of the 3d inst. we recieved a letter from mr King (arrived at N. York) covering one from Livingston & Monroe to him in which they informed him that on the 30th. of April they signed a treaty with France, ceding to us the island of N. Orleans and all Louisiana as it had been held by Spain. the price is not mentioned. we are in hourly expectation of the treaty by a special messenger. Spain has latterly divided the province of Louisiana from N. Mexico by the river Mexicana, from the head of which the line gains the highlands encircling the waters running into the Missisipi; and altho' we do not suppose it defined far North, yet we expect to make those high lands round the head of the Missouri to that of the Missisipi the boundary of this new acquisition with Spain & Gr. Britain. it is something larger than the whole US. probably containing 500 millions of acres, the US. containing 434. millions. this removes from us the greatest source of danger to our peace.

I am very thankful that you mention to me with frankness the situation of your affairs, because as soon as it can be in my power I should share them with you as far as I could, as my feelings entirely identify my own concerns & those of my family. my great object at present is, within the course of my present term of office to get compleatly thro' the old debts of mr Wayles's estate & my own. I hope I shall do it by the aid of this & the next years crop, & what sparings I can put by from my salary, tho' they are very small. perhaps the accomplishment of this may run a year into a second term of office. whenever it is effected I should be in a condition to aid you, which renders it interesting to obtain from mr Wickham as long instalments as possible. tho' as respects the Hendersons the purchase of their lands is nearly all paid, yet is there not one dollar of it actually paid by me, as I am in arrears the whole amount of it to mr Barnes, who happened to be retiring from commerce & able to let his capital lie in my hands a little while. I have to work up therefore against this as well as the old arrearages. and it is quite as much as I can hope, if by the end of my second term of office (which will certainly be my last) I can see all of us out of debt, and my mill & farms in such a state as to supply the expences of living to which the course of my political life will expose me I fear unavoidably. if March 1809. can see me in that condition all my desires will be crowned with contentment to myself, and I hope to leave the public circumstances so much improved from what they were in March 1801. as to carry into retirement the contentment of the public.

Mr. & mrs Peter Carr are now here, and will probably set out on the 7th. and be with you the 9th. or 10th. if they go the lower side of the mountain. Sam is here also, & is to set out at the same time. but I doubt it, as his children are not very well & himself I think not decided. Peter is well, but weak. I fix on the 25th. for my own departure. but the expected arrival of the treaty, of Genl. Bernardotte, & of mr Merry, & arrangements which these may call for, may detain me. yet I shall not be detained easily, as the sickly season will then be on. my tenderest love to my dear Martha, kisses to the young ones, & affectionate attachment to yourself. TH: JEFFERSON

P.S. Capt. Lewis set out on his journey to-day.

RC (DLC); at foot of first page: "T M Randolph"; endorsed by Randolph as received 8 July. PrC (MHi); endorsed by TJ in ink on verso.

RIVER MEXICANA: properly, the Neches River in present-day Texas, although TJ was likely referring to the Sabine River, which was frequently confused with the

Neches (Jedidiah Morse, *The American Gazetteer* [Boston, 1797], s.v., "Mexicano River"; Ron Tyler, ed., *The New Handbook of Texas*, 6 vols. [Austin, Tex., 1996], 4:966-7; TJ to Alexander von Humboldt, 9 June 1804).

Randolph may have discussed his financial SITUATION in a letter of 27 June, recorded in SJL as received 29 June but not found.

From Jonathan Williams

SIR West Point July 5. 1803.

I beg you to excuse one more intrusion relative to my late Station as Lt Col Comdt of Engineers, and the circumstances that caused my Resignation. I am impelled to it from having seen, with equal concern & surprize, a Letter from the Secretary of War to Capt Barron date June 21 (of which you have a Copy inclosed) stating that the reason of my Resignation was "the adherence to the principle *adopted* relative to the question of military command." This Letter, taken in all its parts, proves to me that I have been misunderstood in all that I have said or written upon this Subject, for the Secretary could not otherwise ascribe to me a motive for action, so diametrically opposite to the true one, and his Letter equally proves that my Report of 14th Decemr and the points I put into his hands in April last have not had the good fortune to excite sufficient attention, or that I have not expressed myself intelligibly: As perspicuity is not always the attendant of sensibility, I will suppose the latter.—

I would beg leave Sir to ask the Secretary of War where this *adopted* principle is to be found, and, if it ever has been, when it was promulgated to the Army: Untill I read the Secretary's Letter of the 21st I was ignorant of any new principle, so adopted, respecting the Relation the Corps of Engineers have to the rest of the Army; and I am at this moment ignorant of its nature & extent. There is no such principle in the Law establishing the Corps, on the contrary the Law has stationed the Corps of Engineers at West Point and totally annihilated[1] any other Command of that Territory; the Law also equalises the Rank Pay & Emoluments of the Officers of the Corps with those of the rest of the Army; The Commissions of the Officers of the Engineers are also in the same Words; (enjoining all subordinate officers to obey them) they are under the signature of the President & stamped with the Seal of the War Office; in precisely the same manner that the Commissions of the other Officers of the Army are signed and sealed; those Officers of Engineers who have been transfered from the Artillery, have their Rank expressly taken from the date of the old Commissions; and if anything were wanting to show the precise similarity in the nature of their Authoritys, the Orders to Engineers, & the annunciations of all appointments in the Corps, come from the Office of the Inspector of the Army; & all muster Rolls are transmitted regularly to him, in common with every other military proceeding connected with the War Office.

Since the passing of the Law, no alteration of the principles so established has to my knowledge appeared, and indeed it is difficult to conceive how any such alteration could take place without a new Act of Congress on the Subject.

The Secretary is pleased to state as the Cause of the principle said to be adopted, that it has been considered "incompatible with the duties of the Gentlemen of the Corps of Engineers to have any military command given to the *members* of the Corps over the Troops *in any of the Regiments*." I have never, to my recollection, asked for *Regimental Command* for the *members* of the Corps of Engineers; such an Idea has never occurred to me, and indeed I should be the first to complain if the *members* of the Corps of Engineers had been ordered on regimental Duty, which regimental command implies. The Point No 1 so far as it relates to the member of the Corps individually embraces the principle of military honour & respect; no question of command can occur except an Officer of Engineer at his proper Post or Station, is superior to all other Officers at the same Post or Station; in that case he must command or be commanded; there is no middle line in this respect, except when an Officer is considered as passing or sojourning without being at his Station; he would not in that case interfere in anything relating to either Post or Troops: The question as it relates to the Engineers is more to avoid being commanded by an inferior, than a desire to command at all.—

If there can remain a doubt whether a superior Officer of Engineers ought to command a Post or not, permit me to refer to the Custom of that Nation where such a Corps originated, and where it has been carried to perfection. It will there be found that Engineers have conducted Seiges as Commanders in chief, have defended beseiged Places as Commanders in chief, and Engineers have generally been chosen as Governors of Citadels; but I beleive the military annals of France will furnish no Instance where an Officer of Engineers has been commanded by an inferior Officer of any military Corps. It would indeed be an absurdity in military Ideas, to suppose an officer who by profession is capable to erect a Work or fortify a Camp, at the same time incapable of directing the attack or defense of either.—The true progress of military Science, as it relates to the professions of different Corps, seems to be this; An Officer of Infantry ought to be a compleat master of military tactics; An Officer of Artillery should add to that knowledge that of[2] the composition & combination of every species of military fire work, with the principles & practice of every species of military projectiles; While an Engineer should in addition to all that the preceding officers are acquainted with, be Master of the art of Fortification, of every system of attack & defense, and with almost every branch of Physics; for in some way or other his profession embraces almost the whole: This Picture does not surely place the Engineer below the other parts of the Army, and he claims no Superiority.

The Secretary has been pleased to say that "the adoption of his Principle is in strict conformity with the general practice during the revolutionary War" I confess, Sir, that it appears to me more accurate to say, that untill the Establishment of the present Government, we never had a Corps of Engineers, properly so called; for during our revolutionary contest the Engineers we had were foreign Officers engaged for specific purposes; these officers were always so placed as to have constantly a superior Officer at their Posts: Indeed it was not the Policy of the Revolution to have foreign officers in chief command of Posts. The distinction between regimental & Post Command appears to me this; the first relates wholly to the men, the second to the Territory; the moment an elder or superior officer takes command of the Post, he quits his regimental command. When I was at Wilkinsonville on the Ohio with the 2d & 4th. Regiments of Infantry & 2 Companys of Artillery, the Infantry commanded by Cols Strong & Butler, & the Artillery by myself; Col. Strong commanded the Post, & the command of his Regiment instantly devolved on Major Buel. Col Strong interfered with neither of us, tho' he command us all; in like manner, Sir, if a Battalion was placed at West Point, I should not meddle with the interior command of that Body of men; but I should expect the major commanding it, to report himself to me & take my Orders for everything relating to the Territory. If this were not the case, the contrary would follow, for two independant military commands at the same time, in the same place, appears to me impossible.

It was in this way that I endeavoured to conform to certain regulations which were proposed by the Secretary of War, by way of Experiment for this Post, and while I stiled myself Comdt. of Engineers I endeavoured to preserve entire the command of the Men to the Regimental officer, stiling him Commander of Troops; But these regulations were soon trodden down by the Artillery stationed here, The officer calling himself Commanding officer of the Garrison, al-

though there is no Garrison here, the Fort being in ruin & uninhabitable, & although both officers & men were occupying Territory placed under my Command by act of Congress.
In my last, I stated the reversed propositions of the Points inclosed, & I am confident that the more you consider them, the more you will think my Statement correct; The practice might not go to the full extent mentioned, but the principle, and the power of execution undeniably would.

I have not Sir the vain affectation of saying that I voluntarily resigned my Commission, On the contrary, I avow it to be done with regret, & so the resignation itself expressed.—I have been forced from service, by the painfull conviction that it was, under all circumstances dishonourable to remain; but it was not only a duty to myself that induced the determination, it was also a duty to my Brother Officer Major Wadsworth; four out of five of the Points were made by him, & he left me with a declaration upon honour that if these our legal & just Rights were not granted to us, he would resign his commission; how then Sir could I as chief hold a command upon terms which the officer next in command thought so dishonourable especially as we have no difference in opinion on the Subject. Now Sir that I have explained my motives in a manner not to be misunderstood, I shall go into private Life with that complacency which always attends conscious rectitude.

I have the honour to be with the most perfect deference & respect Your much obliged and most Faithfull Servant

JONA. WILLIAMS

RC (PHi); at foot of text: "The President of the United States"; endorsed by TJ as received 9 July and so recorded in SJL. Enclosure: Henry Dearborn to William A. Barron, 21 June 1803, informing Barron of Williams's resignation and placing direction of the military academy at West Point under him during the absence of Major Decius Wadsworth; Dearborn states that the reason for Williams's unexpected decision was "the adherence to the principle adopted, relative to the question of Military Command" and explains that officers in the Corps of Engineers have not been given command over troops in any of the regiments because it has not been considered compatible with their duties or with the "views of Government in the establishment of the Corps"; Dearborn sees no inconvenience resulting from the adoption of this principle, which has been "in strict conformity with the general practice during our Revolutionary War & in the present Corps from its establishment" (FC in Lb in DNA: RG 107, LSMA).

[1] Word interlined.
[2] Preceding two words interlined.

From Albert Gallatin

Sir

Treasury Department
July 6th: 1803.

I have the honor to submit to your consideration, the draft of a circular to the collectors of customs which has been prepared on the suggestion of the Secretary of State; and will be transmitted if it shall receive your approbation.

I have the honor to be, very respectfully, Sir, Your obed. Servant

Albert Gallatin

RC (DLC); in a clerk's hand, signed by Gallatin; at foot of text: "The President of the United States"; endorsed by TJ as received from the Treasury Department on 6 July and "Circular on roll of Citizen seamen" and so recorded in SJL. Enclosure: Dft of circular not found, but see below.

Gallatin sent a printed circular to the collectors of customs dated 6 July with instructions for carrying out the first section of the 28 Feb. 1803 act for the "further protection of American seamen," which called for masters of vessels bound for foreign ports to provide collectors with a list of persons on their ship. The Treasury Department requested that the list include a column for the seamen composing the crew along with the country of citizenship. After the collector received adequate evidence of citizenship, he provided the seamen with individual certificates "commonly called a protection." Under the new instructions, the collector certified and returned the general list of seaman provided by the master, along with a certified list of those who were citizens of the United States. The master presented the certificate to the consul at the port of delivery. Gallatin stated that the certified list of U.S. citizens would prove beneficial to the seamen in cases of impressment because "a general certificate not being liable to frauds arising from improper transfers" would have a higher degree of credit than single certificates, and seamen would not bear the "risks arising from those certificates being lost, or taken from them." It would put them "more immediately under the care and protection of the Consuls and Agents of the United States abroad" (Gallatin, *Papers*, 8:515; U.S. Statutes at Large, 2:203).

From Mary Heator

Honorable Sir

City Washington July 6th 1803

My present Situation oblidges me to Write these few lines to you hopeing your Honour will be so kind and so Considerate as to help me in my Distressed Situation. My Husband now Deceased, was in the Service for Some time. He was a Serjint. his name was Heator. I am Quiet Destitute and my little Effects are appraised and to be Sold for Rent. without your Honour be so kind as to help me in my present Distress. I have a family of Young Helpless Children and I hope you will consider them and Grant me some present Assistance And I in duty Bound will Ever pray—

Mary Heator

RC (MHi); endorsed by TJ as received 6 July and so recorded in SJL.

To James Madison and Family

Th: Jefferson requests the favour of *Mr. Madison & family* to dine with him —— at half after three.

Wednesday July [6] *1803.*[1]

Many thanks to mrs Madison for the trouble she has been so good as to take.

The favour of an answer is asked.[2]

RC (Charles M. Storey, Boston, Massachusetts, 1958); printed form, with blanks filled by TJ reproduced in italics; damaged.

[1] Date illegible on RC but TJ left Washington on 19 July and the previous Wednesdays that month were 6 and 13 July.

[2] Preceding sentence, part of printed form, canceled, probably by TJ.

From Robert Smith

Navy dept.
July 6. 1803

SIR,

I have the honor to enclose 12 blank commissions to which your Signature is requested.—

They are wanted for Officers who have been heretofore appointed but not properly commissioned, their appointments having been made out on blank warrants.—

With high respect, I am Sir, yr mo: ob: Servt. RT SMITH

RC (DLC); in a clerk's hand, signed by Smith; at foot of text: "The President of the U. States"; endorsed by TJ as received from the Navy Department on 6 July and "blank commns." and so recorded in SJL. FC (Lb in DNA: RG 45, LSP).

From Robert Smith

Navy dept.
July 6. 1803

SIR,

I have the honor to present for your approbation as Midshipmen in the Navy,

Gilbert H. Smith	recommended by Judge Kilty & others—
Francis B. Whiting.—	John Smith Esqr. Va.
Dl. P. Ramsey—	Mr. Strode—
Chs. Jones—	Mr. Merriweather Jones thro' Mr. Madison.—

If you approve the above nominations, the enclosed warrants will require your signature.—

With high respect, I am Sir, yr mo: ob Servt. RT SMITH

RC (DLC); in a clerk's hand, signed by Smith; at foot of text: "The President"; endorsed by TJ as received from the Navy Department on 6 July and "<*Warnts.*> Midshipmen" and so recorded in SJL. FC (Lb in DNA: RG 45, LSP).

On 6 July, Smith forwarded Gilbert H. SMITH, Francis B. WHITING, Daniel P. RAMSEY, and Charles JONES their warrants as midshipmen in the U.S. Navy (FC in Lb in DNA: RG 45, LSO).

To John Strode

DEAR SIR Washington July 6. 1803.

I recieved last night your friendly letter of June 26. and am always happy to learn that my fellow citizens approve of the course which is pursued in their affairs. I trust that such of the late advocates for war as did not expect to get commissions & offices, will now join with us in rejoicing that their clamours & calumnies of the day did not move us out of our course. whether after a long, bloody & expensive war we should have been able to retain New-Orleans would have depended on the final success of the war. we have by pursuing the ways of peace & reason, obtained immediately & permanently, besides the island of N. Orleans, the whole country of Louisiana, including all the Western waters of the Missisipi & Missouri, larger in extent than the whole united states & equal to them in soil & climate. and, altho' I do not yet know the sum we are to pay, yet I am sure it is less than one year's expence of war. so ends the chapter of the 2. millions of dollars put into my private pocket, but every dollar of which has been paid down on the nail for this purchase.

I expect to leave this on the 25th. and shall certainly have the pleasure of being with you the 26th. unless I should be detained by unforeseen emergencies arising out of our late treaty, or the war of Europe. but I shall not for a slight cause be induced to run further into the sickly season here, than the date abovementioned. with respectful salutations to yourself & family, accept assurances of my friendly esteem. TH: JEFFERSON

PrC (DLC); at foot of text in ink: "Mr. Strode."

From Benjamin Austin, Jr.

Honored Sir Boston July 7th 1803

Your much esteem'd Letter of the 28th Utimo, I acknowledge with every sentiment of respect. when the Volume, of which you are pleas'd to express your approbation, was sent you, I did not feel myself at liberty to present it with an immediate Communication, but requested the Honorable Secretary at War to introduce it to your notice in such a mode as He thought most agreable.

The politicks of this Country have for many Years been so serious & important, that they could not but arrest the attention of every Citizen who felt interested to realize the blessings anticipated by the adoption of the Federal Constitution.—It would be presumption in me to retrace the ground for your consideration, but permit me Sir to say, (without the detestable crime of flattery) that the change of the administration has been, under God, our only salvation.—

Your various occupations, especially at *this Crizis*, must peculiarly arrest your Official attention, I can therefore only express my wishes, as a Citizen, that the measures of government under your patronage, may continue to promote the happiness, & Independance of the United States, & that your Enemies may always, as they are at present, be confounded by the wisdom & integrity of your Conduct.—

Any Services which I can render my time will be readily devoted to their accomplishment.—

As you have been pleas'd to read the publications of Old South, I should feel myself under equal Obligations, if you would peruse the *Examiner* in the Chronicle.—

please Sir, to make my respects to Mr. Maddison, & Mr. Gallatine, & such other republican friends as are honor'd with your attention & confidence.—

I am Honored Sir with the highest Sentiments of respect, & with the fullest confidence in your Administration Your Friend, & fellow Citizen Benj. Austin Jr.

PS—As Letters sometimes fail, a bare acknowlegement of the receipt will be agreable.—

RC (DLC); at foot of text: "The President of the United States"; endorsed by TJ as received 15 July and so recorded in SJL.

THE VOLUME: Austin's *Constitutional Republicanism, in Opposition to Fallacious Federalism.*

THE EXAMINER: on 6 June, the Boston *Independent Chronicle* commenced publishing a series of essays under the heading "The Examiner," which were highly critical of Federalism and staunchly defended Republican principles and TJ's administration. Five installments appeared by the end of the month and new contributions were published with regularity throughout the remainder of TJ's presidency, totaling more than eighty installments by early 1808 (*Independent Chronicle*, 6, 9, 16, 23, 30 June 1803, 14 Jan. 1808).

Statement of Account with William Duane, with Jefferson's Order

President of the United States

1802				To William Duane Dr.	
Jany	4	To	1	Glass Inkstand	1
	23	"	1	Box Chessmen & Board	6
	"	"	1	Ream fine English 4to. post paper	7
	"	"	1	paper Red Inkpowder	25
	"	"	1	Marble Note presser	1
	"	"	2	Dozen Middletons pencils	3 50
	"	"	100	Best Quills No 4	4
	"	"	6	Tooth Brushes	75
Feby	3	"	1	Bottle Red Ink	31
	13	"	2	Wedgewood Inkstands	2
	"	"	1	Ream Invitations 2 on a sheet 4to. post	20
Apl.	14	"	1	Bottle Copying Ink	37¼
	22	"	1	Ream Writing Demy	10
	"	"	1	Ream wove 4to. post	6
May	3	"	1	Dressing Case	4 50
Octor	6	"	6	Quires Hotpress'd 4to. post	2 04
	20	"	1	lb. Best Glazed Wafers	2 50
	"	"	1	Ream Hotpress'd 4to. post	7
	"	"	1	Bottle Copying Ink	37¼
Decr.	13	"	1	Copy Precie's Historiqué	1
	20	"	1	Ream Invitations 2 on a sheet 4to. post	20
1803					
Jany	13	"	1	Ream Hotpress'd 4to. post	7
Feby	12	"	1	Nautical Almanac	75
	17	"	1	Copy Boyers French Grammar	1 25
	19	"	2	Nautical Almanacs for 1804-5	2 80
	24	"	1	Copy New Census	75
	"	"	1	Copy Old Census	75
	"	"	1	Copy letter to Th Jefferson	37¼
	"	"	1	Copy letter to Alexr. Hamilton	37¼
Mar	5	"	1	Copy Requisite Tables	3
	"	"	1	Copy Perins French Grammar	1
					$117 65

1803			Amt. Brought forwd.	$117 65
Apr.	6	To	1 Quire folio post got By his Coach Man	50
	19	To	4 Metal Thermomaters @ $6	24
	25	"	2 Reams Copying paper	10
	"	"	2 Bottles Copying Ink	1
May	6	"	600 Invitations	15
	10	"	2 Reams Hotpress'd 4to. post	14
	"	"	1 Copy Ossians poems 2 Vo.	2 50
	"	"	1 Copy History Christianity 2 Vo. 8vo.	5 50
	16	"	½ Ream thin folio post	5 50
June	9	"	1 Ream wove English 4to. post	6
July	5	"	1 Mag N. America	7
	"	"	1 Set Annual Biography 3 Vo. 8vo.	9 75
	"	"	1 Set Voyage En Grece	6
	"	"	1 Set Femeal Biography 6 Vo.	13 50
	7	"	200 Dutch Quills	7
				$244 90

Crt.

1802	Jany 27 By Cash	$22.50	By J Barnes	
	Mar 8 By Cash	25.31		
1802	May 6 By Cash	28.87½		76 86½
			Balance due	$ 168 03½

[*Order by TJ*:]

Sep. 29. 1803

Mr Barnes will be pleased to pay the above

TH: JEFFERSON

MS (CSmH); in a clerk's hand; with receipt below TJ's order in Kean's hand and signed by him: "[Recd] payment in full By the hands of Mr John Barnes this 29th day of Sept. 1803"; faint; endorsed by TJ: "Duane Wm. Sep. 1803"; endorsed at foot of text by John Barnes as paid 29 Sep.

MIDDLETONS PENCILS: the black lead pencils produced in London by John Middleton were frequently advertised for sale in American newspapers (Henry Petroski, *The Pencil: A History of Design and Circumstance* [New York, 1990], 5, 127; *Gazette of the United States*, 27 Mch. 1802; New York *Evening Post*, 24 Nov. 1802).

PRECIE'S HISTORIQUÉ: probably Jean Nicholas Berthe, *Précis Historique de la Maladie qui a Régné dans l'Andalousie en 1800* (Paris, 1802; Sowerby, No. 921).

BOYERS FRENCH GRAMMAR: probably Abel Boyer, *The Compleat French Master for Ladies and Gentlemen*, which enjoyed wide popularity and numerous reprintings since its initial publication in 1694 (DNB, s.v. "Boyer, Abel").

In 1802, Duane published editions of the NEW CENSUS of the United States of 1800 and the OLD CENSUS of 1790 (Sowerby, Nos. 3288, 3289).

LETTER TO TH JEFFERSON: Junius Philænus, *A Letter to Thomas Jefferson, President of the United States* (New York, 1802).

LETTER TO ALEXR HAMILTON: Tom Callender, *Letters to Alexander Hamilton, King of the Feds. Ci-Devant Secretary of the Treasury of the United States of America, Inspector-General of the Standing Armies Thereof, Counsellor at Law. &c. &c. &c.* (New York, 1802; Sowerby, No. 3279).

REQUISITE TABLES: Nevil Maskelyne, *Tables Requisite to be used with the Nautical Ephemeris for finding the Latitude and Longitude at Sea* (London, 1781; Sowerby, No. 3811).

PERINS FRENCH GRAMMAR: possibly *A Grammar of the French Tongue, Grounded Upon the Decisions of the French Academy*, one of several popular educational works on the French language by John Perrin of Dublin (Shaw-Shoemaker, No. 7030; DNB, s.v. "Perrin, Jean Baptiste").

HISTORY CHRISTIANITY: probably Joseph Priestley, *An History of the Corruptions of Christianity*, published in two octavo volumes (Sowerby, No. 1526; TJ to Mary Jefferson Eppes, 25 Apr. 1803).

MAG N. AMERICA: most likely, this entry meant to record the purchase of a map of North America. TJ also purchased one about the same time from James Cheetham (see TJ to Cheetham, 17 June 1803, and Charles Ludlow to TJ, 24 June 1803).

ANNUAL BIOGRAPHY probably refers to William Bingley, *Animal Biography; or, Anecdotes of the Lives, Manners, and Economy, of the Animal Creation, Arranged According to the System of Linnæus*, 3 vols. (London, 1803). The female ("femeal") BIOGRAPHY is probably Mary Hays, *Female Biography; or, Memoirs of Illustrious and Celebrated Women, of All Ages and Countries*, 6 vols. (London, 1803). Advertisements for both new works appeared in Philadelphia newspapers in June 1803, about the time TJ purchased them from Duane (*Poulson's American Daily Advertiser*, 7 June 1803; *Gazette of the United States*, 24 June 1803).

MAY 6 BY CASH: this payment was not recorded in TJ's financial records. To arrive at the total of \$76.86½, this amount should be \$29.05½. For the cash entries of \$22.50 and \$25.31, see MB, 2:1064, 1065. For TJ's final payment of \$168.035, see MB, 2:1109.

From Horatio Gates

DEAR SIR Rose Hill 7th: July, 1803:

From my Heart I congratulate your Excellency, upon the Glorious success of The Embassy you sent to France, it must [. . .]ly strike the Mind of every true Friend to Freedom in the United States, as the Greatest, & most Beneficial Event, that has taken place since the Declaration of Independence. The Fame of Your Political Wisdom is now so permanently Establish'd, that it is past the power of a disappointed Faction, ever to Diminish it. Proceed my Noble Friend in the Steady Course you have invariably Pursu'd; & your Presidency will be as long as you incline to make it. Your Enemies may hide Themselves, and Their Arrogance together, an insulted Country whom they wish'd to Tyrrannize, will no longer be deceived by their Intrigues: I am astonished when I see so great a Business Finish'd, which but a few Months since we whispered to one another about; it has the Air of Inchantment!—presently a New Field will open to your View, New Orleans will be to be taken Possession of, & all Military, & Civil Officers, to be appointed; it is of Importance who you fix upon for the First Station in that City; what do you think of Colonel Smith Ci devant Aid to Gen: Washington; Son in Law to your Predecessor; He has Dignity Sufficient to suit the Spaniard; Military Character, and Tactical Abillities exactly to suit the Frenchman; he has an Establish'd Credit for Thirty Thousand Dollars upon the Debt agreed to be Liquidated by The Treaty; & also a good Office in the Customs here, which will be Vacated by His appointment to be Governour of New Orleans.—Your recommendation of Him to the Senate, will shew you so superior to any petty resentment against his Father in Law, that the World will admire it!

You have Indulged me in this Freedom, and as my Sole motive is your Fame, you will continue that Indulgence. all I ask is your Friendly acknowlegement of this Letter. in return, I will only Tresspass upon your invaluable Time when I think the Subject worthy the doing it. with the Sincerest Sentiments of Esteem & Affection I am

Your Excellencys most Faithfull Friend & Obedient Servant

HORATIO GATES

P.S.

Mrs. Gates presents You Her Compliments.—

RC (DLC); torn; endorsed by TJ as received 9 July and so recorded in SJL.

William Stephens SMITH, John and Abigail Adams's son-in-law, was surveyor and inspector of customs at New York City (Vol. 35:235-8).

AN ESTABLISH'D CREDIT: Smith had invested in ships that were lost to privateers in the 1790s. Gates probably saw reports that American claims against France were to be settled as part of the purchase agreement for Louisiana (ANB; New York *Daily Advertiser*, 4 July).

From Jared Mansfield

SIR, West-Point July 7th. 1803

After I had the honor of my last interview with you at Washington, I repaired to the Secretary of the treasury's Office; In conversation with him on the subject of allowing my account of travelling expences to the seat of government, I found, that he considered himself unauthorized by the law to advance any money, or pay for any expenses which may arise, except that of instruments; & even this, it would appear, was not to be made in advance. At that time I considered my Own personal property as abundantly sufficient to set me forward, even if every expence incident to the business should be derived from it. Accordingly since my arrival in these parts, I have assiduously endeavoured from my own means to prepare for the business, to which you have thought proper to appoint me. I am sorry that circumstances do not afford me much prospect of success, unless aided by something in advance. The expence of travelling with a family must be considerable, & the expence of the instruments more serious. These cannot be procured without money in hand. The credit of the U. States, even If I were authorized to pledge it would not Answer.

I confess, Sir, that I was not sufficiently apprized, while at Washington of these difficulties, otherwise I should have represented them to you in person—I am of opinion however, that you will condescend to enquire into every thing admissible for this service, & that you will grant me every indulgence, consistent with the duties of your high station.

If I am to embark in this undertaking, it is necessary that the instruments be in a state of preparation, particularly those, which it may require time to adjust, as I should by no means risque my own reputation & the honor of the country on those which might be imperfect & inaccurate.

In making this address, I beg to be understood, not as asking any thing extraordinary from the pay allowed by Law, but merely by way of advance, that I may be enabled to procure what is indispensable for such a new employment. I should neither expect, nor desire any emoluments beyond my salary; but advances must be made for the instruments, & they may be made with equal propriety for any other object connected with the service, especially when on account for services past or to come.—

I am sorry to have troubled you thus much on this subject. I feel too sensibly the honor intended me, by your invitation to accept of an office more lucrative, & better suited to my Genius than perhaps any other in the U. States, to admit for a moment any idea of intrusion, or trespassing on your time. It appeared to me necessary that you should be informed of the circumstances relative to this business, both as the fittest judge of what would be proper & right to be pursued, & the only One who can obviate the difficulties which are Opposed to subordinate Officers. I am

Sir, with the sincerest attachment Yours Obet Humbe Servt

JARED MANSFIELD

RC (DLC); endorsed by TJ as received 12 July and so recorded in SJL.

For Mansfield's CONVERSATION with Albert Gallatin and the subject of his EXPENCES relating to his appointment as surveyor general, see TJ to Mansfield, 21 May 1803 and TJ to Gallatin, [7 June 1803].

From John Thomson Mason

Dear Sir George Town 7th July 1803

Since I had last the pleasure to see you I have revolved in my mind the subject we then conversed on, towit the vacancy which Mr Marshall ought and probably would shortly make by his resignation. No man can be generally known as a man eminent in the law unless it be by his success as a practitioner, and it is to be apprehended that a man thus situated would scarcely be prevailed on to accept that office. Indeed it has always been subject of surprize to me that these offices are as well filled as they are in this Country. I then took the liberty to explain to you the propriety indeed necessity that one Judge should reside in Alexandria, this circumstance will I have no doubt increase the difficulty. You will I hope excuse the liberty I take at this time in naming to you a Gentleman who would I have no doubt be pleased with the appointment should you not be able to find one willing to accept and better quallified to fill the office. It is Mr Nicholas Fitzhugh of Fairfax County. He is a man firm and decided in his political principles which are truly republican. He was bred to the law, and tho' not very earnestly he has always practised it in the County in which he lives. He was a contempory of mine at Wm & Mary and is I think a sound lawyer and a man of good sense. He is a man of as nice honor and strict integrety as lives.

It is my duty however to state that he never was thought eminent at the bar, he has no talent for public speaking, indeed he is not by any means fitted for the practice of the law

He has been several years a member of the Virga Legislature and is much respected by those who know him

With sentiments of high respect I have the Honor to be your Obedt Servt John T. Mason

RC (DNA: RG 59, LAR); endorsed by TJ as received 9 July and "Fitzhugh Nichs. to be judge of Columbia" and so recorded in SJL.

James M. Marshall, appointed by Adams during the last days of his presidency, did not officially submit his resignation as judge of the circuit court for the District of Columbia until 16 Nov., when he wrote Madison that it was no longer convenient for him to perform the duties. Marshall was establishing a law practice in Winchester, Virginia (RC in DNA: RG 59, RD, endorsed by TJ: "Marshall James to mr Madison. resigns as judge of Columbia"; DAB; Vol. 33: 52n). For the appointment of Nicholas Fitzhugh, see his letter to TJ of 22 Aug. and TJ to the Senate, 21 Nov. 1803.

From Caesar A. Rodney

Honored & Dear Sir, Wilmington July 7th. 1803.

I had the pleasure of receiving the letter inclosed to Mr. Bringhurst, in which was contained one addressed to my father. To our confidential friends I have communicated the ground on which our Collector stands. The public sentiment is so fixed on this subject that it is[1] difficult to reconcile our leading active politicians. You may rely on it in this State it is not the *interested few* but the disinterested *many* who are extremely anxious about it & manifest the strongest sensations. Time may perhaps overcome them. Reflection & good sense prevail against the strongest desires of the day. At all events patriotism & the sincerest attachment to the Republican cause, to yourself & your administration will induce them to acquiese in what those, whose "positions command a view of the whole ground" may consider upon mature reflection & after full information to be most productive of the Public good. The next election fortunately is of little importance & the necessity of a great struggle will not be so absolutely essential. If it were I should contemplate with serious apprehensions the result. Kent & Sussex I fear will not move, & a Sheriff's election keeps New-Castle alive—The succeeding election will be an important one. It will decide the fate of this State, & I anticipate every aid & assistance consistent with principle from a virtuous administration. By that period I trust the exertions of every man who has a spark of Republicanism will be brought forwd. by principle & genuine [unison?] & that we shall be again victorious.

You are acquainted with my individual sentiments on the subject of removal. I should be deficient in candor if I were not to state that the effects visible from the different policies of Govs. McKean & Bloomfield had not considerably changed them. But The almost unanimous voice of our friends here has weighed in my mind most strongly. Had I been most directly & pointedly opposed to them, I should have been the strongest advocate for their voice being heard & their wishes being gratified

Our annual state tax is but $10,000 the salary commissions & patronage of the Collectors Office is each year nearly that sum—This last is equal to it. This is a serious consideration. In so small a state the weight of such an officer is sufficient to turn the scale.

Judge Chase was extremely moderate here in his charge. I suppose he was ashamed of the one he gave in Maryland. It was to be sure a phenomenon in jurisprudence & a monster in law. I am almost ready to exclaim "How long Cataline will you be permitted to abuse us."

My father informs me in his last letter that he has written to you, that he will accept of the commissions you offer. His friends were averse to it here as we could not well spare him from the bench & I could not reconcile his going so far, & to remain there but he has thought best to do it & wishes to see that new country. It is my desire to accompany him as the journey woud be benificial to my health, if I could return by the time Congress meets, as I wish to be punctual in my attendance there & to exert my feeble efforts in support of you & your administration. Whilst I am speaking of the Western Country permit me most sincerely to congratulate you on the "glad tidings of great joy." The fate of Federalism is sealed I trust. The Hydra with so many heads is [decrepit?].

Delaware has its "little band." [. . .][2] who patiently submitted to a cow-skinning & T. Mendenhall[3] who warmly supported Bayard until the tide changed, with not six others in the County (& they are unknown out of it) under the pretended mask of friends are the most insidious enemies. In the Borough elections they openly join the *Feds* & before my election they used every little low device to rescind it. They failed however in every attempt. They *then* accused me of having deliverd to you a paper I ought not. I acknowledged I had delivered the paper & justified it & exposed them so much at several meetings of the people that they had not a friend left & shrunk from the charge. T. Mendenhall[4] then carried me before the lodge where my brethren with one voice passed sentence in my favor

Now they pretend to have received a letter from you, stating that I never shewed you or delivered a letter addressed to me & signed by the principal Republicans of this place & sent on to me when I was at Washington in July 1801. This they say they have had near five months & the evening preceding the 4th. of July let it out expecting to draw off some from joining in the celebration of the day but how were they mortified when a solitary individual alone was gulled by the maneuvre, who is ashamed of it since

In order however to "take a bond of fate" as it were I will thank you to search your files about the period I mention & to let my friend Mr. Jarvis take a copy of the paper & transmit it to me. The original I wish, & so do all the signers wish, to have left, that it may always rise up in judgt. agt. him. Before my election he wished to make it a condition of supporting me, that I would have it withdrawn but I scorned the idea & rejected the base proposal.

I am really sorry to trouble you on such an occasion, but as I believe my deeds will all bear the light, I wish for that pleasing evidence that will expose them in their true colours.

If they have received a letter from you, I am sure they do not state its contents truly. On [. . .] you will remember, that I read the document alluded to, as the best method of making you acquainted with those sentiments which they wished me to express to you It being their own language. And after I had so done you, yourself requested me to leave it with you which I did.

We have celebrated[5] the anniversary of Independence with *éclat*. Near two hundred respectable citizens & the leading characters, set down to a table under the shade of the trees—With every wish for your health & happiness & the prosperity of your administration I remain Dr. Sir

Yours Most Sincerely C. A. Rodney

RC (DLC); several illegible words; frayed at margin; endorsed by TJ as received 9 July and so recorded in SJL.

LETTER INCLOSED TO MR. BRINGHURST: that is, TJ to Caesar A. Rodney, 17 June, and enclosure.

POSITIONS COMMAND A VIEW OF THE WHOLE GROUND: in his first inaugural address, TJ declared: "When right, I shall often be thought wrong by those whose positions will not command a view of the whole ground" (Vol. 33:151).

In the local SHERIFF's race, Richard C. Dale, the candidate selected by a general meeting of Republicans at the Red Lion Inn, was being challenged by Charles Anderson, who had been endorsed by the party in previous years. Articles by "Plain Dealer" and "Republico" in the *Mirror of the Times* supported the Dale candidacy. Dale won the election (Wilmington *Mirror of the Times, & General Advertiser*, 13, 30 July, 8 Oct. 1803; Vol. 37:467n).

In earlier correspondence, Rodney had noted the difference in the removal policies of Thomas MCKEAN and Joseph BLOOMFIELD as governors (see Vol. 38: 636, 639n).

For Samuel Chase's charge to the MARYLAND grand jury, see TJ to Joseph H. Nicholson, 13 May. HOW LONG CATALINE: Rodney refers to the opening lines of Cicero's first oration against Catiline, which in a 1766 translation reads, "How far wilt thou, O Catiline! abuse our Patience? How long shall thy Madness elude our Justice?" (*The Orations of Marcus Tullius Cicero*, 2 vols. [Dublin, 1766], 2:5).

HE HAS WRITTEN TO YOU: Thomas Rodney to TJ, 1 July. GLAD TIDINGS OF GREAT JOY: Luke 2:10.

Thomas Mendenhall ACCUSED Rodney of delivering a remonstrance to TJ in July 1801 (see Mendenhall to TJ, 12 Feb. 1803). CARRIED ME BEFORE THE LODGE: perhaps Lodge No. 14, where Rodney delivered an oration on 24 June 1803 (Caesar A. Rodney, *An Oration Prepared and Delivered at Wilmington, in the State of Delaware, on the Twenty-Fourth of June, A.D. 1803. At the Request of the Worshipful Master and Brethren of Lodge No. 14* [Wilmington, Del., 1803]; Shaw-Shoemaker, No. 4989). PRETEND TO HAVE RECEIVED A LETTER FROM YOU: see TJ to Thomas Mendenhall, 25 Feb.

TAKE A BOND OF FATE: Shakespeare, *Macbeth*, 4.1.

[1] Word supplied by Editors.

[2] Here a name or names are canceled, perhaps by Rodney, and illegible.

[3] Name canceled, either by Rodney or at a later date.

[4] Name again canceled, either by Rodney or at a later date.

[5] MS: "cebrated."

From James Taylor, Jr.

SIR Norfolk July 7. 1803

Your favour of 18th. June enclosed J Davedsons chick on the Branch Bank here for Seven Hundred and Sixty Six Drs. out of which I have paid Colo: Newton for the Cyder; there will be a balance due you of a few drs which will be settled when I have the pleasure of furnishing you with more Wine—I have received two pipes, for you which I will not dispose of until I hear from you—I have had several applications for them—they are of the same importation of those sent you last—

I am respectfully Yr: ob: Servt. JAS TAYLOR

RC (MHi); endorsed by TJ as received 12 July and so recorded in SJL.

James Davidson, Jr., was cashier of Washington's BRANCH of the Bank of the United States (MB, 2:1128; Vol. 35: 304-5n).

From Joseph Bringhurst

ESTEEMED FELLOW CITIZEN Wilmington Del. 7 Mo. 8th 1803

During my absence, on a journey for the benefit of my health, thy note, of the 17th Ultim., was recd. and opened by my wife. She carefully deliver'd the enclosure, according to its address, without permiting it to be seen by, or known to any other than its owner—Suffer me to remark that this instance of confidence is grateful to my heart, & shall never be violated—

It will be grateful to thee to hear that during my journey into the State of N York, about 100 miles north of that City, I found the majority of Friends, (Quakers) well satisfied with thy administration, & desirous of thy continuance in Office, as a blessing to this Country—

I am with real esteem and affection thy frd

JOSEPH BRINGHURST JR

RC (DLC); endorsed by TJ as received 9 July and so recorded in SJL.

Joseph Bringhurst (1767-1834), son of Philadelphia Quakers James and Anne Pole Bringhurst, attended the Friends Latin School, where he formed a friendship with Charles Brockden Brown. He went on to study medicine and establish a practice in Philadelphia. Bringhurst is credited with carrying on a poetical correspondence with Elihu Hubbard Smith and Brown for several months in 1791 in the *Gazette of the United States* under the nom de plume "Birtha." In 1793, Bringhurst moved to Wilmington, Delaware. Six years later, he married Deborah Ferris, from a prominent Chester County, Pennsylvania Quaker family. Bringhurst carried on his medical practice, established a drugstore, and, after his appointment as postmaster in 1802, operated the post office from his residence on Market Street in Wilmington. He was active in

Republican politics, the Delaware Abolition Society, and in the promotion of domestic manufactures, later becoming the owner of a cotton factory. He frequently corresponded with his friend John Dickinson, caring for him during his final illness and informing TJ of his death (Josiah Granville Leach, *History of the Bringhurst Family with Notes on the Clarkson, De Peyster and Boude Families* [Philadelphia, 1901], 30, 39-41; Charles E. Bennett, "A Poetical Correspondence Among Elihu Hubbard Smith, Joseph Bringhurst, Jr., and Charles Brockden Brown in *The Gazette of the United States*," *Early American Literature*, 12 [1977-78], 277-85; Wilmington *Mirror of the Times, & General Advertiser*, 19 Feb. 1800; Wilmington *Delaware Gazette*, 9 Mch. 1815; John A. Munroe, *Federalist Delaware, 1775-1815* [New Brunswick, N.J., 1954], 217n, 227n; Latrobe, *Correspondence*, 2:7n; Bringhurst to TJ, 16 Feb. 1808).

For TJ's NOTE of 17 June (not found), the ENCLOSURE, and its delivery, see TJ to Caesar A. Rodney, 17 June, and Rodney to TJ, 7 July.

From Meriwether Lewis

12. O,Clock.

DEAR SIR, Harper's Ferry July 8th. 1803.

The waggon which was employed by Mr. Linnard the Military Agent at Philadelphia, to transport the articles forming my outfit, passed this place on the 28th. Ulto.—the waggoner determined that his team was not sufficiently strong to take the whole of the articles that had been prepared for me at this place and therefore took none of them; of course it became necessary to provide some other means of geting them forward; for this purpose on the evening of the 5th. at Fredericktown[1] I engaged a person with a light two horse-waggon who promised to set out with them this morning, in this however he has disappointed me and I have been obliged to engage a second person who will be here this evening in time to load and will go on early in the morning: I shall set out myself in the course of an hour, taking the rout of Charlestown, Frankfort, Uniontown and Redstone old fort to Pittsburgh, at which place I shall most probably arrive on the 15th.

Yesterday I shot my guns and examined the several articles which had been manufactered for me at this place; they appear to be well executed.—

My complyments to Mr. Harvie, & accept the assureance of my sincere wishes for your health and happiness.

Your friend & Obt. Servt. MERIWETHER LEWIS.

RC (DLC); at foot of text: "Mr. Jefferson. Presidt. of US."; endorsed by TJ as received 14 July and so recorded in SJL.

On the way to PITTSBURGH, Lewis expected to pass through Charles Town, west of Harpers Ferry, and Frankfort, in Hampshire County, both in Virginia (now

West Virginia). In Pennsylvania, his intended route went through Uniontown and Brownsville, which was also known as Redstone Old Fort (Jedidiah Morse, *The American Gazetteer*, 2d ed. [Charlestown, Mass., 1804]).

[1]MS: "Fredercktown." Lewis interlined this and the preceding word.

From Blair McClenachan

SIR, Philadelphia 8. July 1803.

Consciousness of your goodness, and the respectability of the recommendation which the Citizens of Philadelphia were pleased to offer in my behalf, induced me to indulge Some hope of receiving the place, which was lately vacated by Mr. Israel Whelen.—I am informed however, that it has been deemed proper to confer it upon Mr. Tench Coxe, whose principles and talents must be allowed to merit this attention.

I Should be Sorry Sir, to Seem importunate, or to consume one moment of that time which you So happily devote to the most weighty concerns, did not the urgency of my circumstances, oblige me once more to obtrude myself on your recollection, and to entreat any Situation, to the faithful discharge of the duties of which, you may do me the honor of considering me competent.

I pray you Sir, to accept the assurance of my most profound respect.

BLAIR MCLENACHAN

RC (DNA: RG 59, LAR); endorsed by TJ as received 10 July and "for office" and so recorded in SJL.

For the RECOMMENDATION signed by 61 CITIZENS OF PHILADELPHIA, see the enclosure listed at McClenachan to TJ, 29 Nov. 1802.

Constitutional Amendment on Louisiana

I. DRAFT AMENDMENT, [ON OR BEFORE 9 JULY 1803]

II. REVISED AMENDMENT, [CA. 9 JULY 1803]

EDITORIAL NOTE

"I think it will be safer not to permit the enlargement of the Union but by amendment of the constitution," Jefferson wrote to his secretary of the Treasury in January 1803. The president was responding to Gallatin's rebuttal of arguments from the attorney general about the desired purchase of New

Orleans and the Floridas. Jefferson, Levi Lincoln knew, thought that an amendment to the Constitution would be necessary for the incorporation of the new territory into the United States. Lincoln believed, however, that proposing an amendment would be a "doubtful attempt" that, if it failed, could bring down the whole enterprise of acquiring New Orleans. While Gallatin dismissed questions about amendment, contending that the necessary powers were already in the Constitution, Lincoln tried to find a means, by the incorporation of land into existing states or territories, of satisfying the president's constitutional concerns without following the dangerous route of seeking approval of an amendment. The president rejected both officers' advice. There might be "no constitutional difficulty as to the acquisition of territory," he maintained, but an amendment was required for incorporation of new areas into the federal system—the "enlargement of the Union" (Vol. 39:302-5, 324-6, 328).

In January, as Jefferson was just determining to send James Monroe to France to join Robert R. Livingston in negotiations for the purchase of New Orleans, the constitutional questions were anticipatory and theoretical. The topic became a more immediate concern on the evening of 3 July, when news reached Washington of the French government's agreement to sell not just New Orleans, but all of Louisiana. Jefferson went right to work: "I have sketched an amendment to the constitution," he informed Gallatin on the 9th. He hastened the project forward, without knowing the details of the cession, because he wanted to leave soon for Monticello and foresaw that the Louisiana transaction would have high priority when Congress returned from its recess (TJ to Gallatin, [9 July], first letter).

Jefferson saw his amendment as an addition to Article 4, Section 3 of the Constitution, which covered the creation of new states and territories (see his heading to Document II below). He proposed something he and his advisers could not have anticipated during their earlier discussions of the constitutionality of acquiring New Orleans: the maintenance of most of the vast province of Louisiana as Indian country to foster the relocation of Native Americans from east of the Mississippi River (Documents I and II). As he explained in a letter to George W. Erving on 10 July, "if we place the new accession of Louisiana on proper grounds, while it secures our peace, it may be the means of confining & condensing our population on the E. side of the Missisipi, instead of diffusing it; and of removing our Indian population to the other side." The purchase of Louisiana gave him, he thought, the means to forward a policy he had explained to William Henry Harrison in February, when he wrote that "our settlements will gradually circumscribe & approach the Indians, & they will in time either incorporate with us as citizens of the US. or remove beyond the Missisipi." A few months before that, he had laid out for the secretary of war a project of making the western edge of the United States—that is, the east bank of the Mississippi River—a "strong front." At that time, with Spanish officials cutting off trade through New Orleans and the French readying a military colony for the Mississippi Valley, he deemed "securing us" on the west to be a goal "now of great importance." To that end, he suggested to Henry Dearborn a policy of filling Mississippi Territory and the Illinois country with agricultural settlements and requiring Native Americans to assimilate into that landscape and culture or move across the Mississippi. With the acquisition of Louisiana the immediate threats to the nation's western flank and to commerce along the Mississippi disappeared. Yet the vision of a rationally managed, neatly consolidated settlement still held Jefferson. As he wrote to John Breckinridge in August, the annexation of Louisiana would provide a way of "filling up" the eastern side of the Mississippi Valley and proceeding with "range after range" of new states, "advancing compactly as we multiply" (Vol. 39:231-4, 590-2; TJ to Breckinridge, 1 Aug.).

In his proposed amendment Jefferson gave little attention to the southern part of Louisiana lying on both sides of the lower Mississippi River, where the majority of the province's inhabitants of French, African, Caribbean, and Spanish origins lived. Congress would simply institute territorial government for that region "whenever they deem expedient" (Documents I and II). Jefferson's focus was on the remainder of the sprawling acquisition, the limits of which were only vaguely understood. Native Americans living there would retain "rights of occupancy in the soil," but all areas deemed abandoned or not "rightfully occupied" by the native inhabitants "shall belong to the US." There would be no land office and no land sales, effectively barring new settlement by non-Indians. Congress, however, would have the power to exchange lands held by Indians east of the Mississippi for rights of occupancy on the west side of the river and to trade land owned by whites in upper Louisiana for land east of the Mississippi. The United States could establish military posts, trading stores, and roads, and could develop sources of minerals and salt, but the native peoples would govern themselves and another constitutional amendment would be required to open the way for the creation of any territorial government.

For his draft, Jefferson used 31 degrees north latitude as the division between the upper and lower parts of Louisiana—the line between the anticipated land preserve to the north and the more densely inhabited areas to the south (Document I). East of the Mississippi River, the 31st parallel was the southern boundary of the United States, separating Spanish and U.S. territory as specified by Article 2 of the Pinckney Treaty (Miller, *Treaties*, 2:319-20). Jefferson kept the division of Louisiana at the 31st parallel as he made a fair copy of the amendment, but at some point he or one of his advisers may have raised some doubt about whether that line was far enough north to serve the intended purpose west of the river. He amended the fair copy, changing the line of latitude from 31 to 32 degrees. Another copy in his hand, which has survived only in the form of a pressed copy, and a copy by Lewis Harvie both specified the 32d parallel (see notes to Document II). Robert Smith placed the line there also in a substitute version of the amendment he proposed, but whether the idea of using that latitude originated with him is not known (Smith to TJ, 9 July). Jefferson apparently had doubts about even the 32d parallel, for he and Harvie enclosed the number in brackets. When Jefferson revised the amendment in August, he put the line even farther north, at the latitude of the mouth of the Arkansas River. Several months later, the March 1804 act of Congress that split Louisiana into a southern territory of Orleans and a northern district of Louisiana set the boundary between them at 33 degrees north latitude (U.S. Statutes at Large, 2:283; TJ to Gallatin, 23 Aug.).

Jefferson showed the amendment to at least some members of the cabinet on 9 July. Gallatin and Smith responded on that day, and Madison, Dearborn, and Lincoln surely saw it at about the same time, although the subject does not appear in Jefferson's surviving correspondence with them around that day. Although Gallatin replied only that he did not understand the matter to be one "for immediate decision," Smith made a detailed response. He advised that it was unnecessary for the amendment to list the powers Congress would have in upper Louisiana, and he cautioned against what would amount to a constitutional guarantee of right of occupancy to Native Americans. Smith drafted a leaner amendment that avoided the pitfalls he saw in the president's more detailed version (Gallatin to TJ, 9 July; Smith to TJ, 9 July, and enclosure).

A penciled addition by Madison at the foot of Jefferson's fair copy of the amendment allowed in general terms for the annexation of any part of the Floridas (see Document II). Whether Jefferson let Madison add that part before the president's other advisers saw the amendment is not known. When Jefferson circulated a revised version of an amendment in August, the new text included a paragraph about Florida similar to Madison's addendum on the earlier version, although differently worded. Jefferson also heeded Smith's advice and omitted the enumeration of the powers of Congress in upper Louisiana. Madison wrote his own version of an amendment, perhaps during the renewed consideration of the question in August, although the president likely did not see it (Madison, *Papers, Sec. of State Ser.*, 5:156; TJ to Gallatin, 23 Aug.; to Madison, 24 Aug.; to Lincoln, 30 Aug.).

One of the changes Jefferson had to make in the new version of the amendment in August pertained to citizenship. Monroe's and Livingston's instructions for the negotiation contained the framework of a proposed treaty for the acquisition of New Orleans and Florida, one article of which read: "To incorporate the inhabitants of the hereby ceded territory with the citizens of the United States on an equal footing, being a provision, which cannot now be made, it is to be expected, from the character and policy of the United States, that such incorporation will take place without unnecessary delay. In the mean time, they shall be secure in their persons and property, and in the free enjoyment of their religion." In the instructions Madison acknowledged "the respect due to the rights of the people inhabiting the ceded territory" but also noted "the delay which may be found in constituting them a regular and integral portion of the union." Jefferson had a similar understanding as he drafted his amendment, which predicated citizenship on the creation of a territorial government, in the southern part of the province only, and at the discretion of Congress. At the time, he had not yet seen the text of the treaty for the Louisiana cession and did not know that his proposed amendment was at odds with the language of the agreement. "The inhabitants of the ceded territory," the treaty's third article stated, "shall be incorporated in the Union of the United States and admitted as soon as possible according to the principles of the federal Constitution to the enjoyment of all the rights, advantages and immunities of citizens of the United States, and in the mean time they shall be maintained and protected in the free enjoyment of their liberty, property and the Religion which they profess." In his August revision of the amendment Jefferson accommodated that provision of the treaty, with some adjustment. Only "white inhabitants" would be citizens, he specified, and their rights would be those of other U.S. citizens "in analogous situations." He used the same language in the clause relating to the potential incorporation of Florida into the union (Madison, *Papers*, *Sec. of State Ser.*, 4:371, 376; Miller, *Treaties*, 2:501; Malone, *Jefferson*, 4:314; TJ to Gallatin, 23 Aug.).

Although the amendment Jefferson proposed to the cabinet in August was very different from the July draft, Paul Leicester Ford printed them side-by-side in his edition of Jefferson's *Writings*. Dumas Malone later identified Ford's source texts as Document I, below, for the July draft and Jefferson's 30 Aug. letter to Levi Lincoln for the later one (Ford, 8:241-9; Malone, *Jefferson*, 4:314n; the two texts, reprinted from Ford, are also in John P. Foley, *The Jeffersonian Cyclopedia* [New York, 1900], 510-11). For the evolution of the amendment in August, see also Jefferson's letters to Gallatin on 23 Aug., to Madison on the 25th, and the draft Jefferson made around or shortly after 30 Aug. For Jefferson's consideration of constitutional issues relating to the acquisition of Louisiana, see Malone, *Jefferson*, 4:311-25; Robert W. Tucker and David C. Hendrickson, *Empire of Liberty: The Statecraft of Thomas Jefferson* (New York, 1990), 163-71, 234-6; Jeremy D. Bailey, *Thomas Jefferson and Executive Power* (Cambridge, 2007), 171-94; Ralph Ketcham, *James Madison: A Biography* (New York, 1971), 420-2; Irving Brant, *James Madison: Secretary of State, 1800-1809* (Indianapolis, 1953), 141-5; Everett Somerville Brown, *The Constitutional History of the Louisiana Purchase, 1803-1812* (Berkeley, Calif., 1920), 17-48; and Stephanie P. Newbold, "Statesmanship and Ethics: The Case of Thomas Jefferson's Dirty Hands," *Public Administration Review*, 65 (2005), 669-77. The relationship between Jefferson's amendment proposals and his Indian policy receives particular attention in Merrill D. Peterson, *Thomas Jefferson and the New Nation: A Biography* (New York, 1970), 771-5, 842-3; Anthony F. C. Wallace, *Jefferson and the Indians: The Tragic Fate of the First Americans* (Cambridge, Mass., 1999), 224-6, 254-6; Bernard W. Sheehan, *Seeds of Extinction: Jeffersonian Philanthropy and the American Indian* (Chapel Hill, 1973), 245-6; Christian B. Keller, "Philanthropy Betrayed: Thomas Jefferson, the Louisiana Purchase, and the Origins of Federal Indian Removal Policy," APS, *Proceedings*, 144 (2000), 58-9; and Jack N. Rakove, "Thinking Like a Constitution," *Journal of the Early Republic*, 24 (2004), 25n.

I. Draft Amendment

[on or before 9 July 1803]

Amendment to the Constitution.

The Province of Louisiana is incorporated with the US. and made part thereof. the rights of occupancy in the soil, and of self government, are confirmed to the Indian inhabitants, as they now exist. Preemption only of the portions rightfully occupied by them, & a succession to the occupancy of such as they may abandon, with the full rights of possession as well as of property & sovereignty in whatever is not rightfully occupied by them or shall cease to be so,[1] shall belong to the US.

The legislature of the union shall have authority to exchange the right of occupancy in portions where the US. have full right, for lands possessed by Indians within the US. on the East Side of the Missisipi:[2] to exchange lands on the East side of the river for those of the White inhabitants on the West side thereof and above the latitude of 31 degrees:[3] to maintain in any part of the Province such military posts as may be requisite for peace or safety: to exercise police over all persons therein, not being Indian inhabitants: to work salt springs, or mines of coal, metals & other minerals within the possessions of the US[4] or in any others with the consent of the possessors: to regulate trade & intercourse between the Indian inhabitants and all other persons: to explore and ascertain the geography of the province, it's productions and other interesting circumstances: to open roads & navigation therein where necessary for[5] beneficial communication; and to establish agencies & factories therein for the cultivation of commerce, peace & good understanding with the Indians residing there.

The legislature shall have no authority to[6] dispose of the lands of the province otherwise than is herein before permitted, until a new amendment of the constitution shall give that authority. Except as to that portion thereof which lies South of the latitude of 31. degrees; which whenever they deem expedient, they may erect into a territorial government, either separate, or as making part with one on the Eastern side of the river, vesting the inhabitants thereof with all the rights possessed by other territorial citizens of the US.

MS (DLC: TJ Papers, 137:23688); undated, but before TJ to Gallatin, [9 July], first letter; entirely in TJ's hand.

[1]Preceding six words interlined.

[2]Word written over "river."

[3]TJ interlined the preceding clause beginning with "to exchange lands."

[4]TJ first wrote "within our own possessions" before altering the phrase to read as above.

[5]Preceding four words interlined in place of "for a more easy &."

[6]TJ here canceled "open a land office for the said."

II. Revised Amendment

[ca. 9 July 1803]

Amendment to the Constitution to be added to Art. IV. section III.

The Province of Louisiana is incorporated with the US. and made part thereof. the rights of occupancy in the soil, & of self-government, are confirmed to the Indian inhabitants, as they now exist. Preemption only of the portions rightfully occupied by them, and a succession to the occupancy of such as they may abandon, with the full rights of possession as well as of property & sovereignty in whatever is not rightfully occupied by them, or shall cease to be so, shall belong to the US.

The legislature of the union shall have authority

to exchange the right of occupancy in portions where the US. have full right, for lands possessed by Indians, within the US. on the East side of the Missisipi:

to exchange lands on the East side of the river for those of the White inhabitants on the West side thereof & North of the latitude of [32][1] degrees:

to maintain in any part of the province such military posts as may be requisite for peace or safety:

to exercise police over all persons therein, not being Indian inhabitants:

to work salt-springs, or mines of coal, metals & other minerals within the possessions of the US. or in any others with the consent of the possessors:

to regulate trade & intercourse between the Indian inhabitants, & all other persons:

to explore & ascertain the geography of the province, it's productions and other interesting circumstances:

to open roads & navigation therein, where necessary for beneficial communication:

and to establish agencies & factories therein for the cultivation of Commerce, peace and good understanding with the Indians residing there.

The legislature shall have no authority to dispose of the lands of the province otherwise than is herein before permitted, until a new amendment of the constitution shall give that authority:

Except, as to that portion thereof which lies South of the latitude of [32.°][2] which, whenever they deem expedient, they may erect into a territorial government, either separate, or as making part with one on the Eastern side of the river, vesting the inhabitants with all the rights possessed by other territorial citizens of the US.

[*In Madison's hand*:]

added by J.M.

Territories Eastwd. of the Mississippi & Southward[3] of the U.S. which may be acquired by the U.S. shall be incorporated as a part thereof;[4] and be subject with their inhabitants[5] including Indians, to the same authorities of the general Govt. as may now be exercised over territories & inhabitants under like circumstances now within the limits of the U. States.

MS (NN: Thomas Jefferson Papers); undated; in TJ's hand, including brackets; addendum by Madison in pencil; endorsed by Madison: "Mem. of proposed Amendment to Constitution T.J & J.M." PrC (DLC: TJ Papers, 10:1606); with 31 degrees as the specified line of latitude (see notes 1 and 2); lacks addendum. PrC (same, 10:1607); from another MS in TJ's hand, not found; with 32 degrees in brackets as the line of latitude; lacks addendum. Tr (same, 10:1605); in Lewis Harvie's hand; with 32 degrees in brackets as the line of latitude; lacks addendum; endorsed by TJ: "Louisiana. Amendmt. constn."

[1]TJ first wrote "31," without brackets, then altered the "1" to "2" and added the brackets. He did not make the changes to the PrC.

[2]TJ first wrote "31.°," without brackets, before altering the "1" to "2" and adding the brackets. He did not make the changes to the PrC.

[3]Madison here canceled "of the present limits."

[4]Preceding word interlined.

[5]Madison here canceled "whether."

To Albert Gallatin

TH:J. TO MR GALLATIN [9 July 1803]

It is but a fortnight before we shall separate, and there will be but a month between our return & the meeting of Congress, & that crowded by the business which will accumulate during our absence. it is well therefore to make up our minds on such subjects as we can before we separate. Louisiana is an important one. it is our duty in the first place to obtain the information supporting it which may enable Congress to decide understandingly as to the footing on which it ought to be placed. for this purpose I have prepared a set of queries which I propose to send immediately to Dunbar, Clarke, and govr. Claiborne, to be answered and returned before November. be so good as to propose such amendments & additions to them as [respects] you. besides this I think it would be well we should make up our own minds as to the proper footing on which that succession should be placed, and to put our plan into the hands of a friend in Congress.[1] with this view I have sketched an amendment to the constitution (for I think that the proper mode) to be proposed by Congress to the states as soon as they meet. I pray you to consider this well and suggest such alterations of form or substance as you would prefer. saluta[tions]

PrC (DLC); undated; blurred and frayed at margin. Recorded in SJL as a letter to the Treasury Department of 9 July with notation "Louisiana." Enclosures: (1) Document I at Queries on Louisiana, printed at 9 July. (2) Document I at Constitutional Amendment on Louisiana, also printed at 9 July.

[1]Preceding two words interlined.

To Albert Gallatin

TH:J. TO MR GALLATIN [9 July 1803]

It is proposed to appoint Rodney & Williams Commrs. for the Natchez district, & Kirby for that of Tombigby. a 2d for that is wanting.

Rob. C. Nicholas (son of George) is recommended. he is not a lawyer; nor has any lawyer offered, but one who is concerned in one of the companies. mr Garrard of Kentucky, who wished to be a judge of Indiana has occurred to me. but I do not know that he would accept it, for tho' he would have given up his business for a less lucrative but permanent office, perhaps he might not interrupt it's course for a temporary one. a lawyer from Connecticut in addition to Kirby has been recommended by mr Granger, but without his own knolege. two from the same state might also be exceptionable. be so good as to consider this, & say whom you would prefer.

RC (NHi: Gallatin Papers); undated; addressed: "The Secretary of the Treasury"; endorsed. PrC (DLC). Recorded in SJL at 9 July with notation "Commrs. for Missisipi territory."

For the recommendation of William GARRARD for the Indiana judgeship, see John Brown to TJ, 5 Dec. 1802.

From Albert Gallatin

DEAR SIR 9th July 1803

As mr Nicholas has, through his Uncle, applied for the office, and it is uncertain whether Mr Garrard would take it, I think he should be preferred. The only objection which presents itself is that to several applications the general answer has been given that lawyers only should be appointed. Amongst others a gentleman from Carolina recommended by Hampton & who came here on purpose. But the office of Register for Mobile should be filled immediately: it is really more pressing than that of Commissr. Would either Mr Garrard or Mr Nicholas take it?

I was preparing, when I received your's, an official letter to Mr Clarke on the subject of Louisiana, but confined of course to the objects immediately connected with this department, to witt the present revenue, & particularly that drawn from duties on imports & exports—and amount of exports principally those articles which pay duty on their importation into the U. States vizt. cotton, indigo, & particularly Sugar. As the revenue we draw from this last article is not less than nine hundred thousand dollars a year, it is important to ascertain the quantity which is now annually exported from New Orleans, in order either to find means of supplying the deficiency of revenue if that article shall be imported from thence duty free, or to devise some method by which the duty may still be collected. My present idea was that until an amendment to the Constitution had been adopted, all the duties on imports now payable in the United States should be likewise paid on importations to New Orleans—all the duties on imports now payable at New Orleans by Spanish laws should cease—and all articles of the growth of Louisiana which when imported into the U. States now pay duty, should continue to pay the same or at least such rate as would on the whole not affect the revenue. But facts are wanted, & I will try by next Monday to have such additional or explanatory queries prepared as will answer my object & give them to be added to those you had prepared.

The amendment to the Constitution is intended, I presume, for deliberation & reflection, but not for immediate decision—

With respectful attachment Your obedt. Servt.

Albert Gallatin

RC (DLC); addressed: "The President of the United States"; endorsed by TJ as received from the Treasury Department on 9 July and "Louisiana.—R. C. Nicholas.—Garrard" and so recorded in SJL.

THROUGH HIS UNCLE: see Wilson Cary Nicholas to TJ, 31 May, and enclosures.

GENTLEMAN FROM CAROLINA: perhaps Thomas Fitzpatrick himself delivered the three letters TJ received on 3 June—including one from Wade Hampton—recommending Fitzpatrick for an office in Mississippi Territory (see Pierce Butler to TJ, 21 Apr.).

To George Jefferson

Dear Sir Washington July 9. 1803.

Not having yet learned from you that my tobo. is sold, I must pray you to sell, as well as you can, as much of it as will discharge my note to Craven Peyton for thirteen hundred dollars payable at your office[1] the [thirteenth next]. I leave to yourself to consider whether it is best to sell the residue now, or to wait as the market I understand is getting better & cannot fail to do so on account of the war. I generally deem it bad policy to sell on a rising market.

Ten packages of different kinds for me, will leave Alexandria within 2. or 3. days for Richmond, which I will pray you to forward by the boats as I shall be there before them, [presuming] to leave this place about the 24th. or 25th. There are also [18.] barrels of fish for S. Carr

& myself, which I believe have not yet been forwarded from Alexandria. Accept assurances of my constant affection.

TH: JEFFERSON

PrC (MHi); blurred; at foot of text: "Mr. George Jefferson."

NOT HAVING YET HEARD: TJ evidently wrote this letter before receiving on this day George Jefferson's letter of 7 June, which was recorded in SJL but has not been found. TJ recorded in his financial memoranda that Jefferson had sold his tobacco to the Richmond firm of Pickett, Pollard & Johnston for a little over $3,330 "of which 1300.D. to be pd. cash for my note ante Mar. 18. The balance paiable Sep. 6" (MB, 2:1102, 1104).

[1]Preceding three words interlined.

Report from John Lenthall

Stone work done to the South wing of the Capitol July 5th to the 9th 1803

— Rough Stone —

To the South & West fronts about 47 Perches
Part of the time employed in erecting Scaffolds fixing Machinary for Setting the Cut Stone &c &c—

— Cut Stone —

Set in South front, of Ashler 60 feet run.
of Base blocks, rung. Measure 91 feet
Ashler Courses 12 Inches thick
Base Block—13 Inches do

for B H Latrobe
JNO LENTHALL

MS (DLC); in Lenthall's hand and signed by him; endorsed by TJ: "Capitol. July 5. to 9. 03."

To James Lyle

DEAR SIR Washington July 9. 1803.

Your favor of June 24. came to hand on the 1st. inst. the impression on my mind is that there were important errors in Richd. Harvie's acct. and that I gave you some years ago a detailed statement of them. Richard and myself had one or more conversations on the subject, and some explanations took place, but what their effect was, my memory does not enable me to say. I think I have probably a note of it at Monticello where those papers all are, and as I shall go there in a fortnight, I will write you from thence. I remember well that he undertook to make further enquiries of one or more individuals; but being soon afterwards called away from the neighborh'd, no final agreement took place.

My tobacco of the last year has been for some time in the hands of Gibson & Jefferson for sale, and they were instructed to sell before this time. but it is possible that an expected rise in the price on the prospect of war in Europe may have induced them to let it lie a while. they informed me they would not sell on credit. the moment I know of the sale I shall send you an order for a thousand dollars. mr Bolling's estate with a reasonable indulgence will pay all it's debt without being much [broke in?] on. I trust therefore it will not be long before you recieve your and my demand [both] from it. Accept my friendly salutations and assurances of continued esteem & attachment.

TH: JEFFERSON

PrC (MHi); faint; at foot of text: "Mr. James Lyle"; endorsed by TJ in ink on verso.

The DETAILED STATEMENT was probably an enclosure in TJ's letter to Lyle of 7 Mch. 1790 (Vol. 16:212), but see also the notes TJ compiled on Richard HARVIE'S ACCOUNT five years later (Vol. 28: 413-17).

Queries on Louisiana

I. JEFFERSON'S DRAFT OF QUERIES, [ON OR BEFORE 9 JULY 1803]

II. ALBERT GALLATIN'S QUERIES, WITH JEFFERSON'S REVISIONS, [9-17 JULY 1803]

III. JEFFERSON'S REVISION OF ORIGINAL DRAFT, [12-17 JULY 1803]

IV. FINAL LIST OF QUERIES, [17 JULY 1803]

EDITORIAL NOTE

The news that had arrived on the evening of 3 July, of the cession of Louisiana to the United States, confirmed for the Jefferson Administration the correctness of its pacific approach to the crisis in the West. Much uncertainty remained, however, on just what the acquisition would entail. The exact boundaries of the vast territory, a very different expanse than that initially sought by the administration, were then unknown (Madison, *Papers*, 4:364-78). If possible, a census of the population in the different areas of the province was needed. Most important perhaps, the administration would have to resolve how the United States was to incorporate a territory that had been governed by an entirely different political, legal, and economic regime. Gaining some understanding of the rules and norms under which citizens of Louisiana lived and of the ways they made a living would help the administration and Congress begin the difficult process of incorporation.

EDITORIAL NOTE

At some point during the next six days, Jefferson compiled a list of queries on Lousiana (see Document I, below). By 9 July, he had completed a list in his own hand and had his secretary, Lewis Harvie, execute at least three transcripts. The pristine quality of Jefferson's own copy suggests that it may have been a fair copy developed from earlier drafts, but if so, no such drafts have been found. Jefferson's questions involved such subjects as the geography and population of the land mass, its administrative divisions, the province's officers and the method of their appointment, sources of revenue for the government, land tenure, the status of religion, legal codes, and agriculture. On the 9th, he forwarded the queries to Albert Gallatin, asking for Gallatin's input but also implying that he considered them ready to be sent to William C. C. Claiborne, governor of the Mississippi Territory; Daniel Clark, the American consul at New Orleans; and Jefferson's Natchez correspondent William Dunbar. Presumably, the three transcripts in Harvie's hand were intended for this purpose.

As he explained in his response that day, Gallatin had already been working on a set of questions to be included in "an official letter to Mr Clarke on the subject of Louisiana." Gallatin's queries (see Document II), which focused largely on aspects of Louisiana's economy and revenue system, were far more detailed than Jefferson's. On 11 July, the secretary of the Treasury indicated in a letter to Jefferson that he would call on the president the following day, when they could discuss the subject. There is no indication that Gallatin sent Jefferson his list before this conference, although that is possible. Either before or during the meeting, Gallatin appears to have added some items to his initial list that he based on Jefferson's queries. He inserted three at the head of the document that, judging from the numbers he assigned to them, he considered analogous to Jefferson's second, fourth, and fifth through seventh queries, respectively. At the bottom of his list, Gallatin added a short question on tithes, which he connected to Jefferson's eighth on the status of clergy and the church. He numbered the two following items, the first on population and the second on feudal rights, "9" and "10" respectively, to connect them to similar queries from Jefferson's list. Below the last of these queries, which spilled onto a new page, Gallatin added six more dealing with judicial and educational issues. He did not number these, and he may have added them at a later time, possibly during his conference with Jefferson.

At this stage, the documents entered a phase of direct collaboration between Jefferson and Gallatin, with Jefferson taking charge of overhauling his original list (see Document III), emending Gallatin's list, and combining the two emended lists into a single document. It is uncertain whether the president made changes during their meeting on the 12th or if they agreed on a general course of action, with Jefferson developing the comprehensive list on his own at a later time. There is nothing to suggest that James Madison had any involvement in developing the list, but given the leading role he took in the incorporation of Louisiana, his participation cannot be ruled out. Nor do other members of the cabinet seem to have contributed to the effort.

Jefferson made several changes to Gallatin's queries, interlining details he considered necessary and canceling some questions entirely. Most notably, he canceled the queries that Gallatin had added in response to his original list, while shifting some but not all of the information contained in these queries to other areas of the comprehensive list. Jefferson also significantly revised his original list. Taking a transcript that was in Harvie's hand, perhaps the one he had forwarded to Gallatin on the 9th, he interlined some new questions of his own or that had been part of Gallatin's list, while canceling some other queries (see Document III). Two of the interlined queries, for example, solicited more detailed geographical information than that solicited in the first query of the original draft. In another instance, Jefferson interlined verbatim Gallatin's question about feudal rights. In the end, the 17 queries in Jefferson's original list became 16 queries, five of which were either new or imported from Gallatin's list.

In compiling and reorganizing the final list of queries, Jefferson adopted a numbering system, which displaced the strategy that Gallatin had pursued in his list. Beginning with the 16 queries in the revision of the transcript discussed in the previous paragraph, Jefferson continued to the third and last page of Gallatin's list. The six queries that Gallatin had added there, possibly at Jefferson's behest, became numbers 17 through 22, after which Jefferson added four of his own, three of which he had shifted from his original list. He next turned to the first two pages of Gallatin's list, there adding numbers 27 through 43. Gallatin had organized his list thematically, using braces to group sets of queries and labeling each group with a word in the left-hand margin. The word "debt," for example, had denoted the items that Jefferson numbered 35 through 37. To avoid confusion and to ensure that his preferred method of organization would be obvious, Jefferson canceled all of Gallatin's marginalia.

No fair copy of the expanded and reorganized list in Jefferson's hand has been found. The president most likely explained all the changes to Lewis Harvie, who then wrote up at least three copies, based exactly on the heavily emended drafts. A press copy in Harvie's hand of the final 43 queries is the only version that has been found (Document IV), but it is clear that Jefferson enclosed these same queries in the letters he sent on 17 July to Claiborne, Clark, and Dunbar (see William C. C. Claiborne to TJ, 24 Aug. 1803).

I. Jefferson's Draft of Queries

[on or before 9 July 1803]

Queries.

1. What are the boundaries of Louisiana, and on what authority does each portion of them rest?
2. What is the distance from New Orleans to the nearest point of the Western boundary
3. into what divisions is the province laid off?
4. what officers civil or military are appointed to each division, and what to the general government, with a definition of their powers?
5. what emoluments have they, and from what source derived?

6. what are the annual expences of the province drawn from the treasury?
7. what are the nett reciepts of the treasury, & from what taxes or other resources are they drawn?
8. on what footing is the church & clergy, what lands have they, and from what other funds are they supported?
9. what is the population of the province, distinguishing between white & black but excluding Indians, on the East side of the Missisipi? of the settlement on the West side next the mouth? of each distinct settlement in the other parts of the province? and what the geographical position and extent of each of these settlements?
10. what are the foundations of their land-titles? and what their tenure?
11. what is the quantity of granted lands as near as can be estimated?[1]
12. what is the quantity ungranted in the island of New Orleans, and in the settlement adjacent on the West side?
13. what are the lands appropriated to public use?
14. what buildings, fortifications, or other fixed property belong to the public?
15. what is the quantity & general limits of the lands fit for the culture of sugar? what proportion is granted & what ungranted?
16. whence is their code of laws derived? a copy of it, if in print.
17. what are the best maps, general or particular, of the whole or parts of the province? copies of them, if to be had in print.

MS (DLC: TJ Papers, 137:23705); undated; entirely in TJ's hand. Tr (same, 137:23706); in Lewis Harvie's hand. Tr (same, 137:23707); in Harvie's hand; with one emendation (see below). Tr (same, 137:23708); in Harvie's hand; endorsed on verso by TJ: "Louisiana Queries." Enclosed in TJ to Albert Gallatin, 9 July (first letter).

[1]Here interlined in the 2d Tr in an unidentified hand: "& in tracts of what size."

II. Albert Gallatin's Queries, with Jefferson's Revisions

[9-17 July 1803]

<2. *What is the distance from Manchac to the Western boundary?*>

<4. *Are any of the officers appointed by the inhabitants?*>

<5. 6. 7. *Are any of the officers paid in whole or in part by fees, or perquisites?*>[1]

27. What are the local taxes paid in each division, for the local expences of such division such as roads, poor, clergy, schools salary of local officers?[2] and by whom are they imposed?

28 What are the duties on imports & exports respectively, the gross amount of each, the manner of collecting them, the place where levied, & the time of paying them

29 How are the officers employed in the collection paid?[3] whether by fees, daily or annual salary, or commission?

30 What is the nett amount of those duties paid in the Treasury

31 Are there any other general taxes levied in the Province whether 1. on land, income, or capitation—2 on transfer of real property wills & inheritances—3 on sales of merchandize <*in the nature of the Spanish*> 4 on stamps or records—5 on manufactures by way of excise. 6 in any other way?[4] the gross and nett amount of each? the time, place, & manner of collecting & whether the collecting officers are paid by fees, commission or salary?

<*revenue*>

<*The same questions as on import & export duties respecting the mode of collection, the collectors & their salary, the gross & nett amount of the taxes*>

32 <*General*> What are the expences of the Province paid from the Treasury under the following heads—1 Salaries of Governor, Intendant, Judges & all other civil officers—2 Military including fortifications, barracks &ca. 3. Erection & repairs of public buildings—4. College & schools—5 Pensions & gratuities—6 Indians. 7 Clergy—8. roads—9. all other expenses.?

<*expenditure*>

33. What are the usual dilapidations of the public treasury 1. before it is collected, by smuggling & bribery—2 in its expenditure by the unfaithfulness of the agents & contractors through which it passes?

34 If the annual expenditure exceeds the annual revenue in what manner is the deficiency made up?

35 What is the nature, amount & depreciation of the paper currency?

36 On what funds does it rest—whether on provincial revenue which will remain pledged for its redemption? or on the credit of the Government? And will Spain remain bound to redeem it, or will[5] it fall as a charge on the existing
<*debts*> Government whatever it may be?

37. Exclusively of paper currency, are there any other debts incurred by the Spanish government? their amount? do they bear interest? are any evidences of the same in circulation?[6] in what proportion are they due to inhabitants <*to persons not*> of the province or of the US.? and to persons not inhabitants of either?

38. What is the annual amount of exports of articles of the growth or produce of the Province under following heads—1 Cotton—2 Sugar & Molasses—3 Indigo—4 Boards, planks, & wood [generally] 5 Lead—6 Corn—7. Furs
<*exports*> & deer skins—8 Horses, cattle, hides—9 all other articles

39. What proportion of those articles were exported to the U. States during the last years of the last war & what to other countries? and what proportion of what was exported to other countries was exported in american vessels

40. What is the annual amount of imports under following heads—1. Articles of the growth of the United States coming down the Mississipi—2. Articles of the growth of the United States coming by sea. 3 Articles of the growth of other countries distinguished as followeth. *Wines*
<*imports*> quantity & quality—*Spirits* & *brandies* do. *Coffee—Teas—Pepper & spices—Cocoa & chocolate—refined Sugar Other West India articles—Salt—Segars & spanish tobacco*—also quantity & quality *All other articles of European & East India manufacture being generally "dry goods & hardware"* their value, & as far as practicable, the quantities of each head.

41 *<re-export >* What portion of all those several importations is for the consumption of the province? what portion for re-exportation? particularly the articles which are *not of the growth of the United States*? where are these last re-exported? by land or by sea? openly or with a design to a contraband trade?

42. *<manufactures>* What is the annual quantity of Cotton, Indigo, Sugar & molasses particularly the two last, made in the province
What are the domestic manufactures? are there any distilleries & sugar refineries?

43. *<shipping>* What number of vessels & tonnage is required for the exportation of New Orleans? what for the importations? Is there any coasting trade? what species of vessels & tonnage employed in do.?

<8. Are there any tythes?>

<9. Is there any land cultivated in the Delta (comprized between Iberville & the Lakes, the Sea, & the most western mouth of the Missisipi called in our maps Piakemines river) besides the Banks of the Mississippi? the population of that tract & of the contiguous settlement on the West bank of the Mississipi from opposite Manshac as high up the Mississippi as the settlements extend—the population, situation & extent of land fit for cultivation of the Apalousa settlement? of the Natchicoches do.? of those on the main red river & Arkansas?>

<10. Are there any feudal rights, such as ground rents—fines of alienation—droits du moulin and any noblesse as in Canada.>

17. What are the courts in existence, & their jurisdiction? Are they corrupt? are they popular? are they tedious in their proceedings

18 What is the number of lawyers, their fees, their standing in society?

19 Are the people litigious? what is the nature of most law suits—are they for right to land—personal contracts—personal quarrels—?

20 What would be the effect of the introduction of the trial by jury in civil & criminal cases?

21. What is the nature of the criminal jurisprudence—number & nature of crimes and punishment?

22. What is the nature of the colleges & schools?[7] Can the inhabitants generally read & write? What degree of information do they possess beyond that? *<Are they moral & religious? Superstitious & bigotted?>*

[*Queries added by TJ*:]

23. On what footing is the church and clergy, what lands or tythes have they, & what other sources of support
24. What officers civil or military are appointed to each division of the province, and what to the general government, with a general definition of their powers?
25. By whom are they appointed? are any chosen by the inhabitants?
26. What emoluments have they & from what source derived?

MS (DLC: TJ Papers, 133:23031-2); undated; in Gallatin's hand, with emendations (see notes below) and last four queries in TJ's hand; TJ also added numerals 17 through 43, probably as he canceled Gallatin's labels at the point of the braces; cancellations are rendered in italics in angle brackets; one word obscured by tape.

PIAKEMINES was a French variation of an Indian word for persimmon and was later standardized by French creoles as Plaquemine. The river Gallatin identified as a western mouth of the Mississippi was most likely the same waterway now called Bayou Plaquemine, a distributary of the Mississippi River. It appears as the Piakemines River in at least two English-language maps published in the 1780s, both of which were based on the work of French cartographer Jean Baptiste Bourgignon d'Anville (William A. Read, *Louisiana Place Names of Indian Origin: A Collection of Words*, ed. George M. Riser [Tuscaloosa, Ala., 2008], 52-3; Thomas Kitchen, Sr., and others, *A General Atlas Describing the Whole Universe. Being a Complete and New Collection of the Most Approved Maps Extant; Corrected with the Utmost Care, and Augmented from the Latest Discoveries, Down to 1782* [London, 1782], map 33; DLC: Map Collection).

[1] Gallatin probably added the preceding questions, now canceled, after receiving TJ's queries (Document I).

[2] Remainder of query in TJ's hand.

[3] TJ emended this query to read: "How are the officers paid who are employed in the collection?"

[4] Remainder of query in TJ's hand.

[5] Word interlined by TJ in place of "shall."

[6] Remainder of query in TJ's hand.

[7] Preceding question emended by TJ to read: "What public colleges & schools have they?"

III. Jefferson's Revision of Original Draft

[12-17 July 1803]

Queries

[1. What are the best maps, general or particular, of the whole or parts of the province? copies of them if to be had in print.][1]

2 What are the boundaries of Louisiana, and on what authority does each portion of them rest?

[3. What is the extent of sea coast from the Western mouth of the Missisipi called Piakemines river?]

<*2. What is the distance from New Orleans to the nearest point of the Western boundary?*>

[4. what the distance from the same mouth due West to the Western boundary?]

5 Into what divisions is the province laid off?

<*4 What officers civil or military are appointed to each division, and what to the general government, with a definition of their powers?*[2] *are any of the officers appointed by the inhabitants? which & how?*>

<*5. What emoluments have they and from what source derived?*>

<*6. What are the annual expences of the Province drawn from the Treasury?*>

<*7. What are the nett receipts of the Treasury, and from what taxes or other resources are they drawn?*>

<*8. On what footing is the church and clergy, what lands have they have they tythes,*[3] *and from what other funds are they supported?*>

6. What is the population of the Province, distinguishing between White and Black but excluding Indians on the East side of the Missisipi? of the settlement on the West side next the mouth? of each distinct settlement in the other parts of the province? and what the geographical position and extent of each of those settlements?

[7 have they a militia? & what their numbers? what may be the number of free males from 18. to 45. y. of age in the different settlements]

[8 As good an estimate as can be had of the nations of Indians, to wit their names, numbers, and geographical position]

9 What are the foundations of their land titles? and what their tenure?

[10 Are there any feudal rights, such as ground rents, fines on alienation, droits de Moulins, or any Noblesse as in Canada?]

11 What is the quantity of granted lands as near as can be estimated?

12 What is the quantity ungranted in the Island of New Orleans, and in the settlement adjacent on the West side?

13 What are the lands appropriated to public use?

14 What [public] buildings, fortifications [barracks] or other fixed property belong to the public?

15 What is the quantity and general limits of the lands fit for the culture of sugar? What proportion is granted and what ungranted?

[<*16. on what footing is the church & clergy, what lands or tythes have they, & what other sources of support?*>]

16 Whence is their code of Laws derived? a copy of it if in print

<*17. What are the best maps general or particular, of the whole or parts of the province? copies of them if to be had in print.*>

MS (DLC: TJ Papers, 133:23030); undated; in Lewis Harvie's hand, with TJ's interlineations, often whole queries, rendered in square brackets; TJ canceled other queries, as rendered in angle brackets in italics above, and renumbered queries 1 though 10; for other emendations, see notes below.

[1] Query in TJ's hand moved here from the bottom of the sheet.

[2] Remainder of query interlined by TJ, but then canceled.

[3] Preceding three words interlined by TJ, but then canceled.

IV. Final List of Queries

[17 July 1803]

Queries 1 What are the best maps general, or particular of the whole or parts of the province? copies of them if to be had in print?

2 What are the boundaries of Louisiana, and on what authority does each portion of them [rest?]

3 What is the extent of the [sea coast from] the western mouth of the Missisipi called Piakemines?

4 What is the distance due West from the same mouth to the Western boundary?

5 Into what divisions is the province laid off?

6 What is the population of the province distinguishing between White and Black but excluding Indians on the East side of the Missisipi? of the settlement on the West side next the mouth? of each distinct settlement in the other parts of the province? and what the geographical position and extent of each of these settlements?

7 Have they a militia? and what their numbers? what may be the number of free males between 18 & 45 years of age in the different settlements?

8 As good an estimate as can be had of the Indian nations to wit their names, numbers and geographical position

9 What are the foundations of their Land titles? and what their tenure?

10 Are there any feudal rights, such as ground rents, fines on alienation [droits de moulins], or any noblesse as in Canada?

11 What is the quantity of granted Lands, as near as can be estimated?

12 What is the quantity ungranted on the Island of New Orleans and in the settlement [adjacent on the West side]?

13 What are the lands appropriated to public use?

14 What public buildings fortifications, barracks or other fixed property belong to the public?

15 What is the quantity and general limits of Lands fit for the culture of sugar? and what proportion is granted and what ungranted?

16 [Whence is their] code of Laws derived? a copy of it if in print

17 [What are the courts in existence] and their jurisdictions? are they corrupt? are they popular? are they tedious in their proceedings?

18 What is the number of lawyers, their [fees &] their standing in society?

19 Are the people litigious? what is the nature of most lawsuits? are they for rights to land, personal contracts, personal quarrels?

20 What would be the effect of the introduction of the trial by jury [in civil and criminal] courts?

21 What is the nature of their criminal jurisprudence [numbers and nature of crimes] punishments?

22 What public colleges and schools have they & can the Inhabitants generally read and write? what degree of information do they possess beyond that?

23 On what footing is the church and clergy? what [lands or] tythes have they? and what other sources of support?

24 What officers civil or military are appointed to each division [of the province] and to the general government, with a general definition of their powers?

25 By whom are they appointed are any [chosen] by the inhabitants?

[26] [What emoluments] have they? and from what source [derived]?

27 What are the local taxes paid in each division for the local expences of each division such as roads poor clergy schools salary of local officers? and by whom are they imposed?

28 What are the duties on imports and exports respectively, the gross amount of each the place where levied? and the manner of paying them?

29 How are the officers paid who are employed in the collection? [whether by fees, daily or annual salary, or commission?]

30 What is the nett amount of those duties paid in the Treasury?

31 Are there any other general taxes levied in the province, whether 1. on land, income, or capitation 2. on transfer of real property, wills and inheritances. 3 on sales of merchandise 4 on [stamps or] records. 5. on manufactures by way of excise. 6 in any other way? the gross and nett amount of each? the time, place and manner of collecting and whether the collecting officers are paid by fees, commission or salary?

32 What are the expences of the province paid from the Treasury under the following heads 1. salaries of Governor Intendant, Judges, all other civil officers. 2. Military including fortifications, barracks &c. 3 [erection] and repairs of public buildings. 4 Colleges and schools. 5 pensions and gratuities. 6 Indians 7 Clergy. 8 roads and all other expences

33 What are the usual dilapidations of the public treasury 1 before it is collected by [smuggling & bribery] 2. in its [expenditure] by the unfaithfulness of the agent and contractors through whom it passes?

[34] If the annual expenditure exceeds the annual revenue, in what manner is the deficiency made up?

[35] [What is the] nature amount and depreciation of the paper currency?

[36] On what funds does it rest? whether on provincial revenues which will remain pledged for its [redemption or on] the credit of the government?

37 Exclusively of paper currency are there any other debts incurred by the Spanish government? their amount? do they bear interest? are any evidences of the same in circulation? in what proportion are they due to inhabitants of the Province or of the U.S.? and to persons not inhabitants of either?

38 What is the annual amount of exports of articles of the growth or produce of the Province under following heads 1 Cotton. 2 Sugar and Molasses. 3 Indigo 4 Board planks, and wood generally 5 Lead. 6 Corn. 7 Furs and deer skins. 8 Horses cattle 9 all other articles

39 What proportion of those articles were exported to the U.S. during the last years of the last war? and what to other countries and what proportion of what was exported to other countries was exported in American vessels.

40 What is the annual amount of imports under following heads 1 Articles of the growth of the U.S. coming down the Missisipi. 2 articles of the growth of other countries distinguished as followeth Wines quantity and quality Spirits & brandies

do Coffee Tea Pepper and spices cocoa and chocolate Refined sugar other West India articles Salt Segars and Spanish tobacco also quantity and quality. All other articles of European and East India manufacture being generally dry goods and hardware their value as far as practicable the quantities of each head.

41 What portion of these several importations is for the consumption of the Province? what portion for exportation particularly the articles which are not of the growth of the US? where are these last exported? by land or by sea? openly or with a design to a contraband trade?

42 What is the annual quantity of Indigo, cotton, sugar, and molasses particularly the two last made in the Province? what are the domestic manufactures [are there any] distilleries and sugar refineries?

43 What number of vessels and tonnage is required for the exportation of New Orleans? what for the importation? Is there any coasting trade? What species of vessels and tonnage imployed in do?

PrC (DLC: TJ Papers, 133:23033-6); undated; entirely in Lewis Harvie's hand; faint and blurred, with words in brackets supplied from previous sets of queries, especially Documents II and III, and William C. C. Claiborne to TJ, 24 Aug.; numbers for queries 13 through 26 and 37 through 43 appear in right margin. Enclosed in TJ to William C. C. Claiborne, TJ to Daniel Clark, Jr., and TJ to William Dunbar, all 17 July 1803.

From Robert Smith

SIR July. 9. 1803.

I am greatly pleased with the ideas suggested in the proposed amendment of the Constitution and I sincerely hope that they will be adopted by the legislature of the Union. But I am rather inclined to think that they ought not all to be ingrafted upon the Constitution. Your great Object is to prevent Emigrations excepting to a certain portion of the ceded territory. This would be effectually accomplished by a Constitutional prohibition that Congress should not erect or establish in that portion of the ceded territory situated North of Lat. 32 degrees any new State or territorial government and that they should not grant to any people excepting Indians any right or title relative to any part of the said portion of the said territory. All other powers of making exchanges, working mines &c would then remain in Congress to be exercised at discretion; and in the exercise of this discretion subject as it would be to the three aforementioned restrictions I do not perceive that any thing could be done which would counteract your present intentions.

The rights of Occupancy in the soil ought to be secured to the Indians and government ought, in my Opinion, to endeavour to Obtain for them the exclusive Occupation of the Northern portion of Louisiana excepting such posts as may be necessary to our trade and intercourse with them. But ought not this to be a subject of legislative provision? If the Indian rights of Occupancy be a part of the Constitution might not the government be hereafter thereby much entangled? Under such a Constitutional guarantee the Indians might harass our military posts or our settlements in the southern portion or elsewhere in the most wanton manner and we could not disturb their rights of Occupancy without a formal alteration of the Constitution.

Under the idea that so many & such undefined restrictions as you have proposed to be ingrafted upon the Constitution might in process of time embarrass the Government and might probably not be acceptable to Congress, I have respectfully submitted to your Consideration the enclosed Sketch.— RT SMITH

RC (DLC); endorsed by TJ as received from the Navy Department on 11 July and "Louisiana" and so recorded in SJL.

ENCLOSURE

Proposed Amendment to the Constitution

An Amendment proposed to the Constitution to be added to S. 3. Art. 4.

Louisiana being in virtue of the Treaty &c incorporated with the U. States and being thereby a part of the Territory thereof, Congress shall have power to dispose of and make all needful rules and regulations respecting the same as fully and effectually as if the same had been at the time of the establishment of the Constitution a part of the Territory of the U. States: provided nevertheless that Congress shall not have power to erect or establish in that portion of Louisiana which is situated North of the latitude of (32) degrees any new state or territorial government nor to grant to any Citizen or citizens or other individual or individuals excepting Indians any right or title relative to any part of the said portion of Louisiana until a new amendment of the Constitution shall give that authority.

MS (DLC); undated; entirely in Smith's hand.

To John Strode

Dear Sir Washington July 9. 1803.

Three days ago I answered your friendly letter of the 26th. June and mentioned that I should probably leave this place on the 25th. I now think I shall leave it on the 24th. & be with you on the 25th. if nothing unforeseen happens. I last night recieved from my daughter Eppes a letter informing me she should then be at the Louisa springs, which will induce me to go by them, and the rather as it may give me an opportunity of exploring the road from the Raccoon ford towards Boswell's old place, & so on to the old well on the 3. notched road, James river &c. I think you once told me you had a friend residing perhaps at Porter's mill or near there, who would know of the ways leading towards Boswell's & the springs, or could easily acquire the knolege. if you could by letter obtain information from him whether there be a road leading from the Raccoon ford towards Boswell's old place or the Louisa springs, and some account of it, before I have the pleasure of seeing you, I could on recieving it when I meet you, decide whether I would attempt to go along it. the state of the road, stages, or farmer's houses distances, whether hilley or level, open or embarrassed with trees &c are the material circumstances. Accept my salutations & respects. Th: Jefferson

PrC (MHi); at foot of text: "John Strode esq."; endorsed by TJ in ink on verso.

From Joseph Yznardi, Sr.

Sir— Cadiz 9th. July 1803—

The verry moment I arrived on this side of the Water last Year, I did myself the honour taking the liberty of advising your Excelly. how very Sensible I was & ever will be to the very Kind attentions & favours I received & meritted from your goodness; requesting the continuation of your Kind protection, without doubting of the faithfull compliance in the duty of my office.—

In my Journey to Madrid I have given evident proofs, as Mr. Graham can acertain your Excelly. in every case that presented, & particularly in the affair of New Orleans; influencing with the Prince & State Minister to send the Vessel of War to give Satisfaction to the just complaints of that Governmt; I also obtained to obviate from the Council the wrong information which they had respecting Quarenteens; and notwithstanding that I do not appear with Public honours nor distinctions, I expect meritorious recompenses for my Conduct in the several Commissions that the King has put under my direction.

I most cordialy congratulate your Excelly. on the happy event of the great Negociations of Mr. Monroe, on which happy issue & in celebration; I on the 4th. inst. gave a Dinner to all the Americans that were in Bay & in this City; reading to them what the Inclosed Paper mentions, as cordial Sentiments of my own; & which I beg that your Excelly. will pardon the Liberty I take in communicating the same; & allthough so very far distant I never will forget the merit I profess your Excy.

Inclosed I hand your Excy. some Gibraltar Chronicles which shews the rancour that exists against France, & likewise Copy of the violation made by the English on the Spanish Terrotory, from which we may suppose that the Spanish neutrality will not last long. Last month I forwarded ℔ Duplicate via Salem & Baltimore the proofs against Israel, in favour of the unjust lawsuit that he carrys on against me in the Court of Philada. which I most earnestly request of your Excy. to have present my Innocence—& to command without reserve—

Sir—Your Excellencys—Most obedt. & most hble. Servt.

JOSEF YZNARDY

RC (DLC); in a clerk's hand, signed by Yznardi; at foot of text: "To His Excellency. Thomas Jefferson President of the United States of America—Washington"; endorsed by TJ as received 5 Sep. and so recorded in SJL. Enclosures: (1) Address expressing the gratitude of America "to Divine Providence," signed "J.Y."; noting that after 28 years of independence the population of the United States has doubled, and the last census shows that the increase is largely due to births rather than immigration; Americans can "with manly pride reflect upon our envious State of Prosperity"; he lauds the acquisition of Louisiana, "by which our Agriculture & Navigation will undoubtedly encrease to the astonishment of all the World," and commends "the Wisdom & Conduct of our actual Administration who has accomplished this grand object, at an expence, which compared to the numerous advantages we shall derive from it, is so very inconsiderable, that it is scarce worth mentioning"; also praising "the able Negociator"—Monroe—"who to serve his Country, left his Seat of quiet, to cross the troubled Ocean, & appear at a Court, where he had before been a favourite Minister to exert his Patriotism in the advantages of his Country"; he expresses gratitude that on "this Memorable Day" of celebration, the United States is "free from the Clashing of Arms, which is now again about to involve all Europe in Blood & Slaughter" (Tr in same, in a clerk's hand; Tr in same, unsigned, in a clerk's hand, in Spanish, expressing the same sentiments). (2) List of 11 toasts given at the dinner at Yznardi's house on 4 July; the third toast is to TJ, "The friend of Man: May we esteem his virtues as freemen, but not adulate him as slaves," and the eighth is to "The tree of liberty: planted by Franklin, cultivated by Washington and preserved by Jefferson" (Tr in same, in a clerk's hand). (3) Extract, likely from the *Gibraltar Chronicle*, dated Gibraltar, 4 July, announcing that a British sloop of war captured two French vessels that were at anchor near a Spanish fort; although this regretful incident could lead to war between Britain and Spain if the prizes are not returned, "the question must be decided by the Admiralty" (Tr in same, in a clerk's hand). Other enclosures not found.

In August 1801, TJ appointed John GRAHAM to be secretary of the U.S. legation in Madrid (Vol. 35:189, 190n).

Manuel Godoy was the PRINCE, Pedro Cevallos the STATE MINISTER (Vol. 38: 207n; Yznardi to TJ, 4 Apr.).

TO SEND THE VESSEL OF WAR: for the dispatch of a Spanish brig to the United States with news of the restoration of the right of deposit at New Orleans, see TJ to DeWitt Clinton, 22 Apr.

CHRONICLES: the *Gibraltar Chronicle* began publication in May 1801. The newspaper published news items and advertisements and served as the printing shop of the British garrison at Gibraltar (Jason R. Musteen, *Nelson's Refuge: Gibraltar in the Age of Napoleon* [Annapolis, Md., 2011], 29, 59, 194n; Stephen Constantine, *Community and Identity: The Making of Modern Gibraltar since 1704* [Manchester, Eng., 2009], 19, 59, 81).

For the prolonged dispute between Yznardi and shipmaster Joseph ISRAEL, see Vol. 36:4, 5, 6n; Vol. 37:80-1, 306-7; Vol. 38:206-7.

To the Earl of Buchan

MY LORD Washington July 10, 1803.

I recieved through the hands of mr Lenox, on his return to the US. the valuable volume you were so good as to send me on the life & writings of Fletcher of Saltoun. the political principles of that[1] patriot were worthy the purest periods[2] of the British constitution. they are those which were in vigour[3] at the epoch of the American emigration. our ancestors brought them here, and they needed little strengthening to make us what we are. but in the weakened condition of[4] English whiggism at this day, it requires more firmness to publish[5] and advocate them, than it then did to act on them. this merit is peculiarly your Lordship's; and no one honours it more than myself; freely admitting, at the same time,[6] the right of a nation to change it's political principles and constitution at will, and the impropriety of any but it's own citizens, censuring that change. I expect your Lordship has been disappointed, as I acknowledge I have been, in the issue of the convulsions on the other side the channel. this has certainly lessened the interest which the Philanthropist warmly felt in those struggles. without befriending human liberty, a gigantic force has risen up which seems to threaten[7] the world. but it hangs on the thread of opinion,[8] which may break from one day to another. I feel real anxiety on the conflict[9] in which your nation is again engaged; and bless the almighty[10] being who in gathering together the waters under the heavens into one place,[11] divided the dry lands of[12] your hemisphere, from the dry lands of ours, and said, "here, at least, be there peace." I hope that peace and amity with all nations will long be the charter of our land,[13] and that it's prosperity under this charter[14] will re-act on the mind of Europe, and profit her by the example. my hope of preserving peace for our country[15] is not founded in the quaker principle of non resistance under every wrong, but in the belief that a just and friendly conduct on our part will procure justice and friendship from others, and that, in the existing contest,[16] each of the combatants will find an[17] interest in our friendship.[18] I cannot say we shall be unconcerned spectators of the combat. we feel for human sufferings; and we wish the good of all.[19] we shall look on[20] therefore with the sensations which these dispositions and the events of the war will produce.

I feel a pride in the justice which your lordship's sentiments render to the character of my illustrious countryman Washington. the moderation of his desires and the strength of his judgment enabled him to calculate correctly[21] that the road to that glory which never dies is to use power for the[22] support of the laws and liberties of our country, not for their destruction, and his[23] will accordingly survive the wreck of every thing now living.

Accept, my Lord, the tribute of esteem from one who renders it with warmth to the disinterested friend of mankind, and assurances of my very high consideration & respect TH: JEFFERSON

PrC (DLC); at foot of first page: "Earl of Buchan." Dft (same); undated. Tr (PPAmP); in Erskine's hand; enclosed in Earl of Buchan to Dugald Stewart, Professor of Moral Philosophy at the University of Edinburgh, 21 Dec. 1803. Tr (CU-BANC); in Erskine's hand and endorsed by him: "considering the state of G. Britain & of Europe & what I believed to be the principles & character of Mr. Jefferson, I sent to him with a short expressive inscription a copy of my Essay on the life & writings of Fletcher of Saltoun; my intention was to defeat as far as my opinion could the prejudices conceived against Mr. J. on both sides of the Atlantic." Enclosed in TJ to George W. Erving, 10 July 1803.

David Steuart Erskine, 11th earl of Buchan (1742-1829), was a Scottish lord, writer, and literary patron who founded the Society of Antiquaries of Scotland in 1780. A supporter of the Americans during the Revolution, he considered moving to the United States after the war but instead purchased Dryburgh Abbey, hoping to make it a Scottish cultural center, and lived there from 1786 until his death. The Scottish agricultural reformer and economist James Anderson transmitted a letter from Buchan to TJ of 22 Oct. 1792. Buchan and Anderson were elected to membership in the American Philosophical Society on 18 Apr. 1794, the same day as TJ's son-in-law, Thomas Mann Randolph. While president of the Agriculture Society in London, Buchan had been a frequent correspondent of George Washington from 1790 to 1798. Buchan quoted the above letter from TJ in an address he delivered to a group of Americans at Edinburgh in 1811 on the occasion of Washington's birthday. TJ's letter and the earl's address were published in a pamphlet and also in numerous American newspapers beginning in the summer of 1811 (DNB; Washington, *Papers, Pres. Ser.*, 5:284-5; same, *Ret. Ser.*, 4:502n; *National Intelligencer*, 9 July 1811; *Richmond Enquirer*, 7 Dec. 1822; Sowerby, No. 3403; RS, 4:150, 153n; Vol. 24:565n; Vol. 27:656n).

VALUABLE VOLUME: Buchan's work on the Scottish patriot Andrew Fletcher, *Essays on the Lives and Writings of Fletcher of Saltoun and the Poet Thomson: Biographical, Critical, and Political*, was published in London in 1792 (Sowerby, No. 437).

[1] In Dft TJ here canceled "worth illustrious."

[2] In Dft word interlined in place of "stages."

[3] TJ here continued in Dft "when the greater part of the emigrants came from thence to this country and which needed but a" before altering the remainder of the sentence to read as above.

[4] TJ first wrote "weakened state of political principles" before altering the Dft to read as above.

[5] In Dft TJ first wrote "them with approbation than it did then to act on them" before altering the remainder of the sentence to read as above.

[6] Dft: "while I freely submit."

[7] In Dft TJ first wrote "which threatens."

[8] In Dft TJ first wrote "did it not hang on the slender thread of a single life" before altering the sentence to this point.

[9] In Dft TJ here continued to semicolon: "to which imperious circumstances seem to call your nation."

[10] Word interlined in Dft.

[11] Preceding three words interlined in Dft.

[12] In Dft TJ first concluded the sentence " 'your hemisphere from the dry lands of the other,' and said 'here let there be peace.' "

[13] Word interlined in Dft in place of "republic."

[14] In Dft word interlined in place of "system."

[15] Preceding three words interlined in Dft.

[16] In Dft TJ interlined the passage from "belief" to this point.

[17] Dft: "their."

[18] In Dft TJ interlined "friendship" in place of "neutrality."

[19] Preceding sentence interlined in Dft.

[20] Remainder of sentence interlined in Dft in place of largely illegible canceled text.

[21] Word interlined in Dft.

[22] Remainder of sentence interlined in Dft in place of "good of those who confide it, & to lay it down when that good <*call for*> requires it. That it is the light which shines longest and not <*the blaze of a moment*> that which blazes most, is the [estimation] of true wisdom."

[23] Tr in PPAmP: "his glory." Tr in CU-BANC: "*His*."

From Jean Dacqueny

New york july 10th. 1803

Since ten years I have been a printer in Charleston and having during six conducted freneau & paine's city gazette, I tooke upon me to offer you my services as such. Lousianna being now ceded to the United States I am thinking that your honor will establish there a government similar to that of the different states of the Union. Therefore a printer there will be useful, and if I am happy enough to get a letter of recommendation from you, I am sure I will get the preference from the gentleman you shall be pleased to send[1] there as governor. The letter which is inclosed in this and directed to citoyen Pichon, is recommendation from a most eminent man in the french government; I beg your honor to have the goodness of sending it to Mr Pichon. Be pleased, sir, to let me know your answer as I am going to New-Orleans in a few weeks, I should like to know your excellency's opinion on this subject.

I am your excellency's most Obedient Servant

J. Dacqueny
409 pearl-street, New-york

N. B. I take also the liberty of sending you one of my Catalogues; if any books could please your honor Let me know of it by your next.

RC (DLC); at head of text: "Thos. jefferson, Esqr. president of the U.S."; endorsed by TJ as received 15 July and so recorded in SJL. Enclosure not found.

Native Frenchman Jean Dacqueny (b. 1777 or 1778) had worked with Peter Freneau and Seth Paine in Charleston, South Carolina, on the daily *City Gazette*, before undertaking the triweekly publication of a French newspaper, *L'Echo du Sud. Moniteur Francais*, from April through July 1801. After moving to the Louisiana Territory, Dacqueny partnered with J. B. Thierry & Co. and published from November 1807 to June or July 1810 a French and English New Orleans newspaper, the *Courrier de la Louisiane*. In the Territory of Orleans, the governor had authority, until 1813, to appoint a public printer whose duties included publishing the laws in French and English. William C. C. Claiborne awarded the lucrative government printing contract in 1809 to Thierry and Dacqueny, describing the latter as "an industrious, inoffensive man." Dacqueny also took control of the *Telegraphe Louisianais and Mercantile Advertiser*, which he published in the city as a bilingual triweekly newspaper from 1810 to 1811 (Brigham, *American Newspapers*, 1:185, 191-2; 2:1024, 1026, 1031; Dunbar Rowland, ed., *Official Letter Books of W. C. C. Claiborne, 1801-1816*, 6 vols. [Jackson, Miss., 1917], 5:16; Florence M. Jumonville, "'The People's Friend—The Tyrant's Foe': Law-Related New Orleans Imprints, 1803-1860," in Warren M. Billings and Mark F. Fernandez, eds., *A Law Unto Itself? Essays in the New Louisiana Legal History* [Baton Rouge, 2001], 43-9; Claiborne to TJ, 10 Jan. 1805).

[1]MS: "sent."

To George W. Erving

Dear Sir Washington July 10. 1803.

I take the liberty of putting under your cover the inclosed letters. two of them contain pamphlets, & I would therefore wish them to be so conveyed as to avoid the expence of postage. that to Sr. John Sinclair can be left at his house in town, from whence he has doubtless regular means of conveyance to his residence in Scotland where he probably is at this season. I do not know that mr Strickland has any particular deposit in London. I must get you to supply whatever is defective in the address of the Earl of Buchan and to forward the letter by post. presuming the intercourse between England & Leghorn is still open, I have also inclosed a letter for mr Appleton, our Consul there, to be forwarded as you shall see best.

The preference we had given to the ways of peace rather than of war for obtaining an easier position on the Missisipi, had already met the approbation of the more candid federalists and had loosened them from their leaders; the happy termination of it has given that party it's coup de grace. those who had made themselves so prominent as to be ashamed to retreat, will still make a noise. but they will be literally a vox et præterea nihil. the mercantile interest indeed, which identifies itself with England, not having yet corrected their belief that this administration has partialities against England, still follow their old file-leaders, and give them the benefit of the numerous newspapers which their advertisements support. the rectification of this error, the employment of proper means to neutralise at least the banking interests, will affect the merchants more favorably. if we place the new accession of Louisiana on proper grounds, while it secures our peace, it may be the means of confining & condensing our population on the E. side of the Missisipi, instead of diffusing it; and of removing our Indian population to the other side. the books you sent are recieved, but not yet opened. on a view of the invoice the prices appear reasonable. Accept my friendly salutations & assurances of great esteem.

Th: Jefferson

PrC (DLC); at foot of text: "George W. Erving esq." Enclosures: (1) TJ to Sir John Sinclair, 30 June. (2) TJ to William Strickland, 30 June. (3) TJ to the Earl of Buchan, 10 July. (4) TJ to Thomas Appleton, 5 July.

vox et præterea nihil: nothing but noise (voice). For a previous use of the expression by TJ, see his letter to Pierre Auguste Adet of 5 Feb.

At TJ's request, Erving was acquiring books for the congressional library; see Vol. 38:472-3 and Erving to TJ, 8 Mch. 1804. A letter from Erving to TJ dated 14 Apr. 1803, recorded in SJL as received from London on 20 June, has not been found.

Statement of Account with John March, with Jefferson's Order

Georgetown, Potomac

The President

1802		To John March	
Decr. 29 To	Binding	Historia Evangelica, Morocco	$1.75
	Binding	Revolution Francoise, 18o: Calf, gilt	0.62½
	Binding	Ossian, 4 vols: 18o: Calf, gilt	2.50
1803			
March 3	Binding	Plutarque, &c. 4 vols: 18o: Calf, gilt	2.50
May 2	Domestic	Encyclopædia, vol: 1, boards	2.50
11	Binding	Derham's Theology, 2 vols: 8vo: Calf, gilt	2.00
	½ Binding	1 vol: Journals of the Senate, 8vo	0.62½

	Binding	Helvetius, 10 vols: Calf, gilt	6.25
June 7	Binding	De L'Homme Physique, &c: 2 vols: 8vo: Calf, gilt	2.00
	Do	Le Dentiste, 1 vol: 8vo: Calf, gilt	1.00
	Do	Randolph on Gardening, 18o: Calf, gilt	0.62½
	Do	Ossian, 2 vols: 18o: Calf. gilt	1.25
	Do	Racine, 2 vols: 18o: Do	1.25
	Do	De Cive—De Justo—Almanack, 3 vols: 18o. Calf, gilt	1.87½
	½ Binding	Connaissance des Tems, 4 vols	2.00
	Do	1 vol: Journals 8vo	0.62½
	Binding	Meridies de Democrat; 12 mo	0.50
20	12 Cases for Writings		4.00
July 5	Canvas, and Pasting and lining 4 Maps		2.00
10	Binding	Barton's Botany, 2 vols: in 1, 8vo: Calf, gilt	1.25
	Do	Lois de la Nature, 8vo: Calf, gilt	1.00
	Do	Priestley's Institutes of Religion, 2 vols: 12 mo; Calf, gilt	1.50
	Do	Linn on Genius, Calf, gilt	0.62½
			$40.25

[*Order by TJ*:]

Mr. Barnes will be pleased to pay this

TH: JEFFERSON
July 16. 1803

MS (CSmH); in March's hand.

HISTORIA EVANGELICA: probably Antoine Arnauld, *Historia et Concordia Evangelica* (Paris, 1653; Sowerby, No. 1491).

REVOLUTION FRANCOISE: possibly Jean Paul Rabaut Saint Étienne, *Précis historique de la Révolution Françoise* (Vol. 28:358).

DE L'HOMME PHYSIQUE: probably *Rapports du physique et du moral de l'homme* by Pierre Jean Georges Cabanis, a copy of which TJ received from the author in May 1803 (Vol. 38:524-5; Sowerby, No. 1246).

LE DENTISTE: possibly Louis Laforgue, *L'art du dentiste, ou manuel des opérations de chirurgie* (Paris, 1802). According to his financial records, on 16 July TJ gave John March an order on John Barnes for $40.25 for bookbinding (MB, 2:1104).

From Thomas Worthington

SIR Chilicothe July 10th 1803

Our election for a representative to Congress took place on the 21st of Last month since then official returns have been receved from 17 counties There is 18 counties in the state—returns are yet to be recd from the 18th which will not materially alter the present state of the poll, which is as follows

Jeremiah Morrow (republican)	3644 votes
Wm McMillan (Fed)	1887
E Langham (professed Rep)	615
Wm Goforth (Rep)	310
Michael Baldwin	764

Mr Morrow is elected by a Large Majority and is a decided republican—I regret he does not possess more general information on political subjects—He is a man of much firmness excellent understanding and of an amiable disposition—With his industry I have no doubt he will soon enable himself to discharge his duty with satisfaction to his constituents Every act has been used by the federalists to divide the republicans and not without its effect—Some indeed Who call themselves republicans have acted in the most shameful manner and have met with a united repulse from the people From the mixed unsetled state of society throughout the state I was fearful we should be so divided that our enemies would succeed but the good sense of the people has caused a union sufficient to carry our point—

You know sir the part I have acted in bringing about the change from a Territorial to a state government. The republicans in Congress through my representations as agent for the people extended to the people of this country those priviledges they wished to enjoy leaving them free to pursue that course in politicks which appeared to them best calculated to promote their own happiness This was generous, it was Just—Although I was satisfied in my own mind as to the course they would pursue Yet I felt very anxious and in some measure responsible for the good or evil which might[1] grow out of a measure I had so strongly advocated—I am now sir in a great measure relieved from anxiety and released from responsibility—Our state government has commenced its operations with much harmony and with the approbation of a very Large majority of the governed The people of the state have elected a representation to Congress decidedly republican Thus sir they have given in every way the strongest proof of their approbation of the measures pursued by the General government In addition to this the representatives of the people have positively instructed their representation in Congress to promote all in their power an alteration of that part of the Constitution relateing to the election of president and vice president In the course I have been obliged to pursue to promote the measures which have taken place and which I believed calculated to promote greatly the interests of the people of this country and the union at Large I have uniformly had the approbation of my own conscience and as far as I could Judge acted a disinterested part. I have been conscious of a want of ability but not of integrity Yet our federalists and some unprincipled republicans (if they may be called republicans) have constantly attempted to misrepresent my conduct and calumniate my private reputation I would not have troubled you with this subject but for a late publication of Mr M Baldwin in the sioto gazette which you have no doubt seen and which so far as it relates to me (except that I was opposed to his election) is false and malicious—A part of this publication is sir within your own knowledge untrue I mean that part which relates to my appointment as superviser—If you recollect sir when you was about to nominate officers for the federal court in this state I mentioned that Mr Baldwin was unsteady but hoped he would as he grew older become more consistant and be a better member of society I fear my hopes will not be realized I wish most heartily he would pursue a course more honourable to himself and satisfactory to society—He has thought proper to accept the appointment you have given him contrary to the expectation of his brother and yourself—I have been informed that the Register and receiver of publick monies at Cincinnati are about to resign their[2] offices—Give me leave to recommend Mr Daniel Symmes of that place as a proper person to fill the office of register of the land office—I have mentioned the same Gentleman to Mr Gallatin—I regret that it is necessary to exclude any *class* of *men* from appointment but when those men use the influence they obtain by their office to thwart misrepresent & counteract the government I cannot think they ought to hold offices—This is the case with several characters in office in this state—Mr Byrd as judge of the federal court and major Zeigler as marshal so far as I can learn give universal satisfaction—It will be necessary ere long to appoint a register of the landoffice and recever of publick monies at Zanesville on the muskingum river by virtue of a law of Last session of Congress Perhaps Mr Gallatin has sufficient information on this subject I wrote him some time since and at the request of two federal Gentlemen & named them as applicants for the appointments. I did not expect they would be appointed If further information should be wanted on this subject if in my power I will afferd it with pleasure—I am fearful I shall not have the pleasure of seeing you this winter If I should resign you may depend on my successor as a decided republican—

Accept sir of My sincere wishes for your health and happiness

T WORTHINGTON

RC (DNA: RG 59, LAR); at foot of text: "The president of the united states"; endorsed by TJ as received 25 July and "Symmes Danl. to be Register Cincinnati" and so recorded in SJL.

Michael Baldwin received an APPOINTMENT as U.S. atttorney for Ohio in March 1803. HIS BROTHER was U.S. Senator Abraham Baldwin of Georgia (TJ to the Senate, 1 Mch. 1803).

REGISTER AND RECEIVER OF PUBLICK MONIES AT CINCINNATI: Israel Ludlow and James Findlay, who had been appointed by John Adams in May 1800 (JEP, 1:353).

LAW OF LAST SESSION: see John Irvin to TJ, 17 May 1803.

[1] MS: "migh."

[2] MS: "their their."

Appendix I

EDITORIAL NOTE

Jefferson kept an ongoing list of appointments and removals that extended throughout his two terms as president, with entries extending from 5 Mch. 1801 to 23 Feb. 1809. For the first installment of this list, from 5 Mch. 1801 to 14 May 1802, see Vol. 33, Appendix I, List 4. Subsequent installments have appeared as Appendix I in Volumes 37, 38, and 39. This segment continues at 4 Apr. 1803, with the president's recording of Levett Harris's appointment to St. Petersburg. It includes the entries for the period covered by this volume, except for the appointment of five bankruptcy commissioners at 4 Mch., which Jefferson entered on his list between those of 1 and 3 Mch.; they are printed in Volume 39. The president's entries at 3 Mch. included Hore Browse Trist, Henry Warren, and Joseph Turner, who received interim appointments after the close of the Seventh Congress but whose entries are printed in the previous volume with the other entries at that date. No entries appear between 4 Mch. and 4 Apr. or 30 June and 10 July. This was a working list, which Jefferson updated as he received information, such as that for James S. Morsell at 3 June, where the president added "declined" at the end of the entry at a later sitting. The bankruptcy commissions for Samuel Knight and the three Worcester appointees were dated 16 June. Jefferson probably signed them the next day and entered the names on his list at the 17th (list of commissions in Lb in DNA: RG 59, MPTPC). Most of the appointments entered below, excluding those for bankruptcy commissioners, were interim appointments requiring the approval of the Senate (see TJ to the Senate, 11 Nov. 1803).

List of Appointments

[4 Apr.-29 June 1803]

Apr. 4. Levitt Harris Pensva to be Consul at St. Petersbg

Isaac Coxe Barnet of New Jersey Commercl. agent Havre vice Peter Dobell resigned

Edward Turner of Kentucky Register of land office at Natchez. new

7. Isaac Briggs Surveyor of the lands of the US. South of the state of Tennissee. new

8. Charles Jones Jenkins Commr. of the US. under the act for the valuan of lands S.C.[1] &c vice[2] Samuel Hay resigned.

11. Cathcart Leander Consul at Tunis. vice Wm. Eaton resigned.

20. Isaac Illsley of Mass. Collector for the district of Portland & Falmouth vice Isaac Illsley junr. by misnomer.

18. blanks for Min. Plen. to London & Paris.

26. James Wilkenson, Benjamin Hawkins & Robert Anderson of S.C. Commrs. to treat with Creeks on a cession of lands.

May 4. to be commercial Agent at Antwerp vice Isaac Coxe Barnet appd to Havre.

10. Samuel Ward of Massachusets to be Naval officer for the district of Salem & Beverly Mass. v. Story declined

Samuel Osgood of N.Y. to be Naval officer for the district of N. York v. Richd. Rogers removed.

Jeremiah Bennet junr. of N.J. to be Collector for the district of Bridgetown N.J. & Inspector of the revenue v. Eli Elmer. delinquent [money][3]

George House of Connecticut to be master of a cutter [at N London restored[4] v. Hindman removd] for incapacity & malpractices

June 3. James S. Morsell of Columbia (Geo.t.) Commr. bkrptcy v Gantt resigned. declined

Wm. Duvall of Virginia (Richmd.) Commr. bkrptcy (reappointed)

7. pro 1st. Robert Brent reappointed Mayor of City of Washington for one year.

10. Tobias Lear Consul general for the city & kingdom of Algiers v. Obrien resigned

17. Samuel Knight Commr. bkrptcy Vermont (Brattleboro') v. James Elliot resigned. (& Oliver Gallop declined acceptg.)

Samuel Flagg
Abraham Lincoln
Francis Blake } Worcester. Commrs. bkrptcy Massach.

Thos. Durfee of R.I. Surveyor & Inspector of port of Tiverton district of Newport R.I. new.

Charles Gibson of Maryld. Surveyor & Inspector of port of Easton district of Oxford. Maryld. new.

Brian Hellen of N.C. to be Collector & Inspector of revenue for the district of Beaufort N.C. new. [not the surveyorship suppressd by law. Benj. Cheney held it]

21. Abraham Ten Wyck to be Commr. bkrptcy at Albany vice Nichs. N. Quackenbush. resd.

24. Richard Henry Lee
John E. Holt } Norfolk Commrs. bkrptcy

29. for Mar. 4. 1803. Nicholas King Surveyor of Washington

MS (DLC: TJ Papers, 186:33097); entirely in TJs hand, including brackets, unless indicated otherwise (see note 3); being the continuation of a list that extends from 5 Mch. 1801 to 23 Feb. 1809; for the installment immediately preceding this one, see Vol. 39: Appendix I.

The interim commission for Levett HARRIS as consul at St. Petersburg is dated 4 Apr. (FC in Lb in DNA: RG 59, PTCC).

On 12 Nov. 1802, Madison wrote ISAAC COXE BARNET, recently appointed commercial agent at Antwerp, inquiring whether he would prefer the position that had opened at Le Havre. Barnet replied on 24 Jan. that he chose the French port, noting, "I should hope, from my acquaintance with the French to make myself more useful to my Country and reap earlier advantages for myself." He recommended Jacob Ridgway of Philadelphia as his successor at Antwerp. Barnet's interim commission is dated 4 Apr. (RC in DNA: RG 59, LAR, endorsed by TJ: "Barnet I. Cox to mr Madison to be Consul at Havre"; FC of commission in Lb in DNA: RG 59, PTCC; Madison, *Papers, Sec. of State Ser.*, 4:117, 280-1; Vol. 37: 697, 699, 700; Vol. 38:60n).

James Leander Cathcart's interim commission as CONSUL AT TUNIS is of 11 Apr. (FC in Lb in DNA: RG 59, PTCC).

BLANKS FOR MIN. PLEN.: see Editorial Note at Preparations to Negotiate an Alliance, 18 Apr.

COMMERCIAL AGENT AT ANTWERP: on 5 May, Madison sent Robert R. Livingston a blank commission for the Antwerp consulate and noted that the president's first choice was Daniel Strobel, but if he declined the commission should go to Jacob Ridgway (Madison, *Papers, Sec. of State Ser.*, 4:573-4). See TJ to the Senate, 9 Dec. 1803, for Ridgway's appointment.

For the appointment of JAMES S. MORSELL, see Samuel Hanson to TJ, 11 Feb. 1803.

[1] Abbreviation interlined.
[2] MS: "vice v."
[3] Brackets supplied by Editors.
[4] Word interlined.

Appendix II

Letters Not Printed in Full

EDITORIAL NOTE

In keeping with the editorial method established for this edition, the chronological series includes "in one form or another every available letter known to have been written by or to Thomas Jefferson" (Vol. 1:xv). Most letters are printed in full. In some cases, the letter is not printed but a detailed summary appears at the document's date (for an example, see E. T. Hadwen to TJ, 3 Jan. 1803). Other letters have been described in annotation, which, for the period covered by this volume, are listed in this appendix. Arranged in chronological order, this list includes for each letter the correspondent, date, and location in the volumes where it is described. Among the letters included here are brief letters of transmittal, multiple testimonials recommending a particular candidate for office, repetitive letters from a candidate seeking a post, and official correspondence that the president saw in only a cursory way. In other instances, documents are described in annotation due to the near illegibility of the surviving text. Using the list in this appendix, the table of contents, and Appendix III (correspondence not found but recorded in Jefferson's Summary Journal of Letters), readers will be able to reconstruct Jefferson's chronological epistolary record from 4 Mch. to 10 July 1803.

To Joseph Hamilton, 21 Mch. Noted at Hamilton to TJ, 3 Mch. 1803.
From S. Smith & Buchanan, 16 Apr. Noted at TJ to S. Smith & Buchanan, 14 Apr. 1803.
From William Short, 3 May. Noted at TJ to Short, 6 May 1803.
From James Ash, 14 May. Noted at Ash to TJ, 29 Apr. 1803.
Frin Jan H.C. Heineken, 23 June. Noted at John Vaughan to TJ, 25 June 1803.
From Albert Gallatin, received 28 June. Noted at TJ to Gallatin, 22 June 1803 (first letter).
From Barnabus McShane, 2 July. Noted at TJ to McShane, 28 June 1803.
From James Wallace, 6 July. Noted at TJ to Wallace, 11 July 1803.
To John Minor, 9 July. Noted at Minor to TJ, 15 July 1803.

Appendix III

Letters Not Found

EDITORIAL NOTE

This appendix lists chronologically letters written by and to Jefferson during the period covered by this volume for which no text is known to survive. Jefferson's Summary Journal of Letters provides a record of the missing documents. For incoming letters, Jefferson typically recorded in SJL the date that the letter was sent and the date on which he received it. He sometimes included the location from which it was dispatched and an abbreviated notation indicating the government department to which it pertained: "N" for Navy, "S" for State, "T" for Treasury, and "W" for War.

From James Jackson, 4 Mch. 1803; received 4 Mch. from Washington with notation "gunboats. Wylly."
From William Pickering, 6 Mch.; received 5 Mch. with notation "jail."
From Caesar A. Rodney, 11 Mch.; received 21 Mch. from Wilmington.
"Dover applicn."; received 18 Mch. with notation "Tilton v. Mclane."
From John B. Magruder; received 19 Mch.
From Wilson Cary Nicholas, 20 Mch.; received 20 Mch. from Warren.
From Marten Wanscher, 21 Mch.; received 25 Mch.
From Burgess Griffin, 23 Mch.; received 28 Mch.
From the Treasury Department, 24 Mch.; received 4 Apr. with notation "Jno. Wallace to be keepr lt. house Cape Hat. & shell."
From William Duane; received 25 Mch. with notation "Freneau's lre. revd. Danl. McCalla. Carpenter alias Cullen."
To Hancock Allen, 26 Mch.
To Joseph Moran and William Maddox, 26 Mch.
From David Higginbotham, 28 Mch.; received 28 Mch.
From David Hall, 29 Mch.; received 6 Apr. from Lewes.
To John Walker, 29 Mch.
To John Walker, 30 Mch.
From John Walker, 30 Mch.; received 30 Mch. from Belvoir.
To Burgess Griffin, 31 Mch.
To Wilson Cary Nicholas, 31 Mch.
From Benjamin Waterhouse, 31 Mch.; received 12 Apr. from Cambridge.
From David Higginbotham, 1 Apr.; received 5 Apr. from Milton.
From John Hooff, 1 Apr.; received 4 Apr. from Alexandria with notation "resigns lieutcy. W."
From James B. Richardson, 2 Apr.; received 17 Apr. from Charleston with notation "S."
From John Walker, 4 Apr.; received 12 Apr. from Belvoir.
From John Whipple and others; received 4 Apr. with notation "Theodore Foster to be loan officer R.I."
From Timothy Alden, Jr., 5 Apr.; received 16 Apr. from New Hampshire.
From Caspar Wistar, 5 Apr.; received 9 Apr. from Philadelphia with notation "Edwd Cutbush hosp. Boston."
From Arthur Fenner, 6 Apr.; received 17 Apr. from Providence with notation "T. Foster loan officer."

From Samuel Houston; received 8 Apr. from Washington with notation "jail. N."
From James McCrea, 11 Apr.; received 26 Apr. from Willsboro, N.Y., with notation "Commrs. bkrptcy."
To John Wayles Eppes, 13 Apr.
To Thomas Mann Randolph, 13 Apr.
From George W. Erving, 14 Apr.; received 20 June from London.
To Gabriel Lilly, 14 Apr.; notation "170. D."
From James Dinsmore, 15 Apr.; received 19 Apr. from Monticello with notation "John Dinsmore. Natchez. to be surveyor."
From Henry Dearborn; received 20 Apr.
To James Dinsmore, 20 Apr.
To Gideon Fitz, 20 Apr.
From David Higginbotham, 21 Apr.; received 26 Apr. from Milton.
From Henry Sheaff, 21 Apr.; received 25 Apr. from Philadelphia.
To James Dinsmore, 22 Apr.
From John Armstrong, 23 Apr.; received 10 May from Cincinnati.
From Abraham Baldwin, James Jackson, and John Milledge, 25 Apr.; received 22 May from Louisville, Georgia, with notation "Jno Clarke Commr. Missipi."
From Benjamin H. Latrobe, 25 Apr.; received 27 Apr. from Philadelphia.
To David Higginbotham, 27 Apr.
From Thomas Eston Randolph, 28 Apr.; received 1 May from Richmond.
From William Jackson, 30 Apr.; received 2 May from Philadelphia with notation "T."
To Henry Sheaff, 30 Apr.
From Thomas Sumter, Sr., April; received 3 June from Stateburg with notation "Fitzpatrick to office."
From James Dinsmore, 1 May; received 8 May from Monticello.
From John Gordon, 1 May; received 13 May from Northumberland with notation "Wm. Montague for Lt. House Smith's point."
From Gideon Fitz, 2 May; received 8 May from Monticello.
To Burgess Griffin, 2 May.
From [. . .], [Jon.] Jones, 2 May; received 6 May from Westmoreland with notation "Fras. Foushee Lt. house O. Pt. Comf."
From Jones & Howell, 2 May; received 4 May from Philadelphia with notation "309.42."
From John Wells, 2 May; received 9 May from Newburyport (see Madison, *Papers, Sec. of State Ser.*, 5:34).
From Anonymous; received 3 May with notation "Pittsbg. postmark. agt. Scull printer of Pittsbg gazette."
To Thomas Eston Randolph, 3 May.
From Gabriel Lilly, 8 May; received 11 May from Monticello.
From James Dinsmore, 9 May; received 11 May from Monticello.
From George Divers, 9 May; received 11 May from Farmington.
From Benjamin H. Latrobe, 9 May; received 11 May from Philadelphia.
From Martha Jefferson Randolph, 9 May; received 11 May from Edgehill.
From DeWitt Clinton, 10 May; received 18 May from Newtown, Long Island, with notation "mr Goetschius. Sacket harb."

From Samuel Latham Mitchill, 10 May; received 18 May from New York with notation "Sacket harbour L. Ontario."
To Gabriel Lilly, 12 May; with notation "5 for 50. D.—inclose 130.—nailrod.—groceries."
From James Oldham, 12 May; received 16 May from Monticello.
From Wade Hampton, 13 May; received 3 June from Charleston with notation "Fitzpatrick to office."
From Lafayette, 13 May; received 13 May 1805 from Paris.
From Jacob Morton, 16 May; received 18 May from New York with notation "with Clarke's papers for mr Madison."
From John Pittman, 16 May; received 19 May from Alexandria with notation "W."
To George Divers, 18 May.
To James Oldham, 18 May.
From Sackets Harbor; received 18 May with notation "petn for port of entrance."
From Leeson Simmons, 18 May; received 20 May from Philadelphia with notation "N."
To Gideon Fitz, 20 May.
From David Higginbotham, 20 May; received 22 May from Milton with notation "rect. of lre to Lilly May 12."
To Gabriel Lilly, 20 May; with notation "fish. Fitz."
From Philip Mazzei, 20 May; received 17 Aug. from Leghorn.
From Thomas Worthington, 21 May; received 31 May from Lancaster, Ohio.
To John Barnes, 22 May.
From Hugh Chisholm, 23 May; received 25 May from Farmington.
From Christopher Ellery, 23 May; received 29 May from Newport with notation "Philip Caswell to keep lighthouse."
From Benjamin H. Latrobe, 26 May; received 28 May from Philadelphia.
From Gideon Granger, 27 May; received 2 June from Suffield with notation "in favr. Jackson Browne."
From Burgess Griffin, 27 May; received 7 June from Poplar Forest.
From William Stewart, 27 May; received 2 June from Monticello.
To Gideon Fitz, 29 May.
To Benjamin H. Latrobe, 29 May.
From George Poindexter, 30 May; received 3 July from Washington, Miss. Terr., with notation "to be judge Missipi."
From John Hollins, 31 May; received 31 May from Baltimore.
From James Oldham, 3 June; received 7 June from Monticello.
From John Perry, 3 June; received 7 June from Shadwell.
From Gideon Fitz, 5 June; received 8 June from Monticello.
From Marten Wanscher, 5 June; received 7 June from Alexandria.
From George Divers, 7 June; received 12 June from Farmington.
To Hugh Chisholm, 8 June.
To Gabriel Lilly, 8 June; with notation "120. D. for Chisolm."
From Jacob Crowninshield and others, 9 June; received 17 June from Salem with notation "Paul Dudley Sarjent to be Collectr. Frenchman's bay, Maine, v. Meletiah Jordan."
From James Dinsmore, 10 June; received 12 June from Monticello.

From David Higginbotham, 10 June; received 12 June from Milton.
From John Jacob Ulrich Rivardi, 11 June; received 14 June from Philadelphia with notation "W."
From James Oldham, 13 June; received 16 June from Monticello.
To James Dinsmore, 14 June.
To Gabriel Lilly, 14 June.
From William Coach, 18 June; received 19 June from Christiana Bridge with notation "to be Collectr. v. Mclane."
From Levi Lincoln, June; received 20 June from Washington with notation "claim of Maryland to lands in Washington."
From George Clinton, 21 June; received 29 June from Albany with notation "Fred. Jenkins to be Coml Agt Havre."
From James Currie, 24 June; received 29 June from Richmond.
From James Oldham, 24 June; received 25 June from Monticello.
From Henry Lee, 26 June; received 28 July from Fincastle.
From Thomas Mann Randolph, 27 June; received 29 June from Edgehill.
To Gabriel Lilly, 28 June; notation "Oldham. Peyton."
To James Oldham, 28 June.
To James Currie, 29 June.
From James Dinsmore, 1 July; received 3 July from Monticello.
From Gabriel Lilly, 1 July; received 3 July from Monticello.
From David Longworth, 2 July; received 4 July from New York.
From John Walker, 3 July; received 6 July from Richmond.
To James Dinsmore, 4 July.
From Robert King, Sr., 4 July; received 30 Sep. from Scarborough.
From David Higginbotham, 7 July; received 10 July from Milton.
From George Jefferson, 7 July; received 9 July from Richmond.
To John Walker, 7 July.
From Martin Dawson, 8 July; received 10 July from Milton.
From James Oldham, 8 July; received 10 July from Monticello.
From Christopher Ellery, 9 July; received 15 July from Providence.
From Hancock Allen, 10 July; received 14 July from Milton with notation "64.73."

Appendix IV

Financial Documents

EDITORIAL NOTE

This appendix briefly describes, in chronological order, the orders and invoices pertaining to Jefferson's finances during the period covered by this volume that are not printed in full or accounted for elsewhere in this volume. The orders for payments to Étienne Lemaire and Joseph Dougherty pertain, for the most part, to expenses associated with running the President's House. The *Memorandum Books* are cited when they are relevant to a specific document and provide additional information.

Order on John Barnes for payment of \$137.04½ to Joseph Dougherty, Washington, 6 Mch. 1803 (MS, Opportunity Shop, New York City, 1955; in TJ's hand and signed by him; signed by Dougherty acknowledging payment). TJ recorded this transaction as payment of Dougherty's accounts for forage and contingencies (MB, 2:1094).

Order on John Barnes for payment of \$34.37½ to Joseph Dougherty, Washington, 6 Apr. (MS in DCU; in TJ's hand and signed by him; signed by Dougherty acknowledging payment). TJ recorded this transaction as payment of Dougherty's accounts for forage, saddlery, smiths, and contingencies (MB, 2:1096).

Order on John Barnes for payment of \$435.47 to Étienne Lemaire, Washington, 6 Apr. (MS, American Museum of Historical Documents, Las Vegas, Nevada, 1989; in TJ's hand and signed by him; signed by Lemaire acknowledging payment; endorsed by Barnes as paid on 11 Apr.). TJ recorded this transaction as payment of Lemaire's accounts from Mch. 6 to Apr. 2 for provisions, stores, fuel, groceries, furniture, servants, and contingencies (MB, 2:1096).

Order on John Barnes for payment of \$75.50 to Étienne Lemaire, Washington, 11 Apr. (MS, Raab Collection, Ardmore, Pennsylvania, 2011; in TJ's hand and signed by him; signed by Lemaire acknowledging payment). TJ recorded this transaction as payment of Lemaire's accounts from Apr. 3 to 9 for provisions, groceries, servants, and furniture (MB, 2:1096).

Order on John Barnes for payment of \$74.53 to Étienne Lemaire, Washington, 2 May (MS in OClWH; in TJ's hand and signed by him; signed by Lemaire acknowledging payment). TJ recorded this transaction as payment of Lemaire's accounts from Apr. 24 to 30 for provisions, servants, and repairs (MB, 2:1098).

Invoice submitted by David Longworth to TJ for \$17.00 for "2 Telemachus" at \$8.50 each, New York, 2 May (MS, Harry L. Dalton, Rosemont, Pennsylvania, 1950).

Order on John Barnes for payment of \$30 to John Christoph Süverman, Washington, 18 May (MS in MHi; in TJ's hand and signed by him; signed by Süverman acknowledging payment; endorsed by Barnes as paid 18 May). TJ recorded this transaction as charity (MB, 2:1101).

Order on John Barnes for payment of $40 to William Stewart, Washington, 2 June (MS in ViU; in TJ's hand and signed by him; signed by William G. Stewart acknowledging payment; endorsed by Barnes as paid on 2 June). See MB, 2:1101.

Order on John Barnes for payment of $14.20 to Joseph Dougherty, Washington, 6 June (MS, Keith A. Nixon, McMurray, Pennsylvania, 2005; in TJ's hand and signed by him; signed by Dougherty acknowledging payment). TJ recorded this transaction as payment of Dougherty's accounts for forage, smiths, and "dress for myself" (MB, 2:1102).

Order on John Barnes for payment of $10 to Alexander Terrasse (MS in ViU; undated; in TJ's hand and signed by him; signed by Terrasse acknowledging payment; endorsed by Barnes as paid on 9 June). TJ recorded this transaction as charity (MB, 2:1102).

Order on John Barnes for payment of $26.56 to Joseph Dougherty, 13 June (MS, Sotheby's, New York City, 1998; in TJ's hand and signed by him; signed by Dougherty acknowledging payment; endorsed by Barnes as paid 14 June). TJ recorded this transaction as payment of Dougherty's account for forage (MB, 2:1102).

Order on John Barnes for payment of $132.33 to Étienne Lemaire, 13 June (MS in CtY; in TJ's hand and signed by him; signed by Lemaire acknowledging payment; endorsed by Barnes as paid on 17 June). TJ recorded this transaction as partial payment of Lemaire's accounts from June 5 to 11 for provisions, contingencies, servants, coal and drayage (MB, 2:1102).

Order on John Barnes for payment of $10 to Marten Wanscher, Washington, 19 June (MS in ViU: Edgehill-Randolph Papers; in TJ's hand and signed by him; signed by John W. Pratt acknowledging payment; endorsed by Barnes as paid on 12 Sep.). See MB, 2:1103.

Order on John Barnes for payment of $53.81 to George Andrews, Washington, 23 June (MS in CtY; in TJ's hand and signed by him; signed by Andrews acknowledging payment; endorsed by Barnes as paid on 23 June). TJ recorded this transaction as payment for ornaments for himself and George Divers (MB, 2:1103).

Order on John Barnes for payment of $114.60 to Étienne Lemaire, 27 June (MS in MHi; in TJ's hand and signed by him; signed by Lemaire and Joseph Dougherty acknowledging payment; endorsed by Barnes as paid on 8 July). TJ recorded this transaction as payment of Lemaire's accounts from June 19 to 25 for provisions, servants, wood, President's House furniture, and contingencies (MB, 2:1103).

Order on John Barnes for payment of $5 to Edward Frethy, 2 July (MS in ViU; in TJ's hand and signed by him; written on invoice from Frethy to TJ, undated, for "one months Dressing"; signed by Frethy acknowledging payment on 1 July; endorsed by Barnes as paid on 1 July).

Order on John Barnes for payment of $13.50 to J. B. Anderson, 8 July (MS in ViU; in TJ's hand and signed by him; written on invoice from Anderson to TJ, dated Washington, 27 June, for making four frames for medallions and one for a "print of Washington"; signed by Samuel Howlett acknowledging payment). See MB, 2:1104.

INDEX

INDEX

INDEX

INDEX

A comprehensive index of Volumes 1-20 of the First Series has been issued as Volume 21. Each subsequent volume has its own index, as does each volume or set of volumes in the Second Series.

THE PAPERS OF THOMAS JEFFERSON are composed in Monticello, a font based on the "Pica No. 1" created in the early 1800s by Binny & Ronaldson, the first successful typefounding company in America. The face is considered historically appropriate for The Papers of Thomas Jefferson because it was used extensively in American printing during the last quarter-century of Jefferson's life, and because Jefferson himself expressed cordial approval of Binny & Ronaldson types. It was revived and rechristened Monticello in the late 1940s by the Mergenthaler Linotype Company, under the direction of C. H. Griffith and in close consultation with P. J. Conkwright, specifically for the publication of the Jefferson Papers. The font suffered some losses in its first translation to digital format in the 1980s to accommodate computerized typesetting. Matthew Carter's reinterpretation in 2002 restores the spirit and style of Binny & Ronaldson's original design of two centuries earlier.

✧

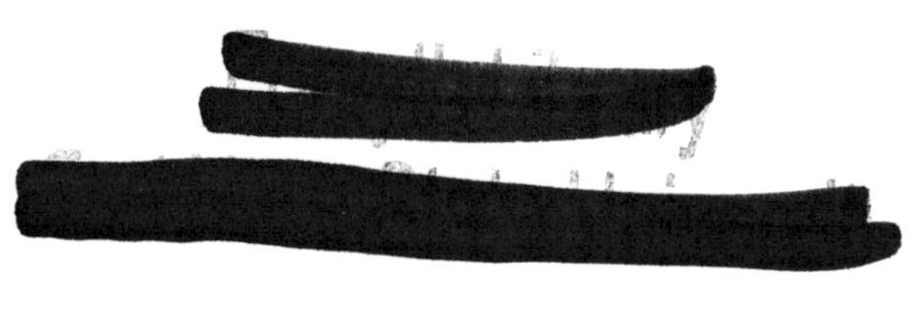